CMT Level I

CMT Level I

An Introduction to Technical Analysis

Readings Selected by

The Market Technicians Association

WILEY

Cover design: Wiley

Published by John Wiley & Sons, Inc., Hoboken, New Jersey.
Published simultaneously in Canada.

ISBN 978-1-119-22269-9 (Paperback)
ISBN 978-1-119-25140-8 (ePub)

Printed in the United States of America
10 9 8 7 6 5 4 3 2

CONTENTS

ABOUT THE MARKET TECHNICIANS ASSOCIATION

The Market Technicians Association is a not-for-profit professional regulatory organization servicing over 4,500 market analysis professionals in over 85 countries around the globe. The MTA's main objectives involve the education of the public, the investment community, and its membership in the theory, practice, and application of technical analysis.

The MTA has the following stated mission:

- Attract and retain a membership of professionals devoting their efforts to using and expanding the field of technical analysis and sharing their body of knowledge with their fellow members.
- Establish, maintain, and encourage the highest standards of professional competence and ethics among technical analysts.
- Educate the public and the investment community of the value and universality of technical analysis.

The MTA mission is accomplished through the effective execution of a wide variety of professional services including, but not limited to, regional seminars, local chapter meetings, the maintenance of an extensive library of technical analysis material, and the regular publication of newsletters and journals.

MTA members and affiliates include technical analysts, portfolio managers, investment advisors, market letter writers, and others involved in the technical aspects of equities, futures, options, fixed income securities, currencies, international markets, derivatives, etc.

Services provided to our members and affiliates are performed by a small NYC-based Headquarter staff, an active Board of Directors, Committee Chairs, and an extensive cadre of volunteers located in both U.S. and non-U.S. markets.

WHAT IS THE CMT® PROGRAM?

The Chartered Market Technician® (CMT) credential is the global standard for practitioners of technical analysis and technical risk management. It is a FINRA-recognized designation which sets apart CMT charterholders as specialists and value-generators among active investment professionals.

The designation is awarded to those who demonstrate mastery of a core body of knowledge in risk management and portfolio management settings. The advanced technical expertise represented by the CMT charter immediately communicates to clients and employers the disciplined approach, academic rigor, and unique professional skill set which CMT charterholders possess.

The objectives of the CMT Program are:

- To promote high ethical standards of education, integrity, and professional excellence
- To guide candidates in mastering a professional body of knowledge
- To professionalize the discipline of technical analysis

Those candidates who successfully complete all three levels of the CMT examination and agree to abide by the MTA Code of Ethics are granted the right to use the CMT credential.

What Will You Learn?

The CMT Program is offered in a self-study format. There are three levels of exams, each one building on the previous. The levels progressively narrow in focus while increasing the emphasis on higher-order reasoning.

The final exam requires candidates to implement critical analysis to arrive at well-supported recommendations in a professional investing/trading context.

The curriculum is organized into exam-specific knowledge domains that provide a framework for recognizing and implementing investment and trading opportunity.

Level I	Level II	Level III
I. Theory & History	I. Theory & History	I. Risk Management
II. Markets	II. Market Indicators	II. Asset Relationships
III. Market Indicators	III. Construction	III. Portfolio Management
IV. Construction	IV. Trend Analysis	IV. Classical Methods
V. Trend Analysis	V. Chart & Pattern Analysis	V. Behavioral Finance
VI. Chart & Pattern Analysis	VI. Confirmation	VI. Volatility Analysis
VII. Confirmation	VII. Cycles	VII. Ethics
VIII. Cycles	VIII. Selection & Decision	
IX. Selection & Decision	IX. System Testing	
X. System Testing	X. Risk Management	
XI. Statistical Analysis	XI. Statistical Analysis	
XII. Ethics	XII. Ethics	

HOW THIS BOOK WAS CREATED

The curriculum for the Market Technician Association's CMT exam level I is comprised of selected readings in the areas of technical analysis and other financial disciplines. The MTA curates each level of the 3-volume curriculum, reviewing the available academic literature as well as practitioner scholarship. The process distills the best readings from all available and applicable works into a concise study tool for CMT Candidates to gain broad understanding of the core body of knowledge and best practice in active money management. The MTA is indebted to the fine work of each author whose work is included in the curriculum.

PREFACE

Congratulations on choosing to prepare yourself for the CMT Level I Exam. The CMT program will put you on a path to develop uncommon insight in your research and analysis as a practitioner in the financial industry. Chartered Market Technicians are found in a variety of roles around the industry, but they share one thing in common: a desire to discover value and opportunity for those who they supply. This is also true of the many men and women who have contributed to the 2015 revision of the new CMT curriculum.

As technical analysis moves further into the mainstream of financial analysis tools, CMTs need the capacity to communicate their insights. They need to show their expertise in using tools that have been validated and have become trusted, acceptable components in a serious practitioner's work. This exam helps you to build a foundation of study in topics recognized as critical or very important to active practitioners today.

The CMT Level I exam measures basic competence of an entry-level analyst. The CMT Level I candidate should have a working knowledge of the terminology used in the required readings, be able to **identify** the concepts discussed in these readings, and have a definitional understanding of the analytical tools presented in the required readings.

Exam time length: 2 hours, 15 minutes

Exam format: Multiple Choice

The curriculum is organized into exam specific knowledge domains that provide a framework for recognizing and implementing investment/trading decisions. The CMT Level I exam tests the candidate's knowledge in 12 domains:

1. Theory and History
2. Markets
3. Market Indicators
4. Construction
5. Trend Analysis
6. Chart and Pattern Analysis
7. Confirmation
8. Cycles
9. Selection and Decision
10. System Testing
11. Statistical Analysis
12. Ethics

Exam Topics & Question Weightings

1. Theory and History	a. history of financial markets	9%	11
	b. history of technical analysis		
	c. Modern Portfolio Theory		
	d. Adaptive Market Hypothesis		
	e. Dow Theory		
	f. behavioral finance		
2. Markets	a. historical market data	5%	6
	b. traditional asset classes		
	c. alternative asset classes		
	d. currencies		
	e. non-U.S. markets		
	f. market indices		
	g. exchanges		
3. Market Indicators	a. breadth indicators	7%	9
	b. index construction		
	c. government/Fed reports		
	d. private money flows		
	e. sentiment measures		
	f. volatility		
4. Construction	a. scaling methods	5%	6
	b. line chart		
	c. bar chart		
	d. candlestick chart		
	e. point and figure chart		
	f. volume		
5. Trend Analysis	a. trendlines	16%	18
	b. regression analysis		
	c. moving averages		
6. Chart and Pattern Analysis	a. classic pattern recognition	23%	28
	b. candlestick pattern recognition		
	c. Elliott Wave principle		
	d. Fibonacci price analysis		
	e. support and resistance		

	f. relative strength index (RSI)		
	g. moving average convergence/ divergence (MACD)		
	h. Bollinger Bands		
	i. stochastics		
7. Confirmation	a. open interest and volume	3%	4
8. Cycles	a. cyclical price patterns	5%	6
9. Selection and Decision	a. relative strength	13%	15
	b. forecasting techniques		
	c. strategic models		
10. System Testing	a. objective testing	5%	6
	b. order execution and slippage		
11. Statistical Analysis	a. descriptive statistics	6%	7
	b. fundamentals of probability		
12. Ethics	a. standards and practices	3%	4

CHAPTER 1

Introduction to the Evolution of Technical Analysis

From Andrew W. Lo and Jasmina Hasanhodzic, *The Evolution of Technical Analysis: Financial Prediction from Babylonian Tablets to Bloomberg Terminals* (Hoboken, New Jersey: John Wiley & Sons, 2010), Introduction.

Technical analysis—the forecasting of prices based on patterns in past market data—is something of a black sheep in modern economics. Some skeptics view it as kissing cousins with sleazy speculation or gambling, while others regard it as a relic that is only slightly more sophisticated than the reading of chicken entrails. Proponents of quantitative analysis, who take physics as the ideal model of how economic science ought to look, view technical analysis as antiquated and contrived in its very foundations. They demand mathematical proofs of its validity and dismiss as exception bias the strong betting averages and impressive bottom lines of successful technicians. We make it no secret, then, that we regard technical analysis as a legitimate and useful discipline, tarred by spurious associations and deserving of further academic study.

Some of this skepticism is understandable in light of the historical origins (and occasional abuses) of technical analysis. Many of its methods come down to us from the days before computers and the number-crunching-intensive theories they made possible, and not all of its methods have been thoroughly explored within the quantitative frameworks now available. Many terms and concepts in technical analysis can seem abstruse or outmoded; it is easy to see how a discipline that involves eyeballing charts for patterns with names like "head and shoulders" and "cup with a handle" might seem at first blush more akin to astrology than science. However, many of these are merely heuristics developed in the precomputer age when calculating a simple statistic was a formidable task. For instance, the 10-day moving average became a fixture of technical analysis not because it was optimal, but because it was trivially easy to compute. Indeed, there are many such concepts in "classical" technical analysis that could benefit from quantitative reformulation.

Ultimately, however, both technical and quantitative analysis serve similar purposes: They both attempt to predict the future based on models of the past. One is statistical, the other is intuitive. Whereas a quant minimizes a sum of squared residuals to find the best-fitting line given the data, a technician estimates it by looking at the charts, searching for tell-tale patterns, and inferring the thoughts and feelings of other market players. Both approaches have merit. This is not to say that they are equal; clearly, quantitative methods have won hands down, dominating the investment industry because of their demonstrable value-added. But technical analysis is surprisingly resilient and persistent, and in some corners of the financial industry—such as the trading of commodities and currencies—it is still the dominant mode of analysis. This state of affairs suggests that technical analysis may have something to contribute, even to the most sophisticated quant. Fortunately, a slow but sure reconciliation is underway.

Though big strides have been made throughout history and in recent years toward developing a more systematic approach to technical analysis, technicians remain ostracized to this day. For evidence, look no further than the Financial Industry Regulatory Authority's official recognition of the Chartered Market Technician designation, which occurred only in 2005. Part of the reason is that technical analysis is often associated with the speculators, bear raiders, and market cornerers of previous eras. As Tony Tabell, a veteran technical analyst and an heir to the technical brokerage business founded by his father Edmund Tabell in the 1930s, explains:

> It's hard to visualize unless you've talked to people who were involved how difficult this was in the atmosphere of [the] 1930s and 1940s. The entire brokerage business was a basket case. Volume on the NYSE was under a million shares. This was the 1930s, the Great Depression, nobody had any money, and if they did, they were very leery about investing. Furthermore, technical analysis had been associated with the excesses of the 1920s. All of the various Securities Acts were designed to get rid of the manipulative market operations that had characterized the '20s. Since technical work to a great degree (certainly point and figure charts) had been originally conceived as a means of detecting pool operations, confessing that you were involved in technical work at that point was sort of equivalent to confessing that you were some kind of a low-level criminal. I saw some [of] this, because the remainder of this attitude was still kicking around when I started in the business in the 1950s, but I can imagine how incredible it must have been in the '30s and '40s.[1]

The efficient markets hypothesis (EMH), formulated in the writings of Samuelson (1965) and Fama (1965a,b; 1970), did not help much.[2] According to this theory, there are no patterns in market data that are exploitable through trading strategies.

Ever since the advent of modern finance—a theory based on rational expectations and market efficiency—technical analysis has been dismissed in academic circles as a mathematical impossibility. As Princeton University economist Burton Malkiel concluded in his influential book *A Random Walk Down Wall Street* (1973), "under scientific scrutiny, chart-reading must share a pedestal with alchemy."

As we recount the premature obituaries for technical analysis, it is worth noting as an aside that recent research has not only documented departures from the EMH—in the form of cognitive biases such as overconfidence, overreaction, loss aversion, and herding—but has also included new theoretical underpinnings for technical analysis and the empirical validation of certain technical patterns and indicators.

Malkiel's lumping of technical analysis with alchemy is not entirely coincidental, for here we come across another historical reason for the field's questionable reputation—technical analysis was used in conjunction with astrology since the earliest times. The ancient Babylonians would methodically record, often intraday, the prices of various commodities, but they would also assign those same commodities to the astrological regions of Pisces and Taurus, depending on whether they were bullish or bearish. Similarly, in addition to the very logical lists of weights, measures, and exchange rates recorded in medieval merchant manuals, they also often contained lengthy astrological appendixes and advised their readers to buy, sell, or begin anything when they were in the region of Virgo. Yet another example is provided by Christopher Kurz, a sixteenth-century Antwerp trader, who claimed to be able to forecast prices of commodities up to 20 days in advance using his technical trading system based on back-tested astrological signals.

Such close links between technical analysis and astrology are naturally a cause for suspicion and skepticism today. But for our ancestors, astrology was a way of life, applied to wide-ranging areas of human endeavor including warfare and medicine. It was no coincidence that Christopher Kurz doubled as a political astrologer—he is known for having forecasted the extinction of the papacy, among other things—while Thales of Miletus, one of the Seven Sages of ancient Greece, made meteorological predictions based on movements of the stars and planets. That societies would base their operations in part on astrology sounds absurd today, but interestingly, if we view astrology as a random number generator of the precomputer age, its prevalence becomes more understandable. Then, as now, forecasting—financial and otherwise—was a business of probabilities. Just as computer-generated random numbers are part of today's statistical forecasting models—for example, the commonly used Markov Chain Monte Carlo method for constructing Bayesian forecasts—astrology may be thought of as a random input in ancient forecasting models.

The evolution of technical analysis did not take place in isolation. The growth of markets provided one stimulus for its development. In ancient Babylon, simply writing down commodity prices on clay tablets was sufficient for tracking market action, but with the advent of financial exchanges, the need for visualizing market data became evident. By the 1830s, price charts emerged and soon became so prevalent that people like William Stanley Jevons and James Wyld made their livelihoods from producing sophisticated charts and selling them to various offices.

Speculation provided another stimulus. Though speculation and technical analysis are not synonymous, they do share a certain awareness of market psychology and of the forces of supply and demand. It was precisely when speculative techniques were ripe that technical analysis became more concrete, such as on the Dojima Rice Exchange in seventeenth-century Japan, where the legendary trader Munehisa Homma developed the "candlestick" charting method to be able to visualize open, high, low, and closing market prices over a certain period, and formulated his version of technical analysis, which remains popular to this day.

Despite the distance created by continents and thousands of years, the market wisdom of Charles Dow, the father of modern technical analysis, is astonishingly similar to that of his earliest predecessors, including the ancient Athenian practice of using price level as an indicator of market sentiment, Homma's rotation of Yang and Yin (bullishness and bearishness), and the emphasis in late imperial China on "the ultimate principle," which is that "when goods become extremely expensive, then they must become inexpensive again."[3] Such similarities reveal technical analysis as a truly universal phenomenon and highlight how deeply ingrained it is in human psychology to reason in technical terms in order to ride and reinforce the trends, as was the case with the humble tulip bulb during the 1633–1637 tulip mania in Amsterdam. As de la Vega put it, "for on this point we are all alike: when the prices rise, we think that they fly up high and, when they have risen high, that they will run away from us."[4] As long as humans, not robots, make the markets, bubbles and crashes will be a reality. This is an especially important lesson in the wake of the 2007–2009 global financial crisis, a time when many fundamentals have crumbled and in some spheres of financial practice there has been nothing left to work with other than technical analysis.

In this book, we present a broad, largely nontechnical historical survey of technical analysis, tracing its roots and evolution from ancient times through the medieval and modern eras. While neither of us is a practicing technical analyst or "technician," as they prefer to be called, we have been fascinated by this strange craft for many years, and this volume is the outgrowth of our own attempt to make sense of the discipline. As outsiders, we hope to bring a somewhat different perspective that can bridge the gap between academia and the technical analysis community. Our previous book, *The Heretics of Finance*, contained interviews with leading technicians in which they described their art in their own words. In this volume, we take a more expansive view and search for the origins of technical analysis throughout history.

This endeavor was more challenging than we anticipated because, in many cases, the historical evidence of technical analysis is indirect, and many ideas were not fully developed by their originators. This is not surprising since, in the past, the concept of technical analysis as a separate discipline did not exist; rather, it was entangled with the intuitive, sometimes whimsical, and rarely systematic way of buying and selling practiced by speculators, bankers, and merchants. Hence when we say that merchants were the liberators of the independent human spirit and the driving force behind the progress of world civilization, we mean technicians, too. It was they who put an end to solely monastic education and the use of Latin in business and private life, and who initiated lay education in the Middle Ages. It is no coincidence that some of history's great scientists were also engaged in investing, their market experiences often motivating their scientific contributions (bonacci being but one example). Sapori once said that medieval merchants "traced for individuals and peoples of all times to come the only way that leads to a full realization of humanity."[5] We hope this book will convey the same for technical analysts across all eras.

Notes

1. A.W. Lo and J. Hasanhodzic, *The Heretics of Finance: Conversations with Leading Practitioners of Technical Analysis* (New York: Bloomberg Press, 2009), 100.
2. Throughout the manuscript, when referencing academic papers in the text, we will use the "author lastname (publication year)" convention commonly followed in the academic finance literature.
3. W. Bingyuan, *Maoyi xuzhi yaoyan* (1900), 15; as quoted in R.J. Lufrano, *Honorable Merchants: Commerce and Self-Cultivation in Late Imperial China* (Honolulu: University of Hawai'i Press, 1997), 133.
4. J. de la Vega, *Confusion de Confusiones* (Boston: Harvard University Printing Office, 1957), 35.
5. A. Sapori, *The Italian Merchant in the Middle Ages* (New York: W. W. Norton, 1970), 38.

CHAPTER 2

A New Age for Technical Analysis

From Andrew W. Lo and Jasmina Hasanhodzic, *The Evolution of Technical Analysis: Financial Prediction from Babylonian Tablets to Bloomberg Terminals* (Hoboken, New Jersey: John Wiley & Sons, 2010), Chapter 5.

At the turn of the nineteenth century the field of technical analysis was made concrete, formal, and even scientific. It was also made popular; Thomas notes that at that time "quite a cult of chartists mushroomed up who based their trading along technical lines."[1] (Technical analysts are sometimes called "chartists" due to their fondness for charts, plots, and diagrams.) The leading figure in this development was Wall Street legend Charles H. Dow. Dow got his start as a financial reporter for the *New York Mail* and *Express*, and then for the Kieran News Agency. He also worked as a broker and a floor trader on Wall Street. With Edward D. Jones he co-founded the Dow Jones and Company news service, and on July 8, 1889, Dow Jones and Company first published *The Wall Street Journal* with Dow as the editor.[2]

Known as the "father of technical analysis," in his editorials in the early 1900s Dow communicated his ideas about stock market dynamics and methods of stock speculation. After his death in 1902 Dow's ideas and observations became known as Dow theory thanks to the writings of Samuel A. Nelson. Dow argued that stock speculation is far removed from gambling, for it is based on the perception of a stock's value and of the underlying market movements.[3] "The market is not like a balloon plunging hither and thither in the wind," Dow used to say.[4] Rather, "it represents a serious, well-considered effort on the part of farsighted and well-informed men to adjust prices to such values as exist or which are expected to exist in the not too remote future."[5]

In this chapter we delve deeper into some of the specifics of Dow theory. We also introduce important theoretical and methodological innovations in market analysis that evolved around the same time as Dow theory and helped establish the full modern tool kit of technical analysis.

Dow Theory

At the core of Dow's theories is an understanding of human psychology and the effect it has on market prices. This may seem unremarkable nowadays, but in early twentieth-century America such thinking was well ahead of its time. "There is always a disposition in people's minds to think the existing conditions will be permanent," Dow wrote, and went on to say: "When the market is down and dull, it is hard to make people believe that this is the prelude to a period of activity and advance. When the prices are up and the country is prosperous, it is always said that while preceding booms have not lasted, there are circumstances connected with this one, which make it unlike its predecessors and give assurance of permanency. The fact pertaining to all conditions is that they will change."[6]

A defining element of Dow theory is the idea of a trend. In the January 4, 1902, edition of *The Wall Street Journal*, Dow communicated his famous principle of successive highs and lows as indicators of a trend: "It is a bull period as long as the average of one high point exceeds that of previous high points. It is a bear period when the low point becomes lower than the previous low points."[7] He further elaborated on the idea of trends in his editorial *Swings within Swings*:

> Nothing is more certain than that the market has three well-defined movements which fit into each other. The first is the daily variation due to local causes and the balance of buying and selling at that particular time. The secondary movement covers a period ranging from ten days to sixty days, averaging probably between thirty and forty days. The third move is the great swing covering from four to six years.[8]

According to Hamilton, this observation *is* Dow theory; while other formulations of the theory may be broader, they all have this idea at their core.[9]

Dow implemented his ideas by computing the Dow Jones Industrial Average, which he published to enable traders to visualize basic market trends. The first averages appeared in the Dow Jones market letters in the early 1880s. They were made up of eleven stocks that were considered to be the most active and representative of the market as a whole; not surprisingly, nine of them were railroad stocks. According to Gartley's research, Dow began computing his industrial average in 1881, first mentioned it in his writings in 1887, and began publishing it regularly after January 1, 1897. At one point he began constructing a separate average specifically for railroad stocks; between 1884 and 1896 he would occasionally mention his railroad average, and he began publishing it regularly after November 2, 1896. Dow argued that the railroad and the industrial averages had to confirm each other for a signal to be conclusive in judging future trends. Later still, in 1929, an average for utilities came into use as well.[10]

Dow viewed the stock market as a natural system and likened the averages to a measuring instrument:

> A person watching the tide coming in and who wishes to know the exact spot which marks the high tide, sets a stick in the sand at the points

> reached by the incoming waves until the stick reaches a position where the waves do not come up to it, and finally recede enough to show that the tide has turned.
>
> This method holds good in watching and determining the flood tide of the stock market. The average of twenty stocks is the peg which marks the height of the waves. The price-waves, like those of the sea, do not recede at once from the top. The force which moves them checks the inflow gradually and time elapses before it can be told with certainty whether the tide has been seen or not.[11]

The averages were meant not only as a measurement of present conditions, but also as an indication of the future ones: "Within limitations, the future can be foreseen. The present is always tending toward the future and there are always in existing conditions signals of danger or encouragement for those who read with care."[12]

According to the theory of averages, in the long run, the number of advancing days for a stock approximately equals the number of declining days. In Dow's words, "if there comes a series of days of advance, there will almost surely come the balancing days of decline."[13]

The extent to which Dow's methods were precisely quantified is illustrated by his law of action and reaction, which establishes that after a primary market move there is generally a secondary move that retraces by a specific amount—at least three-eighths—of the primary move; the longer the primary (or action) move, the greater the secondary (or reaction) move.

The theory of responses demonstrates powerfully that Dow's methods were not short-lived, data-driven rules, but were instead measures of the fundamental reality of market dynamics. According to this theory, the market is always subject to manipulation in the following way: A large operator who wants to advance the market first buys two or three leading stocks, then examines the effect this has on other stocks. Based on the market's response the operator can determine whether the public is bullish or bearish and whether the general market will follow the leading stocks.

With "the intuitiveness of an artist" and "the analytical power of a mathematician," as Rhea would later write, Dow dissected the market organism and wrote about concrete methods for analyzing and forecasting its dynamics. He discussed these "methods of reading the stock market" in his editorials.[14] For example, in his July 20, 1901, editorial he provided one of the earliest descriptions of the so-called book method, which became known as figure charting in the 1920s and acquired its current name—point and figure—in the 1930s. On a point-and-figure chart, price changes are recorded in a succession of columns—ascending columns of x's when prices are rising and descending columns of o's when prices are falling—the column being changed when the price changes direction. If a stock stays within a narrow range (known as the trading range)—that is, after trending downwards (or upwards) it shows little to no price movement—it forms a long horizontal line, which indicates that the stock has been accumulated (or distributed) and that a reversal on the upside (or downside) is likely.

Credited with shaping the point-and-figure charts into what they are today, and using them in ingenious ways to apply and extend the Dow theory, is legendary trader and financial magazine publisher Richard D. Wyckoff. Wyckoff entered the business in 1888 as a 15-year-old "pad shover," but soon became a broker in his own right and a partner in numerous enterprises. By 1907 he was a publisher of the *Ticker Magazine*, later known as the *Magazine of Wall Street*. After his second wife Cecilia—dubbed by the media the "Prima Donna of Wall Street"—seized control of the magazine after he divorced her, he went on to found the Richard D. Wyckoff Analytical Staff, an investment advisory firm. Based on his own experience and conversations with the great speculators of his time, including Jesse Livermore, E.H. Harriman, James R. Keene, Otto Kahn, and J.P. Morgan, Wyckoff formulated the so-called Wyckoff method, for which he is now famous.

In a nutshell, the Wyckoff method is a use of bar charts and point-and-figure charts to study the supply/demand imbalances with the purpose of determining future price trends, and has the following three fundamental laws at its core. The first is the law of supply and demand: When demand exceeds supply, prices will rise, and vice versa, and the relationship between supply and demand can be gauged using bar charts that plot price and volume over time. The second is the law of effort versus results: When volume and price diverge, the price trend is likely to change direction; to measure the relationship between price and volume, Wyckoff developed his "optimism vs. pessimism" index, an on-balance-volume type of indicator (see Chapter 3). Finally, there is the law of cause and effect: The extent of the accumulation or distribution during the trading range (the cause) is directly proportional to the extent of the subsequent price move (the effect); point-and-figure charts are used to count horizontally the units of the cause, and project them into vertical units of effect. This method is used in virtually the same form by traders today, and since 1990 it has been a central part of the Graduate Certificate in Technical Market Analysis at Golden Gate University in San Francisco under the leadership of Henry Pruden, a contemporary expert of the method.[15]

Having amassed a vast fortune in the early 1900s, including a nine-and-a-half-acre Great Neck estate neighboring that of the General Motors boss Alfred P. Sloan, Wyckoff turned his attention to philanthropic and educational endeavors. So in 1931, he formed Richard D. Wyckoff Associates, which became the Stock Market Institute, one of the first institutions to rigorously teach technical analysis.

The ideas from Dow's editorials were compiled and organized by his publisher colleague and admirer Samuel Armstrong Nelson in his 1903 book *The ABC of Stock Speculation*. (Nelson had actually tried to persuade Dow to write such a book himself, but, as he used to say, his attempts were unavailing.[16]) It was in this book that Nelson first referred to Dow's work as Dow theory and elaborated on Dow's idea that market averages and stock prices in general serve as probes and metrics of the stock market and the broader economy: "Stock Exchange prices register values and the state of trade, precisely as a thermometer registers heat or cold."[17]

More generally, in his other two books, *The ABC of Wall Street* and *The Consolidated Stock Exchange of New York*, Nelson strived to represent market activity as emerging from a set of laws. Speculation, in his view, was governed by universal laws such as "never overtrade," meaning you should take a large interest if and only if you have large capital; "never double up," that is, always change your position cautiously and gradually; "run quick or not at all," in other words, take action at the first signs of danger, but otherwise hold onto at least a part of your position; and "sell down to the sleeping point," namely, when worried or in doubt, you should reduce the amount of interest.[18]

Despite his penchant for systematizing, Nelson never lost sight of the fact that human psychology played a big role in investing: While he considered the preceding laws absolute, he also recognized conditional laws, so called because they should be modified to suit a speculator's individual level of greed and fear, as well as his temperament.[19] Indeed, Nelson strongly emphasized that an operator's personality played a big role in his success. A successful operator must possess "the temperament and accurate and swift reasoning powers necessary to cope with the ablest money getters in the world."[20] He must be calm by nature and always seek to preserve "the balance of mind," since when "a fluctuation in the market unnerves the operator," then "his judgment becomes worthless."[21]

Dow theory was further championed by William P. Hamilton, a journalist who immigrated from England and joined *The Wall Street Journal* in 1899. As is evident from his writing, Hamilton enthusiastically embraced Dow's tenet that markets discount everything:

> The farmers say . . . "what does Wall Street know about farming?" Wall Street knows more than all the farmers put together ever knew, with all that the farmers have forgotten. It can, moreover, refresh its memory instantly at any moment. It employs the ablest of farmers, and its experts are better even than those of our admirable and little appreciated Department of Agriculture, whose publications Wall Street reads even if the farmer neglects them.[22]

Moreover, Hamilton believed that the theory was universal and the principles underlying it were so sound that they held true for any market.

Hamilton not only organized but also expanded Dow's ideas. As Gartley pointed out, "the Dow Theory as generally understood was almost entirely the joint work of Dow and Hamilton."[23] In 1922 Hamilton published a book called *The Stock Market Barometer* in which he combined Dow's ideas with his own and put forth a method of predicting a stock market. In particular, Hamilton regarded the stock market as "the barometer of the country's and the world's business."[24] As he put it, "the sum and the tendency of the transactions in the Stock Exchange represent the sum of all Wall Street's knowledge of the past, immediate and remote, applied to discounting of the future."[25]

Hamilton argued that market crises were caused by "too much imagination" and underscored the need for "soulless barometers, price indexes and averages to tell us where we are going and what we may expect."[26] Essential to the predictive power of the barometer is the idea that speculation is based on expectations, rather than on common knowledge: A bear market *anticipates* a contraction, whereas a bull market *anticipates* an expansion in business activities. As a Wall Street maxim puts it, "a movement is over when the news is out."[27] And it is precisely in the objectivity of the barometer where the key to its usefulness lies: "A barometer predicts bad weather, without a present cloud in the sky. It is useless to take an axe to it merely because a flood of rain will destroy a crop of cabbages in poor Mrs. Brown's backyard."[28]

In this light, Hamilton went on to praise Dow's stock market averages: "The best, because the most impartial, the most remorseless of these barometers is the recorded average of prices in the stock exchange."[29] Moreover, he noted that Dow theory is the best tool for reading this barometer. Hamilton is also known for his editorial, "The Turn of the Tide," published in the October 29, 1929, edition of *The Wall Street Journal* (shortly before his death) in which he correctly predicted the end of the great bull market of the 1920s.

Robert Rhea further systematized the theories of Dow and Hamilton. The son of a stock market speculator, Rhea was exposed to Dow's writings from a young age. Plagued by health problems since youth—first tuberculosis, then a plane accident that further damaged his lungs—Rhea spent the latter part of his life bedridden, where he continued to chart the stock market and study Dow theory. He was a Dow historian rather than an innovator. It was Rhea's understanding that "the element of independent judgment or 'art' . . . must accompany all Dow Theory interpretations."[30] Rhea published three books: *Dow's Theory Applied to Business and Banking* (1938), *The Dow Theory* (1932), and *The Story of the Averages* (1932). He also published a complete historical collection of daily charts of the Dow Jones averages.

One of Rhea's signal contributions was to reduce Dow theory (as interpreted by Hamilton) to a set of definite theorems and axioms. These axioms include the "manipulation" axiom, according to which day-to-day movement of the averages can be manipulated, the secondary reaction can be manipulated to a limited degree, but the main movement can never be manipulated; the "averages discount everything" axiom, which says that Dow Jones rail and industrial averages capture the fears, hopes, and knowledge of all market participants, and hence are able to anticipate future events; and the axiom that the "Dow Theory is not infallible," in other words, the market cannot be beaten.

Among the theorems, a special place belongs to the theorem of Dow's three movements. According to this theorem, there exist three distinct and simultaneous movements of the averages: a primary, a secondary, and a day-to-day movement. Primary movements, which refer to major bull and bear markets, are direct reflections of human psychology. For example, the primary bull market evolves in three phases: It starts when people become confident about a bright business future, becomes more pronounced when earnings indeed rise, and finally the top is reached as the stock prices continue to rise. But this rise is founded on hopes and expectations, rather than on value; as Rhea put it, "This is the phase where worthless stocks are bought for no other reason than because they look cheap and because gamblers hope they will double in price."[31] A secondary reaction, or retracement, refers to a significant decline in a bull market or to a significant advance in a bear market, lasting from three weeks to three months. Finally, Rhea advises that day-to-day movements should be charted because they usually develop into a pattern of forecasting value.

Other notable theorems include the "determining a trend" theorem, which says that highs terminating above preceding highs and lows terminating above preceding lows indicate a bull market, while the inverse is bearish; the "relation of volume to price movements" theorem, according to which an overbought market sees light volume on rallies and heavier volume on declines, while the reverse is true for an oversold market; and a theorem about individual stocks, which says that active and well-distributed stocks of great American corporations generally move in tune with the averages.[32]

Dow theory was subjected to a good deal of empirical testing and validation both by academics, such as Brown, Goetzmann, and Kumar (1998) (see Chapter 5), and practitioners, such as Richard Russell, a prominent contemporary Dow theorist. In his work *The Dow Theory Today*, a collection of twelve articles between December 1958 and December 1960, Russell examined market developments by applying Dow theory to current and historical data.[33]

For example, Dow had discussed the particular behavior of low-priced stocks—the so-called "cats-and-dogs" or "fancy stocks"—during a bull market. In 1899, near the peak of the 1896–1899 bull market, Dow wrote about "a perceptible increase in trading in fancy stocks" and noted that "this has not always been the best sign of a continued general upward movement for any great length of time, although it is certainly an accompanying feature of a bull market."[34] Seeking to generalize Dow's remarks, Russell studied the market action data from the 1900s to 1960s. He concluded that, in general, low-priced stocks often undergo significant advances during the third, final phase of a major bull market. Moreover, Russell used the market history to check the validity of Dow's 1902 statement that "when a stock sells at a price which returns 3.5 percent on the investment, it is obviously dear, except there be some special reason for the established price" and that "in the long run, the prices of stocks adjust themselves to the return on investment, and while this is not a safe guide at all times, it is a guide that should never be laid aside or overlooked."[35]

Russell observed that at the top of the 1929, 1937, and 1946 bull markets, the average yield of the Dow Jones industrials was 3.1 percent, 3.7 percent, and 3.3 percent respectively. He concluded that indeed, as Dow had established, the bull markets ended when the average yield on the Dow Jones industrials entered a zone of about 3.5 percent or less.[36] Russell further used historical market data to study the relationship of the Dow Jones Industrial Average to its own 30-week moving average. He concluded that, historically, the industrial average was always above its 30-week moving average in a major bull market and that the industrial average moving below its 30-week moving average for the second time was a sure bearish indication.

Many others have contributed to the Dow theory literature over the years. C.J. Collins, a Dow theorist of the 1930s, helped popularize the theory in his weekly market letter, *Investment Letters*, in which he regularly published his discussions of the technical aspects of the market interpreted in the light of Dow theory. His interpretations of Dow theory also appeared in *The Wall Street Journal*. Gartley recommended Collins's work to technical students, praising it as "clean-cut and dependable."[37] Also worthy of mention is Samuel Moment, who sought to reduce Dow theory to a set of precise and mechanically applicable rules and to thereby eliminate the subjectivity or "art" from technical thinking. In the process he greatly modified the theory, at one point even eliminating the premise that the averages must confirm. In fact, as Gartley suggested, "many followers of Dow feel that Moment has varied the Theory until the founder would no longer recognize it."[38] His most important reports are "The Dow Theory—A Test of Its Value and a Suggested Improvement" and "The Secondary Trend Barometer," both of which were published by Dunnigan's *Forecast Reports*.

Relative Strength

Although Dow theory is largely considered the foundation of the technical approach, other methods for reading and interpreting the market emerged around the same time and evolved in parallel with Dow theory. One of these is the notion of relative strength—a measure of how a stock is performing relative to other stocks in its industry. Though veiled, one of the first references to this concept is due to Nelson, who combined Dow's theory of responses with Dow's proposition that "value has little to do with temporary fluctuations in stock prices, but is the determining factor in the long run," to conclude the following:

> An operator should always keep in mind that big traders and bankers seek to manipulate the price by buying below value and selling above value. If the public follows the lead, temporary movements in the price of a stock occur. However, in the long run, it is the investor who establishes the price of a stock based on its value. An intelligent operator should pay more attention to the value of the stock in which he is dealing, than to prices. He should first study the general market conditions, and then examine the role his stock plays in the improvement or deterioration of those conditions. In this way he can determine whether the value of his stock is rising or falling.[39]

Nelson did not label his idea as relative strength; that distinction belongs to Rhea. In his article "Stock Habits," which appeared in the May 8, 1933, issue of *Barron's*, Rhea gave the first explicit discussion of relative strength in stock market speculation and explained how to compute and interpret the relative-strength ratio. In particular, he described it as the ratio of the price of a stock to the price of the market average; if this ratio is rising over time, then the stock is outperforming the market, and if a given stock consistently outperforms the market over a period spanning several market swings, then it is safe to assume that the stock will continue to outperform.[40]

Russell fully endorsed Rhea's conception of relative strength. He believed that technical analysis of individual stock charts had to be accompanied by relative strength analysis. He proposed the following relative-strength-based stock selection strategy:

> First examine the relative strength for different groups of stocks. Select the groups with best RS, preferably those characterized by a RS that is turning up after a long decline. From the groups selected in step 1, pick

the stocks with the best RS. From the group selected in step 2, pick the stocks that exhibit best technical patterns and buy them. Constantly watch the RS ratio of the stocks you bought. Sell a stock when its RS line reverses.[41]

Market Cycles and Waves

Another development that evolved apart from Dow theory is the theory of market cycles. Seminal research in this direction was conducted by British economist William Stanley Jevons, who proposed his sun-spot theory in a series of papers published in the journal *Nature* between 1878 and 1882. Jevons's thesis was that economic cycles occur as a result of "the varying power and the character of the sun's rays."[42] Specifically, in his paper "Commercial Crises and Sun-Spots," Jevons analyzed two hundred years of English price data on corn, wheat, and other commodities, and documented a market cycle lasting on average 10.466 years. He wrote: "I am perfectly convinced that these decennial crises do depend upon meteorological variations of like period, which again depend, in all probability, upon cosmological variations of which we have evidence in the frequency of sun-spots, auroras, and magnetic perturbations."[43]

Charles Dow was a disciple of Jevons's work. "This ten-year movement is given in detail by Professor Jevons in his attempt to show that sun-spots have some bearing upon commercial affairs," he wrote. And later: "Without going into the matter of sun-spots and their bearing upon crops, commerce, or states of minds, it may be assumed that Professor Jevons has stated correctly the periods of depression as they have occurred in England during the last two centuries."[44] Dow extended Jevons's work by arguing that the 10-year cycle consisted of five to six years of boom or confidence followed by a period of bust or depression of about the same duration. Furthermore, he documented the same cycle in the United States that Jevons had documented in England.

Dow used the sun-spot theory to correctly predict the 1907 financial crisis in the United States, according to Hamilton in his 1922 book *The Stock Market Barometer*.[45] Market participants as a whole have "a tendency to go from one extreme to another,"[46] and the reason it takes time to go from one extreme to the next lies in the fact that "the stock market reflects general conditions and it takes several years for such a change for better or for the worse to work its way through the community,"[47] postulated Dow. Thus, as with his other theories, Dow found a basis for the sun-spot theory in the very nature of crowd psychology.

Another landmark in the theory of market waves and cycles is the wave principle. It was developed by Ralph Nelson Elliott, an accountant who started studying the stock market relatively late in his life—in 1932, at the age of 61. The wave principle postulates that the stock market follows a basic cyclical pattern, where each cycle consists of eight waves (five waves in one direction, followed by three waves in the opposite direction). Elliott's thinking was influenced by Rhea's book, *The Dow Theory*, as well as by Rhea's market letter, *Dow Theory Comment*; however, as Robert

Prechter, an authority on the Elliott wave principle, points out, while Elliott "was undoubtedly directed initially by exposure to the tenets of Dow theory," his "ultimate discovery was all his own."[48] Elliott himself considered his wave principle "a much needed complement to the Dow Theory."[49]

Similarities between Elliott and financial astrologer William D. Gann, Elliott's contemporary, are often raised. Gann, for example, believed in a universal natural order that ruled everything, including the stock market. As he reflected while describing his road to discovery:

> I soon began to note the periodical recurrence of the rise and fall in stocks and commodities. This led me to conclude that natural law was the basis of market movements. After exhaustive researches and investigations of the known sciences, I discovered that the Law of Vibration enables me to accurately determine the exact points to which stocks or commodities should rise and fall within a given time.[50]

Likewise, Elliott believed that "no truth meets more general acceptance than that the universe is ruled by law," and furthermore that "all life and movement consists of vibrations, and the stock market is no exception."[51] For this reason Elliott has often been classified together with Gann and astrology, and denounced as one of those "trader/fanatics who operate mostly on faith and can offer little evidence or logic to support their beliefs."[52] However, Prechter suggests that, except for occasional Gann-like comments, Elliott "stayed focused on his empirical observations," and hence should be given credibility.[53]

Chart Patterns

Technical analysis today is often identified with the subjective practice of detecting with the naked eye certain weird patterns with weird names in past price data—think "head and shoulders" or "ascending triangle." Because it is based on human pattern recognition, rather than on rigorous, fine-grained statistical analysis, it is often disparaged as "voodoo finance." However, in the precomputer age, patterns were a way of processing the data and detecting supply/demand imbalances; furthermore, each pattern had an underlying explanation, a story based on market psychology and crowd action and reaction.

For example, the head-and-shoulders pattern, observed on a price chart in the final stages of market rallies, captures the tug of war between buyers and sellers. As the sellers come in and test the downside market potential, the prices are brought down, leaving behind a peak corresponding to the "left shoulder" in the pattern; as buyers respond in panic, they take the market to a new high—the "head" of the pattern. However, their efforts are only temporary as sellers reemerge and test the downside again; the buyers make another tentative effort leading to another, lower peak—the "right shoulder"—until they are finally overtaken by new sellers who join in at the market top. Similarly, a sequence of successively higher highs and lower lows, which traces the so-called "triangle bottom" pattern in price data, was interpreted as the embodiment of strengthening confidence punctuated by subsiding terror, and hence as the presage of an uptrend.

Chart patterns were pioneered by Richard W. Schabacker—*Forbes Magazine*'s financial editor with previous stints at the Federal Reserve Bank of New York and the Standard Statistics Company (which later became Standard & Poor's)—in his three highly influential books, *Stock Market Theory and Practice* (1930), *Technical Analysis and Market Profits* (1932), and *Stock Market Profits* (1934). Edwards and Magee used Schabacker's writings and theories as a primary source in writing their book *Technical Analysis of Stock Trends*, widely regarded today as a primer of technical analysis instruction. Most prominent among Schabacker's patterns are the common basic formations indicating a major accumulation (distribution). These include head-and-shoulders bottom (top), common upward (downward) turn, triangular bottom (top), ascending bottom (descending top), double bottom (top), complex bottom (top), and broadening bottom (top). There are also types of continuation triangles, such as symmetrical, ascending, and descending triangle, and other types of continuation formations, such as ascending peak and descending bottom. Minor editions of the basic formations indicating a major accumulation (distribution), or a growing irregularity on high volume in a bull move, are examples of reverse formations. In addition, Schabacker identified a number of miscellaneous formations. These include false moves and shake-outs, support points and resistance levels, and gaps. Gaps are observed if today's low is higher than yesterday's high, or if today's high is lower than yesterday's low.[54]

Schabacker recognized that the public tends to judge the day as a whole based on the closing prices they read in the evening paper. Thus, he emphasized that closing prices are largely what govern the public's predictions of the future, and that this insight should be used in charting. However, he was well aware of the limitations of the available price data—"stock price lists had a very bad reputation in the United States (and not only), as being unreliable and manipulated," notes Preda.[55] Hence, Schabacker advised his readers to keep in mind that the closing prices are not always genuine due to the practice of "window dressing"—portfolio managers are known to spruce up the performance of their funds by increasing significantly, through price manipulation, the prices of securities to which they have high exposure—at the close of a day's trading.[56]

Like his patterns, Schabacker's practical advice was deeply rooted in his understanding of the reality of the markets. For example, he observed that stop-loss orders—a popular strategy for cutting losses short—were undermined by bear traders: As the demand of bear traders for such stocks increases, the price of those stocks decreases; this triggers the automatic selling of those stocks and causes prices to decline even further, which allows the bear traders to cover their short positions and make a profit. However, since this collapse in prices is artificial and temporary and prices rebound, stop-loss traders often lose positions in very good stocks. Schabacker therefore advised traders to combine their practice of placing stop-loss orders with the practice of buying at support levels in order to minimize the potential loss and maximize the potential profit.[57]

Volume of Trading

After the 1929 stock market crash, speculative techniques received their fair share of criticism. There was a clear and urgent need for more accurate and objective market statistics. The general view was that detachment and objectivity in financial dealings were not only in the investors' interests, but also in the nation's. This sentiment prompted the New York Stock Exchange (NYSE) economist J. Edward Meeker to proclaim:

> There is today a particular need of statistical yardsticks with which to measure its activities. For only by recourse to definite figures can a basis be provided for a serious and unprejudiced study of the activities and functions of the Stock Exchange. The need of adequate statistics is all the more important because mass psychology is regularly so considerable a cause of most stock market phenomena.[58]

Meeker announced that monthly statistics concerning trading activity on the NYSE and monthly indexes and averages would be made "as promptly and as generally available to the public as possible," and stressed that the statistics would be "entirely without comment, for while the Stock Exchange wishes to make every effort to discover and make public factual evidence concerning stock market conditions, it leaves it to others to interpret and comment upon this material."[59] He went on to say: "It is the beginning of wisdom to recognize quite clearly and frankly the defects of the statistical record we already have, and to purify these necessary economic agents of ours as far as possible by painstaking care in collection and compilation, patient experimentation and critical impersonal analysis. These, after all, are the methods of true science."[60]

As stock market statistics became more readily available, it was only natural to incorporate the new resources into technical reasoning. One such statistic is trading volume—the number of shares involved in a stock sale or purchase. Volume can be decomposed into demand volume, which occurs during advances, and supply volume, which occurs during declines. Hence, volume can be used as a measure of supply and demand for shares. A pioneer in this area was Harold M. Gartley—one of the founders of the New York Society of Security Analysts and later a director of the National Securities and Research Corporation, one of the 10 largest mutual funds at the time. In his 1935 book *Profits in the Stock Market*, Gartley formalized Wall Street's ideas about the volume of trading. Writing in 1966, Schulz noted that Gartley's "famous chapter on Trading Volume . . . [was] a real landmark in technical theory and one of the very few extensive studies on the subject of volume ever published."[61]

Gartley himself acknowledged that the available published information concerning volume was indeed small at the time he undertook his endeavor:

> Many financial writers have, more or less vaguely, referred to the activity on the Stock Exchange (which we call volume), but detailed analyses are, for the most part, lacking. Perhaps the reason is that a detailed

study of volume of trading is a tedious and laborious task, the results of which frequently do not seem worth the effort.[62]

Although technical notions of volume had not been standardized before Gartley's seminal work, volume has been part of Dow theory from the start. Charles Dow introduced his ideas concerning the relationship between volume and trend in the March 7, 1902, edition of *The Wall Street Journal*, where he wrote that "in a bull market, dullness is generally followed by an advance," while "in a bear market by a decline."[63] Furthermore, in the May 29, 1901, edition, Dow observed: "There is a relation between the volume of business and the movement of prices. Great activity means great movements whenever the normal balance between buyers and sellers is violently disturbed."[64] Hamilton continued Dow's studies on volume, but his views on the subject were inconsistent. Until 1910 he clove to the old Wall Street maxim that volume follows a trend—in other words, that volume on rallies indicates strength, while on declines it indicates weakness. As he wrote in the May 21, 1909 edition of *The Wall Street Journal*:

> One of the platitudes most constantly quoted in Wall Street is to the effect that one should never sell a dull market short. That advice is probably right oftener than it is wrong, but it is always wrong in an extended bear swing. In such a swing, the tendency is to become dull on rallies and active on declines.[65]

But in 1910 Hamilton changed his mind, arguing that averages discount everything, including volume. From that point onward he seemed confused on the subject of volume, sometimes saying that he "[preferred] to neglect volume," other times returning to the old maxim he once endorsed.[66]

In his interpretation of Dow theory, Rhea incorporated volume in the discussions of trends, turns, and penetrations. For example, he would say that dullness on declines and activity on rallies indicate strength, while the reverse indicates weakness; that bull markets usually terminate in heavy volume and bear markets terminate in light volume; and that when a critical point is penetrated on high volume, the signal such penetration produces is more valid.[67] C.J. Collins, the author of the *Investment Letters*, also believed in the old volume-follows-a-trend maxim. He discussed volume in virtually every market letter he wrote; on the other hand, Samuel Moment ignored volume altogether in his discussion of Dow theory.[68] Gartley for his part believed that trend analysis cannot be complete without consideration of volume: "It is probably no exaggeration to say that volume is one of the best single indicators of trend," he wrote.[69]

Market Breadth

Gartley is also known as the man who empirically tested and set down in writing Wall Street's wisdom concerning market breadth, or the number of stocks advancing or declining for the day. In fact, when he was writing the famous "Breadth-of-the-Market" chapter of his book *Profits in the Stock Market*, he used no references. This was the case because, as he himself acknowledged, "although this subject has been studied by many market students, with the exceptions of the author's work, [he knew] of no published references."[70]

It was the increased availability of market statistics following the crash of 1929 that allowed Gartley to start his market-breadth research. In 1931 he began collecting data on the number of issues traded, number of advances, declines, and prices unchanged, number of new high and lows, total volume, and the ratio of trading in the 15 most active stocks to total volume, with the objective of determining whether these statistics could be used as means of judging intermediate price reversals. He made the following three observations. First, he found that whenever the seven-day moving averages of the ratio of advances to declines exceeds 60 percent of the total issues traded, it is likely to be the signal of a turning point. Second, he saw that the ratios of advances and declines appear to be more accurate in suggesting buying signals than selling signals. And third, he observed that market-breadth statistics appear to be very useful in judging final phases of major bear markets but not so useful in the bull markets.[71]

Nontechnical Analysis

Financial astrology is often categorized with technical analysis. This is entirely unjustified, of course: It is the use of past market—not cosmic—data that defines technical analysis. Nevertheless, no history of technical analysis would be complete without a survey of this perennial phenomenon. The temptation to invoke mystical aid for predicting the future is strong and deeply rooted in the human psyche.

Starting from the belief that the planets' orbits, the sun, and the moon have an effect on the minds and actions of people, and therefore on the stock market, financial astrologers study the natal horoscopes of markets and companies, as well as the positions of planets in the sky at any given time, and use them to astrologically chart and forecast the cycles and prices of stocks and commodities.[72] A company's natal horoscope (or birth chart) is a map of the heavens that corresponds to its birth data—that is, to the time, place, and date of its incorporation. Just as a personal horoscope describes one's character, talent, and ability, a company's horoscope is a measure of its market potential.[73] The positions of planets in the sky at any given time, also known as the transits, are the main indicators of the likely course of events.[74] More precisely, "it is [the planets'] constantly changing relationship to the natal horoscope chart that is the basis of almost all astrological prediction."[75] Financial astrologers might also consult their own horoscopes, those of their clients and advisors, the first-trade horoscope of a company, and the horoscopes of various countries, stock markets, and central banks.[76]

Financial astrologers generally believe that their craft should be used in conjunction with conventional techniques, rather than in isolation. In fact, "very few financial astrologers use *only* astrological tools to forecast markets, and most likely these are the beginners," suggests Weingarten.[77] Astrology is just one of the three "screens" or "layers" necessary for a successful investment strategy, the other two being fundamental analysis and technical analysis.[78] Along the same lines, Hyerczyk explains that the "knowledge of astrology is necessary to interpret and convert the degrees of the planets, but knowledge of technical analysis techniques is still needed to build charts, interpret tops and bottoms, find support and resistance, and place stop orders."[79]

One legend of the early twentieth-century financial astrology was William D. Gann (mentioned earlier), whose 80 to 90 percent success rate on trades earned him the moniker "master trader."[80] Combining astrology and market data, he predicted several months in advance that September 1909 wheat would sell at $1.20 by the end of the month, which is indeed what happened on the very last trading day and in the very last trading hour of September. Gann wrote eight books, the best known of which are *Wall Street Selector* (1930), *45 Years in Wall Street* (1949), and *Truth of the Stock Tape* (1923).

As Marisch points out, "Gann's trading methods are based on his personal beliefs of a natural order existing for everything in the universe."[81] Or, in Gann's own words: "Everything in existence is based on exact proportion and perfect relationship. There is no chance in nature, because mathematical principles of the highest order lie at the foundation of all things."[82]

Turning to ancient esoteric pseudoscience for direction, he became a student of numerology, astronomical cycles, astrological interpretations, time cycles, Biblical symbology, and sacred geometry.[83] In addition, Gann researched early Egyptian writings and even traveled to India to gain access to the ancient pre-Hindu literature.[84] Moreover, Gann's religious beliefs profoundly influenced his trading. For example, in the book entitled *Tunnel Thru the Air*, Gann advised his readers to "read the Bible to learn about cycles and about the manner in which the Creator reveals nature's universal laws."[85] To explain his general market philosophy, he would often quote Ecclesiastes 1:9–10 from the Bible: "What has been, that will be; what has been done, that will be done. Nothing is new under the sun. Even the thing of which we say, 'See, this is new!' has already existed in the ages that preceded us."[86]

Gann researched the 3½ -day, -week, -month, and -year cycle in the market data. As Hyerczyk explains, the number 3½ fascinated Gann because it occurs several times in the Bible—"for example, in the Book of Revelation, where the woman was sent into the wilderness for three and one-half years; during Daniel's vision of 42 months (3½ years); when the Christ child was hidden in Egypt for three and one-half years; and during Christ's public ministry, which lasted for exactly three and one-half years."[87]

The flavor of Gann's theories is captured by his law of vibration, which he said enabled him "to accurately determine the exact points to which stocks and commodities should rise and fall within a given time," and to "[determine] the cause and [predict] the effect long before the Street is aware of either."[88] Gann used physics as motivation for his law: Stocks were analogous to "electrons, atoms, and molecules, which hold persistently to their own individuality in response to the fundamental Law of Vibration." Science teaches "that an original impulse of any kind finally resolves itself into periodic or rhythmical motion," wrote Gann, and that "just as the pendulum returns again in its swing, just as the moon returns in its orbit, just as the advancing year ever brings the rose to spring, so do the properties of the elements periodically recur as the weight of the atoms rises."[89]

Physics was not only a way of thinking about the stocks; in Gann's mind, the speculative endeavor itself was rendered scientific under his law:

> Through the Law of Vibration, every stock in the market moves in its own distinctive sphere of activities, as to intensity, volume and direction; all the essential qualities of its evolution are characterized in its own rate of vibration. Stocks, like atoms, are really centers of energies, therefore they are controlled mathematically. Stocks create their own field of action and power; power to attract and repel, which in principle explains why certain stocks at times lead the market and "turn dead" at other times. Thus to speculate scientifically it is absolutely necessary to follow natural law.[90]

Gann was one of the first to convert astrological signals into price and incorporate them into a trading system. As he described in his article "Soy Beans: Price Resistance Levels," which appeared in the early versions of the W.D. Gann Commodities Course:

> . . . 67 (cents), add 90 gives 157 or 7 degrees Virgo. Add 135 gives 202 or 22 degrees Libra. Add 120 gives 127 or 7 degrees Leo. Add 180 gives 247 or 7 degrees Sagittarius. Add 225 gives 292 or 22 degrees Capricorn. Add 240 gives 307 or 7 degrees Aquarius. Add 270 gives 337 or 7 degrees Pisces. Add 315 gives 382 or 22 degrees Aries. Add 360 gives 427 or 7 degrees Gemini. Add 271¼ gives 438¼. High on May Beans was 436¾. After that high the next extreme low was 201½. Note that 67 plus 125 gives 202, and that one-half of 405 is 202½, and 180 plus 22½ is 202½, which are the mathematical reasons why May Soy Beans made bottom at 201½. All of the above price levels can be measured in Time Periods of days, weeks and months, and when the time periods come out at these prices, it is important for a change in trend, especially if confirmed by the geometrical angles from highs and lows.[91]

Unfortunately, rather than disclosing his ideas in a systematic way, Gann preferred to make statements such as: "It is impossible here to give an adequate idea of the Law of Vibration as I apply it to the markets."[92] According to Plummer, "it seems that there was a central body of theory underlying Gann's analysis which he was either unable, or unwilling, to reveal."[93] Whether Gann chose to be so obscure because he "simply did not know why his techniques worked" or because "he considered that the underlying theories were too esoteric for general consumption" is an open question.[94] However, one thing for certain is that Gann himself did not lack confidence. This was clearly reflected in his writings; for example, he wrote: "After years of patient study I have proven to my entire satisfaction as well as demonstrated to others that vibration explains every possible phase and condition of the market."[95]

Astrology remains part of unconventional trading systems to this day. Notable contemporary market technicians who openly use astrology in their work include Arch Crawford and Bill Meridian. *Barron's* financial weekly has named Arch Crawford "Wall Street's best known astrologer." Moreover, as Colby points out, "Crawford's combination of astronomical cycles and technical analysis to make market calls has earned him top ratings in market timing in the Hulbert and *Timer Digest* surveys." He is known for having predicted the crash of 1987, the bear markets of July 1990 and March 2000, as well as many minor trend changes. Perhaps the most remarkable of Meridian's findings is his 1994 study of the effect of the lunar cycle on the Dow Jones Industrial Average, which, according to Colby, was confirmed by an analysis at the University of Michigan in 2001. A designer of analytical software, Meridian has developed a program for computing correlations between time series data and planetary cycles.[96]

Proponents of financial astrology argue that it should not be ignored, if for no other reason than for its prevalence. Writing in 1996 Weingarten noted that "currently, over $14,000,000,000 in the United States and Europe follow the stars," and warned his readers that "someday soon astrology was going to become a factor in the market, simply because so many people believe in it, and inevitably that would influence money flows."[97] This is certainly true—as far as it goes. But this is merely the argument that astrology might introduce exploitable inefficiencies into the market simply by dint of rendering predictable the decision-making behavior of some people; it says nothing in favor of astrology's inherent predictive value.

For our predecessors of precomputer eras it may have seemed justifiable to use astrology as an input in their price-based forecasting models. In fact, astrological inputs may have been genuinely useful to prediction insofar as they played the same role that random-number generators play in today's forecasting models. As interesting as this is from a historical perspective, to classify astrology with technical analysis in this day and age is a fallacy. Financial astrology should be called what it is, a distinct branch of esoteric financial decision making with tools and a cult following that are all its own.

Notes

1. D. L. Thomas, *The Plungers and the Peacocks: An Update of the Classic History of the Stock Market*, rev. ed. (New York: William Morrow, 1989), 119.
2. Thomas, *The Plungers*, 121; H. D. Schultz and S. Coslow, eds., *A Treasury of Wall Street Wisdom* (Palisades Park, NJ: Investors' Press, 1966), 3.
3. Schultz and Coslow, *A Treasury*, 10.
4. As quoted in Schultz and Coslow, *A Treasury*, 15.
5. Ibid.
6. As quoted in R. Russell, *Dow Theory Today* (Flint Hill, VA: Fraser Publishing, 1997), 17.
7. As quoted in H. M. Gartley, *Profits in the Stock Market* (Pomeroy, WA: Lambert-Gann Publishing, 1981), 177.
8. As quoted in Schultz and Coslow, *A Treasury*, 11.
9. W. P. Hamilton, *The Stock Market Barometer: A Study of Its Forecast Value Based on Charles H. Dow's Theory of the Price Movement* (New York: Harper and Brothers, 1922), 5.

10. Thomas, *The Plungers*, 120; Gartley, *Profits*, 54.
11. As quoted in de Goede 2005, 104.
12. C. H. Dow, *Scientific Stock Speculation: A Condensed Statement of the Principles upon Which Successful Stock Speculation Must Be Based*, ed. G. C. Selden (New York: The Magazine of Wall Street, 1920), 15; as quoted in de Goede 2005, p. 108.
13. Schultz and Coslow, *A Treasury*, 14.
14. As quoted in Russell, *Dow Theory Today*, 19.
15. For more information about the Wyckoff method see H. Pruden, *The Three Skills of Top Trading: Behavioral Systems Building, Pattern Recognition, and Mental State Management* (Hoboken, NJ: Wiley, 2007) and R. D. Wyckoff, under the pseudonym Rollo Tape, *Studies in Tape Reading* (Burlington, VT: Fraser Publishing Co., 1982 [1910]).
16. S. A. Nelson, *The ABC of Stock Speculation* (Flint Hill, VA: Fraser Publishing, 1997), 7.
17. S. A. Nelson, *The ABC of Stock Speculation*. (Wells, VT: Fraser Publishing, 1964 [1903]), 24; as quoted in de Goede 2005, 105.
18. As quoted in Schultz and Coslow, *A Treasury*, 37–38.
19. Schultz and Coslow, *A Treasury*, 37–38.
20. Nelson, *ABC*, 31.
21. Ibid., 37–38.
22. As quoted in Schultz and Coslow, *A Treasury*, 99–100.
23. Gartley, *Profits*, 174.
24. Schultz and Coslow, *A Treasury*, 46.
25. As quoted in Schultz and Coslow, *A Treasury*, 46.
26. Hamilton, *Stock Market Barometer* 4; as quoted in de Goede 2005, p. 105.
27. Schultz and Coslow, *A Treasury*, 52.
28. Hamilton, *Stock Market Barometer* 4; as quoted in de Goede 2005, p. 105.
29. Ibid.
30. Gartley, *Profits*, 176.
31. Russell, *Dow Theory Today*, 8.
32. Schultz and Coslow, *A Treasury*, 80; Russell, *Dow Theory Today*, 7.
33. Russell, *Dow Theory Today*, 15.
34. Ibid., 116.
35. As quoted in Schultz and Coslow, *A Treasury*, 95–96.
36. Schultz and Coslow, *A Treasury*, 95–96.
37. Gartley, *Profits*, 176.
38. Ibid.
39. As quoted in Schultz and Coslow, *A Treasury*, 34.
40. Schultz and Coslow, *A Treasury*, 90–92.
41. As quoted in Schultz and Coslow, *A Treasury*, 92.
42. W. S. Jevons, "Commercial Crises and Sun-Spots," *Nature* 19 (November 14, 1878), 36; as quoted in de Goede 2005, p. 103.
43. W. S. Jevons, "Sun-Spots and Commercial Crises," *Nature* 19 (April 24, 1879), 588; as quoted in de Goede 2005, 103.
44. Dow, *Scientific Stock Speculation*, 97–98; as quoted in de Goede 2005, 103.
45. Hamilton, *Stock Market Barometer* 27; as quoted in de Goede 2005, 103.
46. Dow, *Scientific Stock Speculation*, 97; as quoted in de Goede 2005, 103.
47. C. H. Dow, "Review and Outlook," *The Wall Street Journal* (April 21, 1899), 1; as quoted in de Goede 2005, 104.
48. R. R. Prechter, ed., *R. N. Elliott's Masterworks: The Definitive Collection* (Gainesville, GA: New Classics Library, 1996), 50.
49. Prechter, *R. N. Elliott's Masterworks*, 52.
50. As quoted in J. A. Hyerczyk, *Pattern, Price and Time* (New York: Wiley, 1998), 9.
51. Prechter, *R. N. Elliott's Masterworks*, 53, 59.

52. C. Lebeau and D.W. Lucas, *Technical Traders Guide to Computer Analysis of the Futures Market* (Homewood, IL: Business One Irwin, 1992), 32.
53. Prechter, *R. N. Elliott's Masterworks*, 53.
54. Schultz and Coslow, *A Treasury*, 239–241; Schabacker 1930, pp. 656–657.
55. Preda 2002, 11.
56. Schultz and Coslow, *A Treasury*, 228–230.
57. Ibid., 235–238.
58. J. E. Meeker, *Measuring the Stock Market*. Address before the American Statistical Association, Cleveland, Ohio, December 30, 1930, 3; as quoted in de Goede 2005, 106.
59. Meeker, *Measuring the Stock Market*, 18; as quoted in de Goede 2005, p. 106.
60. Meeker, *Measuring the Stock Market*, 19–20; as quoted in de Goede 2005, 106.
61. Schultz and Coslow, *A Treasury*, 246.
62. Gartley, *Profits*, 299.
63. As quoted in Gartley, *Profits*, 192.
64. Ibid.
65. Ibid.
66. Ibid.
67. Gartley, *Profits*, 192.
68. Ibid., 193.
69. Ibid.
70. Ibid., 391.
71. Ibid., 325.
72. Hyerczyk, *Pattern, Price*, 19.
73. H. Weingarten, *Investing by the Stars: Using Astrology in the Financial Markets* (New York: McGraw-Hill, 1996), 29–30.
74. Weingarten, *Investing*, 29.
75. Ibid., 31.
76. Ibid., 29–30.
77. Ibid., 45.
78. Ibid., 27.
79. Hyerczyk, *Pattern, Price*, 21.
80. G. Marisch, *The W. D. Gann Method of Trading* (Brightwaters, NY: Windsor Books, 1990), 2–3.
81. Marisch, *Gann Method*, 3.
82. As quoted in Hyerczyk, *Pattern, Price*, 11.
83. Weingarten, *Investing*, 66.
84. Hyerczyk, *Pattern, Price*, 12.
85. Weingarten, *Investing*, 66.
86. As quoted in Marisch, *Gann Method*, 3.
87. Hyerczyk, *Pattern, Price*, 12–13.
88. As quoted in Hyerczyk, *Pattern, Price*, 9.
89. Ibid., 9–11.
90. Ibid.
91. Ibid., 19–20.
92. Ibid., 9.
93. T. Plummer, *Forecasting Financial Markets: The Truth Behind Technical Analysis* (London: Kogan Page, 1989), 233.
94. Ibid.
95. As quoted in Hyerczyk, *Pattern, Price*, 11.
96. R. W. Colby, *The Encyclopedia of Technical Market Indicators*, 2nd ed. (New York: McGraw-Hill, 2003), 109.
97. Weingarten, *Investing*, 20, 24–25.

CHAPTER 3

Technical Analysis Today

From Andrew W. Lo and Jasmina Hasanhodzic, *The Evolution of Technical Analysis: Financial Prediction from Babylonian Tablets to Bloomberg Terminals* (Hoboken, New Jersey: John Wiley & Sons, 2010), Chapter 6.

The world has grown relentlessly more complex over the past several decades, and many fields of science and thought have had to evolve to keep pace. For its part, technical analysis is a far more intricate field than it was a century ago. Nevertheless, the principles on which it is built have remained unchanged since the time of Charles Dow and his immediate successors in the first half of the twentieth century. Then, as now, markets moved in trends and cycles. Now, as then, technical analysts pore over their famous panoply of assorted charts in search of clues, trends, patterns, strength, and cycles in market data. This is not because technical analysis is an anachronism, frozen by traditionalist sensibilities in Edwardian-era amber. Quite the contrary: Technical analysis has had to undergo so little change precisely because it is so robust and so deeply relevant to how markets operate.

We begin this chapter by reviewing some of the main tools technicians use to recognize market developments. The intention of this part is to give unfamiliar readers a flavor of the craft rather than provide an in-depth survey. We then go on to describe how the changes on Wall Street in the second half of the twentieth century have led technicians to reinterpret their craft.

Trends

Price trends are the main tool of technical analysis; indeed, "trend is your friend" is the technician's mantra. An essential trend-following device is the moving average, which is computed by averaging prices over a moving time window in an equally weighted or exponentially weighted manner. Moving averages smooth out the spiky, jittery fluctuations of fine-grained market data to reveal overarching trends or other patterns over various time scales. Moving averages detect trends that are already in place—rather than anticipate them—and are useful to help traders let their profits run and cut their losses short in trending markets. Of course, the shorter the time window over which the average is computed, the faster the recognition of the trend's reversal, but the more likely there will be false signals.

To manage this inherent trade-off between early signal detection and sensitivity to random noise, Perry Kaufman, highly regarded for his work on technical trading systems, developed the "adaptive" moving average. Depending on the relationship between price direction and volatility, this metric allows one to use a faster or a slower moving average depending on the relationship between price direction and volatility. Moving averages are also used in crossover methods—superimposing averages from different time scales to spot tell-tale patterns based on intersections and divergences between each other. For example, the shorter average crossing above the longer indicates a downtrend and produces a sell signal, and vice versa. Furthermore, percentage envelopes—such as 3 percent envelopes around a 21-day moving average for short-term traders, or 5 percent envelopes around a 10-week average for long-term ones—are often placed at fixed percentages above and below a moving average to help identify market extremes. To account for the dynamic nature of volatility, in the early 1980s John Bollinger proposed plotting the market-extreme lines approximately two standard deviations (rather than some fixed percentage) above and below a moving average, a technique known as the Bollinger bands.

More generally, trends are analyzed using indicators, which measure trend momentum and market extremes. We will mention four of them here. First is the momentum line, which is simply a continuously computed difference between the current price and the price a desired number of periods ago. Second is the relative strength index (RSI), developed by J. Welles Wilder and introduced in his 1978 book, *New Concepts in Technical Trading Systems*. RSI is a function of the ratio of the average prices when the market closed up to the average prices when the market closed down during some prespecified period. Third is the rate of change line (ROC), which is a ratio of the current price to the price a desired number of periods ago. Finally, there is the moving average convergence/divergence (MACD), developed by Gerald Appel in the late 1970s and presented in his 1980 book, *Stock Market Trading Systems: A Guide to Investment Strategy for the 1980s*. MACD is modeled through the interaction of a faster signal—which is computed as the difference between two exponential moving averages—and a slower signal, obtained by smoothing the faster signal line with an exponential moving average. When the faster line crosses above the slower one, a buy signal is generated, and vice versa.

The price of a security is not the only quantity technical analysts chart. Volume—the number of shares being traded—is typically tracked alongside price and serves as a confirming indicator of a price trend. Volume tends to expand in an uptrend and contract in a downtrend, and when price and volume diverge it may indicate a coming trend reversal. Technicians have devised a number of heuristics to help them gauge volume trends. One such heuristic is the on-balance volume, which was popularized in the 1963 book *Granville's New Key to Stock Market Profits* by Joseph Granville—who is known as much for his writings on technical analysis as for his extravagant investment seminars, where he would dress up as Moses or appear to walk on the surface of water. On-balance volume is computed as a cumulative total of volume, where volume is added when the price closes higher on a particular day and otherwise is subtracted. Volume is sometimes thought to precede price—that is, the weakening of the buying pressure in an uptrend and of the selling pressure in a downtrend becomes apparent in volume before it shows up as a price trend.

Trends are also frequently studied using point-and-figure charts. The most popular form of point and figure in use today—the three-box reversal—is an extension of the work of Richard D. Wyckoff (see Chapter 2) and is due to Abraham W. Cohen. Cohen, the founder in 1947 and first editor of *Chartcraft* (later known as *Investors Intelligence*), a technical analysis research service, formulated this method in his 1968 book, *How to Use the Three-Point Reversal Method of Point and Figure Stock Market Trading*. As we saw in Chapter 2, on a point-and-figure chart price changes are recorded in a succession of ascending columns of x's (for positive price changes) and descending columns of o's (for negative price changes). Traditionally, all price changes are plotted as they occur (including the intraday ones), and a new column starts forming as soon as the price changes direction—this is called the "one-box reversal" method. However, in the second half of the twentieth century, the ever-increasing speed of the market action and the growing number of stocks to be charted rendered the one-box reversal charts noisy and the manual charting process unsustainable. To solve this problem, Cohen proposed plotting only the high and low prices (readily available in newspapers) and using the "three-box reversal" method, where a new column is started only when the price changes direction by the value of at least three x's or three o's. On the three-box reversal charts, trends are gauged using 45-degree trendlines, drawn by connecting the diagonals of the adjacent x- or o-filled boxes. An upward (downward) sloping trendline being penetrated by a column of o's (x's) is an indication of imminent trend reversal.[1]

Another way to gauge price trends is through the theory of contrary opinion, which says that whatever the majority thinks is likely to be wrong. More precisely, if the majority of traders are on one side of the market, it means that not enough buying or selling pressure is left to continue the present trend. Indicators that assess the bullishness/bearishness of market participants are one vehicle through which technicians apply this theory. Two popular such indicators are the NYSE Bullish Percent and the Advisors Sentiment, created by Abraham W. Cohen in 1955 and 1963, respectively. The NYSE Bullish Percent index is simply the percentage of stocks traded on the New York Stock Exchange (NYSE) that exhibit buy signals on point-and-figure charts, and the Advisors Sentiment is a survey of over a hundred independent investment advisors, summarized as the percentage of those who are bullish, bearish, or expect a market correction.

Patterns

Technicians rely on certain patterns in price and volume to study the behavior of ongoing trends. Traditionally, as cemented in *Technical Analysis of Stock Trends*, the influential 1948 work by Edwards and McGee, patterns have been classified into two main types: reversal patterns, which signal a trend reversal, and continuation patterns, which signal a pause in a prevailing trend. Although widely regarded as misleading by today's technicians, as most patterns occur at both continuation and reversal points without preference, this classification persists as a hangover from the past. Longer patterns have higher failure rates, but if they do materialize, they tend to yield greater subsequent moves than shorter patterns.

Among reversal patterns, "head and shoulders," which we described in the previous chapter, is the most famous. This pattern occurs at market tops and provides a great example of how technicians use volume in conjunction with price to analyze market movements. It starts with the formation of the left shoulder, which is a price peak that is higher than the previous peak and is accompanied at first by expanding volume, and then by contracting volume at the subsequent reaction low. After the left shoulder comes the head, a peak that is even higher than the left shoulder and is accompanied by lighter volume. This lighter volume is the first warning of an approaching trend reversal. The head is then followed by a second reaction low that is lower than the left shoulder, and then by a subsequent rally to a third peak called the right shoulder, which is lower than the previous peak (at the head) while volume continues to contract. After observing the right shoulder, a flat line called the neckline is drawn under the last two reaction lows. The breaking of this neckline completes the price pattern and is accompanied by a burst in volume. After the breaking of the neckline, prices may bounce back to it but typically will not recross it—this is called "a retracement." Often, though not necessarily, the retracement is accompanied by a contraction in volume; after it is over, the volume significantly expands and the downtrend is resumed.

There are variations of head and shoulders. Complex head and shoulders are patterns with double tops or double shoulders. Failed head and shoulders is a pattern that starts out looking like a head and shoulders but then, after breaking the neckline, prices bounce back and recross the neckline.

Other reversal patterns that occur at market tops include "triple tops," "double tops," and "spike tops." Triple tops consist of three peaks at about the same level and two troughs in between them, which are also at about the same level. The patterns are complete when the troughs have been broken with an accompanying burst of volume. Double tops, which are characterized by two peaks that are at about the same level, are complete when a reaction low following the first peak has been broken on a burst of volume. Spike tops are seen when market action suddenly changes direction. This can happen when some unexpected news suddenly becomes available or when markets become extremely overextended.

Each of the foregoing patterns has a mirror-image form: inverse head and shoulders, and triple, double, and spike bottoms, all of which occur at market bottoms.

Among continuation patterns, a prominent place belongs to so-called triangles. The "symmetrical triangle," or "coil," has a declining upper trendline and a rising lower trendline that approach each other as we move from left to right and finally meet at the apex. The "ascending triangle" has a flat upper trendline and a rising lower trendline and most commonly appears in an uptrend. In the "descending triangle," the situation is reversed. The "broadening formation" or "megaphone top" looks like a triangle rotated by 180 degrees (that is, the apex is at the far left of the formation and the trendlines diverge from that point rightwards); this pattern is often seen at the end of major bull markets that are driven by a high degree of public participation, which causes significant volume expansion during the pattern's formation. "Flags" and "pennants" refer to pauses in extremely sharp and almost vertical market moves known as "flagpoles." The "wedge" formation looks like a small symmetrical triangle that slopes against the prevailing trend and is most important as a reversal pattern after a speculative peak or panic bottom. The "rectangle" or "trading range" looks like a rectangle within which the prices move in broad swings.

Strength

The assessment of the continuation or reversal of market trends is aided by the assessment of market strength. The overall health of the marketplace is measured by the so-called advance-decline line, computed as a cumulative total of a normalized difference between the number of stocks that advanced and the number of stocks that declined. As long as this measure is advancing with the major market averages such as the Dow Jones Industrial Average, the market is considered strong, or in technicians' lingo, "the troops are keeping up with the generals."

Other ways of measuring market strength include comparing the number of stocks reaching new highs to the number reaching new lows, or comparing the level of volume in the advancing issues to that in the declining issues—in both cases, the greater the volume on the upside, the stronger the market. Perhaps the best known strength metric is the relative strength ratio (RS ratio), which is obtained by dividing the close of a stock (or a group of stocks) by the S&P 500 or another market index, then plotting this ratio as a line; if the relative strength line is rising, a stock or group is deemed to be acting better than a market as a whole. Robert Levy, a pioneer in the study of relative strength, documented statistical evidence for the validity of the RS ratio as a criterion for stock selection in his 1968 book, *The Relative Strength Concept of Common Stock Price Forecasting*. As with most elements of technicians' craft, the RS ratio is not an innovation of the second half of the twentieth century. George Chestnutt—a prominent technician who in the 1950s not only wrote about this concept but also for nearly 30 years managed the highly successful American Investors Fund, based on this idea—put it this way: "The principle of measuring the strength of a stock in relation to a market average . . . has been in use for many years. I began experimenting with relative performance ratios in the early thirties. The best stock market technicians of that era had been using them for at least a generation before."[2] His adherence to the principle was based not only on statistical evidence but also on intuition:

> Which is the best policy? To buy a strong stock that is leading the advance or to "shop around" for a "sleeper" or "behind-the-market stock" in the hope that it will catch up? . . . On the basis of statistics covering thousands of individual examples, the answer is very clear as to where

the best probabilities lie. Many more times than not, it is better to buy the leaders and leave the laggards alone. This is often difficult from a psychological standpoint. You always want to buy the stock that looks cheap in relation to recent prices. The leader, which will already have advanced, will never look cheap in relation to its price before the advance began. However, too many laggard stocks never do come to life because there is a good reason why they are laggards. The reason may be obscure but your buying will not eliminate the reason. In the market, as in many other phases of life, "the strong get stronger, and the weak get weaker."[3]

Cycles

Some technicians take a philosophical stand, arguing that technical analysis is not only a reflection of human psychology but also directly shaped by the forces of nature. For example, Robert Colby, the author of *The Encyclopedia of Technical Market Indicators*, writes: "Western culture prefers the illusion that each individual can completely control his life. Yet our lives are inevitably shaped, even predetermined, by cycles. Every living being's life is prescheduled and prescripted within actuarially predictable ranges of time."[4]

Market cycles, defined as regularly occurring sequences of events, are influenced by numerous naturally cyclical forces. For example, annual seasonal cycles are reflected in virtually all markets. Seasonality is most obvious in agricultural markets, where, around harvest time, supply increases and prices fall. A well-known phenomenon in the grains market is the "February break": Farmers, who cannot work their fields because of the bad weather, use this time to convert their inventories into the cash they need to prepare for the coming crop season, and consequently, supply increases and prices fall.

Cycles have been a subject of systematic investigations through history. In 1860 the French statistician Clemant Juglar described a 9.25-year cycle in stock prices, now known as the Juglar wave. In 1923 Harvard professor Joseph Kitchin found a four-year cycle, known as the Kitchin wave, in bank clearings, wholesale prices, and interest rates in Great Britain and in the United States for the period 1890 to 1922. The Kondratieff wave, first identified in 1926, refers to a 49- to 58-year cycle of economic activity that is made up of approximately 13 four-year cycles. More recently, in his 1993 Charles H. Dow Award–winning paper, "Charles Dow Looks at the Long Wave," Charles Kirkpatrick, the author of *Technical Analysis: The Complete Resource for Financial Market Technicians*, a standard textbook in the field, observed that from 1700 to 1994, every period that saw both a decline in long-term interest rates and a rise in the stock market has been followed by a major stock market collapse.[5]

Related to the study of cycles in technical analysis is the study of Fibonacci numbers—a sequence constructed such that each successive number is the sum of the two previous numbers (1, 1, 2, 3, 5, 8, . . .)—and their ratios. With the exception of the first four numbers in the sequence, the ratio of any number to its next higher number approaches 0.618—an important mathematical constant, the so-called "golden ratio," which appears in many natural and biological systems (it has also been a favorite of numerologists, mystics, and artists since ancient times). Fibonacci circles, arcs, fans, pentagons, stars, and time zones are but a few visual representations of the Fibonacci ratios that technicians chart. In addition to being useful in and of themselves in gauging price levels, Fibonacci numbers underlie the Elliott wave principle (see Chapter 2). According to this principle, the stock market follows a cyclical pattern consisting of a five-wave stretch in one direction and a subsequent three-wave stretch in the opposite direction; each wave is further subdivided into smaller five- and three-stretch waves.

Wall Street's Reinterpretation of Technical Analysis

A common criticism of technical analysis is that it has not kept up with the changing times. It is true that its tools have remained virtually unaltered for several decades. However, technicians are quick to point out that keeping up with the times does not necessarily require new tools. "[T]echnical analysis has seen a proliferation of a lot more junk out there. What can you say about technical analysis? There's nothing new to say about it. You're testing a previous high or a low, you're buying a retracement and a trend, or you're following a breakout strategy. It's really simple." These words were spoken by Linda Raschke, a highly successful technical trader and one of the interviewees in our book, *The Heretics of Finance*, describing the recent evolution of technical analysis.[6]

What technicians will more readily acknowledge is that changing times call for a *reinterpretation* of some of their tools. The 1950s ushered in an unprecedented transformation of the investing practices on Wall Street, brought on by the rise of institutional trading in large blocks of shares, integration of domestic and worldwide markets, and, most significantly, the widespread use of computers. In this section we survey some of the main developments in these areas and point out how they have prompted leading technical analysts to refine and adapt their craft.

Small Investors

The catalyst of the events of the post–World War II era was the increasing prominence of small investors on the investment scene. During the bull market of the 1950s, the investing business prospered and flourished—so much that its appeal widened beyond its traditional (realms) of institutions and floor traders and began to lure small investors and day traders. The growing popularity of investing came hand-in-hand with the betterment of the social status of its practitioners: While the profession of stockbroker was still considered slightly disreputable through the first half of the twentieth century, by the end of the 1950s its status had risen to the echelon of doctors, lawyers, and CEOs.[7] The same could be said for the reputation of technical analysis. In their 1964 *Financial Analysts Journal* article, a father-and-son team, Edmund and Anthony Tabell, who between them had been doing technical research and consulting with institutions since the early 1930s, wrote: "It was barely a decade ago that the average portfolio manager, if he was aware of technical analysis at all, regarded it as some sort of black magic. Today, almost all professionals have at least a familiarity with the terminology and a good many make such analysis a major part of their decision-making process."[8]

The integration of small investors into the marketplace would continue throughout the decades, aided by technological advances such as the Internet and automated trading platforms. Many of them used technical trading strategies, and their presence waxed and waned with the bull and bear market cycles. John Murphy, author of *Technical Analysis of the Financial Markets*, a standard reference in the field, sums it up with an anecdote:

> Until 2000, we had a lot of people who were day-trading. They were making a fortune. I remember giving a lot of seminars to these people. Then we went into a big downtrend in stocks, and they all went broke. I remember a lot of them saying to me, "Mr. Murphy, these signals did not work anymore." Of course, they didn't work. All they were doing was buying. The short-term buy signals that you get are legitimate if the market is going up. If the market is going down, those little buy signals don't work. You have to look at the environment! So it's not so much the signal; it's the environment.[9]

Seasoned technical analysts such as Laszlo Birinyi, president of Birinyi Associates and a leading authority in the field, argue that the presence of small investors calls for a reinterpretation of their craft. "We should recognize that what worked in an environment in which we had a historical classical long-term investor is totally different from what works in an environment where people are day-trading," says Birinyi, adding, "We still think that charts and indicators work in the same way, when in fact they work differently now."[10]

Institutional Trading

The desire of small investors to take part in the bull markets of the 1950s and 1960s led to a proliferation of mutual funds, specializing not only in the U.S. stock market but also in international investments. Examples of the latter include the Canadian fund, the Japan Fund and ASA (American South Africa) Ltd., the Mexico fund, and the Korea fund.[11]

Boston-based mutual fund management companies Fidelity Investments and Wellington Management maintained (and still do to this day) elaborate chart rooms and based their operations in part on technical analysis. For example, in 1957 the legendary investor Gerald Tsai, then at Fidelity, started managing a hugely successful mutual fund, called the Fidelity Capital Fund, based on broker information and technical analysis (the fund was operated by Tsai but actually run by his boss, Fidelity chairman Ned Johnson). Less than a decade later, after Fidelity refused to give him stock and make him the future chairman, Tsai struck off on his own to launch another mutual fund, the Manhattan Fund, in the same style. Often described as the Pentagon war room for its plethora of sliding and rotating charts, the Manhattan Fund's chart room required "three men to work full time maintaining literally hundreds of averages, ratios, oscillators, and indices, ranging from a 'ten-day oscillator of differences in advances and declines' to charts of several Treasury issues, to 25-, 65-, and 150-day moving averages for the Dow."[12] While serving as a powerful publicity tool, the chart room, however, had little use in the fund's day-to-day operations, causing Chester Pado, a technician who followed Tsai from Fidelity, to quit in frustration. In the market declines in the 1970s, the fund's performance was so dismal that it was ridiculed in the financial press and among professionals. The fund was finally liquidated when Tsai sold it to an insurance company to pay for an expensive divorce.

Another type of mutual funds that were popular with small investors are index funds. These passively managed portfolios mimicking various market indexes captured public attention after "A Study of Mutual Funds"—prepared for the Securities and Exchange Commission (SEC) by the Wharton School of the University of Pennsylvania in 1962—found that average mutual funds do not perform better than an unmanaged portfolio consisting of the same types of securities.[13]

By the mid-1960s the institutional (mutual fund) trading of equities in large blocks of 10,000 shares or more had become commonplace—a far cry from the time when New York Stock Exchange (NYSE) specialists traded round lots of 100 shares of a stock. And the trend continued: While these so-called block trades accounted for 3 percent of the NYSE's volume in 1965, in 1972 they accounted for 19 percent and in 1987 for 50 percent.[14] For example, Walston and Co., Merrill Lynch, and Solomon Brothers had block desks in the late 1960s and early 1970s. Charles Kirkpatrick recounts how while working on the Walston block desk in the late 1960s, at one time he crossed the then largest block ever to be crossed on the American Stock Exchange—276,000 shares of Research Cottrell (no longer an operating company). In fact, in the late 1960s, block trades were so prevalent that some service providers, such as that run by Don Worden, calculated and provided tick and block volume for all stocks. The strong market and the rise of the dollar in the second half of the 1990s led to a renewed explosion of the mutual fund industry, and by the end of 1996 the three largest funds—Fidelity, Vanguard, and Capital Research—controlled $850 billion in assets. This contributed to a surge in trading volume from the beginning to the end of the 1990s, from low hundreds of millions of shares per day to over a billion.[15] Block trading led technical analysts to conceive new ways of measuring market action data, as Laszlo Birinyi recounts:

> In 1979 I introduced into our work the idea of ticker tape analysis. When we first started doing that, it was a very useful indicator. In the first version of it, we would look only at block trading. We would look at every single block trade to see if it was in an uptick or in a downtick, and that proved very helpful. Then we thought that since we were interrogating every single trade to see if it was a block, why not analyze every single trade further, and therefore we developed the idea called "money flows."
>
> Money flows proved to be very useful until 1982, when they did not have quite the predictability that they had previously. We had to

recognize that starting in the early 1980s the dynamics of the trading desk had changed. Before then, when volume was much lower, the specialist on the floor of the New York Stock Exchange controlled the marketplace. You did not really want to antagonize the specialist. He was a partner in what you did. I remember trading Motorola in the early 1970s and putting on a small trade without really checking with the specialist to see if he wanted to participate. The order came from the floor, from John Coleman, who was one of the great powers on Wall Street: "That young man will not trade Motorola again without my permission!"

In the 1980s, institutions grew, commissions were still very significant, and liquidity increased, so upstairs block trading became a bigger and more important force in the marketplace, and the control of the marketplace went from the specialist to the trading desk. Firms like Salomon Brothers, where I worked, would put on large prints—which in those days were twenty thousand to thirty thousand shares—tell the specialists that this was what they were going to do and to move out of the way. Our money flow concept was not as useful as it had been, because with block trading, gradually the information did not seep into the marketplace. More and more prices were being set too often; prices were being set by retail investors. It was a unique circumstance because the NYSE was at that time, and to some degree still is, the only market in the world where retail sets wholesale prices. A hundred shares of Ford up a dime was a new price. Even though there were many millions of shares outstanding, that was the price that showed up on your screen. So we recognized that we had to differentiate between the retail and the wholesale markets, and we started doing money flows on block and nonblock trades, and we looked at them in different marketplaces.[16]

Negotiated Commissions

As pledged in the Buttonwood Agreement of 1792, which founded the exchange, the brokers of the 1950s charged fixed commission rates of no less than one-quarter of 1 percent. This was a great deal for them, especially given the prominence of block trades, and when it came under threat they fought hard to preserve it.[17] In 1969 NYSE chairman and Goldman Sachs CEO Gus Levy went so far as to argue that fixed commissions were "at the very heart" of the financial system. But despite the opposition of Wall Street's elite, the replacement of fixed commissions with flexible ones, which would give the customers power to negotiate the rates and get a discount on large orders, was inevitable.[18]

In 1971 the SEC called for a gradual transition from fixed to negotiated rates—first on trades over $500,000, then over $300,000, until finally on May 1, 1975, so-called "May-day," all commissions were to become fully negotiated. The over-the-counter market NASD (National Association of Securities Dealers) led the way by adopting the automated quotations system known as the Nasdaq, where the prices of various market makers were quoted on a computer and made easily accessible to brokers.[19] (Market makers are specialists on the stock exchange who take the other side of customer orders when there are buy- and sell-side imbalances.) The NYSE had no choice but to follow in Nasdaq's footsteps.[20] This development has had a profound effect on the practice of technical analysis, as Laszlo Birinyi explains:

> There is a cliché, "It's not your grandfather's market anymore." When you have a market that's dominated by traders, when your commissions are one or two cents a share or less, the dynamics are totally different from when you're paying a commission of fifty to sixty cents a share, as people were paying in 1976. In all investing, you look for these wonderful underlying truths, and the more statistically valid they are and the longer they persist, the more confidence you have in them, whereas actually it should be the other way around.[21]

In other words, during the last three decades the market has been evolving so rapidly that the very intuition on which developing technical or quantitative trading strategies is based—the stronger the historical backtest results, the more promising the strategy—got turned on its head. The rate of change has been such that historical viability has become hardly indicative of present success, challenging today's portfolio managers to develop adaptive strategies capable of detecting shifts in the market environment.

Market Integration

The early 1970s saw high inflation and the consequent devaluation of the dollar. Around the same time, markets around the world were becoming highly integrated. In 1971 these two facts came into potent interaction. In August of that year President Nixon took the United States off the gold standard in order to make imports more expensive and exports less expensive; foreign investors, fearing that the dollar was debased, began selling dollars frantically and markets became upset.[22] The lesson was clear: We had entered an era in which investors needed to think about the strength of the dollar. "No longer was talk of currencies a peripheral issue," writes Charles Geisst in *Wall Street*, a popular history of the Street.[23]

The new market environment called for new financial instruments—foreign currency derivatives—that would allow investors to hedge the movements in the dollar; in fact, shortly after President Nixon's announcement, the International Monetary Market (IMM) introduced and started trading currency futures. A few years later, in 1975, futures on Treasury bills, the so-called interest rate futures, emerged.[24] Another major event of that period was the decision of the Organization of Petroleum Exporting Countries (OPEC) to double the price of oil in 1973. This brought Arab and other oil-exporting countries to the forefront of the financial scene and led to a redistribution of wealth from primarily the United States to Europe and later Japan. John Murphy explains the effects these developments have had on the practice of technical analysis:

> I wrote a book on it back in 1991 called *Intermarket Technical Analysis*, and I wrote another one in 2004. This was an outgrowth of my having

> worked in the futures markets, where we were trading bonds, stocks, commodities, and the dollar, and where I started to notice all kinds of correlations. The whole idea of the book is that all these markets are related. For example, if you're trading the stock market, you also have to follow bonds, since what happens in the bond market has an impact on stocks. And bonds are very much affected by commodity prices. For example, when commodities turn up, that's an early sign of inflation. Commodities' turning up pushes interest rates higher, and, in time, that becomes bearish for stocks. Now what pushes commodity prices higher is the falling dollar. You can't look at any one of these markets all by itself—you have to understand the impact they have on one another. Also, global markets are very important. Then there are sector rotations; depending on where you are in the business cycle, you need to understand which sectors of the stock market you should be emphasizing. That comes out of the whole body of intermarket analysis.[25]

Technicians have practiced their craft in conjunction with economic analysis since at least the time of Charles Dow. For example, Dow's emphasis on the importance of confirmation between industrial and railroad averages stemmed from his economic intuition that if the expansion in industrial production were genuine, then the produced goods would start being shipped to customers in greater volume via the railroads. The developments of the second half of the twentieth century underscored the necessity of such an integrated approach, as Murphy suggests:

> When I wrote my book fifteen years ago on the intermarket, most stock market analysts did not pay much attention to the price of gold or the price of oil. Whenever the price of oil moves up close to $40 a barrel, the stock market always goes down. That has happened every time over the last thirty years. So, oil becomes a tremendous factor. Every recession we've had has been caused by a rise in oil prices. Fifteen years ago nobody paid any attention to that, but now you turn on CNBC, and they talk about the impact of the dollar on interest rates, and technical analysts talk about these things. . . . Technical analysis is being recognized as a much broader field. . . . Very often, I write pieces on where the economy is. By knowing where we are in stocks, bonds, and commodities, we are actually doing economic analysis. These markets are leading indicators. The stock market is the leading indicator of the economy. So, technical analysts are actually moving into economic analysis.[26]

The integration of markets leaped forward again in June 1975 with the introduction of the so-called consolidated tape—a system for showing all trades as soon as they are executed regardless of whether they are traded on big exchanges such as the NYSE or small, regional ones. The degree of complex interconnectivity the world's markets had achieved was underscored in October 1987, when the Dow

Jones Industrial Average abruptly collapsed by over 500 points and other markets worldwide suffered even more.[27]

Decimalization

From the eighteenth century through the end of the twentieth, stock prices were quoted in fractions of a point. This practice became problematic because it increasingly caused the bid/ask spreads on the exchanges to be artificially high, and in an era when volume could readily exceed 400 million shares per day, it allowed the market maker to profit substantially. The problem was especially acute for Nasdaq, where the average spread was 1/4 of a point, or 25 cents per share, whereas the spread on the NYSE was 1/8 of a point, or 12.5 cents per share. In 1994, in a *Journal of Finance* paper, William Christie and Paul Schultz argued that wide spreads on Nasdaq were artificially inflated by market makers who avoided the "odd-eight quotes" and changed bids and offers by 1/4 of a point even if such an amount was not justified.[28] The article spurred the Justice Department and the SEC to conduct an investigation, which confirmed the allegation that spreads were artificially inflated. At the end of 1997, 30 market makers settled a class action antitrust civil lawsuit. This spurred Wall Street to start quoting prices in decimals, rather than in fractions, and by 2001 both the NYSE and Nasdaq followed suit.[29] Together with lower commissions, decimalization has driven out of business a number of market makers and may well have reduced market liquidity. The effect of decimalization on the practice of technical analysis is pointed out by Alan Shaw, whose luminous career in the technical research departments of Wall Street's elite firms throughout the second half of the twentieth century has established him as one of the technical gurus of that time:

> Decimalization has not only affected the advance/decline line; it has affected the high/low statistics as well. Nowadays it's possible for a stock to go up one cent and make a twelve-month high. Decimalization has distorted these statistics somewhat, but we still keep them on the wall. However, whereas in the past we used to give them the strength of 10, we now give them the strength of 6. We may not pay as much attention to these high/low statistics as we used to, but they're still worth doing.[30]

Electronic Markets

In the early 1990s, the reputations of both Nasdaq and the NYSE were tainted—Nasdaq's by the artificial inflation of the bid-ask spreads described in the previous section, and the NYSE's by a widespread front-running scandal. Front running is an illegal practice by which a floor trader trades his own accounts before customer orders and thereby makes a profit since he knew how the customer's order would affect the price once executed. As a result, investors became disgruntled with traditional exchanges and turned to more transparent electronic communications networks (ECNs) to trade with a measure of assurance.[31]

ECNs, which came about in the 1990s, are stock markets where buyers and sellers get matched up to transact their orders without a market maker or a specialist. They would soon capture one-third of the Nasdaq trading volume.[32] Providing streamlined procedures, fast execution, reduced commissions, and the convenience of after-hours trading, the ECNs quickly became favorites among institutional investors and large block traders, and gained some popularity among day traders, too.[33] Gail Dudack, a long-time leader in technical analysis, points out that ECNs have had a major effect on measurements of volume, a crucial ingredient in the practice of the craft:

> As technicians, we have to be alert to the fact that the actual execution of a trade has changed. Trading used to be done either on the New York and American stock exchanges or on the over-the-counter market. Today, volume is found on the Nasdaq Composite Index, on multiple electronic communication networks, in global twenty-four-hour trading, and on upstairs desks that never hit the system. This change means we can *no longer* define volume. If we're talking about an NYSE stock, volume could be defined as exchange-only volume or exchange plus after-hours volume, or it could be composite volume. If I'm trying to get one consistent series of volumes on five hundred stocks, it can be a nightmare. For each individual stock, I have three different sets of volumes and three different sets of numbers. Why? The trading structure has changed. Trading no longer starts at 9:30 a.m. on the New York Stock Exchange and ends at 4:00 p.m. Volume is a very important ingredient since it is a measure of conviction.
>
> Thirty years ago the market structure was simple, and we did not have these questions. When I'm buying a volume series, I have too many choices to make. I have to ask myself if after-hours trading is relevant to my project because a different kind of trader is involved there. Is using only the NYSE volume good enough, or do I really want composite volume? How about ECN volume? Some trading takes place today that is not measured, and we never see or hear about it. Since the charts are looking at price and volume, these choices are important. You can come to a wrong conclusion if you inadvertently chose the volume series that doesn't relate to your study. You *must* understand your data to make good decisions. It's better to use a smaller number of indicators, use them really well, and really understand them.[34]

Dudack's point should be understood in the context of volume analysis as confirmation of chart patterns and trends. In effect, it is no longer useful because it is unreliable and in the case of large cap stocks overly influenced by their inclusion in so many exchange-traded funds (ETFs) baskets, and hedge trades.

The Use of Computers

If one development of the second half of the twentieth century had to be singled out for its transformational effect on the practice of technical analysis, that would be the rise of the computer. Its revolutionary potential was apparent from the beginning. In 1965 *Barron's* wrote that "the age of the computer unmistakably is dawning on Wall Street" and that "the potential rewards of the computer, properly used, promise to be immeasurable."[35] "Because it can perform millions of statistical calculations in seconds and recall almost instantaneously hundreds of thousands of details stored for years on its magnetic tapes, the giant brain can relieve an analyst of all such dreary labor, freeing him for more creative activity," the article continued.[36]

Similarly, *The Wall Street Journal* articles at that time emphasized the power of the computer to rank and filter a large number of stocks. "There are more than 6,700 corporations with 300 or more shareholders each, whose shares are traded on one or more exchanges, or are otherwise available to the public. Using human analysts, not even the biggest brokerage house can hope to do a comprehensive job of analysis on more than a small fraction of these," one such article wrote.[37]

The adoption of computers in the years to come and the ensuing Internet age allowed for automated data collection. "When I first started in business on my own in 1980, my main data source was a VCR hooked to a television set that recorded the stock market channel. . . . Now, with the Internet, all the information is available for free and instantaneously," recounts Walter Deemer, a highly regarded technical analyst with almost half a century of experience in financial industry.[38]

Computers provided automatic ranking and filtering from a large universe of securities. As John Murphy sums it up, "with two clicks the computer will show me a chart of the strongest sector of that day, as well as a chart of the strongest stock, [and] within twenty seconds, I can be looking at the five best-performing stocks in the best sector."[39]

Computers meant instantaneous communication. In Alan Shaw's words, "When I was starting out in the business, it used to take me twenty minutes to get a quote. . . . [Now] we send out a 'tech fax,' and all the brokers and all the clients see it immediately; it goes right to their computers."[40]

One of the first computers on Wall Street devoted solely to technical analysis was at Walston and Co., led by Anthony Tabell, where in the late 1960s Charles Kirkpatrick began the data accumulation that would be used for technical research later on. In those days, the usual programming language was Basic, and the computer was an IBM typewriter terminal linked to a remote computer service provider through a dial-up telephone connection. Anthony Tabell remembers how his interest in applying computers to technical analysis originated:

> In the late '50s, early '60s, one of the things that moved me personally was the use of the computer. I liked computers. I liked sitting down and writing computer programs in assembly language. But it was a natural marriage with what I was doing with technical analysis, because technical analysis is analysis of data. I can tell many stories about fighting my way through Wall Street in my efforts to merge computers with the practice of technical analysis. The whole idea of doing research on them was foreign to everyone involved with technical analysis. I'm probably one of the first people who tried to evaluate stock price returns on a

> computer, necessarily a mainframe. The PC was still twenty-five years in the future. This was an interest I pursued when my father was still alive, but I got involved in it more deeply when we started our own firm in 1970. I went out and bought a Digital Equipment PDP-11. This was to my knowledge the first computer to be 100 percent devoted to doing technical research. I regard the computer as a watershed in technical analysis.[41]

It was around the same time that computers gave rise to quantitative hedge funds, blurring the lines between technical and quantitative analysis (which would soon become a force to be reckoned with in its own right). In his 1967 book, *The Money Game*, Goodman, under the pseudonym Adam Smith, provides an entertaining account of the emergence of highly quantitative and aggressive trading on the Wall Street scene:

> I have a friend called Irwin the professor at one of our nation's leading universities who must rank as one of the top architects of computer-based technical analysis. . . . Irwin's computer system . . . is on line, real time, and all that. It is hooked up to the tickers of the New York and American stock exchanges, and it doesn't even have to read the tapes optically; it picks up the original electrical impulse which drives the stock tickers and whisks it right into the memory. . . . I wanted to know how Irwin's computer worked on the Technical side of the market. "The first thing it does is to monitor every stock transaction, the price, the volume, and the percentage move," Irwin said. "We have a Behavior Pattern for every stock. When a stock is behaving out of its pattern, the monitor flashes on."[42]
>
> "Most buying and selling is still done by individuals and institutions," Irwin said, "just as it was in the old days." (The old days to Irwin are 1962 or so, when computers were still doing only clerical chores.) "But," Irwin went on, "there are a couple of sophisticated funds that have computers like ours on the air. Then it really gets to be fun. Our computer scans the pattern of the other computer on the air, what its buying and selling programs seem to be. Once we get its pattern, we can have all kinds of fun. We can chase the stock away from it. Or even better, we can determine where the other computer wants to buy."[43]

Although in principle well developed, as late as the 1980s computer technology did not exist in a format that would make it accessible to the investment masses. Michael Bloomberg, the originator of the Bloomberg terminals, recalls how systems that would let users do even simple statistical analysis were lacking in those days. "A few large underwriting firms had internal systems that tried to fill this need, but each required a PhD to use and weren't available off the shelf to the little guy," he reminisces, and further elaborates:[44]

> Merrill wanted its traders to be able to enter a transaction and automatically update the firm's positions themselves. That wasn't a big

deal, you would think. But the only systems Merrill had for trade entry used massive, unreliable, and complex terminals that wouldn't fit on regular-size desks, much less in the typical sales-person/trader's small cubicle. They connected these terminals to a single, large mainframe without backup. This wasn't what the market needed.[45]

No one has left a bigger mark in the drive toward computerization on Wall Street than Bloomberg. In his irreverent autobiography, Michael Bloomberg describes how the situation in the 1980s led him to conceive his product:

> When it came to knowing the relative value of one security versus another, most of Wall Street in 1981 had pretty much remained where it was when I began as a clerk back in the mid-1960s: a bunch of guys using No. 2 pencils, chronicling the seat-of-the-pants guesses of too many bored traders. Something that could show instantly whether government bonds were appreciating at a faster rate than corporate bonds would make smart investors out of mediocre ones, and would create enormous competitive advantage over anyone lacking these capabilities. At a time when the U.S. budget deficit (financed by billions of dollars of new Treasury bonds and notes) was poised to explode, such a device would appeal to everyone working in finance, securities, and investments—combined, a very big potential market for my proposed product.[46]

Bloomberg not only filled that need but also exploited the computer's capabilities in other ways, such as providing integrated charting, system testing, and trading platforms, as well as making news reporting almost instantaneous. In the process he set industry-wide standards.

Although computers have become standard tools of technical analysts, they have not yet replaced them—on that, the leading practitioners of technical analysis interviewed in our book *The Heretics of Finance* unanimously agree. For example, Robert Farrell, a founder and the first president of the Market Technicians Association, who enjoyed an illustrious career at Merrill Lynch spanning the entire second half of the twentieth century, notes that technical analysis is "still a human game."[47] The Elliott wave expert Robert Prechter further elaborates: "The best thing a computer does is save plotting time. I don't think much of the analytical software programs I've seen. The market is so complex to model that you can't use equations and statistics to do it. You can only model aspects of it. I think the future will be in getting computers to recognize patterns and forms despite quantitative variation."[48]

The human eye may have a crucial advantage over computer algorithms in this endeavor. It is well known that computers still struggle with many image-recognition and classification tasks that are trivial for humans. The same may be true for the task of analyzing financial markets, something that would explain the gulf separating technical analysis—still a largely human endeavor—and quantitative financial analysis, a more analytical and algorithmic approach, and why the former practice persists despite the lack of support from the latter. If the human eye does have an advantage over computers in analyzing financial markets, the possibility is raised of using human-computer interfaces to *systematically* harness human skills for financial trading, while avoiding subjective inconsistency and emotional biases to which traditional chart reading is prone. Such an interface—think of it as a starship video game in which trajectories of the starships are given by market prices—would not necessitate the human participant to be aware of the financial context behind the patterns he or she is implicitly recognizing, or to have any financial background, for that matter.

Some of our own work, co-authored with Emanuele Viola and discussed in more detail in Chapter 4, may pave the way toward making this possibility a reality. We conducted an experiment, implemented as an online video game, in which players were challenged to distinguish actual financial market returns from random temporal permutations of those returns.[49] We found very strong statistical evidence that subjects could consistently distinguish between the two types of time series.[50] These results demonstrate that human beings can distinguish market returns from their randomized counterpart—in other words, that market returns carry a unique signature that human beings are able to detect.

Such results, coupled with the fact that human pattern recognition skills outstrip those of any known algorithm, open the door to the development of human-computer interfaces that allow us to translate certain human abilities into other domains and functional specifications. For example, with the proper interface, it may be possible to translate the hand-eye coordination of highly skilled video-gamers to completely unrelated pattern-recognition and prediction problems such as weather forecasting or financial trading. Laszlo Birinyi has warned that "more and more, because the market has changed so much, because we have hedge funds, exchange-traded funds, electronic communication networks, we find that there is no precedent" for current market conditions.[51] Interfaces, such as video games, that allow human subjects to systematically harness their own abilities to recognize, and even predict, market changes better than any computer is currently capable of doing, may prove useful in the face of the fast-evolving market environment.

Notes

1. For more information about the point-and-figure charting methods, see A. W. Cohen, *How to Use the Three-Point Reversal Method of Point and Figure Stock Market Trading* (Larchmont, NY: Chartcraft, 1968) and J. du Plessis, *The Definitive Guide to Point and Figure: A Comprehensive Guide to the Theory and Practical Use of the Point and Figure Charting Method* (Petersfield: Harriman House Publishing, 2005).
2. G. A. Chestnutt, Jr., *Stock Market Analysis: Facts and Principles* (Larchmont, NY: American Investors Corporation, 1965), 19; as quoted in R. A. Levy, *The Relative Strength Concept of Common Stock Price Forecasting* (Larchmont, NY: Investors Intelligence, 1968), 89.
3. Chestnutt, *Stock Market Analysis*, 28; as quoted in Levy, *The Relative Strength Concept*, 89–90.
4. R. W. Colby, *The Encyclopedia of Technical Market Indicators*, 2nd ed. (New York: McGraw-Hill, 2003), 177.
5. C. Kirkpatrick, "Charles Dow Looks at the Long Wave," *Journal of Technical Analysis* 57 (Winter–Spring 2002), 6–8.
6. Lo and Hasanhodzic 2009, 148.

7. C. R. Geisst, *Wall Street: A History: From Its Beginings to the Fall of Enron* (New York: Oxford University Press, 2004), 280–281.
8. E. W. Tabell and A. W. Tabell, "The Case for Technical Analysis," *Financial Analysts Journal* 20, no. 2 (March–April 1964), 67.
9. Lo and Hasanhodzic 2009, 244–245.
10. Ibid., 14–15.
11. R. Sobel, *The New Game on Wall Street* (New York: Wiley, 1987), 20.
12. *The Institutional Investor*, as quoted in J. Brooks, *The Go-Go Years* (New York: Weybright and Talley, 1973), 147.
13. I. Friend, F. E. Brown, E. S. Herman, and D. Vickers, *A Study of Mutual Funds* (Washington, DC: Government Printing Office, 1962), x–xi; as quoted in R. A. Levy, *The Relative Strength Concept*, 245.
14. Sobel, *The New Game*, 7.
15. Geisst, *Wall Street: A History*, 366–368.
16. Lo and Hasanhodzic 2009, 15–16.
17. Cf. Chapter 4.
18. Sobel, *The New Game*, 15.
19. Geisst, *Wall Street: A History*, 306.
20. Sobel, *The New Game*, 15.
21. Lo and Hasanhodzic 2009, 14.
22. Geisst, *Wall Street: A History*, 303.
23. Ibid., 305.
24. Ibid., 307.
25. Lo and Hasanhodzic 2009, 68.
26. Ibid., 146–147.
27. Geisst, *Wall Street: A History*, 308.
28. W. Christie and P. Schultz, "Why Do NASDAQ Market Makers Avoid Odd-Eighth Quotes?" *Journal of Finance* 49, no. 5 (1994), 1813–1840.
29. Geisst, *Wall Street: A History*, 368–369, 384.
30. Lo and Hasanhodzic 2009, 98.
31. Geisst, *Wall Street: A History*, 383.
32. Ibid., 370.
33. Ibid., 384.
34. Lo and Hasanhodzic 2009, 145–146.
35. D. L. Thomas, "Calculating Risks," *Barron's* XLV, no. 26 (June 28, 1965), 3, 19; as quoted in Levy, *The Relative Strength Concept*, 13.
36. Thomas, "Calculating Risks," 3, 19; as quoted in Levy, *The Relative Strength Concept*, 13.
37. R. E. Blodgett, "Wall Street Computers Begin Analyzing Stocks to Select 'Best' Buys," *The Wall Street Journal* (August 10, 1965), 1; as quoted in Levy, *The Relative Strength Concept*, 14.
38. Ibid., 144.
39. Ibid., 156.
40. Ibid., 149.
41. Ibid., 102.
42. Smith 1968, 172–173.
43. Ibid., 176.
44. Bloomberg 1997, 42.
45. Ibid., 51–52.
46. Ibid., 42.
47. Lo and Hasanhodzic 2009, xxi.
48. Ibid., 156.
49. The game is available at http://arora.ccs.neu.edu.
50. J. Hasanhodzic, A. W. Lo, and E. Viola, "Is It Real, or Is It Randomized? A Financial Turing Test". Available online at http://ssrn.com/abstract=1558149 (2010).
51. Ibid., 237.

CHAPTER 4

A Brief History of Randomness and Efficient Markets

From Andrew W. Lo and Jasmina Hasanhodzic, *The Evolution of Technical Analysis: Financial Prediction from Babylonian Tablets to Bloomberg Terminals* (Hoboken, New Jersey: John Wiley & Sons, 2010), Chapter 7.

Ever since the emergence of modern finance theory in the mid-twentieth century, the followers of technical analysis have found themselves marginalized by the financial establishment. This ostracism is partly based on misunderstanding, since the technical jargon of head-and-shoulders, wedges, and pennants sounds odd to minds steeped in physics and statistics. It is also based on great faith in the efficient markets hypothesis (EMH), an academic theory which states that in a properly functioning market, changes in market prices are fundamentally unpredictable—in a word, random—if markets are operating as they should. The EMH is based on the idea that in a frictionless competitive market with many self-interested participants, current stock market activity will reflect *all relevant factors* determining value; thus, no factors can possibly be left over that might create useful (exploitable) patterns or trends in market data, otherwise they would have been exploited already. Consequently, even though stock market activity is not *generated* randomly, to an outside observer it is *indistinguishable* from what mathematicians call a "random walk." Thus, disciples of the EMH reject out of hand the possibility of exploitable patterns in historical market prices—the very basis of technical analysis.

Despite recent proposals of alternative hypotheses, the EMH remains deeply ingrained in the culture of academic finance, a rigorous and highly mathematical discipline that has become central to the financial industry. This state of affairs stands in sharp contrast to technical analysis, which attempts to divine market direction based on past prices and volume. As we saw in the previous two chapters, this involves searching with the naked eye for certain patterns in price histories that are believed to embody the prime mover of all market action: crowd psychology.

The EMH was formally developed in the 1960s, but its roots go back much further in time. Its earliest beginnings can be traced back to the 1565 manuscript *Liber de Ludo Aleae* (*The Book of Games of Chance*) in which the prominent Italian mathematician Girolamo Cardano (1501–1576) first proposed an elementary theory of gambling. In this remarkably prescient volume, Cardano described the basic logic of the "martingale"—a precursor to the EMH—in the following way:

> The most fundamental principle of all in gambling is simply equal conditions, e.g., of opponents, of bystanders, of money, of situation, of the dice box, and of the die itself. To the extent to which you depart from that equality, if it is in your opponent's favour, you are a fool, and if in your own, you are unjust.[1]

This notion of a "fair game," a gamble that is neither in your favor nor your opponent's, has the interesting implication that the best forecast of either party's total wealth tomorrow is simply equal to today's total wealth, which sounds a lot like the EMH.

When the martingale hypothesis is applied to the prices of financial securities, some rather surprising implications follow. For example, if stock prices are a martingale, it can be mathematically proven that no linear forecasting rule based solely on historical prices can forecast future price changes—thus ruling out the efficacy of moving-average rules, regression models, trendlines, and other staples of technical analysis. Such are the sweeping statements of academic finance that have become anathema to the practicing technician.

A more modern version of the EMH originated in the mid-nineteenth century in the French popular investment literature. It was formalized mathematically by Louis Bachelier half a century later (see Chapter 5), five years before Albert Einstein proposed essentially the same model for Brownian motion, and six decades before Paul Samuelson and Eugene Fama formulated the version used today.

More recently, departures from the EMH have been documented in the behavioral finance literature, providing theoretical grounding for technical analysis and paving the way for its formalization and synthesis. Nevertheless, efforts to incorporate technical analysis into the theory of financial markets are in many ways just getting underway. This is due not only to cultural biases but also to historical limitations in areas other than finance that help bring financial ideas to fruition. In the mid-twentieth century, two theories of financial markets were proposed roughly simultaneously—Simon's theory of bounded rationality and Paul Samuelson's and Eugene Fama's theory of market efficiency. Both had merit, but only the latter had a clean mathematical representation; the former would require greater understanding of human psychology and computation that simply didn't exist at the time. Now that the notion of adaptative markets and computationally bounded algorithms are available, though not yet fully developed, reinterpreting market efficiency in computational and evolutionary terms might well be able to bridge the gap between academic finance and technical analysis.

In the next chapter we will look at some of the reasons to doubt strong interpretations of the EMH, as well as evidence supporting the methods of technical analysis and a theoretical framework in which such techniques can add value. In the present chapter we recount the rise of academic finance and how it eclipsed other approaches, including technical analysis and behavioral approaches. And because the EMH implies that the stock market's ups and downs are indistinguishable from randomness, at the end of the chapter we reexamine the very meaning of "random."

Prices as Objects of Study

As we saw in the early chapters, the history of technical analysis is inextricably tied to the history of behavioral finance—the use of social, cognitive, and emotional factors to explain and predict market activity. Such practices originated in the price diaries of the ancient Babylonians 2,700 years. They evolved through centuries and civilizations, with ancient Athenians devising price-based market sentiment measures; with medieval merchants relying on a combination of prices and planets' orbits, which they believed had an effect on human behavior, to forecast future price; and with sophisticated speculative techniques that took into account human psychology flourishing on the seventeenth-century Bourse of Amsterdam. This long, folkloristic tradition of recognizing prices as a reflection of minds and actions of people and using them to forecast the future price was formalized to some extent in the eighteenth century by Munehisa Homma in Japan and in the early twentieth century by Charles Dow and his successors in the United States, molding the legacy of times past into a distinct craft of technical analysis.

All these, however, are popular developments—practical solutions to concrete everyday problems, which were often passed on from generation to generation through word of mouth, and sometimes documented in the astronomical price diaries, newspaper articles, and merchant and investor manuals. These practices belong to the realm historians of economic thought call "low" or vernacular economics. This stands in contrast with its "high" or academic counterpart, of which the EMH is a central element. While academic economics is "a body of homogeneous, abstract, and formalized explanations of economic processes," vernacular economics "is understood to comprise heterogeneous sets of practices, know-how techniques, and rationalization procedures that help social actors make sense of their economic environment and of the economic consequences of their own actions," Preda explains.[2]

As we saw in Chapter 2, the nineteenth century witnessed a general shift in worldview toward systematic, formal modeling, and as part of this shift, the economy came to be seen as a natural, law-based system that can be mathematically rationalized. People had been recording prices since ancient times, but price had always stood on an equal footing with other types of data, such as political, climatic, and even astronomical, on which it was often superimposed with the goal of detecting causal relationships. For example, James Vansommer, the secretary of the Committee of the London Stock Exchange, in 1843 published a collection of charts in which he correlated bond price movements with political events over a 44-year period, and nineteenth-century

British geographers would routinely superimpose the prices of wheat and bonds with measures of temperature.[3] It comes as no surprise that at the time when price recording was difficult and unreliable, as was especially the case with higher frequency intraday records, prices were often tied to political events in the popular press; newsletter writers would simply add an additional column in the table of price quotations to indicate the political event that happened on a day when the price reached a particular level.[4] As Preda points out, if economic and political events occurred less frequently than price variations, they could not have explained them.[5]

But by the end of the nineteenth century prices had come to be regarded as more than just a useful lens on the market; they increasingly came to be seen as the ultimate embodiment of every possible kind of information that influenced them, including investor psychology, market sentiment, and all other behavioral factors. With the advent of technology it became possible to record and accurately disseminate prices in real time, the causal explanation of price movements fell by the wayside, and technical analysis, which stresses pure price movements, advanced.

Financial markets are to be "approached in a functionalist, not in a causal, manner," argued investment writers of that time.[6] For example, in his 1874 investor manual, *Principles of the Science of the Stock Exchange*, Henri Lefevre depicted prices themselves as autonomous, living organisms by defining them via biological analogies, as opposed to focusing on causal explanations of price movements; what mattered was "to explain the functions fulfilled by markets in the society at large":[7]

> The stock exchange is a circulation organ; its function is to make [things] circulate, not to appraise the quality of the materials submitted to its action. When you introduce poison, venom, in the veins of an animal, the heart makes it circulate through the entire organism. More or less grave disorders result, and the heart becomes a victim, but, again, its role is to produce movement, and not to make chemical analyses. This is why most criticisms of the bourse are off the mark, like the legal dispositions they pretended to impose upon [the bourse]. It will go on like that as long as we continue to believe that society is a mechanism whose movements and wheels can be controlled at will, when in fact it is a natural *organism* whose spontaneous functioning must be studied with the aim of supporting its development.[8]

In rejecting the causal explanation of price movements, the functionalists highlighted the importance of their visual representation: "The public does not need definitions and formulas; it needs images that are fixed on its mind [esprit], and with the help of which it can direct its actions. Images are the most powerful auxiliary of judgment; thus, whatever properties of a geometric figure result from its definition and are implicitly contained within, it would be impossible to extract them without the help of the eyes, that is, of images, in order to help the mind," wrote Lefevre. He further emphasized that "especially in the case of stock exchange operations, where the developments are so rapid, where the decisions must sometimes be so prompt, it matters if one has in his mind clear images instead of more or less confused formulas, because the slightest hesitation or a false movement may cause considerable damage in some cases."[9] This insistence on visualization naturally gave an impetus to technical analysis, which together with the ticker ushered in what Preda calls "cognitive standardization," where price charts serve as a standardized mode of visualization and technical analysis jargon as the standardized language of chartists.[10]

By the 1900s, technical analysis became institutionalized, with investor magazines regularly publishing detailed charts, chart rooms growing into fixtures of brokerage houses, and technical analysis jargon of head and shoulders, triangles, and rectangles becoming commonplace.[11] "This self-styled 'science of financial markets' promoted the notion that financial markets are governed by principles that are not controlled by any single individual or group," explains Preda.[12] That markets are governed by universal principles had been well recognized for hundreds of years. By the early twentieth century, this attitude was reinforced in technical analysis circles. Although big traders and bankers might be able to manipulate prices, the movements they induce were deemed only temporary, it was believed; as Nelson argued, "in the long run, it is the investor who establishes the price of a stock based on its value."[13]

Similarly, Pierre-Joseph Proudhon's realization of the ubiquitous and omniscient nature of the markets inspired him in 1854 to proclaim that restricting market operations would be absurd and even unfeasible:

> Let the press be muzzled, a tariff be put on the library, let the post be spied on, the telegraph exploited by the state, but speculation, by the anarchy that constitutes its essence, escapes all state and police regulations. To try putting a control on this last and infallible interpreter of opinions would mean to govern in the darkness of Egypt, which, according to the rabbis, was so thick that even candles and lanterns went out. How, for example, to forbid *options markets*? To forbid options markets, they should stop the oscillations of *demand* and *supply*, that is, guarantee to the trade the production, the quality, the placement, and the invariability of commodities' prices and at the same time eliminate all the aleatory conditions of the production, circulation, and consumption of goods, which is impossible and even contradictory.[14]

The popular science of financial markets provided practical solutions to everyday problems; the point was to reach the masses, not elite academic circles. But as a side effect, argues Preda, popular financial writers prepared the ground for rigorous theoretical treatment of financial markets. The EMH, he continues, was a result of a "slow evolution of popular knowledge into an academic, formalized science," not due to bursts of isolated genius.[15]

The Emergence of Efficient Markets

In describing how the movement of investing toward science led to the EMH, Preda notes that "irrational mass psychology was superseded as an explanatory variable by the informed decisions of individuals."[16] While this conclusion is largely justified given the enormous success of the EMH both in academia and in industry, it does a disservice to the technical analysts of the early twentieth century, many of whom acknowledged the forces of irrationality explicitly, and dissected these forces and developed heuristics for dealing with them. Eventually, these practical rules of thumb took on a life of their own without reference to the psychological and economic milieu that gave rise to them.

Interestingly, the EMH came to France first, where the ticker was slow to be adopted and, as a result, the uncertainty about prices was especially high. For example, in the unofficial French bond options markets, traders would often negotiate directly with each other, without an auctioneer acting as a central clearinghouse, causing conflicting prices to be posted simultaneously for the same securities and rendering detailed price charts an impossible endeavor.[17] In the absence of charts, speculators relied on abstract models to reduce market risks. While, in France, the absence of the ticker gave an impetus to theoretical models of market behavior, its presence in the United States made it possible to understand investor behavior by charting and analyzing the price data through which it was reflected.

Moreover, just as "the popular science of financial investments provided the cognitive and cultural background against which elaborate theories and models, like Louis Bachelier's [model of market efficiency], could appear" in the early twentieth century, as Preda suggests, we argue that technical analysis has provided the background against which a rigorous theory of behavioral finance could take shape.[18] When Nobel Prize–winning economist Herbert Simon in 1955 proposed his model of financial markets based on the idea of bounded rationality—according to which humans are naturally limited in their computational resources and therefore bound to make choices that are merely satisfactory and not necessarily optimal—he was not working in a vacuum. Simon's ideas were as much a product of the cognitive and cultural background in which he operated as they were of his genius; the long legacy of technical analysts lies precisely in their recognition of human inability to consistently make optimal decisions and in the heuristics they developed to deal with that inability. However, the lack of appropriate technology inhibited the materialization of Simon's ideas. Though immediately compelling—even earning Simon a Nobel Prize—his work has not yet been operationalized nor made rigorous. One possible cause was the lack of the necessary concepts in the economics and computer science literatures: The notions of adaptive markets (see Chapter 5) and computationally constrained algorithms (see below) did not exist in his time, and still have not been fully developed to this day.

Around the same time as Simon, the now-familiar ideas of market efficiency were taking shape. While Paul Samuelson and Eugene Fama are credited with this important milestone in financial economics, the notion of efficiency began taking shape in the 1950s and 1960s. For example, a British statistician by the name of Maurice G. Kendall (1953) presented a paper, *The Analysis of Economic Time-Series—Part I: Prices*, to the Royal Statistical Society, in which he insisted that "there [was] no hope of being able to predict movements on the exchange for a week ahead without extraneous information."[19] Rather, it was "almost as if once a week the Demon of Chance drew a random number from a symmetrical population of fixed dispersion and added it to the current price to determine the next week's price."[20] In other words, predicting future stock prices based on past prices alone, without insider information or knowledge of a company's fundamentals, was deemed a futile endeavor. It is from this rediscovery that the EMH stems.[21]

Also, in Paul Cootner's classic 1964 volume *The Random Character of Stock Market Prices*, a collection of academic studies by a number of prominent economists and statisticians, he summarizes Harry Roberts's (1959) motivation for the random walk model for stock prices in the following passage:

> The basic proposition depends upon a characteristic of competition in perfect markets: That participants in such a market will eliminate any profits above the bare minimum required to induce them to continue in the market, except for any profits which might accrue to someone who can exercise some degree of market monopoly. There is, for example, no reason why a trader with special information about future events cannot profit from that monopolized knowledge. On the other hand, we should not expect, in such a market, that traders could continue to profit from the use of a formula depending only upon past price data and generally available rules of "technical analysis." If this is so, all changes in prices should be independent of any past history about a company which is generally available to the trading public.[22]

This summary is a strikingly contemporary and practical view of market efficiency that anticipates Samuelson's (1965) and Fama's (1970) more formal analyses. And note that even as the EMH was being developed, disdain for technical analysis was already building!

The concept of market efficiency has a counter-intuitive and Zen-like contradictory flavor to it: the more efficient the market, the more random the sequence of price changes generated by such a market must be, and the most efficient market of all is one in which price changes are completely random and unpredictable. Unlike the motivation for Brownian motion in the physical and biological sciences—typically a weak statement of general ignorance regarding the dynamics of interactions—the motivation for randomness in financial markets is the direct outcome of many active participants attempting to profit from their information. Unable to curtail their greed, an army of investors aggressively pounces on even the smallest informational advantages at their disposal, and in doing so, they impound their information into market prices and quickly eliminate the profit opportunities that gave rise to their actions. If this occurs instantaneously, which it must in an idealized world of "frictionless" markets and costless trading, then prices must always fully reflect all available information and no profits can be garnered from information-based trading (because such profits have already been captured).

With the benefit of hindsight and the theoretical insights of LeRoy (1973) and Lucas (1973), it is now clear that efficient markets and the random walk hypothesis are two distinct ideas, neither one necessary nor sufficient for the other. The reason for this distinction comes from one of the central ideas of modern financial economics: the necessity of some trade-off between risk and expected return. If a security's expected price change is positive, it may be just the reward needed to attract investors to hold the asset and bear the corresponding risks. Indeed, if an investor is sufficiently risk averse, he might gladly *pay* to avoid holding a security that has unforecastable returns. In such a world, prices do not need to be perfectly random, even if markets are operating efficiently and rationally.[23]

Cootner and the other early contributors can hardly be faulted for not appreciating the distinction between efficient markets and the random walk. By itself, the notion of market efficiency is not a well-posed and empirically refutable hypothesis. To make it operational, we must specify additional structure, such as investors' preferences, the information they each possess, their current financial circumstances, and so on. But then a test of market efficiency becomes a test of several auxiliary hypotheses as well, and a rejection of such a joint hypothesis tells us little about which aspect of the joint hypothesis is inconsistent with the data. The hypothesis that investors are fully rational agents that instantaneously and correctly process all available information is clearly unrealistic—rationality is difficult to define, human behavior is often unpredictable, information can be difficult to interpret, technology and institutions change constantly, and there are significant "frictional" costs to gathering and processing information, and to transacting. But how can we take all the complexities of the real world into account? We tackle this issue in the next chapter. Before doing so, however, we take a short detour to review the historical origins of randomness, a concept that is central not only to quantitative finance, but also to the skepticism surrounding technical analysis.

What Is Random?

The concept of randomness is directly related to the evolution of the probability theory, and here again, popular science paved the way for its academic counterpart. The nineteenth-century popular financial writer Henri Lefevre was also an inventor of instruments for conducting probabilistic calculations for gamblers, such as the *autocompteur*, his 1871 creation intended as an aid in horse-race betting.[24] Probabilistic modeling was not limited to gambling outcomes, but was also applied to financial speculation with the aim of reducing the risks and making it more acceptable to investors. As Preda points out, "While investor behavior was reduced to decisions according to certain given situations, decisions were reduced to calculations. In order to decide, the investor needs to compute possible outcomes."[25] Lefevre, for example, in addition to his horse-race gambling device, also invented the "abacus of the speculator," a wooden board divided into squares and equipped with movable letters, where by moving the letters one could see the outcomes of decisions for different options contracts.[26] And in his 1891 business manual *The Mathematical Theory of Long-Term Investing*, Adolphe Pierre Brasilier presented a framework in which French corporate bonds were to be treated as a lottery problem because of their structure—periodically a certain number of bonds would be drawn by lottery and reimbursed at a premium above the issue price, and the rest of the bonds would continue to receive interest until the next drawing date—and analyzed Parisian bonds from 1855 to 1860 in that framework.[27]

Using past prices, business manuals also suggested computing the probabilities that the securities would attain certain price levels in the future. One method was to take the difference between the yield of a given security and the state bond yield—the latter was used as a reference point because it was guaranteed and slow varying; then, based on past variations of these differences, future variations were predicted.[28] As the probability theory was making the inroads into the analysis of price fluctuations, it provoked hot debates in the investor manuals, such as the 1854 *La Bourse de Paris*:

> I do not know about the power of probabilistic calculus applied to the operations of the stock exchange, but I know that Condorcet and the Marquis of Laplace failed on all their calculations on the probability of moral events, on judgments on a plurality of votes, and on the results of parliamentary votes. A moral event depends on a thousand unknown causes that cannot be submitted to any calculus. If we would want to try our fortune by some calculus, the method of the Viscount Saint-André would be better. The Marquis of Laplace has made a science out of probability calculus. This science can be applied to life insurance, to ship insurance; it has a basis in the mortality tables and the number of ships that are stranded every year, but it is impossible to find it in the lows and highs of bonds. What produces the movements of these bonds is as variable as the golden arrow on the palace of the bourse.[29]

The credit for the first formal study of the mathematics of probability belongs to the same Italian mathematician who gave us the martingale, Girolamo Cardano. His treatise *Liber de Ludo Aleae* went far beyond simple games of chance, and also contained many of the basic concepts of formal probability theory. As was the case with many of his contemporaries, Cardano's interest in this subject was sparked by his passion for gambling; he believed that there was a sense in which, when throwing a pair of dice, some numbers were more likely to come up than others, and that he could use this insight to make money. However, the addiction for gambling proved stronger than his rationality, apparently driving him to squander the money his family had left him, and, on one occasion, cutting with a knife the opponent whom he thought had cheated at cards.

A century later the study of probability was taken over by the French. Chevalier de Méré, another gambler, devised in 1654 a system for gambling which he thought would win him money; when it did not, he asked the mathematician Blaise Pascal (1623–1662) why. After some analysis, Pascal noticed that, in fact, Chevalier's system would lose more often than not. This event fostered Pascal's interest in probability theory, leading to an intense correspondence with Pierre de Fermat (1601–1665) which laid the foundations of probability theory. After having learned of this correspondence, a Dutch scientist, Christiaan Huygens, published *De Ratiociniis in Ludo Aleae*, the first book on probability. The theory was further developed in the seventeenth and eighteenth centuries by Daniel Bernoulli and Abraham de Moivre. Then in 1812 Pierre de Laplace published his *Théorie Analytique des Probabilités*, which, unlike previous works, did not focus on games of chance but developed a general theory of probability applicable to many practical problems, even catching the eye of Napoleon.

According to Laplace's notion of probability—which we term the "classical approach to randomness"—a certain probability is assigned to each possible outcome of an experiment. For example, when tossing a coin, heads has probability 1/2, and tails has the same. Classical probability theory develops many sophisticated ways to compute these probabilities, but at the core is the underlying assumption that the outcomes of experiments have certain inherent or fundamental probabilities: The fact that heads has probability 1/2 is axiomatic, and the theory allows us to compute more complicated probabilities, such as that of obtaining heads 10 times in a row, which is $(1/2).^{10}$

This classical notion of probability is used today in nearly every branch of science. However, it is in some sense unsatisfactory because it does not capture people's intuitive notion of "random." This is best understood by considering the following paradox. Suppose a friend tells you: "I have tossed a die 10 times and I have gotten 6, 6, 6, 6, 6, 6, 6, 6, 6, 6." You would probably think he is lying, or that he was using a nonstandard die. But what if the same friend tells you: "I have tossed a die 10 times and I have gotten 1, 3, 4, 3, 6, 2, 5, 4, 2, 5"? You would probably harbor no suspicions about that sequence; it "looks random." Intuitively, the second sequence of outcomes looks more random than the first. The paradox is that, according to the classical theory of probability, both sequences have the same probability: $(1/6)^{10} = 0.00000001653\ldots$. Thus, the classical notion of randomness does not match human intuition.

A solution to this paradox had to wait until the beginning of the twentieth century, when what we refer to as "the ontological approach to randomness" emerged. The idea is to note that 6, 6, 6, 6, 6, 6, 6, 6, 6, 6 is very regular—it is the repetition of the number 6—whereas the second sequence, 1, 3, 4, 3, 6, 2, 5, 4, 2, 5, appears irregular. The ontological approach to randomness declares a sequence of outcomes random if the outcomes are not regular. This notion is indeed ontological because it refers to a quality that is intrinsic to an object: A fixed string can be random or not. At first sight, it seems problematic to make sense of this approach, since it is not clear what "regular" may mean. One person might see regularity in 2, 3, 5, 7, 11, 13, recognizing the sequence of prime numbers, but others may not. Arbitrarily complicated regularity may be created. Thus, how can we be sure that the second sequence our friend shows us—1, 3, 4, 3, 6, 2, 5, 4, 2, 5—is indeed random?

To answer this question, one needs a precise definition of "regular." This definition was made possible in the first half of the twentieth century with the development of computer science. The work of Gödel (1931), Church (1936), Kleene (1936), Post (1936), and Turing (1937) gave strong evidence that computers form a universal language in which every possible regularity can be programmed (this is known as the Church-Turing thesis). This computational framework is central to the ontological definition of randomness, which appeared in the 1960s, most notably in the works of Ray Solomonoff (1960, 1964) and Andrey Kolmogorov (1965).[30]

According to this theory, we consider a string regular, and so nonrandom, if there is a way to generate the string with a computer program that is shorter than the string itself; in other words, the program is "compressing" the string. For example, the 20-character string 6, 6, 6, 6, 6, 6, 6, 6, 6, 6, 6, 6, 6, 6, 6, 6, 6, 6, 6, 6 is nonrandom because the computer program "Print '6' 20 times" generates it and is much shorter than the string itself. Conversely, the string 1, 3, 4, 3, 6, 2, 5, 4, 2, 5, 2, 6, 4, 4, 3, 2, 1, 4, 2, 3 is random because the shortest computer program generating it is "Print 1, 3, 4, 3, 6, 2, 5, 4, 2, 5, 2, 6, 4, 4, 3, 2, 1, 4, 2, 3," which contains the string inside it and in particular is longer than the string it outputs. The shorter the computer program generating the string, the more regular and less random the string is.

The need for a third definition of randomness is clear. Modern computer systems routinely need large amounts of random numbers to carry through simulations of probabilistic models in a variety of fields including finance, physics, and biology—a paradigm known as Monte Carlo simulation. Moreover, the explosion of electronic commerce also requires a large quantity of random numbers, which are used to encrypt our credit card numbers every time we make a purchase online. As it turns out, neither the classical definition of random nor the ontological one are of much use to generate these numbers. The classical definition of random gives no way to generate randomness, but rather assumes that certain experiments, such as tossing a coin, have random outcomes; certainly we don't expect computers to toss coins to obtain random numbers. Even other experiments whose outcomes are believed to be random, for example, those involving radioactive decay, usually cannot be performed sufficiently fast by computers to be of use in applications (though sometimes they are used as the starting point or "seed" for the procedures we describe in Note 31); today we use procedures, or algorithms, that quickly output a stream of pseudorandom numbers. The ontological approach to randomness does not help either in this enterprise: It declares a string to be random precisely when there is no way to generate it using a computer program!

The way around this is given by what we call the modern or "behavioral" approach to randomness. This approach comes with a twist on our original question: Rather than asking what "is" random, we should ask what "looks" random. We have already encountered an example of how such a reformulation could make a difference. A mathematician could spot the prime numbers in the sequence 2, 3, 5, 7, 11, 13, and because of this regularity would deem the sequence to be nonrandom. But somebody who is not familiar with prime numbers might very well think of this sequence as random; the sequence may not be random, but looks random to him.[31]

This behavioral perspective on randomness suggests that a more direct "test" of the efficacy of technical analysis might be to ask whether humans can distinguish actual market data from randomly generated numbers. Now this is a horse race that technicians should care about!

The conviction that humans cannot distinguish market returns from randomly generated ones is widespread.[32] It is clearly at odds with technicians, who study past returns with the aim of forecasting future returns—a task that is impossible for randomly generated returns and, therefore, should not be possible for market returns either.

As we briefly discussed in Chapter 3, in an experimental study co-authored by us and Emanuele Viola, we test this simple hypothesis by recruiting human subjects to play a Web-based video game (http://arora.ccs.neu.edu) in which individuals are shown two dynamic price series side by side, both evolving in real time (a new price is realized each second)—but only one of which is a "replay" of actual historical price series, the other series being constructed from a random shuffling of the actual series (see Figure 4.1).[33] On each trial, subjects are asked to press a button indicating which price series they think is the real one, and they are given immediate feedback as to whether they were correct or incorrect. In a sample of 78 subjects participating in up to 8 different contests (using different types of financial data), with each contest lasting two weeks and concluding with prizes awarded to top performers, we obtained 8,015 human-generated guesses for this real-time choice problem. The results provided overwhelming statistical evidence (less than 1 percent probability of the findings being generated by pure chance) that humans can quickly learn to distinguish actual price series from randomly generated ones.

This experiment can be viewed as the financial version of the Turing test, an idea proposed by Alan Turing (1950) for deciding whether a computer program can be considered truly intelligent. In Turing's scenario, a human subject interacts with two other agents—one machine, one human—via written correspondence; the computer will have passed the test if the subject cannot correctly identify which correspondent is artificial. To date, no computer has passed the Turing test. Similarly, our video-game experiments show that financial markets have not passed the financial Turing test either, which is encouraging news for technical analysis.

The financial Turing test is just one example of how computer science can change the way we think about economics and finance. More broadly, the notion of

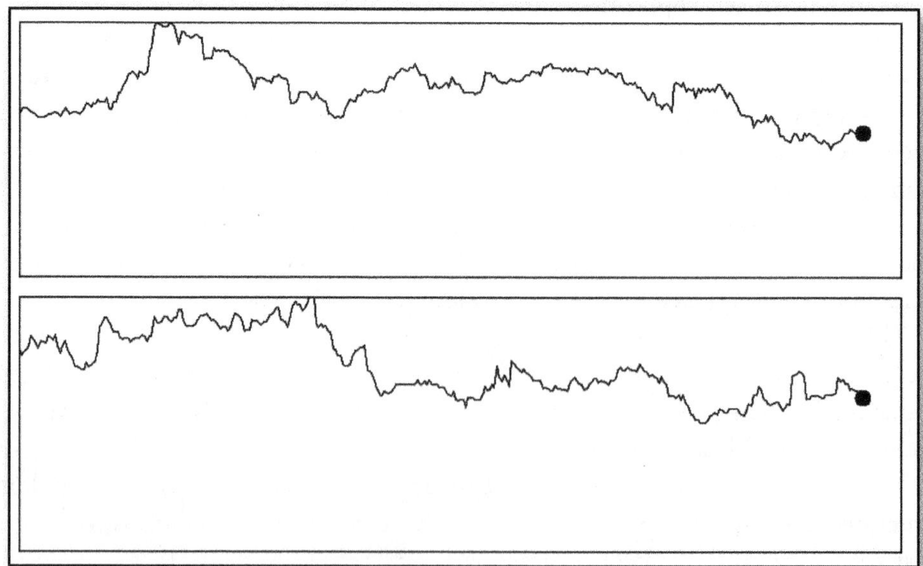

FIGURE 4.1 Real and Simulated Financial Prices—Can You Tell Which One Is Which? See Note 34 for the Answer.

computationally bounded algorithms may be an important missing piece in Simon's theory of bounded rationality. Although there are many early examples of scientists distinguishing between "efficient" and "inefficient" algorithms—where efficiency is now used in a completely different sense than the EMH—it was not until the 1960s that Cobham (1964), Edmonds (1965), and Hartmanis and Stearns (1965), as part of the early development of computational complexity theory, identified the class of computationally bounded algorithms today known simply as "P" (for polynomial-time algorithm).[35] To model Simon's bounded rationality, we need to understand what can be computed efficiently; in other words, how good a decision can be made in a limited amount of time and/or with a limited amount of memory. This amounts to understanding what algorithms lie in P. Although the class P was put forth already in the 1960s, its understanding still baffles researchers to this day.

The study of the power of algorithms that use limited resources has proved a daunting task that has arguably seen very little progress. It is, in fact, one of the seven "millennium problems" for which the Clay Mathematics Institute offers a prize of one million dollars to the first person to come up with a solution. Undoubtedly, progress in the theory of bounded rationality in economics will go hand-in-hand with the progress in the theory of computationally bounded algorithms. And tagging right along will be the analytical future of technical analysis.

Notes

1. O. Ore, *Cardano: The Gambling Scholar, with a Translation from the Latin of Cardano's Book on Games of Chance by Sydney Henry Gould*, Princeton: Princeton University Press, 1953.
2. Preda 2004, 354.
3. Ibid., 367–368, footnote 12.
4. Ibid., 370–371.
5. Ibid., 371.
6. Preda 2004, 371. Over a century later, the functional approach to finance has become a reality with R. Merton and Z. Bodie, 1993, "Deposit Insurance Reform: A Functional Approach", Carnegie-Rochester Conference Series on Public Policy 38, 1–34, and R. Merton and Z. Bodie, 1995, "Financial Infrastructure and Public Policy: A Functional Perspective", in D. Crane, K. Froot, S. Mason, A. Perold, R. Merton, Z. Bodie, E. Sirri, and P. Tufano, 1995, *The Global Financial System: A Functional Perspective* (Boston, MA: Harvard Business School Press), Chapter 8.
7. Preda 2004, 371.
8. H. Lefevre, *Principes de la science de la Bourse: Méthode approuvée par la chamber syndical des agents de change de la Bourse* [Principles of the science of the stock exchange: A method approved by the Union of Stock Brokers] (Paris: Publications de l'Institut Polytechnique, 1874), 13; as quoted in Preda 2004, 371.
9. H. Lefevre, *Traité des valeurs mobilières et des operations de Bourse: Placement et speculation* [Treatise of financial securities and stock exchange operations] (Paris: E. Lachaud, 1870), 184–185; as quoted in Preda 2004, 372.
10. Preda 2002, 27.
11. Preda 2004, 368.
12. Ibid., 360.
13. As quoted in Schultz and Coslow, *A Treasury*, 34.

14. P.-J. Proudhon, *Manuel du spéculateur à la Bourse* (Paris: Garnier frères, 1854), 31; as quoted in Preda 2004, 375.
15. Preda 2004, 356.
16. Ibid., 363.
17. Ibid., 367.
18. Ibid., 380.
19. M. G. Kendall and A. Bradford Hill, "The Analysis of Economic Time Series Part I: Prices," *Journal of the Royal Statistical Society* 116, no. 1 (1953), 11–34, 11.
20. Ibid., 13.
21. R. A. Brealey and S. C. Myers, *Principles of Corporate Finance* (New York: McGraw Hill Higher Education, 2000), 354.
22. P. H. Cootner, ed., *The Random Character of Stock Market Prices* (Cambridge, MA: MIT Press, 1964).
23. Although this distinction between efficient markets and the random walk may seem to be a subtle one, it underscores an important current in the finance literature that has become even more pronounced today—the increasing gulf between purely statistical and mathematical models of financial markets (now known as "mathematical finance"), and models firmly grounded in economic theory. Classic examples of the latter approach are the equilibrium models of Sharpe (1964) and Lintner (1965) in which risk and expected return are related to each other through the forces of supply and demand—expected return being the necessary reward to cause investors to bear undiversifiable risk. It is notable and curious that Cootner did not see fit to include either of these papers in his volume, and it is one of the few gaps in the volume's coverage of the most important research topics of that era. Indeed, although many of the chapters make oblique references to risk aversion, the dynamics of buyers and sellers, and market competition, it is apparent that the notion of an equilibrium trade-off between risk and expected return was still in its embryonic stages. The more typical world view was the kind espoused by Bachelier (1900) in his doctoral dissertation in which he developed the mathematics and statistics of Brownian motion without delving into the economic underpinnings.
24. Preda 2004, 352.
25. Ibid., 362–363.
26. Ibid., 374.
27. Ibid., 379.
28. Ibid., 377.
29. A. G. de Mériclet, *La Bourse de Paris: Moeurs, anecdotes, speculations, et conseils* (Paris: D. Giraud, 1854), 88–89; as quoted in Preda 2004, 377.
30. See also M. Li and P. Vitanyi, *An Introduction to Kolmogorov Complexity and Its Applications* (New York: Springer Verlag, 2008).
31. This twist is closely related to the development, in the second half of the twentieth century, of computational complexity theory, which is the study of what can be solved by a computer in a limited amount of time. A striking outcome of recent research is that (assuming widely believed conjectures) it is possible to generate strings that look random for all practical purposes, in the sense that no human being nor computer could tell the strings apart from coin tosses in less than, say, a billion years. In other words, the task of distinguishing one of these strings from a hypothetical string made of truly random coin tosses is infeasible for computers, even in an astronomical amount of time. Such are the strings used in all computer systems mentioned before, such as Monte Carlo simulations or online purchases; their adequacy for these simulations precisely relies on the fact that no computer can tell them apart from coin tosses. The computer will behave as if it were tossing coins to obtain random numbers. See also O. Goldreich, *Foundations of Cryptography: Volume 1, Basic Tools* (Cambridge: Cambridge University Press, 2001).
32. For example, Malkiel (1973) discusses an experiment in which students were asked to generate returns by tossing fair coins, which yielded observations that were apparently indistinguishable from market returns (p. 143). Kroll, Levy, and Rapoport (1988) conduct an experiment of a portfolio selection problem, where 40 subjects are asked to choose between two assets whose

returns are sampled randomly and independently from normal distributions, and given the option of viewing the assets' past return series. The authors find that "even in the extreme case of our experiment, where the subjects were instructed and could actually verify that the stock price changes were random, many of them still developed, maintained for a while, discarded, and generated new hypothesis about nonexistent trends" (p. 409). The same conclusions are reached by De Bondt (1993), who in a series of experiments about forecasting stock prices and exchange rates, including what he calls a "technical analysis game," finds that "people are prone to discover 'trends' in past prices and to expect their continuation," even when "stock prices changes are highly unpredictable" as is the case over short horizons (p. 357). Similar experiments were reported in Roberts (1959), Keogh and Kasetty (2003), and Swedroe (2005), and summarized in Warneryd (2001).

33. Shuffling the actual historical price series preserves the marginal distribution of the returns but eliminates any time-series properties, effectively creating a random walk for prices.
34. Gold spot price tick data (1–60 sec.), June–October 2009. Real data is in the top panel. See also Hasanhodzic, Lo, and Viola (2009).
35. For an introduction to this exciting active area of research see J. E. Hopcroft and J. D. Ullman, *Introduction to Automata Theory, Languages and Computation* (Reading, MA: Addison-Wesley Publishing Company, 1979); M. Sipser, *Introduction to the Theory of Computation* (Boston: PWS Publishing Company, 1997); O. Goldreich, *Computational Complexity: A Conceptual Perspective* (New York: Cambridge University Press, 2008); S. Arora and B. Barak, *Computational Complexity: A Modern Approach* (New York: Cambridge University Press, 2009).

CHAPTER 5

Academic Approaches to Technical Analysis

From Andrew W. Lo and Jasmina Hasanhodzic, *The Evolution of Technical Analysis: Financial Prediction from Babylonian Tablets to Bloomberg Terminals* (Hoboken, New Jersey: John Wiley & Sons, 2010), Chapter 8.

Big strides have been made toward the standardization of technical analysis in recent years.[1] The impetus for statistically evaluating technical analysis naturally comes from academia, with studies yielding evidence of its validity in wide-ranging areas, such as moving averages (Brock, Lakonishok, and LeBaron, 1992), genetic algorithms to discover optimal trading rules (Neely, Weller, and Dittmar, 1997), and the Dow theory (Brown, Goetzmann, and Kumar, 1998), to name a few. In their quest to quantify technical analysis, academics have turned, too, to the most controversial of its techniques: geometric patterns. Finding patterns in price charts is a subjective endeavor that relies on the natural smoothing filter of the human eye (which, needless to say, is vastly more sophisticated than a moving average); therefore, a main challenge in quantifying the patterns lies in modeling the way in which eyes smooth the data they view. Academics such as Chang and Osler (1994) and Lo, Mamaysky, and Wang (2000) take on this challenge by smoothing the data using statistical filtering techniques. They then develop algorithms to automatically identify technical patterns in those data and finally evaluate the information content of the patterns thus found; these works, too, find proof of the potential value of technical analysis.

In this chapter we survey these and other relevant works. Our purpose is to review the main trends rather than provide an all-inclusive encyclopedia of academic research.

Theoretical Underpinnings

While the idea that stock market prices follow a random walk was anticipated in the nineteenth-century popular investment literature by French authors such as Henri Lefevre, the steps toward its mathematical formalization were first made in 1900 by the French graduate student Louis Bachelier (1870–1946) in his doctoral dissertation, *Théorie de la Spéculation*. Unfortunately, the dissertation, now deemed the "origin of mathematical finance," fell into oblivion until the statistician L.J. Savage rediscovered his thesis and contacted Paul A. Samuelson, who immediately recognized its significance.[2]

As we saw in Chapter 3, a great deal of research has been devoted ever since to formulating theoretically the efficient market hypothesis, building up market efficiency—the idea that "prices fully reflect all available information"—into one of the most important concepts in economics. Since Samuelson's and Fama's landmark papers, many others extended their original framework, yielding a "neoclassical" version of the efficient market hypothesis, where price changes, properly weighted by aggregate marginal utilities, must be unforecastable.[3] In markets where, according to Lucas (1978), all investors have "rational expectations," prices do fully reflect all available information and marginal-utility-weighted prices follow martingales. Market efficiency has been extended in many other directions, including the incorporation of nontraded assets such as human capital, state-dependent preferences, heterogeneous investors, asymmetric information, and transaction costs.[4] But the general thrust is the same: Individual investors form expectations rationally, markets aggregate information efficiently, and equilibrium prices incorporate all available information instantaneously.[5]

But the EMH is not the unassailable edifice it is often made out to be. For example, consider situations of asymmetric information. It has been argued that even if market inefficiencies could be induced by asymmetric informedness of market participants, they would be instantly eliminated. In Fischer Black's (1986) presidential address to the American Finance Association, he argued that financial market prices were subject to "noise," which could temporarily create inefficiencies that would ultimately be eliminated through intelligent investors competing against each other to generate profitable trades. Since then, many authors have modeled financial markets by hypothesizing two types of traders—informed and uninformed—where informed traders have private information better reflecting the true economic value of a security, and uninformed traders have no information at all, but merely trade for liquidity needs.[6] In this context, Grossman and Stiglitz (1980) suggest that market efficiency is impossible because if markets were truly efficient, there would be no incentive for investors to gather private information and trade, and DeLong et al. (1990, 1991) provide a more detailed analysis in which certain types of uninformed traders can destabilize market prices for periods of time even in the presence of informed traders.[7]

More direct evidence against the EMH and in favor of technical analysis emerged in the work of Treynor and Ferguson (1985), who show that it is not only the past prices, but the past prices plus some valuable nonpublic information, that can lead to profit. A more basic challenge to market efficiency was proposed by Lo and MacKinlay (1988), who strongly reject the efficient market hypothesis for weekly stock market returns by using a simple volatility-based specification test.

Empirical Evaluation

The early empirical testing of the EMH turned out in its favor, though this was as much due to the cultural attitudes toward technical analysis as to the scientific results. For example, in their important study, Fama and Blume (1966) investigate whether one can exploit the degree of dependence between successive price changes of individual securities by following a mechanical trading rule. Independence here refers to a situation where successive price changes are independent in a probabilistic sense. For example, if today's price is higher than yesterday's, that makes it neither more nor less likely for tomorrow's price to be higher than today's. If, on the other hand, a positive price change increases the likelihood of observing a positive (negative) price change in the future, that is called positive (negative) dependence. The trading rule they consider is known as Alexander's filter technique, and they measure its profitability by comparing its expected returns to those of a passive buy-and-hold strategy. More precisely, in their 1966 paper, "Filter Rules and Stock-Market Trading," Fama and Blume investigate whether the random walk model of price movements is meaningful from an investor's viewpoint. They start by noting that the degree of dependence between successive price changes of individual securities may simultaneously be meaningful to some and insignificant to others—it all depends on the specific case. For example, for an investor, the independence assumption becomes meaningful if it can make expected profits from some mechanical trading rule greater than those of a buy-and-hold strategy.

With this in mind, the authors evaluate Alexander's filter technique, a mechanical trading rule developed by Sidney Alexander to test whether or not prices move in trends. According to the filter of size *x* percent, if the daily closing price of a particular security moves up at least *x* percent, one buys and holds the security until its price moves down at least *x* percent from a subsequent high, at which time one sells and goes short and maintains the short position until the price moves up at least *x* percent above a subsequent low, at which time one covers and buys.

The authors apply Alexander's filter technique to a series of daily closing prices for each of the individual securities of the Dow Jones Industrial Average from 1956 to 1962 using various values for *x*. They find that even when the commissions are omitted, the average returns from the filter rules are inferior to the returns from the buy-and-hold strategy. This stands in contrast to the findings of Alexander, who, according to the authors, wrongly concluded that the filter rule was superior to the buy-and-hold rule. The reason for his misinterpretation lies in his improper adjustment for dividends, Fama and Blume explain. They also point out that even if the filter technique were restricted to the more profitable long positions, it would not consistently outperform the buy-and-hold strategy, and that, naturally, the inclusion of commissions further emphasizes the superiority of the buy-and-hold strategy.

Fama and Blume hence conclude that "even on extremely close scrutiny" the results "[do] not yield evidence of dependence."[8]

The authors do find, however, that slight amounts of both positive and negative dependence are present in the price changes. Specifically, for the filter sizes of 0.5 percent, 1.0 percent, and 1.5 percent, the average returns per security on long positions are greater than the average return from buy-and-hold, and the average losses on short positions are smaller than the gains from buy-and-hold. The opposite is true for filter sizes that are larger than 1.5 percent and smaller than 5 percent, constituting evidence for positive dependence in very small movements of stock prices and for the negative dependence in the intermediate movements. However, the authors deemphasize this evidence by arguing that the degree of the dependences is so small that it is easily offset by the transaction costs, making it impossible, even for a floor trader, to profit from the filter rule. Since the marginal transaction costs of the floor trader are the minimum trading costs, the authors again conclude that the market is indeed efficient and that, even from an investor's viewpoint, the random walk model is an adequate description of the price behavior. Such conclusions rule out the possibility that technical analysts, whose principal assumption is that past prices contain information for predicting future returns, can add value to the investment process. Consequently, for a long time technical analysis has been largely discredited in the academic world, with Burton G. Malkiel, the author of the influential *A Random Walk Down Wall Street* (1973), concluding that "under scientific scrutiny, chart-reading must share a pedestal with alchemy."

To this day many academics remain critical of the discipline. However, an increasing number of studies suggest, either directly or indirectly, that "technical analysis may well be an effective means for extracting useful information from market prices."[9] A growing number of finance academics are coming to recognize that efficient markets are not an adequate model of reality. Thus, a crack in the door has been opened for academic considerations of technical analysis.

An early (though in its time largely ignored) study by Granger and Morgenstern (1963) finds that the random walk model ignores the possibly important low-frequency (long-run) components of the time series of stock market prices. Specifically, in their 1963 paper, "Spectral Analysis of New York Stock Market Prices," Granger and Morgenstern test how well the random walk model fits the specified sample of New York Stock Exchange prices and also promote the idea that "the most appropriate statistical techniques to be used [in the analysis of stock market data] are the recently developed spectral methods."[10] Spectral analysis, in this case, refers to a statistical procedure known as the Fourier transform, which, loosely speaking, decomposes a time series into cycles of different frequencies. This procedure is used to obtain a frequency spectrum of the time series—its representation in the frequency domain—which shows how much of the series lies within different frequency bands over a range of frequencies.

The authors start by suggesting that the random walk model may ignore the possibly important low-frequency (long-run) components of the time series. For example, let $\{X_t\}$ denote a time series of prices generated by a random walk model, ω a small frequency value, and a some constant term. Then, the first differences of $\{X_t\}$

are virtually indistinguishable from the first differences of $\{Y_t\}$, where $Y_t = X_t + a\cos(\omega t)$, even though the latter contains a low-frequency (long-run) component specified by a cosine of a small ω. The authors then test whether their data contain long-run components of greater importance than the random walk hypothesis would imply. They hence estimate the frequency spectrum of the data and compare them to the expected spectrum if the random walk hypothesis were true. They find that, while most of the frequency bands of the estimated spectra parallel their expected counterparts, certain bands are significantly greater than what the random walk model would lead us to expect. The authors conclude that the random walk model, "although extremely successful in explaining most of the spectral shape, does not adequately explain the strong long-run (24 months or more) components of the series."[11]

The controversy of the EMH in the theoretical literature has also paved the way for more direct studies of the validity of various technical analysis techniques and systems: The natural starting point was the most readily quantifiable of them, such as technical trading systems and moving averages. For example, Pruitt and White (1988) test the performance of a technical trading system and conclude that it does better than a simple buy-and-hold strategy to an extent that could not be attributed to chance alone.

And in their 1992 paper, "Simple Technical Trading Rules and the Stochastic Properties of Stock Returns," Brock, Lakonishok, and LeBaron test "two of the simplest and most popular trading rules"—moving average and trading range break—based on the data of the Dow Jones Index from 1897 to 1986. Two moving average varieties are considered: the "variable length moving average," which initiates buy (sell) signals when the short moving average is above (below) the long moving average by an amount larger than the specified band, and the "fixed length moving average," which initiates buy (sell) signals when the short moving average cuts the long moving average from below (above) and keeps that position for the next 10 days. In a trading range break-out rule, a buy (sell) signal is generated when the price penetrates the resistance (support) level, as defined by a local maximum (minimum). It is found that the buy signals select periods with higher conditional returns and lower volatilities, while the sell signals select periods with lower conditional returns and higher volatilities; the fact that the higher returns for buys do not arise during riskier periods indicates that the difference in returns between buys and sells is not easily explained by risk.

Overall, these results indicate that the technical rules explored do possess some predictive power. Consistently, buy (sell) signals provided by the trading rules generate returns that are higher (lower) than unconditional returns. Moreover, the returns generated from the buy and sell signals are unlikely to be generated by the random walk or other popular null models, suggesting that the empirical foundations of the EMH may not be as strong as is generally believed.

Attention turned next to the most controversial of technical analytic practices, chart-pattern reading, for patterns are the most subjective and hardest to quantify of technical indicators. One of the first rigorous studies of patterns was initiated by Charles Kirkpatrick, who convinced his then employer, Arthur Little Corporation, to hire Robert Levy to conduct the study. The results are summarized in Levy's 1971 paper, "The Predictive Significance of Five-Point Chart Patterns." Studying 32 possible forms of five-point chart patterns in the daily closing prices of 548 New York Stock Exchange securities from 1964 to 1969, Levy finds that after accounting for transaction costs none of the patterns show profitable forecasting ability. He concedes that changing the parameters of his pattern definitions and the type of data on which they are based, and most significantly specifying patterns not only in terms of price but also in terms of volume, may alter the conclusions.

The next important step in this direction was made by Chang and Osler, who in their pioneering work, "Evaluating Chart-Based Technical Analysis: The Head-and-Shoulders Pattern in Foreign Exchange Markets," evaluate the predictive power of the head-and-shoulders pattern using daily dollar exchange rates of the dollar vs. the yen, mark, Canadian dollar, Swiss franc, French franc, and pound during what at the time constituted the entire floating rate period, from March 1973 to June 1994. Chang and Osler's head-and-shoulders pattern identification algorithm starts by tracing out a zigzag pattern in the data, then scans the thus smoothed data for the evidence of the defining characteristics of the head-and-shoulders pattern (see Chapter 3). Importantly, the position is entered after the breaking of the neckline and exited when a new peak or a new trough is reached, and the profits are calculated as the gain or loss between entry and exit. The results indicate that the profits are significantly greater than what a random walk model would suggest, albeit only for the mark and the yen. Nonetheless, this suggests that the head-and-shoulders pattern has some predictive power. The authors also note that while profitable for the mark and the yen, the head-and-shoulders pattern is "extremely risky." Namely, the standard deviation of returns across positions ranged from 2 to 4 times the mean return. However, Chang and Osler argue that it is still likely that investors would find the profits from the head-and-shoulders pattern attractive in the context of a diversified portfolio, given that they are often more concerned with systematic risk than with absolute risk.

Further work in the pattern quantification was done by Lo, Mamaysky, and Wang (2000), who in an attempt to transform the "art" of technical analysis into more of a science, propose in their paper, "Foundations of Technical Analysis: Computational Algorithms, Statistical Inference, and Empirical Implementation," an algorithm which aims to formalize and automate the highly subjective and controversial practice of detecting, with the naked eye, the geometric patterns that appear in price charts and are believed to have predictive value. They start by recognizing that the evolution of prices over time is not random, but that it contains certain regularities or patterns, and they then attempt to identify, or extract, these nonlinear patterns from the historical time series of prices. Here it is important to realize that identifying patterns directly from the raw price data would not be sensible. When professional technicians study a price chart, their eyes naturally smooth the data, while their cognitive faculties discern regularities. Moreover, many would argue that much of this process takes place on an intuitive and subconscious level, making it even harder to quantify. Hence, natural candidates for modeling the process by which technicians look for patterns in a price chart are pattern-recognition techniques known as smoothing estimators, which estimate nonlinear relationships by averaging the data in sophisticated ways to reduce the observational errors. In particular, Lo, Mamaysky, and Wang (2000) automate technical analysis using a smoothing estimator known as kernel regression.

In an attempt to answer the question of whether or not this aspect of technical analysis "works," they apply kernel regression to the daily returns of individual NYSE/AMEX and Nasdaq stocks from 1962 to 1996. The kernel regression function is then analyzed for the occurrence of each of the 10 technical patterns under consideration in the experiment: head-and-shoulders, triangles, rectangles, broadening and double formations, and their inverse or "bottom" counterparts. After the technical patterns have been obtained, their information content is examined by comparing the unconditional empirical distribution of returns with the corresponding conditional empirical distribution, conditioned on the occurrence of a technical pattern. If technical patterns are informative, conditioning on them should alter the empirical distribution of returns; in other words, if the information contained in such patterns has already been incorporated into returns, there should not be much difference between the conditional and unconditional distribution of returns.[12]

They find that certain technical patterns, when applied to many stocks over many time periods, do provide incremental information, especially for Nasdaq stocks, supporting the claim that technical analysis can add incremental value to the investment process.[13] The authors conclude that although there will probably always be demand for talented technical analysts, the benefits of transparency and low cost associated with its automation suggest that algorithms should play some role in an investor's portfolio and may also bring technical analysis closer to other forms of systematic financial analysis. The same conclusions are reached by Hasanhodzic (2007), who conducts the robustness test of the Lo, Mamaysky, and Wang results by replacing the kernel regression smoothing algorithm with the neural network one.

"The proof is in the pudding," respond successful technicians when faced with skepticism about their craft. Rather than simply dismissing as exception bias the track records of winning technicians, some academics have evaluated them statistically. One such technician, the legendary early-twentieth-century Dow theorist William Hamilton, is the subject of Brown, Goetzmann, and Kumar's 1998 paper, "The Dow Theory: William Peter Hamilton's Track Record Reconsidered." In particular, Brown, Goetzmann, and Kumar reevaluate Alfred Cowles's (1933) test of the Dow theory, which provided "strong evidence" against the ability of the theory to forecast stock market prices. The authors test whether Hamilton's interpretation of the Dow theory can predict stock market movements and attempt to uncover the rules of the Dow theory (as interpreted by Hamilton) and to understand its implications for the EMH. To this end, they label as bullish, bearish, neutral, or indeterminate the 255 editorials Hamilton published in *The Wall Street Journal* during his tenure as its editor from 1902 to 1929, and then calculate the frequency with which the Dow theory beats the risk-free rate (assumed to be at 5 percent per annum) over the interval following an editorial, conditional upon bull or bear call.

Brown, Goetzmann, and Kumar (1998) find that the proportion of successful up calls is greater than the proportion of the failed up calls, and that the proportion of successful down calls is much greater than the proportion of failed down calls. In fact, their contingency table analysis shows strong evidence of an association between Hamilton's calls and subsequent market performance. In addition, the proportion of correct bear calls is found to be much higher than what could be attributed to chance alone. To make these observations more concrete, they simulate a trading strategy based on Hamilton's editorials—going long the market on a bullish signal and shorting the market on a bearish one. They find that over the 27-year period under consideration, the Hamilton strategy yields a very similar average annual return to the Standard & Poor's Composite Index but with lower volatility, resulting in a superior risk-adjusted return.

To test the validity of Hamilton's forecasts out of sample (that is, for the Dow Jones Industrial Average from 1930 to 1997 for which Hamilton did not generate any forecasts), Brown, Goetzmann, and Kumar (1998) first reduce the dynamics of past price series to basic trend shapes such as rising trends, falling trends, head-and-shoulders, and resistance levels. These trend shapes are then used as inputs to a neural network that is trained on the 27 years' worth of Hamilton editorials data to identify a nonlinear mapping from features to Hamilton's recommendation.

The success of the in-sample performance (that is, for the 1902–1929 period for which Hamilton's forecasts are available) of the neural network indicates that Hamilton did rely on structures that resemble positive and negative trends and reversals. The out-of-sample performance is evaluated on the September 1930–December 1997 period, and returns of the buy-and-hold strategy are compared to those of the "next day Hamilton strategy" and the "second day Hamilton strategy." The "next day Hamilton strategy" refers to investing at the opening-of-the-day prices of the day on which the neural network forecast comes out—for example, an investor who bought the paper before the opening of the market can take advantage of the signal immediately or as soon as the market opens. And the "second day Hamilton strategy" refers to investing at the close-of-the-day prices of the day on which the neural network forecast comes out—for example, an investor who bought the paper before the opening of the market cannot take advantage of the signal until the end of the day. The authors find that while the returns of the second day strategy are almost exactly equal to the buy-and-hold returns (but would be less than that after transaction costs), they do exhibit less variance and lower systematic risk compared to the buy-and-hold.

Such results are comparable to those obtained during Hamilton's lifetime: returns that are close to a buy-and-hold strategy, but that are characterized with lower levels of risk. The next-day Hamilton strategy has much higher returns than the second-day Hamilton strategy; however, even the next-day strategy does not dominate buy-and-hold in the 1980s. The results suggest that the Dow theory is not entirely consistent, and it would not be able to generate large excess returns due to transaction costs and other trading frictions. However, these results also indicate that the Dow theory was more than random decision making on the part of Hamilton. In particular, the Hamilton strategy appears to reduce portfolio volatility and, in the case where the immediate execution of the sell signal is possible, to yield profits that are higher than those of the buy-and-hold. Again, this implies that the empirical foundations of the EMH may not be as strong as long believed.

The observation that human nature never changes, and that consequently technical indicators designed to measure the reflection of human nature in market prices never change either, is a notable argument in favor of technical analysis, but one that at the same time underscores its main shortcoming: Technical analysis has not kept up with technological advances. Of course, charting and data collection have become automated, but most popular patterns and heuristics of today were developed in the precomputing age when calculating a simple moving average was a formidable task. For example, the 10-day moving average became popular not because it was optimal, but simply because it was trivial to compute. The 10-day moving average remains in common use today in spite of the fact that computers can calculate a moving average for *any* time scale with equal ease.

Suboptimal parametrization is only a symptom of a chronic disease afflicting technical analysis: Its static nature cannot account for the ever-changing character of financial markets. In the past, when execution was manual and costly, and financial systems were far less connected and complex, "static" used to be a prerequisite for practical use; now it is more often a recipe for failure. As markets evolve and trading strategies become more sophisticated, the need for new, dynamic indicators is apparent. Never has this need been more urgent than now, in the wake of the financial crisis of 2007–2009.

Some authors have taken steps in this regard by investigating the form of an optimal trading rule that can be revealed by the data themselves, rather than evaluating the commonly used technical indicators. For example, in their 1997 paper, "Is Technical Analysis on the Foreign Exchange Markets Profitable? A Genetic Programming Approach," Neely, Weller, and Dittmar use genetic programming to discover trading rules that are most profitable given the data with which they are dealing. The purpose of such an approach is to reduce the risk of the out-of-sample bias, which arises when the trading rules are selected ex post, rather than at the beginning of the sample period (the authors claim that the results of previous studies that sought to document the existence of excess returns to various types of trading rules in the foreign exchange market are all biased in this way). Six exchange rate time series are considered: dollar/German mark, dollar/yen, dollar/pound, dollar/Swiss franc, German mark/yen, and pound/Swiss franc, and the rules are obtained over the period 1975–1980.

When the performance of these rules is examined over the period 1981–1995, strong evidence of economically significant out-of-sample excess returns after the adjustment for transaction costs is found for each of the six exchange rates. Since technical analysts commonly claim that their rules exploit general features of financial markets, rather than being specific to any particular market, the authors run the dollar/German mark rules on the data of other markets under consideration and conclude that there is a significant improvement in performance in the vast majority of cases.

Finally, the trading rules that emerge from their research approximate well the rules commonly used by technical analysts, they argue. The rules that at first sight might appear complicated are often highly redundant; for example, the rule that was represented by a tree with 10 levels and 71 nodes turned out to be equivalent to the following simple advice: "Take a long position at time t if the minimum of the normalized exchange rate over periods $t-1$ and $t-2$ is greater than the 250-day moving average."[14]

Adaptive Markets and Technical Analysis

Even though the craft of technical analysis is deeply rooted in human civilization, serious efforts to formalize and statistically evaluate it have been launched only in the last two decades. The cultural biases of finance academics are, at least in part, responsible. In his autobiography, *Education of a Speculator*, the renowned trader and one-time finance professor, Victor Niederhoffer, paints an irreverent picture of the kind of forces at work in creating such biases at the University of Chicago where he was a finance Ph.D. student in the 1960s:

> This theory and the attitude of its adherents found classic expression in one incident I personally observed that deserves memorialization. A team of four of the most respected graduate students in finance had joined forces with two professors, now considered venerable enough to have won or to have been considered for a Nobel Prize, but at that time feisty as Hades and insecure as kids on [their] first date. This elite group was studying the possible impact of volume on stock price movements, a subject I had researched. As I was coming down the steps from the library on the third floor of Haskell Hall, the main business building, I could see this Group of Six gathered together on a stairway landing, examining some computer output. Their voices wafted up to me, echoing off the stone walls of the building. One of the students was pointing to some output while querying the professors, "Well, what if we really do find something? We'll be up the creek. It won't be consistent with the random walk model." The younger professor replied, "Don't worry, we'll cross that bridge in the unlikely event we come to it."
>
> I could hardly believe my ears—here were six scientists openly hoping to find no departures from ignorance. I couldn't hold my tongue. "I sure am glad you are all keeping an open mind about your research," I blurted out. I could hardly refrain from grinning as I walked past them. I heard muttered imprecations in response.[15]

One reason the EMH took such a stronghold in the academic community is because it was the first to be formalized and operationalized; although economists, including Nobel laureates, have proposed behavioral theories of financial markets—such as Simon's theory of bounded rationality (see Chapter 4)—over half a century ago, their ideas were not as directly implementable using the mathematical and computational tools available at the time. Now that the notions of adaptive markets and computationally bounded algorithms are available, a reinterpretation of market efficiency in evolutionary and computational terms might be the key to reconciling this theory with the possibility of making profits based on past prices alone. From an engineer's perspective, the efficiency of a device or system is rarely an all-or-nothing condition, but is more likely to be a continuum that captures the degree to which energy is transformed from one type to another. Just as air conditioners and hot-water heaters have efficiency ratings that fall somewhere between 0 and 100 percent—with higher ratings implying better cooling and heating abilities per unit of input power—financial markets differ in their ability to transform information into market prices, with more efficient markets impounding greater information into prices over a fixed time interval. The relevant question is not whether a market is efficient, but rather what its *relative degree of efficiency* is when compared to other alternatives.

Moreover, it makes little sense to talk about market efficiency without taking into account that market participants have bounded resources and adapt to changing environments. Instead of saying that a market is "efficient," we should say, borrowing from theoretical computer science, that a market is efficient with respect to certain resources, such as time or memory, if no strategy using those resources can generate a substantial profit. Similarly, it may be misleading to say that investors act optimally given all the available information; rather, they act optimally within their resources. This allows for markets to be efficient for some investors but not for others; for example, a computationally powerful hedge fund may extract profits from a market that looks very efficient from the point of view of a day trader who has fewer resources at his disposal—arguably the status quo.[16]

Human behavior is central to the limitations of the EMH, but the debate between disciples of market efficiency and proponents of behavioral finance have created a false dichotomy between the two schools of thought—in fact, both perspectives contain elements of truth, but neither is a complete picture of economic reality. Markets do function quite efficiently most of the time, aggregating vast amounts of disparate information into a single number—the price—on the basis of which millions of sound decisions are made. This remarkable feature of capitalism is an example of Surowiecki's (2004) "wisdom of crowds." But every so often, markets can break down, and the wisdom of crowds can quickly become the "madness of mobs."

Why do markets break down? Animal spirits! Recent neuroscientific research has shown that what we consider to be "rational" behavior is the outcome of a delicate balance among several distinct brain functions, including emotion, logical deliberation, and memory.[17] If that balance is upset—say, by the strong stimulus of a life-threatening event—then reason may be cast aside in favor of more instinctive behaviors like herding or the fight-or-flight response. Although few of us encounter such threats on a daily basis, much of our instincts are still adapted to the plains of the African savannah 50,000 years ago, where survival was a full-time occupation. Brain scans have shown that these same instincts can be triggered by more modern threats such as shame, social rejection, and financial loss. And as social animals, humans will react en masse if the perceived threat is significant enough, occasionally culminating in lynch mobs, riots, bank runs, and market crashes. Markets are not always efficient, nor are they always irrational—they are adaptive.

This "adaptive markets hypothesis" of Lo (2004, 2005)—essentially an evolutionary biologist's view of market dynamics—is at odds with the current economic orthodoxy, which has been heavily influenced by mathematics and physics (see, for example, Lo and Mueller, 2010). This orthodoxy has emerged for good reason: Economists have made genuine scientific breakthroughs, including general equilibrium theory, game theory, portfolio optimization, and derivatives pricing models. But any virtue can become a vice when carried to an extreme. The formality of mathematics and physics, in which mainstream economics is routinely dressed, can give outsiders—especially business leaders, regulators, and policymakers—a false sense of precision regarding our models' outputs (recall Samuelson's admonition that "macroeconomists have predicted 5 out of the past 3 recessions"). From an evolutionary perspective, markets are simply one more set of tools that *Homo sapiens* has developed in his ongoing struggle for survival. Occasionally, even the most reliable tools can break or be misapplied.

The adaptive markets hypothesis offers an internally consistent framework in which the EMH and behavioral biases can coexist. Behavior that may seem irrational is, instead, behavior that has not yet had sufficient time to adapt to modern contexts. For example, the great white shark moves through the water with fearsome grace and efficiency, thanks to 400 million years of natural selection. But take that shark out of water and onto a sandy beach, and its flailing undulations will look . . . irrational! The origins of human behavior are similar, differing only in the length of time we have had to adapt to our environment (about 2 million years) and the speed with which that environment is now changing.

Like the six blind monks who encountered an elephant for the first time—each monk grasping a different part of the beast and coming to a wholly different conclusion as to what an elephant is—disciples of the EMH and behavioral finance have captured different features of the same adaptive system.

The implications of the adaptive markets hypothesis for technical analysis are significant. Markets can be trusted to function properly during normal times, but when humans are subjected to emotional extremes (either pleasure or pain), animal spirits may overwhelm rationality, even among seasoned investors. Therefore, fixed investment rules that ignore changing environments will almost always have unintended consequences, and pattern recognition—in any form—may yield important competitive advantages.

Languishing for too long in the murky waters of part art, part science, technical analysis is finally starting to develop a more rigorous foundation. Although the fortress walls separating technicians from the adherents of modern finance still stand tall, they are not insurmountable, and we hope that the recognition of the thousands-of-years-long legacy of technical analysis and the role it has played in shaping the behavioral theory of financial markets will awaken some of the skeptics and open the door for a more constructive dialogue between the two communities.

Notes

1. See, for example, D. Aronson, *Evidence-Based Technical Analysis: Applying the Scientific Method and Statistical Inference to Trading Signals* (Hoboken, NJ: Wiley, 2007) and C. Kirkpatrick and J. Dahlquist, *Technical Analysis: The Complete Resource for Financial Market Technicians* (Upper Saddle River, NJ: FT Press, 2006).

2. J.-M. Courtault, Y. Kabanov, B. Bru, P. Crepel, I. Lebon, and A. Le, "Louis Bachelier: On the centenary of 'Théorie de la Spéculation,'" *Mathematical Finance* 10, no. 3 (2000) 339–353.
3. See, for example, S. F. LeRoy, "Risk aversion and the martingale property of stock returns," *International Economic Review* 14 no. 2 (1973), 436–446; M. Rubinstein, "The valuation of uncertain income streams and the pricing of options," *Bell Journal of Economics* 7 (1976), 407–425; R. Lucas, "Asset Prices in an Exchange Economy," *Econometrica* 46 (1978), 1429–1446.
4. See A. W. Lo, ed., *Market Efficiency: Stock Market Behaviour In Theory and Practice, Volumes I and II.* (Cheltenham, UK: Edward Elgar Publishing Company, 1997), 50–67 for a representative collection of papers in this literature.
5. See A. W. Lo, "Effcient Markets Hypothesis," in L. Blume and S. Durlauf, eds., *The New Palgrave: A Dictionary of Economics*, 2nd ed., (New York: Palgrave McMillan, 2007) for a more detailed summary of the market efficiency literature in economics and finance.
6. See, for example, S. Grossman and J. Stiglitz, "On the Impossibility of Informationally Efficient Markets," *American Economic Review* 70 (1980), 393–408; D. W. Diamond and R. E. Verrecchia, "Information Aggregation in a Noisy Rational Expectations Economy," *Journal of Financial Economics* 9 (1981), 221–235; A. R. Admati, "A Noisy Rational Expectations Equilibrium for Multi-Asset Securities Markets," *Econometrica* 53, no. 3 (1985), 629–657; A. S. Kyle, "Continuous Auctions and Insider Trading," *Econometrica* 53, no. 6 (1985), 1315–1336.; and J. Y. Campbell and A. S. Kyle, "Smart Money, Noise Trading and Stock Price Behavior," *Review of Economic Studies* 60 (1993), 1–34.
7. More recently, studies by G. Luo, "Evolution and Market Competition," *Journal of Economic Theory* 67 (1995), 223–250; G. Luo, "Market Efficiency and Natural Selection in a Commodity Futures Market," *Review of Financial Studies* 11 (1998), 647–674; G. Luo, "Natural Selection and Market Efficiency in a Futures Market with Random Shocks," *Journal of Futures Markets* 21 (2001), 489–516; G. Luo, "Evolution, Efficiency and Noise Traders in a One-Sided Auction Market," *Journal of Financial Markets* 6 (2003), 163–197;), D. Hirshleifer and G. Luo, "On the Survival of Overconfident Traders in a Competitive Securities Market," *Journal of Financial Markets* 4 (2001), 73–84; and L. Kogan, S. A. Ross, J. Wang, and M. M. Westerfield, "The price impact and survival of irrational traders," *Journal of Finance* 61 (2006), 195–229 have focused on the long-term viability of noise traders when competing for survival against informed traders. While noise traders are exploited by informed traders as expected, certain conditions do allow them to persist, at least in limited numbers, these authors argue.
8. E. Fama and M. Blume, "Filter Rules and Stock Market Trading," Journal of Business 39 (1966), 236.
9. A. W. Lo, H. Mamaysky, and J. Wang, "Foundations of Technical Analysis: Computational Algorithms, Statistical Inference, and Empirical Implementation," *Journal of Finance* LV, no. 4 (August 2000), 1705.
10. C. W. J. Granger and O. Morgenstern, "Spectral Analysis of New York Stock Market Prices," *Kyklos* XVI (1963), 3.
11. Granger and Morgenstern, "Spectral Analysis," 11.
12. The distance between the two distributions is measured in two ways: (1) by a goodness-of-fit test, which compares the deciles of conditional returns with their unconditional counterparts, and (2) by the Kolmogorov-Smirnov test.
13. It is important here to distinguish between evaluating the "profitability" of technical trading rules and evaluating the "information content" of technical analysis; the former necessitates the modeling of the trading implementation and risk management, whereas the latter detects supply/demand imbalances regardless of whether one can profitably act on that information.
14. C. Neely, P. Weller, and R. Dittmar, "Is Technical Analysis in the Foreign Exchange Market Profitable? A Genetic Programming Approach," *Journal of Financial and Quantitative Analysis* 32 (1997), 405–426, p. 420.
15. V. Niederhoffer, *Education of a Speculator* (New York: Wiley, 1997), 270.
16. J. Hasanhodzic, A. W. Lo, and E. Viola, "A Computational View of Market Efficiency," Available online at http://arxiv.org/abs/0908.4580 (2009).
17. A. Damasio, *Descartes' Error: Emotion, Reason, and the Human Brain* (New York: Avon Books, 1994).

CHAPTER 6

The New High–New Low Index

From Dr. Alexander Elder, *The New Trading for a Living* (Hoboken, New Jersey: John Wiley & Sons, 2014), Part 6, Chapter 34.

Stocks that reach their highest level in a year on any given day are the leaders in strength. Stocks that fall to their lowest point for that year on the same day are the leaders in weakness. The New High–New Low Index (NH-NL) tracks the behavior of market leaders by subtracting the number of New Lows from the New Highs. In my experience, NH-NL is the best leading indicator of the stock market.[1]

How to Construct NH-NL

The New High–New Low Index is easy to calculate, using information that appears in many online sources and in major newspapers.

$$\text{NH-NL} = \text{New Highs} - \text{New Lows}$$

Most data services in the United States report the daily numbers of New Highs and New Lows, but it is shocking how loosely they define their data. Some are too narrow and track only the NYSE stocks, ignoring other exchanges. Others are too broad and track everything, including interest rate ETFs. My favorite source of reliable data is www.barchart.com. I take their data, subtract New Lows from New Highs, and plot the result underneath the daily chart of the S&P 500.

The task of constructing NH-NL is harder for traders outside the United States, in countries where such data isn't reported. There you'll need to do a bit of programming. First, run a daily scan of the database of all stocks in your country to find those that have reached the highest high and the lowest low for the year during the day. Once you have those two lists, take the above formula and apply it to the numbers you found.

[1] In 2012, I wrote an e-book with Kerry Lovvorn on the New High–New Low Index. We publish nightly updates on its signals on SpikeTrade.com.

On the days when there are more new highs than new lows, NH-NL is positive and plotted above the centerline. On the days when there are more new lows than new highs, NH-NL is negative and plotted below the centerline. If the numbers of new highs and new lows are equal, NH-NL is zero. We normally plot the New High–New Low Index as a line, with a horizontal reference line at a zero level.

While I plot NH-NL underneath the S&P 500, keep in mind that it has a much broader reach than the S&P—NH-NL includes data from the NYSE, AMEX, and NASDAQ, excluding only ETFs, unit investment trusts, closed-end funds, warrant stocks, and preferred securities. The chart of the S&P 500 is there simply for a comparison.

Crowd Psychology

A stock appears on the list of new highs when it's the strongest it's been in a year. It means that a herd of eager bulls is chasing its shares. A stock appears on the list of new lows when it's the weakest it's been in a year, showing that a crowd of aggressive bears is selling its shares.

The New High–New Low Index compares the numbers of the strongest and the weakest stocks on the exchange. It reveals the balance of power between the leaders in strength and the leaders in weakness.

You can visualize all stocks on the New York Stock Exchange, the NASDAQ, or any other exchange as soldiers in a regiment. The new highs and new lows are their officers. The new highs are the officers who lead an attack uphill. The new lows are the officers who are deserting and running downhill.

The quality of leadership is a key factor in any conflict. When I was in officer training, they kept telling us that there are no bad soldiers, only bad officers. The New High–New Low Index shows whether more officers are leading an attack uphill or deserting downhill. Where the officers lead, soldiers follow. The broad indexes, such as the S&P 500, tend to follow the trend of NH-NL (Figure 6.1).

When NH-NL rises above its centerline, it shows that the bullish leadership is dominant. When NH-NL falls below its centerline, it shows that bearish leadership is in charge. If the market rallies to a new high and NH-NL climbs to a new peak, it shows that bullish leadership is growing and the uptrend is likely to continue. If the market rallies but NH-NL shrinks, it shows that the leadership is becoming weak and the uptrend is in danger. A regiment whose officers are starting to desert is likely to retreat.

A new low in NH-NL shows that the downtrend is well led and likely to persist. If officers are running faster than the men, the regiment is likely to be routed. If stocks fall but NH-NL turns up, it shows that officers are no longer running. When officers regain their morale, the whole regiment is likely to rally.

Trading Rules for NH-NL

Traders need to pay attention to three aspects of NH-NL: the level of NH-NL above or below its centerline, the trend of NH-NL, and divergences between the patterns of NH-NL and prices.

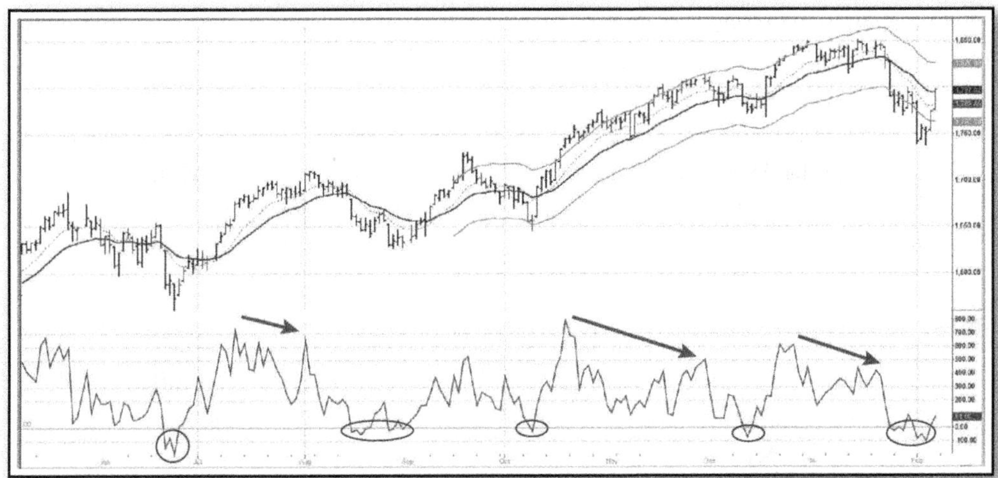

FIGURE 6.1 S&P 500 Daily, 26- and 13-Day EMAs, Autoenvelope, NH-NL Daily. ***(Chart by TradeStation)***

NH-NL—Daily Chart, Yearly Look-Back

This chart tracks daily NH-NL during a mostly bullish year in the stock market. Still, every bullish trend gets interrupted by pullbacks. Bearish deterioration patterns of NH-NL, marked here by diagonal red arrows, warn you of coming declines. These signals emerge because officers start shifting towards the rear before the soldiers retreat.

Declines end and rallies begin when NH-NL rallies from negative into positive territory, marked here by purple circles. Those signals work especially well when the S&P is oversold, i.e., near its lower channel line. As always, trading messages are especially strong when independent signals confirm each other.

NH-NL Zero Line

The position of NH-NL in relation to its centerline shows whether bulls or bears are in control. When NH-NL is above its centerline, it shows that more market leaders are bullish than bearish and it is better to trade from the long side. When NH-NL is below its centerline, it shows that bearish leadership is stronger, and it's better to trade from the short side. NH-NL can stay above its centerline for months at a time in bull markets and below its centerline for months in bear markets.

If NH-NL stays negative for several months but then rallies above its centerline, it signals that a bull move is likely to begin. It is time to look for buying opportunities, using oscillators for precise timing. If NH-NL stays positive for several months but then falls below its centerline, it shows that a bear move is likely to begin. It is time to look for shorting opportunities using oscillators for precise timing.

NH-NL Trends

When the market rallies and NH-NL rises, it confirms uptrends. When NH-NL declines together with the market, it confirms downtrends.

1. A rise in NH-NL shows that it's safe to hold long positions and add to them. If NH-NL declines while the broad market stays flat or rallies, it is time to take profits on long trades. When NH-NL falls below zero, it shows that bearish leadership is strong and it's safe to hold short positions and even add to them.

If the market continues to fall but NH-NL rises, it shows that the downtrend is not well led—it's time to cover shorts.

2. If NH-NL rises on a flat day, it flashes a bullish message and gives a buy signal. It shows that officers are going over the top while the soldiers are still crouching in their foxholes. When NH-NL falls on a flat day, it gives a signal to sell short. It shows that officers are deserting while the troops are still holding their positions. Soldiers aren't stupid—if their officers start running away, they will not stay and fight.

NH-NL Divergences

If the latest market peak is confirmed by a new high of NH-NL, that rally is likely to continue, even if punctuated by a decline. When a new market low is accompanied by a new low in NH-NL, it shows that bears are well led and the downtrend is likely to persist. On the other hand, divergences between the patterns of NH-NL and broad market indexes show that leaders are deserting and the trends are likely to reverse.

1. If NH-NL traces a lower peak while the market rallies to a new high, it creates a bearish divergence. It shows that bullish leadership is weakening even though the broad market is higher. Bearish divergences often mark the ends of uptrends, but pay attention to the height of the second peak. If it is only slightly above zero, in the low hundreds, then a big reversal is probably at hand and it's time to go short. If, on other hand, the latest peak is in the high hundreds, it shows that the upside leadership is strong enough to prevent the market from collapsing.
2. If the market declines to a new low, but NH-NL traces a shallower bottom than its previous decline, it creates a bullish divergence. It shows that bearish leadership is shrinking. If the latest low of NH-NL is shallow, in the low hundreds, it shows that the bearish leadership is exhausted and a major upside reversal is near. If the latest low sinks deep, then bears still have some strength, and the downtrend may pause but not reverse. Keep in mind that bullish divergences at stock market bottoms tend to develop faster than bearish divergences at market tops: buy fast and sell slowly.

NH-NL in Multiple Timeframes and Look-Back Periods

Markets move simultaneously in different timeframes. My original work on the NH-NL focused on the daily charts with a one-year look-back period—counting stocks that have reached a new high or a new low for their latest 52-week range. I have since added several dimensions for a deeper understanding of this key indicator.

Weekly NH-NL

The weekly NH-NL helps confirm major stock market trends and identify major reversals. I build it from the daily data of barchart.com, mentioned above, by running a five-day moving total. I plot the result underneath a weekly chart of the S&P 500.

The weekly NH-NL gives its most important signals when it reaches extreme levels and also by divergences. To understand its logic, keep in mind how the weekly NH-NL is constructed. For example, if the weekly NH-NL rises to a +1,500 level, it means that in each of the past five trading days there were on average 300 more New Highs than New Lows. It takes a period of sustainable bullishness or bearishness to push the weekly NH-NL to an extreme.

These are the most important signals of weekly NH-NL:

- When it drops below minus 4,000 and then rallies above that level, it delivers major buy signals.
- When the weekly NH-NL rises above plus 2,500, it confirms bull markets.
- When the tops or bottoms of weekly NH-NL diverge from price patterns, they signal important reversals.

A drop below −4,000 reflects an unsustainable market panic. To fall that low, the market has to deliver an average of 800 more daily New Lows than New Highs for five days in a row. Such massive panic is not going to last. When the weekly NH-NL rises above −4,000, it flashes a buy signal I call a Spike. It's so powerful and effective in both bull and bear markets that I named our SpikeTrade group after it. This signal misfired only once in several decades, as you'll see on the chart in Figure 6.2.

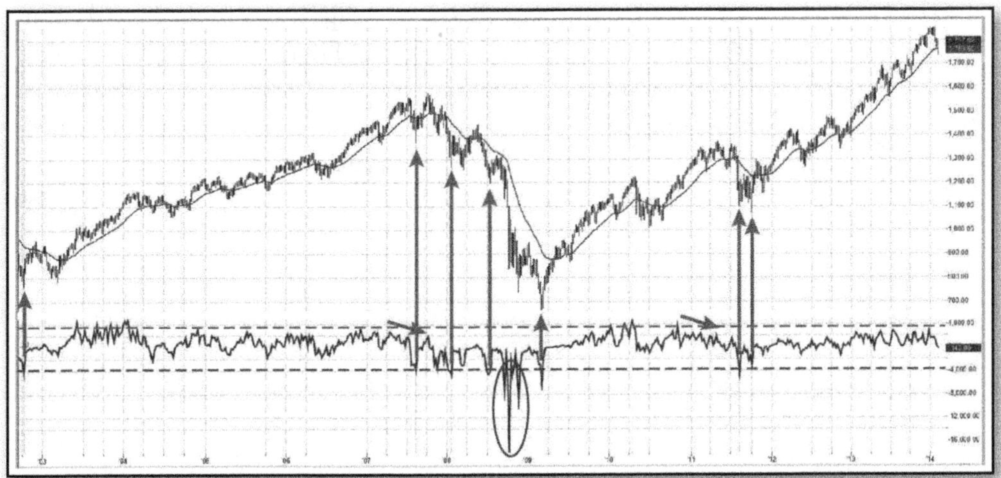

FIGURE 6.2 S&P 500 Weekly, 26-Week EMA, NH-NL Weekly. Green Line at +2,500, Purple Line at −4,000. ***(Chart by TradeStation)***

NH-NL—Weekly Chart

When the weekly NH-NL falls below −4,000 and then rises above that level, it nails important bottoms, marked here with vertical green arrows. This chart covers 11 years—the signal works in bull and bear markets. There was only one exception—in October and November 2008, during the worst bear market of a century (marked by a purple oval). Let this serve as a reminder that no market signal works 100% of the time, making risk management essential for survival and success.

Red diagonal arrows mark major bearish divergences. Weekly NH-NL touching the +2,500 level confirms bull markets and calls for higher prices ahead, even if interrupted by a correction.

When the weekly NH-NL rises to the +2,500 level, it confirms bull markets. This indicator never rises this high during bear market rallies. When you see it above that level, you know you're in a bull market, with higher prices likely ahead.

The 65-day and 20-day NH-NL

One of the great innovations in the New High–New Low analysis in recent years was the addition of two new look-back windows: a 20-day and a 65-day. While the regular daily NH-NL compares each day's high and low to the high-low range for the preceding year, a 20-day NH-NL compares it only to the preceding month and a 65-day NH-NL to the preceding quarter. These shorter-term views of the NH-NL are useful for short-term timing.

These two new time windows deliver more sensitive signals than the standard year-long NH-NL. The logic is simple: before a stock reaches a new high for the year, it must first make a new high for the month and then for the quarter. If a stock has been in a downtrend, it may take a long time to recover and reach a new yearly high, but it can reach monthly and quarterly highs much sooner.

In addition to the usual signals, such as trends and divergences, a very sharp short-term buy signal occurs when the 20-day NH-NL drops below minus 500 and then rallies above that level. It shows that the market has touched and rejected a short-term bearish extreme, and afterwards it usually launches a short-term rally. We call this a "Spike bounce" signal.

Tracking market leaders with the help of NH-NL helps improve timing. There are two ways to utilize the New High–New Low signals. First, since individual stocks largely depend on broad market trends, we can use NH-NL signals to decide when to buy or sell our stocks. Furthermore, we can use NH-NL signals to trade vehicles that track the broad market, such as the S&P e-mini futures.

For more information regarding Dr. Alexander Elder's work, please visit www.elder.com.

CHAPTER 7

Stocks above 50-Day MA

From Dr. Alexander Elder, *The New Trading for a Living* (Hoboken, New Jersey: John Wiley & Sons, 2014), Part 6, Chapter 35.

This broad stock market indicator is based on the key concepts regarding prices and moving averages (Figure 7.1). Each price represents a momentary consensus of value among market participants, while a moving average represents an average

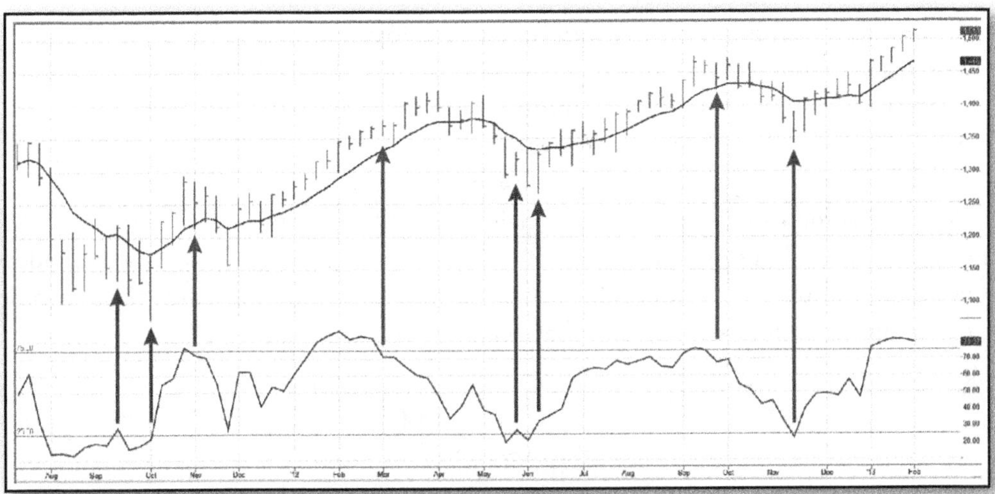

FIGURE 7.1 S&P 500 Weekly and 26-Week MA; Stocks above 50 MA with Reference Lines at 75% and 25%. ***(Chart by TradeStation)***

Stocks above 50-Day MA

When the "stocks above their 50-day MA" indicator reaches an extreme—above 75% or below 25% and then moves away from that level, it shows that the intermediate-term trend has reached a likely turning point. A reversal of this indicator flashes a signal for the entire market: buy when it turns up and sell when it turns down. In the latter part of 2013, as the market started going up with almost no pullbacks, buy signals from upside reversals began to occur at levels higher than 25%. These signals don't mark every reversal—no indicator does—but when it flashes its signal, we had better pay attention.

consensus of value during its time window. This means that when a stock trades above its MA, the current consensus of value is above average—bullish. When a stock trades below its MA, the current consensus of value is below average—bearish.

When the market is trending higher, the percentage of stocks above their moving averages keeps growing. In a broad downtrend, the number of stocks above their MAs keeps shrinking.

This indicator tracks all stocks traded on the New York Stock Exchange, American Exchange, and NASDAQ and calculates how many of them trade above their moving averages. It plots that percentage as a line that fluctuates between 0% and 100%. We can use the pattern of this line to confirm market trends and anticipate reversals.

The indicator for tracking the number of stocks above their 50-day MAs is included in many software packages. I like to view it on a weekly chart, where it helps catch intermediate reversals—market turns that augur in trends that last anywhere from several weeks to several months. You don't need to look at this indicator daily, but it can be an important part of weekend homework.

In theory, the highest possible reading of this indicator would be 100%, if all stocks rallied above their MAs. Its lowest possible reading of 0% would occur if all stocks were to fall below their MAs. In practice, only exceptional market moves swing it near the 90% or 10% extremes. Normally, this indicator tends to top out near 75% and bottom out near 25%. I draw two reference lines on its chart at 75% and 25% and start looking for the market turn as this indicator approaches those levels.

The percentage of stocks above their 50-day MA gives its trading signals not by reaching any certain levels but rather by reversing near those levels. It signals the completion of a top by rising to or above the upper reference line and then sinking below that line. It signals that a bottom has been formed when it falls below or even near the lower reference line and then turns up.

Notice that the tops of this indicator tend to be broad, while its bottoms are sharper. Tops are formed by greed, which is a happier, longer-lasting emotion. Bottoms are formed by fear—a more intense and shorter-lived emotion.

While some of this indicator's signals are right on time in catching reversals, others mark only temporary pauses in major trends. Let this serve as a reminder never to rely on a single indicator for trading decisions. Use multiple tools: when they confirm each other's signals, they reinforce one another.

For more information regarding Dr. Alexander Elder's work, please visit www.elder.com.

CHAPTER 8

Other Stock Market Indicators

From Dr. Alexander Elder, *The New Trading for a Living* (Hoboken, New Jersey: John Wiley & Sons, 2014), Part 6, Chapter 36.

Only a handful of general market indicators have stood the harsh test of time. Many that used to be popular in previous decades have been swept away by the flood of new trading vehicles. The New High–New Low Index and Stocks Above 50-day MA, reviewed above, continue to work because of their clear logic. Several other indicators are listed below. Whatever tools you choose, be sure to understand how they work and what exactly they measure. Select a few and track them on a regular basis, until you come to trust their signals.

Advance/Decline

The Advance/Decline line (the A/D line) tracks the degree of mass participation in rallies and declines. Each day it adds up the number of stocks that closed higher and subtracts the number of stocks that closed lower.

While the Dow Jones Industrials track the behavior of the generals and the New High–New Low Index focuses on the officers, the A/D line shows whether soldiers are following their leaders. A rally is more likely to persist when the A/D line rises to a new high, while a decline is likely to deepen if A/D falls to a new low in step with the Dow.

The A/D line is based on the day's closing prices for each stock at any exchange: take the number of advancing stocks, subtract the number of declining stocks, and ignore unchanged stocks. The result will be positive or negative, depending on whether more stocks advanced or declined during the day. For example, if 4,000 stocks were traded, 2,600 advanced, 900 declined, and 500 were unchanged, then Advance/Decline equals +1,700 (2,600−900). Add each day's Advance/Decline figures to the previous day's total to create a cumulative A/D line (Figure 8.1).

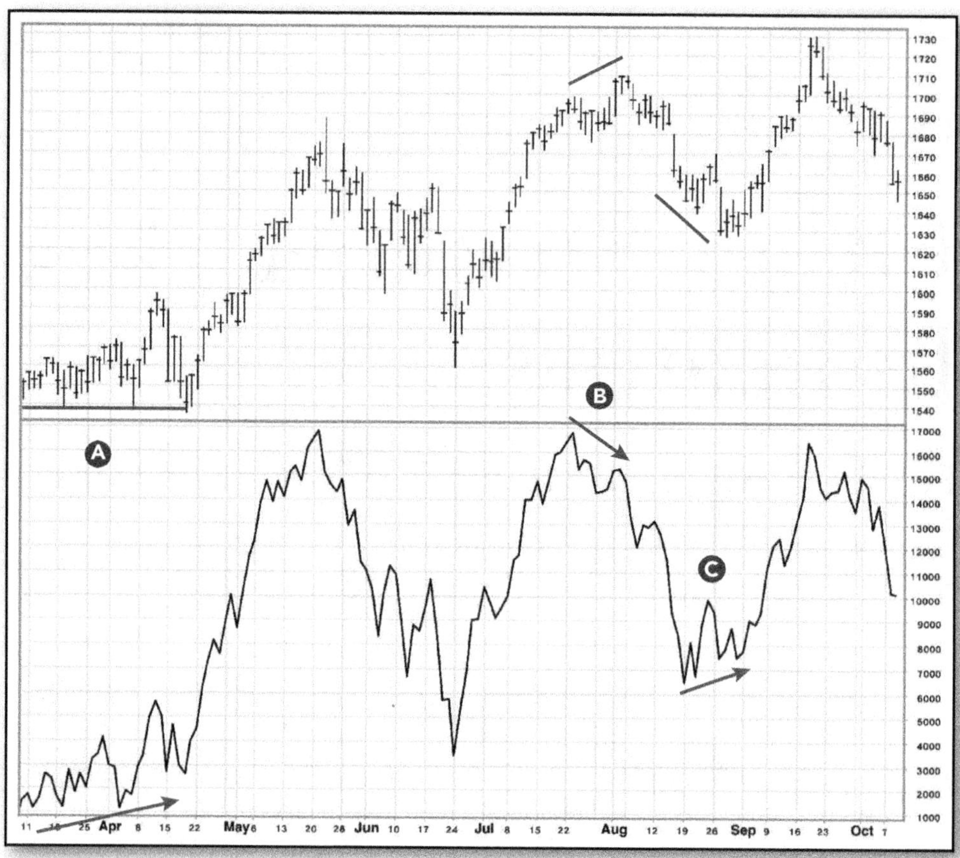

FIGURE 8.1 S&P 500 Daily and the Advance/Decline Line. *(Chart by Stockcharts.com)*

Advance/Decline Line

The turns of this indicator usually coincide with price turns, but occasionally precede them. This ability to give early warnings makes A/D line worth following. In area A, prices are scratching the bottom and make a new low, while the uptrend of the A/D line calls for a rally. In area B, the opposite occurs—prices press higher, while a downturn of the A/D line calls for a decline. In area C, prices continue to decline, while the A/D line turns up and calls for a rally. Those warnings don't occur at every turning point.

Traders should watch for new peaks and valleys in the A/D line rather than its absolute levels, which depend on its starting date. If a new high in the stock market is accompanied by a new high of the A/D line, it shows that the rally has broad support and is likely to continue. Broadly based rallies and declines have greater staying power. If the stock market reaches a new peak, but the A/D line reaches a lower peak than during the previous rally, it shows that fewer stocks are participating, and the rally may be near its end. When the market falls to a new low but the A/D line traces a shallower bottom than during the previous decline, it shows that the decline is narrowing down and the bear move is nearing an end. These signals tend to precede reversals by weeks if not months.

The **Most Active Stocks indicator** (MAS) is an Advance/Decline line of the 15 most active stocks on the New York Stock Exchange. It used to be listed daily in many newspapers. Stocks appeared on this list when they caught the public's eye. MAS was a big money indicator—it showed whether big money was bullish or bearish.

When the trend of MAS diverged from the price trends, the market was especially likely to reverse.

Hardly anyone today uses an indicator called **TRIN**, which was important enough to have its own chapter in the original Trading for a Living. Very few people track another formerly popular indicator called **TICK**. Old stock market books are full of fascinating indicators, but you have to be very careful using them today. Changes in the market over the years have killed many indicators.

Indicators based on the volume of **low-priced stocks** lost their usefulness when the average volume of the U.S. stock market soared and the Dow rose tenfold. The **Member Short Sale Ratio** and the **Specialist Short Sale Ratio** stopped working after options became popular. Member and specialist short sales are now tied up in the intermarket arbitrage. **Odd-lot** statistics lost value when conservative odd-lotters bought mutual funds. The **Odd-lot Short Sale Ratio** stopped working when gamblers discovered puts.

CHAPTER 9

Consensus and Commitment Indicators

From Dr. Alexander Elder, *The New Trading for a Living* (Hoboken, New Jersey: John Wiley & Sons, 2014), Part 6, Chapter 37.

Most private traders keep their opinions to themselves, but financial journalists, letter writers, and bloggers spew them forth like open hydrants. Some writers may be very bright, but the financial press as a whole has a poor record of market timing.

Financial journalists and letter writers tend to overstay trends and miss turning points. When these groups become intensely bullish or bearish, it pays to trade against them.

It's "monkey see, monkey do" in the publishing business, where a journalist's or an advisor's job may be endangered by expressing an opinion that differs too sharply from his group. Standing alone feels scary, and most of us like to huddle. When financial journalists and letter writers reach a high degree of bullish or bearish consensus, it's a sign that the trend has been going on for so long that a reversal is near.

Consensus indicators, also called contrary opinion indicators, are not suitable for precision timing, but they draw attention to the fact that a trend is near its exhaustion level. When you see that message, switch to technical indicators for more precise timing of a trend reversal.

A trend can continue as long as bulls and bears remain in conflict. A high degree of consensus precedes reversals. When the crowd becomes highly bullish, get ready to sell, and when it becomes strongly bearish, get ready to buy. This is the contrary opinion theory, whose foundations were laid by Charles Mackay, a Scottish barrister. His classic book, *Extraordinary Popular Delusions and the Madness of Crowds* (1841) describes the infamous Dutch Tulip Mania and the South Seas Bubble in England. Humphrey B. Neill in the United States applied the theory of contrary opinion to stocks and other financial markets. In his book, *The Art of Contrary Thinking*, he made it clear why the majority must be wrong at the market's turning points: prices are established by crowds, and by the time the majority turns bullish, there aren't enough new buyers to support a bull market.

Abraham W. Cohen, an old New York lawyer whom I met in the early 1980s, came up with the idea of polling market advisors and using their responses as a proxy for the entire body of traders. Cohen was a skeptic who spent many years on Wall Street and saw that advisors as a group performed no better than the market crowd. In 1963, he established a service called *Investors Intelligence* for tracking letter writers. When the majority of them became bearish, Cohen identified a buying opportunity. Selling opportunities were marked by strong bullishness among letter writers. Another writer, James H. Sibbet, applied this theory to commodities, setting up an advisory service called *Market Vane*.

Tracking Advisory Opinion

Letter writers follow trends out of fear of losing subscribers by missing major moves. In addition, bullishness helps sell subscriptions, while bearish comments turn off subscribers. Even in a bear market, we rarely see more bears than bulls among advisors for more than a few weeks at a time.

The longer a trend continues, the louder the letter writers proclaim it. They are most bullish at market tops and most bearish at market bottoms. When the mass of letter writers turns strongly bullish or bearish, it's a good idea to look for trades in the opposite direction.

Some advisors are very skilled at doubletalk. The man who speaks from both sides of his mouth can claim that he was right regardless of what the market did, but editors of tracking services have plenty of experience pinning down such lizards.

When the original *Trading for a Living* came out, only two services tracked advisory opinions: *Investors Intelligence* and *Market Vane*. In recent years, there has been an explosion of interest in behavioral economics, and today many services track advisors. My favorite resource is SentimenTrader.com, whose slogan is "Make emotion work for you instead of against you." Jason Goepfert, its publisher, does a solid job of tracking mass market sentiment.

Signals from the Press

To understand any group of people, you must know what its members crave and what they fear. Financial journalists want to appear serious, intelligent, and informed; they are afraid of appearing ignorant or flaky. That's why it's normal for them to straddle the fence and present several sides of every issue. A journalist is safe as long as he writes something like "monetary policy is about to push the market up, unless unforeseen factors push it down."

Internal contradiction is the normal state of affairs in financial journalism[1]. Most financial editors are even more cowardly than their writers. They print contradictory articles and call this "presenting a balanced picture."

For example, an issue of a major business magazine had an article headlined "The Winds of Inflation Are Blowing a Little Harder" on page 19. Another article on page 32 of the same issue was headlined "Why the Inflation Scare Is Just That." It takes a powerful and lasting trend to lure journalists and editors down from their fences. This happens only when a tide of optimism or pessimism sweeps up the market near the end of a major trend. When journalists start expressing strongly bullish or bearish views, the trend is ripe for a reversal.

This is why the front covers of major business magazines serve as contrarian indicators. When a leading business magazine puts a bull on its cover, it's usually a good time to take profits on long positions, and when a bear graces the front cover, a bottom cannot be too far away.

Signals from Advertisers

A group of three or more ads touting the same "opportunity" in a major newspaper or magazine warns of an imminent top. This is because only a well-established uptrend can break through the inertia of several brokerage firms. By the time all of them recognize a trend, come up with trading recommendations, produce ads, and place them in a newspaper, that trend is very old indeed.

The ads on the commodities page of *The Wall Street Journal* appeal to the bullish appetites of the least-informed traders. Those ads almost never recommend selling; it is hard to get amateurs excited about going short. You'll never see an ad for an investment when its price is low. When three or more ads on the same day tout gold or silver, it is time to look at technical indicators for shorting signals.

A more malignant breed of promoters appeared on the scene in the past decade: thanks to the Internet, "pump and dump" operators have migrated online. The scammers touting penny stocks know that they need to wait for an uptrend to hook their victims. Whenever a higher than usual number of promo pitches starts showing up in my spam filter, the top can't be too far away (Figure 9.1).

Commitments of Futures Traders

Government agencies and exchanges collect data on buying and selling by various groups of traders and publish summary reports of their positions. It pays to trade with the groups that have a track record of success and against those with track records of persistent failure.

[1]And not only journalism: in 2013 three academicians shared a Nobel Prize in economics. The work of one of them showed that the market was efficient and couldn't be timed; the work of another showed that the market was irrational and could be timed. Take your pick and wait for next year's prize.

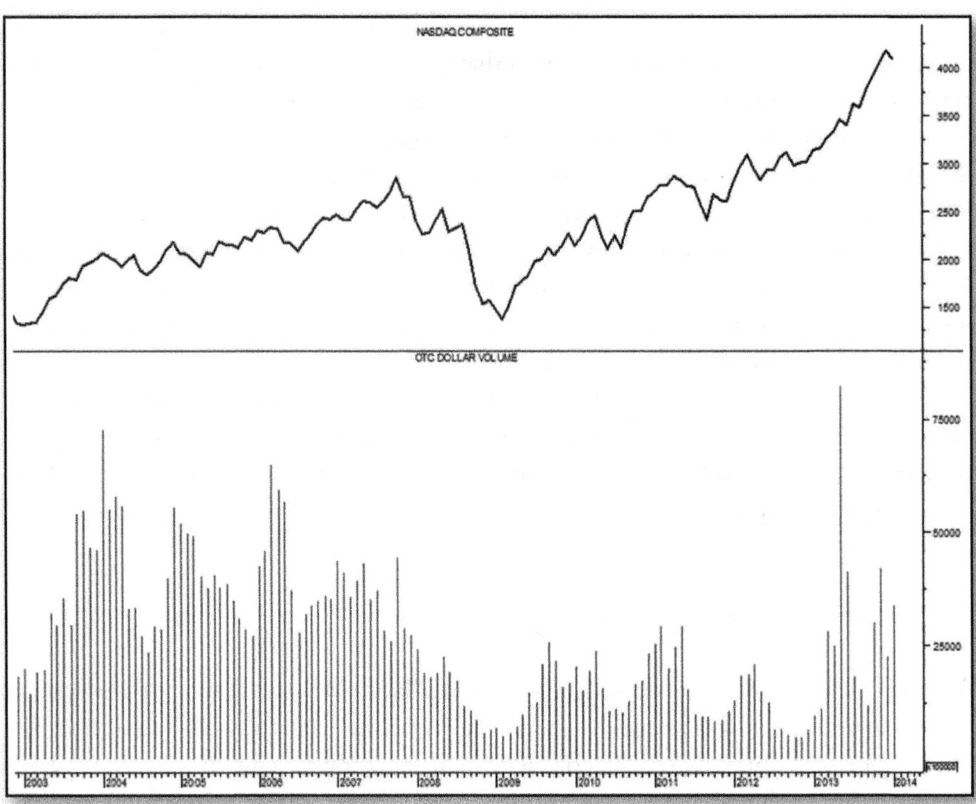

FIGURE 9.1 Monthly Total Dollar Value of OTC Stocks. ***(Courtesy SentimenTrader.com)***

Money pours into penny stocks when the market is up, dries up when it is down. This is reflected in the monthly reports of penny stock volume at the NASDAQ. After markets have hit new highs and the news is good, volume often spikes up for these "lottery ticket" stocks. When the stock market hits the skids, their volume dries up.

For example, the Commodity Futures Trading Commission (CFTC) reports long and short positions of hedgers and big speculators. Hedgers—the commercial producers and consumers of commodities—are the most successful market participants. The Securities and Exchange Commission (SEC) reports purchases and sales by corporate insiders. Officers of publicly traded companies know when to buy or sell their shares.

Positions of large futures traders, including hedge funds, are reported to the CFTC when their sizes reach the so-called **reporting levels.** At the time of this writing, if you are long or short 250 contracts of corn or 200 contracts of gold, the CFTC classifies you as a big speculator. Brokers report those positions to the CFTC, which compiles the data and releases summaries on Fridays.

The CFTC also sets up the maximum number of contracts a speculator is allowed to hold in any given market— these are called **position limits.** Those limits are set to prevent very large speculators from accumulating positions that are big enough to bully the markets.

The CFTC divides all market participants into three groups: commercials, large speculators, and small speculators. **Commercials**, also known as **hedgers**, are firms or individuals who deal in actual commodities in the normal course of their business. In theory, they trade futures to hedge business risks. For example, a bank trades interest rate futures to hedge its loan portfolio, while a food processing company trades wheat futures to offset the risks of buying grain. Hedgers post smaller margins and are exempt from speculative position limits.

Large speculators are those whose positions have reached reporting levels. The CFTC reports buying and selling by commercials and large speculators. To find the positions of **small traders**, you need to take the open interest and subtract from it the holdings of the first two groups.

The divisions between hedgers, big speculators, and small speculators are somewhat artificial. Smart small traders grow into big traders, dumb big traders become small traders, and many hedgers speculate. Some market participants play games that distort the CFTC reports. For example, an acquaintance who owns a brokerage firm sometimes registers his wealthy speculator clients as hedgers, claiming they trade stock index and bond futures to hedge their stock and bond portfolios.

The commercials can legally speculate in the futures markets using inside information. Some of them are big enough to play futures markets against cash markets. For example, an oil firm may buy crude oil futures, divert several tankers, and hold them offshore in order to tighten supplies and push up futures prices. They can take profits on long positions, go short, and then deliver several tankers at once to refiners in order to push crude futures down a bit and cover shorts. Such manipulation is illegal, and most firms hotly deny that it takes place.

As a group, commercials have the best track record in the futures markets. They have inside information and are well-capitalized. It pays to follow them because they are successful in the long run. Big speculators used to be successful wealthy individuals who took careful risks with their own money. That has changed, and today most big traders are commodity funds. These trend-following behemoths do poorly as a group. The masses of small traders are the proverbial "wrong-way Corrigans" of the markets.

It is not enough to know whether a certain group is short or long. Commercials often short futures because many of them own physical commodities. Small traders are usually long, reflecting their perennial optimism. To draw valid conclusions from the CFTC reports, you need to compare current positions to their historical norms.

Legal Insider Trading

Officers and investors who hold more than 5 percent of the shares in a publicly traded company must report their buying and selling to the Securities and Exchange Commission. The SEC tabulates insider purchases and sales, and releases this data to the public.

Corporate insiders have a long record of buying stocks when they're cheap and selling them high. Insider buying emerges after severe market drops, and insider selling accelerates when the market rallies and becomes overpriced.

Buying or selling by a single insider matters little: an executive may sell shares to meet major personal expenses or he may buy them to exercise stock options. Analysts who researched legal insider trading found that insider buying or selling was meaningful only if more than three executives or large stockholders bought or sold within a month. These actions reveal that something very positive or negative is about to happen. A stock is likely to rise if three insiders buy in one month and to fall if three insiders sell within a month.

Clusters of insider buying tend to have a better predictive value than clusters of selling. That's because insiders are willing to sell a stock for many reasons (diversification, buying a second home, sending a kid to college) but they are willing to buy for one main reason—they expect their company's stock to go up.

Short Interest

While the numbers of futures and options contracts held long and short is equal by definition, in the stock market there is always a huge disparity between the two camps. Most people, including professional fund managers, buy stocks, but very few sell them short.

Among the data reported by exchanges is the number of shares being held short for any stock. Since the absolute numbers vary a great deal, it pays to put them into a perspective by comparing the number of shares held short to that stock's float (the total number of publicly owned shares available for trading). This number, **"Short Percent of Float,"** tends to run about one or two percent. Another useful way to look at short interest is by comparing it to the average daily volume. By doing this, we ask a hypothetical question: if all shorts decided to cover, while all other buyers stood aside and daily volume remained unchanged, how many days would it take for them to cover and bring short interest down to zero? This **"Days to Cover"** number normally oscillates between one and two days.

When planning to buy or short a stock, it pays to check its Short Percent of Float and Days to Cover. If those are high, they show that the bearish side is overcrowded. A rally may scare those bears into panicky covering, and send the stock sharply higher. That would be good for bulls but bad for bears.

Fear is a stronger emotion than greed. Bulls may look for bargains but try not to overpay, while squeezed bears, facing unlimited losses, will pay any price to cover. That's why short-covering rallies tend to be especially sharp.

Whenever you look for a stock to buy, check its Short Percent of Float and Days to Cover. The usual, normal readings don't provide any great information, but the deviations from the norm often deliver useful insights (Figure 9.2).

High shorting numbers mark any stock as a dangerous short. By extension, if your indicators suggest buying a stock, its high short interest becomes an additional positive factor—there is more fuel for a rally. It makes sense for swing traders to include the data on shorting when selecting which of several stocks to buy or sell short. I always review these numbers when working up a potential trade.

Apple Incorporated	$ 534.97	Green Mountain Coffee Roasters	$ 119.74
AAPL	-1.00	GMCR	0.34
Daily Short Sale Volume	view	Daily Short Sale Volume	view
Short Interest (Shares Short)	16,538,900	Short Interest (Shares Short)	32,931,300
Days To Cover (Short Interest Ratio)	0.9	Days To Cover (Short Interest Ratio)	15.1
Short Percent of Float	1.86 %	Short Percent of Float	25.76 %

FIGURE 9.2 AAPL and GMCR Shorting Data. *(Source: Shortsqueeze.com)*

Short Interest and Days to Cover

Compare short interest data for two popular stocks on the day I'm editing this chapter. "Short Percent of Float" is 1.86% for Apple, Inc. (AAPL), but nearly 26% for Green Mountain Coffee Roasters, Inc. (GMCR). "Days to Cover" are 0.9 for AAPL but over 15 for GMCR. These numbers reflect much more aggressive shorting of GMCR. Not to forget, each and every one of those shorts at some point will need to buy in order to cover his short position.

Perhaps savvy shorts know something very bad about GMCR, but what if its stock rallies even a little? Many bears will run for cover, and as they scramble to cover shorts, the stock may soar. Whatever its long-term prospects, it could be sent flying in the near term.

CHAPTER 10

Basic Candlestick Charting

From Michael C. Thomsett, *Bloomberg Visual Guide to Candlestick Charting* (Hoboken, New Jersey: John Wiley & Sons, 2012), Chapters 1–6.

Types of Charts

Traders can use a variety of charts. Today, candlesticks are recognized as the most practical, simple, and easy-to-use charting formats. The structure of the candlestick provides all of the information traders require, not only in a single session but also over as long a period as a trader wants to analyze.

Many other kinds of charts have been used in the past.

The **line chart** consists of data points, all connected into a continuous line from one session to the next. The line usually represents each session's closing price (although line charts may include multiple lines to indicate both opening and closing price).

The greatest problem of the line chart is that it does not provide important data such as price gaps, momentum changes, or distinctions in session-to-session trading range. It is very simple, but it does not give analysts many of the rich forms of insight about the nature of trading in an issue. In comparison, the candlestick chart is very valuable in what it provides.

A comparison between the candlestick and the line charts demonstrates the difference in what can be gleaned from each. The next figure shows the candlestick chart of Yahoo! (YHOO) over a three-month period (Figure 10.1). Note the variations in candlestick length, color, and especially the extension of shadows. For example, the very visible upper shadow early in November precedes the downtrend, visually showing that buyers were not able to create upward momentum. The long candlestick of November 30 is followed by a white soldiers pattern leading to an uptrend. These short-term indicators are among the most valuable candlestick signals.

KEY POINT:
Candlestick charts are the most useful, practical, and visual of all charting systems. Older-style charts like the line chart and OHLC chart are no longer practical and are more limited.

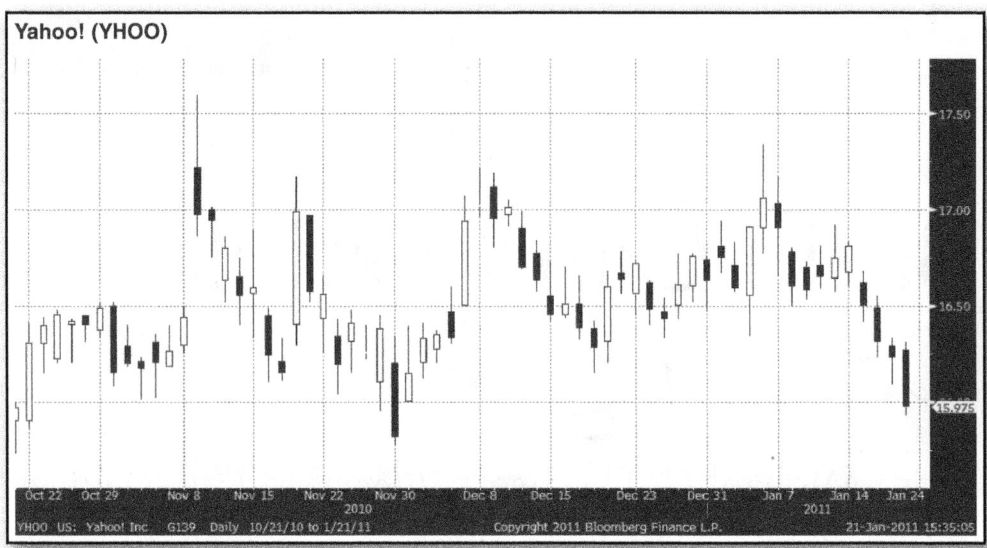

FIGURE 10.1

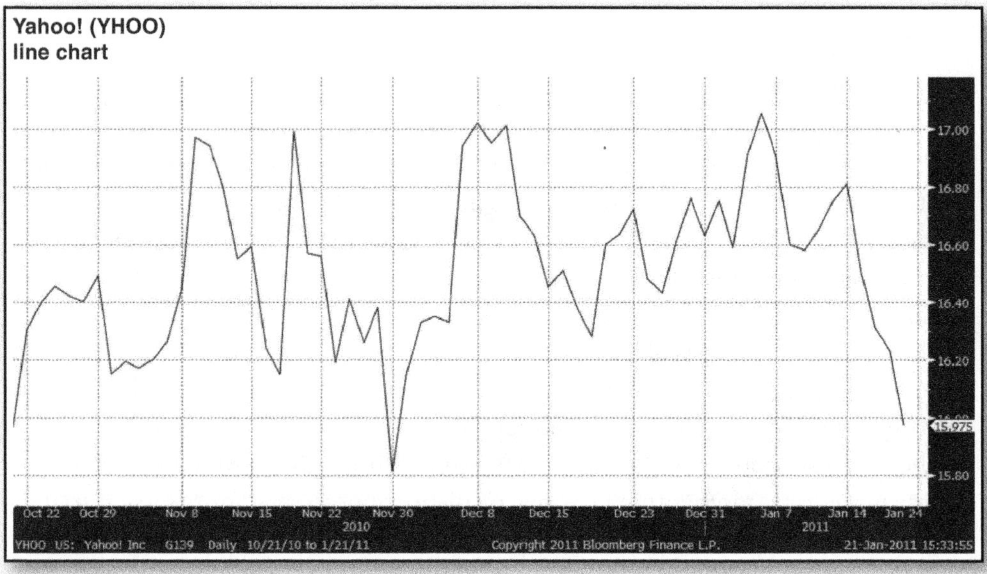

FIGURE 10.2

In comparison, the line chart (Figure 10.2) for the same period provides very little information concerning reversals. The price movement is the same as that on the candlestick, but very little can be taken from this line chart to anticipate where price is likely to move next, nor does the line chart provide any daily breadth or momentum signals.

Example of chart construction:

On May 1 through 5, the following closing values were found:

5/1	$34.00
5/2	32.15
5/3	28.50
5/4	36.00
5/5	35.50

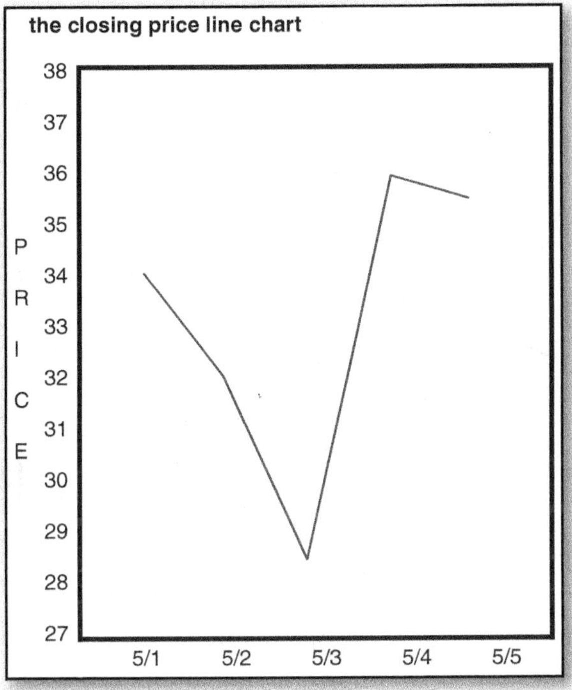

FIGURE 10.3

To construct a line chart based on five closing values, you need only to connect a series of lines representing those closing prices.

> **KEY POINT:**
> Line charts are not as effective as candlesticks in spotting entry and exit signals, notably for reversals that are very visible on candlestick charts.

The completed version of the line chart is shown in Figure 10.3.

Expanded example

The line chart can be expanded to include two separate lines, one each for opening and closing prices. A second line chart can also be created based on the following values:

	Opening Prices	Closing Prices
5/1	$31.75	$34.00
5/2	$35.50	32.15
5/3	$33.00	28.50
5/4	$29.25	36.00
5/5	$36.75	35.50

A two-line version of the line chart shows both opening and closing prices. The completed two-line version of the line chart follows in Figure 10.4.

Another popular form of chart is the **OHLC chart** (open, high, low, close) chart (Figure 10.5). This is a simplified tracking system in which each session contains four

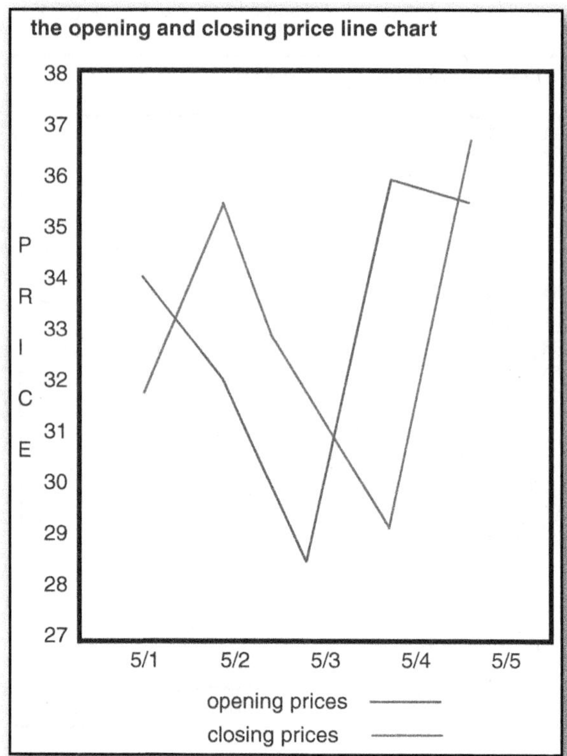

FIGURE 10.4

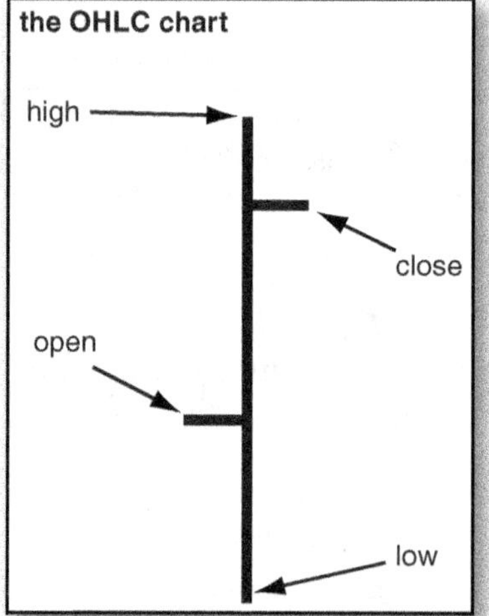

FIGURE 10.5

specific markets. The session begins with a vertical line extending from the high at the top, down to the low at the bottom. The session's opening price is represented by a smaller horizontal extension attached to the left of the range stick; and the closing price is found in a similar horizontal extension to the right.

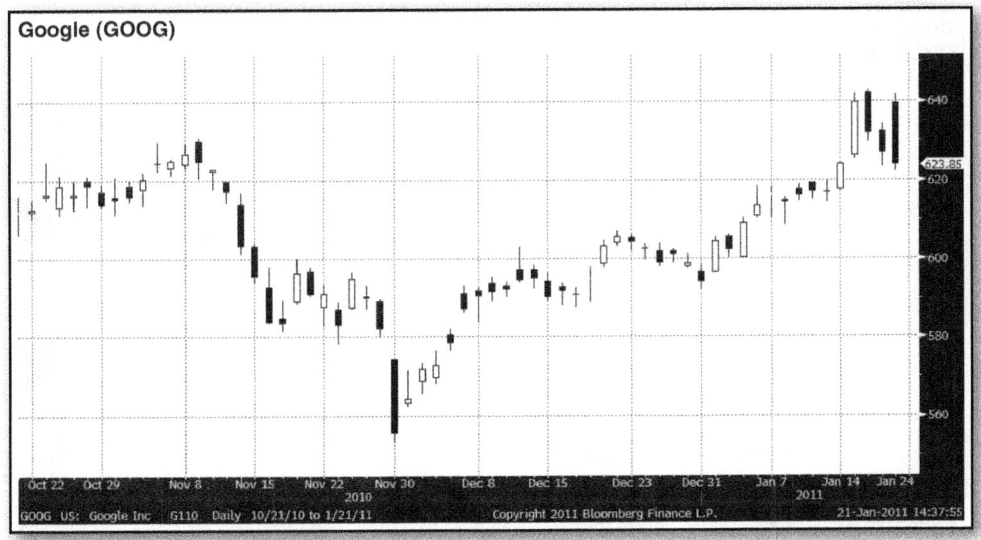

FIGURE 10.6

The OHLC chart is an improvement over the more primitive line chart, even though it is not as visually as easy to follow as the candlestick chart. It provides all of the same data (open, close, range, and direction) but is more difficult to track. Gaps do show up, but overall the OHLC chart is a difficult tracking device compared to the candlestick. It is possible to find and identify the same reversal and continuation indicators that candlesticks provide, but it takes greater effort to spot them.

KEY POINT:

The OHLC chart includes the same information as that on a candlestick chart. However, it is nowhere near as visible as the indicators reflected through candlesticks.

The candlestick chart for Google (GOOG) shows clearly the directional trends and strength of momentum, notably at the turns (Figure 10.6). Figure 10.6 contains several clear candlestick indicators (black crows occurring at the middle of November, and doji followed by gaps in the third week of December, for example).

An OHLC chart (Figure 10.7) for the same period provides identical information, but it is more difficult to read. For example, the many gaps occurring between sessions with overlapping trading ranges (hidden gaps) are very hard to spot and even harder to interpret. Even though the same data are found on the OHLC chart, the candlestick version is an easier analytical tool.

An OHLC chart can be constructed based on the following values:

	Opening Prices	Closing Prices	Daily High	Daily Low
5/1	$31.75	$34.00	$36.00	$30.00
5/2	$35.50	32.15	36.50	29.00
5/3	$33.00	28.50	33.50	28.00
5/4	$29.25	36.00	37.75	27.50
5/5	$36.75	35.50	37.50	29.00

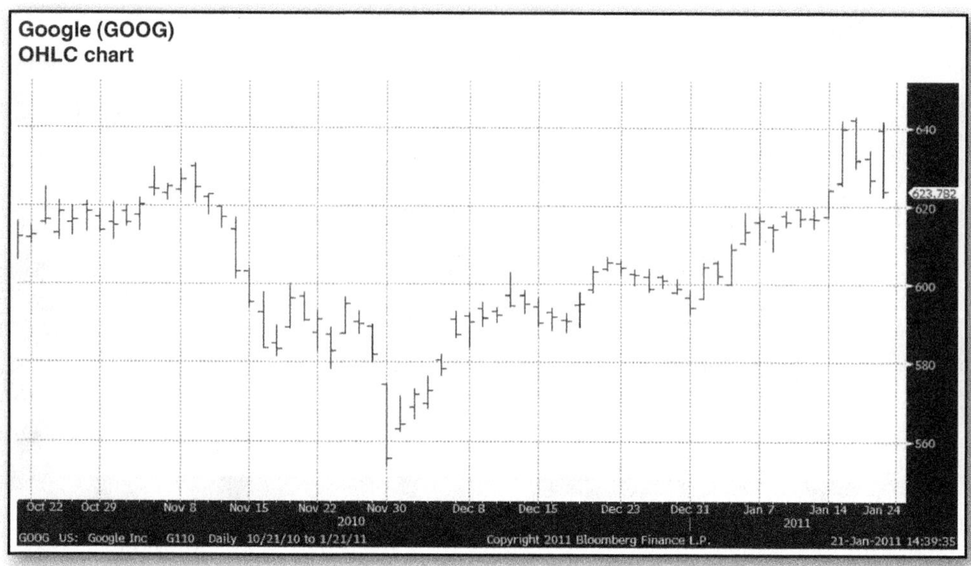

FIGURE 10.7

The OHLC chart reveals all of the information shown on the candlestick chart, but with less visual value. The completed OHLC chart reflecting these daily values is shown in Figure 10.8.

Charts can be created and saved in many formats, including bar charts, point and figure charts, and other creative variations. The appeal of alternate charting systems is a throwback to the days before the Internet, when charts had to be created by hand

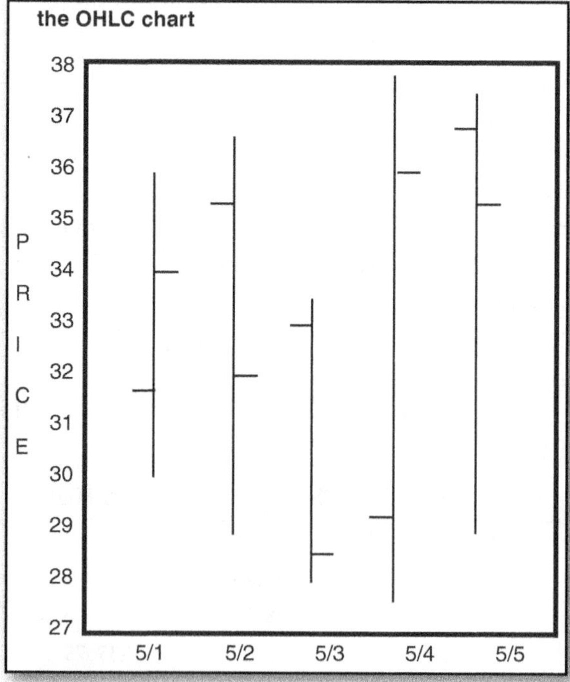

FIGURE 10.8

or bought from charting services. In that environment, simplified chart creation made sense. Today, charts are easily and automatically created in any format desired. The candlestick chart is visually the most revealing and easiest to use among the many charting formats.

The History of Candlesticks

Mokarimakka? This traditional greeting among business people in Japan means, "Are you profiting?" The culture of investing and trading goes back centuries in Japan, and at the core of this tradition is the candlestick.

This is a device for visually expressing movement of price, in terms of direction, strength, and the more subtle price range versus opening and closing price levels. A single candlestick of one session (a day or other increment of time) is revealing by itself. When combined with two, three, or more consecutive sessions, a candlestick chart reveals a pattern of trading, likely reversal points, and momentum.

Candlestick terminology employs phrasing that is both descriptive and, in many cases, warlike. When candlesticks were originally developed, Japan was in a long-term era of war and conflict, and this was reflected throughout the culture of the 16th and 17th centuries.

An Era of Commerce and Growth

By the early 17th century, Japan's warlike culture had settled into a commercial alternative. Osaka, due to its location near the ocean, became the cultural and trading center of the country. Called the "kitchen of Japan" due to its central location for moving products to and from markets, Osaka also evolved into a trading center for commodities, notably rice.

In the 17th century, Japan recognized four classes of citizens: soldiers, farmers, artisans, and merchants. One prominent merchant was Yodoya Keian, whose influence enabled him to set the price of rice. The first rice exchange in Japan was in his front yard in the late 17th century and was named the Dojima Rice Exchange, the first commodities exchange in Japan. However, because the Japanese government was keenly interested in maintaining class distinctions, Keian's success as a merchant drew attention to him. He had become wealthy, but all of his assets were taken from him by the government, which was led by the military and, especially, by the **Shogunate** warrior class. A wealthy merchant was not acceptable under the rigid class system of 17th century Japan.

KEY POINT:

"Are you profiting?" is said in Japan. Even today, this is a common greeting among traders in Osaka.

DEFINITION:

Shogunate

A Shogunate was a warrior class in Japan, in which the ruling military created a rank of general (Shogun, an abbreviated name of the seii taishōgun, or force commander) to control various tribes within the country.

Keian was accused of living a lifestyle above his rank of merchant, and this reflected a general distrust among the military of the entire merchant class. When a group of merchants had tried to corner the rice market, the government reacted by executing their children, exiling the merchants, and seizing all of their wealth.

The importance of rice (and rice futures) enabled merchants to organize and price their product even under threat from their military rulers. It was essential to grade rice by quality in order to set prices and to create an orderly market. By 1710, storage houses were issuing receipts called **"rice coupons"** *(also called "empty rice" coupons)* fixing prices of the grain, and these became the first form of a rice futures contract.

DEFINITION:

Rice coupons

The "rice coupon" (also called the "empty rice" coupon), which originated in 1710, was the first instrument for fixing rice prices, and became the first futures contract.

This system of orderly pricing and rice futures created the wealth of Osaka, which also led to rice being used as a form of currency. At the time, Japanese coinage was not reliable as an exchange medium, so rice futures provided a reasonable alternative monetary system. A farmer could fix the future value of his rice production, often for many years in advance. The futures system was very successful; in 1749, the exchange transacted 110,000 bales of rice, even though only 30,000 bales existed at the time. Several future crop years had been priced through the "empty rice" contracts, and today the worldwide commodities market functions on the same methods.

The God of the Markets

By the mid-18th century, trading in rice futures was formalized and the first appearance of the *candlestick* occurred. Munehisa Homma (also called Sakata) was called "the god of the markets" because he was the most successful trader of the time. He moved his family's firm to Edo (Tokyo), where he began researching and correlating price movements, crop yield, and weather conditions. Recognizing repetitive patterns in rice commodities pricing, he devised a system for identifying trends, with what is known today as the candlestick. The entire Japanese investing philosophy was based on Homma's observations.

In the Western world, candlesticks have been used in charting and technical analysis only since 1989. Prior to that time, traders in the United States based their methods on the tradition of bulls and bears and the ideas of Charles Dow. Even when candlesticks were introduced, they were perceived as difficult to understand, and little interest in Japanese methods was evident. Today, candlestick charts can be viewed with the click of a mouse and adjusted for trading periods and even for sessions of different durations. The automation of charting and the ability to overlay as many indicators as desired have brought candlestick analysis into the mainstream of Western technical analysis. Today, traders do not need to choose between Western and Eastern analysis; both can be used to make the overall process of analysis and confirmation very dynamic. Entry and exit timing is vastly improved by using both systems together.

Candlesticks Come to America

In 1989 in *Futures Magazine,* Steve Nison published his first article about candlestick analysis. He is the founder of Candlecharts.com but is better known as the pioneer of candlestick charting outside of Japan. He authored the first U.S. book about candlesticks, *Japanese Candlestick Charting Techniques* (1991) and also wrote *The Candlestick Course* (2003).

Although Nison was the first modern analyst to introduce candlesticks to the West, it was Charles Dow who first noted their value. In 1900, Dow observed that there were many ways to express price trends, including the Japanese methods. However, the time required to construct each day's session prevented this initial research from progressing further. The Dow Theory and pre-Internet charting techniques survived, but candlesticks went dormant for the next century. The Dow Theory forms the basis of modern technical analysis, also called "Western" analysis (compared with candlestick charting, or "Eastern" analysis). The Dow Theory is based on a set of six observations about price trends. These are (1) the market has three kinds of movements: primary, secondary, and minor; (2) market trends have three phases: accumulation, public participation, and distribution; (3) the stock market discounts all news; (4) stock market averages must confirm each other before a trend or change in trend is accepted; (5) trends are confirmed by trading volume; and (6) trends continue until a specific signal ending a trend is discovered.

Candlesticks were not popular in the United States until the Internet made it possible for traders using online systems such as the Bloomberg Professional terminal and its Launchpad platform to automate charting and to create immediate value in candlesticks and other types of technical data.

Nison's early work in candlestick research formed the basis for candlesticks as they are used today. Now, most online services provide candlestick charting as the default format for research. Most traders understand the basic concept of the candlestick itself and of how charting appears based on price movement and trends; however, the intricacies of candlestick analysis are not widely known among traders, whose reliance on Western charting techniques often excludes consideration of the candlestick as a valuable indicator for spotting and confirming the same price trends that Western indicators provide.

KEY POINT:

The introduction of candlesticks to the West was by Charles Dow. In 1900, he observed the Japanese method as one of many ways to report price trends, but it was a century before the Internet and the system did not catch on.

KEY POINT:

Launchpad delivers all the rich content of the Bloomberg Professional service in a customizable and persistent desktop format, so you see the realtime information that's relevant to you and your strategies. The result? You can make quicker, smarter investment decisions.

(This text from Bloomberg's website, www.bloomberg.com/professional/charts_launchpad/)

Candlesticks use and report the same daily information as other charting systems—the opening and closing price, and the daily high and low—but they are far more visual not only for each session but over many periods. This makes it possible to visualize trends as they evolve and to *see* changes in momentum as price moves from day to day. Even though there are dozens of candlestick indicators of one, two, or three sessions, learning to interpret and apply candlesticks is not difficult. As a visual system, it is far easier to interpret than the less visual line or OHLC charts that were used widely in the past.

The combination of Nison's research and publications, aided by subsequent mainstream acknowledgement of candlestick analysis, have made candlesticks popular as one of many systems for tracking prices. As a charting method, candlesticks are clearly the best system available, explaining their widespread use among technicians and chartists. The Internet has overcome the problems of constructing charts from scratch; it has also made it possible to pass information among traders about using candlesticks to find and confirm price continuation and reversal. Today, candlesticks are not foreign, complex, or mystical. They have become the mainstream charting tool for most Western price analysis.

Candlesticks and Their Attributes

Candlestick attributes features and trend indicators found on every candlestick (Figure 10.9). The value to this form of charting is found in the fact that all pricing data for a session is easily identified at first glance and that viewing a series of sessions helps traders easily identify momentum, direction, and reversal.

The attributes of every candlestick are defined in three areas:

1. **Opening and closing price.** Each session's opening and closing prices are found at the horizontal borders of the rectangular box for the session. The opening price is at the bottom of a white candlestick or at the top of a black candlestick. The closing price is at the top of a white candlestick or at the bottom of a black candlestick. The rectangular box is called the real body. When the opening and closing price are identical or very close, the real body is replaced by a horizontal line. This type of formation is among the most revealing of candlestick sessions and is called a doji (in Japanese, "doji" means "mistake").
2. **Trading range from high to low.** The full trading range for each session is represented by the upper and lower extensions from the real body. These are called the upper shadow and lower shadow (also called tails or wicks). The complete lack of shadow has significance in many candlestick formations, and an exceptionally long shadow also reveals failed momentum by buyers (long upper shadow) or sellers (long lower shadow), signaling potential reversal of the existing trend.
3. **Direction of movement.** One of the most powerful visual attributes of candlestick charting is the ability to immediately see the overall direction that price is moving. While line charts and OHLC charts reveal direction through the shape and duration of each session, the candlestick short-term trend is easily spotted. A white candlestick reveals that the session moved upward, and a black candlestick reveals a downward-moving session.

KEY POINT:

Every candlestick provides price information in three major areas: opening and closing prices, trading range, and direction.

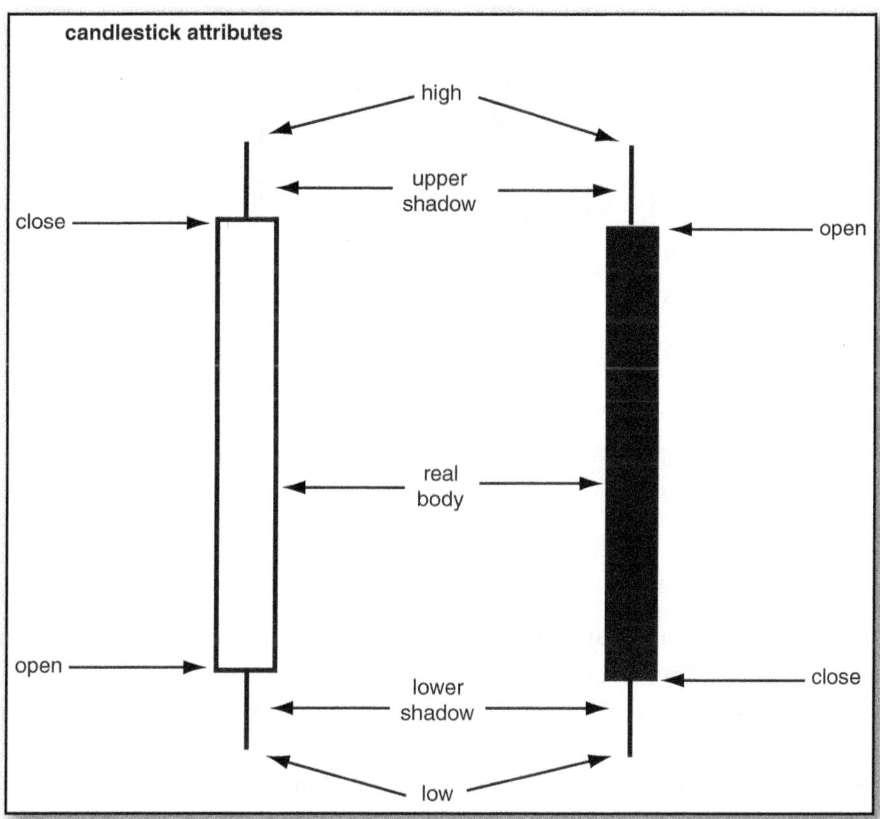

FIGURE 10.9

A candlestick chart for five sessions requires the following values:

	Opening Prices	Closing Prices	Daily High	Daily Low
5/1	$31.75	$34.00	$36.00	$30.00
5/2	$35.50	32.15	36.50	29.00
5/3	$33.00	28.50	33.50	28.00
5/4	$29.25	36.00	37.75	27.50
5/5	$36.75	35.50	37.50	29.00

The attributes of candlesticks include the opening and closing prices, the high and low for the session, and the direction (white for upward sessions and black for downward sessions). A candlestick chart for these is shown in Figure 10.10.

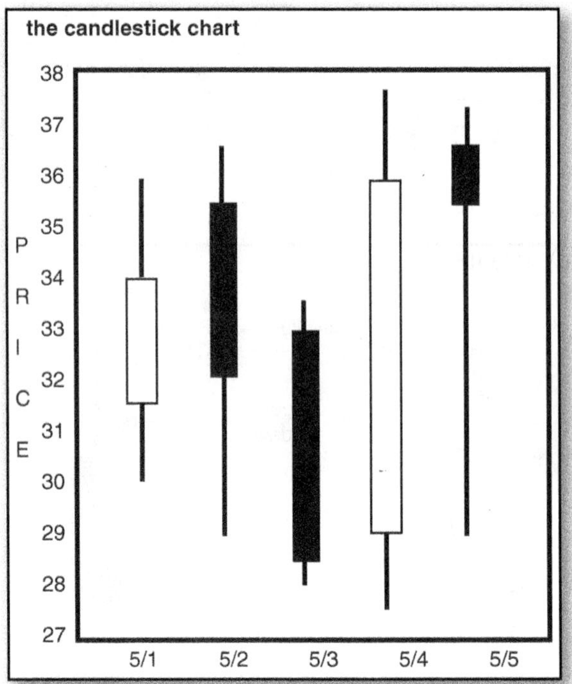

FIGURE 10.10

The Importance of Long Candlesticks

Beyond the revealing attributes of the candlestick's color and extensions, its shape and size are equally important. The longer the real body, the more struggle there is between buyers and sellers. So long candlesticks often signal continuation or reversal. When the long body appears in the same direction as the existing trend (white in uptrends or black in downtrends) it indicates continuation. When the long session is opposite, it often serves as a signal of reversal, either by itself or as part of a multisession reversal indicator. This is especially true when the long session also marks or touches resistance or support, or when price breaks through those levels and then retreats.

One form of the long candlestick is the **marubozu**, which has little or no upper or lower shadow. The lack of extension above or below the session's open or close

DEFINITION:

Marubozu

"Marubozu" is a Japanese word meaning "little hair." This is a long candlestick with little or no upper or lower shadow. As significant as a long candlestick is, the marubozu is exceptionally revealing; the lack of shadows identifies momentum and control on one side or the other.

DEFINITION:

Doji

The doji (Japanese for "mistake") is a session in which opening and closing prices are identical or very close.

indicates exceptional strength in the direction the long session moves. This reveals which side (buyers or sellers) are in control of price movement and which side manages the momentum in price.

Although shorter than average candlesticks signal less volatility and even consolidation—a form of "agreement" between buyers and sellers, a very narrow range (doji) session can signal more volatility.

KEY POINT:

Doji significance (like marubozu significance) is a relative matter based on price levels of the stock. For example, a one-point move in an $80 stock is a 1.25 percent change, but the same one-point change in a $10 stock is a 10 percent move.

The Opposite: The Extremely Narrow-Range Session

As important as long candlesticks are in identifying momentum and control issues between buyers and sellers, a different kind of importance is attached to very short sessions. The **doji** session is one in which the real body is so narrow that it consists only of a horizontal line (identical price or very thin range between high and low).

Swing traders look for the narrow-range day (NRD) as an important turning point in a short-term trend. Candlestick terminology is different, but analysis recognizes the same significance. The doji is the candlestick name for the NRD.

The upper and lower shadows on doji sessions vary and provide different signals, based not only on the size of the shadow but also on where the doji appears in the current short-term trend. A doji might look like a cross (with both upper and lower shadows) or contain upper shadows only or lower shadows only. The most important attribute of the doji is that it indicates a very tight struggle between buyers and sellers. The fact that neither side was able to move price off the open during the session is revealing to the analyst; the more shadow movement occurring within the session, the more important the doji becomes in how the current trend has to be interpreted.

The meaning of candlestick breadth varies in importance based on sessions surrounding the change. For example, when a doji is found after a period of very low volatility, it probably does not contain a lot of meaning. However, when it follows a very volatile period of long candlestick sessions, price gaps, and tests of resistance or support, a doji has greater meaning, especially if one or both of its shadows are also long.

Attributes Missing in Candlestick Analysis

No form of charting is perfect and, like all types of charts, candlestick charts have flaws. To truly understand how a session's price action has developed and what it reveals, the sequence of events has to be tracked throughout the session (Figure 10.11). Candlesticks show the range between open and close, and the distance between high and low, but they do not reveal the sequence in which that occurs.

KEY POINT:

A daily session is summarized by a candlestick, but this does not disclose the sequence of price change during the day. For that you need shorter-duration charts, because sequence can be as revealing as open, close, high, and low prices.

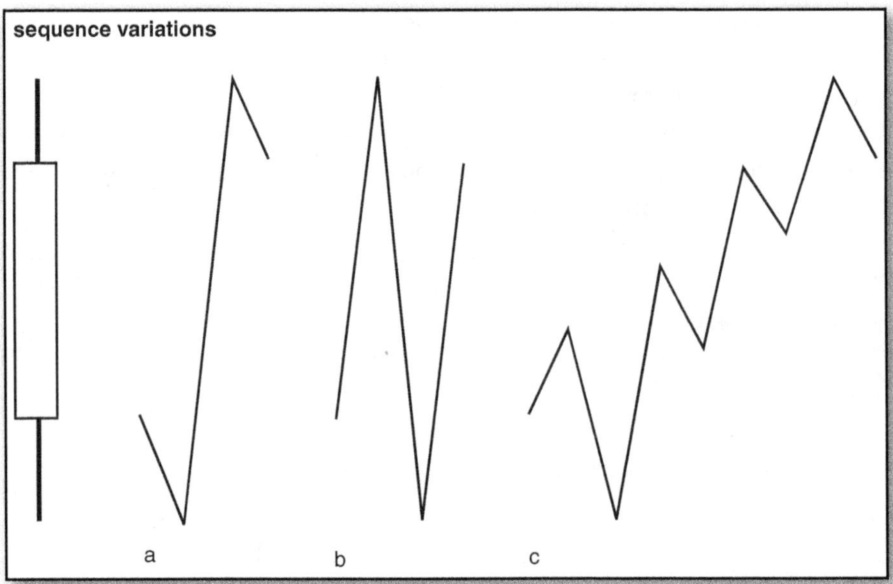

FIGURE 10.11

This is why chartists like to compare daily candlesticks to charts with higher frequency duration, such as one-hour or 20-minute charts. These more-frequent-duration charts track the sequence of price history throughout the session, revealing more price action and improving entry and exit timing.

KEY POINT:

Many possible sequencing variations are possible. Studying a full day's sequence is likely to affect a trader's opinion about momentum, volatility, and overall trend strength.

A session's change can take many forms. This is demonstrated in the preceding figure. The candlestick chart reveals an upward-moving session with moderate upper and lower shadows, but that is the extent of what it discloses.

In variation a, the session price falls to the low of the day, moves to the high, and retreats to the close.

In variation b, the price moves first to the high, retreats to the low, and then rises to the closing price.

In the final variation, c, the price moves upward and downward in a series of exchanges that reveal a more robust struggle between buyers and sellers.

With these three examples of possible sequencing of price during the day (and keeping in mind that many more variations are also possible), it is clear that the daily session's summary does not reveal all that a trader might need to know. The solution to the problem of hidden sequencing is to combine daily session analysis with intraday charts of varying duration. This enables the trader to see how quickly price levels change and how much volatility is taking place, factors that are likely to be invisible in the candlestick summarizing the entire day's trading.

Pitfalls of Candlesticks

Most traders understand that no system can provide complete accuracy. All signals fail some of the time, and some may even provide opposite indicators based on what follows. One purpose of this chapter is to present the various types of candlestick formations and to demonstrate how interpretation is supposed to take place. This means checking for confirmation as well as understanding the degree of reliability to a particular indicator.

Traders using multiple disciplines (Eastern as well as Western technical analysis) may expect to improve their reading of charts and, as a result, an improved level of timing. This means that the accuracy of entry and exit will also improve, but no one will pinpoint the perfect entry and exit all the time. If a trader is able to increase the percentage of well-timed decisions, then overall improvement in trading experience results.

Eastern indicators (candlesticks) are revealing and often pinpoint reversal or continuation. However, these are most effective when confirmed by other indicators, notably Western ones (tests of resistance and support, gapping price trends, triangles, and signals that track volume, momentum, and moving averages).

The use of any technical system relies on an understanding of how technical analysis works, either apart from the fundamentals or as part of a coordinated strategic approach. A pure chartist tracks the patterns of price movement and momentum among buyers and sellers. The belief in this approach is that price movement is very predictable.

It would be a mistake to believe that candlestick charting ensures 100 percent accuracy or guarantees the timing of entry and exit. Candlesticks are among many tools that technicians use. The chart itself does not lead price into reversal or continuation; it simply reflects an ever-changing market environment. In that sense, any particular price pattern is not "caused" by candlesticks but instead is a response to an infinite number of possible causes within the public markets. A candlestick indicator forms based on these factors and becomes a visual representation of more subtle forces at work: supply and demand, momentum, and public perceptions about markets—as well as economics, politics, and global trade, to name only a few.

This reality points out the importance of coordinating many sources of information, including:

- Western technical analysis, including familiar and popular charting techniques based on observations of trading range, resistance, and support, and the patterns and features of price movement.
- Eastern technical analysis, a range of price patterns and likelihood of reversal or continuation represented by candlestick signs, moves, and patterns.
- Fundamental analysis, the study of recent financial results as a means for identifying trends in operations, working capital, and competitive strength.

This chapter shows candlestick indicators at work in actual charts. The ideal candlestick formation is rare, so analysts must settle for close approximations, and even for accepting and acting on indicators that do not contain all of the desired attributes. Just as it is important to demonstrate that candlesticks lead to a predictable outcome, it is equally important to show that in some cases the prediction does not come true. These failed signals are crucial to recognize because, just as successful ones lead to a well-timed decision, a failed signal helps prevent an ill-timed decision.

Hindsight is easy because a price trend can be reviewed in its full context and outcome. However, in the moment, there is no way to know how price will move. An analyst or chartist may only use skills to recognize patterns and then seek confirmation. The goal is never to achieve total accuracy in timing, but to improve timing to increase the frequency of profitable outcomes and reduce the frequency of unprofitable ones. The candlestick may confirm other indicators or be confirmed by what follows. Like all technical indicators, candlestick formations are only reflections of market and external factors that collectively move prices in one direction or the other. From there, the quest for certainty has to rest with confirmation, a gathering of more and better information.

Pitfalls are going to apply in all analytical systems, especially in the short-term chaos of the markets. Price movement has a random character in the moment, so the challenge of technical analysis is to identify signals that are meaningful and then seek confirmation of what those signals predict. There are four specific types of pitfalls that traders need to watch for in any technical system. These are:

1. *Charting philosophy*. A practical point of view about all forms of charting is that price patterns are reflections of change. Thus, fundamentals (earnings reports or dividend announcements, for example) have an immediate impact on price, and that is going to show up in how price moves on the chart. Price patterns do not cause reversals or continuation patterns; they are symptoms of a broader effect that is caused by marketwide or company-specific events, some obvious and others subtle. It is easy to fall into the pitfall of viewing indicators, both Eastern and Western, in a cause and effect manner. This is a mistake. Price patterns occur in reaction to other matters.
2. *Scaling and possible misleading conclusions.* Charts are constructed to scale price movement based on the size of the chart itself. So if a selected time period involves a price movement of 40 points, the scale of the chart is adjusted to center the price activity during that period. The chart of a different company might involve a price movement of only three points. Thus, scaling will again center price activity, but the results may be misleading. For example, on a three-point scale, a one-point move will appear much more volatile than the same point change on a 40-point scale. A long candlestick (one with more range than typical) will appear more often in the smaller scale, creating the appearance of volatility on a higher level than that of a company whose chart is scaled much differently.

   An example of this scaling problem can be seen between two sample charts. The chart of Yahoo! (YHOO) covers only three points (Figure 10.12), and the

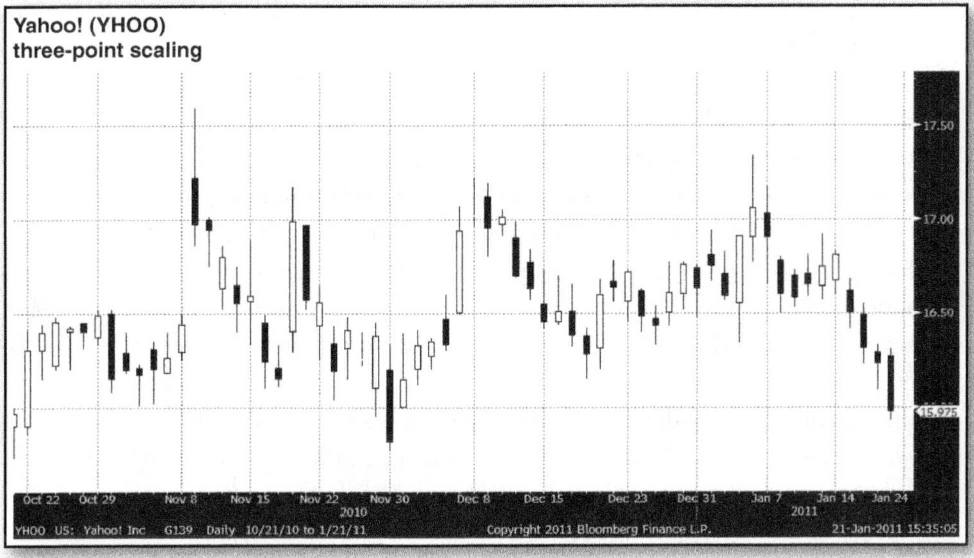

FIGURE 10.12

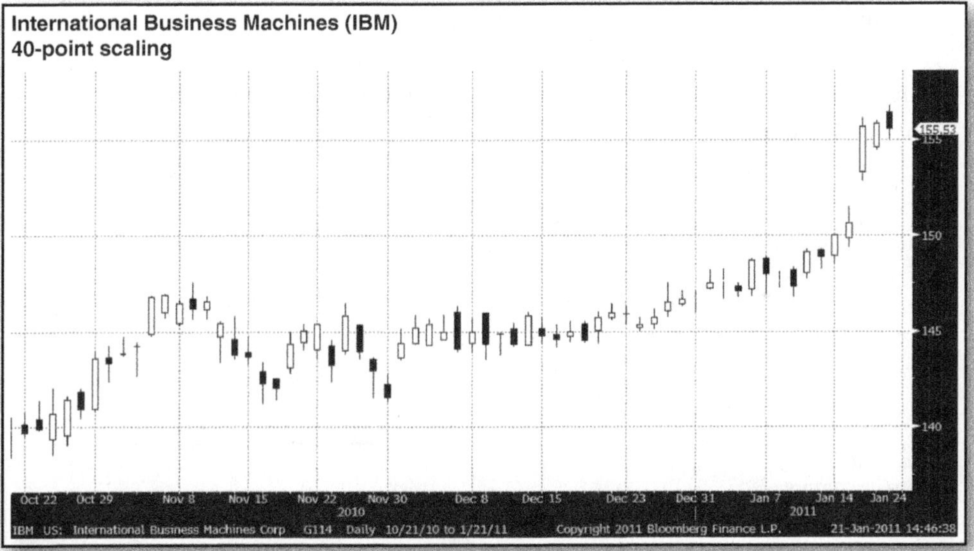

FIGURE 10.13

chart for the same period for International Business Machines (IBM) involves a 40-point range (Figure 10.13). Although IBM's price movement covered a much wider range, Yahoo!'s chart appears more volatile.

3. *Blending that may distort rather than enlighten*. One technique in candlestick analysis is called blending. In this technique, candlesticks from two or more periods are blended and recalculated to present a different view of the price trend. So a three-session change that provides no insight may be blended into a single candlestick that provides a strong indication. Properly applied, blending is nothing other than a change in the period analyzed. Just as traders may study charts on the basis of an hour or 20 minutes rather than a full day, the definition of a session can be expanded to cover several days.

Blending is an effective technique if used cautiously and only in circumstances justifying it. However, it is crucial to observe that a period-to-period comparison is going to be distorted if the blended candlestick is compared to previous single sessions. When the sessions are dissimilar, the outcome has to be viewed with the distortion in mind.

It is also possible to blend any set of candlestick outcomes in a way that distorts the true meaning of the indicator, so that the insight expected is obscured. For example, one of the more interesting three-session indicators is called a squeeze alert. This involves a long candle session followed by two sessions each smaller on both the opening and closing (they are squeezed within the range of the first session). A bear squeeze alert starts out with a white session, but it predicts a coming price decline. If all three of these are blended, it looks like a long white candlestick, which is bullish. In this example, the blending of a strong bearish signal creates a bullish signal.

4. *Forcing indicators*. The quest for "good" and "reliable" information is a constant struggle for chartists. Knowing how to interpret a signal is never easy, and one pitfall is to seek information where none exists. During sideways price movement, for example, it is quite possible that no important information is going to develop. Traders have to wait out the indecision between buyers and sellers before a new trend develops. Any indicator must be confirmed before acting on apparent signals.

   For example, the chart for Apple (AAPL) displayed a long period of sideways movement and indecision (Figure 10.14). At such times, any indicator must be confirmed by other indicators before taking action. Three examples of this are shown in the next figure.

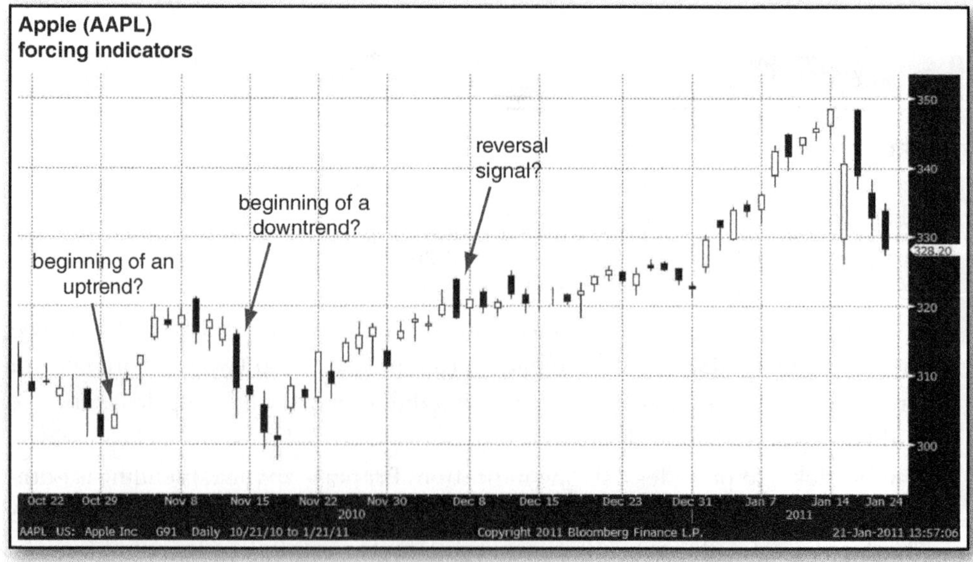

FIGURE 10.14

The first looks like a strong uptrend. Four sessions move upward with price gaps and it would be easy to assume that the price direction is likely to continue. As it turns out, this would have been a forced assumption. Without confirmation, some signals—like this one—are false leads. The same is true for the second signal, an apparent start of a downtrend. After four black sessions, traders might easily assume that prices will continue moving south. Finally, the black session might appear to provide a reversal and pending downtrend, but prices continues to drift sideways.

This example demonstrates how easily indicators can be forced. Traders in long positions may find themselves seeking bullish signals because, if price does turn upward, they will make a profit. However, in some cases a bullish signal will not be found because price is going to move sideways or down. The pitfall is a form of wishful thinking, and as a matter of gaining experience traders will benefit from knowing about this danger and striving for objectivity. In other words, it is more rational to study the signals to judge price movement, rather than seeking the type of price movement a trader desires.

Traders struggle will these pitfalls every time they look at a chart. Maintaining objectivity is difficult because everyone has specific biases toward bullish or bearish movement, as well as toward stocks they love or hate (often not for rational reasons). The truth, however, is that a trader will maintain objectivity by ignoring the emotional tendency to like or dislike a particular company or trend, and to recognize the one universal truth about technical analysis: It is possible to achieve profits in all types of markets, including bullish, bearish, and sideways trends. However, in order to be able to position themselves to profit, traders are going to have the best results when they remain analytical and avoid following the crowd or reacting the way most traders do, emotionally.

The overall pitfall to trading is to "gut react" to price changes. When prices rise strongly, the emotion of greed causes a majority of people to jump into long positions. This often takes place right as prices peak. When prices fall, a majority tends to panic and sell to avoid further losses, and this is most likely to happen at the price bottom. So instead of applying the "buy low and sell high" approach, the outcome of this broad pitfall is to "buy high and sell low."

The contrarian approach to trading is the best way to avoid following the crowd and timing entry and exit poorly. By recognizing that the emotions of greed and panic dominate short-term trading, traders can adopt a smart strategic approach and move opposite of the majority. A market adage summarizes this approach well: "Bulls and bears can make money, but pigs and chickens get slaughtered."

Confirmation

Confirmation is an important aspect of technical analysis, notably when analyzing candlestick formations. It is the observation of separate and independent signals that verify what the candlestick pattern predicts. For example, a candlestick reversal may be confirmed by tests of resistance or support, momentum indicator changes, or moving average-based analysis. Two or more candlestick indicators may occur in proximity, providing very strong confirmation.

Confirmation is the core concept of technical analysis. Candlestick patterns and indicators are valuable additions to other technical signals, either as confirming indicators or as leading indicators that may be confirmed separately. A test of resistance or support, for example, may be first made by a familiar technical signal (such as head and shoulders or double top or bottom) and then confirmed by strong reversal candlestick signals. Or a candlestick reversal may first appear and then be confirmed by failed tests of resistance or support. There are many possible combinations of cross-confirmation between Western and Eastern (candlestick) signals.

KEY POINT:

Confirmation is the central theme and base of all technical analysis. Properly used, it is likely to vastly improve entry and exit timing.

Traders rely on confirmation to improve their timing of entry and exit. The concept is necessary because no single indicator is always reliable. Even confirmed signals may fail; however, with the use of confirmation, the ratio of successful trade timing improves and failed signals are more easily spotted when secondary indicators contradict rather than confirm what the initial signal indicates.

Confirming indicators are those indicators occurring immediately after an initial indicator, or at the same time, when both point to the same price action expected to follow. A confirming indicator may be based on Western technical analysis or on Eastern (candlestick) signals or both.

A confirming indicator may also consist of a second sign of the same type. For example, an initial candlestick reversal may be followed by an equally strong but different candlestick revealing the same potential. When this occurs, the reliability of the dual signal is exceptionally strong.

The initial purpose of confirmation is to improve timing for trades. Another value is found in how a confirming indicator identifies and confirms a broader trend. A price trend may last only a few sessions, or extend for weeks or even months. Confirmation relying on moving averages, volume trends, and relative strength are valuable in identifying the likelihood of a trend continuing or ending. In this respect, confirmation not only affects the turning point in price, but it also can anticipate an overall weakening in momentum or development of a period of consolidation after a strong or rapid trend has run its course.

KEY POINT:

Confirmation does not require two separate types of indicators. It can also involve two candlesticks both indicating the same continuation or reversal in price.

Confirmation is also valuable when used to time entry and exit within the context of existing resistance and support levels. Traders recognize the tendency for price to remain within the trading range until a signal changes current conditions. In traditional technical analysis, a failed attempt to break out of the trading range is likely to lead to a price trend in the opposite direction. When this occurs and separate confirmation is found in candlestick formations, the reversal has a better than average likelihood of taking place.

> **KEY POINT:**
> A trendline is a dynamic variety of falling resistance (in a downtrend) or rising support (in an uptrend). It is simply a line drawn to track movement of price, which reverses once the trendline runs into a directional trend in the price range.

If price does break through resistance or support, traders face an immediate decision point. Will the trend continue and establish a new trading range? Or will the breakout fail, any gaps reverse and fill, and price levels return to previously set levels? The uncertainty of the outcome of a breakout can be clarified with confirmation, notably through candlestick formations that accompany or follow the breakout itself. Augmenting the dual analysis of breakouts and candlestick patterns, further confirmation may also be found in momentum oscillators and studies of indicators based on changes in volume, moving average convergence and divergence, and other specialized technical signals.

The short-term changes in price direction and strength can further be confirmed and tracked with the use of trendlines and other visual tools. Following a trendline helps identify when a short-term trend is likely to reverse, and if confirmed with candlestick reversal signals, is a reliable method for tracking and confirming price and momentum. An uptrend is marked with a trendline drawn under the price levels from a low point, and it continues until it runs into price that has peaked and reversed. A downtrend is marked with a trendline drawn above the price levels starting from a high point and continuing downward until price reaches its low and then turns.

Confirmation comes in many forms and is applied to short-term or intermediate trends, evolving trading ranges, and momentum. Just as important as confirming an indicated change to make well-timed entry and exit is the opposite theory of contradiction. When two normally reliable indicators do not agree, the significance is uncertain. In this instance, traders have to choose one of several courses of action:

1. Seek confirmation from a new set of indicators.
2. Take no action until the indication is clarified.
3. Select one indicator as more reliable and act based on what it shows.
4. Expand the analysis for more time, sessions of a different duration, or using multiple indicators.

The Six Basic Candlesticks

Among the dozens of candlestick formations, there exist many combinations of the six basic candlesticks. These are:

1. **Long candlesticks.** The long candlestick indicates a lot of momentum among buyers (long white) or sellers (long black). When there is little or no shadow,

the long candlestick is defined as a marubozu. The lack of shadow indicates exceptional strength for one side or the other, because price opens or closes at the opening or closing price without further extension. A marubozu may have no shadows, or a small one at the top or at the bottom of the real body. (See Figure 10.15.)

The significance of the long candlestick relies completely on placement. For example, a long white candlestick appearing within an uptrend is a strong reversal indicator, but if the same candlestick appears after a downtrend, it is more likely to act as a reversal signal. The same is true for long black candlesticks. Within a downtrend, it tends to confirm, and when it follows an uptrend, it is more likely to signal reversal.

2. **Short candlesticks.** A candlestick with average or relatively small extension signals (Figure 10.16) indicates a general agreement between buyers and sellers that the current price is reasonable, especially when short candlesticks appear in a series of sideways-moving sessions. However, when short candlesticks appear following a period of strong trend in either direction, especially when long candlesticks have shown up, the short candlestick can indicate a struggle between buyers and sellers and a likely reversal in the trend, or a slowing down in price momentum.

> **KEY POINT:**
> A long candlestick does not always mean the same thing; it depends on where it appears. If it contradicts the direction of the prevailing trend, it signals reversal; if it conforms to the direction of that trend, it is a continuation indicator.

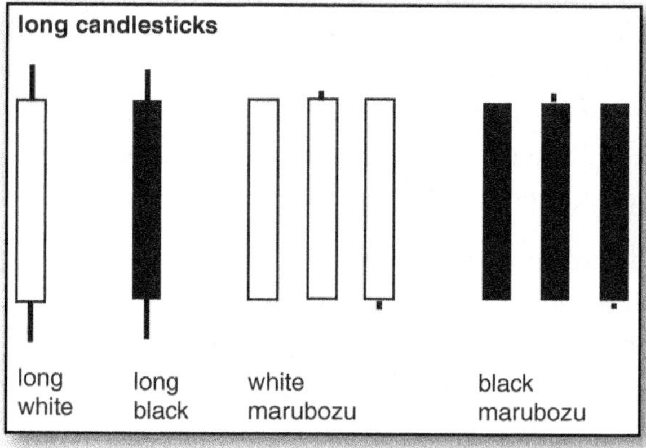

FIGURE 10.15

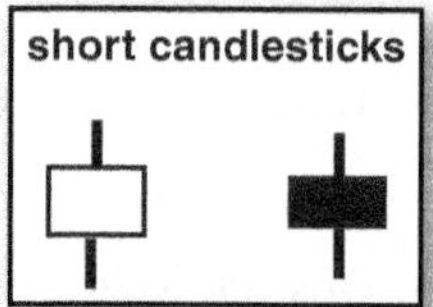

FIGURE 10.16

KEY POINT:
The appearance of a single short candlestick is not a signal at all, just part of the normal trading pattern. However, when a series of short candlesticks appears after a period of relatively long sessions, it implies falling momentum.

The appearance of a single short candlestick is not meaningful by itself. When a series of short candlesticks sets a pattern, it may show declining momentum in the current trend or be a symptom of sideways movement. The lack of decisive control by either buyers or sellers in such a series may be viewed as showing that the next price movement is not clear and will not be until one side or the other takes control.

KEY POINT:
A doji to the candlestick analyst is the same thing as the narrow-range day (NRD) to the swing trader. The power of the doji is not only in its identical or close open and close, but also in the length and placement of its shadows.

3. **Doji sessions.** The session with no real body (Figure 10.17)—one in which open and close are the same—is a very significant development if the session appears at the end of a current trend. Also called a narrow-range day (NRD) in swing trading, the fact that price opens and closes at the same place has even greater significance when the doji also has exceptionally long upper or lower shadows, or both. The longer shadows reveal an attempt by buyers (upper shadow) or sellers (lower shadow) to move price in the desired direction. However, the effort failed when price retreat to close at the same price as the open.

   The meaning of the failure on one side or the other, or on both sides, affects how the current trend is viewed and what it means in terms of likely reversal. For example, when a doji appears at the bottom of a downtrend and also has an exceptionally long lower shadow, it shows that sellers tried to move price lower but could not; this hints at the likely reversal in direction and a coming trend to the upside. If a doji appears at the top of an uptrend and also has a very long upper shadow, the same failed attempt is shown, this time among buyers. This foreshadows a likely reversal and subsequent downtrend.

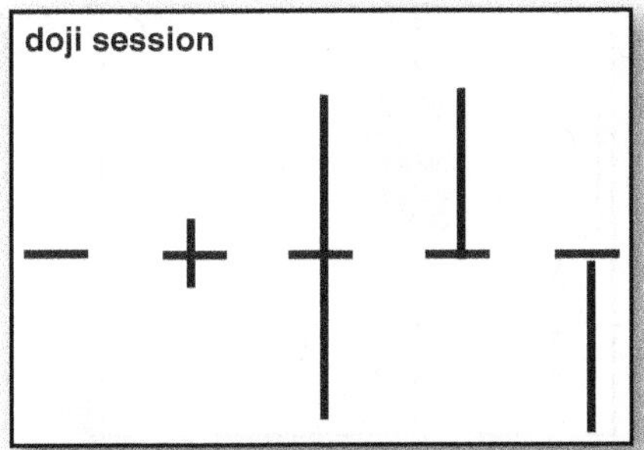

FIGURE 10.17

Confirmation is essential to these interpretations, which are only generalizations unless confirmation agrees with the interpretation of the doji session. However, just as long candlesticks indicate exceptional strength on one side of the buyer/seller equation, doji sessions indicate a loss of momentum and, based on the appearance of any shadows, provide strong reversal signals.

4. **Long upper and lower shadows.** One of the most interesting signals in all of candlestick analysis is an exceptionally long shadow appearing on both sides of the real body (Figure 10.18). When such shadows are found in both upper and lower realms in comparison to the real body, it shows that neither buyers nor sellers had enough power to move price beyond the opening and closing range. This failure of both sides to control price movement is seen at times as the advent to a period of consolidation. When a candlestick shows up with long shadows on both sides and a current trend has been underway, it most often signals the end of that trend, even though both sides were unable to create more movement.

   Long shadows both above and below the real body may be better understood when analysis is aided with a study of intraday charts in addition to daily charts. Based on the level of volatility within the session, a trader may conclude that the volatility has little meaning as a reversal signal or that the chaotic nature of the trading day has created an environment of uncertainty. Clearly, any existing trend will have most likely ended once this candlestick appears; what is not as certain is whether the trend will pause and continue, or fall apart and reverse.

5. **Long upper shadow only.** When a session contains an unusually long upper shadow (Figure 10.19), it signals that buyers have lost momentum or failed in an effort to take momentum away from sellers. If this pattern unfolds at the top of an uptrend, it is very likely a signal that the trend is about to end. If it shows up within a downtrend, it may confirm or establish continuation; buyers tried to reverse the downtrend, but failed.

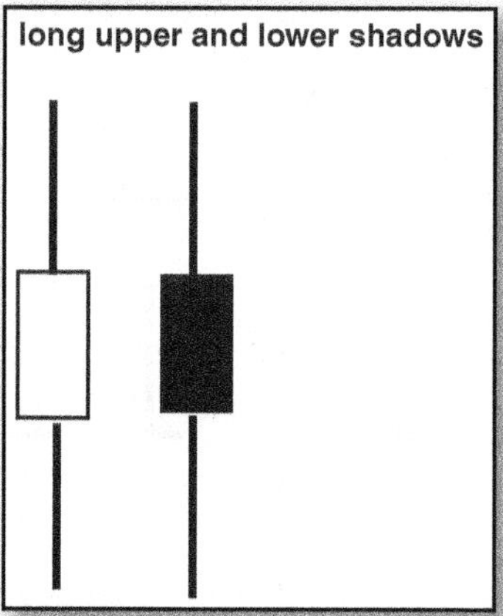

FIGURE 10.18

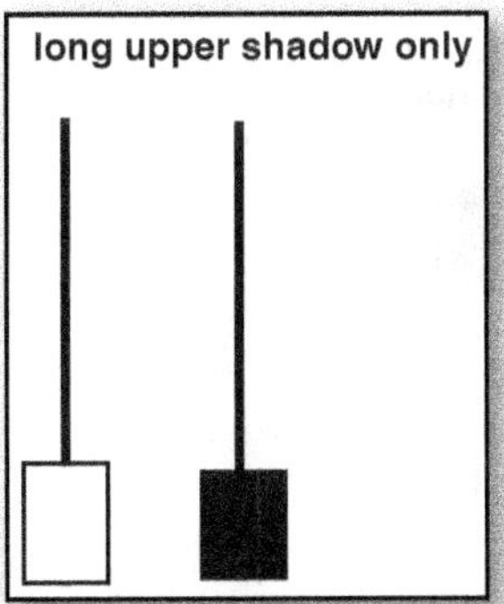

FIGURE 10.19

> **KEY POINT:**
> When a session includes long upper and lower shadows, it usually means momentum in the current trend is ending. Both sides—buyers and sellers—were unable to move price beyond the real body range.

> **KEY POINT:**
> A long upper shadow demonstrates that buyers were not able to move price higher. This reveals weak or weakening buyer-driven momentum.

This pattern also works in many two-stick or three-stick candlestick patterns as one of the elements that makes up that pattern. For example, the inverted hammer is a bullish indicator after a long black candlestick and a downside gap, followed by the black or white session with a long upper shadow, a sign that the downtrend is reversing direction. A bearish version follows a long white candlestick, an upside gap, and then the inverted session—a smaller session with a long upper shadow, foreshadowing the highest point in the uptrend, to be followed next by a reversal and downtrend.

> **KEY POINT:**
> A long lower shadow demonstrates that sellers were not able to move price lower. This reveals weak or weakening seller-driven momentum.

6. **Long lower shadow only.** The appearance of a candlestick with a long lower shadow (Figure 10.20) has significance opposite of the session with a long upper shadow. It indicates a failure by sellers to move price lower, which leads to the immediate conclusion that either the current downtrend is ending, or an existing uptrend is continuing. However, the pattern can have either a bullish or a bearish interpretation.

> **KEY POINT:**
> Not every development forms up as an indicator. To paraphrase Sigmund Freud, sometimes a candlestick is just a candlestick.

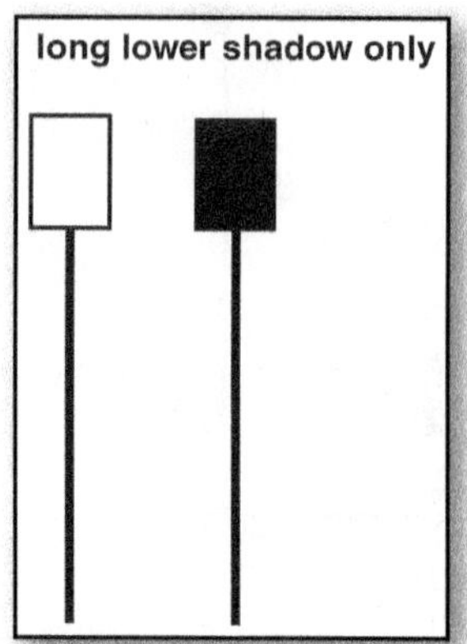

FIGURE 10.20

The single session of this shape is either a hammer or a hanging man. The interesting thing about this pattern is that it can be bullish or bearish, depending on where it appears. The real body may also be either white or black, without affecting the interpretation of the session. A hammer appears at the bottom of a downtrend and is recognized as a relatively small real body of either color and an unusually long lower shadow. A hanging man is often the highest point in the uptrend and signals the reversal point. It consists of a small real body of either color and a long lower shadow, signaling the turn of direction and the beginning of a downtrend.

With all forms of candlesticks, "significance" is a matter of content. The importance of a shape or pattern changes based on what occurred before the candlestick, and it may have either reversal or continuation ramifications. Remember, also, that candlestick patterns do not always have to mean anything of interest. In the daily trading pattern, some apparent signals are really not signals at all; this is why confirmation is so important.

CHAPTER 11

Basic Indicators Reference A to C

From Michael C. Thomsett, *Bloomberg Visual Guide to Candlestick Charting* (Hoboken, New Jersey: John Wiley & Sons, 2012), Chapter 8, A-C.

Accumulation/Distribution (AD) a **momentum oscillator** based on price trends, developed by Marc Chaikin, a trader who recognized the importance of whether current price movement of a stock is controlled by buyers (accumulation phase) or by sellers (distribution phase).

DEFINITION:

momentum oscillator

A momentum oscillator is a type of price-based indicator. Momentum measures the rate of change in price; an oscillator shows how value changes in relation to a set value or values over time.

The A/D indicator is based on a single day's prices and it identifies whether buyers or sellers determined the price levels and movements. A series of A/D days expressed in a moving average and divided by volume for the averaged period (usually 21 days) is called the Chaikin Money Flow (CMF), a strong technical sign that often provides reversal signals in advance of the turnaround and that may be confirmed by candlestick signals.

DEFINITION:

The A/D indicator

The A/D indicator is a momentum oscillator. Its value goes beyond the initial calculation, however. The moving average of A/D serves as the basis for the more revealing signal, the Chaikin Money Flow (CMF).

The A/D trend is important because it reveals what may be an otherwise invisible or subtle change in momentum. A focus on the **breadth indicators** may assume that as long as prices remain within the established trading range, no change is on the horizon. A/D may demonstrate than even when prices remain below resistance and above support, a developing shift in control precedes a turnaround in the trend and, often, a breakout from the established trading range. When the basic A/D formula is expanded into CMF and included on a candlestick chart, it provides a meaningful additional form of technical information and trend development.

> **DEFINITION:**
> **breadth indicators**
> A breadth indicator measures advances and declines in price to identify participation among traders in a specific issue or in the market in general.

The chart for American Express (AXP) shows both price movement and A/D (Figure 11.1). Note how A/D often precedes changes in price. For example, at the end of the first week in December, the price appears to be continuing upward, but the A/D line begins falling, anticipating the price decline that does not follow until one week later. This indicates that the uptrend was ending. A few days later, price

> **DO IT YOURSELF**
> A/D is calculated by finding the sum of differences between the close/low and the close/high of a session:
>
> ([(close – low) – (high – close)] ÷ (high – low)) = A/D
> The formula produces a numerical value between +1 (maximum accumulation) and –1 (maximum distribution).

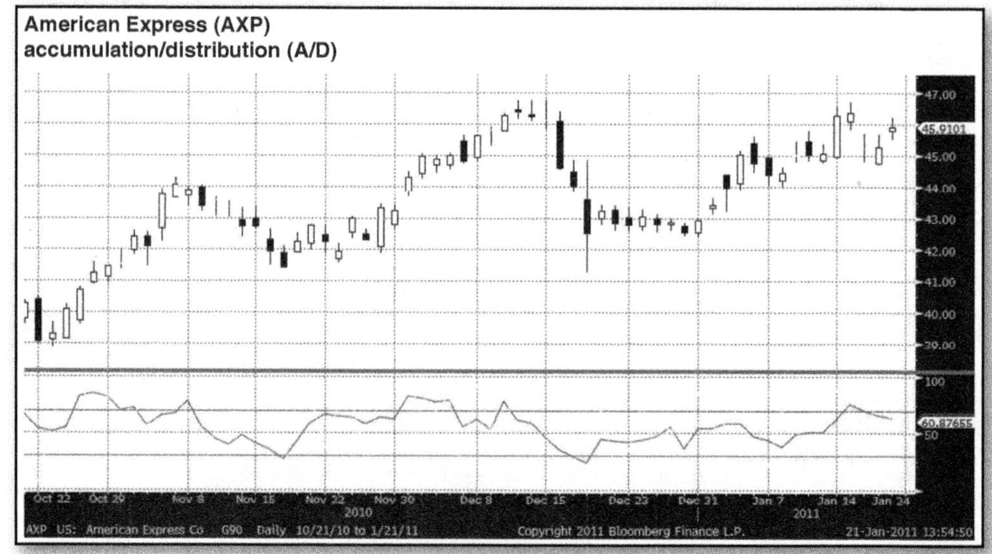

FIGURE 11.1

STEP-BY-STEP

Follow these steps to calculate A/D:

1. Subtract the session's low from the close.
2. Subtract the session's close from the high.
3. Find the net difference between the results of steps 1 and 2.
4. Subtract the session's low from the session's high.
5. Divide the result of step 3 by the result of step 4.
6. The answer is the A/D. If step 1 produced a negative result, A/D will also be negative.

DO IT YOURSELF

An example of A/D calculation: One session's high was $38, its low was $31, and its close was $37. A/D was:

([(37 – 31) – (38 – 37)] ÷ (38 – 31)) = +0.71

DO IT YOURSELF

When the net difference in the first side of the A/D formula is negative, A/D is also negative. One session's outcome was $55 high, $46 low, and $48 close. A/D was:

([(48 – 46) – (55 – 48)] ÷ (55 – 46)) = –0.56

reached the bottom of its downtrend when A/D fell below the zero line. However, A/D began moving upward a session before price followed. Once more, the reversal in A/D preceded the reversal in price.

Average True Range (ATR) At times confused with the simpler true range, which is a form of blending between two consecutive sessions, ATR is the averaging of 14 periods intended to smooth out short-term volatility. Originally developed by J. Welles Wilder and featured in his 1978 book, *New Concepts in Technical Trading Systems* (Trend Research), the indicator recognizes that volatility may prevent traders from recognizing the real trend underway and becoming too focused on the short-term price volatility instead.

The outcome of ATR relies on the starting point. Because the calculation of current and all future ATR levels is going to be affected by the level of volatility in the initial 14 periods, the outcome is also going to be affected by whether those periods are quite volatile, or very smooth. With this in mind, accuracy may be improved by calculating ATR based on an initial longer period, perhaps even a 52-week range instead of only 14 days. Even with the longer period, the volatility during that period compared to more recent levels of volatility may also distort ATR.

A second problem grows from the fact that lower-priced securities tend to move in a narrower range than higher-priced securities. As a result, lower-priced securities tend to have lower ATR and higher-priced securities tend to have higher ATR, because the calculation is based on the point range. An alternative may be to use percentage changes over the period being averaged. However, the combination of trading price levels of different securities, with the issue of the starting point for the calculation, make ATR a difficult indicator to rely upon for timing of decisions. The study of candlestick patterns to confirm price patterns and volume is a more accurate method for measuring price volatility.

DO IT YOURSELF

To calculate ATR, the prior ATR is multiplied by 13 and added to the current trading range; the sum is then divided by 14.

$[(ATR_p \times 13) + TR] \div 14 = ATR_n$

where: ATR_p = Prior ATR

TR = current period's trading range

ATR_n = new ATR

KEY POINT:

There are two problems with ATR. First, the outcome varies depending on the volatility of the starting point. Second, calculation is based on point range, so lower-priced securities tend to have lower ATR than higher-priced ones with larger point spreads in their range.

Blending Candles (Bear) Candlestick indicators created by combining several sessions into a single indicator pointing to the downside. Blending may lead to trouble if not used sparingly; any series of candlesticks may be blended to create an effect. Blending is best used when a reversal trend is uncertain and blending can clarify the picture. It may apply in blending several days into a single indicator; it may also be used to summarize shorter trade intervals during one session into a blended version of the trend. The illustration of a bearish blending demonstrates how black crows can be restated to a blended long black candle (Figure 11.2).

A true blend extends from the open to the close of all of the candlesticks within the blended range, from the open of the first session to the close of the last, and should also reflect the high and low shadows of the entire range.

Blending may become quite complex and involve a number of sessions. The chart for Wal-Mart (WMT) provides an example of this blending process (Figure 11.3). The long black blend is a summary of 10 sessions. The blend clearly reflects the bearish reversal. However, the 10 sessions collectively are less clear in their significance. As long as the blending clarifies or simplifies the trend, it is a useful tool.

To create a blended chart, combine several consecutive sessions. The following three sessions were found on the accompanying chart:

	Open	Close	High	Low
Day 1	46	39	52	37
Day 2	43	41	49	36
Day 3	42	39	44	34

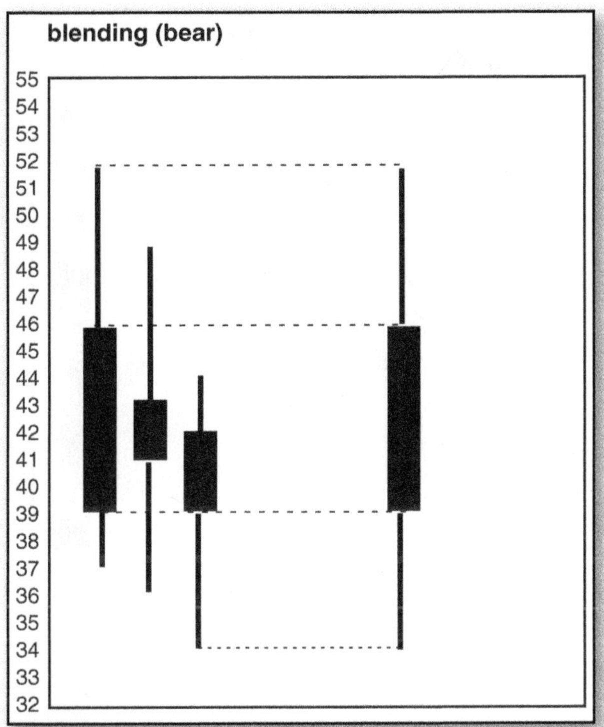

FIGURE 11.2

> **KEY POINT:**
> Blending combines a consecutive set of sessions into a single candlestick. This can clarify the picture, or it can obscure it.

Calculate the following:

a. The three days' candlesticks, showing the direction, high, low, open, and close of each.
b. A blending candlestick combining all of the price features into a single session.

The answers are shown in Figure 11.4.

Blending Candles (Bull) Blending can also be done on the bullish side. Any series of candlestick can be summarized in a blend to improve understanding of what a trend means. This is especially true when reversal seems to be underway, but chaotic price movement within the blended candlesticks obscures the signals. Blending is usually used to describe summaries of several days into a single candle; it can also be applied to shorter trade intervals during one session to create a blended version of the trend.

The next illustration shows how white soldiers can be blending into a single long white candlestick. In determining whether the blended version or individual candlesticks are most revealing, traders need to compare both. The white soldiers indicator is a strong bullish signal; so is a long white candlestick.

blending (bear)
black crows
=
long black
Wal-Mart (WMT)
blending (bear)
blend
56.50
56.00
55.80
55.50
55.00
54.50
54.00
53.50
53.00
Oct 22
Oct 29
Nov 8
Nov 15
Nov 22
Nov 30
2010
Dec 8
Dec 15
Dec 23
Dec 31
Jan 7
Jan 14
Jan 24
2011
WMT US: Wal-Mart Stores Inc G137 Daily 10/21/10 to 1/21/11
Copyright 2011 Bloomberg Finance L.P.
21-Jan-2011 15:30:19

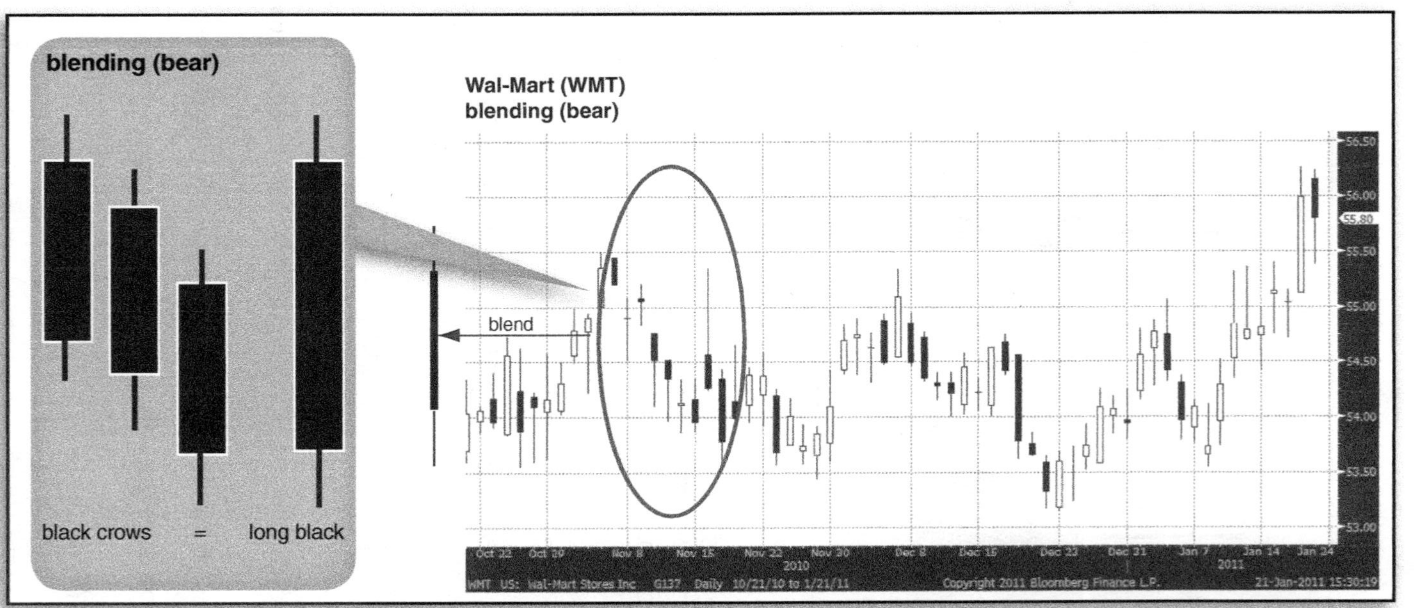

FIGURE 11.3

KEY POINT:
At first glance, the belt hold does not seem especially important. But the real key to understanding the belt hold is the invisible gap that forms between the two sessions. This gap, combined with the reversal in direction, makes the belt hold an important reversal signal.

The chart for Exxon Mobil (XOM) shows how this comparison may be useful or confusing (Figure 11.5). The series of six white candlesticks provides a good bull trend indication; traders need to determine whether this is more or less useful than a blended long white session. The sideways movement that came next was followed by a resumption of the uptrend. With this in mind, the blended candlestick may have provided a stronger indication than the six individual sessions.

A blended candlestick combines consecutive sessions into a single one. For example, the following three sessions were found on the accompanying chart:

	Open	Close	High	Low
Day 1	46	48	52	37
Day 2	46	41	49	36
Day 3	42	51	56	34

Calculate the following:

a. The three days' candlesticks, showing the direction, high, low, open, and close of each.
b. A blending candlestick combining all of the price features into a single session.

The answers are shown in Figure 11.4.

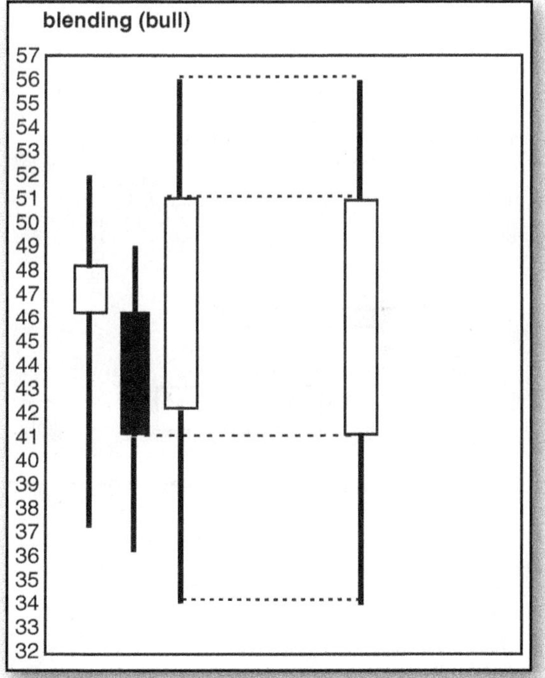

FIGURE 11.4

blending (bull)
white crows = long white
Exxon Mobil (XOM)
blending (bull)
blend
80.00
78.985
78.00
76.00
74.00
72.00
70.00
68.00
66.00
64.00
Oct 22 Oct 29 Nov 8 Nov 15 Nov 22 Nov 30 Dec 8 Dec 15 Dec 23 Dec 31 Jan 7 Jan 14 Jan 24
2010
2011
XOM US: Exxon Mobil Corp G105 Daily 10/21/10 to 1/21/11
Copyright 2011 Bloomberg Finance L.P.
21-Jan-2011 14:26:16

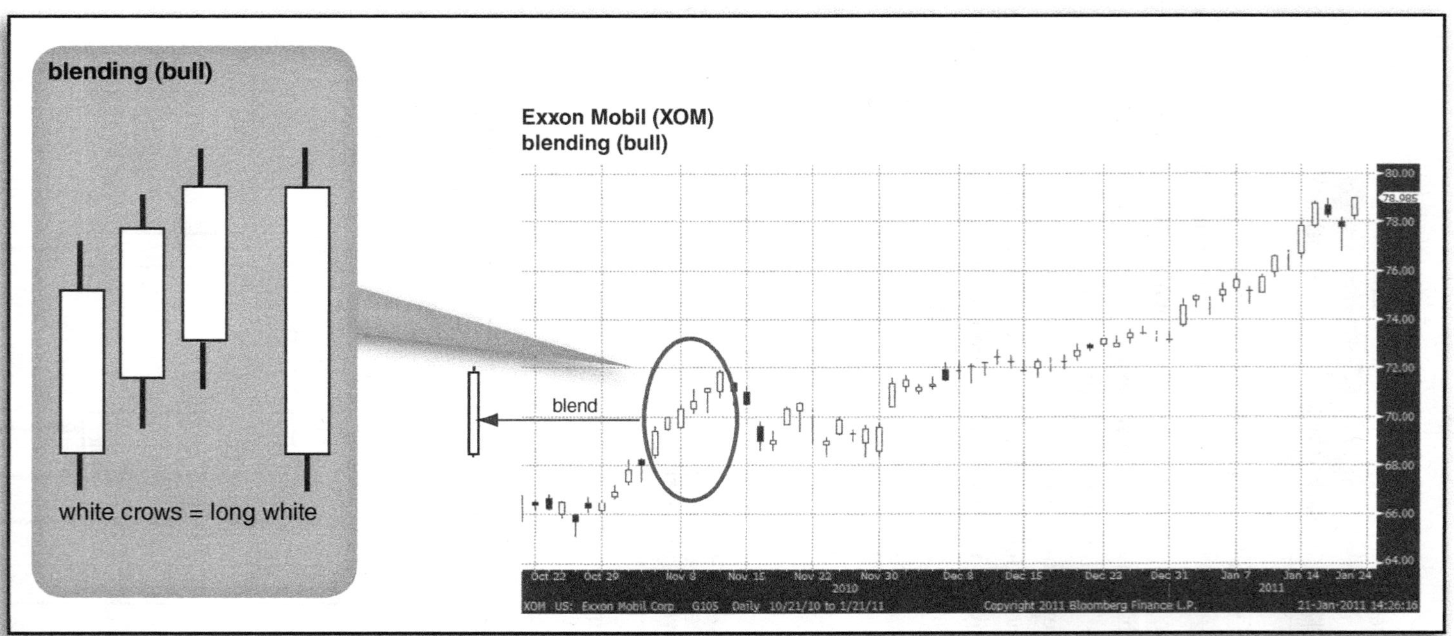

FIGURE 11.5

Bollinger Bands A useful technical indicator developed by John Bollinger in the early 1980s. Bollinger, a chartered financial analyst and chartered market technician, created the bands as a means for anticipating price trends in a systematic way before price reversals occur.

> **KEY POINT:**
> Bollinger bands show variations above and below a simple moving average. The indicator is valuable for anticipating reversals and works nicely with confirming candlesticks.

The indicator consists of three separate bands or curves. The middle, or intermediate band, represents a simple moving average of price. Bands two and three are found above and below and are calculated by price volatility (plotted as two standard deviations of 20 periods' moving average in default settings, which can be adjusted for more or fewer periods as desired).

Bollinger bands can be used in conjunction with candlestick indicators, either to confirm those indicators or as a lead indicator to be independently confirmed by subsequent candlestick patterns.

Bollinger devised this indicator in the belief that volatility levels are dynamic and rarely static for a particular security. Changes in volatility levels, whether attributed to a specific security or responsive to larger market causes, anticipates changes in price direction and momentum. This concept—that volatility acts in a dynamic manner—went against the popular technical thinking of the 1980s, when the bands were introduced.

The use of three bands is crucial because the span between top and bottom to the middle simple moving average expands and contracts as volatility changes. The bands place relative values on high and low volatility and help traders recognize emerging price patterns, also improving the timing of entry and exit. When combined with candlestick patterns as confirming indicators, Bollinger bands add the element of changing volatility to the study of the price trend.

Bollinger bands display changes in momentum, volume, and trader sentiment that collectively strengthen the use of candlestick signals in spotting and timing reversals, or in noting continuation indicators. Because the bands test both momentum and direction, they are valuable tools for testing overall sentiment about the security. The indicator is valuable in confirming double tops or bottoms, head and shoulders, and other tests of trading range borders, especially when candlestick indicators reveal the same changes as the bands.

The chart for Coca-Cola (KO) tracks the three bands in the illustration (Figure 11.6). Note how the range between the bands begins to narrow during the second half of December. This signals the slowing down of momentum in the prevailing uptrend, even though this was not indicated in any immediate candlestick patterns. However, the combination of the narrowing Bollinger bands and the sideways price pattern foreshadowed the subsequent reversal and downtrend.

Breadth of Trading A class of technical indicators that measure price volatility over time. The indicators include the 52-week high/low, advance/decline index

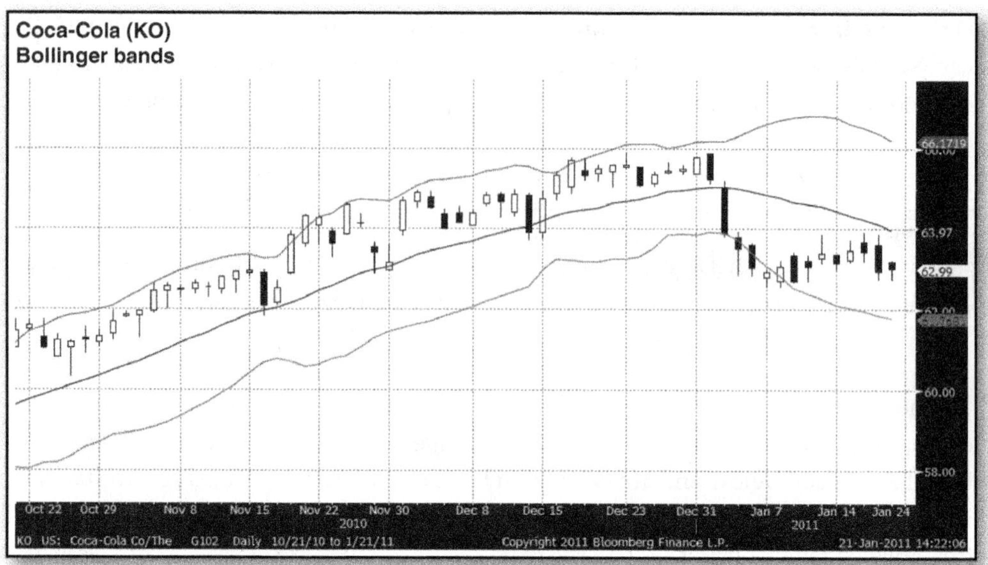

FIGURE 11.6

or line, absolute breadth index, and cumulative volume index, among others. The term also applies to the longer-term tendency within price volatility. As the trading range's breadth broadens, volatility grows; as it narrows, volatility declines. The trend toward increasing or decreasing volatility is one of many signals of changes in momentum.

> **KEY POINT:**
> Breadth—a visual representation of volatility—is the measurement of market risk based on movement of price within the trading range.

Divergence among technical indicators lead to major indices moving contrary to what breadth indicators reveal. Popular indices such as the Dow Jones Industrial Average (DJIA) reflect current price trends as the average of only 16 issues, for example. So the trends are not only reflective of averages among bullish and bearish trends; these indices may also diverge from the broader market's trend and sentiment. This is why indicators focused on breadth of trading help clarify or contradict trends coming solely from weighted indices. Breadth of an overall market can be measured using several indicators. These include:

- **issues traded,** the number of stocks listed on an exchange during a single day. The greater the level of activity, the higher trading volume tends to be. A flaw in issues traded is that the number is usually going to closely approximate the number of total issues available for trading on each exchange.
- **large block trades,** a test of institutional trader participation. These are single trades of 10,000 shares or more of a single issue. This is a test of market interest as well as a directional indicator within market breadth.

- **advancing, declining, and unchanged issues,** a test of breadth based on stocks rising or falling in a single day. On notably bullish days, advancing issues will outpace declining, and on bearish days, the opposite is expected. However, the relationships are not specific, so the advance/decline ratio may predict growing or shrinking trend momentum. When major indices, such as the DJIA, reflect advance/decline trends opposite the overall market, it is a sign of weak breadth.
- **advance/decline line,** a value derived by subtracting the number of declines from the number of advances. The result is then plotted over a number of sessions to spot the bullish (rising) or bearish (falling) trend represented by the net difference between the two. A noncumulative variation of the advance/decline line is the sum of the net difference between advancing and declining issues, divided by the number of issues traded on the session.
- **overbought/oversold index,** an indicator closely related to advancing and declining tests. In this index, the number of advancing stocks is divided by the number of declining stocks. A higher ratio reflects a bullish sentiment, and a lower ratio is bearish. This is a useful breadth test when tracked over time.
- **unchanged issues index,** calculated by dividing the number of unchanged stocks by the total issues traded. The resulting percentage reflects possible turning points in the market breadth, pointing to potential reversals from the current trend. Unchanged issues is a low number when the market is trending strongly in either direction. As the market moves toward a period of consolidation (which often precedes a turn in the trend direction), unchanged issues are likely to increase.
- **absolute breadth index,** a test of participation in the market without distinguishing between rising and falling prices. It is the sum of subtracting declines

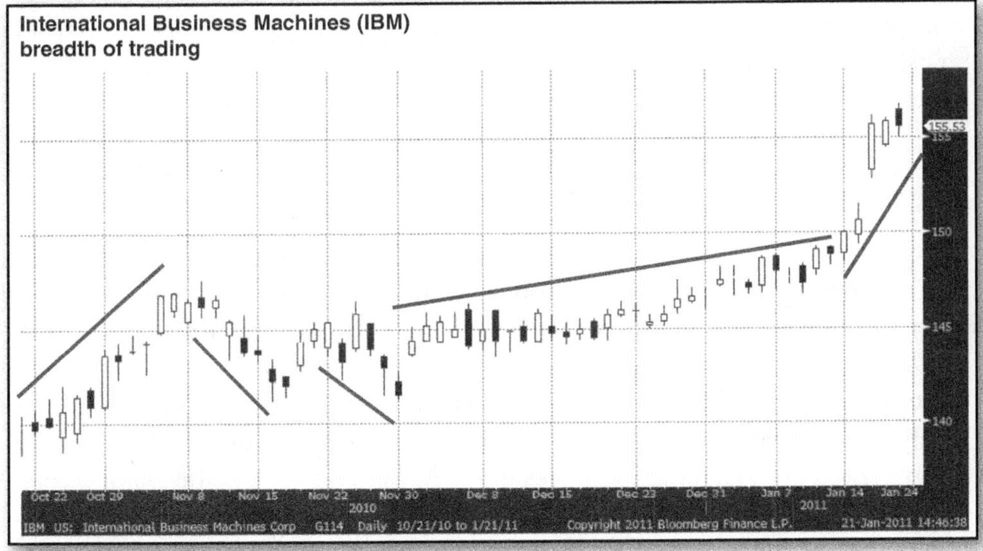

FIGURE 11.7

from advances and dividing the difference by the number of shares traded on the exchange. This percentage will be the opposite of the unchanged issues index. It is termed "absolute" because the outcome is identical whether more issues advance or decline.

- **new high and new low prices,** the number of stocks attaining these levels based on the past 52 weeks. More new highs are expected to appear in bull markets, and more new lows during bear markets.
- **volume trends,** a summary of total shares traded during a session. When price movement is high, the direction is confirmed by correspondingly higher than average volume. This is a strong test of breadth due to the confirmation of moving trading ranges that accompany high volume in strongly dynamic markets.
- **advancing and declining volume,** a further distinction of market breadth and what it means. Many technical tests of daily volume controlled by either buyers or sellers provide valuable confirmation of both candlestick-based and other technical signals.
- **traders index (TRIN),** also called the ARMS Index, is computed by dividing the advance/decline ratio (A ÷ D) by the ratio of advancing volume (AV) to declining volume (DV).

Candlesticks may confirm indicated changes in market breadth, just as breadth trends may confirm what candlestick indicators are showing. For example, IBM's range remained within a five-point spread throughout most of the period shown on its chart. However, the last leg demonstrated a significant jump in breadth, with price climbing 10 points in less than two weeks. The sudden rise in breadth and accompanying accelerated momentum was confirmed by consecutive upward-moving candlesticks and price gaps.

DO IT YOURSELF

To calculate TRIN, divide the advance/decline ratio by the ratio for advancing volume to declining volume:

(A ÷ D) ÷ (AV ÷ DV) = TRIN

Breakaway Gap A price pattern starting with a gap that becomes the beginning of a new trend; the price gap may also be part of a pattern of gapping action with recurring gaps in an especially strong upward or downward trend.

The breakaway gap may confirm a candlestick indicator of reversal from a previous trend, or the candlestick indicator may confirm what the gap appears to indicate. Likely to be accompanied with a period of higher than usual volume, the breakaway gap is a signal of momentum. It breaks through resistance on the way up or through support on the way down.

The gap and direction are not enough to qualify a gap as a breakaway, however. It requires that the movement continues in the indicated direction and that price does not retreat to fill the gap and return to its previous trading range. The significance of the breakaway gap is that it moves into new trading range territory.

The volatility associated with breakaway gaps is a confirming signal that the breakaway is going to hold. When a breakaway pattern is not accompanied by volume spikes or repetitive gapping price patterns, it probably means the apparent breakaway will fail in the near future, and prices will retreat. The breakaway is just as likely to signal reversal as a decision point moving price above or below a trend of sideways movement. In that instance, the breakaway marks the end of the congestion price range and a firm decision granting control to either buyers or sellers. During congestion, temporary and often narrow resistance and support levels are established and then finally broken by the breakaway gap.

The dramatic increase in volume reflects two important changes after the sideways trend. First is the volume created by those controlling the direction of the breakaway. Second is volume generated by traders covering or closing positions entered when the expectation was for price to move in the opposite direction. Long traders sell when the breakaway moves downward, and short traders cover their short positions to curtail losses as price moves upward. Both of these actions create additional volume. In the case of traders exiting previous positions, the increased volume is most likely to occur after the breakaway gap. These traders are less likely to anticipate the gap and more likely to respond to it.

Confirmation is likely to be found in triangles or in previous resistance establishing new support in an uptrend, or previous support becoming new resistance in a downtrend. Candlestick formations indicating reversal and then followed by clear trending price patterns further confirm that a breakaway gap will not turn into a failed breakout.

For example, in the chart of Bristol-Myers Squibb (BMY), two breakaway gaps were found, each marking the beginning of a new trend (Figure 11.8). First was an upside

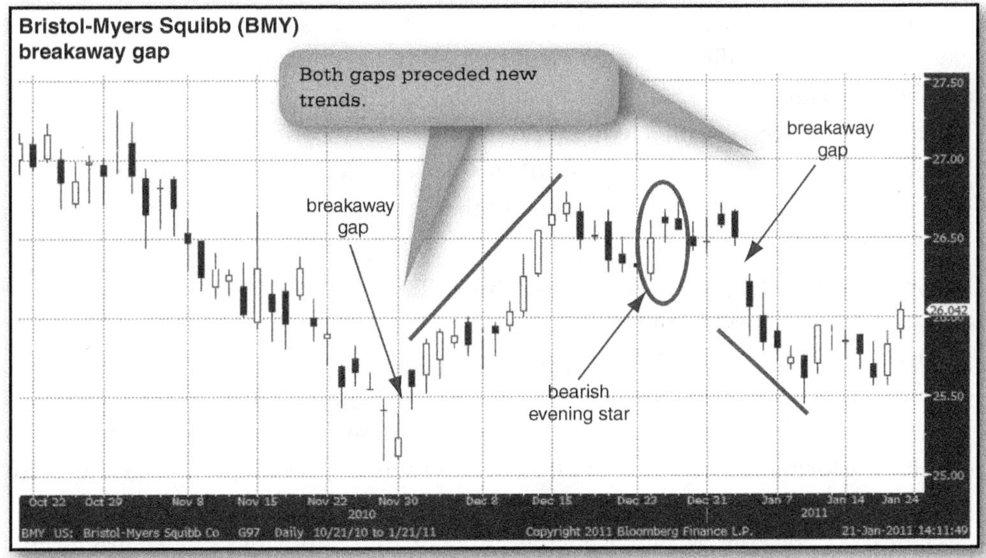

FIGURE 11.8

gap on the first trading day of December. Second was a downside gap in the first week of January. Both of these were the starting points of a reversal and new trend.

> **KEY POINT:**
> A breakaway gap presents a challenge in interpretation. It might be a signal of a new trend and higher or lower trading range. It might also end up failing when price reverses and fills.

The first, upward reversing breakaway gap confirmed a strong indicator in preceding days. First were consecutive doji sessions (narrow-range days), with the second showing an unusually long lower shadow. This indicated weakening of seller-side momentum. Then a white inverted hammer day clearly signaled that an uptrend was about to occur. The following session began with the breakaway gap to the upside.

The second, downward reversing breakaway gap was preceded by a three-stick evening star pattern. This is a rare but very strong signal; in this situation, the candlestick pattern was followed by four uncertain sessions before the downward breakaway gap occurred.

These two breakaway gaps are good examples of a technical pattern and candlestick cross-confirmation of reversals.

> **KEY POINT:**
> With price patterns like breakaway gaps, you have to rely on strong confirmation before deciding what is going on. This is where candlestick formations are valuable.

Breakout A significant technical price move, in which the price level trends above resistance or below support. Breakout may signal a new trend leading to the establishment of higher or lower trading range, or it may fail and prices retreat back to the previously established trading range.

A successful breakout may be foreshadowed by candlestick formations, in which case the breakout confirms what the candlestick indicator predicted. A breakout may also be confirmed or contradicted by subsequent candlestick indicators. For example, a breakout accompanied by long candlesticks (single stick), engulfing or harami patterns (double stick) or white soldiers, black crows or abandoned baby (three stick) provide exceptional confirmation of the direction established by the breakout. If the momentum weakens after the breakout, similar candlestick patterns in the opposite direction indicate failure of the breakout and likely retreat of prices back to the previously set trading range.

The chart for Caterpillar (CAT) provides an example of a bullish breakout (Figure 11.9). The previous resistance level is passed and a new trading range established. The legitimacy and permanence of the breakout is confirmed by a very strong bullish candlestick formation in the form of the white soldiers (three or more sessions with consecutively higher high prices and higher low prices).

A bearish breakout is shown in the chart of Best Buy (BBY) in Figure 11.10. In this case, a very strong breakout through support was predicted by two factors.

FIGURE 11.9

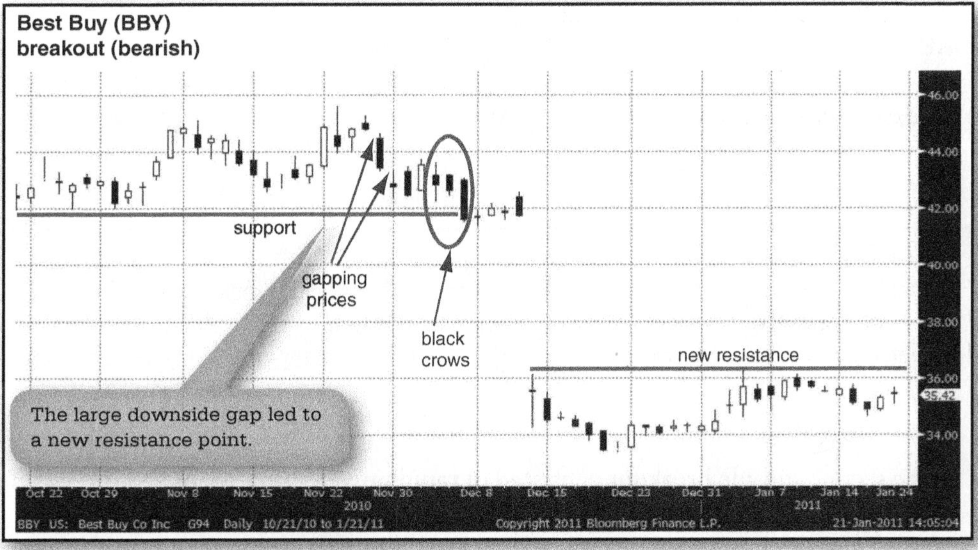

FIGURE 11.10

First was the strong and consecutive downside gapping price action. Second was the black crows. This is an exceptionally strong indicator and the third leg of the pattern moved price beneath support—this was a slight downward move, but it proved to be significant.

For a final look at breakouts, look at the chart for AT&T (T) in Figure 11.11. This chart contains three failed breakouts. The first downside attempt at breakout was not strong, and the patterns, even in the downward candle series, were erratic. The final entry in this reversal consisted of an upside gap and then a white candlestick, a signal that the breakout had failed.

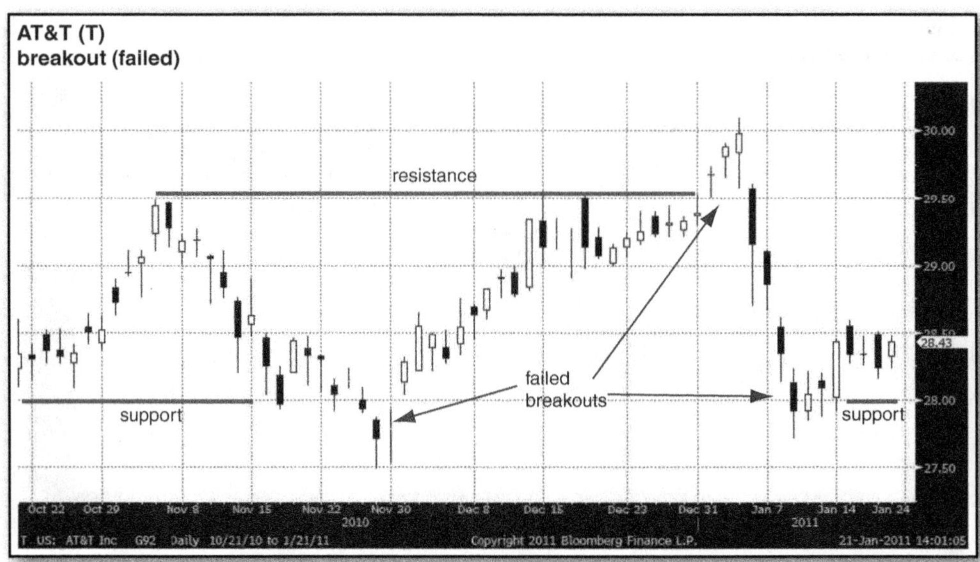

FIGURE 11.11

> **KEY POINT:**
> A breakout is the first step in establishing a new trend. But its success or failure can be predicted only when confirming signals reveal whether it is succeeding or failing.

> **KEY POINT:**
> Repetitive failed breakout patterns reveal that the side trying to break out (sellers on the downside, buyers on the upside) lacks the requisite momentum to move price permanently out of the current trading range.

The second, upside breakout consisted of rapid upward movement and three consecutive sessions with upside gapping action. Movement in one direction was strong and fast, but the last white candle also had long shadows on both sides, indicating a slowing of momentum. The subsequent downward trend, including four sessions with price gaps, was as troubling on the downside as the previous, similar pattern was on the upside. The final analysis shows, however, that the established trading range held even with the volatility both attempted breakouts revealed.

The third example, a failed breakout below support, dipped below that level on three consecutive sessions, with the third forming the first half of an exceptionally strong bullish engulfing pattern. The second session, a long white candlestick, demonstrated that the attempted breakout had failed.

Chaikin Money Flow (CMF) A technical indicator based on volume and comparing buyer and seller activity. The CMF is the basis for calculation of accumulation/

distribution (AD), a momentum oscillator. CMF, developed by Marc Chaikin, summarizes a cumulative total of volume for a period, usually 20 sessions. The indicator produced is calculated either above or below a zero point so that traders can judge the relative strength of volume and identify whether it is being influenced more by buyers or by sellers. The indicator changes any time it crosses the zero line, demonstrating that the pressure from buyers has switched to pressure by sellers, or vice versa.

The CMF result will be above zero if buyers had greater influence during the 20-day period, and below zero if sellers dominated. The maximum range of the indicator is between 1 and –1.

The calculation can be chosen as a technical selection in developing price charts, with CMF usually shown below the price tables. The value to this indicator is that it often reflects changes in momentum before price moves, and confirms what candlestick formations show. For example, the chart of Johnson & Johnson (JNJ) showed CMF moving above and below zero several times during the three-month period (Figure 11.12). The short-term price swings often were predicted early by CMF. In the last week of November, for example, the price fell dramatically while CMF rose. The doji session at November 30 marked a turning point based on candlestick analysis, but CMF had been rising for a week by that point. During the first week of December, traders might have expected an uptrend, but CMF contradicted this as it fell below zero. The rest of December and all of January was a period of uncertainty. If traders relied only on candlestick analysis, failed indicators were possible. The combined analysis of candlestick indicators and CMF provided a more reliable set of timing signals.

KEY POINT:

The appeal of CMF is its simplicity. It ranges from 1 to –1 with a zero line as the point defining which side is in control.

DO IT YOURSELF

To calculate CMF, four steps are required:

1. Calculate the multiplier for each of the 20 sessions.

   [(close – low) – (high – close)] ÷ (high – low)

2. Multiply the result by the session's volume.

   Multiplier × Volume for the session = Money flow volume

3. Add the totals for all 20 periods.

   Money flow volume × 20 periods – 20-period volume

4. Divide by 20 to find the average.

   20-period volume ÷ 20 = CMF

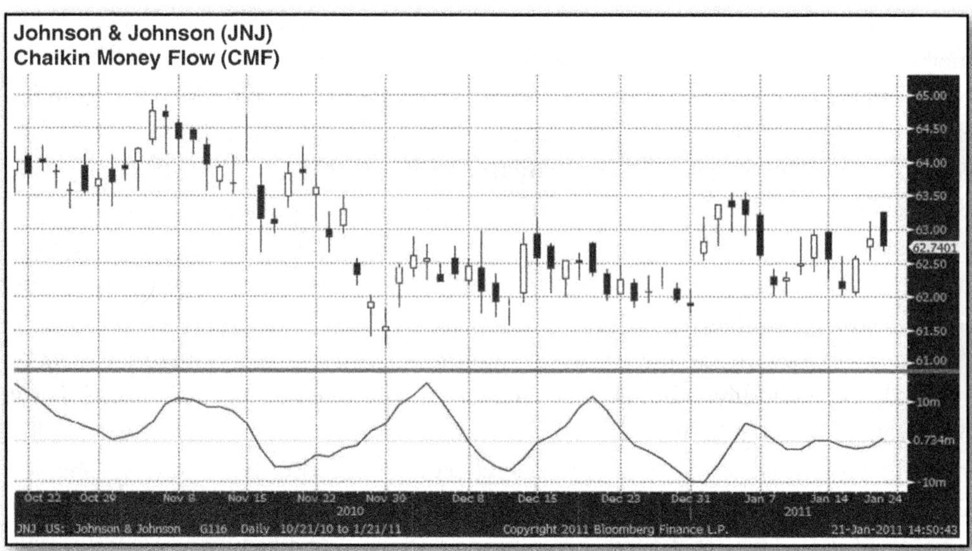

FIGURE 11.12

Channel Lines A visual device used to identify trends in prices and also to provide confirmation or contradiction of candlestick reversal indicators. The lines are drawn above and below the trading range in parallels, marking resistance and support in all types of trend movements.

There are three possible trends: upward, downward, and sideways. Channel lines identify all three and also act as confirmation of candlestick indicators; this is especially important when momentum in an existing trend begins to weaken and traders attempt to identify the reversal point. This may be first seen in a price decline in the uptrend through the bottom of the rising channel lines, or in a price increase in the downtrend through the top of the falling channel lines.

The chart for Google (GOOG) showed both falling and rising channel lines (Figure 11.13). At the end of the falling channels, the long black candlestick is followed by an upward-moving gap and then three uptrend days.

Even though subsequent sessions were black, they continued moving upward in a gapping pattern. This also marked the beginning of the upward-moving channel lines.

The channel lines identify resistance and support, which may each remain at the same levels or change dynamically. In these examples, Google's price history was characterized by dynamic movement in both directions. The identification of the trading range, when this strong, may also serve as a visual representation of price volatility.

> **KEY POINT:**
> Channel lines are expanded versions of trendlines. They border the current trend and identify likely reversal through the simplicity of two straight lines.

Common Gap A recurring and regular aspect of price movement, in which price in one session opens at a gap either above or below the close of the previous session. As long as the trading range remains intact, a common gap should not be considered

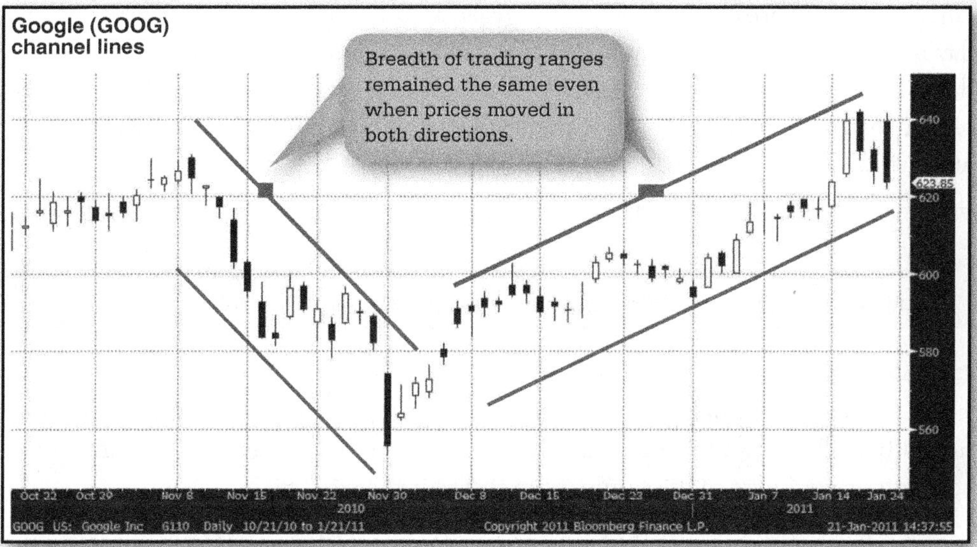

FIGURE 11.13

as any type of signal of reversal or breakout. When viewed as part of a candlestick formation that indicates reversal, gaps are often exhibited.

If and when the common gap develops into a trend and a pattern of gaps, it is no longer a common occurrence. Recognition of the differences between the common gap and the gap taking place as part of reversal may be based on recognition of candlestick reversal patterns, momentum, and tests of resistance or support. Some common gaps are also hidden gaps, meaning they are not immediately recognized because candlesticks between sessions overlap.

Common gaps are identified on the chart of Visa (V), and 10 instances are marked with arrows (Figure 11.14). Many additional gaps are observed as well; however, these may be part of developing trends or reversals and are not common. Two spe-

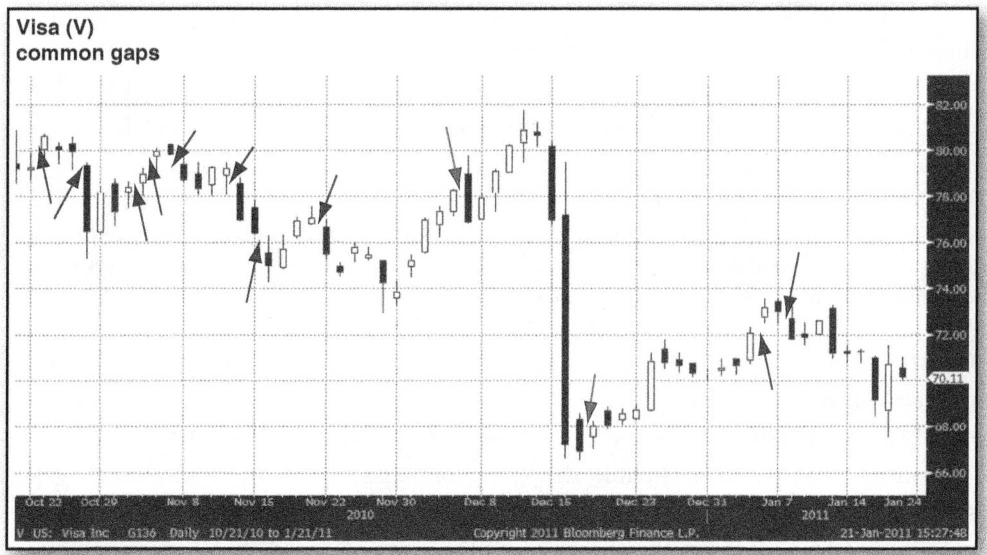

FIGURE 11.14

cific hidden gaps are also marked by the green arrows. In the first one, a white candle day is followed by a black candle day that opened higher than the close of the white day. In the second one, a black candle was followed by a white candle that opened higher than the previous close. Both of these examples are common gaps, but they are not visible immediately.

> **KEY POINT:**
> The important fact to remember about common gaps is that they are common. They occur as part of normal price movement but by themselves are not significant.

Complex Gap Trends Types of gapping action seen as part of candlestick formations. In these indicators of three or more sessions, the gap plays an important role, not only in defining the importance of the price trend but also in identifying the strength or weakness of the momentum that is involved.

Examples of complex gap trends are the tasuki gap (both downside and upside) and the gap filled (downside and upside). These types all contain gaps. The tasuki is characterized by gaps not being filled, which distinguishes it from the gap filled.

Consolidation A trading pattern in which the price movement is sideways rather than in either an uptrend or a downtrend. Also called congestion, this is interpreted as a time of indecision in which neither buyers nor sellers are able to move price out of the current narrow range.

Consolidation often follows a strong trend and represents a period of rest before the trend either resumes or is reversed. The time may be limited to part of a day or last for weeks or months. Volume during consolidation may be quite low, and the range from high to low may be low as well.

Once a breakout occurs from the consolidation range, a new trend begins. A study of the price pattern alone does not reveal the likely direction of the new trend. However, a combination of analysis including momentum indicators and candlesticks may foreshadow the actual move by a few sessions. The direction is quite uncertain and may go either way, so the use of any signal indicator is not wise. Confirmation of any indicator implying a coming breakout is essential before orders are placed.

> **KEY POINT:**
> Traders find consolidation frustrating; they want to see movement. However, periods of sideways movement are necessary in order for buyers and sellers to decide who will be in control in the next trend.

Continuation Any indicator anticipating that the current trend will continue in the same direction. In comparison, a reversal is an indicator pointing to the current trend ending and then a new trend starting in the opposite direction.

Continuation patterns include the rising or falling three methods, tasuki gaps, side-by-side lines, neck lines, and thrusting lines. The continuation may be bullish or bearish, depending on the direction of the current trend. In Western technical analysis, continuation is found in triangles and wedges.

CHAPTER 12

Basic Indicators Reference D to H

From Michael C. Thomsett, *Bloomberg Visual Guide to Candlestick Charting* (Hoboken, New Jersey: John Wiley & Sons, 2012), Chapter 8, D-H.

Day Trading The practice of moving in and out of positions very quickly, with the primary characteristic closing of all open positions by the end of the trading day.

> **KEY POINT:**
> As long as trades are opened and closed within a single trading day, no margin maintenance applies, since that is based on balances at the end of a session. This leverage opportunity can be abused, which is why active traders are likely to fall under the definition of a pattern day trader.

This achieves two goals. First, it avoids the risk that securities may open significantly higher or lower than the previous day's closing price, in which case a trader is not able to control or time an exit strategy. Second, margin requirements are circumvented by closing leveraged positions, since margin requirements are computed based on open trades at the end of the trading day.

> **REGULATORY AGENCIES CAN BE CONTACTED AT:**
> Financial Industry Regulatory Authority (FINRA)—www.finra.org
>
> Securities and Exchange Commission (SEC)—www.sec.gov

Frequent trading may lead to a trader being classified as a pattern day trader, a status defined by the Financial Industry Regulatory Authority (FINRA) and the Securities and Exchange Commission (SEC). A pattern day trader is any trader who buys and sells a specific security or position four or more times in any five consecutive market sessions. An individual fitting this criterion is required to maintain an equity balance of no less than $25,000 in a margin account.

The key to day trading is timing of both entry and exit. For this reason, many day traders rely on candlestick chart analysis in conjunction with confirming momentum indicators and other technical price and volume patterns, to improve chances of timing trades profitably.

Double Bottom A familiar pattern seen in technical analysis, in which support is tested twice, followed by a trend moving in the opposite direction and often moving through resistance to create a new trading range.

The pattern may be confirmed by candlestick patterns or by a combination of independent indicators. It often also occurs that the level of previous resistance marks the beginning of a newly established support level in the uptrend that follows.

The chart of United Technologies (UTZ) demonstrates a double bottom and several subsequent signals (Figure 12.1). The second downward move forms a hammer, a bullish reversal signal. This is quickly followed by a very strong upward price gap and a long white session that moves rapidly through previous resistance. This also sets up a rising support level.

> **KEY POINT:**
> Double bottoms can be single-day spiked, forming a "W" shape, or more rounded. These may also be distinguished by what Thomas Bulkowski terms Adam or Eve formations, in his book *Encyclopedia of Chart Patterns* (Wiley, 2005).

Double Top A pattern in technical analysis in which resistance is tested twice, but no breakthrough holds. It is followed by a strong downward movement and often by the establishment of a lower resistance level.

> **KEY POINT:**
> Like double bottoms, double tops may form as sharp price patterns (like an "M") or as more rounded shapes.

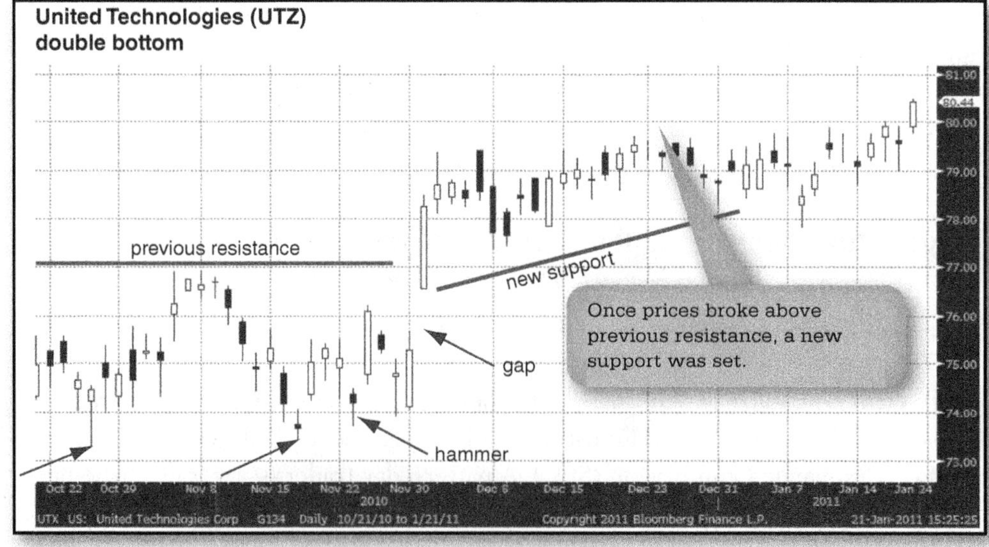

FIGURE 12.1

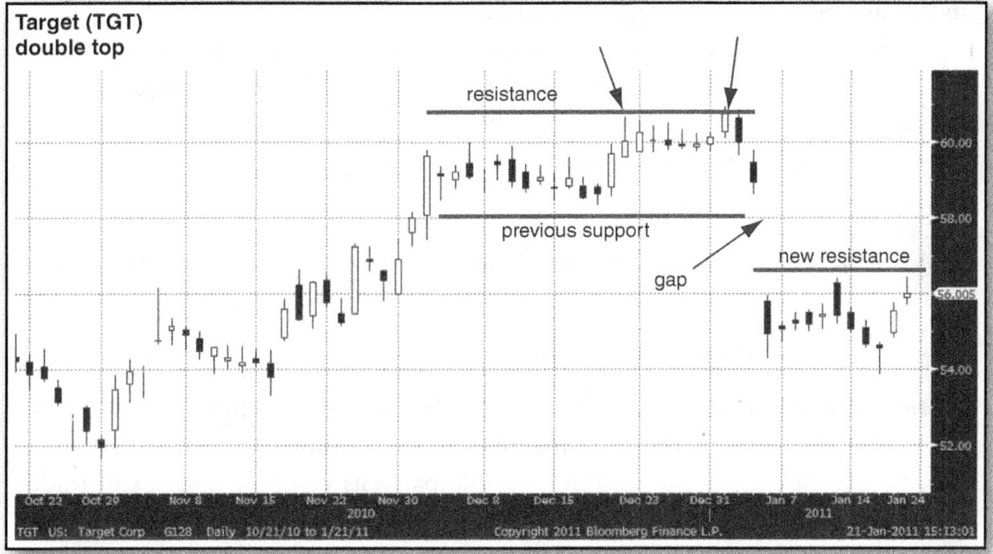

FIGURE 12.2

Confirmation may be found in candlestick or separate technical price patterns. The chart of Target (TGT) shows a clear double top (Figure 12.2). The reversal is anticipated by several doji sessions preceding the reversal itself. This is further confirmed by the large downward gap, which violates support and then forms a new resistance level.

Downtrend Any movement toward lower prices, which may include specific characteristics and duration. The definition relies on which system is in play. As a general observation a downtrend is likely to favor the declining price, but it may also include interim peaks or offsets in price levels, which may be single sessions or small uptrends within the longer-duration downtrend, a pattern called retracement.

A downtrend defined as part of a swing trading strategy requires three or more consecutive sessions with lower high prices and lower low prices than the previous day. A short-term downtrend is normally marked by entry and exit signals including doji days (narrow range days), volume spikes, or upward sessions identifying the trend's specific reversal.

Under the principles of the Dow Theory, a distinction is made between market movements and trends. There are three movements: a primary or major trend, which may last several months or years; a second reaction or swing period lasting up to three months and characterized by a retracement of a portion of the primary trend; and a short swing or minor movement lasting a month or more.

Market trends under the Dow Theory occur in three phases. In a bear market in which the downtrend dominates, the first phase is distribution, then public participation, and finally panic. Distribution involves active trading which, in a downtrend, means selling of shares; this occurs contrary to popular opinion, which tends to be buying while the downtrend's distribution phase is underway. Public participation begins when technical traders recognize the change and add to the selling pressure. Public participation takes place once the downtrend has been established and is well underway. By this time, the downtrend may be losing momentum; however, astute traders have made their moves ahead of the market and may be searching for the end to the downtrend and potential timing for reversal. The third phase is panic, where the majority of traders believe the downtrend will continue. So selling activity accelerates even as the downtrend comes to an end.

> **KEY POINT:**
> A downtrend may involve as few as three sessions under a swing trader's definition, or it may extend months or even years as a technical primary trend. It may also be a retracement within a larger uptrend.

Eastern Technical Analysis Reference to Japanese candlesticks as the basis for chart analysis, trend spotting, and identification of continuation or reversal indicators. Candlesticks tend to create identifiable patterns based on a series of trading ranges, gaps, and breadth. In comparison, Western indicators rely on patterns created by ranges of price movement.

Eastern (candlestick-based) methodology is most effective when the price-specific indicators are employed in cross-confirmation with Western indicators based on broader charting patterns. The two in combination provide not only confirmation or contradiction of what any one indicator points to as the next leg in a trend, but they also augment the overall recognition of trends, continuation or reversal, momentum, and volatility.

> **KEY POINT:**
> Eastern methods, candlesticks, are traced back centuries ago to rice future tracking in Japan. The modern trend is to combine Eastern with Western methods to expand and improve confirmation techniques.

Entry Signal Any indicator pointing to reversal of a previous trend or to the initiation of a new one, used when a trader is not in an open position and seeks the sign that timing is right to create a new position. Swing traders and day traders look for entry based on overreaction by price to immediate news and developments, recognizing that short-term price movements tend to pause and retreat within a few sessions. The interim reaction presents many entry opportunities.

Many systems are used by traders to time entry into either open long or short positions. These include the use of stop-loss orders at the time of entry. A trade position can also be left open to ride using a trailing stop.

Another entry system mixes entry with the timing of exit. For example, the 50 percent rule states that once a position gains a predetermined percentage of profit, one-half of a long position is sold, or one-half of a short position is bought to close.

> **KEY POINT:**
> There is no single entry signal or system used by traders to time trades. The important feature of price movement is to recognize that the entry price is not a starting point, but the current price within a longer-term timeframe.

A third entry system is based on repetitive and unusually strong gapping action. For example, if a stock gaps in one direction three times in five consecutive sessions, a trader may expect some filling action and will make entry in the direction opposite of the gaps. If an open position exhibits the same kind of gapping movement in a desired direction, it will be taken as an exit signal based on the same rationale and expectation of reversal.

Exhaustion Gap A type of gap in price that comes after a strong move in one direction or the other. It signals the closing out of the trend, a loss of momentum, and very likely reversal to follow soon.

> **KEY POINT:**
> Recognizing exhaustion by gapping action and higher than average volume creates a valuable reversal signal and confirmation device.

This type of gap signals the end of the trend and may also serve as part of a candlestick reversal pattern. It may also confirm separate reversal indicators, providing a valuable form of Western confirmation of other Western signals or of Eastern signals. However, exhaustion gaps can be confused with the beginning of a trend of runaway gaps. Exhaustion can be distinguished by unusually high volume at the point of the gap, a situation not likely to accompany runaway gaps.

The most important aspect of the exhaustion gap is the degree to which it confirms reversal. For example, Verizon (VZ) experienced a long uptrend, and then price had a double exhaustion gap (Figure 12.3). This signaled the end to the uptrend and was followed by a downturn in price. The long black session that followed confirmed the gaps as exhaustion gaps and set up the reversal.

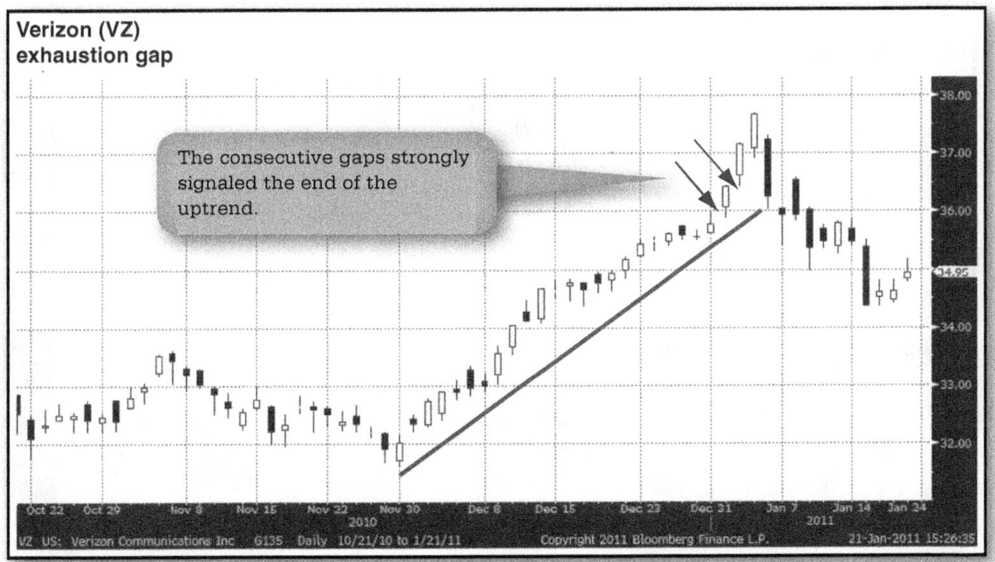

FIGURE 12.3

Chevron (CVX) experienced an exhaustion gap after a short downtrend (Figure 12.4). The exhaustion gap also marked a failed breakout move below support; this example shows how price may turn immediately and move in the opposite direction after the exhaustion gap appears.

Exit Signal Any system, indicator, or method applied by traders to identify when to exit from an open position. Many exit signals employ candlestick indicators, either alone or as confirmation for other technical turning points.

One method for creating exit is through the use of specialized orders such as a stop loss order (or the trailing stop, a variation of the stop loss). This automates the action of exiting a position, although actual execution can be delayed. As a consequence, the action begins at a specified price point, but it does not ensure that the trader closes the position at the desired price. If a security's price is changing rapidly, it invariably means that order volume is high, so a stop loss order may be delayed in execution.

Another system involves closing part of a position in order to take profits while leaving the remainder of the position open, in the hope that additional profits will be earned in future price movement (or that by taking part of the profits, future losses are minimized).

The most reliable form of exit order is the use of price patterns to identify changes in momentum. Dozens of candlestick indicators provide traders with reliable signals anticipating reversal. These include patterns emerging due to change in momentum within the current trend. When candlestick indicators are used in cross-confirmation with other technical signals, timing of exit is vastly improved.

> **KEY POINT:**
> Various exit signals are developed and applied by traders and no one system ensures good timing. Finding a method that improves the percentages is a worthwhile goal.

FIGURE 12.4

Candlestick indicators may be coordinated with price approaching, testing or crossing resistance, or support levels. These trading range borders may serve either as targets to take profits or cut losses; they may also be used to confirm turning points found in either candlestick indicators or other technical signs. Among these are any that are associated with resistance and support, such as head and shoulders or double top/bottom price movement. A breakout may lead to a new trading range, or it may retreat and fill. The uncertainty of a breakout in the immediate sessions after it occurs make exit signals valuable, especially if they can also be independently confirmed. Another possible outcome is testing of the borders with failure, which most technicians see as a prelude to price movement in the opposite direction. This may also serve as a strong exit point, especially if the shift in momentum is confirmed by candlestick patterns.

Exponential Moving Average (EMA) A method of weighting a moving average and calculating each new entry in an abbreviated manner. This is used in many technical indicators using multiperiod averaging. The EMA is calculated and added to charts automatically on many websites offering charting services. The following brief explanation of EMA is intended to explain how it is calculated, but it does not imply that it needs to be done by hand in every situation.

KEY POINT:

EMA is an efficient method for weighting a moving average. It is built in automatically on charts employing EMA and does not have to be manually calculated.

The first step is to calculate the exponent to be used. The value 2 is divided by the number of values in the field (the value of n). For example, for a 50-day moving average, the exponent is:

$$2 \div 50 = 0.04$$

DO IT YOURSELF

To calculate EMA:

1. $2 \div n = e$ (where n is the number of values in the field being averaged)
2. $t \div n = a$ (where t is the total of field values, n is the number of values in the field, and a is the resulting average)
3. $ve = c$ (where v is the next value in the series, e is the exponent calculated in step 1, and c is the sum of step 2)
4. $c + a = EMA$ (where c is the sum of step 3 and a is the sum of step 2)

The complete formula:

$[(Vp - [(V_1 - V_2 + \ldots V_n) \div n]) \times (2 \div n)] + P = EMA$

where Vp = previous EMA
V1 = first value in the field
V2 = second value in the field
Vn = final value in the field
n = number of values in the field
p = previous EMA
EMA = new EMA

In this case, the exponent is 0.04. All of the values in the field are added together for the first entry, and the sum is then divided by the number of entries in the field. Once this average is calculated, it is easy to calculate EMA for each new field. The net difference between the new value and the average is multiplied by the exponent (0.04 in the example), and the resulting value is added to the previously set average.

For example, a 50-day field adds up to a total of 97,400. The first step is to divide this by the number of values to find the average:

$$97{,}400 \div 50 = 1{,}948$$

The next entry, for example, may be 2,106. Multiply this by the exponent:

$$2{,}106 \times 0.04 = 84$$

Add this to the previous average:

$$84 + 1{,}948 = 2{,}032$$

This is the new moving average entry. Once you have a moving average, calculation is a two-step process: Multiply the new field by the exponent, and add that to the previous average (if negative, subtract it).

EMA is an important method used in many technical indicators, so traders benefit by understanding that it is a weighted total, adding more influence to the latest entry in the field than to previous entries.

Failed Pattern Any indicator pointing to a change that does not materialize. Any indicator can fail, including both candlesticks and traditional Western signals for reversal or continuation. Failed patterns occur often enough in price chart analysis, pointing to the importance of confirmation.

Even confirmation does not guarantee that a promised reversal will occur as the indicator shows. However, it does improve the accuracy of both entry and exit to rely on strong patterns and confirmation of them. Candlestick indicators may be confirmed by other candlestick patterns or by price changes such as gapping, narrowing trading ranges, or tests of resistance and support. All of the traditional Western indicators can also be confirmed by one another or by candlestick signals occurring at or near the same trading point. Any of these price-based indicators including a session's activity is also confirmed by momentum oscillators, price-based moving averages (especially analysis including convergence and divergence of two separate moving averages), and finally by specific indicators based on analysis of volume trends.

KEY POINT:

Any signal can fail, even those that are confirmed strongly. The purpose to using indicators and confirmation is to improve timing, but timing is never going to work at 100 percent. That is the reality of any charting system.

Confirming indicators do not always agree. It is equally important to note that in some instances, mixed signals result from seeking confirmation. When this occurs, traders must decide which side of the contradiction to follow. If the planned action is entry, it makes sense in cases of contradictory indicators to wait out the trend and see what emerges in coming sessions. If the planned action is exit, it is most prudent to take profits or cut losses whenever the next movement cannot be identified due to contradictory indicators.

Failed patterns occur in varying percentages. Some indicators are clearly stronger and more reliable than others. Traders who rely on single indicators may lose more from failed patterns than those who wait for confirmation and act only when the same action is indicated from separate signals.

Falling Wedge A bullish trend that may last only a few sessions or extend over a wider time period. It is characterized by a decreasing range over time with its origin wider and its conclusion narrower, and the trading range trending downward. The actual bullish trend is realized only when prices move above the wedge range and move to the upside in a breakout above resistance.

Chevron (CVX) experienced a falling wedge that lasted approximately three weeks (Figure 12.5). It fits the definition because of the strong breakout above resistance that marked the end of the wedge. This was the start of a sustained uptrend.

Confirmation consisted of the breakout and gapping price action that recurred for two weeks in a strong uptrend. The long white candlestick appeared two sessions after the breakout provided more immediate confirmation, revealing that it was unlikely that price direction would reverse and fill to the downside.

Fibonacci Retracement A series of ratios used in some technical indicators to predict price movement or reversal. It is one of many indicators that adds to both initial and confirming information about continuation of reversal of a current price direction.

KEY POINT:

The Fibonacci retracement is mathematically interesting, but it is more. It is used to estimate point where price is likely to reverse. The features found in the levels of 62 percent and 38 percent derived from this mathematical oddity are the key.

The retracement is used most often for identifying likely reversal points within price trends. The sequence consists of the sum of the previous two numbers in a series. Thus, beginning with zero and 1, the Fibonacci retracement sequence is:

0, 1, 1, 2, 3, 5, 8, 13, 21, 34, 55, 89, 144, 233, 377, 610 ...

Chartists identify likely reversal following a price trend. The retracement level is equal to a specific percentage move from the base, after which a pullback and reversal is expected.

The most popular percentages used to estimate retracement are 62 and 38. These are rounded values. The 62 percent is the approximate value of each entry in the series, of the value that precedes it. For example:

$$55 \times 62\% = 34$$
$$89 \times 62\% = 55$$

falling wedge
Chevron (CVX)
falling wedge
93.85
92.00
90.00
88.00
86.00
84.00
82.00
80.00
Oct 22
Oct 29
Nov 8
Nov 15
Nov 22
Nov 30
2010
Dec 8
Dec 15
Dec 23
Dec 31
Jan 7
Jan 14
Jan 24
2011
CVX US: Chevron Corp G100 Daily 10/21/10 to 1/21/11
Copyright 2011 Bloomberg Finance L.P.
21-Jan-2011 14:16:39

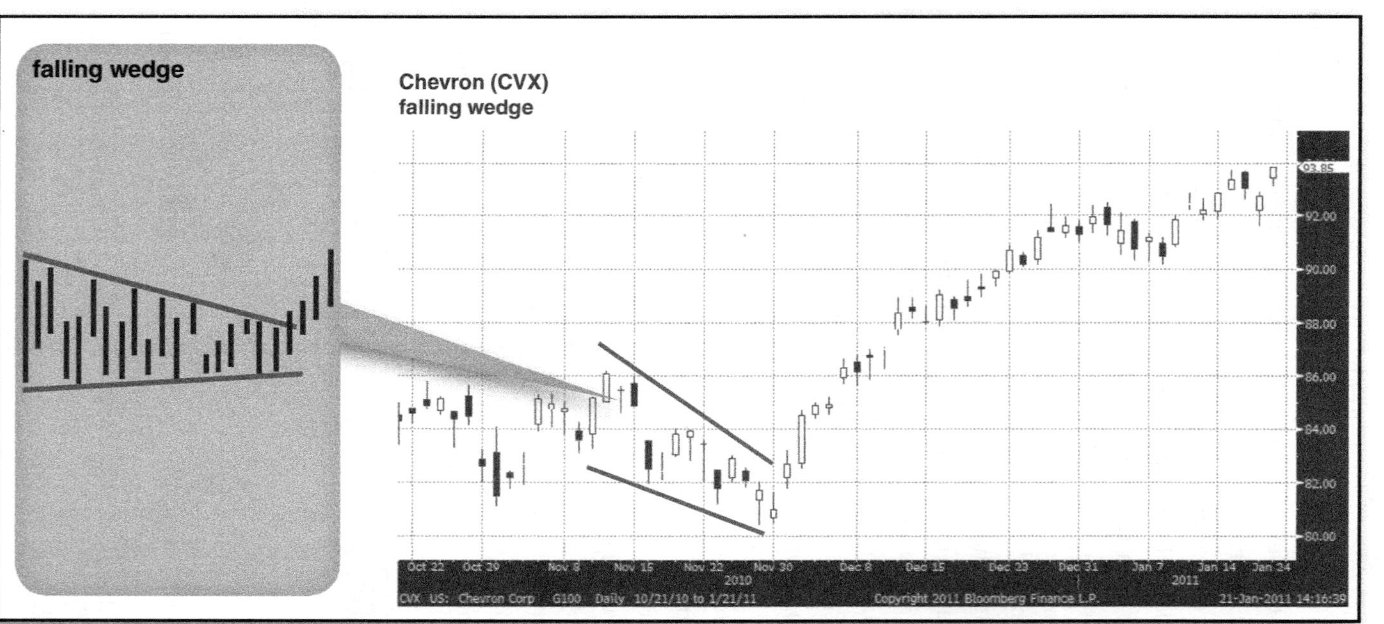

FIGURE 12.5

The 38 percent value is the approximate value of any sum of the value of two entries preceding it in the sequence. For example:

$$55 \times 38\% = 21$$
$$89 \times 38\% = 34$$

Chartists employing retracement may estimate the degree of move from one point to another in the opposite direction, representing correction or pullback of the price peak or valley. The technique is named for Italian mathematician Leonardo of Pisa (Leonardo Pisano), also called "Fibonacci," the name derived from *filius Bonacci,* or "son of Bonaccio." However, the sequence was known in mathematics before Fibonacci's life (1170–1250), for example in India.[1]

For many technicians, this retracement method identifies likely levels of existing or evolving resistance or support, based on degrees of price movement and reversal tied to the 62 percent and 38 percent levels.

Fundamental Analysis A form of analysis based on the study of a range of ratios and trends of companies apart from price and volume tracking. Fundamental analysis is restricted to historical indicators found on the balance sheet and income statement and related financial results.

Some indicators combine fundamental and technical input. The best know of these is the price/earnings ratio (P/E). This is a comparison between a technical indicator (price per share) and a fundamental one (earnings per share).

Strictly fundamental indicators include tests of working capital (current ratio and debt ratio); capitalization tests (total shareholders' equity compared among companies to identify the difference between large-cap, mid-cap, and small-cap companies); return testing of many types (return on equity or net worth, or return on revenue, for example); and trends measuring changes in revenue, net profits, or net return.

For technicians, fundamental indicators are used as an initial method for stock selection apart or in conjunction with technical tests. Investors may identify exit points for stock ownership based on changes in fundamental tests, or rely strictly on price and volume trends. Both approaches may use candlestick indicators and other technical trends to determine entry and exit points.

KEY POINT:
Fundamentals do not have to be chosen to the exclusion of technical indicators. Portfolio selections can be used as a means for narrowing down selections of securities based on profitability, capital strength, dividend yield, and working capital. The price is then tracked with technical indicators.

Gap differences between the closing price of one session and the opening price of the one that follows. Gaps often act as part of a larger indicator, notably as part of candlestick signals. They may also accompany strong breakouts or trend reversals. If a gap is created and continues, it implies strength in the direction of movement.

[1] Susantha Goonatilake, *Toward a Global Science* (Bloomington IN: Indiana University Press, 1998).

If price reverses and fills the gap, it is a sign that the attempted movement of price lacked adequate momentum.

> **KEY POINT:**
> Gaps are very common, and the study of most price charts demonstrates this. The difficulty is distinguishing between the often-occurring common gaps from those that form as part of a significant signal.

Many gaps are common gaps and have no special significance other than in the way they form or become part of a large indicator. Among the kinds of gaps are:

- common gaps, recurring and frequent spaces between close and open of sessions that do not have any trend-based meaning.
- exhaustion gap, a gap showing up at the end of a trend and representing the last move prior to reversal.
- breakaway gap, one that represents growing momentum in a trend and the potential for setting a new trading range, usually accompanied with exceptionally high volume.
- runaway gaps, a series of gapping price movement in one direction and a symptom of a strong or growing trend.
- hidden gap, one that forms between sessions but is not immediately visible.

Several candlestick formations involve gaps and the distinction between those that do not get filled (such as upside or downside tasuki gaps) and those that are filled (upside or downside gap filled).

Gaps occur often in many charts, and many are hidden. The chart of Yahoo! (YHOO) in Figure 12.6 identifies many common gaps (in red) as well as hidden gaps

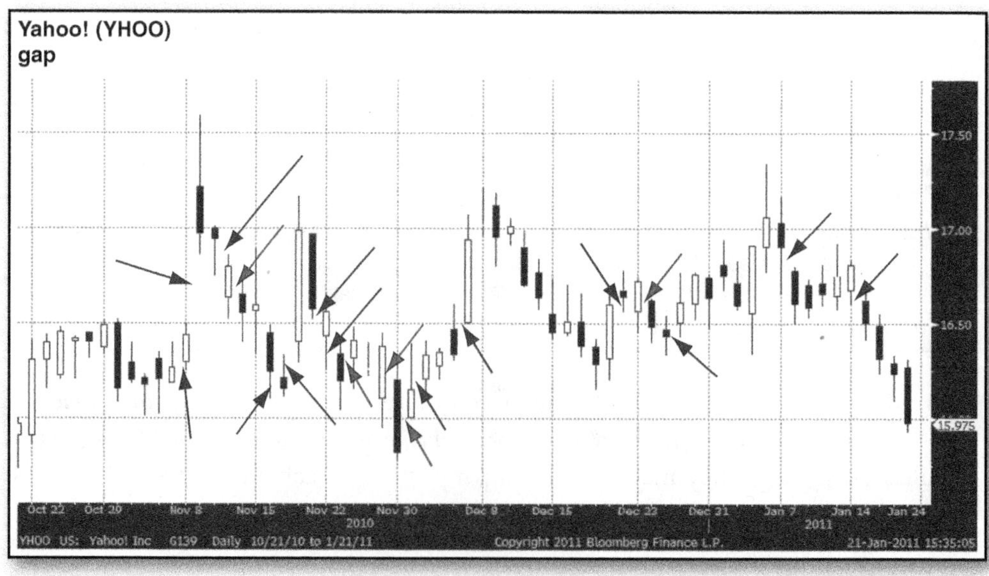

FIGURE 12.6

(in blue). These are hidden because the real bodies of each session overlap; however, there is a gap between close and open even with the overlapping trading range.

Gap Opening A gap, often significant, between one session's closing price and the next one's opening price. This may occur due to unusually news or rumor, especially after the first session's close. If the gap does not close within the session, it indicates that the price direction is likely to continue.

In the case of Toyota (TM), the gap opening moved to the upside (Figure 12.7). Although the point movement was not wide, the size of the gap relative to price movement both before and after the gap was large. Subsequent price direction was also upward, and after sideways adjustment the uptrend continued to the conclusion of the period charted.

Gapping Trend A series of sessions in which several sessions display gaps in one direction. This may be an uptrend or a downtrend. The occurrence of numerous gaps may represent a breakout above resistance or below support, or the trend may lose momentum and prices later fill all or part of the gapping trend.

Coca-Cola (KO) showed two gapping trends on its chart, one in each direction (Figure 12.8). The two patterns are quite similar, with consecutive gaps revealed in three sessions and then a fourth nongapping session moving in the same direction. The duration of the gapping trend varies. The more gaps occurring in a single direction, the greater the momentum.

Head and Shoulders A price pattern that tests resistance without breaking through, often followed by price movement in the opposite direction. It consists of three peaks. The first and third are the shoulders, and the middle (second) is the head. This highest of the three price spikes may test or momentarily break through resistance.

The loss of momentum represented in this pattern is bearish and, especially when confirmed with candlestick reversal signals, is reliable as a signal of the conclusion in the uptrend.

The chart of SPDR Gold Shares (GLD) patterned a head and shoulders over a period of nearly two months (Figure 12.9). The price dips in between the three peaks defines the shape clearly. Confirmation of the bearish reversal is found in the large downside gap immediately after the second shoulder and then again 10 sessions later.

Hidden Gaps Patterns in which real bodies of consecutive sessions overlap but create a price gap that is not immediately visible. This may occur in any pattern type (white-white, white-black, black-black, or black-white) and in either an upward or a downward direction.

The hidden gap occurs often in the normal course of trading and is most likely to represent one of several common gaps. However, when its significance in terms of price direction, reversal, or momentum has greater meaning, it is easy to overlook the hidden gap as one of the important factors in timing entry or exit.

The chart for DuPont (DD) shows 12 hidden gaps on the three-month chart (Figure 12.10). None of these is visible at first glance, but all present a case in which a price gap was found between the first day's close and the second day's open.

gap opening
uptrend
downtrend
Toyota (TM)
gap opening
85
02.23
80
75
70
Oct 22 Oct 29 Nov 8 Nov 15 Nov 22 Nov 30 Dec 8 Dec 15 Dec 22 Dec 31 Jan 7 Jan 14 Jan 24
2010
2011
TM US: Toyota Motor Corp G129 Daily 10/21/10 to 1/21/11
Copyright 2011 Bloomberg Finance L.P.
21-Jan-2011 15:15:39

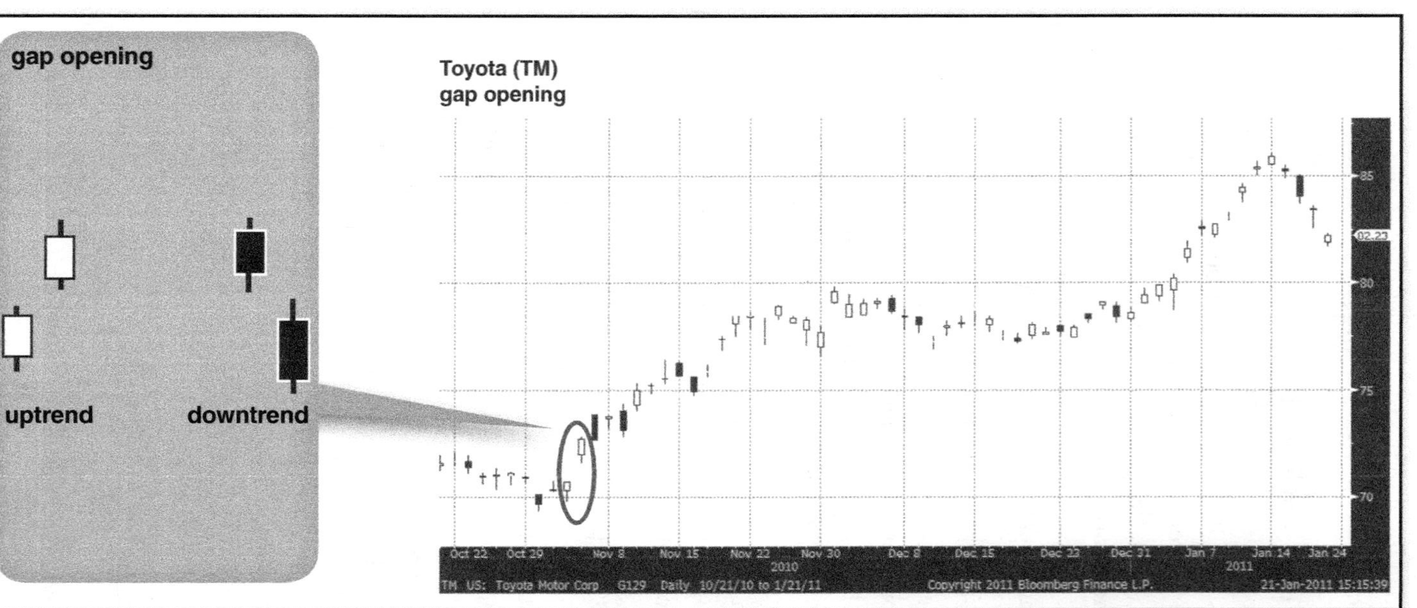

FIGURE 12.7

gapping trend
uptrend
downtrend
Coca-Cola (KO)
gapping trend
The trends in both directions consisted of specific colors of sessions as well as gaps.
66.00
65.00
64.00
62.97
62.00
61.00
60.00
Oct 22 Oct 29 Nov 8 Nov 15 Nov 22 Nov 30 Dec 8 Dec 15 Dec 23 Dec 31 Jan 7 Jan 14 Jan 24
2010
2011
KO US: Coca-Cola Co/The G102 Daily 10/21/10 to 1/21/11
Copyright 2011 Bloomberg Finance L.P.
21-Jan-2011 14:20:40

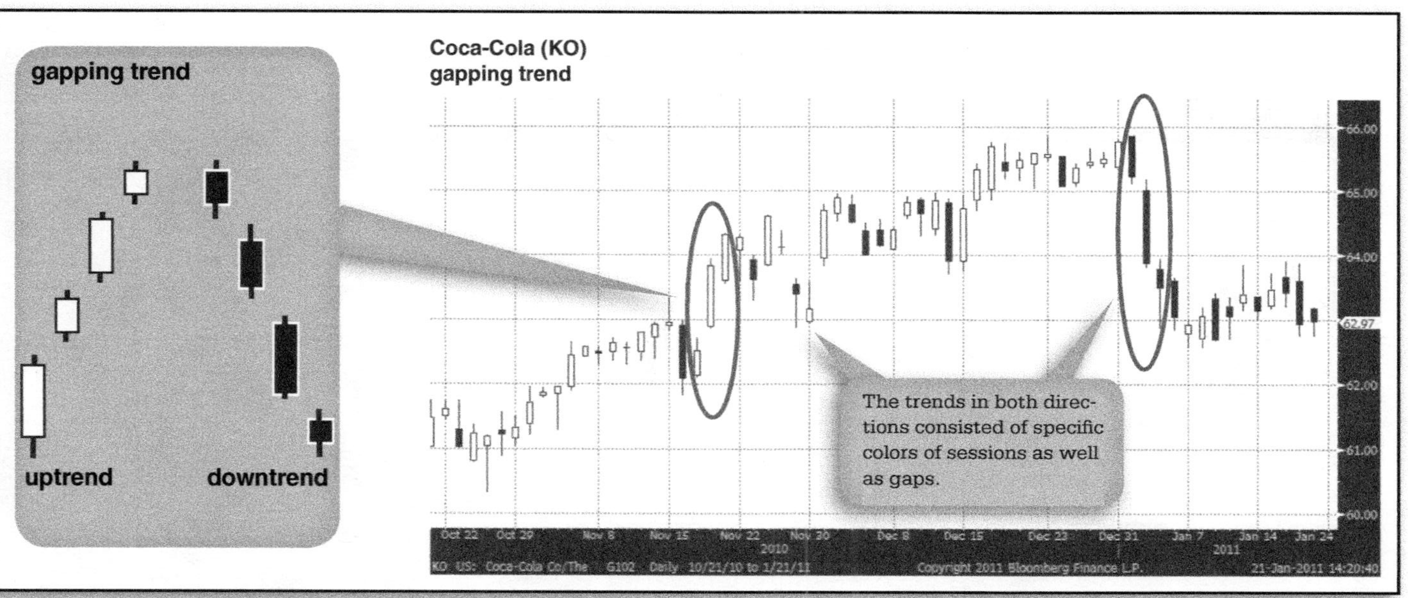

FIGURE 12.8

head and shoulders
SPDR Gold Shares (GLD)
head and shoulders
shoulder
head
shoulder
140.00
138.00
136.00
134.00
132.00
131.02
130.00
128.00
Oct 22 Oct 29 Nov 8 Nov 15 Nov 22 Nov 30 Dec 8 Dec 15 Dec 23 Dec 31 Jan 7 Jan 14 Jan 24
2010
2011
GLD US: SPDR Gold Shares G109 Daily 10/21/10 to 1/21/11
Copyright 2011 Bloomberg Finance L.P.
21-Jan-2011 14:36:38

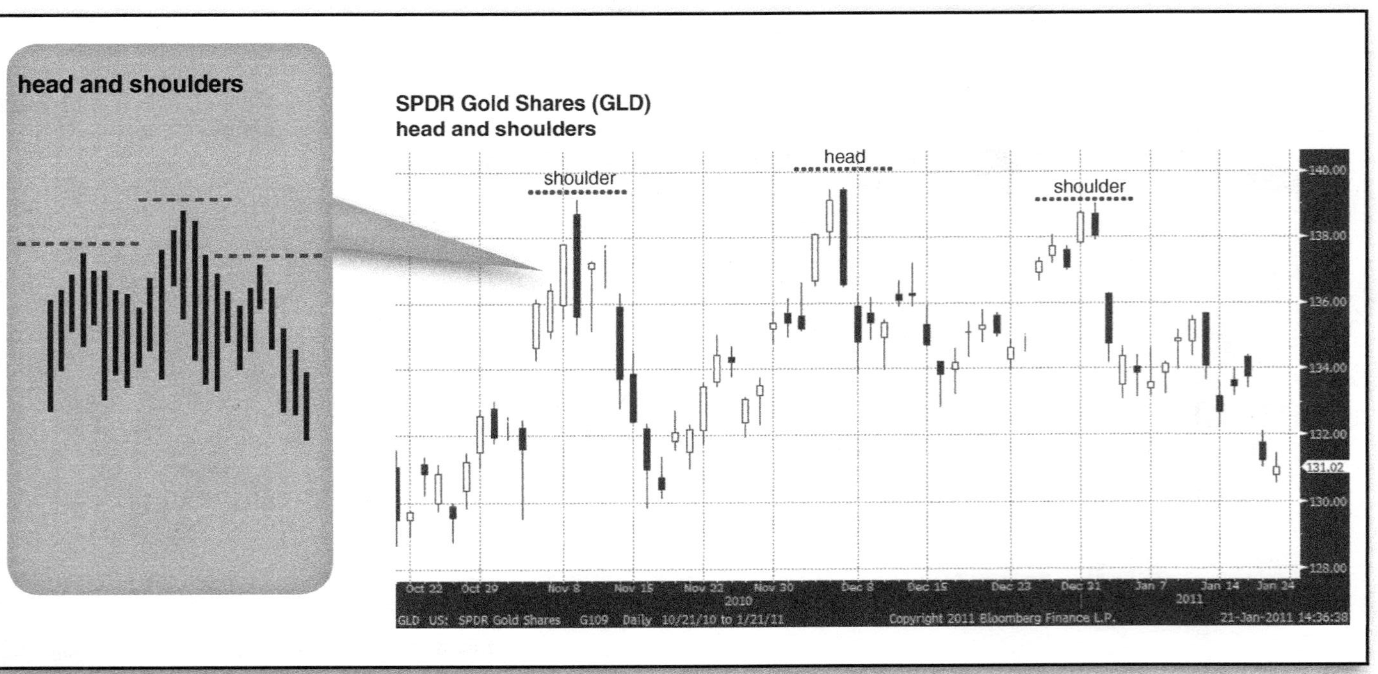

FIGURE 12.9

hidden gaps
DuPont (DD)
hidden gaps
51.00
50.00
49.00
48.64
48.00
47.00
46.00
45.00
Oct 22
Oct 29
Nov 8
Nov 15
Nov 22
Nov 30
2010
Dec 8
Dec 15
Dec 23
Dec 31
Jan 7
Jan 14
Jan 24
2011
DD US: EI du Pont de Nemours & Co G104 Daily 10/21/10 to 1/21/11
Copyright 2011 Bloomberg Finance L.P.
21-Jan-2011 14:24:46

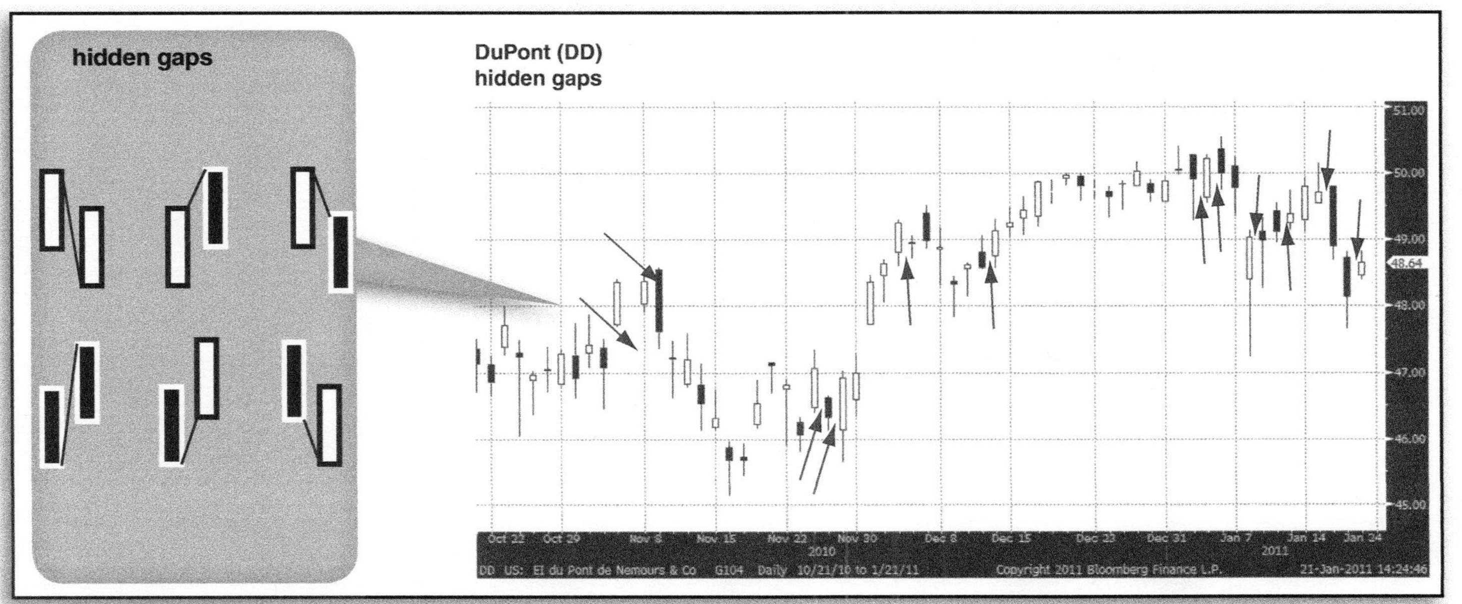

FIGURE 12.10

CHAPTER 13

Basic Indicators Reference I to O

From Michael C. Thomsett, *Bloomberg Visual Guide to Candlestick Charting* (Hoboken, New Jersey: John Wiley & Sons, 2012), Chapter 8, I-O.

Ichimoku Clouds An Eastern technical indicator developed by Goichi Hosada, a newspaper reporter. The cloud chart predicts coming resistance and support levels and changes, strength or weakness in the existing trend, and candlestick-based advanced signals.

KEY POINT:
In Japan the cloud is called Ichimoku kinko hyo, which means "at a glance equilibrium chart."

The Ichimoku cloud chart is constructed using not only moving averages of price, but daily high and low price levels as well. It develops five separate lines. The first two are the highest high and the lowest low over nine sessions. The third line is an average of these two lines, calculated over 26 sessions. The fourth and fifth are leading span lines. The first leading span is the base line average of 26 sessions, divided by two and plotted for 26 periods forward (beyond the latest price data). The second is the highest high and the lowest low for the past 52 sessions, divided by two and plotted for 26 future periods.

KEY POINT:
The complexity of calculating Ichimoku clouds leads many traders to overlook the cloud's significance: the combined indicators predict momentum based on evolving support and resistance, a powerful combination of price predictions.

The space between the fourth and fifth forward estimates is the cloud portion of this chart. The cloud itself can be adjusted by changing the 26 session and 52 session periods used to create it. The two future-plot lines are a representation of the relationship between the 9-session and the 26-session moving averages.

The calculation is a complex one to perform by hand, since it demands not only moving averages but also forward estimates of price changes. However, online sites provide automatic Ichimoku cloud chart calculations. For example, the illustration shows how this calculation is applied to the chart for McDonald's (MCD) in Figure 13.1. The perimeters of the calculated future price trends reveal the future convergence and divergence of the averages. However, unlike technical indicators like moving average convergence/divergence (MACD), the Ichimoku technique carries the estimates into the future by approximately one month.

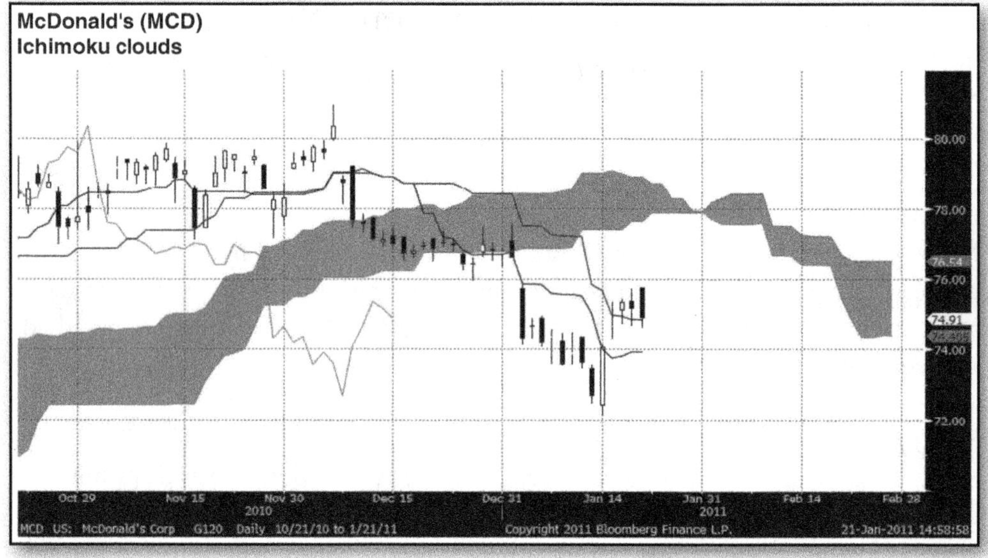

FIGURE 13.1

Inverse Head and Shoulders A pattern of price changes and reversal of an existing downtrend. This may confirm candlestick indicators or those indicators may be confirmed by the development of the inverse head and shoulders.

Like the bearish head and shoulders, this is a bullish signal in which an attempt to break below support level fails, and it is followed by price movement in the opposite direction. It may lead to a breakout above resistance and replacement of prior resistance as a new level of support.

KEY POINT:

The inverse head and shoulders is one of the most reliable bullish reversal signals. The failed attempt at breakout below support is a visual signal of lost momentum among sellers, and this leads to a bullish reaction.

There are three distinct sections in the inverse head and shoulders. First is a fall in price followed by an upward reversal. Second is another price decline below the bottom of the first, a test of support, followed by another reversal to the upside. Third is the second shoulder, a decline in price that does not move as low as the middle decline, followed by a rise that continues moving upward. Prices then approach resistance and may break through its neckline to establish a new trading range and strong uptrend.

The chart of Pfizer (PFE) met all of the criteria in its reversal of a downtrend (Figure 13.2). The inverse head and shoulders fell below the prior support, and that level created a new resistance line. The inverse head and shoulders tested the new support but failed to break through. Prices then rose and surpassed resistance, and the success of the breakthrough was confirmed over the five sessions after the upward gap, which did not retreat but instead resulted in a strong uptrend.

Momentum The degree and speed of changes in price or volume of a security. The causes of momentum may be fundamental (earnings announcements, sales growth, or improved market share) or technical (shifts between buyer and seller activity or changes in moving averages due to institutional buying or selling, for example).

> **KEY POINT:**
> Momentum is a measurement of a trend's strength or weakness. It forms the basis for reversal and, as it slows, tracking momentum improves entry and exit timing.

Traders are likely to respond more immediately to technical momentum than to more subtle changes in fundamental strength or weakness. As a result, momentum most often is applied to price and volume than to revenues and earnings. Momentum is measured in dozens of ways through Western indicators, as well as through candlestick patterns and indicators. Extremely long candlesticks, for example, demonstrate a wide range between opening and closing price. However, equally important is the extension of upper and lower shadows, which reflect failed attempts by buyers (upper shadow) or sellers (lower shadow) to move price further. Once trading occurs above or below and then retreats to close within the lower range, the shadow extension is a signal of changes in momentum.

Momentum Oscillator An indicator that measures the speed or change in price or volume, or changing rates of acceleration and deceleration in those movements. Momentum is a key measure of trends, so oscillators are the most important measurements in technical analysis. When combined with studies of price movement in relation to resistance and support, it is possible to gauge the likelihood of breakout or retreat. Trends tend to lose momentum when breakout is attempted but fails, and price often moves in the opposite direction after testing the trading range's edges.

Oscillators also work well with candlestick indicators. Candlesticks are visual representations of changes in trends, most notably in how momentum increases or decreases. An oscillator may indicate that momentum is weakening, and candlestick

Pfizer (PFE)
Inverse head and shoulders
Inverse head and shoulders
The flip from support to resistance is one of the signals that this pattern will lead to an uptrend.
breakout
new resistance
prior support
shoulder
new support
head
shoulder
18.50
18.3615
18.00
17.50
17.00
16.50
Oct 22 Oct 29 Nov 8 Nov 15 Nov 22 Nov 30 Dec 8 Dec 15 Dec 23 Dec 31 Jan 7 Jan 14 Jan 24
2010
2011
PFE US: Pfizer Inc G123 Daily 10/21/10 to 1/21/11
Copyright 2011 Bloomberg Finance L.P.
21-Jan-2011 15:03:20

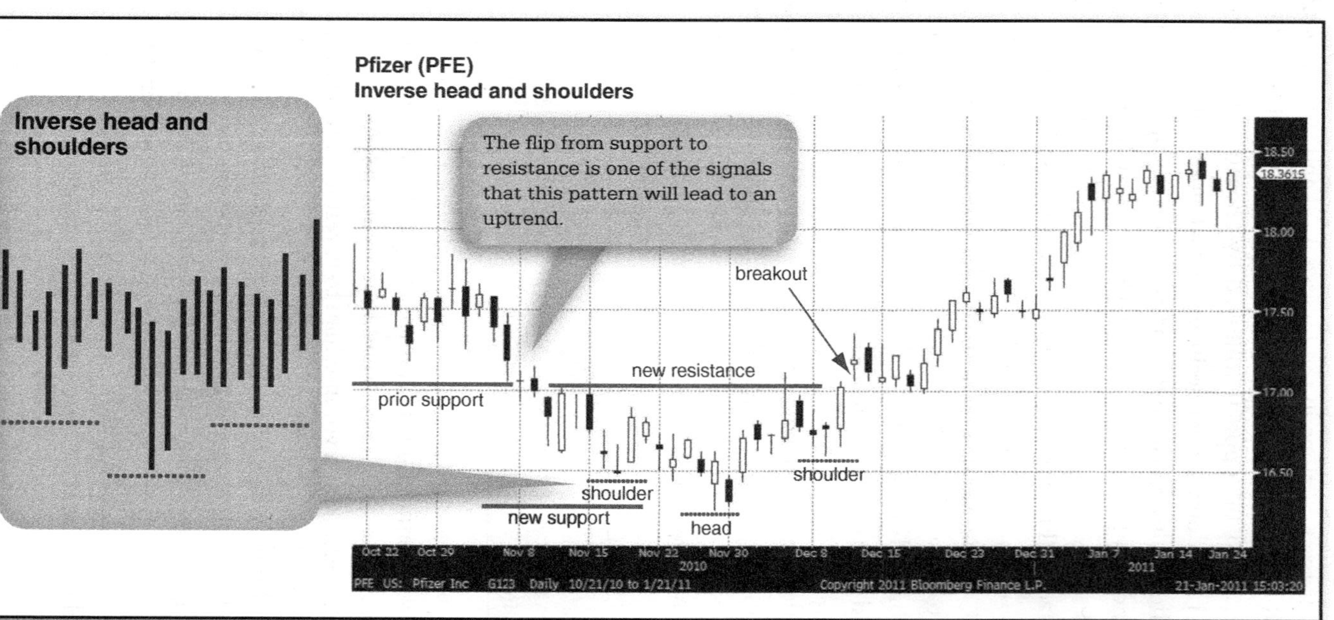

FIGURE 13.2

reversal indicators identify the turning point when momentum is likely to begin moving in the opposite direction. Momentum oscillators may also confirm what candlestick indicators forecast in the immediate future.

Two additional price patterns are significant: candlestick shadows and price gaps. A candlestick's shadows are further measures of declining momentum. The longer the shadow, the higher the possibility that the indicated side of the trade is losing momentum (buyers with upper shadows, or sellers with lower shadows). Price gaps work both within specific indicators and separately as part of Western technical analysis demonstrating increasing momentum. Interpretation is a matter of understanding how the strength of oscillators affects price movement. For example, rapid gapping prices may lead to retreat and fill patterns, especially if this occurs close to resistance or support. Or, when momentum is growing along with gapping trends, it may point to a coming breakout and establishment of a new trading range. Both of these possibilities have to be considered, and the likelihood of each can be confirmed by observing how candlestick indicators interact with the Western signals.

> **KEY POINT:**
> Oscillators have two important attributes for traders. First, they work very well in cross-confirmation with candlestick signals. Second, they may be the best entry and exit timing devices because slowing momentum is itself a powerful predictor of pending reversal.

When momentum indicators are used as initial, or leading indicators, they are expected to be confirmed by candlesticks or by other Western-based technical signals. Popular among those momentum indicators serving as leading indicators are relative strength index (RSI), which compares buyer and seller momentum to judge which is in control; various forms of price moving averages; and moving average convergence/divergence (MACD), which tracks two moving averages and looks for crossover points as a means of anticipating near-term changes in momentum. Additional momentum indicators are designed to identify overbought and oversold conditions for trading and trying to time the market. Some are also based on changes in volume. For example, on-balance volume (OBV) is cumulative as it adds or subtracts volume control over several periods.

Money Flow A measurement of changes in stock price based on studies of price range and trading volume. The purpose is to identify whether buyers or sellers controlled the direction of change, and to what degree. This is different from the easily observed direction of price movement because it further studies the momentum of price beyond the point changes. Most technical indicators based on money flow create an index to measure change. The purpose is to not only identify whether buyers or sellers are in command, but to anticipate and recognize when a security is overbought or oversold.

Money Flow Index (MFI) An oscillator combining price and volume to measure strengths or weaknesses (and evolving changes in each) among buyers and sellers. The indicator is also called volume-weighted RSI (relative strength index), because the initial calculation of rising or falling prices is then used to create an oscillator based on the RSI formula. The resulting oscillator ranges between zero and 100. This is a valuable indicator for anticipating coming reversals. It may either confirm reversal indicators in candlesticks or be relied upon as confirmation for what the same candlestick patterns predict.

DO IT YOURSELF

To calculate MFI:

1. (H + L + C) ÷ 3 = T

   where: H = daily high
   L = daily low
   C = daily close
   T = typical price

2. T × V = R

   where: V = daily volume
   R = raw money flow

3. Calculate the sum of both positive and negative money flow over the past 14 periods:

   PR × pp = PRMF
   NR × np = NRMF
   where: PR = positive raw money flow periods
   NR = negative raw money flow periods
   pp = number of positive periods in the past 14
   np = number of positive periods in the past 14

(note: the sum of n periods must equal 14)

   PRMF = positive raw money flow
   NRMF = negative raw money flow

4. PRMF ÷ NRMF = MFR

   where: MFR = money flow ratio

5. 100 − (100 ÷ (1 + MFR)) = MFI

   where: MFI = money flow index

KEY POINT:

MFI is an oscillator that is easily understood and used to confirm reversal. It ranges between zero and 100 with key signals above 80 or below 20.

The calculation of MFI is typically based on a 14-period study, with each new period added as the oldest is subtracted. The formula creates a "typical" price, which is the average of the daily high, low, and close, and then multiplies the average by the daily volume.

MFI is employed to identify when a security is overbought or oversold. The index ranges from zero to 100. When the level is greater than 80, the security is assumed to be overbought; when it falls below 20, it is undersold. However, the reliability of the index by itself is questionable as the indicator may lag behind rapidly developing price changes. Because of this, analysts often wait for the level to exceed 90 before acknowledging an overbought signal, or below 10 on the undersold side.

Chaikin Money Flow (CMF) provides a more accurate summary of the money flow trend, because it calculates the range of changes each day rather than relying on the "typical" price average between high, low, and close.

Moving Average (MA) Also called a rolling or running average, a method of tracking stock prices or any other factor, in which a set of values (the field) are added together and then added by the number of values. For example, if there are five values in a field, they are added together and then divided by 5 to find a simple moving average.

> **KEY POINT:**
> Moving average is a valuable tool for managing trends in price. However, like all statistical stools, it is easily misused and misunderstood.

> **DO IT YOURSELF**
> To calculate a simple moving average:
> (V1 + V2 + ... Vn) ÷ N = SMA
> when: V = value
> N or $_n$ = total number of values in the field
> SMA = simple moving average

Many technical indicators rely on averaging to track evolving trends over time. The field (number of values) remains set and as each new value is added, the oldest is dropped off. For example, a 20-day moving average always consists of the past 20 periods. The field of 20 periods is averaged by adding the 20 values together and then dividing the sum by 20.

The value of using averages to track stock prices and other trends is to smooth out the short-term and nonrecurring value spikes and fluctuations. In reviewing the latest price data, chartists will discover that variations between sessions make it difficult to identify the trend or how it is growing or weakening over time. The MA solves this problem.

The simple moving average described above may also be termed a nonweighted simple moving average. This means that each value in the field is given the identical value. A field of 20, for example, is added together and divided by 20. In a weighted moving average, one of several methods is used to provide more influence to the latest data than to the oldest data. A basic form of weighted moving average is to count the latest value twice. For example, in a field of 20 closing prices, the most recent price would be counted twice, and the entire field divided by 21. This weights the most recent entry by twice the weight of the previous 19.

Another form of weighting is called the sum-of-the-digits method. In this form of weighting, the oldest value is counted once, the second-oldest twice, and so on. The final and most recent would be counted based on the full number of periods; in a five-field data set, the most recent value is multiplied by 5 and the period just before by 4. The total is added and divided by 15:

$$1 + 2 + 3 + 4 + 5 = 15$$

This provides five times more weight, or influence, on the most recent value, and the weighting is reduced for each period. There are many ways to weight a moving average to provide more weight on the most recent information; one of the most efficient of these is exponential moving average (EMA). This calculation is based on calculating an exponent based on the size of the field (for example, a 20-period moving average involves calculating an exponent based on 20 periods). Each new entry is calculated to adjust the EMA up or down without having to recalculate the moving average each time.

MA is used in many technical formulas, as a means for smoothing out price or volume data and for identifying changes in the prevailing trend. Western technical analysis relies on MA as a core basis for understanding how those trends gather momentum or lose momentum as time passes.

Moving Average Convergence Divergence (MACD) A popular momentum oscillator that tracks two separate moving averages to anticipate points when changes in price are likely to occur.

MACD was developed by Gerald Appel in the late 1970s. MACD lines change as they move above and below an identified "zero line." Key moments occur when these lines approach each other (converge), cross over one another, and move away (diverge). The calculation of MACD begins with a subtraction of the longer-term moving average from the shorter-term. These are 26-day and 12-day calculations, although the averages can be adjusted.

These averages are calculated using exponential moving average, which is a simplified method for weighting an average. The field consists of each day's closing price. In addition to the two EMA lines, a "signal line" serves as a base for comparison. This is a nine-day EMA, and the two additional moving averages are compared to this signal line. The signal line is the key, because when the net MACD (26-day minus 12-day moving average) is above that line, it is positive, and when below, it is negative.

On an MACD chart, two primary lines representing the two EMAs are at work. On some charts, a third factor, presented in the form of a histogram, tracks the net difference in the two EMAs; however, MACD analysis can be accomplished with only the two lines, as the convergence, divergence, and crossover are the key signals traders look for.

Convergence—the two EMA lines approaching one another or approaching the price from above or below—anticipates crossover and the possibility of a change in trend direction. Divergence—the two lines moving away from one another or away from the price level itself—indicates changes in momentum. Crossover—when the two lines cross one another or when one of the lines crosses the price trend itself—may signal and precede a reversal in price.

KEY POINT:
The daunting name of moving average convergence/divergence (MACD) should not prevent an appreciation of the predictive value it provides. Convergence and divergence of averages in relation to price is an excellent visual device for predicting and confirming reversal trends.

All of these key changes in MACD confirm candlestick indicators or may lead the trend to be confirmed by candlestick formations after the MACD trend develops. No indicator, including MACD, may be used by itself to time entry or exit. MACD is especially complex to use for timing because at times it leads, but at other times, it follows the price trend. Using averages makes interpretation difficult, and MACD is based on the use of two separate weighted averages.

DO IT YOURSELF
The primary MACD line is a net of two separate EMAs:

12-day EMA – 26-day EMA = MACD line

In general, whenever the price records a new high and MACD is lower than the price, it is a bearish signal. When the price forms a new low and MACD is above that level, it is considered bullish. However, the timing and time duration of these signals is not certain, and because MACD is based on backward-looking indicators (moving averages of past sessions) the strength of a bearish or bullish signal will rely on the speed and extent of movement within the averages.

For example, the three-month chart of Exxon Mobil (XOM) shows the two MACD lines below the price. The shorter 12-session EMA is shown with the black line and the longer 26-session EMA is found on the red line. The shorter EMA is the most responsive, and in this chart that line tracks the price trend very closely. The value of EMA is found in the manner in which the two EMAs interact.

The 26-session EMA begins declining in mid-November, when the price trend was sideways. Both averages fell to a low and remained quite close together even as the price began moving upward. This is an example of how MACD may lag rather than lead. MACD's bullish move did not occur until the first week in January, more than a month after the subtle and gradual uptrend began. The price gap that occurred after November 30 was a bullish signal that led to this slow uptrend. It was confirmed by a 12-session MACD turn upward that occurred at the same time; however, interpretation of this is not clear. It may be seen as nothing more than an adjustment of the average *caused* by the price gap and not confirming it. The crossover on December 31 signaled the increase in bullish momentum. In this case, MACD led the trend even without clear confirmation from any candlestick formations. Throughout this period, the trading range remained very small, meaning there was little to rely on in candlestick indicators.

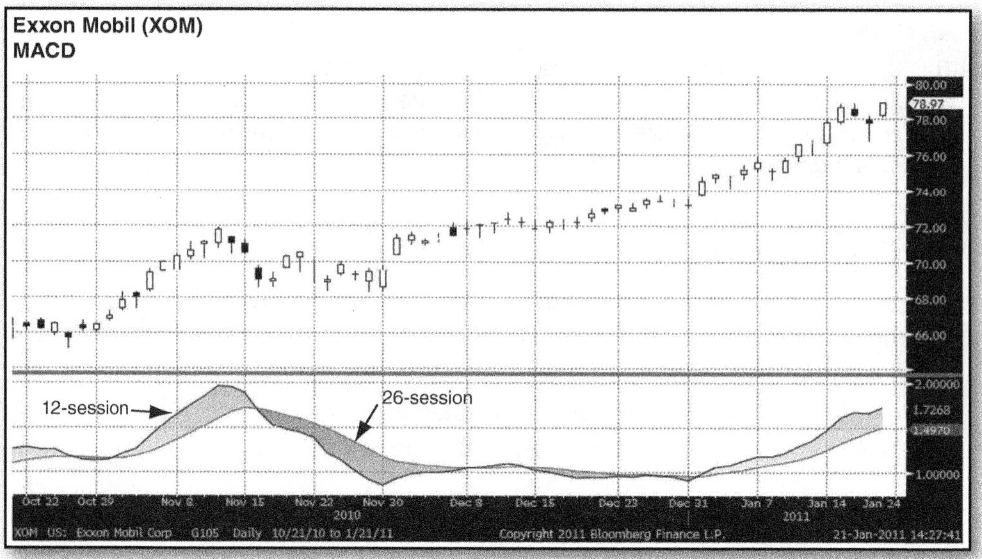

FIGURE 13.3

Narrow-Range Day (NRD) In swing trading and day trading, a likely reversal session. It is a near-doji or doji session, in which the range between open and close is very small, or when the close is the same price as the open.

> **KEY POINT:**
> What swing traders call an NRD is the same as the candlestick term doji or near-doji. Its value as a signaling session is found in translation. In Japanese, "doji" means "mistake."

Timing of entry and exit often is based on the appearance of an NRD. In charts where this occurs frequently, no clear signal is possible. But when an NRD follows a series of broader-range trading, it is a valuable leading or confirming signal. An NRD (doji) also serves as part of a several multisession candlestick indicator.

Confirmation of the NRD consists of not only candlestick formations, but several other changes observed by active traders. These include:

- a reversal session immediately before or after the NRD, or a session moving in the direction opposite the trend. This applies when a trend is underway, defined as three or more consecutive sessions moving in the same direction.
- a volume spike, a day in which volume is significantly higher than average. The combination of a volume spike and an NRD is among the strongest of reversal indicators based solely on Western technical analysis.
- approach to resistance (in an uptrend) or support (in a downtrend) and an unsuccessful attempt at breakout, which anticipates a retreat in the opposite direction.
- confirmation through candlestick reversal indicators that include the NRD (doji or near-doji) as part of its formation.

On-Balance Volume (OBV) A cumulative indicator developed by market writer, speaker, and forecaster Joseph Granville. OBV was first introduced in Granville's

1964 book, *New Key to Stock Market Profits* (Prentice Hall). The concept is to measure both positive and negative volume on the theory that changes in volume predict price movement.

The running calculation assigns each day as either positive or negative. If a stock's price closes higher, the day's OBV is positive, and if it closes lower, OBV is negative. One flaw in OBV is that it makes no distinction between slight changes and significant changes. A day whose price increases by one-quarter point is given the same weight as one whose price increases by six points. In both cases, the OBV is given a positive mark. Each day's positive entry is added to the previous cumulative total, and negative entries are subtracted.

The basis of OBV is the belief that volume precedes price and that the current price projection can be used to measure changes in volume as positive (up days) or negative (down days). However, it is not the level of volume that matters but the behavior of the OBV line. OBV may precede and thus predict price changes, although it does not always do so. The uncertainty is augmented by price behavior near resistance and support, or on days in which volume spikes. These factors and the effect on trading behavior may distort OBV and provide a false indicator.

OBV is believed to turn bullish when the cumulative line moves high as prices move lower, especially as price forms a new low. A bearish divergence results when prices move higher but OBV moves lower. This is especially compelling if price level reaches a new high.

DO IT YOURSELF

Calculation of each day's OBV:

1. Positive price change:
   prior OBV + current volume = new OBV
2. Negative price change:
   prior OBV – current volume – new OBN

KEY POINT:

OBV has two drawbacks. First, it defines a session as either positive or negative even when the direction is very slight. Second, because it is a cumulative indicator, its current level varies based on the starting point.

OBV is a useful indicator of buying and selling pressure over time. However, it serves best as a confirming indicator or when it is independently confirmed by other formations, notably candlesticks. Considering the assignment of all volume as either positive or negative regardless of the degree of change in price, each session's change in OBV is neither as reliable as other Western signals, nor as strong a reversal indicator as many candlestick formations.

For example, the chart of Chevron (CVX) tracks OBV below the price over three months (Figure 13.4). The price trend was sideways for the first month and then began moving up. There were two moments in which OBV precedes the price move accurately. The first was during the first week of November, when price direction was far from clear but the OBV line moved sharply upward. This upward change began even as the price trend was downward, including a strong downside gap. How-

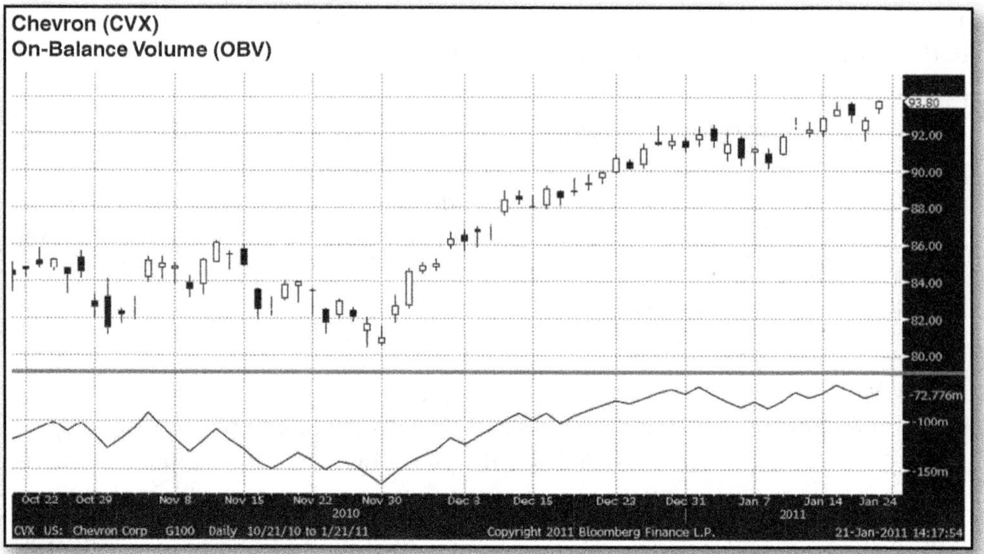

FIGURE 13.4

ever, this was followed immediately with a reversal, upside gap, and strong but brief uptrend. The second forecast showed up in the first week of January. OBV moved upward, and price followed a few sessions later.

Confirmation that the November OBV moved was found in two changes. First was the near-doji, and second was the very strong upside gap. In the second, January move, the sequence was reversed. First came a very strong bullish harami ending on January 7, preceding the OBV move two sessions later. In this case, OBV confirmed the candlestick reversal signal.

Overbought/Oversold (OB/OS) The condition of the overall market, when prices have been driven too high through excessive buying (overbought) or too low as the result of selling (oversold). The circumstance may be an aspect of the advance/decline ratio, relative strength index (RSI), and other oscillators. Or it is the result of a calculation based on comparisons between advancing and declining issues. In treating this as an indicator, a 10-session moving average is most often used to calculate the net difference between advancing and declining stocks on a particular exchange.

The number of the OB/OS is a matter of interpretation. When the 10-day average is higher than +200 (very overbought market), OB/OS is very bearish, and when the 10-day average is under –200 (oversold), the signal is very bullish. However, based on volume levels for the market, traders may decide to use this indicator to identify reversal points in the market rather than relying on a specific number of advancing and declines issued averaged in this manner.

DO IT YOURSELF

To calculate the overbought/oversold indicator:

10MA (AI – DI) = OB/OS

where: 10MA = moving average

AI = advancing issues

DI = declining issues

OB/OS – overbought/oversold indicator

OB/OS is expected to act as a leading indicator, so price movement and, specifically, reversals are expected to follow the point where they are identified as overbought or oversold. However, it is important to find confirmation in candlesticks and other indicators before making entry or exit decisions.

KEY POINT:

OB/OS provides confirmation of pending reversal, but identifying the point of extremes is a matter of opinion and interpretation.

CHAPTER 14

Basic Indicators Reference P to R

From Michael C. Thomsett, *Bloomberg Visual Guide to Candlestick Charting* (Hoboken, New Jersey: John Wiley & Sons, 2012), Chapter 8, P-R.

Paper Trading Also called "virtual trading," a system for simulating trades without placing funds at risk. The purpose is to learn how trading works or to try out specific strategies. For example, a trader interested in testing the effectiveness of using candlestick reversal signals to time entry and exit may employ paper trading to determine actual risk levels and the usefulness of specific signals to better time trades.

KEY POINT:
Paper trading systems are offered by several online brokerage companies as well as by the Chicago Board Options Exchange (CBOE) (www.cboe.com/ tradtool/virtualtrade.aspx) and other exchanges

Although paper trading is safe (no actual funds are placed at risk), a danger in employing this strategy to test a theory is that it does not provide actual experience. As a trading "game," it may have the unintended consequence of insulating traders from risk awareness and convincing them that risks are lower than they are, or even nonexistent. In addition, traders using "virtual money" do not act in the same manner as those with actual capital at risk. Paper trading is a valuable learning tool, but its usefulness is limited. Paper trading is useful for learning to recognize candlestick formations and to then time entry or exit in response.

Percentage Swing System A device used to confirm the timing of entry or exit. Developed by market expert Marty Zweig and first discussed in his 1985 book, *Winning on Wall Street,* the system is based on tracking price changes in both directions and making a move if and when a predetermined percentage of change has been reached. Zweig favored 4 percent moves to create buy and sell signals, but this is a matter of judgment for each trader. Even small changes in underlying assumptions may cause a model to work less effectively or even to fail altogether.

Price retracement may also be based on the observation of how prices move and then reverse, either temporarily or to return to a prevailing trend. One well-known percentage swing system tracks retracement based on the Fibonacci sequence, in which trendlines are used to predict price movement and reversal.

KEY POINT:

Applying a universal percentage to every security is not always an accurate method for timing of trades. It may need to be adjusted based on levels of price volatility for the security versus typical volatility among other securities.

A percentage swing system should not be considered as a sole means for timing of trades. However, it is an excellent confirmation tool for other reversal indicators, notably those found in strong candlestick patterns. The percentage swing system, along with other trend and momentum indicators, is effective in improving the timing of entry and exit based primarily on both candlestick and Western methods.

Price Oscillator Also called percentage price oscillator (PPO), a measurement of momentum based on the trend between two separate exponential moving averages (EMAs). This is used in conjunction with MACD to assign a percentage value to monitor convergence and divergence. It requires a calculation of the net difference in the 12-day and 26-day EMA, dividing by the longer average and then multiplying the result by 100 to arrive at the percentage value.

DO IT YOURSELF

Formula for the price oscillator:

$[(12_{ma} - 26_{ma}) \div 26_{ma}] \times 100 = PO$

where: 12_{ma} = 12-day EMA

26_{ma} = 26-day EMA

PO = price oscillator

KEY POINT:

Price oscillators are two separate calculations working together. They mark evolving trends as a powerful means for anticipating points of reversal.

The price oscillator is useful in employing MACD to identify buy and sell signals. The indications are similar to MACD, but expressed as percentages above or below the signal line (a 9-day EMA of the price oscillator).

The price oscillator is a valuable confirmation tool for what candlestick reversal indicators signal. Like MACD, this is a track of moving averages, so it is backward-looking. Any large moves in price may distort the price oscillator, meaning that before acting on a buy or sell signal, traders using the price oscillator need independent confirmation from candlestick patterns in agreement, or from Western technical signals.

Price Spikes A tendency for prices to move dramatically above or below the accepted range. As a statistical standard, spikes are distortions and should be removed from the analysis as long as they meet two specific criteria. These are the following:

- the spike must be one-time and nonrecurring.
- price levels must return to the prevailing trading range immediately.

Primary Trend Under the Dow Theory, the basis of technical analysis, the long-term trend of the market (trends moving upward are bull trends and those moving downward are bear trends).

Every primary trend has three parts: accumulation or distribution phase, public participation, and panic (or excess).

> **KEY POINT:**
> Primary trends have three predictable phases: accumulation or distribution, public participation, and panic or excess. Understanding behavior during each trend helps improve timing and strengthens a contrarian approach.

In a bull market, the primary trend begins with accumulation. The Dow Theory states that this earliest phase is when knowledgeable investors begin acquiring long positions. The timing of accumulation is associated with the last segment of a downtrend, when most traders are fearful and expect further downward movement. At the beginning, accumulation also marks a period of consolidation, and only toward the end do prices begin moving upward.

The second bull market phase is public participation. Traders recognize that prices are moving higher, so a big move into long positions occurs. Gradually, the previous negative opinion is replaced with optimism, which in turn accelerates the bull market. Public participation is likely to also be the longest period within the trend, as well as the one with the most significant degree of upward price movement.

The third and final bull market phase is called excess. In this phase, the most knowledgeable traders begin selling shares and moving out of long positions, recognizing that the bull market is beginning to lose momentum. However, most traders do not recognize this and continue to acquire larger long positions. At this point, a growing number of new traders also enter the market in the belief that the uptrend will continue. This buying activity is at its greatest at the peak of the bull market.

Primary bear markets also involve three parts. First is the distribution phase, in which knowledgeable traders and investors begin selling shares to close long positions or may open short positions. At this point, most traders continue to view the trend optimistically, not realizing that the previous bull market has ended.

The second phase is public participation, when the majority realizes that a bear market is underway. Selling activity grows as prices continue to fall. New short positions accelerate as traders believe prices will continue to move downward.

The third and final phase of a bear market is called the panic phase. Traders sell shares to avoid further losses and pessimism rules the market. The selling activity reaches its height at the same time that the bear trend bottoms out.

The timing of all phases in both bull and bear markets often is very difficult to spot. However, contrarians recognize the tendency to "buy high and sell low" instead of to "buy low and sell high." They use many technical devices not only to improve the timing of trades, but also to recognize the type of market trend underway. These include a range of momentum oscillators, evaluation of evolving trading ranges for specific issues, and the types of candlestick patterns showing up in price movement. Sideways movement over an extended period hints at a switch point between primary bull and bear markets, and traders using candlesticks will look for breakout and reversal patterns to determine when the market is about to move once again. While candlestick indicators provide clues about short-term reversal or continuation, a recurring candlestick pattern may confirm or lead a new trend direction within the primary trend.

Pullback A reversal in price, found at either the top or the bottom of a short-term trend. When prices have risen quickly, a pullback is expected, especially to fill gaps that developed during the price rise. When prices have fallen rapidly, the same tendency to reverse and fill gaps will be found.

Deciding when to use pullbacks to time entry or exit should rely on the use of candlestick indicators. Pullbacks are examples of price adjustments for which candlesticks are exceptionally useful. When confirmed by tests of resistance and support, the candlestick indicators are excellent methods of confirmation. For example, if price rises and breaks through resistance, a candlestick reversal signal anticipates a pullback to fill the gap and retreat into the previous trading range. The same is true for breakouts below support. If the candlestick formation is bearish, then it is more likely that prices are going to continue falling; a bullish reversal makes reversal more likely.

Reaction Swing Also called retracement, a tendency for price to move in the direction away from the primary trend, as a temporary adjustment that is followed by a resumption of price movement in the trend direction.

Securities do not trade in a straight line, but tend to be dominated by a direction for a period of time (the trend) and to experience reaction swings within that trend. Traders may take advantage of these short-term swings as part of a timing strategy.

KEY POINT:

No trend moves in a straight line. They slow down, retreat, consolidate, and then resume. The range of candlestick signals and confirming indicators help manage the chaotic nature of short-term price movement.

Candlestick indicators are very effective at timing of trades based on reaction swings. Most traders understand that even when a long-term trend is underway, shorter-term reaction swings are found frequently within that trend. A swing-based strategy relies on reversal signals that appear often within a primary trend and point to short-term entry and exit opportunities. When traders rely on candlestick indicators and separate confirmation, timing will be improved. However, the trader does not know whether a change of direction is a reaction swing or the beginning of a reversal to a new trend moving in the opposite direction. For this reason, continued monitoring of candlesticks and other technical patterns is the only method for ensuring that positions entered will be closed based or reliable signals. This applies both to newly established trends and to reaction swings.

Rectangle Bottom A formation in price in which a decline leads to upside reversal, but only after a short period of sideways movement. This formation has two aspects. First, it is a reversal but is not V-shaped like so many other reversals. Second, it often will be found as a test of support, which also confirms the reversal when a breakout attempt below support fails.

Confirmation through support holding up may be further confirmed through strong candlestick reversal signals. For example, U.S. Oil Fund (USO) followed the pattern precisely (Figure 14.1). The downtrend concluded with a clear rectangle bottom that also tested support. The conclusion of the rectangle bottom was found in the closing white marubozu.

This rectangle bottom also conformed to the expectations for behavior of support and resistance. This began with the test of support within the rectangle bottom and then an upward movement that broke through the previously established resistance level. The chart overall presents an example of how Western indicators such as rectangle bottom at support are effectively confirmed with easily spotted candlestick signals.

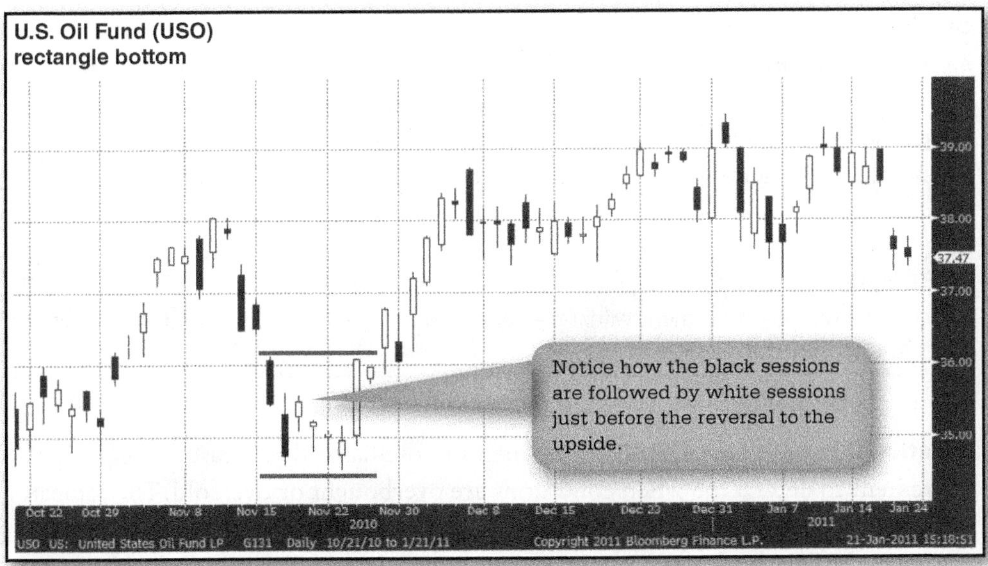

FIGURE 14.1

Rectangle Top A price pattern in which an uptrend ends and then reverses, not in a V formation but after a brief period of sideways movement. This occurrence often is found in conjunction with a failed test of resistance, leading to a new downtrend.

The test of resistance is not an essential matter in order for the rectangle top to appear. However, when it does, that serves as confirmation of the reversal in the

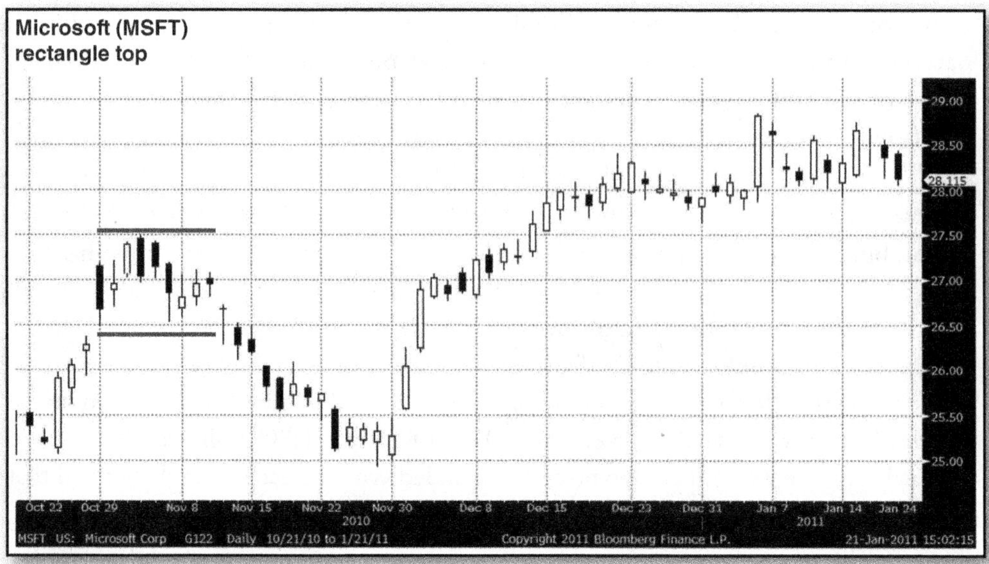

FIGURE 14.2

same manner that other tests of resistance do. For example, the three-month chart of Microsoft (MSFT) included a rectangle top that briefly broke through resistance established the previous June at $26.50 (Figure 14.2).

Rectangles are valuable charting tools when they not only conform to the requirements of Western technical price movements but also provide compelling candlestick confirmation. At the end of the rectangle top, a two-session bearish meeting lines signal preceded the reversal and marked the end of the rectangle top. That was followed by an easily spotted doji and then the downside price retreat. Much later, beginning on December 14, the temporary resistance level set by the rectangle top at $27.50 became the new support level after a successful upside breakout.

> **KEY POINT:**
> The brief sideways movement within the rectangle identifies resistance and foreshadows an offsetting downside reversal.

Relative Strength Index (RSI) A momentum oscillator that measures recent price movement to determine when conditions are overbought or oversold. The indicator was developed by J. Welles Wilder, a market expert, researcher, and author who introduced RSI in his book, *New Concepts in Technical Trading Systems* (Trend Research, 1978).

RSI measures not only the amount of movement and its meaning, but also the speed of price change. The indicator creates a measurement between zero and 100. When it moves above 70, conditions are defined as overbought; when it moves below 30, the security is oversold. When RSI reaches the extreme of zero, it reveals that price moved lower during all 14 periods. When it reaches 100, it means that price moved higher during all 14 periods.

The set period does not have to be left at 14 days. By lowering the number of days, sensitivity to change increases and overbought or oversold conditions will be reached more often. With an increase in the number of days, more smoothing occurs in the average and overbought or oversold conditions will occur less often.

The index values can also be adjusted from 30 and 70. For example, when expanded to a 20–80 range, the occurrences of oversold or overbought will occur less often. Some traders employ two separate RSI calculations. The first is the traditional 14-period RSI based on a 30–70 range. The second is a shorter-term averaging (two-period, for example) using the 20–80 range; the latter identifies short-term oversold and overbought conditions and helps find reaction swings in price within day-trading and swing-trading strategies.

In two-part systems such as this, effectiveness is greatly improved when traders seek confirmation between RSI levels and candlestick indicators. When oversold and overbought conditions appear, candlestick formations are likely to provide useful confirming signals.

KEY POINT:

RSI is a popular indicator because of its effectiveness in anticipating price changes before reversal occurs. Its outcome is simple: a range between zero and 100, with key indicators above 70 (overbought) or below 30 (oversold).

RSI is useful in identifying not only overbought and oversold conditions, but also failure swings and centerline crossover (such as the key change in momentum found in indicators like MACD). RSI also identifies the primary trend's direction, which is not always apparent, especially in very volatile markets. In situations of sudden price change, the long-term meaning is not always clear. RSI helps provide perspective in such times (for example, when a large price gap occurs or when resistance or support levels are broken and a new trend begins).

DO IT YOURSELF

The formula for RSI is:

$100 - [\,100 \div (1 + \{U \div D\})] = RSI$

where: U = average of days closing higher (up) over a set period

D = average of days closing lower (down) over a set period

(the set period used in most RSI calculations is 14 days)

RSI can be used to spot reversals as well as overbought or oversold conditions. A divergence between price and RSI provides a strong signal and one most likely to find candlestick-based confirmation. As RSI's originator pointed out, directional momentum does not confirm price movement by itself. A divergence is always possible. A bullish divergence is the combination of a lower low in the price at the same time as a higher low in RSI. A bearish divergence is the opposite: a higher high in the price along with a lower high in RSI.

Tracking divergences is not an exact science. Many interim divergences are likely to appear within a trend, moving opposite the primary price direction. This is where candlesticks are valuable in identifying whether a divergence is a true reversal or a temporarily movement opposite of the prevailing trend. A failure swing offers the same kind of information but also the same kind of danger. RSI analysts recognize that an RSI swing occurs independently of price swings. This occurs when the RSI line moves below 30 or above 70, comes back, and then hovers at or near the line before breaking in one direction or the other. This occurs most often immediately before a strong reversal. Candlestick signals confirm the potential reversal and may actually lead RSI. In that instance, the price reversal trend has greater strength than the RSI trend, because RSI lags due to the smoothing in the use of an average, whereas price reversal is raw, immediate information.

> **KEY POINT:**
> Even when prices are on the move, RSI makes a distinction between the trend and overbought or oversold. A trend may progress without moving into the extremes, and RSI makes this a visual outcome.

Two examples of RSI provide a look at how the indicator performs in different levels of volatility. First is the three-month chart of Home Depot (HD) in Figure 14.3.

The first observation in this chart is that RSI never moves into either overbought or oversold ranges. Although the stock price was trending upward, traders who tracked RSI did not find any sell signals because RSI remained in the middle zone for the entire period. Even the strong upward movement during the first week of December did not set off any alarms about possible reversal. In this example, RSI provided a degree of certainty for traders in long positions that no reversal was likely in the immediate future.

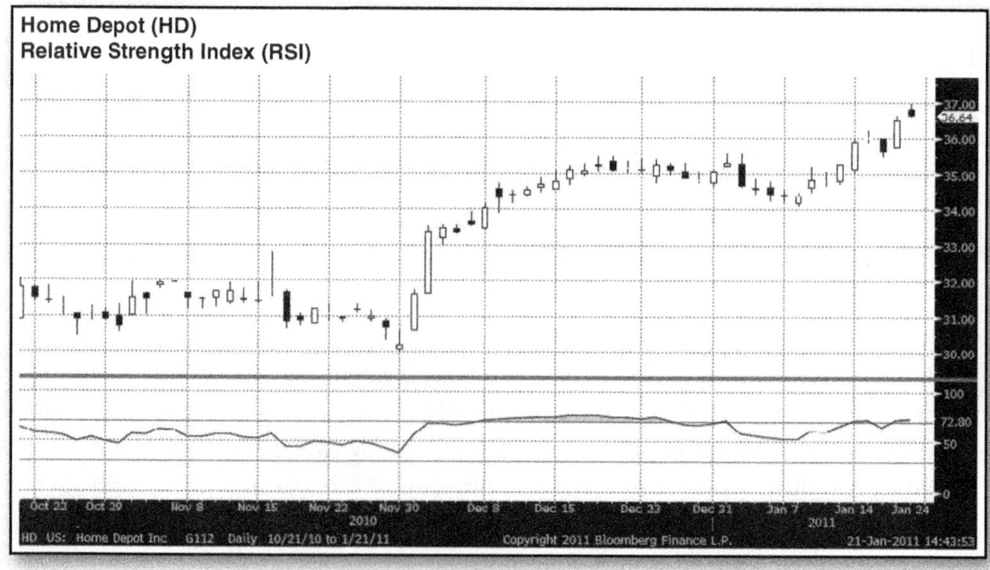

FIGURE 14.3

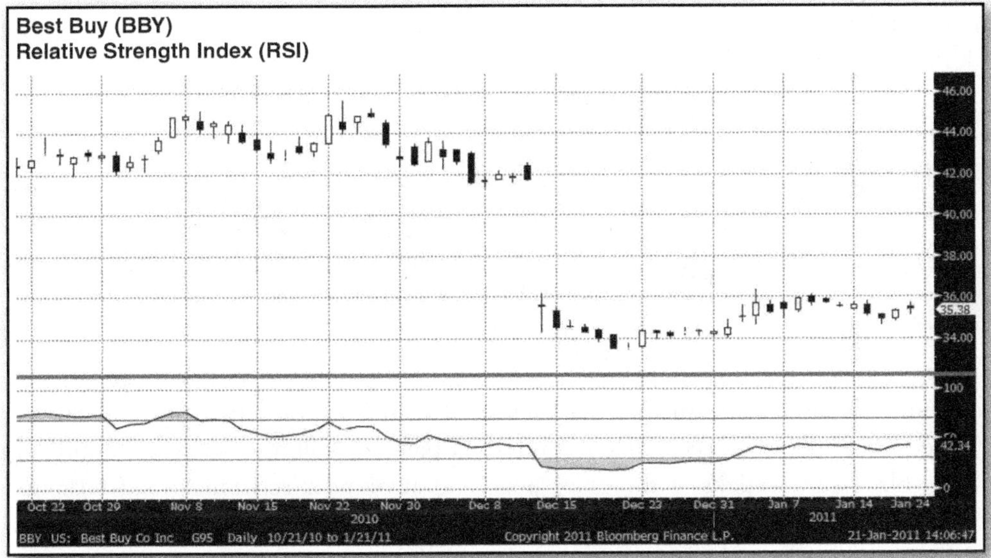

FIGURE 14.4

The second chart is for Best Buy (BBY) in Figure 14.4 This situation is quite different. The stock was experiencing a sideways trend for its first six weeks. Then a strong downside gap occurred, dropping the price six points in a single session. At this point, RSI also fell and moved into the oversold range, but only slightly. It remained below 30 but did not continue to fall. RSI rose back into the middle zone in early January. Even though price continued to decline, dropping to $28 by April, RSI stayed above 30 for the entire period (beyond this chart) except for some very brief dips under that level.

This second chart reveals that RSI is not an indicator of price direction within the immediate future. It identifies instances when the security is overbought or oversold, but the trend moves independently. BBY was one such case. Between December and April, price dropped 17 points while RSI moved very little. As a confirming indicator of overbought or oversold conditions, RSI is valuable; it points to those moments when traders will want to enter a trade. But RSI is not a trend indicator. Before acting on what RSI predicts, traders need confirmation from other Western technical signals or from candlesticks.

Resistance The price level representing a limit on price moving any higher, due to the strength among sellers (as an offset to the strength among buyers). As price approaches resistance, selling pressure grows and buying pressure shrinks. At resistance, the supply of shares meets or exceeds demand and halts further price growth.

Once this changes, prices may break through resistance and establish a higher trading range. So resistance (like its opposite, support) defines the current trading range, but that may change in the future. When price breaks above resistance, one of two patterns follow. If the breakout holds, prices move higher and set a new trading range. But prices may also retreat back into the established range, declining below resistance as a consequence of lost buyer momentum.

When breakout succeeds, a new trading range will set a higher resistance price, as well as a new support level. New support often is going to be found at the previous level of resistance.

KEY POINT:

The level of resistance may be flat, rising, or falling. The shape it creates in relation to support is used to anticipate continuation or reversal, even in very volatile conditions.

As price levels approach resistance, many traditional Western indicators provide insight to price behavior, especially involving downward reversal and decline. These include double tops and head and shoulders, for example. The failure to break through resistance leads to reversal and downtrend.

These price tendencies are confirmed by candlestick patterns that occur when price tests resistance. Seek strong reversal signals and confirmation through Western technical signs. Strong price reversal may also include gapping price movement, especially as part of a recognized candlestick pattern; volume spikes; exceptionally long black candlesticks at the price peak and at or near resistance; and near-doji or doji sessions, especially those with very long upper shadows (a symptom of lost buyer momentum, which anticipates a downward turn).

Retracement A short-term move in price in the direction opposite that of the prevailing trend. Chartists recognize that trends do not move indefinitely in a straight line, tending instead to experience retracements within the longer-term trend. Candlestick formations are valuable in narrowing down a distinction between a retracement and a true reversal.

Reversal A turn in price trend, when an uptrend halts and then moves into a downtrend, or when a downtrend stops and subsequent price movement creates an uptrend.

Reversal in Western technical analysis includes many well-known price patterns, such as head and shoulders or inverse head and shoulders, double tops, double bottoms, and falling or rising wedges. Among candlesticks, reversal indicators take many forms, including hammer and hanging man, engulfing patterns, harami, belt holds, doji star, meeting and piercing lines, white soldiers and black crows, inside up and down, outside up and down, abandoned baby, squeeze alert, and concealing baby swallow.

Reversal Formation Any indicator in price that predicts a reversal in direction. These are found in both Western and Eastern signals and are best interpreted when confirmed independently. A reversal formation may fail, so confirmation is required before acting. Confirmation of a reversal formation may include other reversal formations, candlesticks, or Western price patterns. They may also include volume spikes of volume-based indicators and measurements.

Most reversal formations work in conjunction with changes in momentum among the dominant side in the current trend. So one of the most important reversal formation confirming indicators is a momentum oscillator that changes the indicated strength and weakness of the trend.

Reversal Session A single trading session in which price movement is in a direction opposite that of the prevailing trend. This appears at random in some cases, or it may be part of a more complex candlestick pattern. For example, numerous two-session candlestick reversals begin with a directional session but then follow with a reversal session. Notably strong examples include engulfing patterns, harami, meeting lines, and piercing lines.

Reversal sessions also are found in Western technical signals, notably exhaustion gaps, failed breakouts, double tops and bottoms, and narrow-range sessions (in candlesticks, called doji or near-doji sessions).

> **KEY POINT:**
> An isolated reversal session may have no particular significance within the broader trend. Before a trader acts on such a signal, the larger trend and related candlestick formations should be studied carefully.

Rising Wedge A bearish formation developing over several periods of trading. It begins with a wide range that narrows. As the range narrows, prices rise. It provides a reversal indication in most instances. The rising price levels combined with the narrowing range usually leads to a decline once the wedge is complete; however, this needs confirmation from other signals such as candlestick patterns or Western signals such as a failed test of resistance just prior to the reversal. The rising wedge may develop as a continuation pattern in a minority of cases. In continuation situations, the rising wedge will often appear as a short-term upward price trend moving counter to the prevailing downtrend.

> **KEY POINT:**
> The rising wedge is usually very bearish because, even as price trends upward, the range narrows. This is a subtle but compelling leading indicator for a downturn at the end of the wedge period.

To work as a reversal, there must first be an uptrend in effect. The chart for Visa (V) shows a good example of a rising wedge (Figure 14.5). The uptrend was

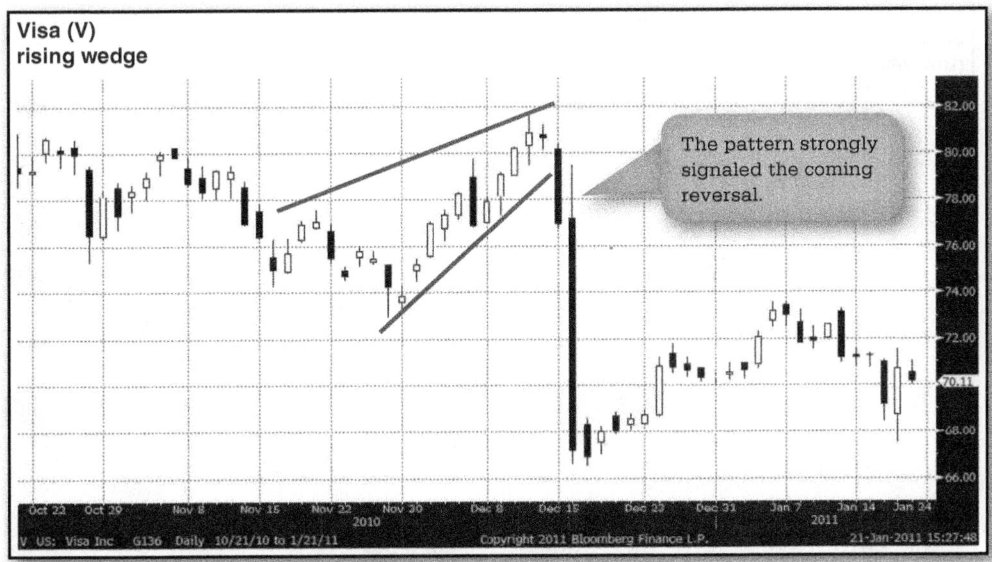

FIGURE 14.5

clear, but the narrowing price was a symptom of falling momentum during the period. Confirmation of a coming reversal was found in the last two sessions of the uptrend, in which a bearish harami appeared. This was the action point, especially since the rising wedge had narrowed considerably by this point. The following session gapped down and then a very strong long black session with a long upper shadow (a symptom of lost buyer momentum) made a convincing case for the lower trading range.

Runaway Gaps A series of price movements with recurring gapping action. It is a signal of growing interest in the stock among buyers (during an upward runaway gap pattern) or a widespread sense that the security is overbought, leading to downside runaway gapping prices.

> **KEY POINT:**
> Runaway gaps are difficult to interpret and require strong confirmation. When the gapping action includes a lot of doji or near-doji sessions, especially if volume also spikes, it signals almost certain reversal.

Runaway gaps may be a symptom of strong directional interest, but they may also show up during a period of excess (upside) or panic (downside). This means that the meaning of the price pattern needs to be confirmed independently before acting. This may consist of candlestick continuation or reversal patterns as well as Western technical indicators. When any of these are accompanied by volume spikes, the meaning of the runaway becomes clearer. Volume growth often is seen in conjunction with narrow-range days (near-doji or doji sessions) and is a strong sign of a coming reversal.

Johnson & Johnson (JNJ) experienced a very strong but short-lived drop in prices, including five distinct runaway gaps, all moving down (Figure 14.6). The

FIGURE 14.6

pattern ended once price settled into a sideways-moving range for two months before beginning to move upward. However, the seemingly upward reversal seen at the end of the chart turned out to be a disappointment. JNJ's price trend remained uncertain until late April (beyond this chart) before it moved strongly upward.

The opposite pattern was found on the chart of Walt Disney (DIS) in Figure 14.7. This uptrend involved only three runaway gaps, but interpretation based on what happened afterward was difficult. Considering the month-long sideways movement preceding the runaway gap pattern, the change looked very much like an upward movement. Prices continued upward beyond the charted period, confirming that this example of a runaway gap was bullish (prior to the preceding sideways movement, the price trend had been bullish, making this a continuation indicator). However, the candlestick signals were contradictory. Immediately after the brief runaway gap to the upside, a bearish harami cross appeared. Considering that the runaway gap may be found during a period of bearish reversal after excess on the part of buyers, this looked very much like a reversal signal. However, as later price movement revealed, there was no downtrend. This is an example of a combined runaway gap and bearish reversal signal, which failed.

FIGURE 14.7

CHAPTER 15

Basic Indicators Reference S to Z

From Michael C. Thomsett, *Bloomberg Visual Guide to Candlestick Charting* (Hoboken, New Jersey: John Wiley & Sons, 2012), Chapter 8, S-W.

Setup Session A signal applying both to swing trading and to candlestick analysis. In swing trading (and day trading), the setup is the first hint that a turning point has arrived. This may consist of a volume spike, a narrow-range day (NRD, or in candlesticks, a near-doji or doji), or a reversal day after a short-term trend. The setup is expected to be followed by a confirming signal or execution.

Candlestick setup refers to a specific session, the first one in a multistick signal or indicator. It is followed by a signal session. The combined signal is found in both reversal and continuation candlestick formations, and the setup often forms the final entry in an existing trend before it reverses. The second signal session (or sessions) create the pattern first entered by the setup.

KEY POINT:
Setup has more than one definition. In swing trading, a setup is the first part of reversal. In candlestick indicators, it is the first session of a multisession indicator that may predict reversal or continuation.

The swing trading and candlestick indicators are closely related and should be employed as part of a comprehensive strategy based on signal recognition and the search for confirmation. Setup in this regard consists of testing resistance or support, unusual gapping action, volume spikes, exceptionally strong candlestick signals (doji or long sessions, for example), and confirmation through technical patterns and index changes.

Short-Term Gapping Behavior Commonly occurring price changes characterized by repetitive gaps between sessions for a limited period of time. Unlike running gaps or breakouts, short-term gapping price patterns are likely to occur within the current trend, but they offer no specific signal of a change. This is most likely a random event.

To distinguish between running gaps and short-term random gapping price movement, the pattern has to be analyzed in the context of existing price direction, growing or shrinking momentum, and direction or change that other signals predict. If the price is acting within an established trend and no confirming indicators are found, the pattern is likely to be short-term gapping behavior. However, if other signals are found, such as growing momentum in the direction of the gapping action, it may be the beginning of a runaway gap trend.

Signal Session The indicator that completes a setup. In swing trading, the signal confirms the initial setup (volume spike, NRD or reversal day, for example). In candlestick analysis, the signal session (or sessions) follow the first session (the setup) and complete the pattern.

The signal session is the completion of a candlestick indicator in both reversal and continuation roles. The indicator cannot exist without both sides except in the single-session candlestick. All indicators, even very strong candlestick patterns, need independent confirmation. Using both the swing trading and candlestick definitions of a signal session, traders may use both disciplines to identify and then confirm entry and exit points, especially at moments when the signs point to reversal.

KEY POINT:

Signal has more than one meaning. To swing traders, it is the reversal followup confirming a setup day. In candlestick terminology, it is the completion of a multisession indicator and predicts either reversal or continuation.

Simple Moving Average (SMA) In statistics, a calculation that smoothes a series of changing values or trends or that identifies the mean of a field of values. In trading applications, the SMA is a starting point for the more complex weighted moving average, including the exponential moving average (EMA), which is used in popular price tracking indicators such as MACD.

DO IT YOURSELF

To calculate simple moving average (SMA), add together the values in a field and then divide by the number of values:

$(V_1 + V_2 + \ldots V_n) \div N = SMA$

where: V = value

N or$_n$ = total number of values in the field

DEFINITION:

time series

In a moving average, reference to a fixed number of periods to be averaged, which advances with each new value; the new value is added and the oldest is dropped off, so the time series involves calculation for a fixed number of values.

SMA, also termed a rolling or running average or the mean of the values in a field, is rarely a fixed calculation. In trading, a set number of fields are used to calculate averages of price, for example. A particular calculation may involve 14 sessions or as many as 200. This **time series** requires recalculation with each subsequent entry. The oldest field is dropped off and the newest is added to extend the moving average forward.

A cumulative moving average is an exception. It begins with a set number of values and adds more values, so the field expands with each new value. For example, on-balance volume (OBV) adds new data as volume sessions develop, and a previous numerical index is adjusted based on new information, without dropping off any previous values.

Spike A nonrecurring entry within a trend that is far above or below the norm. To ensure accuracy of a moving average, a spike should be excluded from the calculation.

In order to ensure the accuracy of any moving average, value spikes will distort the calculation. By definition, a spike occurs when one value is unusually higher or lower than the typical value. However, the subsequent entries must return to the established range of values in order for the exceptionally low or high value to meet this definition. For example, in tracking a security's trend based on closing prices, a single session far above or below the established trading range is excluded as long as it is isolated and nonrecurring.

Stochastic Oscillator A momentum indicator that computes a relationship between a security's current price and its recent price range. This indicator was introduced in the 1950s by George C. Lane, who has been nicknamed the "Father of Stochastics."

KEY POINT:

Stochastics provides a relative value to current price. It expresses a trend in relationship to a 14-period range of price extremes. It does not track price or volume, but the momentum of price movement.

DO IT YOURSELF

The stochastic oscillator consists of two separate lines termed %K, which is a 14-period value, and %D, a 3-session moving average of %K:

$100\,[(C - L14) \div (H14 - L14)] = \%K$

$\%K_3 \div 3 = \%D$

where: C = most recent closing price

L14 = lowest price among the previous 14 sessions

H14 = highest price among the previous 14 sessions

%K = 14-period stochastic value line

$\%K_3$ = %K for the three most recent sessions

%D = three-session moving average of %K

The word "stochastic" is derived from a concept in probability theory. A stochastic process is a family of random variables that may include price and time, as well as a potentially random sequence of price movement. The oscillator developed by Lane was based on a comparison between the most recent closing price and a 14-period analysis of the lowest close and the highest close. The outcome of the calculation places the most recent close in proximity to the 14-period extremes. Lane described the oscillator as one that does not track price or volume, but that instead calculates the momentum of price movement. As a result of the trend found in the stochastic oscillator, traders can discover bullish or bearish reversals. Because the indicator is found between zero and 100, it is also valuable for identifying overbought or oversold conditions.

The calculation is designed to track 14 prior periods, usually representing days or other increments of trading sessions. This can be increased or decreased to adjust what it reveals, or to alter the responsiveness of the calculation to price movement. When the line moves above 80, it is a signal that price is overbought and is due for a downward reversal. When below 20, it signals a bull reversal and oversold condition. Like other range-bound oscillators, the periods employed and the assumed overbought/oversold levels can be adjusted.

The chart of Boeing (BA) provides the oscillator below price (Figure 15.1). The black line represents %K and the orange line is %D. The frequent crossovers between the two lines are the result of averaging and are not significant on their own. However, when both lines move above 80 or below 20, a signal results. On about November 15 and again on December 15, stochastics provided a buy signal as both lines dipped below the 20 threshold. From November 15 through to the end of the period shown, the trend was clearly bullish. However, from December 23 onward, the stochastic level moved briefly above 80 several times, indicating overbought conditions. This tendency continued beyond the period shown; however, the price trend continued a gradual upward movement.

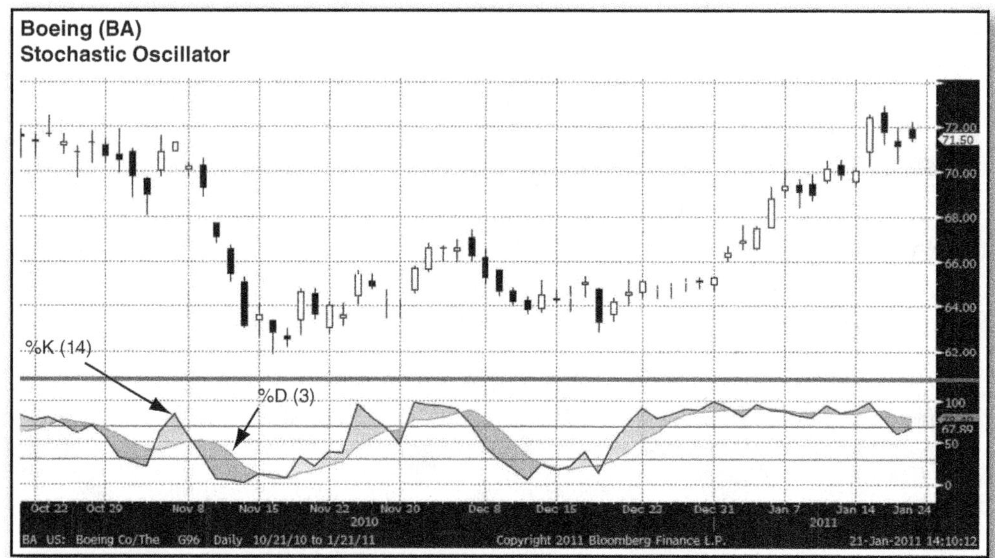

FIGURE 15.1

Support The lower price that securities will trade based on the current trading range; the price where buying interest meets or exceeds seller momentum. As price approaches the support price level, buying pressure grows, preventing sellers from taking the price lower.

KEY POINT:
Support may be flat, rising, or falling. It is one of two important test lines (the other is resistance) that displays changes in momentum.

Price levels may eventually break below support, which leads to one of two outcomes. First, a lower trading range is set. Second, prices may turn and retreat into the previously set trading range and then continue upward. The failed seller momentum is likely to be followed by a price rally. When price does break below support, that price may become the resistance level in a new trading range. The flip between support and resistance is one pattern that occurs frequently when trading ranges move.

At the point that price approaches and tests support, Western indicators provide strong clues about the potential for declining momentum and a following uptrend. These include inverse head and shoulders or double bottoms. When these patterns are found, price is likely to turn and move upward, away from support.

The movement of price, notably after a failed breakout below support, is confirmed effectively with candlestick reversal patterns. Seek those patterns with reversal gaps, long white candlesticks, or doji and near-doji sessions with exceptionally long lower shadows (a sign of failed seller momentum). Also look for gapping price patterns and volume spikes as signals of bullish reversal.

Swing Trading A short-term trading method, also termed "active trading," based on opening positions for periods usually not exceeding three to five sessions. The theory in swing trading is based on the observation that a majority of traders act and react emotionally to market news, causing prices to move in an exaggerated fashion and then reverse to compensate for the initial move. Swing traders seek short-term trends in the three- to five-session timeframe, and then enter positions to create short-term profits.

The short-term trend has to be established in order for reversal to occur. This consists of three or more sessions moving strongly in the same direction. An uptrend is made up of consecutive higher high prices and higher lows. A downtrend requires consecutive lower lows offset by lower highs.

Swing trading entry and exit is based on reversal signals of many types. Among these are the narrow-range day (NRD), known also as the near-doji or doji session. Another is the basic reversal session, when the direction moves opposite that of the short-term trend. Finally, a volume spike is a compelling signal of potential reversal. When any two of the three popular signals occur in the same session, reversal is very likely.

KEY POINT:
Swing traders are not concerned with primary or even secondary trends; they look for retracements based on overreaction to immediate information. This translates to entering and exiting trades on very short timeframes, usually three to five days.

These reversal signals are powerful timing mechanisms. However, they are made even stronger when confirmed by either Western or candlestick formations as well. These confirming indicators include price gaps, tests of resistance or support, doji or near-doji (NRD) sessions with exceptionally long shadows (lower shadows at the end of downtrends or upper shadows at the top of uptrends are signs of lost momentum), and well-known strong candlestick reversal formations.

A combination of Western technical signals with candlestick reversal indicators is a powerful tool for timing entry and exit, notably within a swing trading strategy. This is a natural approach, not only because swings occur as part of a larger trend, but also because short-term reversal is easily spotted and, given the appropriate degree of confirmation, is a reliable method to improve timing of swing trades.

Technical Analysis A range of analysis designed to anticipate price movement, speed, and direction based on a study of charts, momentum, volume, and price patterns.

> **DEFINITION:**
> **efficient market theory**
> A belief that the prices of all securities reflect all publicly known information at any given time, meaning that markets reflect fair pricing efficiently.

In comparison, fundamental analysis is based strictly on the study of financial reports and related information in the belief that capitalization, working capital control, and profitability determine stock prices. The fundamentals are backward looking in the sense that they rely on published summaries of recent operating results. Technical analysis is a study of the current price and recent trends, including moving averages to plot momentum, combining price and volume analysis, and specific price movements and patterns, in order to estimate a likely next step in price.

> **DEFINITION:**
> **random walk hypothesis**
> A belief that all short-term price movement is completely random and will not be affected by outside influences.

> **KEY POINT:**
> Both efficient market and random walk concepts are interesting. But real-life market activity defies these ideas. Anyone who has seen how price moves understands that the market is neither efficient nor random.

A foundation of technical analysis is the concept of resistance and support, the top and bottom of the current trading range. If price movement approaches either of these borders but does not break through, the price direction is likely to reverse and move in the opposite direction. This occurs because a failure to move price beyond the current trading range is a symptom of lost momentum among buyers (failed resistance breakout) or sellers (failed support breakout), after which the other side of the supply-and-demand interaction takes control.

Opponents of technical analysis (who may also be dubious about the fundamental approach) may hold one of two academically based points of view. The **efficient market theory** is a belief that the current prices of all securities reflects all known information about the company, and that price is always efficient and correct as a result. Closely related is the **random walk hypothesis**, a belief that all short-term price movement is random and will not be affected by news, information, earnings, and other market developments.

Both technical and fundamental analysts are likely to reject both of these theories based on observations about news and reaction in price. It is true that price reaction often is irrational, but forces like momentum and moving average trends cannot be discounted completely. Even a pessimistic market observer will acknowledge that technical principles do play a role in affecting price movement.

Technical analysis is divided into two primary schools of thought. Western technical analysis is based on chart analysis as well as price and volume trend analysis, relying on momentum oscillators and moving averages to identify specific price behavior. Remember that the trading range and interaction between price and range (resistance and support) defines many technical patterns. These include head and shoulder, double top or bottom, trendlines, and a variety of triangles and wedges.

In addition to tracking price, Western technical analysis relies on moving average analysis and momentum oscillators studying price as well as volume to identify when securities are overbought or oversold, indicators that act as initial reversal warnings. Such indicators include the relative strength index (RSI), moving average convergence/divergence (MACD), Chaikin Money Flow (CMF), accumulation/distribution (AD), and on-balance volume (OBV). The modeling resulting from these tools may be expanded to an advanced level of study of price behavior, using indicators like Bollinger bands or the stochastic oscillator. Although technical analysis is based to an extent on the principles of trends within the Dow Theory, the practical application of its tools are usually very short term, and designed to improve the timing of entry and exit into speculative trades, with little intent to employ a buy-and-hold strategy more closely associated with fundamental analysis.

The second school is Eastern, and it involves primarily the study of candlesticks. Among the many candlesticks are a range of formations of varying strength that may forecast continuation or reversal. The most effective use of candlesticks is to seek confirmation from other indicators. When Eastern and Western signals are used together to cross-confirm price movement anticipated in the signals, the charting technique is vastly improved.

Some critics believe that technical analysis is simply a method of trying to predict the future in a random world; however, analysis of momentum and moving averages belies this assumption. The purpose of all forms of chart analysis is to improve the timing of entry and exit based on developing trends in price and momentum and to be able to spot radical change (such as strong gapping price action moving through resistance or support, for example) or, equally important, failed attempts at moving price (often seen at resistance and support when the breakout fails, and prices retreat along with reversal confirmation from candlestick indicators).

Technical analysis covers a broad range of techniques and indicators, and candlestick charting has become a standard for analysis. Even chartists focusing on Western price patterns and volume trends tend to rely on candlestick charts as the best visual summaries of price performance. A distinction should be made between the charting of price and the use of candlestick indicators. The chart itself is useful in both Western and Eastern approaches. The specific continuation and reversal candlestick indicators are valuable confirmation tools or leading signals, and they are most effective within a program of analysis using both Western and Eastern techniques.

Trading Range The price area in which a security currently trades, marked by resistance at the top and support at the bottom. Resistance represents the price at which sellers are able to prevent the price from rising any higher; support is the level at which demand has enough strength to prevent further decline.

> **KEY POINT:**
> Trading range, the area between resistance and support, defines the entire study of technical analysis including volatility and momentum. When trading range analysis is combined with candlesticks, the result is a powerful set of predictive and confirming tools.

As long as resistance and support maintain this balance, the trading range does not change. However, price level is not always a flat line. A trading range may maintain the same breadth between the levels of resistance and support, even while price levels trend higher or lower. Resistance and support may also move toward or away from each other to create patterns known as triangles or wedges. In these instances, the trading range changes as the pattern develops and may foreshadow either continuation or reversal in the near future.

Trend A tendency for price to move in one direction for a period of time, based on momentum and interaction between buyers and sellers. Trends rarely move in a straight line and are characterized by short-term retracements. Unlike a reversal, which is the end of one trend and the beginning of another moving in the opposite direction, a retracement is a temporary adjustment to the trend and normally does not last for more than a few trading sessions.

Trends may move upward, downward, or sideways. An uptrend, also known as a bull trend, is characterized by a combination of progressively higher high prices and higher low prices. Swing traders recognize short-term trends by this definition. A downtrend, also called a bear trend, is defined as consecutive sessions with lower low prices offset by lower highs.

Within an uptrend or downtrend, it is possible to also experience a pattern of short retracements within the broader trend. Candlestick formations are valuable in identifying the differences between these retracements and actual trend ends and reversals.

In addition to uptrends and downtrends, a sideways trend occurs whenever prices do not move beyond a defined trading range. The range often is quite small since this is a period of indecision, when neither buyers nor sellers have momentum adequate to move price beyond the current narrow range. In this sense, a sideways trend may be called a nontrend because prices remain within a fixed and narrow range.

> **KEY POINT:**
> All price movement is about trends and their momentum. Even in the most chaotic of price movements, trends emerge and provide a sense of order . . . for the moment.

Any of the three trend types may last for as short a period as three sessions or as long as several months. The time a trend continues further distinguishes it as long term (one year or more), intermediate (one to three months), or short term. A short-term trend may represent a retracement of long-term or intermediate trends. However, swing traders and day traders rely on short-term trends to time their entry and exit, considering movements as short as three days to be trends for the purpose of trading.

Chartists and other technicians rely on trends to track momentum and follow price and volume as a means of anticipating when the trend will weaken. Augmenting this analysis is the study of moving averages, notably two separate moving averages, to seek trend evolution characterized by convergence or divergence of the averages, or the use of moving average lines crossing over each other or moving back and forth above and below the price as a means for quantifying the trend and anticipating reversal.

Trendline A method for tracking a current trend and identifying the likely end point. It involves drawing a straight line beneath the uptrend or above the downtrend. The line begins at the start of the trend and concludes when price levels meet or pass into the path of the line.

> **KEY POINT:**
> Trendlines are simple but powerful. A single straight line helps find likely reversal points in the current trend.

The chart for Kellogg (K) was characterized by a specific pattern: sharp but brief trends ending with sideways movement and then a new trend (Figure 15.2). The first of these sharp movements was a downtrend lasting just under two weeks. This ended with a strong bullish reversal signal, a three-session morning star (black session, downside gap, small white session, and a larger white session). Although this indicates a bullish reversal, prices moved sideways for the following month.

The second trendline was to the upside and lasted approximately two weeks. The sideways trend preceding this sharp price rise ended when the long black session was followed by an even larger long white. The uptrend ended with another sideways trend just like the first one.

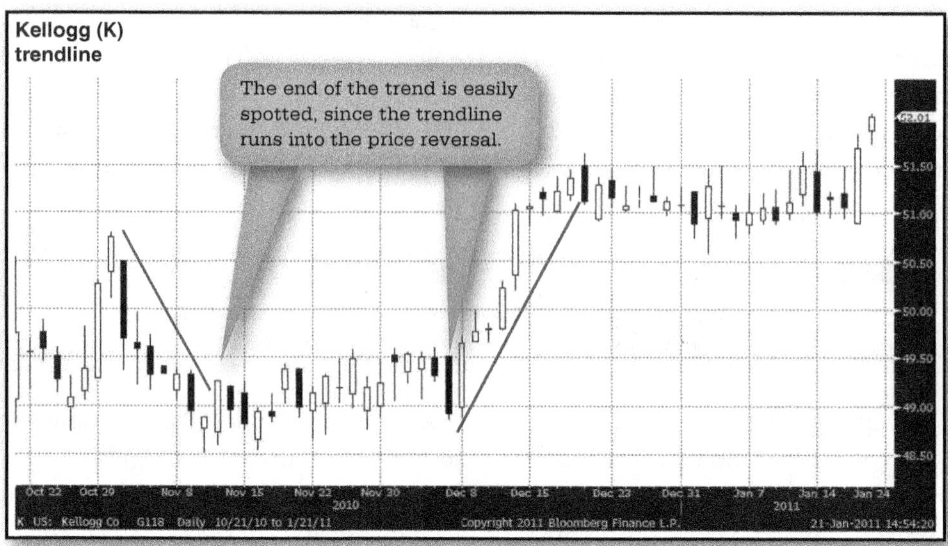

FIGURE 15.2

The trendlines on this chart are clear in the sense that they mark the strength of the downtrend and uptrend. Even though they were very brief, the momentum of each was robust.

Triangle (Ascending) A bullish continuation chart pattern in which prices continue rising, with support climbing higher against a level resistance price, as a sign of accumulation. As a result, the trading range narrows as the triangle closes.

As the support level climbs, price eventually breaks out above resistance and a new trading range is set. The prior resistance level often forms a new support as the higher trading range develops. For example, the chart of Walt Disney (DIS) included an ascending triangle that extended for seven weeks (Figure 15.3). The prior trend had been bullish, and the triangle represented a pause in the trend that then

FIGURE 15.3

resumed. It further appeared that once resistance was broken, that price formed new support. Analysis of DIS for the three months after this period confirmed this.

Triangle (Descending) A bearish pattern seen during an existing downtrend and visually reflecting a period of distribution. Although the descending triangle may provide reversal after an uptrend, it is most often a continuation formation. In both cases, looking for confirmation in the form of bearish candlesticks is prudent. The support level remains fixed while resistance moves downward, forming a narrowing range. At the point where the triangle is at its thinnest, prices continue the previous downward movement.

> **KEY POINT:**
> The fixed support level combined with a narrowing trading range is a powerful predictor of a downside breakout.

For example, Sears Holdings (SHLD) displayed a descending triangle that continued a short-term downtrend (Figure 15.4). After completion of the triangle, prices continued downward as expected. Confirmation that the downtrend was going to continue was convincing and involved three separate two-session candlestick signals.

1. The first confirmation signal was found five and six sessions prior to the end of the triangle, where the price gapped upward but then formed a bearish harami. This confirmed the triangle and also foreshadowed the continuing downward trend.
2. A second bearish signal appeared next, a thrusting lines signal. This confirmed both the descending triangle and the bearish harami.

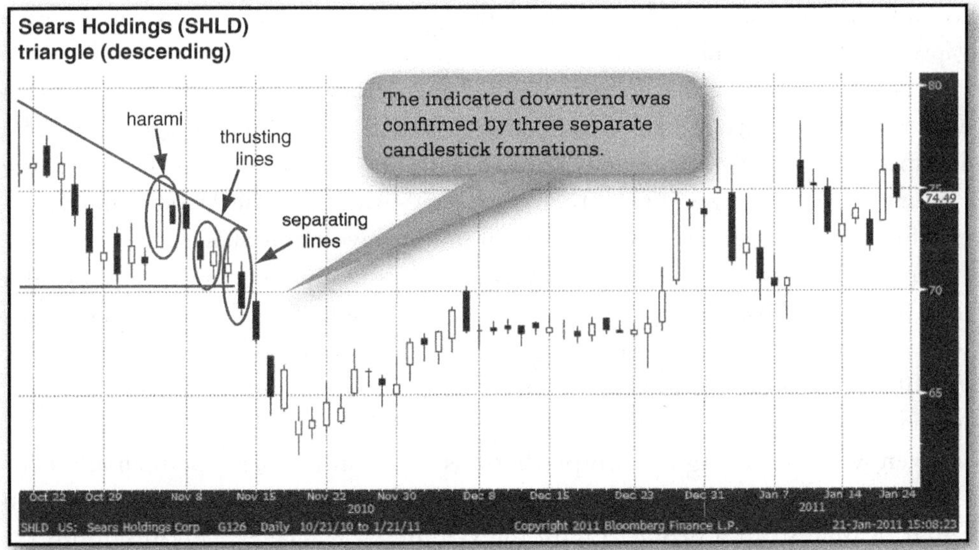

FIGURE 15.4

3. Third, the last session in the triangle and the first downward session that followed formed a bearish separating lines signal, adding to the strong downward confirmation.

These three candlestick signals were all bearish and anticipated the strong downward movement that quickly followed. Although the trends themselves were quite short term, the patterns displaying before, during, and after the descending triangle demonstrated how price patterns and confirmation work together effectively.

Triangle (Symmetrical) Also called a coil, a continuation pattern that is found in either an uptrend or a downtrend. It may also narrow the range of a sideways price pattern. In this type of triangle, resistance trends downward while support trends upward so that the trading range narrows, often rapidly, a sign of consolidation in the price movement. The two offsetting trendlines are trading range barriers found at the same time, which is unusual but revealing. Price is prevented from heading higher *or* lower. Most technicians observe that once the stalemate has been broken, it leads to an exceptionally strong trend; however, the direction is not foreshadowed by the pattern and must be the result of independent confirming data.

KEY POINT:

The symmetrical triangle is unusual because both resistance and support move closer together; during its development, price is prevented from moving higher or lower. Buyers and sellers are in a stalemate until the range narrows completely.

When the price breaks below the narrowing range, it often precedes a downtrend, and when it breaks higher, it is viewed as a signal of a coming uptrend. However, remembering that at the point a symmetrical triangle ends the range is very narrow, any move after the formation needs to be confirmed by volume spikes, price gaps, or candlestick indicators.

Hewlett-Packard (HPQ) went through a period of volatility after a failed attempt at an uptrend, an offset, and then the expected consolidation. The symmetrical triangle lasted only three weeks and then broke to the downside (Figure 15.5). However, prices then moved sideways again before starting an exceptionally strong uptrend. The problem in this development is that two bearish confirmation signals appeared immediately. This confirmed the likelihood of a new downtrend based on price breaking below. The first of these bearish signals was a clear and distinct black crows indicator. This concluded with a downside gap filled (consisting of the last two black crows session and the session that followed, filling the previous gap).

Even with the strong bearish predictions found in the price pattern and confirmed with two of the strongest bearish candlestick signals, this prediction failed. It points out a problem with the symmetrical triangle. Because both resistance and support are moving to a narrower range, it creates a great deal of

FIGURE 15.5

uncertainty and, at times, even strong signals are not reliable. The final outcome of this was that after the last sideways movement of less than three weeks, an exceptionally strong uptrend completed the charted period, but lacked any obvious bullish signals.

True Range A calculation of the distance between the opening price of the first session and the closing price of the one following. It may also be calculated based on the extension of the opening-side shadow of the first session and the closing-side shadow of the second. Applying this definition, the true range combination may shrink or extend the trading range, and may also create signals not found with the sessions separately.

KEY POINT:

True range is a form of two-session price blending intended to clarify the significance of candlestick signals. This is not the same as average true range (ATR), a form of moving average developed to smooth out volatility and to measure movement but not price direction.

KEY POINT:

Finding true range may help clarify the current price situation; however, it can also obscure it or create the desired but inaccurate effect.

The calculation is often thought to be the same as average true range (ATR), but it is quite different, representing the two-session blending of prices to either absorb or accent the true trading ranges. It often occurs that this volatility between two sessions actually is far less volatile when the two are combined, and this aids in the analysis of the current price trend.

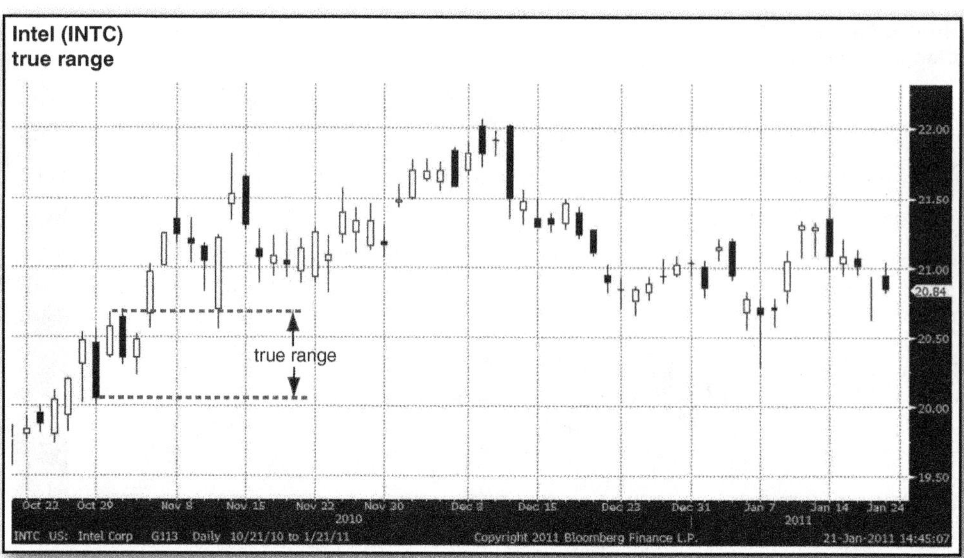

FIGURE 15.6

The chart of Intel (INTC) included an example of an upward-moving true range (Figure 15.6). Two sessions were involved. First was a black session and second was a white session opening well above the previous close. However, the gap between the two sessions was invisible. By blending the two sessions into a true range, the distance between session one's opening price and session two's closing price was quite small.

An example of a downward-moving true range is seen in the chart of Google (GOOG) in Figure 15.7. Two consecutive black sessions include a wide gap between, extending from the close of the first to the opening price of the second. When viewed apart, the downside gap implies that the downtrend will continue. However, when combined, the new true range including both sessions creates a strong bullish

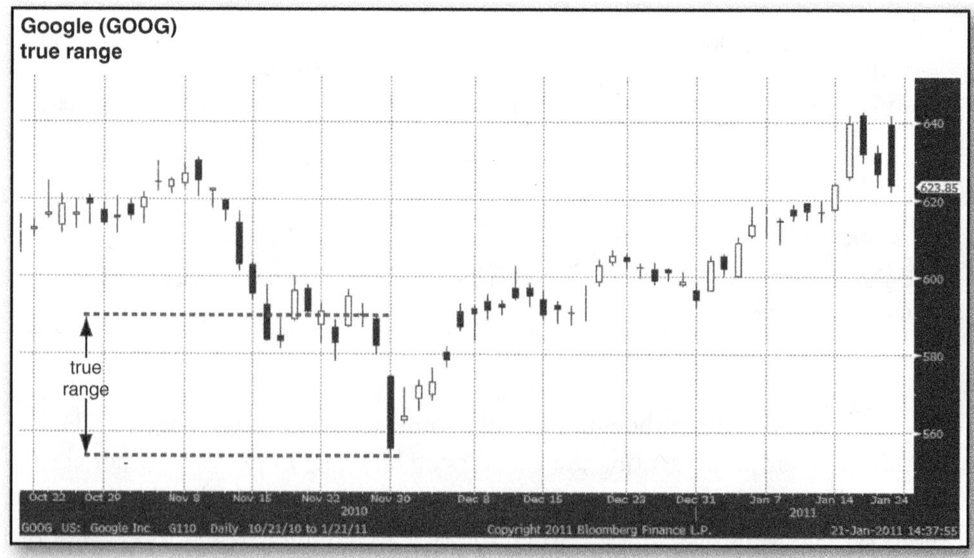

FIGURE 15.7

signal. The existing black session followed by a very small white session is a bullish harami; the true range session makes this bullish harami even stronger. Furthermore, extending the harami to one additional session forms a bullish three-day inside up signal. Finally, the three white sessions beginning at the same point form a modified white soldiers. Note the strength of the uptrend: Upside gaps follow in several of the sessions, including upside gapping black days. This downside true range example collectively serves as a nicely confirmed reversal signal.

All forms of blending, including true range, are troubling in the sense that they can easily distort the signals to create a desired outcome. The intention of the true range is to restate volatility so that traders can better read what is taking place over a limited timeframe. However, it can easily mislead. The Google chart is a good example. By making two black sessions into a single long black indicator, it would be easy to conclude that the signal was strongly bearish. This would be confused by the double bullish confirmation that followed. The use of true range must be undertaken with caution, and candlestick analysis and confirmation of Western signals provide a more reliable method for managing short-term price volatility.

Uptrend A trend in which price movement is higher, which also includes degrees of momentum and duration. An uptrend may represent the primary trend underway or an interim move away from the primary trend. Such short-term retracement is common and expected; however, this reversal movement may easily mislead traders. Recognizing the difference between a primary trend's reversal and a retracement is difficult. The meaning of an uptrend is best understood through confirmation, especially when a long-term indication based on Western technical analysis is confirmed with candlestick formations.

Swing trading and day trading strategies are based on short-term movement, so long-term uptrends are not as important as a movement of three days or more. The definition of an uptrend in a swing strategy is three or more days with consecutively higher highs and higher lows. Swing traders seek this strict definition as a means of identifying reversal. Once a reversal day appears, the trend is probably over in the swing trading view. Confirmation is sought through narrow-range days (doji or near-doji) or through volume spikes. However, in addition to the swing reversal signals, candlestick patterns also confirm the swing trading short-term reversal and provide valuable additional confirmation.

The Dow Theory, serving as a basis for technical analysis, recognizes three distinct types of movements. A primary or major trend extends several months or even years; a second reaction or swing period may last several months and is a retracement against the primary trend, and many uptrends fit this definition. Finally, a short swing or minor movement may last up to a month.

> **KEY POINT:**
> An uptrend may last as few as three sessions (swing trading) or many months or even years (primary trend). It may also be a short-term retracement within a prevailing downtrend.

The Dow Theory also acknowledges that uptrends occur over three specific phases. First is accumulation, then public participation, and finally distribution. Accumulation is a period of active trading by knowledgeable traders, which in an uptrend means buying activity. Public participation occurs when the majority of traders recognize that the uptrend is underway. This adds to buying pressure, which tends to move prices higher and, as a result, expand public participation. However, by this time, the knowledgeable trader is beginning to look for signs that the uptrend may be ending. This is the distribution phase.

An uptrend follows these tendencies over the long term, meaning that analytical and professional traders lead the trend, both at its initial phase and at its conclusion. Recognizing a coming reversal relies not only on the observable price momentum, but also on confirmation through Western indicators and patterns, and through candlestick signals.

Weighted Moving Average A form of smoothing, most often represented by exponential moving average (EMA), and used in many moving average indicators such as moving average convergence/divergence (MACD).

KEY POINT:

The purpose to weighting a moving average is to provide more importance to the most recent information, and less to possibly outdated, older information.

Any form of calculation that adds greater weight to the most recent values in a field is a weighted average, and as long as the number of periods remains fixed (older fields are dropped off as newer ones are added), it is a weighted moving average. These may take many forms beyond EMA, including simply adding the latest value twice. Thus, in a field of 14 periods, the most recent would be counted twice and the sum divided by 15. This doubles the weight of the latest value.

The need for weighting arises from problems with simple moving averages. Price action and the trend, especially long-term, may not be representative of current price momentum or movement. For example, a 200-day moving average that is equally weighted is overly smoothed in favor of outdated price, but weighting the more recent entries to the field is viewed as more accurate.

Western Technical Analysis Forms of analysis based on price and volume, or the study of trends, duration, and momentum. No single trading session is by itself used in Western technical analysis, but it serves as an entry into a larger charting price and volume trend. The evolving price trend is used to predict continuation or reversal, based on the recognition of the current trading range and its borders, resistance at the top and support at the bottom. Many Western reversal signals are based on failed attempts by buyers or sellers to break through these barriers. The trading range is the framework and reference point for momentum as well as for a majority of technical signals.

These are called Western signals because they have been used for many decades in North America and Europe as primary measurements of price movement and momentum. In contrast, Eastern technical analysis is the term for candlestick analysis, which is based on the shapes of sessions—the opening and closing prices—as well as trading range extensions (shadows) above and below those opening and closing levels. Eastern analysis is less concerned with trading ranges or with resistance and support, and more focused on single session, double session, or multiple session indicators, defined as reversal or continuation signals.

Western technical analysis is most effective when it relies on additional Western signals or candlestick formations to confirm what an initial indicator predicts. Because any signal can fail or provide false predictions, confirmation is essential in both Western and Eastern analysis. The most effective method for improving timing of entry and exit is to combine both disciplines and use them to confirm each other.

CHAPTER 16

Overview

From David Wilson, *Visual Guide to Financial Markets* (Hoboken, New Jersey: John Wiley & Sons, 2012), Chapter 1.

Financial markets offer you two basic investment choices: debt or equity. You can lend money to a government or company for some amount of time, or you can buy at least a share of companies and hard assets.

Debt represents a promise to pay. A borrower is required to make interest payments, if any, according to a schedule that's set when the loan is made. The borrower eventually has to repay the full amount and possibly a little extra.

Equity means full or partial ownership. Entire companies are bought and sold in the stock market along with their shares. Gold, other commodities, and real estate change hands through markets as well.

Debt payments and equity investments vary from one market to the next, as you'll find out later. What's constant is that governments, companies, and producers of hard assets play a role in these markets directly. They are more than names that are attached to contracts.

Financial markets enable borrowers to find lenders and equity owners to locate investors. This first takes place in what's known as the primary market, where new securities and assets are sold.

Borrowers usually rely on competitive auctions for fundraising, though some sales are negotiated. Companies can sell stock publicly for the first time in initial public offerings (IPOs). They can sell additional shares as needed.

Commodity markets that focus on the buying and selling of raw materials, rather than derivative contracts, can be labeled primary markets. In real estate, marketplaces for new buildings can be described the same way.

KEY POINT:
Governments and companies raise money from investors in primary markets. Investors buy from and sell to each other in secondary markets.

In secondary markets, investors trade with each other rather than governments, companies, and owners of hard assets. Most buying and selling happens in these markets if only because they tend to be far bigger than primary markets.

The longer the life of a security or asset, the greater the role of secondary trading. Debt maturing in a few months is less likely to change hands than a security with years left until it comes due. Equity has no maturity date by definition. Gold and other commodities can be stored indefinitely. Buildings typically last for decades, and land is eternal.

> **KEY POINT:**
> There are three main approaches to market analysis. Fundamentals provide insight into a government, company, or hard asset. Technicals reflect a security's price moves. Quantitative analysis relies on data.

Investors who own a security or hard asset are said to have a long position. The holding becomes more valuable as the price increases. The opposite is a short position, established by selling a security or asset borrowed from another investor. Anyone with a short position stands to gain when the price drops, and vice versa.

Three basic types of analysis help investors decide whether to go long or short. Some investors rely on one type, and others combine them in search of investments most likely to rise or fall.

1. **Fundamental analysis** focuses on the prospects for governments, companies, or hard assets. The analysis can take what's known as a top-down or a bottom-up approach. Top-down analysis begins by looking at overall economic and business conditions. Bottom-up analysis begins by considering the outlook for a specific government, company, or asset.
2. **Technical analysis** is the study of prices and other data to determine trading patterns. If a chart shows that a stock fell to $20 and rebounded twice in six months, then a technical analyst may conclude that the next retreat to $20 will attract enough buyers to lead to a rebound. Sales, earnings, and other fundamental data aren't part of the picture.
3. **Quantitative analysis** relies on number crunching. Financial and trading statistics and other data are collected and run through mathematical formulas programmed into computers. The results are used to guide investment decisions. The people doing the analysis are known as rocket scientists or quants, because their work is relatively complex.

Quotations

Whether you're looking at governments, companies, or hard assets, you'll need to know something about prices and trading to understand what's happening to their value.

The key details vary by market as we'll learn later. The data presented in Figure 16.1, a stock quotation for International Business Machines Corp., differs from what you see in Figure 16.2, a quote for one of IBM's bonds.

IBM US $ ↑ 200.83 +1.02 T 1s K 200.81/200.83 T 1x2 Equity
At 13:26 Vol 1,719,826 Op 199.98 T Hi 201.1 N Lo 199.72 P ValTrd 345.084m

FIGURE 16.1 An IBM Stock Quote.

IBM 1.95 07/16 $ ↓ 103.373 -.137
At 09:47 Vol 2,000 Op 103.373 Hi 103.373 Lo 103.373 YLD 1.153 TRAC

FIGURE 16.2 An IBM Bond Quote.

Yet some facts and figures are usually included, no matter what the security, and they are worth knowing now. Let's take a closer look at them.

Security symbol: This code, known as **a ticker,** is the first thing you'll see in any quote. Some symbols identify only the original seller or the issuer. Others include details about the security itself.

Uptick/downtick arrow: The direction of the arrow shows the last change, usually in the price. It's known as an uptick/downtick arrow because each price move in a security is called a tick. ▲▼

Latest price: This is the most basic piece of data in any quote. It's usually taken from trades. Some investments aren't quoted at a price as we'll see later.

Change on the day: By comparing this figure with the latest price, you'll know how much the market value has moved during the day.

Bid price: This is the highest price that anyone is willing to pay. It's shown because a seller would rather get as much money as possible, all other things being equal.

Ask price: This is the lowest price at which anyone is willing to sell. It's known as the offer price. By either name, it's the flip side of the bid price, as a buyer would rather pay as little as possible. The difference between the bid and ask prices is known as the bid-ask spread. The narrower the spread, the easier it is for investors to buy and sell without moving the price, and vice versa.

Time: This shows whether the latest price is a reasonable indication of market value. If it's a minute or two old, then the answer is probably yes. If it's an hour or two old, then maybe not. Times are presented in 24-hour format. This means that a stock price posted at the close of U.S. stock exchanges, 4 p.m. Eastern time, would appear as 16:00.

Price range: Opening, high, and low prices for the day's trading put the current price in context. How much have prices moved during the day? Is the current price closer to the high or the low? It's easier to answer these questions when the data are readily available. For the same reason, many quotes include the previous day's closing price.

You may have noticed that volume, or the amount of trading, isn't part of this list. That's no accident. Volume is available mainly for stocks and other securities that trade on exchanges. For currencies, bonds, and hard assets, they often are hard to find or undisclosed.

> **KEY POINT:**
> Returns, risks, and relative value are the three Rs of investing. Returns are based on price changes and any payments that investors receive. Risks can be general, specific to an investment, or somewhere in between. Relative value refers to what's cheap, expensive, or fairly valued.

Three Rs

Now that you have gone this far, it's time to address a basic question: What's in it for me? Put another way, how would markets for investing in governments, companies, and hard assets affect me? To find the answer, you have to focus on the three Rs of returns, risks, and relative value.

The first two Rs, returns and risks, go together. If one investment produces higher returns than another, then it's usually riskier as well. Investors who pay too much attention to the returns can end up suffering unexpected losses when a change in market direction highlights the risks.

> **STEP-BY-STEP:**
> **REAL RETURN MATH**
> 1. The Standard & Poor's 500 Index fell 0.003 percent in 2011.
> 2. Dividends paid during the year equaled 2.089 percent of the index's value.
> 3. Add price changes and dividends to calculate the nominal return of 2.086 percent, or 2.1 percent after rounding.
> 4. Inflation was 3.4 percent, based on the change in the Consumer Price Index (CPI) for the 12 months ended in November.
> 5. Subtract inflation from the nominal return to calculate the real return of minus 1.3 percent.

Relative value, the third R, begins with understanding the relationship between the first two. If the price of a security or hard asset falls, it's possible the move might be temporary and the potential returns may rise accordingly. It's also possible the investment has become more speculative. Returns in the future may be the same or lower after adjusting for the added risk.

These kinds of judgments are essential in determining whether an investment is cheap, expensive, or fairly priced, the goal of relative-value analysis. They can be made for a specific security, between securities in a single market, between market segments, and among markets as we'll see again later.

Returns

Price changes usually make the biggest contribution to returns on an investment. Their effect depends on the direction of the move and on whether an investor owns the security or asset or is betting on a decline.

The first point is obvious enough. Investors in a government, company, or hard asset want to make money. The same goes for anyone who's betting against them. The second point refers to whether someone has a long or short position.

Investors can go long through the primary or secondary market. Either way, the price they pay for a security or asset becomes the starting point for determining their returns.

To go short, investors borrow securities or assets and sell them as mentioned earlier. The borrowing is usually conducted in a securities-lending market, where investors are paid for making their holdings available.

The price of the second transaction, or short sale, is the basis for calculating returns. If the price declines, then short sellers can make money by buying back whatever was sold and by repaying the lender. Their profit comes from the gap between the short sale and market prices. If the security or asset rises, then the short seller loses.

When we study returns later, we'll focus on what investors in governments, companies, and hard assets will earn. Remember, though, that rising prices don't lead to gains for everyone invested in a market. Lower prices don't hurt everyone either.

We'll consider what else affects returns besides changes in price. Anyone who lends money to governments and companies typically earns interest. Stocks often pay dividends. Gold and other commodities don't provide either type of payment, which means returns are more closely tied to price moves. Real estate owners receive lease payments or rental income.

Inflation reduces returns by making these payments less valuable before they are received. Investors take this effect into account by tracking real returns, which are adjusted for inflation. Figures that don't have any adjustment are known as nominal returns.

Costs and expenses hurt returns. Buying and selling securities and hard assets requires the payment of trading fees. Having someone hold them in an account adds to the cost. You incur storage and transportation expense for commodities and maintenance expenses for real estate. Taxes are imposed on interest and dividend payments and investment gains as a rule.

Because the costs can vary considerably from one investor to the next, we'll keep the discussion of them to a minimum in later chapters. Even so, you should learn about the tax benefits that go with investing in some markets.

Risks

Investors probably wouldn't bother putting money into governments, companies, and hard assets if they knew the prices of their holdings would fall rather than rise. Yet that's a risk they inevitably take when they buy securities, commodities, or real estate.

> **KEY POINT:**
> For owners of a security or hard asset, market risk is the possibility of a drop in value. For short sellers, it's the opposite.

The short sellers we encountered earlier have the opposite risk. When their asset's price increases, the value of their short position declines, and vice versa. Their losses can be infinite. Buyers can only lose what they paid for their holdings plus investment fees and expenses.

Either way, prices may go in the wrong direction. This is called market risk. It's a concern for anyone who's invested in a security or market, whether the holding is direct or indirect.

Another universal risk is the threat that investors won't be able to sell an asset at the current market price because there aren't enough potential buyers around. This is known as **liquidity** risk. The phrase refers to the ability to raise cash, known as a liquid asset. Some investments are more liquid than others because there's more trading in them. It's probably much easier to sell a 10-year Treasury note, for example, than a 10-year corporate note. That's the case because the government security changes hands all day, and the company debt might trade occasionally.

DEFINITION:

Liquidity

Liquidity is the ease of buying and selling without causing price changes.

Demand for actively traded securities sometimes evaporates. Shares of some of the biggest U.S. companies changed hands for as little as one cent a share on May 6, 2010, when the Standard & Poor's 500 Index plunged as much as 10 percent before rebounding. That's liquidity risk in the extreme.

Risks found outside the markets can trip up investors in governments, companies, and hard assets as well. Four of them are worth a closer look.

We'll start with economic risk, or the possibility that slower growth or contraction—in the worst case, a recession or depression—will cut government tax revenue along with corporate sales and earnings. Risk exists when growth accelerates, as companies must pay more for workers or raw materials. Companies most vulnerable to this risk are known as cyclicals because their fortunes are closely linked to the economy's up-and-down cycles.

KEY POINT:

Currency-market moves can affect the value of any investment. When the dollar is rising, demand for investments priced in the U.S. currency tends to increase. When the dollar is falling, assets denominated in other currencies become more valuable.

Political risk is the potential for legislative actions to deter or prevent governments and companies from reaching their goals. This risk was especially pronounced for the United States in July and August 2011 when President Barack Obama and Congress were unable to agree on raising the country's debt ceiling until the limit was almost reached.

Policy risk is a specific type of political risk, which isn't limited to the executive and legislative branches. It's focused on monetary policy, controlled by the Federal

Reserve (Fed) and other central banks, and fiscal policy, defined by taxing and spending decisions made by the president and Congress.

Monetary policy affects the amount of funds available to the economy as well as their cost, otherwise known as interest rates. The Fed's version is designed to meet two goals: containing inflation and maximizing employment. The central bank pursues these objectives by adjusting the amount of money in the economy from day to day and by setting benchmark rates.

Additional moves are made when necessary, as they were during the 2008 financial crisis and its aftermath. The Fed added hundreds of billions of dollars to the economy through bond purchases, a practice known as quantitative easing, and started paying interest on funds that banks kept on deposit.

Fiscal policy shapes the way a government takes in and spends money, which in turn affects the economy's performance. The types of taxes that households and businesses must pay and the rates they are charged affect the revenue side. Outlays are linked to decisions about national defense, social programs, and other areas that the government manages.

Policy decisions can explain why the U.S. federal budget was balanced for part of the 1990s, for instance. They can account for the deficits that reached more than $1 trillion annually during the next decade.

Investors have to concern themselves with currency risk. Because U.S. stocks and bonds are priced in dollars, their value is affected by the dollar's value against other currencies. If the dollar is dropping, then demand from non-U.S. investors may decline, causing prices to fall.

Currency risk can cut the opposite way as well. A rising dollar makes U.S. exports more costly to overseas buyers, which tends to reduce international trade and curtail economic growth. Gains in the dollar reduce the value of sales and profits that U.S. companies make outside the country.

We'll examine more specific risks in later chapters. Credit risk, or the ability of a government or company to keep up payments on its debt, is one of them. Another is business risk, or the threat that a company's operations or finances may falter.

Relative Value

U.S. government bills, maturing in one year or less, paid next to nothing after the Fed began targeting near-zero interest rates at the end of 2008. Earlier in the 2000s, the securities rewarded investors with rates of 6 percent or more. During the 1980s, rates exceeded 10 percent.

The historical comparisons show Treasury debt is far less lucrative than it used to be. They provide a starting point for determining whether the securities are cheap, expensive, or fairly priced in relative terms. Similar analysis is done on all the other types of securities we'll cover.

History only tells part of the story. Investors have to determine how much risk there is today for a government, company, or hard asset. Then they have to decide whether the potential returns are high enough to justify taking that risk.

The opinions of credit-rating services, especially Standard & Poor's, Moody's Investors Service, and Fitch Ratings, are often part of that process. These companies assess the risks that go with debt securities. Their judgments help shape the views of investors, for better or worse.

Investors may study two securities that are essentially the same except for the maturity date or another key detail. Relative-value analysis would help them decide whether the difference matters, based on the potential returns.

> **KEY POINT:**
>
> Rating services are private companies though they are often called agencies, and some of them have official recognition from U.S. and international regulators.

The same issue arises when looking at similar securities from different entities. Suppose investors can choose between a three-month government bill and a corporate security maturing at about the same time. The company probably will be a riskier bet than the government. If the corporate security provides enough additional income to compensate for the greater risk, it may be worth buying. If not, it's the other way around.

Different securities from the same entity can be studied this way. Consider the example of a company that has publicly traded bonds and shares. It's possible to decide which is cheaper by comparing interest payments on the debt with dividends on the stock even though the payments aren't identical.

> **STEP-BY-STEP:**
>
> **RISK AND RETURN**
>
> 1. Suppose a three-month Treasury bill has a 0.1 percent rate.
> 2. Suppose a three-month corporate security has a 0.5 percent rate.
> 3. Subtract the Treasury bill rate from the corporate rate, and what's left is 0.4 percent.
> 4. The 0.4 percent is what an investor gets paid for lending money to the company, rather than the government.
> 5. The investor has to determine whether the additional amount is worth the risk.
> 6. Relative-value analysis guides the decision-making.

Relative-value comparisons like these can be extended to entire markets. They help investors decide whether to focus on stocks or bonds, how much cash to keep on hand, and whether to put money into hard assets, among other things.

The criteria used to determine what's cheap, expensive, and fairly priced vary by market. For bills, notes, bonds, and other types of debt, interest rates are important. Though the rates differ, as we'll learn later, there's a common thread to how they are interpreted. Investors want to know how much they stand to earn for lending out money, and rates are the guidepost.

Investors in debt securities are concerned with a borrower's ability to pay interest on time and repay the money when it's due. This leads them to focus on cash: where it's coming from, where it's going, how much exists, and how fast it's growing. The less a borrower needs the money, the more secure someone will be with owning its debt.

Stock investors also concentrate on cash. For one thing, they're interested in a company's ability to pay dividends. For another, companies with cash can buy back shares, which can increase returns on the remaining stock. These payouts help determine relative value as do revenue and earnings, which indicate how well the business is doing.

Relative-value comparisons are more basic for hard assets, if only because less data are available. For commodities, history and supply-demand analysis play larger roles than they would in securities. There aren't any interest, dividends, and earnings to use in deciding what's cheap and expensive.

In real estate, it's possible to assess value through comparisons between a property and similar ones that have been sold recently. That said, the analysis isn't as straightforward as finding rates on bonds or financial ratios for stocks. Real estate doesn't change hands that often, so the right numbers can be elusive.

CHAPTER 17

Government

From David Wilson, *Visual Guide to Financial Markets* (Hoboken, New Jersey: John Wiley & Sons, 2012), Chapter 2.

Can you imagine an investment that carries no risk? No worries about markets, liquidity, or anything else? What kind of an interest rate would you expect this investment to provide? Put another way, what kind of a return would you need to be a buyer?

For many investors, the answer to the first two questions is "yes." That's because a risk-free rate is often used in evaluating returns and in making relative-value judgments. The rate is theoretical because every investment carries some risk.

The third and fourth questions can be answered by looking at the interest rate on three-month Treasury bills. It's reasonably close to a risk-free U.S. rate for a couple of reasons. First, the government can require many of the more than 300 million Americans to pay taxes, and the revenue is a source of funds for making payments on the securities. Second, the government has the ability to pay with new money.

Other borrowers don't have the two advantages working for them. This means government securities markets are a relatively sure bet for investors. The three-month period provides an additional margin of safety as there isn't much time for risks to surface. The promise to pay goes with bills, a form of debt. The government can't sell equity, a riskier type of investment.

Some safety exists in cash, as suggested by the image of people stuffing their money under a mattress during times of economic turmoil. Government is responsible for sustaining the value of that cash as it makes decisions on a country's borrowing.

KEY POINT:

Rates on government securities are sometimes called risk-free rates because the debt carries little risk for investors.

Remember, though, that risk-free remains a relative term. Government debt can lose value as interest rates rise and inflation accelerates, as do other securities. Investors who turn over their money for longer periods can suffer bigger losses when rates or inflation go against them. We'll explore the risks later in this chapter. For now, let's take a closer look at currencies.

Currencies

We often measure the value of money by how far it goes at the supermarket, the shopping mall, the online store, and other retail locations. Another barometer serves as the foundation for a multitrillion-dollar market: the amount of a foreign currency we can purchase.

STEP-BY-STEP: FROM DOLLARS TO YEN

1. Assume the dollar is trading at 80 yen.
2. The yen's value is the inverse, so divide 80 by 100.
3. One yen is equal to 80/100 of a dollar, or 0.8 cent.

Money comes in pairs in the foreign exchange markets. Pairs that include the dollar tend to be watched most closely. The dollar is a reserve currency, held by central banks and used internationally to set the price of goods and services. Because the United States is the world's largest economy, there are plenty of dollars crossing borders each day.

Each pair has two values, based on buying or selling one unit of the currency. There's a value, for instance, that shows Japanese tourists en route to the United States how many dollars they can buy with their yen. Another exists for the U.S. businessman going to Tokyo, who has the opposite concern. The values are mirror images of each other, as shown in Figure 17.1.

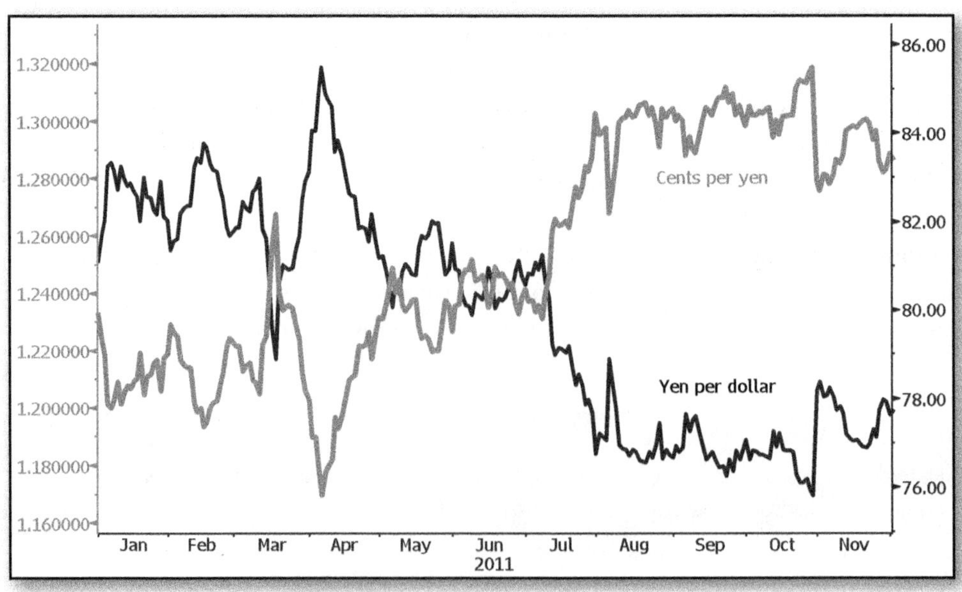

FIGURE 17.1 Dollar's Value in Yen and Yen's Value in Dollars.

STEP-BY-STEP: FROM POUNDS TO DOLLARS

1. Assume the pound is trading at $1.60.
2. The dollar's value is the inverse, so divide 100 by 1.60.
3. One dollar is equal to 100/1.60, or 62.5 pence.

Only one of the values in any currency pair is front and center on traders' computer screens. Usually, it's the amount of another currency you can buy for a dollar. That's the case with the yen.

There are prominent exceptions. The euro, Europe's common currency, is among them. Traders focus on the number of dollars and cents required to buy one euro and not the reverse. Others include British Commonwealth currencies, especially the British pound and the Australian and New Zealand dollars.

Currency pairs that exclude the dollar get some attention. Their exchange rates are called cross rates because they reflect each currency's value against the dollar. This assumes someone will go across the dollar—buying dollars with one currency and selling those dollars for the other currency—to complete a trade. If the dollar trades at 80 yen and the pound is at $1.60, the pound-yen cross rate is 80 times 1.60, or 128 yen to the pound.

Regardless of the pairing, currency moves can affect economies and financial markets. A declining currency makes a country's goods and services cheaper in international markets, and vice versa. This may encourage more people to visit, like those Japanese tourists, and to invest in government securities, companies, and hard assets.

Foreign exchange swings can be a double benefit or a double whammy for investment returns. If a stock or bond rises, a strengthening of the currency in which it's denominated will enhance the gain. If the price drops, a weaker currency will magnify the loss.

Trillions of dollars changes hands daily in the global currency markets. The latest available figure is $4 trillion, taken from an April 2010 survey by the Bank for International Settlements (BIS). The BIS, which assists central banks and monetary authorities worldwide, canvasses them every three years on trading in currencies and related contracts.

Practically all this buying and selling takes place over the counter, or away from exchanges. Banks, brokers, and other financial companies connect over electronic networks to carry out their trading. This approach means the amount of information available about foreign exchange trading from day to day is relatively sparse, as we'll see shortly.

Quotations

Suppose you were that businessman who traveled to Tokyo from New York and needed to exchange currency. You could go to an automated teller machine (ATM) and withdraw the number of yen you wanted. You may stop at a bank branch, a foreign-exchange kiosk at the airport, or a hotel's front desk.

If you choose one of these other locations, you'll run across a table with three columns. The first has the names of currencies, including the dollar. The second shows how much you would receive in return for each currency, and the third shows how much you would have to pay to buy them. The line for the dollar might look like this: **JPY 76.25 78.75**.

> **KEY POINT:**
> Foreign-exchange quotes always show the value of one currency against another. Moves in the two currencies over time are mirror images of each other.

The first number is the bid price, and the second is the ask, or offer, price. The gap between them, 17.5 yen, is the bid-ask spread. The wider the spread, the greater the profits for a bank, money changer, or hotel from currency exchange.

> **KEY POINT:**
> USD is the three-letter code for the U.S. dollar. Others include AUD (Australian dollar), CAD (Canadian dollar), CHF (Swiss franc), EUR (euro), and GBP (British pound), along with JPY for the yen.

Bid and ask prices are all that are disclosed in the global foreign exchange market. Prices at which currencies trade aren't made public, which means there's little detail available to show in quotes. Take the Japanese yen as an example (see Figure 17.2).

There's no way to tell how many yen changed hands during the day, or the exact price at which dollars were sold for yen. Let's find out what is available.

JPY: The quote's first line begins with a three-letter code for the yen. Each currency has a code. Some of the more popular ones are EUR for the euro, GBP for the British pound, CAD for the Canadian dollar, and CHF for the Swiss franc. When only three letters are included, the other currency is the dollar. Six-letter codes are used for cross rates, where the dollar isn't involved in the trade. EURJPY, for example, shows the value of one euro in yen.

76.33: This is the number of yen one dollar will buy. It's known as the **mid price** because it's halfway between the bid and ask prices.

–.13: Change from the previous day's last price, recorded at 5 p.m. New York time in this case. Currency markets don't open and close during the week, as trading happens worldwide 24 hours a day. The last price might be based on trading in London, home to the world's biggest foreign exchange market, or in Tokyo, another currency trading hub, for some market participants.

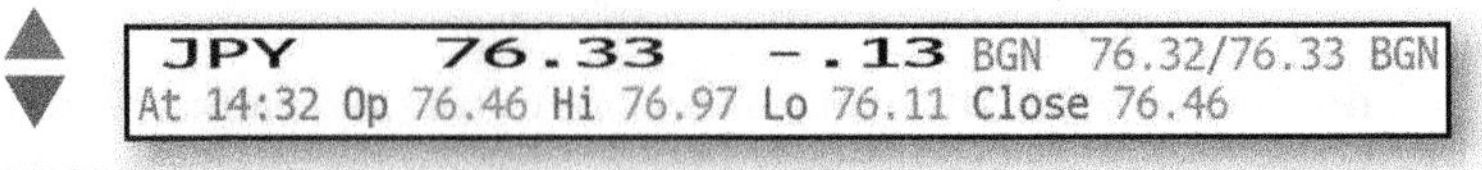

FIGURE 17.2 Yen Quote.

BGN 76.32/76.33 BGN: Highest bid and lowest ask prices, along with the source of each. BGN stands for Bloomberg generic pricing, which combines quotes from a number of banks. In other cases, a code for a specific bank may appear.

The spread between them is 0.01 yen, far narrower than the 2.5-yen differential in our earlier example. That's the case because there's far more currency bought and sold in the market than at bank branches, currency kiosks, and hotels.

At 14:32: The second line begins with the time at which the mid price was recorded. This is as common as the uptick/downtick arrow in quotes, as you'll see later. It's essential because currency values, like security prices, are constantly changing.

Op 76.46: Opening price, recorded shortly after 5 p.m. New York time the day before.

Hi 76.97: High price for the current trading day.

Lo 76.11: Low price for the current trading day.

Close 76.46: Closing price for the previous day. It's the basis for the day's change of –.13, shown in the first line.

Three Rs

The Japanese tourists and the U.S. businessman introduced earlier are exchanging currency to cover expenses rather than to turn a profit. The same might be said about companies doing business internationally. They may need to buy another currency to complete a purchase or to make an exchange for their local currency to bring revenue home.

Many investors make foreign exchange trades for similar reasons. Funds that invest outside their home country need the local currency to purchase stocks, bonds, and other assets. Some of these funds trade to reduce the risk that currency moves will affect their profits.

Currency **speculators** have another goal in mind. They want to make money as one currency rises or falls in value against another. We'll look at the three Rs of returns, risks, and relative value from their perspective.

Returns

Speculators buy and sell currencies in anticipation of changes in exchange rates over time. Returns from making these bets depend on how rates move. The potential for swings reflects the willingness of governments to allow markets to set the value of their currencies.

Some rates are fixed, which means they don't move. Argentina, for example, set the value of its peso at $1 between 1991 and 2002. The fixing of the exchange rate helped the country bounce back from years of economic contraction.

Fixed exchange rates are an example of pegging, known as linking, in which governments determine the value of currencies. In other cases, monetary authorities set the range in which the value can fluctuate and buy and sell currency to maintain the range. In 2005, Hong Kong pegged its dollar at HK$7.75 to HK$7.85 to the U.S. dollar and China let its currency—the renminbi, denominated in yuan—float within a band tied to a basket of currencies.

Then there are the freely floating currencies, where the value is almost entirely determined in markets. The "almost" is included because central banks occasionally stage what's known as an intervention. They buy and sell currencies when values get too far out of line for their liking.

> **DEFINITION:**
> **Speculators**
> Speculators buy and sell to profit from changes in market value.

Central banks can set lower exchange rates through currency devaluations. The dollar was last devalued in 1934, when the amount of gold that the U.S. currency could buy was cut by 41 percent. The pound's value tumbled 4 percent on Sept. 16, 1992, when the United Kingdom withdrew from an agreement that fixed its exchange rate. Several emerging market currencies have been devalued more recently.

Generally, the daily movements in floating currencies—the dollar, euro, yen, British pound and Swiss franc, to name a few—reflect what tourists, businessmen, companies, speculators, and others are buying and selling. This means they provide the greatest potential for returns.

> **KEY POINT:**
> Governments can directly affect the value of their currencies in three ways. They can establish a fixed rate or peg, intervene in foreign exchange markets by buying or selling, or officially devalue the currency.

Exchange rate changes aren't entirely tied to returns though. Speculators don't buy currencies and hide them under a mattress or in a corner office. Instead, they deposit the funds in a bank and earn interest.

Banks dominate currency trading worldwide, so it makes sense that they would end up with the money. Deposits are the investment of choice because their market and liquidity risk is low. This reduces the odds of investment losses that would cut into returns if the currency moves the right way.

Put this all together, and it's understandable that deposit rates would affect the flow of funds into and out of currencies, as well as their returns. Money tends to flow into a country as rates increase and flow out as rates fall.

Banks take their lead on what to pay for deposits from a central bank, such as the Fed. They're guided by a rate that the central bank sets directly. The United States has a target rate for overnight loans between banks that's known as the federal funds rate. The Fed's policy makers set the target, and the central bank adjusts the amount of money in the banking system each business day to control the market rate.

Speculators can deposit funds in the country that printed the money or elsewhere. Interest rates for deposits made outside the country are known as Eurodollar rates. Although the name originally referred to European bank deposits of dollars, the Euro-prefix has come to mean foreign. There are Eurodollar rates in Tokyo and Euroyen rates outside of Japan.

Risks

We've seen how market and liquidity risks affect the currency market. Anyone buying stocks, bonds, or hard assets with their money, rather than depositing the funds in a bank, is more likely to sustain losses. They may be large enough to wipe out any gains from exchange-rate moves.

Political, economic, and policy risks are part of the territory as well. After all, U.S. paper money says "The United States of America" and "Federal Reserve Note." This means the president, Congress, and the Fed each has a role to play in determining its value.

Market-specific issues also exist, beginning with interest rate risk. Because money obtained through the currency market goes into bank deposits, the rate is set for a certain period. If the central bank raises rates during that time, the deposit won't earn as much money as it might have otherwise. Currency moves tied to the rate increase may not make up for this lost opportunity.

Inflation risk is another concern. When prices are rising, the money on a deposit will buy less than it might have otherwise. If the inflation rate exceeds the deposit rate, the funds will buy less. Put another way, inflation reduces the purchasing power of money, whether it's in your wallet, your pocketbook, or a bank.

In extreme cases, inflation turns into hyperinflation. Prices rise so far and fast that the increases essentially wipe out a currency's value. This took place in Germany after World War I and in several emerging markets more recently.

The African country of Zimbabwe provided a worst-case scenario during the 2000s, as shown in Figure 17.3. Soaring prices prompted Zimbabwe's central bank

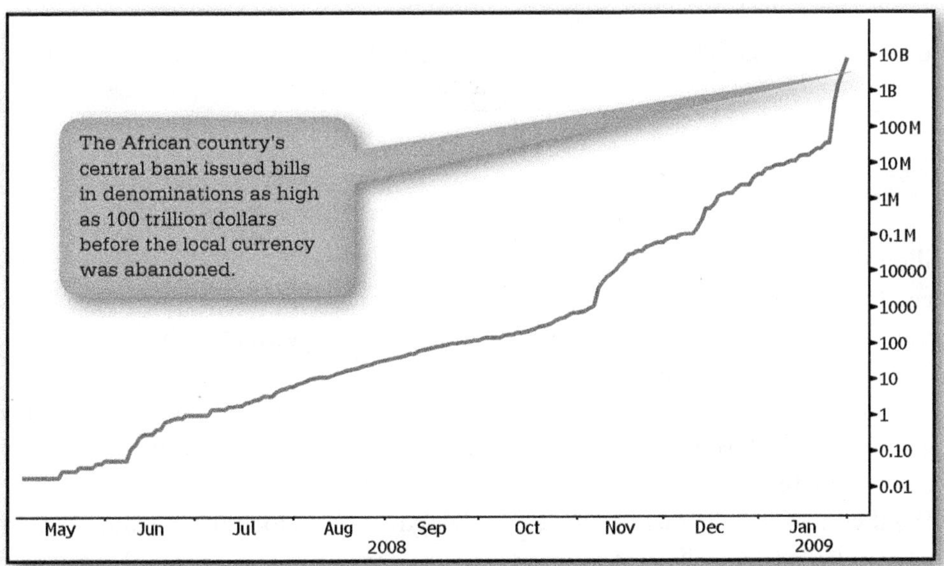

FIGURE 17.3 **Number of Zimbabwe Dollars per U.S. dollar during Hyperinflation.**

to redenominate its currency, the dollar, multiple times. The central bank resorted to printing bills with face values as high as Z$100 trillion before doing away with the local currency in 2009.

Relative Value

What does the same item cost in different locations? The answer provides a way to determine the value of one currency against another. McDonald's Big Mac sandwiches and Starbucks lattes have been used in these kinds of comparisons because they're so widely available.

The analysis is based on the principle that people should be able to buy goods and services for the same price anywhere. Economists refer to this as purchasing power parity. Ideally, exchange rates would maintain parity, though it doesn't quite work out that way in currency markets.

STEP-BY-STEP: PURCHASING POWER

1. Assume Big Macs cost $3 at McDonald's restaurants in the United States and 12.5 yuan in China.
2. Divide the Chinese Big Mac price by the exchange rate to translate into dollars. If the yuan is at 6.25 to the dollar, then the price is 12.5/6.25 = $2.
3. At $2, the Big Mac is 33 percent cheaper in China. This suggests the yuan is 33 percent undervalued relative to the dollar.

There's another relative-value gauge that was mentioned earlier: deposit rates. The gap in rates between two countries influences the movement of money between them, which in turn affects exchange rates. For currency speculators, the rate differential counts for more than Big Macs and lattes.

DEFINITION:

Treasury bills

Treasury bills are securities that the U.S. government sells to borrow funds for a year or less. Investors and companies classify them as cash equivalents.

Bills

Trillion-dollar budget gaps have to be closed somehow. The U.S. government has learned this lesson the hard way in the past few years. Increased spending to help sustain the country's economy and fluctuations in tax revenue swelled the federal deficit to more than $1 trillion annually.

Investors made up the shortfall. The government stepped up fundraising in the money market, where money is made available for as long as a year. It leaned more heavily on the bond market to borrow for two to 30 years.

We'll visit the government bond market shortly, so let's focus on the money market. The U.S. Treasury sells debt securities maturing in one, three, six, or 12 months on a regular schedule, and for other periods as needed. They are known as Treasury bills.

The word "bills" may make you think about the $1, $5, $10, and $20 bills in your wallet or pocketbook. That's an idea worth keeping in mind. Treasury bills play much the same role as paper money even though the government doesn't print and distribute them. Accountants consider them the same as cash, like other money market securities we'll run across later. Companies refer to them as cash equivalents in financial statements.

Treasury bills are as safe an investment as you'll find in financial markets, for a couple of reasons. First, consider the government's power to impose taxes on tens of millions of people and millions of companies to pay its debts. No other borrower is in that position. Second, the government can create money through the central bank. If worse came to worst, it would be possible to obtain the money by cranking up the Fed's printing presses. That's an option no one else has.

The relative safety of government bills is tied to their maturity date. There's less potential for things to go wrong in a year than there is in five, 10, or 30 years. What might happen? We'll find out when we examine the three Rs.

Investors can buy bills in the primary or secondary market. The primary market consists of auctions conducted by the Federal Reserve Bank of New York (New York Fed) on the Treasury's behalf. The secondary market is run by the largest banks and securities firms, along with the brokers that connect them.

The Treasury currently sells one-month, three-month, and six-month bills each week, along with one-year bills each month. Some banks and securities firms are required to bid at every auction, ensuring the government will have buyers for whatever bills are sold. These bidders are known as primary dealers, a title that fits their position within the primary market.

Primary dealers compete at auctions by submitting bids, based on the interest rate they're willing to accept. The New York Fed then sells the bills at the lowest possible rate, which translates into the highest price. This enables the Treasury to borrow as cheaply as possible.

Investors can buy new bills through primary dealers or straight from the Treasury. If they go through a dealer, the firm's auction bid will largely determine what they have to pay. They can go through Treasury Direct, a program that lets smaller investors buy securities at the average rates set in auctions.

These rates are known as discount rates because Treasury bills are bought for less than their face value. The securities don't pay interest before they mature, so the size of the discount has much to do with their returns, the first of the three Rs. They are stated as annual rates for consistency's sake even for bills maturing in less than a year, as most of them do.

As 2008 ended, discount rates at bill auctions dropped to almost zero. The decline resulted from the Fed's efforts to prop up the U.S. economy through monetary policy. Put another way, the government could pay almost nothing to borrow money. Figure 17.4 places the borrowing costs in perspective.

Discount rates are the focus in the secondary market, where the primary dealers and others trade bills sold at past auctions. There isn't an exchange where the securities are bought and sold. Instead, trades are made between firms electronically in the over-the-counter (OTC) market.

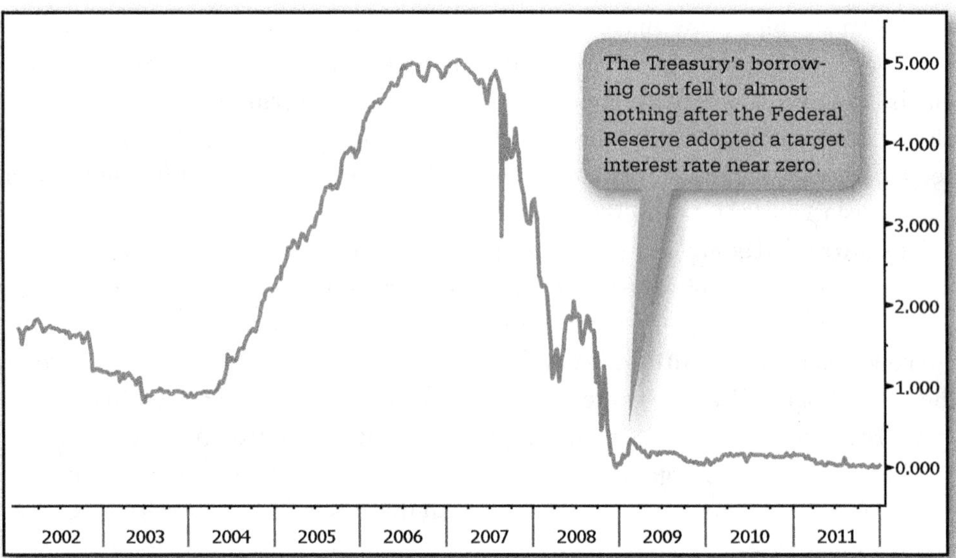

FIGURE 17.4 Three-Month Treasury Bill's High Discount Rate at Auction.
Sources: U.S. Treasury, Bloomberg.

Securities firms operate their own electronic trading networks. Similar systems are provided by independent firms, including Bloomberg, which has one called Bloomberg BondTrader for Treasury bills and other debt securities.

Dealers may use brokers to carry out trades. Cantor Fitzgerald LP, ICAP Plc, and Tullett Prebon Plc operate three of the biggest brokerages for bills and other government securities, including the notes and bonds we'll study later in this chapter.

Quotations

Prices are nowhere to be found in quotes on Treasury bills. Instead, they are quoted at discount rates, in keeping with how they're sold at auctions. This rate determines the price that a buyer will pay.

DEFINITION:
Basis points
Basis points are hundredths of a percentage point.

The number or dollar amount of bills traded during the day won't be found in quotes either. They're omitted because the OTC markets where they trade don't make the data widely available.

Now that we know what isn't in Treasury bill quotes, let's look at what is (see Figure 17.5).

B 09/20/12 ↑ .090 – .005 .095/.090
At 14:33 Op .095 Hi .100 Lo .080 Prev .095 CBBT

FIGURE 17.5 A Treasury Bill Quote.

B: Symbol for Treasury bills.

9/20/12: Maturity date, when the holder receives face value from the Treasury. It's shown in month/day/year format.

Up arrow: Direction of the most recent change in the discount rate. Because the rate moved up, this is known as an uptick. A down arrow would signify a decline in the rate, or a downtick. You'll see arrows like this in many other quotes.

This uptick/downtick arrow tracks the discount rate rather than the price. Higher rates mean lower prices, and vice versa. Keep that in mind, as it's true for other types of debt securities.

.090: Discount rate in percentage points. Investors buying this bill would earn 0.09 point on their investment by keeping it until the maturity date. That amounts to nine cents for every $1,000 invested. Percentages like this are so small that traders and investors move the decimal point two places to the right and talk about **basis points**. Each basis point amounts to 0.01 percentage point, so the bill's discount rate is 9 basis points.

.005: Today's rate change in percentage points. For the bill, it's 0.005 point. We might as well move the decimal point again and refer to the drop as half a basis point.

.095/.090: Bid and ask rates. The bid rate is higher because the resulting price will be lower. For the ask rate, it's the other way around.

At 14:33: Time of the quote, using the 24-hour clock.

Op .095, Hi .100, Lo .080, Prev .095: Opening, high, and low rates for the current day and closing rate for the previous day.

CBBT: Source of the current rate. This is a composite quote from Bloomberg BondTrader.

Three Rs

Safety comes with a price in the government bill market. It's measured by the potential return, which usually won't come close to matching what's available on other investments. On the other hand, the risks are relatively low as well. The United States has paid its debts on time for decades and isn't poised to follow companies and some local governments into bankruptcy court.

The relative safety explains why the rate the United States pays to borrow has historically been known as a risk-free rate. The phrase isn't quite accurate, as noted earlier, because investors face risks even when the government's finances are sound. We'll explore them as we go through the three Rs, and learn how investors find relative value.

Returns

Because government bills don't pay interest before maturity, their returns depend mainly on the difference between the purchase price and face value. The price, in turn, results from the quoted discount rate.

As an example, let's assume you bought Treasury bills maturing in one year at a 0.1 percent rate. Based on how the math works out, you would pay about $999 for every $1,000 face amount of the securities.

STEP-BY-STEP: BASIS POINTS

1. Start with a value in percentage points, such as the .090 in Figure 17.5.
2. Multiply by 100, which is the same as shifting the decimal point two places to the right.
3. In this case, .090 × 100 = 9.0, or 9 basis points. Each basis point equals 0.01 percentage point.

These bills are bound to rise in value as the number of days to maturity, or the amount of time until that final $1,000 payment is due, gets smaller. Changes in market rates will affect how and when the increase occurs. In the end, the price will equal $1,000 as long as the Treasury is paying its debts on time.

Risks

Bills are a type of fixed-income security, as the timing and amount of the payment are preset. Investors in the securities are taking the same kinds of risks as they do with government bonds, corporate debt, and related securities as we'll see later.

KEY POINT:

The price of a Treasury bill is less than the face value as long as the discount rate exceeds zero. How much less depends on the rate and the time to maturity.

The most basic concern is whether a borrower, in this instance the government, will be able to pay on time. This is known as credit risk. The discount rate is a gauge of the amount of risk that investors see. The higher the rate, the greater the concern, and vice versa. Bond yields, which we'll learn about shortly, play a similar role.

Judging credit risk is the business of credit-rating services, often called agencies even though they are companies. Standard & Poor's, Moody's Investors Service, and Fitch Ratings are the three largest services. They analyze governments, or sovereigns, and companies, and they assign ratings to their debt. Although the borrower usually pays for the ratings, there are exceptions for sovereign debt. When a government doesn't pay, the rating is said to be unsolicited.

Bill ratings start at A-1+ for S&P, P-1 for Moody's, and F1+ for Fitch. The companies use fewer tiers, or levels, than they do for notes and bonds, which we'll see later. Only borrowers with high ratings typically can raise funds in the money market.

KEY POINT:
MONEY-MARKET RATINGS

Each of the three main creditrating services has its own scale.
S&P uses A-1+, A-1/2/3, B, B-1/2/3, C, D, Not Rated.
Moody's uses Prime-1/2/3, Not Prime.
Fitch uses F1+, F1/2/3, B, C, D, Not Rated.

Interest rate risk is another concern, as higher rates translate into lower prices for bills and other debt securities. If the one-year Treasury bill rate in the earlier example climbed to 0.2 percent the next day from 0.1 percent, the price would fall by about $10 for every $1,000 face amount. Investors who sell the security or have to reflect its value in their financial statements would suffer losses.

Lower rates, on the other hand, pose reinvestment risk. This refers to the inability to earn as much on a similar investment when payments are received. The risk is minimal in our example, because the one-year bill rate can't fall too far from 0.1 percent. If the rate was 1 percent, or perhaps 10 percent, then the risk would be far greater.

Inflation risk, or the threat that price increases will reduce the buying power of whatever money you receive, is present as well. This would turn into a reality in our 0.1 percent example as long as the Consumer Price Index (CPI), the most widely followed gauge of inflation, increases at a faster rate. If the pace accelerates, then the risk will rise as well.

Government bills have relatively little risk by comparison with other fixed-income securities. First, the government can raise taxes or print more money if needed to pay its debts. Other borrowers don't have those options. That's why bill rates are often called risk-free even if that isn't exactly the case.

Second, the bills mature in no more than a year. This means there isn't much time for interest rates or inflation to cut into the value of the final payment or the potential return from reinvesting the money.

Relative Value

Is that 0.1 percent bill in our example, or some other security like it, worth buying or something to avoid? We can make relative-value comparisons to help us answer the question.

Let's consider how the 0.1 percent rate stacks up against one-year Treasury bill rates over time. For the 10-year period that ended in 2008, the rate was about 4.5 percent on average. By that standard, the bills earn next to nothing. Then again, the bill rate fell below 1 percent from 2009 onward, which means the gap with 0.1 percent isn't so wide. Figure 17.6 shows the historical rates.

Then you can look at how the discount rate compares with similar rates for three- and six-month bills. Let's assume the three-month rate is 0.005 percent, and the six-month rate is 0.05 percent. This means the one-year bill will return 20 times as much if you tie up your money for four times longer or twice the amount for investing twice as long. The comparisons may make the 0.1 percent rate look better.

Investors can plot each rate on a graph and connect the dots between them. The result is a **rate curve**, used to compare government bills with other types of securities. We'll revisit this topic when we run across another type of curve for notes and bonds.

Suppose you shunned the one-year Treasury bills and bought one-year securities sold by some other government, or a company. The borrower might well be a bigger credit risk than the U.S. government. If that turns out to be the case, you ought to earn more for turning over your money.

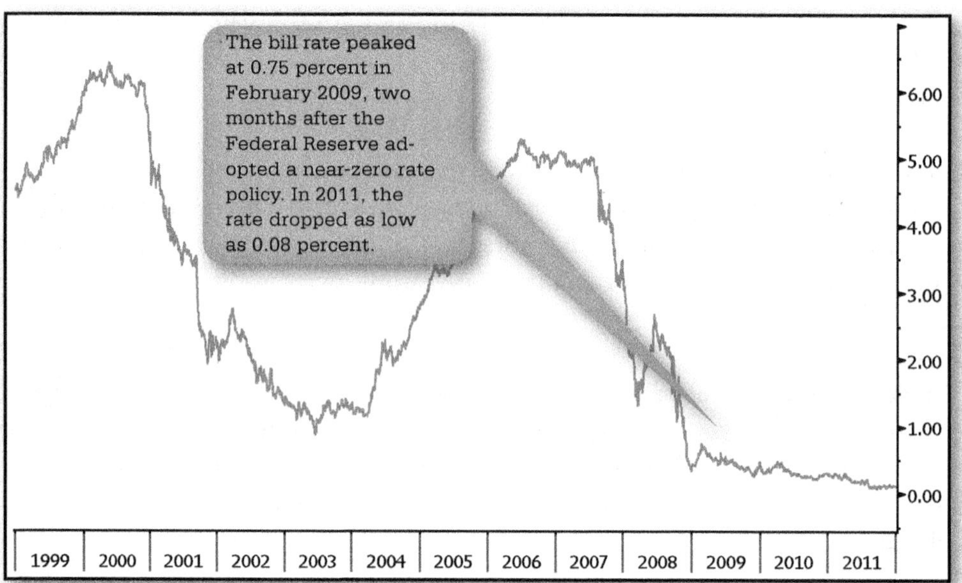

FIGURE 17.6 One-Year Treasury Bill Rates.
Source: U.S. Federal Reserve.

How much more? The answer provides another way to judge relative value. Let's assume the other investment has a 0.5 percent discount rate. Subtract the 0.1 percent bill rate to calculate the gap between them: 0.4 percentage point. The figure is known as a rate spread and is expressed in basis points. So, you'll be able to earn another 40 basis points for your trouble.

To determine if 40 basis points is a little or a lot, you can look at whether the spread has widened or narrowed over time. You can determine how much more credit risk you would be taking with the other borrower, rather than the government.

DEFINITION:

Rate curve

Rate curves show borrowing costs over time by displaying discount rates as dots on a graph and then connecting the dots. Rate spreads are differences in rates between two securities, or two points on a curve.

Notes and Bonds

Considering how much money the United States borrows these days, could you possibly imagine that the country didn't sell bonds regularly during its first two centuries? Well, it's true if only technically.

There's a distinction made in the Treasury market and elsewhere between notes, which mature in two to 10 years, and bonds, which last for longer periods. The only U.S. securities that fit into the latter category are 30-year bonds.

Regular sales of 30-year Treasuries started in February 1977, more than two centuries after the Declaration of Independence was adopted. They were suspended in October 2001 because the country had budget surpluses and resumed in February 2006.

Along the way, the government raised money from bond investors through sales of notes as well as bills. These days, notes maturing in two, three, five, seven, and 10 years are sold on a set schedule.

The price the government pays to borrow in note and bond sales is called the **yield**. The yield is set by financial companies who buy the securities when they're first sold and by the investors who trade them afterward. It's based on the price of the notes and bonds and the rate at which they pay interest. Lower yields translate into higher prices, and vice versa.

> **DEFINITION:**
> **Yield**
> Yield is the projected annual return on a bond, based on the current price and future interest payments.

We'll take a closer look at yield shortly. For now, it's enough to know that Treasury yields are a benchmark, or point of reference, for the cost of borrowing. Yields for notes and bonds sold by U.S. agencies, other countries, and companies are tied to the yield on Treasuries that mature at about the same time. The gap in yields largely determines which securities investors want to buy, sell, or hold.

To understand why Treasury notes and bonds are benchmarks—and Treasury bills, too—let's review the reasons why the bills can be a safe investment. The federal government has the power to impose taxes, which other governments don't have to the same extent and companies don't have at all. The central bank has the ability to create money, which sets apart the government from every other borrower.

Auctions are the primary market for Treasury notes and bonds. It's been this way since the 1970s, when the government dropped an earlier practice of selling securities at fixed prices. The New York Fed handles auctions on behalf of the Treasury as it does for bill sales.

Yields at these auctions are like discount rates for bills since they represent the Treasury's cost of borrowing. The government has generally been able to raise funds more cheaply since the 1980s. Yields are still well above zero as the 10-year note shown in Figure 17.7 illustrates.

Treasury notes are sold monthly. Each auction of two-year, three-year, five-year, and seven-year notes consists of new securities with their own maturity date. For 10-year notes, that's only true in February, May, August, and November. In other months, additional amounts of the most recent 10-year security are sold. These sales are called reopenings because they reopen an opportunity for investors to buy the notes. Thirty-year bond auctions work the same way as 10-year sales.

Regardless of the schedule or the maturity that's being sold, the government can count on offers from primary dealers. These firms make bids that specify a dollar amount and a yield, rather than the discount rate used for bills. The New York Fed accepts the lowest bids at which the sale can be completed.

Investors can buy notes and bonds from dealers or through the Treasury Direct program, as they can with bills. Other similarities exist between the auctions, based on details left out of the earlier discussion of bill sales.

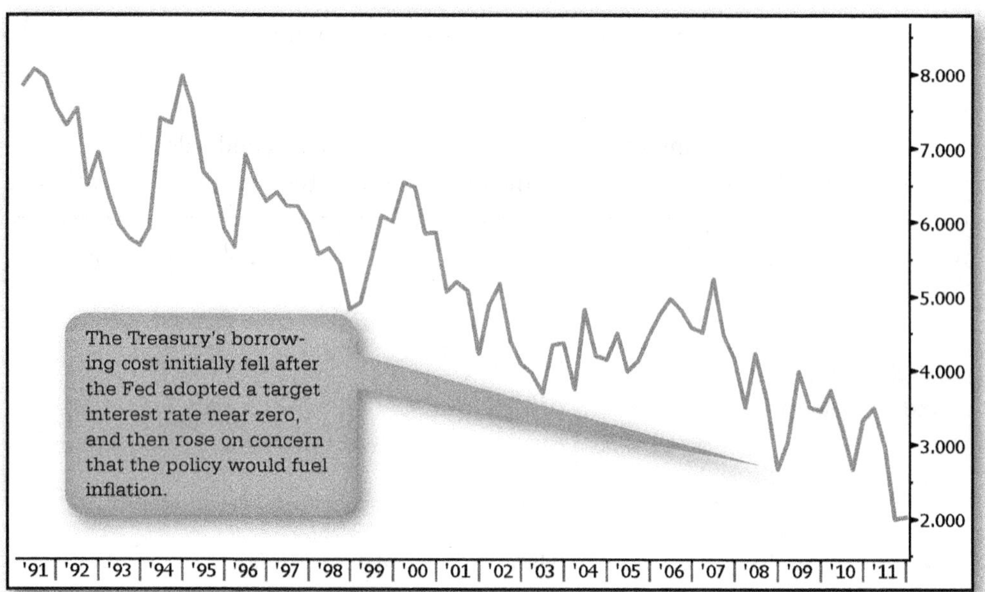

FIGURE 17.7 Ten-Year Treasury Note's High Yield at Auction.
Sources: U.S. Treasury, Bloomberg.

Bids are competitive or noncompetitive, depending on whether there's a yield specified. Primary dealers may submit competitive bids on their own behalf and noncompetitive offers for clients. Treasury Direct bids are noncompetitive as successful bidders have to accept the average yield.

Bidders are direct or indirect. Primary dealers and Treasury Direct participants make their bids directly. Indirect bidders must go through primary dealers, and foreign central banks are in this category. Auction results show the percentage of bids made indirectly and the percentage of bonds sold to indirect bidders.

The bid-to-cover ratio, an indicator of demand, is made available for each auction. It's calculated by dividing the dollar value of bids by the dollar value of securities sold. If the ratio for a $10 billion note sale was 3.25, the ratio would mean investors sought to buy $32.5 billion of the securities. By comparing the 3.25 with previous ratios for similar note sales, you can assess how motivated the bidders were.

Once the notes and bonds are sold, they begin trading in the secondary market. Trades are made over the counter through the same electronic networks that handle the buying and selling of bills. Exchanges aren't part of the Treasury market though they play a role in other countries' debt markets.

Quotations

There's more than one type of quotation for Treasury notes and bonds, and it's worth looking at a couple of formats to find out what we'll see (see Figures 17.8 and 17.9).

The prices in the two quotes are about the same as they show the same Treasury note. The first one resembles the bill quote in Figure 17.5 except that the numbers differ. To find out why, let's go through the details.

```
T 2⅛ 08/15/21   ↑ 103-20 +1-07  103-19+/103-20
At 14:42  Op 102-13¾   Hi 103-28+   Lo 102-13   Prev 102-13  CBBT
```

FIGURE 17.8 **A Treasury Note Quote, Part 1.**

```
US TREASURY N/B   T 2⅛ 08/15/21  103-19¾/103-20¼  ( 1.73 /72) CBBT @14:41
```

FIGURE 17.9 **A Treasury Note Quote, Part 2.**

T: Symbol for Treasury notes and bonds.

2 1/8: Annual interest rate, or **coupon rate, in percentage** points. The note's owner will receive 2 1/8 percent of face value, or $2.125 for every $1,000 invested, each year until maturity.

08/15/21: Maturity date in month/day/year format.

Up arrow: The uptick/downtick arrow tracks prices this time around. When it's up, the last price change was an increase, and vice versa.

103-20: Price of the note as a percentage of face value. Here, it's 103 percent and then some. The 20 means 20/32 of a percentage point, as Treasury notes and bonds are quoted in fractions, and the standard denominator is 32. The price is 103 20/32 percent, which is the same as 103 5/8 percent.

+1-07: Change on the day in fractions of a point. The note rose 1 7/32, or about $1.22 for every $1,000 invested.

103-19+/103-20: Bid and ask prices for the note, in percentages of face value. The + sign that ends the bid price indicates that it's halfway between 103 19/32 and 103 20/32. (The second quote's bid price ends with 19 3/4 divided by 32, which means the full number is 103 79/128. The ask price ends with 20 1/4, making the number 103 81/128. Bond-market fractions get even smaller sometimes.)

At 14:42: Time of the quote, using the 24-hour clock.

Op 102-13 3/4, Hi 103-28+, Lo 102-13, Prev 102-13: Opening, high, and low prices for the current day, and the close from the previous day. The opening price is 102 55/128, as the fraction equals 13 3/4 divided by 32. The high is between 103 28/32 and 103 29/32, as the + indicates.

CBBT: Source of the price information. This is a composite quote from Bloomberg BondTrader, as the Treasury bill quote was earlier.

> **KEY POINT:**
> When a bond's price is greater than 100, the yield is lower than the coupon rate, and vice versa. The yield accounts for the gap between the purchase price and face value.

A pair of figures appears only in the second quote: **1.73/1.72.** This shows the bond's yield at the bid and ask prices. Yield is based on the note's annual interest rate—in this case, 2 1/8 percent—and the difference between the market price and face value.

Why would the note yield less than 2 1/8 percent, as it does here? Go back and look at the 103–20 price. Any investor who pays that much will lose 3 5/8 percent of the security's face value at maturity. If the price was less than 100 instead, then the yield would exceed 2 1/8 percent.

Three Rs

Returns, the first of the three Rs, and yields are much the same for government notes and bonds. If investors buy a security and put it away until maturity, it's a safe bet the interest will be paid on time and the principal amount, or face value, will be paid off. Changes in yield won't affect returns unless they sell the security before the maturity date.

Even so, the risks confronting buy-and-hold investors rise over time. Inflation has more of an opportunity to cut into the value of note and bond payments. Interest rates have more room to fall, reducing the income from reinvesting those funds when they're received. There's more time for the government's finances to worsen, hurting its ability to borrow.

Relative-value comparisons are built around yields in the same way that the analysis of bills started with discount rates. It's possible to include bills in the analysis by calculating bond-equivalent yields, based on the assumption that they paid interest.

DEFINITION:

Treasury Inflation-Protected Securities

Treasury Inflation-Protected Securities, or TIPS, are bonds whose principal is adjusted as consumer prices increase. TIPS are a form of inflation-indexed debt.

Returns

Our discussion of yield touched on the two main components of bond returns. The first is interest, which is paid according to a set schedule. The second is the purchase price relative to the face amount, or principal, repaid at the maturity date.

Not all government notes and bonds pay interest and principal the same way. Some account for inflation, which otherwise reduces the value of bond payment. Others have a single payment at maturity, like government bills. Let's find out how these differences affect returns.

Fixed-rate debt accounts for most of the Treasury's borrowing. The 10-year note is a perfect example. The annual interest rate and the face amount stay the same until maturity. In other words, they're fixed. Anyone who bought the note at the quoted price and kept the security until August 15, 2021, would be assured of a 1.73 percent annual yield at current market rates.

The 1.73 percent figure represents a nominal return, as it doesn't take inflation into account. The real return can only be estimated because it's ultimately based on price changes for the next 10 years. Consumer prices would have to increase about 1.75 percent a year to send the real return below zero. The higher the inflation rate, the more a bond investor suffers.

Inflation-indexed notes and bonds are designed to adjust for shifts in inflation rates. **Treasury Inflation-Protected Securities**, called TIPS, are the U.S. government's version. The principal amount changes along with the CPI, and the government pays the adjusted principal at maturity as long as the CPI has risen. Quotes on TIPS show the real yield rather than the nominal yield. If 10-year TIPS have a 0.48 percent yield, for instance, anyone buying and holding them can expect to earn 0.48 percent after inflation each year for the next decade, based on current market rates.

To gauge the outlook for inflation, subtract TIPS yields from those on fixed-rate Treasuries maturing about the same time. The 10-year note yield of 1.73 percent minus our 10-year TIPS yield, 0.48 percent, equals 1.25 percentage points. That's how much consumer prices may increase each year, on average, in the next decade. Figure 17.10 shows how the gap between fixed-rate yields and TIPS, an implied inflation rate, compares with changes in consumer prices over time.

TIPS are a variation on floating-rate bonds, where the interest payments vary or float along with a specified market interest rate. We'll have more on these later, as the Treasury doesn't sell floating-rate debt.

Zero-coupon securities aren't sold directly by the U.S. government either. Securities firms create them from fixed-rate and inflation-indexed notes and bonds. Each interest payment is transformed into a separate security as is the principal payment. The result is Separate Trading of Registered Interest and Principal Securities (STRIP or STRIPS).

STRIPS are similar to government bills, except that most of them take longer than a year to mature. The buyer pays less than face value and receives the full amount at maturity in a single payment. The gap between market price and face value closes over time, which means an investor has to pay income taxes on STRIPS each year even though income isn't paid out.

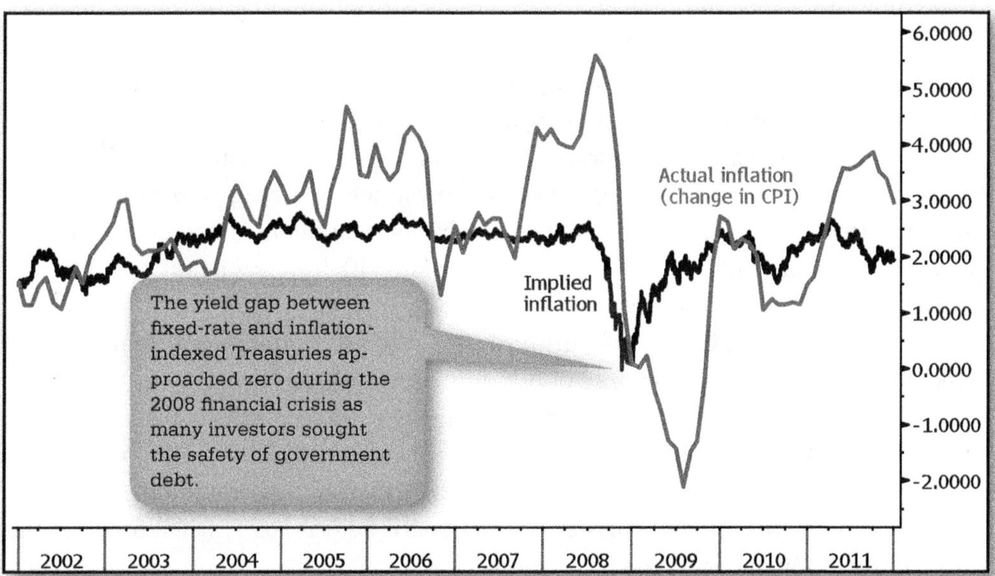

FIGURE 17.10 Ten-Year Implied Inflation Rate and 12-Month Change in Consumer Price Index.

Companies raise money by selling fixed-rate debt, along with other types of notes and bonds. We'll look at the possibilities in more detail later.

Risks

The risks of owning government notes and bonds increase over time. They depend on the amount of money you receive as an investor and the amount of time that passes until each payment arrives.

To illustrate, let's compare a 10-year Treasury note and a 10-year STRIP as investments. Assume that both securities have a face value of $1,000 and a coupon of 2 percent.

Owners of the note receive $10 every six months, as it pays interest twice a year, plus $1,000 at maturity. This means they get a total of $1,200. If they buy the security at an auction, they will only have to wait six months before the money starts rolling in.

The interest payments make the note less risky than the STRIP even though they mature at the same time. They amount to $200, or one-sixth of the $1,200 total, and all but the last one arrives before the 10 years are up. Investors in the STRIP receive $1,000, and all the money comes at maturity.

> **KEY POINT:**
>
> Note and bond ratings differ from money-market ratings.
>
> S&P and Fitch use AAA, AA, A, BBB, BB, B, CCC, CC, C, D. S&P's ratings can add + or – from AA to CCC, and Fitch's can do so from AAA to B.
>
> Moody's uses Aaa, Aa, A, Baa, Ba, B, Caa, Ca, C.

An indicator called duration shows the note is a safer bet. Duration is the time period investors will have to wait for the amount they initially invested to be returned. It's based on what all the payments are worth today, or their present value.

The note's duration is about nine years, thanks to the 2 percent annual interest rate. The STRIP has a 10-year duration, matching its maturity date.

Modified duration, a similar figure, shows how much the note's price would rise or decline if the yield changed by one percentage point. This figure is a percentage rather than a number of years. The modification has to do with how interest is calculated.

Now that you've seen how bond investors gauge risk, let's remind ourselves where it comes from. Credit risk, interest rate risk, inflation risk, and reinvestment risk affects government notes, and bonds, as well as bills.

S&P, Moody's, and Fitch, the largest rating services, are among those assessing credit risk. AAA ratings have become synonymous with the least risky borrowers, and we have S&P to thank for that. Moody's has a different top rating, Aaa. Fitch uses AAA. Treasuries had these ratings across the board before 2011, when S&P cut the United States for the first time.

All three companies use the letters A, B, and C in their bond-rating systems. S&P's scale includes plus and minus signs as well. Moody's uses the small "a" along with the number 1, 2, or 3 for several ratings below Aaa. Fitch uses pluses and minuses in much the same way as S&P does, and both include a fourth letter in their scales, D, meaning default.

We'll revisit the credit ratings later when we look at corporate notes and bonds. For the moment, it's enough to know there's more time for them to worsen while notes and bonds are outstanding than there is with bills. The same holds true for investors' outlook, which may or may not be in line with the assessments made by rating companies.

Risk and time are linked for interest rates, inflation, and reinvestment as well. Let's take inflation as an example. If consumer prices increase 2 percent a year, the value of a $1,000 payment on a note or bond will be about $780 after 10 years. That's far below the $980 value after one year, the longest maturity date for a Treasury bill.

Relative Value

When investors consider whether a note or bond is cheap, expensive, or fairly priced, they inevitably look at yield. It's a common denominator for debt securities regardless of who sold them, which currency they are denominated in, when and how they pay interest, or any other detail.

There are yields at two, three, five, seven, and 10 years to consider for Treasury notes, along with yields on 30-year bonds. We can add one-month, three-month, six-month, and one-year bills to the mix by assuming they paid interest and by adjusting their discount rates accordingly.

Graphs come in handy to see how they compare as they did for bills. There's a dot for each security, whose position depends on the yield and the amount of time to maturity. The dots are joined into a yield curve, which shows how much it might cost to borrow for other periods (see Figure 17.11).

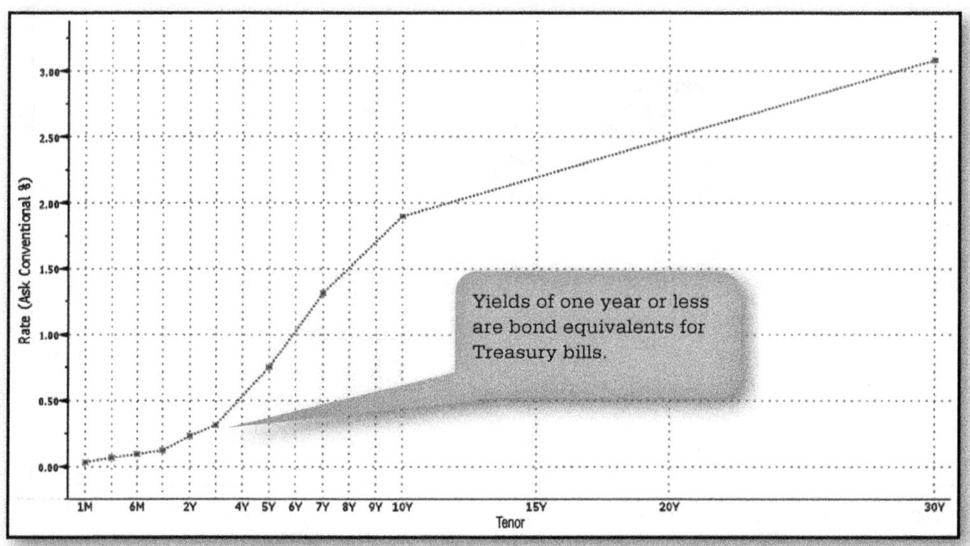

FIGURE 17.11 Treasury Yield Curve.

The line in this graph rises along with the time to maturity. This means the yield curve is upward sloping, which is usually the case. Investors get paid more for lending money to the government for longer.

Curves don't always look this way. When the central bank is raising interest rates to restrain inflation, yields may fall over time rather than rise. That can happen because bill yields are more closely linked to Fed policy than note and bond yields, which are more influenced by the inflation outlook.

When curves slope downward, they are said to be inverted. This kind of shape has historically pointed toward slower economic growth at best, and a recession at worst, because it signals the central bank wants to discourage borrowing.

At other times, there's little difference in bill, note, and bond yields. The curve looks like a straight line, and it's said to be flat. Curves can flatten as they shift from being upward sloping to inverted, and vice versa.

Regardless of how the curve appears, differences in yield will occur among the depicted bills, notes, and bonds. This leads to another way of judging relative value: looking at those gaps, or yield spreads, the bond market's equivalent of rate spreads.

We can do this with securities on the curve. Ten-year Treasury notes yielded about 2 percent, while two-year notes yielded about 0.25 percent. In other words, bond investors stood to earn about 175 basis points by lending money to the government for eight more years. The differential was in line with historical standards as shown in Figure 17.12.

The spread narrowed to about zero in February 2006 and turned negative for much of the following year, as the chart depicts. When two-year and 10-year yields are about the same, the **yield curve** flattens. When their spread is less than zero, the result is an inverted curve.

Similar comparisons can be made among Treasuries and other types of U.S. government debt, and between the United States and other countries. Investors do so regularly as they search for what's cheap, expensive, and fairly priced.

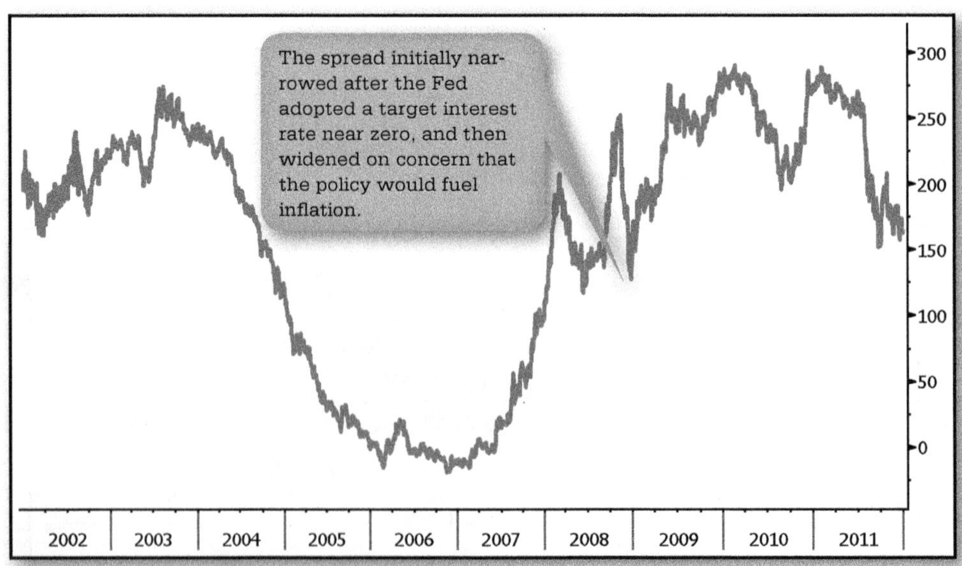

FIGURE 17.12 Two-Year/Ten-Year Treasury Note Yield Spread.

There's more to relative-value comparisons than yield curves and yield spreads as you might imagine. We'll see the effect of credit ratings, for example, when we look at corporate notes and bonds. For the moment, it's enough to know the central role that curves and spreads have to play.

DEFINITION:

Yield curve

Yield curves show borrowing costs over time by displaying yields as dots on a graph and then connecting the dots. Yield spreads are differences in yields between two securities, or two points on a curve.

Test Yourself

Answer the following multiple-choice questions:

1. Currencies quoted in dollars per unit, rather than units per dollar, include:
   a. Euro.
   b. British pound.
   c. Australian dollar.
   d. All of the above.
   e. a and b only.
2. Governments affect the value of currencies through:
   a. Pegging.
   b. Intervention.
   c. Devaluation.
   d. All of the above.
   e. b and c only.
3. Treasury-bill returns come from:
   a. Price changes.
   b. Interest payments.
   c. Dividend payments.
   d. All of the above.
   e. a and b only.
4. Treasury note and bond returns come from:
   a. Price changes.
   b. Interest payments.
   c. Dividend payments.
   d. All of the above.
   e. a and b only.
5. The Treasury yield curve is usually:
   a. Flat.
   b. Inverted.
   c. Upward sloping.
   d. Humped.
   e. All of the above.

Answers: 1. d; 2. d; 3. a; 4. e; 5. c

CHAPTER 18

Companies

From David Wilson, *Visual Guide to Financial Markets* (Hoboken, New Jersey: John Wiley & Sons, 2012), Chapter 3.

Companies have more ways to raise money than the government does. They can borrow by selling the equivalent of Treasury bills and by making other arrangements to borrow funds for a year or less. They can sell notes and bonds, occasionally or regularly. They can sell shares, which enables them to bring in new owners and allows current investors to increase their stakes.

Each of these investments can be riskier than handing over money to a government. Companies can't compel anyone to buy their products or services, as the government can. There isn't any printing press that can come to their aid during business slumps.

These investments have degrees of risk as well. Equity holders can't count on receiving payments from the company, as the owners of corporate notes and bonds usually can. Companies aren't required to pay dividends on their shares, and some of the most successful ones don't. Owners of the stock can only hope the value of their holdings will rise over time.

The ultimate risk is that a company will be unable to meet its financial obligations and go bankrupt. Investors in U.S. government debt don't have to worry about that prospect. Let's look at how one bankruptcy shut down the money market, where the shorter-term borrowing is done.

KEY POINT:
Companies compete with government to borrow money from investors. They can raise additional funds by selling stock, which government can't do.

Money Markets

Companies turn to the money market to borrow money for days, weeks, or months, typically to finance day-to-day operations. Lehman Brothers Holdings Inc., which filed for bankruptcy in September 2008, was among the financial companies that tapped the market by selling securities.

Lehman's collapse caused the value of investments in the firm to plunge. The losses hurt many investors who had seen the money market securities as a safe bet. The casualties included the Reserve Primary Fund, which was the country's oldest money market mutual fund.

KEY POINT:

Companies compete with government to borrow money from investors. They can raise additional funds by selling stock, which government can't do.

Many investors responded by refusing to buy similar securities, regardless of the company selling them. Their retreat left the money market unable to function and forced a number of companies that raised money there to turn to bank borrowings and bond sales, which are more costly and time consuming. The U.S. government had to provide hundreds of billions of dollars in financial support to money funds, among the biggest buyers of the debt.

DEFINITION:

Libor

Libor is the London Interbank Offered Rate, which banks in London charge each other to borrow. Libor varies by maturity, 1 to 12 months, and by currency. It's a benchmark for commercial and consumer loans.

Fortunately, instances like this are rare. Companies can use the money market to borrow from investors as well as each other. They can gain access to financing in many ways, and they're all worth a look.

Banks can borrow directly from other banks in the United States through the federal funds market. The money comes from funds that have to be held in reserve under federal regulations. When a bank's reserves are too low, it's able to borrow to meet the minimum standard. When a bank has excess reserves, it can earn money by lending them.

The rate on overnight loans of federal funds, or fed funds for short, is significant. The Federal Reserve (Fed) sets a target for this rate through monetary policy, designed to contain inflation and maximize employment. Though the market rate will fluctuate from day to day, the Fed ensures it stays near the target. To meet this goal, the central bank adds and removes money from the banking system as needed through open market operations.

International banks borrow from and lend to each other in several financial centers, especially London, where rates are set for one-month to 12-month loans of dollars and other currencies. The British Bankers' Association surveys these rates each day and compiles averages. Each average is known as a London Interbank Offered Rate (**Libor**). The cost of borrowing for financial and non-financial companies alike is often tied to Libor, as we'll see later. Libor is available for several currencies and maturities, and Figure 18.1 illustrates rates in dollars.

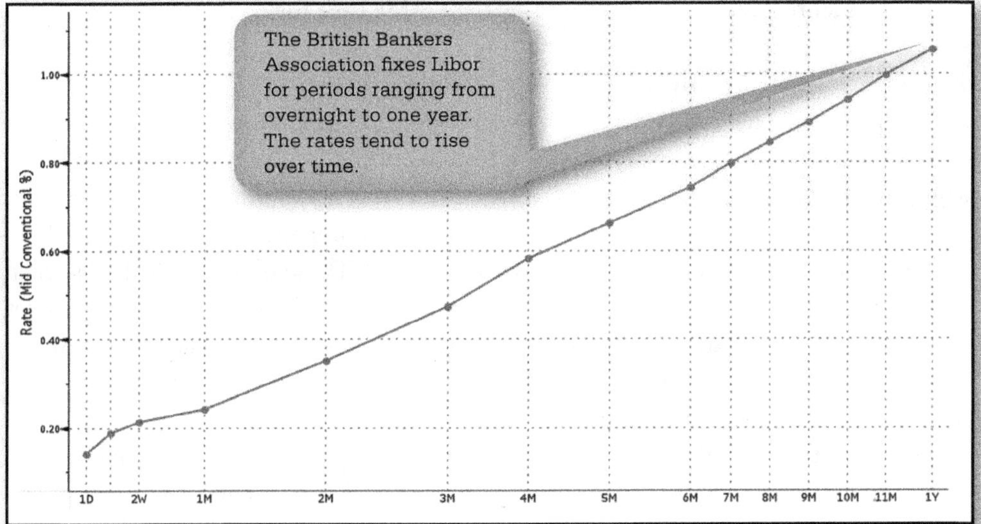

FIGURE 18.1 A Dollar Libor Curve.

Certificates of deposit (CDs) are another way for banks to raise money-market funds. These aren't the kind of CDs you'll see advertised at your local bank branch. They have denominations of $100,000 or more, which explains why they're often described as jumbo CDs. Larger investors and companies buy them to earn some money on their excess cash.

Bankers' acceptances (BAs) are part of the money market mix as well. They are used in international trade to help ensure a future payment will be made on time. Banks create them when an importer with enough money in its accounts asks the institution to take responsibility for the payment. The importer sends the acceptance to its supplier, which has the ability to raise cash right away by selling the agreement for less than face value.

Repurchase agreements (repos or RPs) enable securities firms as well as banks to finance investments. These agreements have two components, a sale of securities and a contract that requires the seller to buy them back later. The gap between the sale and repurchase prices provides a return to the buyer, who is effectively a lender. The buyer may seek higher returns by selling the borrowed security in a short sale.

Many of these agreements go through another bank or a clearinghouse, which ensures that both sides live up to their obligations. These are known as tri-party repos because there are three participants rather than two.

Repos are a type of secured financing, in which the securities serve as collateral. Many companies rely on unsecured financing, or borrowing that's based on a promise to pay. Investors lose if a company fails to keep the promise, as Lehman's lenders found out the hard way.

Even so, demand exists for securities that enable companies to borrow for as long as nine months without having to put up collateral. This type of debt is called commercial paper (CP), and it represents the corporate equivalent of Treasury bills.

Financial companies run CP programs to provide cash for daily operations. Automakers' finance units raise money this way as well because CP is a flexible way for these companies to borrow money.

Companies can file for U.S. regulatory approval to sell CP up to a specified dollar limit. Once they have clearance, they are free to choose which maturities to sell and when to sell them. Some companies sell securities daily, and others do so less often.

Not all CP is unsecured. Some banks and financial companies sell asset-backed paper through specially created units known as conduits. These units, also called special investment vehicles (SIVs), are set up to own assets that the company wants to get off its books. Many of them collapsed in the 2008 financial crisis because they owned mortgage-related securities. When the SIVs failed, the companies that started them had to take back the assets and suffered as a result.

The crisis took a toll on the CP market, especially because of Lehman's failure. Many investors shunned the market to avoid a similar disaster in the future. Many companies that sold the securities turned to bond sales so they wouldn't lose access to financing.

KEY POINT:

Companies sometimes provide security to lenders by putting up collateral. Other times they don't. Investors must depend on what's known as the company's full faith and credit, or promise to pay.

Combine fed funds, Libor, BAs, CDs, RPs, and CP, and you end up with a bowl of money market alphabet soup. You won't find this on a menu of investments for individuals. It's made for brokerage firms, banks, pension and endowment funds, money managers, and other institutional investors.

There's an emphasis on the primary market because it's easier to track than the secondary market for the securities. Companies that sell CP, for instance, regularly post discount rates for different maturities. After the securities are sold, finding their market rates may be difficult to do, if not impossible.

CP sellers can choose to adopt a do-it-yourself (DIY) approach or to have a securities firm do the work on their behalf. Securities that are sold without a middleman are labeled as direct issue, and those going through brokerages are dealer placed.

Quotations

Less detail is in quotes on companies' money market securities than there was earlier on Treasury bills. As an example, take a look at Figure 18.2, a quote on CP sold by General Electric's finance unit, GE Capital.

FIGURE 18.2 A GE Capital Commercial-Paper Quote.

Rather than complain about what's missing, be thankful for what you have: a quote on an individual company that provides something more than the current discount rate. With that in mind, let's see what's here.

DIGE090D: DI stands for direct issue. GE Capital is among the companies that go directly to investors for funds, rather than having dealer-placed paper. GE designates the seller, General Electric Capital, GE's finance unit. The three numbers followed by a D stand for 90 days, the period from the initial sale to the maturity date. CP is sold for as long as 270 days, so the 0 before the 90 would be 1 or 2 in some cases.

Up arrow: The uptick/downtick arrow refers to the rate, as it did with Treasury bills, rather than price.

.14: Current rate of 0.14 percent, or 14 basis points.

unch: Rate change on the day. There wasn't one in this case.

At 10:20: Time of the quote, using the 24-hour clock. Companies usually make CP sales early in the day, as this quote suggests.

Op .14, Hi .14, Lo .14: Opening, high, and low rates for the current day. Here they show the rate was unchanged throughout the day.

Three Rs

Lehman's collapse showed that corporate money market investments can be riskier than government bills. At worst, investors may end up with unexpected losses on their holdings. Many investors are willing to take the additional risk anyway because of the potential for higher returns. They make relative-value comparisons similar to those we saw earlier for government securities. With that in mind, let's go through the three Rs.

Returns

Companies follow the government's example by avoiding interest payments on money market debt. Investors buy these securities at a discount to the face value, which they get at maturity. This means the difference between the purchase price and face amount counts the most in returns.

The discount is larger than it would be for a government security with the same terms. Otherwise, investors would lack a financial incentive for buying the corporate debt. CP sold directly by top-rated companies for three months might have a 0.2 percent discount rate, for example, when the comparable Treasury bill rate is near zero. That way, the securities will provide some income, unlike the government's debt.

KEY POINT:

The higher the discount rate, the riskier the investment. Rates on CP and other money market investments generally exceed those on government bills.

The 0.2 percent figure may vary over time even if the government keeps paying next to nothing to borrow because the rate reflects supply and demand. Specifically, it's based on the value of securities being sold and the amount that investors are willing to put into them.

Risks

Now that we have moved to companies from governments, it's worth reviewing the risks that investors take in markets. The clearest is market risk, or the potential for prices to fall rather than rise. There's also liquidity risk, which is the inability to sell at the market price when raising cash.

CP and other money market investments are affected by these risks, along with those tied to the economy, politics, policy, and currency swings. Interest rate risk, inflation risk, and reinvestment risk are a concern though they're less of an issue than for notes and bonds because these securities mature in a short time.

Credit risk, on the other hand, takes on greater meaning. There's plenty of room for differences among companies as the rating scales from S&P, Moody's, and Fitch indicate. Investors have to take them into account in determining which securities are worth owning. The analysis is more complex than it is for Treasury bills, where they can focus on the U.S. government's ability to pay its debts.

Investors must deal with concerns that specifically affect corporate securities, starting with business risk, or the possibility that a company's performance will worsen. As the risk increases, so does the potential for a drop in cash flow, or the amount of money the company can use to cover debt payments and other expenses.

Event risk is a specific type of business risk, tied to an occurrence that may affect the company's ability to operate or to pay debts. Mergers and acquisitions can add to a company's debt burden and hinder its ability to compete. Splitting up a company or spinning off a business may mean less cash is available to meet obligations.

Industry risk can affect the value of companies and their securities as well. This is the threat that a company may suffer because of what's happening in its industry rather than its own actions. Consider what happened to photography, for example, when digital cameras replaced film cameras as the industry standard. The shift hurt Eastman Kodak Co. so badly that the company, once the world's largest maker of film, filed for bankruptcy. Fujifilm Holdings Inc. and other competitors also were affected.

Business risk, event risk, and industry risk are lower for corporate money market securities than for notes and bonds because of their shorter time to maturity. That said, the risks must be examined, as the Lehman example shows. They do much to explain the return gap between companies and governments.

Relative Value

Let's turn our attention to that 0.2 percent rate on CP. Considering that Treasury bill rates are close to zero, the two-tenths of a percentage point may be enough to draw some investors to the company's securities. Others might look at that additional return and conclude it isn't enough to compensate for the risk.

This is the kind of relative-value judgment that money market investors make daily. Others are similar to those cited with government bills, so let's run through the comparisons in summary form.

History: The 0.2 percent rate is tiny by historical standards. Top-rated U.S. companies paid three times as much to borrow in the CP market in mid-2010, according to data compiled by Bloomberg. In 2006 and 2007, the rate was more than 5 percent, or 25 times as high.

Different maturities: Companies sell CP for one to 270 days, so many other rates and time periods are available. Rate curves are more useful for this analysis than they are for Treasury debt, with four maturities sold regularly. Figure 18.3 shows how a curve might look for the highest-rated, directly placed CP.

Rate spreads may provide insight into what's cheap, expensive, or fairly valued as yield spreads did in the previous chapter. It's possible to compare spreads for any two maturities included on the curve.

> **KEY POINT:**
> Rate curves are available for asset-backed commercial paper, fed funds, and repurchase agreements, as well as unsecured commercial paper and Treasury bills. All of them can be used in relative-value analysis.

Different credit ratings: CP is classified by rating. Borrowers rated A1+ by S&P and P1 by Moody's get the best deal. The rates they pay can be shown on a curve and compared with those of lower-rated companies.

Direct issue vs. dealer placed: Companies that run their own CP sales pay lower rates on their borrowing than those who work with dealers. By tracking them separately, it's possible to compare their curves.

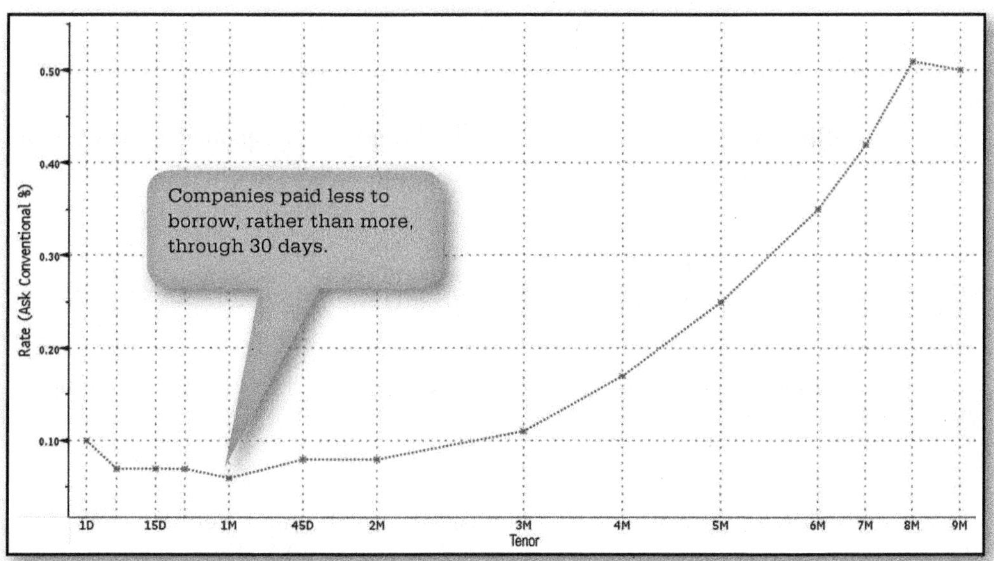

FIGURE 18.3 Commercial Paper A1+/P1 Direct Issue Rates.

Different security types: Money market investors can buy asset-backed CP, rather than securities that carry only a promise to pay. They can dig into the alphabet soup we made earlier and come up with CDs or repos. These investments have rate curves, so it's possible to compare them with others or to look at specific rate spreads.

Notes and Bonds

Microsoft Corp. doesn't need to borrow money. The world's largest software maker once paid out $32.6 billion to investors because too much money was sitting around. Microsoft piled up billions of dollars more cash each year, thanks to the dominance of its Windows operating system and Office collection of word processing, spreadsheet, and presentation software for personal computers.

None of this stopped Microsoft from raising funds in the bond market. The first sale of debt, totaling $3.75 billion, was completed in May 2009. The company later borrowed billions of dollars more through additional sales.

Why would Microsoft go this route? Borrowing money didn't cost that much since the company received the highest possible credit ratings. Some of the funds were used to buy back stock, a way to reward shareholders. Some went to pay for an expansion of the company's business.

Companies without Microsoft's financial stability can raise money from bond investors for similar purposes. They may sell debt securities to help pay for takeovers, to refinance more costly borrowing, and to pay off earlier obligations, among other reasons.

Investors buy them, secured or unsecured, because they can provide higher returns than lending money to the government. To calculate how much higher, they compare yields on the securities with those on government notes or bonds that mature at about the same time. The difference between them is a yield spread, or premium, and shows what investors will earn for taking the added risk of lending to a company.

This risk can be small when a borrower's credit exceeds minimum ratings, defined as BBB– by S&P and Fitch and Baa3 by Moody's. Companies in the category are described as **investment-grade** borrowers, and the notes and bonds they sell are called investment-grade securities.

DEFINITION:

Investment-grade

Investment-grade bonds exceed rating thresholds set by S&P, Moody's, and Fitch. High-yield, or junk, bonds are below them.

Ratings below the thresholds put companies into the high-yield category. They have to borrow in the non-investment-grade, or junk bond, market, which Michael Milken popularized at Drexel Burnham Lambert in the 1970s and 1980s.

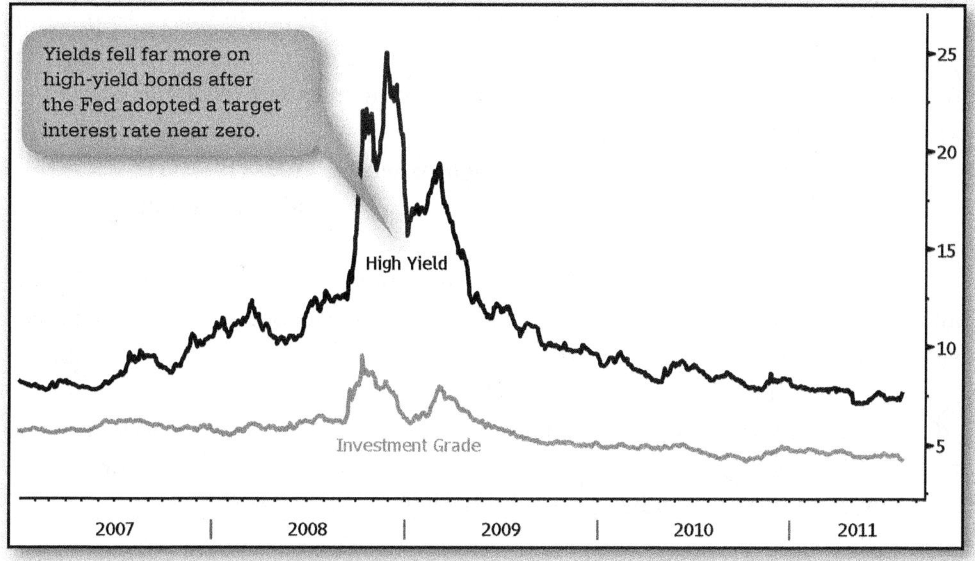

FIGURE 18.4 FINRA-Bloomberg Corporate Bond Yield Indexes.

Some investors avoid buying junk-rated debt on principle. Others are willing to invest as long as the potential returns are high enough. Either way, high-yield notes and bonds are prone to bigger gains and losses than investment-grade issues. Figure 18.4, a chart of yield indexes compiled by the Financial Industry Regulatory Authority (FINRA), an independent regulator, and Bloomberg, shows the volatility.

As you can see, high-yield securities can be more lucrative than their investment-grade counterparts as long as the borrower makes payments on time. That's a bigger if, as we'll find out later.

Financial companies are among the biggest sellers of notes and bonds because their business is all about money. They raise funds to make loans and investments, and they profit by earning more than enough to cover their financing costs. Industrial, media and telephone companies and utilities also turn to bond investors regularly. They spend relatively large amounts of money on plants and equipment, and their businesses produce the kind of cash needed to make debt payments.

Some companies that borrow regularly to finance daily operations sell medium-term notes (MTNs). These securities are created and sold in much the same way as CP even though MTNs usually mature in one to 10 years and can last as long as 30 years.

Most corporate notes and bonds are **debentures**, or unsecured loans. This means investors only have a company's promise to pay interest and repay the principal, or borrowed money, on time. If the promise isn't kept, they can't come and repossess any of its assets, as a bank can when people fail to keep up with mortgage and car payments.

DEFINITION:

Debentures

Debentures are notes and bonds without any collateral backing them other than a company's full faith and credit.

Owners of secured corporate debt, on the other hand, are in the same position as the bank. The notes and bonds are backed by buildings, equipment, property, and other collateral. As an example, transportation companies sell securities backed by airplanes and railcars.

Many corporate notes and bonds are bought when they first go on sale and rarely, if ever, are traded later. This means bond investors pay considerable attention to what they can buy in the primary market.

Some companies raising money in the United States register each bond sale individually with regulators. Registrations can cover more than one type of security. For example, a company looking to sell five-year and 10-year notes and 30-year bonds at the same time can file one statement for all of them.

Once the documents are approved, one or more securities firms conduct the sale on the company's behalf. These firms, called underwriters, line up investors to buy the bonds and arrange for other banks and brokers to do the same.

STEP-BY-STEP:
BORROWING RATES

1. ABC Inc. wants to sell bonds maturing in 30 years.
2. The 30-year Treasury bond yields 3 percent.
3. Investors demand a premium of 255 basis points to buy ABC's bonds. That's 2.55 percentage points.
4. Add the yield to the spread to determine ABC's borrowing cost, 5.55 percent.
5. The coupon will be set at 5.5 percent and the bonds will be sold at less than face value to provide the 5.55 percent yield.

Others use a different approach, especially for MTNs. These companies lay the groundwork for future sales by filing a document called a shelf registration. They can then sell securities on a daily basis, as they would with CP, to provide funds as needed. They can also sell notes and bonds more quickly later on, which allows them to take advantage of favorable market moves.

Either way, yields and yield spreads provide a basis for setting prices and interest payments. Let's assume that XYZ Co. wants to sell 10-year notes and investors demand a yield spread of 205 basis points to buy them. One basis point equals 0.01 percentage point. So, if the 10-year Treasury note's yield is 2 percent, the XYZ yield will have to be 4.05 percent.

The bond's annual interest rate, or coupon, and price would be adjusted to produce the required yield. The coupon might be set at 4 percent a year for the sake of rounding. To lift the yield to 4.05 percent, the buyer would pay a bit less than face value.

Once corporate notes and bonds are sold, they trade in a secondary market that's primarily over the counter. Though it's possible to buy and sell some securities on the New York Stock Exchange (NYSE) or the Nasdaq Stock Market (NASDAQ), the amount of debt changing hands there is small.

Price information is easier to obtain for corporate debt than for government bonds because of the Trade Reporting and Compliance Engine (TRACE).

TRACE was introduced in 2002 to collect secondary market trading data from securities firms, compile the figures, and send out the results. These days, it's run by FINRA, which oversees the firms and ensures they provide the required information.

Many corporate debt securities aren't displayed on TRACE. Finding prices for the notes and bonds can be difficult at best because they rarely trade. Bloomberg provides price estimates based on yields for similar securities, and we'll see one further on.

Quotations

There's quite a disparity in the amount of detail that bond quotes provide, as you may have guessed by now. The two-for-one display in Figures 18.5 and 18.6 provides an illustration.

For starters, these quotes are for two separate bonds. Their main similarity is they were sold by units of General Electric. The first quote is for a note from GE's finance unit, GE Capital, which started out as a 10-year security. The statistics include the first figure we have seen so far for volume, or the amount of trading. It's here because of TRACE, which provides real-time prices for a fee and delayed prices free.

The second is for a bond sold by a GE unit, Security Capital Group, which originally matured in 30 years. The price is an estimate made by Bloomberg, using the yield on comparable securities as a guide.

Let's go through these quotes and find out what they have to offer. We'll focus on the first and mention the second along the way.

GE: Symbol for General Electric, which begins the first quote and follows Security Capital's name in the second.

4 5/8: Annual interest rate of 4 5/8 percent, or 4.625 percent. The comparable rate for the bond is 7.7 percent. Rates can be stated as fractions or decimals, as these two examples suggest.

01/21: Month and year of maturity for the GE Capital note. The Security Capital quote has an exact date, 06/15/28, in the month/day/year format.

$: Dollar-denominated security. GE sells bonds in several currencies, so the dollar sign is more than a formality.

Up arrow: The uptick/downtick arrow, tied to price changes this time.

104.310: Price of the note as a percentage of face value. It's in decimals rather than the fractions used for Treasuries. A buyer would have to pay $1,043.10 for every $1,000 face amount. The price for the Security Capital bond would be $1,440.237, as it's valued at 144.0237 percent of the face amount.

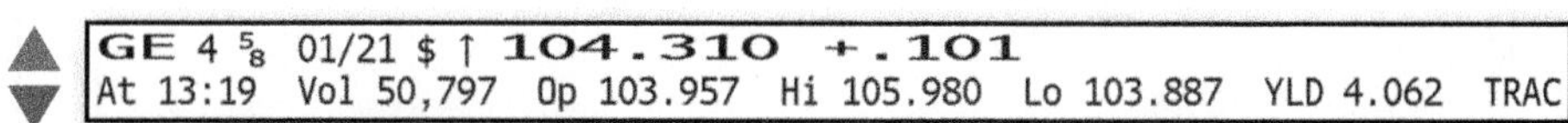

FIGURE 18.5 **A GE Capital Bond Quote.**

SECURITY CAP GRP GE 7.7 06/15/28 144.0237/144.0237 (4.04/4.04) BFV @16:55

FIGURE 18.6 **A GE Unit's Bond Quote.**

+.101: Change from the previous day's close in percent.

At 13:19: Time of the quote, using the 24-hour clock.

Vol 50,797: Number of notes traded today. Each note has a face value of $1,000, which means about $50.8 million of the securities were traded. Other quotes show a dollar amount in place of this kind of number.

Op 103.957, Hi 105.980, Lo 103.887: Opening, high, and low prices for the current day.

Yld 4.062: Yield, rounded to three decimal places, at the current price.

TRAC: TRACE, the source of the GE note's price. The Security Capital bond was priced using Bloomberg Fair Value (BFV), which compares the bond with similar securities and estimates the yield, then the price. This kind of estimate often has to be made because many securities are bought and held, rather than traded.

There's another piece of data that might have appeared in the quote for GE's note: **233 bp vs T2.625 11/15/20.** It's the difference in yield between the security and a 10-year Treasury maturing at about the same time.

The bp stands for basis points, which means the GE yield is 233 basis points higher than the Treasury note yield. The spread is the additional amount you're paid as an investor to take the risk of lending money to the company, which can't impose taxes or print money as the government can.

The gap is equivalent to 2.33 percentage points. Subtract that amount from the 4.06 percent yield on GE's security after rounding, and you'll be left with the Treasury note's yield at the time: 1.73 percent, in line with what we saw earlier. The yield differential usually fluctuates over time, as Figure 18.7 illustrates.

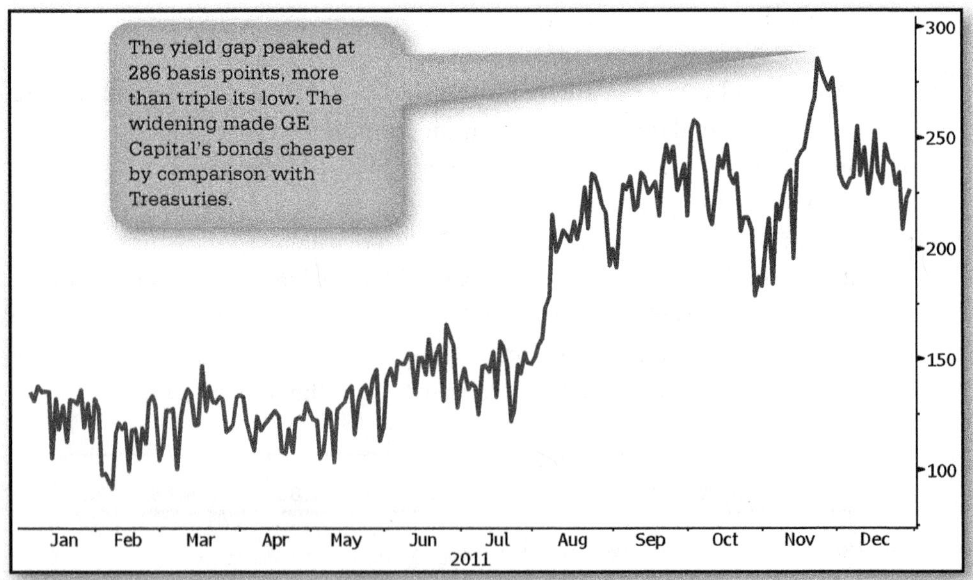

FIGURE 18.7 Yield Gap between GE Capital Bond and Treasuries (in Basis Points).

Three Rs

When we looked at government notes and bonds, we started with the idea that yields and returns are similar. This may not be true for corporate debt, as these securities are designed to give companies more flexibility in managing their finances.

Interest payments on many corporate securities are linked to a market interest rate. This means they will fluctuate from one period to the next rather than staying the same. Investors can't be sure how much interest they will receive while owning the debt.

In some cases, investors don't know how long they will be able to own the debt either. The issue arises because companies sell notes and bonds they can buy back before the maturity date at a set price. This feature allows them to take advantage of future declines in interest rates by refinancing at a lower cost.

These kinds of bells and whistles have to be built into return calculations and relative-value comparisons, which makes them more difficult. They heighten some risks we have seen before and introduce others we haven't. Let's look at the three Rs with those points in mind.

Returns

Investors make money on corporate notes and bonds in two ways as they do with government debt. They are assured of receiving interest payments, based on a schedule that's set when the securities are first sold. They stand to benefit from any market-price increases though the debt will be repaid at face value when the maturity date rolls around.

Fixed-rate corporate debt pays the same amount of interest every time. The market price of the note or bond fluctuates to keep the yield in line with current interest rates. When rates rise, companies benefit from having lower-cost financing. When they decline, investors profit because the future interest payments become more valuable.

Companies also sell **floating-rate** notes and bonds, where only the timing of interest payments is preset. The amount that's paid each time depends on a market rate such as Libor, which we discussed earlier. Payments are usually based on a spread to Libor for a specified currency and maturity date, often three months.

DEFINITION:
Floating-rate
Floating-rate debt pays interest that varies along with Libor or another market rate.

Floating-rate debt makes sense for companies whose income rises and falls along with interest rates. Banks are among them because they provide credit cards, make commercial loans, and buy securities whose interest payments float. Companies looking for rates to fall may favor floating-rate notes and bonds, which assure them of lower interest expense as long as their outlook is accurate.

STEP-BY-STEP:
FLOATING-RATE INTEREST

1. ABC Inc. sells 10-year floating-rate notes. They pay interest twice a year at three-month dollar Libor plus 75 basis points.
2. Six months after the sale, Libor is 0.5 percent. Add the spread, and the note's annual interest rate is 1.25 percent.
3. ABC's first payment is half the annual rate. That's 0.625 percent, or 62.5 cents for every $1,000 borrowed.
4. One year after the sale, Libor is 0.75 percent. The annual rate rises to 1.5 percent.
5. ABC's second payment is 0.75 percent, or 75 cents per $1,000.

Some companies sell inflation-indexed securities, similar to the U.S. government's Treasury Inflation-Protected Securities (TIPS). Changes in an inflation gauge such as the Consumer Price Index (CPI) replace Libor, or some other market rate, in the formula for calculating interest.

Returns on corporate notes and bonds depend on whether they remain outstanding until maturity. Some of these securities are callable, which means companies are allowed to buy them back in advance. A 30-year bond that can be called after five years would effectively turn into a five-year note if the company repurchases the debt.

Callable securities have what's called a yield to worst, which assumes they are bought back at the first possible opportunity. This yield can be calculated because call prices are set when the notes and bonds are first sold.

Corporate debt can be putable. Investors owning these securities would be able to sell them back to the company at predetermined prices before they mature. This feature sets a floor under the price of the notes and bonds, which aids returns. Call provisions have the opposite effect, as they give companies the right to buy their debt at what may be below-market prices.

Companies can sell convertible notes and bonds, which can be exchanged for common stock at a set price for each share. The ability to convert may belong to the investor, the company, or both, depending on the terms of the security. We'll revisit convertibles later, when we look more closely at variations on investing in companies.

Risks

We have seen three levels of risk that investors take in buying corporate notes and bonds. The first is the broadest, consisting of market risk, liquidity risk, economic risk, political risk, policy risk, and currency risk. The second combines credit risk, interest rate risk, inflation risk, and reinvestment risk, which are concerns for anyone owning debt securities. Real returns, adjusted for inflation, take this level of risk into account.

Business risk, event risk, and industry risk amount to a third level, focused on companies. A more specific business risk for note and bond investors is worth adding: bankruptcy risk, which Lehman's investors learned about the hard way. If a company's performance suffers enough, it may be unable to stay in business without seeking court protection from creditors. The reorganization that follows often results in losses for note and bond investors, among others.

While we're at it, we might add a bankruptcy-related threat to the second level: default risk. It's the most extreme form of credit risk. Companies default when they don't pay interest or repay principal on their debt as required. This can take place because they don't have the money or because they decide to keep their cash instead. Bankruptcy risk and default risk increase with the amount of time until corporate debt matures. That's why they're especially relevant here. We could have mentioned them in the discussion of money market securities, based on the Lehman example.

Call risk deserves a mention because of the earlier reference to callable notes and bonds. When interest rates fall, companies have more of an incentive to refinance or repay the debt to reduce interest expense. This would cause bond investors to lose years of interest payments at above-market rates. They would get back their original investment sooner than they wanted and would have to settle for lower returns if the funds were reinvested in similar securities.

Relative Value

Yield, especially in the form of curves and spreads, is a guidepost for determining whether corporate notes and bonds are cheap, expensive, or fairly valued. The same kinds of analysis we learned about earlier for government debt can be done with company securities. Let's run through them in summary form.

KEY POINT:

Corporate bonds can have options built into them. Callable bonds give companies the option to buy them back before maturity. Putable bonds give investors the option to sell them back early. Convertible bonds provide investors with the option to swap debt for equity.

History: The easiest way to judge whether a yield is low, high, or somewhere in between is to look at where it's been. This usually has to be done on a security-specific basis because most companies don't sell securities with the consistency of the U.S. government. This means benchmark maturities are unavailable for comparisons.

Similar companies: Yield curves are available for categories of corporate notes and bonds that provide a benchmark for specific securities. If a bank note yields 4 percent and matures in five years, for example, the five-year yield on a curve of bank debt would shed light on the note's relative value.

Corporate curves are created differently than the Treasury curve. The connect-the-dots approach cited earlier won't work because there are too many maturities and yields to consider, including some for cheap or expensive securities.

KEY POINT:

Corporate yield curves aren't created through a connect-the-dots approach. Instead, a group of similar bonds is identified and a curve is calculated that comes closest to fitting them all.

Instead, the first step in creating a corporate curve is defining a debt category. Industry groups and credit ratings are among the criteria. Financial, industrial, media and telephone companies, and utilities can have their own curves. There may be one curve for companies with top ratings from S&P and Moody's, another for ratings one level lower, and so on.

Once the category is created, a group of corporate notes and bonds is compiled. Their yields and maturity dates are run through a mathematical formula to calculate the curve, which comes closest to fitting them all.

Different industries: Financial companies can be broken down into banks, broker-dealers, insurance companies, and real estate owners. Relative-value comparisons among these segments are made possible through industry-specific yield curves. It's possible, for instance, to track the spread between five-year notes on banks and insurers and decide which offers more value.

Different credit ratings: This kind of analysis can focus on yields for investment-grade and high-yield securities as a group. Spreads between the two categories enable investors to determine how much more they would earn by putting money into companies rated below BBB- at S&P and Baa3 at Moody's.

Investors can compare yields for similar corporate borrowers at different rating levels. S&P and Moody's ratings provide a basis to create rating-specific curves for banks, industrial companies, and others.

Different borrowers: Corporate yield curves are directly comparable to those on government debt even though they are compiled differently. The Treasury curve is a benchmark for gauging the relative value of companies' notes and bonds.

There's a comparison between top-rated industrial debt and Treasuries in the following chart. As you might expect, yields on the corporate securities are higher (see Figure 18.8).

Similar comparisons are possible between companies and other government-related borrowers that we have yet to cover. We'll touch on those later. Now it's time to shift our focus toward equity, as in stock, and away from debt.

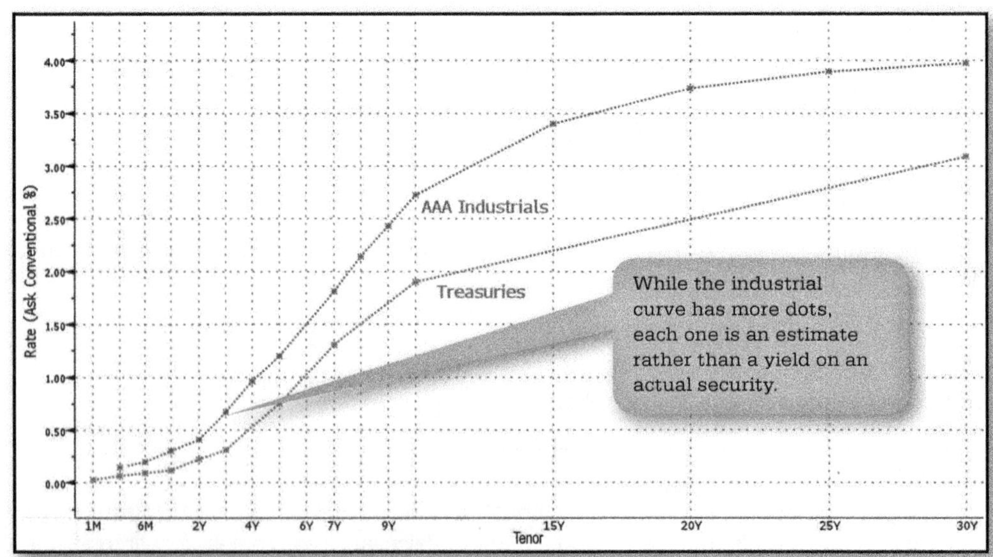

FIGURE 18.8 AAA Industrial and Treasury Yield Curves.

Stocks

"How's the market doing?" The question could refer to any of the financial markets we have examined or any of the ones we'll consider in later chapters, but it doesn't. You could insert "stock" before "market" by default.

This is true because individuals and institutional investors have bought and sold shares in the United States for more than two centuries. Stocks tend to account for a bigger percentage of their holdings than any other asset. Share prices tend to fluctuate more than bond prices and money market rates each day.

All the interest in stocks works to the benefit of companies looking to raise money. They can sell shares and obtain funds they don't have to repay. It's good for corporate executives, financial backers, and others with stakes in a company because it gives them the opportunity to turn their holdings into cash.

The fewer shares there are, the greater the percentage of ownership that each share provides, and vice versa. If a company had 1,000 shares outstanding, for instance, then each share would amount to a 0.1 percent stake. If there are a million instead, then a share is only 0.0001 percent of the total.

Any other benefits of owning shares are up to the company that sells them. Voting rights and dividend payments are two of the most widely available perks.

Stockholders select the members of a company's board of directors, approve the outside accounting firm that audits its financial statements, accept or reject takeover bids, and decide other issues. Some companies ensure a smaller number of holders make these decisions by creating non-voting and voting shares. Others accomplish the same goal by having a separate class of stock with extra votes for each share.

Dividends are taken out of a company's profits, and the payments are usually made quarterly. Companies can go without them if they need the funds to finance expansion or sustain their business. Those that make the distributions set a payout ratio, or a percentage of earnings, they want to maintain each year.

Companies can return cash to holders by buying back stock as well as paying dividends. The repurchases increase earnings per share by reducing the amount of outstanding stock. Let's suppose the company with 1 million shares posted a $1 million profit. The earnings would amount to $1 a share. If the company bought back 100,000 shares and reported the earnings, the $1 million would be divided among only 900,000 shares. That works out to $1.11 a share.

STEP-BY-STEP:
OWNERSHIP STAKES

1. Apple Inc. had 929.4 million shares outstanding in October 2011 when co-founder Steve Jobs died.
2. Jobs owned about 5.6 million shares at the time of his death.
3. Divide 5.6 into 929.4. The result shows Jobs left behind a 0.6 percent stake.

There's no obligation for companies to repurchase stock. They can do the opposite. Sales of stock and related securities, takeovers of other companies, and grants to executives are among the moves that increase the number of outstanding shares.

> **KEY POINT:**
> Secondary offerings are sales of existing stock even though the phrase is often used to describe sales of new shares after an IPO.

These kinds of actions can dilute earnings, or spread them over a greater number of shares. That $1 million profit would be 91 cents a share, for instance, if the company had 1.1 million shares outstanding. Increase the share count to 2 million, and the profit drops to 50 cents a share.

The number of shares outstanding often rises because a company sells new stock as mentioned earlier. These sales are done in the primary market, where companies make initial public offerings (IPOs) and sell additional shares.

IPOs result from a company's decision to become publicly traded. The company selects one or more securities firms to be underwriters. These firms work with the company to determine the sale's timing, the number of shares to be sold, and the price to charge for them. Underwriters line up other firms to take part in the share sale and investors to buy the stock.

Investors and executives can sell shares when a company goes public. This portion of the sale is a secondary offering even though it's occurring in the primary market. The difference is that the proceeds will go to whoever sells the shares, rather than the company. In some cases, secondary offerings account for an entire IPO.

Going public lays the foundation for companies to sell additional shares and raise more money. While these sales are sometimes called secondary offerings, the phrase doesn't apply when they involve new stock.

Newly public companies can be more rewarding than older ones. This was the case during the 2000s, when a Bloomberg index of U.S. companies in their first year of trading rose as the Standard & Poor's 500 Index fell. Figure 18.9 compares the indexes.

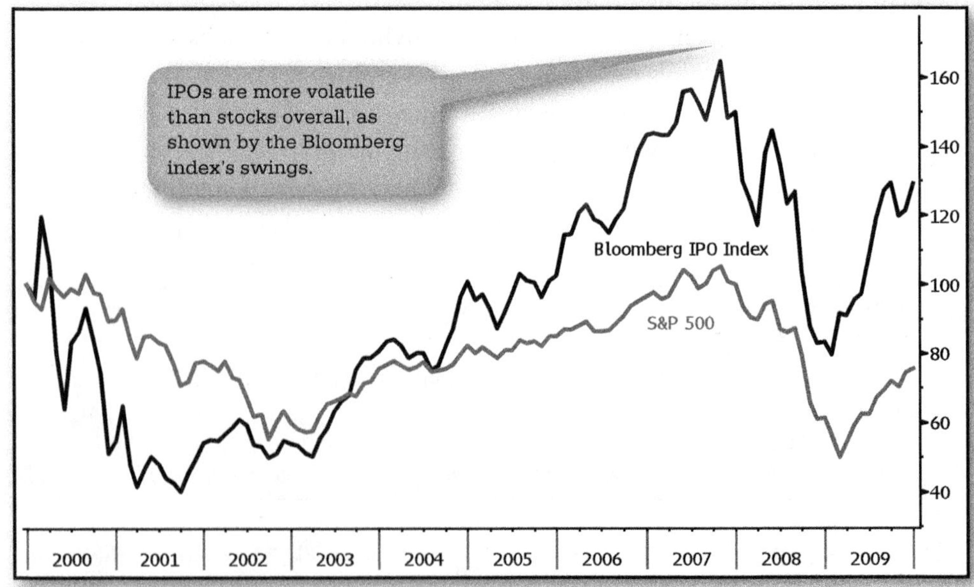

FIGURE 18.9 Initial Public Offerings versus Standard & Poor's 500 Index (December 31, 1999 = 100).

IPOs bring companies into the secondary market, where their stock trades daily. U.S. companies usually list their shares on the NYSE or the NASDAQ. The NYSE's roots go back to 1792 when brokers gathered under a buttonwood tree in New York to set rules for stock and bond trading. NASDAQ, an electronic market, followed in 1971.

The NYSE and NASDAQ compete for stock trading with BATS Global Markets Inc. and Direct Edge Holdings LLC, which own exchanges. All four companies operate multiple markets, which are linked electronically to help investors make the best possible deal on their trades. The NYSE is the only one with floor trading, where brokers buy and sell on an exchange floor.

The development of all-electronic markets has led to high-frequency trading, in which firms use computer-based buying and selling to profit from instantaneous market moves. The firms may own stock for a few seconds. Estimates of their share of trading in U.S. markets have been as high as 70 percent. Institutional investors can bypass exchanges and trade through dark pools, run by securities firms and others, where large blocks of stock change hands. The pools get their name because participants and public investors are kept in the dark about who's buying and selling and how many shares they have to trade.

Quotations

Stock quotes provide a level of detail we haven't run across before. Exchanges collect, consolidate, and distribute all kinds of trading data, including details about purchases and sales taking place on other markets. Let's check a quote for Apple Inc., which became the world's biggest company by market value in 2011, to see this for ourselves (see Figure 18.10).

AAPL: Apple's ticker, or stock symbol. U.S. tickers are no more than five letters. Use of one- to three-letter tickers was restricted to companies listed on the NYSE or the American Stock Exchange (AMEX) and four-letter tickers were reserved for listings on NASDAQ until 2007.

Companies can use one to four letters regardless of where they're listed, including the AMEX, now NYSE Amex. NASDAQ stocks with traditional tickers can have a fifth letter, which designates the type of security, a company in bankruptcy, or other conditions.

US: U.S. composite trading. Individual markets each have their own two-letter code on the Bloomberg terminal. The first letter is always U, designating a U.S. market. The second can appear alone in quotes.

$: Dollar-denominated security.

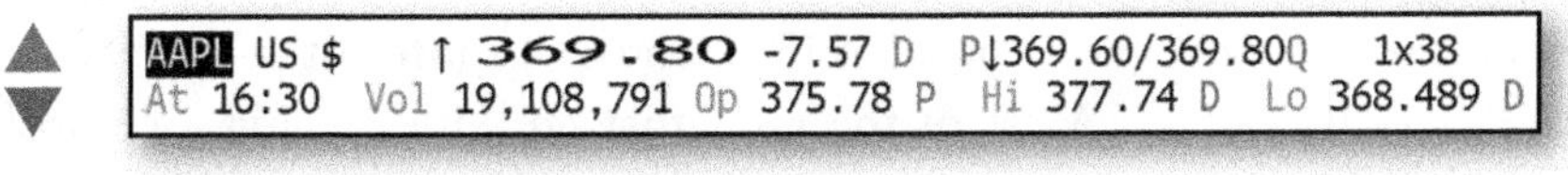

```
AAPL US $    ↑ 369.80 -7.57 D  P↓369.60/369.80Q   1x38
At 16:30  Vol 19,108,791 Op 375.78 P  Hi 377.74 D  Lo 368.489 D
```

FIGURE 18.10 An Apple Inc. Stock Quote.

Up arrow: Uptick/downtick arrow, displaying the latest change in the stock price.

369.80: Price of the latest trade. U.S. share prices have been quoted in dollars and cents since 2001. Before then, they were quoted in fractions, just like Treasury notes and bonds.

–7.57: Change from the previous close. At the time of the quote, Apple was $7.57 lower on the day.

D: Second letter of the code for the Alternative Display Facility, where the latest price was posted. FINRA runs the facility to report on stock trades made outside NASDAQ.

P: Second letter of the exchange code for NYSE Arca, an electronic market owned by NYSE Euronext, where the bid price was posted. The letter originally stood for the Pacific Stock Exchange, a regional market with historical ties to NYSE Arca.

Down arrow: Uptick/downtick arrow, referring this time to the latest change in Apple's bid price.

369.60: Highest price that any potential buyer is willing to pay for Apple's shares.

/: Separator for the bid and ask price.

369.80: Lowest price that any potential seller will accept for Apple's shares.

Q: Second letter of UQ, the two-letter code for NASDAQ.

1 × 38: Number of round lots associated with the bid and ask prices. When combined with the earlier details, here's what the quote says: Someone wants to buy 100 shares of Apple at $369.60 each on NYSE Arca. Someone else is looking to sell 3,800 shares at $369.80 apiece on NASDAQ. This is known as the inside market, because the bid and ask prices are inside the range set by prices available in other markets.

At 16:30: Time of the latest price. In this case, it's the official close for the stock. Prices between 09:30 and 16:00, or 9:30 a.m. and 4 p.m. Eastern, are from the trading day.

Vol 19,108.791: Volume, or the number of shares changing hands during the current day. The total consists of round lots, or trades in multiples of 100 shares, and odd lots, or trades of fewer than 100 shares. Round lots are the standard for U.S. stocks.

Op 375.78 P, Hi 377.74 D, Lo 368.489 D: Opening, high, and low prices for the current day, along with the markets on which they were recorded. On this day, Apple opened at $375.78 on NYSE Arca. The high of $377.74 and the low of $368.489 both appeared on FINRA's facility. Note that the low price goes out to three decimal places, rather than two.

Quotes posted during the trading day would end the second line with a number like this: **ValTrd 4780.216m**. It's the dollar value of shares traded. The m is for $1 million, so the figure shows $4.78 billion of Apple shares changed hands.

Three Rs

Stocks are similar to corporate notes and bonds when it comes to returns and risks, the first two Rs that we'll consider. Dividends, like interest payments, are included in return calculations. Most of the risks that go with owning a company's shares affect its debt's value.

Relative value is where they part company. Though yields can show whether shares are cheap, expensive, and fairly priced, they aren't as encompassing a gauge as they are for bonds. For instance, yields based on dividends aren't meaningful for companies that don't pay them.

Earnings carry more weight with stock investors than bond investors, who are more concerned with a company's ability to pay debts. One of the most widely used relative-value gauges for stocks is the **price-earnings ratio** (P/E). It's calculated by dividing the stock's price by earnings per share, which can be historical or estimated.

> **DEFINITION:**
> **Price-earnings ratio**
> The price-earnings ratio (P/E) is the share price divided by earnings per share. The calculation is based on past or projected profits.

Before we go any further, let's go through the three Rs in sequence to ensure we don't miss anything.

Returns

Dividends contribute to returns on stocks in the same way that interest affects bond returns, as mentioned earlier. The biggest difference is that there isn't any time limit on how long investors can receive payouts because stocks don't have a maturity date.

The role that dividends play in returns increases with the amount of time an investor owns shares. Payouts accounted for 90 percent of U.S. stock returns between 1871 and 2009, according to a study done by Grantham, Mayo, Van Otterloo & Co. (GMO), a money management firm. The figure reflected dividend yields as well as inflation-adjusted growth in payouts, which James Montier, a member of GMO's asset allocation team, noted in an August 2010 report.

Investors don't make a habit of studying stock returns for 138-year intervals. They're more likely to focus on the latest quarter, the latest year, and some other relatively short period. Price changes affect returns far more than dividends for these periods.

When stocks don't pay dividends, investors can only make money if the price rises. Dividend-paying stocks, by contrast, can have positive returns even when the price drops. That's possible as long as the loss is smaller than the payout.

Dividends provide a financial cushion against losses. They enable investors to earn additional income by reinvesting the payouts. Shareholders in companies that keep their cash have to go without those benefits.

Risks

Shareholders can be perched at either end of the three levels of risk cited earlier. The first level consists of market risk, liquidity risk, economic risk, political risk, policy risk, and currency risk. The third touches on business risk, event risk, and industry risk along with the threat of bankruptcy.

Currency risk can be linked to a company's business rather than its shares. Many companies based outside the U.S. have American Depositary Receipts (ADRs), representing some number of shares. ADRs trade on the NYSE, NASDAQ, and other markets. They are also known as American Depositary Shares (ADSs).

Though ADRs are dollar-denominated, their owners still have to deal with currency risk. If the company is based in a country whose currency is losing value, then its shares are likely to fall as many international investors move their money elsewhere. The U.S.-listed securities will decline as well.

Currency risk can cut the other way because of its effect on a company's business. If the local currency rises in value, international sales and earnings may count for less when they're translated into that currency. The increase might lead to slower growth in revenue and profit, or even declines, as the company's products become more costly.

Bankruptcy risk is worth highlighting because it's more acute for shareholders than for any other investors in a company. When a company reorganizes, the holders have to settle for what remains after payments to banks, bondholders, and suppliers. In many cases, the shares are canceled, leaving the holders with nothing to show for their investment.

The second level of risk hasn't been mentioned because it's less of an issue for equity investors. Credit risk and default risk don't affect the value of securities directly. Inflation may be more of an opportunity than a risk as price increases can lead to higher sales, earnings, and share values. Interest rate risk and reinvestment risk are less of a concern because an investor can put dividend payments back into the stock, as opposed to settling for a lower-yielding investment.

Relative Value

Price has taken a back seat in our searches for relative value. That's no accident. Prices of government bills and other money market securities are an afterthought, designed to produce a specified discount rate. Note and bond prices are tied to the securities' face value, which the borrowers are obligated to pay at maturity. Little room exists for them to move without a substantial change in market interest rates.

Stock prices don't have these kinds of constraints. Though shares can have a face amount, known as a par value, they don't have to. When they do, it's often a fraction of a cent. That's fine for accounting purposes because par value isn't a sum of money that investors will receive in a few months or years.

Instead, the company's share price is driven by what's happening to sales, earnings, and dividend payments over time. Faster growth usually brings bigger gains for the stock, and declines can send the price lower.

The P/E ratio is one way to value stocks. Investors may use historical or projected earnings in their analysis, and each approach has merit. Historical earnings have the advantage of being more definite than estimates, which may not prove to be accurate. Then again, anyone buying a stock has to rely on future profits to push the share price higher. The past is useful as a guide to the future.

For the fastest-growing companies, historical P/Es will be higher than those based on projected earnings. For those growing more slowly, there may be little difference between the ratios.

STEP-BY-STEP:
PRICE-EARNINGS RATIO

1. ABC Inc.'s shares trade at $30.
2. ABC's earnings in the previous four quarters equaled $3 a share.
3. Divide the profit into the stock price for the P/E ratio, which is 10.

Finding cheap, expensive, and fairly priced stocks may involve price-to-sales and price-to-cash flow ratios, calculated by dividing share prices by sales or cash flow per share rather than earnings. Another yardstick is book value, or the value of what a business owns minus what it owes. More precisely, book value shows what the company's assets are worth after subtracting liabilities.

We need to give yields their due as well, starting with dividend yields. They can be historical or estimated, like the earnings figures in P/E ratios. If the company with the $30 stock paid $1 a share in the past 12 months, then the shares have a dividend yield of 3.3 percent, or 1 divided by 30. If the company raised its payout rate to $1.20 a share, the projected dividend yield would be 4 percent.

STEP-BY-STEP:
ESTIMATED P/E RATIO

1. ABC Inc.'s shares trade at $30.
2. Analysts expect next year's earnings to be $3.33 a share on average.
3. Divide the projection into the stock price for the estimated P/E ratio, which is nine.

There's a yield for earnings as well as dividends, which is useful for studying stocks without payouts. The earnings yield is the inverse of the P/E, or 100 divided by the ratio. Our $30 stock yields 10 percent, based on the $3 in profit during the past 12 months.

Similar ratios and yields for industry groups and market indexes are available. Investors use these indicators as benchmarks when looking at specific stocks. This approach is worthwhile because moves in these gauges over time can be substantial. The P/E for the Standard & Poor's 500 Index, displayed in Figure 18.11, provides an example.

Now that we have an idea how to determine relative value, it's time to look at some comparisons that help investors decide what stocks to buy, sell, or hold. This analysis can be done for individual shares or broader categories, as we saw earlier for money-market securities, notes, and bonds. Here's a summary.

History: Maybe the shares of a company are trading at record prices. Maybe they lost half their value during the past three months. Maybe they haven't changed all that much in the past three years. The only way to know is to look at historical prices, a starting point for relative-value judgments.

Historical data is available for the P/E, price-to-sales ratio, price-to-cash-flow ratio, price-to-book-value (or book) ratio and more gauges, along with dividend and earnings yields. These can shed light on the significance of price moves. If a stock has risen to a record and the P/E ratio has changed little during the past year, the price move may mean the business is doing well. If the P/E has climbed, the gain may have more to do with speculation than the company's results.

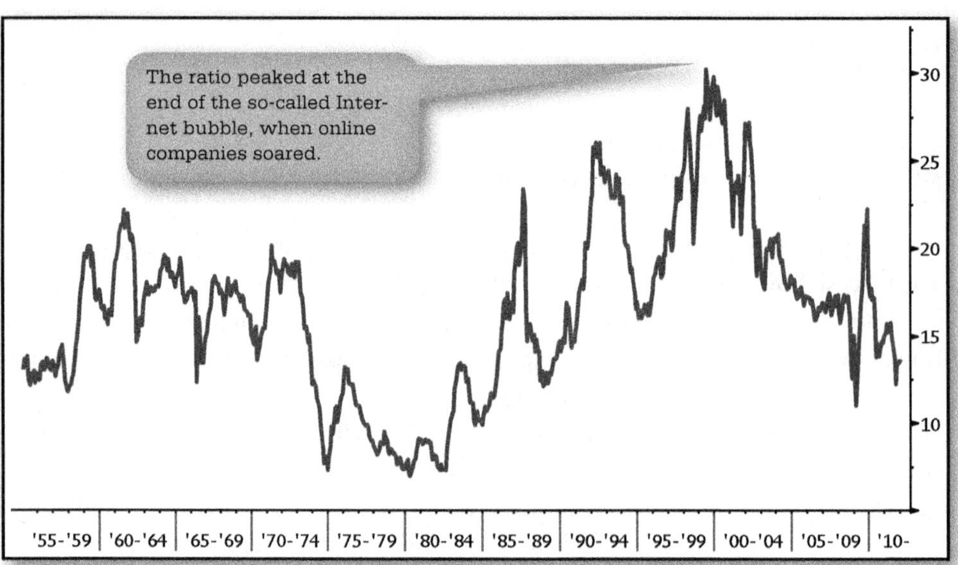

FIGURE 18.11 **Standard & Poor's 500 Index Price-Earnings Ratio.**

Different companies: Comparisons based on financial ratios provide the most insight when they involve shares of a company and its competitors. Dividend yields are an example. Utilities and telephone companies have the highest payouts because their businesses are stable, leaving them with plenty of money to distribute. There's little to be gained by comparing yields on a utility stock and shares of a technology company, which may be growing much faster and need cash for expansion.

Different industries: Money managers make judgments about the companies in which they invest and about the industries represented in their holdings. They may have a preference for some industry groups over others that affects their weightings, or percentage of assets. In coming to these conclusions, they look at ratios, yields, and other indicators for industry groups. They're the same as the gauges used for individual stocks except that they're based on averages.

Different categories: Industry groups are one of many ways to categorize stocks. Others include market value, growth rates, economic ties, and location. Relative-value comparisons make it possible to sort through them and determine what's worth buying, selling, or holding.

Market value is known as market capitalization (cap). Stocks can be large-cap, mid-cap, or small-cap, depending on the company's value. Some investors describe the largest companies as mega-caps and refer to the smallest as micro-caps. The dollar values used for each category depend on who's doing the categorizing and how stocks are performing. It's enough to know that these breakdowns exist and can serve as a starting point for determining relative value.

Sales, earnings, assets, and other financial barometers can define companies as growth or value. Growth stocks are tied to the biggest increases in revenue and profit. Value stocks have some of the lowest price-to-book ratios. Beyond that, the criteria are as variable as the market cap thresholds. That doesn't stop investors from looking for value in one or the other.

Industries can be classified as cyclical or defensive, based on how vulnerable they are to slower economic growth and recession. Commodity, energy, industrial, and technology stocks are cyclical. Health-care, telephone, and utility shares are defensive. Consumer companies are in both categories. Cyclicals include media companies, retailers, automakers, and homebuilders, which depend on consumers' discretionary income. The makers of food, beverages, and other consumer staples are defensive stocks. By combining economic and relative-value analysis, investors can decide how heavily to bet on either category.

> **KEY POINT:**
> Secondary offerings are sales of existing stock even though the phrase is often used to describe sales of new shares after an IPO.

Location refers to countries, regions, or economic areas. The broadest distinction made globally is between developed markets and emerging markets, as defined by the pace of economic growth and other criteria. Investors may favor one geographic region over another or concentrate on countries or markets where the outlook is most promising. These kinds of investment decisions rely on the ability to assess value worldwide, and that's made possible by the kind of analysis we have just explored.

Test Yourself

Answer the following multiple-choice questions:

1. The federal funds rate is set by:
   - a. Banks.
   - b. The Federal Reserve.
   - c. The U.S. Treasury.
   - d. All of the above.
   - e. a and b only.
2. Companies can borrow for one year by selling:
   - a. Corporate bonds.
   - b. Medium-term notes.
   - c. Commercial paper.
   - d. All of the above.
   - e. a and b only.
3. Bonds of companies with relatively low credit ratings are labeled as:
   - a. Non-investment grade.
   - b. High yield.
   - c. Junk.
   - d. All of the above.
   - e. a and b only.
4. Returns on stocks always reflect:
   - a. Price changes.
   - b. Dividend payments.
   - c. Share repurchases.
   - d. All of the above.
   - e. a and b only.
5. Underwriters sell:
   - a. Stocks.
   - b. Corporate bonds.
   - c. Treasury securities.
   - d. All of the above.
   - e. a and b only.

Answers: 1. e; 2. b; 3. d; 4. a; 5. e

CHAPTER 19

Hard Assets

From David Wilson, *Visual Guide to Financial Markets* (Hoboken, New Jersey: John Wiley & Sons, 2012), Chapter 4.

All the investments we have examined so far fit into one of three categories: stocks, bonds, and cash. Investors also can pick from a number of alternative investments, or strategies and assets other than buying stocks and bonds or holding onto cash.

Alternative can refer to hedge funds, or private partnerships that rely on investment strategies besides buying and holding securities. Private-equity funds, which acquire entire companies mainly with borrowed money, are another alternative.

We'll take a closer look at these funds and others later. For the moment, we'll focus on alternative assets. Commodities and real estate are two of the most popular types. Because of their physical presence, they're described as real assets, tangible assets, and hard assets. They are more than pieces of paper or entries on computer screens. They can protect investors against inflation risk, as their value tends to increase during periods when prices are rising more broadly.

Let's start by considering gold, a precious metal that's sometimes seen as its own asset class. This distinction exists because gold's value depends on the amount of confidence that investors have in financial assets, not just the industrial demand that matters for most raw materials.

Gold

"Do you think gold is money?"

Representative Ron Paul, a Republican from Texas, asked that question to Federal Reserve (Fed) Chairman Ben Bernanke at a congressional hearing in July 2011.

Bernanke's answer was no. "It's a precious metal," he said.

The reply prompted Paul to note that gold has been seen as money for 6,000 years. He asked, "Has somebody reversed that, eliminated that economic law?" He then questioned why central banks owned gold and concluded, "Some people still think it's money."

This exchange shows why gold differs from other commodities. Few would argue a barrel of crude oil, a pound of copper, or a bushel of corn is money as Paul did with gold at the hearing. Yet many investors share his view of the metal's role.

Gold is often described as a store of value or a way to preserve wealth. Historically, the Fed and other central banks followed the gold standard. Their currencies were backed by the metal, resulting in what's known as hard money.

This standard has been replaced by a system of fiat money, in which currencies have value primarily because of their legal status. Fiat money has been the standard since August 1971, when the United States ended trading of gold at a fixed price of $35 an ounce. Figure 19.1 shows what has happened to the price.

Gold prices reflect the dollar's value because the commodity is bought and sold in dollars worldwide. They indicate the level of concern among investors about the future of the global financial system. Many investors consider gold to be a better investment than stocks, bonds, and cash during times of financial turmoil because its value extends beyond national borders. Some own gold bullion, in the form of bars or coins, to hedge against this kind of upheaval.

Bullion is called physical gold, a phrase used to distinguish the metal from the securities and derivatives linked to its value. Physical gold is a hard asset, which explains its popularity among many investors.

Individuals can own gold directly, which isn't possible for many other commodities because of the quantities and costs involved. They have the option of buying allocated gold, which banks store on behalf of the owners. There's also unallocated gold, which banks and investment funds own. Gold certificates and other securities can be backed by allocated or unallocated metal.

Central banks own gold, as Paul's questioning of Bernanke suggested. European central banks have limited gold sales under a series of five-year agreements since

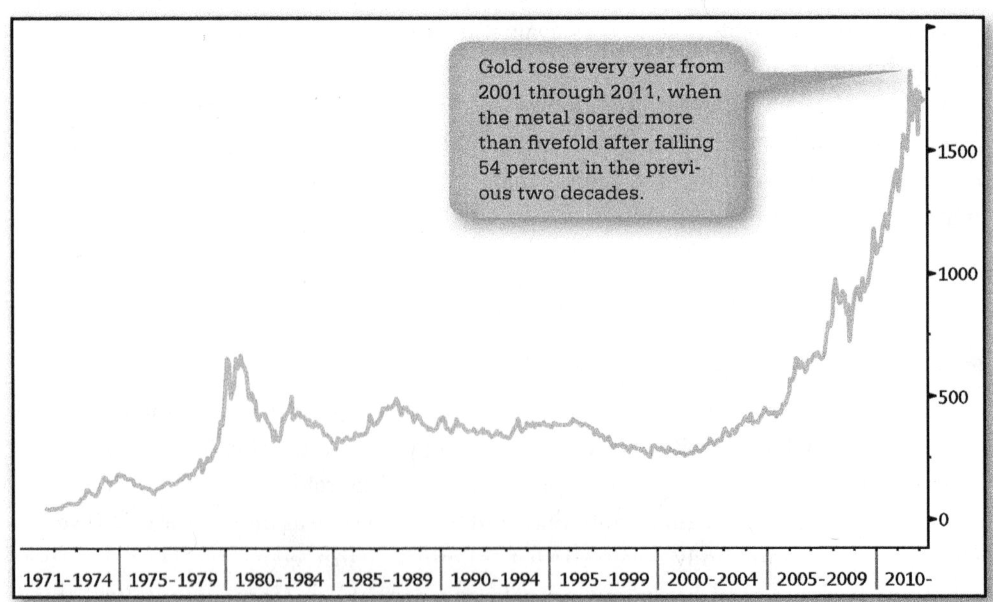

FIGURE 19.1 Gold Prices Since the United States Ended Trading at $35/Ounce.

1999. The International Monetary Fund (IMF), which promotes global financial stability and economic development, owns the metal as part of its official reserves for international payments.

All this means investment demand plays a larger role in setting the price of gold than it does with other commodities. Industrial demand is tied to the production of gold jewelry as well as dental fillings and electronic components.

The primary market for gold consists of sales by mining companies to their customers. Investors aren't active in that market because there aren't any initial public offerings (IPOs) for newly produced metal. Instead, they do business in secondary markets, which are split between spot and futures trading.

In **spot markets**, gold changes hands for immediate delivery. Buying and selling takes place over the counter. While you won't find data about the price and quantity of gold traded on a given day, market quotes are available from brokerage firms and precious-metal dealers. Spot prices are a benchmark for gold's market value.

> **DEFINITION:**
> **Spot markets**
> In spot markets, gold and other commodities are sold for immediate delivery. Futures markets set prices for later deliveries.

Another benchmark is the London gold fixing, a price provided by a group of five dealers. The price comes from a spot market, dating back to 1919, which operates each weekday morning and afternoon. The group consists of the Barclays Capital unit of Barclays Plc, Deutsche Bank AG, HSBC Holdings Plc, Bank of Nova Scotia's ScotiaMonetta unit, and Societé Generale.

Gold futures prices are followed as well. Futures contracts lock in the price for a later delivery. They trade on exchanges, which specify the amount and quality of gold as well as other contract terms. Exchanges provide data on trades as they take place. This makes the futures market easier to follow than the spot market.

As the delivery date draws closer, any price gap between gold futures and spot markets will usually shrink. There's less of a difference over time between estimates of the metal's future price, which affect the market value of the contract, and its current price.

We'll take a closer look at futures later, when we delve into derivatives. Let's focus on spot trading.

Quotations

When you look for a quote on spot gold, Figure 19.2 shows what you might find. Prices are quoted in dollars worldwide, which explains why the dollar sign we have seen in other quotes is missing.

```
GOLDS ↑    1743.22 -39.13    DBFX 1743.2/1743.25 ANON
At 14:50 Op 1782.3   Hi 1786.47   Lo 1722.03   Prev 1782.35
```

FIGURE 19.2 **A Spot Gold Quote.**

GOLDS: Symbol for spot gold.

Up arrow: Uptick/downtick arrow, pointing in the direction of the latest price change.

1743.22: Price of latest trade in dollars and cents.

-39.13: Change from previous day's close. As with currencies, the market never formally closes during the week. The last trade at a specified time and place, such as 6 p.m. Eastern time in New York, represents the closing price.

DBFX: Symbol for the gold dealer with the highest bid price. In this case, it's Deutsche Bank. The FX in the symbol isn't an accident, as some of the largest securities firms have fixed income, currency, and commodity (FICC) trading desks.

1743.2/1743.25: Highest bid price, $1,743.20 an ounce, and lowest ask price, $1,743.25 an ounce.

ANON: Symbol showing the dealer with the lowest ask price has chosen to remain anonymous.

At 14:50: Time of the latest update.

Op 1782.3, Hi 1786.47, Lo 1722.03: Opening, high, and low prices for the current day.

Prev 1782.35: Closing price for the previous day, based on the specified time and place.

Three Rs

Returns are easier to figure out for gold than for stocks, bonds, and cash. Gold has no discount rate, and you can avoid any payments in the calculations. This means gold investors can't count on income they would otherwise receive. They're at the mercy of swings in spot and futures markets.

Gold's risks differ from those of financial assets. Owning the metal provides investors with insurance against extreme outcomes, according to the late Peter Bernstein, a market historian. The price of gold is the premium charged for that insurance. When investors become more concerned that the outcomes might occur, the price or the premium tends to rise even as the value of stocks, bonds, and cash falls.

Relative value is less obvious with gold as well. Deciding how much an ounce of the metal should cost is more difficult than comparing prices in different markets. The kind of supply-and-demand analysis done with other commodities is less useful because of the larger role played by investment demand, which can be volatile.

Returns

Gold bullion doesn't pay interest. Gold bars don't pay dividends. Gold coins don't generate any reinvestment income. This means returns from owning bullion, bars, and coins depend on price changes.

Storage and insurance costs reduce the returns. Owners of allocated gold have to pay annual fees for keeping the metal in bank vaults and insuring against theft. These costs, along with management fees, are also borne by investors who have claims on unallocated gold.

Gold futures add more variables to the return equation as we'll touch on later. Contracts end on a regular schedule, and investors who want to maintain their bets must sell expiring contracts and buy new ones. Price differences between futures can increase or cut into returns. Investors have to keep money on deposit to own futures, and those funds earn interest.

Risks

There's a saying that every problem is an opportunity in disguise. If that's true, it might be said that gold investors see through the costume.

> **KEY POINT:**
> Investors in gold and other commodities give up the interest they would receive from bonds and the dividends that go along with stocks.

Risks to financial, economic, and political stability represent opportunities to make money in gold. Many investors turn to the metal as a haven from these kinds of threats. The phrase "safe haven" is often used even though a haven would be safe by definition.

Because of this tendency, growing investor confidence represents the biggest risk in owning gold. Investment demand may decline as countries and regions resolve issues that might lead to extreme outcomes.

Currency risk takes on a different meaning with gold. A stronger dollar makes the metal more costly for international investors, who must exchange their local currencies for dollars before they can make purchases. This may reduce investment demand and bring down the price.

Relative Value

Gold traded for less than $300 an ounce when the 2000s began. The market price was about $1,100 when the decade ended and approached $2,000 within the next two years. Did that surge make the precious metal too costly?

This kind of relative-value question isn't easily answered. Gold lacks a yield that can be compared with the yields on bonds or dividend paying stocks. The metal doesn't produce any revenue or earnings by sitting in a vault, so there are no price ratios to work with either.

Supply and demand figures can provide some insight. The World Gold Council, an industry trade group, presents them in quarterly reports. Gold buying is split into three categories: investment, jewelry, and technology. Even though jewelry makers are the biggest purchasers, investors have been gaining on them.

In the end, anyone trying to find out whether the metal is cheap, expensive, or fairly valued has to focus on the price of gold itself. Here are some comparisons that are worth making in the analysis.

History: The price comparisons and the chart in this chapter show that gold costs far more these days than it did when the 1990s began. The chart illustrates that a surge in the late 1970s gave way to two decades of declines. That's perspective worth having.

> **KEY POINT:**
> The price of gold depends on demand from jewelry makers, electronic equipment producers, and investors.

Other markets: Gold trades in several markets worldwide beyond the ones already mentioned. Investors with the ability to buy and sell in multiple markets can look at prices to determine where they can get the best deals. Similar opportunities may be available by comparing spot and futures prices.

Other precious metals: Silver attracts some buying from investors seeking a haven, and a ratio of gold and silver prices can serve as a guide to their decision making. The ratio show how many ounces of silver would cost as much as one ounce of gold. When gold trades at $1,800 an ounce and silver changes hands at $30, the number would be 60. Ratios can be calculated for gold versus platinum and palladium, two other precious metals.

Commodities

China's emergence as one of the world's largest economies has bolstered demand for raw materials. Imports of steel, iron ore, coal, copper, aluminum, and other industrial products have risen as the country has gone through a building boom. Oil imports have increased as China's energy needs have grown faster than production. Corn, wheat, soybeans, and other agricultural items have been shipped in growing numbers as the Chinese standard of living increases, giving consumers more money to spend on food.

Price increases spurred by the Chinese buying have fueled growth in investment demand for commodities. Greater interest in owning assets that perform differently than stocks and bonds and protect against inflation has contributed as well. Another catalyst has been the development of new ways to invest in them, such as exchange-traded funds (ETFs), which we'll cover later.

Commodities can be split into five categories: precious metals, base or industrial metals, energy, agriculture, and livestock. Growing demand for them has led to higher prices in each category, as Figure 19.3 shows.

Gold fits into the precious-metal category along with silver, platinum, and palladium. The latter two metals are largely limited to industrial use. They go into catalytic converters, which reduce auto pollution, and other products.

Copper is an example of a base metal. It's sometimes described as Dr. Copper, the metal with a Ph.D. in economics, because its gains and losses are a barometer of

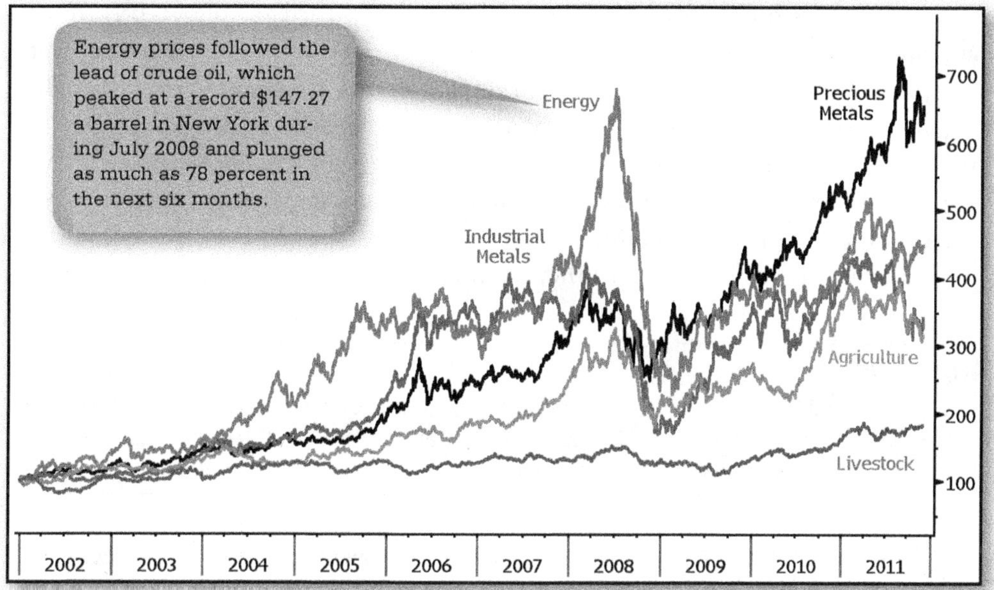

FIGURE 19.3 **Commodity Market Performance (December 31, 2001 = 100).**

the economy's prospects. Aluminum, lead, nickel, tin, and zinc are part of this group as well.

Crude oil dominates energy trading even though it's only part of a bigger picture. Heating oil and gasoline, two commodities made from crude, change hands actively. So do natural gas, coal, and electricity.

Grains such as corn, wheat, and soybeans are mainstays of agricultural commodity markets, as are foodstuffs, or food and beverages in raw form. Cocoa, coffee, sugar, and orange juice are all foodstuffs. The category can be stretched to include cotton, which comes from plants, and lumber, which begins with trees.

Cattle and hogs are examples of the livestock that change hands in commodity trading. Pork bellies, used to make bacon and featured in the 1983 movie "Trading Places," were in this group. Contracts on frozen bellies stopped trading in 2011 after restaurants shifted toward bacon made from fresh bellies.

All these products can be identified as **commodities** because they are widely available, essentially the same regardless of where they're produced, and raw materials rather than finished goods. Even gasoline is processed before it's sold at the pump.

Gold, oil wells, corn fields, or cattle herds are identical in terms of trading. The key difference in trading is between spot and futures markets, as opposed to primary and secondary markets.

DEFINITION:

Commodities

Commodities are raw materials. There are five main categories: precious metals, base or industrial metals, energy, agriculture, and livestock.

Spot markets on many commodities are small and hard to follow. Base metals are one exception because there's a spot market operated by the London Metal Exchange, which reports trading data. Precious metals are another, as spot trading occurs in gold, silver, platinum, and palladium. Futures markets are more active and widely followed than spot markets as a rule. When people discuss oil prices, they're more likely to refer to New York or London futures trading than spot prices in West Texas or the North Sea, two oil-producing regions that are closely followed. Futures can serve as price references for other commodities.

> **KEY POINT:**
> West Texas Intermediate, or WTI, is one of many grades of U.S. crude oil. Others include Bakken UHC (U.S. High Sweet Crude) and Louisiana Light Sweet. Crude is classified as light or heavy by its density, and as sweet or sour based on its sulfur content.

We'll concentrate on spot markets because we haven't looked at futures. When we do, we will feature commodities prominently.

Quotations

Even though spot prices for commodities aren't always benchmarks, it's worth taking a look at one that's closely tracked (see Figure 19.4).

The quote is for a grade of crude oil called West Texas Intermediate (WTI). It's a benchmark for oil contracts because it's plentiful, flows more easily than other grades, and is low in sulfur, which costs extra to remove.

WTI spot trading takes place over the counter, which means there's little data available. The quote is based on the price of the WTI futures contract closest to expiring, and anyone seeking a more detailed look at the market would have to focus on futures. Here are the components of the spot quote:

- **USCRWTIC:** Symbol for WTI on the Bloomberg terminal. USCR stands for U.S. crude, as there's more than one grade. The C at the end refers to Cushing, Oklahoma, where deliveries are made.
- **Down arrow:** Uptick/downtick arrow, showing the direction of the latest price change.
- **80.00:** Latest price. There's no dollar sign included before the amount because oil, like gold, is priced in dollars worldwide.
- **–5.75:** Change from the previous day, $5.75.
- **80.00/80.00:** Bid and ask prices, which are the same here.
- **At 13:52:** Time of the quote, using the 24-hour clock.
- **Op 80.39, Hi 80.98, Lo 80.00:** Opening, high, and low prices for the current day.

USCRWTIC ↓80.00 –5.75 80.00/80.00
At 13:52 Op 80.39 Hi 80.98 Lo 80.00

FIGURE 19.4 A West Texas Intermediate Crude-Oil Quote.

Three Rs

Metals, energy, agriculture, and livestock are the same as gold from an investor's perspective. The interest payments made on notes and bonds and the dividends available from stocks are nowhere to be found. Unless the price moves the right way, the commodity investment doesn't make any money.

The risks differ because demand for commodities is tied to economic growth rather than instability. There's a greater need for metals used in buildings, machinery, cars, appliances, electronics, and other products as the economy accelerates. Oil, natural gas, and other forms of energy provide the power to keep them running. Grains, meats, and other foods gain popularity as household income increases, especially in emerging markets.

Additionally, you can assess relative value in commodities in ways that are less relevant for gold. Investors can look at whether to sell them now or to store them for sale later. They can compare the cost of raw materials, such as crude oil, with the price of products to gauge processing profits.

Returns

Chances are that no one will offer a chance to buy 1,000 barrels of crude oil unless you're an institutional investor, a brokerage, or an energy company. Let's suspend disbelief for a moment and pretend the opportunity arose.

Assuming you made the deal, changes in the price of crude would determine if you turned a profit. Any gain would have to exceed storage and transportation costs for the oil, along with trading fees and expenses.

Returns for commodity futures work the same way as those for gold futures, so price changes aren't the whole story. Many investors sell contracts as the expiration date approaches and buy contracts that mature at a later date. This process is called a **futures roll**, and we'll learn more about it when we focus on futures. For now, it's enough to know that the price gap between contracts has an effect on returns.

DEFINITION:

Futures roll

In a futures roll, traders sell contracts about to come due and buy contracts with a later expiration date.

Interest on deposits has to be accounted for. The funds, known as margins, vary from one contract to the next. We'll revisit them in our look at futures.

Risks

Economic risk stands out as a concern for commodity investors as noted earlier. These days, the biggest risk is related to the Chinese economy. China is the world's largest buyer of many commodities, and slower growth in the country could send shock waves through markets for raw materials.

Market and liquidity risks are present, especially for investors owning commodities rather than futures. There may be less demand for 1,000 barrels of oil than for a contract on the same amount of crude. The oil buyer would have to take delivery, unlike the futures buyer, who can sell the contract later without owning the crude.

Commodity investors have to be mindful of event risk. Floods, droughts, and other natural disasters can cause price swings, tied to changes in supply. Shipping lane closures, pipeline breakdowns, and refinery shutdowns can have the same effect.

KEY POINT:
Like gold, oil is priced in dollars worldwide. This means WTI and Brent can be compared directly even though Brent is produced in a region where the dollar isn't the local currency.

Relative Value

Commodities offer more opportunity to analyze what's cheap, expensive, or fairly priced than gold if only because more than one product is available to consider. Each has its own balance of supply and demand, which can be tracked through industry data. For instance, U.S. government statistics influence prices for energy, farm products, and livestock.

Though equivalents for bond yields and stock price ratios are unavailable, that's less of an issue than it was for gold. Prices and price moves can be more telling, as you'll see from these possible comparisons.

History: Energy soared far more than other commodities during the 2000s and tumbled before the end of the decade, as the chart in this chapter shows. Precious metals ended up in a similar position more recently. Anyone making the comparison might conclude that history would repeat itself, a signal that gold and other precious metals were too expensive. That's the kind of insight available from studying past pricing.

Other markets: Oil, like gold, is traded around the world. Though crude varies more than gold in its makeup, investors can make judgments about relative value that account for those differences. As a price gap between two grades of crude widens or narrows, one or the other may become cheap. That happened in 2011 with WTI, a benchmark for U.S. trading, as Figure 19.5 illustrates. WTI changed hands for about $28 a barrel less than its European counterpart, North Sea Brent (Brent), during the year as shipments failed to keep pace with production.

Similar commodities: Five categories were defined in the chart. It's possible to split grains from food and fiber, namely cotton, in the agricultural products group. Prices for the commodities within each group provide a basis for making buying and selling decisions.

Raw material versus products: Oil markets have crack spreads. Crack refers to a catalytic cracker, a piece of refining equipment that turns crude into gasoline, heating oil, and other products. Spreads track the difference between the cost of crude and the market price of the products, a gauge of relative value.

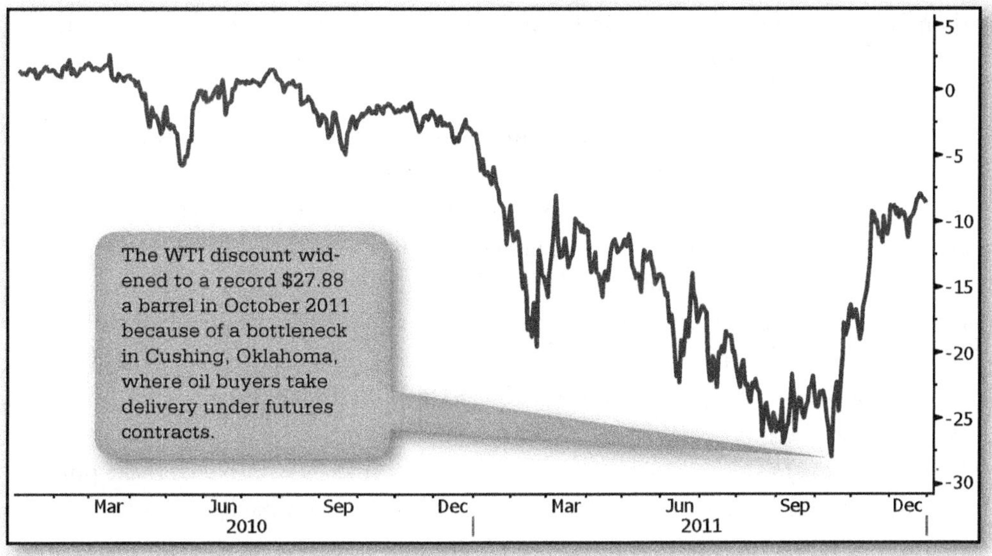

FIGURE 19.5 **Price Gap between WTI and Brent (in $/barrel).**

Refiners make more money when these spreads widen and less when they narrow. Similarly, crush spreads compare the cost of soybeans with the price of soybean oil and soybean meal, produced by crushing the beans.

Real Estate

Yale University's endowment fund became a model for its peers by making investments well beyond stocks, bonds, and money market securities. Under David Swensen, who was named chief investment officer in 1985, the endowment posted an average annual return of 13.1 percent for the 20 years ending in June 2010.

Near the end of the period, the fund had the biggest chunk of its money in "real assets," as defined in financial reports. Oil and gas fields and farmland, which benefited from commodity price increases, were among them. There was also real estate.

When Yale's endowment and other institutional investors put money into real estate, they have two choices at their disposal. First, they can buy properties themselves, hire managers to run them, and earn the income they produce. Second, they can invest in real estate funds and leave all the work to the fund manager.

KEY POINT:
The Moody's/REAL index is based on commercial real estate sales valued at more than $2.5 million. The S&P/Case-Shiller indexes reflect home sales across the U.S. and in 20 metropolitan areas.

Most individual investors don't have the same kinds of opportunities because the price tag for real estate is too high. They might be able to buy a home or two and rent them, but that's about it. Real estate funds are a less costly investment along with real estate investment trusts (REITs), which are specifically created to own property and are governed by different rules than the average company.

We'll look at REITs more closely later, when we revisit the investments covered so far. For now, let's focus directly on the real estate.

There are three main types of investment properties: commercial, residential, and land. Shopping malls and stores, office buildings, warehouses, self-storage facilities, hotels and motels, and hospitals are examples of commercial real estate. Apartment buildings are in the residential category along with mobile home parks. The oil and gas fields and farms that Yale's endowment fund owns take their place alongside timberland, mine sites, and undeveloped land as investment choices.

The value of commercial property has much to do with the economy's performance. When consumers are spending more, the value of the places where they make purchases is likely to rise. When corporate profits are increasing, companies are more likely to expand, which means they may have to add office and warehouse space. They are more likely to send employees on business trips, benefiting the hotel and motel industry.

U.S. commercial real estate values went through a bigger boom and bust than home prices in the 2000s and beyond, as the chart below shows. The swings in commercial prices are reflected in an index from Moody's Investors Service and another company, Real Estate Analytics LLC. The housing index comes from S&P, working with economists Robert Shiller and Karl Case (see Figure 19.6).

Though economic growth influences residential real estate values, the two don't move in tandem. Demand for rental housing may rise when the economy falters because fewer people can afford to buy homes. This was the case during the 2007–2009 recession and its aftermath, a period in which apartment demand rose as falling house prices deterred many potential buyers.

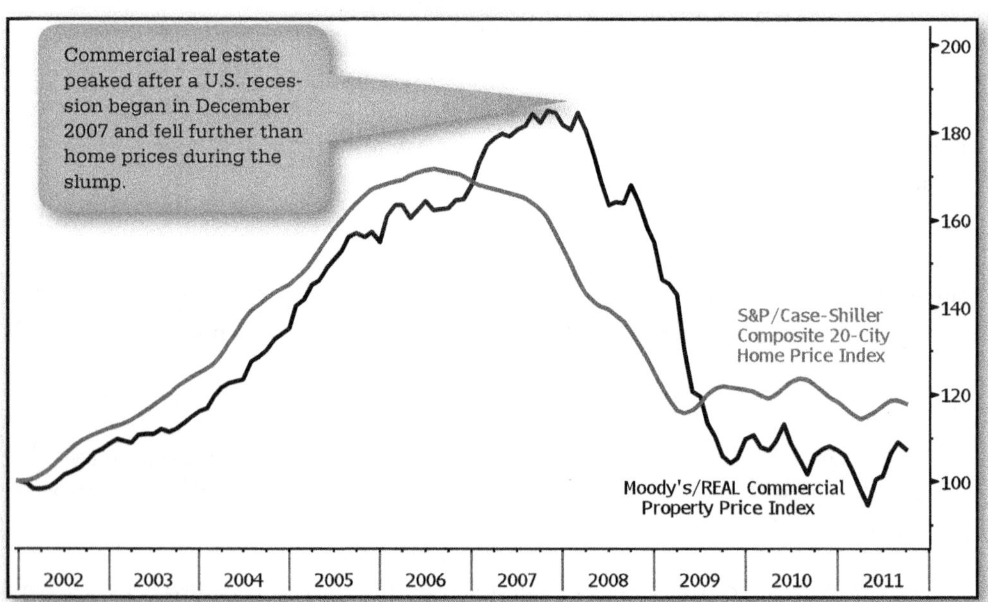

FIGURE 19.6 U.S. Commercial Real Estate, Home Prices (December 2001 = 100).

Land values mirror the economy more closely because the pace of growth influences the value of the commodities produced there. The housing bubble that ended in 2007 meant higher prices for lumber and the timberland where the wood came from. China's increasing demand for crop imports has had a similar effect on farmland. Higher energy and metals prices have meant rising values for oil and gas leases and mining rights.

The primary market for real estate is composed of sales, leases, and rentals that property developers make. When a building or piece of land gets bought, the purchase takes place in the secondary market.

Specific properties seldom change hands, and there isn't an exchange where they are bought and sold. Instead, real estate brokers line up property listings and work with potential purchasers to arrange sales. Investment banks take the place of brokers for more costly deals.

Quotations

Price quotes on real estate are about as simple as it gets. They consist of an offer price, which is the dollar amount that a seller wants for the property.

There are no symbols, market prices, volume figures, or any other details we have become used to seeing for securities. Properties don't change hands often enough to generate those kinds of data.

Three Rs

When we looked at notes and bonds earlier, we saw yield was a common denominator for deciding what was cheap, expensive, and fairly valued. Real estate has a similar gauge, known as capitalization (cap) rates.

Cap rates indicate how much an investor stands to earn on a property. They're based on income, operating expenses, and purchase prices. Only purchase prices are fixed, which means the rates may be more volatile than bond yields. We'll see how they're put together shortly.

DEFINITION:

Cap rates

Capitalization (cap) rates indicate the annual return from owning a property. They can be calculated for specific buildings and land and for real estate companies.

Real estate owners face the same kind of business-related risks as holders of a company's debt and equity. They must make relative-value judgments, complicated by a lack of publicly available data. Let's spend some time looking at how the three Rs apply to them.

Returns

As yields are a starting point for note and bond returns, cap rates show the potential gains from real estate. They provide a way to evaluate properties and to determine if deals are worth doing or avoiding.

Cap rate calculations begin with rent or lease payments, depending on the type of building. For example, let's consider a shopping center that receives $12,000 a month from the retail stores located there. Multiply the amount by 12 and you end up with $144,000 a year in income.

We have to subtract the costs of maintenance, repairs, and other expenses of running the building. Let's assume they totaled $24,000 for the latest year. Subtract that amount and we're left with $120,000, which real estate investors would define as net operating income.

There's one more detail to add to this scenario: the property is up for sale with a $1.5 million asking price. Prospective buyers would have to evaluate its worth. As part of that process, they would want to know how much they stand to make on the deal.

Cap rates indicate what's possible. The rate for our example is 8 percent, or $120,000 divided by $1.5 million. If a buyer pays less for the shopping center, the rate will increase accordingly. If multiple bidders are competing and the price rises, the rate will drop. The relationship is the same as the link we saw earlier between note and bond prices and yields.

Differences between cap rates and yields exist that are worth noting. Net operating income isn't guaranteed. Next year's earnings may decline as retailers close and stores go unoccupied, or as maintenance costs pile up. Either of these events would reduce the cap rate. On the other hand, income may increase as store leases expire and the owner raises rates. The cap rate would rise accordingly.

The 8 percent figure may not be comparable to cap rates for other shopping centers. Data used to calculate the rates often aren't publicly available, and accounting differences among property owners may affect the results. Less room for discrepancies is available with 10-year note yields, for instance, as security prices and payment amounts can be verified.

Financing costs are another variable to consider though they weren't included in our example. The 8 percent figure assumed the buyer paid cash for the property, which is seldom done. Any interest expense on debt would have to be subtracted from net operating income to calculate returns.

Risks

When we revisit the first level of risks, we can see two significant ones for investors in real estate. Liquidity risk is relatively high because offices, apartments, and other buildings often carry price tags in the millions of dollars and can take months or years to sell. Economic risk is an issue for owners of commercial properties, as their success in finding tenants and producing income depends on how well businesses are performing.

Business risk, event risk, and industry risk apply. Real estate investors may end up with properties that are less lucrative or are in less desirable locations, as the market changes over time. Disputes may occur with leaseholders or tenants that result in lost payments and legal costs.

Fires, floods, and other disasters can destroy and damage buildings, which reduces income and increases expenses at the same time. And when the industry takes a turn for the worse, there's plenty of suffering to go around, as Figure 19.6 makes clear.

Relative Value

The similarity between cap rates and note and bond yields carries over to their use in evaluating what's cheap, expensive, or fairly priced. Comparing rates is similar to studying yield spreads. The higher the rate, the more value there may be in a property, and vice versa.

Cap rates provide a way to compare returns on real estate and other types of investments. Blackstone Group LP carried out a $39 billion buyout of Equity Office Properties at a 5.3 percent cap rate, as noted in a February 2007 story from Bloomberg News. That was a record low, according to Green Street Advisors Inc., a research firm that came up with the figure. Ten-year Treasury notes yielded about 4.7 percent, which indicated the additional return on the deal was only about 0.6 percentage point.

STEP-BY-STEP:
CAP RATE MATH

1. Suppose an office building is up for sale at $3 million.
2. Income from rents and leases is $25,000 a month. Multiply the monthly amount by 12 for the annual income: $300,000.
3. Maintenance and repair costs are $120,000 a year. Subtract the expenses from annual income for the net operating income: $180,000.
4. Divide $180,000 into $3 million to calculate the cap rate, expressed as a percentage: 6 percent.

KEY POINT:
Cap rates can vary more than note and bond yields over time because a property's cash flow and maintenance costs have more room to fluctuate than interest payments.

Even so, this analysis has limits. Cap rates aren't turned into the equivalent of yield curves as the time element isn't the same. Instead of maturity dates, the timing of deals matters. More recent sales are usually a better gauge of value than those completed months earlier, when the real estate market may have differed.

To address the issue, brokers and investment banks obtain data on comparable properties (comps) that have changed hands. Looking at the comps helps the firms set selling prices along with aiding potential buyers.

Replacement value and income potential provide a basis for judging if real estate is worth buying. The first gauge is based on the projected cost of a new building that's similar to the one being sold. The second focuses on how much money the property could generate, as opposed to the current income.

Test Yourself

Answer the following multiple-choice questions:

1. Investors seeking to own gold can buy:
   a. Jewelry.
   b. Bullion.
   c. Futures.
   d. All of the above.
   e. a and b only.
2. These organizations own gold:
   a. The Federal Reserve.
   b. The World Bank.
   c. The United Nations.
   d. All of the above.
   e. a and b only.
3. The benchmark grade of U.S. crude oil is commonly called:
   a. USCR.
   b. WTI.
   c. Brent.
   d. All of the above.
   e. a and b only.
4. Commodity-related properties that investors can buy include:
   a. Farms.
   b. Timberland.
   c. Oil and gas fields.
   d. All of the above.
   e. a and b only.
5. Cap-rate calculations for real estate exclude:
   a. Rental income.
   b. Maintenance costs.
   c. Interest payments.
   d. All of the above.
   e. a and b only.

Answers: 1. d; 2. e; 3. b; 4.d; 5. c

CHAPTER 20

Indexes

From David Wilson, *Visual Guide to Financial Markets* (Hoboken, New Jersey: John Wiley & Sons, 2012), Chapter 5.

The 2000s have been called a lost decade for U.S. stock investors because they lost money even after taking dividends into account. Figure 20.1 shows how stocks fared relative to the dollar, bonds, commodities, and real estate in the 10-year period.

This kind of comparison is made possible by market indexes, which track performance over time. Indexes provide a way to gauge the daily performance of currency, debt, equity, and hard asset markets and a way to assess their moves during the day.

Each market has indicators that provide more specific data. Stock indexes, for example, can be used to compare larger companies with those that are mid-sized and smaller. They track industry groups and other market segments.

Money managers use indexes to show whether they're beating the market. Funds specializing in the largest U.S. companies may focus on how their returns compare with those of the Standard & Poor's 500 Index, a gauge of similar stocks. Bond funds may use debt indexes for the same purpose.

Indexes provide a basis for the derivatives and funds that we'll come across in looking at indirect investing. Various contracts are tied to an index's value, and hundreds of funds are designed to mirror a benchmark's moves.

Put another way, indexes let you follow markets and provide a way for you to invest in them. This dual purpose is more than enough reason to take a closer look at these indicators.

KEY POINT:

Indexes are gauges of market performance. They serve as the underlying assets for some derivatives and as benchmarks for funds.

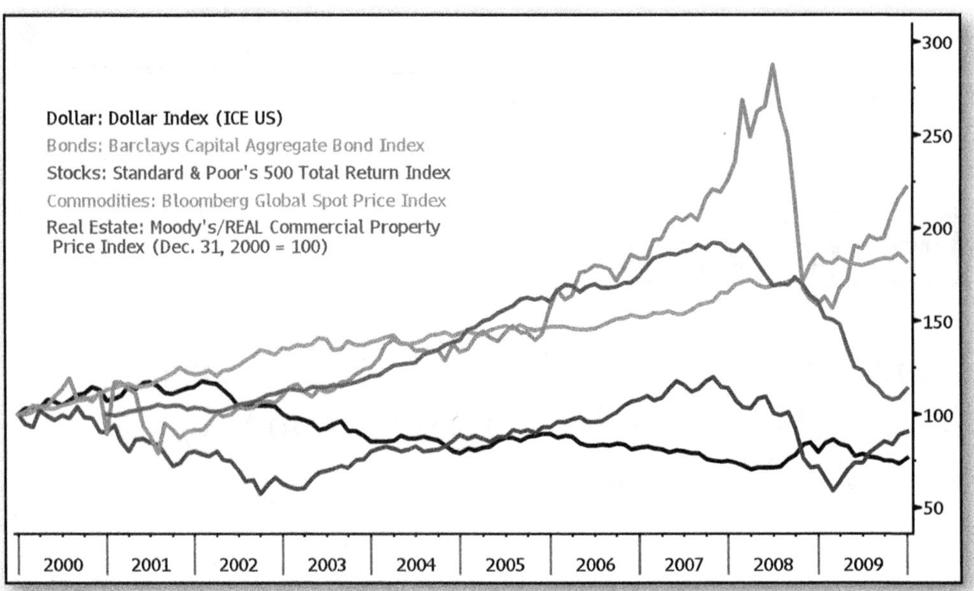

FIGURE 20.1 Market Performance during the 2000s (December 31, 1999 = 100).

Currency

When people talk about a weaker or stronger dollar, they might be referring to another specific currency, like the yen. In many cases, they're talking about a gain or loss of value against a number of currencies.

Indexes are the easiest way to track the broader moves. Figure 20.2 compares the performance of three indicators during the 2000s.

FIGURE 20.2 Currency Index Performance (December 31, 1999 = 100).
Sources: ICE US, Federal Reserve, Bloomberg.

The Dollar Index is among them. The indicator, calculated by the IntercontinentalExchange (ICE), is based on the value of the U.S. currency against the euro, Japanese yen, British pound, Canadian dollar, Swedish krona, and Swiss franc.

Trade is taken into account in determining each currency's share of the index. The euro accounts for more than half of its value. That's based on the amount of imports and exports moving between the United States and countries using the European currency.

Two **trade-weighted indexes** are compiled by the Federal Reserve (Fed). One of them shows the dollar's value against major currencies, defined by the Fed as the Australian dollar and the components of the Dollar Index. The other is broader, including the Chinese yuan, Mexican peso. and other emerging market currencies.

DEFINITION:

Trade-weighted indexes

A trade-weighted index is based on the value of a country's currency against several others. Each currency's weighting in the index is tied to the share of trade with the country.

These indexes, and others compiled by firms such as Barclays Capital and Goldman Sachs, are based on the dollar's swings against other currencies. Deposit rates, mentioned earlier as an influence on investment returns, aren't part of the calculations.

Debt

Lending money to governments and companies produced the kinds of returns in the 2000s that were associated with stocks in past decades. Figure 20.3 shows the relative performance of government debt, corporate debt, mortgage-backed debt, and municipal debt, as well as Treasury bills, during the 10-year period.

In Figure 20.3, the four bond indexes were relatively close to each other when a crisis began to sweep through the financial system in 2007. At that point, many investors bought Treasury securities for their relative safety and sold riskier types of debt, especially corporate securities.

KEY POINT:

Indexes can track price changes or total returns, which include interest or dividend income. Bond benchmarks reflect returns, while the most widely followed stock-market indicators are price-based.

It's worth noting that these indexes weren't provided by exchanges, which play a minor role in bond trading. The government bond indicator is compiled by Bloomberg, along with the European Federation of Financial Analysts Societies (EFFAS), a regional trade group.

The corporate, mortgage, and municipal indexes come from Barclays Capital, a unit of Barclays Plc that's among the biggest dealers in U.S. bonds. The Treasury-bill index is from Standard & Poor's and a market data unit of BGC Partners Inc., a bond broker.

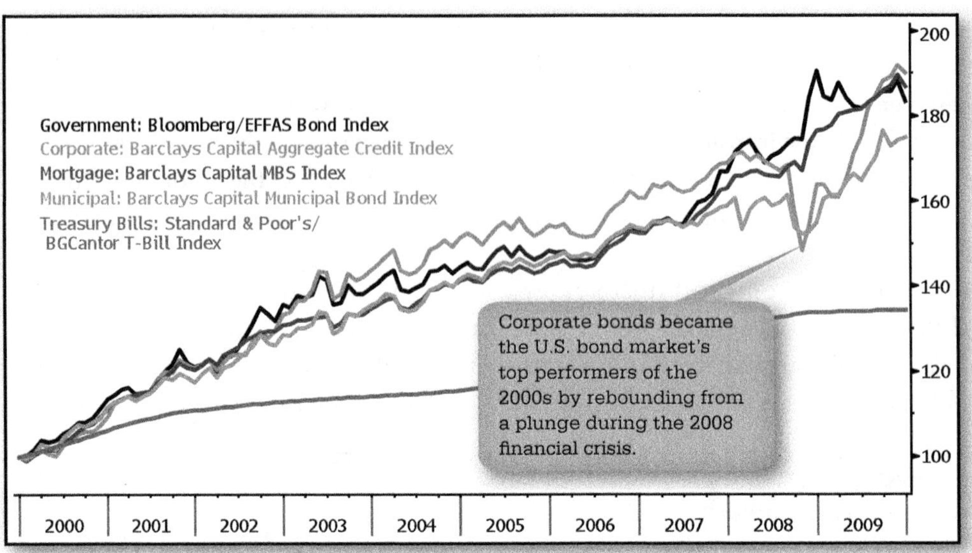

FIGURE 20.3 Bond Index Performance (December 31, 1999 = 100).

BGC is a recent entrant into the world of bond data, as the bill index made its debut in March 2010. The Barclays Capital indicators have been around for longer, as they were produced by Lehman Brothers Holdings Inc. before that firm went into bankruptcy in September 2008.

Bond indexes from securities firms have traditionally served as market benchmarks. Bank of America Corp.'s Merrill Lynch unit and JPMorgan Chase & Co. are among the providers of index series similar to Barclays Capital's.

S&P and other independent providers compile bond indexes as well. Bloomberg produces gauges for Treasuries and government bonds in 25 other countries through an agreement with EFFAS.

Regardless of who puts them together and calculates their value, bond indexes are based on total returns, which account for interest payments and price changes. This feature sets them apart from the most widely followed stock indexes.

Other indexes track the average yield spread between a specific category of bonds and U.S. Treasuries. These are called **option-adjusted spreads (OAS)** because they account for the value of any options built into the bonds. A borrower might be able to buy back the debt before maturity at a set price, or an owner may be able to sell it back the same way. Taking them out of the equation ensures the bonds are comparable to each other.

DEFINITION:

Option-adjusted spreads

Option-adjusted spreads (OAS) exclude the estimated value of options to call, put, or convert individual securities. They are used to calculate some bond indexes.

Indexes may focus on bond-market segments, especially for government debt. The Bloomberg and EFFAS indexes, for instance, break down Treasury bills, notes, and bonds into six categories based on the amount of time to maturity. There are indexes for securities maturing in less than a year, 1 to 3 years, 3 to 5 years, 5 to 7 years, 7 to 10 years, and more than 10 years.

Equity

U.S. stock-market reports in newspapers, online, and on radio and television cite three indexes as a matter of course. They are the Dow Jones Industrial Average (DJIA or Dow), the Standard & Poor's 500 Index, and the NASDAQ Composite Index.

The Dow average is the oldest of these indicators. It has been calculated since 1896 and has been composed of 30 stocks since 1928. The average's members are among the biggest U.S. companies. Not all of them are industrials these days as financial stocks are included.

Standard & Poor's introduced the S&P 500 in 1957, and data for the index go back to 1928. The S&P 500 tracks more of the largest U.S. companies than the Dow industrials and is more widely used as a gauge of money managers' performance. Funds with trillions of dollars in assets use the S&P 500 as a benchmark. Some are created specifically to mirror the index, and we'll learn more about them later.

The NASDAQ Composite tracks all of the shares listed on the NASDAQ Stock Market. Technology companies account for the bulk of its value. Two of the biggest ones are Microsoft Corp. and Intel Corp., which became the first NASDAQ companies to join the Dow industrials in 1999.

Figure 20.4 shows how the lost decade of the 2000s looked for each of the three indicators.

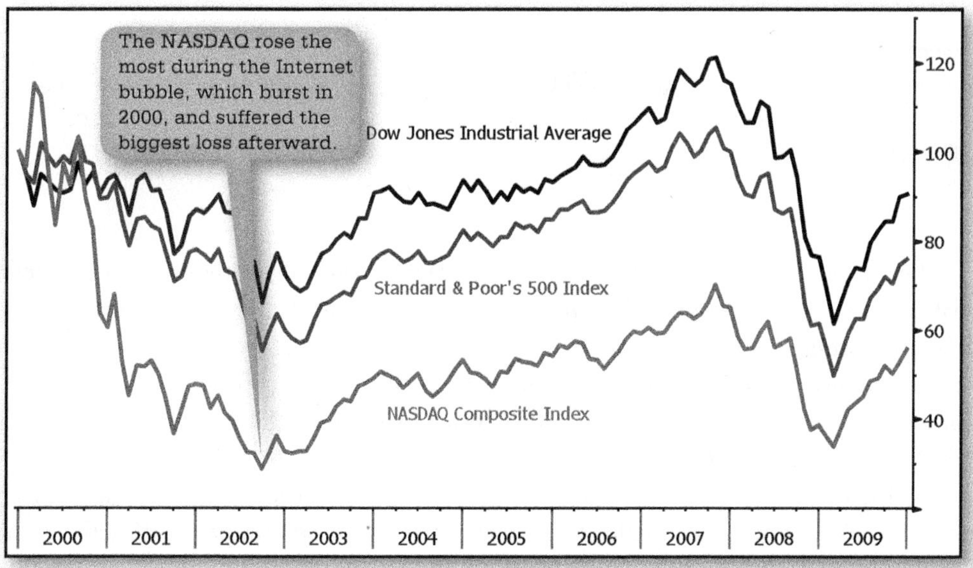

FIGURE 20.4 Stock Index Performance (December 31, 1999 = 100).

Stock indexes can be defined by three criteria, starting with their coverage. The Dow industrials and the S&P 500 cover the entire U.S. market, but the NASDAQ Composite is tied to a specific exchange.

Other indexes focus on market segments. The Russell 2000 Index, compiled by Russell Investments, is a good example. The Russell 2000 is a popular indicator for small-cap companies, which have less market value than those in the Dow average or the S&P 500.

S&P has four levels of indexes that track industry groups. The broadest consists of 10 categories, including two for consumer-related companies. Energy, financial, health care, industrial, raw material, technology, and telephone and utility companies round out the lineup. The narrowest has about 130 industries, including some that consist of only one or two companies.

The second criteria is the method of weighting or determining each stock's effect on the value of an index. Share prices are used for the Dow industrials. The company whose stock costs the most to buy counts the most in the average, and vice versa. Company size doesn't matter, so the smallest member of the average could have the biggest effect on its performance.

Weighting stocks by market capitalization (market cap) addresses the size issue. The S&P 500 was calculated this way, and the NASDAQ Composite still is. A drawback emerged as funds made greater use of indexes to gauge their performance and guide their trading. Their decision making was influenced by shares they couldn't buy because insiders and major investors owned them. Those shares counted toward market value even though they were off the market.

Index providers resolved this concern by using **float**, or the number of shares available for trading, in place of market cap to weight each company. The S&P 500 became a float-adjusted index, and others followed.

DEFINITION:

Float

A float is the number of shares available for trading. Shares owned by founders and their families, officers, directors, other insiders, and related companies are excluded because they generally don't trade.

These changes weren't enough to please everyone. Another method was developed that took market value out of the equation entirely. Robert Arnott, the founder of the Research Affiliates LLC investment firm, created indexes that weighed companies by sales, earnings, dividends, and other company-specific gauges. Arnott's approach, fundamental indexing, reflects his view that a company's market value is often out of line with the performance of its business.

Finally, there's the role of dividends. The most popular stock indexes are based only on price changes as a rule. This means they can't be compared directly with bond indexes, which include interest payments. To overcome this hurdle, stock index providers compile total return versions of their indicators.

Hard Assets

Although gold, commodities, and real estate are similar because of their hard-asset status, their markets differ. Indexes that track them all aren't readily available. Figure 20.5 shows each one separately by comparing gold with commodity and real estate indexes.

Gold's spot price plays the role of an index in the chart. That's the case in the precious metals market, where it's a widely followed benchmark.

> **KEY POINT:**
> The three main benchmarks for U.S. stocks are each calculated differently. The Dow average is price weighted, the S&P 500 is float weighted, and the NASDAQ Composite is market-cap weighted.

Commodities are represented by the Bloomberg Spot Commodity Index, based on price quotes on 24 raw materials for immediate delivery. They are divided into six categories, including energy, precious metals, and base metals. Corn, soybeans, and wheat comprise the crops category. Sugar, coffee, cocoa, and cotton are classified as food and fiber. A livestock group consists of steers and hogs.

Other commodity gauges that are called spot indexes are based on futures prices. For those indicators, "spot" refers to market performance, the main component of total returns. Other sources of returns are included in some commodity futures indexes as we'll learn when we examine indexes based on derivatives.

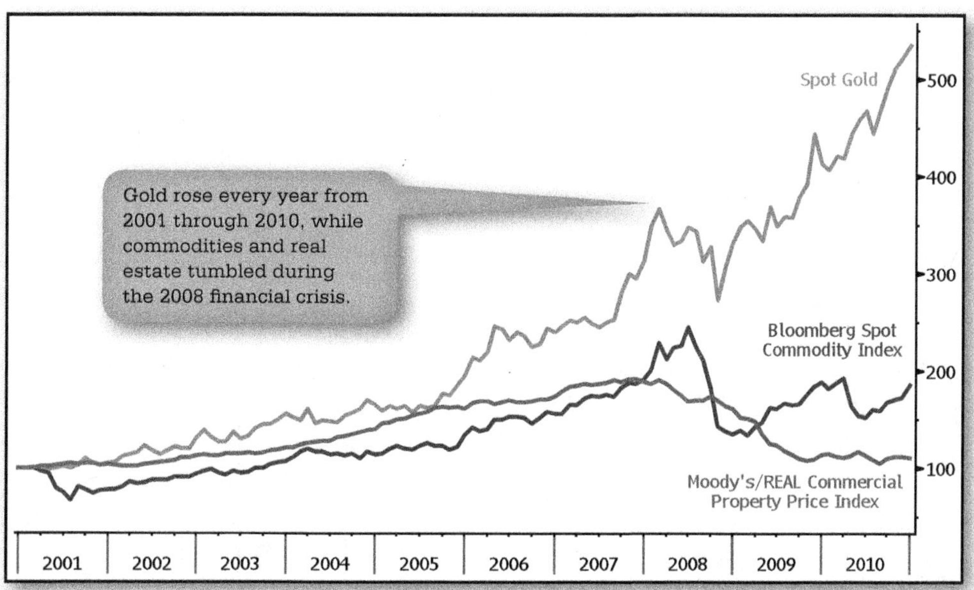

FIGURE 20.5 Hard Asset Performance (December 31, 2000 = 100).

The Moody's/REAL index represents commercial real estate. Moody's and Real Estate Analytics work with two other organizations on the index. The data are compiled by Real Capital Analytics Inc., and the methodology comes from the Massachusetts Institute of Technology's Center for Real Estate.

Moody's publishes the index, based on sale prices, every month. Indicators for apartments, offices, industrial buildings, and retail stores are available every quarter. There are gauges for metropolitan areas as well.

Quarterly indexes are also available from the National Council of Real Estate Investment Fiduciaries (NCREIF), a trade group that serves institutional investors. The council tracks farmland and timberland prices and the performance of private equity funds specializing in real estate.

CHAPTER 21

Basic Concepts and Calculations

From Perry J. Kaufman, *Trading Systems and Methods, + Website,* 5th edition (Hoboken, New Jersey: John Wiley & Sons, 2013), Chapter 2.

Economics is not an exact science: it consists merely of Laws of Probability. The most prudent investor, therefore, is one who pursues only a general course of action which is "normally" right and who avoids acts and policies which are "normally" wrong.

—L. L. B. Angas

New technology gives us a sense of security. There is data from everywhere in the world at our fingertips, programs that perform sophisticated calculations instantly, and access to anyone at any time.

As Isaac Asimov foretold, there will come a time when we will no longer know how to do the calculation for long division because miniature, voice-activated computers will be everywhere. We might not even need to be able to add; it will all be done for us. We will just assume that the answer is correct, because computers don't make mistakes.

In a small way this is happening now. Not everyone checks their spreadsheet calculations by hand to be certain they are correct before going further. Nor does everyone print the intermediate results of computer calculations to verify their accuracy. Computers don't make mistakes, but people do.

With computer software and trading platforms making price analysis easier and more sophisticated, we no longer think of the steps involved in a moving average or linear regression. A few years ago, we looked at the correlation between investments only when absolutely necessary because they were too complicated and time-consuming to calculate. It would even be difficult to know if you had made a mistake without having someone else repeat the same calculations. Now we face a different problem: If the computer does it all, we lose our understanding of why a moving average trendline differs from a linear regression. Without looking at the data, we don't see an erroneous outlier or that the stock wasn't adjusted for splits. By not reviewing each hypothetical trade, we miss seeing that the slippage can turn a profit into a loss.

To avoid losing the edge needed to create a profitable trading strategy, the basic tools of the trade are explained in this chapter. Those of you already familiar with these methods may skip over it; others need to be confident that they can perform these calculations manually even while they use a spreadsheet.

Helpful Software

In Excel, many of the functions, such as the standard deviation, are readily accessible at any time. The more advanced statistical functions require that you install the Add-Ins, which also come free with Excel. These include histograms, regression analysis, *F*-test, *t*-test, *z*-test, Fourier analysis, and various smoothing techniques. To install these add-ins in Excel 2010, go to File/Options/Add-Ins and select the *Analysis Toolpak*. You will also want the *Solver Add-in*. Once installed, which takes only a few seconds, these functions can be accessed in the Data menu at the top of the screen. You should find the Data Analysis and Solver options at the far right on the menu bar.

There are other very useful and user-friendly statistical programs available at a wide range of sophistication and price. One of the best values is *Pro-Stat* by Poly Software (polysoftware.com). The examples in this chapter will use both Excel and Pro-Stat.

About Data and Averaging

The Law of Averages

We begin at the beginning, with the law of averages, a greatly misunderstood and misquoted principle. In trading, the law of averages is most often referred to when an abnormally long series of losses is expected to be offset by an equal and opposite run of profits. It is equally wrong to expect a market that is currently overvalued or overbought to next become undervalued or oversold. That is not what is meant by the law of averages. Over a large sample, the bulk of events will be scattered close to the average in such a way that the typical values overwhelm the abnormal events and cause them to be insignificant.

This principle is illustrated in Figure 21.1, where the number of average items is extremely large, and the addition of a small abnormal grouping to one side of an average group of near-normal data does not affect the balance. It is the same as being the only passenger on a jumbo jet. Your weight is insignificant to the operation of the airplane and not noticed when you move about the cabin. A long run of profits, losses, or an unusually sustained price movement is simply a rare, abnormal event that will be offset over time by the overwhelming large number of normal events.

In-Sample and Out-of-Sample Data

Proper test procedures call for separating data into *in-sample* and *out-of-sample* sets. For now, consider the most important points. All testing is overfitting the data, yet

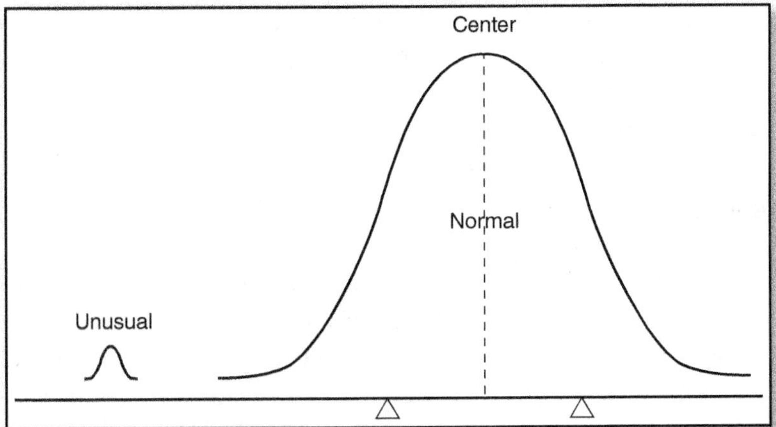

FIGURE 21.1 The Law of Averages. The normal cases overwhelm the unusual ones. It is not necessary for the extreme cases to alternate—one higher, the next lower—to create a balance.

there is no way to find out if an idea or system works without testing it. By setting aside data that you have not seen to use for validation, you have a better chance that your idea will work before putting money on it.

There are many ways to select in-sample data. For example, if you have 20 years of price history, you might choose to use the first 10 years for testing and reserve the second 10 years for validation. But then markets change over time; they become more volatile and may be more or less trending. It might be best to use alternating periods of in-sample and out-of-sample data, in 2-year intervals, provided that you never look at the data during the out-of-sample periods. Alternating these periods may create a problem for continuous, long-term trends.

The most important factor when reserving out-of-sample data is that you get only one chance to use it. Once you have done your best to create the rules for a trading program, you then run that program through the unseen data. If the results are successful, then you can trade the system, but if it fails, then you are also done. You cannot look at the reasons why it failed and change the trading method to perform better. You would have introduced *feedback,* and your out-of-sample data is considered contaminated. The second try will always be better, but it is now overfitted.

How Much Data Is Enough?

Statisticians will say, "More is better." The more data you test, the more reliable your results. Technical analysis is fortunate to be based on a perfect set of data. Each price that is recorded by the exchange, whether it's IBM at the close of trading in New York on May 5, or the price of Eurodollar interest rates at 10:05 in Chicago, is a confirmed, precise value.

Remember that when you use in-sample and out-of-sample data for development, you need more data. You will only get half the combinations and patterns when 50% of the data has been withheld.

Economic Data Most other statistical data are not as timely, not as precise, and not as reliable as the price and volume of stocks, futures, ETFs, and other exchange-traded products. Economic data, such as the Producer Price Index or Housing Starts, are released as monthly averages, and can be seasonally adjusted. A monthly average represents a broad range of numbers. In the case of the PPI, some producers may have paid less than the average of the prior month and some more, but the average was +0.02. The lack of a range of values, or a standard deviation of the component values, reduces the usefulness of the information. This statistical data is often revised in the following month; sometimes those revisions can be quite large. When working with the Department of Energy (DOE) weekly data releases, you will need to know the history of the exact numbers released as well as the revisions, if you are going to design a trading method that reacts to those reports. You may find that it is much easier to find the revised data, which is not what you really need.

If you use economic data, you must be aware of when that data is released. The United States is very precise and prompt but other countries can be months or years late in releasing data. If the input to your program is monthly data and comes from the CRB Yearbook, be sure that you check when that data was actually available.

Sample Error When an average is used, it is necessary to have enough data to make that average accurate. Because much statistical data is gathered by sampling, particular care is given to accumulating a sufficient amount of representative data. This holds true with prices as well. Averaging a few prices, or analyzing small market moves, will show more erratic results. It is difficult to draw an accurate picture from a very small sample.

When using small, incomplete, or representative sets of data, the approximate error, or accuracy, of the sample can be found using the standard deviation. A large standard deviation indicates an extremely scattered set of points, which in turn makes the average less representative of the data. This process is called the *testing of significance*. Accuracy increases as the number of items becomes larger, and the measurement of *sample error* becomes proportionately smaller

$$Sample\ error = \frac{1}{\sqrt{Number\ of\ items\ sampled}} = \frac{1}{\sqrt{N}}\ or\ \frac{1}{sqrt(N)}$$

Therefore, using only one item has a sample error of 100%; with four items, the error is 50%. The size of the error is important to the reliability of any trading system. If a system has had only four trades, whether profits or losses, it is very difficult to draw any reliable conclusions about future performance. There must be sufficient trades to assure a comfortably small error factor. To reduce the error to 5%, there must be 400 trades. This presents a dilemma for a very slow trend-following method that may only generate two or three trades each year. To compensate for this, the identical method can be applied across many markets and the number of trades used collectively.

Representative Data. The amount of data is a good estimate of its usefulness; however, the data should represent at least one bull market, one bear market, and some sideways periods. More than one of each is even better. If you were to use 10 years of daily S&P Index values from 1990 to 2000, or 25 years of 10-year Treasury notes through 2010, you would only see a bull market. A trading strategy would be profitable whenever it was a buyer, if you held the position long enough. Unless you included a variety of other price patterns, you would not be able to create a strategy that would survive a downturn in the market. Your results would be unrealistic.

Data That Is No Longer Useful There are clear cases when a stock or futures market has undergone a structural change and the current data is different from historic data. The evolution of General Electric from a manufacturer of light bulbs to a massive financial institution represents a structural change. Its transformation back to a manufacturing company, announced in 2010, may be another structural change. A company that began in the United States, such as McDonald's, but expanded to have large international exposure also shows a structural change in its price patterns. In foreign exchange, we have seen the individual European currencies first tied together by agreement, then finally merged into a single unit, the euro.

Is it important to include historic data in your testing when that data represents a different company profile or a different geopolitical situation? Ideally, your strategy is robust if it can adapt to these changing profiles and show consistently profitable returns over a long test period. The statisticians have that point in their favor—longer really is better. These companies and markets will continue to evolve, and your program will need to continue to adapt.

As a very fast trader, you may think about limiting your testing to much shorter periods. If you trade once each day, then in 5 years you would generate 1,250 trades; in 10 years, 2,500 trades. If your trading strategy is profitable over 2,500 trades, then you've satisfied the issue of the sampling error. However, you may not have included data that is representative of different types of markets and a variety of price patterns. Even with a large number of trades, tests spanning many years will be needed to show robustness.

Safety First It is important to remember that the accuracy of your testing depends on both the amount of data used and the number of trades generated by the system. If your estimates of loss are not reliable, you put your investment at risk.

On Average

In working with numbers, it is often necessary to use representative values. The range of values or the average may be substituted to change a single price into a general characteristic in order to solve a problem. The average (arithmetic mean) of many values can be a preferable substitute for any one value. For example, the average retail price of one pound of coffee in the Northeast is more meaningful to a cost-of-living calculation than the price at any one store. However, not all data can be combined or averaged and still have meaning. The average of all prices taken on the same day would not say anything about an individual market that was part of the average. Averaging the prices of unrelated items, such as a box of breakfast cereal, the hourly cost of automobile repair, and the price of the German DAX index, would produce a number of questionable values. The average of a group of numbers must have some useful meaning.

The average can be misleading in other ways. Consider coffee, which rose from \$0.40 to \$2.00 per pound in one year. The average price of this product may appear to be \$1.20; however, this would not account for the time that coffee was sold at various price levels. Table 21.1 divides the coffee price into four equal intervals, then shows that the time spent at these levels was uniformly opposite to the price rise. That is, prices remained at lower levels longer and at higher levels for shorter time periods, which is very normal price behavior.

When the time spent at each price level is included, it can be seen that the average price should be lower than \$1.20. One way to calculate this, knowing the specific number of days in each interval, is by using a weighted average of the price

$$W = \frac{a_1 d_1 + a_2 d_2 + a_3 d_3 + a_4 d_4}{d_1 + d_2 + d_3 + d_4}$$

and its respective interval

$$W = \frac{6000 + 8000 + 8400 + 7200}{280}$$

$$W = 105.71$$

This result can vary based on the number of time intervals used; however, it gives a better idea of the correct average price. There are two other averages for which time is an important element—the geometric mean and the harmonic mean.

Geometric Mean

The *geometric mean* represents a growth function in which a price change from 50 to 100 is as important as a change from 100 to 200. If there are *n* prices, $a_1, a_2, a_3, \ldots, a_n$, then the geometric mean is the *n*th root of the product of the prices

$$G = (a_1 \times a_2 \times a_3 \times \cdots \times a_n)^{1/n}$$

or

$$\texttt{product}(a_1, a_2, a_3, \ldots, a_n)^{1/n}$$

TABLE 21.1 Weighting an Average

Prices Go From	To	Average During Interval	Total Days for Interval	Weighted	1/a
40	80	$a_1 = 60$	$d_1 = 100$	6000	0.01666
80	120	$a_2 = 100$	$d_2 = 80$	8000	0.01000
120	160	$a_3 = 140$	$d_3 = 60$	8400	0.00714
160	200	$a_4 = 180$	$d_4 = 40$	7200	0.00555

To solve this mathematically, rather than using a spreadsheet, the previous equation can be changed to either of two forms:

$$\ln(G)=\frac{\ln(a_1)+\ln(a_2)+\cdots+\ln(a_n)}{n}$$

or

$$\ln(G)=\frac{\ln(a_1\times a_2\times a_3\times\cdots\times a_n)}{n}$$

The two solutions are equivalent. The term *ln* is the natural log, or log base *e*. (Note that there is some software where the function *log* actually is *ln*.) Using the price levels in Table 21.1,

$$\ln(G)=\frac{\ln(40)+\ln(80)+\ln(120)+\ln(160)+\ln(200)}{5}$$

Disregarding the time intervals, and substituting into the first equation:

$$\ln(G)=\frac{3.689+4.382+4.787+5.075+5.298}{5}$$

Then:

$$\ln(G)=4.6462$$
$$G=104.19$$

While the arithmetic mean, which is time-weighted, gave the value of 105.71, the geometric mean shows the average as 104.19.

The geometric mean has advantages in application to economics and prices. A classic example compares a tenfold rise in price from 100 to 1000 to a fall to one tenth from 100 to 10. An arithmetic mean of the two values 10 and 1000 is 505, while the geometric mean gives

$$G=(10\times1000)^{1/2}=100$$

and shows the relative distribution of prices as a function of comparable growth. Due to this property, the geometric mean is the best choice when averaging ratios that can be either fractions or percentages.

Quadratic Mean

The *quadratic mean* is most often used for estimation of error. It is calculated as:

$$Q=\sqrt{\frac{\sum a^2}{N}}$$

The quadratic mean is the square root of the mean of the square of the items (*root-mean-square*). It is most well known as the basis for the standard deviation. This will be discussed later in this chapter in the section "Moments of the Distribution: Variance, Skewness, and Kurtosis."

Harmonic Mean

The *harmonic mean* is another time-weighted average, but not biased toward higher or lower values as in the geometric mean. A simple example is to consider the average speed of a car that travels 4 miles at 20 mph, then 4 miles at 30 mph. An arithmetic mean would give 25 mph, without considering that 12 minutes were spent at 20 mph and 8 minutes at 30 mph. The weighted average would give

$$W = \frac{(12\times20)+(8\times30)}{12+8} = 24$$

The harmonic mean is

$$\frac{1}{H} = \frac{\frac{1}{a_1}+\frac{1}{a_2}+\cdots+\frac{1}{a_n}}{n}$$

which can also be expressed as

$$H = n/\sum_{i=1}^{n}\left(\frac{1}{a_i}\right)$$

For two or three values, the simpler form can be used:

$$H_2 = \frac{2ab}{a+b} \qquad H_3 = \frac{3abc}{ab+ac+bc}$$

This allows the solution pattern to be seen. For the 20 and 30 mph rates of speed, the solution is

$$H_2 = \frac{2\times20\times30}{20+30} = 24$$

which is the same answer as the weighted average. Considering the original set of numbers again, the basic form of harmonic mean can be applied:

$$\frac{1}{H} = \frac{\frac{1}{40}+\frac{1}{80}+\frac{1}{120}+\frac{1}{160}+\frac{1}{200}}{5}$$

$$H = 87.59$$

$$= \frac{0.5708}{5} = 0.01142$$

We might apply the harmonic mean to price swings, where the first swing moved 20 points over 12 days and the second swing moved 30 points over 8 days.

Price Distribution

The measurement of distribution is very important because it tells you generally what to expect. We cannot know what tomorrow's S&P trading range will be, but if the current price is 1200, then we have a high level of confidence that it will fall between 900 and 1500 this year, but less confidence that it will fall between 1100 and 1300. We have much less confidence that it will fall between 1150 and 1250, and we have virtually no chance of picking the exact range. The following measurements of distribution allow you to put a probability, or confidence level, on the chance of an event occurring.

In all of the statistics that follow, we will use a limited number of prices or—in some cases—individual trading profits and losses as the sample data. We want to measure the characteristics of our sample, finding the shape of the distribution, deciding how results of a smaller sample compare to a larger one, or how similar two samples are to each other. All of these measures will show that the smaller samples are less reliable, yet they can still be used if you understand the size of the error or the difference in the shape of the distribution compared to the expected distribution of a larger sample.

Frequency Distributions

The *frequency distribution* (also called a *histogram*) is simple yet can give a good picture of the characteristics of the data. Theoretically, we expect commodity prices to spend more time at low price levels and only brief periods at high prices. That pattern is shown in Figure 21.2 for wheat during the past 25 years. The most frequent occurrences are at the price where the supply and demand are balanced, called *equilibrium*. When there is a shortage of supply, or an unexpected demand, prices rise for a short time until either the demand is satisfied (which could happen if prices are too high)

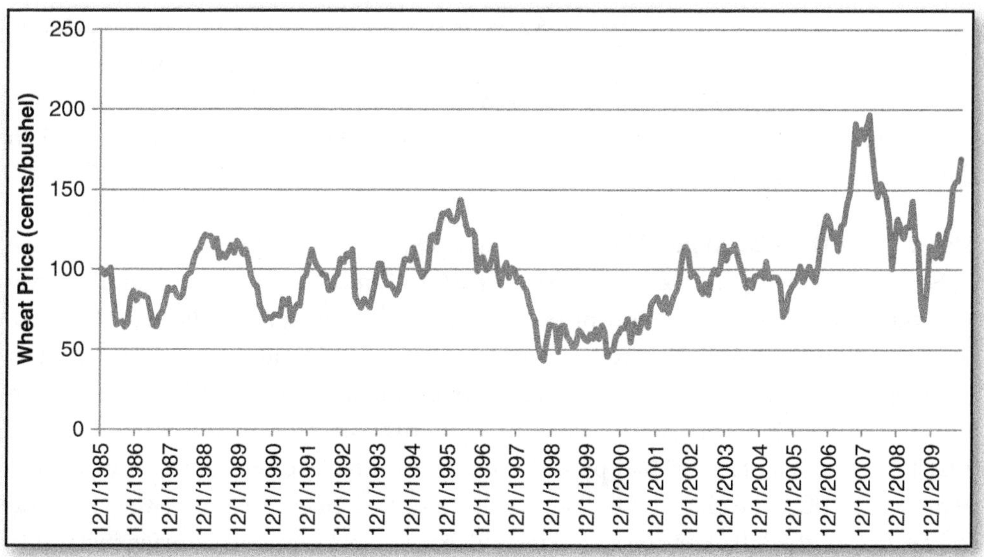

FIGURE 21.2 Wheat Prices, 1985–2010.

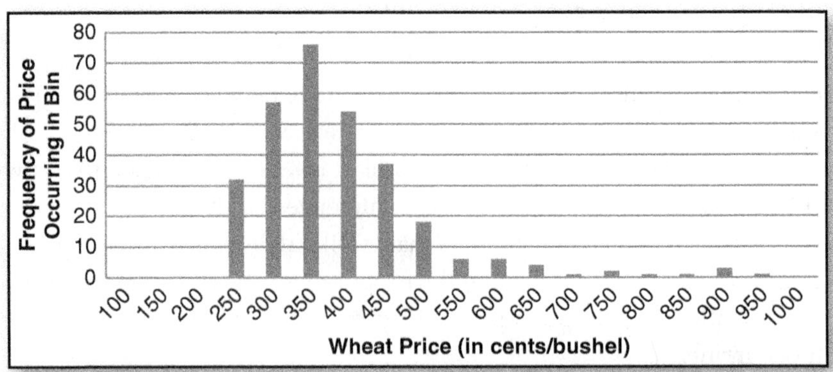

FIGURE 21.3 Wheat Frequency Distribution Showing a Tail to the Right.

or supply increases to meet demand. There is usually a small tail to the left where prices occasionally trade for less than the cost of production, or at a discounted rate during periods of high supply.

To calculate a frequency distribution with 20 bins, we find the highest and lowest prices to be charted, and divide the difference by 19 to get the size of one bin. Beginning with the lowest price, add the bin size to get the second value, add the bin size to the second value to get the third value, and so on. When completed, you will have 20 bins that begin at the lowest price and end at the highest price. You then can count the number of prices that fall into each bin, a nearly impossible task, or you can use a spreadsheet to do it. In Excel, you go to Data/Data Analysis/Histogram and enter the range of bins (which you need to set up in advance) and the data to be analyzed, then select a blank place on the spreadsheet for the output results (to the right of the bins is good) and click OK. The frequency distribution will be shown instantly. You can then plot the results seen in Figure 21.3.

The frequency distribution shows that the most common price fell between $3.50 and $4.00 per bushel but the most active range was from $2.50 to $5.00. The tail to the right extends to just under $10/bushel and clearly demonstrates the *fat tail* in the price distribution. If this was a normal distribution, there would be no entries past $6. The absence of price data below $2.50 is due to the cost of production. Below that price farmers would refuse to sell at a loss; however, the U.S. government has a price support program that guarantees a minimum return for farmers.

The wheat frequency distribution can also be viewed net of inflation or changes in the U.S. dollar. This will be seen at the end of this chapter.

Short-Term Distributions The same frequency distributions occur even when we look at shorter time intervals, although the pattern is more erratic as the time interval gets very small. If we take wheat prices for the calendar year 2007 (Figure 21.4), we see a steady move up during midyear, followed by a wide-ranging sideways pattern at a higher level; however, the frequency distribution in Figure 21.5 shows a pattern similar to the long-term distribution, with the most common value at a low level and a fat tail to the right. If we had picked the few months just before prices peaked in September 2007, the chart might have shown the peak price further to the right and the fat tail on the left. For commodities, this represents a period of price instability and expectations that prices will fall.

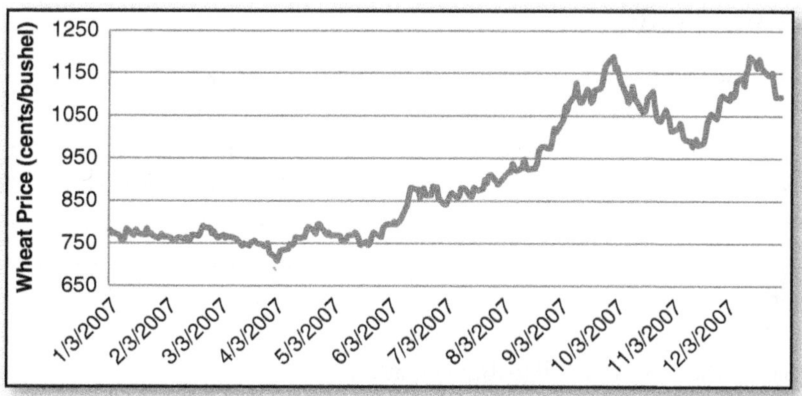

FIGURE 21.4 Wheat Daily Prices, 2007.

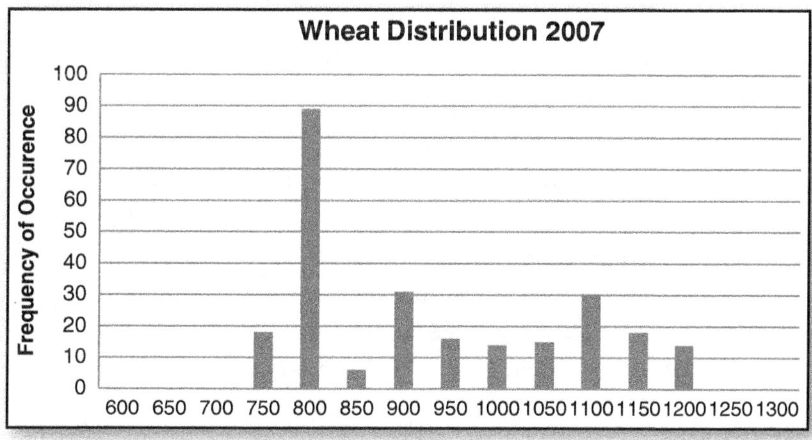

FIGURE 21.5 Frequency Distribution of Wheat Prices, Intervals of $0.50, During 2007.

It should be expected that the distribution of prices for a physical commodity, such as agricultural products, metals, and energy, will be *skewed* toward the left (more occurrences at lower prices) and have a *long tail* at higher prices toward the right of the chart. This is because prices remain at relatively higher levels for only short periods of time while there is an imbalance in supply and demand. In the stock market, history has shown that stocks will not sustain exceptionally high price/earnings (P/E) ratios indefinitely; however, the period of adjustment can be drawn out over many years, unlike an agricultural product that begins again each year. When observing shorter price periods, patterns that do not fit the standard distribution may be considered in transition.

The measures of *central tendency* discussed in the previous section are used to describe the shape and extremes of price movement shown in the frequency distribution. The general relationship between the three principal means when the distribution is not perfectly symmetric is

$$\text{Arithmetic mean} > \text{Geometric mean} > \text{Harmonic mean}$$

Median and Mode

Two other measurements, the median and the mode, are often used to define distribution. The *median*, or "middle item," is helpful for establishing the "center" of the data; when the data is sorted, it is the value in the middle. The median has the advantage of discounting extreme values, which might distort the arithmetic mean. Its disadvantage is that you must sort all of the data in order to locate the middle point. The median is preferred over the mean except when using a very small number of items.

The *mode* is the most commonly occurring value. In Figure 21.5, the mode is the highest bar in the frequency distribution, at bin 800.

In a normally distributed price series, the mode, mean, and median all occur at the same value; however, as the data becomes skewed, these values will move farther apart. The general relationship is:

$$\text{Mean} > \text{Median} > \text{Mode}$$

A normal distribution is commonly called a *bell curve*, and values fall equally on both sides of the mean. For much of the work done with price and performance data, the distributions tend to be skewed to the right (toward higher prices or higher trading profits) and appear to flatten or cut off on the left (lower prices or trading losses). If you were to chart a distribution of trading profits and losses based on a trend system with a fixed stop-loss, you would get profits that could range from zero to very large values, while the losses would be theoretically limited to the size of the stop-loss. Skewed distributions will be important when we measure probabilities later in this chapter. There are no "normal" distributions in a trading environment.

Characteristics of the Principal Averages

Each averaging method has its unique meaning and usefulness. The following summary points out their principal characteristics:

The *arithmetic mean* is affected by each data element equally, but it has a tendency to emphasize extreme values more than other methods. It is easily calculated and is subject to algebraic manipulation.

The *geometric mean* gives less weight to extreme variations than the arithmetic mean and is most important when using data representing ratios or rates of change. It cannot be used for negative numbers but is also subject to algebraic manipulation.

The *harmonic mean* is most applicable to time changes and, along with the geometric mean, has been used in economics for price analysis. It is more difficult to calculate; therefore, it is less popular than either of the other averages, although it is also capable of algebraic manipulation.

The *mode* is the most common value and is only determined by the frequency distribution. It is the location of greatest concentration and indicates a typical value for a reasonably large sample. With an unsorted set of data, such as prices, the mode is time-consuming to locate and is not capable of algebraic manipulation.

The *median* is the middle value, and is most useful when the center of an incomplete set is needed. It is not affected by extreme variations and is simple to find; however, it requires sorting the data, which causes the calculation to be slow. Although it has some arithmetic properties, it is not readily adaptable to computational methods.

Moments of the Distribution: Variance, Skewness, and Kurtosis

The *moments of the distribution* describe the shape of the data points, which is the way they cluster around the mean. There are four moments: *mean*, *variance*, *skew*, and *kurtosis*, each describing a different aspect of the shape of the distribution. Simply put, the mean is the center or average value, the variance is the distance of the individual points from the mean, the skew is the way the distribution leans to the left or right relative to the mean, and the kurtosis is the peakedness of the clustering. We have already discussed the mean, so we will start with the 2nd moment.

In the following calculations, we will use the bar notation, $\overline{P}$, to indicate the average of a list of *n* prices. The capital *P* refers to all prices and the small *p* to individual prices.

$$\overline{P} = \frac{\sum_{i=1}^{n} p_i}{n}$$

The *mean deviation (MD)* is a basic method for measuring distribution and may be calculated about any measure of central location, such as the arithmetic mean.

$$MD = \frac{\sum_{i=1}^{n} |p_i - \overline{P}|}{n}$$

Then *MD* is the average of the differences between each price and the arithmetic mean of those prices, or some other measure of central location, with all differences treated as positive numbers. This formula will be seen often throughout the book.

Variance (2nd Moment)

Variance (Var), which is very similar to mean deviation, the best estimation of dispersion, will be used as the basis for many other calculations. It is

$$Var = \frac{\sum_{i=1}^{n} (p_i - \overline{P})^2}{n-1}$$

Notice that the variance is the square of the standard deviation, $var = s^2 = \sigma^2$, one of the most commonly used statistics. In Excel, the variance is the function *var(list)* and in TradeStation's *EasyLanguage* it is *variance(series,n)*.

The *standard deviation (s),* most often shown as σ (sigma), is a special form of measuring average deviation from the mean, which uses the root-mean-square

$$\sigma = \sqrt{\frac{\sum_{i=1}^{n} (p_i - \overline{P})^2}{n}}$$

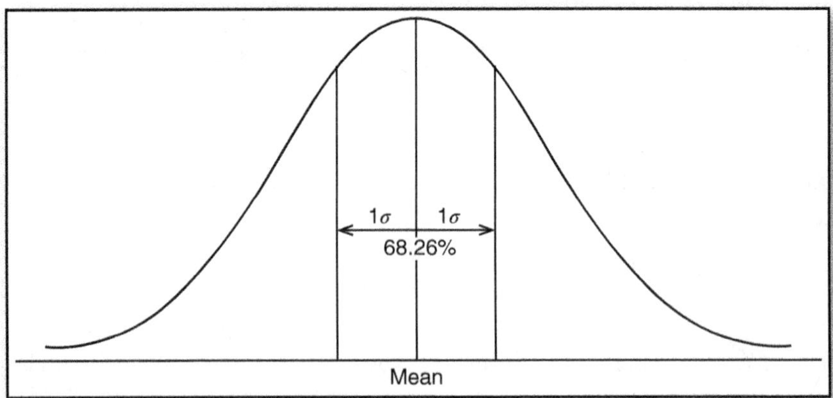

FIGURE 21.6 Normal Distribution Showing the Percentage Area Included Within One Standard Deviation About the Arithmetic Mean.

where the differences between the individual prices and the mean are squared to emphasize the significance of extreme values, and then the total value is scaled back using the square root function. This popular measure, used throughout this book, is the *Excel* function *Stdevp* and the TradeStation function *StdDev(price,n)*, for *n* prices.

The standard deviation is the most popular way of measuring the dispersion of data. The value of 1 standard deviation about the mean represents a clustering of about 68% of the data, 2 standard deviations from the mean include 95.5% of all data, and 3 standard deviations encompass 99.7%, nearly all the data. While it is not possible to guarantee that all data will be included, you can use 3.5 standard deviations to include 100% of the data in a normal distribution. These values represent the groupings of a perfectly *normal* set of data, shown in Figure 21.6.

Skewness (3rd moment)

Most price data, however, are not normally distributed. For physical commodities, such as gold, grains, energy, and even interest rates (expressed at yields), prices tend to spend more time at low levels and much less time at extreme highs. While gold peaked at $800 per ounce for one day in January 1980, it remained between $250 and $400 per ounce for most of the next 20 years. If we had taken the average at $325, then it would be impossible for the price distribution to be symmetric. If 1 standard deviation is $140, then a normal distribution would show a high likelihood of prices dropping to $185, an unlikely scenario. This asymmetry is most obvious in agricultural markets, where a shortage of soybeans or coffee in one year will drive prices much higher, but a normal crop the following year will return those prices to previous levels.

The relationship of price versus time, where markets spend more time at lower levels, can be measured as *skewness*—the amount of distortion from a symmetric distribution, which makes the curve appear to be short on the left and extended to the right (higher prices). The extended side is called the *tail*, and a longer tail to the right is called *positive skewness*. *Negative skewness* has the tail extending toward the left. This can be seen in Figure 21.7.

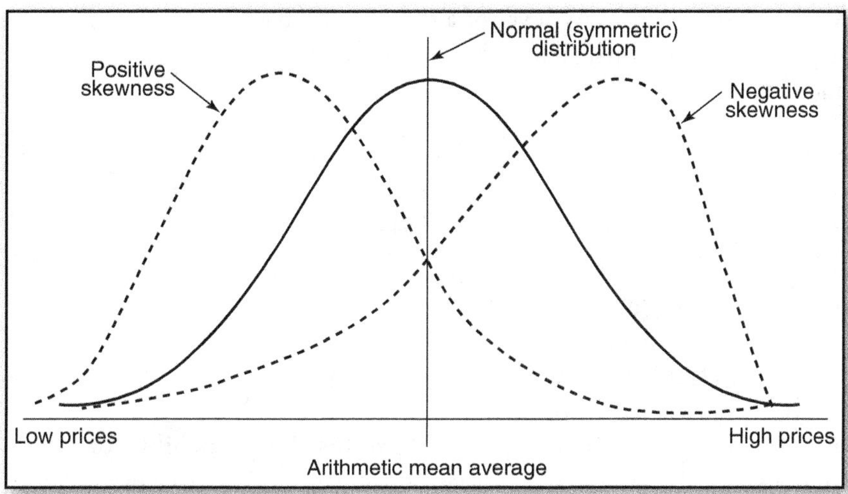

FIGURE 21.7 Skewness. Nearly all price distributions are positively skewed, showing a longer tail to the right, at higher prices.

In a perfectly normal distribution, the mean, median, and mode all coincide. As prices become positively skewed, typical of a period of higher prices, the mean will show the greatest change, the mode will show the least, and the median will fall in between. The difference between the mean and the mode, adjusted for dispersion using the standard deviation of the distribution, gives a good measure of skewness.

$$\text{(Skewness)}\, S_K = \frac{\text{Mean} - \text{Mode}}{\text{Standard deviation}}$$

The distance between the mean and the mode, in a moderately skewed distribution, turns out to be three times the difference between the mean and the median; the relationship can also be written as:

$$(Skewness)\, S_K = \frac{3 \times (Mean - Median)}{Standard\ deviation}$$

To show the similarity between the 2nd and 3rd moments (variance and skewness) the more common computational formula is

$$S_K = \frac{\sum_{i=1}^{n} \left(p_i - \bar{P}\right)^3}{(n-1)\sigma^3}$$

where n is the number of prices in the distribution, and σ is the standard deviation of the prices. The functions for skew can be found in Excel and TradeStation.

Transformations The skewness of a data series can sometimes be corrected using a *transformation*. Price data may be skewed in a specific pattern. For example, if there are 3 occurrences at twice the price, and 1/9 of the occurrences at 3 times the price, the original data can be transformed into a normal distribution by taking the square root of each data item. The characteristics of price data often show a logarithmic, power, or square-root relationship.

To calculate the probability level of a distribution based on the skewed distribution of price, we can convert the normal probability to the *exponential probability* equivalent, P_E, using

$$P_E = \frac{\bar{X}\log_{10}\left(\frac{1}{1-P}\right)}{\log_{10}e}$$

where $\bar{X}$ = the average of all prices
P = the normal probability
$\log_{10}e = .434294482$

While the normal probability, P, understates the probability of occurrence in a price distribution, the exponential distribution, P_E, will overstate the probability. Whenever possible, it is better to use the exact calculation; however, when calculating risk, it might be best to err on the side of slightly higher than expected risk.

Skewness in Distributions at Different Relative Price Levels Because the lower price levels of most commodities are determined by production costs, price distributions show a clear tendency to resist moving below these thresholds. This contributes to the positive skewness in those markets. Considering only the short term, when prices are at unusually high levels, they can be volatile and unstable, causing a negative skewness that can be interpreted as being top heavy. Somewhere between the very high and very low price levels, we may find a frequency distribution that looks normal. Figure 21.8 shows the change in the distribution of prices over, for example, 20 days as prices move sharply higher. The mean shows the center of the distributions as they change from positive to negative skewness.

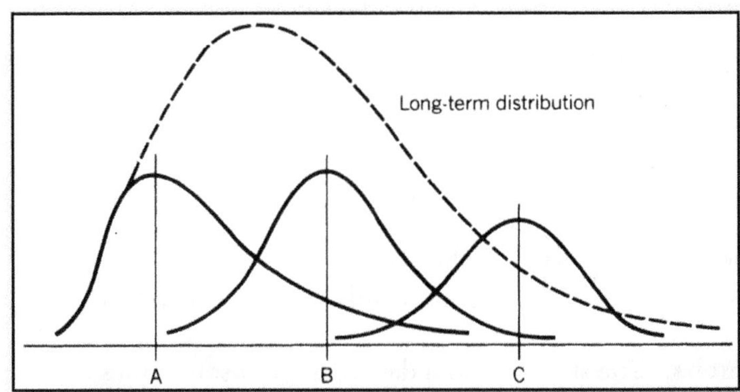

FIGURE 21.8 Changing Distribution at Different Price Levels. A, B, and C are increasing mean values of three shorter-term distributions and show the distribution changing from positive to negative skewness.

This pattern indicates that a normal distribution is not appropriate for all price analysis and that a log, exponential, or power distribution would only apply best to long-term analysis.

Kurtosis (4th Moment)

One last measurement, *kurtosis*, is needed to describe the shape of a price distribution. *Kurtosis* is the peakedness or flatness of a distribution as shown in Figure 21.9. This measurement is good for an unbiased assessment of whether prices are trending or moving sideways. If you see prices moving steadily higher, then the distribution will be flatter and cover a wider range. This is call *negative kurtosis*. If prices are rangebound, then the frequency will show clustering around the mean and we have *positive kurtosis*. Steidlmayer's *Market Profile* uses the concept of kurtosis, with the frequency distribution accumulated dynamically using real-time price changes.

Following the same form as the 3rd moment, skewness, kurtosis can be calculated as

$$K = \frac{\sum_{i=1}^{n}\left(p_i - \overline{P}\right)^4}{(n-1)\sigma^4}$$

An alternative calculation for kurtosis is

$$K = \frac{n(n+1)}{(n-1)(n-2)(n-3)}\sum\left(\frac{p_i - \overline{P}}{\sigma}\right)^4 - \frac{3(n-1)^2}{(n-2)(n-3)}$$

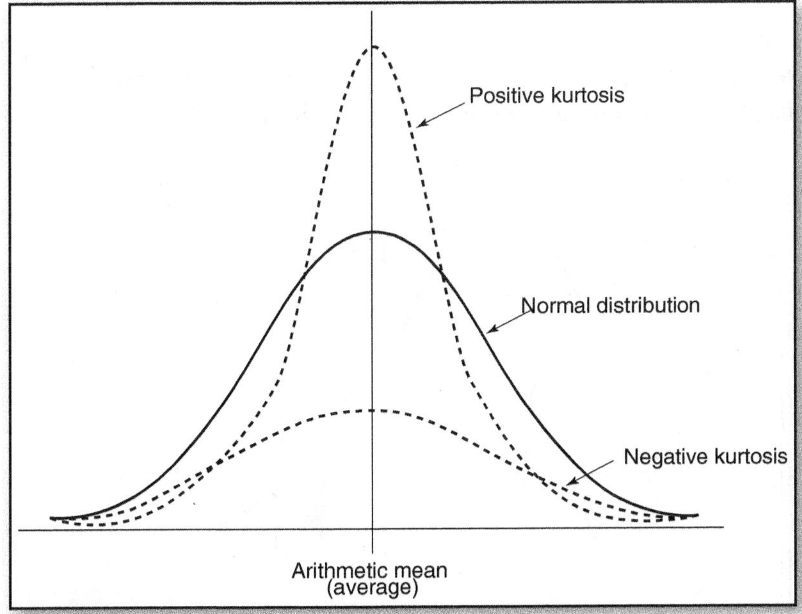

FIGURE 21.9 Kurtosis. A positive kurtosis is when the peak of the distribution is greater than normal, typical of a sideways market. A negative kurtosis, shown as a flatter distribution, occurs when the market is trending.

where n = the number of prices in the distribution
pi = the individual prices
$\bar{P}$ = the average of n prices
σ = the standard deviation of prices

Most often the *excess kurtosis* is used, which makes it easier to see abnormal distributions. Excess kurtosis, $KE = K - 3$ because the normal value of the kurtosis is 3.

Kurtosis is also useful when reviewing system tests. If you find the kurtosis of the daily returns, they should be somewhat better than normal if the system is profitable; however, if the kurtosis is above 7 or 8, then it begins to look as though the trading method is overfitted. A high kurtosis means that there are an overwhelming number of profitable trades of similar size, which is not likely to happen in real trading. Any high value of kurtosis should make you immediately suspicious.

Choosing between Frequency Distribution and Standard Deviation

Frequency distributions are important because the standard deviation doesn't work for skewed distributions, which is most common for most price data. For example, if we look back at the histogram for wheat, the average price over the past 25 years was \$3.62 and the standard deviation of those prices was \$1.16, then 1 standard deviation to the left of the mean is \$2.46, a bin that has no data. On the right side, 3.5 standard deviations, which should contain 100% of the data, is \$7.68, far below the actual high price.

Then using the standard deviation can fail on both ends of the distribution for highly skewed data, while the frequency distribution gives a very clear and useful picture. If we wanted to know the price at the 10% and 90% probability levels based on the frequency distribution, we would sort all the data from low to high. If there were 300 monthly data points, then the 10% level would be in position 30 and the 90% level in position 271. The median price would be at position 151. This is shown in Figure 21.10.

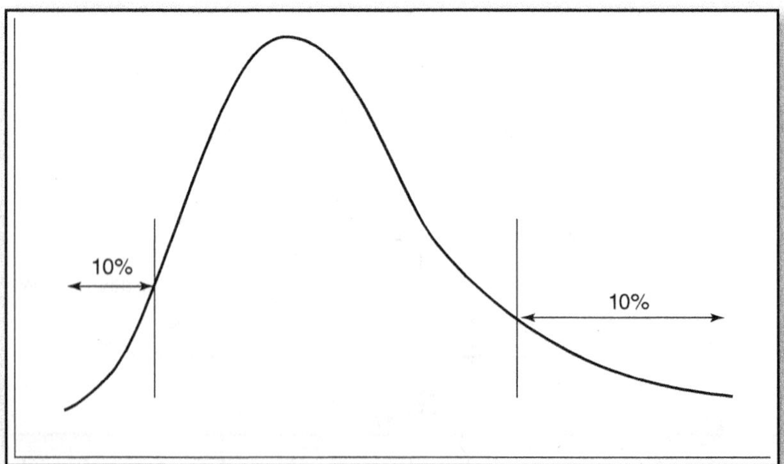

FIGURE 21.10 Measuring 10% from Each End of the Frequency Distribution. The dense clustering at low prices will make the lower zone look narrow, while high prices with less frequent data will appear to have a wide zone.

When there is a long tail to the right, both the frequency distribution and the standard deviation imply that large moves are to be expected. When the distribution is very symmetric, then we are not as concerned. For those markets that have had extreme moves, neither method will tell you the size of the extreme move that could occur. There is no doubt that, given enough time, we will see profits and losses that are larger than we have seen in the past, perhaps much larger.

Autocorrelation *Serial correlation* or *autocorrelation* means that there is persistence in the data; that is, future data can be predicted (to some degree) from past data. Such a quality could indicate the existence of trends. A simple way of finding autocorrelation is to put the data into column A of a spreadsheet, then copy it to column B while shifting the data down by 1 row. Then find the correlation of column A and column B. Additional correlations can be calculated shifting column B down 2, 3, or 4 rows, which might show the existence of a cycle.

A formal way of finding autocorrelation is by using the Durbin-Watson test, which gives the *d*-statistic. This approach measures the change in the errors (e), the difference between N data points and their average value.

$$e_t = r_t - \frac{\sum_{t-N+1}^{t} r_i}{N}$$

$$d = \frac{\sum_{t-N+1}^{t} \left(e_i - e_{i-1}\right)^2}{\sum_{t-N+1}^{t} e_i^2}$$

The value of d always falls between 0 and 4. There is no autocorrelation if d=2. If d is substantially less than 2, there is positive autocorrelation; however, if it is below 1, then there is more similarity in the errors than is reasonable. The farther d is above 2 the more negative autocorrelation appears in the error terms.

A *positive autocorrelation*, or serial correlation, means that a positive error factor has a good chance of following another positive error factor.

Probability of Achieving a Return

To be uncertain is to be uncomfortable, but to be certain is to be ridiculous.

—Chinese proverb

If we see the normal distribution (Figure 21.6) as the annual returns for the stock market over the past 50 years, then the mean is about 8%, and one standard deviation is 16%. In any one year, we can expect the returns to be 8%; however, there is a 32% chance that it will be either greater than 24% (the mean plus one standard deviation) or less than –8% (the mean minus one standard deviation). If you would like to know the probability of a return of 20% or greater, you must first rescale the values,

$$\textit{Probability of reaching objective} = \frac{\textit{Objective} - \textit{Mean}}{\textit{Standard deviation}}$$

If your objective is 20%, we calculate

$$Probability = \frac{20\% - 8\%}{16\%} = 0.75$$

Looking up the standard deviation of 0.75 gives 27.34%, a grouping of 54.68% of the data. That leaves one half of the remaining data, or 22.66%, above the target of 20%.

Calculating the Probability Automatically It is inconvenient to look up the probability values in a table when you are working with a spreadsheet or computer program, yet the probabilities are easier to understand than standard deviation values. You can calculate the area under the curve that corresponds to a particular z value (the standard deviation) using the following approximation.[1]

Let $z' = |z|$, the absolute value of z. Then

$$r = 1 + z' \times \left(c_1 + z' \times \left(c_3 + z' \times \left(c_5 + z' \times c_6\right)\right)\right)$$

Where $c_1 = 0.049867347$
$c_2 = 0.0211410061$
$c_3 = 0.032776263$
$c_4 = 0.0000380036$
$c_5 = 0.0000488906$
$c_6 = 0.000005383$

Then the probability, P, that the returns will equal or exceed the expected return is

$$P = 0.5 \times e^{[\ln(r) \times (-16)]}$$

Using the example where the standard deviation z = 0.75, we perform the calculation

$$r = 1 + 0.75 \times (0.049867347 + 0.75 \times [0.0211410061 + 0.75 \times (0.0032776232 + 0.75 \times [0.0000380036 + 0.75 \times (0.0000488906 + 0.75 \times [0.000005383])])])$$

$$r = 1.0507$$

Substituting the value of r into the equation for P, we get

$$P = 0.5 \times e^{[\ln(1.0507) \times (-16)]} = 0.226627$$

Then there is a 22.7% probability that a value will exceed 0.75 standard deviations (that is, fall on one end of the distribution outside the value of 0.75). The chance of a value falling inside the band formed by ±0.75 standard deviations is 1 – (2 × 0.2266) = 0.5468, or 54.68%.

[1] Stephen J. Brown and Mark P. Kritzman, *Quantitative Methods for Financial Analysis*, 2nd ed. (Dow Jones-Irwin, 1990), 238–241.

For those using Excel, the answer can be found with the function *normdist (p, mean, stdev, cumulative)*, where

p is the current price or value
mean is the mean of the series of *p*'s
stdev is the standard deviation of the series of *p*'s, and
cumulative is "true" if you want the *z* value.

Then the result of *normdist*(35,20,5,true) is 0.99865, or a 99.8% probability, and if cumulative is "false," then the result is 0.000866.

Standard Error

Throughout the development and testing of a trading system, we want to know if the results we are seeing are as expected. The answer will always depend on the size of the data sample and the amount of variance that is typical of the data during this period.

One descriptive measure of error, called the *standard error* (*SE*), uses the variance, which gives the estimation of error based on the distribution of the data using multiple data samples. It is a test that determines how the sample means differ from the actual mean of all the data. It addresses the *uniformity* of the data.

$$SE = \sqrt{\frac{Var}{n}}$$

where Var = the variance of the sample means
n = the number of data points in the sample means

Sample means refers to the data being sampled a number of times, each with *n* data points, and the means of these samples are used to find the variance. In most cases, we would use a single data series and calculate the variance as shown earlier in this chapter.

t-Statistic and Degrees of Freedom

When fewer prices or trades are used in a distribution, we can expect the shape of the curve to be more variable. For example, it may be spread out so that the peak of the distribution will be lower and the tails will be higher. A way of measuring how close the sample distribution of a smaller set is to the normal distribution (of a large sample of data) is to use the *t-statistic* (also called the *student's t-test*, developed by W. S. Gossett). The *t*-test is calculated according to its degrees of freedom (*df*), which is $n - 1$, where *n* is the sample size, the number of prices used in the distribution.

$$t = \frac{\textit{Average of price changes}}{\textit{Standard deviation of price changes}} \times \sqrt{n}$$

The more data in the sample, the more reliable the results. We can get a broad view of the shape of the distribution by looking at a few values of *t* in Table 21.2, which gives the values of *t* corresponding to the upper tail areas of 0.10, 0.05, 0.025, 0.01, and 0.005. The table shows that as the sample size *n* increases, the values of *t* approach those of the standard normal values of the tail areas.

TABLE 21.2 Values of t Corresponding to the Upper Tail Probability of 0.025

Degrees of Freedom (df)	Value of t
1	12.706
10	2.228
20	2.086
30	2.042
120	1.980
Normal	1.960

For example, if we had 20 prices in our sample and wanted the probability of the upper tail to be 0.025, then the value of t would need to be 2.086. For smaller samples, the value of t would be larger in order to have the same confidence.

When testing a trading system, degrees of freedom can be the number of trades produced by the strategy. When you have few trades, the results may not represent what you will get using a longer trading history. When testing a strategy, you will find a similar relationship between the number of trades and the number of parameters, or variables, used in the strategy. The more variables used, the more trades are needed to create expectations with an acceptable confidence level.

2-Sample t-Test You may want to compare two periods of data to decide whether the price patterns have changed significantly. Some analysts use this to eliminate inconsistent data, but the characteristics of price and economic data change as part of the evolving process, and systematic trading should be able to adapt to these changes. This test is best applied to trading results in order to decide if a strategy is performing consistently. This is done with a 2-sample t-test:

$$t = \frac{\overline{P}_1 - \overline{P}_2}{\sqrt{\frac{var_1^2}{n_1} + \frac{var_2^2}{n_2}}}$$

where $\overline{P}_1$ and $\overline{P}_2$ = the averages of the prices for periods 1 and 2
var_1 and var_2 = the variances of the prices for periods 1 and 2
n_1 and n_2 = the number of prices in periods 1 and 2

and the two periods being compared are mutually exclusive. The degrees of freedom, df, needed to find the confidence levels can be calculated using Satterthwaite's approximation, where s is the standard deviation of the data values:

$$df = \frac{\left(\frac{s_1^2}{n_1} + \frac{s_2^2}{n_2}\right)}{\frac{\left(\frac{s_1^2}{n_1}\right)^2}{(n_1 - n_2)} + \frac{\left(\frac{s_2^2}{n_2}\right)^2}{(n_2 - n_1)}}$$

When using the t-test to find the consistency of profits and losses generated by a trading system, replace the data items by the net returns of each trade, the number of data items by the number of trades, and calculate all other values using returns rather than prices.

Standardizing Risk and Return

In order to compare one trading method with another, it is necessary to standardize both the tests and the measurements used for evaluation. If one system has total returns of 50% and the other 250%, we cannot decide which is best unless we know the duration of the test and the volatility of the returns, or risk. If the 50% return was over 1 year and the 250% return over 10 years, then the first one is best. Similarly, if the first return had an annualized risk of 10% and the second a risk of 50%, then both would be equivalent. The return relative to the risk is crucial to performance. For now it is only important that returns and risk be annualized or standardized to make comparisons valid.

Calculating Returns

The calculations for both 1-period returns and annualized returns will be an essential part of all performance evaluations. In its simplest form, the *1-period rate of return, R,* or the *holding period rate of return* is often given as

$$Return = \frac{Ending\ value - Starting\ value}{Starting\ value} = \frac{Ending\ value}{Starting\ value} - 1$$

For the stock market, which has continuous prices, this can be written

$$r_1 = \frac{p_1 - p_0}{p_0} = \frac{p_1}{p_0} - 1$$

where p_0 is the initial price and p_1 is the price after one period has elapsed. The securities industry often prefers a different calculation,

$$r_n = \ln\left(\frac{P_t}{P_{t-1}}\right)$$

Both methods have advantages and disadvantages. Neither one is the "correct" calculation. Note that in some software, the function *log* is actually the natural log, and *log10* is the log base 10. It is best to always check the definitions. In order to distinguish the two calculations, the first method will be called the *standard method* and the second the *ln method*.

In the following spreadsheet example, shown in Table 21.3 over 22 days, the standard returns are in column D and the ln returns in column E. The differences seem small, but the averages are 0.00350 and 0.00339. The standard returns are better by 3.3% over only one trading month. At this rate, the standard method would have yielded returns that were nearly 40% higher after one year. The *net asset value* (*NAV*),

TABLE 21.3 Calculation of Returns and NAVs from Daily Profits and Losses						
Date	PL	Cum PL	Standard Return	Return using LN	NAV	NAV using LN
9/10/2010		100000			100.00	100.00
9/13/2010	1154	101154	0.01154	0.01147	101.15	101.15
9/14/2010	1795	102949	0.01774	0.01759	102.95	102.91
9/15/2010	–1859	101090	–0.01806	–0.01822	101.09	101.08
9/16/2010	–1603	99487	–0.01585	–0.01598	99.49	99.49
9/17/2010	449	99936	0.00451	0.00450	99.94	99.94
9/20/2010	1090	101026	0.01090	0.01084	101.03	101.02
9/21/2010	2949	103974	0.02919	0.02877	103.97	103.90
9/22/2010	1346	105320	0.01295	0.01286	105.32	105.18
9/23/2010	64	105384	0.00061	0.00061	105.38	105.24
9/24/2010	–2051	103333	–0.01946	–0.01966	103.33	103.28
9/27/2010	3269	106602	0.03164	0.03115	106.60	106.39
9/28/2010	1795	108397	0.01684	0.01670	108.40	108.06
9/29/2010	–1154	107243	–0.01064	–0.01070	107.24	106.99
9/30/2010	128	107372	0.00120	0.00119	107.37	107.11
10/1/2010	–705	106666	–0.00657	–0.00659	106.67	106.45
10/4/2010	1090	107756	0.01022	0.01016	107.76	107.47
10/5/2010	–449	107307	–0.00416	–0.00417	107.31	107.05
10/6/2010	2308	109615	0.02150	0.02128	109.62	109.18
10/7/2010	–769	108846	–0.00702	–0.00704	108.85	108.48
10/8/2010	–256	108589	–0.00236	–0.00236	108.59	108.24
10/12/2010	–1218	107372	–0.01122	–0.01128	107.37	107.11
Average			0.00350	0.00339		
Std Dev			0.01502	0.01495		
Ann StdDev			0.23846	0.23730		
AROR					125.85%	119.69%

used extensively throughout this book, compounds the periodic returns and most often has a starting value, $NAV_0 = 100$.

$$NAV_t = NAV_{t-1} \times (1 + r_t)$$

Annualizing Returns In most cases, it is best to standardize the returns by *annualizing*. This is particularly helpful when comparing two sets of test results, where each covers a different time period. When annualizing, it is important to know that

- Government instruments use a 360-day rate (based on 90-day quarters).
- A 365-day rate is common for most other data that can change daily.
- Trading returns are best with 252 days, which is the typical number of days in a trading year for the United States (262 days for Europe).

The following formulas use 252 days, which will be the standard throughout this book except for certain interest rate calculations; however, 365 or 360 may be substituted, or even 260 for trading days in other parts of the world.

The annualized rate of return (AROR) on a simple-interest basis for an investment over n days is

$$AROR_{\text{simple}} = \frac{E_n}{E_0} \times \frac{252}{n}$$

where E_0 is the starting equity or account balance, E_n is the equity at the end of the nth period, and $252/n$ are the years expressed as a decimal. When the 1-period returns are calculated using the standard method, the *annualized compounded rate of return* is

$$AROR_{\text{compounded}} = \left(\frac{E_n}{E_0}\right)^{\frac{252}{n}} - 1$$

Note that *AROR* or *R* (capital) refers to the annualized rate of return while *r* is the daily or 1-period return. Also, the form of the results is different for the two calculations. An increase of 25% for the simple return will show as 0.25 while the same increase using the compounded returns will be 1.25.

When the 1-period returns use the ln method, then the annualized rate of return is the sum of the returns divided by the number of years

$$AROR_{\text{ln method}} = \frac{\sum_{i=1}^{n} r_i}{n}$$

An example of this can be found in column F, the row labeled AROR, in the previous spreadsheet. Note that the annualized returns using the ln method are much lower than those using division and compounding. The compounded method will be used throughout this book.

Probability of Returns The standard deviation and compounded rate of return are combined to find the probability of a return objective. In the following calculation,[2] the arithmetic mean of continuous returns is $\ln(1 + Rg)$, and it is assumed that the returns are normally distributed.

$$z = \frac{\ln\left(\frac{T}{B}\right) - \ln(1+R_g)n}{\sqrt{s \times n}}$$

where z = standardized variable

T = target value or rate-of-return objective

B = beginning investment value

R_g = geometric average of periodic returns

n = number of periods

s = standard deviation of the logarithms of the quantities 1 plus the periodic returns

[2] This and other very clear explanations of returns can be found in Peter L. Bernstein, *The Portable MBA in Investment*.

Risk and Volatility

While we would always like to think about returns, it is even more important to be able to assess risk. With that in mind, there are two extreme risks. The first is *event risk*, which takes the form of an unpredictable price shock. The worst of these is *catastrophic risk*, which will cause fatal losses or ruin. The second risk is self-induced by *overleverage*, or *gearing up* your portfolio, until a sequence of bad trades causes ruin.

The standard risk measurement is useful for comparing the performance of two systems. It is commonly applied to the returns of a single stock or an entire portfolio compared to a benchmark, such as the returns of the S&P 500 or a bond fund. The most common estimate of risk is the standard deviation, σ, of returns, r, shown earlier in this chapter. For most discussions of risk, the standard deviation will also be called *volatility*. When we refer to the *target volatility* of a portfolio, we mean the percentage of risk represented by 1 standard deviation of the returns, annualized. For example, in the previous spreadsheet, columns D and E show the daily returns. The standard deviations of those returns are shown in the same columns in the row "Std Dev" as 0.01512 and 0.01495. Looking only at column D, 1 standard deviation of 0.01502 means that there is a 68% chance of a daily profit or loss less than 1.502%. However, target volatility always refers to annualized risk, and to change a daily return to an annualized one, we simply multiply by $\sqrt{252}$. Then the daily standard deviation of returns of 1.512% becomes an *annualized volatility* of 23.8%, also shown at the bottom of the spreadsheet example. Because we only care about the downside risk, there is a 16% chance that we could lose 23.8% in one year. The greater the standard deviation of returns, the greater the risk.

Beta *Beta* (β) is commonly used in the securities industry to express the relationship of a single market to an index or portfolio. If beta is zero, then there is no relationship; if it is positive, then the single series tends to move with the index, both above and below. As beta gets larger, the volatility of the single market tends to be increasingly greater than the index. Specifically,

$0 < \beta < 1$, the volatility of the single market is less than the index
$\beta = 1$, the volatility of the single market is the same as the index
$\beta > 1$, the volatility of the single market is greater than the index

A negative beta is similar to a negative correlation, where the moves of the market are generally opposite to the index.

Beta is found by calculating the linear regression of the single market with the index. It is the slope of the single market divided by the slope of the index. *Alpha*, the added value, is the y-intercept of the solution. A general formula for beta is

$$Beta(\text{A}) = \text{cov}(returns\ \text{A}, returns\ \text{B}) / \text{var}(returns\ \text{B})$$

where A is the single market and B is a portfolio or index.

Adjusting to the Target Volatility If we have a target volatility of 12%, that is, we are willing to accept a 16% chance of losing 12% in one year, but the actual returns show an annualized volatility of 23.8% based on an investment of $100,000, then to correct to a 12% target we simply increase the investment by 23.8/12.0, or a factor of 1.98 to \$198,000, while holding the same position size. This is essentially deleveraging your positions by trading a smaller percentage of your account value. Alternatively, we can reduce the position size by dividing by 1.98 and keeping the investment the same.

All results in this reading will be shown at the target volatility of 12% unless otherwise stated. This is considered a modest risk level, which can be as high as 18% for some hedge funds. It will allow you to compare various systems and test results and see them at a level of risk that is most likely to represent targeted trading results.

Annualizing Daily and Monthly Returns The previous examples used daily data and an annualization factor of $\sqrt{252}$. For monthly data, which is most common in published performance tables, we would take the monthly returns and multiply by $\sqrt{12}$. In general, annualizing can be done by multiplying the data by the square root of the number of data items in a year. Then we use 252 for daily data, 12 for monthly, 4 for quarterly, and so on.

Monthly Data Always Appears Less Volatile Although monthly performance results are common in financial disclosure documents, this convention works to the advantage of the person publishing the performance. It is unlikely that the highest or lowest daily *net asset value* (NAV) will occur on the last day of the month, so the extremes will rarely be seen, and the performance statistics will appear smoother than when using daily returns. Those responsible for due diligence before investing in a new product will often require daily return data in order to avoid overlooking a large drawdown that occurred mid-month.

Using the S&P index as an example, the annualized volatility of the daily returns from 1990 through 2010 was 18.6%, but based on monthly returns it was only 15.3%. The risk based on monthly returns is 17.7% lower, but the annualized rate of return would be the same because it only uses the beginning and ending values.

Downside Risk Because the standard deviation is symmetric, a series of jumps in profits will be interpreted as larger risk. Some analysts believe that it is more accurate to measure the risk as limited to only the downside returns or drawdowns. The use of only losses is called *lower partial moments*, where *lower* refers to the downside risk, and partial means where only one side of the return distribution is used. The easiest way to see this is *semivariance*, which measures the dispersion that falls below the mean, $\overline{R}$, or some target value,

$$Semivariance = \frac{\sum_{i=1}^{n}\left(\overline{R} - r_i\right)^2}{n}, \text{ where each } ri < \overline{R}$$

However, the most common calculation for system performance is to take the daily drawdowns, that is, the net loss on each day that the total equity is below the peak equity. For example, if the system returns had produced an equity of \$25,000 on day *t*, followed by a daily loss of \$500, and another loss of \$250, then we would have two values as input 500/25000 and 750/25000, or 0.02 and 0.03. Only those net returns below the most recent peaks are used in the semivariance calculation. Alternatively, you could just take the standard deviation of these daily drawdowns to find the probable size of the drawdowns.

One concern about using only the drawdowns to predict other drawdowns is that it limits the number of cases and discards the likelihood that higher-than-normal profits can be related to higher overall risk. In situations where there are limited amounts of test data, using both the gains and losses will give more robust results. When there is a large amount of data, the use of drawdowns can be a very good measurement.

The Index

The purpose of an average is to transform individuality into classification. In doing that, the data is often smoothed, and useful information is gained. Indexes have attracted enormous popularity in recent years. Where there was only the Value Line and S&P 500 trading as futures markets in the early 1980s, now there are stock index futures contracts representing the markets of every industrialized country. The creation of trusts, such as SPDRs (called "Spyders," the S&P 500), Diamonds (DIA, the Dow Jones Industrials), and Qs (QQQ, the NASDAQ 100), has given stock traders a familiar vehicle to invest in the broad market rather than pick individual shares. Industrial sectors, such as pharmaceuticals, health care, and technology, first appeared as mutual funds, then as ETFs, and now can also be traded as futures. These index markets all have the additional advantage of not being constrained by having to borrow shares in order to sell short, or by the uptick rule (if it is reinstated) requiring all short sales to be initiated on an uptick in price.

Index markets allow both individual and institutional participants a number of specialized investment strategies. They can buy or sell the broad market, they can switch from one sector to another (sector rotation), or they can sell an overpriced sector while buying the broad market index (statistical arbitrage). Institutions find it very desirable, from the view of both costs and taxes, to temporarily hedge their cash stock portfolio by selling S&P 500 futures rather than liquidating stock positions. They may also hedge using options on the S&P futures or SPYs. An index simplifies the decision-making process for trading. If an index does not exist, one can be constructed to satisfy most purposes.

The index holds an important role as a benchmark for performance. Most investors believe that a trading program is only attractive if it has a better return-to-risk ratio than a portfolio of 60% stocks (as represented by the S&P 500 index) and 40% bonds (the Lehman Brothers Treasury Index). Beating the index is called *creating alpha*, proving that you're smarter than the market.

Constructing an Index

An index is a standardized way of expressing price movement, normally an accumulation of percentage changes. Most indexes have a starting value of 100 on a specific date. The selection of the base year is often "convenient" but can be chosen as a period of price stability. The base year for U.S. productivity and for unemployment is 1982; for consumer confidence, 1985; and for the composite of leading indicators, 1987. The CRB Yearbook shows the Producer Price Index (PPI) from as far back as 1913. For example, the PPI, which is released monthly, had a value of 186.8 in October 2010 and 185.1 in September 2010, a 0.9184% increase in one month. An index value less than 100 means that the index has less value than when it started.

Each index value is calculated from the previous value as:

$$\textit{Current index value} = \textit{Previous index value} \times \left(\frac{\textit{Current price}}{\textit{Previous price}} \right)$$

and the 1-period returns are calculated in the same way as shown previously in this chapter.

Calculating the Net Asset Value—Indexing Returns

The last calculations shown in the spreadsheet, Table 21.3, are the *net asset value* (NAV), calculated two ways. This is essentially the returns converted to an index, showing the compounded rate of return based on daily profit and losses relative to a starting investment. In the spreadsheet, this is shown in column F using standard returns and G using ln returns.

The process of calculating NAVs can be done with the following steps:

1. Establish the initial investment, in this case $100,000, shown at the top of column C. This can be adjusted later based on the target volatility.
2. Calculate the cumulative account value by adding the daily profits or losses (column B) to the previous account value (column C).
3. Calculate the daily returns by either (a) dividing today's profit or loss by yesterday's account value to get r, or (b) taking the natural log of $1 + r$.
4. If using method (a), then each subsequent $NAV_t = NAV_{t-1} \times (1 + r)$, and if using method (b), then each $NAV_t = NAV_{t-1} + \ln(1 + r)$.

The final values of the NAV are in the last dated rows. The U.S. government requires that NAVs be calculated this way, although it doesn't specify whether returns should be based on the natural log. This process is also identical to indexing, which turns any price series into one that reflects percentage returns.

Leveraged Long or Short Index Funds

As index markets have become more popular, financial engineering has created a wide range of innovative trading vehicles. Mutual funds, such as Rydex and ProFunds, cater to market timers, a group of money managers that may trade in and out of the funds each day. These funds track the major index markets closely, but offer unique variations. There are both long and short funds, and each may be leveraged. When you buy a long fund that tracks the S&P 500 (called *Nova* by Rydex), you are simply long the equivalent of the S&P 500. However, when you buy a short S&P fund, called *Ursa*, you profit when the S&P index price drops. In addition, both Rydex and ProFunds offer leverage of 1.5 or 2.0 on these funds, so that a gain of 1.0% in the S&P 500 translates into a gain of 2.0% in ProFunds' *UltraBull S&P fund*; a drop of 1.0% in the S&P would generate a profit of 2.0% in ProFunds' *UltraBear fund*. The motivation behind the short funds, or *inverse funds*, is to circumvent the U.S. government rule that does not permit short sales in retirement accounts.

The calculation for leveraged long funds is very similar to a simple index; however, a short fund (where you profit from a decline in prices) is compounded to the upside, in the same way as a long fund. The following calculation will create a long and short index that closely approximates those used by Rydex and ProFunds. In addition, it includes the calculation of the daily high and low index values. If you intend to create a leveraged S&P index, start with the cash S&P price. Use the cash index equivalent for each of the mutual fund indexes that you plan to duplicate.

In the following calculations, *leverage* is the leverage factor of the fund. Initial index values for both long and short funds are

$$XC_1 = 100$$

$$XH_1 = XC_1 + 100 \times \left(\frac{H_1}{C_1} - 1.0 \right) \times Leverage$$

$$XL_1 = XC_1 + 100 \times \left(\frac{L_1}{C_1} - 1.0 \right) \times Leverage$$

Each subsequent index value for long funds is

$$XC_i = XC_{i-1} \times \left(\left(\frac{C_i}{C_{i-1}} - 1.0 \right) \times Leverage + 1.0 \right)$$

$$XH_i = XC_{i-1} \times \left(\left(\frac{H_i}{C_{i-1}} - 1.0 \right) \times Leverage + 1.0 \right)$$

$$XL_i = XC_{i-1} \times \left(\left(\frac{L_i}{C_{i-1}} - 1.0 \right) \times Leverage + 1.0 \right)$$

For each subsequent value for the short funds invert the middle term:

$$XC_i = XC_{i-1} \times \left(\left(\frac{C_{i-1}}{C_i} - 1.0 \right) \times Leverage + 1.0 \right)$$

$$XH_i = XC_{i-1} \times \left(\left(\frac{H_{i-1}}{C_i} - 1.0 \right) \times Leverage + 1.0 \right)$$

$$XL_i = XC_{i-1} \times \left(\left(\frac{L_{i-1}}{C_i} - 1.0 \right) \times Leverage + 1.0 \right)$$

where XC, XH, and XL = the leveraged index closing, high, and low prices
C, H, and L = the underlying close, high, and low prices or index values.

If there is no leverage, then substitute the value 1 for leverage in the equations.

Cross-Market and Weighted Index

It is very convenient to create an index for two markets that cannot normally be compared because they trade in different units. For example, if you wanted to show the spread between gold and IBM, you could index them both beginning at the same date. The new indexes would then be in the same units (percent) and would be easy to compare.

Most often, an index combines a number of related markets into a single number. A *simple aggregate index* is the ratio of unweighted sums of market prices in a specific year to the same markets in the base year. Most of the popular indexes, such as the New York Stock Exchange Composite Index, fall into this class. A *weighted aggregate index* biases certain markets by weighting them to increase or decrease their effect on the composite value. The index is then calculated as in the simple aggregate index. When combining markets into a single index value, the total of all the weights will equal 1 and all weights are expressed as a percentage.

U.S. Dollar Index

A practical example of a weighted index is the U.S. Dollar Index, traded as DX on the New York Board of Trade (NYBOT) and USDX on the Intercontinental Exchange (ICE). It is a trade-weighted geometric average of six currencies: the euro, 57.6%; the Japanese yen, 13.6%; the UK pound, 11.9%; the Canadian dollar, 9.1%; the Swedish krona, 4.2%; and the Swiss franc, 3.6%. The Dollar Index serves as a valuable economic indicator, but shows only 13.6% representing Asia. It is not a good substitute for a diversified world market portfolio.

The Dollar Index rises when the U.S. dollar increases in value relative to the other currencies. In the daily calculation of the Dollar Index, each price change is represented as a percent. If, for example, the euro rises 50 points from 1.2500 to 1.2550, the change is 1.2550/1.2500 = .004; this is multiplied by its weighting factor 0.576 and contributes –0.002304 to the index (a rising euro is a falling dollar).

Standard Measurements of Performance

As important as standardizing risk and return is the need to compare the performance of two funds or two trading models in order to decide which is best. That decision is normally made based on a combination of return and risk. The simplest and most practical of these measurements is the *information ratio* (IR)

$$Information\ ratio = \frac{Annualized\ returns}{Annualized\ risk}$$

where both annualized returns and annualized risk (the same as annualized volatility) have been given in the previous section of this chapter.

When you compare performance using any return/risk ratio, you are looking for the optimum point on the efficient frontier. That is, any fund with a higher return but the same risk will be preferable, and any fund with the same return but a lower risk will be preferable.

Sharpe Ratio The *Sharpe ratio*, presented by William F. Sharpe, is the most popular of all performance measures. It differs from the more generic information ratio in that it isolates excess return by subtracting the risk-free rate of return from the fund performance

$$Sharpe\ ratio = \frac{Annualized\ returns - Risk\text{-}free\ returns}{Annualized\ risk}$$

Treynor Ratio The *Treynor ratio* also isolates excess return; however, it replaces the annualized risk of the fund or trading program with the beta of the portfolio. Beta is the volatility (risk) of a stock relative to a benchmark index, for example, the S&P. The portfolio beta is the sum of the weighted individual stock betas within the portfolio. If the fund has a beta of 1.2, then it has 20% more volatility than the overall market and moves generally in the same direction (see the previous section on *beta*). The Treynor ratio is

$$Treynor\ ratio = \frac{Annualized\ returns - Risk\text{-}free\ returns}{Program\ beta}$$

Other Performance Measurements There are numerous variations on performance measures of varying degrees of usefulness. Most often the simplest ones are the best. The value of any measurement is to rank one trading system or fund above another in terms of risk and reward; that is, to help make the decision that one is better. The developers of each performance measure believe that all others are flawed, yet the most popular ratios will usually rank the candidate programs in similar order.

The most common performance measure after the information ratio is simply the maximum drawdown relative to the investment size. The maximum drawdown should always be measured as a percentage from a highest NAV to the lowest subsequent NAV. The maximum drawdown is important because, in a long performance record, a single, large drawdown can be lost in the standard deviation when there are an overwhelming number of "normal" drawdowns. A statistician might be satisfied saying that there is a very, very small chance of that large drawdown occurring again, but an investor might want to know that it did happen and understand why it happened. One measure that accounts for this is the *Calmar ratio*

$$Calmar\ ratio = \frac{Annualized\ return}{Maximum\ drawdown}$$

Another measure that tries to focus on the drawdowns is the *Sortino ratio*. It uses downside volatility as the risk, which is the lower partial moment of degree 2, but can also be substituted with the standard deviation of those days in which the NAV was lower than the previous high NAV (see the section on *semivariance*).

$$Sortino\ ratio = \frac{Annualized\ return - Risk\text{-}free\ return}{Downside\ volatility}$$

These performance measures will be used when comparing different systems.

Probability

Calculation must measure the incalculable.

—Dixon G. Watts

Change is a term that causes great anxiety. However, the effects and likelihood of a chance occurrence can only be measured—not predicted. The area of study that deals with uncertainty is probability. Everyone uses probability in daily thinking and actions. When you tell someone that you will "be there in 30 minutes," you are assuming:

- Your car will start.
- You will not have a breakdown.
- You will have no unnecessary delays.
- You will drive at a predictable speed.
- You will have the normal number of green lights.

All these circumstances are extremely probabilistic, and yet everyone makes the same assumptions. Actually, the 30-minute arrival is intended only as an estimate of the average time it should take for the trip. If the arrival time were critical, you would extend your estimate to 40 or 45 minutes to account for unexpected events. In statistics, this is called *increasing the confidence interval*. You would not raise the time to 2 hours because the likelihood of such a delay would be too remote. Estimates imply an allowable variation, all of which is considered normal.

Probability is the measuring of the uncertainty surrounding an average value. Probabilities are measured in percent of likelihood. For example, if M numbers from a total of N are expected to fall within a specific range, the probability P of any one number satisfying the criteria is

$$P = \frac{M}{N}, \quad 0 < P < 1$$

When making a trade, or forecasting prices, we can only talk in terms of probabilities or ranges. We expect prices to rise 30 to 40 points, or we have a 65% chance of a \$400 profit from a trade. Nothing is certain, but a high probability of success is very attractive.

Laws of Probability

Two basic principles of probability are easily explained by using examples with playing cards. In a deck of 52 cards, there are 4 suits of 13 cards each. The probability of drawing a specific card on any one turn is $1/52$. Similarly, the chances of drawing a particular suit or card number are ¼ and 1⁄13, respectively. *The probability of any one of these three possibilities occurring is the sum of their individual probabilities.* This is known as the *law of addition*. The probability of success in choosing a numbered card, suit, or specific card (that is, either a 10, or a spade, or the queen of hearts) is

$$p = \frac{1}{13} + \frac{1}{4} + \frac{1}{52} = \frac{18}{52} = 35\%$$

The other basic principle, the law of multiplication, states that the probability of two occurrences happening simultaneously or in succession is equal to the product of their separate probabilities. The likelihood of drawing a 3 and a club from the same deck in two consecutive turns (replacing the card after each draw) or of drawing the same cards from two decks simultaneously is

$$p = \frac{1}{13} \times \frac{1}{4} = \frac{1}{52} = 2\%$$

Joint and Marginal Probability

Price movement is not as clearly defined as a deck of cards. There is often a relationship between successive events. For example, over two consecutive days, prices must have one of the following sequences or joint events: (up, up), (down, down), (up, down), (down, up), with the joint probabilities of 0.40, 0.10, 0.35, and 0.15, respectively. In this example, there is the greatest expectation that prices will rise. The marginal probability of a price rise on the first day is shown in Table 21.4, which concludes that there is a 75% chance of higher prices on the first day and a 55% chance of higher prices on the second day.

Contingent Probability

What is the probability of an outcome "conditioned" on the result of a prior event? In the example of joint probability, this might be the chance of a price increase on the second day when prices declined on the first day. The notation for this situation (the probability of *A* conditioned on *B*) is

$$P(A|B) = \frac{P(A \text{ and } B)}{P(B)} = \frac{\textit{Joint probability of } A \text{ and } B}{\textit{Marginal probability of } B}$$

then

$$P(\text{up Day 2}|\text{down Day 1}) = \frac{\textit{Joint probability of } (\text{down, up})}{\textit{Marrginal perobability of } (\text{down Day 1})}$$

$$= \frac{0.15}{0.25} = 0.60$$

The probability of either a price increase on Day 1 or a price increase on Day 2 is

$$P(\text{either}) = P(\text{up Day 1}) + P(\text{up Day 2}) - P(\text{up Day 1 and up Day 2})$$
$$= 0.75 + 0.55 - 0.40$$
$$= 0.90$$

TABLE 21.4 Marginal Probability

		Day 2 Up	Day 2 Down			
Day 1	Up	.40	.35	.75	Up	Marginal probability on Day 1
	Down	.15	.10	.25	Down	
		.55	.45			
		Up	Down			
		Marginal probability on Day 2				

Markov Chains

If we believe that today's price movement is based in some part on what happened yesterday, we have a situation called *conditional probability*. This can be expressed as a *Markov process*, or *Markov chain*. The results, or outcomes, of a Markov chain express the probability of a state or condition occurring. For example, the possibility of a clear, cloudy, or rainy day tomorrow can be related to today's weather.

The different combinations of dependent possibilities are given by a *transition matrix*. In our weather prediction example, a clear day has a 70% chance of being followed by another clear day, a 25% chance of a cloudy day, and only a 5% chance of rain. In Table 21.5, each possibility today is shown on the left, and its probability of changing tomorrow is indicated across the top. Each row totals 100% and accounts for all weather combinations. The relationship between these events can be shown as a continuous network (see Figure 21.11).

TABLE 21.5 Transition Matrix

		Tomorrow Clear	Tomorrow Cloudy	Tomorrow Rainy
Today	Clear	0.70	0.25	0.05
	Cloudy	0.20	0.60	0.20
	Rainy	0.20	0.40	0.40

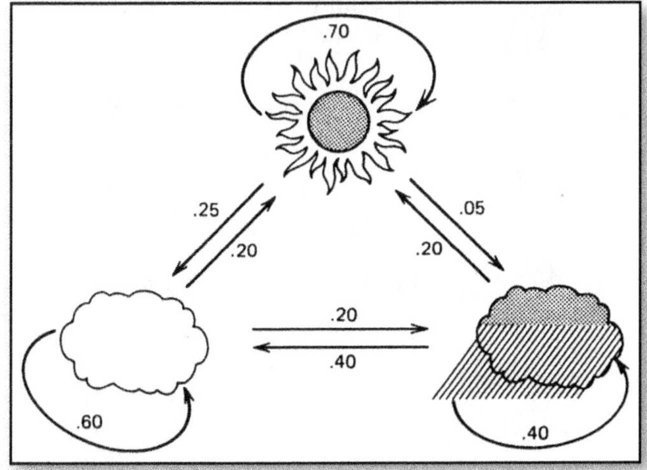

FIGURE 21.11 Probability Network.

The Markov process can reduce intricate relationships to a simpler form. First, consider a two-state process. Using the markets as an example, what is the probability of an up or down day following an up day, or following a down day? If there is a 70% chance of a higher day following a higher day (which we can say is an uptrend) and a 55% chance of a higher day following a lower day, what is the probability of any day within an uptrend being up?

Start with either an up or down day, and then calculate the probability of the next day being up or down. This is done easily by simply counting the number of cases, given in Table 21.6a, then dividing to get the percentages, as shown in Table 21.6b.

Because the first day may be designated as up or down, it is an exception to the general rule and therefore is given the weight of 50%. The probability of the second day being up or down is the sum of the joint probabilities

$$\begin{aligned} P(\text{up})_2 &= (0.50 \times 0.70) + (0.50 \times 0.55) \\ &= 0.625 \end{aligned}$$

The probability of the second day being up is 62.5%. Continuing in the same manner, use the probability of an up day as 0.625, the down as 0.375, and calculate the third day,

$$\begin{aligned} P(\text{up})_3 &= (0.625 \times 0.70) + (0.375 \times 0.55) \\ &= 0.64375 \end{aligned}$$

and the fourth day,

$$\begin{aligned} P(\text{up})_4 &= (0.64375 \times 0.70) + (0.35625 \times 0.55) \\ &= 0.64656 \end{aligned}$$

which can now be seen to be converging. To generalize the probability of an up day, look at what happens on the *i*th day:

$$P(\text{up})_{i+i} = [P(\text{up})_i \times 0.70] + [(1 - P(\text{up})_i) \times 0.55]$$

TABLE 21.6a Counting the Occurrences of Up and Down Days

		Today		
		Up	**Down**	**Total**
Previous day	Up	75	60	135
	Down	60	65	125

TABLE 21.6b Starting Transition Matrix

		Today		
		Up	**Down**	**Total**
Previous day	Up	0.555	0.444	1.00
	Down	0.480	0.520	1.00

Because the probability is converging, the relationship

$$P(\text{up})_{i+1} = P(\text{up})_i$$

can be substituted and used to solve the equation

$$P(\text{up})_i = [P(\text{up})_i \times 0.70] + [0.55 - P(\text{up})_i \times 0.55]$$

giving the probability of any day being up within an uptrend as

$$P(\text{up})_i = 0.64705$$

We can find the chance of an up or down day if the 5-day trend is up simply by substituting the direction of the 5-day trend (or *n*-day trend) for the previous day's direction in the example just given.

Predicting the weather is a more involved case of multiple situations converging and may be very representative of the way prices react to past prices. By approaching the problem in the same manner as the two-state process, a ⅓ probability is assigned to each situation for the first day; the second day's probability is

$$\begin{aligned} P(\text{clear})_2 &= (0.333 \times 0.70) + (0.333 \times 0.20) + (0.333 \times 0.20) \\ &= 0.3663 \end{aligned}$$

$$\begin{aligned} P(\text{cloudy})_2 &= (0.333 \times 0.25) + (0.333 \times 0.60) + (0.333 \times 0.40) \\ &= 0.41625 \end{aligned}$$

$$\begin{aligned} P(\text{rainy})_2 &= (0.333 \times 0.05) + (0.333 \times 0.20) + (0.333 \times 0.40) \\ &= 0.21645 \end{aligned}$$

Then, using the second day results, the third day is

$$\begin{aligned} P(\text{clear})_3 &= (0.3663 \times 0.70) + (0.41625 \times 0.20) + (0.21645 \times 0.20) \\ &= 0.38295 \end{aligned}$$

$$\begin{aligned} P(\text{cloudy})_3 &= (0.3663 \times 0.25) + (0.41625 \times 0.60) + (0.21645 \times 0.40) \\ &= 0.42791 \end{aligned}$$

$$\begin{aligned} P(\text{rainy})_3 &= (0.3663 \times 0.05) + (0.41625 \times 0.20) + (0.21645 \times 0.40) \\ &= 0.18815 \end{aligned}$$

The general form for solving these three equations is

$$\begin{aligned} P(\text{clear})_{i+i} &= [P(\text{clear})_i \times 0.70] + [P(\text{cloudy})_i \times 0.20] + [P(\text{rainy})_i \times 0.20] \\ P(\text{cloudy})_{i+i} &= [P(\text{clear})_i \times 0.25] + [P(\text{cloudy})_i \times 0.60] + [P(\text{rainy})_i \times 0.40] \\ P(\text{rainy})_{i+i} &= [P(\text{clear})_i \times 0.05] + [P(\text{cloudy})_i \times 0.20] + [P(\text{rainy})_i \times 0.40] \end{aligned}$$

where each $i + 1$ element can be set equal to the corresponding ith value. There are then three equations in three unknowns, which can be solved directly or by matrix multiplication.[3] Otherwise, it will be necessary to use the additional relationship

$$P(\text{clear})_i + P(\text{cloudy})_i + P(\text{rainy})_i = 1.00$$

The results are

$$P(\text{clear}) = 0.400$$

$$P(\text{cloudy}) = 0.425$$

$$P(\text{rainy}) = 0.175$$

Bayes' Theorem

Although historic generalization exists concerning the outcome of an event, a specific current market situation may alter the probabilities. *Bayes' theorem* combines the *original probability* estimates with the *added-event probability* (the reliability of the new information) to get a *posterior* or *revised probability*:

$$\frac{P(\text{Original and added-event})}{P(\text{Added-event})}$$

Assume that the price changes $P(\text{up})$ and $P(\text{down})$ are both original probabilities, and an added-event probability, such as an unemployment report, trade balance, crop report, inventory stocks, or Federal Reserve interest rate announcement, is expected to have an overriding effect on tomorrow's movement. Then the new probability $P(\text{Up} \mid \text{added-event})$ is:

$$\frac{P(\text{Up and added-event})}{P(\text{Up and added-event}) + P(\text{Down and added-event})}$$

where *up* and *down* refer to the original historic probabilities, and $P(A \text{ and } B)$ is a joint probability.

Bayes' theorem finds the conditional probability even if the joint and marginal probabilities are not known. The new probability $P(\text{up} \mid \text{added-event})$ is:

$$\frac{P(\text{Up}) \times P(\text{Added-event} \mid \text{up})}{P(\text{Up}) \times P(\text{Added-event} \mid \text{up}) + P(\text{Down}) \times P(\text{Added-event} \mid \text{down})}$$

where $P(\text{Added-event} \mid \text{up})$ = the probability of the new event being a correct predictor of an upwards move

$P(\text{Added-event} \mid \text{down})$ = the probability of prices going down when the added news indicates up

[3] A full mathematical treatment of Markov chains can be found in John G. Kemeny and J. Laurie Snell, *Finite Markov Chains* (New York: Springer-Verlag, 1976).

For example, if a quarter percent decline in interest rates has a 90% chance of causing stock prices to move higher, then

$$P(\text{Added-event} \mid \text{up}) = 0.90$$

and

$$P(\text{Added-event} \mid \text{down}) = 0.10$$

Supply and Demand

Price is the balancing point of supply and demand. In order to estimate the future price of any product or explain its historic patterns, it will be necessary to relate the factors of supply and demand and then adjust for inflation, technological improvement, and other indicators common to econometric analysis. The following sections briefly describe these factors.

Demand

The demand for a product declines as price increases. The rate of decline is always dependent on the need for the product and its available substitutes at different price levels. In Figure 21.12a, *D* represents normal demand for a product over some fixed period. As prices rise, demand declines fairly rapidly. *D′* represents increased demand, resulting in higher prices at all levels.

Figure 21.12b represents the actual demand relationship for potatoes from 1929 to 1939. Although this example is the same as the theoretical relationship in Figure 21.12a, in most cases the demand relationship is not a straight line. Production costs and minimum demand prevent the curve from going to zero; instead, it approaches a minimum price level. This can be seen previously in the frequency distribution

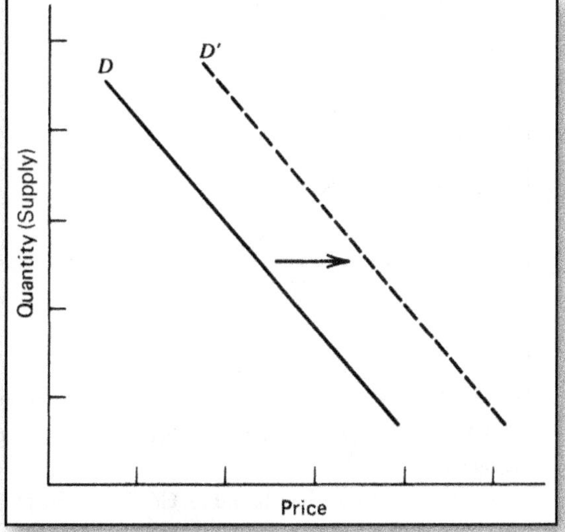

FIGURE 21.12a Shift in Demand.

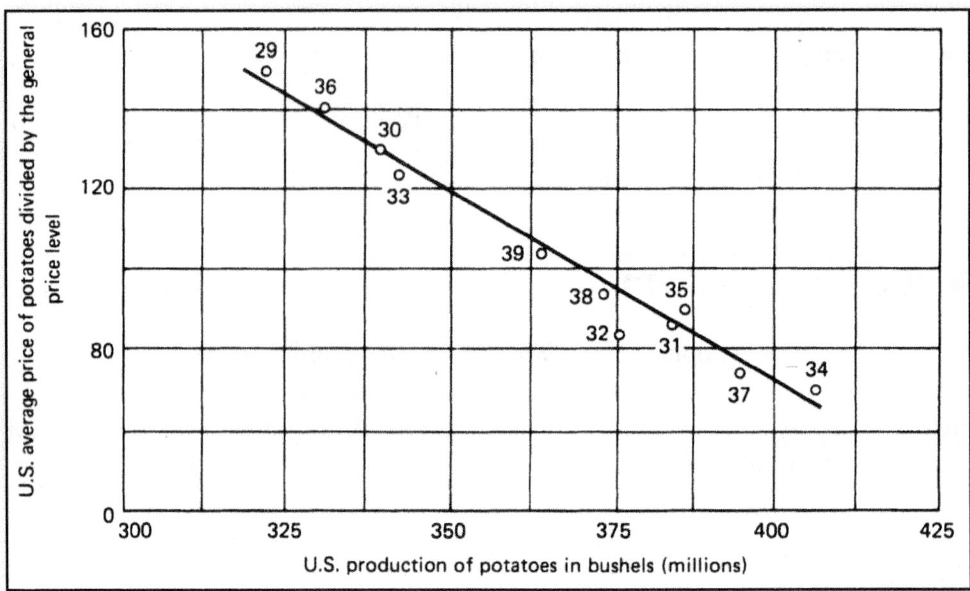

FIGURE 21.12b Potatoes: U.S. Average Farm Price on December 15 versus Total Production: 1929–1939.

for wheat, Figure 21.3, where the left side of the distribution falls (lower price) off sharply. On the higher end of the scale, there is a lag in the response to increased prices and a consumer reluctance to reduce purchasing even at higher prices (called "inelastic demand"). Coffee is well known for having inelastic demand—most coffee drinkers will pay the market price rather than consume less. Figure 21.12c shows a

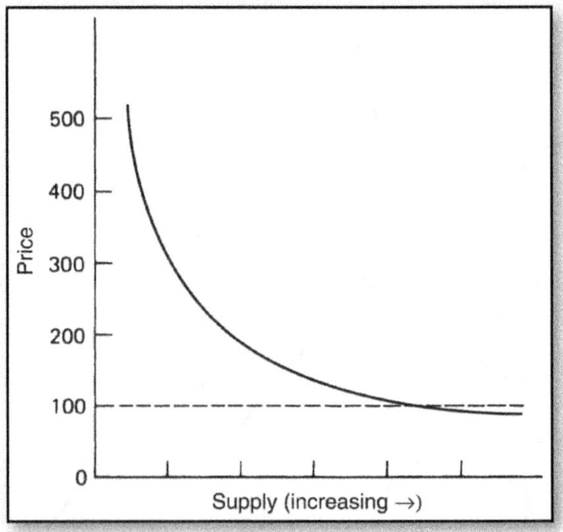

FIGURE 21.12c Demand Curve, Including Extremes.

Source: (for Figures 21.12a, b, and c): Geoffrey S. Shepherd and G. A. Futrell, *Agricultural Price Analysis* (Ames: Iowa State University, 1969), 53.

more representative demand curve, including extremes, where 100 represents the cost of production for a producer. The demand curve, therefore, shows the rate at which a change in quantity demanded brings about a change in price. Note that, although a producer may lose money below 100, lack of demand and the need for income can force sales at a loss.

Elasticity of Demand *Elasticity* is the key factor in expressing the relationship between price and demand and defines the shape of the curve. It is the relative change in demand as price increases:

$$E_D = \frac{\textit{Relative change}(\%)\textit{in demand}}{\textit{Relative change}(\%)\textit{in price}}$$

A market that always consumes the same amount of a product, regardless of price, is called *inelastic*; as price rises, the demand remains the same, and *ED* is negatively very small. An elastic market is just the opposite. As demand increases, price remains the same and *ED* is negatively very large. Figure 21.13 shows the demand curve for various levels of demand elasticity.

If supply increases for a product that has existed in short supply for many years, consumer purchasing habits will require time to adjust. The demand elasticity will gradually shift from relatively inelastic (Figure 21.13b) to relatively elastic (Figure 21.13a).

Supply

The supply side of the economic equation is the normal counterpart of demand. Figure 21.14a shows that, as price increases, the supplier will respond by offering greater amounts of the product. Figure 21.14b demonstrates the supply at price extremes. At low levels, below production costs, there is a nominal supply by those producers who must maintain operations due to high fixed costs and difficulty restarting after a shutdown (as in mining). At high price levels, supply is erratic. There may be insufficient supply in the short term, followed by the appearance of new supplies or substitutes, as in the case of a location shortage.

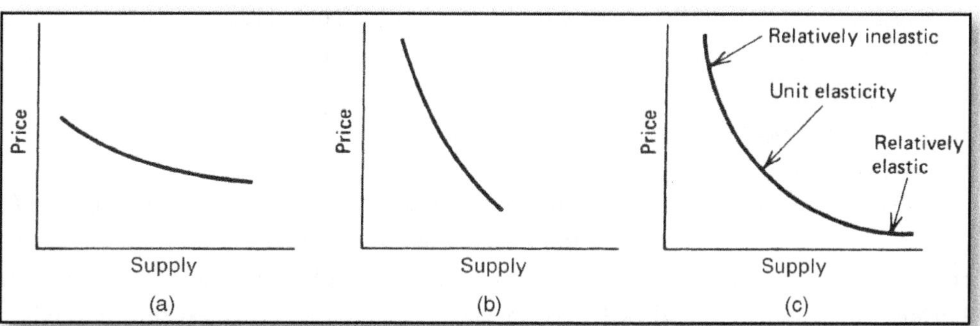

FIGURE 21.13 Demand Elasticity: (a) Relatively Elastic; (b) Relatively Inelastic; (c) Normal Market.

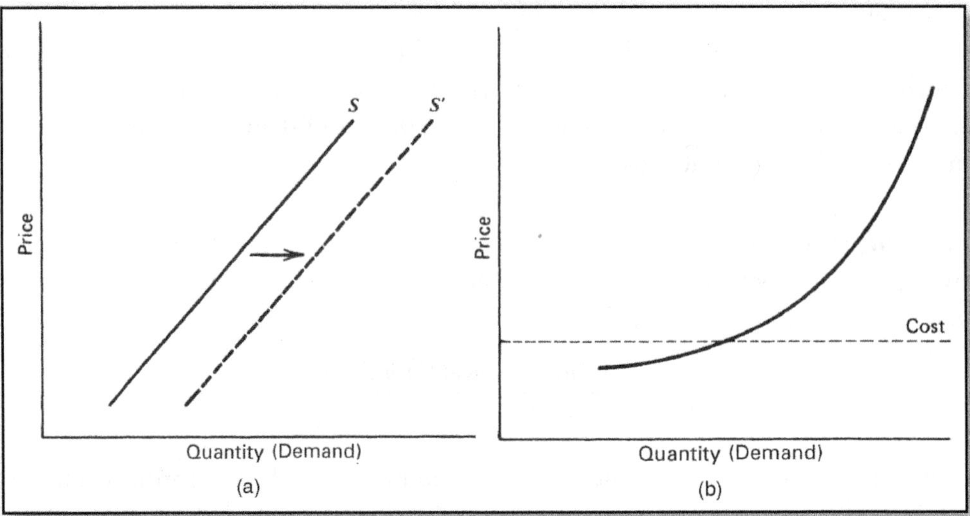

FIGURE 21.14 Supply-Price Relationship: (a) Shift in Supply; (b) Supply Curve, Including Extremes.

When there is a shortage of orange juice, South American countries are willing to fill the demand; when there is an oil disruption, other OPEC nations will increase production. In most cases, however, it is reduced demand that brings price down.

Elasticity of Supply The *elasticity of supply* E_S is the relationship between the change in supply and the change in price:

$$E_S = \frac{\textit{Relative change}(\%)\textit{in supply}}{\textit{Relative change}(\%)\textit{in price}}$$

The elasticity of supply, the counterpart of *demand elasticity*, is a positive number because price and quantity move in the same direction at the same time.

Equilibrium

The demand for a product and the supply of that product cross at a point of *equilibrium*. The current price of any product, or any security, represents the point of equilibrium for that product at that moment in time. This is the basis for the technical assessment that the price, at any moment in time, represents the netting of all fundamental information. Figure 21.15 shows a constant demand line D and a shifting supply increasing to the right from S to S'.

The demand line D and the original supply line S meet at the equilibrium price P; after the increase in supply, the supply line shifts to S'. The point of equilibrium P' represents a lower price, the consequence of larger supply with unchanged demand. Because supply and demand each have varying elasticities and are best represented by curves, the point of equilibrium can shift in any direction in a market with changing factors.

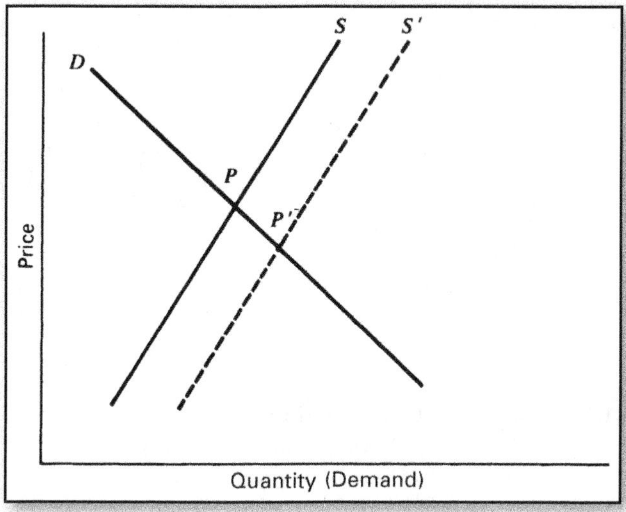

FIGURE 21.15 Equilibrium with Shifting Supply.

Equilibrium will be an important concept in developing trading strategies. Although the supply and demand balance may not be calculated, in practical terms equilibrium is a balance between buyers and sellers, a price level at which everyone is willing to trade, although not always happy to do so at that price. Equilibrium is associated with lower volatility and often lower volume because the urgency to buy or sell has been removed. Imbalance in the supply-demand-price relationship causes volatility. Readers interested in a practical representation of equilibrium, or price-value relationships, should study "Price Distribution Systems" in Steidlmayer's *Market Profile*, Chapter 18.

Cobweb Charts

The point at which the supply and demand lines cross is easily translated into a place on a price chart where the direction is sideways. The amount of price volatility during this sideways period (called noise) depends upon the price level, market participation, and various undertones of instability caused by other factors. Very little is discussed about how price patterns reflect the shift in sentiment between the supply and demand lines, yet there is a clear representation of this action using cobweb charts.

Figure 21.16a shows a static (symmetric) supply-demand chart with dotted lines representing the "cobweb." A shift in the perceived importance of supply and demand factors can cause prices to reflect the pattern shown by the direction of the arrows on the cobweb, producing the sideways market represented by Figure 21.16b. If the cobweb were closer to the intersection of the supply and demand lines, the volatility of the sideways price pattern would be lower; if the cobweb were further away from the intersection, the pattern would be more volatile.[4]

[4] Curtis McKallip, Jr., "Fundamentals behind Technical Analysis," *Technical Analysis of Stocks & Commodities* (November 1989).

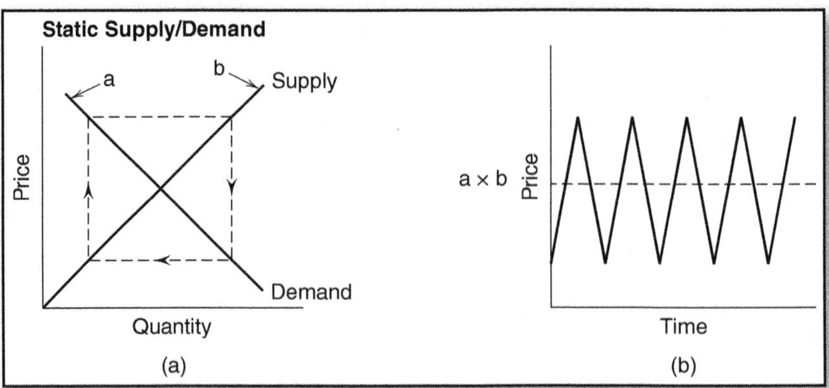

FIGURE 21.16 Static Supply/Demand Cobweb. (a) Dotted lines represent a shift of sentiment from supply to demand to supply, and so forth; (b) the price pattern likely to result from the cobweb in (a).
Source: Curtis McKallip, Jr., "Fundamentals Behind Technical Analysis," *Technical Analysis of Stocks & Commodities* 7, no. 11 (November 1989). © 1989 by Technical Analysis, Inc. Used with permission.

Most supply/demand relationships are not static and can be represented by lines that cross at oblique angles. In Figure 21.17a, the cobweb is shown to begin near the intersection and move outwards, each shift forming a different length strand of the web, moving away from equilibrium. Figure 21.17b shows that the corresponding price pattern is one that shifts from equilibrium to increasing volatility. A reversal in the arrows on the cobweb would show decreasing volatility moving toward equilibrium.

Building a Model

A model can be created to *explain* or *forecast* price changes. Most models explain rather than forecast. Explanatory models analyze sets of data at concurrent times;

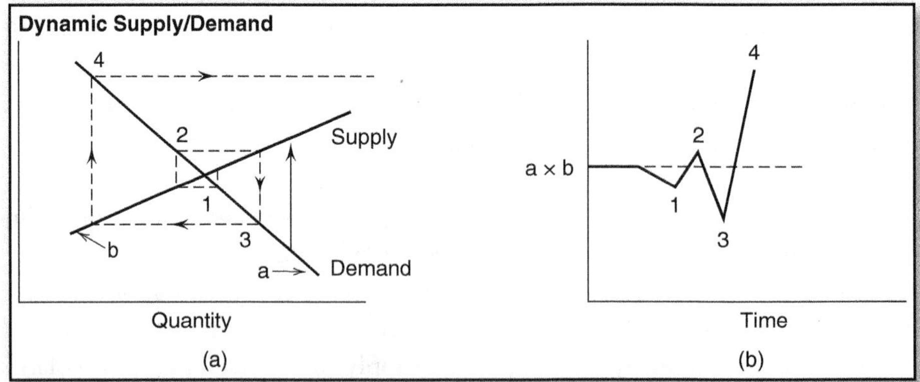

FIGURE 21.17 Dynamic Supply/Demand Cobweb. (a) Dotted lines represent a cobweb moving away from equilibrium; (b) the price pattern shows increasing volatility.
Source: Curtis McKallip, Jr., "Fundamentals Behind Technical Analysis," *Technical Analysis of Stocks & Commodities* 7, no. 11 (November 1989). © 1989 by Technical Analysis, Inc. Used with permission.

that is, they look for relationships between multiple factors and their effect on price at the same moment in time. They can also look for *causal*, or lagged relationships, where prices *respond* to other factors after one or more days. It is possible to use the explanatory model to determine the normal price at a particular moment. Although not considered forecasting, any variation in the actual market price from the normal or expected price could present a trading opportunity.

Methods of selecting the best forecasting model can affect its credibility. An *analytic* approach selects the factors and specifies the relationships in advance. Tests are then performed on the data to verify the premise. Many models, though, are refined by *fitting* the data, using regression analysis or some mass testing process, which applies a broad selection of variables and weighting factors to find the best fit. These models, created with perfect hindsight, are far less likely to be successful at forecasting future price levels. Even an analytic approach that is subsequently fine-tuned could be in danger of losing its forecasting ability.

The factors that comprise a model can be both numerous and difficult to obtain. Figure 21.18 shows the interrelationship between factors in the cocoa industry. Although this chart is comprehensive in its intramarket relationships, it does not emphasize the global influences that have become a major part of price movement since the mid-1970s. The change in value of the U.S. dollar and the volatility of interest rates have had far greater influence on price than some of the "normal" fundamental factors for many commodities. Companies with high debt may find the price fluctuations in their stock are larger due to interest rate changes than increases or decreases in revenues.

Models that explain price movements must be constructed from the primary factors of supply and demand. A simple example for estimating the price of fall potatoes[5] is

$$P/PPI = a + bS + cD$$

where P = the average price of fall potatoes received by farmers
PPI = the Producer Price Index
S = the apparent domestic free supply (production less exports and diversions)
D = the estimated deliverable supply
a, b, and c = constants determined by regression analysis

This model implies that consumption must be constant (that is, inelastic demand); demand factors are only implicitly included in the estimated deliverable supply. Exports and diversion represent a small part of the total production. The use of the *PPI* gives the results in *relative* terms based on whether the index was used as an *inflator* or *deflator* of price.

[5] J. D. Schwager, "A Trader's Guide to Analyzing the Potato Futures Market," *1981 Commodity Yearbook* (New York: Commodity Research Bureau, 1981).

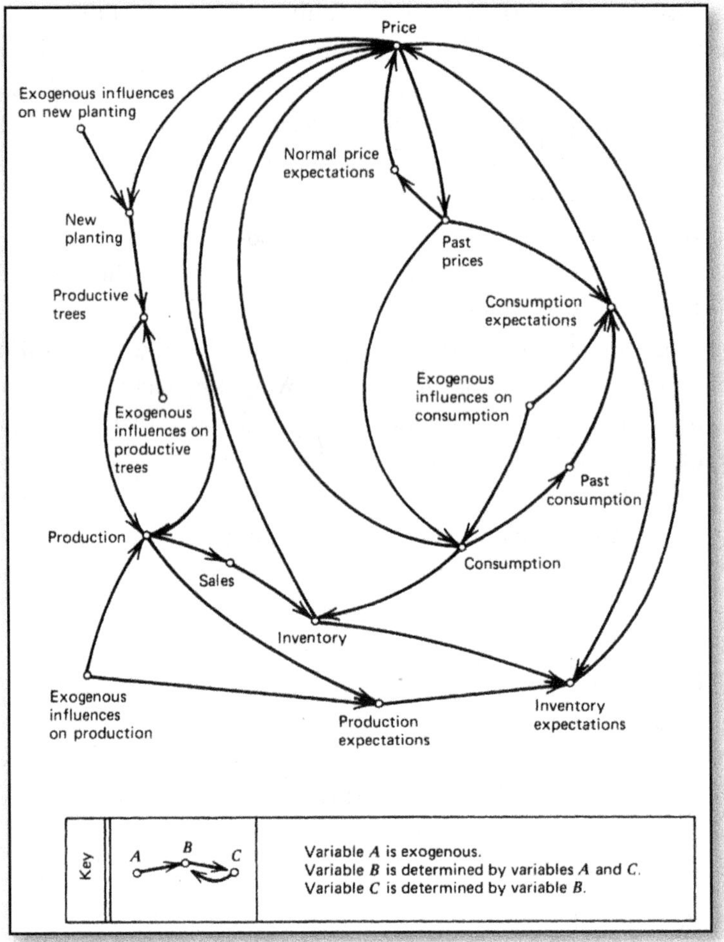

FIGURE 21.18 Cocoa Factors.
Source: F. H. Weymar, *The Dynamics of the World Cocoa Market* (Cambridge: MIT Press, 1968), 2. Use by permission ofThe MIT Press.

A general model, presented by Weymar,[6] may be written as three behavior-based equations and one identity:

Consumption

$$C_t = f_C(P_t, P_t^L) + e_{C_t}$$

Production

$$H_t = f_H(P_t, P_t^L) + e_{H_t}$$

Inventory

$$I_t = I_{t-1} + H_t - C_t$$

[6] F. H. Weymar, *The Dynamics of the World Cocoa Market* (Cambridge: MIT Press, 1968).

Supply of storage

$$P'_t - P_t = f_p(I_t) + e_p$$

where C = the consumption
P = the price
P^L = the lagged price
H = the production (harvest)
I = the inventory
P' = the expected price at some point in the future
e = the corresponding error factor

The first two equations show that both demand and supply depend on current and/or lagged prices, the traditional macroeconomic theory; production and consumption are therefore dependent on past prices. The third equation, *inventory level*, is simply the total of previous inventories, plus new production, less current consumption. The last equation, *supply of storage*, demonstrates that people are willing to carry larger inventories if they expect prices to increase substantially. The inventory function itself, the third equation, is composed of two separate relationships: manufacturers' inventories and speculators' inventories. Each reacts differently to expected price change.

Changing Factors

Although the PPI was always considered the component of inflation and used in forecasting prices, the value of the U.S. dollar has not been an input. Currency values have always fluctuated but have taken on more significance following the dropping of the gold standard by most countries. The value of a currency is based on the health of the economy as measured by production output and inflation, among other factors.

Wheat is a good example to show the impact of these changes. As an export market for the United States, the price of wheat reflects the world value, that is, what other countries are willing to pay. Wheat is *fungible*, in other words, a country in need will buy from any source with the lowest price, and that keeps all prices competitive.

Rather than the complex analysis of factors shown in the previous section on cocoa, we will only look at the impact of inflation and currency changes on the price of wheat. Figure 21.19 shows the monthly price of cash wheat, along with the PPI and the U.S. dollar index (DX). The dollar index shows the relative value of the U.S. dollar; therefore, a decline in DX indicates a weaker U.S. dollar. Both the PPI and DX have been indexed to begin 1985 with the value of 100.

In Figure 21.19 the PPI nearly doubles from 1.0 to 1.8 while the U.S. dollar halves to 0.51. At the same time wheat prices rise 69% from 100 to 169 (the cash price from \$3.56 to \$7.13). If we are only concerned with the big picture, the macro factors rather than the seaonality of price, then the rise in wheat prices over this 25-year interval can be completely explained by either the PPI or the DX. In fact, they are clearly related because inflation (PPI) has a negative effect on the currency value.

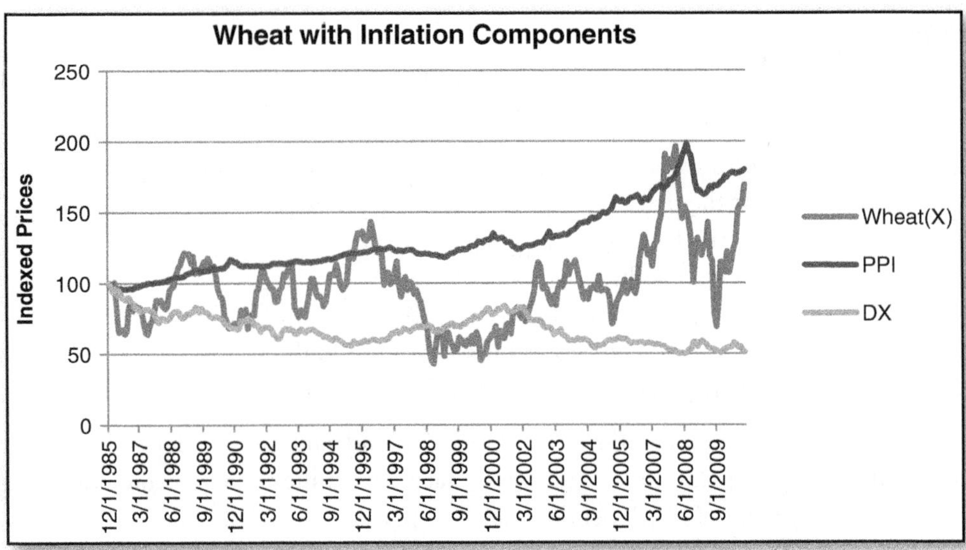

FIGURE 21.19 **Cash Wheat with the PPI and Dollar Index (DX), from 1985 through October 2010.**

By dividing the indexed price of wheat by the PPI or multiplying wheat by the DX value, Figure 21.20 shows that the long-term price of wheat is unchanged. By observation, we can conclude that the rise in wheat prices is attributed to inflation, the decline in the value of the U.S. dollar, or both.

If we then want to look at the effect of seasonality, or supply and demand, factors that cause wheat prices to lose 75% of its value or gain 100%, we need to remove the effects of inflation first. For trading, this means selling DX in the same dollar value

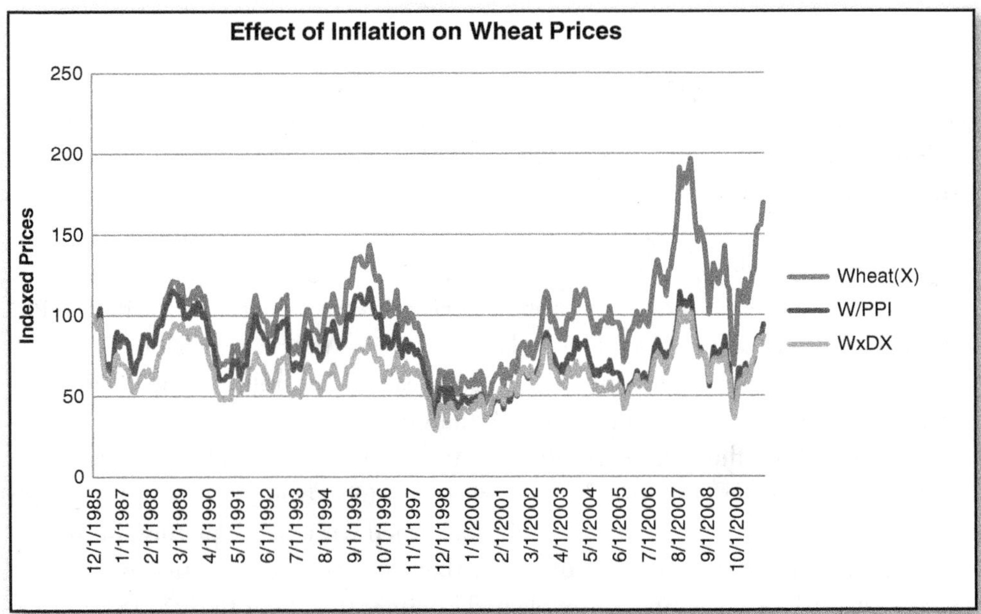

FIGURE 21.20 **Wheat Prices Adjusted for PPI and Dollar Index.**

as buying wheat so that, if the price of wheat rises due to the U.S. dollar falling, the change in value of the hedge position is close to zero.

In the case of wheat, it is clear that the price is affected by inflation. It may be that the success of most wheat trading strategies depends on the trend of inflation, rather than the underlying wheat factors. However, if the intent is to profit from seasonal moves, then a rally in May when a good crop is being harvested may be obscured by a rise in the U.S. dollar. Without hedging the potential effects of the dollar, you leave the results of the strategy to chance.

Economic Reports

Economic reports are released nearly every day. Based on the economic condition of the nation, investor focus shifts from one report to another. Since 2008 the focus has been on the employment reports, the ultimate solution to recovery; GDP, a measure of that recovery; and of less importance housing, consumer confidence, and various manufacturing data. The Leading Economic Index (LEI), released by the Conference Board each month, tries to anticipate the direction of the economy about six months ahead based on

- Average weekly hours, manufacturing
- Average weekly initial claims for unemployment insurance
- Manufacturers' new orders, consumer goods, and materials
- Index of supplier deliveries—vendor performance
- Manufacturers' new orders, nondefense capital goods
- Building permits, new private housing units
- Stock prices, 500 common stocks
- Money supply, M2
- Interest rate spread, 10-year Treasury bonds less federal funds
- Index of consumer expectations

Most of these seem reasonable, but the weighting of them is not clear. It has been said that the direction of the stock market plays a relatively large part in the index.

Can these and other indicators be used for trading? Are they timely, or are the expectations of their impact in the market even before the reports are released? With many reports, the market anticipates the numbers. If unemployment was expected to increase, then the stock market tends to sell off ahead of the report, or if economists anticipate the Fed lowering rates, then the yield curve will adjust to that expectation ahead of the announcement. Therefore, it is the difference between the expectation and the actual report that moves the market, and only secondarily is it the actual numbers released. For example, if the GDP was expected to rise from 3.5% to 4.0% and the actual number came in at 3.6%, the market would sell off. But then it would rally again because 3.6% is still a good number indicating growth.

While large, unexpected changes move the market, the cumulative effect of small changes could also be significant.

Ruggiero has quantified the significance of some of these indicators, concentrating on predicting the direction of yields, which is key to much of the financial market price moves.[7]

Interest rates

$$Ratio = 1 - \frac{Rate\ of\ Inflation}{Yield}$$

$$Inflation\ \ yield\ Oscilator\ (IYO) = R - \overline{R}$$

where *Yield* is the 3-month Treasury bill and $\overline{R}$ is the 20-day average of the ratio, *R*.

- If ($R < 0.2$ or IYO < 0) and $Yield_t > Yield_{t-3mo}$, then rates will rise.
- If ($R > 0.3$ or IYO > 0.5) and $Yield_t < Yield_{t-3mo}$, then rates will fall.

Money Supply Using monthly data for *M2* and the 3-month Treasury bill yields, where *m* is the current month,

If $(M2_m - M2_{m-1}) > (M2_m - M2_{m-6})$ and $Yieldt > Yield_{t-11mo}$, then rates will rise.
If $(M2_m - M2_{m-1}) < (M2_m - M2_{m-6})$ and $Yield_t < Yield_{t-11mo}$, then rates will fall.

Consumer Sentiment Using the University of Michigan's *Consumer Sentiment Survey* (*CS*), and where *m* is the month it is released,

If $CS_m > CS_{m-12}$ and $CS_m > CS_{m-11}$ and $Yield_t > Yield_{t-4mo}$, then rates will rise.
If $CS_m < CS_{m-12}$ and $CS_m < CS_{m-11}$ and $Yield_t < Yield_{t-4mo}$, then rates will fall.

Unemployment Claims Using monthly *unemployment claims* (*UC*) released on the first Friday of each month,

If $UC_m < UC_{m-11}$ and $UC_m > UC_{m-14}$, then rates will rise.
If $UC_m > UC_{m-11}$ and $UC_m < UC_{m-14}$, then rates will fall.

The big picture of price direction is very important, and an accurate forecast can greatly improve results. Using fundamental data in a systematic way is perfectly consistent with other algorithmic approaches.

[7] Murray A. Ruggiero, Jr., "Fundamentals Pave Way to Predicting Interest Rates," *Futures* (September 1996).

CHAPTER 22

Point-and-Figure Charting

From Perry J. Kaufman, *Trading Systems and Methods, + Website*, 5th Edition (Hoboken, New Jersey: John Wiley & Sons, 2013), Chapter 5.

Point-and-Figure Charting

There does not appear to be any record of which came first, swing charting or point-and-figure charting. Both methods are very similar; however, point-and-figure has developed a much more extensive following. Point-and-figure charting is credited to Charles Dow, who is said to have used it just prior to the turn of the twentieth century. It has three important characteristics:

1. It has simple, well-defined trading rules.
2. It ignores price reversals that are below a minimum price move as determined by the *box size*.
3. It has no time factor (it is event-driven). As long as prices fail to change direction by the reversal value, the trend is intact.

When point-and-figure charting first appeared, it did not contain the familiar boxes of *X*s and *O*s. The earliest book containing the subject is reported to be *The Game in Wall Street and How to Play it Successfully*, published by Hoyle (not Edmond Hoyle, the English writer) in 1898. The first definitive work on the subject was by Victor De Villiers, who in 1933 published *The Point and Figure Method of Anticipating Stock Price Movement*. De Villiers worked with Owen Taylor to publish and promote a weekly point-and-figure service, maintaining their own charts; he was impressed by the simple, scientific methodology. As with many of the original technical systems, the application was intended for the stock market, and the rules required the use of every price change appearing on the ticker. It has also been highly popular among futures traders in the grain and livestock pits of Chicago. The rationale for a purely technical system has been told many times, but an original source is often refreshing. De Villiers said:[1]

[1]Victor De Villiers, *The Point and Figure Method of Anticipating Stock Price Movements* (1933; reprint New York: Trader Press, 1966), 8.

Silver

854.0	X									
853.0	X	O	X							
852.0	X	O	X	O						
851.0		O	X	O	X					
850.0		O		O	X	O				
849.0				O	X	O				
848.0				O	X	O				
847.0				O						
846.0										

FIGURE 22.1 **Point-and-Figure Chart.**

The Method takes for granted:

1. That the price of a stock at any given time is its correct valuation up to the instant of purchase and sales (a) by the consensus of opinion of all buyers and sellers in the world and (b) by the verdict of all the forces governing the laws of supply and demand.
2. That the last price of a stock reflects or crystalizes everything known about or bearing on it from its first sale on the Exchange (or prior), up to that time.
3. That those who know more about it than the observer cannot conceal their future intentions regarding it. Their plans will be revealed in time by the stock's subsequent action.

The unique aspect of the point-and-figure and swing methods is that they ignore the passage of time. The point-and-figure chart differs from the swing chart in that each column representing an upswing is a series of boxes containing *X*s, and each downswing is shown as a string of *O*s (Figure 22.1), and a mark is not placed unless a minimum price change occurs.

The original *figure charts* were traditionally plotted on graph paper with square boxes, and only dots, or the exact price, were written in each box. The chart evolved to have prices written on the left scale of the paper, where each box represented a minimum price move. Some point-and-figure chartists then used a combination of *X*s and occasional digits (usually 0s and 5s every five boxes) to help keep track of the length of a move. In some cases the top of an upswing column was connected to the start of a downswing in the next column with a crossbar, and the bottom of a downswing column was connected to the beginning of the next upswing column. This gave the point-and-figure chart an appearance similar to the swing chart. Charts using 1, 3, and 5 points per box were popular, where each point represented a minimum price move. In the 5-point method, no entry was recorded unless the price change spanned 5 points.

Point-and-figure charts, which were commonly used on the floor of the Chicago Mercantile Exchange and the Chicago Board of Trade up to the late 1990s, are intended to show the greatest detail. Each box represents the minimum allowable price move, and reversals of direction use the traditional 3-box criteria. Floor traders use the charts to show only the short-term price moves, and leave a lot to the interpretation of patterns.

Plotting Prices Using the Point-and-Figure Method

To plot prices on a point-and-figure chart, start with a piece of square-box graph paper and mark the left scale using a conveniently small price increment. For example, each box may be set at $0.25 for Microsoft, $0.50 for IBM, 5.0 points for S&P 500 index, $1 for gold and platinum, 4/32 for 30-year bond futures, 1¢ for soybeans and silver, and so forth (as in Figure 22.1). The choice of a box size will make the chart more or less sensitive to changes in price direction as will be seen in later examples. The smaller the box size, the more changes in direction will be seen. This also corresponds to longer and shorter trends or major and minor trends. Therefore, a point-and-figure chartist looking for a long-term price movement will use a larger box size. Box sizes are often related to the current volatility of the markets.

Once the graph paper has been scaled and the prices entered along the left side, the chartist can begin. The first box is entered with the current closing price of the market. If the price of silver is 852.50 and a 1¢ (1¢ = 1.00) box is being used, a mark is placed in the box beside the value 852. An *X* or an *O* is used to indicate that the current price trend is up or down, respectively. Either an *X* or *O* may be used to begin—after that, it will be determined by the method.

The rules for plotting point-and-figure charts are easily shown as a flowchart in Figure 22.2. Preference is given to price movements that continue in the direction of the current trend. Therefore, if the trend is up (represented by a column of *X*s), the new high price is tested first; if the trend is down, the low price is given preference. The opposite price is checked only if the new price fails to increase the length of the column in the direction of the current trend.

The traditional point-and-figure method calls for the use of a *3-box reversal*, that is, the price must reverse direction by an amount that fills 3 boxes from the most extreme box of the last column before a new column can begin (it actually must fill the fourth box because the extreme box is left blank). The importance of keeping the 3-box reversal has long been questioned by experienced point-and-figure traders. It should be noted that the net reversal amount (the box size times the number of boxes in the reversal) is the critical value. For example, a 5-point box for the NASDAQ 100 ETF (QQQ) with a 3-box reversal means that QQQ prices must reverse from the lows of the current downtrend by 15 points to indicate that an uptrend has started. The opposite combination, a 3-point box and a 5-box reversal, would signal a new trend at the same time, after a 15-point reversal. The difference between the two choices is that the smaller box size would recognize a smaller continuation of a price move by filling more boxes. Ultimately, the smaller box size

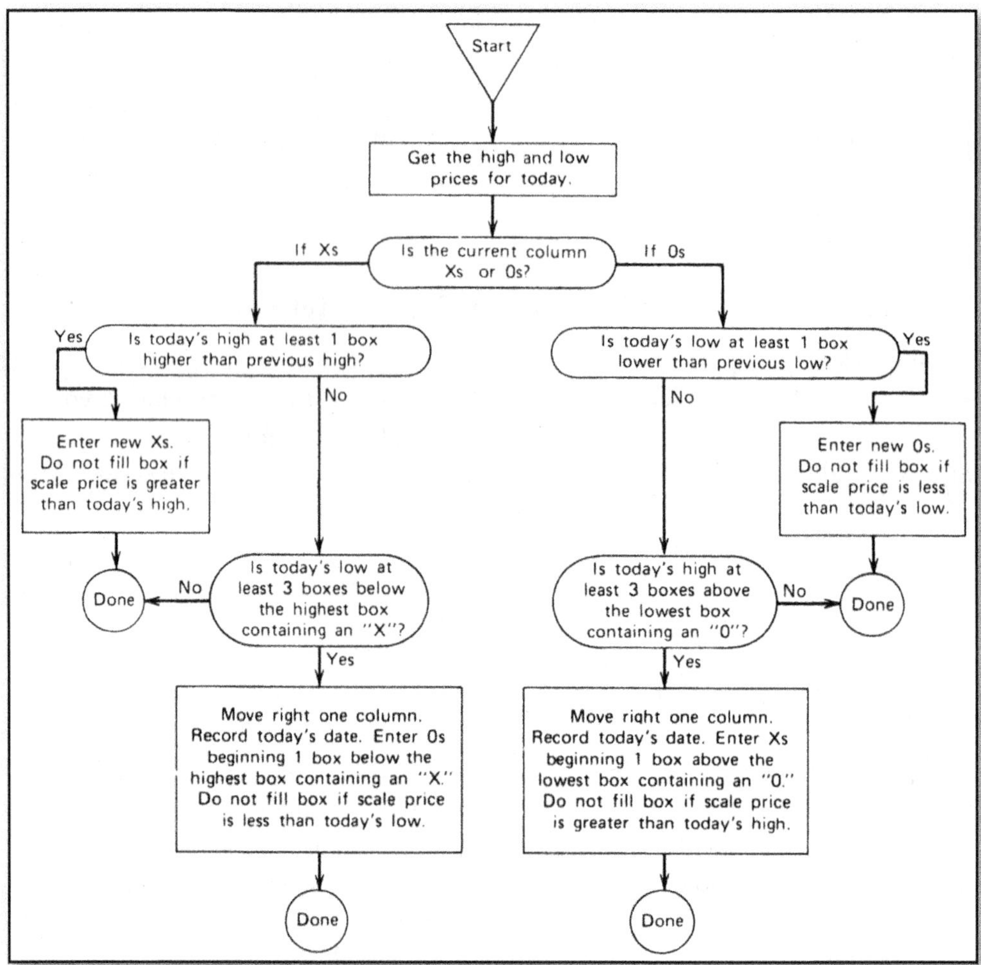

FIGURE 22.2 Point-and-Figure Daily Rules.

will capture more of the price move; it is considered the preferable alternative. The choice of box size and reversal boxes will be considered later in more detail.

Painless Point-and-Figure Charts There are a number of graphic charting and quote systems that allow a simple bar chart to be converted to point-and-figure automatically. It is still necessary to specify the box size and the reversal size. The reason for showing the construction in detail is that none of these services provide trading signals or performance results based on point-and-figure charting. For that, it will be necessary to code the instructions into a spreadsheet or a strategy development platform.

Point-and-Figure Chart Formations

It would be impossible for the average speculator to follow the original method of recording every change in price. When applied to stocks, these charts became so lengthy and covered so much paper that they were unwieldy and made interpretation

```
Ascending Triple Top          Breakout of a Triple Bottom
        X ←BUY                   X   X
     X  X                      O X O X O
  X  X O X                     O X O X O
  X O X O X                    O   O   O
  X O X O                              O ←SELL
    O
```

FIGURE 22.3 Best Formations from Davis's Study.

difficult. In 1965, Robert E. Davis published *Profit and Profitability*, a point-and-figure study that detailed eight unique buy and sell signals. The study covered two stocks for the years 1914–1964, and 1100 stocks for 1954–1964. The intention was to find specific bull and bear formations that were more reliable than others. The study concluded that the best buy signal was an *ascending triple top* and the best sell signal was the *breakout of a triple bottom*, both shown in Figure 22.3 and with the other patterns studied in Figure 22.4.

Plotted using daily data, futures prices do not offer the variety of formations available in the stock market. The small number of markets and the high correlation of movement between many of the index and interest rate markets make the limitations of signal selection impractical. Instead, the most basic approach is used, where a buy signal occurs when an *X* in the current column is one box above the highest *X* in the last column of *X*s, and the simple sell signal is an *O* plotted below the lowest *O* of the last descending column. The flexibility of the system lies in the size of the box; the smaller the size, the more sensitive the chart will be to price moves. In 1933, Wyckoff noted that it was advisable to use a chart with a different box size when the price of the stock varied substantially.[2]

Point-and-Figure Trendlines

Bullish and bearish trendlines are commonly used with point-and-figure charts. The top or bottom box that remains blank when a reversal occurs can form the beginning of a descending or ascending pattern at a 45° angle (diagonally through the corners of the boxes, providing the graph paper has square boxes). These 45° lines represent the major anticipated trends of the market. Once a top or bottom has been identified, a 45° line can be drawn down and to the right from the upper corner of the top boxes of *X*s, or up and towards the right from the bottom of the lowest box of *O*s (Figure 22.5). These trendlines are used to *confirm* the direction of price movement and are often used to filter the basic point-and-figure trading signals so that only long positions are taken when the 45° trendline is up and only shorts sales are entered when the trendline is down.

[2] Richard D. Wyckoff, *Stock Market Technique, Number One* (New York: Wyckoff, 1933), 89.

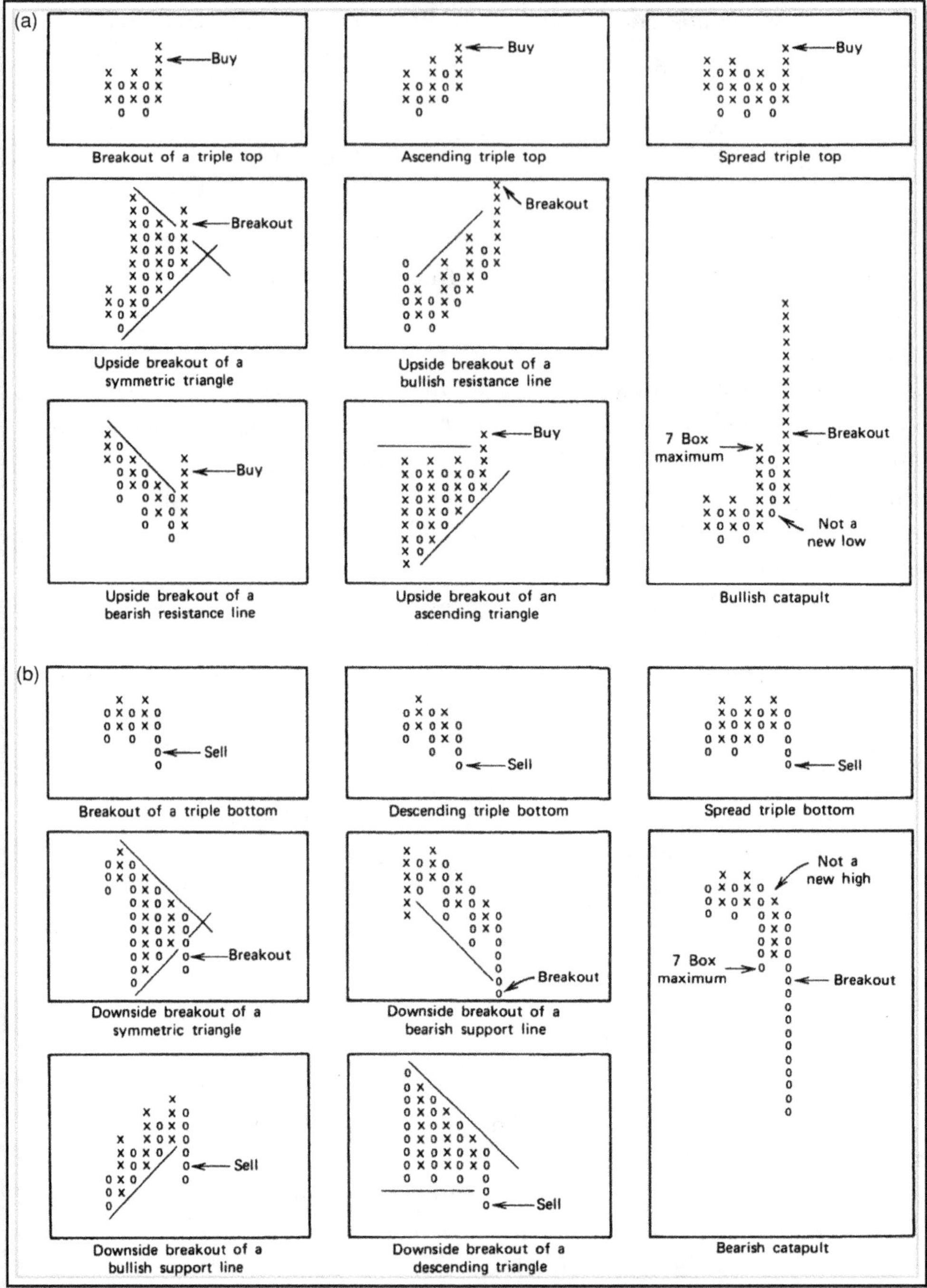

FIGURE 22.4 (a) Compound Point-and-Figure Buy Signals. (b) Compound Point-and-Figure Sell Signals.

More Point-and-Figure Studies In 1970, Charles C. Thiel, Jr., with Robert E. Davis, completed the first purely futures market point-and-figure study[3] that calculated

[3] Charles Thiel and R. E. Davis, *Point and Figure Commodity Trading: A Computer Evaluation* (West Lafayette, IN: Dunn & Hargitt, 1970).

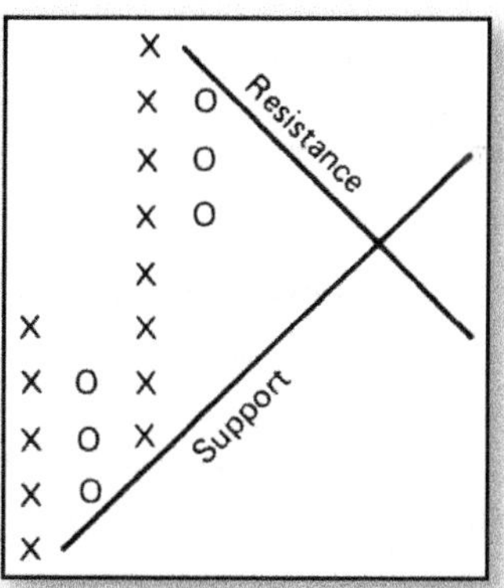

FIGURE 22.5 Point-and-Figure Trendlines.

profitability of a reasonably large sample of markets by varying both the value of a box and the reversal criteria. With the standard 3-box reversal and only simple buy and sell formations, the tests showed 799 signals, of which 53% were profitable; the average net profit on all trades was $311 realized in approximately 50 days. The period studied was 1960 through 1969. In the mid-1970s, Zieg and Kaufman[4] performed a computerized study using the same rules but limiting the test period to six months ending May 1974, an extremely active market period. For the 22 commodities tested, 375 signals showed 40% of the trades were profitable; the net profit over all the trades was $306 and the average duration was 12.4 days. It is interesting to note that the most significant difference in the results of the two studies is in the average length of a trade, from 50 in the Thiel and Davis study to 12.4 days in the Zieg and Kaufman tests, indicating a change apparently induced by more volatile markets. Although the two tests varied in many of the details, the results are a strong argument for the consistency of the point-and-figure method as a trading tool.

In its current role, point-and-figure differs from traditional charting because it provides a rigid set of trading rules. Many of the formations are still subject to interpretation and are frequently used that way by floor traders. For the more systematic trader, it will tell exactly what penetration of a resistance or support level is necessary to generate a buy or sell signal and exactly where the stop-loss order should be placed to limit risk. It is this well-defined nature of point-and-figure charting that allows computer testing and evaluation.

A complete study of the point-and-figure method includes rules of charting, buy and sell signals, trendlines, geometric formations, and price objectives. They apply equally to point-and-figure charting. They have also been covered effectively in a book by Cohen and another by Zieg and Kaufman.[5] The following sections cover more advanced point-and-figure topics, including its relationship to bar charting, alternate plotting rules, risk-limited trading, and varying box size.

---

[4] Kermit C. Zieg, Jr., and Perry J. Kaufman, *Point and Figure Commodity Trading Techniques* (Larchmont, NY: Investors Intelligence, 1975). This book contains complete tabularized results of both point-and-figure tests.

[5] A.W. Cohen, *How to Use the Three-Point Reversal Method of Point and Figure Stock Market Trading* (Larchmont, NY: Chartcraft, 1972); and Kermit C. Zieg and Perry J. Kaufman, *Point & Figure Commodity Trading Techniques* (Larchmont, NY: Chartcraft, 1975).

Point-and-Figure Box Size The box size used in a point-and-figure chart determines the sensitivity, or frequency of signals. The selection of the box size is critical to successful trading. For many years Chartcraft (Investors Intelligence) was the only major service that produced a full set of point-and-figure charts for the futures markets. A history of their box sizes is shown in Table 22.1. There are now a number of services providing these charts, and they can easily be found by searching the Internet for "point-and-figure charts."

Since the 1970s, every traded commodity has had at least one major price move taking it to levels often greater than twice the normal price. Sugar and silver each topped at 10 times their value in 1970. By 2000 many technology stocks had surged 20 times their 1990 value only to retreat by as much as 90% in the next few years. These moves necessitate changes in box size in order to control the impact of the increased, and later decreased, volatility.

TABLE 22.1 Point-and-Figure Box Sizes*

		Prior to 1975†		1975‡	1977‡	1977§	1986‡	2002–2003
Futures Market	Units	Year	Box Size	Box Size	Box Size	Box Size	Box Size	Box Size
				Grains				
Corn	cents	1971	½	2	2	2	1	2
Oats	cents	1965	½	1	1		1	½
Soybeans	cents	1971	1	10	10	5	5	4¼
Soybean meal	pts	1964	50	500	500		100	200
Soybean oil	pts	1965	10	20	20		10	20
Wheat	cents	1964	1	2	2	2	1	1.5
				Livestock and Meats				
Live cattle	pts	1967	20	20	20		20	10
Live hogs	pts	1968	20	20	20		20	40
Pork bellies	pts	1965	20	20	20		20	75
				Other Agricultural Products				
Cocoa¶	pts	1964	20	100	100	50	10	2
Coffee	pts		(20)†	100	100	50	100	
Cotton	pts		(20)†	100	100		50	90
Lumber	pts		(100)†	100	100		100	170
Orange juice	pts	1968	20	20	100	20	100	100
Sugar	pts	1965	5	20	20		10	16
				Metals				
Copper	pts	1964	20	100	100	50	50	100
Gold	pts			50	100		400	200
Platinum	pts	1968	200	100	200	200	400	
Silver	pts	1971	100	200	200	400	1000	150

*All box sizes use a 3-box reversal and are in points (decimal fractions treated as whole numbers) unless otherwise indicated.
†Cohen (1972); parentheses indicate approximate values.
‡Courtesy of Chartcraft Commodity Service, Chartcraft, Inc., Larchmont, New York.
§Chart Analysis Limited, Bishopgate, London. Values are for long-term continuation charts.
¶Cocoa contract changed from cents/pound to dollars/ton.

Table 22.2 shows the performance of the point-and-figure method from 2000 through 2010 for a selection of widely traded futures markets. When testing these markets, the first problem that surfaces is that each market needs its unique box size. For example, soybeans trading at $15/bushel will need a box size smaller than the DAX, trading at 6000. The box size reflects a sensitively to volatility during the period of the test data.

To solve that problem as simply as possible, the box sizes were initialized to a percentage of the price at the beginning of the test. These centered around 1%, so that gold at $1000/oz would have a box size of $10. All gold signals used the $10 box size and a 3-box reversal for a total directional reversal of $30. In Table 22.2a, all negative net profits are shaded in grey, and the best results for each market are outlined.

Results show inconsistency. The more trending markets, the interest rates and the euro, are generally profitable for all box sizes. The noisier markets, primarily the equity index markets, show consistent losing results. Eurodollar interest rates show few trades because a percentage of the price at 99.00 is far too big for a box size. To get the right box size, the series would need to be converted to yields. The same is true of the longer-term rates, even though both 10-year notes and 30-year bonds showed good returns. The grains were also inconsistent, with soybeans showing too many trades (see Table 22.2b) while wheat appears normal. This reflects the volatility of the individual markets.

Even during this 10-year test, the volatility of each market would have changed considerably. Systems that are event driven, such as swings, point-and-figure, and breakouts, are not bothered by low volatility for moderate periods of time. They typically hold the same position until something new happens. However, if at the start of the test the volatility was much lower than at the end, there will be few trades at the beginning and much more at the end. Results will be distorted, with greater importance given to the more volatile periods.

It seems reasonable to conclude that the change in price and, consequently, the change in volatility determine the most practical choice of box size. As an example, if we look at the best choice of box size for a selection of stocks and industrial groups for 2003, we get the results shown in Table 22.3. These are plotted as a scatter diagram in Figure 22.5. They show a clear relationship between price level and box size. We will use this pattern to create a more dynamic point-and-figure chart. Rules for varying box sizes and risks associated with these price and volatility changes are discussed later in the section, "Point-and-Figure with Variable Box Size."

Point-and-Figure Trading Techniques

The basic point-and-figure trading signals are triggered on new highs and new lows:

Buy when the filled column of *X*s, the current upswing, rises above the previous column of *X*s by one box.

Sell when the filled column of *O*s, the current downswing, falls below the low of the previous column of *O*s by one box.

TABLE 22.2a Net Profits for the Point-and-Figure Method Initial box sizes range from 0.10% to 2.0% for a selection of futures markets, 2000–2010. Negative results are in grey, and the best results for each market are outlined.

Box (%)	Crude Oil	Cotton	DAX	EUR	Bund	Euro-dollars	S&P	Gold	Heating Oil	Japanese Yen	NASDAQ	Soy-beans	10-Year Notes	30-Year Bonds	Wheat
2.0	3540	-12540	31450	54538	0	0	-6838	-10200	-22142	-925	4895	-8725	19641	-5188	-26200
1.9	-10510	-22970	80800	74600	0	0	-11325	3450	-10580	14413	-2165	11150	16484	14813	-28813
1.8	-42370	-44990	186225	74875	14360	0	11975	-24610	-55797	-9563	-11730	650	34672	2906	-32288
1.7	-9840	-45610	133513	89763	7240	0	-11500	25300	-122653	14100	-13985	18275	13953	26156	-32750
1.6	-28630	-67010	42425	104875	14580	0	-6875	-740	-97297	-14363	-21930	9700	24766	-3438	-26688
1.5	-34170	-47705	-4738	88325	2840	0	12225	-2860	-82555	-31538	-1215	8650	8328	17156	-7663
1.4	26410	-42895	74125	89125	-9120	0	2400	12480	-60967	-1263	-21130	10900	-2953	49563	-13363
1.3	6860	-53445	123688	105038	-6350	0	-25850	16080	-60955	-11725	-29685	8000	-1766	20219	-13225
1.2	-13150	-53080	105950	128650	-9260	0	-20000	19980	-40110	-3488	-29150	-18000	16	2719	-1013
1.1	46420	-39220	92313	119838	710	0	-37300	33020	-23822	-5150	-43535	-5275	-1328	33688	2750
1.0	46420	-33535	175338	107063	20890	0	-41250	-15280	-57464	-9175	-24410	-12550	-9609	23313	-15113
0.9	87410	-6700	-16375	117800	31980	0	-46500	9820	-61828	-66838	-12890	-22025	1828	10875	2538
0.8	32520	-3920	-15975	111700	22820	0	1250	-13020	-48313	-57213	-350	-7000	2078	60688	-24475
0.7	30770	2310	-8888	90063	16360	0	-1363	2500	-56268	-90025	15010	1925	1016	52500	-14963
0.6	-27060	25630	888	47263	21830	0	-40763	120	-82870	-50163	-16020	-11325	22766	31063	-2375
0.5	22460	31090	-21313	50988	-6380	0	-42388	23880	-118335	-76950	-5540	-5575	16188	16188	20825
0.4	-31900	20820	22263	9000	17290	0	-55688	33300	-65814	-48463	-14380	-3950	17813	24500	13350
0.3	-46300	6060	18913	34075	11760	0	-56163	12020	-71665	-25863	-25310	12875	-4063	-10375	20838
0.2	6640	13160	-48988	51250	-17960	7175	-54538	14340	-86684	-9213	-23160	14400	16031	3063	25788
0.1	-19020	9620	-15288	55525	-19500	8012.5	-44638	22920	-95848	25513	-27340	15700	-10438	10063	26663

TABLE 22.2b The Number of Trades Associated with the Performance in Table 22.2a

Box (%)	Crude Oil	Cotton	DAX	EUR	Bund	Euro-dollars	S&P	Gold	Heating Oil	Japanese Yen	NASDAQ	Soybeans	10-Year Notes	30-Year Bonds	Wheat
2.0	53	41	74	9	0	0	17	53	59	4	17	193	4	16	17
1.9	61	47	76	7	0	0	19	51	59	4	19	203	6	16	21
1.8	71	51	80	11	2	0	17	69	67	8	21	209	4	18	23
1.7	65	51	90	11	2	0	23	64	79	6	27	221	6	16	29
1.6	69	59	106	11	2	0	23	71	81	10	33	225	8	24	31
1.5	83	57	120	17	4	0	23	73	91	12	29	231	14	22	33
1.4	79	63	126	19	6	0	27	82	99	10	41	245	14	24	35
1.3	91	67	134	23	6	0	37	92	111	14	47	251	14	32	41
1.2	109	82	152	23	8	0	39	100	135	14	51	267	18	42	41
1.1	117	88	168	27	6	0	47	112	145	20	67	273	20	44	45
1.0	139	100	188	33	10	0	55	125	163	22	69	297	24	54	55
0.9	141	100	236	37	10	0	61	142	183	32	79	313	32	66	61
0.8	175	116	276	49	14	0	65	154	199	38	97	303	38	76	83
0.7	195	150	314	65	18	0	79	162	229	50	107	307	48	102	97
0.6	225	174	358	101	26	0	117	184	241	60	157	319	52	130	111
0.5	227	198	394	129	38	0	149	192	275	92	187	325	78	169	135
0.4	255	228	418	186	61	0	189	208	273	127	235	325	120	217	167
0.3	273	268	470	231	103	0	241	250	297	179	261	309	172	267	199
0.2	277	290	520	275	187	4	283	278	297	247	287	309	239	289	251
0.1	285	290	546	293	285	8	299	282	297	293	293	307	294	297	285

TABLE 22.3	Point-and-Figure Box Sizes—Stocks and Sectors 2003	
Market	**Box Size**	**Average Price**
AMZN	13	25
AMR	38	20
AOL	6	13.5
GE	25	27
IBM	143	72
INTC	80	17.5
MRK	162	52
XOM	50	34
Aerospace	17.5	1,800
Biotech	15	700
Large banks	8	1,000
Life Insurance	22	1,450
Semiconductors	1.6	300

Using the basic rules, you are always in the market, reversing from long to short and from short to long, unless you only trade stocks from the long side.

There are alternate methods for selecting point-and-figure entry and exit points that have become popular. Buying or selling on a pullback after an initial point-and-figure signal is one of the more common system entries because it can limit risk and still maintain a logical stop-loss point. Of course, there are fewer opportunities to trade when only small risk is allowed, and there is a proportionately greater chance that the trade will be stopped out because the entry and exit points are close together. There are three approaches recommended for entering on limited risk:

1. *Wait for a reversal back to within an acceptable risk, then buy or sell immediately with the normal point-and-figure stop.* Figure 22.6 shows various levels of risk in IBM with $2.00 boxes. The initial buy signal is at $150, with the simple sell signal for liquidation at $134, giving a risk of $16 per share. Instead of buying as prices reach new highs, wait for a reversal after the buy signal, then buy when the low for the day penetrates the box corresponding to your acceptable level of risk. Three possibilities are shown in Figure 22.7. Buying into a declining market assumes that the support level (at $134 in this example) will hold, preventing the stop-loss level from being reached. To increase confidence, the base of the formation should be as broad as possible. The test of a triple bottom or a spread triple bottom after a buy signal is a more reasonable place to go long than a simple buy after a small reversal in the middle of a move.

   It is not advisable to reduce risk by entering on the simple buy signal and placing a stop-loss at the point of the first reversal (3 boxes below the highs). The advantage of waiting for the pullback is that it uses the logical support level as a stop. A stop-loss placed nearby following a breakout has no logical basis and will quickly result in a losing trade.

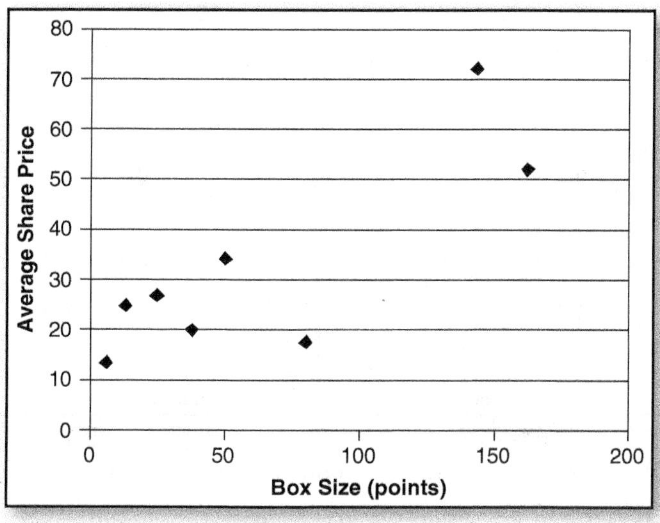

FIGURE 22.6 Point-and-Figure Box Sizes Are Larger When Prices Are Higher or Volatility Is Greater.

Price								
160								
158	O							
156	O							
154	O							
152	O	X						
150	O	X	O			X	<-----	Simple buy signal, standard risk of $16
148	O	X	O	X		X		
146	O	X	O	X	O	X	<-----	Enter on pullback to 146, risk $12
144	O	X	O	X	O	X		
142	O	X	O	X	O	X	<-----	Enter on pullback to 142, risk $8
140	O	X	O	X	O	X		
138	O		O	X	O	X	<-----	Enter on pullback to 138, risk $4
136			O		O			
134							<-----	Stop-loss and reversal at $134

FIGURE 22.7 Entering IBM on a Pullback with Limited Risk.

2. *Enter the market on the second reversal back in the direction of the original signal.* As shown in Figure 22.8, the first reversal following a signal may not reach the target risk level. Price movement does not often accommodate our expectations; therefore, a more flexible rule is needed. One technique is to enter a long position on the second upswing. That is, do not enter a long position on the initial buy signal but wait until a 3-box reversal has caused a downswing. As the downswing continues, place a trailing buy order at the point where the next upswing would begin, at the fourth box above the lowest box of *O*s. If the order is executed, then there is a new position in the direction of the trend; however, the risk has been limited to the value of four boxes, which is the new trend reversal point. In a wide-ranging, volatile market, this entry may be better than the original point-and-figure buy signal.

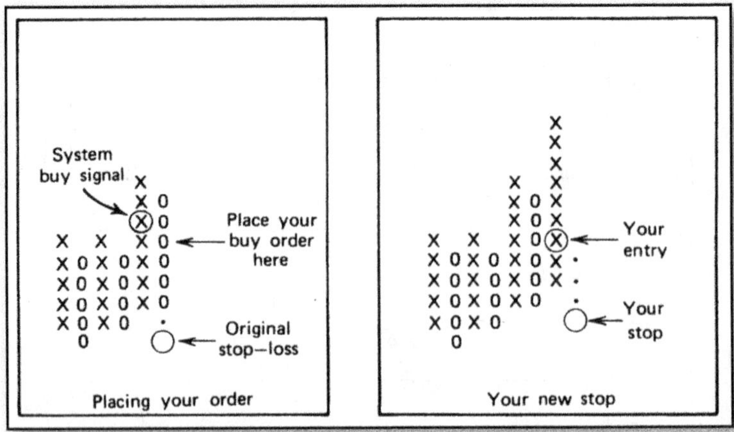

FIGURE 22.8 Entering on a Confirmation of a New Trend after a Pullback.

This technique is frequently used by traders, who firmly believe that a reversal follows immediately after a breakout, to prevent both high risk and false signals. If the pullback that follows the breakout continues in an adverse direction, penetrates the other support or resistance level, and triggers the original system stop-loss, then no entry occurs, thus saving a substantial whipsaw loss. These traders are essentially looking for a confirmation of direction. However, if prices continue upward, without a pullback, the trade may be missed entirely. You can read more on this topic in the section "Individual Trade Risk" in Level III, Chapter 12.

The reversal principle in Step 2 can also be effective for building positions. In bar charting, a pullback to a bullish support line or a bearish resistance line is a point for adding to a position with a risk limited to penetration of the major trendline. The equivalent procedure using point-and-figure is to add on each reversal back in the direction of the trend using the newly formed stop-loss point to exit the entire position (as shown in Figure 22.9).

3. *Allowing for irregular patterns*. Price patterns are not always orderly, and the price activity at the time of a trend change can be very indecisive. One basic trading

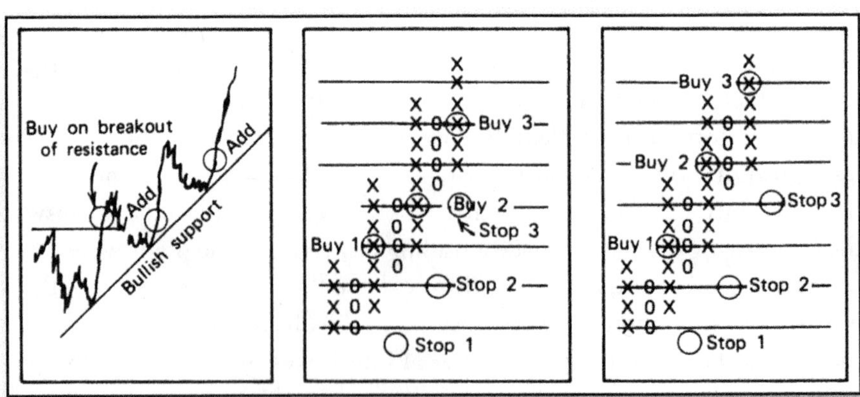

FIGURE 22.9 Three Ways to Compound Positions.

principle demands that the market confirm a new high before buying; the first new high might simply occur during an erratic sideways pattern, or an expanding formation after a period of low volatility. If prices are required to make a new high by more than one box on the next upward thrust, and raise the lowest point of the reversal by another box on the third upward thrust, we are actually demanding that the momentum, or speed of price movement, increase before a position is set.[6] The pattern of higher highs and higher lows is similar to upwards acceleration.

This technique, which tends to minimize false breakouts, may be modified to increase the confirmation threshold from two to three or four boxes as market volatility increases. If the box size is changed according to volatility, as discussed later in this chapter, confirmation can remain at two boxes.

Point-and-Figure Trading Risk

I go long or short as close as I can to the danger point, and if the danger becomes real I close out and take a small loss.

—Jesse Livermore to Richard Wyckoff[7]

The point-and-figure method is a simple trend-following concept, yet in its normal use it is subject to interpretation using trendlines and geometric formations. Why is that necessary? The answer involves the risk of an individual trade. In the previous section, the risk of a trade was changed by using alternate entry points based on pullbacks; however, there are other choices.

The treatment of the same price move can be seen by looking at both a bar chart and a corresponding point-and-figure chart for the same period (Figure 22.10). The

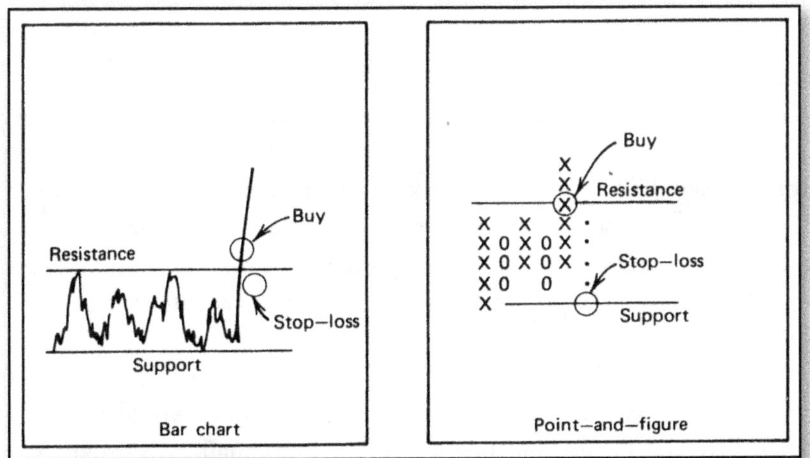

FIGURE 22.10 Placement of Point-and-Figure Stops.

[6] Adam Hewison, "The Will Rogers Theory of Point & Figure Trading," *Technical Analysis of Stocks & Commodities* (August 1991).

[7] Richard D. Wyckoff, *Stock Market Technique, Number One* (New York: Wyckoff, 1933), 2.

most basic bar chart trading method uses horizontal support and resistance lines to define a trading range; when the resistance line is penetrated, a long position is entered. This is the same concept used in the swing method. A stop-loss is placed below the resistance line in order to close out the trade in the event of a false breakout. An alternate placement of the stop-loss could have been below the support line, allowing the new bull move some latitude to develop.

Viewing this chart pattern in retrospect makes the selection of the entry point and the placement of stops or reversal of position seem obvious; however, when trading, the choice of the support and resistance lines is not usually as clear. The time to enter a trade after a breakout is never quite certain, and the position for the stop or reversal depends on the volatility of prices and the risk that you are willing to take. In contrast to the ambiguity of the bar chart, the point-and-figure method defines the support and resistance levels exactly, establishes a place to buy in advance, and designates the position for the stop-loss below the rectangular congestion area, always at the place where a long position would turn to a short sale. The rigidity of the method allows only one place for the stop-loss and fixes the risk as the difference between the support and resistance lines, a total of five boxes in the example shown in Figure 22.10. In the bar chart, the risk might have been held to the equivalent of two boxes using the closer stop-loss, where the trade is exited on a pullback into the range; however, a very small risk often results in being stopped out of the trend prematurely.

Take It and Run! From time to time, you find yourself the beneficiary of a substantial price move where there is an uncomfortably large profit. It is normal to consider how much of the unrealized profits will be returned before the system finally generates an exit signal. At these times, some traders prefer to take the profits. These are decisions that go beyond the area of technical analysis, although they could be rigorously tested. If the profit currently held in open positions is enough to sustain a life of leisure, a home in the mountains, membership in a country club, and a small investment in a hotel or restaurant to occupy your time, then take it and run! A trading system should not depend on a single, very large profit to work over time. It should have a steady, successful profile. We can therefore reason that any extremely large profit is a windfall and should be taken. Occasionally, a price shock gives you a windfall profit that has nothing to do with a well-designed system or astute trading. It is another opportunity to take profits. If you are correct, prices will reverse after you have gotten out, and there will be an opportunity to reenter the trade at a much better level.

If you cannot sleep nights and the unrealized profits are just enough to satisfy some important obligations, but one or two adverse days would ruin the opportunity, then take the profits and begin again with a small investment. While it is important to follow a system in order to benefit from the long-term expectations, investor "risk preference" preempts the act of blindly following all rules. Sometimes you need to reduce the market exposure, whether the current position is a profit or a loss. If you have some risk latitude, a logical place to capture most of the current open profits and still have a chance of increasing those profits is to use the

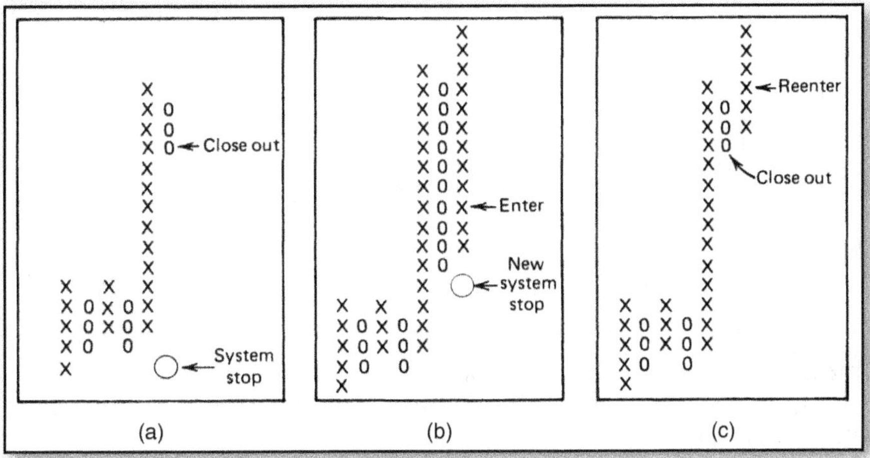

FIGURE 22.11 **Cashing in on Profits.**

point-and-figure reversal value for your exit. If the 3-box reversal represents only 10% of the open profits, then you have a significant chance of profiting from a continuation of the price move. The *reversal value*, the box size times the number of boxes in a reversal (usually 3), is meant to indicate a significant contrary move and can be used as an objective indication of a change of direction. One approach to taking profits is shown in Figure 22.11.

In Figure 22.11a, a trailing 3-box reversal value is used for the stop-loss once there is a sustained move of at least 10 boxes. To reenter the move in the same direction, the same technique is used (Figure 22.11b), adding another 4 boxes of profits while keeping the new risk small. In Figure 22.11c, this method lost 4 boxes of the potential profits when the reversal was short lived.

In general, taking small profits in this way does not improve overall profitability because it most often misses the biggest moves. It may, however, reduce the risk of loss at a rate even faster than the reduction in profits, yielding a better reward-to-risk ratio. A new rule should be carefully tested to know its effect on different market conditions before it is used. This topic is covered thoroughly in Level III, Chapter 10.

Control of risk can also be accomplished effectively using *volatility stabilization* methods. These continually adjust your position size to maintain a *target volatility*. If the volatility of either a market or your portfolio increases sharply, volatility stabilization will cause positions to be cut in order to bring your risk down to an acceptable level. See Level III, Chapter 12, for more about this.

Alternate Treatment of Reversals Traditional point-and-figure charting favors the continuing trend. On highly volatile days, *broad ranging days* (also called *outside days*), it is possible for both a trend continuation and a 3-box reversal to occur. Point-and-figure rules require that the trend continuation be recorded and the reversal ignored. Figure 22.12 shows a comparison of the two choices. In the example, prices are in an uptrend when a new 1-box high and a 3-box reversal both occur on Day 6, as seen in Figure 22.12a. In Figure 22.12b, the traditional approach is taken,

Day	High	Low									
1	$8.02	$7.90	$8.40			X					X
2	$8.11	$7.95	$8.35			X					X
3	$8.13	$7.92	$8.30			X					X
4	$8.18	$7.96	$8.25			X			X		X
5	$8.25	$8.10	$8.20			X			X	O	X
6	$8.32	$8.08	$8.15			X			X	O	X
7	$8.40	$8.25	$8.10	X		X	X		X	O	
			$8.05	X	O	X	X	O	X		
			$8.00	X	O	X	X	O	X		
			$7.95	X	O		X	O			
			$7.90	X			X				
	(a)			(b)					(c)		

FIGURE 22.12 Alternate Methods of Plotting Point-and-Figure Reversals. (a) Sample Prices for Plotting. (b) Traditional Method. (c) Alternate Rule Taken on Day 6.

resulting in a continuous upward trend with a stop-loss at 7.90. Taking the reversal first as an alternate rule, Figure 22.12c shows the same trend with a stop-loss now at 8.05, 15 points closer.

Plotting the reversal first usually works to the benefit of the trader; both the stop-loss and change of trend will occur sooner. Subsequent computer testing proved this to be true. This alternative does not work when the reversal value is small and broad ranging days (that trigger the optional reversals) occur frequently.

Selecting Trades

Not all trades are profitable in any trading system. Some analysts prefer point-and-figure charts because both the profit objective and the risk can be identified at the time of entry. The profit objective can be calculated using the vertical or horizontal count, and the risk is the size of the price reversal needed to cause the opposite signal. Trades are then taken only if the return to risk ratio is greater than 2.0.

As with other trending systems, 45° trendlines can be drawn to identify the current dominant trend. Trades may be taken only in the direction of that trend. In a bull market, new short signals are ignored until the box is filled that penetrates the upwards bullish trendline. Then the bias switches to the short side.

Price Objectives

Point-and-figure charting has two unique methods for calculating price objectives: *horizontal counts* and *vertical counts*. These techniques do not eliminate the use of the standard bar charting objectives, such as support and resistance levels, which apply here as well.

The Horizontal Count The time that prices spend in a consolidation area is considered directly related to the size of the subsequent price move. One technique for calculating price objectives is to measure the width of the consolidation (the number of columns on a bar chart) and project the same measurement up or down as the target of the move. The point-and-figure horizontal count method is a more exact approach to the same idea.

The upside price objective is calculated as

$$H_U = P_L + (W \times R)$$

where H_U = the upside horizontal count price objective
P_L = the price of the lowest box of the base formation
W = the width of the bottom formation (number of columns)
R = the reversal value (number of boxes times the value of one box)

To use this formula, the *base* (width of the bottom or top formation) needs to be identified. Count the number of columns, W, not including the breakout column and multiply that width by the value of a minimum reversal, R; then add that result to the bottom point of the base to get the upper price objective. The base can always be identified after the breakout has occurred. For example, Figure 22.13 shows the March 74 contract of London Cocoa (£4 box) forming a very long but clear base. The reversal value is £12, and the width of the base is 19 columns (not counting the last column, which included the breakout). Added to the lowest point of the base (£570) this gives an objective of £798, reached on the left shoulder of the topping formation. Another alternative is the wider base, marked as $W_2 = 25$. Using this selection results in a price objective of £870, by adding 25 × £12 = £300 to £570, the lowest point of the base.

The downside objective is calculated in the same manner as the upside objective:

$$H_D = P_H - (W \times R)$$

where H_D = the downside horizontal count price objective
P_H = the price of the highest box of the top formation
W = the width of the top formation (number of columns)
R = the reversal value

Some examples are given for downside objectives in the same Cocoa diagram (Figure 22.13). A small correction top could be isolated at the £720 level and two possible top widths, W_3 and W_5, could be chosen. The broader top, W_3, has a width of nine and a downside objective of £632. The shorter top, W_5, has a width of five and a downside objective of £680. Although the closer objective, calculated from W_5, is easy to reach, the farther one is reasonable because it coincides with a strong intermediate support level at about £640.

The very top formation, W_4, was small and only produced a nearby price objective similar to the first downside example; there would be no indication that prices were ready for a major reversal. The top also forms a clear head-and-shoulders pattern, which could be used in the same manner as in bar charting to find an objective. Using that technique, the distance from the top of the head to the point on the neckline directly below is 20 boxes; then downside price objective is 20 boxes below the point where the neckline was penetrated by the breakout of the right shoulder, at £776, giving £696 as the objective.

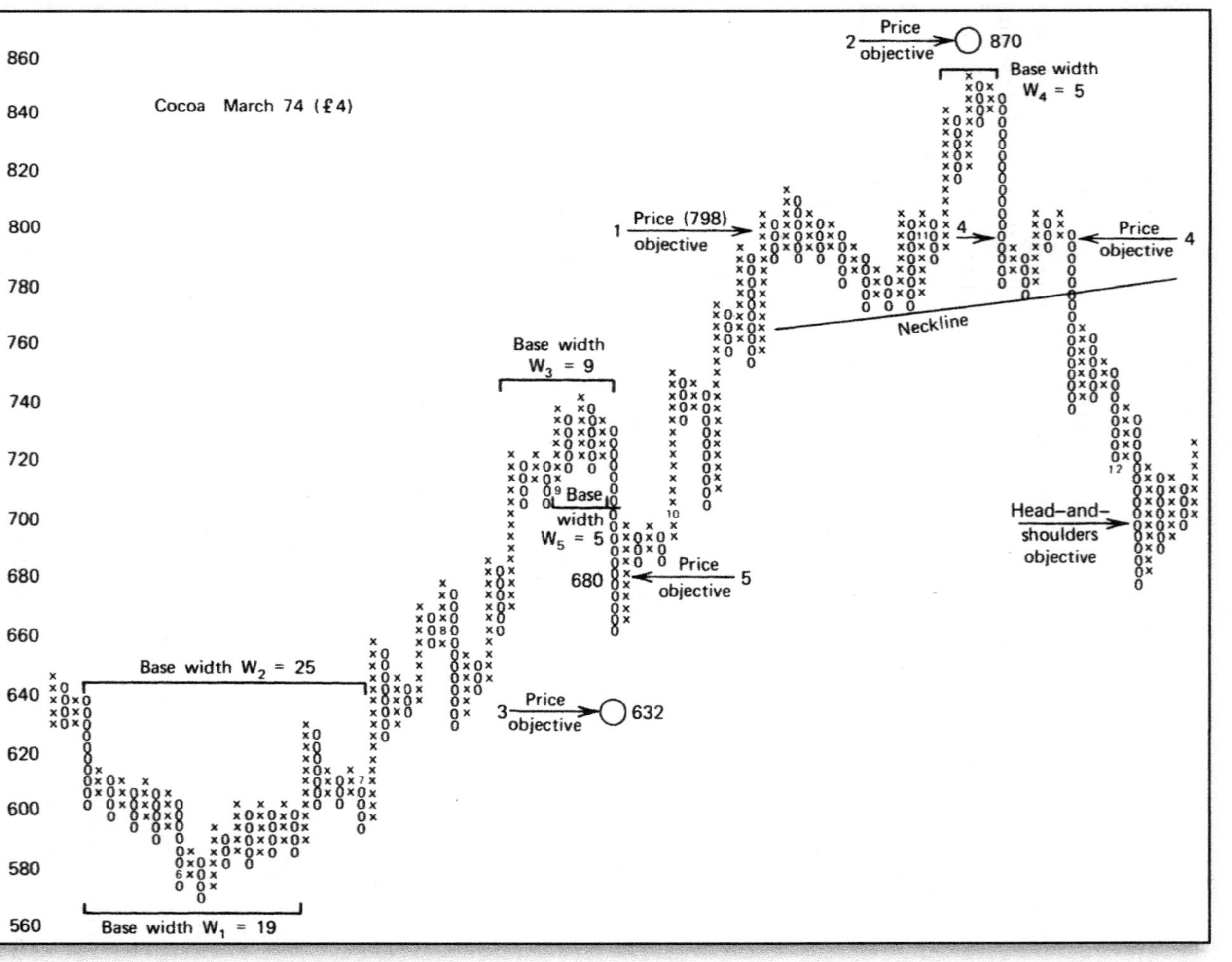

FIGURE 22.13 Horizontal Count Price Objectives.

The horizontal count can also be applied to a breakout from a triangular formation, similar to the one on the very far right in Figure 22.13 (marked "Head-and-shoulders objective"). The width of the formation is the widest point in the center of the triangle, and the upwards objective is also measured from the center, rather than from the bottom of the triangle.

The Vertical Count The vertical count is a simpler and more definitive calculation than the horizontal count. As with the horizontal count, there is adequate time to identify the formations and establish a price objective before it is reached. The vertical count is a measure of volatility (the amount of rebound from a top or bottom) and can be used to determine the size of a retracement after a major price move. To calculate the upside vertical count price objective, locate the first reversal column after a bottom formation. To do this, a bottom must be established with one or more tests, or a major resistance line must be broken to indicate that a bottom is in place. The vertical count price objective is then calculated:

$$V_{up} = \textit{Lowest box} + (\textit{First reversal boxes} \times \textit{Minimum reversal boxes})$$

The downside vertical count price objective is just the opposite:

$$V_{down} = \textit{Highest box} - (\textit{First reversal boxes} \times \textit{Minimum reversal boxes})$$

where *First reversal boxes* = the number of boxes in the first reversal
Minimum reversal boxes = the number of boxes needed for a chart reversal

Examples illustrating the vertical count are easy to find. In the QQQ chart (Figure 22.14), the NASDAQ low is clearly in early October 2002, followed by an upwards reversal of 13 boxes. Each box is \$0.25, giving a total reversal of \$3.25. Multiply the reversal amount by 3, the number of boxes in a reversal, and add that value, 9.75, to the low of \$20.00 to get the target of \$29.75. That value was reached during May 2003.

A secondary low in the QQQ chart occurs in February 2003 at \$23.50. The first reversal that follows is seven boxes, or \$1.75. Multiple 1.75 by 3 and add the result to the low to get the target of \$28.75. The two objectives confirm each other. As a simple measurement tool based on recognizing key highs or lows, the vertical count relies on volatility to determine the extent of the move that follows. It can be quite accurate at times; otherwise it is likely to understate the expected price move.

In Figure 22.15, Intel is used to show frequent possibilities for the point-and-figure vertical count. As with QQQ, the chart uses a box size of 25 points (\$0.25) and a 3-box reversal. The low in August 2002 at \$19.00 gives a target of \$27.25 reached at the end of October. The high in early January 2003 points to a very nice interim low in April, but falls far short of the actual low. Two other midrange price reversals could be used to find additional downside targets, each of which is successful but also fall short of predicting the true low of the stock. The vertical count can be very reliable but should not be expected to be a magic wand.

FIGURE 22.14 Point-and-Figure Vertical Count for Qqq. The major low in October 2002 had a reversal of 13 boxes, each with a value of 0.25, for a total of 3.25. Multiplying by 3 and adding the result, 9.75, to the lowest value $20.00, gives the price objective of 29.75. The second bottom in February 2003 shows a reversal of 7 boxes and gives a target of 28.75.

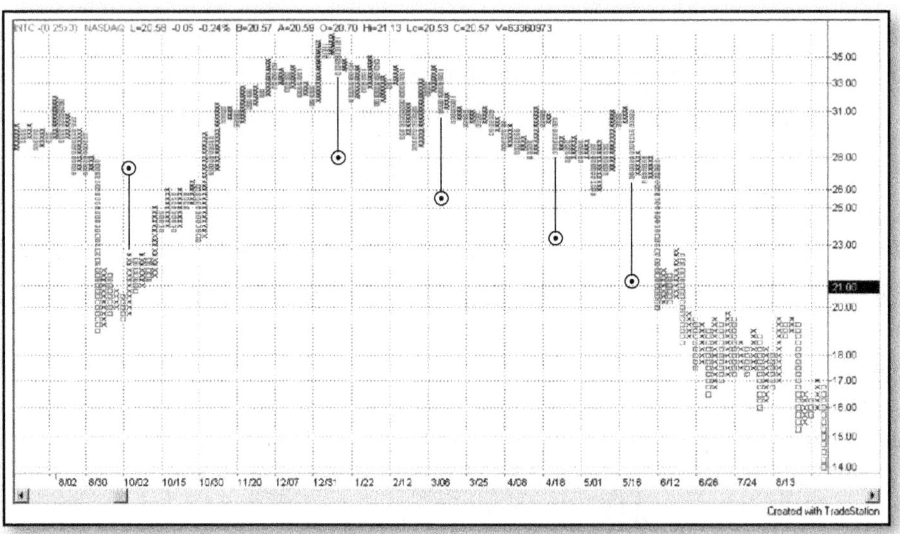

FIGURE 22.15 Intel Vertical Count Examples. This chart of Intel had many possibilities for the point-and-figure vertical count, all of which understate the actual price move. The vertical count is a good tool for setting initial objectives, but it is not a magic wand.

Point-and-Figure with Variable Box Sizes

In the section "Point-and-Figure Box Size," we looked at the results of various fixed point box sizes for a selection of markets. An optimization showed the net profits from boxes varying from 0.10% to 2.0%, all using a 3-box reversal (see Table 22.2).

The inconsistency of results shows that each market must be treated uniquely, or that a more general approach to volatility-adjusting the box sizes is needed. Volatility will be discussed in detail in Level III, Chapter 9; however, some simple principles can be used here. Two possible solutions that would change the box size daily (or periodically) are based on

1. A fixed percentage of the current price
2. A fixed multiple of the average true range

These two methods will be applied to three futures markets, the euro, S&P, and gold, for the period from 2000 through 2010. That interval had every combination of price movement, strong trends, both down (after the tech bubble) and up, as well as the most severe economic crisis in many years. The price of gold more than tripled as well. Each showed very different results in Table 22.2.

To further support the need for a more flexible approach, consider crude oil, shown in Figure 22.16. The right scale shows the price of continuous futures (the cash price peaked near $150/bbl) and the left scale the annualized volatility in percent. With a price range of $30 to $150 during the past 10 years, and a volatility of less than 10% to near 60%, no one choice of box size will work. If you find a successful box size for 2007, it would be too large to generate any orders before 2000. If you used the best box size for the 1990s, it would be changing signals every day in 2007.

Boxes Based on a Fixed Percentage of Price Volatility is directly related to price; therefore, we can use a percentage of the current price to adjust the box size. For gold at $500, a 0.5% box size gives a $2.50 box and a $7.50 reversal criteria. At $1500, the box size is $7.50 and the reversal $22.50. With gold highly volatile, and daily ranges greater than $22.50, that seems a bit sensitive, so a 1% box size might be better. Prices may also have been represented on a log scale.

When the box size is varied each day, and the point-and-figure chart is essentially redrawn, rising price will tend to hold the position longer because the reversal criteria get larger. On the other side, falling price will shorten the reversal and may generate a new signal where there was none yesterday.

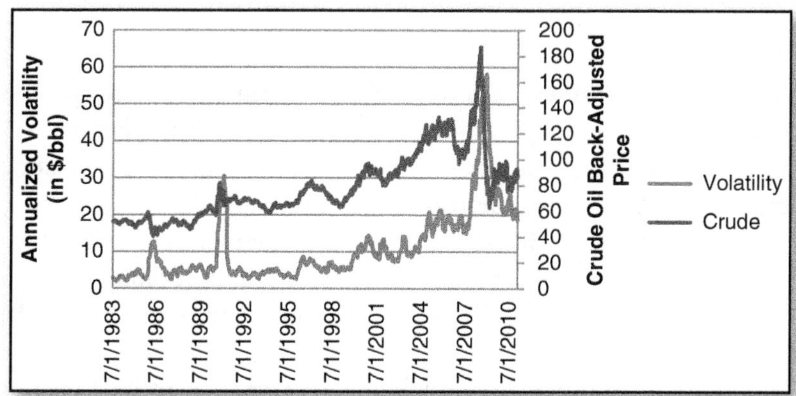

FIGURE 22.16 Annualized Volatility of Crude Oil in $/bbl Using Back-Adjusted Futures.

TABLE 22.4	Results of Using Point-and-Figure with Variable Box Size Based on a Fixed Percentage Futures Data from 2000 through 2010					
	Net Profits or Losses			Number of Trades		
Box (%)	EUR	S&P	Gold	EUR	S&P	Gold
2.0	0	19,538	13,770	0	21	6
1.9	0	30,650	51,160	0	19	8
1.8	0	–28,875	41,260	0	23	8
1.7	0	–29,038	11,4440	0	28	10
1.6	0	7,150	6,100	0	37	16
1.5	0	11,625	55,120	0	45	22
1.4	0	–14,300	89,540	0	45	24
1.3	54,900	56,050	–52,000	1	57	30
1.2	57,988	85,450	9,180	3	71	31
1.1	49,250	54,800	–33,800	4	77	42
1.0	71,013	58,875	45,520	7	101	62
0.9	15,575	81,525	–57,740	9	129	78
0.8	–100,200	100,200	–54,120	17	149	102
0.7	–73,000	85,400	–46,240	29	185	130
0.6	–30,288	111,500	–61,520	61	245	158
0.5	110,863	93,275	–87,640	110	305	230
0.4	–47,438	115,800	–13,8550	196	385	292
0.3	–55,750	89,075	–13,4300	317	449	380
0.2	46,475	106,650	–13,5380	461	553	498
0.1	46,225	111,100	–12,9900	553	593	556

Results in Table 22.4 are very different from those in Table 22.2. Where the euro was profitable everywhere in the original test, it has no trades for higher percentages and is profitable in only half of the remaining trades. The S&P, however, has the opposite result. Instead of erratic, mostly losing results, it is highly profitable for box sizes less than 1.4%. Gold has both better and worse results. Overall, this method changes the shape of the results but seems inconsistent.

Boxes Based on a Multiple of the Average True Range A clear problem with the percentage method in the previous section is that each market has a different level of volatility and that volatility changes. A percentage of the closing price is not sufficient to capture these variations. One measure that has proved valuable is the average true range. In this strategy, the average true range over the past 50 days was multiplied by a factor, shown in the first column of Table 22.5. While the factor does not change, the volatility will vary considerably causing the box sizes to vary.

Results can be seen as much more uniform in both net profits and the number of trades. Rather than no trades in the euro, the three markets all show about the same pattern of trades based on the factor size. Profits also cluster. That is, the losing results

TABLE 22.5 Results of Using Point-and-Figure with Variable Box Size Based on a Multiple of the Average True Range (Factor) Futures Data from 2000 through 2010

	Net Profits or Losses			Number of Trades		
Factor	EUR	S&P	Gold	EUR	S&P	Gold
3.0	42,900	−1,800	85,590	5	9	8
2.8	24,913	−2,925	73,070	7	9	10
2.6	38,888	−9,563	76,410	7	11	12
2.4	38,788	3,625	71,030	7	9	8
2.2	−9,313	1,088	23,350	11	11	13
2.0	−77,363	−88	18,740	11	13	14
1.8	−17,538	−5,013	58,440	13	15	18
1.6	−23,688	4,763	33,980	13	15	22
1.4	12,538	5,713	24,070	21	17	24
1.2	31,088	21,150	19,30	31	21	26
1.0	16,963	39,538	−490	33	27	44
0.8	46,463	25,463	31,940	39	41	50
0.6	30,838	14,113	53,170	75	61	68
0.4	55,513	−18,163	14,320	121	127	126
0.2	18,538	−4,588	30,270	253	203	223

are mostly adjacent to one another. All markets, on average, did very well. While this is intended to be an example of the way a strategy can adapt to changing volatility, it seems to show that there are some techniques that will succeed.

Finding the True Price-Volatility Relationship One other method must be discussed. The fixed percentage and ATR approaches were convenient and easy to program. But perhaps the best results will come from finding the true price-volatility relationship. As an example, we calculated the rolling 20-day annualized volatility of crude oil using futures from 1983 to 2010. Figure 22.17 shows that relationship as a scatter diagram. While there are sets of points near the top of the chart, the underlying relationship is very clear, clustering at about 7% when crude was $20 and reaching about 50% when crude was $140. This cannot be found using a linear regression because the higher outliers will cause the regression line to have a steeper ascending angle.

Stock Dividends and Splits When using point-and-figure charts for stocks, an adjustment must be made whenever a stock dividend is issued or the stock splits, because the chart represents the price of one share. Splits and dividends result in stock multiplying factors:[8]

[8] William G. S. Brown, "Logarithmic Point & Figure Charting," *Technical Analysis of Stocks & Commodities* (July 1995).

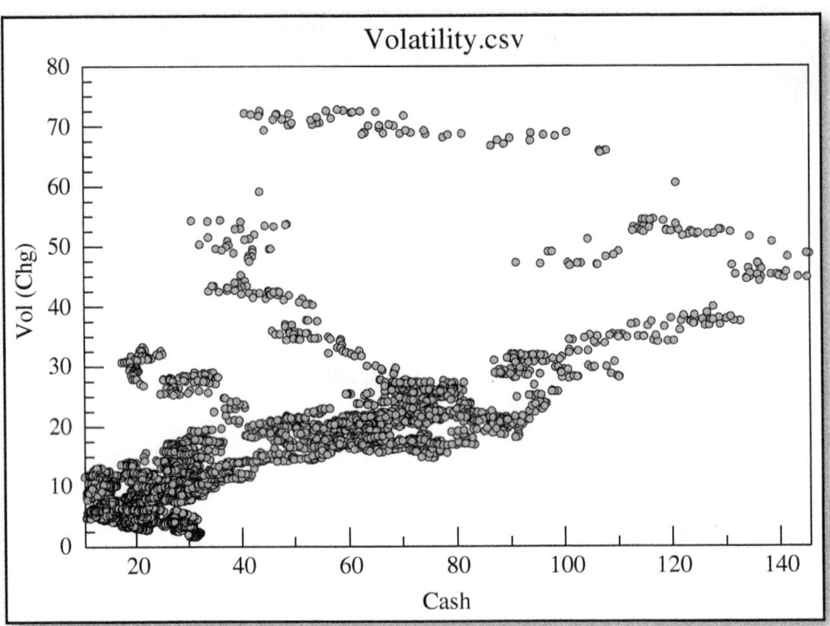

FIGURE 22.17 Volatility Relationship for Crude Oil, 1983–2010 (Using PSIplot).

Activity	Stock Multiplication Factor
10% stock dividend	1.1
30% stock dividend	1.3
2 for 1 stock split	2.0
3 for 2 stock split	1.5

These multiplication factors can be used to correct the box size of a percentage or logarithmic point-and-figure chart by dividing all the boxes by the multiplication factor; therefore, the new box sizes represent the value of one share.

Recent Applications of Point-and-Figure

Not much new has happened to point-and-figure during the past 100 years; however, there has been renewed interest in using it. Two new books, *Power Investing with Sector Funds* by Peter Madlem and *Point & Figure Charting,* second edition, by Thomas Dorsey, show more recent examples of how this technique applies to stocks and sector indexes. There are also a number of websites with instructions and examples, most combined with advertising.

CHAPTER 23

Technical Analysis as a Science

From David Aronson, *Evidence-Based Technical Analysis* (Hoboken, New Jersey: John Wiley & Sons, 2006), Introduction.

Technical analysis (TA) is the study of recurring patterns in financial market data with the intent of forecasting future price movements.[1] It is comprised of numerous analysis methods, patterns, signals, indicators, and trading strategies, each with its own cheerleaders claiming that their approach works.

Much of popular or traditional TA stands where medicine stood before it evolved from a faith-based folk art into a practice based on science. Its claims are supported by colorful narratives and carefully chosen (cherry-picked) anecdotes rather than objective statistical evidence.

This book's central contention is that TA must evolve into a rigorous observational science if it is to deliver on its claims and remain relevant. The scientific method is the only rational way to extract useful knowledge from market data and the only rational approach for determining which TA methods have predictive power. I call this evidence-based technical analysis (EBTA). Grounded in objective observation and statistical inference (i.e., the scientific method), EBTA charts a course between the magical thinking and gullibility of a true believer and the relentless doubt of a random walker.

Approaching TA, or any discipline for that matter, in a scientific manner is not easy. Scientific conclusions frequently conflict with what seems intuitively obvious. To early humans it seemed obvious that the sun circled the earth. It took science to demonstrate that this intuition was wrong. An informal, intuitive approach to knowledge acquisition is especially likely to result in erroneous beliefs when phenomena are complex or highly random, two prominent features of financial market behavior.

Although the scientific method is not guaranteed to extract gold from the mountains of market data, an unscientific approach is almost certain to produce fool's gold.

This book's second contention is that much of the wisdom comprising the popular version of TA does not qualify as legitimate knowledge.

Key Definitions: Propositions and Claims, Belief and Knowledge

I have already used the terms *knowledge* and *belief* but have not rigorously defined them. These and several other key terms will be used repeatedly in this book, so some formal definitions are needed.

The fundamental building block of knowledge is a *declarative statement*, also known as a *claim* or a *proposition*. A declarative statement is one of four types of utterances that also include exclamations, questions, and commands. Declarative statements are distinguished from the others in that they have truth value. That is to say, they can be characterized as either true or false or probably true or probably false.

The statement "Oranges are on sale at the supermarket for five cents a dozen" is declarative. It makes a claim about a state of affairs existing at the local market. It may be true or false. In contrast, the exclamatory statement "Holy cow, what a deal," the command "Go buy me a dozen," or the question "What is an orange?" cannot be called true or false.

Our inquiry into TA will be concerned with declarative statements, such as, "Rule X has predictive power." Our goal is to determine which of these declarative statements warrant our belief.

What does it mean to say, "I believe X."? "With regard to states of affairs in general (i.e., 'matters of fact' or 'what will happen') believing X amounts to expecting to experience X if and when we are in a position to do so."[2] Therefore, if I believe the claim that oranges are on sale for five cents a dozen, it means that I expect to be able to buy oranges for five cents a dozen if I go to the store. However, the command to buy some oranges or the exclamation that I am happy about the opportunity, set up no such expectation.

What does all this mean for us? For any statement to even be considered as a candidate for belief, it must "assert some state of affairs that can be expected.[3] Such statements are said to have *cognitive content*—they convey something that can be *known*. "If the statement contains nothing to know then there is nothing there to be believe."[4]

Although all declarative statements presumably have cognitive content, not all actually do. This is not a problem if the lack of cognitive content is obvious, for example, the declaration "The square root of Tuesday is a prime number."[5] This utterance is, on its face, nonsense. There are other declarative statements, however, whose lack of cognitive content is not so obvious. This can be a problem, because such statements can fool us into thinking that a claim has been made that sets up an expectation, when, in fact, no claim has really been put forward. These pseudo-declarative-statements are essentially *meaningless claims* or *empty propositions*.

Although meaningless claims are not valid candidates for belief, this does not stop many people from believing in them. The vague predictions made in the daily astrology column or the nebulous promises made by promoters of bogus health cures are examples of meaningless claims. Those who believe these empty propositions simply do not realize that what they have been told has no cognitive content.

A way to tell if a statement has cognitive content and is, thus, a valid candidate for belief is the *discernible-difference* test[6] described by Hall. "Utterances with cognitive content make claims that are either true or false; and whether they are true or false makes a difference that can be discerned. That is why these utterances offer something to believe and why there is no point in trying to believe an utterance that makes no such offer"[7] In other words, a proposition that passes the discernible-difference test sets up an expectation such that the state of affairs, if the statement were true, is recognizably different from the state of affairs, if the statement were false.

The discernible-difference criterion can be applied to statements purporting to be predictions. A prediction is a claim to know something about the future. If a prediction has cognitive content, it will be clearly discernible in the outcome if the prediction was accurate or not. Many, if not most, of the forecasts issued by practitioners of popular TA are devoid of cognitive content on these grounds. In other words, the predictions are typically too vague to ever determine if they were wrong.

The truth or falsity of the claim *oranges are on sale for five cents a dozen* will make a discernible difference when I get to the market. It is this discernible difference that allows the claim to be tested. As will be described in Level II, Chapter 39, testing a claim on the basis of a discernible difference is central to the scientific method.

Hall, in his book *Practically Profound*, explains why he finds Freudian psychoanalysis to be meaningless when examined in light of the discernible-difference test.

"Certain Freudian claims about human sexual development are compatible with all possible states of affairs. There is no way to confirm or disconfirm either 'penis envy' or 'castration complex' because there is no distinguishable difference between evidence affirming and evidence denying these interpretations of behavior. Exactly opposite behaviors are equally predictable, depending on whether the alleged psychosexual stress is overt or repressed." The requirement of "cognitive content rules out all utterances that are so loose, poorly formed or obsessively held (e.g., conspiracy theories) that there is no recognizable difference between what would be the case if they were so, and what would be the case if they were not."[8] In a like vein, the Intelligent Design Theory carries no cognitive freight in the sense that no matter what life form is observed it is consistent with the notion that it manifests an underlying form specified by some intelligent designer.[9]

What then is *knowledge?* Knowledge can be defined as *justified true belief*. Hence, in order for a declarative statement to qualify as *knowledge*, not only must it be a candidate for belief, because it has cognitive content, but it must meet two other conditions as well. First, it must be true (or probably true). Second, the statement must be believed with justification. A belief is justified when it is based on sound inferences from solid evidence.

Prehistoric humans held the false belief that the sun moved across the sky because the sun orbited the earth. Clearly they were not in possession of knowledge, but suppose that there was a prehistoric person who believed correctly that the sun moved across the sky because of the earth's rotation. Although this belief was true, this individual could not be described as possessing knowledge. Even though they believed what astronomers ultimately proved to be true, there was no evidence yet to justify that belief. Without justification, a true belief does not attain the status of knowledge. These concepts are illustrated in Figure 23.1.

From this it follows that *erroneous beliefs* or *false knowledge* fail to meet one or more of the necessary conditions of knowledge. Thus, an erroneous belief can arise either because it concerns a meaningless claim or because it concerns a claim that, though meaningful, is not justified by valid inferences from solid evidence.

Still, even when we have done everything right, by drawing the best possible inference from sound evidence, we can still wind up adopting erroneous beliefs. In other words, we can be justified in believing a falsehood, and honestly claim to know something, if it appears to be true according to logically sound inferences from the preponderance of available evidence. "We are entitled to say 'I know' when the target of that claim is supported beyond reasonable doubt in the network of well-tested evidence. But that is not enough to guarantee that we do know."[10]

Falsehoods are an unavoidable fact of life when we attempt to know things about the world based on observed evidence. Thus, knowledge based on the scientific method is inherently uncertain, and provisional, though less uncertain than knowledge acquired by less formal methods. However, over time, scientific knowledge improves, as it comes to describe reality in a progressively more accurate manner. It is a continual work in progress. The goal of EBTA is a body of knowledge about

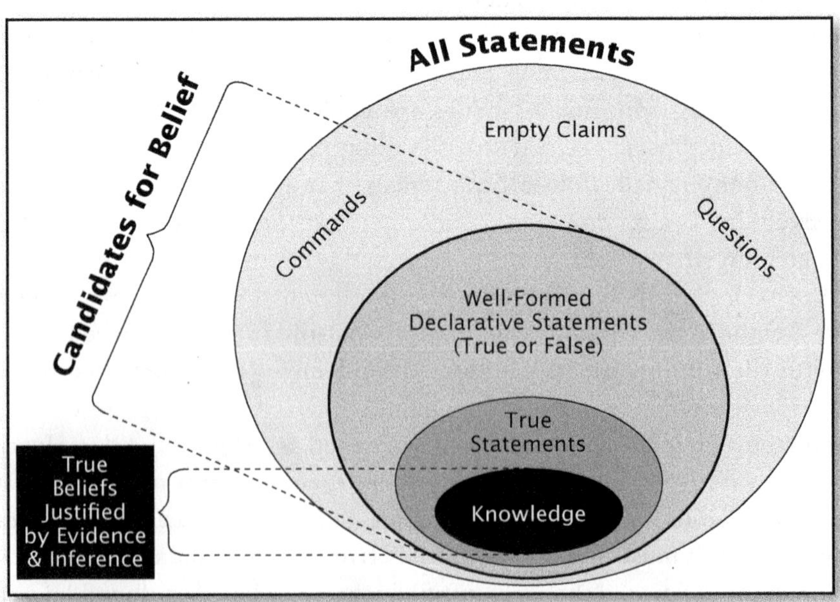

FIGURE 23.1 Knowledge: Justified True Belief.

market behavior that is as good as can be had, given the limits of evidence gathering and the powers of inference.

Erroneous TA Knowledge: The Cost of Undisciplined Analysis

To understand why the knowledge produced by the popular version of TA is untrustworthy, we must consider two distinct forms of TA: subjective and objective. Both approaches can lead to erroneous beliefs, but they do so in distinct ways.

Objective TA methods are well-defined repeatable procedures that issue unambiguous signals. This allows them to be implemented as computerized algorithms and back-tested on historical data. Results produced by a back test can be evaluated in a rigorous quantitative manner.

Subjective TA methods are not well-defined analysis procedures. Because of their vagueness, an analyst's private interpretations are required. This thwarts computerization, back testing, and objective performance evaluation. In other words, it is impossible to either confirm or deny a subjective method's efficacy. For this reason they are insulated from evidentiary challenge.

From the standpoint of EBTA, subjective methods are the most problematic. They are essentially meaningless claims that give the illusion of conveying cognitive content. Because the methods do not specify how they are to be applied, different analysts applying it to the same set of market data can reach different conclusions. This makes it impossible to determine if the method provides useful predictions. Classical chart pattern analysis,[11] hand-drawn trend lines, Elliott Wave Principle,[12] Gann patterns, Magic T's, and numerous other subjective methods fall into this category.[13] Subjective TA is religion—it is based on faith. No amount of cherry-picked examples showing where the method succeeded can cure this deficiency.

Despite their lack of cognitive content and the impossibility of ever being supported by sound evidence, there is no shortage of fervent believers in various subjective methods. Flaws in human thinking can produce strong beliefs in the absence of evidence or even in the face of contradictory evidence.

Objective TA can also spawn erroneous beliefs but they come about differently. They are traceable to faulty inferences from objective evidence. The mere fact that an objective method has been profitable in a back test is not sufficient grounds for concluding that it has merit. Past performance can fool us. Historical success is a necessary but not a sufficient condition for concluding that a method has predictive power and, therefore, is likely to be profitable in the future. Favorable past performance can occur by luck or because of an upward bias produced by one form of back testing called data mining. Determining when back-test profits are attributable to a good method rather than good luck is a question that can only be answered by rigorous statistical inference. This is discussed in Level III, Chapter 23. Level III, Chapter 24, considers the problem of data-mining bias. Although I will assert that data mining, when done correctly, is the modern technician's best method for knowledge discovery, specialized statistical tests must be applied to the results obtained with data mining.

How EBTA Is Different

What sets EBTA apart from the popular form of TA? First, it is restricted to meaningful claims—objective methods that can be tested on historical data. Second, it utilizes advanced forms of statistical inference to determine if a profitable back test is indicative of an effective method. Thus, the prime focus of EBTA is determining which objective methods are worthy of actual use.

EBTA rejects all forms of subjective TA. Subjective TA is not even wrong. It is worse than wrong. Statements that can be qualified as wrong (untrue) at least convey cognitive content that can be tested. The propositions of subjective TA offer no such thing. Though, at first blush, they seem to convey knowledge, when they are examined critically, it becomes clear they are empty claims.

Promoters of New Age health cures excel at empty claims. They tell you that wearing their magic copper bracelet will make you will feel better and put more bounce in your step. They suggest your golf game will improve and maybe even your love life. However, the claim's lack of specificity makes it impossible to nail down exactly what is being promised or how it can be tested. Such claims can never be confirmed or contradicted with objective evidence. On these same grounds, it can be said that the propositions of subjective TA are empty and thus insulated from empirical challenge. They must be taken on faith.

In contrast, a meaningful claim is testable because it makes measurable promises. It states specifically how much your golf game will improve or how bouncy your steps will be. This specificity opens the claim to being contradicted with empirical evidence.

From the perspective of EBTA, proponents of subjective methods are faced with a choice: They can reformulate the method to be objective, as one practitioner of the Elliott Wave Principle has done,[14] thus exposing it to empirical refutation, or they must admit the method must be accepted on faith. Perhaps Gann lines actually provide useful information. In their present form, we are denied this knowledge.

With respect to objective TA, EBTA does not take profitable back tests at face value. Instead, they are subjected to rigorous statistical evaluation to determine if profits were due to luck or biased research. As will be pointed out in Level III, Chapter 24, in many instances, profitable back tests may be a data miner fool's gold. This may explain why many objective TA methods that perform well in back testing perform worse when applied to new data. Evidence-based technical analysis uses computer-intensive statistical methods that minimize problems stemming from the data-mining bias.

The evolution of TA to EBTA also has ethical implications. It is the ethical and legal responsibility of all analysts, whatever form of analysis they practice, to make recommendations that have a reasonable basis and not to make unwarranted claims.[15] The only reasonable basis for asserting an analysis method has value is objective evidence. Subjective TA methods cannot meet this standard. Objective TA, conducted in accordance with the standards of EBTA can.

EBTA Results from Academia

Evidence-based technical analysis is not a new idea. Over the past two decades, numerous articles in respected academic journals[16] have approached TA in the rigorous manner advocated by this book.[17] The evidence is not uniform. Some studies show TA does not work, but some show that it does. Because each study is confined to a particular aspect of TA and a specific body of data, it is possible for studies to reach different conclusions. This is often the case in science.

The following are a few of the findings from academic TA. It shows that, when approached in a rigorous and intellectually honest manner, TA is a worthwhile area of study.

- Expert chartists are unable to distinguish actual price charts of stocks from charts produced by a random process.[18]
- There is empirical evidence of trends in commodities[19] and foreign exchange markets that can be exploited with the simple objective trend indicators. In addition, the profits earned by trend-following speculators may be justified by economic theory[20] because their activities provide commercial hedgers with a valuable economic service, the transference of price risk from hedger to speculator.
- Simple technical rules used individually and in combinations can yield statistically and economically significant profits when applied to stock market averages composed of relatively young companies (Russell 2000 and NASDAQ Composite).[21]
- Neural networks have been able to combine buy/sell signals of simple moving-average rules into nonlinear models that displayed good predictive performance on the Dow Jones Average over the period 1897 to 1988.[22]
- Trends in industry groups and sectors persist long enough after detection by simple momentum indicators to earn excess returns.[23]
- Stocks that have displayed prior relative strength and relative weakness continue to display above-average and below-average performance over horizons of 3 to 12 months.[24]
- United States stocks, selling near their 52-week highs, outperform other stocks. An indicator defined as the differential between a stock's current price and its 52-week high is a useful predictor of future relative performance.[25] The indicator is an even more potent predictor for Australian stocks.[26]
- The head-and-shoulders chart pattern has limited forecasting power when tested in an objective fashion in currencies. Better results can be had with simple filter rules. The head-and-shoulders pattern, when tested objectively on stocks, does not provide useful information.[27] Traders who act on such signals would be equally served by following a random signal.

- Trading volume statistics for stocks contain useful predictive information[28] and improve the profitability of signals based on large price changes following a public announcement.[29]
- Computer-intensive data-modeling neural networks, genetic algorithms, and other statistical learning and artificial-intelligence methods have found profitable patterns in technical indicators.[30]

Who Am I to Criticize TA?

My interest in TA began in 1960 at the age of 15. During my high-school and college years I followed a large stable of stocks using the Chartcraft point and figure method. I have used TA professionally since 1973, first as a stock broker, then as managing partner of a small software company, Raden Research Group Inc.—an early adopter of machine learning and data mining in financial market applications—and finally as a proprietary equities trader for Spear, Leeds & Kellogg.[31] In 1988, I earned the Chartered Market Technician designation from the Market Technicians Association. My personal TA library has over 300 books. I have published approximately a dozen articles and have spoken numerous times on the subject. Currently I teach a graduate-level course in TA at the Zicklin School of Business, Baruch College, City University of New York. I freely admit my previous writings and research do not meet EBTA standards, in particular with regard to statistical significance and the data-mining bias.

My long-standing faith in TA began to erode in response to a very mediocre performance over a five-year period trading capital for Spear, Leeds and Kellogg. How could what I believed in so fervently not work? Was it me or something to do with TA in general? My academic training in philosophy provided fertile grounds for my growing doubts. My concerns crystallized into full fledged skepticism as a result of reading two books: *How We Know What Isn't So* by Thomas Gilovich and *Why People Believe Weird Things*, by Michael Shermer. My conclusion: Technical analysts, including myself, know a lot of stuff that isn't so, and believe a lot of weird things.

Technical Analysis: Art, Science, or Superstition?

There is a debate in the TA community: Is it an art or a science? The question has been framed incorrectly. It is more properly stated as: Should TA be based on superstition or science? Framed this way the debate evaporates.

Some will say TA involves too much nuance and interpretation to render its knowledge in the form of scientifically testable claims. To this I retort: TA that is not testable may sound like knowledge, but it is not. It is superstition that belongs in the realm of astrology, numerology, and other nonscientific practices.

Creativity and inspiration play a crucial role in science. They will be important in EBTA as well. All scientific inquiries start with a hypothesis, a new idea or a new insight inspired by a mysterious mixture of prior knowledge, experience, and a leap of intuition. Yet, good science balances creativity with analytical rigor. The freedom to propose new ideas must be married to an unyielding discipline that eliminates ideas that prove worthless in the crucible of objective testing. Without this anchor to reality, people fall in love with their ideas, and magical thinking replaces critical thought.

It is unlikely that TA will ever discover rules that predict with the precision of the laws of physics. The inherent complexity and randomness of financial markets and the impossibility of controlled experimentation preclude such findings. However, predictive accuracy is not the defining requirement of science. Rather, it is defined by an uncompromising openness to recognizing and eliminating wrong ideas.

I have four hopes for this book: First, that it will stimulate a dialogue amongst technical analysts that will ultimately put our field on a firmer intellectual foundation; second, that it will encourage further research along the lines advocated herein; third, that it will encourage consumers of TA to demand more "beef" from those who sell products and services based upon TA; and fourth, that it will encourage TA practitioners, professional and otherwise, to understand their crucial role in a human-machine partnership that has the potential to accelerate the growth of legitimate TA knowledge.

No doubt some fellow practitioners of TA will be irritated by these ideas. This can be a good thing. An oyster irritated by a grain of sand sometimes yields a pearl. I invite my colleagues to expend their energies adding to legitimate knowledge rather than defending the indefensible.

Notes

1. Data typically considered by TA includes prices of financial instruments; trading volume; open interest, in the case of options and futures; as well as other measures that reflect the attitudes and behavior of market participants.
2. J. Hall, *Practically Profound: Putting Philosophy to Work in Everyday Life* (Lanham, MD: Rowman & Littlefield Publishers, 2005).
3. Ibid., 4.
4. Ibid., 4.
5. Ibid., 5.
6. Ibid., 5.
7. Ibid., 5.
8. Ibid., 6.
9. Ibid., 5.
10. Ibid., 81.
11. R.D. Edwards and J. Magee, *Technical Analysis of Stock Trends*, 4th ed. (Springfield, MA: John Magee, 1958).
12. For a complete description of Elliott wave theory see R.R. Prechter and A.J. Frost, *Elliott Wave Principle* (New York: New Classics Library, 1998).
13. Any version of these methods that has been made objective to the point where it is back testable would negate this criticism.
14. The professional association of technical analysts, the Market Technicians Association (MTA), requires compliance with the National Association of Securities Dealers and the New York Stock

Exchange. These self-regulating bodies require "*that research reports have a reasonable basis and no unwarranted claims.*" Going even further, the MTA requires of its members that they "*shall not publish or make statements concerning the technical position of a security, a market or any of its components or aspects unless such statements are reasonable and consistent in light of the available evidence and the accumulated knowledge in the field of technical analysis.*"

15. Some peer-reviewed academic journals include *Journal of Finance*, *Financial Management Journal*, *Journal of Financial Economics*, *Journal of Financial and Quantitative Analysis*, and *Review of Financial Studies*.
16. Outside of academia, there has been a move to greater emphasis on objective methods of TA, but often the results are not evaluated in a statistically rigorous manner.
17. F.D. Arditti, "Can Analysts Distinguish Between Real and Randomly Generated Stock Prices?," *Financial Analysts Journal* 34, no. 6 (November/December 1978), 70.
18. J.J. Siegel, *Stocks for the Long Run*, 2nd ed. (New York: McGraw-Hill, 1998), 243.
19. G.R. Jensen, R.R. Johnson, and J.M. Mercer, "Tactical Asset Allocation and Commodity Futures: Ways to Improve Performance," *Journal of Portfolio Management* 28, no. 4 (Summer 2002).
20. C.R. Lightner, "A Rationale for Managed Futures," *Technical Analysis of Stocks & Commodities* (2003). Note that this publication is not a peer-reviewed journal but the article appeared to be well supported and its findings were consistent with the peer-reviewed article cited in the prior note.
21. P.-H. Hsu and C.-M. Kuan, "Reexamining the Profitability of Technical Analysis with Data Snooping Checks," *Journal of Financial Economics* 3, no. 4 (2005), 606–628.
22. R. Gency, "The Predictability of Security Returns with Simple Technical Trading Rules," *Journal of Empirical Finance* 5 (1998), 347–349.
23. N. Jegadeesh, "Evidence of Predictable Behavior of Security Returns," *Journal of Finance* 45 (1990), 881–898.
24. N. Jegadeesh and S. Titman, "Returns to Buying Winners and Selling Losers: Implications for Stock Market Efficiency," *Journal of Finance* 48 (1993), 65–91.
25. T.J. George and C.-Y. Hwang, "The 52-Week High and Momentum Investing," *Journal of Finance* 59, no. 5 (October 2004), 2145–2184.
26. B.R. Marshall and R. Hodges, "Is the 52-Week High Momentum Strategy Profitable Outside the U.S.?" awaiting publication in *Applied Financial Economics*.
27. C.L. Osler, "Identifying Noise Traders: The Head and Shoulders Pattern in U.S. Equities," *Staff Reports, Federal Reserve Bank of New York* 42 (July 1998), 39 pages.
28. L. Blume and D. Easley, "Market Statistics and Technical Analysis: The Role of Volume," *Journal of Finance* 49, no. 1 (March 1994), 153–182.
29. V. Singal, *Beyond the Random Walk: A Guide of Stock Market Anomalies and Low-Risk Investing* (New York: Oxford University Press, 2004). These results are discussed in Chapter 4, "Short Term Price Drift." The chapter also contains an excellent list of references of other research relating to this topic.
30. A.M. Safer, "A Comparison of Two Data Mining Techniques to Predict Abnormal Stock Market Returns," *Intelligent Data Analysis* 7, no. 1 (2003), 3–14; G. Armano, A. Murru, and F. Roli, "Stock Market Prediction by a Mixture of Genetic-Neural Experts," *International Journal of Pattern Recognition & Artificial Intelligence* 16, no. 5 (August 2002), 501–528; G. Armano, M. Marchesi, and A. Murru, "A Hybrid Genetic-Neural Architecture for Stock Indexes Forecasting," *Information Sciences* 170, no. 1 (February 2005), 3–33; T. Chenoweth, Z.O. Sauchi, and S. Lee, "Embedding Technical Analysis into Neural Network Based Trading Systems," *Applied Artificial Intelligence* 10, no. 6 (December 1996), 523–542; S. Thawornwong, D. Enke, and C. Dagli, "Neural Networks as a Decision Maker for Stock Trading: A Technical Analysis Approach," *International Journal of Smart Engineering System Design* 5, no. 4 (October/December 2003), 313–325; A.M. Safer, "The

Application of Neural-Networks to Predict Abnormal Stock Returns Using Insider Trading Data," *Applied Stochastic Models in Business & Industry* 18, no. 4 (October 2002), 380–390; J. Yao, C.L. Tan, and H.-L. Pho, "Neural Networks for Technical Analysis: A Study on KLCI," *International Journal of Theoretical & Applied Finance* 2, no. 2 (April 1999), 221–242; J. Korczak and P. Rogers, "Stock Timing Using Genetic Algorithms," *Applied Stochastic Models in Business & Industry* 18, no. 2 (April 2002), 121–135; Z. Xu-Shen and M. Dong, "Can Fuzzy Logic Make Technical Analysis 20/20?," *Financial Analysts Journal* 60, no. 4 (July/August 2004), 54–75; J.M. Gorriz, C.G. Puntonet, M. Salmeron, and J.J. De la Rosa, "A New Model for Time-Series Forecasting Using Radial Basis Functions and Exogenous Data," *Neural Computing & Applications* 13, no. 2 (2004), 100–111.

31. This firm was acquired by Goldman Sachs in September 2000.

CHAPTER 24

Objective Rules and Their Evaluation

From David Aronson, *Evidence-Based Technical Analysis* (Hoboken, New Jersey: John Wiley & Sons, 2006), Chapter 1.

This chapter introduces the notion of objective binary signaling rules and a methodology for their rigorous evaluation. It defines an evaluation benchmark based on the profitability of a noninformative signal. It also establishes the need to detrend market data so that the performances of rules with different long/short position biases can be compared.

The Great Divide: Objective versus Subjective Technical Analysis

Technical analysis (TA) divides into two broad categories: objective and subjective. Subjective TA is comprised of analysis methods and patterns that are not precisely defined. As a consequence, a conclusion derived from a subjective method reflects the private interpretations of the analyst applying the method. This creates the possibility that two analysts applying the same method to the same set of market data may arrive at entirely different conclusions. Therefore, subjective methods are untestable, and claims that they are effective are exempt from empirical challenge. This is fertile ground for myths to flourish.

In contrast, objective methods are clearly defined. When an objective analysis method is applied to market data, its signals or predictions are unambiguous. This makes it possible to simulate the method on historical data and determine its precise level of performance. This is called back testing. The back testing of an objective method is, therefore, a repeatable experiment which allows claims of profitability to be tested and possibly refuted with statistical evidence. This makes it possible to find out which objective methods are effective and which are not.

The acid test for distinguishing an objective from a subjective method is the *programmability criterion: A method is objective if and only if it can be implemented as a computer program that produces unambiguous market positions (long,*[1] *short,*[2] *or neutral*[3]). All methods that cannot be reduced to such a program are, by default, subjective.

TA Rules

Objective TA methods are also referred to as mechanical trading rules or trading systems. In this book, all objective TA methods are referred to simply as *rules*.

A rule is a function that transforms one or more items of information, referred to as the rule's input, into the rule's output, which is a recommended market position (e.g., long, short, neutral). Input(s) consists of one or more financial market time series. The rule is defined by one or more mathematical and logical operators that convert the input time series into a new time series that consists of the sequence of recommended market position (long, short, out-of-the-market). The output is typically represented by a signed number (e.g., +1 or −1). This book adopts the convention of assigning positive values to indicate long positions and negative values to indicate shorts position. The process by which a rule transforms one or more input series into an output series is illustrated in Figure 24.1.

A rule is said to generate a *signal* when the value of the output series changes. A signal calls for a change in a previously recommended market position. For example a change in output from +1 to −1 would call for closing a previously held long position and the initiation of a new short position. Output values need not be confined

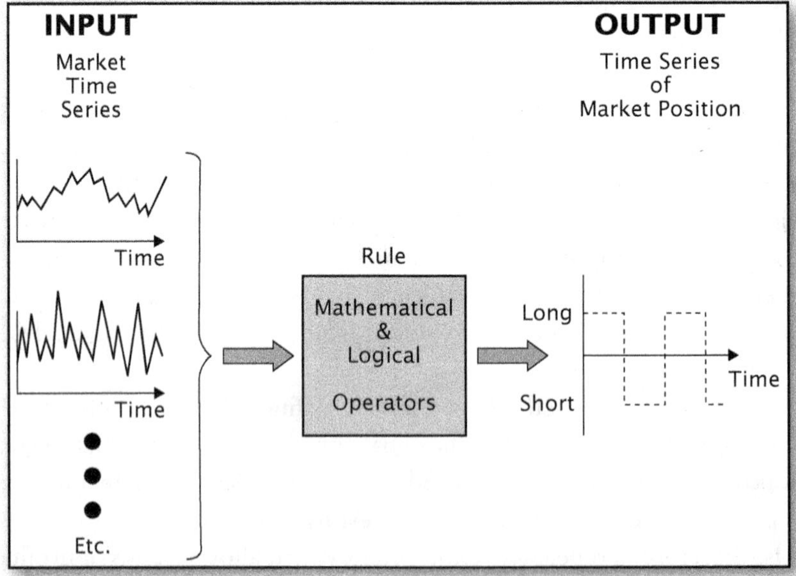

FIGURE 24.1 TA Rule Transforms Input Time Series into a Time Series of Market Position.

to $\{+1, -1\}$. A complex rule, whose output spans the range $\{+10, -10\}$, is able to recommend positions that vary in size. For example, an output of $+10$ might indicate that 10 long positions are warranted, such as long 10 contracts of copper. A change in the output from $+10$ to $+5$ would call for a reduction in the long position from 10 contracts to 5 (i.e., sell 5).

Binary Rules and Thresholds

The simplest rule is one that has a *binary output*. In other words, its output can assume only two values, for example $+1$ and -1. A binary rule could also be designed to recommend long/neutral positions or short/neutral positions. All the rules considered in this book are binary long/short $\{+1, -1\}$.

An investment strategy based on a binary long/short rule is always in either a long or short position in the market being traded. Rules of this type are referred to as *reversal rules* because signals call for a reversal from long to short or short to long. Over time a reversal rule produces a time series of $+1$'s and -1's that represent an alternating sequence of long and short positions.

The specific mathematical and logical operators that are used to define rules can vary considerably. However, there are some common themes. One theme is the notion of a *threshold*, a critical level that distinguishes the informative changes in the input time series from its irrelevant fluctuations. The premise is that the input time series is a mixture of information and noise. Thus the threshold acts as a filter.

Rules that employ thresholds generate signals when the time series crosses the threshold, either by the rising above it or falling beneath it. These critical events can be detected with logical operators called *inequalities* such as *greater-than* (>) and *less-than* (<). For example, if the time series is greater than the threshold, then rule output $= +1$, otherwise rule output $= -1$.

A threshold may be set at a fixed value or its value may vary over time as a result of changes in the time series that is being analyzed. Variable thresholds are appropriate for time series that display trends, which are large long-lasting changes in the level of the series. Trends, which make fixed threshold rules impractical, are commonly seen in asset prices (e.g., S&P 500 Index) and asset yields (AAA bond yield). The moving average and the Alexander reversal filter, also known as the zigzag filter, are examples of time series operators that are commonly used to define variable thresholds. The operators used in the rules discussed in this book are detailed in Level II, Chapter 42.

The moving-average-cross rule is an example of how a variable threshold is used to generate signals on a time series that displays trends. This type of rule produces a signal when the time series crosses from one side of its moving average to the other. For example:

If *the time series is above its moving average,* then *the rule output value* $= +1$, *otherwise the rule output value* $= -1$.

This is illustrated in Figure 24.2.

Because it employs a single threshold, the signals generated by the moving-average-cross rule are, by definition, mutually exclusive. Given a single threshold, there are only two possible conditions—the times series is either above or below[4]

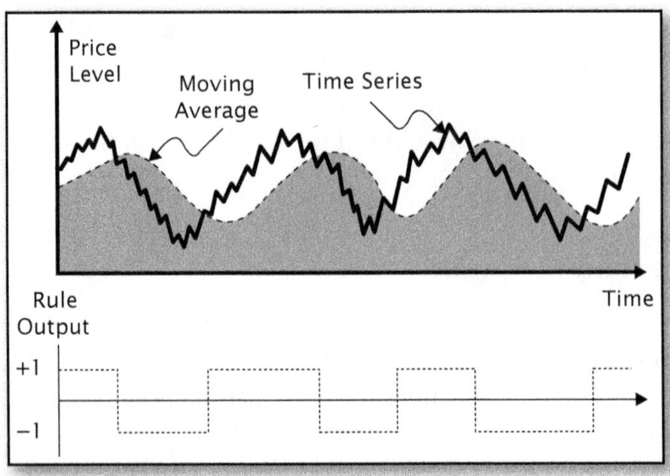

FIGURE 24.2 Moving-Average-Cross Rule.

the threshold. The conditions are also exhaustive (no other possibilities).[5] Thus, it is impossible for the rule's signals to be in conflict.

Rules with fixed value thresholds are appropriate for market time series that do not display trends. Such time series are said to be *stationary*. There is a strict mathematical definition of a stationary time series, but here I am using the term in a looser sense to mean that a series has a relatively stable average value over time and has fluctuations that are confined to a roughly horizontal range. Technical analysis practitioners often refer to these series as *oscillators*.

Time series that display trends can be *detrended*. In other words, they can be transformed into a stationary series. Detrending, which is described in greater detail in Level II, Chapter 41, frequently involves taking differences or ratios. For example the ratio of a time series to its moving average will produce a stationary version of the original time series. Once detrended, the series will be seen to fluctuate within a relatively well-defined horizontal range around a relatively stable mean value. Once the time series has been made stationary, fixed threshold rules can be employed. An example of a fixed threshold rule using a threshold of value of 75 is illustrated in Figure 24.3. The rule has an output a value of +1 when the series is greater than the threshold and a value of −1 at other times.

Binary Rules from Multiple Thresholds

As pointed out earlier, binary rules are derived, quite naturally, from a single threshold because the threshold defines two mutually exclusive and exhaustive conditions: the time series is either above or below threshold. However, binary rules can also be derived using multiple thresholds, but employing more than one threshold creates the possibility that the input time series can assume more than two conditions. Consequently, multiple threshold rules require a more sophisticated logical operator than the simple inequality operator (greater-than or less-than), which suffices for single threshold rules.

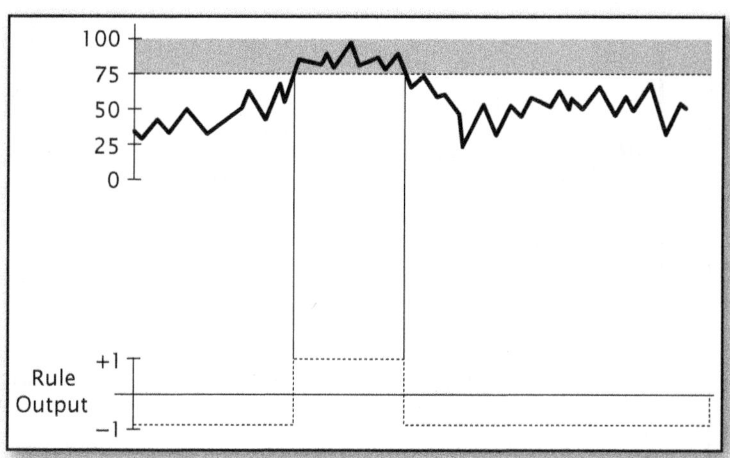

FIGURE 24.3 Rule with a single Fixed Threshold.

When there are two or more thresholds, there are more than two possible conditions. For example, with two thresholds, an upper and lower, there are three possible conditions for the input time series. It can be above the upper, below the lower, or between the two thresholds. To create a binary rule in this situation, the rule is defined in terms of two mutually exclusive events. An event is defined by the time series crossing a particular threshold in a particular direction. Thus, one event triggers one of the rule's output values, which is maintained until a second event, which is mutually exclusive of the first, triggers the other output value. For example, an upward crossing of the upper threshold triggers a +1, and a downward crossing of the lower threshold triggers a −1.

A logical operator that implements this type of rule is referred to as a *flip-flop*. The name stems from the fact that the rule's output value *flips* one way, upon the occurrence of one event, and then *flops* the other way, upon the occurrence of the second event. Flip-flop logic can be used with either variable or fixed threshold rules. An example of a rule based on two variable thresholds is the moving average band rule. See Figure 24.4. Here, the moving average is surrounded by an upper and lower band. The bands may be a fixed percentage above and below the moving average, or the deviation of the bands may vary based on of the recent volatility of the times, as is the case with the Bollinger Band.[6] An output value of +1 is triggered by an upward piercing of the upper threshold. This value is retained until the lower threshold is penetrated in the downward direction, causing the output value to change to −1.

Obviously, there are many other possibilities. The intent here has been to illustrate some of the ways that input time series can be transformed into a time series of recommended market positions.

Hayes[7] adds another dimension to threshold rules with *directional modes*. He applies multiple thresholds to a stationary time series such as a diffusion[8] indicator. At a given point in time, the indicator's mode is defined by the zone it occupies and its recent direction of change (e.g., up or down over the most recent five weeks). Each zone is defined by an upper and lower threshold (e.g., 40 and

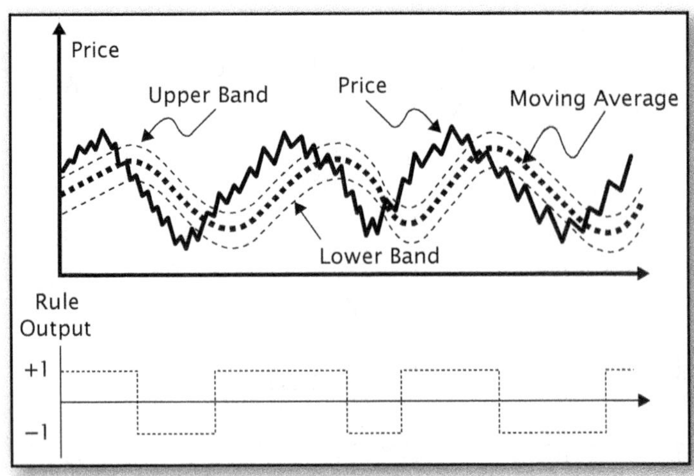

FIGURE 24.4 **Moving Average Bands Rule.**

60). Hayes applies this to a proprietary diffusion indicator called Big Mo. With two thresholds and two possible directional modes (up/down), six mutually exclusive conditions are defined. A binary rule could be derived from such an analysis by assigning one output value (e.g., +1) to one of the six conditions, and then assigning the other output value (i.e., −1) to the other five possibilities. Hayes asserts that one of the modes, when the diffusion indicator is above 60 and its direction is upward, is associated with stock market returns (Value Line Composite Index) of 50 percent per annum. This condition has occurred about 20 percent of the time between 1966 and 2000. However, when the diffusion indicator is > 60, and its recent change is negative, the market's annualized return is zero. This condition has occurred about 16 percent of the time.[9]

Traditional Rules and Inverse Rules

Part Two of this book is a case study that evaluates the profitability of approximately 6,400 binary long/short rules applied to the S&P 500 Index. Many of the rules generate market positions that are consistent with traditional principles of technical analysis. For example, under traditional TA principles, a moving-average-cross rule is interpreted to be bullish (output value +1) when the analyzed time series is above its moving average, and bearish (output value of −1) when it is below the moving average. I refer to these as *traditional* TA rules.

Given that the veracity of traditional TA maybe questionable, it is desirable to test rules that are contrary to the traditional interpretation. In other words, it is entirely possible that patterns that are traditionally assumed to predict rising prices may actually be predictive of falling prices. Alternatively, it is possible that neither configuration has any predictive value.

This can be accomplished by creating an additional set of rules whose output is simply the opposite of a traditional TA rule. I refer to these as *inverse* rules. This is

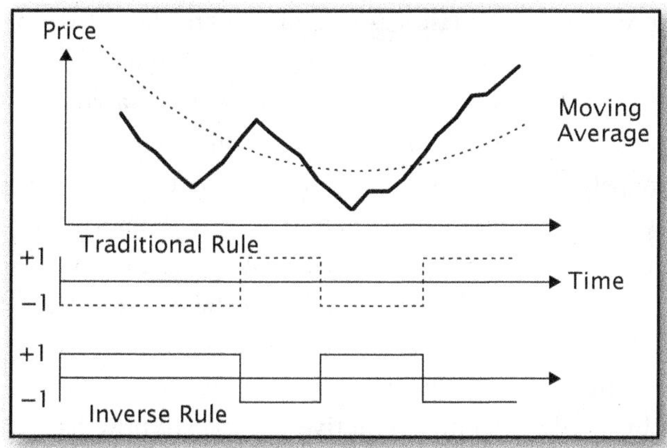

FIGURE 24.5 **Traditional Rules and Inverse Rules.**

illustrated in Figure 24.5. The inverse of the moving-average-cross rule would output a value of −1 when the input time series is above its moving average, and +1 when the series is below its moving average.

There is yet another reason to consider inverse rules. Many of the rules tested in Part Two utilize input series other than the S&P 500, for example the yield differential between BAA and AAA corporate bonds. It is not obvious how this series should be interpreted to generate signals. Therefore, both up trends and down trends in the yield differential were considered as possible buy signals. The details of these rules are taken up in Level II, Chapter 41.

The Use of Benchmarks in Rule Evaluation

In many fields, performance is a relative matter. That is to say, it is performance relative to a benchmark that is informative rather than an absolute level of performance. In track and field, competitors in the shot-put are compared to a benchmark defined as best distance of that day or the best ever recorded in the state or world. To say that someone put the shot 43 feet does not reveal the quality of performance, however if the best prior effort had been 23 feet, 43 feet is a significant accomplishment!

This pertains to rule evaluation. Performance figures are only informative when they are compared to a relevant benchmark. The isolated fact that a rule earned a 10 percent rate of return in a back test is meaningless. If many other rules earned over 30 percent on the same data, 10 percent would indicate inferiority, whereas if all other rules were barely profitable, 10 percent might indicate superiority.

What then is an appropriate benchmark for TA rule performance? What standard must a rule beat to be considered good? There are a number of reasonable standards. This book defines that standard as the performance of a rule with no predictive power (i.e., a randomly generated signal). This is consistent with scientific practice in other fields. In medicine, a new drug must convincingly outperform a placebo (sugar pill) to be considered useful. Of course, rational investors might reasonably choose a higher standard of performance but not a lesser one. Some other benchmarks that could make sense would be the riskless rate of return, the return of a buy-and-hold strategy, or the rate of return of the rule currently being used.

In fact, to be considered good, it is not sufficient for a rule to simply beat the benchmark. It must beat it by a wide enough margin to exclude the possibility that its victory was merely due to chance (good luck). It is entirely possible for a rule with no predictive power to beat its benchmark in a given sample of data by sheer luck. The margin of victory that is sufficient to exclude luck as a likely explanation relates to the matter of *statistical significance*. This is taken up in Level III, Chapters 23 and 24.

Having now established that the benchmark that we will use is the return that could be earned by a rule with no predictive power, we now face another question: How much might a rule with no predictive power earn? At first blush, it might seem that a return of zero is a reasonable expectation. However, this is only true under a specific and rather limited set of conditions.

In fact, the expected return of a rule with no predictive power can be dramatically different than zero. This is so because the performance of a rule can be profoundly affected by factors that have nothing to do with its predictive power.

The Conjoint Effect of Position Bias and Market Trend on Back-Test Performance

In reality, a rule's back-tested performance is comprised of two independent components. One component is attributable to the rule's predictive power, if it has any. This is the component of interest. The second, and unwanted, component of performance is the result of two factors that have nothing to do with the rule's predictive power: (1) the rule's long/short position bias, and (2) the market's net trend during the back-test period.

This undesirable component of performance can dramatically influence back-test results and make rule evaluation difficult. It can cause a rule with no predictive power to generate a positive average return or it can cause a rule with genuine predictive power to produce a negative average return. Unless this component of performance is removed, accurate rule evaluation is impossible. Let's consider the two factors that drive this component.

The first factor is a rule's *long/short* position bias. This refers to the amount of time the rule spent in a +1 output state relative to the amount of time spent in a −1 output state during the back test. If either output state dominated during the back test, the rule is said to have a position bias. For example, if more time was spent in long positions, the rule has a long position bias.

The second factor is the *market's net trend* or the average daily price change of the market during the period of the back test. If the market's net trend is other than zero, and the rule has a long or short position bias, the rule's performance will be impacted. In other words, the undesirable component of performance will distort back-test results either by adding to or subtracting from the component of performance that is due to the rule's actual predictive power. If, however, the market's net trend is zero or if the rule has no position bias, then the rule's past profitability will be strictly due to the rule's predictive power (plus or minus random variation). This is demonstrated mathematically later.

To clarify, imagine a TA rule that has a long position bias but that we know has no predictive power. The signals of such a rule could be simulated by a roulette wheel. To create the long position bias, a majority of the wheel's slots would be allocated to long positions (+1). Suppose that one hundred slots are allocated as follows: 75 are +1 and 25 are −1. Each day, over a period of historical data, the wheel is spun to determine if a long or short position is to be held for that day. If the market's average daily change during this period were greater than zero (i.e., net trend upward), the rule would have a positive expected rate of return even though the signals contain no predictive information. The rule's expected rate of return can be computed using the formula used to calculate the expected value of a random variable (discussed later).

Just as it is possible for a rule with no predictive power to produce a positive rate of return, it is just as possible for a rule with predictive power to produce a negative rate of return. This can occur if a rule has a position bias that is contrary to the market's trend. The combined effect of the market's trend and the rule's position bias may be sufficient to offset any positive return attributable to the rule's predictive power. From the preceding discussion it should be clear that the component of performance due to the interaction of position bias with market trend must be eliminated if one is to develop a valid performance benchmark.

At first blush, it might seem as if a rule that has a long position bias during a rising market trend is evidence of the rule's predictive power. However, this is not necessarily so. The rule's bullish bias could simply be due to the way its long and short conditions are defined. If the rule's long condition is more easily satisfied than its short condition, all other things being equal, the rule will tend to hold long positions a greater proportion of the time than short positions. Such a rule would receive a performance boost when back tested over historical data with a rising market trend. Conversely, a rule whose short condition is more easily satisfied than its long condition would be biased toward short positions and it would get a performance boost if simulated during a downward trending market.

The reader may be wondering how the definition of a rule can induce a bias toward either long or short positions. This warrants some explanation. Recall that binary reversal rules, the type tested in this book, are always in either a long or short position. Given this, if a rule's long (+1) condition is relatively easy to satisfy, then it follows that its short condition (−1) must be relatively difficult to satisfy. In other words, the condition required for the −1 output state is more restrictive, making it likely that, over time, the rule will spend more time long than short. It is just as possible to formulate rules where the long condition is more restrictive than the short condition. All other things being equal, such a rule would recommend short positions more frequently than long. It would be contrary to our purpose to allow the assessment of a rule's predictive power to be impacted by the relative strictness or laxity of the way in which its long and short conditions are defined.

To illustrate, consider the following rule, which has a highly restrictive short condition and, therefore, a relatively lax long condition. The rule, which generates

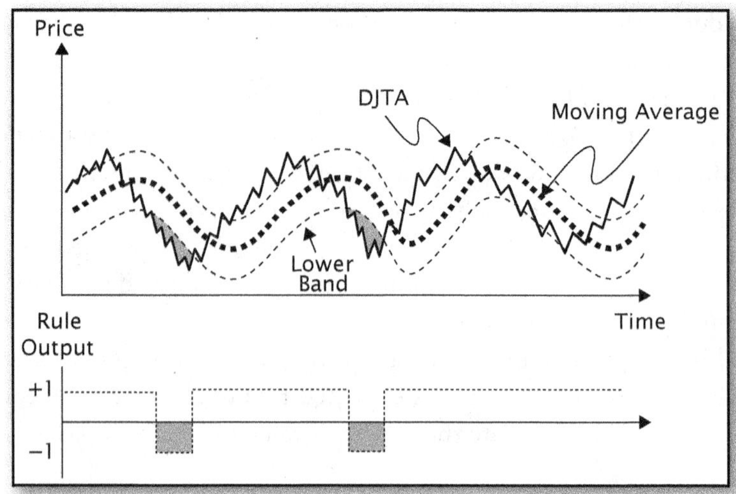

FIGURE 24.6 Rule with Restrictive Short Condition and Long Position Bias.

positions in the S&P 500 index, is based on the Dow Jones Transportation Average.[10] Assume that a moving average with bands set at +3 percent and −3 percent is applied to the DJTA. The rule is to be short the S&P 500 while the DJTA is below the lower band, by definition a relatively rare condition, and long at all other times. See Figure 24.6. Clearly, such a rule would benefit if the S&P were in an uptrend over the back-test period.

Now let's consider the back test of two binary reversal rules which are referred to as rule 1 and rule 2. They are tested on S&P 500 data over the period January 1, 1976 through December 2004. During this period of approximately 7,000 days, the S&P 500 had an average daily return of +0.035 percent per day compounded, or +9.21897 percent annualized. Assume that rule 1 was in a long state 90 percent of the time and rule 2 was in a long state 60 percent of the time. Also, suppose that neither rule has predictive power—as if their output values were determined by a roulette wheel with 100 slots. The output for rule 1 is based on a roulette wheel with 90 slots assigned a value of +1 and the remaining 10 assigned a value of −1. The output for rule 2 is based on a wheel with 60 slots assigned a +1 value and 40 a value of −1. By the Law of Large Numbers,[11] it is reasonable to expect that over the 7,000 days, rule 1 will be long very close to 90 percent of the time and rule 2 will be long approximately 60 percent of the time. Although the rules have different long/short biases, they have equal predictive power—none. However, their expected rates of return will be quite different over this segment of market history.

The expected return of a rule depends upon three quantities: (1) the proportion of time the rule spent in long positions, (2) the proportion of time spent in short positions (1 minus the proportion of time long), and (3) the market's average daily price change during the historical test period. The expected return (ER) is given by the following equation.

Expected Return

$$ER = [p(L) \times ADC] - [p(S) \times ADC]$$

Where
p(L) – probability of long position (proportion long)
p(S) – probability of short position (proportion short)
ADC: average daily change in market traded

Based on this calculation, the expected return for rule 1 is .028 percent per day or 7.31 percent annualized.[12] The expected return for rule 2 is 0.007 percent per day or 1.78 percent annualized.[13] This demonstrates that the rules' historical performance misleads us in two ways. First, both rules generate positive returns, yet we know that neither has any predictive power. Second, rule 1 appears to be superior to rule 2 even though we know they have equal predictive power—none.

When testing actual trading rules, one way to remove the deceptive effect due to the interaction of position bias and market trend would be to do the following: Subtract the expected return of a nonpredictive rule with the same position bias as the rule tested from the observed return of the tested rule. For example, assume that we did not know rules 1 and 2 had no predictive power. Simply by knowing their historical position bias, 90 percent long for rule 1 and 60 percent for rule 2, and knowing the market's average daily return over the back-test period, we would be able to compute the expected returns for rules with no predictive power having these position biases using the equation for the expected return already shown. The expected returns for each rule and would then be subtracted from each rule's observed performance. Therefore, from rule 1's back-tested return, which was 7.31 percent, we would subtract 7.31 percent, giving a result of zero. The result properly reflects rule 1's lack of predictive power. From rule 2's return of 1.78 percent, we would subtract a value of 1.78 percent, also giving a value of zero, also revealing its lack of predictive power.

The bottom line is this: by adjusting the back-tested (observed) performance by the expected return of a rule with no predictive power having an equivalent position bias, the deceptive component of performance can be removed. In other words, one can define the benchmark for any rule as the expected return of a nonpredictive rule with an equivalent position bias.

A Simpler Solution to Benchmarking: Detrending the Market Data

The procedure just described can be quite burdensome when many rules are being tested. It would require that a separate benchmark be computed for each rule based on its particular position bias. Fortunately there is an easier way.

The easier method merely requires that the historical data for the market being traded (e.g., S&P 500 Index) be detrended prior to rule testing. It is important to point out that the detrended data is used only for the purpose of calculating daily rule returns. It is not used for signal generation if the time series of the market being traded is also being used as a rule input series. Signals would be generated from actual market data (not detrended).

Detrending is a simple transformation, which results in a new market data series whose average daily price change is equal to zero. As pointed out earlier, if the market being traded has a net zero trend during the back-test period, a rule's position bias will have no distorting effect on performance. Thus, the expected return of a rule with no predictive power, the benchmark, will be zero if its returns are computed from detrended market data. Consequently, the expected return of a rule that does have predictive power will be greater than zero when its returns are computed from detrended data.

To perform the detrending transformation, one first determines the average daily price change of the market being traded over the historical test period. This average value is then subtracted from each day's price change.

The mathematical equivalence between the two methods discussed, (1) detrending the market data and (2) subtracting a benchmark with a equivalent position bias, may not be immediately obvious. A detailed mathematical proof is given in the Appendix, but if you think about it, you will see that if the market's average daily price change during the historical testing period is equal to zero, then rules devoid of predictive power must have an expected return of zero, regardless of their long/short position bias.

To illustrate this point, let's return to the formula for computing the expected value of a random variable. You will notice that if the average daily price change of the market being traded is zero, it does not matter what p(long) or p(short) are. The expected return (ER) will always be zero.

$$ER = [p\ (\text{long}) \times \text{avg. daily return}] - [p\ (\text{short}) \times \text{avg. daily return}]$$

For example, if the position biases were 60 percent long and 40 percent short, the expected return is zero.

$$0 = [0.60 \times 0] - [0.40 \times 0] \text{ Position Bias: 60 percent long, 40 percent short}$$

If, on the other hand, a rule does have predictive power, its expected return on detrended data will be greater than zero. This positive return reflects the fact that the rule's long and short positions are intelligent rather than random.

Using Logs of Daily Price Ratio Instead of Percentages

Thus far, the returns for rules and the market being traded have been discussed in percentage terms. This was done for ease of explanation. However, there are problems with computing returns as percentages. These problems can be eliminated by computing daily returns as the logs of daily price ratios which is defined as:

$$\text{Log}\left(\frac{\text{current day's price}}{\text{prior day's price}}\right)$$

The log-based market returns are detrended in exactly the same way as the percentage changes. The log of the daily price ratio for the market being traded is computed for each day over the back-test period. The average is found, and then this average is deducted from each day. This eliminates any trend in the market data.

Other Details: The Look-Ahead Bias and Trading Costs

It is said the devil lives in the details. When it comes to testing rules, this truth applies. There are two more items that must be considered to ensure accurate historical testing. They are (1) the look-ahead bias and the related issue, assumed execution prices, and (2) trading costs.

Look-Ahead Bias and Assumed Execution Prices

Look-ahead bias,[14] also known as "leakage of future information," occurs in the context of historical testing when information that was not truly available at a given point in time was assumed to be known. In other words, the information that would be required to generate a signal was not truly available at the time the signal was assumed to occur.

In many instances, this problem can be subtle. If unrecognized, it can seriously overstate the performance of rule tests. For example, suppose a rule uses the market's closing price or any input series that only becomes known at the time of the close. When this is the case, it would not be legitimate to assume that one could enter or exit a position at the market's closing price. Assuming this would infect the results with look-ahead bias. In fact, the earliest opportunity to enter or exit would be the following day's opening price (assuming daily frequency information). All of the rules tested in Part Two of this book are based on market data that is known as of the close of each trading day. Therefore, the rule tests assume execution at the opening price on the following day. This means that a rule's daily return for the current day (day_0) is equal to the rule's output value (+1 or −1) as of the close of day^0 multiplied by the market's change from the opening price of the next day (open day_{+1}) price to the opening price on day after that (open day_{+2}). That price change is given as the log of the ratio defined as opening price of day_{+2} divided by the opening price on day_{+1}, as shown in the following equation:

$$Pos_0 \times Log\left[\frac{O_{+2}}{O_{+1}}\right]$$

Where:

Pos_0 = Rule's market position as of the close of day_0

O_{+1} = Open S&P 500 on day_{+1}

O_{+2} = Open S&P 500 on day_{+2}

This equation does not show the detrended version of rule returns, as shown here:

$$\text{Pos}_0 \times \left[\text{Log}\left[\frac{O_{+2}}{O_{+1}}\right] - \text{ALR} \right]$$

Where:

Pos_0 = Rule's market position as of the close of day_0

O_{+1} = Open S&P 500 on day_{+1}

O_{+2} = Open S&P 500 on day_{+2}

ALR = Average Log Return over Back Test

Look-ahead bias can also infect back-test results when a rule uses an input data series that is reported with a lag or that is subject to revision. For example, the back-test of a rule that uses mutual fund cash statistics,[15] which is released to the public with a two-week delay, must take this lag into account by lagging signals to reflect the true availability of the data. None of the rules tested in this book use information reported with a lag or that is subject to revision.

Trading Costs

Should trading costs be taken into account in rule back-tests? If the intent is to use the rule on a stand-alone basis for trading, the answer is clearly yes. For example, rules that signal reversals frequently will incur higher trading costs than rules that signal less frequently and this must be taken into account when comparing their performances. Trading costs include broker commissions and slippage. Slippage is due to the bid-asked spread and the amount that the investor's order pushes the market's price—up when buying or down when selling.

If, however, the purpose of rule testing is to discover signals that contain predictive information, then trading costs can obscure the value of a rule that reverses frequently. Since the intent of the rule studies conducted in this book are aimed at finding rules that have predictive power rather than finding rules that can be used as stand-alone trading strategies it was decided not to impose trading costs.

Notes

1. A long position in a security means the investor owns the security and hopes to benefit by selling it in the future at a higher price.
2. A short position in a security means the investor has sold the security without owning it but is obligated to buy it back at a later point in time. The holder of a short position therefore benefits from a subsequent price decline, thereby permitting the repurchase at a lower level than the selling price, earning a profit.

3. *Neutral* refers to the case where the investor holds no position in the market.
4. It is assumed that all market information required by the method is known and publicly available at the time the method produces the recommendation.
5. The possibility of the time series being equal to the moving average is eliminated by computing the value of the moving average to a greater degree of precision than the price level.
6. J. Bollinger, *Bollinger on Bollinger Bands* (New York: McGraw-Hill, 2002).
7. T. Hayes, *The Research Driven Investor: How to Use Information, Data and Analysis for Investment Success* (New York: McGraw-Hill, 2001), 63.
8. A diffusion indicator is based on an analysis of numerous market time series within a defined universe (e.g., all NYSE stocks). The same rule, such as a moving average cross, is applied to all the series comprising the universe. Each series is rated as in an uptrend or downtrend, depending on its position relative to its moving average. The value of the diffusion indicator is the percentage of time series that are in an upward trend. The indicator is confined to the range 0 to 100.
9. This analysis does not make clear how many rule variations were explored to attain this level of discrimination. As will be pointed out in Chapter 6, it is impossible to evaluate the significance of these findings without information on the amount of searching that led to the discovery of a rule.
10. Many of the rules tested in this book use data series other than the S&P 500 to generate signals on the S&P 500.
11. This law of statistics is discussed in detail in Chapter 4.
12. $(0.9) \times 0.035\% - (0.1) \times 0.035\% = 0.028\%$ per day or 7.31% annualized.
13. $(0.60) \times 0.035\% - (0.40) \times 0.035\% = 0.007\%$ per day or 1.78% annualized.
14. The look-ahead bias is discussed by Robert A. Haugen, *The Inefficient Stock Market: What Pays Off and Why* (Upper Saddle River, NJ: Prentice-Hall, 1999), 66.
15. The percentage of fund portfolios invested in interest-bearing cash instruments such as T-bills, commercial paper, and so forth.

CHAPTER 25

Being Right or Making Money

From Ned Davis, *Being Right or Making Money*, 3rd edition (Hoboken, New Jersey: John Wiley & Sons, 2014), Chapter 1.

Bad News about Forecasting (Being Right)

There are a number of factors—including a potential cyclical bear market, demographics, and the U.S. energy renaissance—that could be game changers, and might help forecast the future. I hope you will find my perspectives useful, even though after studying forecasting for over 40 years I realize I do not always know what the market is going to do.

You may have heard of the Texan who had all the money in the world but who had an inferiority complex because he felt he wasn't very bright. When he heard about a brilliant doctor who was offering brain transplants, he immediately consulted him to find out if it were true and how much it would cost. The doctor told him it was indeed true that he could boost intelligence quotient (IQ) levels. The doctor had three types of brains in inventory: lawyer brains for $5 an ounce, doctor brains at $10 an ounce, and stock-market guru brains for $250 per ounce. The Texan asked, "Why in the world are the stock-market guru brains so much more expensive or valuable than those of doctors or lawyers?" And the doctor replied, "Do you have any idea how many gurus it takes to get an ounce of brain?"

People laugh at that joke because unfortunately there is a lot of truth to it. I don't know in what direction the markets will go, and neither does Janet Yellen or Barack Obama. Even George Soros, whose modest $1 billion take-home pay of a few years ago qualifies him as a bona fide market guru, says in his book *The Alchemy of Finance*,[1] "My financial success stands in stark contrast with my ability to forecast events . . . all my forecasts are extremely tentative and subject to constant revision in the light of market developments."

While 95 percent of the people on Wall Street are in the business of making predictions, the super successful Peter Lynch, in his book *Beating the Street*,[2] says, "Nobody can predict interest rates, the future direction of the economy, or the stock market. Dismiss all such forecasts. . . ." And as Mark Twain once observed, "The art of prophecy is difficult, especially with respect to the future."

I think it was Alan Shaw, one of the more successful practitioners of technical analysis, who said, "The stock market is man's invention that has humbled him the most." Fellow legendary technician Bob Farrell warned, "When all the experts and forecasts agree—something else is going to happen."[3]

Economist John Kenneth Galbraith put it this way, "We have two classes of forecasters: those who don't know and those who don't know they don't know."

Financial theorist William Bernstein described it similarly, but with an even darker message: "There are two types of investors, be they large or small: those who don't know where the market is headed, and those who don't know that they don't know. Then again, there is a third type of investor—the investment professional, who indeed knows that he or she doesn't know, but whose livelihood depends upon appearing to know."[4]

Despite my realization that forecasting is difficult, I haven't become a spoilsport and turned away from predicting the market's course entirely, because I've had my share of really good forecasts. Perhaps recounting how I came to distrust "being right" and instead embraced techniques that allowed me to make money consistently will be helpful.

Like nearly all novice investors and analysts, back in 1968 I was convinced that all I had to do was discover the way the investment world worked, develop the best indicators available to forecast changes in the markets, have the conviction to shoot straight, and gather my profits. And my record of forecasting stock prices from 1968 to 1978 was so good that during a *Wall $treet Week* broadcast in 1978 Louis Rukeyser said, "Ned Davis has had an outstanding record in recent years . . . and has been absolutely right about most of the major ups and downs. . . ."

The only problem was that at the end of each year, I would total up my capital gains and unfortunately I would not owe Uncle Sam much money. Before someone else could question me, I asked myself, "If you are so smart, why aren't you rich?" It was about that time (1978–1980) that I began to realize that smarts, hard work, and even a burning desire to be right were really not my problems, or the solution to my problems. My real problems were a failure to cut losses short, a lack of discipline and risk management, letting my ego color my market view (which made it difficult to admit mistakes), and difficulty controlling fear and greed. *It was thus a lack of proper investment strategy and good money management techniques, not poor forecasting, that was holding me back.*

I dealt with those problems, and by 1985 *Barron's* magazine was interviewing me and saying on its cover: "No Bum Steers from This Raging Bull: Ned Davis Has Been Dead Right on the Market."

Over the years I have seen scores of very bright investment advisors turn into hugely successful gurus who blaze into the investment business with spectacular forecasts. Yet, I've watched each and every one of them crash back to earth when a big subsequent forecast inevitably proved wrong. The Bible says, "Live by the sword, die by the sword." As my late friend Marty Zweig and I watched these forecasting gurus fail, we often said to each other, "Live by the forecast, die by the forecast."

Before examining indicators, I'd like to discuss the record of some professional forecasters. Perhaps the biggest myth in financial markets is that experts have expertise or that forecasters can forecast. The reality is that flipping a coin would produce a better record. Therefore, relying on consensus economic forecasts to provide guidance for investment strategy is almost certain to fail over the long run.

What is my evidence? Consider forecasts from the Survey of Professional Forecasters released by the Federal Reserve Bank of Philadelphia and shown in Figure 25.1 (solid line). The dashed line shows real GDP. The chart shows seven recessions (shaded zones) since 1970. As a group, professional economic forecasters did not correctly call a single one of these recessions. In fact, they have never predicted a recession, period. Since the first edition of *Being Right or Making Money* was published in 2000, on average economists have been 59 percent too high in their 12-month forecasts (predicted growth: 3.1 percent; actual growth: 1.9 percent).

Well, what about the experts at the Federal Reserve? They are supposed to be independent. They have a lot of money to spend on research, a full professional staff, and they have expanded their projections from a year or so to five years ahead. Two years ago the initial projection for 2013 was 4.15 percent real growth. In Figure 25.2 we plot the wide range of projections by the Fed (not the central tendency or specific point forecast) and then see how real GDP performed since 2000. And as shown, the Fed was actually correct (actual GDP fell within the Fed's wide range) just 26.3 percent of the time!

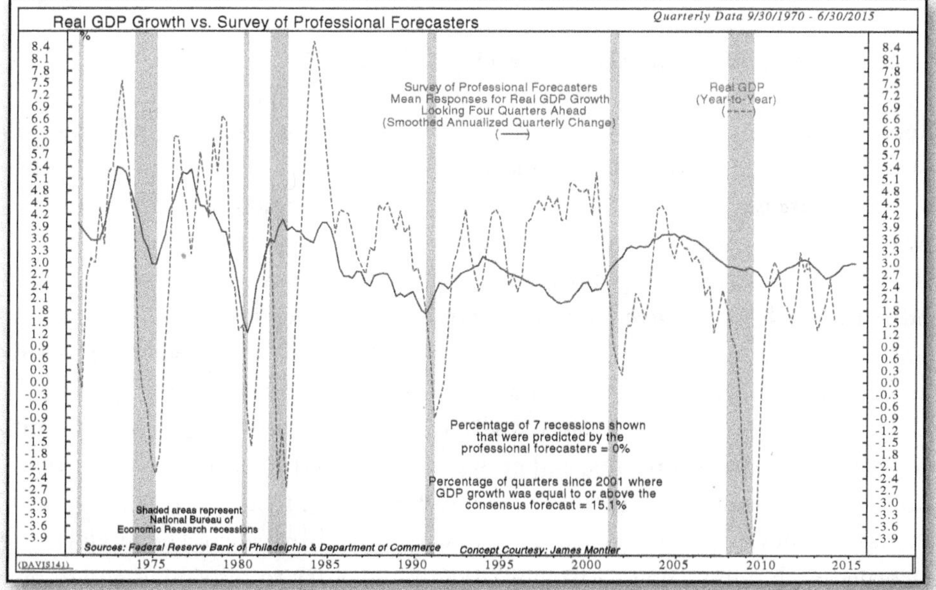

FIGURE 25.1 Real GDP Growth versus Survey of Professional Forecasters.

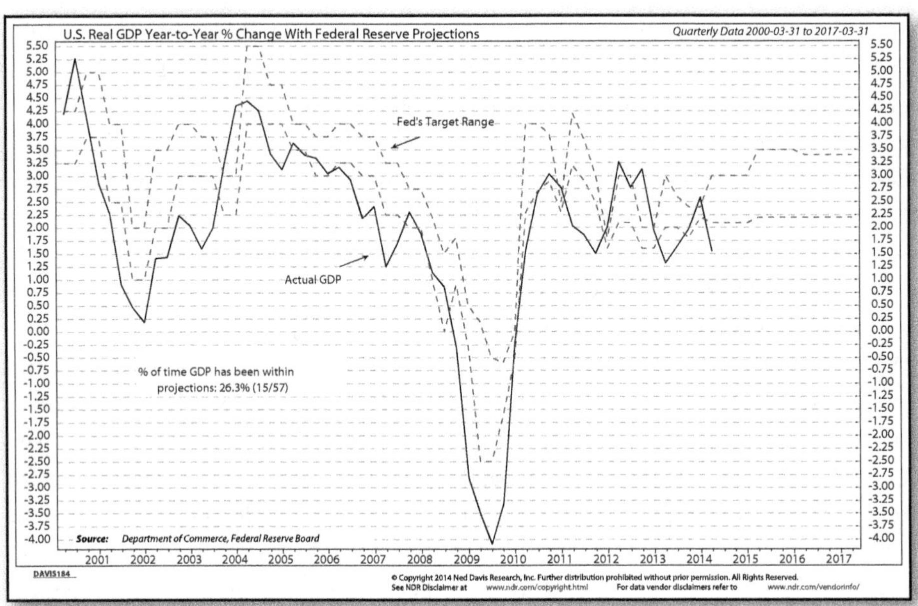

FIGURE 25.2 Real Year-to-Year Percentage Change in U.S. GDP versus Federal Reserve Projections.

The last word I'll offer on predictions is from the Fed's leader during much of the period covered by the chart. In October 2013 Alan Greenspan said, "We really can't forecast all that well. We pretend we can, but we can't."

Forecasting the economy and the investment markets consistently and reliably is very difficult. In fact, consensus predictions often contain the seeds of their own destruction by altering human actions. Most crowds are usually wrong at sentiment extremes as I will discuss later in this chapter.

Good News about Making Money

After studying winners in the investment world over many years, I found some good news. While *nobody was right* year in and year out, a number of advisors and investors did in fact *make money* year in and year out. I decided I would follow their advice on how to make money consistently.

In 1980 I acquired a computer and a good program, and started building timing models that I felt would give me the objectivity, discipline, flexibility, and risk management that I needed to make consistent profits. And since 1980 the Ned Davis Research Group has been dedicated to building timing models that do not forecast, but are simply designed to make money. These models have made a real and substantial change in my investment profits, and both Uncle Sam and I are now much better off. As far as my forecasting of the market goes: if anything, it suffered. Timing models that make money invariably are less cocky than a crystal-ball guru. The models are so concerned with minimizing disastrous risks that they try to hit singles and doubles rather than home runs. And they definitely limit the number of strikeouts.

Again, my financial well-being improved significantly, and the humility and discipline that the timing models forced upon me relieved me of a lot of stressful anxiety. I shifted my focus from gaining glory and prestige to designing a business focused on making money while managing risk.

Timing models have permitted me to make money on a more consistent basis. Throughout my career I have followed a number of renowned market winners, and though their methods do not all include timing models, these winners share certain investment-strategy characteristics that we have tried to incorporate into our models.

I found winners such as Marty Zweig, Dan Sullivan of *The Chartist*,[5] and Value Line,[6] who have consistently made money since 1980 (according to Mark Hulbert, who rates advisors). I found investment legends who consistently win, including John Templeton, Warren Buffett, Peter Lynch, George Soros, Stan Druckenmiller, Paul Tudor Jones, Bill Gross, and Jim Stack. What commonalities do these winners share?

Being Right and Other Investment Techniques Are Overrated and Are Not the Keys to Success

It's not the markets they trade or even the techniques they use. These are people who rely on different philosophies, ranging from Ben Graham's long-term valuation techniques to in-and-out technical commodity trading . . . from dollar-cost averaging to market timing . . . from buying high-yielding stocks to buying relatively strong stocks with almost no yield. Clearly, a variety of techniques can make money. I find it exciting that numerous techniques can make money, as investors can choose the technique that best fits their own psyches.

The winning methods of successful professional investors are even sometimes contradictory. For example, in the book *Market Wizards*[7] the successful pro Jim Rogers is quoted as saying that he often examines charts for signs of "hysteria," and also that "I haven't met a rich technician." In the same book an equally successful pro, Marty Schwartz, is quoted as saying, "I always laugh at people who say, 'I've never met a rich technician.' I love that! It is such an arrogant, nonsensical response. I used fundamentals for nine years and then got rich as a technician." If you think that is confusing, in the book *What I Learned Losing a Million Dollars*[8] the legendary John Templeton is quoted as saying, "Diversify your investments." In the same book, the equally legendary Warren Buffett says, "Concentrate your investments. If you have a harem of forty women, you never get to know any of them very well."

So as I studied other long-term winners on Wall Street, I found that instinctively or otherwise, they had come to the same conclusions that I had. While the methods of Warren Buffett, Peter Lynch, and John Templeton are very different from my risk-management, asset-allocation, market-timing orientation, all of these men have been exceedingly humble, made multiple mistakes, and rarely (if ever) get headlines about a spectacular call. Yet they all use objective methods for picking stocks, their investment philosophy is disciplined and designed to limit risks, and they are flexible when they must be.

This book is not designed to challenge those of you who are long-term fundamentalists or short-term technicians. Instead, we offer some tools that hopefully will help you to be more right more often. But much more importantly, this book will show you that being right is not really where it's at, since at least as much of your focus should be on risk management, a disciplined strategy, and flexibility.

The Four Real Keys to Making Money

As I continued studying legendary investors, I discovered that all of these winners shared four key characteristics, some of which I had already learned by the time I completed kindergarten.

1. **Objective indicators:** These legendary investors all used ***objectively determined indicators*** rather than gut emotion. We have a little riddle about this. In a room there were three people: a high-priced lawyer, a low-priced lawyer, and the tooth fairy. In the middle of the room was a $100 bill. Suddenly the lights went out, and when they came back on the $100 bill was gone. Who took it? The answer, of course, is the high-priced lawyer—because the other two are figments of the imagination. We want to make sure that what our indicators say is factual and not a figment of our imaginations. As our teachers tried to help us understand in kindergarten, it is critical to learn what is real and what is imaginary.

What is an objective indicator? It must be mathematical, with long historical analysis to demonstrate its effectiveness. One example might be the rate of inflation. Perhaps it is because the Fed is supposed to control inflation, or perhaps it is because bond yields have an inflation premium, but inflation is one of the best macroeconomic indicators to use to call the stock market.

But in all of the noisy data, how much does inflation need to rise or fall on a monthly basis to be important? The chart in Figure 25.3 looks at the year-to-year rate of inflation relative to a five-year moving average. In the 41.3 percent of the time since 1952 that the year-to-year inflation rate was at least 0.5 of a percentage point below the five-year average, the S&P 500 shot up at a 13.5 percent annual rate—almost double the 62-year buy-and-hold average of 7.2 percent. And when inflation was more than one percentage point above the five-year average, one actually lost money in stocks.

2. **Discipline:** All the winners are very ***disciplined***, remaining faithful to their systems through good and bad times. I sometimes compare investing to classical Greek tragedies, in which the hero is inevitably ruined by some character flaw. My own biggest flaw in investing, as noted earlier, is letting my ego get involved in my market view. This makes it very difficult to admit mistakes. Thus, to shift from concentrating on being right to making money, I had to learn discipline. That is how I came up with the idea of using computer-derived mathematical models for stock-market timing that would *force* discipline upon me. That discipline may not have made me more right over the past 40 years, but it did control my mistakes and allowed me to be a much more successful investor. In June 1998 Dan Sullivan said in his *The Chartist* newsletter, "Successful investors

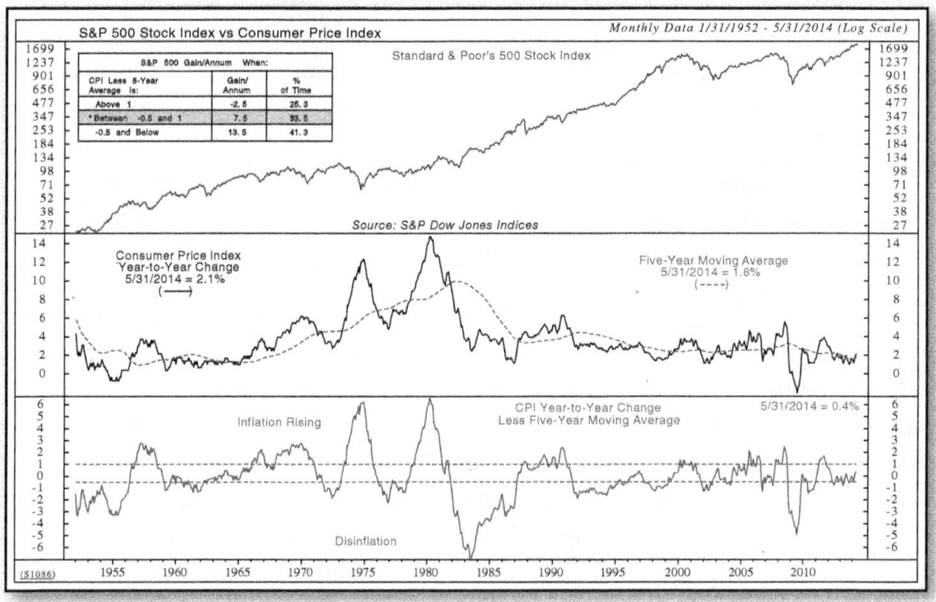

FIGURE 25.3 S&P 500 Index versus Consumer Price Index.

have several things in common. First, they have patience. Second, successful investors are like great athletes, they adhere to a strict discipline." As my teacher taught me in kindergarten, there will be chaos if you don't have discipline.

3. **Flexibility:** While disciplined, these winners were ***flexible*** enough to change their minds when the evidence shifted, even if they did not understand why. In his book *Winning on Wall Street*,[9] Marty Zweig talks about how bearish he was during a sell-off in February and March 1980: "I was sitting there looking at conditions and being as bearish as I could be—but the market had reversed. Things began to change as the Fed reduced interest rates and eased credit controls. Even though I had preconceived ideas that we were heading toward some type of 1929 calamity, I *responded* to changing conditions." In conclusion he states, "The problem with most people who play the market is that they are not flexible . . . to succeed in the market you must have discipline, flexibility, and patience."

Barton Biggs once called Stan Druckenmiller "the investment equivalent of Michael Jordan. . . . He is the best consistent macro player." Biggs said, "He is a combination of being very intellectual and analytical, but also using technical analysis." In *Market Wizards*, author Jack Schwager writes of Druckenmiller:

> Another important lesson . . . is that if you make a mistake, respond immediately! Druckenmiller made the incredible error of shifting from short to 130 percent long on the very day before the massive October 19, 1987, stock crash, yet he finished the month with a net gain. How? When he realized he was dead wrong, he liquidated his entire long position during the first hour of trading on October 19 and actually went short. . . . The *flexibility* [emphasis added] of Druckenmiller's style . . . is obviously a key element of his success.

So as I learned in kindergarten: expect surprises. Things change.

4. **Risk Management:** Finally, all of these successful investors were ***risk managers***. I asked Paul Tudor Jones once what he does at work all day, and he answered, "The first thing I do is try to figure out what is going to go wrong, and then I spend the rest of the day trying to cover my butt." In *Market Wizards*, Paul says, "I am always thinking about losing money as opposed to making money." And he is widely known as a risk taker!

Nearly all of the pros I have studied are clear about one thing: *they want to control their losses*. In *Market Wizards*, fundamentalist Jim Rogers says, "Whenever I buy or sell something, I always try to make sure I'm not going to lose any money first . . . my basic advice is don't lose money." In the same book, technician Marty Schwartz says, "Learn to take the losses. The most important thing in making money is not letting your losses get out of hand." In his book, *Pit Bull*,[10] Schwartz says, "Honor thy stop . . . exiting a losing trade clears your head and restores your objectivity." Controlling losses is one lesson I wished I had learned in kindergarten. They did tell me to be careful, but it wasn't until much later that it sunk in. I learned this from Warren Buffett, who once stated his two favorite rules for successful investing: Rule #1: Never lose money. Rule #2: Never forget Rule #1. In *What I Learned Losing a Million Dollars*, the legendary Bernard Baruch is quoted as saying, "Don't expect to be right all the time. If you have a mistake, cut your loss as quickly as possible."

In *Reminiscences of a Stock Operator*,[11] the hero (widely believed to be the legendary trader Jesse Livermore) says, "A loss never bothers me after I take it. I forget it overnight. But being wrong—not taking the loss—that is what does the damage to the pocketbook and to the soul." Echoing that sentiment, Druckenmiller in *The New Market Wizards*[12] says of George Soros, "Soros is also the best loss taker I've ever seen. He doesn't care whether he wins or loses on a trade. If a trade doesn't work, he's confident enough about his ability to win on other trades that he can easily walk away from the position." Finally, the last word on the subject of taking losses (and making money) goes to Leo Melamed, chairman emeritus of the Chicago Mercantile Exchange. In the book *The Inner Game of Trading*,[13] in response to the question, "What do you think are the primary psychological barriers that prevent most traders from being successful?" Leo answered: "One of them is the ability to take a loss. You've got to know that no risk taker is going to be right all the time. As a matter of fact, I figured out when I was trading that I could be wrong 60 percent of the time and come out a big winner. The key is money management. You must take your losses quickly and keep them small and let your profits run and make them worthwhile. . . ."

In the December 12, 2013, edition of *The Chartist Mutual Fund Letter* was a list of seven insights from John Bogle, founder of the Vanguard Mutual Fund Group, that I found helpful in making money. He says:

1. Balancing of return and risk is the task of intelligent investing.
2. Predicting stock-market returns has a very high margin of error.
3. Impulse is your enemy.

4. There is no escaping risk; a well-diversified portfolio should provide remarkable growth over the long term.
5. Investing is simple, but it is not easy. It requires discipline, patience, steadfastness, and common sense.
6. Be patient and ignore the crowd. If you can't resist temptation, you absolutely must not manage your own money.
7. The secret to investing is there is no secret.

So, in conclusion, what I've learned after all these years is that *we are in the business of making mistakes*. I've never heard Peter Lynch give an interview where he didn't point out some mistake he has made. And he has said, "If you are right half of the time (in the markets), you have a terrific score. It is not an easy business." So if we all make mistakes, what separates the winners from the losers? The answer is simple—*the winners make small mistakes*, while the losers make big mistakes.

The Battle for Investment Survival and Handling Mistakes

When I first became professionally involved in the stock market, a book by Gerald M. Loeb, who was called "the dean of Wall Street," made a big impression on me. The book is *The Battle for Investment Survival*.[14] I have battled in the marketplace daily for over 40 years and in my opinion Loeb was right—*investment survival* is everything. In 1994, the hugely successful George Soros said in his book *The Alchemy of Finance*, "If I had to sum up my practical skills, I would use one word: survival." He writes about how his father, who lived through the Russian Revolution as an escaped prisoner of war, taught his son "the art of survival." I don't think you need to be a prisoner of war to be successful on Wall Street, but I do think you often need to react as a survivor would.

In a recent *Business Week Investor* interview, successful money manager Michael Orkin said, "Have caution and respect for the market. The first job is survival."

I feel I have been a fairly high achiever in my life, and yet as I reflect on my successes, I also see failure after mistake after failure. Being a survivor means you must be able to handle these mistakes. I usually pick myself up and say: you have done the best you can; that's all you can ask of yourself—period, end of discussion. I also tell myself that failure is just the opportunity to start over with a lot of important new information. Another lesson I have learned during the ups and downs of my career is that when someone criticizes me, I let it go to my head because there may be something constructive I can learn from it. But I never ever let criticism go to my heart, where it can hurt me. Likewise, when people compliment me, I let it go to my heart, but I try not to let praise go to my head. Being caught up in the manic-depressive crowd psychology world of the stock market, it is important to have a balanced view of both successes and mistakes.

Here is a recent example of my personal struggle with making mistakes. On March 12, 2013, I authored a commentary *Hotline* entitled "Stubborn on Gold." I said:

> This is a commentary *Hotline*, as it is not my usual objective, disciplined analysis. As you know, I like to have both the Fed and the tape together

to make a strong bet. I also look at sentiment and macro factors, like inflation.

In the case of gold, I've largely lost the tape. Gold is in a major consolidation. It has not broken support around 1530, but it sure rallies poorly. I think it would need to break its downtrend line to get a more hopeful tape message. Moreover, while I think of gold as a currency hedge, history also argues it has served as an inflation hedge, and inflation has been very, very quiet. It may not stay quiet, but for now it is not at all a trigger for gold.

So I am left with just the friendly Fed and some sentiment factors. Nevertheless, I am a little stubborn on gold, and I am convinced that it is going quite a bit higher in the long run . . . [due to Fed monetary-base growth] . . . my opinion is that a gold insurance position, relative to *global* money-printing, is still a prudent investment.

I bring up this mistake in hopes that eating some humble pie will prove a useful lesson. Even after 40 years in this business and preaching about being open-minded and disciplined, it is still very easy and very human, to fall into a stubborn desire to be right. Ouch!

In listing the personal qualities it takes to succeed in his book, *One Up on Wall Street*,[15] Peter Lynch does not mention being smart or being right, but rather he lists things like patience, persistence, humility, flexibility, and a *willingness to admit to mistakes*.

Paul Tudor Jones puts a positive spin on mistakes in *Market Wizards*, saying, "One learns the most from mistakes, not successes." He talks about a very intense gut-wrenching loss on a disastrous cotton trade he made early in his career, saying that his experience altered his whole trading style in terms of risk. He first called himself Mr. Stupid and said, "I am not cut out for this business; I don't think I can hack it much longer." But "that was when I first decided I had to learn discipline and money management. It was a cathartic experience for me, in the sense that I went to the edge, questioned my very ability as a trader, and decided that I was not going to quit. I was determined to come back and fight. I decided that I was going to become very disciplined and businesslike about my trading."

I have heard Paul tell another story that contains a critical message. He says that one time when he was trapped in a losing trade, he went to a pro for advice as to whether he should honor his stops. The pro said, "The markets are going to be here 20 and 30 years from now; the real question is, will you be?"

Stories of Five Successful Winners

I thought about calling this section of the book "Being Wrong and Making Money." My experience tells me investors will be right enough that the profits will take care of themselves (being right and making money), but the key is how you handle your losses and your mistakes. So I thought telling stories about five successful winners in the investment world might help illustrate the point. I talked about three of them in the previous edition of this book, when all were near the top of their fields. Also, all five are and were successful money managers who approach the market as I do, as a market timer or tactical asset allocator. All have been hugely successful on Wall Street. They are Marty Zweig, Paul Tudor Jones, Dan Sullivan, Chris Cadbury, and James Stack.

Before and during the 1987 crash, Marty Zweig was widely labeled as a prominent gloom-and-doomer due to his vocal warnings that there might be a 1929-style crash, followed by an economic depression. His forecasts were ubiquitous on television and in major media newsmagazines. I had talked to Marty several times during the crash, and if anything, he was more bearish than he was being portrayed.

Thus, I was surprised when a few days after the crash he told me he was going to turn all out bullish. I asked him why, given his concerns about a depression. He said, "I have spent the last 20 years of my life building indicators and most of them are flashing buys—what is the use of building them if you aren't going to follow them?" Thus, his keen mind was so *flexible* that he was able to forget his *deep-seated worries* and follow his indicator rules, correctly turning bullish very quickly. This kind of flexibility, an ability to let his prior stance be and thus shift with the indicators, made Marty one of the top investment advisors from July 1980 until he quit publishing his investment newsletter in December 1997. He never had a down year. When I asked Marty why he changed a position, he simply said, "I'm just trying to stay out of trouble." He turned his nervous, worrying nature into a profitable risk-management virtue. To sum up, Marty was hardly ever 100 percent in or out of the stock market, rarely forecasted where stocks were going, rarely achieved the number one advisory spot in a single year, only took small risks, and paid a lot of commissions since he often shifted his stance. Yet over the long run, he ended up well ahead of other advisors and many hedge funds.

As for Paul Tudor Jones, $1,000 invested in his Tudor Futures Fund on September 18, 1984, would have been worth $669,670 on December 31, 2013, a gain of 668.67 percent in just over 29 years, or a whopping 24.8 percent per annum, perhaps one of the greatest money-management success stories ever achieved. The Tudor Futures Fund has *never* had a losing calendar year since its launch in September 1984. This record led *Barron's* to feature Paul in its year-end list of experts for many years. In a *Barron's* Roundtable discussion at the start of 1989, Paul was quoted as being very bearish on both the U.S. stock market ("The fact is I think the stock market is a low-risk short.") and the Japanese market ("I couldn't sleep at night if I were long the Japanese market.") However, he was very wrong on both counts (although a year later, his call on Japan proved prophetic). But this super speculator was so good at money management, flexibility, and cutting losses short, and so adept at being objective and disciplined, that he ended 1989 making 42 percent for his investors and returning some $200 million to his partners.

Lest you think that was a fluke, Paul spoke at a Ned Davis Research (NDR) investment conference in early 1991. His number one trade for the year was to short the Dow and buy gold. Again, he was wrong. Paul recently told me *the* reason for *all* the Wall Street success stories he knew was clear—"money management, money management, money management." I am certain that Paul has been right many times and has made much money when he was right, but these stories show that the top pros can be wrong and still make money!

The Chartist has been highly ranked by the *Hulbert Financial Digest*[16] for returns for over 21 years. In a letter, Dan Sullivan, *The Chartist*'s editor, once said:

> For the year-to-date, the Actual Cash Account, which buys and sells in sync with our consensus Model, has lost $22,525, –3.71 percent. The Aggressive Account has lost $12,849, –6 percent. . . . To be absolutely candid, the losses we have sustained, given the high standards we have always set for ourselves, border on disastrous. . . . While no one enjoys taking losses, there are times when to do so is absolutely essential. One of the main planks in our stock-market methodology is the preservation of capital. This involves taking losses quickly, before they become unmanageable.

The September 12, 2013, issue of *The Chartist* newsletter listed four negative behaviors and attitudes that can lead to poor investment returns:

1. Failing to take losses.
2. Being overly fearful at market bottoms and overly optimistic at market tops.
3. Failing to take responsibility for your own money.
4. Not following a disciplined strategy.

And it has worked. *The Chartist Mutual Fund Letter* (February 13, 2014) says:

> The Actual Cash Account now stands at $1,327,947, still another record high on a monthly basis. Per our usual policy, a month-by-month performance of the Actual Cash Account since its inception is available to any subscriber. The Actual Cash Account has outperformed the benchmark S&P 500 with dividends factored in since we started it with an original $100,000 back in August of 1988. What we are most proud of is the fact that the profitable results have been accomplished with considerably less risk than buy and hold because this real money account has the ability to move to the sidelines during adverse periods. We are using basically the same methodology that we deployed when we started this newsletter some 25 years ago. It has stood the test of time.

Since our philosophy is somewhat like Sullivan's, I'd like to quote a few of the things he has written. On January 17, 1991, after having just sold a group of stocks at a loss and before correctly turning bullish again to catch the 1991 bull market, Sullivan observed:

> Here's what you get with *The Chartist*. We are not going to be right all of the time, but be assured that we back our recommendations with our

own money. We're not going to ask our subscribers to take any risks that we are not willing to take ourselves. When we are wrong, we are going to admit it flat out. You're not going to see us loaded up with a portfolio of losing stocks for an extended period of time, hoping that the market is going to bail us out.

As stated previously, our philosophy is to cut losses quickly. At the outset of a buying campaign, we think 'short-term'. If the stocks we select are not living up to their expectations, we act quickly to cut losses. However, once we find ourselves on the profit side of the ledger, you will not find us all that anxious to sell. In essence, we are quite willing to risk paper profits. Most investors are too slow to cut losses and too quick to take profits, which is the exact opposite of our approach to the market.

The market is going to be there tomorrow and it will present us with many opportunities in the future. It is not the slightest blow to our ego or self-esteem to tell you that our timing was off the mark. We were wrong. But, that is how we do it here at *The Chartist*.

Winners like Dan Sullivan are very flexible and very disciplined, and they're risk managers. While I am not trying to knock the importance of study, hard work, and being right in terms of investment success, the key is how to make money. If you choose not to follow my exact rules, or even if you decide to throw out market timing altogether, I still believe that objectivity, flexibility, discipline, and risk management are the keys to making money, and this book can help your understanding of the importance of those factors.

I am including two advisors who did not appear in the last edition. Only one is still practicing. But I wanted to include both because their general approach is similar to mine. Again, I am not trying to push my investment strategy on anyone. It just so happens that I have the psyche of a hedge-fund trader, and so I sought out winners who used tools similar to those I use to make money consistently.

The differences between Chris Cadbury and Jim Stack are striking. Cadbury's approach was very short-term, and Stack's is more cyclical. Cadbury, who recently retired, was more focused on mean reversion, sentiment, and overbought/oversold indicators, while Stack is more technical-trend and macro-oriented. Personally, I try to fuse all of these factors. Yet, both have made money by cutting risks short and letting profits run.

Cadbury was ranked number one in the United States by *Timer Digest* at some point each year from 2002 to 2011, according to the one-year performance metrics used by that publication. He had more than 45 years of trading experience. In 2011 *Timer Digest* said:

> In terms of performance, as measured by *Timer Digest*, Chris Cadbury has distinguished himself across multiple time horizons and in response to various market environments.

He ranked No. 1 for both 5- and 10-year periods ending on December 31, 2010, as well as No. 2 for 3 years and No. 3 for 8 years. Over the 10-year horizon, the market has essentially gone nowhere. And within that time period, there have been several difficult bull and bear cycles to negotiate.

When the market gets oversold and excessive pessimism exists, Cadbury likes to go contrary to sentiment extremes with buy signals. But once he buys (for example, the S&P 500 futures), he generally sets a five-point stop-loss. I have seen him be wrong with several five-point losing trades in a row, but he will stay with his indicators. I've seen him go from three or four small losses to a 100-point gain. Cadbury is also quite flexible. He can lean bearish for an extended period (1987 and 2007–2008) and then flip and lean bullish (since 2009). This flexibility is rare for market-letter writers.

Jim Stack publishes a newsletter called *InvesTech Research* and conducts his research from Whitefish, Montana, far from the madding crowd on Wall Street. He uses objective indicators, historical research, and a disciplined safety-first approach to investing that has been successful for over 30 years.

Besides "objectivity," Stack lists "humility" and "integrity" as fundamental principles for survival in this business. Mark Hulbert rates Stack as a market timer, but Stack prefers to think of himself as more of a risk manager (as I prefer to think of myself). Stack says:

> The April [2013] issue of the *Hulbert Financial Digest* released its latest Stock Market Timers Honor Roll. As described by Mark Hulbert, making it onto their honor roll requires producing above-average performance in both up and down markets.
>
> In our view, managing risk through portfolio and sector allocation isn't the same as market timing, so we don't consider ourselves to be market timers. Yet we are honored to be included in the 4 percent of advisors who made this respected list. In the performance Scoreboard of the same issue, the InvesTech Research Portfolio Strategy was the only service to make it into the top five in risk-adjusted ranking over the past 5-, 10-, and 15-year time periods.[17]

While Cadbury and Marty Zweig both used stop-loss strategies effectively to move into cash and manage risks, Jim Stack does not use published stops and feels he manages risks simply by following his indicators in a disciplined, patient manner. He basically uses the trend as a stop-loss. I saw him turn mostly optimistic too soon, before the 2009 lows, but he maintained his position, thanks to numerous historical studies that showed an "upcoming buying opportunity of a lifetime."[18] Again, after seeing him squirm in the tumultuous year of 2012, I thought his description of risk management was insightful and useful:

> Managing risk will be increasingly important as this bull market matures. But risk management does not mean jumping into a high-cash position

every time fearful headlines appear or one becomes nervous because of a market correction. If that was the case, one would have moved to cash and been whipsawed at least four times since this bull market began.

Managing risk requires setting aside one's emotions and relying on discipline. That's easy to say, but very difficult to do without time-tested technical models and extensive historical knowledge. This bull market, like every predecessor, will someday draw to a close. And while there are no guarantees, we are confident that our tools and 33 years of analytical experience will help us recognize the warning flags when they start to appear.

Objective risk management can take different forms, but it works.

Making Our Own Reality

I've often wondered why the crowd and popular forecasts are so often wrong. My favorite theory is that crowd psychology and liquidity (potential demand) are inversely related. For another explanation, in the foreword to Charles Mackay's book *Extraordinary Popular Delusions and the Madness of Crowds*,[19] the legendary Bernard Baruch says that "all economic movements by their very nature, are motivated by crowd psychology. . . . Without due recognition of crowd thinking (which often seems crowd-madness) our theories of economics leave much to be desired." But listen to how he views crowd thinking, "Schiller's dictum: Anyone, taken as an individual, is tolerably sensible and reasonable—as a member of a crowd, he at once becomes a blockhead."

Baruch, who wrote this foreword in October of 1932, prescribes a "potent incantation" to use against crowd thinking:

> I have always thought that if, in the lamentable era of the "New Economics," culminating in 1929, even in the very presence of dizzily spiraling prices, we had all continuously repeated, "two and two still make four," much of the evil might have been averted. Similarly, even in the general moment of gloom in which this foreword is written, when many begin to wonder if declines will never halt, the appropriate abracadabra may be: They always did.

Some other quotes I like regarding crowds, reality, and human nature are these:

Jonathan Swift: "Truths languish, while myths flourish."

Bennett Goodspeed: "Man is extremely uncomfortable with uncertainty. To deal with his discomfort, man tends to create a false sense of security by substituting certainty for uncertainty. It becomes the herd instinct."

Edwin Lefèvre, *Reminiscences of a Stock Operator*: "The speculator's chief enemies are always boring from within. It is inseparable from human nature to hope and to fear."

Or as Shakespeare put it in *Julius Caesar*: "The fault, dear Brutus, is not in our stars / But in ourselves, that we are underlings." Or as Pogo said, "We have met the enemy and they are us."

Additionally, I have become fascinated with the concept that we all *create our own realities*.

An important truth is that people will view reality according to how they *want* to perceive it or believe it *should be*. I found a powerful illustration of this principle in a human-relations class I was taking, in which we read a quote from a long-serving warden of New York's infamous Sing Sing prison. According to the warden, "Few of the criminals in Sing Sing regard themselves as bad men. They are just as human as you and I. So they rationalize, they explain. . . . Most of them attempt by a form of reasoning, fallacious or logical, to justify their anti-social acts even to themselves . . . the desperate men and women behind prison walls *don't blame themselves for anything*." *Rationalization is a powerful coping mechanism.*

People who seemingly *have to* gamble provide another good example of the human tendency to create our own realities. Despite the fact that casinos make hundreds of millions of dollars every year, I've almost never met a gambler who claimed to have been a loser. Gamblers will look you straight in the eye when they tell you that. It is my belief that the pain of losing is so great, they actually forget the losses. *Denial is a powerful defense mechanism.*

Yet another illustration: in listening to the sexual harassment testimony given during the Clarence Thomas confirmation hearing, I found that it was impossible for me to discern who was telling the truth and who was lying, but clearly, I believed, he or his accuser had to be lying. That is, until I heard a wise psychiatrist say that she thought that both of them were telling the truth. At least it was the *truth as far as each of them saw it. Illusion or delusion is a powerful psychological force.*

Some time ago I read a fascinating magazine interview with actor Ralph Fiennes, who played the evil Nazi Amon Goeth in the film *Schindler's List*. He said, *It's not a rational thing, but it's an instinctive thing*. . . . If you're playing a role, you are immersing yourself in thinking about that character—how he moves, how he thinks. In the end he *becomes an extension of your own self. You like him.* It just throws up all kinds of question marks about acting, about human behavior, about how evil is probably a lot closer to the surface than we like to think."

When asked whether there was an emotional residue from the experience of playing a character he views as obscene and sick, after a long pause Fiennes answered softly, "I think there was a price to pay for this one. When you're investigating behavior that is so negative, so intensely for three months, then you feel sort of peculiar because you might have at moments enjoyed it and at the same time you feel slightly soiled by it. . . . "[20]

A person's mind can sometimes get badly twisted under intense emotional pressure.

Then there's the O. J. Simpson case. Was he guilty? Two-thirds of whites said yes. Three-fifths of blacks said no. William Raspberry, the black Pulitzer Prize-winning journalist, asked: "How can that be? Are white people, less invested in Simpson's fate, being objective, while blacks are being emotional? Have we come to the point where color is of such importance as to override every other consideration, to render us, black and white, *incapable* of a *shared reality*?"[21]

The recent trial of George Zimmerman, a white man, for the death of Trayvon Martin, a black teenager, provides similar examples:

> *Washington Post*, July 22, 2013
>
> Among African Americans, 86 percent say they disapprove of the verdict—with almost all of them saying they strongly disapprove—and 87 percent saying the shooting was unjustified. In contrast, 51 percent of whites say they approve of the verdict while just 31 percent disapprove. There is also a partisan overlay to the reaction among whites: 70 percent of white Republicans but only 30 percent of white Democrats approve of the verdict.
>
> Gallup, April 5, 2012
>
> U.S. public opinion about the Trayvon Martin case in Florida reflects the same type of racial divide found in 1995 surveys asking about the murder trial of O. J. Simpson in Los Angeles. In one Gallup poll conducted Oct. 5–7, 1995, for example, 78 percent of blacks said the jury that found Simpson not guilty of murder made the right decision, while only 42 percent of whites agreed.
>
> Pew Research Center poll, July 22, 2013
>
> Younger Americans express far more dissatisfaction over the Zimmerman trial verdict than do older Americans. Among those under 30, 53 percent say they are dissatisfied with the verdict and just 29 percent are satisfied. The balance of opinion is the reverse among those ages 65 and older: 50 percent are satisfied and just 33 percent dissatisfied.

Finally, as an avid basketball fan, my favorite example of imagination distorting reality comes while watching games. And I'm willing to admit to being guilty of succumbing to this particular distortion myself. Almost always, the vast majority of home fans at a game will swear that the referees favored the opposing team (many even proclaiming that the other team has paid off the refs), even though their home team won the game, and even though objective statistics generated by academics based upon NBA games show that if there is a bias, the calls in an average game favor the home team. Crowd psychology is contagious and can influence even what we see with our own eyes. *One's perception equals one's reality.*

So the bottom line is that *people often create their own realities*, based upon things that may have happened to them as far back as the very early years of life. We are all subject to that condition. We are human. This means what feels right and easy and obvious in your gut is quite often wrong.

The reason I believe people make their own realities and see and hear what they want to see and hear is not that they are not looking for reality, but rather that they are hardwired to have a certain nature. Shown a half glass of water, many people simply will describe it as half full while others insist it is half empty. A lot of us just get up in the morning as natural-born optimists or pessimists. On the other hand, I would probably look at the glass and ask, are we sure that is indeed water? I am a natural-born skeptic. One needs to know one's nature, but to make money consistently in stocks, one must also be able to be an optimist or a pessimist when the objective indicator evidence so dictates.

The Ned Davis Research Response to All This

To avoid being swept up by the crowd, and to prevent our own reality from becoming badly distorted, we need an unbiased, objective standard that weighs the evidence and passes judgment devoid of emotionalism. In applying this concept to the financial markets, Ned Davis Research builds *objective, mathematical timing models*, which we believe are the best tools to overcome emotional rationalizations.

Ned Davis Research has two mandates—we are trying to make money and we are trying to stay out of big trouble. Thus, we tell our clients that the *art* of forecasting is something we do only for fun, but that making money is something about which we are serious, and we approach it in as *scientific* and *quantitative* a manner as is possible.

I like to think of *money management* today as similar to the beginning of the European Renaissance. While there were many invaluable contributions to the arts during that period from men such as Michelangelo and Rembrandt, much of what has shaped the world since then came from those who were bold enough to venture forward with scientific investigation, including da Vinci, Galileo, and Newton.

So while we are in an industry that often blends art and science, our preference is to have a strongly objective, scientific, and quantitative bias to our work.

Most technicians look at stock charts and see patterns that, unfortunately, exist only in the eyes of the beholder (just as many observers of art can find many different meanings in a painting). Most fundamentalists look at a company and profess to be able to envision earnings way into the future. We simply try to get into harmony with the impartial reality from the numbers (the weight of the evidence) available today.

Timing Models

I developed my basic approach to the stock market when studying high school economics. The teacher said that prices are determined by supply and demand. So when I got into the business, I tried to focus on areas of analysis that give one clues about the forces that drive those variables. The three areas I found were the tape, the Fed, and crowd psychology.

Since prices are the equilibrium points between supply and demand, it follows that if prices are rising broadly, demand must be stronger than supply, and vice versa. Since it controls interest rates and the amount of money available, the Fed should never be ignored when trying to ascertain supply and demand. Likewise, extremes in crowd sentiment can tell us if demand is largely satisfied or if nervous holders of stock have mostly sold out.

In an effort to make money, we build timing models that we will explain in this book. But first, let's discuss five key rules we use when we build our models, which include the three areas that give clues about supply and demand.

The primary rule that we use in our models is something I modestly call Davis' Law.

> Davis' Law
>
> The degree of unprofitable anxiety in an investor's life corresponds directly to the amount of time one spends dwelling on how an investment should be acting, rather than the way it actually is acting.

Rule No. 1. Don't fight the tape. We do not like to fight the harsh reality of the tape (market trend), and we try to get in harmony with the cold, bloodless verdict of the market. To enforce Davis' Law, our models are at least 50 percent price- or trend-sensitive, which we believe means we can never be fully invested during a vicious bear market or never miss the bulk of a roaring bull market.

As Marty Zweig said in *Winning on Wall Street*: "To me, the tape is the final arbiter of any investment decision. I have a cardinal rule: never fight the tape. . . . I'm a trend follower, not a trend fighter." We think our emphasis on trend- and price-sensitive indicators means that if we make a mistake, the trend will change and bail us out with a small mistake, and if we are right and it turns out to be a big move, we are almost guaranteed to get a good part of that large gain. In other words, dwell on the reality of market action rather than hopes, wishes, and imagination.

A key point on the tape/trend. In the 2010 edition of *Reminiscences of a Stock Operator*, there are some thoughts from Paul Tudor Jones. He talks about many of the disasters from the bubbles over the past decade or so, but he ends up with this conclusion: "The whole point of *Reminiscences* was that all of those very serious economic issues should be largely irrelevant to a great operator. Yes, they are interesting to debate, important to know, but always secondary to the tale the tape tells us on a continual basis."

Later in this book, we will feature many of the indicators in our timing models. But, in each section, I also wanted to illustrate what I am talking about through indicator examples that are not in the models. For example, Figure 25.4 looks at price trends in the Dow Jones Industrial Average (DJIA) and Dow Jones Transportation Average (DJTA). The results, shown in the box in the top clip, go back 114 years, to 1900. As can be seen, the market has advanced at double-digit rates of gain (dividends not included) in the 53 percent of the time demand was above supply, as measured by when both the DJIA and DJTA are above their respective 200-day average prices. One actually lost money on the DJIA when both were below their smoothed 200-day trend.

As I learned in kindergarten: don't pick fights with bullies (the tape).

Rule No. 2. Don't fight the Fed. We are not pure technicians. Why stand on one foot, when two feet give you better balance? So we also try not to fight city hall—the Federal Reserve Board. The Fed often writes the script for Wall Street.

In *Winning on Wall Street*, Marty Zweig said, "The major direction of the market is dominated by monetary considerations, primarily Federal Reserve policy and the

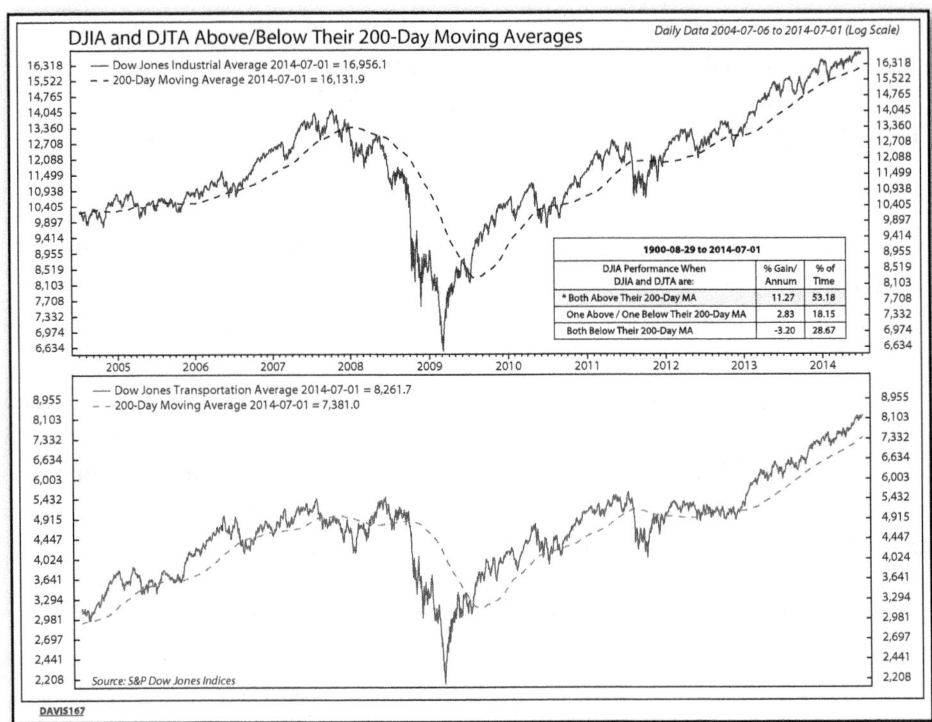

FIGURE 25.4 DJIA and DJTA Above/Below Their 200-Day Moving Averages.

movement of interest rates." Like Zweig and Ned Davis Research, Dan Sullivan of *The Chartist*, who along with Zweig has consistently outperformed in the Hulbert Advisory Service rankings since 1980, puts most of his emphasis on market trends, market momentum, and monetary conditions. Sullivan says, "The Monetary Model gauges the direction of interest rates. There is a direct correlation between the movement of interest rates and stock prices. Favorable monetary conditions (declining rates) provide the catalyst for bull markets. Conversely, rising rates hinder the upward movement of stock prices as fixed-rate investments become more attractive to investors."

One classic indicator of Fed easing or tightening is the yield curve, featured in Figure 25.5. By forcing the T-bill yields (which the Fed largely controls) above T-bond yields, the Fed can push up long-term interest rates that compete with stock dividend yields. And in the 58.5 percent of the time in which the central bank has pushed short-term rates well below long-term rates, the S&P 500 has shot ahead at double-digit rates, as you can see on the chart.

One example of the availability of money can be seen on Figure 25.6. All of the net gains in stocks since 1925 have come when the Fed was providing monetary-base growth above 0.5 of a percentage point on a real basis (above inflation). The Fed has a definite impact on supply and demand for stocks.

As we learned in kindergarten, try to be friends with the biggest kid in class—in this case, the Fed.

Rule No. 3. Be wary of the crowd at extremes. I believe that the stock market is a fairly efficient mechanism. If you are good at controlling your losses, the market presents

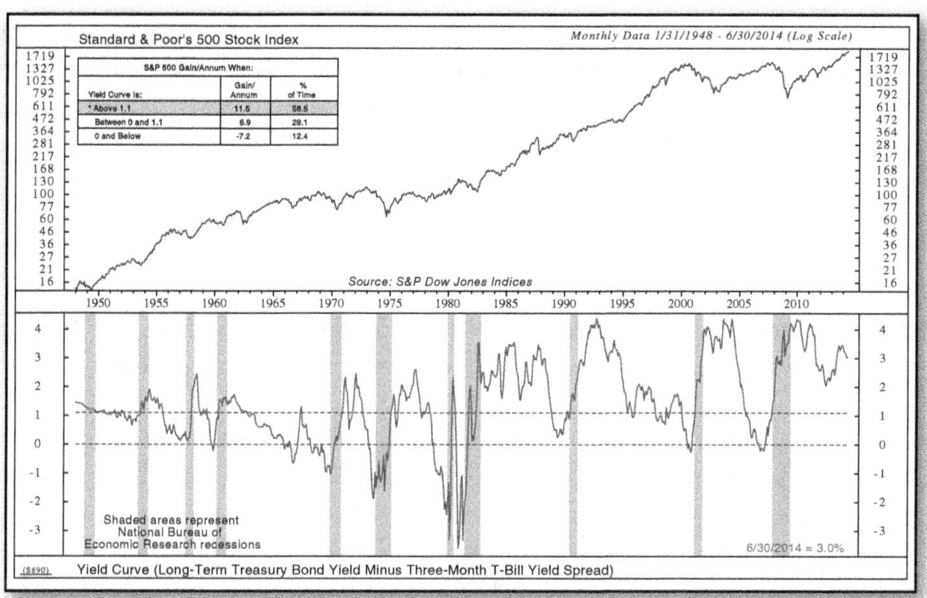

FIGURE 25.5 ***Top*, S&P 500 Index; *Bottom*, Yield Curve (Long-Term Treasury Bond Yield minus Three-Month T-Bill Yield Spread).**

you with the likelihood of about a 9 to 10 percent gain per year over the long run. To beat that return—to beat the efficient market—you are going up against not only some of the smartest people around, but also some of the most sophisticated technology.

Much of the time, the crowd is right. Yet almost by definition, the only way to beat the majority is by selectively taking a position against them. So we use numerous

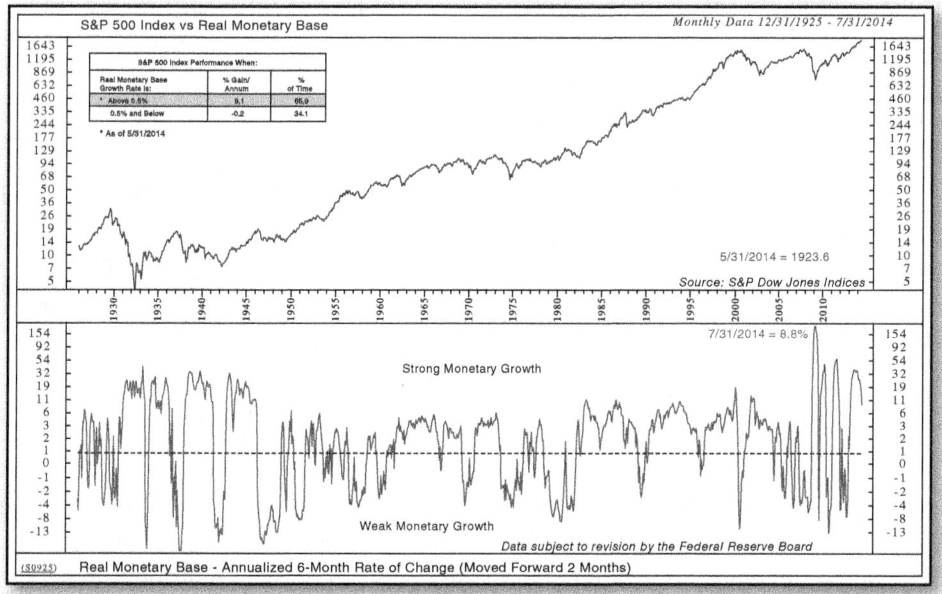

FIGURE 25.6 ***Top*, S&P 500 Index; *Bottom*, Real Monetary Base: Annualized Six-Month Rate of Change (Moved Forward Two Months).**

ways to measure majority crowd sentiment, to gauge market risk. For example, we monitor valuation and sentiment indicators, such as new-issue speculation, advisory-service sentiment, put/call ratios, the Dow earnings yield, and mutual fund cash/assets ratios to measure emotional moves in and out of the market. What distinguishes our philosophy from others is that our indicators are generally built to go *with* the majority flow until the indicators reach extreme readings and begin to *reverse*. It is at that point that it usually pays to be contrary.

In *Beating the Street* Peter Lynch said, "Over the past three decades, the stock market has come to be dominated by a herd of professional investors. Contrary to popular belief, this makes it easier for the amateur investor. You can beat the market by ignoring the herd."

Even Max Lucado, best-selling author, writer, and preacher, points out, "A man who wants to lead the orchestra must turn his back on the crowd."

In *Winning on Wall Street* Marty Zweig said, "Just because 51 percent of the crowd is bullish and 49 percent bearish is no reason the market cannot go higher. In fact, it probably will advance at that point. The time to be wary of crowd psychology is when the crowd gets extraordinarily one-sided. . . . The idea is: Beware of the crowd when the crowd is too one-sided."

Warren Buffett said one of his secrets to success is "we simply attempt to be fearful when others are greedy and to be greedy only when others are fearful." And this value investor explains the connection between sentiment and values:

> The most common cause of low prices is pessimism—sometimes pervasive, sometimes specific to a company or industry. We want to do business in such an environment, not because we like pessimism, but because we like the prices it produces.[22]

Technical analyst Joe Granville said, "If it is obvious, it is obviously wrong." I think what he meant is that what everybody knows is already priced into stocks (discounted), and it is, thus, not worth knowing.

The last word on sentiment goes to another very successful investor, Sir John Templeton, who ostensibly invested based upon fundamentals and values. He said, "Bull markets are born on pessimism, grow on skepticism, mature on optimism, and die on euphoria."

As I learned in kindergarten, if you want good reports or the teacher's praise, you need to be able to stand out from the crowd. It is not always good to follow the other kids, especially when they're really emotional.

What Is Contrary Opinion and How to Use It

If you want to try to be a genius and catch major market turning points, you can start with contrary opinion—wait for majority opinion to reach an extreme and then assume the opposite position. At turning points, contrary sentiment indicators are nearly always right. Almost by definition, *a top in the market is the point of maximum optimism and a bottom in the market is the point of maximum pessimism*.

To better understand how contrary opinion operates, think of money as financial liquidity. And think of an extreme in liquidity as the direct opposite of an extreme in psychology. If everyone decided that the Dow Industrials would rise by 25 percent, for instance, they would rush out and buy stocks. Everyone would become fully invested, the market would be overbought, and nobody would be left to buy, in which case the market wouldn't be able to go any higher. *When optimism is extreme, liquidity is low.*

On the other hand, if everyone was pessimistic and thought the Dow would drop by 25 percent, the weak and nervous stockholders would sell, the market would be sold out, and nobody would be left to sell, in which case the market wouldn't go down any more. Whereas increasing optimism and confidence produce falling liquidity, rising pessimism and fear result in rising liquidity.

My favorite way to describe this inverse relationship is to compare liquidity to a car's shock absorbers. As you drive down the road, you will inevitably encounter some potholes—some random, unpredictable, negative events. If your car has good shocks (abundant liquidity), you will be able to continue merrily along your journey after encountering a pothole. But if your car has poor shocks (no liquidity), you may crash.

Another way of looking at contrary opinion is to compare stockholders to nuts in a tree. An investor once wrote to me, asking, "How do you get nuts out of a nut tree?" The answer, he said, is through a nut-shaking machine, which is hooked to the nut tree. The machine rattles the tree, and the nuts drop until all of the nuts have fallen out. In other words, when there is enough fear in the market, all of the weak holders are shaken out, and there is no selling left to be done. "Have the nuts been shaken out," the contrarian asks, "or are all of the speculative traders fully invested?"

The impact of contrary opinion can also be illustrated by comparing the market to a theater. If someone yelled "*fire*" in a theater full of people, panic would break out and people would get crushed in the ensuing rush to the door. But if someone yelled "*fire*" in a theater with very few people, the people would be more likely to walk out in an orderly manner. In looking at any market, it is important to determine the degree to which it is crowded.

What makes contrary opinion really valuable is that it opens your mind and keeps you from being swept up in the crowd. With an open mind, you can say to yourself, "I know the majority is right, and I know the world is going to hell in a handbasket, but what if the minority is right? What if there is a silver lining in the cloud out there?" *Contrary opinion allows you to be flexible, enabling you to turn your emotions inside out, and to act when you need to act.*

Psychology plays into the supply-demand equation through valuation and emotional buying and selling when greed or fear takes over. To show clients why they should be wary of the crowd at extremes, many years ago I put together a composite of seven sentiment indicators and called it the NDR Crowd Sentiment Poll. The record can be seen in Figures 25.7 and 25.8, and in Table 25.1.

When I built the NDR Crowd Sentiment Poll, my main goal was to prove to clients that the crowd was *usually* wrong at extremes in sentiment. We tried to judge the extremes objectively by defining certain levels as excessive and looking for big

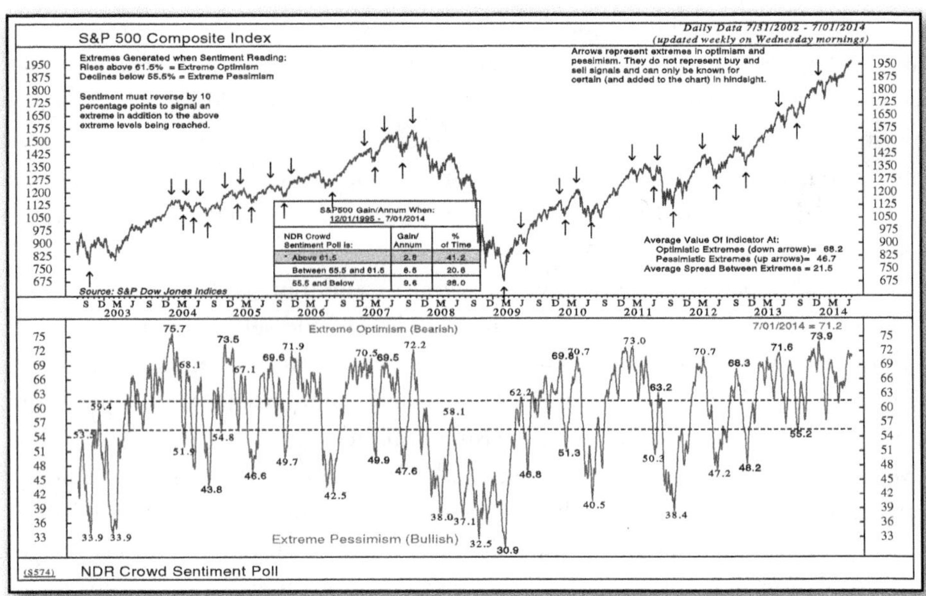

FIGURE 25.7 *Top*, **S&P 500 Composite Index;** *Bottom*, **Crowd Sentiment Poll (2002–2014).**

shifts. But as proven by the historical record (1996–2013), shown in Table 25.1, the crowd has yet to be right even *once* at extremes in sentiment. In fact, following the crowd at extremes would have cost one over 10,000 S&P 500 points since 1996.

To be fair, the extremes can *only* be known for certain in hindsight, and the optimistic extreme of 71.6 percent bulls on May 22, 2013, was almost correct. More importantly, the extreme pessimism in 2008 and early 2009 was largely correct, even if the *exact* extreme was wrong. Sentiment indicators are not perfect in runaway

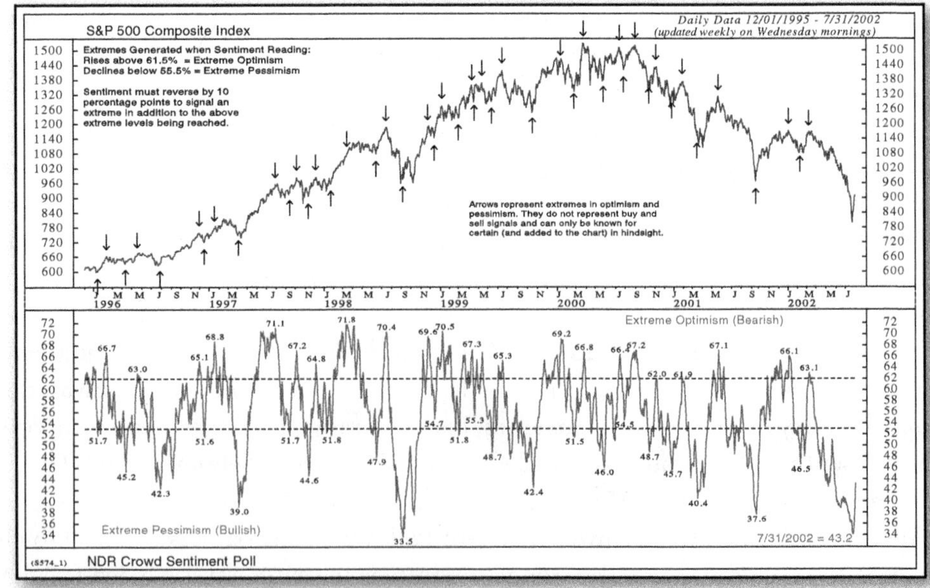

FIGURE 25.8 *Top,* **S&P 500 Composite Index;** *Bottom,* **Crowd Sentiment Poll (1995–2002).**

TABLE 25.1 Crowd Sentiment Poll

NDR CROWD SENTIMENT POLL (S574)													
Date	Extreme Pessimism	Extreme Optimism	S&P 500	S&P Point Profit/Loss	Crowd Right	Crowd Wrong	Date	Extreme Pessimism	Extreme Optimism	S&P 500	S&P Point Profit/Loss	Crowd Right	Crowd Wrong
1/15/1996	51.7		600	-61		x	9/21/2001	37.6		966	-207		x
2/12/1996		66.7	661	-24		x	1/4/2002		66.1	1173	-77		x
4/12/1996	45.2		637	-32		x	2/8/2002	46.5		1096	-68		x
5/17/1996		63.0	669	-38		x	3/8/2002		63.1	1164	-387		x
7/29/1996	42.3		631	-126		x	10/9/2002	33.9		777	-371		x
11/29/1996		65.1	757	-36		x	1/21/2004		75.7	1148	-39		x
12/16/1996	51.6		721	-56		x	3/25/2004	51.9		1109	-36		x
1/20/1997		68.8	777	-19		x	4/12/2004		68.1	1145	-51		x
4/4/1997	39.0		758	-194		x	5/21/2004	47.3		1094	-47		x
7/30/1997		71.1	952	-32		x	6/30/2004		66.6	1141	-76		x
9/15/1997	51.7		920	-63		x	8/13/2004	43.8		1065	-119		x
10/7/1997		67.2	983	-77		x	11/18/2004		73.5	1184	-13		x
11/12/1997	44.6		906	-78		x	1/28/2005	55.4		1171	-39		x
12/5/1997		64.8	984	-27		x	2/15/2005		67.1	1210	-57		x
1/26/1998	51.8		957	-122		x	4/19/2005	46.6		1153	-91		x
3/16/1998		71.8	1079	-2		x	8/2/2005		69.6	1244	-66		x
6/15/1998	47.9		1077	-107		x	10/18/2005	49.7		1178	-90		x
7/16/1998		70.4	1184	-210		x	11/25/2005		71.9	1268	-28		x
9/4/1998	33.5		974	-214		x	7/21/2006	42.5		1240	-191		x
11/23/1998		69.6	1188	-47		x	1/17/2007		70.5	1431	-44		x
12/14/1998	54.7		1141	-134		x	3/16/2007	49.9		1387	-126		x
1/8/1999		70.5	1275	-49		x	5/9/2007		69.5	1513	-102		x
3/2/1999	51.8		1226	-124		x	8/16/2007	47.6		1411	-151		x
4/13/1999		67.3	1350	-44		x	10/12/2007		72.2	1562	-879		x
4/20/1999	55.3		1306	-62		x	3/6/2009	30.9		683	-262		x
5/13/1999		66.8	1368	-74		x	6/11/2009		62.2	945	-44		x
6/14/1999	48.7		1294	-125		x	7/13/2009	46.8		901	-246		x
7/16/1999		65.3	1419	-165		x	1/11/2010		69.8	1147	-71		x
10/18/1999	42.4		1254	-196		x	2/12/2010	51.3		1076	-136		x
1/13/2000		69.2	1450	-97		x	4/15/2010		70.7	1212	-152		x
2/24/2000	51.5		1353	-174		x	7/7/2010	40.5		1060	-283		x
3/24/2000		66.8	1527	-145		x	2/18/2011		73.0	1343	-71		x
5/25/2000	46.0		1382	-128		x	6/17/2011	50.3		1272	-72		x
7/17/2000		66.4	1510	-90		x	7/8/2011		63.2	1344	-220		x
7/28/2000	54.5		1420	-101		x	10/4/2011	38.4		1124	-286		x
9/1/2000		67.2	1521	-147		x	3/19/2012		70.7	1410	-124		x
10/13/2000	48.7		1374	-58		x	6/5/2012	47.2		1286	-175		x
11/6/2000		62.0	1432	-117		x	9/19/2012		68.3	1461	-108		x
12/26/2000	45.7		1315	-59		x	11/15/2012	49.5		1353	-302		x
1/30/2001		61.9	1374	-223		x	5/22/2013		71.6	1655	-15		x
3/16/2001	40.4		1151	-158		x	9/3/2013	55.2		1640	-201		x
5/22/2001		67.1	1309	-343		x	12/30/2013		73.9	1841		?	
							Average	46.7	68.2	Total	-10501		
Ned Davis Research Group													*S574_IND.RPT*

momentum moves, but they can help one keep a clear head when the crowd is fearful or euphoric.

History and Risk Management

Two other rules we use in building timing models are these:

1. When I asked in kindergarten why we needed to study boring old history, the teacher said, "Those who do not study history are condemned to repeat its mistakes." Ned Davis Research takes great pride in our large historical database. We are able to take our models back as far in history as possible, so they have a chance to adjust to as many different environments as possible.

We also conduct many historical studies for investor perspective. Two real-time examples follow.

Table 25.2 is a little subjective for my taste, but it is also one of the studies of which I am proudest. I put it out on the morning of 9/11, right after the horrible attacks on the World Trade Center. It shows how the study of history can provide perspective and help one stay grounded.

Using history for perspective and keeping one's mind open and flexible is critical for investment success. Nearly all surveys of Wall Street investors show that they lean Republican, so it is widely believed that the stock markets prefer Republicans. And, in fact, the market and economy performed very well under Eisenhower and Reagan.

When President Obama was elected in late 2008, many wealthy investors got out of stocks, predicting disaster. They were particularly upset with Obama's calls to sharply raise taxes on the top 2 percent, a group that happens to be large

TABLE 25.2 Crisis Events, DJIA Declines, and Subsequent Performance

NED DAVIS RESEARCH, INC. CHART OF THE DAY 11 SEPTEMBER 2001

Our updated table of crisis events is featured in the table below (study T_900). It shows that the DJIA has dropped by a median of 5% during crisis events, but has rallied afterwards. The table's implication is that after an initial negative reaction to today's tragic events, a recovery could be expected. Of course, the list is subjective, and even the reaction dates are subject to interpretation in some cases. Please let us know if you would like to see the table modified in any way. Future NDR publications will have more details and perspectives, including statistics on the performance of other assets during and after previous crises.

CRISIS EVENTS, DJIA DECLINES AND SUBSEQUENT PERFORMANCE

Event	Reaction Dates	Date Range % Gain/Loss	DJIA Percentage Gain Days After Reaction Dates 22	63	126
Fall of France	05/09/1940 - 06/22/1940	-17.1	-0.5	8.4	7.0
Pearl Harbor	12/06/1941 - 12/10/1941	-6.5	3.8	-2.9	-9.6
Truman Upset Victory	11/02/1948 - 11/10/1948	-4.9	1.6	3.5	1.9
Korean War	06/23/1950 - 07/13/1950	-12.0	9.1	15.3	19.2
Eisenhower Heart Attack	09/23/1955 - 09/26/1955	-6.5	0.0	6.6	11.7
Sputnik	10/03/1957 - 10/22/1957	-9.9	5.5	6.7	7.2
Cuban Missile Crisis	10/19/1962 - 10/27/1962	1.1	12.1	17.1	24.2
JFK Assassination	11/21/1963 - 11/22/1963	-2.9	7.2	12.4	15.1
U.S. Bombs Cambodia	04/29/1970 - 05/26/1970	-14.4	9.9	20.3	20.7
Kent State Shootings	05/04/1970 - 05/14/1970	-4.2	0.4	3.8	13.5
Arab Oil Embargo	10/18/1973 - 12/05/1973	-17.9	9.3	10.2	7.2
Nixon Resigns	08/09/1974 - 08/29/1974	-15.5	-7.9	-5.7	12.5
U.S.S.R. in Afghanistan	12/24/1979 - 01/03/1980	-2.2	6.7	-4.0	6.8
Hunt Silver Crisis	02/13/1980 - 03/27/1980	-15.9	6.7	16.2	25.8
Falkland Islands War	04/01/1982 - 05/07/1982	4.3	-8.5	-9.8	20.8
U.S. Invades Grenada	10/24/1983 - 11/07/1983	-2.7	3.9	-2.8	-3.2
U.S. Bombs Libya	04/15/1986 - 04/21/1986	2.6	-4.3	-4.1	-1.0
Financial Panic '87	10/02/1987 - 10/19/1987	-34.2	11.5	11.4	15.0
Invasion of Panama	12/15/1989 - 12/20/1989	-1.9	-2.7	0.3	8.0
Gulf War Ultimatum	12/24/1990 - 01/16/1991	-4.3	17.0	19.8	18.7
Gorbachev Coup	08/16/1991 - 08/19/1991	-2.4	4.4	1.6	11.3
ERM U.K.Currency Crisis	09/14/1992 - 10/16/1992	-6.0	0.6	3.2	9.2
World Trade Center Bombing	02/26/1993 - 02/27/1993	-0.5	2.4	5.1	8.5
Russia Mexico Orange County	10/11/1994 - 12/20/1994	-2.8	2.7	8.4	20.7
Oklahoma City Bombing	04/19/1995 - 04/20/1995	0.6	3.9	9.7	12.9
Asian Stock Market Crisis	10/07/1997 - 10/27/1997	-12.4	8.8	10.5	25.0
U.S. Embassy Bombings Africa	08/07/1998 - 08/10/1998	-0.3	-11.2	4.7	6.5
Russian LTCM Crisis	08/18/1998 - 10/08/1998	-11.3	15.1	24.7	33.7
Mean		**-7.1**	**3.8**	**6.8**	**12.5**
Median		**-4.6**	**3.9**	**6.7**	**12.1**

Days = Market Days T_900 9/11/2001

TABLE 25.3 Percentage Gain per Annum for Stocks, Industrial Production, Inflation, Bonds, and the U.S. Dollar by Party of President and Majority Party in Congress, 1901–2014

GAIN/ANNUM (%) FOR STOCKS, INDUSTRIAL PRODUCTION, INFLATION, BONDS, AND U.S. DOLLAR ($) BY PARTY OF PRESIDENT AND MAJORITY PARTY* IN CONGRESS (03/04/1901 - 07/01/2014)

	Stocks (DJIA)	Industrial Production	Inflation (CPI)	Since: Real Stock Returns	1925 Long-Term Gov't Bonds	1971 Fed's U.S. Dollar
Democratic President	7.97	5.18	4.35	3.47	3.53	-0.25
Republican President	3.02	1.80	1.80	1.20	7.74	-1.39
Democratic Congress	6.21	4.45	4.29	1.85	5.28	-1.21
Republican Congress	3.62	1.45	0.65	2.95	6.39	-0.23
Dem. Pres., Dem. Congress	7.53	6.14	4.48	2.92	2.57	-2.38
Dem. Pres., Rep. Congress	9.76	1.11	3.78	5.76	8.12	3.93
Rep. Pres., Rep. Congress	1.70	1.56	-0.37	2.07	5.48	-4.24
Rep. Pres., Dem. Congress	4.46	2.05	4.01	0.43	8.99	-0.52
All Periods Buy/Hold	5.28	3.38	2.99	2.22	5.57	-0.94

**Majority Party = Party with average of % control in House and % control in Senate greater than 50%.*

Ned Davis Research, Inc. T_50.RPT

holders of stock. The market did continue to decline sharply in early 2009. However, I wrote a *Hotline* arguing that in order to make money in stocks consistently, I believed that one should analyze them with an apolitical mindset. In fact, I featured Table 25.3, and wrote, "The historical record shows the stock market doing better under Democratic presidents, but also with more inflation."

No matter how things eventually turn out or what one thinks about President Obama, certainly a study of history provides a useful perspective. I believe the record since 1901 suggests stressing factual reality over Wall Street myths. Also, while people fret about a gridlocked government, the limited historical examples suggest that this, too, has not been a big problem for stocks.

President Harry S. Truman once said, "My choice early in life was either to be a piano player in a whorehouse or a politician. And to tell the truth, there's hardly any difference." Regardless of what people think about politicians, I still try to respect people's political beliefs. But the study of history tells me that investing based upon politics is a poor way to make money.

2. Despite all our efforts to build models that will provide good gains going forward, we realize that we will never find the Holy Grail, and thus, we try to build *good money management* into our timing models by attempting to cut losses short and letting profits run. There are periods, historically, in which model indicators tend to fail or stay wrong against a major move. Accordingly, we put stop-losses in the indicators, where the indicator weight goes to zero until the indicator gives a new signal. As we learned in kindergarten, sometimes doo-doo happens, so we need to be prepared.

Finally, we see ourselves as risk managers. Here's a story about risk management I want to share with you.

Two cowboys, having lost their jobs, went into a bar to drown their sorrows. Over the bar was a sign that said, Bear Hides $25. When they asked the bartender what that meant he said, "It means what it says," so the two cowboys went out, came back with two bear hides, and received $50. One of the cowboys was a capitalist and he said, "All we need now is inventory," so they got on their horses and rode deep into bear country. It was dark out, so they put up their tent and went to sleep. Early the next morning they heard a rumble, so one cowboy looked outside to see what it was.

When he opened the tent he saw 10,000 growling bears. He looked at all the bears and then looked at the other cowboy, and with a grin said, "We're rich!"

One good definition of the difference between professionals and amateurs is that amateurs ask what the potential rewards are, while professionals ask what the risks are. Take our composite timing models, for example. If we have a model composed of 10 indicators, all of which are bullish, we would obviously be extremely bullish. But let's say two of these 10 reliable indicators turn bearish. Obviously, with eight bullish indicators and just two bearish indicators, we would stay with the investment, but we might take 20 percent of our chips off the table out of respect for the higher risks. This is not a black-and-white world that we live in. It's beautifully composed of shades of gray and degrees of bullishness and bearishness.

Thus, the bottom line at Ned Davis Research is that our timing models, at every stage of development, are designed with one thought foremost in mind, and that is *controlling big mistakes*.

The Nine Rules of Ned Davis Research Group

The nine rules that follow are a teaching aid for new NDR employees.

1. Don't Fight the Tape

   The tape provides a stop-loss for should-be beliefs.

   The trend is your friend (smoothings, slopes, and stop-losses).

   Go with Mo (momentum, breadth thrusts, signs of churning).

   Listen to the cold, bloodless verdict of the market (pay special notice to indicators on the leading edge of the market like volume, new highs or lows, the Dow Utilities, bonds, relative strength, etc.).

   Moves with a lot of confirmation are the healthiest, and huge moves are often global in nature.

2. Don't Fight the Fed

   Remain in harmony with interest-rate trends (rates dropping is good; rates rising is bad).

   Money moves markets. Stay in line with monetary trends (especially money less economic demands equals liquidity left over for financial markets).

   Economic strains: inflationary pressures lead to Fed tightness (up commodities, up gold, down dollar, rising real interest rates).

   Economic ease: disinflation leads to Fed ease.

3. Beware of the Crowd at Extremes

   Go with the flow until it reaches a psychological extreme and begins to reverse. At that point, it pays to take a contrary approach (reverse inverted brackets).

   Key relationship: liquidity and psychology are inversely related.

   Extreme optimism equals low cash. Extreme fear equals high cash.

Liquidity is like shock absorbers on a car.

Is the theater crowded or empty?

Top is the point of maximum optimism. Bottom is the point of maximum pessimism.

Valuation measures long-term extremes in psychology.

4. Rely on Objective Indicators

   Rather than using gut emotions to determine the supply and demand balance, use the weight-of-the-evidence approach (computer-derived mathematical measurements).

5. Be Disciplined

   Our mandate is to follow our models, forcing us to be *disciplined*.

   Benchmark or anchor composite model determines core invested position.

6. Practice Risk Management

   We are in the business of making mistakes. Winners make small mistakes, losers make big mistakes. We focus on a risk management strategy to keep mistakes small (use stop-losses and a heavy dose of technical trend-sensitive indicators).

7. Remain Flexible

   Indicators change and data is revised. Scenarios change. Use dynamic modeling, such as standard deviation brackets. Review models on an objective and timely basis.

8. Money Management Rules

   We are more interested in making money than being right.

   Be humble and flexible (be ready to turn emotions upside down and thus be open-minded).

   Let profits run, cut losses short.

   Think in terms of risks, including the risk of missing a bull market.

   Buy on the rumor, sell on the news.

   Consider cyclical, seasonal, progressive trading patterns that do not add to models (for fun).

9. Those Who Do Not Study History Are Condemned to Repeat Its Mistakes

   Go back as far as possible. Use bull, bear, and neutral cycles.

Notes

1. George Soros, *The Alchemy of Finance* (New York: John Wiley & Sons, 1987).
2. Peter Lynch and John Rothchild, *Beating the Street* (New York: Simon & Schuster, 1993).
3. Jonathan Burton, "Learn a Lesson—Before You Get One" summarized from Bob Farrell's 10 "Market Rules to Remember," *MarketWatch* (June 11, 2008).
4. William Bernsetin, *The Intelligent Asset Allocator* (New York: McGraw-Hill, 2000).
5. *The Chartist*, P.O. Box 758, Seal Beach, CA 90740.
6. Value Line, 220 East 42nd Street, New York, NY 10017.
7. Jack D. Schwager, *Market Wizards* (New York: New York Institute of Finance, 1989).
8. Brendan Moynihan and Jim Paul, *What I Learned Losing a Million Dollars* (Nashville: Infrared Press, 1994).

9. Martin Zweig, *Winning on Wall Street* (New York: Warner Books, 1986).
10. Martin Schwartz, *Pit Bull* (New York: Harper Business, 1998).
11. Edwin Lefèvre, *Reminiscences of a Stock Operator* (Larchmont, NY: George H. Doran, 1923).
12. Jack D. Schwager, *The New Market Wizards* (New York: Harper Business, 1992).
13. Howard Abell and Robert Koppel, *The Inner Game of Trading* (Chicago: Probus Publishing, 1994).
14. Gerald M. Loeb, *The Battle for Investment Survival* (New York: Simon & Schuster, 1935).
15. Peter Lynch and John Rothchild, *One Up on Wall Street* (New York: Simon & Schuster, 1989).
16. *Hulbert Financial Digest*, 8001 Braddock Road #107, Springfield, VA 22151.
17. James B. Stack, *InvesTech Research* (May 31, 2013).
18. James B. Stack, "A Buying Opportunity of a Lifetime?," *InvesTech Research* (March 13, 2009).
19. Charles Mackay, *Extraordinary Popular Delusions and the Madness of Crowds* (New York: Barnes & Noble 1989).
20. John Darnton, "Self-Made Monster: An Actor's Creation," *New York Times*, February 14, 1994.
21. William Raspberry, "Does This Poll Mean That Skin Color Is Everything?" (Washington Post Writers Group, 1994).
22. Warren Buffett, "1990 Chairman's Letter," Berkshire Hathaway Chairman's Letters to Shareholders.

CHAPTER 26

The Model-Building Process

Sam Burns

Updated by Ned Davis from, *Being Right or Making Money*, 3rd edition (Hoboken, New Jersey: John Wiley & Sons, 2014), Chapter 2.

Chapter 25 described the types of indicators we use to try to manage risk in the stock market in general. This chapter will further outline our model-building process.

The Model-Building Process

A market-timing model can form the basis of an investor's market outlook by providing a benchmark for adjusting exposure to different types of assets. By using objective, quantitative information and testing its predictive value against historical data, an investor can avoid making decisions based on emotion, gut feel, or the pronouncements of the market guru *du jour*. A model with a variety of indicators, which individually have value in highlighting risk and reward, can offer a more stable, predictable, and reliable reflection of the market than any single indicator can. Such a model can anchor the investment/asset-allocation process.

Where to Start: Model Inputs

Any model is only as good as its inputs, and if those inputs contain errors, aren't timely, or are simply irrelevant, the model will provide little benefit. So the first thing investors who want to build or maintain a quantitative timing model must do is make sure that they have clean (error-free), reliable data that is updated regularly.

One must also take into account data revisions, which are common in economic reports, and make sure that the information used is consistent over time. At Ned Davis Research, we devote a lot of time and effort to making sure our data is as clean, as reliable, and as up-to-date as possible.

The next thing an investor building a timing model should investigate is which data series, out of the innumerable possible sets out there, are the most useful or relevant for asset-allocation and market-timing purposes. Some data is best suited for aggressive, short-term trading, while other data is best suited for long-term asset allocation and risk control. Finding out what is useful is the biggest challenge the investor faces and is a primary goal of our analysts. To help narrow the possibilities and provide some structure for those looking to use or develop models, we offer some of the results of our research and the ways we categorize data.

One distinction we often make is between "internal" and "external" indicators.

Internal indicators are based on the market itself. They include price trend and momentum, as well as corollary indicators, such as the number of stocks rising versus the number falling on a given day (a.k.a. *breadth*). Internal indicators are generally designed to ensure that we keep our eye on the ball by focusing the model on the actual market whose future we are trying to predict, and that we do not allow the model to become too far removed from that market's primary underlying trend. Our goal is to be in harmony with that trend. Because we have found that the trend in market prices is perhaps the most important factor to consider, internal measures typically account for half (or more) of the indicators in our timing models.

External indicators aren't derived from the market directly, but are known (or thought) to significantly influence it. The best example of an important external indicator is interest rates. History shows that their level and direction have a major impact on the direction of stock prices. So we try to include indicators based on interest rates in our stock-timing models.

The following sections describe the various categories of indicators we have found useful in constructing models.

Sentiment and Valuation Indicators

While many analysts consider sentiment and valuation indicators to be quite separate and distinct, we put the two together because we often view valuation indicators as simply another way of measuring investor sentiment. As noted in other chapters, investor psychology plays a crucial role in how stock prices behave, and so monitoring what most investors are thinking and doing is very important. There are several regularly updated polls or surveys of various investors, including market newsletter writers, futures traders, and individuals. These polls typically just ask the respondents whether they have a bullish (positive) or a bearish (negative) view on stocks and then aggregate the responses to give the percentage of the group that is bullish or bearish at any given time. When a great majority of investors have the same view of the market, it is typically a warning to expect a reversal contrary to the majority opinion. In addition to watching the surveys, we also consider data related to valuation, such as price/earnings (P/E) ratios, as a sentiment indicator. Why? Because the price investors are willing to pay for a stock, relative to its underlying assets or earnings, indicates their level of confidence or optimism about the prospects for that stock (or in the aggregate, the market). When investors are very optimistic they will pay higher prices, as reflected in high price/earnings or price/book value ratios, while pessimistic investors will buy only at low valuation levels. We see how much investors are paying for current valuations and compare that to historical norms. This has the added benefit of reflecting what investors are actually *doing*, as opposed to what they are *saying* in response to polls.

An example of a sentiment and valuation indicator is the results of the weekly poll of its members by the American Association of Individual Investors, and the price/earnings ratio of the S&P 500 (see Figures 26.1 and 26.2).

Monetary Indicators

Some of the most important external indicators are monetary indicators. These reflect what is happening to the *price* of money (interest rates) and the *supply* (availability) of money. Interest rates are a primary driver of stock returns, because high rates make debt securities relatively more attractive than equities to investors, and also drive up businesses' cost of raising capital. So indicators based on the level and trend of interest rates (or bond prices, which are inversely related to rates) are common in our stock-market models. Of course, bond prices and interest rates appear in our bond-market models as well, but they are considered internal indicators in that context. We also use indicators based on the growth of the money supply, since

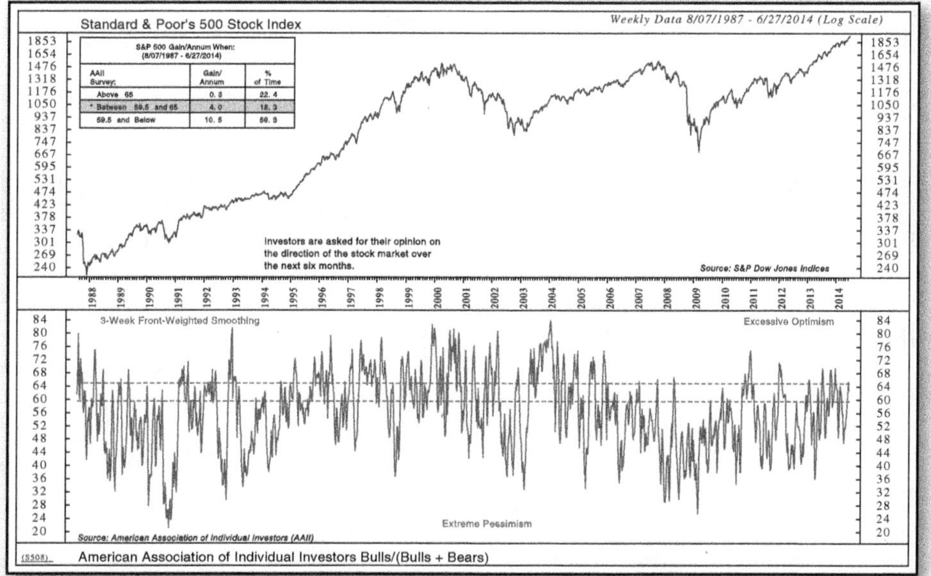

FIGURE 26.1 *Top*, **S&P 500 Index;** *Bottom*, **American Association of Individual Investors: Bulls/(Bulls + Bears).**

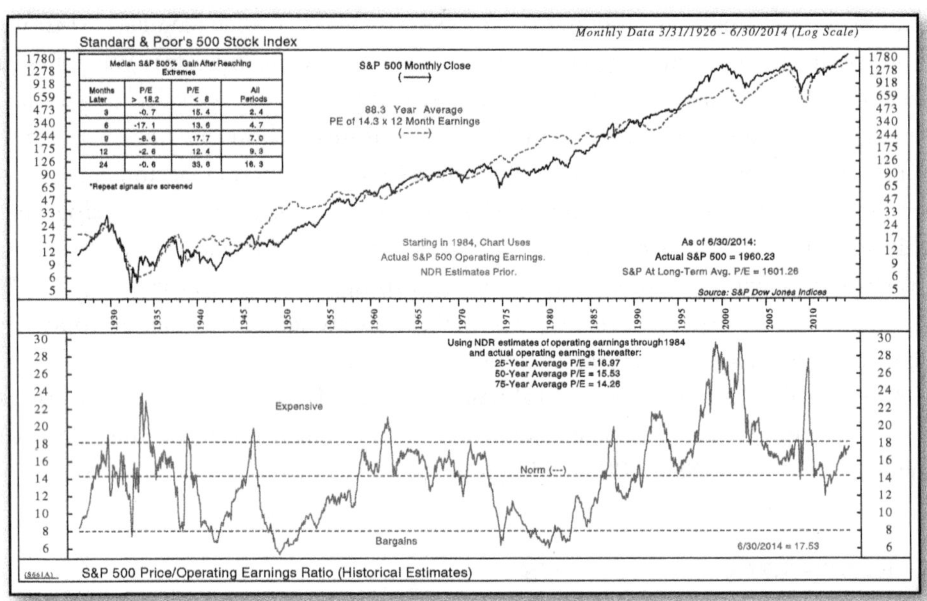

FIGURE 26.2 *Top*, **S&P 500 Index;** ***Bottom***, **S&P 500 Price/Operating Earnings Ratio (Historical Estimates).**

changes in that often influence interest rates, the stock market, and the economy as a whole. We do this by tracking M1, M2, and M3, which are monetary aggregates defined and watched carefully by the Federal Reserve. Figure 26.3 shows how such indicators can be used.

One of the principles that we adhere to at Ned Davis Research (as noted in Chapter 28) is *don't fight the Fed*. The Fed, of course, is the Federal Reserve Board, which acts as the nation's central bank and largely controls the money supply and short-

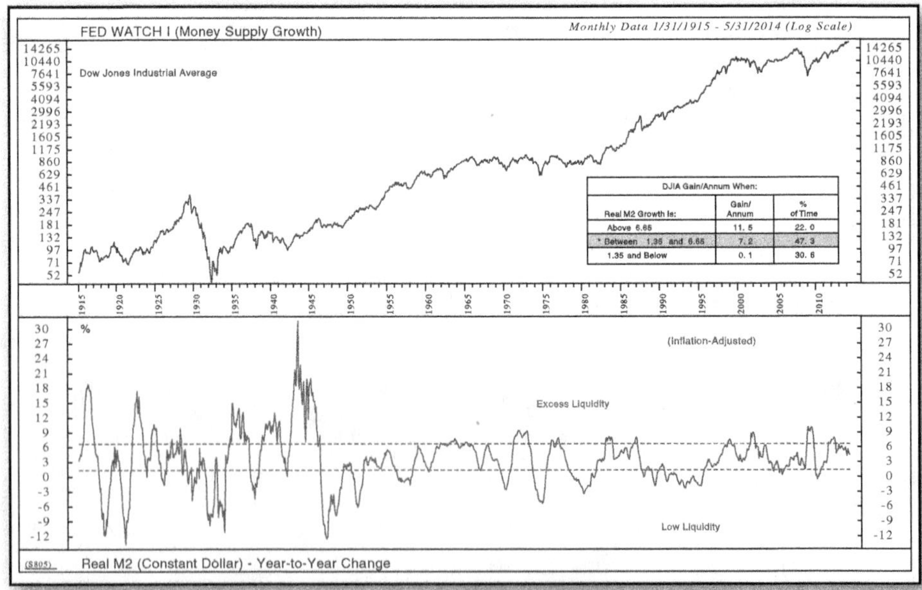

FIGURE 26.3 Fed Watch I (Money Supply Growth): *Top*, **DJIA;** ***Bottom***, **Year-to-Year Change in Real M2 (Constant Dollars).**

term interest rates. It has a great deal of influence over the banking system, the economy, and the financial markets, and its primary goal is to achieve price stability (a very low inflation rate) and sustainable economic growth. Because it is concerned, first and foremost, with keeping inflation low and economic growth reasonable (not too strong and not too weak), the Fed uses its influence on interest rates and the money supply to stimulate the economy when it is too weak and restrain the economy when it appears to be growing at an unsustainable rate. Excessively high growth often leads to higher inflation, as demand for goods and services exceeds the economy's ability to produce them. The resulting scarcity boosts prices. Thus, when the Fed decides it needs to restrain the economy, it raises rates and reduces the money supply to limit consumers' purchasing power. But higher interest rates and slower money-supply growth are bad for stock prices. So whenever the Fed is in a restrictive monetary posture, it also ends up restraining stock prices as well. When we see evidence that the Fed is turning more restrictive we become more cautious toward stocks. This is why we place considerable weight on the monetary indicators in our stock-market timing models.

A simple but effective monetary indicator can be constructed by determining the momentum, or rate of change, of interest rates. For example, one can simply compute the year-to-year change in the average yield on Baa-rated corporate bonds, as shown in Figure 26.4. When the current yield is materially higher than it was one year earlier it sends a negative warning signal for stock prices, as it implies that interest rates have risen enough to become restrictive. Conversely, when rates have fallen noticeably below the level of a year earlier that's a positive for stocks, because falling rates can stimulate the economy and offer less competition for investors' capital. For a more sensitive indicator, one could use a six-month, rather than a one-year, rate of change. This simple kind of monetary indicator can go a long way toward making sure that an investor is not swimming against the tide . . . and the Fed.

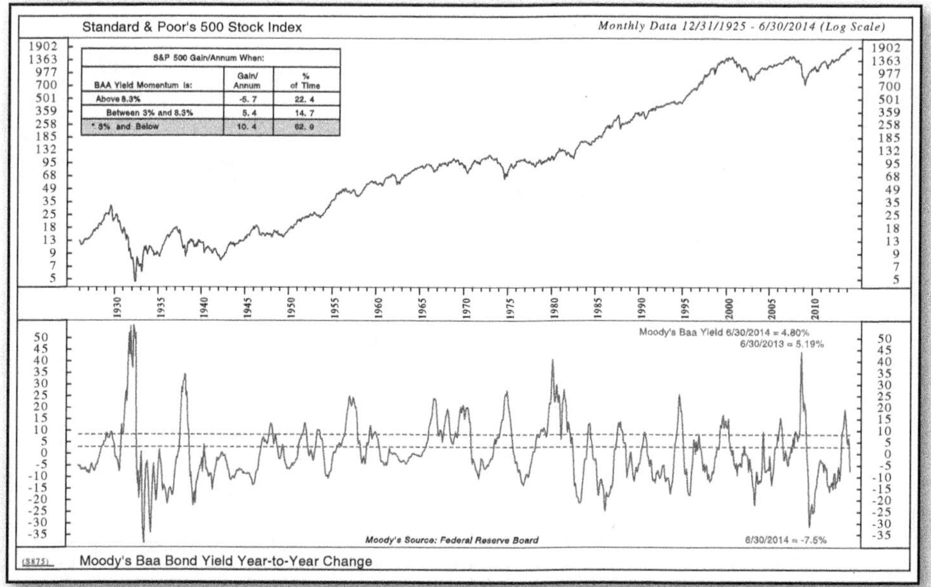

FIGURE 26.4 *Top*, **S&P 500 Index;** *Bottom*, **Moody's Year-to-Year Change in Baa Bond Yield.**

Economic Indicators

A broader category of external indicators can be classified simply as economic indicators. These track economic vitality or inflation. Examples are gross domestic product (GDP), the consumer price index (CPI), and surveys showing current and expected economic conditions (such as the monthly polls underlying The Conference Board's index of consumer confidence and the Institute for Supply Management's report on business activity). These indicators typically have the most effect on bond prices and interest rates, and thus on the actions of the Federal Reserve and on stock prices. In many cases, good economic news—such as high growth, high employment, or high confidence—is bad for bonds and stocks. Conversely, news of slower economic, wage, or employment growth, or lower consumer confidence can be good for both. Why this perverse reaction? Because strong economic reports are likely to prompt the Fed to worry about rising inflation, leading it to cool off the economy by raising rates and curbing money-supply expansion. That, in turn, would make stocks and bonds less attractive (see Figure 26.5).

Internal Indicators

All of these external indicators can be useful when applied correctly, but because they are, in effect, once or twice removed from the stock market itself, we don't rely exclusively on them. Because economic data is often revised, subject to estimation errors, or released with a lag, we typically want to anchor our models with data straight from the source—the price, breadth, and volume readings from the market itself. As noted earlier, we call all of the indicators based on stock prices and volume

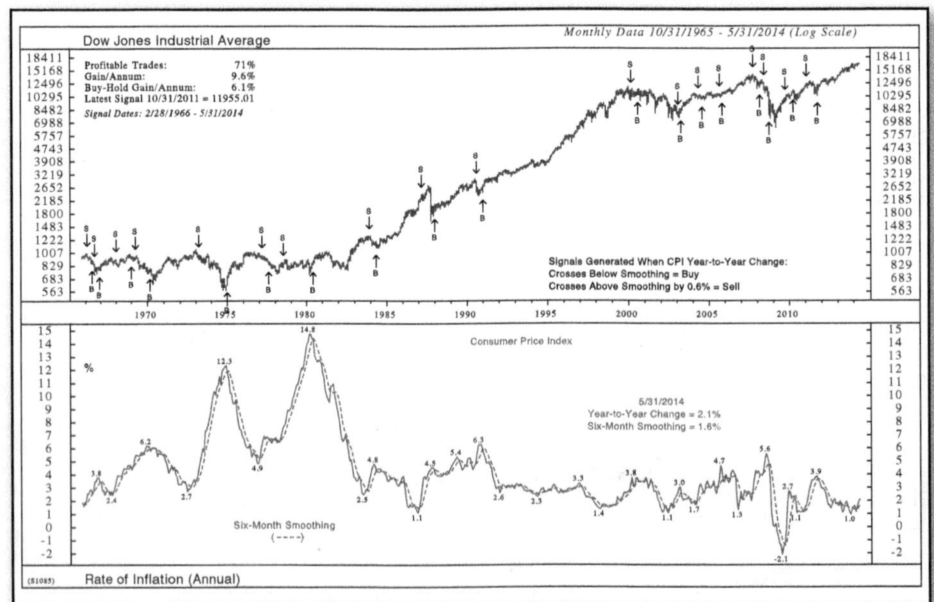

FIGURE 26.5 *Top*, **DJIA with Buy/Sell Signals;** *Bottom*, **Annual Rate of Inflation.**

internal. But to get a really solid view of what is happening in the market, we might also use other types of internal indicators, along with various signal-generation techniques. The same principles apply to indicators for any other market as well (bonds, commodities, and so on).

Moving Averages

One well-known way to get a handle on the underlying trend in stock prices is to use a *moving average (MA)*. This is simply an average of the last, say, 50 days of prices. It's updated each day, by dropping the price from 51 days earlier and adding in the most recent day's quote. Then the average is recalculated.

When plotted on a chart, this continuously updated fixed-period average *moves*, along with the actual price data; hence the name. What this technique does is smooth out the largely random short-term wiggles in the price of a stock or a market index, revealing the underlying trend. One can calculate a moving average using any number of periods. But the longer the time frame is, the more smoothing will occur and the less sensitive the results will be to the latest price changes. A short-term trader might use a five-day moving average to pick up the near-term trend, while a long-term investor might use a six-month moving average to pick up only larger, longer term moves and ignore shorter term fluctuations.

The moving average I just described (known as a simple moving average) has a potential drawback in that it applies equal weight to all of the prices it includes. But if the more recent data is the most important, one may want to use an average that applies more weight to the newest information and less to the older numbers. This is achieved by using a weighted moving average or an exponential moving average. Both calculate a moving average by placing more weight on recent observations. The actual calculations are a bit complicated and are available in many reference books. The important point is that, in some cases, variations on an indicator can improve performance. So, we use variations in our models as well.

Crossings and Slopes

Once we have calculated a moving average, how can it be used to objectively generate signals about the direction of prices? One way is to just see if the current stock or index price is above or below the current moving average value. If it is above that value the trend can be considered up, and if the current price is below the moving average the trend can be considered down. We call this a *crossing* indicator. However, the price can whip back and forth around the moving average and thus change its signal too frequently. To get around that, a model can be built that recognizes signals, up or down, only if they're based on moves of a certain minimum size. Or, one can use both short- and longer term averages together. The short-term average smooths out the very short-term blips in prices but remains responsive to the latest price action, while the longer term average indicates the underlying trend. A change in trend is signaled when the short-term average (rather than the price itself) crosses

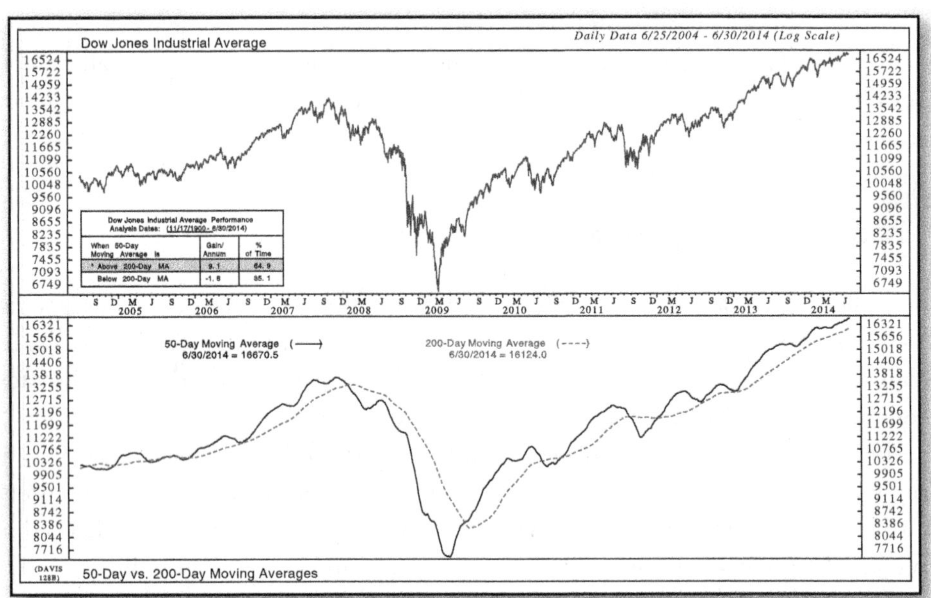

FIGURE 26.6 *Top*, **DJIA 2004–2014;** *Bottom*, **50-Day versus 200-Day Moving Averages.**

above or below the longer term average. This reduces the frequency of *whipsaws*, or short-term signals caused by random volatility in prices (see the table in the top section of Figure 26.6, which shows how the 50- and 200-day moving averages impact DJIA performance going back to 1900).

Another approach is to ignore the latest price and just watch the direction of the moving average itself. We consider this a *slope* indicator because we are measuring the moving average's direction or slope (when plotted on a chart). When the moving average rises a specified amount from a low (say, 5 percent), an uptrend is in place, while a decline of a specified amount from a peak indicates a downtrend. (Figure 26.7 shows a moving-average direction with a small slope for the NASDAQ.) By varying the length of the moving average and the amount that it must rise or fall to give a signal, the analyst can dictate the indicator's sensitivity (e.g., by making it send frequent signals for short-term traders or less frequent signals for longer term investors). We often use some combination of these moving-average indicators in our models.

Two other indicators that illustrate slope signals are very useful. Figure 26.8 uses a 5.5 percent rise on the NASDAQ 100 Index (NDX) to get a buy signal, and a 6.8 percent decline from a high to get a sell signal. Only 48 percent of the trades made with this indicator were profitable, but it cuts losses short and lets profits run, so it has made good money. Figure 26.9 uses a similar slope analysis on interest rates to generate buy and sell signals on the S&P 500.

One breadth indicator I have had good luck with is shown in Figure 26.10. I featured this on January 7, 2013, following a buy signal from a breadth thrust on January 4. Historically, it showed *no* losses one year after the buy signal. The indicator gives a buy whenever 90 percent of our database of institutional grade common stocks rises above their 50-day moving average. We call this a *breadth-thrust*

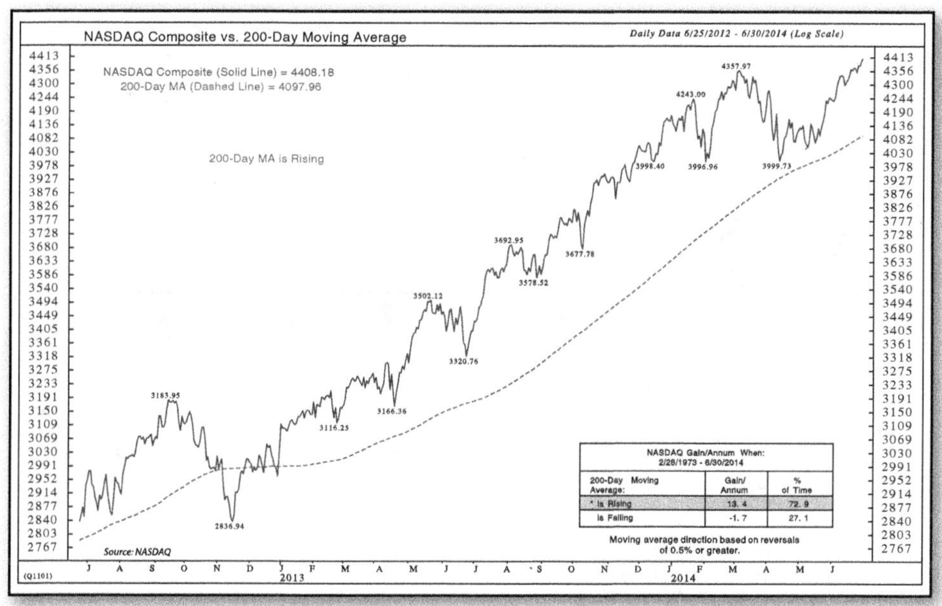

FIGURE 26.7 **NASDAQ Composite versus 200-Day Moving Average.**

buy signal. In my *Hotline* I said, "I generally try to 'trust the thrust' with such strong momentum, and I am very careful with overbought readings or excessive optimism when big momentum is strong on the upside." As can be seen on the chart, that January 4 buy signal hit a real bull's-eye!

Perhaps the granddaddy of breadth indicators, which uses things like advance and decline lines, new highs or new lows, up and down volume, and so on, is shown on Figure 26.11. It just tracks the number of NYSE issues at new 52-week lows each

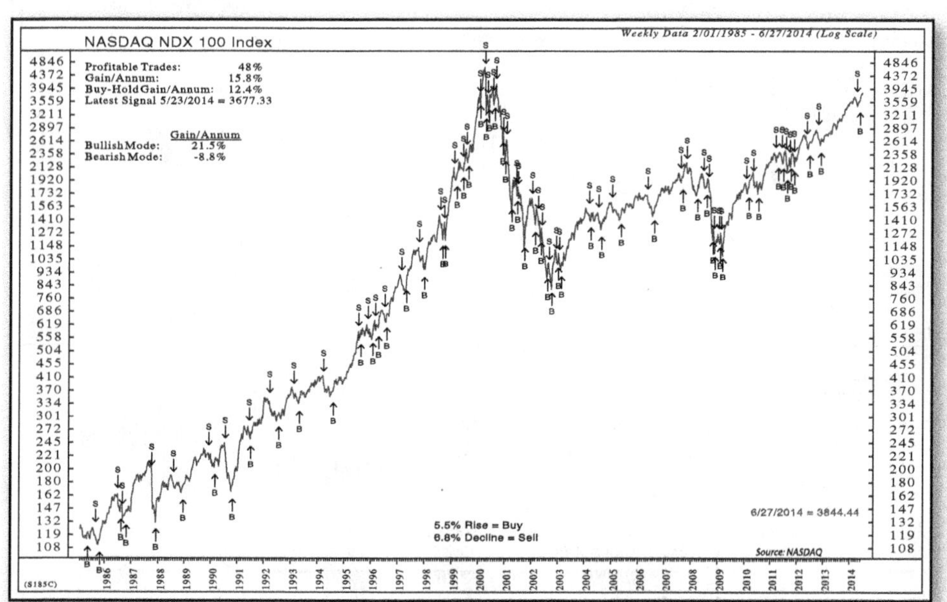

FIGURE 26.8 **NASDAQ NDX 100 Index.**

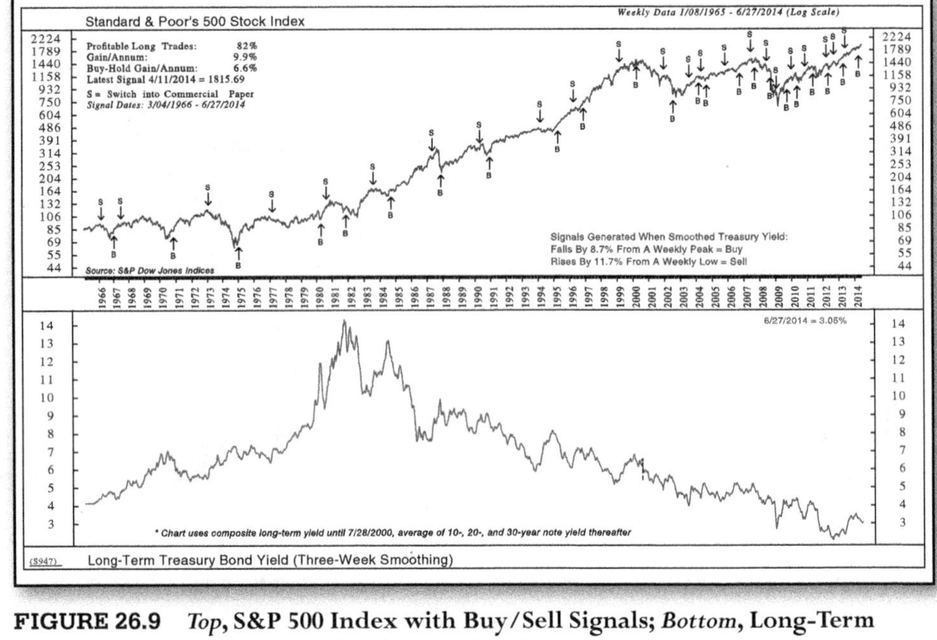

FIGURE 26.9 *Top*, **S&P 500 Index with Buy/Sell Signals;** *Bottom*, **Long-Term Treasury Bond Yield (Three-Week Smoothing).**

week as a percentage of issues traded. It goes back all the way to 1940! When there are a lot of new lows, the market has declined, on average. And when there are very few new lows, the market has little downside leadership and good breadth; in that case, the S&P 500 has advanced at double-digit rates more than 50 percent of the time. Make the breadth trend your friend.

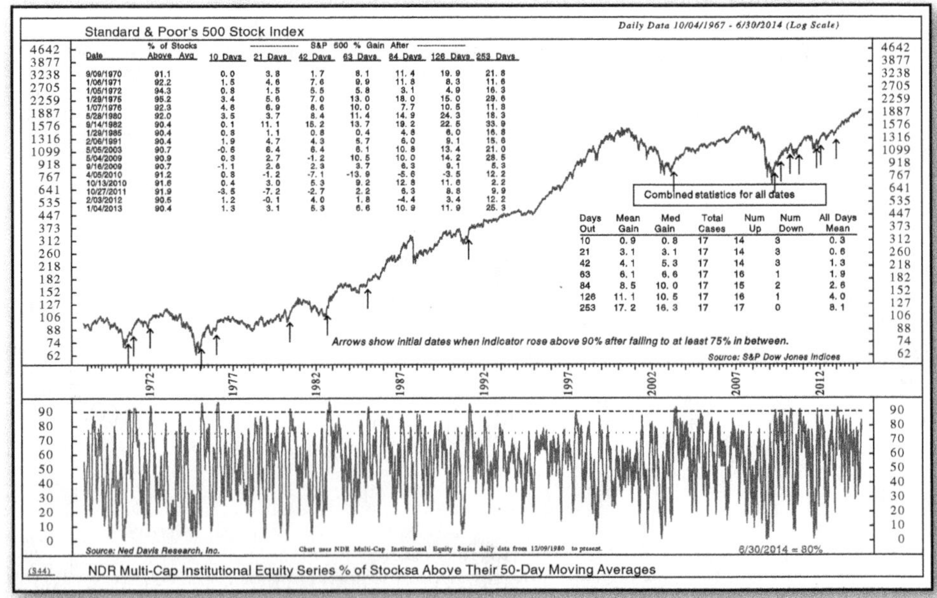

Date	% of Stocks Above Avg	S&P 500 % Gain After 10 Days	21 Days	42 Days	63 Days	84 Days	126 Days	253 Days
9/09/1970	91.1	0.0	3.8	1.7	8.1	11.4	19.9	21.8
1/06/1971	92.2	1.5	4.6	7.6	9.9	11.8	8.3	11.6
1/05/1972	94.3	0.8	1.5	5.5	5.8	3.1	4.9	16.3
1/29/1975	95.2	3.4	5.6	7.0	13.0	18.0	15.0	29.6
1/07/1976	92.3	4.6	6.9	6.6	10.0	7.7	10.5	11.8
5/28/1980	92.0	3.5	3.7	8.4	11.4	14.9	24.3	18.3
9/14/1982	90.4	0.1	11.1	15.2	13.7	19.2	22.5	33.9
1/29/1985	90.4	0.8	1.1	0.8	0.4	4.8	6.0	16.8
2/06/1991	90.4	1.9	4.7	4.3	5.7	6.0	9.1	15.6
5/05/2003	90.7	-0.6	6.4	6.4	6.1	10.8	13.4	21.0
5/04/2009	90.9	0.3	2.7	-1.2	10.5	10.0	14.2	28.5
9/16/2009	90.7	-1.1	2.6	2.3	3.7	6.3	9.1	5.3
4/05/2010	91.2	0.8	-1.2	-7.1	-13.9	-5.6	-3.5	12.2
10/13/2010	91.6	0.4	3.0	5.3	9.2	12.8	11.6	2.2
10/27/2011	91.9	-3.5	-7.2	-2.7	2.2	6.3	8.8	9.9
2/03/2012	90.5	1.2	-0.1	4.0	1.8	-4.4	3.4	12.2
1/04/2013	90.4	1.3	3.1	5.3	6.6	10.9	11.9	25.3

Combined statistics for all dates

Days Out	Mean Gain	Med Gain	Total Cases	Num Up	Num Down	All Days Mean
10	0.9	0.8	17	14	3	0.3
21	3.1	3.1	17	14	3	0.6
42	4.1	5.3	17	14	3	1.3
63	6.1	6.6	17	16	1	1.9
84	8.5	10.0	17	15	2	2.6
126	11.1	10.5	17	16	1	4.0
253	17.2	16.3	17	17	0	8.1

FIGURE 26.10 *Top*, **S&P 500 Index;** *Bottom*, **Multi-Cap Institutional Equity Series Percentage of Stocks above Their 50-Day Moving Averages.**

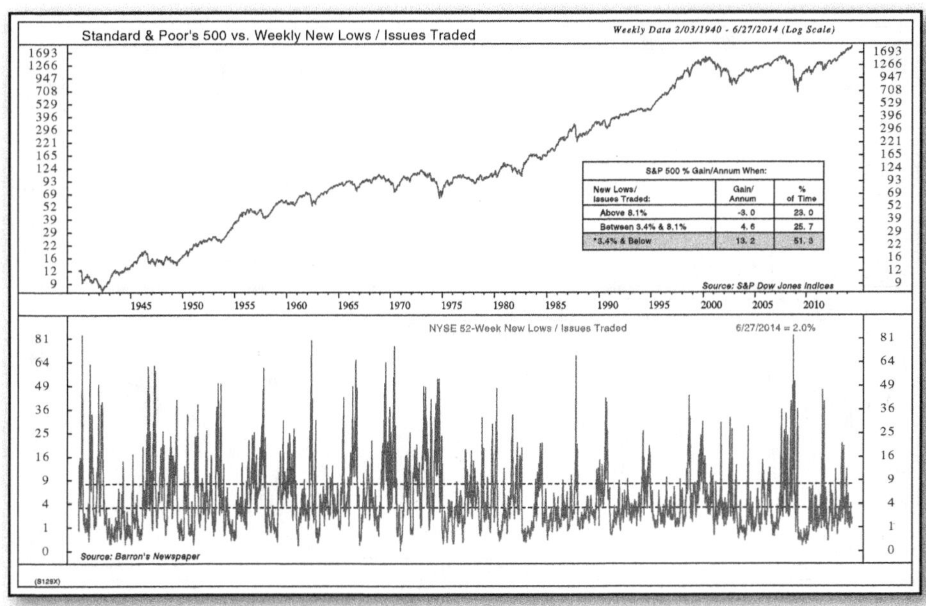

FIGURE 26.11 *Top*, **S&P 500 Index;** *Bottom*, **NYSE 52-Week New Lows/Issues Traded.**

Momentum

Another important type of internal indicator is *momentum*. The term typically applies to physical objects, and, indeed, stock prices exhibit characteristics similar to those of objects that are in motion. Momentum is typically measured as a rate of change, as in the distance an object travels in a given period, or the amount by which stock prices rise or fall in a given time span. To calculate a 10-day momentum, simply divide the current price by the price 10 days ago and subtract 1 from the result. A positive value indicates that the price trend is up, and a negative value implies a downtrend. We also look at how high or low the momentum is, because when a market shows a significant *thrust*, or sharp movement in one direction (an extremely high or low momentum reading), it often indicates that prices will continue in the same direction for a while, much as an object hurled into the air will keep rising for a while due to its momentum before it slows and tumbles back to earth (see Figure 26.10). So a very high momentum reading implies that prices will continue on an upward path for some time, while a very low (negative) reading implies that a downtrend is under way. The chart waits for a clear reversal from extreme readings to show an objective change in momentum (see Figure 26.12).

Momentum can be applied to external indicators, too. We can use the momentum of bond prices to give signals for stocks, or the momentum of the CRB (Commodity Research Bureau) Commodity Price Index to give signals for bonds or stocks. Also, because extreme momentum cannot be maintained indefinitely, and extreme readings are often followed later by reversals, we can use *brackets*, or specified levels of momentum (up or down), to indicate when an extreme has been reached. An extreme by itself may be useful for signals, or we can set up the indicator so that it gives a signal when an extreme has been hit *and then reverses*

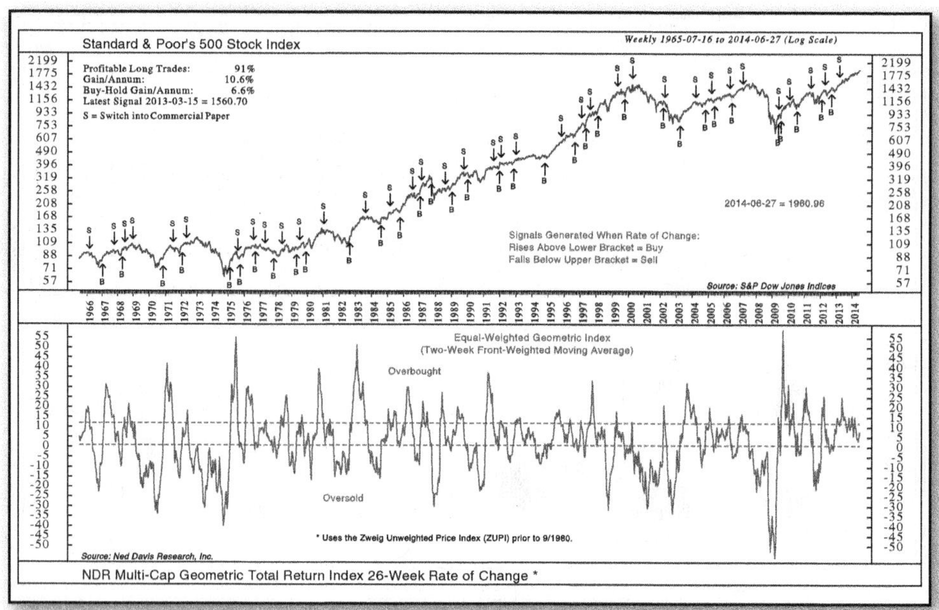

FIGURE 26.12 NASDAQ Composite versus 200-Day Moving Average.

back below the bracket level to indicate that the momentum has been spent and a reversal is likely.

Putting Indicators Together

We've now seen a variety of indicators that can be used in a market-timing or asset-allocation model. As mentioned, no single indicator or data series can consistently provide a reliable view of something as complex as the stock or bond market. So in the same way that companies are often run by a group of informed directors, we put a variety of individual indicators into a model to produce a *consensus* (composite) view of the market. That way, if any one indicator is ineffective or gets out of sync with the market it won't throw the investor completely off course, since the other indicators in the model will likely override the erroneous one.

The simplest way to create a model from a collection of separate indicators, and the way we often do it at Ned Davis Research, is to just determine whether each indicator is bullish, bearish, or neutral. Then we assign a +1 for each bullish indicator, a –1 for each bearish indicator, and 0 for the neutral indicators, and add up the results. If a model has 20 individual indicators and 12 are bullish, 6 are bearish, and 2 are neutral, the composite model reading would be +6. The analyst could then test the model's readings over time against the market's performance and determine if it provides good signals and what the optimum parameters are for taking action. For example, testing might indicate that it's best to buy shares when the model rises to +2 or more, and to sell only when it falls to –2 or below.

Ideally, a composite model will include a variety of indicators, including trend, monetary, and sentiment gauges, so that a complete picture of market conditions emerges, and no single type of indicator carries too much weight. Thus, building a model is a bit like building an investment portfolio; it's generally wise to diversify. At Ned Davis Research, our experience and long-standing focus on risk control and avoiding major losses has led us to usually require that at least half of a composite model's indicators be trend-oriented, or internal. This ensures that the model will always be forced to stay with the trend of the market itself.

One key issue that a model builder must consider is *overoptimization* or excessive *curve-fitting*. With enough data and many permutations and combinations of indicators, a determined analyst with a computer can find some mixture of indicators that appears to predict the stock market (or almost anything else) with very high accuracy *in hindsight* (meaning the information *fits the curves* of past stock price movements very closely). But because the future never looks exactly like the past, indicators or models that are created (*fitted*) based on the exact sequence of prices seen in the past invariably perform much worse in the future, as they haven't picked up a real, repeatable pattern or trend. Because computers can try literally millions of possible data combinations and match them to a set of historical prices, a few indicators will pop up, purely by chance, that will show extraordinarily good results and seem to be the holy grail of investing. But any results that fit the past too perfectly are unlikely to fit the future nearly so well. They should be examined very carefully or discarded.

One way to try to avoid over-fitting indicators or models is to analyze and test them on a subset of the available historical data (such as the first 10 years of a 20-year span), set the indicator's parameters, and then test it on a different subset (the next 10 years) to see if both results are similar. If they are, the indicator is more likely to be reliable. If they aren't, the correlation with past data probably has been found by chance. The indicator is more lucky than good.

Other ways to determine if an indicator's or model's results are likely to be repeated in the future is to examine all of the signals it gives. One thing to check is whether a good performance is due entirely to one or a few big gains. An example would be an indicator that just happened to be out of the stock market, or short the market, during the historic stock market crash of October 19, 1987. If the indicator's other signals weren't particularly good, one would have much less confidence in its ability to provide consistently accurate future results. Similarly, any indicator that gives only a very few signals over the historical testing period must be used with caution, even if the results look good. The fewer the signals, the higher the probability that the results are due to luck.

Ideally an indicator or model should provide useful information during *any* period of reasonable length, rather than just in certain periods or under specific conditions. However, an indicator that works only under certain circumstances can still be useful, so long as one does not rely on it too much. Measures designed to highlight extremes, for example, such as very high or low price momentum or investor sentiment readings, can be very valuable *when they are flashing a signal*. But during periods when the indicator is not at an extreme and is just sitting in the middle of its typical range, it should be ignored. This is why it's important to create a composite model that aggregates the readings of many different indicators, and why we often allow individual indicators within a model to be neutral or have no influence when they have nothing to say.

Conclusion

Our primary goal in creating a model is to offer investors a testable anchor for measuring risk and reward and making sound asset-allocation decisions. Using objective, quantitative information limits the potential for letting psychological biases (which everyone has) block the correct choices. Subjective opinions and gut feel are often erroneous, inconsistent, and unreliable over time. It's very easy for an individual to get trapped in a subjective market view and stubbornly refuse to do the smart thing. A good model can provide the discipline and confidence needed to navigate the perilous waters of investing.

In summary, the main elements of creating and using a market-timing/asset-allocation model are:

- Gather as much objective, quantitative data as possible.
- Make certain that the information is accurate and can be updated in a relatively timely manner.
- Test individual data series and the various manipulations of the data mentioned above against the market to determine if they have any potential predictive value. Make sure not to over-fit the data to historical prices.
- Select different types of indicators (e.g., trend, monetary, sentiment, etc.) based on their historical reliability and their ability to complement one another.
- Combine the indicators into a model that gives a single composite reading. The indicators can be weighted equally or by their relative importance or historical accuracy.
- Test the resulting model to see if it provides reliable results.
- *Use the model as the basis for disciplined investing.*

CHAPTER 27

What Is Price?

From Dr. Alexander Elder, *The New Trading for a Living* (Hoboken, New Jersey: John Wiley & Sons, 2014), Part 2, Chapter 11.

Traders can be divided into three groups: buyers, sellers, and undecided. Buyers want to pay as little as possible, and sellers want to charge as much as possible. Their permanent conflict is reflected in bid-ask spreads. "Ask" is what a seller asks for his merchandise. "Bid" is what a buyer offers for that merchandise.

A buyer has a choice: to wait until prices come down or pay what the sellers demand. A seller has a similar choice: wait until prices rise or accept a lower offer for his merchandise.

A trade occurs when there is a momentary meeting of two minds: an eager bull agrees to a seller's terms and pays up, or an eager bear agrees to a buyer's terms and sells a little cheaper.

The presence of undecided traders puts pressure on bulls and bears. Buyers and sellers move fast because they know that they're surrounded by a crowd of undecided traders who may step in and snatch away their deal at any moment.

The buyer knows that if he thinks too long, another trader can step in and buy ahead of him. A seller knows that if he tries to hold out for a higher price, another trader may step in and sell at a lower price. The crowd of undecided traders makes buyers and sellers more willing to deal with their opponents. A trade occurs when there is a meeting of two minds.

A Consensus of Value

Each tick on your quote screen represents a deal between a buyer and a seller.

Buyers are buying because they expect prices to rise. Sellers are selling because they expect prices to fall. Buyers and sellers are surrounded by crowds of undecided traders who put pressure on them because they may become buyers or sellers themselves.

Buying by bulls pushes markets up, selling by bears pushes them down, and undecided traders make everything happen faster by creating a sense of urgency among buyers and sellers.

Traders come to the markets from all over the world: in person, via computers, or through their brokers. Everybody has a chance to buy and to sell. *Each price is a momentary consensus of value of all market participants, expressed in action*. Prices are created by masses of traders—buyers, sellers, and undecided people. The patterns of prices and volume reflect mass psychology of the markets.

Behavior Patterns

Huge crowds trade on stock, commodity, and option exchanges. Big money and little money, smart money and dumb money, institutional money and private money, long-term investors and short-term traders, all meet at the exchange. *Each price represents a momentary consensus of value between buyers, sellers, and undecided traders at the moment of transaction. There is a crowd of traders behind every pattern on the screen*.

Crowd consensus changes from moment to moment. Sometimes it gets established in a very low-key environment, and at other times the environment turns wild. Prices move in small increments during quiet times. When a crowd becomes either spooked or elated, prices begin to jump. Imagine bidding for a life preserver aboard a sinking ship—that's how prices leap when masses of traders become emotional about a trend. An astute trader aims to enter the market during quiet times and take profits during wild times. That, of course, is the total opposite of how amateurs act: they jump in or out when prices begin to run, but grow bored and not interested when prices are sleepy.

Chart patterns reflect swings of mass psychology in the financial markets. Each trading session is a battle between bulls, who make money when prices rise, and bears, who profit when they fall. The goal of a serious technical analyst is to discover the balance of power between bulls and bears and bet on the winning group. If bulls are much stronger, you should buy and hold. If bears are much stronger, you should sell and sell short. If both camps are about equal in strength, a wise trader stands aside. He lets bulls and bears fight with each other, and enters a trade only when he is reasonably sure which side is likely to win.

Prices and volume, along with the indicators that track them, reflect crowd behavior. Technical analysis is similar to poll taking. Both combine science and art: They are partly scientific because we use statistical methods and computers; they are partly artistic because we use personal judgment and experience to interpret our findings.

CHAPTER 28

What Is the Market?

From Dr. Alexander Elder, *The New Trading for a Living* (Hoboken, New Jersey: John Wiley & Sons, 2014), Part 2, Chapter 12.

What's the reality behind market quotes, numbers, and graphs? When you check prices in your newspaper, follow ticks on your screen, or plot an indicator on a chart, what exactly are you looking at? What *is* this market that you want to analyze and trade?

Amateurs act as if the market is a giant happening, a ball game in which they can join the professionals and make money. Traders from a scientific or engineering background often treat the market as a physical event and apply the principles of signal processing, noise reduction, etc. By contrast, all professional traders know full well that the market is a huge mass of people.

Every trader tries to take money from others by outguessing them on the probable direction of the market. The members of the market crowd live on different continents, but are brought together by modern telecommunications in the pursuit of profit at each other's expense. *The market is a huge crowd of people. Each member of the crowd tries to take money from others by outsmarting them.* The market is a uniquely harsh environment because everyone is against you, and you are against everyone.

Not only is the market harsh, you have to pay whenever you enter and exit. You have to jump over the barriers of commissions and slippage before you can collect a dime. The moment you place an order, you owe your broker a commission—you're behind the game the moment you enter. Market makers try to hit you with slippage when your order arrives for execution. They try to take another bite out of your account when you exit. *In trading, you compete against some of the brightest minds in the world, while fending off the piranhas of commissions and slippage.*

Worldwide Crowds

In the old days, markets were small, and many participants knew one another. The New York Stock Exchange was formed in 1792 as a club of two dozen brokers. On sunny days, they used to gather under a cottonwood tree, and on rainy days, they moved to

Fraunces Tavern. As soon as those brokers organized the New York Stock Exchange, they stuck the public with fixed commissions, which lasted for the next 180 years.

These days, the few remaining floor traders are on the way out. Most of us are linked to the market electronically. Still, as we watch the same quotes on our screens and read the same articles in the financial media, we become members of the market crowd—even if we live thousands of miles away from one another. Thanks to modern telecommunications, the world is becoming smaller, while the markets are growing. The euphoria of London flows to New York, and the gloom of Tokyo infects Frankfurt.

When you analyze the market, you are looking at crowd behavior. Crowds behave alike in different cultures on different continents. Social psychologists have uncovered several laws that govern crowd behavior, and a trader needs to understand them in order to see how the market crowd influences him.

Groups, Not Individuals

Most people feel a strong urge to join the crowd and "act like everybody else." This primitive urge clouds your judgment when you put on a trade. A successful trader must think independently. He needs to be strong enough to analyze the market alone and carry out his trading decisions.

Crowds are powerful enough to create trends. The crowd may not be too bright, but it is stronger than any of us. Never buck a trend. If a trend is up, you should only buy or stand aside. Never sell short just because "the prices are too high"—never argue with the crowd. You do not have to run with the crowd—but you shouldn't run against it.

Respect the strength of the crowd—but don't fear it. Crowds are powerful, but primitive, their behavior simple and repetitive. A trader who thinks for himself can take money from crowd members.

The Source of Money

Do you ever stop to wonder where your expected profits will come from? Is there money in the markets because of higher company earnings, or lower interest rates, or a good soybean crop? *The only reason there is money in the markets is that other traders put it there. The money you want to make belongs to other people who have no intention of giving it to you.*

Trading means trying to take money from other people, while they are trying to take yours—that's why it is such a hard business. Winning is especially difficult because brokers and floor traders take money from winners and losers alike.

Tim Slater compared trading to a medieval battle. A man used to go on a battlefield with his sword and try to kill his opponent, who was trying to kill him. The winner took the loser's weapons, his chattels, and his wife, and sold his children into slavery. Now we go to the exchanges instead of an open field. When you take money away from a man, it is not that different from drawing his blood. He may lose his house and his chattels, and his wife and his children will suffer.

An optimistic friend of mine once snickered that there are plenty of poorly prepared people on the battlefield: "Ninety to ninety-five percent of the brokers don't know the first thing about research. They don't know what they're doing. We have the knowledge, and some poor people who do not have it are just giving their money away to charity." This theory sounds good, but he soon found out that it was wrong—there is no easy money in the market.

Sure enough, there are plenty of dumb sheep waiting to be fleeced or slaughtered. The sheep are easy—but if you want a piece of their meat, you've got to fight some very dangerous competitors. There are mean professionals: American gunslingers, English knights, German landsknechts, Japanese samurai, and other warriors, all going after the same hapless sheep. Trading means battling crowds of hostile people, while paying for the privilege of entering the battle and leaving it, whether alive, wounded, or dead.

Inside Information

There is at least one group of people who get information before us. Records show that corporate insiders as a group consistently make profits in the stock market. And those are legitimate trades, reported by insiders to the Securities and Exchange Commission. They represent the tip of the iceberg—but there is a great deal of illegitimate insider trading.

People who trade on inside information are stealing our money. The insider trials have landed some of the more notorious insiders in prison. Convictions for insider trading continue at a steady pace, especially after bull markets collapse. After the 2008 debacle, a group of executives from the Galleon fund, led by its CEO, have been sentenced to lengthy jail terms, while a former board member of several leading U.S. corporations got two years behind bars, and recently a money manager from SAC Capital was convicted.

People convicted during the insider trials were caught because they became greedy and careless. The tip of the iceberg has been shaved down, but its bulk continues to float, ready to hit any account that comes in contact with it.

Trying to reduce insider trading is like trying to get rid of rats on a farm. Pesticides keep them under control, but do not root them out. A retired chief executive of a publicly traded firm explained to me that a smart man does not trade on inside information but gives it to his golfing buddies at a country club. Later they give him inside information on their companies, and both profit without being detected. The insider network is safe as long as its members follow the same code of conduct and don't get too greedy. Insider trading is legal in the futures markets, and until recently it was legal for congressmen, senators, and their staff.

Charts reflect all trades by all market participants—including insiders. They leave their footprints on the charts just like everyone else—and it is our job as technical analysts to follow them to the bank. Technical analysis can help you detect insider buying and selling.

CHAPTER 29

The Trading Scene

From Dr. Alexander Elder, *The New Trading for a Living* (Hoboken, New Jersey: John Wiley & Sons, 2014), Part 2, Chapter 13.

Humans have traded since the dawn of history—it was safer to trade with your neighbors than raid them. As society developed, money became the medium of exchange. Stock and commodity markets are among the hallmarks of an advanced society. One of the key economic developments in Eastern Europe following the collapse of communism was the establishment of stock and commodity exchanges.

Today, stock, futures, and options markets span the globe. It took Marco Polo, a medieval Italian merchant, 15 years to get from Italy to China and back. Now, when a European trader wants to buy gold in Hong Kong, he can get his order filled in seconds. There are hundreds of stock and futures exchanges around the world. All exchanges must meet three criteria, first developed in the agoras of ancient Greece and the medieval fairs of Western Europe: an established location, rules for grading merchandise, and defined contract terms.

Individual Traders

Private traders usually come to the market after a successful career in business or in the professions. An average private futures trader in the United States is a 50-year-old, married, college-educated man. The two largest occupational groups among futures traders are farmers and engineers.

Most people trade for partly rational and partly irrational reasons. Rational reasons include the desire to earn a large return on capital. Irrational reasons include gambling and a search for excitement. Most traders are not aware of their irrational motives.

Learning to trade takes time, money, and work. Few individuals rise to the level of professionals who can support themselves by trading. Professionals are extremely serious about what they do. They satisfy their irrational goals outside the markets, while amateurs act them out in the marketplace.

The major economic role of a trader is to support his broker—to help him pay his mortgage bills and keep his children in private schools. In addition, the role of a speculator is to help companies raise capital in the stock market and to assume price risk in the commodities markets, allowing producers to focus on production. These lofty economic goals are far from a speculator's mind when he places his orders to buy or sell.

Institutional Traders

Institutions are responsible for a huge volume of trading, and their deep pockets give them several advantages. They pay low institutional commissions. They can afford to hire the best researchers and traders. A friend of mine who headed a trading desk at a bank based some of his decisions on a service provided by a group of former CIA officers. He got some of his best ideas from their reports, while the substantial annual fee was small potatoes for his firm compared to its huge trading volume. Most private traders do not have such opportunities.

Some large firms have intelligence networks that enable them to act before the public. One day, when oil futures rallied in response to a fire on a platform in the North Sea, I called a friend at an oil firm. The market was frantic, but he was happy, having bought oil futures half an hour before they exploded. He got a telex from an agent in the area of the fire before the reports appeared on the newswire. Timely information is priceless, but only a large company can afford an intelligence network.

An acquaintance who traded successfully for a Wall Street investment bank felt lost when he quit to trade for himself. He discovered that a real-time quote system in his Park Avenue apartment didn't give him news as fast as the squawk box on the trading floor of his old firm. Brokers from around the country used to call him with the latest ideas because they wanted his orders. "When you trade from your house, you are never the first to hear the news," he says.

The firms that deal in both futures and cash markets have two advantages. They have true inside information, and they are exempt from speculative position limits that exist in many futures markets. I went to visit an acquaintance at a multinational oil company; after passing through security barriers tighter than at an airport, I walked down a glass corridor that overlooked rooms where clusters of men huddled around monitors trading oil products. When I asked my host whether his traders were hedging or speculating, he looked me straight in the eye and said, "Yes." I asked again and received the same answer. Companies crisscross the thin line between hedging and speculating, using inside information.

In addition to the informational advantage, employees of trading firms have a psychological one—they can be more relaxed because their own money isn't at risk. When young people tell me of their interest in trading, I tell them to get a job with a trading firm and learn on someone else's dime. Firms almost never hire traders past their mid-twenties.

How can an individual coming later to the game compete against institutions and win?

The Achilles heel of most institutions is that they *have* to trade, while an individual trader is free to trade or stay out of the market when he wants. Banks have to be active in the bond market and grain producers have to be active in the grain market at almost any price. An individual trader is free to wait for the best opportunities.

Most private traders fritter away this fantastic advantage by overtrading. An individual who wants to succeed against the giants must develop patience and eliminate greed. *Remember, your goal is to trade well, not to trade often.*

Successful institutional traders receive raises and bonuses. Even a high bonus can feel puny to someone who earns millions of dollars for his firm. Successful institutional traders often talk of quitting and going to trade for themselves. Very few of them manage to make this transition.

Most traders who leave institutions get caught up in the emotions of fear, greed, elation, and panic when they start risking their own money. They seldom do well trading for their own accounts—another sign that psychology is at the root of trading success or failure. Few institutional traders realize to what a large extent they owe their success to their trading managers, who control their risk levels. Going out on your own means becoming your own manager—we'll return to this in a later chapter, when we focus on how to organize your trading.

The Sword Makers

Just as medieval knights shopped for the sharpest swords, modern traders shop for the best trading tools. The growing access to good software and declining commission rates are creating a more level playing field. A computer allows you to speed up your research and follow more leads. It helps you analyze more markets in greater depth. We'll return to computers and software in "Computers in Trading," but here it is in brief.

There are three types of trading software: toolboxes, black boxes, and gray boxes. A **toolbox** allows you to display data, draw charts, plot indicators, change their parameters, and test your trading systems. Toolboxes for options traders include option valuation models. Adapting a good toolbox to your needs can be as easy as adjusting the seat of your car.

In 1977, I bought the first ever toolbox for computerized technical analysis. It cost $1,900 plus monthly data fees. Today, inexpensive, and even free, software places powerful tools at everyone's fingertips. I illustrated most of the concepts in this book using Stockcharts.com because I wanted my new book to be useful to as many traders as possible.

Stockcharts.com evens out the playing field for traders. It is clear, intuitive, and rich in features. Its basic version is free, although I used its inexpensive "members' version" for higher quality charting. I still remember how hard it was in the beginning and want to show you how much analytic power you can have for free or at a very minimal cost.

What goes on inside a **black box** is secret. You feed it data, and it tells you what and when to buy and sell. It is like magic—a way to make money without thinking. Black boxes are usually sold with excellent historical track records. This is only natural because they were created to fit old data. Markets keep changing, and black boxes keep blowing up, but new generations of losers keep buying them. If you're in the market for a black box, remember that there is a guy in Brooklyn who has a bridge for sale.

Gray boxes straddle the fence between toolboxes and black boxes. These packages are usually put out by prominent market personalities. They disclose the general logic of their system and allow you to adjust some of their parameters.

Advisors

Some newsletters provide useful ideas and point readers in the direction of trading opportunities. A few offer educational value. Most sell an illusion of being an insider. Newsletters are good entertainment. Your subscription rents you a pen pal who sends often amusing and interesting letters and never asks you to write back, except for a check at renewal time. Freedom of the press in the United States allows even a convicted felon to go online and start sending out a financial advisory letter. Quite a few of them do.

The "track records" of various newsletters are largely an exercise in futility because hardly anybody takes every trade suggested by a newsletter. Services that rate newsletters are for-profit affairs run by small businessmen whose well-being depends on the well-being of the advisory industry. Rating services may occasionally tut-tut an advisor, but they dedicate most of their energy to loud cheerleading.

I used to write an advisory newsletter decades ago: worked hard, delivered straight talk, and received good ratings. I saw from the inside a tremendous potential for fudging results. This is a well-kept secret of the advisory industry.

After looking at my letters, a prominent advisor told me that I should spend less time on research and more on marketing. The first principle of letter writing is: "If you have to make forecasts, make a lot of them." Whenever a forecast turns out right, double the volume of promotional mail.

CHAPTER 30

The Market Crowd and You

From Dr. Alexander Elder, *The New Trading for a Living* (Hoboken, New Jersey: John Wiley & Sons, 2014), Part 2, Chapter 14.

Markets are loosely organized crowds whose members bet that prices will rise or fall. Since each price represents crowd consensus at the moment of transaction, traders are betting on the future opinion and mood of the crowd. The crowd keeps swinging from hope to fear and from indifference to optimism or pessimism. Most people don't follow their own trading plans because they get swept up in the crowd's feelings and actions.

As bulls and bears battle in the market, the value of your open positions soars or sinks, depending on the actions of total strangers. You can't control the markets. You can only set your position size and decide whether and when to enter or exit your trades.

Most traders feel jittery entering a trade. Their judgment becomes clouded after they join the crowd. Caught up in crowd emotions, many traders deviate from their plans and lose money.

Experts on Crowds

Charles Mackay, a Scottish barrister, wrote his classic book, *Extraordinary Popular Delusions and the Madness of Crowds,* in 1841. He described several mass manias, including the Tulip Mania in Holland in 1634 and the South Seas investment bubble in England in 1720.

The tulip craze began as a bull market in tulip bulbs. The long bull market convinced the prosperous Dutch that tulips would continue to appreciate. Many abandoned their businesses to grow tulips, trade them, or become tulip brokers. Banks accepted tulips as collateral and speculators profited. Finally, that mania collapsed in waves of panic selling, leaving people destitute and the nation shocked. Mackay sighed, "Men go mad in crowds, and they come back to their senses slowly and one by one."

In 1897, Gustave LeBon, a French philosopher and politician, wrote *The Crowd.* A trader who reads it today can see his reflection in a century-old mirror.

LeBon wrote that when people gather in a crowd, "Whoever be the individuals that compose it, however like or unlike be their mode of life, their occupations, their character, or their intelligence, the fact that they have been transformed into a crowd puts them in possession of a sort of collective mind which makes them feel, think, and act in a manner quite different from that in which each individual of them would feel, think, and act were he in a state of isolation."

People change when they join crowds. They become more credulous and impulsive, anxiously search for a leader, and react to emotions instead of using their intellect. An individual who becomes involved in a group becomes less capable of thinking for himself.

Group members may catch a few trends, but they get killed when trends reverse. Successful traders are independent thinkers.

Why Join?

People have been joining crowds for safety since the dawn of time. If a Stone Age hunter encountered a saber-toothed tiger, he had a very slim chance of coming out alive, but if hunters went as a group, most were likely to survive. Loners got killed and left fewer offspring. Since group members were more likely to survive, the tendency to join groups appears to have been bred into our genes.

Our society glorifies free will, but we carry many primitive impulses beneath the thin veneer of civilization. We want to join groups for safety and be led by strong leaders. The greater the uncertainty, the stronger our wish to join and to follow.

No saber-toothed tigers roam the canyons of Wall Street, but your financial survival is at risk. The value of your position rises and falls because of buying and selling by total strangers. Your fear swells up because you can't control prices. This uncertainty makes most traders look for a leader who will tell them what to do.

You may have rationally decided to go long or short, but the moment you put on a trade, the crowd starts sucking you in. You start losing your independence when you watch prices like a hawk and become elated when they go your way or depressed if they go against you. You are in trouble when you impulsively add to losing positions or reverse them. You lose your independence when you start trusting gurus more than yourself and don't follow your own trading plan. When you notice this happening, try to come back to your senses. If you can't regain your composure, exit your trades and go flat.

Crowd Mentality

When people join crowds, their thinking becomes primitive and they become more prone to act on impulse. Crowds swing from fear to glee, from panic to euphoria. A scientist can be cool and rational in his lab but make harebrained trades after being swept up in the mass hysteria of the market. A group can suck you in, whether you trade from a crowded brokerage office or a remote mountaintop. When you let others influence your trading decisions, your chance of success goes up in smoke.

Group loyalty was essential for a prehistoric hunter's survival. Joining a union can help even an incompetent performer keep his job. The market is different: joining a group tends to hurt you.

Many traders are puzzled why markets reverse immediately after they dump their losing position. This happens because crowd members are gripped by the same fear—and everybody dumps at the same time. Once the selling fit has ended, the market has nowhere to go but up. Optimism returns to the marketplace, and the crowd forgets fear, grows greedy, and goes on a new buying binge.

The crowd is bigger and stronger than you. No matter how smart you are, you cannot argue with the crowd. You have only one choice—to join the crowd or to act independently.

Crowds are primitive, and your trading strategies should be simple. You don't have to be a rocket scientist to design a winning trading method. If the trade goes against you—cut your losses and run. Never argue with the crowd—simply use your judgment to decide when to join and when to leave.

Your human nature leads you to give up your independence under stress. When you put on a trade, you feel the desire to imitate others, overlooking objective signals. This is why you need to write down and follow your trading system and money management rules. They represent your rational individual decisions, made before you entered a trade.

Who Leads?

An inexperienced trader may feel intense joy when prices move in his favor. He may feel angry, depressed, and fearful when prices move against him, anxiously waiting to see what the market will do to him next. Traders become crowd members when they feel stressed or threatened. Battered by emotions, they lose their independence and begin imitating other group members, especially the group leader.

When children feel frightened, they want their parents and other grown-ups to tell them what to do. They transfer that attitude to teachers, doctors, ministers, bosses, and assorted experts. Traders turn to gurus, trading system vendors, newspaper columnists, and other market leaders. But, as Tony Plummer brilliantly pointed out in his book, *Forecasting Financial Markets,* the main leader of the market is price.

Price is the leader of the market crowd. Traders all over the world follow the upticks and downticks. Price seems to say to traders, "Follow me, and I'll show you the way to riches." Most traders consider themselves independent. Few of us realize how strongly we focus on the behavior of our group leader.

A trend that flows in your favor symbolizes a strong and generous parent calling you to share a meal. A trend that goes against you feels like dealing with an angry and punishing parent. Being gripped by such feelings, it's easy to overlook objective signals that tell you to stay or to exit a trade. You may feel happy or frightened, bargain or beg forgiveness—while avoiding the rational act of accepting reality and getting out of a losing trade.

Independence

You need to base your trades on a carefully prepared plan instead of jumping in response to price changes. A proper plan is a written one. You need to know exactly under what conditions you will enter and exit a trade. Don't make decisions on the spur of the moment, when you are vulnerable to being sucked in by the crowd.

You can succeed as a trader only when you think and act as an individual. The weakest part of any trading system is the trader himself. Traders fail when they trade without a plan or deviate from their plans. Plans are created by reasoning individuals. Impulsive trades are made by sweaty group members.

You have to observe yourself and notice changes in your mental state as you trade. Write down your reasons for entering a trade and the rules for getting out of it, including money management rules. You may not change your plan while you have an open position.

Sirens were sea creatures of Greek myths who sang so beautifully that sailors jumped overboard and swam to them, only to be killed. When Odysseus wanted to hear the Sirens' songs, he ordered his men to seal their ears with beeswax but to tie him to the mast. Odysseus heard the Sirens' song but survived because he couldn't jump overboard. You ensure your survival as a trader when on a clear day you tie yourself to the mast of a trading plan and money management rules.

A Positive Group

You don't have to be a hermit—steering clear of the crowd's impulsivity doesn't mean you have to trade in total solitude. While some of us prefer doing it that way, intelligent and productive groups can exist. Their key feature has to be independent decision making.

This concept is clearly explained in a book, *The Wisdom of Crowds,* by a financial journalist James Surowiecki. He acknowledges that members of most groups constantly influence one another, creating waves of shared feelings and actions. A smart group is different: all members make independent decisions without knowing what others are doing. Instead of impacting each other and creating emotional waves, members of an intelligent group benefit from combining their knowledge and expertise. The function of a group leader is to maintain this structure and to bring individual decisions up for a vote.

In 2004, a year prior to reading *The Wisdom of Crowds,* I organized a group of traders along those lines. I continue to manage it with my friend Kerry Lovvorn—the SpikeTrade group.

We run a trading competition, with each round lasting one week. After the market closes on Friday, the stock picks section of the website becomes closed to viewing by members until 3 p.m. on Sunday. During that time, any group member may submit one favorite pick for the week ahead—without knowing what other group members are doing. The picks section of the website re-opens on Sunday afternoon, allowing all members to see all picks. The race begins on Monday and ends on Friday, with prizes to winners.

Throughout the week members exchange comments and answer questions. The site is built to encourage communication—except for weekends, when everyone must work independently. The results of leading group members, posted on the site, have been spectacular.

The key point is that all decisions about stock selection and direction must be made in solitude, without seeing what the leaders or other members are doing. The sharing begins after all votes are in. This combination of independent decision making with sharing brings forth "the wisdom of crowds," tapping the collective wisdom of the group and its leaders.

CHAPTER 31

Psychology of Trends

From Dr. Alexander Elder, *The New Trading for a Living* (Hoboken, New Jersey: John Wiley & Sons, 2014), Part 2, Chapter 15.

Each price represents a momentary consensus of value among market participants. Each tick reflects the latest vote on the value of a trading vehicle. Any trader can "put in his two cents worth" by giving an order to buy or sell, or by refusing to trade at the current level.

Each price bar or candle reflects a battle between bulls and bears. When buyers feel strongly bullish, they buy more eagerly and push markets up. When sellers feel strongly bearish, they sell more actively and push markets down.

Charts are a window into mass psychology. When you analyze charts, you analyze the behavior of trading masses. Technical indicators help make this analysis more objective.

Technical analysis is for-profit social psychology.

Strong Feelings

Ask a trader why prices went up, and you'll probably get a stock answer—more buyers than sellers. This isn't true. The number of shares or futures contracts bought and sold in any market is always equal.

If you want to buy 100 shares of Google, someone has to sell them to you. If you want to sell 200 shares of Amazon, someone has to buy them from you. This is why the number of shares bought and sold is equal in the stock market. Furthermore, the number of long and short positions in the futures markets is always equal. Prices move up or down not because of different numbers but because of changes in the intensity of greed and fear among buyers and sellers.

When the trend is up, bulls feel optimistic and don't mind paying up. They buy high because they expect prices to rise even higher. Bears feel afraid in an uptrend, and they agree to sell only at a higher price. When greedy and optimistic bulls meet fearful and defensive bears, the market rallies. The stronger their feelings, the sharper the rally. The rally ends only when bulls start losing their enthusiasm.

When prices slide, bears feel optimistic and don't quibble about selling short at lower prices. Bulls are fearful and agree to buy only at a discount. While bears feel like winners, they continue to sell at lower prices, and the downtrend continues. It ends when bears start feeling cautious and refuse to sell at lower prices.

Rallies and Declines

Few traders are purely rational human beings. There is a great deal of emotion in the markets. Most participants act on the principle of "monkey see, monkey do." The waves of fear and greed sweep up bulls and bears.

The sharpness of any rally depends on how traders feel. If buyers feel just a little stronger than sellers, the market rises slowly. When they feel much stronger than sellers, the market rises fast. It is the job of a technical analyst to find when buyers are strong and when they start running out of steam.

Short sellers feel trapped by rising markets, as their profits melt and turn into losses. When short sellers rush to cover, a rally can become parabolic. Fear is a much stronger emotion than greed.[1] Rallies driven by short covering are especially sharp, although they do not last very long.

Markets fall because of fear among bulls and greed among bears. Normally bears prefer to sell short on rallies, but if they expect to make a lot of money on a decline, they don't mind shorting on the way down. Fearful buyers agree to buy only below the market. As long as short sellers are willing to meet those demands and sell at a bid, the decline will continue.

As bulls' profits melt and turn into losses, they panic and sell at almost any price. They are so eager to get out that they hit the bids under the market. Markets can drop fast when hit by panic selling.

Price Shocks

Loyalty to the leader is the glue that holds groups together. Group members expect leaders to inspire and reward them when they are good but punish them when they are bad. Some leaders are very authoritarian, others quite democratic and informal, but every group has a leader—a leaderless group can't exist. Price functions as the leader of the market crowd.

Winners feel rewarded when price moves in their favor, and losers feel punished when it moves against them. Crowd members remain blissfully unaware that by focusing on price they create their own leader. Traders who feel mesmerized by prices create their own idols.

When the trend is up, bulls feel rewarded by a bountiful parent. The longer an uptrend lasts, the more confident they feel. When a child's behavior is rewarded, he continues to do what he did. When bulls make money, they add to long positions.

[1] Fear is three times stronger than greed, according to research cited by Prof. Daniel Kahneman, a Nobel Prize winning behavioral economist, whose findings we'll return to again in this book.

While new bulls enter the market, bears feel they are being punished for selling short. Many of them cover shorts, go long, and join the bulls.

Buying by happy bulls and covering by fearful bears pushes uptrends higher. Buyers feel rewarded, while sellers feel punished. Both feel emotionally involved, but few traders realize that they are creating the uptrend and setting up their own leader.

Eventually a price shock occurs—a major sale hits the market, and there aren't enough buyers to absorb it. The uptrend takes a dive. Bulls feel mistreated, like children whose father slapped them during a meal, but bears feel encouraged.

A price shock plants the seeds of an uptrend's reversal. Even if the market recovers and reaches a new high, bulls feel more skittish and bears become bolder. This lack of cohesion in the dominant group and growing optimism among its opponents makes the uptrend ready to reverse. Several technical indicators identify tops by tracing a pattern called bearish divergence. It occurs when prices reach a new high but the indicator reaches a lower high than it did on the previous rally. Bearish divergences mark the ends of uptrends and some of the best shorting opportunities.

When the trend is down, bears feel like good children, praised and rewarded for being smart. They feel increasingly confident, add to short positions, and the downtrend continues. New bears come into the market. People admire winners, and the financial media keeps interviewing bears during bear markets.

Bulls lose money in downtrends, making them feel bad. They start dumping their positions, and some of them switch sides to join bears. Their selling pushes markets lower.

After a while, bears grow confident and bulls feel demoralized. Suddenly, a price shock occurs. A cluster of buy orders soaks up all available sell orders and lifts the market. Now bears feel like children whose father has lashed out at them in the midst of a happy meal.

A price shock plants the seeds of a downtrend's eventual reversal because bears become more fearful and bulls grow bolder. When a child begins to doubt that Santa Claus exists, he'll seldom believe in Santa again. Even if bears recover and prices fall to a new low, several technical indicators will help identify their weakness by tracing a pattern called a bullish divergence. It occurs when prices fall to a new low but an indicator traces a shallower bottom than during the previous decline. Bullish divergences identify some of the best buying opportunities.

Social Psychology

Free will makes individual behavior hard to predict. Group behavior is more primitive and easier to track. When you analyze markets, you analyze group behavior. You need to identify the direction in which groups are running and their changes of speed.

Groups suck us in and cloud our judgment. The problem for most analysts is that they get caught in the emotional pull of the groups they try to analyze.

The longer a rally continues, the more analysts get caught up in mass bullishness, ignore danger signs, and miss the eventual reversal. The longer a decline goes on, the more analysts get caught up in bearish gloom and ignore bullish signs. This is why it helps to have a written plan for analyzing markets. We have to decide in advance what indicators we will watch, how we will interpret them, and how we'll act.

Professionals use several tools for tracking the intensity of the crowd's feelings. They watch the crowd's ability to break through recent support and resistance levels. Floor traders used to listen to the changes in pitch and volume of the roar on the exchange floor. With floor trading rapidly receding into history, you'll need special tools for analyzing crowd behavior. Fortunately, your charts and indicators reflect mass psychology in action. *A technical analyst is an applied social psychologist, usually armed with a computer.*

For more information regarding Dr. Alexander Elder's work, please visit www.elder.com.

CHAPTER 32

Managing versus Forecasting

From Dr. Alexander Elder, *The New Trading for a Living* (Hoboken, New Jersey: John Wiley & Sons, 2014), Part 2, Chapter 16.

I once ran into a very fat surgeon at a seminar. He told me that he had lost a quarter of a million dollars in three years trading stocks and options. When I asked him how he made his trading decisions, he sheepishly pointed to his ample gut. He gambled on hunches and used his professional income to support his habit. There are two alternatives to "gut feel": One is fundamental analysis; the other is technical analysis.

Fundamental analysts study the actions of the Federal Reserve, follow earnings reports, examine crop reports, and so on. Major bull and bear markets reflect fundamental changes in supply and demand. Still, even if you know those factors, you can lose money trading if you are out of touch with intermediate- and short-term trends, which depend on the crowd's emotions.

Technical analysts believe that prices reflect everything known about the market, including fundamental factors. Each price represents the consensus of value of all market participants—large commercial interests and small speculators, fundamental researchers and technicians, insiders and gamblers.

Technical analysis is a study of mass psychology. It is partly a science and partly an art. Technicians use many scientific methods, including mathematical concepts of game theory, probabilities, and so on. They use computers to track indicators.

Technical analysis is also an art. The bars or candles on our charts coalesce into patterns and formations. The movement of prices and indicators produces a sense of flow and rhythm, a feeling of tension and beauty that helps us sense what is happening and how to trade.

Individual behavior is complex, diverse, and difficult to predict. Group behavior is primitive. Technicians study the behavior patterns of market crowds. They trade when they recognize patterns that preceded previous market moves.

Poll-Taking

Politicians want to know their chances of being elected or re-elected. They make promises to voters and have poll-takers measure a crowd's response. Technical analysis is similar to political poll-taking, as both aim to read the intentions of masses. Poll-takers do it to help their clients win elections, while technicians do it for financial gain.

Poll-takers use scientific methods: statistics, sampling procedures, and so on. They also need a flair for interviewing and phrasing questions; they have to be plugged into the emotional undercurrents of their party. Poll-taking is a combination of science and art. If a poll-taker says he is a scientist, ask him why every major political poll-taker in the United States is affiliated with either the Democratic or Republican party. True science knows no party.

A market technician must rise above party affiliation. Be neither a bull nor a bear, but only seek the truth. A biased bull looks at a chart and says, "Where can I buy?" A biased bear looks at the same chart and tries to find where he can go short. A topflight analyst is free of bullish or bearish biases.

There is a trick to help you detect your bias. If you want to buy, turn your chart upside down and see whether it looks like a sell. If it still looks like a buy after you flip it, then you have to work on getting a bullish bias out of your system. If both charts look like a sell, then you have to work on purging a bearish bias.

A Crystal Ball

Many traders believe that their aim is to forecast future prices. The amateurs in most fields ask for forecasts, while professionals simply manage information and make decisions based on probabilities. Take medicine, for example. A patient is brought to an emergency room with a knife wound—and the anxious family members have only two questions: "will he survive?" and "when can he go home?" They ask the doctor for a forecast.

But the doctor isn't forecasting—he is managing problems as they emerge. His first job is to prevent the patient from dying from shock, and so he gives him painkillers and starts an intravenous drip to replace lost blood. Then he sutures damaged organs. After that, he has to watch against infection. He monitors the trend of the patient's health and takes measures to prevent complications. He is managing— not forecasting. When a family begs for a forecast, he may give it to them, but its practical value is low.

To make money trading, you don't need to forecast the future. You have to extract information from the market and find out whether bulls or bears are in control. You need to measure the strength of the dominant market group and decide how likely the current trend is to continue. You need to practice conservative money management aimed at long-term survival and profit accumulation. You must observe how your mind works and avoid slipping into greed or fear. A trader who does all of this will succeed ahead of any forecaster.

Read the Market, Manage Yourself

A tremendous volume of information pours out of the markets during trading hours. Changing prices reflect the battles of bulls and bears. Your job is to analyze this information and bet on the dominant market group.

Whenever I hear a dramatic forecast, my first thought is "a marketing gimmick." Advisors issue them to attract attention in order to raise money or sell services. Good calls attract paying customers, while bad calls are quickly forgotten. My phone rang while I was writing the first draft of this chapter. A famous guru, down on his luck, told me that he had identified a "once-in-a-lifetime buying opportunity" in corn. He asked me to raise money for him and promised to multiply it a hundredfold in six months! I do not know how many fools he hooked, but dramatic forecasts have always been good for fleecing the public. Most people do not change. While working on this update 21 years later, I read in *The Wall Street Journal* that this same "guru" was recently punished for professional misconduct by the National Futures Association.

Use common sense in analyzing markets. When some new development puzzles you, compare it to life outside the markets. For example, indicators may give you buy signals in two markets. Should you buy the one that declined a lot before the buy signal or the one that declined a little? Compare this to what happens to a man after a fall. If he falls down a few steps, he may dust himself off and run up again. But if he falls out of a second-story window, he's not going to run anytime soon; he needs time to recover.

Successful trading stands on three pillars. You need to analyze the balance of power between bulls and bears. You need to practice good money management. You need personal discipline to follow your trading plan and avoid getting high or depressed in the markets.

CHAPTER 33

Charting

From Dr. Alexander Elder, *The New Trading for a Living* (Hoboken, New Jersey: John Wiley & Sons, 2014), Part 3, Chapter 17.

Chartists study market data to identify price patterns and profit from them. Most chartists work with bar or candlestick graphs that show open, high, low, and closing prices and volume. Futures traders also watch open interest. Point-and-figure chartists track only price changes and ignore time, volume, and open interest.

Classical charting requires only a pencil and paper. It appeals to visually oriented people. Those who plot data by hand can develop a physical feel for prices. One of the costs of switching to computerized charting is losing some of that feel.

The biggest problem with classical charting is wishful thinking. Traders seem to identify bullish or bearish patterns, depending on whether they're in a mood to buy or sell.

Early in the twentieth century, Herman Rorschach, a Swiss psychiatrist, designed a test for exploring a person's mind. He dropped ink on 10 sheets of paper and folded each in half, creating symmetrical inkblots. Most people who peer at these sheets describe what they see: parts of the anatomy, animals, buildings, and so on. In reality, there are only inkblots! Each person sees what's on his mind. Most traders use charts as a giant Rorschach test. They project their hopes, fears, and fantasies onto the charts.

Brief History

The first chartists in the United States appeared at the turn of the twentieth century. They included Charles Dow (1851–1902), the author of a famous stock market theory, and William Hamilton, who succeeded Dow as the editor of *The Wall Street Journal*. Dow's famous maxim was "The averages discount everything," by which he meant that the Industrial and Rail Averages reflected all knowledge about the economy.

Dow never wrote a book, only his *Wall Street Journal* editorials. Hamilton took over the job after Dow died and laid out the principles of Dow theory in his book, *The Stock Market Barometer*. He wrote a famous "The Turn of the Tide" editorial following the 1929 crash. Robert Rhea, a newsletter publisher, brought the theory to its pinnacle in his 1932 book, *The Dow Theory.*

The decade of the 1930s was the Golden Age of charting. Many innovators found themselves with time on their hands after the crash of 1929. Schabacker, Rhea, Elliott, Wyckoff, Gann, and others published their books during that decade. They went in two distinct directions. Some, such as Wyckoff and Schabacker, saw charts as a graphic record of supply and demand. Others, such as Elliott and Gann, searched for a perfect order in the markets—a fascinating but ultimately futile undertaking.

In 1948, Edwards (a son-in-law of Schabacker) and Magee published *Technical Analysis of Stock Trends,* in which they popularized such concepts as triangles, rectangles, head-and-shoulders, and other chart formations, as well as support, resistance, and trendlines. Other chartists applied these concepts to commodities.

Markets have changed a great deal since the days of Edwards and Magee. In the 1940s, the daily volume of an active stock on the New York Stock Exchange was only several hundred shares, while now it is measured in millions. The balance of power in the stock market has shifted in favor of bulls. Early chartists wrote that stock market tops were sharp and fast, while bottoms took a long time to develop. That was true in their deflationary era, but the opposite has been true since the 1950s. Now bottoms tend to form quickly, while tops tend to take longer.

The Meaning of a Bar Chart

Chart patterns reflect the sum of buying and selling, greed and fear among investors and traders. Many charts in this book are daily, with each bar representing one trading day, but the rules for understanding weekly, daily, or intraday charts are remarkably similar.

Remember this key principle: "*Each price is a momentary consensus of value of all market participants expressed in action.*" Based on it, each price bar provides several important pieces of information about the tug-of-war between bulls and bears (Figure 33.1).

The **opening price** of a daily bar tends to reflect the amateurs' opinion of value. They read morning papers, find out what happened the day before, perhaps ask for a wife's approval to buy or sell, and place their orders before driving to work. Amateurs are especially active early in the day and early in the week.

Traders who researched the relationship between opening and closing prices found that opening prices most often occur near the high or the low of the daily bar. Buying or selling by amateurs early in the day creates an emotional extreme from which prices tend to recoil later in the day.

In bull markets, prices often make their low for the week on Monday or Tuesday, when amateurs take profits from the previous week, then rally to a new high on Thursday or Friday. In bear markets, the high for the week is often set on Monday or Tuesday, with a new low toward the end of the week.

The **closing prices** of daily and weekly bars tend to reflect the actions of professional traders. They watch the markets throughout the day, respond to changes, and tend to dominate the last hour of trading. Many of them take profits at that time to avoid carrying trades overnight.

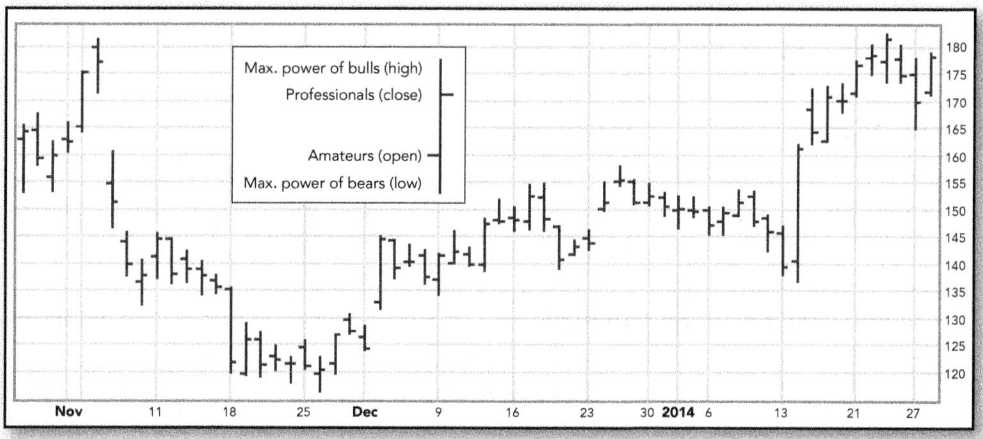

FIGURE 33.1 TSLA Daily. *(Chart by Stockcharts.com)*

The Meaning of a Bar Chart

Opening prices are set by amateurs, whose orders accumulate overnight and hit the market in the morning. Closing prices are largely set by market professionals who trade throughout the day. You can see a reflection of their conflict in how often opening and closing prices occur at the opposite ends of price bars.

The high of each bar marks the maximum power of bulls during that bar. The low of each bar marks the maximum power of bears during that bar. Slippage tends to be less when you enter or exit positions during short bars.

Professionals as a group usually trade against the amateurs. They tend to buy lower openings, sell short higher openings, and unwind their positions as the day goes on. Traders need to pay attention to the relationship between opening and closing prices. *If prices closed higher than they opened, then market professionals were probably more bullish than amateurs. If prices closed lower than they opened, then market professionals were probably more bearish than amateurs.* It pays to trade with the professionals and against the amateurs. Candlestick charting is based, to a large extent, on the relationship between the opening and closing prices of each bar. If the close is higher, the candle is white, but if it is lower, the candle is black.

The **high of each bar** represents the maximum power of bulls during that bar. Bulls make money when prices go up. Their buying pushes prices higher, and every uptick adds to their profits. Finally, bulls reach a point where they cannot lift prices—not even by one more tick.[1] The high of a daily bar represents the maximum power of bulls during the day, while the high of a weekly bar marks the maximum power of bulls during the week.

The highest point of a bar represents the maximum power of bulls during that bar.

The **low of each bar** represents the maximum power of bears during that bar. Bears make money when prices decline. They keep selling short, their selling pushes prices lower, and every downtick adds to their profits. At some point they run out of either capital or enthusiasm, and prices stop falling. The low of a daily bar marks the

[1] A tick is the smallest price change allowed for any given trading vehicle. It may be one cent or even one hundredth of a cent (depending on the stock), a quarter point for S&P e-minis, 10 cents for gold futures, etc.

maximum power of bears during that day, and the low of a weekly bar identifies the maximum power of bears during that week.

The low of each bar shows the maximum power of bears during that bar.

The **closing price of each bar** reveals the outcome of the battle between bulls and bears during that bar. If prices close near the high of the daily bar, it shows that bulls won the day's battle. If prices close near the low of the day, it shows that bears won the day. Closing prices on the daily charts of futures are especially important because your account equity is "marked to market" each night.

The **distance between the high and the low** of any bar reflects the intensity of conflict between bulls and bears. An average bar marks a relatively cool market. A bar that's only half as tall as average reveals a sleepy, disinterested market. A bar that's two times taller than average shows a boiling market where bulls and bears battle all over the field.

Slippage (see the Introduction) tends to be less in quiet markets. It pays to enter trades during short or normal bars. Tall bars are good for taking profits. Trying to enter a position when the market is running is like jumping onto a moving train. It would be safer to wait for the next one.

Japanese Candlesticks

Japanese rice traders began using candlestick charts some two centuries before the first chartists appeared in America. Instead of bars, their charts had rows of candles with wicks at both ends. The body of each candle represents the distance between the opening and closing prices. If the closing price is higher than the opening, the body is white, but if the closing price is lower, the body is black.

The tip of the upper wick represents the high of the day, while the bottom of the lower wick represents the low of the day. The Japanese consider highs and lows relatively unimportant, according to Steve Nison, author of *Japanese Candlestick Charting Techniques.* They focus on the relationship between opening and closing prices and on patterns that include several candles.

The main advantage of a candlestick chart is its focus on the struggle between amateurs who control openings and professionals who control closings. Unfortunately, many candlestick chartists neglect Western tools, such as volume and technical indicators.

Candlesticks have become quite popular worldwide, and some traders ask me why I continue to use bar charts. I am familiar with candlesticks, but I've learned to trade using bar charts, and I believe that using open-high-low-close bars plus technical indicators gives me more information.

Your choice of a bar or a candlestick chart is a matter of personal preference. All concepts expressed in this book can be used with candlestick as well as bar charts.

Efficient Markets, Random Walk, Chaos Theory, and "Nature's Law"

Efficient Market theory is an academic notion that nobody can outperform the market because any price at any given moment incorporates all available information. Warren Buffett, one of the most successful investors of the century, commented: "I think it's fascinating how the ruling orthodoxy can cause a lot of people to think the earth is flat. Investing in a market where people believe in efficiency is like playing bridge with someone who's been told it doesn't do any good to look at the cards."

The logical flaw of Efficient Market theory is that it equates knowledge with action. People may have knowledge, but the emotional pull of the crowd often leads them to trade irrationally. A good analyst can detect repetitive patterns of crowd behavior on his charts and exploit them.

Random Walk theorists claim that market prices change at random. Sure, there is a fair bit of randomness or "noise" in the markets, just as there is randomness in any crowd. Still, an intelligent observer can identify repetitive behavior patterns of a crowd and make sensible bets on their continuation or reversal.

People have memories; they remember past prices, and their memories influence their decisions to buy or sell. Memories help create support under the market and resistance above it. Random Walkers deny that memories influence our behavior.

As Milton Friedman pointed out, prices carry information about the availability of supply and the intensity of demand. Market participants use that information when deciding to buy or sell. For example, consumers buy more merchandise when it is on sale and less when prices are high. Financial traders are just as capable of logical behavior as homemakers. When prices are low, bargain hunters step in. A shortage can lead to a buying panic, but high prices choke off demand.

Chaos Theory has achieved prominence in the recent decades. Markets are largely chaotic, and the only time you can have an edge is during orderly periods.

In my view, markets are chaotic much of the time, but out of that chaos, islands of order and structure keep emerging and disappearing. The essence of market analysis is recognizing the emergence of orderly patterns and having enough courage and conviction to trade them.

If you trade during chaotic periods, the only ones to benefit will be your broker, who'll collect his commission, and a professional day-trader, who'll scalp you. The key point to keep in mind is that once in a while a pattern emerges from chaos. Your system should recognize this transition, and that's when you should put on a trade! Earlier we spoke about the one great advantage of a private trader over professionals—he may wait for a good trade instead of having to be active each day. The Chaos Theory confirms that message.

The Chaos Theory also teaches us that orderly structures that emerge from chaos are fractal. The sea coast appears equally jagged whether you look down on it from space or an airplane, from a standing position or on your knees through a magnifying glass. Market patterns are fractal as well. If I show you a set of charts of the same market, having removed time markings, you will not be able to tell whether it is monthly, weekly, daily, or a 5-minute chart. Later, we'll return to this theme, and you'll see why it is so important to analyze markets in more than one timeframe. We'll have to make sure that buy or sell messages in both timeframes confirm each other, because if they don't it means that the market is too chaotic and we should stand aside.

Nature's Law is the rallying cry of a clutch of mystics who claim there is a perfect order in the markets (which they'll reveal to you for a price). They say that markets move like clockwork in response to immutable natural laws. R. N. Elliott even titled his last book *Nature's Law.*

The "perfect order" crowd gravitates to astrology, numerology, conspiracy theory, and other superstitions. Next time someone talks to you about natural order in the markets, ask him about astrology. He'll probably jump at the chance to come out of the closet and talk about the stars.

The believers in perfect order in the markets claim that tops and bottoms can be predicted far into the future. Amateurs love forecasts, and mysticism is a great marketing gimmick. It helps sell courses, trading systems, and newsletters.

Mystics, Random Walk academics, and Efficient Market theorists have one trait in common. They are equally divorced from the reality of the markets.

CHAPTER 34

Support and Resistance

From Dr. Alexander Elder, *The New Trading for a Living* (Hoboken, New Jersey: John Wiley & Sons, 2014), Part 3, Chapter 18.

A ball hits the floor and bounces. Toss it up, and it'll drop after hitting the ceiling. Support and resistance are like a floor and a ceiling, with prices sandwiched between them. Understanding support and resistance is essential for understanding price trends. Rating their strength helps you decide whether the trend is likely to punch through or to reverse.

Support is a price level where buying is strong enough to interrupt or reverse a downtrend. When a downtrend hits support, it bounces like a diver who hits the bottom and pushes away from it. Support is represented on a chart by a horizontal line connecting two or more bottoms (Figure 34.1).

Resistance is a price level where selling is strong enough to interrupt or reverse an uptrend. When an uptrend hits resistance, it acts like a man who hits his head on a branch while climbing a tree—he stops and may even tumble down. Resistance is represented on a chart by a horizontal line connecting two or more tops.

It is better to draw support and resistance lines across the edges of congestion areas where the bulk of the bars stopped rather than across extreme prices. Those congestion zones show where masses of traders have changed their minds, while the extreme points reflect only panic among the weakest traders.

Minor support or resistance causes trends to pause, while major support or resistance causes them to reverse. Traders buy at support and sell at resistance, making their effectiveness a self-fulfilling prophecy.

How do we identify trends? Not by **trendlines.** My favorite tools are exponential moving averages that we'll review in the next section. Trendlines are wildly subjective—they are among the most self-deceptive tools. Trend identification is an area in which computerized analysis is miles ahead of classical charting.

FIGURE 34.1 **NFLX Weekly.** *(Chart by StockCharts.com)*

Support and Resistance

Draw horizontal lines across the upper and lower edges of congestion areas. The bottom line marks the level of support at which buyers overcome sellers. The upper line identifies resistance, where sellers overpower buyers. Support and resistance areas often switch roles. Note how after a decisive upside breakout in area 1 prices hit resistance, but when they broke above that level it turned into a zone of support (marked 2). The strength of these barriers increases each time prices touch them and bounce away.

Beware of false breakouts from support and resistance. They are marked by letter "F" on this chart. Amateurs tend to follow breakouts, while professionals tend to fade (trade against) them. At the right edge of the chart NFLX is rallying from support at the level where its previous rally ran into resistance.

Memories, Pain, and Regret

Our memories of previous market turns prompt us to buy and sell at certain levels. Buying and selling by crowds create support and resistance. *Support and resistance exist because people have memories.*

If traders remember that prices have recently stopped falling and turned up from a certain level, they are likely to buy when prices approach that level again. If traders remember that an uptrend has recently reversed after rising to a certain peak, they tend to sell and go short when prices approach that level again.

For example, all major rallies in the stock market from 1966 until 1982 ended whenever the Dow Jones Industrial Average rallied into the area between 950 and 1050. That resistance zone was so strong that traders named it "a graveyard in the sky." Once the bulls rammed the market through that level, it became a major support area. In recent years, we saw a similar occurrence in gold, whose chart is shown here (Figure 34.2). It hit the level of $1,000/oz four times, dropping after each attempt. After the price of gold broke above that level on its fifth attempt, the level of $1,000/oz turned into a massive support level.

Support and resistance exist because masses of traders feel pain and regret. Traders who hold losing positions feel intense pain. Losers are determined to get out as soon as the market gives them another chance. Traders who missed an opportunity to buy or sell short feel regret and also wait for the market to give them a second

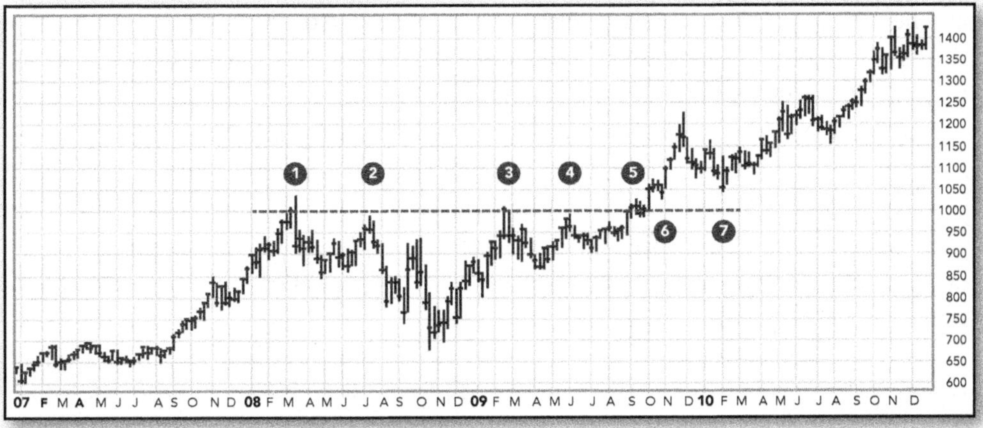

FIGURE 34.2 Gold Weekly. *(Chart by StockCharts.com)*

Resistance Turns into Support

Notice how gold hit its overhead resistance at the $1,000/oz. level five times. Usually, reversals occur on the first, second, or third hit. When a market hits the same level for the fourth time, it shows that it really wants to go that way. Gold broke above $1,000/oz. on its fifth attempt.

Afterwards, gold made two attempts to pull down to its old resistance level, in areas marked 6 and 7. Its inability to decline to that level showed that bears were weak, marking the start of a major bull market in gold.

chance. Feelings of pain and regret are mild in trading ranges when swings are relatively small and losers do not get hurt too badly. Breakouts from those ranges create much more intense pain and regret.

When the market stays flat for a while, traders get used to buying near the lower edge of its range and selling or even shorting near the upper edge. When an uptrend begins, bears who sold short feel a great deal of pain. At the same time bulls feel an intense regret that they didn't buy more. Both are determined to buy if the market declines to the breakout point and gives them a second chance to cover shorts or to get long. The pain of bears and regret of bulls makes them eager to buy, creating **support** during reactions in an uptrend.

When prices break down from a trading range, bulls who bought are in pain: they feel trapped and wait for a rally to get out even. Bears, on the other hand, regret that they haven't shorted more: they wait for a rally as a second chance to sell short. Bulls' pain and bears' regret create **resistance**—a ceiling above the market in downtrends. The strength of support and resistance depends on the strength of feelings among masses of traders.

Strength of Support and Resistance

The longer prices stay in a congestion zone, the stronger the emotional commitment of bulls and bears to that area. A congestion area hit by several trends is like a battlefield with craters from explosions: its defenders have plenty of cover and are likely to slow down any attacking force. When prices approach that zone from above, it serves as support. When prices rally into it from below, it acts as resistance. A congestion area can reverse those roles, serving as either support or resistance.

The strength of those zones depends on three factors: their length, height, and the volume of trading that has taken place in them. You can visualize these factors as the length, the width, and the depth of a congestion zone.

The longer a support or resistance area—its length of time or the number of hits it took—the stronger it is. Support and resistance, like good wine, become better with age. A 2-week trading range provides only minimal support or resistance, a 2-month range gives people time to become used to it and creates intermediate support or resistance, while a 2-year range becomes accepted as a standard of value and offers major support or resistance.

As support and resistance levels grow very old, they gradually become weaker. Losers keep washing out of the markets, replaced by newcomers who don't have the same emotional commitment to very old price levels. People who lost money only recently remember full well what happened to them. They are probably still in the market, feeling pain and regret, trying to get even. People who made bad decisions several years ago may well be out of that market, and their memories matter less.

The strength of support and resistance increases each time that area is hit. When traders see that prices have reversed at a certain level, they tend to bet on a reversal the next time prices reach that level.

The taller the support and resistance zone, the stronger it is. A tall congestion zone is like a tall fence around a property. If a congestion zone's height equals one percent of current market value, it provides only minor support or resistance. If it's three percent tall, it provides intermediate support or resistance, and a congestion zone that's seven percent tall or higher can grind down a major trend.

The greater the volume of trading in a support and resistance zone, the stronger it is. High volume shows active involvement by traders—a sign of strong emotional commitment. Low volume shows that traders have little interest in transacting at that level—a sign of weak support or resistance.

You can measure the strength of support and resistance in dollars if you multiply the number of days a stock spent in its congestion zone by its average daily volume and price. Of course, when making such comparisons, we should measure support and resistance zones for the same stock. You can't compare apples with oranges or AAPL with some $10 stock that trades a million shares on a good day.

Trading Rules

1. Whenever the trend you're riding approaches support or resistance, tighten your protective stop.

   A **protective stop** is an order to sell below the market when you are long or to cover shorts above the market when you are short. A stop protects you from getting badly hurt by a reversal.

   A trend reveals its health by how it acts when it hits support or resistance. If it's strong enough to penetrate that zone, your tight stop will not be triggered. If a trend bounces away from support or resistance, it reveals its weakness. In that case, your tight stop will salvage a good chunk of profits.

2. Support and resistance are more important on long-term charts than on short-term charts.

   A good trader monitors his market using several timeframes, but assigns more weight to the longer ones. Weekly charts are more important than dailies. If the weekly trend is strong, it is less alarming that the daily trend is hitting resistance. When a weekly trend approaches major support or resistance, you should be more inclined to exit.
3. Support and resistance levels point to trading opportunities.

   The bottom of a congestion area identifies the bottom line of support. As prices decline towards it, be alert to buying opportunities. One of the best patterns in technical analysis is a **false breakout**. If prices dip below support and then rally back into the support zone, they show that bears have lost their chance. A price bar closing within a congestion zone after a false downside breakout marks a buying opportunity; set a protective stop in the vicinity of the bottom of the recent false downside breakout.

Similarly, a true upside breakout should not be followed by a pullback into the range, just as a rocket is not supposed to sink back to its launching pad. A false upside breakout gives a signal to sell short as a price bar returns into the congestion zone. When shorting, place a protective stop near the top of the false breakout (Figure 34.3).

On Placing Stops Experienced traders tend to avoid placing them at round numbers. If I buy a stock near $52 and want to protect my position in the area of 51, I'll put a stop a few cents below $51. If I go long at 33.70 in a day-trade and want to protect my position in the area of $33.50, I'll put that stop a few cents below $33.50. Because of a natural human tendency to use round numbers, clusters of stops accumulate there. I prefer to place my stops at the far ends of such clusters.

True and False Breakouts

Markets spend more time in trading ranges than in trends. Most breakouts from trading ranges are false breakouts. They suck in trend-followers just before prices return into their ranges. False breakouts hurt amateurs, but professional traders love them.

Professionals expect prices to fluctuate most of the time, without going anywhere far. They wait until an upside breakout stops reaching new highs or a downside breakout stops making new lows. Then they pounce—fade the breakout (trade against it) and place a protective stop near the latest extreme point. It's a tight stop, and their monetary risk is low, with a big profit potential from prices returning towards the middle of the congestion zone. The risk/reward ratio is so good that professionals can afford to be wrong half the time and still come out ahead of the game.

The best time to buy an upside breakout on a daily chart is when your analysis of the **weekly** chart suggests that a new uptrend is developing. True breakouts are confirmed by heavy **volume,** while false breakouts tend to have light volume. True

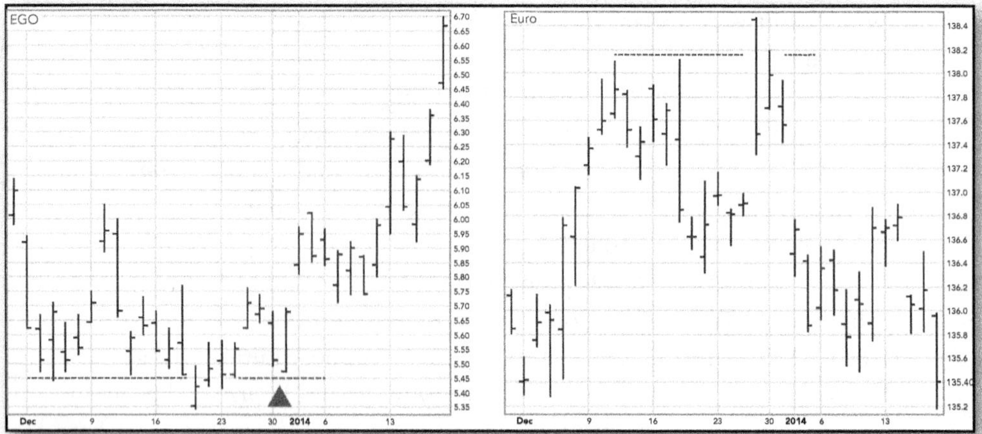

FIGURE 34.3 EGO and the Euro Daily. *(Chart by StockCharts.com)*

False Breakouts

On the left, a chart of Eldorado Gold Corp. (EGO) shows a false downside breakout during gold bears' final attempt to push gold stocks lower in December 2013. Prices opened sharply below support, having gapped down from the previous day's close. From there, a rally began. Notice a pullback to the support line a week later, marked by a green arrowhead. Such pullbacks don't always occur, but when they do, they offer an excellent opportunity to hop aboard a new trend.

On the right, a chart of the Euro (represented here by $XEU) shows how an uptrend culminated in a false upside breakout. Prices gapped above the line of resistance, triggering stops and shaking out weak shorts, and that's when the downtrend began. There was no second chance pullback in this market.

breakouts are confirmed when technical **indicators** reach new extremes in the direction of the new trend, while false breakouts are often marked by divergences between prices and indicators, which we'll discuss later in the book.

CHAPTER 35

Trends and Trading Ranges

From Dr. Alexander Elder, *The New Trading for a Living* (Hoboken, New Jersey: John Wiley & Sons, 2014), Part 3, Chapter 19.

A **trend** exists when prices keep rising or falling over a period of time. In a perfect **uptrend**, each rally reaches a higher high than the preceding rally,. while each decline stops at a higher level than the preceding decline. In a perfect **downtrend**, each decline falls to a lower low than the preceding decline and each rally tops out at a lower level than the preceding rally. In a **trading range**, most rallies stop at about the same high level, and declines peter out at about the same low level. Perfect patterns, of course, aren't that common in financial markets, and multiple deviations make life harder for analysts and traders (Figure 35.1).

Even a quick look at most charts reveals that markets spend most of the time in trading ranges. Trends and trading ranges call for different tactics. When you go long in an uptrend or sell short in a downtrend, you have to give that trend the benefit of the doubt and use a wider stop, so as not to be shaken out easily. In a trading range, on the other hand, you have to use tight stops, be nimble and close out positions at the slightest sign of a reversal.

Another difference in trading tactics between trends and ranges is the handling of strength and weakness. You have to follow strength during trends—buy in uptrends and short in downtrends. When prices are in a trading range, you aim to do the opposite—buy weakness and sell strength.

Mass Psychology

When the trend is up, bulls are more eager than bears, and their buying forces prices higher. If bears manage to push prices down, bulls return to bargain hunt. They stop the decline, and force prices to rise again. A downtrend occurs when bears are more aggressive and their selling pushes markets down. Whenever a flurry of buying lifts prices, bears sell short into that rally, stop it, and send prices to new lows.

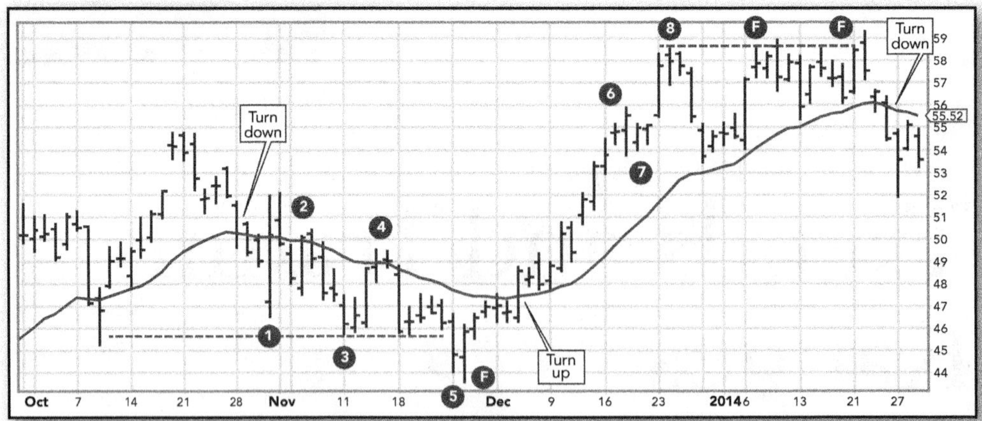

FIGURE 35.1 FB Daily, 22-Day EMA. *(Chart by StockCharts.com)*

Trend and the Trading Range

A pattern of higher tops and higher bottoms defines uptrends, while a pattern of lower bottoms and lower tops defines downtrends. In the middle of this chart of Facebook, Inc. (FB), you see a downtrend defined by three lower lows, marked 1, 3, and 5, and two lower highs, marked 2 and 4. Notice the downtrend of a slow 22-day exponential moving average (which we'll review in Chapter 12, Level II) confirming the price downtrend. Its upturn signaled an upside reversal, confirmed by new price peaks 6 and 8.

We've looked at false breakouts in the previous chapter, and you can see them again in action here. False breakouts occur when prices cross their support or resistance lines, spend one or two days beyond that line, and then return, marking a failed move in the direction of the breakout; afterwards prices tend to turn in the opposite direction. Here, a false downside breakout, followed by the upturn of a moving average gave a strong buy signal.

We see a mirror image of this pattern after the top 8. There are two false upside breakouts, and after the second one, the moving average turns down, giving a sell signal. At the right edge of the chart, prices are pulling back up to their declining moving average. Such patterns tend to create good opportunities for selling short.

When bulls and bears are about equal in strength, prices stay in a trading range. When bulls manage to push prices up, bears sell short into that rally and prices fall. As they decline, bargain hunters step in and buy. Then, as bears cover shorts, their buying helps fuel a rally. This cycle can go on for a long time.

A trading range is like a fight between two equally strong street gangs. They push one another back and forth, but neither can control the city block. A trend is like a fight in which a stronger gang chases the weaker gang down the street. Every once in a while the weaker gang stops and puts up a fight but then turns and runs again.

Crowds spend most of their time aimlessly milling around, which is why markets spend more time in trading ranges than in trends. A crowd has to become agitated and surge to create a trend. Crowds do not stay excited for long—they go back to aimlessness. Professionals tend to give the benefit of the doubt to trading ranges.

The Hard Right Edge

Trends and ranges are easy to see in the middle of a chart, but as you get close to its right edge, the picture becomes increasingly foggy. The past is fixed and clear, but the future is fluid and uncertain. Trends are easy to recognize on old charts, but, unfortunately, our brokers don't allow us to trade in the past—we have to make trading decisions at the hard right edge.

By the time a trend becomes perfectly clear, a good chunk of it is already gone. Nobody will ring a bell when a trend dissolves into a trading range.

Many chart patterns and indicator signals contradict one another at the right edge of the chart. You have to base your decisions on probabilities in an atmosphere of uncertainty.

Most people feel very uncomfortable dealing with uncertainty. When their trade doesn't go the way their analysis suggested, they hang onto losing positions, waiting for the market to turn and make them whole. Trying to be right is an unaffordable luxury in the markets. Professional traders get out of losing trades fast. When the market deviates from your analysis, you have to cut losses without fuss.

Methods and Techniques

Keep in mind that there is no single magic method to clearly and reliably identify all trends and trading ranges. It pays to combine several analytic tools. None of them is perfect, but when they confirm each another, a correct message is much more likely. When they contradict one another, it's better to pass up a trade.

1. Analyze the pattern of highs and lows. When rallies keep reaching higher levels and declines keep stopping at higher levels, they identify an uptrend. The pattern of lower lows and lower highs identifies a downtrend, and the pattern of irregular highs and lows points to a trading range (Figure 35.1).
2. Plot a 20- to 30-bar exponential moving average (see Chapter 12, Level II). The direction of its slope identifies the trend. If a moving average has not reached a new high or low in a month, then the market is probably in a trading range.
3. When an oscillator, such as MACD-Histogram (see Chapter 13, Level II) rises to a new peak, it identifies a powerful trend and suggests that the latest market top is likely to be retested or exceeded.
4. Several market indicators, such the Directional system (see Chapter 14, Level II), help identify trends. The Directional system is especially good at catching early stages of new trends (Figure 35.2).

Trade or Wait

Having identified an uptrend, you need to decide whether to buy immediately or wait for a dip. If you buy fast, you'll get in gear with the trend, but on the minus side, your stops are likely to be farther away, increasing your risk.

If you wait for a dip, your risk will be smaller, but you'll have four groups of competitors: longs who want to add to their positions, shorts who want to get out even, traders who never bought (such as yourself), and traders who sold too early but are eager to buy again. The waiting areas for pullbacks are notoriously crowded! Furthermore, a deep pullback may signal the beginning of a reversal rather than a buying opportunity. The same reasoning applies to shorting in downtrends.

FIGURE 35.2 UNP Daily, 22-Day EMA, Directional System, MACD-Histogram. ***(Chart by StockCharts.com)***

Trend Identification

The single most important identifier of any trend is the pattern of its highs and lows. Look, for example, at this daily chart of Union Pacific Corp (UNP). Once it broke out of its trading range, its highs, marked by horizontal green lines, kept reaching higher and higher. Similarly, its reaction lows, marked by red horizontal lines, kept bottoming out at higher and higher levels. Trying to draw a trendline would be a very subjective exercise because the bottoms of UNP did not line up in a straight line.

The 22-day exponential moving average (EMA), represented by a red line superimposed on prices, confirms the uptrend by its steady rise. Notice excellent buying opportunities, signaled by quick price dips to their moving average (we'll return to this pattern in Chapter 12, Level II).

The Directional system (described in Chapter 14, Level II) signaled the start of a new trend when the Average Directional Index (ADX) fell below 20 and then rallied above that level and penetrated above the lower Directional Line (marked by a vertical green arrow). MACD-Histogram (described in Chapter 13, Level II) identified a very powerful trend when it rallied to its highest peak in several months (marked by a diagonal green arrow). Near the right edge of the chart the trend is up, while prices are slightly below their recent high. A pullback to the EMA is likely to create a fresh buying opportunity.

If the market is in a trading range and you're waiting for a breakout, you'll have to decide whether to buy in anticipation of a breakout, during a breakout, or on a pullback after a valid breakout. If you aren't sure, consider entering in several steps: buy a third of the planned position in anticipation, a third on a breakout, and a third on a pullback.

Whatever method you use, remember to apply the key risk management rule: the distance from your entry to the protective stop, multiplied by position size can never be more than 2 percent of your account equity. No matter how attractive a trade, pass it up if it would require putting more than 2 percent of your account at risk.

Finding good entry points is extremely important in trading ranges. You have to be very precise and nimble because the profit potential is limited. A trend is more forgiving of a sloppy entry, as long as you trade in the right direction. Old traders chuckle: "Don't confuse brains with a bull market."

Specific risk management tactics are different for trends and trading ranges. When trend trading, it pays to put on smaller positions with wider stops. You'll be less likely to get shaken out by any counter-trend moves, while still controlling risk. You may put on bigger positions in trading ranges but with tighter stops.

Conflicting Timeframes

Markets move in several timeframes at the same time (see Chapter 33, Level II). They move simultaneously, and sometimes in the opposite directions on 10-minute, hourly, daily, weekly, and monthly charts. The market may look like a buy in one timeframe but a sell in another. Even indicator signals in different timeframes of the same stock may contradict one another. Which will you follow?

Most traders ignore the fact that markets move in different directions at the same time in different timeframes. They pick one timeframe, such as daily or hourly, and look for trades there. That's when trends from other timeframes sneak up on them and wreak havoc with their plans.

Those conflicts between signals in different timeframes of the same market are one of the great puzzles in market analysis. What looks like a trend on a daily chart may show up as a blip on a flat weekly chart. What looks like a flat trading range on a daily chart shows rich uptrends and downtrends on an hourly chart, and so on.

The sensible course of action is this: before examining a trend on your favorite chart, step back to explore the charts in a timeframe one order of magnitude greater than your favorite. This search for a greater perspective is one of the key principles of the Triple Screen trading system, which we'll discuss in a later chapter.

When professionals are in doubt, they look at the big picture, while amateurs tend to focus on the short-term charts. Taking a longer view works better—and is a lot less nerve-wracking.

CHAPTER 36

Volume-Based Indicators

From Dr. Alexander Elder, *The New Trading for a Living* (Hoboken, New Jersey: John Wiley & Sons, 2014), Part 5, Chapter 29.

Several indicators help clarify volume's trading signals. For example, a 5-day EMA of volume can identify volume's trends. A rising EMA of volume affirms the current price trend, while a declining one points to the price trend's weakness.

This and other volume-based indicators provide more precise timing signals than volume bars. They include On-Balance Volume and Accumulation/Distribution, described below. Force Index combines price and volume data to help identify areas where prices are likely to reverse.

On-Balance Volume

On-Balance Volume (OBV) is an indicator designed by Joseph Granville and described in his book, *New Strategy of Daily Stock Market Timing*. Granville used OBV as a leading indicator of the stock market, but other analysts applied it to futures.

OBV is a running total of volume. Each day's volume is added or subtracted, depending on whether prices close higher or lower than on the previous day. When a stock closes higher, it shows that bulls won the day's battle; that day's volume is added to OBV. When a stock closes lower, it shows that bears won the day, and that day's volume is subtracted from OBV. If prices close unchanged, OBV stays unchanged. On-Balance Volume often rises or falls before prices, acting as a leading indicator.

Crowd Psychology

Prices represent the consensus of value, but volume represents the emotions of market participants. It reflects the intensity of traders' financial and emotional commitments, as well as pain among losers, which is what OBV helps to track.

A new high of OBV shows that bulls are powerful, bears are hurting, and prices are likely to rise. A new low of OBV shows that bears are powerful, bulls are hurting, and prices are likely to fall. When the pattern of OBV deviates from the pattern of prices, it shows that mass emotions aren't in gear with mass consensus. A crowd is more likely to follow its gut than its mind, and that's why changes in volume often precede price changes.

Trading Signals

The patterns of OBV tops and bottoms are much more important than the absolute levels, which depend on the starting date of your calculations. It is safer to trade in the direction of a trend that is confirmed by OBV (Figure 36.1).

1. When OBV reaches a new high, it confirms the power of bulls, indicates that prices are likely to continue to rise, and gives a buy signal. When OBV falls below its previous low, it confirms the power of bears, calls for lower prices ahead, and gives a signal to sell short.
2. OBV gives its strongest buy and sell signals when it diverges from prices. If prices rally, sell off, and then rise to a new high, but OBV rallies to a lower high,

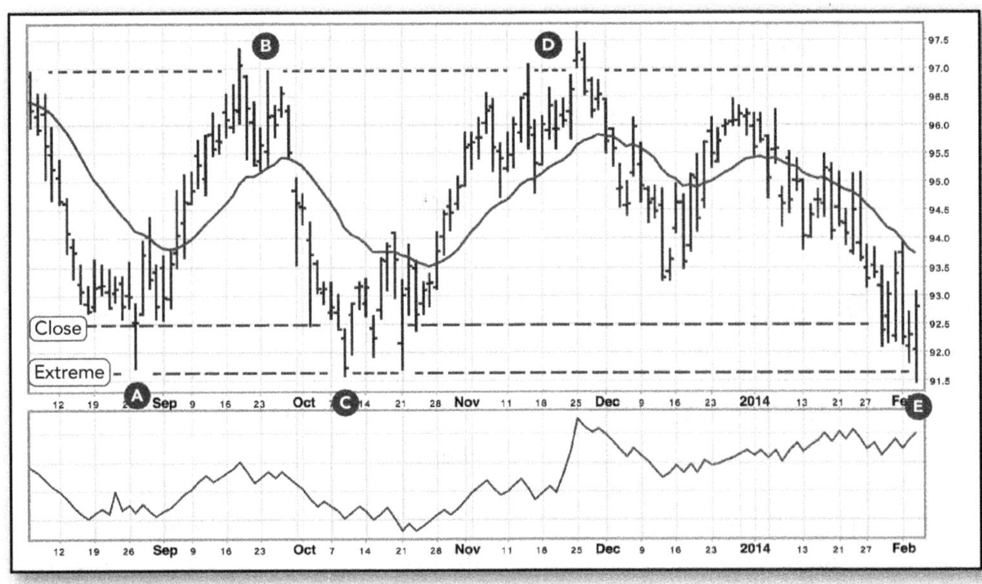

FIGURE 36.1 MCD daily, 22-day EMA, On-Balance volume (OBV). ***(Chart by StockCharts.com)***

On-Balance Volume

McDonald's Corp. (MCD) is a stable, slow-moving stock. You can see a fairly tight trading range, marked with dashed lines (two lines at the lows, one tight and the other loose). Notice the tendency of MCD towards false breakouts (bottoms A and C and tops B and D). Notice a kangaroo tail in area A.

At the right edge of the chart, the stock market is in a free-fall, but while MCD trades near its recent lows, its OBV indicator is trading near the highs. It points to strength and suggests buying rather than selling.

it creates a bearish divergence and gives a sell signal. If prices decline, rebound, and then fall to a new low, but OBV falls to a more shallow bottom, it traces a bullish divergence and gives a buy signal. Long-term divergences are more important than the short-term ones. Divergences that develop over the course of several weeks give stronger signals than those created over a few days.

3. When prices are in a trading range and OBV breaks out to a new high, it gives a buy signal. When prices are in a trading range and OBV breaks down and falls to a new low, it gives a signal to sell short.

More on OBV

One of the reasons for Granville's success in stock market timing was that he combined OBV with two other indicators—the **Net Field Trend indicator** and the **Climax indicator**. Granville calculated OBV for each stock in the Dow Jones Industrial Average and rated its OBV pattern as rising, falling, or neutral. He called that a Net Field Trend of a stock: It could be +1, −1, or 0. Climax indicator was a sum of the Net Field Trends of all 30 Dow stocks.

When the stock market rallied and the Climax indicator reached a new high, it confirmed strength and gave a buy signal. If the stock market rallied but the Climax indicator made a lower top, it gave a sell signal.

You can look at the Dow Jones Industrial Average as a team of 30 horses pulling the market wagon. The Climax indicator shows how many horses are pulling uphill, downhill, or standing still. If 24 out of 30 horses pull up, 1 down and 5 are resting, then the market wagon is likely to move up. If 9 horses pull up, 7 pull down, and 14 are resting, that wagon may soon roll downhill.

Remarkably, Granville did his calculations by hand.[1] Now, of course, OBV, the Net Field Trend indicator, and the Climax indicator can be easily programmed. It would be worthwhile to apply them to a database that includes all stocks of the S&P 500 index. This method may produce good signals for trading the S&P 500 futures and options.

Accumulation/Distribution

This indicator was developed by Larry Williams and described in his 1973 book, *How I Made One Million Dollars*. It was designed as a leading indicator for stocks, but several analysts applied it to futures. The unique feature of Accumulation/Distribution (A/D) is that it tracks the relationship between opening and closing prices, in addition to volume. Its concept is similar to that of Japanese candlesticks, which at the time Williams wrote his book weren't known to Western traders.

[1] I visited Granville in 2005 in Kansas City. Not only did he do all his calculations by hand, he avoided going online, as he was suspicious of pervasive snooping—and that was years before the disclosures of government spying. He disconnected his computer from the Internet until it was time to send out his newsletter. Granville monitored intraday prices by tuning his TV into CNBC with the sound turned off and a towel draped over the upper portion of the screen, so that all he could see was the tape, running along the bottom of his screen.

Accumulation/Distribution is more finely calibrated than OBV because it credits bulls or bears with only a fraction of each day's volume, proportionate to the degree of their win for the day.

$$A/D = \frac{\text{Close} - \text{Open}}{\text{High} - \text{Low}} \bullet \text{Volume}$$

If prices close higher than they opened, then bulls won the day, and A/D is positive. If prices close lower than they opened, then the bears won, and A/D is negative. If prices close where they opened, then nobody won, and A/D is zero. A running total of each day's A/D creates a cumulative A/D indicator.

For example, if today's high-low spread was five points but the distance from the open to the close was two points, then only 2/5 of today's volume is credited to the winning camp. Just as with OBV, the pattern of A/D highs and lows is important, while its absolute level simply depends on the starting date.

When the market rises, most people focus on new highs, but if prices open higher and close lower, then A/D, which tracks their relationship, turns down. It warns that the uptrend is weaker than it appears. If, on the other hand, A/D ticks up while prices are down, it shows that bulls are gaining strength.

Crowd Behavior

Opening prices reflect pressures that have built up while the market was closed. Openings tend to be dominated by amateurs who read their news in the evening and trade in the morning.

Professional traders are active throughout the day. They often trade against the amateurs. As the day goes on, waves of buying and selling by amateurs as well as slow-moving institutions gradually subside. Professionals tend to dominate the markets at closing time. Closing prices are especially important because the settlement of trading accounts depends on them.

A/D tracks the outcomes of daily battles between amateurs and professionals. It ticks up when prices close higher than they opened—when professionals are more bullish than amateurs. It ticks down when prices close lower than they opened—when professionals are more bearish than amateurs. It pays to bet with the professionals and against the amateurs.

Trading Rules

When the market opens low and closes high, it moves from weakness to strength. That's when A/D rises and signals that market professionals are more bullish than amateurs, and the upmove is likely to continue. When A/D falls, it shows that market professionals are more bearish than amateurs. When the market weakens during the day, it's likely to reach a lower low in the days to come.

The best trading signals are given by divergences between A/D and prices.

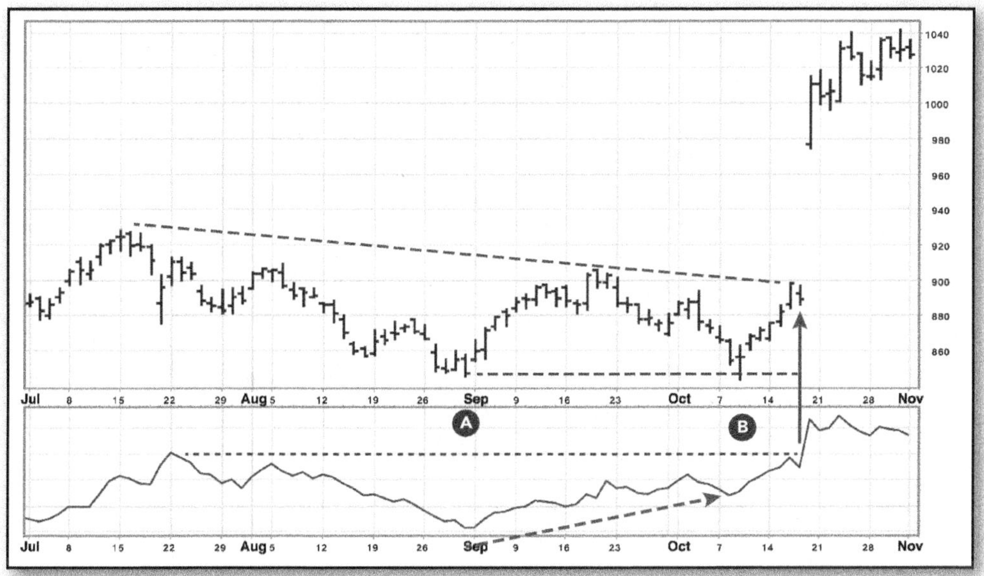

FIGURE 36.2 GOOG daily, Accumulation/Distribution Index. *(Chart by StockCharts.com)*

Accumulation / Distribution

"Coming events cast their shadows before" is an old proverb with a lot of meaning for technical analysts. Google Inc. (GOOG) was trending lower for months, but the uptrend of the Accumulation/Distribution Index (A/D) showed that big money was buying. The stock has fallen lower at point B than at A, but the A/D Index traced out a much higher bottom. Just as important, it broke out to a new high (marked with a vertical green arrow) before prices gapped up following a surprisingly good earnings announcement. Somebody knew what was coming, and their massive buying was identified by the A/D accumulation pattern and its upside breakout. Technical analysis helps even out the imbalance of knowledge between outsiders and insiders.

1. If prices rally to a new high but A/D reaches a lower peak, it gives a signal to sell short. This bearish divergence shows that market professionals are selling into the rally.
2. A bullish divergence occurs when prices fall to a new low but A/D bottoms out at a higher low than during its previous decline. It shows that market professionals are using the decline for buying, and a rally is coming (Figure 36.2).

More on Accumulation/Distribution

When you go long or short, following a divergence between A/D and price, remember that even market professionals can go wrong. Use stops and protect yourself by following the **Hound of the Baskervilles** rule (see Level II, Chapter 24).

There are important parallels between A/D and Japanese candlestick charts, since both focus on the differences between opening and closing prices. A/D goes further than candlesticks by taking volume into account.

CHAPTER 37

Force Index

From Dr. Alexander Elder, *The New Trading for a Living* (Hoboken, New Jersey: John Wiley & Sons, 2014), Part 5, Chapter 30.

Force Index is an oscillator developed by this author. It combines volume with prices to discover the force of bulls or bears behind every rally or decline. Force Index can be applied to any price bar for which we have volume data: weekly, daily, or intraday. It brings together three essential pieces of information—the direction of price change, its extent, and the volume during that change. It provides a practical way of using volume for making trading decisions.[1]

Force Index can be used in its raw form, but its signals stand out much more clearly if we smooth it with a moving average. Using a short EMA of Force Index helps pinpoint entry and exit points. Using a longer EMA helps confirm trends and recognize important reversals.

How to Construct Force Index

The force of every move is defined by three factors: direction, distance, and volume.

1. If prices close higher than the close of the previous bar, the force is positive. If prices close lower than the close of the previous bar, the force is negative.
2. The greater the change in price, the greater the force.
3. The bigger the volume, the greater the force.

$$\text{Force Index} = \text{Volume}_{\text{today}} \cdot (\text{Close}_{\text{today}} - \text{Close}_{\text{yesterday}})$$

A raw Force Index can be plotted as a histogram, with a horizontal centerline at a zero level. If the market closes higher, Force Index is positive and rises above the centerline. If the market closes lower, Force Index is negative and extends below the centerline. If the market closes unchanged, Force Index is zero.

[1] Remember, we're talking about the force of market crowds, not the formula in physics.

The histogram of a raw Force Index is very jagged. This indicator gives much better trading signals after being smoothed with a moving average (Level II, Chapter 23). A 2-day EMA of Force Index provides a minimal degree of smoothing. It is useful for finding entry points into the markets. It pays to buy when the 2-day EMA is negative and sell when it's positive, as long as you trade in the direction of the trend.

A 13-day EMA of Force Index tracks longer-term changes in the force of bulls and bears. When the 13-day EMA crosses above the centerline, it shows that bulls are in control and suggests trading from the long side. When the 13-day EMA turns negative, it shows that bears are in control and suggests trading from the short side. Divergences between a 13-day EMA of Force Index and prices identify important turning points.

Trading Psychology

When the market closes higher, it shows that bulls won the day's battle, and when it closes lower, it shows that bears carried the day. The distance between today's and yesterday's closing prices reflects the margin of victory by bulls or bears. The greater this distance, the larger the victory achieved.

Volume reflects the degree of emotional commitment by market participants (see Level II, Chapter 29). High-volume rallies and declines have more inertia and are more likely to continue. Prices moving at high volume are like an avalanche that gathers speed as it rolls. Low volume, on the other hand, shows that the supply of losers is thin, and a trend is probably nearing an end.

Prices reflect what market participants think, while volume reflects the strength of their feelings. Force Index combines price and volume—it shows whether the head and the heart of the market are in gear with each other.

When Force Index rallies to a new high, it shows that the force of bulls is high and the uptrend is likely to continue. When Force Index falls to a new low, it shows that the force of bears is intense and the downtrend is likely to persist. If the change in prices is not confirmed by volume, Force Index flattens and warns that a trend is about to reverse. It also flattens and warns of a nearing reversal if high volume generates only a small price move.

Trading Rules

Short-Term Force Index

A 2-day EMA of Force Index is a highly sensitive indicator of the short-term force of bulls and bears. When it swings above its centerline, it shows that bulls are stronger, and when it falls below the centerline, it shows that bears are stronger.

Since the 2-day EMA of Force Index is a sensitive tool, we can use it to fine-tune signals of other indicators. When a trend-following indicator identifies an uptrend, the declines of the 2-day EMA of Force Index below zero pinpoint the best buying points: buying pullbacks during a long-term rally (Figure 37.1). When a trend-following tool identifies a downtrend, rallies of a 2-day EMA of Force Index mark the best shorting areas.

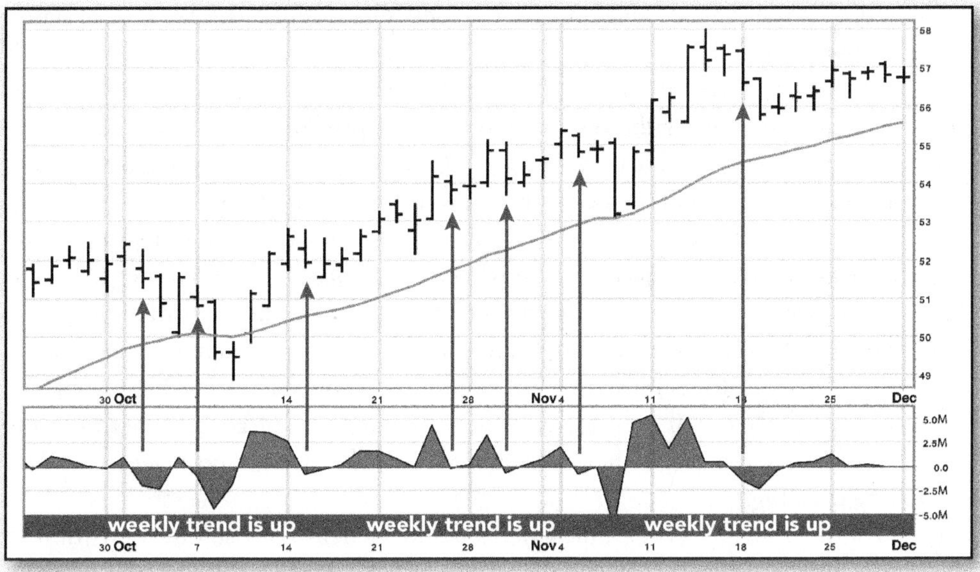

FIGURE 37.1 ADBE daily, 26-day EMA, 2-day Force Index. *(Chart by StockCharts.com)*

Short-Term Force Index

Later in this book we'll return to the all-important topic of using multiple timeframes to make trading decisions. For example, you may make your strategic decision—to be a bull or a bear—on a weekly chart and then make your tactical decisions on where to buy or sell short using a daily chart.

In the case of Adobe Systems, Inc. (ADBE), there is a steady uptrend on the weekly chart, confirmed by its rising EMA (not shown). When the weekly trend is up, a 2-day Force Index on the daily chart provides an ongoing series of signals that identify buy points. Instead of chasing strength and buying high, it's better to buy during short-term pullbacks, when a wave goes against the tide. Those waves are marked by the 2-day Force Index dropping below zero. Once the 2-day Force Index goes negative, it makes sense to start placing buy orders above the latest bar's high. This will ensure you'll be stopped into a long trade as soon as the downwave loses its power.

1. Buy when a 2-day EMA of Force Index turns negative during uptrends.

   Even a fast and furious uptrend has occasional pullbacks. If you delay buying until the 2-day EMA of Force Index turns negative, you'll buy closer to a short-term bottom. Most people chase rallies and then get hit by drawdowns they find hard to tolerate. Force Index helps find buying opportunities with lower risks.

   When a 2-day EMA of Force Index turns negative during an uptrend, place a buy order above the high price of that day. When the uptrend resumes and prices rally, you'll be stopped in on the long side. If prices continue to decline, your order will not be executed. Keep lowering your buy order to near the high of the latest bar. Once your buy stop is triggered, place a protective stop below the latest minor low. This tight stop is seldom touched in a strong uptrend, but it'll get you out early if the trend is weak.
2. Sell short when a 2-day EMA of Force Index turns positive in a downtrend.

   When trend-following indicators identify a downtrend, wait until the 2-day EMA of Force Index turns positive. It reflects a quick splash of bullishness—a shorting opportunity. Place an order to sell short below the low of the latest price bar.

If the 2-day EMA of Force Index continues to rally after you place your sell order, raise your order the next day to near the previous bar's low. Once prices slide and you enter a short trade, place a protective stop above the latest minor peak. Move your stop down to a break-even level as early as possible.

Additionally, a 2-day EMA of Force Index helps decide when to pyramid positions. You can add to longs in uptrends each time Force Index turns negative; you can add to shorts in downtrends whenever Force Index turns positive.

Force Index even provides a glimpse into the future. When a 2-day EMA of Force Index falls to its lowest low in a month, it shows that bears are strong and prices are likely to fall even lower. When a 2-day EMA of Force Index rallies to its highest level in a month, it shows that bulls are strong and prices are likely to rise even higher.

A 2-day EMA of Force Index helps decide when to close out a position. It does it by identifying short-term splashes of mass bullishness or bearishness. A short-term trader who bought when this indicator was negative can sell when it turns positive. A short-term trader who went short when this indicator was positive can cover when it turns negative. A longer-term trader should get out of his position only if a trend changes (as identified by the slope of a 13-day EMA of price) or if there is a divergence between the 2-day EMA of Force Index and the trend.

3. Bullish divergences between the 2-day EMA of Force Index and price give strong buy signals. A bullish divergence occurs when prices fall to a new low while Force Index makes a more shallow low.
4. Bearish divergences between the 2-day EMA of Force Index and price give strong sell signals. A bearish divergence occurs when prices rally to a new high while Force Index traces a lower second top.
5. Whenever the 2-day EMA of Force Index spikes down to five times or more its usual depth and then recoils from that low, expect prices to rally in the coming days.

Markets fluctuate between overbought and oversold, and when they recoil from a down spike, we can expect a rally. Note that this signal doesn't work well in uptrends—markets recoil from down spikes but not from up spikes. Spikes that point down reflect intense fear, which doesn't persist for very long. Spikes that point up reflect excessive enthusiasm and greed, which can persist for quite a long time.

A 2-day EMA of Force Index fits well into the Triple Screen trading system (see Level III, Chapter 1). Its ability to find short-term buying and selling points is especially useful when you combine Force Index with a longer-term trend-following indicator.

Intermediate-Term Force Index

A 13-day EMA of Force Index identifies longer-term changes in the balance of power between bulls and bears. When it rises above zero, the bulls are stronger, and when it falls below zero, the bears are in charge. Its divergences from prices identify intermediate and even major turning points (Figure 37.2). Its spikes, especially near the bottoms, mark approaching trend reversals.

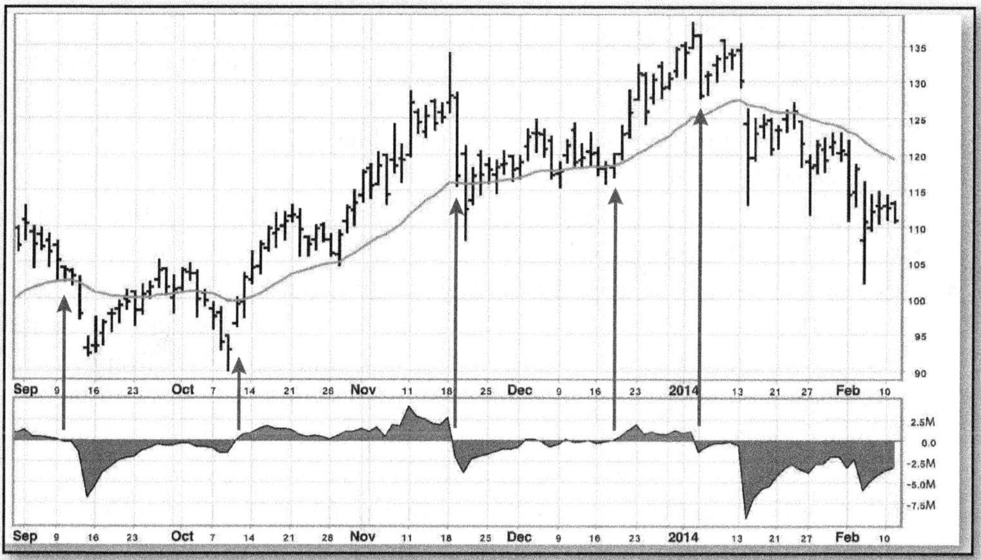

FIGURE 37.2 SSYS daily, 26-day EMA, 13-day Force Index. ***(Chart by StockCharts.com)***

Long-Term Force Index

Stratasys, Inc. (SSYS) is one of the two leading companies in the rapidly emerging additive manufacturing (AM) market. In the two years since I wrote the world's first popular e-book on investing in this technology, AM stocks have become investors' favorites. A technical pattern has emerged, with rallies driven by amateurs piling in and sharp declines as they panic and bail out. The 13-day Force Index does a good job of catching those waves.

When the 13-day Force Index crosses above its zero line (marked by vertical green arrows), it shows that buying volume is coming in. That's where a longer-term trader buys and holds. When the 13-day Force declines below its zero line and stays there, it shows that bears predominate.

Near the right edge of the screen, we see a record low of Force Index, but then bears begin to weaken, as Force Index starts inching towards zero. Keep your powder dry as you wait for an accumulation pattern to emerge and be confirmed by Force Index crossing above zero. This see-saw movement of stocks passing from strong hands into weak ones near the tops and back again near the lows goes on forever. Force Index can help you position yourself with the right group.

The raw Force Index identifies the winning team in the battle between bulls and bears in any price bar, be it weekly, daily, or intraday. We get much clearer signals by smoothing the raw Force Index with a moving average.

1. When a 13-day EMA of Force Index is above the centerline, bulls are in control of the market. When it is below the centerline, bears are in charge.

   When a rally begins, prices often jump on heavy volume. When a 13-day EMA of Force Index reaches a new high, it confirms the uptrend. As an uptrend grows older, prices tend to rise more slowly, and volume becomes thinner. That's when a 13-day EMA of Force Index starts tracing lower tops. When it drops below its zero line, it signals that the back of the bull has been broken.

2. A new peak of the 13-day EMA of Force Index shows that bulls are very strong and a rally is likely to continue. A bearish divergence between a 13-day EMA of Force Index and price gives a strong signal to sell short. If prices reach a new high but this indicator traces a lower peak, it warns that bulls are losing power and bears are ready to take control.

   Note that for a divergence to be legitimate, this indicator must make a new peak, then fall below its zero line, and then rise above that line again, but tracing a lower peak, which creates a divergence. If there is no crossover, then there is no legitimate divergence.

3. A new low in the 13-day EMA of Force Index shows that a downtrend is likely to continue. If prices fall to a new low but this indicator rallies above zero and then falls again, but to a more shallow low, it completes a bullish divergence. It reveals that bears are losing power and gives a buy signal.

   When a downtrend begins, prices usually drop on heavy volume. When a 13-day EMA of Force Index falls to a new low, it confirms the decline. As the downtrend grows old, prices fall more slowly or volume dries up—that's when a reversal is in the cards.

   Adding an envelope to the chart of Force Index can help you detect its extreme deviations from the norm, which tend to lead to price trend reversals. This method for catching deviations and potential reversals works well with weekly charts, but not with the daily and intraday charts. This is truly a longer-term tool.

CHAPTER 38

Open Interest

From Dr. Alexander Elder, *The New Trading for a Living* (Hoboken, New Jersey: John Wiley & Sons, 2014), Part 5, Chapter 31.

Open interest is the number of contracts held by buyers or owed by short sellers in any derivative market, such as futures or options.

Stock market shares are traded for as long as the company that listed them stays in business as an independent unit. Most shares are held as long positions, with only a small percentage of shorts. In futures and options, on the other hand, the total size of long and short positions is always identical, due to the fact that they are contracts for future delivery. When someone wants to buy a contract, someone else has to sell it to them, i.e., go short. If you want to buy a call option for 100 shares of Google, another trader has to sell you that option; in order for you to be long, someone else has to be short. **Open interest equals the total long or the total short positions**.

Futures and options contracts are designed to last for only a set period of time. A futures or options buyer who wants to accept delivery and a seller who wants to deliver have to wait until the first delivery day. This waiting period ensures that the numbers of contracts held long and short are always equal. In any case, very few futures and options traders plan to deliver or accept delivery. Most traders close out their positions early, settling in cash long before the first notice day. We'll return to the topic of futures and options in Part Eight of this book on trading vehicles.

Open interest rises when new positions are being created and falls when positions are being closed. For example, if open interest in April COMEX gold futures is 20,000 contracts, it means that bulls are long and bears short 20,000 contracts. If open interest rises to 20,200, it means that the net of 200 new contracts have been created: both bought and sold short.

Open interest falls when a bull who is long sells to a bear who is short but wants to cover his short position. As both of them get out, open interest falls by the size of their trade, since one or more contracts disappear from that market.

If a new bull buys from an old bull that is getting out of his long position, open interest remains unchanged. Nor does the open interest change when a new bear sells to an old bear who wants to buy to cover his short position. In summary, open interest rises when "fresh blood" enters that market and falls as current bulls and bears start leaving that market, as illustrated in the table below:

Buyer	Seller	Open Interest
New buyer	New seller	Increases
New buyer	Former buyer sells	Unchanged
Former seller buys to cover	New seller	Unchanged
Former seller buys to cover	Former buyer sells	Decreases

Technicians usually plot open interest as a line below price bars (Figure 38.1). Open interest in any market varies from season to season because of massive hedging by industrial users and producers at different stages of the annual production cycle. Open interest gives important messages when it deviates from its seasonal norm.

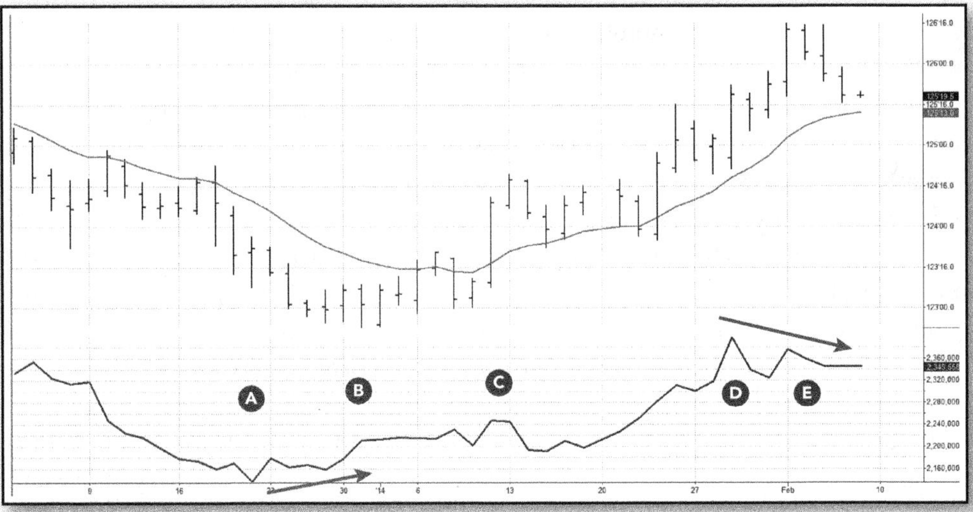

FIGURE 38.1 TYH14 daily, 13-day EMA, open interest. ***(Chart by TradeStation)***

Open Interest

Open interest (OI) reflects the number of all short or long positions in any futures or options market. Since the two are equal in the derivatives markets, OI reflects the degree of conviction among bulls and bears.

Rising OI shows that the conflict between bulls and bears is becoming more intense and confirms the existing trend. Falling OI, on the other hand, shows that losers are leaving the market, while the winners are cashing in—it signals that the trend is nearing its end.

Near the left edge of this chart of March 2014 Treasury Notes futures (TYH14), the trend is down, but the declining OI warns bears not to overstay the downtrend. OI bottomed out in area A, T-Notes in area B, and in area C, both were in clear uptrends, with rising OI calling for higher prices ahead. OI topped out in area D, and while prices continue to rise in area E, the new downtrend of OI serves up a warning to the bulls near the right edge of the chart.

Not all charts of open interest look as smooth and clear as this one. Serious traders don't expect to find a magic tool of a single indicator—they use several indicators and act only when their messages confirm one another.

Crowd Psychology

It takes one bull and one bear to create a futures or options contract. A bull who believes that prices will rise buys a contract. A bear who thinks that prices are going to drop goes short by selling a contract for future delivery. With a trade between a new bull and a new bear, open interest rises by the number of contracts they traded. A single trade is unlikely to move any market, but when thousands of traders make similar trades, they propel or reverse market trends.

Open interest reflects the intensity of conflict between bulls and bears. It depends on their willingness to maintain long and short positions. When bulls and bears don't expect the market to move in their favor, they close out their positions, reducing open interest.

There are two people on the opposite sides of every trade, and one of them will be hurt when prices change. In a rally, bears will get hurt, and in a decline, bulls will suffer. As long as the losers hold on, hoping and hanging on to their positions, open interest doesn't change.

A rise in open interest shows that a crowd of confident bulls is facing down a crowd of equally confident bears. It points to a growing disagreement between the two camps. One group is sure to lose, but as long as potential losers keep pouring in, the trend will continue. These ideas have been clearly put forth in L. Dee Belveal's classic book, *Charting Commodity Market Price Behavior*.

It takes conviction among both bulls and bears to maintain a trend. Rising open interest shows that both camps keep adding to their positions. If they strongly disagree about the future course of prices, then the supply of losers is growing, and the current trend is likely to persist. An increase in open interest gives a green light to the existing trend.

If open interest rises during an uptrend, it shows that longs are buying while bears are shorting because they believe that the market is overvalued. They are likely to run for cover when the uptrend squeezes them harder—and their buying will propel prices higher.

If open interest rises during a downtrend, it shows that shorts are aggressively selling, while bottom pickers are buying. Those bargain hunters are likely to bail out when falling prices hurt them, and their selling will push prices even lower.

When a bull is convinced that prices are going higher and decides to buy, but a bear is afraid to sell short, that bull can buy only from another bull who bought earlier and now wants to cash out. Their trade creates no new contract, and open interest stays unchanged. When open interest goes flat during a rally, it shows that the supply of losers has stopped growing.

When a bear is convinced that prices are going lower and wants to sell short, but a bull is afraid to buy from him, that bear can sell only to another bear who shorted earlier and now wants to cover, take profits, and leave. Their trade creates no new contract, and open interest does not change. When open interest stays flat during a decline, it shows that the supply of bottom pickers isn't growing. Whenever open interest flattens out, it flashes a yellow light—a warning that the trend is aging and the best gains are probably behind.

When a bull decides to get out of his long position, a bear decides to cover his short position, and the two trade with one another, a contract disappears, and open interest shrinks. Falling open interest shows that losers are bailing out, while winners are taking profits. When the disagreement between bulls and bears decreases, the trend is ripe for a reversal. Falling open interest shows that winners are cashing in and losers are giving up hope. It signals that the trend is approaching its end.

Trading Rules

1. When open interest rises during a rally, it confirms the uptrend and gives a green light to add to long positions. It shows that more short sellers are coming into the market. When they bail out, their short covering is likely to push the rally higher.

   When open interest rises as prices fall, it shows that bottom pickers are active in the market. It gives a green light to shorting because those bargain hunters are likely to push prices lower when they throw in the towel.

   If open interest rises when prices are in a trading range, it's a bearish sign. Commercial hedgers are much more likely to sell short than speculators. A sharp increase in open interest while prices are flat shows that savvy hedgers are probably shorting the market. You want to avoid trading against those who likely have better information than you.
2. If open interest falls while prices are in a trading range, it identifies short covering by major commercial interests and gives a buy signal. When commercials start covering shorts, they show that they expect the market to rise.

   When open interest falls during a rally, it shows that winners and losers alike are becoming cautious. Longs are taking profits, and shorts are covering. Markets discount the future, and a trend that is accepted by the majority is ready to reverse. If open interest falls during a rally, consider selling and getting out.

   When open interest falls during a decline, it shows that shorts are covering and buyers are taking losses and bailing out. If open interest falls while prices slide, take profits on short positions.
3. When open interest goes flat during a rally, it shows that the uptrend is getting old and the best gains have already been made. This gives you a signal to tighten stops on long positions and avoid new buying. When open interest goes flat during a decline, it warns you that the downtrend is mature and it is best to tighten stops on short positions. Flat open interest in a trading range does not contribute any new information.

More on Open Interest

The higher the open interest, the more active the market, and the less **slippage** you risk when getting in and out of positions. Short-term traders should focus on the contracts with the highest open interest. In the futures markets, the highest open interest tends to be in the front months. As the first notice day approaches and open interest of the front month begins to drop, while open interest in the next month begins to rise, it signals to roll over your position into the next month.

For more information regarding Dr. Alexander Elder's work, please visit www.elder.com.

CHAPTER 39

Introduction to the Wave Principle

From Wayne Gorman, Jeffrey Kennedy, and Robert R. Prechter, Jr., *Visual Guide to Elliott Wave Trading* (Hoboken, New Jersey: John Wiley & Sons, 2013), Appendix A.

In the 1930s, R. N. Elliott discovered that market price movements adhere to a certain pattern composed of what he called *waves*. He called the pattern's characteristics the Wave Principle. Every wave has a starting point and ending point in price and time. The pattern is continuous in that the end of one wave marks the beginning of the next wave. The basic pattern consists of five individual waves that are linked together and achieve progress as market prices move up or down (see Figure 39.1).

This five-wave sequence, labeled with numbers 1 through 5, is called a *motive wave*, because it propels the market in the direction of the main trend. Subwaves 1, 3, and 5 are also motive waves. Subwaves 2 and 4 are called *corrective waves*, because they interrupt the main trend and travel in the opposite direction.

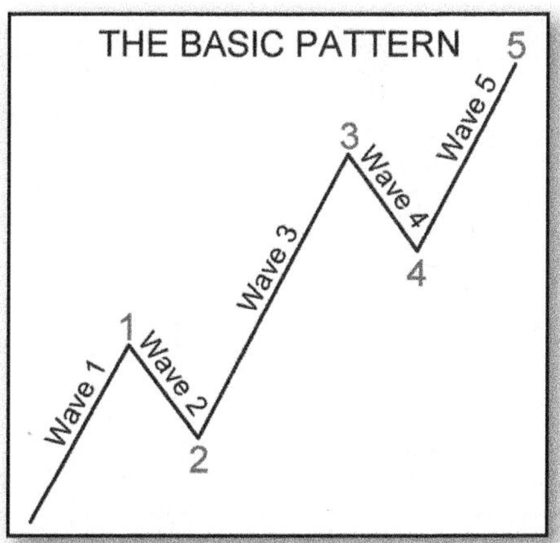

FIGURE 39.1
Source: Adapted from Elliott Wave Principle.

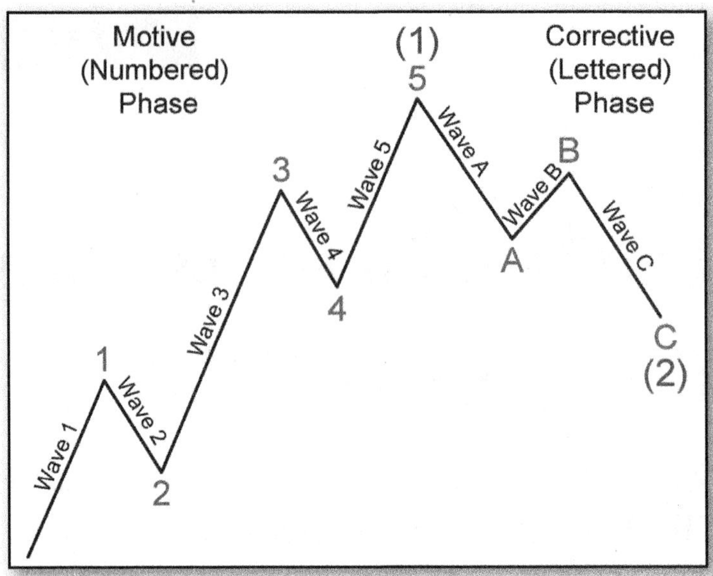

FIGURE 39.2
Source: Adapted from Elliott Wave Principle.

Two Elliott wave rules govern motive waves: Wave 2 always retraces less than 100 percent of wave 1, and wave 3 can never be the shortest motive subwave (although it does not have to be the longest).

After a five-wave sequence is complete, the corrective wave begins. The corrective wave partially retraces the progress made by the motive wave. It follows a three-wave sequence or a specific combination of three-wave structures. Its waves are labeled using letters, for example A, B, and C (see Figure 39.2).

All waves are part of other waves at larger degree. They are also divisible into waves at lower degree, as shown in Figure 39.3. Motive and corrective waves can move up or down.

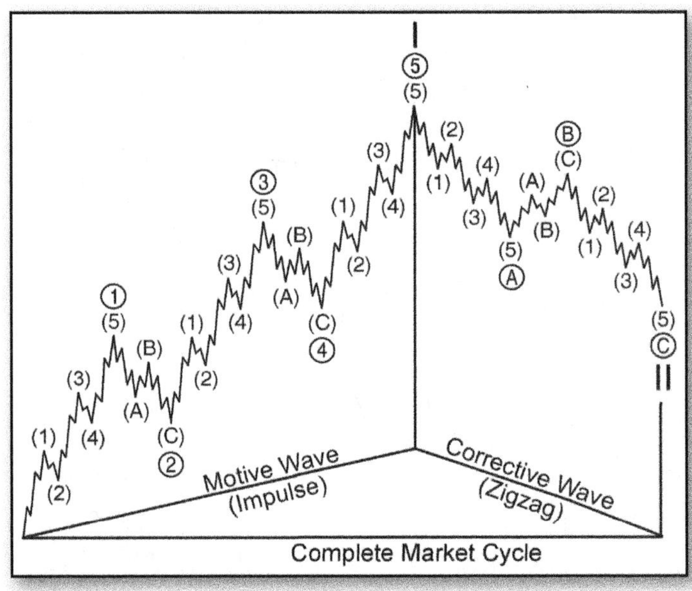

FIGURE 39.3
Source: Adapted from Elliott Wave Principle.

A number of rules and guidelines apply to wave formations. Guidelines differ from hard-and-fast rules in that they describe what is most likely to occur, even though it may not always occur.

Motive Waves

The two types of motive waves are *impulse* and *diagonal*.

Impulse

The impulse wave, which is the strongest form of motive wave, follows these three rules:

1. Wave 2 never moves beyond the start of wave 1. In other words, it always retraces less than 100 percent of wave 1.
2. Wave 3 is never the shortest motive subwave, but it does not have to be the longest.
3. Wave 4 never enters the price territory of wave 1.

Add to these rules one strong guideline: Wave 4 should not enter the price territory of wave 2.

Rules are crucial to real-time application. In Figure 39.4, the first wave count is incorrect, because the end of wave 4 enters the price territory of wave 1. The second wave count is incorrect, because wave 3 is the shortest motive wave. The third wave count correctly displays the first three subdivisions of wave 3. The next wave count is correct because, even though wave 3 is not the longest motive wave, it is also not the shortest one. The last wave count is incorrect, because wave 2 here retraces more than 100 percent of wave 1.

In an impulse wave, waves 1 and 5 are always motive waves (that is, either impulse or diagonal), while wave 3 is always an impulse wave. Waves 2 and 4 are always corrective waves. Therefore, we call an impulse wave a 5-3-5-3-5 structure.

Extension

In an impulse wave, often one of the motive waves, usually wave 3 or wave 5, is extended. An *extended wave* is an elongated impulse wave whose motive subwaves at

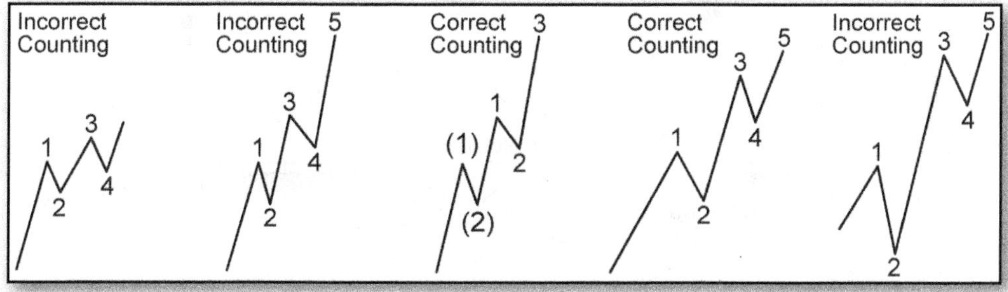

FIGURE 39.4
Source: Adapted from Elliott Wave Principle.

next lower degree are as large as or larger than the nonextended motive wave(s) of the same impulse wave.

Figure 39.5 shows diagrams of extensions for waves 1, 3, and 5. Sometimes the initial subwaves of an impulse wave are all about the same length, and therefore it is difficult to determine which motive wave is extended. This aspect is displayed in the diagram at the bottom, where the extended wave could be 1, 3, or 5. For all practical purposes, it does not matter which one is extended, as long as there is a total of nine waves. Third-wave extensions are often seen in the stock market, while fifth-wave extensions are often seen in commodity markets.

If wave 1 is extended, expect waves 3 and 5 to be about equal in length. If wave 3 is extended, expect wave 5 to be about equal to wave 1. If waves 1 and 3 are about equal, expect wave 5 to be extended. After a fifth-wave extension terminates, expect a swift and sharp reversal back to the second subwave of the extension. Rarely do two motive waves extend, but if that does happen, it is usually waves 3 and 5. We call that structure a *double extension*.

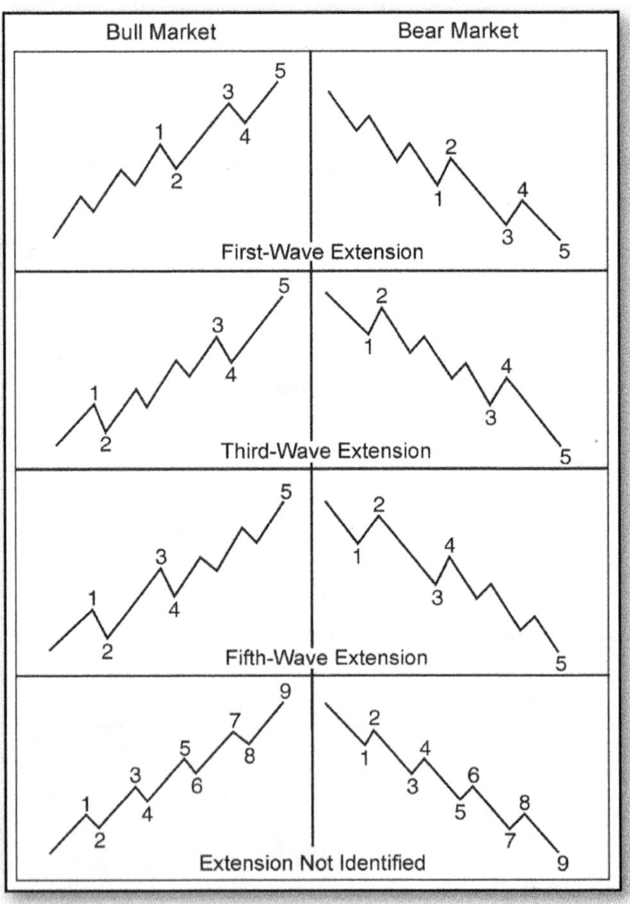

FIGURE 39.5

Source: Elliott Wave Principle.

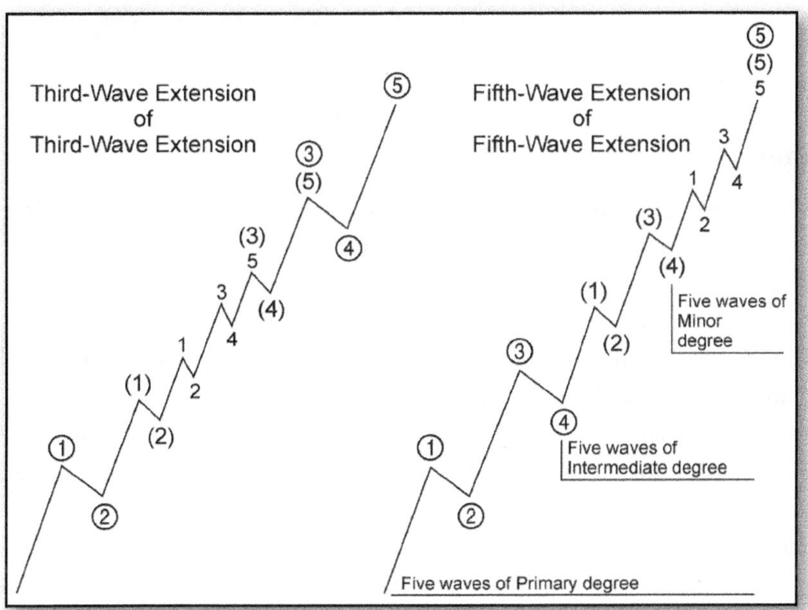

FIGURE 39.6
Source: Elliott Wave Principle.

When an extension occurs within an extended wave, it is common for the extension at lower degree to be in the same wave position as the extension of which it is a part. For example, in a wave 3 extension, subwave 3 is often extended (see Figure 39.6).

Truncation

In an impulse wave, a *truncation* occurs when wave 5 fails to terminate beyond the end of wave 3. A truncated fifth wave still unfolds as a five-wave structure (see Figure 39.7). A truncated fifth wave, which is a sign of exhaustion in the main

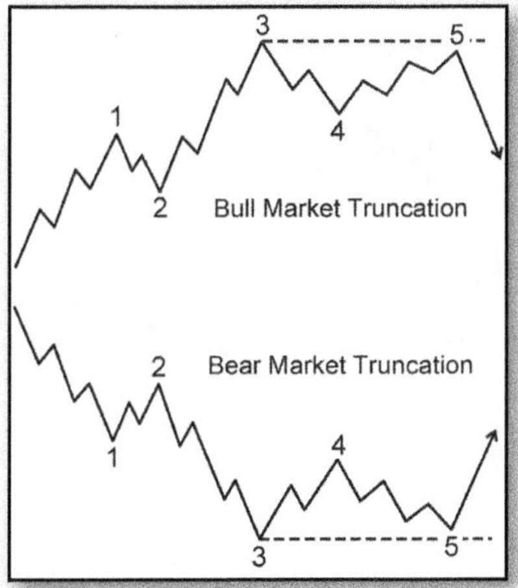

FIGURE 39.7
Source: Elliott Wave Principle.

trend at next higher degree, is often preceded by an exceptionally strong third wave of the same degree. A truncated fifth wave is often followed by a swift and sharp reversal.

Diagonal

Although diagonal and impulse waves are both motive waves, diagonals differ significantly from impulse waves in that they follow the first two rules but not the third rule about wave 4 never entering in the price territory of wave 1. In a diagonal, in fact, wave 4 almost always enters in the price territory of wave 1.

A diagonal is typically contracting but, in rare occasions, expanding. In the contracting variety, wave 3 is shorter than wave 1, wave 5 is shorter than wave 3, and wave 4 is shorter than wave 2. In the expanding variety, wave 3 is longer than wave 1, wave 5 is longer than wave 3, and wave 4 is longer than wave 2. Since expanding diagonals are so infrequent, we will confine the rest of our discussion to the contracting variety.

The two types of diagonals are leading diagonal and ending diagonal, with the ending diagonal being more common. Within an ending diagonal, subwaves 1, 2, 3, 4, and 5 always take corrective-wave form, specifically either a single or multiple zigzag. Ending diagonals can form only as fifth waves of impulse waves and C waves of zigzags and flats. (We will cover zigzags and flats in the section on corrective waves.)

In Figure 39.8, wave (5) is a contracting ending diagonal. It is bounded by two converging trendlines, which gives the diagonal a wedge shape. One trendline connects the termination points of waves 1 and 3, and the other trendline connects the termination points of waves 2 and 4. Wave 5 can end either on or slightly above or below the 1-3 trendline. If wave 5 moves beyond that trendline, it is called a throw-over. A swift and sharp reversal usually brings prices at least back to where the diagonal began and usually far further. The

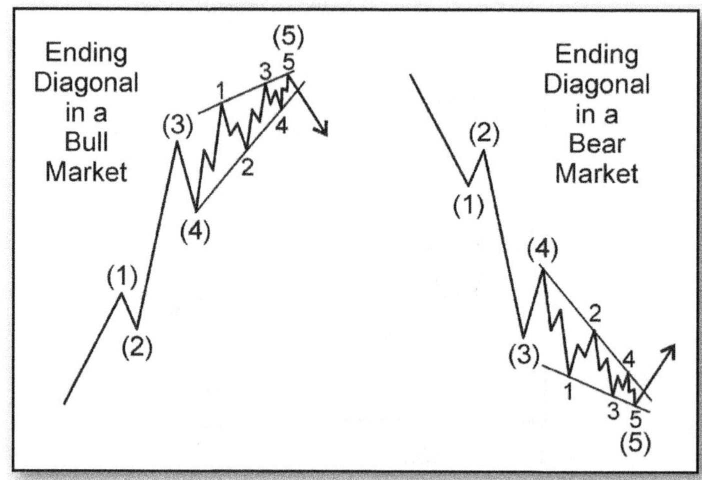

FIGURE 39.8

Source: Adapted from Elliott Wave Principle.

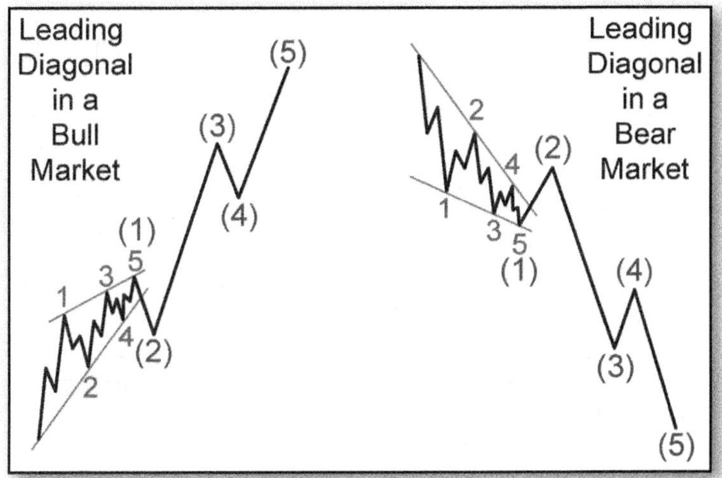

FIGURE 39.9
Source: Adapted from Elliott Wave Principle.

reversal usually takes anywhere from one-third to one-half the time that it took the diagonal to form.

In a leading diagonal, waves 1, 3, and 5 are all impulse waves or all corrective waves in the form of zigzags. Waves 2 and 4 are always zigzag patterns. A leading diagonal can form wave 1 of an impulse wave and the first wave of a zigzag, which we call wave A. This formation is exceptionally rare.

In Figure 39.9, wave (1) is a contracting leading diagonal and has the same structural characteristics as the contracting ending diagonal. After a wave 1 leading diagonal terminates, expect wave 2 to retrace a significant portion of wave 1.

Corrective Waves

In markets, we have all heard the old adage, "nothing moves in a straight line." The Elliott wave model incorporates this observation. Market trends invariably encounter interruptions. In Elliott wave terms, we refer to these interruptions as corrective waves.

Corrective waves are either *sharp* or *sideways*. A sharp corrective wave usually has a relatively steep angle, never registering a new price extreme beyond the previous wave that it is retracing. A sideways correction's boundaries are closer to horizontal and, before terminating, it usually records a new price extreme beyond the previous wave that it is retracing. All corrective waves achieve some partial retracement of the preceding wave of the same degree. Because corrective waves come in many variations, it is a challenge to identify them in real time and to know when they are complete.

The three basic types of corrective wave patterns are *zigzag*, *flat,* and *triangle*. Elliotticians often use the word "three" as a noun, meaning a corrective pattern. When two or more of these patterns link together to form a sideways correction, they are called a *combination*.

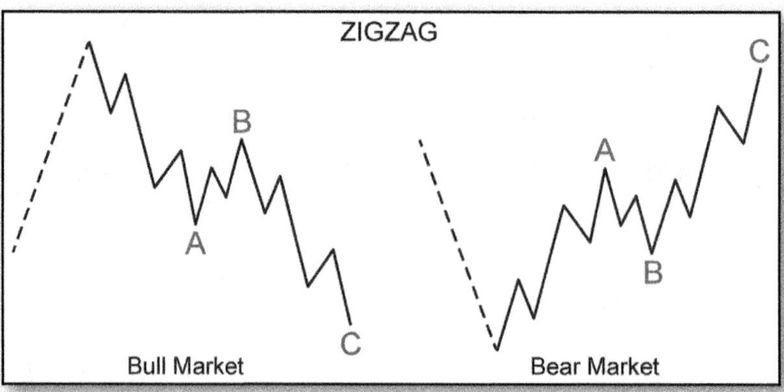

FIGURE 39.10
Source: Adapted from Elliott Wave Principle.

Zigzag

A zigzag is a sharp, three-wave corrective pattern, labeled A-B-C. Wave A is always an impulse or leading diagonal, and wave C is always an impulse or ending diagonal. Wave B is always a corrective wave, that is zigzag, flat, triangle or combination. Therefore, we call the zigzag a 5-3-5 structure (see Figure 39.10).

In a zigzag, wave B can never go beyond the start of wave A, and wave C almost always goes beyond the end of wave A. If wave C does not go beyond the end of wave A, it is called a truncated wave C.

Zigzag corrections can take the form of one, two, or three zigzags. Three zigzags appear to be the limit. Whenever there is more than one zigzag, another corrective wave forms in order to link one zigzag to the other. In a double zigzag, the first zigzag is labeled W, the second zigzag is labeled Y, and the corrective wave that links the two zigzags together is labeled X. In a triple zigzag, the third zigzag is labeled Z. Wave X can form any corrective structure but is usually a zigzag. It always moves in the opposite direction of wave W (see Figure 39.11).

Flat

A flat is a sideways, three-wave corrective pattern, also labeled A-B-C. Waves A and B are always corrective waves, and wave C is always a motive wave. Therefore, we call

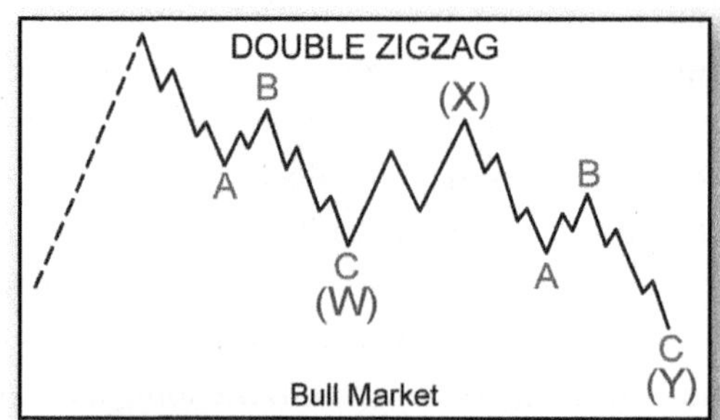

FIGURE 39.11
Source: Adapted from Elliott Wave Principle.

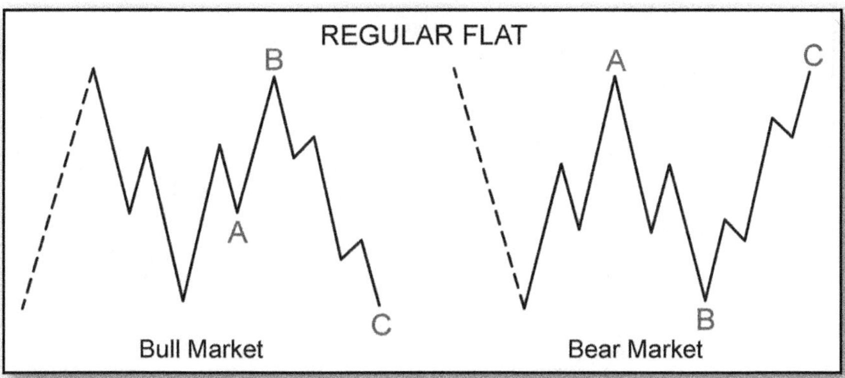

FIGURE 39.12
Source: Adapted from Elliott Wave Principle.

the flat a 3-3-5 structure. In flats, waves A and B are never triangles and rarely flats. Wave B usually retraces at least 90 percent of wave A. There are three types of flats: regular, expanded, and running. The most common type of flat is the expanded flat. Running flats are rare.

In a regular flat, wave B ends at about the same level as the beginning of wave A, and wave C ends slightly past the end of wave A (see Figure 39.12).

In an expanded flat, wave B ends beyond the start of wave A, and wave C ends substantially beyond the end of wave A (see Figure 39.13).

In a running flat, wave B ends beyond the start of wave A, and wave C fails to reach the end of wave A (see Figure 39.14).

Triangle

A triangle is a sideways corrective wave with subwaves labeled A-B-C-D-E. In most cases, all the subwaves of a triangle are zigzags or multiple zigzag patterns. Therefore, we call the triangle a 3-3-3-3-3 structure. On occasion, one of these subwaves takes the form of another triangle, and that subwave is usually wave E. Only one of

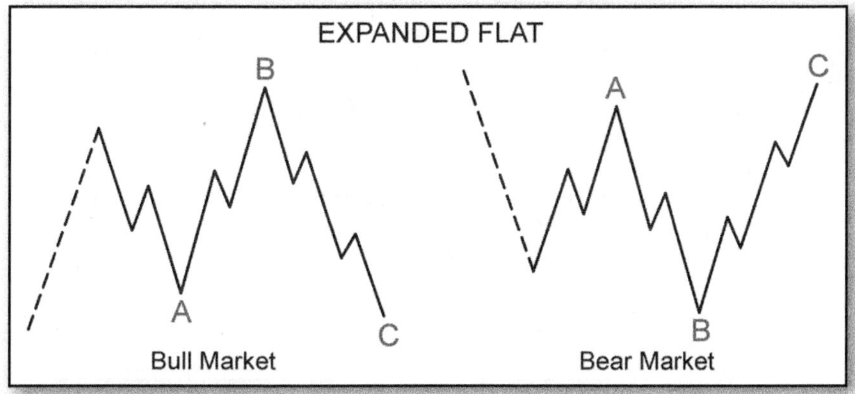

FIGURE 39.13
Source: Adapted from Elliott Wave Principle.

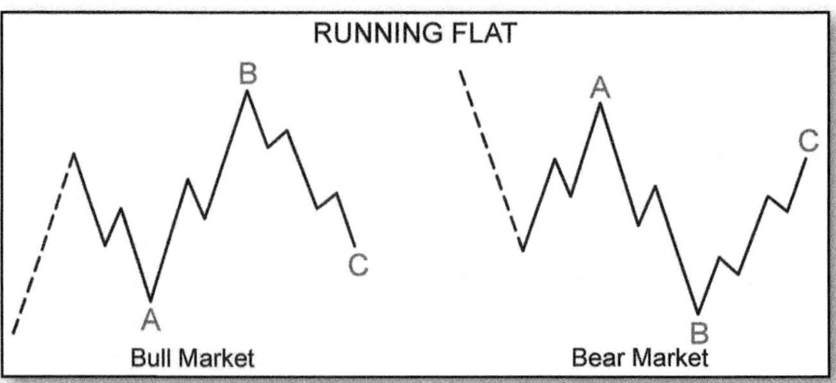

FIGURE 39.14
Source: Adapted from Elliott Wave Principle.

these subwaves can be complex, meaning strung out over time, and that subwave is normally wave C, D, or E. Figure 39.15 shows the three types of triangles: contracting, barrier, and expanding.

In a triangle, the line that connects the termination points of waves A and C is called the A-C trendline, and the line that connects the termination points of waves B and D is called the B-D trendline. Wave E may terminate at, short of, or beyond the A-C trendline.

In contracting and barrier triangles, the A-C and B-D trendlines converge. In barrier triangles, the B-D trendline is horizontal, and the A-C trendline points in the

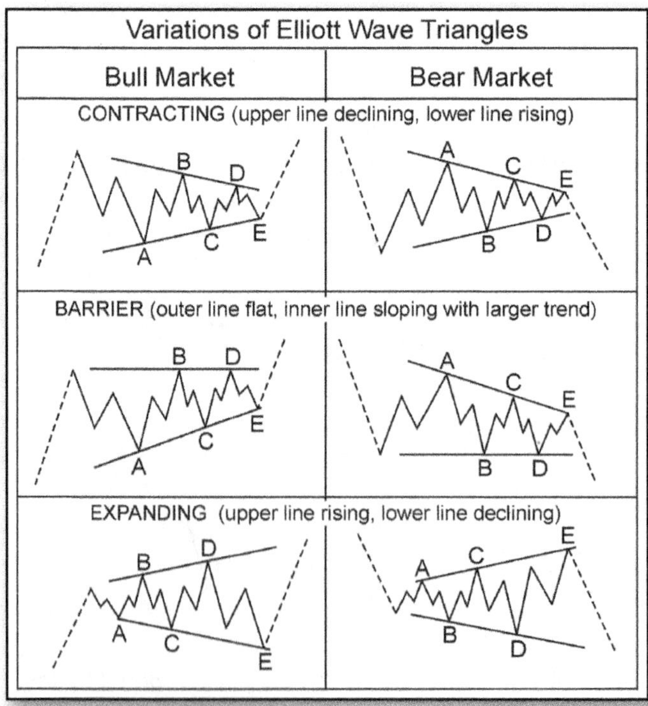

FIGURE 39.15
Source: Elliott Wave Principle.

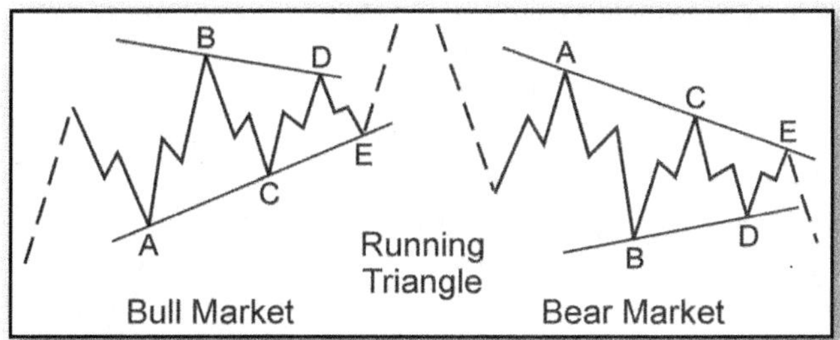

FIGURE 39.16
Source: Elliott Wave Principle.

direction of the main trend at next higher degree. In expanding triangles, the A-C and B-D trendlines diverge.

In a contracting triangle, wave C never moves beyond the end of wave A, wave D never moves beyond the end of wave B, and wave E never moves beyond the end of wave C. Wave B may or may not move beyond the start of wave A. As shown in Figure 39.16, if wave B moves beyond the start of wave A, the triangle is called a running contracting triangle. Running triangles are common.

A barrier triangle has the same characteristics as a contracting triangle, with the following exception: In a barrier triangle, wave D ends at about the same level as wave B. In an expanding triangle, after completion of wave A, each new subwave moves beyond the starting point of the previous subwave.

A triangle always precedes the final motive wave in the direction of the main trend at next higher degree. That final motive wave normally makes a swift and sharp move, which is called the *post-triangle thrust* (see Figure 39.17).

For a contracting or barrier triangle, we can estimate the minimum termination point of the thrust by extending the A-C and B-D trendlines back to the start of wave A and then drawing a vertical line that connects those two trendlines. That vertical distance defines the "width" of the triangle. We then apply the width of the triangle to the end of wave E to give us an estimate for the next move in the direction of the main trend at next higher degree.

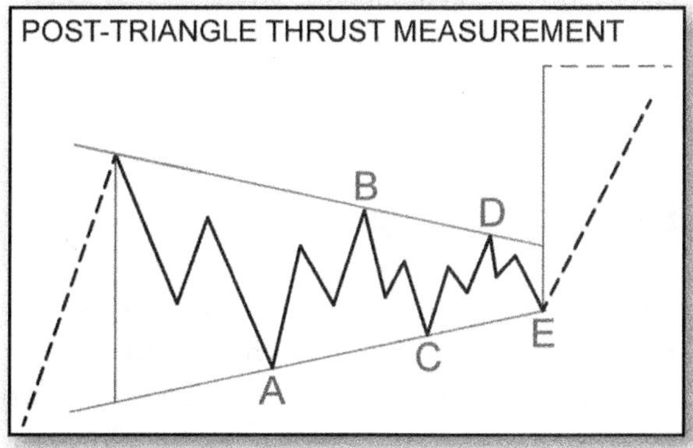

FIGURE 39.17
Source: Elliott Wave Principle.

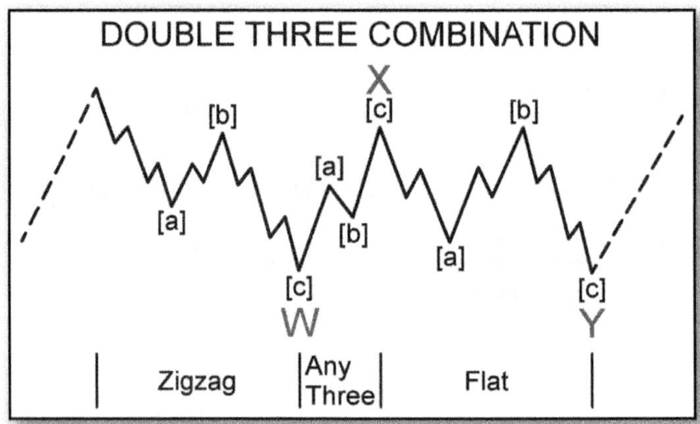

FIGURE 39.18
Source: Elliott Wave Principle.

Within an impulse wave, a post-triangle thrust measurement estimates the minimum length for wave 5. If wave 5 goes beyond the estimated termination point, expect a prolonged fifth wave.

Combination

A combination is a sideways corrective pattern that includes two or more corrective structures. Three corrective structures appear to be the limit. Each corrective structure is linked by an X wave, which has three characteristics: It can be any corrective pattern; it always moves in the opposite direction of the previous corrective pattern; and it is usually a zigzag. There never appears to be more than one triangle in a combination, and, when one appears, it always seems to be the final corrective structure in the combination. The two types of combinations are double three and triple three.

A double three combination includes two corrective patterns—the first labeled W and the second labeled Y—that are linked by an X wave. Figure 39.18 represents one of many variations of a double three correction. A triple three combination includes three corrective patterns, labeled W, Y, and Z, each linked by X waves. Triple threes are rare. Within double and triple threes, X waves are usually zigzags and never triangles.

Fibonacci Relationships

Price and time aspects of wave patterns often reflect *Fibonacci ratios*. In wave formations, the key Fibonacci ratio is .618, which is known as the Golden Ratio or Golden Mean. It is represented by the Greek letter *phi* (ϕ), pronounced "fie." Its inverse is 1.618. *Phi* is the only number which, when added to one, is also equal to its inverse. If we square *phi* or subtract *phi* from 1, the result is .382, which is another Fibonacci ratio.

Fibonacci Ratios and Multiples		
Ratio	Inverse	Φ^N
.618	1.618	$(1.618)^1$
.382	2.618	$(1.618)^2$
.236	4.236	$(1.618)^3$
.146	6.854	$(1.618)^4$
.090	11.089	$(1.618)^5$

FIGURE 39.19

Figure 39.19 displays a number of Fibonacci ratios.

Each ratio can be expressed as *phi*—either .618 or its inverse 1.618—raised to a power. Other important Fibonacci numbers related to wave formation are 0.5 (1/2), .786 (square root of .618), 1.0 (1/1), and 2.0 (2/1).

In Elliott wave patterns, the key types of Fibonacci relationships are *retracements*, *multiples,* and *dividers*. Although these relationships are more commonly used to estimate the length of certain waves with respect to price, they can also be used to estimate the length of waves with respect to time.

Retracements

In impulse waves, second waves usually make deep retracements near .618 times the length of wave one. Fourth waves usually make shallow retracements that are often close to .382 times the length of wave three (see Figure 39.20).

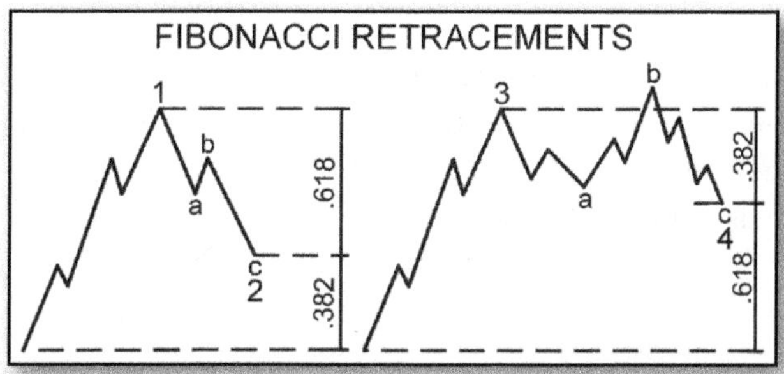

FIGURE 39.20
Source: Elliott Wave Principle.

Guidelines for Typical Retracements of Wave A by Wave B in Zigzags	
Wave B	Net Retracement (%)
Zigzag	50–79
Triangle	38–50
Running Triangle	10–40
Flat	38–79
Combination	38–50

FIGURE 39.21

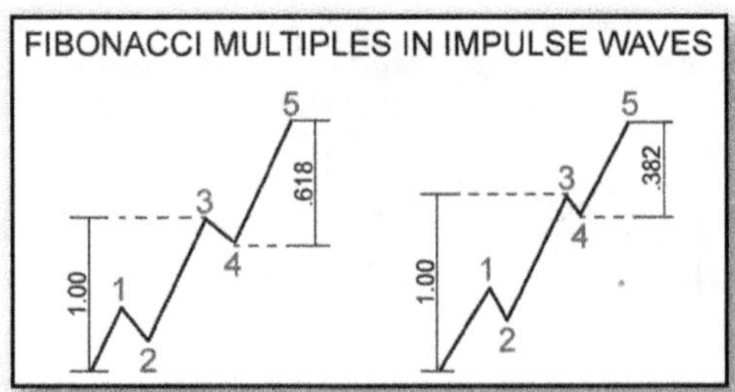

FIGURE 39.22
Source: Elliott Wave Principle.

In a zigzag, the retracement of wave A by wave B will depend on the structure of wave B. For example, in Figure 39.21, if wave B is a zigzag, it should retrace 0.5 to .786 of wave A. If wave B is a triangle, it should retrace .382 to 0.50 of wave A.

Multiples

In an impulse wave, wave 5 will often equal .618 or .382 times the net distance traveled of waves 1 through 3 (see Figure 39.22).

When wave 3 is extended, expect wave 5 to be related to wave 1 by equality or .618. When wave 5 is extended, expect wave 5, in price terms, to travel 1.618 times the net distance traveled of waves 1 through 3. If that length is exceeded, look for larger multiples as shown in Figure 39.22. When wave 1 is extended, expect the net distance traveled of waves 3 through 5 to equal .618 times the length of wave 1 (see Figure 39.23).

The most common Fibonacci relationship in single zigzags and multiple zigzag structures is *equality*—for example, C = A in the single zigzag, and Y = W in the double zigzag (see Figure 39.24).

When equality is not present, look for the other Fibonacci relationships, as shown in Figure 39.25.

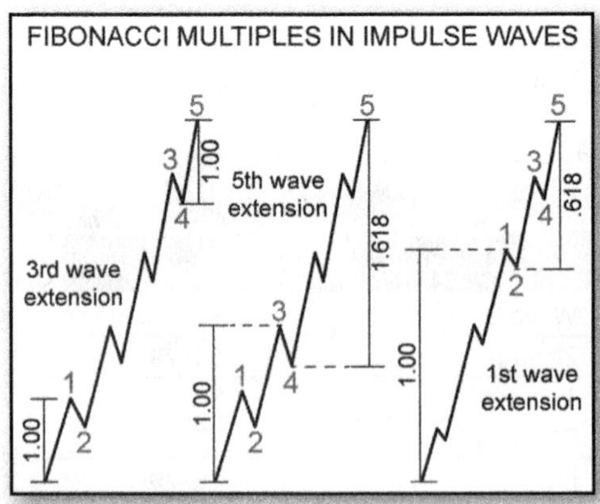

FIGURE 39.23
Source: Adapted from Elliott Wave Principle.

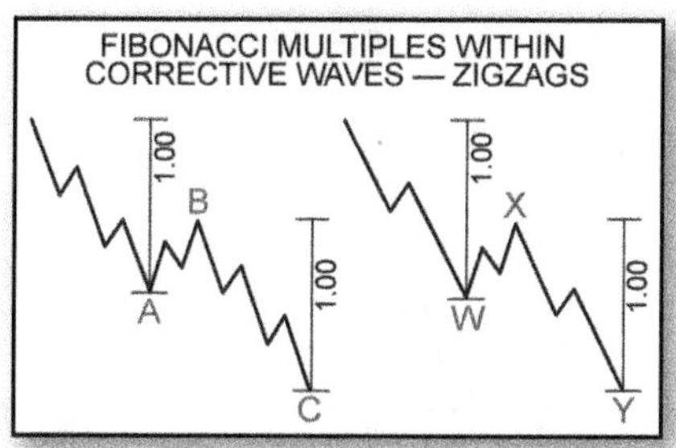

FIGURE 39.24
Source: Adapted from Elliott Wave Principle.

Fibonacci Relationships
Single Zigzag
Wave C = Wave A
Wave C = .618 Wave A
Wave C = 1.618 Wave A
Wave C = .618 Wave A past Wave A
Double Zigzag
Wave Y = Wave W
Wave Y = .618 Wave W
Wave Y = 1.618 Wave W
Wave Y = .618 Wave W past Wave W
Triple Zigzag
Equality for W, Y, and Z
Ratio of .618, i.e., Wave Z = .618 Wave Y

FIGURE 39.25

The relationships for multiple zigzags are analogous to those for a single zigzag.

In a regular flat, waves A, B, and C are generally equal to each other (see Figure 39.26).

In an expanded flat, expect wave C either to equal 1.618 times the length of wave A or to terminate at a price equal to .618 times the length of wave A past wave A. Expect wave B to equal 1.236 or 1.382 times the length of wave A (see Figure 39.27).

The alternate waves of a contracting triangle are often related to each other by the Fibonacci ratio of .618 (see Figure 39.28).

For expanding triangles, that ratio is 1.618.

Dividers

If we divide any length in such a way that the ratio of the smaller part to the larger part is equal to the ratio of the larger part to the whole, that ratio will always be .618 (see Figure 39.29).

This is called the *Golden Section*, which results in a .382/.618 split. Certain wave termination points will often divide wave patterns into the Golden Section or sometimes a .50/.50 split.

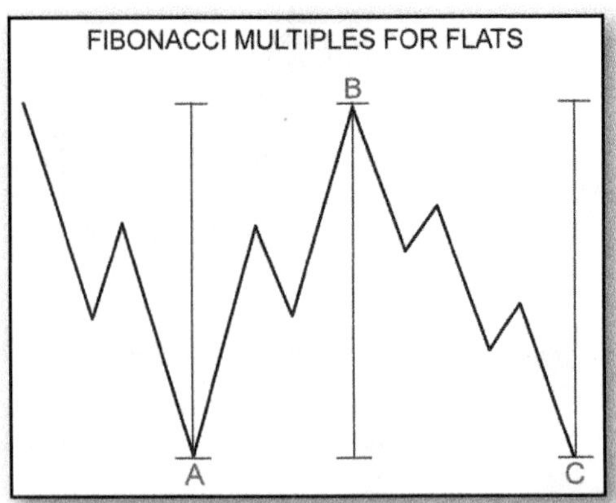

FIGURE 39.26

Source: Adapted from Elliott Wave Principle.

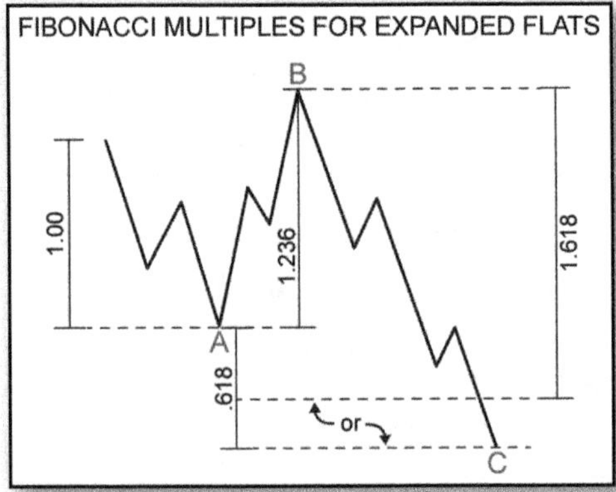

FIGURE 39.27

Source: Adapted from Elliott Wave Principle.

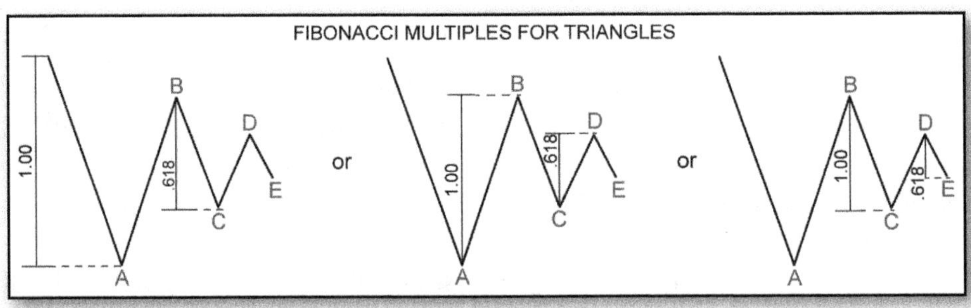

FIGURE 39.28

Source: Adapted from Elliott Wave Principle.

In an impulse wave, wave 4 (usually its origin or termination point) will often divide the entire wave into the Golden Section or into two equal parts (see Figure 39.30).

Clusters

Whenever possible, we prefer not to rely on just one Fibonacci relationship in forecasting market movements. The most powerful application of Fibonacci analysis is the identification of *Fibonacci clusters*. A Fibonacci price cluster occurs when two or

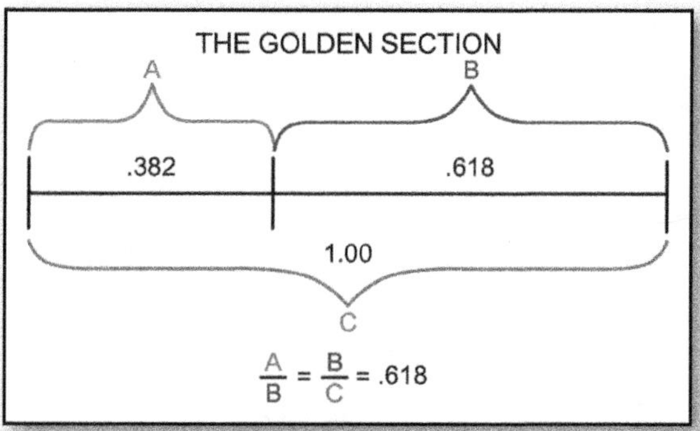

FIGURE 39.29
Source: Adapted from Elliott Wave Principle.

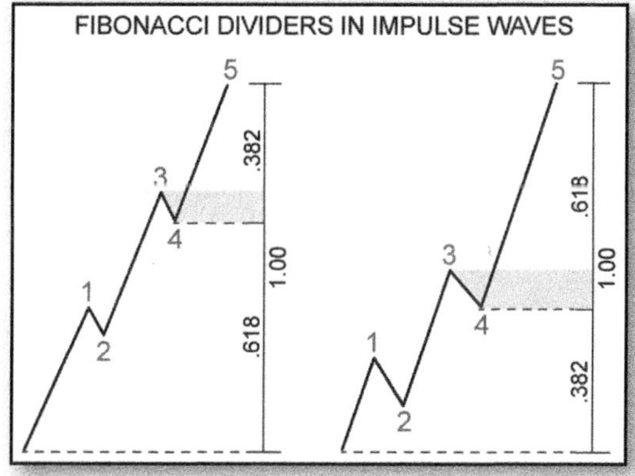

FIGURE 39.30
Source: Adapted from Elliott Wave Principle.

more Fibonacci price relationships project to approximately the same price level. (A Fibonacci time cluster occurs when two or more Fibonacci time relationships project to approximately the same time.) Since wave patterns unfold at all time frames simultaneously, there is often an opportunity to spot a Fibonacci cluster. The diagram in Figure 39.31 illustrates a Fibonacci price cluster.

Figure 39.31 identifies, at the same general price level, the following three Fibonacci relationships:

1. Primary wave [2] retraces .618 of Primary wave [1].
2. In the expanded flat, Intermediate wave (C) equals 1.618 times the length of Intermediate wave (A).
3. Within the Intermediate wave (C) impulse wave, Minor wave 5 equals Minor wave 1.

For More Information

Learn more at your exclusive Reader Resources site. You will find a free online edition of *Elliott Wave Principle* by Frost and Prechter, plus lessons on Elliott wave

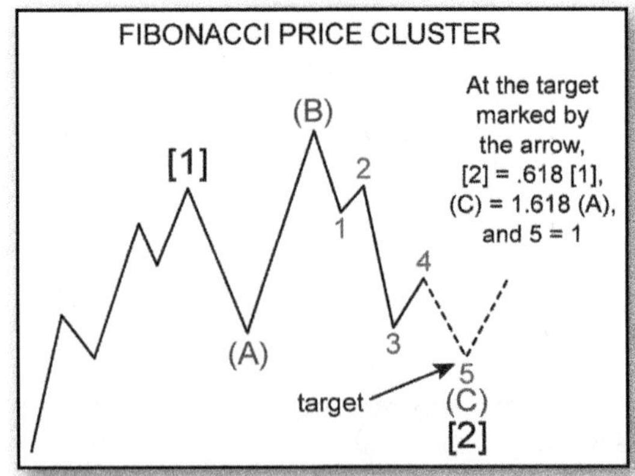

FIGURE 39.31

Source: Adapted from Elliott Wave Principle.

analysis, how to trade specific patterns, and how to use Fibonacci and other technical indicators to increase your confidence as you apply the Wave Principle in real time. Go to: www.elliottwave.com/wave/ReaderResources.

CHAPTER 40

The Anatomy of Elliott Wave Trading

From Wayne Gorman, Jeffrey Kennedy, and Robert R. Prechter, Jr., *Visual Guide to Elliott Wave Trading* (Hoboken, New Jersey: John Wiley & Sons, 2013), Chapter 1.

When teaching the Wave Principle, I begin each class by stating that analysis and trading represent two different skill sets. Although you may be a talented analyst, that does not mean you will be a successful trader and vice versa. I learned the hard way over many years that skilled analysis is a mastery of observation, while successful trading is a mastery of self.

When it comes to trading, there is no right way or wrong way—only your way. One trader's tolerance for risk will be starkly different from another's, just as time frame, portfolio size, and markets traded will also be different. Thus, the guidelines offered within this chapter on how to trade specific Elliott wave patterns are just that—guidelines, but ones that have served me well for many years.

My best advice to you as you look for a trading opportunity is to start your search by asking the question, "Do I see a wave pattern I recognize?" You should look for one of the five core Elliott wave patterns: impulse wave, ending diagonal, zigzag, flat, or triangle. These forms will become the basis of all your trade setups once you learn to identify them quickly and with confidence.

An even simpler question to ask is, "Do I see either a motive wave or a corrective wave?" Motive waves define the direction of the trend. There are two kinds of motive waves: impulse waves and ending diagonals. Corrective waves travel against the larger trend. The three kinds of corrective waves are zigzags, flats, and triangles. If all you do is identify a motive wave versus a corrective wave correctly, you can still identify some useful trade setups.

KEY POINT

Analysis is a mastery of observation, while successful trading is a mastery of self.

In this chapter, we will examine how to use key components of analysis and trading to help you become a better Elliottician and a consistently successful trader. Specifically, we will examine how the Wave Principle improves trading, which waves are the best to trade, which guidelines to use for trading specific Elliott wave patterns, and why the psychology of trading and risk management—what I call the neglected essentials—are important.

How the Wave Principle Improves Trading

Every trader, every analyst, and every technician has favorite techniques to use when trading. Let's go over why the Wave Principle is mine.

How the Wave Principle Improves Upon Traditional Technical Studies

There are three categories of technical studies: trend-following indicators, oscillators, and sentiment indicators. Trend-following indicators include moving averages, Moving Average Convergence-Divergence (MACD), and Directional Movement Index (ADX). A few of the more popular oscillators many traders use today are stochastics, rate-of-change, and the Commodity Channel Index (CCI). Sentiment indicators include put-call ratios and Commitment of Traders report data.

Technical studies like these do a good job of illuminating the way for traders, yet they each fall short for one major reason: They limit the scope of a trader's understanding of current price action and how it relates to the overall picture of a market. For example, let's say the MACD reading in XYZ stock is positive, indicating the trend is up. That's useful information, but wouldn't it be more useful if it could also help to answer these questions: Is this a new trend or an old trend? If the trend is up, how far will it go?

Most technical studies simply don't reveal pertinent information such as the maturity of a trend and a definable price target—but the Wave Principle does.

Five Ways the Wave Principle Improves Trading

Here are five ways the Wave Principle can benefit you and improve your trading:

1. The Wave Principle identifies the trend.
2. It identifies countertrend price moves within the larger trend.
3. It determines the maturity of the trend.
4. It provides high-confidence price targets.
5. It provides specific points of invalidation.

1. Identifying the Trend

> ". . . action in the same direction as the one larger trend develops in five waves. . . ."
>
> —*Elliott Wave Principle* by Frost and Prechter

The Wave Principle identifies the direction of the dominant trend. A five-wave advance identifies the overall trend as up. Conversely, a five-wave decline determines that the larger trend is down. Why is this information important? Because it is easier to trade in the direction of the dominant trend, since it is the path of least resistance and undoubtedly explains the saying, "The trend is your friend." I find trading in the direction of the trend much easier than attempting to pick tops and bottoms within a trend, which is a difficult endeavor and one that is virtually impossible to do consistently.

2. Identifying the Countertrend

> ". . . reaction against the one larger trend develops in three waves. . . ."
>
> —*Elliott Wave Principle by Frost and Prechter*

The Wave Principle also identifies countertrend moves. The three-wave pattern is a corrective response to the preceding impulse wave. Knowing that a recent move in price is merely a correction within a larger trending market is especially important for traders because corrections give traders opportunities to position themselves in the direction of the larger trend of a market.

Being aware of the three basic Elliott wave corrective patterns—zigzags, flats, and triangles—enables you to buy pullbacks in an uptrend and to sell bounces in a downtrend, which is a proven and consistently successful trading strategy. Know what countertrend price moves look like, and you can find opportunities to rejoin the trend.

3. Determining the Maturity of a Trend As R. N. Elliott observed, wave patterns form larger and smaller versions of themselves. This repetition in form means that price activity is a fractal, as illustrated in Figure 40.1. Wave (1) subdivides into five small waves yet is part of a larger five-wave pattern. How is this information useful? It helps traders recognize the maturity of a trend. If, for example, prices are advancing in wave 5 of a five-wave advance and wave 5 has already completed three or four smaller waves, a trader knows that this may not be the best time to add long positions. Instead, it may be time to take profits or at least to raise protective stops.

Since the Wave Principle identifies trend, countertrend, and the maturity of a trend, it's no surprise that the Wave Principle also signals the return of the dominant

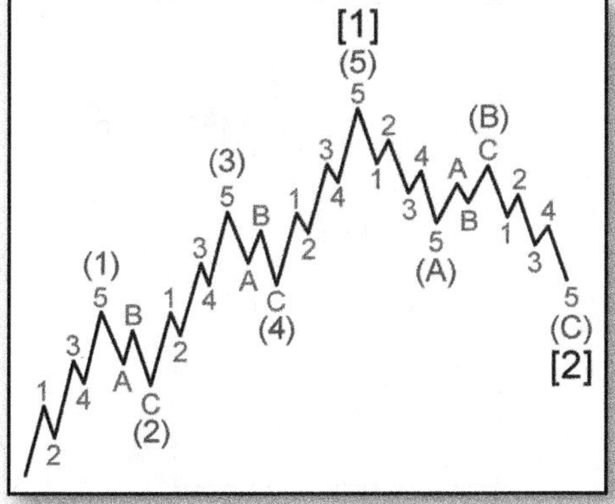

FIGURE 40.1
Source: Elliott Wave Principle.

trend. Once a countertrend move unfolds in three waves (A-B-C), this structure can signal the point where the dominant trend has resumed, namely, once price action exceeds the extreme of wave B. Knowing precisely when a trend has resumed brings an added benefit: It increases the likelihood of a successful trade, which is further enhanced when accompanied by traditional technical studies.

4. Providing Price Targets What traditional technical studies simply don't offer—high-confidence price targets—the Wave Principle again provides. When R. N. Elliott wrote about the Wave Principle in *Nature's Law*, he stated that the Fibonacci sequence was the mathematical basis for the Wave Principle. Elliott waves, both impulsive and corrective, adhere to specific Fibonacci proportions. For example, all three motive waves tend to be related by Fibonacci mathematics, whether by equality, 1.618, or 2.618 (whose inverses are .618 and .382). See Figures 40.2, 40.3, and 40.4.

Also, corrections often retrace a Fibonacci percentage of the preceding wave. These Fibonacci-derived regions allow traders to set profit-taking objectives and identify areas where the next turn in prices will likely occur (see Figures 40.5 and 40.6).

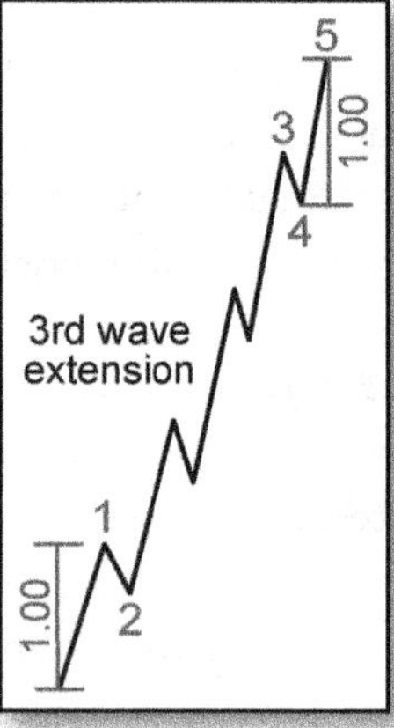

FIGURE 40.2
Source: Elliott Wave Principle.

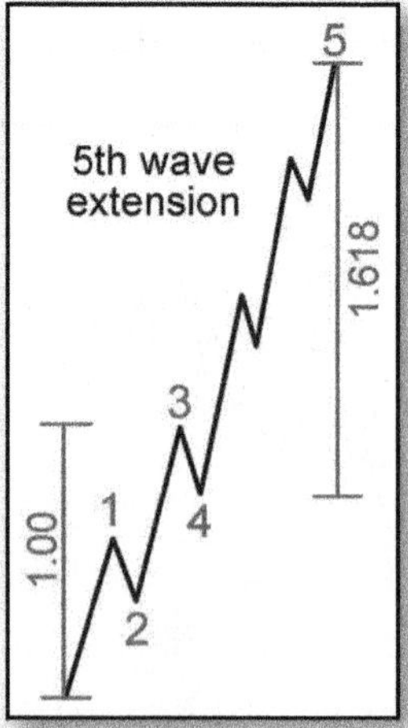

FIGURE 40.3
Source: Elliott Wave Principle.

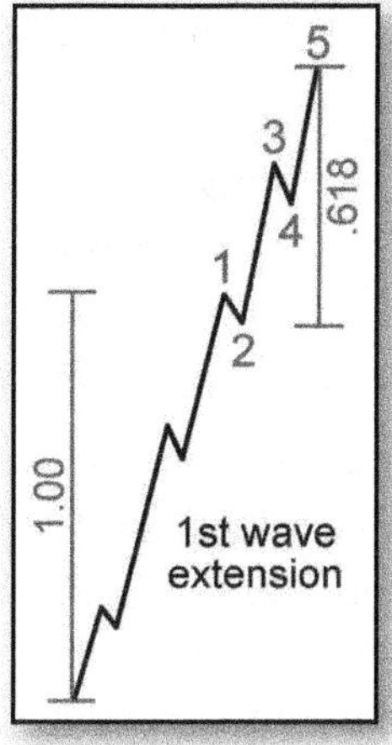

FIGURE 40.4
Source: Elliott Wave Principle.

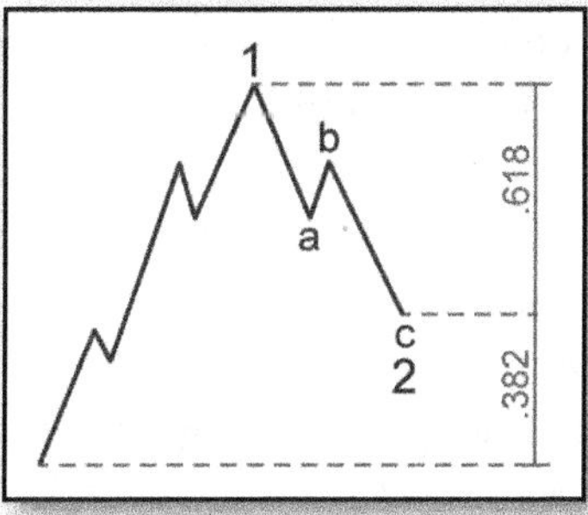

FIGURE 40.5
Source: Elliott Wave Principle.

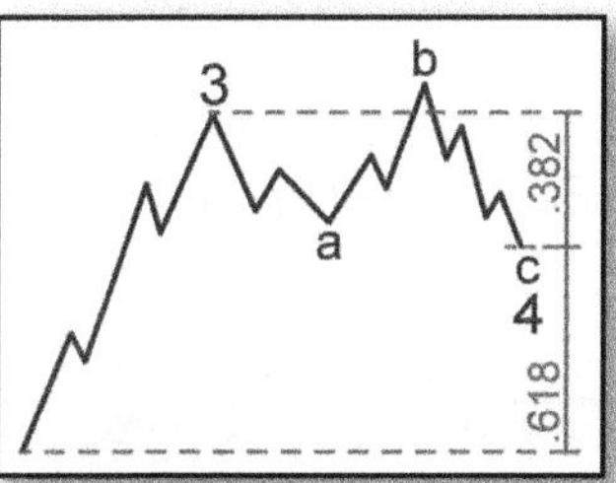

FIGURE 40.6
Source: Elliott Wave Principle.

> **KEY POINT**
> Knowing when you're wrong on a trade is as important as knowing when you're right.

5. Providing Specific Points of Invalidation Wave analysis provides a specific point of invalidation, which is the level at which an interpretation is no longer viable. Knowing when you are wrong is perhaps a trader's most important piece of information.

At what point does a trade fail? Many traders use money management rules to determine the answer to this question, because technical studies simply don't offer the answer. Yet the Wave Principle does—in the form of these three Elliott wave rules for impulse waves:

Rule 1: Wave 2 can never retrace more than 100 percent of wave 1.
Rule 2: Wave 4 may never end in the price territory of wave 1.
Rule 3: Out of the three impulse waves (waves 1, 3, and 5), wave 3 can never be the shortest.

A violation of any of these rules implies that the operative wave count is incorrect. How can traders use this information? If a technical study warns of an upturn in prices, and the wave pattern is a second-wave pullback, the trader knows specifically at what point the trade will fail: a move beyond the origin of wave 1. That kind of guidance is difficult to come by without a framework such as the Wave Principle.

The Four Best Waves to Trade

Here's where the rubber meets the road. Waves 3, 5, A, and C are the most advantageous to trade, because they are oriented in the direction of the one larger trend. Odds favor traders who are long in bull markets (and short in bear markets) versus short sellers in bull markets (and buyers in bear markets). Overall, trading in the direction of the trend is the path of least resistance.

The Wave Principle helps to identify these high-confidence trades in place of lesser-confidence setups that traders should ignore. Remember, five-wave moves determine the direction of the larger trend, while three-wave moves offer traders an opportunity to join the trend. So in Figure 40.7, waves (2), (4), (5), and (B) are actually setups for high-confidence trades exploiting waves (3), (5), (A), and (C).

For example, a wave (2) pullback provides traders an opportunity to position themselves in the direction of wave (3), just as a wave (5) rally offers them a shorting opportunity for wave (A). By combining the Wave Principle with traditional technical analysis, traders can improve their trading by increasing the likelihood of a successful trade.

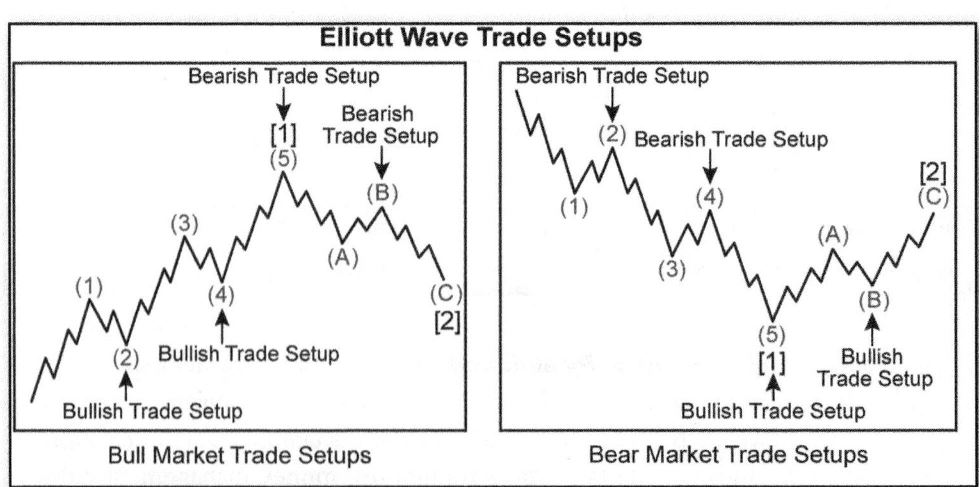

FIGURE 40.7

Technical studies can pick out many trading opportunities, but the Wave Principle helps traders discern which ones are more likely to be successful. This is because the Wave Principle is the framework that provides history and context, current information, and a peek at the future.

Elliott Wave Trade Setups

This next chart (see Figure 40.7) shows bullish and bearish versions of trade setups. In each, waves (2), (4), (5), and (B) are trade setups that introduce the four primary Elliott-based trading opportunities. These corrective waves offer the trader an opportunity to rejoin the larger trend. In such trend trading, a trader buys pullbacks in uptrends and sells bounces in downtrends.

When to Trade Corrections

Corrective waves offer less desirable trading opportunities because of their potential complexity. Impulse waves are trend-defining price moves in which prices typically travel far. Conversely, corrective wave patterns fluctuate more and can unfold slowly while taking a variety of shapes, such as a zigzag, flat, expanded flat, triangle, double zigzag, or combination. Corrections generally move sideways and are often erratic, time-consuming, and deceptive. Thus, it is emotionally exhausting to trade corrections, and the odds of executing a successful trade during this type of price action are low.

Even though I view corrective waves and patterns as providing low-confidence trade setups, there are times when I would consider trading them—but it depends on the potential duration of the correction. If I count five waves up, for example, on a 15-minute price chart of Crude Oil, I do not consider waves 2 or 4 to be viable trading opportunities. I prefer, instead, to wait for waves 2 and 4 to terminate before entering a position. Let's say, though, that we have a market that has also formed an impulse wave, but it has taken weeks or months to do so. In this instance, waves 2 and 4 would form over many weeks and might offer traders many short-term trading opportunities.

Guidelines for Trading Specific Elliott Wave Patterns

Before we review guidelines for trading specific Elliott wave patterns, here is my most important analytical and trading rule: **Let the market commit to you before you commit to the market**. In other words, look for *confirming price action*. Just as it is unwise to pull out in front of an oncoming car on the basis of its turn signal alone, it is equally unwise to take a trade without confirmation of a trend change.

The following guidelines incorporate this idea and benefit the trader in two ways. First, waiting for confirming price action tends to decrease the number of trades executed. One of the biggest mistakes traders make is overtrading. Second, it focuses attention on higher-confidence trade setups. If a trader believes that a particular market is topping—and appropriate price action does indeed corroborate this belief—then the trader is more likely to execute a successful trade.

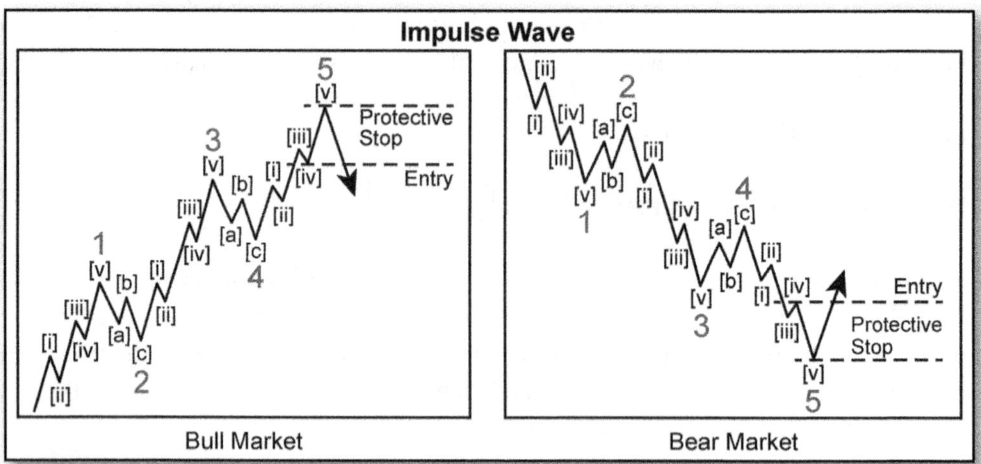

FIGURE 40.8

Smart Investor Tip

Let the market commit to you before you commit to the market.

Smart Investor Tip

Waiting for confi rming price action allows traders to use an evidence-based approach and to focus their attention on higherconfidence trade setups.

Impulse Waves

Whenever an impulse wave is complete, the Elliott wave guideline regarding the depth of corrective waves applies:

> "[C]orrections, especially when they themselves are fourth waves, tend to register their maximum retracement within the span of travel of the previous fourth wave of one lesser degree, most commonly near the level of its terminus."
>
> —*Elliott Wave Principle* by Frost and Prechter

Although that guideline may sound complicated, it's easy to follow in real trading. The trading technique is to enter on a break below the extreme of wave (iv) of 5 (see Figure 40.8). Doing so prevents top picking and requires the market to take out a prior swing low to act as initial evidence that the impulse wave is indeed finished. Set the initial protective stop at the extreme of the price move.

Ending Diagonal

The guidelines for entry and initial protective stops for ending diagonals are similar to those for impulse waves: Wait for a break of the extreme of wave 4 before taking a position, and place the initial protective stop at the extreme of the price move (see Figure 40.9).

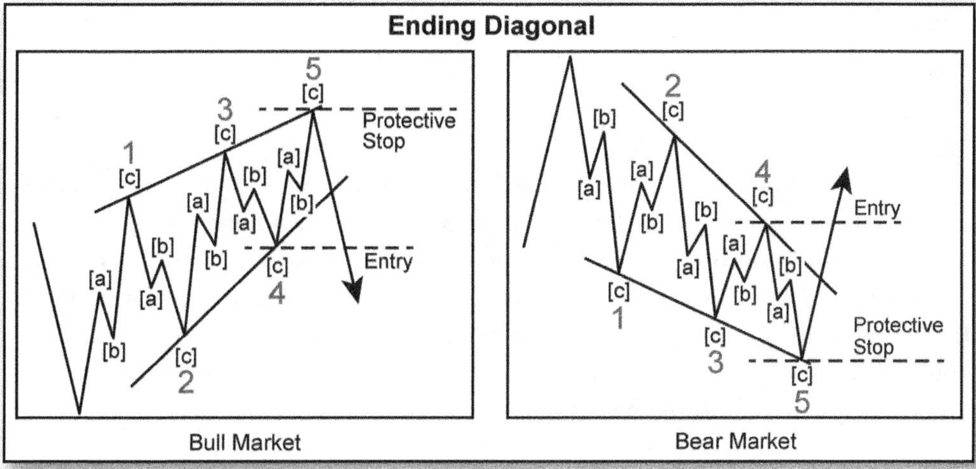

FIGURE 40.9

Remember, these entry techniques demonstrate a conservative approach that I think of as "ready, aim, aim, aim . . . fire" trading. But if you are a more aggressive trader, how do you enter an ending diagonal trade setup? One approach is to enter on a decisive close beyond the trendline that connects the extreme of waves 2 and 4. In this instance, the initial protective stop placement is the same, the extreme of the pattern (see Figure 40.10).

If you define yourself as an out-and-out aggressive trader, here's an entry technique for you. More often than not, wave 3 of an ending diagonal is shorter than wave 1. When this is the case, the rules state that wave 5 cannot be longer than wave 3, since even within an ending diagonal, wave 3 may never be the shortest wave among waves 1, 3, and 5. Thus, you can begin acquiring positions or scale into a position as wave 5 is forming. The protective stop under this aggressive entry technique would be the point at which wave 5 becomes longer than wave 3, since the Wave Principle identifies that as a specific point of invalidation.

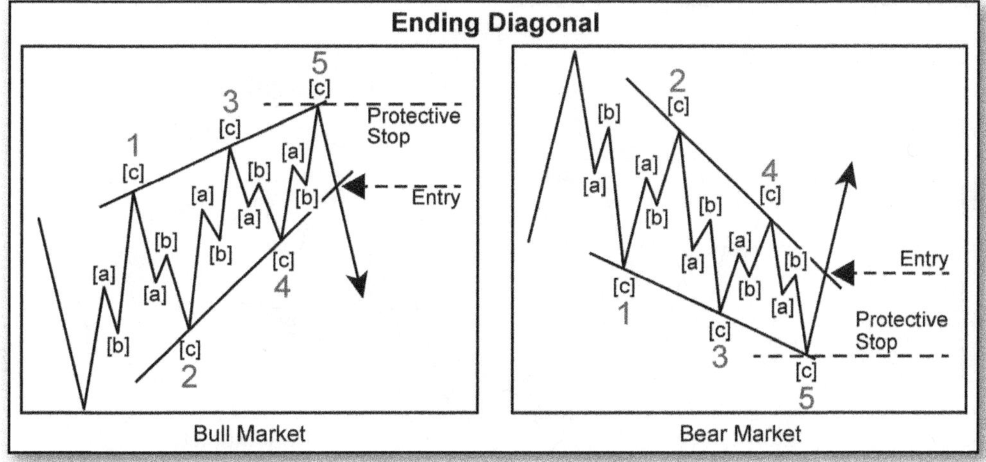

FIGURE 40.10

Zigzag

The first of two guidelines for entering a trade during a zigzag is on a break of the extreme of wave [iv] of C, provided this level is beyond the termination of wave A (see Figure 40.11).

A second entry guideline is to wait for the extreme of wave B to give way before taking action (see Figure 40.12). The initial protective stop is then the extreme of wave C. This conservative approach prevents picking tops or bottoms without sufficient evidence.

Ideally, traders will take these guidelines and adapt them to their own specific trading style. In fact, using a zigzag as an example, an even more conservative trader could wait a bit longer before entering and demand a five-wave move through the extreme of wave B followed by a corrective wave pattern.

Flat

Since the final wave of a flat correction subdivides into five waves, the recommended entry technique is similar to that of an impulse wave: Wait until prices exceed the

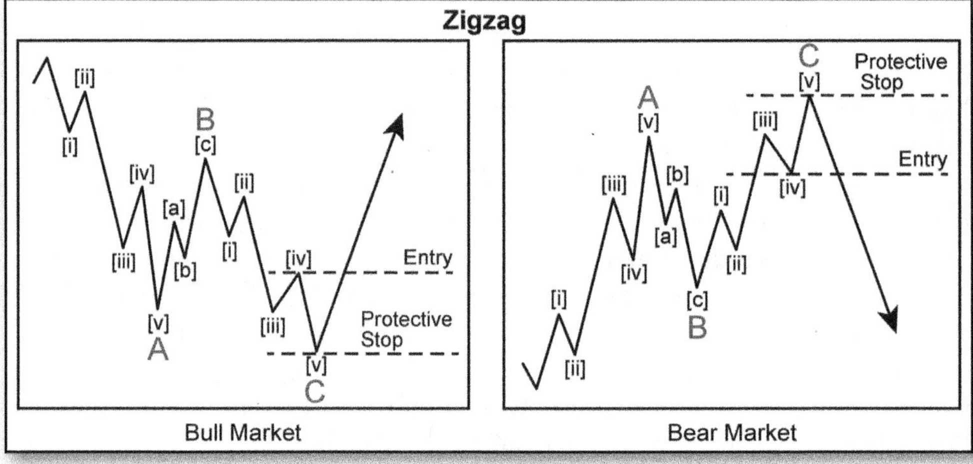

FIGURE 40.11

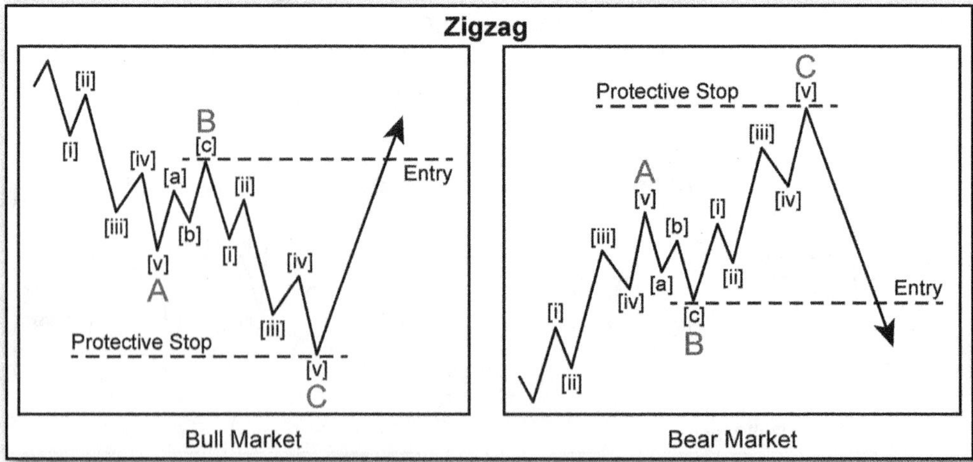

FIGURE 40.12

extreme of wave (iv) of C to enter a trade (see Figure 40.13). This approach is not used with zigzags—where wave C also subdivides into five waves—because in a bullish zigzag, for instance, wave (iv) of a C terminates *below* the extreme of wave A, whereas in a bullish flat, it tends to form *above* the extreme of wave A.

Triangle

The final guideline applies to triangles (see Figure 40.14). A triangle is a sideways price move—typically bounded by converging trendlines—that subdivides into waves A, B, C, D, and E. The entry guideline is to wait for prices to break the extreme of wave D and place an initial protective stop where wave E terminates. I do not endorse a more aggressive entry technique because triangles are sometimes deceptive: Since they can form in the wave 4, B, or X wave positions, what may appear to be a bullish fourth-wave triangle could actually be a bearish triangle B wave.

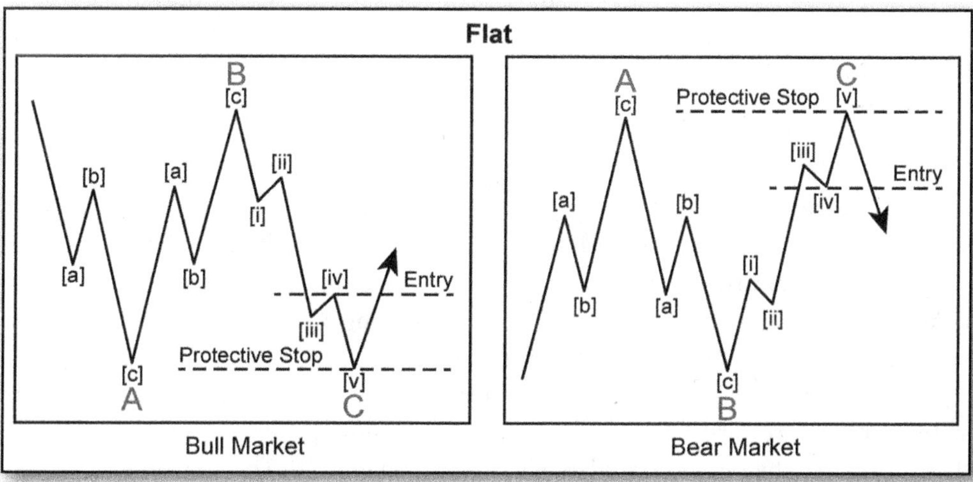

FIGURE 40.13

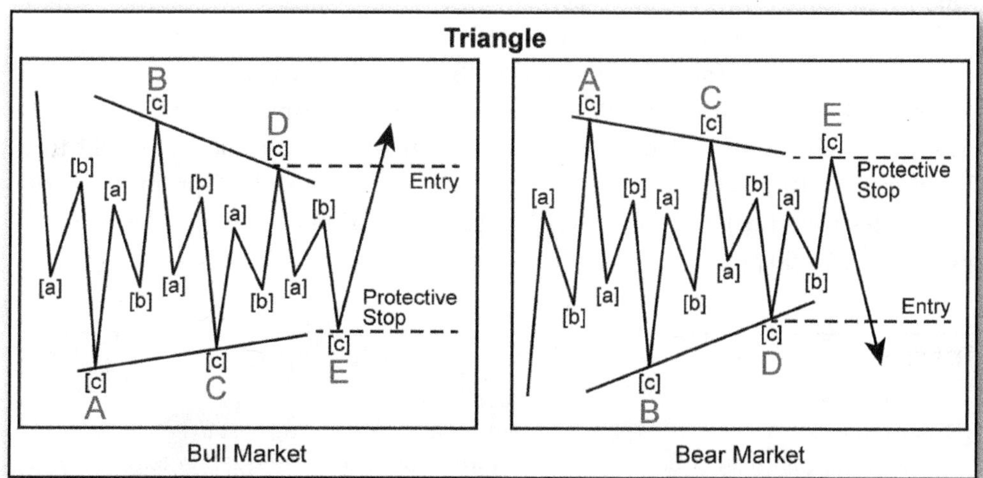

FIGURE 40.14

Smart Investor Tip

The psychology of the individual is the key to becoming a consistently successful trader.

A trader with a more aggressive trading style will most likely enter a position well before prices penetrate the termination point of wave D. If so, I recommend using the extreme of wave A as an initial protective stop rather than the end of wave C. It is not uncommon in equities or thinly traded markets for intraday price action to exceed the extreme of wave C and reverse.

The Neglected Essentials—Risk Management and the Psychology of Trading

When discussing how to become a consistently successful trader, two subjects you don't hear enough about are risk management and the psychology of trading.

Because the topic of risk management is critically important to the success and longevity of a trader, let's briefly discuss risk-reward ratios and trade size.

Risk-Reward Ratio

Risk to reward is a ratio that quantifies the risk versus the reward of a trade. If you buy XYZ stock at $50.00 with the expectation that it will appreciate to $51.00, your expected reward is $1.00. If the protective stop on this position is $49.00, the risk-reward ratio for this trade is 1:1—you're risking $1.00 to make $1.00. If the protective stop is $49.90, then the risk-reward ratio is 10:1.

Note: Even though it's called a risk-reward ratio, the ratio is conventionally stated with the reward figure first. So, in this example, even though risk is 1 and the reward 10, the ratio is stated as 10:1, rather than 1:10. This explains why a 3:1 risk-reward ratio is desirable. It's actually a reward-risk ratio.

A high risk-reward ratio is desirable as a function of probabilities. Let's say that you're right about the market 70 percent of the time, and the risk-reward ratio on each of your trades is 1:1. Thus, out of 10 trades, seven trades were closed with a $1.00 profit, while three were exited with a $1.00 loss. The bottom line is that you walked away with $4.00. What do you think will happen if we increase the risk-reward ratio from 1:1 to 3:1 and decrease the probability of being right from 70 percent to 40 percent? With this 3:1 ratio, for the same $1.00 profit, four winning trades would net $12.00. If we then subtract $6.00 in losing trades, we walk away with a $6.00 profit.

DEFINITION:

Risk to reward

Risk-Reward Ratio is a ratio used to compare expected returns against the amount of risk taken. In line with market convention, risk-reward ratios are expressed in terms of total reward per one unit of risk.

This difference shows how important the risk-reward ratio is—by decreasing the probability of winning trades from 70 percent to almost half (i.e., 40 percent) while increasing the risk-reward ratio, you increase profitability by 50 percent. A misconception about trading is that a trader need be right only on the direction of the market to make money. This is not entirely correct. As you've just seen, a trader can be right as little as 40 percent of the time and still succeed, provided he or she keeps an eye on the risk-reward ratio.

> **Smart Investor Tip**
> Trades that offer less than a 3:1 risk-reward ratio should be avoided.

Trade Size

How large a position should a trader take? The risk on a single trade should never exceed 1 to 3 percent of the total portfolio size. Retail traders tend to balk at these small percentages, while professional traders embrace them. Thus, at 1 percent, for every $5,000 a trader has in a trading account, he or she should risk only $50 on each position. For example, a trader with $10,000 in his account can take either two trades where the risk is $50 apiece or one trade in which the risk is $100. Many traders fail at trading because they simply don't have sufficient capital in their trading accounts to take the positions they want to take.

If you do have a small trading account, though, you can overcome this challenge by trading small. You can trade fewer contracts, trade e-mini contracts, or even penny stocks. Bottom line, on your way to becoming a consistently successful trader, you must realize that *longevity* is key. If your risk on any given position is small relative to your total capital, then you can weather a losing streak. Conversely, if you risk 25 percent of your portfolio on each trade, after four consecutive losers, you're out of business.

The Psychology of Trading

While I consider risk management to be an essential component of successful trading, the true key is psychology—that is, your individual psychology. Let's review a number of psychological factors that prevent traders from becoming consistently successful: lack of methodology, lack of discipline, unrealistic expectations, and lack of patience.

Whether you are a seasoned professional or just thinking about opening your first trading account, it is critically important to your success that you understand how your personal psychology affects your trading results.

Lack of Methodology

If you aim to be a consistently successful trader, then you *must* have a defined trading methodology—a simple, clear, and concise way of looking at markets. In fact, having a method is so important that EWI founder Robert Prechter put it at the top of his list in his essay, "What a Trader Really Needs to Be Successful." Guessing or going by gut instinct won't work over the long run. If you don't have a defined trading methodology, then you don't have a way to know what constitutes a buy or sell signal.

> **Smart Investor Tip**
> Successful trading requires a methodology and the discipline to follow the methodology.

How do you overcome this problem? The answer to this question is to write down your methodology. Define in writing what your analytical tools are and, more important, how *you* use them. It doesn't matter whether you use the Wave Principle, point and figure charts, stochastics, RSI, or a combination of all of these. What *does* matter is that you actually make the effort to define what constitutes a buy, a sell, your trailing stop, and instructions on exiting a position. The best hint I can give you about defining your trading methodology is this: If you can't fit it on a 3" × 5" card, it's probably too complicated.

Lack of Discipline

Once you have clearly outlined and identified your trading methodology, you *must* have the discipline to follow the system. A lack of discipline while trading is the second common downfall of many aspiring traders. If the way you view a price chart or evaluate a potential trade setup today is different from how you did it a month ago, then you either have not identified your methodology or you lack the discipline to follow the methodology you have identified. The formula for success is to consistently apply a proven methodology.

> **Smart Investor Tip**
> Stick with realistic expectations. For instance, the goal for every trader the fi rst year should be not to lose money . In other words, shoot for a 0 percent return during your fi rst year.

Unrealistic Expectations

Nothing makes me angrier than those commercials that say something like, "$5,000 properly positioned in Natural Gas can give you returns of over $40,000." Advertisements like this are a disservice to the financial industry as a whole and end up costing uneducated investors a lot more than $5,000. In addition, they help to create the psychologically sabotaging mind-set of having unrealistic expectations.

Yes, it is possible to experience above-average returns trading your own account. However, it's difficult to do it without taking on above-average risk. So, what is a realistic return to shoot for in your first year as a trader—50 percent, 100 percent, 200 percent? Whoa, let's rein in those unrealistic expectations. In my opinion, the goal for every trader the first year out should be *not to lose money*. In other words, shoot for a 0 percent return your first year. If you can manage that, then in year two, try to beat the Dow or the S&P. These goals may not be flashy, but they are realistic.

Lack of Patience

The fourth psychological pitfall that even experienced traders encounter is a lack of patience. According to Edwards and Magee in their seminal book, *Technical Analysis of Stock Trends*, markets trend only about 30 percent of the time. This means that the other 70 percent of the time, financial markets are not trending.

This small percentage may explain why I believe that, for any given time frame, there are only two or three really good trading opportunities. For example, if you're a long-term trader, typically only two or three compelling tradable moves in a market present themselves during any given year. Similarly, if you are a short-term trader, only two or three high-quality trade setups present themselves in a given week.

All too often, because trading is inherently exciting (and anything involving money usually is exciting), it's easy to feel that you're missing something if you're not in a trade. As a result, you start taking trade setups of lesser and lesser quality and begin overtrading.

How do you overcome this lack of patience? Remind yourself that every week there will be another "trade of the year." In other words, don't worry about missing an opportunity today, because there will be another one tomorrow, next week, and next month . . . I promise.

For More Information

Learn more at your exclusive Reader Resources site. You will find a free online edition of *Elliott Wave Principle* by Frost and Prechter, plus lessons on Elliott wave analysis, how to trade specific patterns, and how to use Fibonacci and other technical indicators to increase your confidence as you apply the Wave Principle in real time. Go to: www.elliottwave.com/wave/ReaderResources.

Test Yourself

Answer the following True/False questions:

1. Analysis and trading employ the same skill set.
2. Wave analysis identifies the direction of the trend, based on the direction of the impulse wave.
3. The Wave Principle offers traders points of invalidation where they can re-evaluate where their analysis may have gone wrong.
4. Wave 2 can sometimes retrace more than 100 percent of wave 1.
5. A complete Elliott wave cycle consists of nine waves.
6. From origin to termination, waves 2 and 4 offer high-confidence trading opportunities.
7. An aggressive approach to trading an ending diagonal is to wait for the extreme of wave 4 to give way.
8. If you look for confirming price action, then you are letting the market commit to you before you commit to the market.
9. The entry guideline for trading a zigzag is to wait for the extreme of wave **B** to give way.

10. A risk to reward ratio of 1:1 is ideal.

Answers: 1. False 2. True 3. True 4. False 5. False 6. False 7. False 8. True 9. True 10. False

CHAPTER 41

What Is the Efficient Market Hypothesis?

From Edwin T. Burton and Sunit N. Shah, *Behavioral Finance* (Hoboken, New Jersey: John Wiley & Sons, 2013), Chapter 1.

The efficient market hypothesis (EMH) has to do with the meaning and predictability of prices in financial markets. Do asset markets "behave" as they should? In particular, does the stock market perform its role as economists expect it to? Stock markets raise money from wealth holders and provide businesses with that money to pursue, presumably, the maximization of profit. How well do these markets perform that function? Is some part of the process wasteful? Do prices reflect true underlying value?

In recent years, a new question seems to have emerged in this ongoing discussion. Do asset markets create instability in the greater economy? Put crudely, do the actions of investment and commercial bankers lead to bubbles and economic catastrophe as the bubbles unwind? The great stock market crash of October 19, 1987, and the financial collapse in the fall of 2008 have focused attention on bubbles and crashes. These are easy concepts to imagine but difficult to define or anticipate.

Bubbles usually feel so good to participants that no one, at the time, really thinks of them as bubbles; they instead see their own participation in bubbles as the inevitable payback for their hard work and virtuous behavior—until the bubbles burst in catastrophe. Then, the attention turns to the excesses of the past. Charges of greed, corruption, and foul play accompany every crash.

If the catastrophe and the bubble that precedes it are the result of evil people doing evil things, then there is no reason to suppose that markets are themselves to blame. Simple correctives, usually through imposition of legal reforms, are then proposed to correct the problem and eliminate future bubbles and catastrophes. Casual empiricism suggests this approach is not successful.

What if markets are inherently unstable? What if bubbles and their accompanying catastrophes are the natural order of things? Then what? If prices do not, much of the time, represent true value and if the markets themselves breed excessive optimism and pessimism, not to mention fraud and corruption, then the very existence and operation of financial markets may cause instability in the underlying economy. Prices may be signaling "incorrect" information and resources may be allocated inefficiently. The question of whether asset markets are efficiently priced, then, is a fundamental question. The outcome of this debate could shed light on the efficiency of the modern, highly integrated economies in which a key role is played by financial institutions.

It is important to agree on a definition of market efficiency, but there are many such definitions. Practitioners in the everyday world of finance often use market efficiency in ways that are different than the textbook definitions. We delimit the most common definitions in the next two sections of this chapter.

Information and the Efficient Market Hypothesis

The EMH is most commonly defined as the idea that asset prices, stock prices in particular, "fully reflect" information.[1] Only when information changes will prices change. There are different versions of this definition, depending on what kind of information is assumed to be reflected in current prices. The most commonly used is the "semi-strong" definition of the EMH: *Prices accurately summarize all publicly known information.*

This definition means that if an investor studies carefully the companies that he/she invests in, it will not matter. Other investors already know the information that the studious investor learns by painstakingly poring over public documents. These other investors have already acted on the information, so that such "public" information is already reflected in the stock price. There is no such thing, in this view, as a "cheap" stock or an "expensive" stock. The current price is always the "best estimate" of the value of the company.

In particular, this definition implies that knowing past prices is of no value. The idea that past stock price history is irrelevant is an example of the weak form of the EMH: *Knowledge of past prices is of no value in predicting future stock prices.*

The semi-strong form implies the much weaker version of the EMH embodied in the weak form of the EMH. It is possible that the weak form is true but that the semi-strong form is false.

The weak form of the EMH is interesting because it directly attacks a part of Wall Street research known as "technical" research. In technical research, analysts study past prices and other historical data in an attempt to predict future prices. Certain patterns of stock prices are said by "technicians" to imply certain future pricing paths. All of this means, of course, that by studying past prices you can predict when stock prices are going to go up and when they are going to go down. Put another way, technical research is an attempt to "beat the market" by using historical pricing data. The weak form says that this cannot be done.

[1] See Eugene Fama's definition in "Random Walks in Stock Market Prices," *Financial Analysts Journal* 21, no. 5 (May 1965):55–59.

Unlike other versions of the EMH, the weak form is especially easy to subject to empirical testing, since there are many money managers and market forecasters who explicitly rely on technical research. How do such managers and forecasters do? Do they perform as well as a monkey randomly throwing darts at a newspaper containing stock price names as a method of selecting a "monkey portfolio"? Do index funds do better than money managers who utilize technical research as their main method of picking stocks? These questions are simple to put to a test and, over the years, the results of such testing have overwhelmingly supported the weak form version of the EMH.

The semi-strong version of the EMH is not as easy to test as the weak form, but data from money managers is helpful here. If the semi-strong version is true, then money managers, using public information, should not beat the market, which means that they should not beat simple indexes that mirror the overall market for stocks. The evidence here is consistent and overwhelming. Money managers, on average, do not beat simple indexes. That doesn't mean that there aren't money managers who seem to consistently outperform over small time samples, but they are in the distinct minority and hard to identify before the fact. Evidence from institutional investors, such as large pensions funds and endowments, are consistent with the view that indexing tends to produce better investment results than hiring money managers.

If this were all we knew, then the EMH would be on solid ground. But we know more. There is growing evidence that there are empirical "regularities" in stock market return data, as well as some puzzling aspects of stock market data that seem difficult to explain if one subscribes to the EMH.

We can identify three main lines of attack for critics of the semi-strong form of the EMH:

1. Stock prices seem to be too volatile to be consistent with the EMH.
2. Stock prices seem to have "predictability" patterns in historical data.
3. There are unexplained (and perhaps unexplainable) behavioral data items that have come to be known as "anomalies," a nomenclature begun by Richard Thaler.[2]

The evidence that has piled up in the past 20 years or so has created a major headache for defenders of the EMH. Even though money managers don't necessarily beat the indexes, the behavioralists' research suggests that perhaps they should.

There is a third form of the EMH that is interesting but not easy to subject to empirical validation. The third form is known as the strong form of the EMH: *Prices accurately summarize all information, private as well as public.*

The strong form, of course, implies both the semi-strong and the weak forms of the EMH. However, both the semi-strong and weak forms can be true while the strong definition can be false. The strong form includes information that may be illegally obtained—or, perhaps, information that is legally obtained but illegal to act upon. Needless to say, those breaking the law are not likely to provide performance data to researchers attempting to ascertain whether they are beating the market.

[2] See Richard Thaler, *Winner's Curse: Paradoxes and Anomalies of Economic Life* (New York: Free Press, 1992).

There seems to be a general consensus that the strong form of the EMH is not likely to be true, but one should not rush to such a conclusion simply because relevant data may be hard to come by. What little data we have from those who have obtained illegal information and then acted upon it is mixed. Sometimes crooks win; sometimes they appear to lose. When Ivan Boesky, probably the most famous insider information trader in history, concluded his investment activities and was carted off to jail, it was clear that investors who owned index funds made better returns than investors in Boesky's fund, even before the legal authorities got wise to Boesky's activities. If Boesky couldn't beat the market with inside information, it does give one pause.

Of the three informational definitions of the EMH, it is the semi-strong hypothesis that commands most interest. It is widely believed that the weak form is likely to be true, and it is commonly assumed that the strong form is not likely to be true, so interest focuses mainly on the semi-strong hypothesis. Information determines prices and no one can really exploit publicly known information—that is the content of the semi-strong EMH hypothesis.

Random Walk, the Martingale Hypothesis, and the EMH

There is an alternative, mathematical view of the stock market related to the EMH. The mathematical version begins with the idea that stock prices follow a process known as *random walk*. The idea of the random walk is sometimes taken by wary observers as the idea that stock price behavior is simply arbitrary, but that is not what random walk means.

Imagine a coin flip where the coin is completely "fair" in the sense that a heads or tails flip is equally likely to occur. Suppose you start with $100 in wealth before beginning a series of coin flips. Suppose further that if you flip a heads, you receive $1, and if you flip a tails, you have to give up $1. After the first flip, for example, you will have either $101 (if you flip a heads) or $99 (if you flip a tails). Your total wealth over time, in this simple example, is following a process known as a random walk. A random walk is a process where the next step (flip outcome, in this example) has a fixed probability that is independent of all previous flips.

What does random walk rule out? If knowing the results of previous coin flips is useful in predicting future coin flips, then the process is not a random walk. Imagine that there have been five flips of heads in a row with no flips of tails. Does this mean it is more likely that the next coin flip will be tails? If so, then the process is not a random walk. The likelihood of a heads or a tails on the next coin flip must be independent of the history of previous flips for the process to be a random walk.

Does this mean, as some assume, that the results are arbitrary? No. We know a lot about this process. What we can't do, however, is predict the next coin flip with any high degree of certainty. If the coin is a fair coin, the heads or tails are equally likely on the next flip regardless of its history.

The coin-flipping game is a good example of a *martingale*. A martingale has the following property:

$$E[X_{t+s} | X_1, X_2, \ldots, X_t] = X_t \text{ for any } t, s > 0 \tag{41.1}$$

What does the above equation mean? X_t is the value at time t of some variable X. It might be helpful to think of X as your wealth, so that X_t is the value of your wealth at time t. X_{t+s} is then your wealth at some future date, $t+s$. The E in the equation is the expectation operator. The simplest way to think about E is that $E[X_{t+s} | X_1, X_2, \ldots, X_t]$ is what, on average, you expect the value of your wealth to be at a future date, $t+s$, given your knowledge of your wealth historically.

So, back to our example. You start on date t with $100 and you flip a coin that is equally likely to be a heads flip as a tails flip. What do you expect your wealth to be s periods from today, t? Since you are just as likely to gain $1 as to lose $1 on each flip, your wealth at any future period is expected to be the same as it is today. Thus, this process satisfies the martingale property. If your wealth is totally in stocks, and if stocks follow a martingale, so will your wealth. On average, you will neither make nor lose money.

But this is not a very satisfying theory of how stocks behave. Why would anyone own stocks if, on average, they could not be expected to increase their wealth? We need to modify our simple coin-flipping experiment to allow for wealth to increase, but in a way consistent with our martingale assumption. Suppose your wealth grows at $0.20 per period on average, so that $E[X_{t+s} | X_1, X_2, \ldots, X_t] = X_t + \$0.20 \times s$. Then, your wealth is no longer a martingale.

To transform it into a martingale, define a new variable, Y_t:

$$Y_t = X_t - \{t \times \$0.20\} \tag{41.2}$$

Y_t is a martingale since:

$$\begin{aligned} E[Yt{+}s] &= E\,[Xt{+}s] - \{(t+s) \times \$0.20\} \\ &= X_t + \{s \times \$0.20\} - \{(t+s) \times \$0.20\} \\ &= X_t - \{t \times \$0.20\} = Y_t \end{aligned} \tag{41.3}$$

Even though wealth is growing over time, we have converted the wealth variable into another variable that is a martingale.

If stock prices follow a random walk, then past stock prices cannot be used to predict future stock prices. Random walk doesn't mean we know nothing or that the result of the process is arbitrary. Instead, one of the implications of random walk is that the outcome on any specific future date cannot be known with certainty. By a simple conversion, similar to what was shown earlier, we can convert the wealth accumulation process into a martingale.

Why all the effort? A martingale is a process whose value at any future date is not predictable with certainty. While X_t is the best estimate of any future value of X after X_t, we still cannot know with any degree of certainty what that value will be.

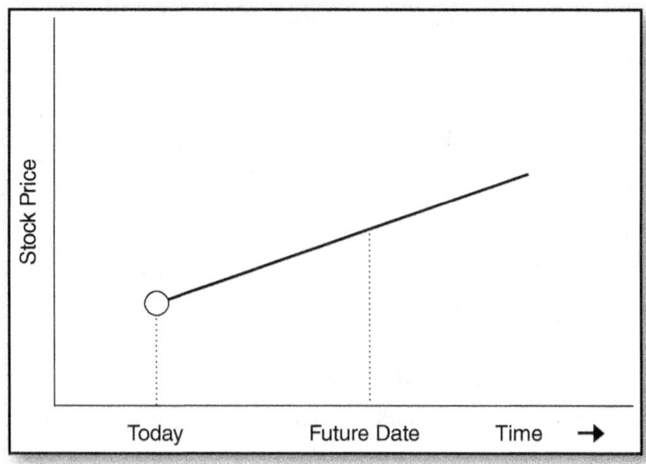

FIGURE 41.1 **Expected Future Stock Price.**

The idea of a martingale captures the informational definitions given in the previous section in a mathematical statement. Given the information available today, the best estimate of a future stock price is today's price (possibly with a risk-adjusted trend over time). This process is described in Figure 41.1.

Of course, the actual prices will not be on the solid line in Figure 41.1. Instead, they will bound around randomly, but trend upward in a pattern suggested by the bold solid line. The actual price movement might appear (or be expected to appear) as the lighter line that bounces around the solid line in Figure 41.2.

What makes the martingale an appropriate model for the EMH is that on any date, past information offers no real clue to predicting future prices. It is the absence of predictability that is the single most important feature of the martingale process.

False Evidence against the EMH

There are always, at any point in time, legendary money managers who have arguably beaten the market over their respective lifetimes. Warren Buffett comes to mind

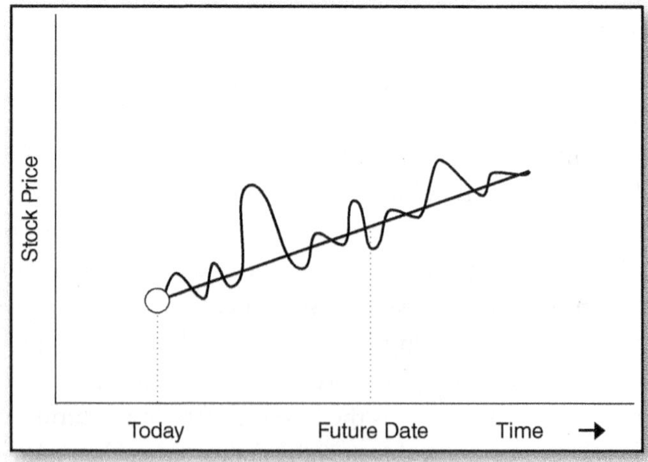

FIGURE 41.2 **Actual Future Stock Price.**

as one of the more prominent examples. Is the existence of money managers with long track records of having beaten indices evidence against the EMH? To give this question some perspective, conduct a simple thought experiment. Imagine a group of 10,000 people engaged in a coin-flipping experiment. In each period, each of these 10,000 people flips a coin and notes the result. What would we expect if the coins were, in all cases, fair coins? The likelihood of heads or tails is identical and equal to 50 percent on each and every coin toss.

In the first trial, you would expect, on average, about half of the 10,000 folks to flip heads and about half to flip tails. This would mean 5,000 flipped heads and 5,000 flipped tails. This wouldn't be the exact outcome, but it serves as a useful approximation to the actual outcome. Now, flip again. After the second trial, you would expect about one-fourth of the participants (2,500) to have flipped two heads in a row and one-fourth (2,500) to have flipped two tails in a row. Continue on in this manner through eight coin flips and what would you have? On average, you would expect about 39 flippers to have flipped eight heads in a row and about the same to have flipped eight tails in a row. Are these 39 flippers evidence that there is something to the science of coin flipping?

What about the number of folks who flipped heads seven out of eight times? There should be about 312 of those folks on average. That makes over 350 people who flipped heads at least seven out of eight times. Isn't that evidence that these people are good head flippers?

No, clearly such evidence is useless. If coin flipping is completely random, with a 50 percent chance each time of either flipping heads or tails, you will still get a significant number of extreme outcomes, even after repeated trials. In fact, failure to get the extremes of eight in a row or seven out of eight a reasonable number of times would be evidence that the flipping was not truly random. The same is true of evidence from money management. If money management outcomes are completely random and no one is really any good at stock picking, then a small percentage of money managers will, nevertheless, appear to be good on the basis of their track records.

One of the anomalies the behavioralists have uncovered is that things that are random often appear not to be random. That is, they don't look random. There seems to be an expectation by observers that if a random process is creating a data series, then that data series should have a random appearance. It turns out that there are many more ways for the outcome of a randomly generated data series to look like a pattern than there are ways for it to look random. Put another way, output from a randomly generated process will typically exhibit trends, repetition, and other patterns even though the results are generated by a truly random process.

What Does It Mean to Disagree with the EMH?

Behavioral finance argues that the EMH is false and that academic finance needs to rethink its foundations. What does it mean for the EMH to be false? There are three different ways that behavioralists have waged warfare against the EMH: the first is logical, the second is psychological, and the third is empirical. The logical argument is what economists call *economic theory*. The psychological arguments are derived mostly from experiments in human psychology that throw doubt on the realism of the assumptions that underlie finance theory. Finally, the empirical arguments exhibit patterns of "predictability" in financial data that belie the assumed "nonpredictability" of future asset prices.

The three different ways to confront the EMH correspond to casual observations that have persisted and echoed through financial markets since their beginning. These observations were dismissed just as casually by finance economists as minor and unscientific. Until very recently, the preponderant view among finance economists was that markets were efficient and that casual observers were wrong. Sometimes, it was argued the casual observers had a vested interest in their assertions that the market was inefficient. After all, virtually the entire money management industry is built on the proposition that intelligent and diligent research and thinking can produce investment returns that exceed random stock picking or indexing, contrary to the semi-strong hypothesis of the EMH.

In the chapters that follow, we consider each of the three ways that the EMH has been challenged in the academic literature. A natural question is: if not the EMH, then what? What paradigm would supplant the EMH if the behavioralists succeed in undermining it? We look at that question after considering the behavioralist critique.

CHAPTER 42

The EMH and the "Market Model"

From Edwin T. Burton and Sunit N. Shah, *Behavioral Finance* (Hoboken, New Jersey: John Wiley & Sons, 2013), Chapter 2.

Risk and Return—the Simplest View

If stocks don't earn positive returns over time, why would anyone own them? This commonplace observation suggests that stocks with high risk, however that may be defined, should earn higher returns than stocks with lower risk. This observation leads to a fairly simple model of stock prices. Under this simple view, stock prices should be such that riskier stocks, over time, make higher returns on average than less risky stocks. Some of those risky stocks will blow up, but the risky stocks that do well will compensate owners for taking the risk by producing larger returns. This theory is interesting as far as it goes, but it doesn't tell us much about what we should own in a portfolio of stocks. It suggests that folks who like to take on risk should buy the riskier stocks and more conservative investors should own less risky stocks.

A number of economists tackled this "portfolio" problem in the 1950s and 1960s. Harry Markowitz formulated the portfolio problem as an optimization problem for an individual investor.[1] Markowitz assumed that each stock could be described by the mean and variance of its returns. Consequently, any portfolio of stocks could be considered an asset itself based on its mean and variance of returns. A stock's return in each period consists of the gain or loss in price plus any dividends received during the period. This sum was then divided by the price at the beginning of the period to give the percentage return during the period.

It is assumed that all investors prefer a portfolio with higher mean returns but are averse to higher variance in return. This latter property is known as *risk aversion.* It is also assumed that all investors have identical information. That means that each investor is looking at the same set of stocks and has common information regarding

[1] Harry Markowitz, "Portfolio Selection," *Journal of Finance* 7, no. 1 (March 1952): 77–91.

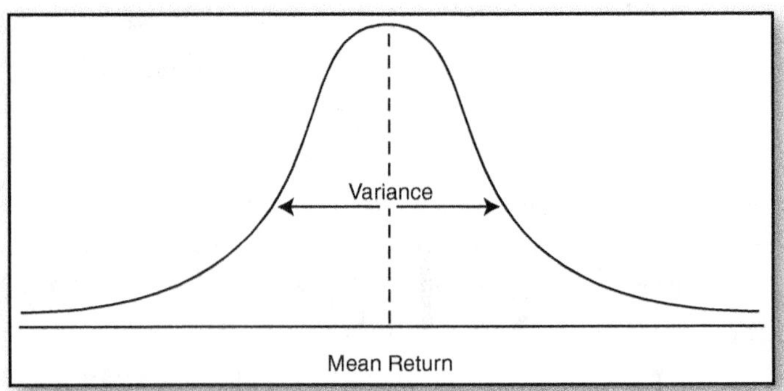

FIGURE 42.1 A Normal Return Distribution.

the means and variances of these stocks. Implicitly, the Markowitz model was identified with normal distributions, such as that pictured in Figure 42.1.

Assuming that each stock can be characterized by such a return distribution, Markowitz was able to derive an optimal portfolio for any risk-averse investor that would be a combination of two fundamental portfolios. If at least one of the assets has a zero variance of return, then the Markowitz result has an investor always choosing one or both of only two assets: the asset with a zero variance of return (the riskless asset) and another portfolio of assets that contains risky assets (ones with nonzero variance of return).[2] This latter portfolio does not depend upon the investor but results strictly from a consideration of the assets. In this sense, this risky portfolio is an outcome of the mathematics of the various asset combinations and is the most efficient combination of the risky assets. A simple diagram in Figure 42.2 shows the Markowitz result when at least one of the assets is riskless.

The two small dots in the diagram represent the two portfolios that all investors will own. Each investor owns some combination of the risk-free asset and the efficient portfolio of risky assets. The thick line that begins at the risk-free asset and passes through the efficient portfolio of assets is the collection of possible outcomes

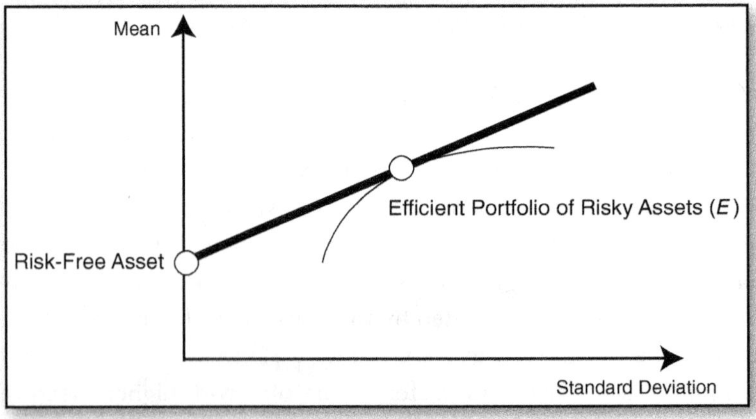

FIGURE 42.2 The Markowitz Result with a Single Riskless Asset.

[2] This result was first pointed out by James Tobin in "Liquidity Preference as Behavior Toward Risk," *Review of Economic Studies* 25, no. 2 (February 1958): 65–86.

for different investors who differ only by their preferences (how they feel about return versus risk). Those who want little or no risk end up near the vertical axis, owning mostly the risk-free asset. Those who prefer more risk move accordingly up the heavy line, up and to the right. Once you pass the efficient portfolio, such investors are borrowing to buy even more of the *E* portfolio. In effect, portfolios to the right of the *E* portfolios are portfolios that employ an increasing amount of leverage. They are implicitly borrowing at the risk-free rate.[3]

The remarkable conclusion of Markowitz's analysis is that all risk-averse investors, with any tolerance for risk at all, should purchase identical portfolios of risky assets. Such investors should generally hold some cash (the riskless asset) and some of the *E* portfolio. This means that if one investor likes risk and the other doesn't, both should still hold the same "mutual fund" of risky assets (the *E* portfolio). The investor who doesn't like much risk should hold less of *E,* relatively, than the investor who prefers more risk. The significance of this conclusion cannot be overstated. What Markowitz is saying is that the common adage that folks who don't like risk should buy less risky stocks and folks who like more risk should by risky stocks is flat wrong. Both of these sets of investors should buy the identical portfolio of risky assets—it's just that one should buy relatively more of it than the other. This means that the portfolio *E* is the most efficient way to own risky assets, regardless of the investor's preference for risk. That makes *E* almost an engineering outcome that simply falls out of the mathematics.

What is behind Markowitz's important result? In a word: diversification. The mathematics in Markowitz's analysis is combining assets into a diversified portfolio. *Given the riskless rate of interest (the return of the riskless asset), there will be only one efficient portfolio of risky assets and it will be the same for all investors.* That shows the power of diversification in a world where assets can all be described by a simple mean-variance characterization.

The Capital Asset Pricing Model (CAPM)

Markowitz's analysis was extended to a general equilibrium setting by several economists. The names Sharpe, Lintner, Mossin, and Black are all associated with the general equilibrium version of Markowitz's analysis, known as the capital asset pricing model (CAPM). Imagine a large number of investors who face a Markowitz situation—a set of assets with normally distributed returns with known means and variances. The outcome is identical to the Markowitz solution. Each investor chooses between the risk-free asset and some portfolio, *E*, that is the most efficient portfolio of risky assets. (This portfolio *E* will be different if there is a different risk-free rate on the risk-free asset.)

The CAPM Equation

The CAPM asks the question: what happens in a world of many investors who are choosing assets in the manner of the Markowitz model, by looking at their statistical

[3]This assumption can be altered to provide for the more realistic assumption that borrowing rates will be higher than the risk-free rate, but that is a detail we can ignore for present purposes.

return distributions (which need not be assumed normal for the CAPM conclusions to hold). *Equilibrium* is defined as a situation where the total quantity bought equals the total quantity sold for each asset at its currently prevailing price. Equilibrium, then, means that there is no tendency for prices to deviate from current prices because investors are satisfied with their current portfolios given their wealth constraints. The conclusion that emerges is:

$$E[R_i] = R_f + \beta_i(E[R_M] - R_f) \tag{42.1}$$

This forbidding-looking equation is actually fairly simple to interpret. Let's begin with the left hand side of this equation, $E[R_i]$. R_i is the return of the stock i and the $E[]$ simply means $E[R_i]$ is the expected future return (the average of what might occur in the future)—something like the statement, "On average, I expect stock i to have a return of 6 percent." This would mean that $E[R_i]$ is 6 percent, but that doesn't mean the actual future return in any particular period is 6 percent. It means the average of future returns is expected to be 6 percent. The actual return might be higher or lower. Equivalently, the "expected" number of head flips in two coin tosses is expected to be one, but could be zero or two.

What is R_f? R_f is the risk-free rate. It represents what an investor can earn without taking any risk. In the real world such an asset might be approximated by three-month U.S. Treasury bills. So far, the equation says that asset i will, on average, produce a return equal to what I can earn risklessly plus something else. This something else is known as the equity risk premium for stock i.

Let's look inside the brackets. What is the meaning of the following expression?

$$E[R_M] - R_f \tag{42.2}$$

$E[R_M]$ is the expected return of M, a portfolio. What is contained in portfolio M? That we shall discover shortly, but for now, let's just assume we know what portfolio M is and proceed. What $E[R_M] - R_f$ represents is the average (future) return of portfolio M after deducting the certain return of the risk-free asset. This is also known as the risk premium of portfolio M. It is the average return in excess of the risk-free rate that is attributable to the risk of owning portfolio M.

Finally, what is beta for asset i?

$$\beta_i$$

β_i represents the relationship between the returns of asset i and the returns of the portfolio M. If the returns of asset i perfectly mirror the returns of portfolio M, then beta is equal to +1. If the returns of asset i are exactly the opposite of the returns of the portfolio M, then beta is equal to –1. In the case where the returns are completely unrelated to one another, beta is equal to zero.

Betas are different for different stocks (assets). Some stocks are perfectly correlated to portfolio M, but others are not. A stock's beta can be an arbitrary number. The interesting question is, what is the portfolio M?

Now let's repeat the fundamental equation of the CAPM:

$$E[R_i] = R_f + \beta_i (E[R_M] - R_f) \quad (42.3)$$

We can now give a full interpretation to the CAPM equation. The equation says: the average future return of stock i will be the risk-free return plus the stock's beta multiplied by the amount by which the return on portfolio M exceeds the risk-free rate on average.

What is the mysterious portfolio M? M, in casual usage, is referred to as "the market portfolio," often approximated by a large stock index such as the Standard & Poor's (S&P) 500, the Wilshire 5000, or some international stock index. But in the theory, M has a very specific meaning: M consists of every single stock (asset) that has value (i.e., has a positive price). The proportions of M that each stock represents are determined by their *market capitalization*. That is, if you take the quantity of stock outstanding for a particular company and multiply that amount by the price of the stock, the result is the market capitalization of the company (the market value of the equity in the company).

Take all the stocks that have positive market capitalizations and add up all of their market capitalizations to get a total market capitalization:

$$\text{Total Market Capitalization} = P_1Q_1 + P_2Q_2 + \cdots + P_NQ_N = M \quad (42.4)$$

This portfolio is M and the weight of each stock in the portfolio is equal to its market capitalization divided by the total market capitalization of M:

$$\text{Weight of } i^{\text{th}} \text{ stock in the portfolio } M \text{ is equal to } \frac{P_iQ_i}{M} \quad (42.5)$$

The Interpretation of CAPM

The key variable in the CAPM equation is beta. Beta measures how much the individual stock's return is related to the return of the market. In mathematical terms:

$$\text{Beta (for stock } i) = \beta_i = \frac{\text{cov}(i, M)}{\text{var}(M)} \quad (42.6)$$

where cov(i, M) measures how closely related the return of stock i is to portfolio M and var(M) measures the volatility (or average fluctuations in value) of the market basket of all stocks, M.

If a stock behaves exactly like the market—goes up the same percentage as the market when the market goes up and goes down the same percentage as the market when the market goes down—then beta will equal 1. If a stock's beta is greater than 1, then it tends to go up faster than the market when the market goes up and tends to go down faster than the market when the market goes down. Betas can be negative. Gold stocks are often cited as an example of a negative beta stock, since gold often goes up when the market goes down and vice versa. A beta of zero means that the

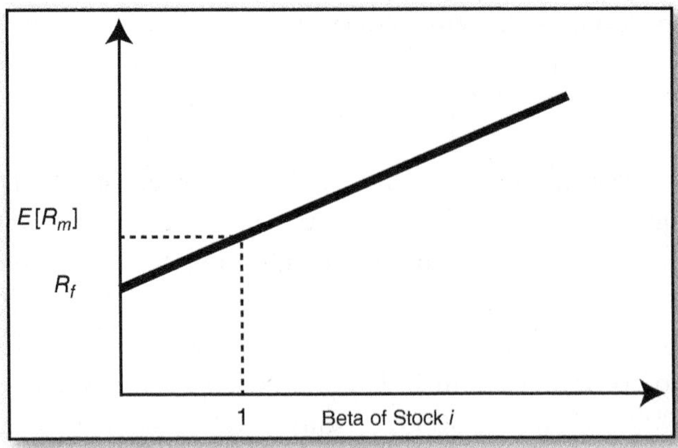

FIGURE 42.3 Expected (Future) Return of Stock *i*.

returns of the stock behave in a way quite independent of the behavior of the overall market. The vast majority of stocks have betas between 0.5 and 1.5.

Now, let's repeat the fundamental CAPM equation:

$$E[R_i] = R_f + \beta_i\,(E[R_M] - R_f) \qquad (42.7)$$

What this equation says is that a stock's future return, on average, should be the risk-free return plus an additional amount for the risk taken in owning stock *i*. A graphic representation of this result is shown in Figure 42.3.

The higher the beta, the higher the future expected return of stock *i*. Notice that how volatile a stock's price may be is irrelevant. A stock's price might have wide fluctuations and be considered risky as an individual stock, but it will not necessarily be risky from a CAPM point of view. In CAPM, investors will choose to diversify and hold a fully diversified portfolio (*M,* in fact). Thus, the risk of an individual stock depends on how it influences the behavior of the portfolio, not how it behaves on its own. This is the heart of CAPM. That beta, not volatility, determines the risk of a single asset as well as its future expected return is a consequence of *diversification*.

Diversification is the true theme of CAPM. Diversification by individual investors leads them to own the entire market basket (think here of a mutual fund that is the entire market basket and individuals own shares in the mutual fund). An investor who likes risk will own more of *M;* an investor who doesn't like risk will own less of *M*. One of the principal conclusions of CAPM, in addition to the CAPM equation, is the conclusion that each investor's portfolio will turn out to consist of at most two assets: (1) the risk-free asset, and (2) shares in an *M* mutual fund. An extremely risk-averse investor might own only the risk-free asset and none of *M*. An extremely risk-loving investor would own more and more *M,* perhaps even more than his entire net worth (which would mean that investor employs leverage to own more *M* than his net worth would normally permit).

CAPM as an "Accepted" Theory

It should already be apparent to the reader that the CAPM, as a theory of how financial markets work, leaves a lot to be desired. To begin with, we don't see many investors owning the entire market, *M*. Instead, most households don't own stock, in the United States or anywhere else in the world. When households do own stock, they don't tend to own portfolios anywhere near as diversified or as universal as the *M* portfolio of the CAPM.

Yet the CAPM dominates the financial landscape as the "language" of modern finance. *Beta* is a widely used term to describe the risk of an individual stock and is commonly used to describe the exposure of a portfolio to broad stock market movements. Measures of covariance of returns with "the market" are used in asset allocation studies for institutional investors—pension funds, endowments, and foundations. Measures of portfolio performance are also thoroughly infused with CAPM terminology, techniques, and methodology. So, in a real sense, the CAPM rules.

However, the CAPM has never been validated empirically. There is simply no empirical support for the notion that a stock's beta can predict its future returns. There is a lot of evidence, in fact, that no such relationship exists between an individual stock's beta and its future returns. In 1977, Richard Roll published a critique of the CAPM, arguing that the theory was not even testable in practice.[4] Roll's argument was that the CAPM was a completely vacuous tautology that could not be tested unless one could successfully delineate all the assets that are theoretically contained in the portfolio *M*. Roll especially criticized the widespread use of the CAPM in portfolio management and in the performance measurement of money management.

The famous "Cross-Section" paper by Eugene Fama and Kenneth French put to rest any claims of validity of the CAPM.[5] Their analysis argued that other factors, such as book-to-market, were far more important than any CAPM measures. They noted that a stock's beta, the cornerstone of CAPM, appeared to be unrelated to future expected returns.

Summarily, the CAPM is a theory unsupported by evidence, and it may not even be possible to subject it to evidence. Nonetheless, the CAPM still controls the language and the methodology of much of practical day-to-day finance, especially in the arena of institutional investing.

What Is the Market Model?

The efficient market hypothesis (EMH) is the broad statement that information determines prices and that no one can predict future stock returns outside of the simple idea that risk creates reward. High expected returns can be achieved only by taking large risks. There is no simple arbitrage strategy that permits an investor to make returns (beyond the risk-free rate) without taking risk. We saw in Chapter 41 that there is a variety of ways of formally stating the EMH, but basically they all lead to the idea of information determining prices and an absence of predictability in asset prices.

[4] Richard Roll, "A Critique of the Asset Pricing Theory's Tests; Part I: On Past and Potential Testability of the Theory," *Journal of Financial Economics* 4, no. 2 (March 1977): 129–176.

[5] Eugene Fama and Kenneth French, "The Cross-Section of Expected Stock Returns," *The Journal of Finance* 47, no. 2 (June 1992): 427–465.

A *market model* is a much more specific characterization of asset prices than that given by the broad EMH dictum. The CAPM would be one such model. The CAPM focused on the role of beta in determining expected returns (as opposed to a stock's own price-volatility) and reshaped and clarified the meaning of diversification in asset pricing theory. Another market model is that of Fama and French, which we will not discuss in this chapter. Book-to-market plays a prominent role in the Fama-French market model. There are numerous other market models, mostly parented by the groundbreaking Fama-French 1992 paper.

Why do we care about the market model? In most tests of the EMH, we are forced to use some market model to describe the asset return-generating process. When testing the EMH and employing a market model, one can never be sure what is being tested—the EMH or the model? The tests tend to simultaneously test both the CAPM and the researcher's employed market model.

CHAPTER 43

The Forerunners to Behavioral Finance

From Edwin T. Burton and Sunit N. Shah, *Behavioral Finance* (Hoboken, New Jersey: John Wiley & Sons, 2013), Chapter 3.

Academics were reasonably content with the efficient market hypothesis (EMH) until sometime toward the end of the twentieth century. The year 1987 was critical in undermining faith in the EMH. U.S. stock market behavior in 1987 was bizarre. The year began with the Dow Jones Industrial Average at slightly above 2,200, and it ended the year in that general area. If all you knew were the beginning and ending stock market averages, then 1987 would seem to be a ho-hum type of year. But in between the beginning and ending averages, there was an incredible rally and a historic collapse. The market's behavior can be summarized in Figure 43.1.

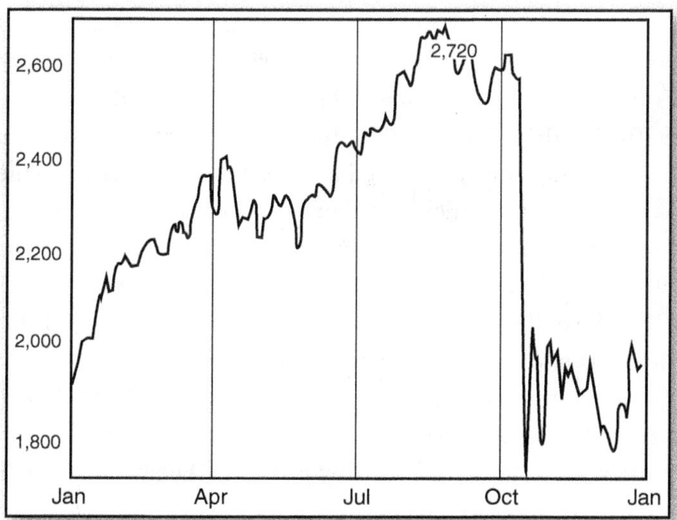

FIGURE 43.1 Summary of Market Behavior.

The interesting question about 1987's stock market performance is: why? What news and information were there that led to a 30 percent rally in the first half of the year, followed by October 19, 1987, the worst single-day percentage loss in U.S. equity market history? The year 1987 should be called the "Rip Van Winkle" year. If you fell asleep in early January and awoke in late December, you would not know that much of anything had happened.

When you ask observers what happened to cause the big rally and big decline, almost everyone will provide an answer, especially those who consider themselves savvy about financial markets. But the answers are all over the map, and no single explanation has gained enough currency to gain widespread acceptance. There are plenty of one-off explanations, but none that command any real authority. The *Wall Street Journal* had a special edition the day after the 509-point, 22 percent historic sell-off on October 19, 1987. In that edition, they surveyed the various top executives of the largest and most prestigious Wall Street firms as to their opinions regarding the cause of the stock market crash. The opinions varied widely with no particular consistency. Even among market professionals who commune with one another regularly and drink at the same watering holes, there was no consensus as to what had happened and a blithering variety of different views espoused.

If you lived through the 1987 crash, then you are likely still wondering what happened. The very few who guessed that the crash was coming (and predictably there should be a few who guessed right) built careers and fortunes out of their prescient views. Paul Tudor Jones was one such individual and created the highly successful Tudor Management on the back of his accurate prediction of the 1987 crash. But did he really know what caused it? Perhaps.

The Folklore of Wall Street Traders

The first modern bull market in common stocks was in the United States in the 1920s. This was also the first time that nonprofessional investors, ordinary citizens, began to take an active participatory role in the public financial markets. A lot of speculative activity took place during this period and financial "traders" became mythic actors on the Wall Street stage. There were a number of books published during the 1920s that described "trading the market" that suggested that the market was "predictable," if one simply followed a few set and time-tested rules. Of course, different books had different rules, but there were some common themes.

The most famous of these books grew out of a series of articles that began appearing in 1922 in the *Saturday Evening Post* written by financial journalist Edwin Lefèvre. In 1923, the collection of articles was recast as a book published that year by Lefèvre entitled *Reminiscences of a Stock Operator*.[1] The book chronicles the trading activity of a fictitious character named Lawrence Livingston. It has long been assumed that the real trader, whose activities are described in this book, was Jessie Livermore, known early in his career as the "Boy Plunger." The book described all sorts of

[1] Edwin Lefèvre, *Reminiscences of a Stock Operator* (New York: John Wiley & Sons, 2006; originally published in 1923).

trading activities including the use of short selling and conducting short squeezes. For our purposes, the significance of Lefèvre's book and others of this genre is that the book suggests that there are ways for the speculative trader to "beat the market." Some of the activities spelled out in this book became illegal under reform legislation in the 1930s. But many of the strategies discussed were based on understanding the emotional sentiment factors that, according to the book, create important stock market moves.

In the 1920s, there wasn't any real academic interest in the stock market, so ideas like the EMH were not discussed in any serious way. Indeed, one of the leading academic economists in the United States, Yale's Irving Fisher, published a book in 1929 (bad timing) that suggested that stocks were unlikely to ever go down again. John Maynard Keynes, one of the most famous economists in history, was, in the 1920s, busily speculating on currency markets, the metals markets, and stock markets. Keynes was to later describe the market as being dominated by "waves of pessimism and optimism" in his classic *The General Theory of Employment, Interest and Money,* published in 1935.[2] Even leading economists suggested, by their behavior, that financial markets were predictable. Behavioral finance did not exist as an academic discipline, nor did any particular finance curriculum exist anywhere in academia during this period, but it is clear from what economists were saying that the EMH would not have ruled the roost among academic economists.

What is interesting about all of this is that trading folklore and the activities of leading academic economists fit the behavioral finance point of view, not the EMH point of view. Economists who were actively discussing and acting in financial markets seemed of the opinion that markets were predictable, which is a key tenet of modern behavioral finance.

There were generally two trading strategies that circulated in the folklore. The first strategy was what we today call a *momentum* strategy. If you see a stock going up dramatically, then hop on board because it will likely continue going up. If everyone hops on board and you can perceive that everyone is on board, then you should hop off. The "hopping off" is more akin to what we call today *mean reversion.* Mean reversion is the idea that if a stock has been doing really well for a long time and people seem to love the stock, then you should sell on the premise that the stock will not do well in the future. So, two trading strategies, mildly conflicting, permeated a lot of the folklore, including Lefèvre's book:

1. In the short term, stocks that are going up will continue that trend; stocks that are going down will continue that trend.
2. In the long run, stocks that have done well for a long time will do poorly in the future, and vice versa.

The first strategy is known today as *short-term momentum,* and the second strategy is still known as *mean reversion.* The central ideas behind these strategies were known and discussed openly by traders in the 1920s. Sixty and 70 years later, academic

[2] John Maynard Keynes, *The General Theory of Employment, Interest and Money* (New York: Harcourt, Brace and World, Inc., 1935). See especially Chapter 12, pages 154 and 155.

economists would pick up these ideas and begin to research their validity under the banner of behavioral finance. Because of the ready availability of data, by the time these researchers began to look at the data, it was relatively easy to document data trends such as those suggested by momentum and mean reversion. We look at this in some detail later in this book. Our point here is that Wall Street trading folklore had long believed in these strategies, even if there was no serious research to test their validity.

The Birth of Value Investing: Graham and Dodd

In 1934, Benjamin Graham and David Dodd, both business school professors, coauthored a book entitled *Security Analysis*[3] that focused investor attention on the financial statements of public companies. The timing for publishing this book could not have been better. The Securities Acts of 1933 and 1934 required all public companies to publish detailed financial statements at least every three months (10-Q quarterly filings). This meant that investors had ready access to the data that Graham and Dodd were now saying could be used to beat the market.

Graham and Dodd argued in their famous book that investors could profit by studying a company's financial statements, income statements, and balance sheet statements to ascertain its value. They implicitly and explicitly decried the "horse race" character of the public markets and said the conscientious investor could beat the crowd by painstakingly studying the "true value" of a company, which could, they argued, be gleaned from the company's financial statements.

The Graham and Dodd approach came to be known as *value investing.* Many modern-day investors hearken back to Graham and Dodd as their inspiration. Warren Buffett is one such Graham and Dodd admirer. The idea is that an investor should buy out-of-favor stocks with strong "fundamentals." The fundamentals are ascertained by poring over income statements and balance sheets to uncover what could best be described as diamonds in the rough. The clear message was don't buy the stocks that other people like; buy the stocks that other people shun. Look for value among the stocks beaten down and overlooked.

This theme meant that markets could be beaten, which is the opposite of the theme of the EMH. Value investing also seemed to be similar to the message of mean reversion. Stocks that had not done well might be the best "values" because investors overreact emotionally to a string of bad news without necessarily considering the underlying fundamentals. Stocks that had done well for a long time were likely to not be good buys because market participants may not have looked closely at deteriorating fundamentals.

The 1930s destroyed much of the public's interest in the stock market, but when interest returned in the 1950s, value investing became a big business, with money managers professing adherence to Graham and Dodd's message. Over time, empirical support seemed to develop for value investing, culminating in a landmark

[3] Benjamin Graham and David Dodd, *Security Analysis* (New York: Whittlesey House, 1934).

research paper published in 1992 by two academic economists, Eugene Fama and Kenneth French. The research by Fama and French appeared to validate the idea that value investing could beat the market.

The main message of Graham and Dodd reinforced the common perception in the 1930s and 1940s that there were ways to beat the market and that stock price movements were, in principle, predictable.

Financial News in a World of Ubiquitous Television and Internet

In modern financial markets, there is constant news reporting on television and the Internet describing the ups and downs of individual securities and aggregated indices as well as all the news that seems relevant to their movements. Traders, eager to have the latest information, keep tuned minute-by-minute to the constant barrage of information that emanates from modern electronic sources. But what kind of information is being conveyed? Most often, the information is opinion as opposed to facts, and the facts that are reported are typically already publicly known facts. One word that could aptly fit the modern financial news that is reported is *noise*. What about the audience? No doubt, many in the audience could be described as "noise traders." If listeners rush out and buy and sell stocks based on outdated facts or random opinions, then such listeners are—by definition—noise traders, because they are not trading on true information but, much of the time, on stale and bogus information.

These news outlets are constantly trumpeting ideas such as "year-end rallies" and the like, which have no relationship to the fundamental drivers of company value. Rational traders would have no interest in year-end rallies. Notions of "support" and "resistance" levels of prices permeate the daily drumbeat of financial news. But a rational trader would find no meaning in these concepts. Yet someone is listening, and no doubt, someone is trading off the noise that is ever-present in the financial news reporting media.

CHAPTER 44

Noise Traders and the Law of One Price

From Edwin T. Burton and Sunit N. Shah, *Behavioral Finance* (Hoboken, New Jersey: John Wiley & Sons, 2013), Chapter 4.

One of the very first things a student learns in beginning economics is that if two commodities are identical, then they will command identical prices in the marketplace. If the price of the two commodities should ever diverge, buyers will buy the cheaper of the two, and sellers will sell the more expensive of the two, pushing the divergent prices toward each other. It is likely that someone will try to buy the commodity in the cheap market and sell it in the more expensive market and earn an arbitrage profit. Thus, the law of one price emerges: two identical commodities must have the same price almost all the time.

The Law of One Price and the Case of Fungibility

All of this seems simple enough, as long as we are comfortable with the definition of identical. What if two things are identical, but we refer to them by different names? Are they still identical? Do they still command the same price in the marketplace? Imagine a factory that produces baseballs. Suppose that every second baseball produced is called a hardball, whereas all others produced are called *baseballs*. But suppose in every respect there is absolutely no physical difference between a hardball and a baseball. They are the exact same thing except for their differing names. Can a hardball have a different price than a baseball? (See Figure 44.1.)

The two items above are not strictly identical because they have different names. This difference in name allows for the possibility that market participants may see

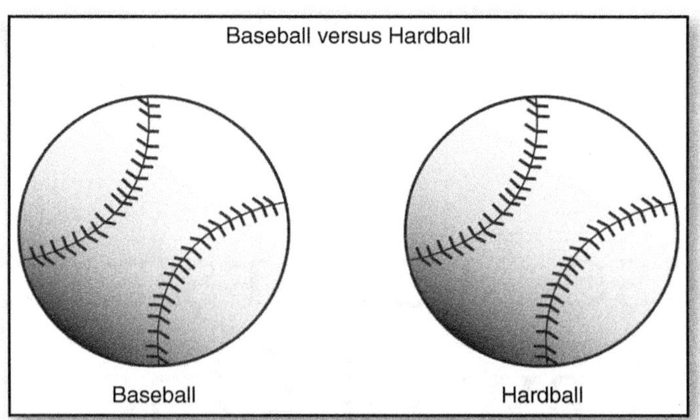

FIGURE 44.1 Can These Two Have Different Prices?

them as truly different and that it may be possible for these two physically identical items to have different prices. If we think of these as assets, then we could say that the efficient market hypothesis (EMH) requires that these two items have identical prices since all information about them is the same. A *behavioral economist* might argue otherwise. The different names might lead to different prices, even when the items themselves are physically indistinguishable.

Imagine a baseball-hardball machine that costlessly converts hardballs into baseballs and baseballs into hardballs, one for one in each case. If the price of baseballs and hardballs were to differ, then one should buy the cheaper of the two, feed it into the machine, and out would come the other, which could then be sold at a profit. This is a simple example of arbitrage. This type of costless conversion is known as *fungibility*.

There are many examples of fungibility in financial markets. Options in certain combinations and most futures contracts are completely fungible into the underlying instruments from which they derive their value. Owning a gold future is simply another way of owning gold, and if the owner of a gold future does not sell the future, then delivery of gold will take place on the future's delivery date. In this manner, the gold future owner becomes the owner of actual gold. This is an example of fungibility. The simple arbitrage of the baseball-hardball machine example is possible in the options and futures markets, though in a more complicated fashion.

What happens if the hardball and the baseball are not fungible? An easy way to make them not fungible is to put an indelible label on each. Each hardball would have the label *hardball* imprinted on it, and each baseball would have the label *baseball* imprinted on it. Then the arbitrage process might fail.

Suppose hardballs have the higher price. A buyer of hardballs might hold out for the product with the preferred label, even though, except for labeling, there is absolutely no physical difference. In the absence of fungibility, there is a clear possibility that the prices of two "identical" things might command different prices (almost all the time). There is no simple arbitrage that produces a guaranteed profit in finite time by buying one and selling the other. In principle, nothing forces the prices to equality, absent fungibility.

The reason fungibility is an important issue is that many seemingly identical pairs of securities are not fungible. The most famous example is the stock pair consisting of Royal Dutch common stock (a Netherlands corporation) and Shell common stock (a British corporation).[1] This pair represents different amounts of ownership in the same company. The former is entitled to 40 percent of all the earnings of the company, while the latter is entitled to 60 percent of all of the earnings of the company. The price of three shares of Royal Dutch should always be approximately equal to the price of two shares of Shell, if the law of one price holds. There simply is no difference between three shares of Royal Dutch and two shares of Shell regarding their economic claims on the company. But, as is well known, Royal Dutch and Shell rarely trade at a 1.5 ratio and can diverge from that ratio by substantial margins and for indefinite periods of time.

Why doesn't the law of one price work in this case? The answer is lack of fungibility. You cannot buy three shares of Royal Dutch Shell and convert those shares into two shares of Shell (British). If you buy shares in either company, the only available method of disposal is to sell them.

If you could convert the cheaper shares into the more expensive shares at a three-to-two ratio, then simple arbitrage would bring the prices together, but you cannot do the conversion. No machine is available. The only thing available is the marketplace. That lack of fungibility has, in practice, meant that those who purchase the cheaper of the Shell stocks and an offsetting position[2] in the more expensive (on a three-to-two ratio) have lingered in that transaction with no particular tendency for the prices to equalize.

If two commodities are identical and fungible (in the sense that one could be converted into the other and vice versa at minimal cost), then the law of one price should hold. But if fungibility is not present, then it is an open question whether the prices of two identical but not fungible assets will converge. The famous example of Royal Dutch and Shell is a very public example of identical things that lack fungibility for which the law of one price doesn't seem to hold.

What If Identical Things Are Not Fungible?

Now let us imagine two identical assets that cannot be transformed one into another except by selling one and buying the other. This is the truly interesting case for the EMH. The fungibility case has a mechanical way of resolving itself and is more an exception than the norm in financial markets. Things that seem almost identical in financial markets are typically not fungible one into the other.

Can prices of two identical, but not fungible, things, like our baseball and hardball, diverge and maintain that divergence for a significant period of time, perhaps even indefinitely? The EMH would say that the prices of two things, even if not fun-

[1] See the exposition of the twin Shell stocks by Andrei Shleifer in *Inefficient Markets* (New York: Oxford University Press, USA, 2000), Chapter 2.

[2] Offsetting position means a short sale, or borrowing the stock from a holder and selling it, planning to repurchase the stock at a later date and return it to its original owner.

gible, should be identical or virtually identical most of the time. That sounds vague, but it is nonetheless a demanding requirement, as we shall see.

If prices in the marketplace are not right, then someone has to be buying and selling at these incorrect prices. There have to be buyers willing to pay too much or sellers willing to sell for too little in order to keep prices from being the right prices. What does the phrase "right prices" mean? It means the prices that rational, knowledgeable participants would be willing to buy or sell something for.

One can easily imagine that there might be individuals who think that our baseballs and hardballs are different things. Individuals perhaps lack the knowledge to know that the baseball and hardball are identical. But, in time, surely they would learn that they are not truly different. Then, it becomes hard to imagine that anyone would pay more for one than the other. But what if there were people who could never be convinced that these two identical items were identical? Perhaps they don't learn, or perhaps they think the fact that they are labeled differently is enough to constitute a true difference.

Can two identical things with different names be different? For our purposes, the answer is no. They should be considered the same thing. But the deeper question is: can they have different prices? If they cannot have different prices, then the EMH, at least for this case, is validated. If different prices can prevail for products that differ only by label, then much other economic theorizing, not just the EMH, could be challenged as well.

How could these prices be different? Someone has to be willing to pay a higher price for one than for the other.

The Friedman View

Milton Friedman provided an argument in the context of currency markets that amounted to a defense of the EMH:

> Despite the prevailing opinion to the contrary, I am very dubious in fact that speculation in foreign exchange would be destabilizing. . . . People who argue that speculation is generally destabilizing seldom realize that this is largely equivalent to saying that speculators lose money, since speculation can be destabilizing only if speculators on the average sell when the currency is low in price and buy when it is high.[3]

Friedman was discussing whether speculators were a destabilizing influence in currency markets. He is arguing that speculators, traders who move prices away from efficiency, will lose money, suggesting that *smart* traders will push prices back toward efficiency while they take the opposite positions and that such speculators will eventually lose all of their capital.

The modern version of Friedman's argument introduces the notion of noise traders, which would include not only Friedman's speculators but other market

[3] Milton Friedman, *Inefficient Markets* (Chicago, University of Chicago Press: 1953), 175.

participants as well. Friedman's argument, updated, would be that noise traders as a group would lose money as they foolishly buy at high prices and sell at low prices.

But Noise Traders, if Sufficiently Diverse, May Not Matter

Imagine some individuals who are irrationally willing to pay more for a baseball than a hardball. Isn't it reasonable to suppose that there may be other individuals who are irrationally willing to pay more for a hardball than a baseball? Perhaps degrees of irrationality are randomly distributed about the true rational outcome. Then, such irrational individuals may offset one another. A kind of law of large numbers might come into play that has the baseball lovers counterbalanced by the hardball lovers so that the prices of the two remain approximately identical—offsetting irrationality, we might suppose. Eugene Fama made precisely this argument in his defense of the EMH[4] against the argument that noise traders would disrupt matters.

The Noise Trader Agenda

It has long been known that there are many, often silly, reasons that people buy and sell stocks. No one pretends that all traders and investors are completely rational; common observation suggests that is not the case. But the very existence of noise traders is not sufficient to invalidate the EMH. In order to show that the EMH is in trouble, at least two conditions must be met. We will call these two conditions the *noise trader agenda*:

1. Noise trader behavior must be systematic. Noise traders must be shown not to simply cancel one another out. If some are too optimistic and others are too pessimistic, then one group may simply cancel out the effect of the other. Instead, there must be something like herd activity, such that a large group of noise traders, or a small group with a large amount of assets, behave in a similar manner.
2. Noise traders need to survive economically for a significant period of time. If all noise traders do is lose money through their noise trading, then their impact will be limited. Noise traders need to make substantial and persistent profits under some conditions. Otherwise, noise traders are simply cannon fodder, as Friedman suggests, for the smart traders.

Noise

Where does the term *noise trader* come from, and what does it mean? Noise trading is normally defined by what it is not. A noise trader is not the rational, knowledgeable trader or investor who is commonly assumed in finance theory. The noise trader is doing something else. A noise trader could be as harmless as a year-end tax seller,

[4] Eugene Fama, "Efficient Capital Markets: A Review of Theory and Empirical Work," *Journal of Finance* 25, no. 2 (May 1970): 383–417.

paying no attention to values at the moment of sale. It could be a grandmother buying a present of stock for a grandchild, where the main interest in the stock is that the company produces something appealing to children, regardless of the inherent investment merits of the company itself.

Fischer Black's 1985 Presidential Address to the American Finance Association

The concept of noise in a financial market context has its first modern expression in Fischer Black's address to the American Finance Association meetings in December 1985. Black's talk on that occasion was simply entitled "Noise."[5] Noise, in a scientific context, almost invariably refers to "white noise" or "Brownian motion." Intuitively, this notion of noise is describing something that bounces around with no particular direction. But the bouncing around is stable. Figure 44.2 is a typical depiction of white noise.

Notice that the pattern is continuous but erratic. Modern financial theory uses white noise to characterize the pattern of stock prices,[6] so Black's lecture was aimed at an audience that was familiar with this notion of noise.

Fischer Black was both an academic and a practitioner. At least half of his working days were spent in Wall Street or Chicago security trading operations. Black was intimately familiar with the diversity of trader motives and activities. He describes a variety of different types of noise traders. The definition of a noise trader is elusive in Black's talk (as it is in the entire literature), but Black provides the following definition: "Noise trading is trading on noise as if it were information."[7] That definition

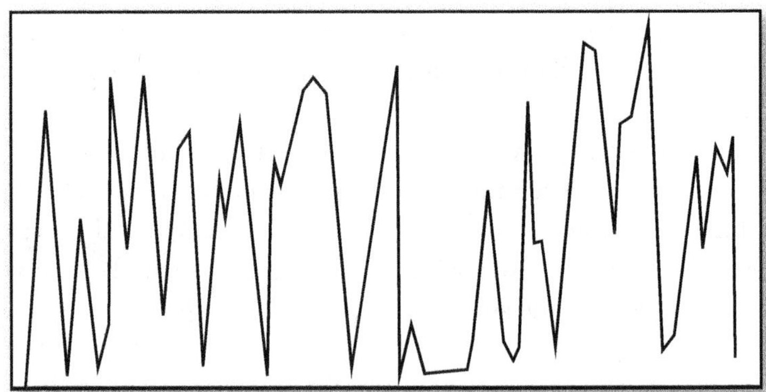

FIGURE 44.2 White Noise.

[5] See Fischer Black, "Noise," *The Journal of Finance* 41, no. 3 (July 1986); Papers and Proceedings of the Forty-Fourth Annual Meeting of the American Finance Association, New York, NY, December 28–30, 1985, 529–543.

[6] Salih Neftci, *An Introduction to the Mathematics of Financial Derivatives* (New York, Academic Press, 1996). Neftci gives a simple explanation of Brownian motion and its equivalent, a Wiener process, on pages 148–149. Neftci's book is an intuitive and easy-to-read description of the role that white noise plays in modern finance.

[7] Black, "Noise," 531.

begs the question as to what exactly is noise, which Black elsewhere in the talk describes as something characterized by "a large number of small events." It is not completely clear what Black means here, but the talk is descriptive of many aspects of trading markets that those who trade for a living would quickly recognize.

Following are the opening lines of Black's presentation:

> I use the word "noise" in several senses in this paper. In my basic model of financial markets, noise is contrasted with information. People sometimes trade on information in the usual way. They are correct in expecting to make profits from these trades. On the other hand, people sometimes trade on noise as if it were information. If they expect to make profits from noise trading, they are incorrect.[8]

Black defines noise traders indirectly by what they are not. A noise trader is someone who is not trading on *information*. By information, Black implicitly means relevant and true information such as might be useful in predicting the future earnings of a publicly traded company. It is not clear from Black's description what a noise trader actually does, but it is clear what a noise trader doesn't do. Black's noise trader is not the rational, information-seeking investor that is typically portrayed in the efficient market paradigm.

In the preceding section, we defined a noise trader as someone willing to buy or sell at "incorrect" prices. In the hardball/baseball story, a noise trader would be someone willing to pay a different amount for a hardball than for a baseball even though they are the same asset. Someone who doesn't use information would fit both Black's definition and our definition. There is no way around the idea that if you want the EMH to be violated, you will need to have models that incorporate noise traders. Without them, you simply can't get identical, nonfungible things to trade at different prices.

As the father of the noise-trading concept, Black seemed little bothered by the implications of noise trading: "Noise makes financial markets possible, but also makes them imperfect."[9]

But Black goes on to say, "With a lot of noise traders in the market, it now pays for those with information to trade. . . . Most of the time, the noise traders will lose money by trading, while the information traders as a group will make money."[10]

After a description of how information traders move prices back to their correct value, Black concludes: "I think almost all markets are efficient almost all of the time. 'Almost all' means at least 90 percent."[11]

Fischer Black's talk paradoxically introduced the notion of noise trading, but concludes that the EMH withstands the impact of noise traders. But Black was not the first to see things this way.

---

[8] Black, "Noise," 529.

[9] Ibid., 530.

[10] Ibid., 530.

[11] Ibid., 533.

It is clear that Black shares the Friedman view, outlined earlier, and that his talk in 1985 can be interpreted as an update of the earlier Friedman position with one important caveat. Black left open the door to critics of the EMH when he observed: "In other words, I do not believe it makes sense to create a model with information trading but no noise trading where traders have different beliefs and one trader's beliefs are as good as any other trader's belief."[12]

Behavioral finance would look back to the following remark as a prescient preview of the direction noise trader research would take: "Noise makes financial markets possible, but also makes them imperfect."[13]

Friedman would not have agreed with Black that noise traders played a positive and essential role in financial markets. Friedman saw such activity as foolish and mostly as a nuisance. Friedman seemed to feel that noise traders were simply sitting ducks for rational traders to take money from. Other than that, noise traders need not be considered and could not influence asset prices in any significant way. It is clear that Black's presidential address moves away from Friedman by asserting that noise traders are essential to financial markets, that they impact prices constantly, and that they cannot be left out of any serious financial market theorizing.

The Friedman-Black Path for Noise Traders

The arguments advanced by Milton Friedman and Fischer Black suggest the pathway ahead for critics of the EMH. Inserting noise traders into models of the financial system, as Black insisted upon, and dealing with what we earlier referred to as the *noise trader agenda,* could enable the existence of noise traders to pose a challenge to the presumed efficiency of financial markets.

[12] Black, "Noise," p. 531.

[13] Ibid., 530.

CHAPTER 45

Noise Traders as Technical Traders

From Edwin T. Burton and Sunit N. Shah, *Behavioral Finance* (Hoboken, New Jersey: John Wiley & Sons, 2013), Chapter 7.

When watching contemporary news accounts of financial market activity, one frequently hears expressions that have no explicit role in traditional finance theory but seem to mean something to the audience of the news commentators. Examples include:

"The market is forming a bottom."
"A very oversold market rallied today."
"The market broke through resistance today."
"The market dropped through support today."
"The market acts well."
"The market looks tired."

These expressions have meaning in the trading world, but they are not part of the received financial theory, and the efficient market hypothesis (EMH) predicts that none of these remarks has any real truth embodied in them. All of these expressions and many more like them are descriptions of technical analysis. If *fundamental analysis* can be defined as basing stock analysis on things taken from accounting statements and projections of accounting statements, then *technical analysis* is based on things that explicitly eschew considerations of profits, cash flow, dividends—any of the tools of fundamental analysis.

The most popular form of technical analysis is the charting of stock prices. There is a big business in providing investors with stock price charts both in printed form and in computer-accessible online form. Armed with pricing history, many traders base their stock buys and sells on how they interpret stock price patterns from historical data. An example of a stock price chart is given in Figure 45.1.

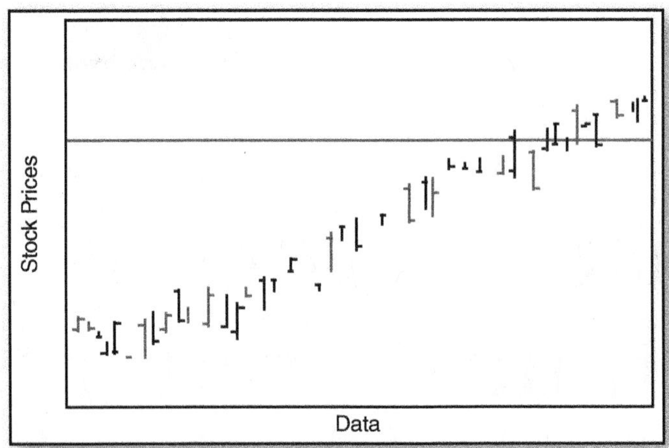

FIGURE 45.1 Stock Price Chart.

Dates are plotted on the horizontal axis and stock prices are plotted vertically. The horizontal line indicates a particular stock price that the charting pattern suggests is significant. That stock prices have surpassed the value indicated by the horizontal line is taken to be important in determining the future path of the price of the stock.

Academics once scoffed at technical traders as akin to believing in voodoo dolls, but technical trading by the turn of the twenty-first century had gone mainstream. The Market Technicians Association (MTA), by 2012, boasted a membership of 4,500 "market analyst professionals in over 85 countries around the globe."[1] The MTA boasts that it offers a certification program to become a Chartered Market Technician (CMT), achievable by passing a set of examinations that test applicants on their knowledge of technical analysis. It has three levels of the CMT exam, much like its much revered ancestor, the Chartered Financial Analyst certification, pioneered by the CFA Institute.[2]

Besides attracting the interest of individual traders, technical analysis was available from mainstream stockbrokers for their clients' usage. Large pools of hedge fund money, by 2012, were invested in trading strategies solely based on past stock price histories. The National Futures Association counts among its members 4,500 firms and 55,000 associates, the vast majority of whom are actively involved in some form of technical trading. All of this activity, of course, runs counter to the EMH, which says that technical analysis activity represents wasted motion and wasted money. But regardless of the calumny heaped upon technical analysis by adherents of the EMH, it is an undeniable fact that technical trading underlies a very large amount of actual trading in modern financial markets.

Many common strategies in technical trading involve projecting past pricing trends into the future. This type of trading, if widespread, can create and sustain a pricing bubble. We will refer to such occurrences as *herd instinct* trading. In the latter part of this chapter, we consider some examples of the herd instinct and bubble literature.

[1] Information taken from www.mta.org on June 9, 2012.

[2] Details available at www.cfainstitute.org.

Technical Traders as Noise Traders

Since technical traders are not rational traders in the sense of the EMH, they can instead be thought of as a specific type of noise trader. To simplify matters, think only about that subset of technical analysis that involves nothing more than the use of stock price charts. There are two things that are intriguing about stock price chart analysis: (1) stock price charting is widely used, and (2) users tend to agree on what many stock price chart patterns mean. The first of these considerations implies that noise traders who are price chart traders represent a significant part of the actual trading community. The second suggests that their behavior in the marketplace may be systematic.

Trend-Following Noise Traders

One of the most widely believed patterns observable in stock price charts is that if a trend is portrayed by the chart, the trend will continue. If the stock price has been rising over time, then the prediction is that it will continue to rise. If the stock price has been falling over time, then the prediction is that it will continue to fall. This idea that price trends, once in place, will continue seems to be a prevailing view in other markets besides financial markets. Many participants in the housing market seem to have expectations of future prices that are a straightforward projection of recent pricing trends.

One simple way to model a noise trader would be an extrapolative model that forecasts future prices as a straightforward projection of the trend implicit in most recent prices (see Figure 45.2). A noise trader using the extrapolative expectations, such as depicted in Figure 45.2, might pay little or no attention to fundamentals. Bad news would not matter to such a noise trader, unless the bad news changed the pattern of stock prices so the extrapolation would lead to some different forecast.

If there is a large number of noise traders defined in this way, then one would expect some self-fulfilling aspect of such trading behavior. Expecting current trends to continue could lead to a higher or lower demand for a stock than might be warranted by the fundamentals. This characterization of a noise trader is consistent with the

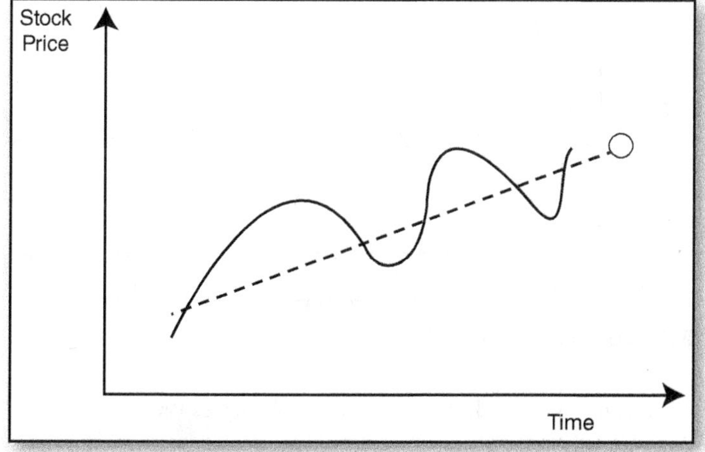

FIGURE 45.2 Predicted Stock Price Based on Trend Projection.

Shleifer model since overoptimism or overpessimism could easily result from trend following. Such traders might even be more profitable than rational traders, at least for a while, for the reasons given in that model.

Reversal Patterns in Stock Prices

Somewhat more complicated is what stock price charts might tell us about market reversals. A market reversal takes place when a rising (falling) price trend becomes a falling (rising) price trend. What stock price patterns predict reversals? There are many.

One of the most interesting stock price patterns that technical traders subscribe to is known as the *island reversal*. The island reversal requires that a stock price jumps from one price to a substantially different price either immediately or during a trading halt, which could be nothing more than close of market on one day and the opening of the market on the next trading day. The gap in the price creates an island, as shown in Figure 45.3.

According to some versions of the island reversal signal, whenever a stock price gaps it must go back and fill in the gap, so that some future reversal in price is predicted by the island reversal phenomenon.

Another popular reversal pattern is the *head-and-shoulders* pattern. Sometimes this is called either a head-and-shoulders top or a head-and-shoulders bottom, depending on whether it is forecasting a fall in future stock prices or an increase in future stock prices. A head-and-shoulders top is pictured in Figure 45.4, together with its forecast of declining prices. In Figure 45.4, the head-and-shoulders pattern has formed and is now suggesting that stock prices will fall, reversing the previous uptrend in prices that had been in place before the formation of the head-and-shoulders pattern.

Head-and-shoulders patterns were studied extensively by Carol Osler[3] and later by Osler and Kevin Chang.[4] Osler's 1998 study reported that strategies based on head-and-shoulders patterns in U.S. equity markets proved to be unprofitable. The

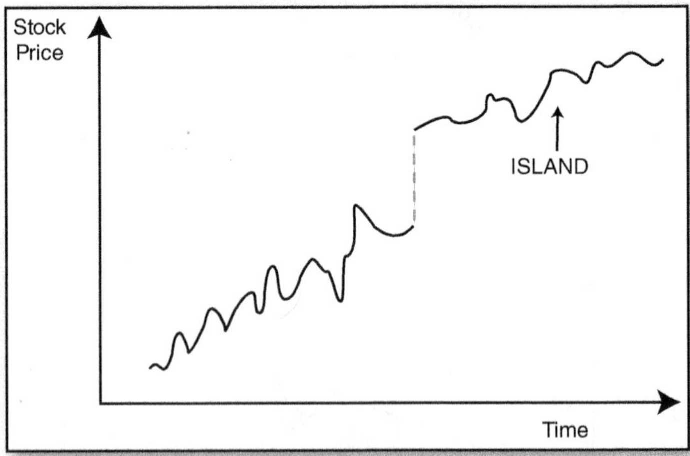

FIGURE 45.3 Price Island.

[3] Carol Osler, "Identifying Noise Traders: The Head-and-Shoulders Pattern in U.S. Equities," Federal Reserve Bank of New York, 1988.

[4] Kevin P. H. Chang and Carol Osler, "Methodical Madness: Technical Analysis and the Irrationality of Exchange-Rate Forecasts," *Economic Journal* 109, no. 458 (October 1999): 636–661.

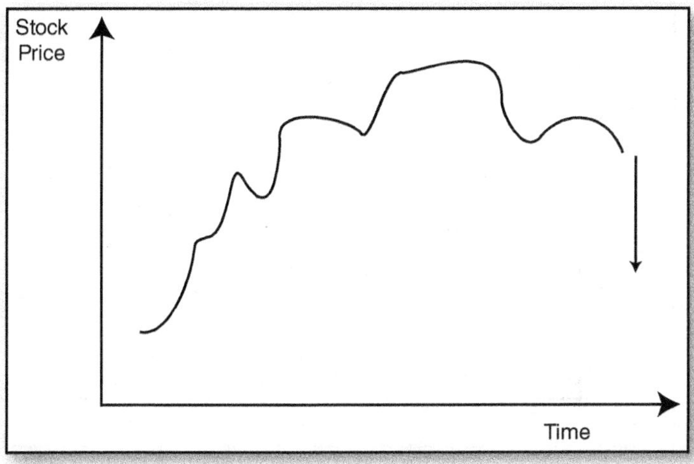

FIGURE 45.4 **A Head-and-Shoulders Top.**

Osler-Chang results, published a year later and based on data from currency markets, found the opposite. Head-and-shoulders trading in currency markets was profitable, according to Osler and Chang.

> The head-and-shoulders trading rule appears to have some predictive power for the German mark and yen but not for the Canadian dollar, Swiss franc, French franc, or pound. Taken individually, profits in the markets for yen and marks are also substantial when adjusted for transactions costs, interest differentials, or risk. These results are inconsistent with virtually all standard exchange rate models, and could indicate the presence of market inefficiencies.[5]

A final example of reversal patterns are the twin concepts of *base building* and *forming a top.* Base building occurs when a stock has dropped over a period of time but seems to have stabilized at a lower level and has traded in a narrow range around that lower level (see Figure 45.5).

The dotted line represents the base that is forming. Forming a top is a similar pattern, flipping the chart upside down so that forming a top is ultimately predicting a future decline in prices, while base building is suggested to lead to prices headed higher at some future date.

The Systematic Issue

Stock price charts are easy to construct and the simple patterns that we just discussed can be discerned from the data with minimal effort. Simple algorithms can be employed—not necessarily all identical—to take advantage of any profit opportunities that stock price charts might have embedded in them. Trend following can be seen as a version of herd mentality. A price is going up rapidly, and everyone jumps on board and buys the stock whose price is rising. A frenzy develops as the price rises higher and higher, and future prices are extrapolated to be even higher still. This line of reasoning suggests that trend

[5] Ibid., abstract.

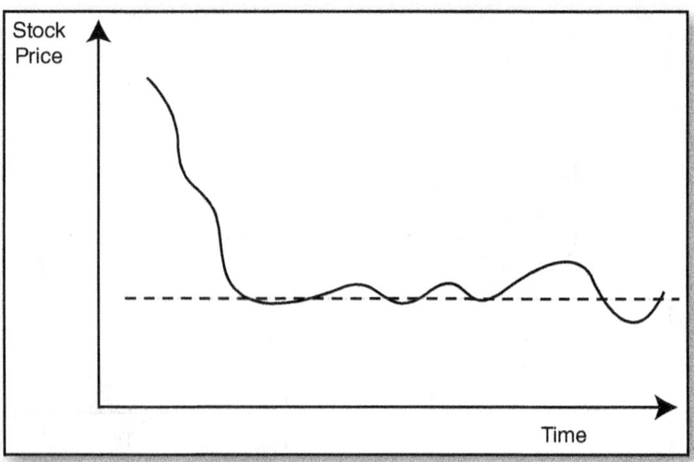

FIGURE 45.5 Base Building.

following is likely to be systematic. Defenders of the EMH argue that noise traders will tend to cancel one another out, and something like the Law of Large Numbers will take hold, so that, in the aggregate, noise trader activity won't matter. But if the noise traders are all doing pretty much the same thing, then the cancel-out argument no longer applies.

Technical trading is a broader approach than simply stock price charting. Besides other stock market information such as volume, various trading statistics, seasonal trading patterns, and the like, technical trading also encompasses many other considerations with the common characteristic that none of these considerations involve fundamental company information such as dividends, earnings, and so forth. Since there is such a variety of different things that are encompassed under the umbrella of technical trading, the cancel-out criticism is likely to apply to much of technical trading. But the cancel-out phenomenon will not apply to strategies that are widely followed by a large number of traders and investors and for which there are not some obvious counterstrategies that seek to do the opposite.

The term *herd instinct* has been applied to models that have systematic behavior. This could be one application of the technical trading strategies, when such strategies are characterized by a large number of investors and traders pursuing similar strategies. Robert Shiller developed a herd instinct model in 1984 that was overlooked until much later, when the idea of systematic noise trading behavior found a more accepting home in the finance literature.

Herd Instinct Models

Herd instinct models[6] are motivated by observing financial market booms and busts. They are typically highly aggregative, and the herd behavior is usually summarized by a single-agent model representing the herd. Market practitioners have observed

[6] These models are normally part of bubble models. For an excellent account of what we know and don't know about bubbles, see Rodney Sullivan, "Taming Global Village Risk II: Understanding and Mitigating Bubbles," *Journal of Portfolio Management* 35, no. 4 (2009): 131–141.

cycles in financial markets that are often described as a "feeding frenzy." A price of a particular asset begins to rise then develops a momentum of its own, seemingly independent of any real fundamental change in the things that should determine its price.

The Shiller Model

Shiller builds his model of stock returns on the back of two different observations. First, he notes that the prevailing thought at that time (the mid-1980s) was that the lack of forecastability in stock returns implied investor psychology could not have much impact in financial markets. The logic was that investor fads should be predictable, so if they impacted stock prices, price movements should be somewhat predictable as well.

Second, he notes that firms generally announce dividend movements in advance, implying that dividend movements are somewhat forecastable. Since dividends should certainly have some impact on stock prices, but price movements are not very forecastable, the prices themselves must anticipate future dividend movements. With investor psychology already ruled out as a factor, that leaves an optimal forecast of dividends as the only possible determinant of stock prices.

Consequently, he models returns on stock prices as:

$$E_t R_t = \delta \tag{45.1}$$

where δ represents a constant, E_t represents the mathematical expectation conditional on all known information at time t, and R_t is defined as

$$R_t = \frac{P_{t+1} - P_t + D_t}{P_t} \tag{45.2}$$

with P_{t+1} and P_t representing next period's and this period's prices, respectively, and D_t representing this period's dividend. The fact that δ is a constant reflects the idea that, in equilibrium, prices adjust so as to equate all stocks' expected returns.

One can solve this equation recursively to obtain a representation of a given stock's price at any time t:

$$P_t = \sum_{k=0}^{\infty} \frac{E_t D_{t+k}}{(1+\delta)^{k+1}} \tag{45.3}$$

In other words, Shiller argues that the EMH implies that the price of a stock at any point in time is simply an optimal forecast of the future stream of dividends. Consequently, if the price of a given stock moves, more often than not that movement should reflect movement in future dividends from that stock.

However, the data does not bear out such a finding. If investor psychology cannot be a factor in price movements according to the EMH, Shiller argues that that leaves only anticipation of dividend movements as a driver of stock prices, so that stock price movements should generally be followed by changes to dividends. The fact that empirical evidence does not support that conclusion, he argues, casts doubt on the EMH as a complete model of stock price movements.

In response, Shiller proffers a slightly adapted version of the EMH that includes irrational investors. This model has rational, or smart-money, investors, as well as investors Shiller calls "ordinary," which represent noise traders. Smart-money investors have the following demand for a given stock as a proportion of total shares outstanding:

$$Q_t = \frac{(E_t R_t - \rho)}{\varphi} \tag{45.4}$$

where $E_t R_t$ is defined as above, ρ is the expected return level at which there is no smart-money demand for the asset, and ϕ represents the risk premium smart-money investors would require to hold all the shares of the given stock.

Ordinary investors, however, are assumed to demand a total value of stock defined as Y_t. Market equilibrium requires that

$$Q_t + \frac{Y_t}{P_t} = 1 \tag{45.5}$$

from which one can solve recursively to arrive at the expression for the price of the stock:

$$P_t = \sum_{k=0}^{\infty} \frac{E_t D_t + \varphi E_t Y_{t+k}}{(1 + \rho + \varphi)^{k+1}} \tag{45.6}$$

This is simply an adjusted form of equation (45.3). Noise traders have their impact through the Y_t terms, so that as ϕ goes to zero, noise traders have no impact and the formula reverts to (45.3), and as ϕ goes to infinity, noise traders drown out smart-money investors and the market price is $P_t = Y_t$.

Shiller then goes through several specifications for Y_t and examines the resulting effect on price. First, he postulates what would happen if ordinary investors are driven by fads for stocks. Y_t would then have a hump-shaped pattern, rising as the stock comes into fashion, leveling off for a while, and then tapering back down towards its original level. The effect on price would depend on the how long the pattern takes to evolve. A relatively short fad would have little effect, since price includes a weighted sum of all future ordinary investor demands, so that a brief fad would get attenuated significantly in its effect on price. Essentially, smart-money investors would simply take the opposite position of ordinary investors, selling the stock high while it is in vogue and then buying it back at lower prices as it goes out of style, so that overall price movements would be minimal.

However, a long-developing fad would have a significant impact on price, with smart-money investors slowly buying in as Y_t rises toward its peak, knowing prices will be higher in the future. The price would peak shortly before Y_t does, then decline as future Y_t values are set to decline as well. Shiller argues that such a phenomenon could explain the lack of forecastability in stock prices.

He then looks at a couple of extreme views on Y_t, namely that Y_t responds directly to either past returns or current and past dividends, and argues that both would imply that a stock's price might overreact to dividends relative to what the EMH would predict. To test this theory, he looks at historical data on the relevant metrics for the Standard & Poor's Index, and finds that stock prices have historically overreacted to dividends. The excess volatility of prices relative to dividends could therefore be explained by an irrational investor model such as this one.

Shiller does, however, caution about reading too much into his results. The specifications of his model are rather restrictive and make strong assumptions about the impact of irrational investors. Further, even if the model's assumptions are correct, Shiller admits that the observed relationship could have other explanations, such as firm dividend behavior responding to the same social dynamics that influence the society at large. Regardless, it is difficult to look at the evidence presented and come away without some additional doubt about the validity of the EMH.

Abreu-Brunnermeier Model

Abreu and Brunnermeier (2003)[7] provide a noise trader model designed to deal specifically with bubbles and crashes. The Abreu-Brunnermeier (AB) model has the interesting feature that even arbitrage traders may find it in their interest to ride the wave of the bubble. Arbitrage traders, the so-called rational traders, are aware that there are noise traders out there and that they can impact prices, perhaps in the manner suggested by Shiller in his model. AB assume that prices begin to diverge from efficient prices without any particular reason and the arbitrageurs observe the divergence. Not all arbitrageurs notice the divergence at the same time. Once an arbitrageur observes the divergence, the arbitrageur will not necessarily trade against the divergence. Some will trade against it, but others might be tempted to ride the wave. The model permits the bubble to be burst by the combined action of the arbitrageurs, but it doesn't provide any certainty that the combined action of the arbitrageurs will ever successfully burst the bubble. Instead, AB use an arbitrary stopping time by which the bubble will burst, no matter what actions the noise traders and the arbitrageurs may be taking. The authors describe this arbitrary stopping date as based on "exogenous reasons." The interpretation of the arbitrary stopping date is that an unforeseen event of significance occurs that changes things and bursts the bubble.

The AB model is successful in capturing the idea that people join bandwagons and get off of bandwagons and such herding activity can prolong a bubble as well as end it. The model is less successful in explaining why this herding activity takes place. The model is descriptive more than insightful. The idea that arbitrageurs might ride the wave of the bubble even when they are perfectly aware that the market is in a bubble phase is an interesting feature of the AB model. There seems some casual evidence that even those who are aware that market prices are beyond what can be supported by fundamentals often will participate anyway on the grounds that they can rationally expect the bubble to continue. This changes the usual definition of an arbitrageur in a way that could prove troublesome for supporters of the EMH.[8]

---

[7] Dilip Abreu and Markus K. Brunnermeier, "Bubbles and Crashes," *Econometrica* 71, no. 1 (January 2003): 173–204.

[8] A similar point is made in Taisei Kaizojiand and Didier Sornette, "Market Bubble and Crash," reprinted in Rama Cont, *Encyclopedia of Quantitative Finance* (Hoboken, NJ: Wiley, 2009).

AB assumes that a divergence between market price and efficient price emerges and then is observed. An econometric study by Gurkaynak[9] suggests that such observations may be difficult to accomplish in practice. The old adage that you only know you were in a bubble when it is over seems borne out by Gurkaynak's statistical tests.

Conclusion

Bubbles are still not well understood. As Reinhart and Rogoff[10] note in their landmark work on financial crises, most economists treat bubbles largely as narratives, as if they are a part of economic history but not much a part of economic theory. We don't really understand how bubbles begin or end, and we are not sure how one can detect bubbles until after the fact. What we do seem to know is that technical trading and herd instinct trading likely play a role in bubbles. Technical traders who herd together and follow simple trend-following strategies can serve to prolong a bubble by simple feedback from price increases to expectations of future price increases.

One of the most interesting questions about bubbles is whether bubbles are an inherent feature of modern financial systems. Are the seeds of the next bubble ever present? Minsky[11] is the most well-known proponent of the view that bubbles inevitably arise from financial markets. Minsky argues that Keynesian economics, properly interpreted, is about bubbles and collapses and quotes Keynes extensively in his own research. Policy makers seem to have the opposite view. After bubble crashes, policy makers rush to enact reforms that will prohibit future bubbles. This may be foolhardy if Minsky's inevitability arguments are correct.

[9] Refet S. Gurkaynak, "Econometric Tests of Asset Price Bubbles: Taking Stock," *Journal of Economic Surveys* 22, no. 1 (2008): 166–186.

[10] Carmen M. Reinhart and Kenneth Rogoff, *This Time Is Different: Eight Centuries of Financial Folly* (Princeton, NJ: Princeton University Press, 2009).

[11] Hyman Minsky, "The Financial Instability Hypothesis," The Jerome Levy Economics Institute of Bard College, Working Paper No. 74, May 1992.

CHAPTER 46

Understanding Chart Patterns

From Thomas N. Bulkowski, *Visual Guide to Chart Patterns* (Hoboken, New Jersey: John Wiley & Sons, 2002), Chapters 1–3.

The Basics

This section of the book reviews the basics: minor highs and lows, trendlines, gaps,. throwbacks, pullbacks, support, and resistance. I provide many exhibits so that we agree on terms and techniques. The basics will become important when we move to identifying chart patterns and then using them to signal trades.

Pattern Recognition Made Easy

While working at Tandy Corporation, I hung on my office wall a price chart of the company's stock. I did not know if the head-and-shoulders top I found was one or not, but it looked like a person's head in the middle of a pair of shoulders. To the left and right of that pattern, price dropped back to earth, making it seem like the pattern was a ghost rising from a moat.

That was my first attempt at finding a chart pattern. Since that time, I taught myself to recognize chart patterns—a skill almost anyone can learn. Let us begin looking at a few charts to see how to recognize patterns.

The Empty Chart

The empty chart is not empty at all, is it? Price bars form a mountain range that climbs higher until July after which a hiker walking on those bars would probably fall to their death. (See Figure 46.1.)

In that brief description, we have learned two things: Price rises until July and then dies. If you owned this stock, you would be looking for chart patterns that predict the coming decline. Why? Because you might want to sell before the tumble or act to protect your position.

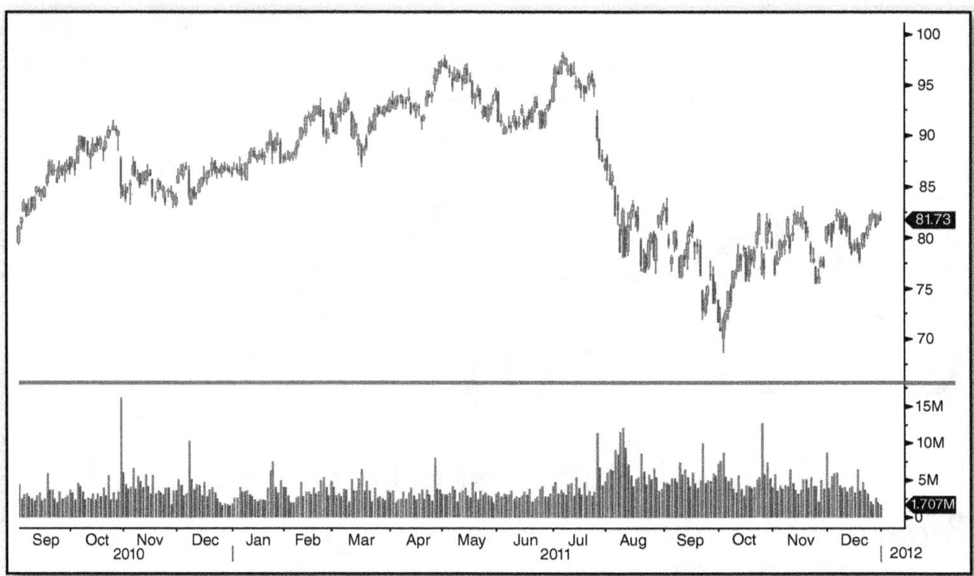

FIGURE 46.1 MMM US Equity (3M Co).

In October, in addition to searching for the remains of our dead hiker, you would be looking for signs that the downward price trend had reversed. If it had, then you might want to buy the stock or buy more to capture the recovery.

How do you find patterns that predict a decline? Begin with peaks.

Finding Peak Patterns

When I look at a price chart, my eyes find peaks that stop at or near the same price. At line A, for example, several peaks approach or touch the upper red line. That line represents **overhead resistance**. When price finally breaks through that ceiling, it signals a change in trend from moving sideways to up. (See Figure 46.2.)

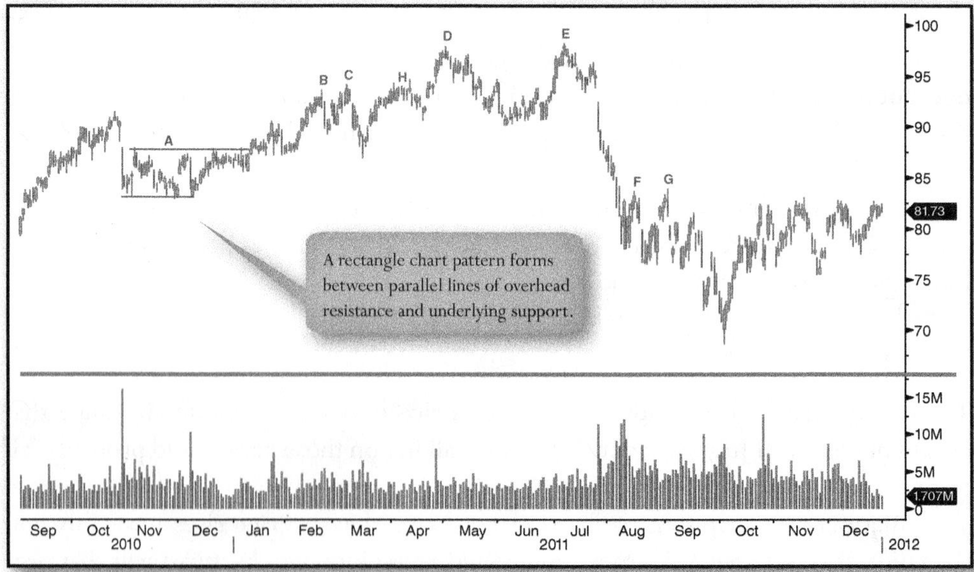

FIGURE 46.2 MMM US Equity (3M Co).

DEFINITION:

Overhead resistance

Overhead resistance, or just resistance, occurs when a stock stalls in an uptrend or reverses, creating a peak, often near the same price as it has in the past. Resistance is always above price.

After finding the top horizontal red line, look for a corresponding line parallel to the top one, but drawn along the valleys. I show that as the lower red line. The two lines form a rectangle chart pattern. The name of the chart pattern is not as important as how I found it. Just imagine a horizontal line that touches several peaks and another line that touches several valleys.

Peaks B and C also exhibit overhead resistance. How do I know that? Because they top out near the same price. An imaginary ceiling exists above those peaks, holding the stock down—for a time. Peak H slams its head against that ceiling, too.

Compare the BCH trio with peaks D and E. The DE pair form twin tops, but further apart—larger. Larger patterns tend to be more important than smaller ones. Price will tend to drop further after a large pattern than after a small one. In this case, the stock declines more after DE than after BC.

Peaks F and G are another pair showing overhead resistance. In this case, a downward price trend leads to this pair whereas BC and DE appeared in an upward price trend.

Peak pairs BC, DE, and FG show the major ingredient of double top chart patterns, that of two peaks finding overhead resistance near the same price.

Smart Investor Tip

Chart patterns tall and wide (large patterns) tend to perform better than narrow and short ones (small patterns).

Finding Valley Patterns

Figure 46.3 highlights price valleys. In a manner similar to peaks, look for two or more valleys that bottom near the same price. Those valleys may rest upon a floor where support is strong enough to launch another move up. One example is CD.

I highlight this pair because it forms **underlying support**. Price finds a floor at C and bounces off it at D. Eventually, though, the stock tunnels its way through support at E, and plummets like a stone through water.

DEFINITION:

Underlying support

Underlying support, or just support, occurs when a falling stock stalls or reverses, creating a valley, often at the same price as it has in the past. Support is always below price.

Valley patterns are useful for determining when a downward price trend changes to horizontal or upward.

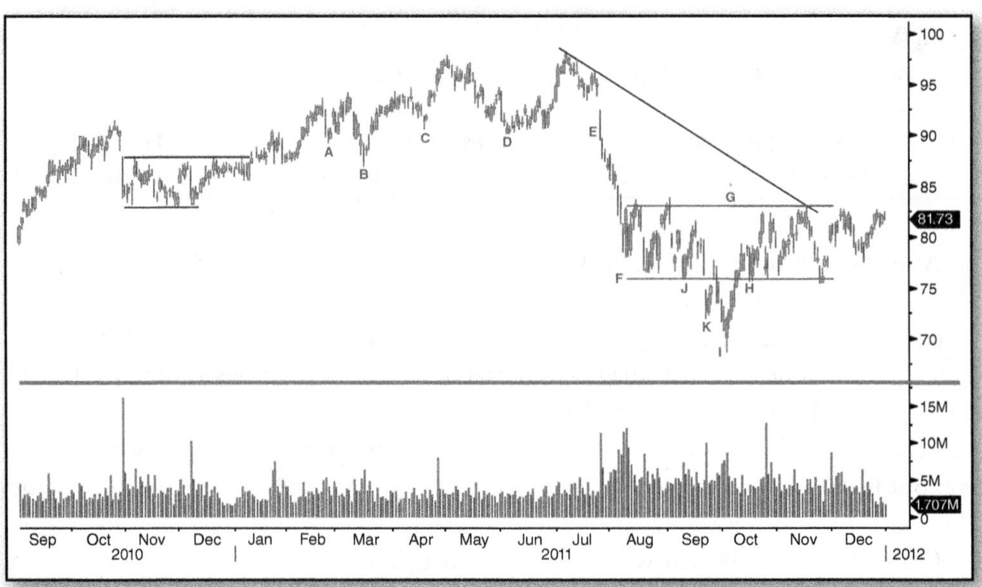

FIGURE 46.3 MMM US Equity (3M Co).

Notice the peaks that bump up against line G, shown in red. The first two poke through the line, but that is fine since rarely will peaks or valleys stop at exactly the same price. The line represents a temporary barrier to an upward move.

For the moment, ignore the V-bottom at I. Search below line G for valleys that bottom near the same price. I found them and drew line F. It represents a support area connecting bottoms J and H, and extending to the right with additional touches along the way.

Does the GF trading range mean price is changing trend from down to up? Perhaps. It is too early to tell for sure.

What about the emergency dive to I? That submarine plunge may have been panic selling, forcing the stock down to a level low enough that it represented a steal to value investors. The needle shape of the V bottom supports this theory (that is, price remained at I for just one day before dumping its ballast and rising).

Notice pattern HIJ. It is an inverted (upside down) **head-and-shoulders pattern**. H and J represent shoulders and I is the head. K could be a cancerous growth on the neck, but lab results have not come back yet. It is not important to the survival of the pattern.

DEFINITION:

Head-and-shoulders pattern

A head-and-shoulders bottom and inverted head-and-shoulders are synonyms.

Another head-and-shoulders bottom (a synonym for an inverted head-and-shoulders) occurs at ABC. This one is unusual—and rarer—because price trends upward into the pattern, not downward.

For now, though, the inbound price trend is not important. What is important is to train your eyes to find peaks that top out near the same level and find valleys that bottom near the same price. When you can do that, you can find chart patterns. It is that simple.

> **Smart Investor Tip**
> In a rising price trend, try forming curved patterns beneath price bars. In a falling price trend, curves often appear smoother along the tops. Either method works.

> **Smart Investor Tip**
> Train your eyes to find peaks that top out near the same price and valleys that bottom near similar prices.

Curved Patterns

After finding peaks and valleys that align, try imagining price tracing curves. I show two examples in Figure 46.4.

Notice that the price bars at A begin rising, following a straight line of trend, but then curve at the top. Connecting the underside of price bars in a rising price trend often shows the curve better than connecting the tops. Either way is fine.

Pattern A is called an inverted and ascending scallop. The chart pattern appears often on the charts, but it is not popular or well known. The fishy sounding name refers to the bowl shape and not the mollusk. If you find one, never eat it.

The rounding turn at B forms another curved pattern. The B turn would be a rounding bottom, but price needs to enter the pattern trending down and not up. B is an example of a failed cup with handle pattern. The handle is at C. Cups have many qualifications, so strictly speaking, this is not one. However, the pattern does show the important parts: a rising price trend followed by a rounded turn and a short handle.

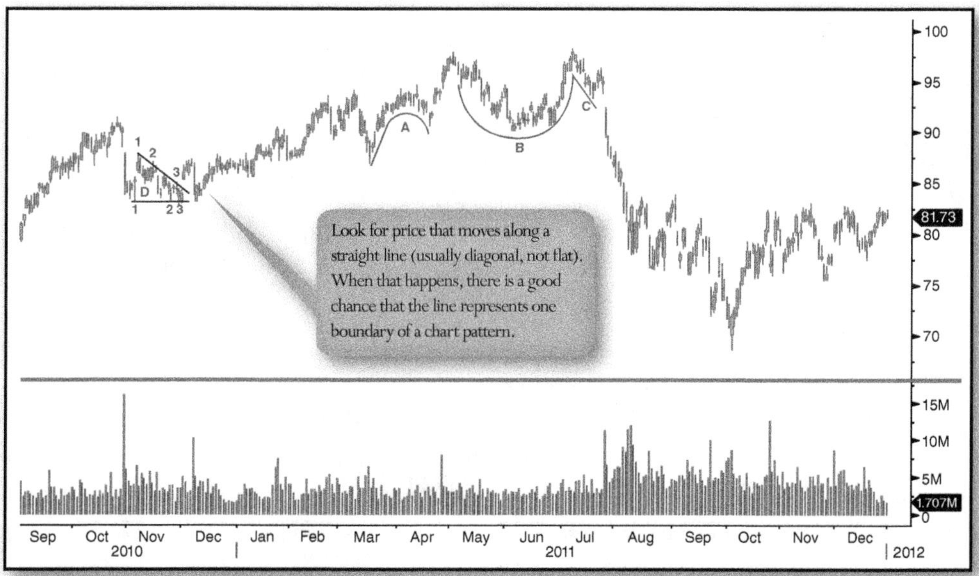

FIGURE 46.4 MMM US Equity (3M Co).

Diagonal Patterns

Staying with the same chart, look at pattern D on the left. What happened to the rectangle bottom identified in an earlier chart? It is still there, of course, but the new lines form a different chart pattern. Chart patterns can nest (one inside the other) and the same pattern can appear as two different types. Think of it as explaining the words "there," "their," and "they're" to someone learning English. They sound the same, but are different.

Look on the chart where price forms diagonals. I show one as a slanting blue trendline above D. The line touches price three times as marked. Another trendline touches the pattern's bottom, also three times. The blue pattern is an example of a descending triangle.

> **Smart Investor Tip**
> Chart patterns can nest—one inside the other. The same price pattern can also appear as two (or more) differently named patterns.

Constructing Patterns

When you look at a price chart, train your eyes to search for peaks that top out near the same price. They may form chart patterns (double tops) that warn of a coming trend change from up to down.

Train your eyes to find valleys that bottom near the same price (double bottoms). Bottoming patterns can alert you to a stock ready to fly like the model rockets I launched as a kid (not the homemade gasoline one that ignited a water puddle—sorry about that, Mom).

Patterns that form diagonals (descending triangle, for example) or curves (scallops, rounding bottoms, or cup with handles) also foretell the direction that price may take.

Visually connect peaks, valleys, curves, and diagonals to form chart patterns.

Figure 46.5 highlights the valid patterns identified so far.

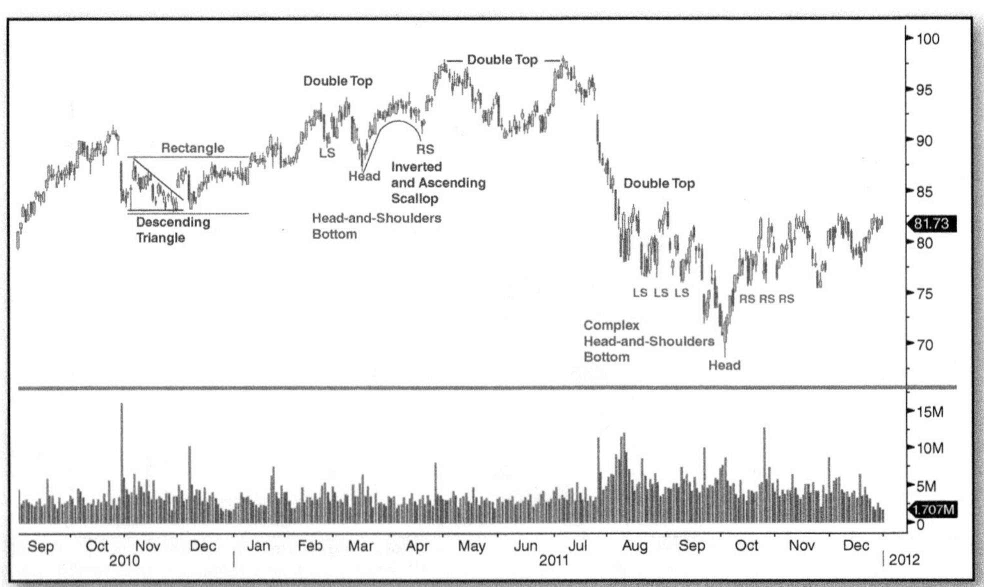

FIGURE 46.5 MMM US Equity (3M Co).

LS means left shoulder and RS means right shoulder. A complex head-and-shoulders bottom (lower right) takes the place of the rectangle bottom. A complex head-and-shoulders bottom has multiple shoulders and multiple heads, but rarely both.

Think of pattern recognition as like trying to find the Big Dipper or Cassiopeia in the heavens at night.

In the next section, I begin to develop a common language, starting with minor highs and lows. Do not be alarmed. This is not as hard as learning French. However, I could be lying because I never learned French.

Test Yourself

Decide which of the following statements are true or false.

1. Overhead resistance occurs when price stalls or reverses, and is always below price.
2. Underlying support happens when price stalls at the same level as it has in the past. Support is never above price.
3. A rectangle forms between underlying resistance and overhead support.
4. On the same price scale (daily scale or weekly scale, but not mixed), tall chart patterns tend to outperform smaller ones.
5. The same price pattern can have multiple names.
6. Like an expectant mother, one price pattern can be inside another.

Answers: 1. False; 2. True; 3. False; 4. True; 5. True; 6. True

Minor Highs and Lows

Minor highs and lows are synonyms for peaks and valleys except that they have strict definitions that can help with pattern recognition. I will use these terms throughout this book, so we might as well go through the pain of learning what they mean and how to recognize them.

A minor high does not refer to an overdose, and a minor low is not lingo for a bad trip. Rather, they represent the building blocks of pattern recognition. If you can program a computer to find them, then you can automate pattern recognition. For example, a triple top has three minor highs near the same price.

Since you are a human computer, I have created definitions for minor highs and lows to help you find them until your eyes become trained to spot them. String them together in your mind and patterns will emerge, patterns that repeat, patterns that can make you money.

Peaks: Minor Highs

A minor high is a significant peak on the price chart. What does *significant* mean? I had to answer that question when I wrote Patternz—free software that automatically finds chart patterns. I discovered that peaks between three and five days apart led to the best pattern recognition (the exact number is pattern specific).

Use five days between peaks for **minor highs**, but be flexible.

> **DEFINITION:**
> **Minor highs**
> A minor high is a peak separated by about five days from a higher high. It should represent a significant peak.

Figure 46.6 shows each peak highlighted with an asterisk that is at least five days away from a higher peak. For example, point A is the highest high from at least five days before to five days after the peak.

Notice that peak B does not have an asterisk. According to my computer, it is not a minor high. Why? Because C has a high that is above peak B, and C is five days away from B.

The same situation occurs at D with a higher high occurring three days later. Nevertheless, I consider peaks B and D to be minor highs. Grasp the concept that a minor high is a significant peak in a price trend and worry less about counting days between peaks. Once you train your eyes to see minor highs, you will not need to count. It also helps if you are sober.

Valleys: Minor Lows

In a manner similar to minor highs, **minor lows** are valleys separated by at least five days from a lower low. That means five days before to five days after the minor low.

Figure 46.7 shows an example, with asterisks highlighting minor lows.

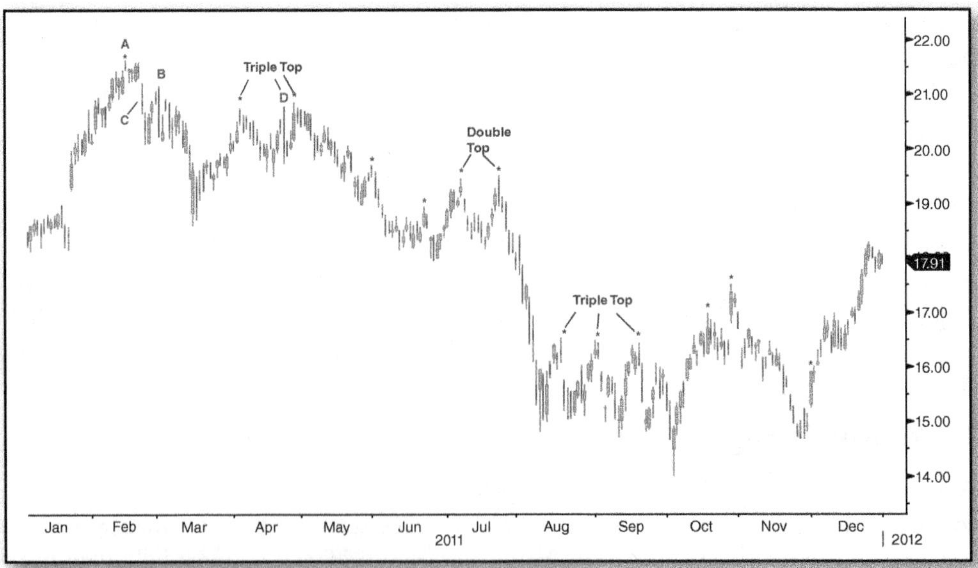

FIGURE 46.6 GE US Equity (General Electric Co).

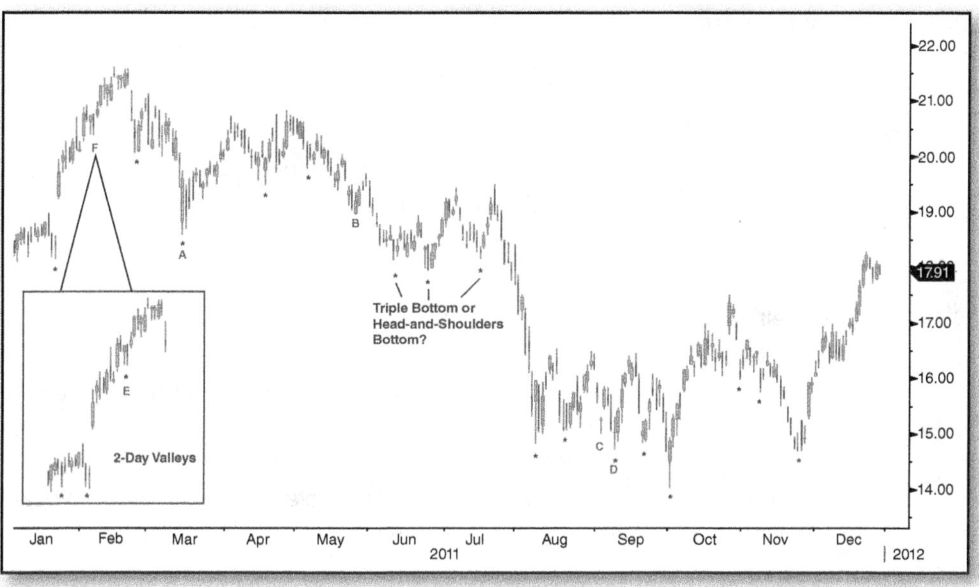

FIGURE 46.7 GE US Equity (General Electric Co).

> **DEFINITION:**
> **Minor lows**
> A minor low is a valley separated by about five days from a lower low. It should represent a significant bottom.

For example, valley A is below the adjacent price bars such that none are lower than it is for at least five days on either side.

Look at B. Notice the absence of an asterisk. If you count five candles to the right of B, you will see that a price bar is slightly lower than B (it may be hard to tell, so just take my word for it). Candle B is not strictly a minor low, but I consider it one anyway.

Candle C is another example of a bottom that is not strictly a minor low because it is too close to lower candles. However, if this were the left shoulder of a head-and-shoulders bottom, then I would probably consider it a valid minor low.

In other words, be flexible when searching for minor lows. If it looks like price is making a turn, then it is a minor low. If you need to count the price bars to be sure it is a minor low, then do so.

The inset shows bottoms with two days of separation instead of five, highlighted with asterisks. Notice that point E qualifies, but does it look like a minor low? No. It appears as part of the upward price trend and not a significant turning point. It is not a minor low.

In the next section, I discuss trendlines, and there are three types. Can you name them?

Need a hint? One is curved, but the others are not straight and diagonal. Wait until you read my exercises. You may find it easier to eat a bowling ball than to get them right!

For Further Reading

You may find my free website useful, including the link to Patternz:

Over 500 articles on chart patterns: www.thepatternsite.com
Free pattern recognition software that finds 66 chart patterns and 105 candlesticks: www.thepatternsite.com/patternz.html

Test Yourself

Answer the following.

1. True or false: As used in this book, a minor high can represent a *major* turning point.
2. True or false: A minor low represents a *minor* turning point.
3. A minor high is the highest peak from five days before to five days after the peak. If peak A is the highest price four days from a higher peak, is peak A still a minor high?

   A. Always.
   B. Never.
   C. Sometimes.

Answers 1. True; 2. True; 3. C

Trendlines

Trendlines are to technical analysis as hammers are to carpentry. Knowing how to use trendlines properly can save you money and allow you to enter a new trade with confidence.

Earlier in this chapter, I asked if you could name the three types of trendlines. They are internal, external, and curved. Before I get to that, let us discuss scaling (this is not a fish joke).

Figure 46.8 shows a chart on the logarithmic price scale. Notice that the price divisions at A (lower right) are spaced further apart than they are at B (upper right). On charts that show price making large moves (such as charts using weekly or monthly data), the log scale will make chart patterns taller at the lower end of the scale so you can see them better.

I drew a line connecting the peaks. The line slopes downward and touches each peak using a straight line.

The same figure on the linear scale looks warped, but it could be your eyeglasses. Check for scratches. (See Figure 46.9.)

A curved line touches the same peaks. Why? Each vertical division is the same height whereas in the prior figure, price was on the log scale.

Which scale should you use to view chart patterns? Hint: I prefer the log scale. Most of the charts in this book are on the linear scale.

For an example of why scaling is important, look at Intel during the technology bubble of 2000 (monthly, linear scale). Figure 46.10 shows a price mountain that would make Tenzing Norgay pause.

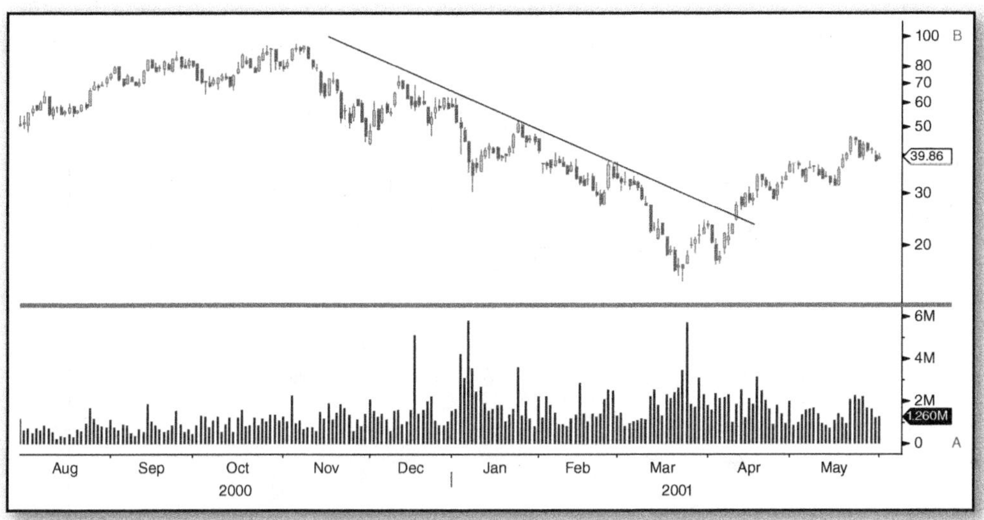

FIGURE 46.8 ABGX US Equity (Abgenix Inc).

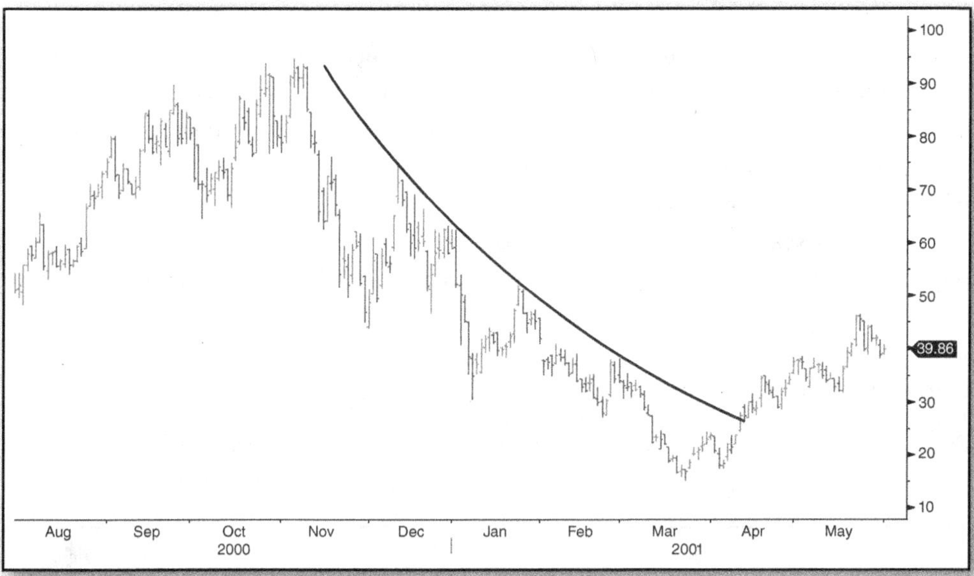

FIGURE 46.9 ABGX US Equity (Abgenix Inc).

A descending triangle appears in 1998. Notice that at the lower price ranges, you cannot see any other chart patterns. The price looks smooth as if a giant stomped on the foothills (until 1995, anyway).

Compare the same chart using a log scale. (See Figure 46.11.)

The rugged terrain becomes apparent. Other chart patterns appear, too, such as a rising wedge and a second descending triangle. Which scale would you rather use?

> **KEY POINT:**
> The logarithmic price scale gives a clearer view of historical price data when the stock makes a large vertical move. Chart patterns are easier to see on the log scale.

FIGURE 46.10 INTC US Equity (Intel Corp).

However, whenever you need to physically measure the height of a chart pattern (like using a ruler held up to a computer screen), use the linear scale. For example, measuring one inch on the linear scale may mean a \$10 rise, but on the log scale, that same one inch could measure \$50. Height becomes important for the measure rule, which I will discuss later in the book.

Whichever scale you decide to use, do not go flipping from log to linear to log. It will only confuse you. Pick one scale and stay with it when searching for chart patterns. Only switch when needed.

Uptrend Connections

Price forms trends. Sometimes, you can connect those trends with lines, called **trendlines**. Most often those lines will be diagonal and straight, but not always.

FIGURE 46.11 INTC US Equity (Intel Corp).

> **DEFINITION:**
> **Trendlines**
> When price trends, a line connecting them is called a trendline.

When you look at a price chart, look for places where price trends. In your mind, connect the valleys with a straight line, highlighting an up-sloping trend.

For example, Figure 46.12 shows price trending at blue line A (far left). The line works well, meaning it follows the minor lows until F, G, and H. Those candles poke through the line. In fact, H begins a new trend downward.

Line B shows a horizontal price trend, also drawn along the minor lows. Trendlines C and D are about the same length as A and at nearly the same slope.

As you experiment with drawing trendlines, you may discover that steep, up-sloping trendlines do not last long. Why? Because traders take profits if the stock rises too fast. That selling pressure will force the stock to move sideways or down, piercing the trendline—at least temporarily.

> **Smart Investor Tip**
> Use the linear/arithmetic scale when physically (think inches, not price) measuring the height of a chart pattern.

Shallower trendlines tend to be powerhouses. From them, strong moves are born. In between the shallow and vertical trendlines are the also-rans. They show breaks in the prevailing short- to intermediate-term trend only to see a new trend emerge, perhaps at a shallower angle.

> **Smart Investor Tip**
> In a rising price trend, draw trendlines along the valleys to detect a change in trend, from up to down.

Look at trendline E, drawn in red. It is the longest on the chart, and it is also the most important. Why? Because price plunges through it in July, signaling the end of the uptrend.

Notice that I have drawn each up-sloping trendline along the valleys and not the tops. Why? To signal a trend change. Up-sloping trendlines drawn along peaks will not do that.

Trendline Types: Internal, External, and Curved

Trendline A (Figure 46.12) is called an **internal trendline** because it slices through price at F and G (H does not count because it ends the trend).

> **DEFINITION:**
> **Internal trendline**
> An internal trendline slices through price.

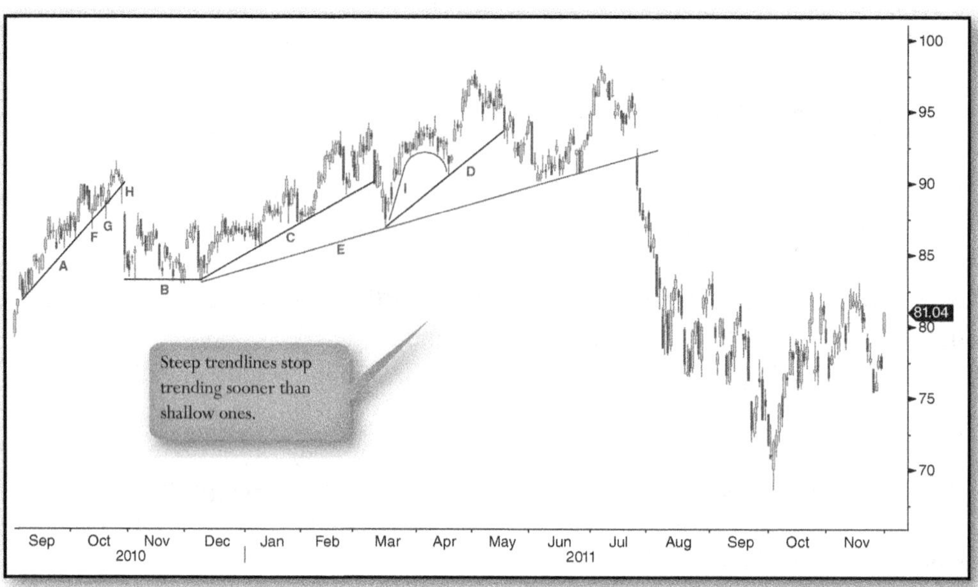

FIGURE 46.12 MMM US Equity (3M Co).

The thinking behind drawing internal trendlines is that the line best represents the majority of traders. Few will receive a fill at the day's exact high or low, so why draw a trendline connecting those outliers?

I have a different view. If I were to place a stop below the trendline, I do not want to be stopped out because my trendline sliced through price and an outlier hit my stop. I prefer to draw my trendlines like line C. This line follows the price bottoms as it trends. Line C is an example of an **external trendline**. An external trendline connects only the price ends; it does not slice through price.

Line I represents the third type of trendline: a **curved trendline**. It begins straight, but curves over at the top of the inverted and ascending scallop chart pattern. Curved trendlines become important for some chart patterns and for parabolic moves (curved moves that resemble a biplane flying level then going vertical).

DEFINITION:

External trendline

An external trendline hugs the end of price.

DEFINITION:

Curved trendline

A curved trendline also hugs price, but it is curved (although a curved trendline can be external or internal, too).

Draw trendlines for the best fit. If a trendline happens to slice through price, do not get your knickers in a twist. If a curved line better represents a trend, then use it.

KEY POINT:

Draw trendlines for the best fit, whether they look curved or slice through price.

FIGURE 46.13 **ACET US Equity (Aceto Corp).**

Downtrend Connections

Down trendlines are the same as up trendlines except you draw them along peaks. Why? To detect a trend change.

Figure 46.13 shows an example of several trendlines highlighting a falling stock. Line A is short and steep. It is an external trendline that touches the candle tops three times.

I originally drew line B from the start in May until point B, but then extended it. It touched another candle at the line's end, forming a chart pattern called a bump and run reversal bottom. The pattern predicts an upward breakout, which is what happened. I used to call them bump and run formations but changed it because of the acronym (BARF).

Line C, drawn in red, is a major trendline not only for its length, but also because it signals a trend change. Price not only slices through the line at E, but closes above it. A new up trend may be underway.

Minor low D finds support near the trendline, too, although price pierced the trendline for a day before reversing. The E to D move is a throwback, a pattern I will discuss in a later chapter.

Notice the two chart patterns outlined in blue on the far left of the chart. Those are broadening tops. A top trendline connects the peaks and a bottom trendline connects the valleys, creating a megaphone appearance.

If you know how to draw trendlines, you probably could have found these two patterns. Not only do trendlines signal a trend change, but they also outline pattern boundaries.

On a price chart, look for peaks that align. Draw trendlines connecting them to see what they reveal. Draw trendlines along valleys and see what they show, too. This is especially significant along the hard right edge (the right side of the chart) because trends there suggest where price is going in the future.

Trendline Guidelines

Now that we have experimented with drawing trendlines, what are the guidelines and tips for their use? Here is a nine-item list.

1. Trendlines should connect at least two peaks (minor highs) or two valleys (minor lows), preferably three or more.
2. Like horseshoes and hand grenades, closeness counts. Price need not touch the trendline, but it should come close.
3. To detect a trend change, draw trendlines along the valleys when price is trending up. Draw trendlines along the peaks in a declining stock.
4. Trendlines with widely spaced touches are more significant than are those with narrow ones (I proved this).
5. In 2006, I wrote in my book *Getting Started in Chart Patterns*, "Trendlines are like diving boards. You get a bigger bounce from a longer diving board than a shorter one."
6. Steep trendlines underperform shallow ones. That means larger moves occur after a trendline pierce from a shallow trendline than a steep one.
7. Rising volume along an up-sloping trendline *powers* (a larger decline) price downward after a trendline break more than does a receding volume trend leading to the breakout.
8. For downward sloping trendlines, receding volume leads to better performance after price pierces the trendline, moving up.
9. Just because price closes above a down-sloping trendline or below an up-sloping one is no reason to believe that the trend has changed. It is only a hint of a trend change, not a guarantee.

The next chapter discusses one of the most important topics: support and resistance. If you can determine when price is going to reverse, you can make a bundle. If you save wisely and invest carefully, you can retire at 36 just as I did. Learning about support and resistance is a good first step to achieving that goal.

This just in: All you have to do is turn the page!

DEFINITION:

Trendlines

Trendlines not only follow trends, but also outline chart patterns.

For Further Reading

Bulkowski, Thomas N. *Getting Started in Chart Patterns*. Hoboken, NJ: John Wiley & Sons, 2006.

Bulkowski, Thomas N. *Trading Classic Chart Patterns*. Hoboken, NJ: John Wiley & Sons, 2002.

Test Yourself

Decide which of the following statements are true or false.

1. To detect a trend change in a rising price trend, draw trendlines along the peaks.
2. To detect a trend change in a falling price trend, draw trendlines along the valleys.
3. When price closes above a down-sloping trendline or below an up-sloping one, it hints of a coming trend change.
4. An internal trendline cuts through price.
5. You should avoid using internal trendlines.
6. A straight trendline on the logarithmic scale will appear curved on the linear scale.
7. When trying to measure physical distances, use the linear scale.

Answers: 1. False; 2. False; 3. True; 4. True; 5. False; 6. True; 7. True

CHAPTER 47

Understanding Chart Pattern Breaks

From Thomas N. Bulkowski, *Visual Guide to Chart Patterns* (Hoboken, New Jersey: John Wiley & Sons, 2002), Chapters 4–6.

Support and Resistance

If trendlines are like hammers, then support and resistance (SAR) are like boards. Price stalls or even reverses at SAR areas, and that makes predicting future price trends easier. Fortunately, there are many techniques that show SAR, and this chapter discusses them.

In the fall of 1987, a friend of mine said that she had purchased shares in a mutual fund. This was her first time investing in the stock market, and she was excited!

On black Monday, October 19, 1987, the Dow Jones industrials lost over 22 percent of their value in *one* session.

She was not excited! In fact, she vowed to sell as soon as she got her money back, which she did.

Her behavior is typical of novices. Imagine that others acted the same way. Their emotional selling would force price down. People buying the stock just before the drop or as the selling begins also get upset as the stock tumbles. They vow to sell when they get their money back, too.

If you were to plot this behavior on a chart, you would see the stock peak and then peak again near the same price. That concerted selling forms a barrier to upward movement called **overhead resistance**. Price will eat through that resistance, so it is not made of concrete.

DEFINITION:

Overhead resistance

Overhead resistance occurs when selling pressure overcomes buying demand, sending price lower—at least for a time.

A similar behavior pattern exists for valleys. People want to buy a stock at $10, but price gaps higher and zooms away from them, rising to $15. They missed the move and vow to buy the stock if it ever gets back to $10.

When the stock drops to $10, they buy, joining others doing the same thing. That buying demand builds a floor underneath the stock, which we call **support**. The floor is not made of concrete either, so price can act as termites do and eat its way through.

> **DEFINITION:**
> **Support**
> Underlying support occurs when buying demand overcomes selling pressure, putting a temporary floor beneath the stock.

Support and resistance is human nature at work—a pictorial representation of emotion.

Support and resistance represent *areas* or *bands* where price is likely (but not guaranteed) to stall or reverse. Price can motor through a support zone and a week later, it will stop there as if taking a snooze at a roadside rest stop.

> **KEY POINT:**
> Support areas can act as resistance and resistance areas can act as support.

Trendline SAR

Trendlines highlight and act as SAR areas. For example, Figure 47.1 shows a trendline connecting the valleys beginning at A, touching B, C, D, and E. At F, however, price pierces the trendline, heading down.

Notice that at G, H, and I, price bumps up against a ceiling formed by the same trendline. The trendline that once acted as support now acts as resistance.

The blue trendline shows the same principle, but not as clearly. The trendline acts as support from J to M and as overhead resistance at N and O.

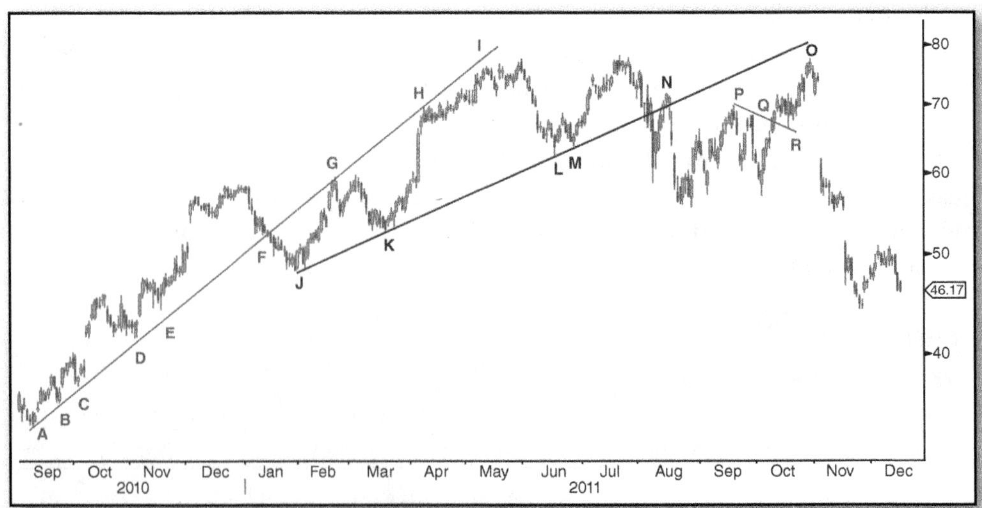

FIGURE 47.1 ANF US Equity (Abercrombie & Fitch Co).

After drawing a trendline, imagine what price might do in the future. By extending trendline AF, a trader can guess where price might reverse when it hits the trendline.

Trendlines can be powerful prediction tools, but they do not always work.

Down-sloping trendlines show the same behavior by acting as support or resistance at any time. An example of this is trendline PQR. Down-sloping trendline PQ acts as overhead resistance at the two peaks, and at R it acts as underlying support.

SAR at Gaps

Price gaps when the day's low remains above the prior day's high, leaving a bullish gap on the daily chart. A bearish gap forms when the day's high remains below the prior day's low.

> **DEFINITION:**
>
> **Price gaps**
>
> A price gap is a blank area on the chart that shows the high price below the prior day's low, or the low price above the prior day's high. Gaps do not work well as support or resistance areas.

Figure 47.2 shows examples of several gaps that act as support and resistance. I measured how often gaps show SAR (support: 20 percent, resistance: 25 percent) and found them to be as reliable as a coworker who promised to pick me up at the airport and then forgot.

Gap A has difficulty supporting price at valley B. At peak C, it does provide overhead resistance to block the upward move.

Gap D shows support at valley E (notice that price pierces the gap but soon reverses) and resistance at peak F before the effect wears off.

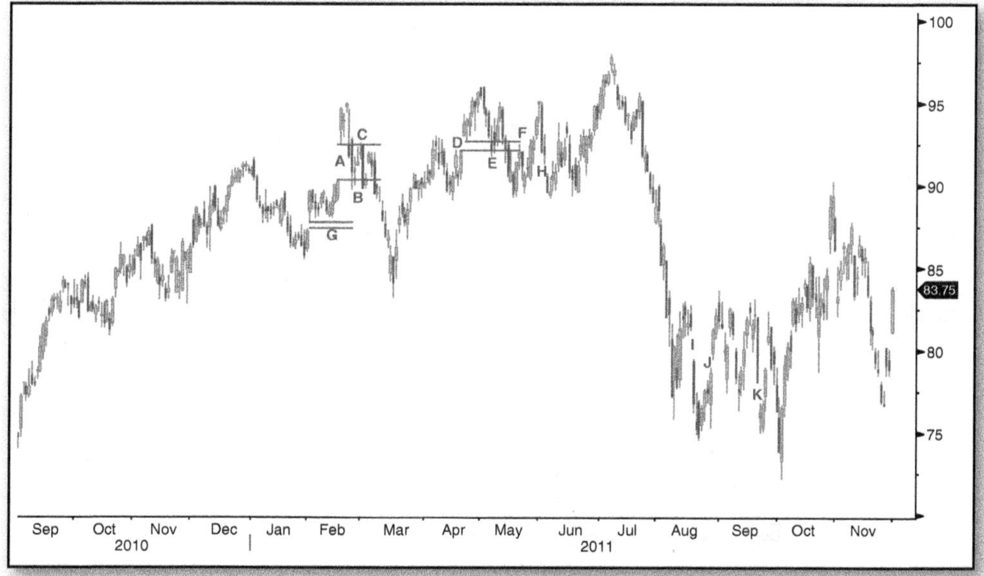

FIGURE 47.2 **APD US Equity (Air Products & Chemicals Inc).**

In February, gap G supports price, but the support melts like snow in spring during the strong downtrend in March.

Now look at gaps H, I, J, and K. Those gaps do not impede price at all.

In candlestick land, gaps are called windows probably because traders that depend on gaps climb out windows and jump.

Horizontal Consolidation Regions

Unless you have read my other books, you probably have never heard of **horizontal consolidation regions (HCRs)**, and yet they are some of the most powerful SAR areas (they work 41 percent to 55 percent of the time). Figure 47.3 shows examples.

> **DEFINITION:**
>
> **Horizontal consolidation regions (HCRs)**
>
> A horizontal consolidation region is an area of horizontal price movement that has lots of price overlap with a flat bottom, flat top, or both. When price bumps against it, the stock often reverses direction or stalls. Long and tight HCRs (lots of price overlap) work better than do short or loose ones (meandering price).

An HCR is an *area* on the price chart where the stock crawls horizontally. The best HCRs have flat tops, flat bottoms, or both. When an HCR appears in the path leading to a chart pattern, any breakout that takes price back into the path of the HCR will often run into support or resistance.

To explain this, the inset shows the ideal case. A horizontal consolidation region appears as the grey box. Price drops out of this area and heads down, eventually forming a symmetrical triangle chart pattern. After an upward breakout from the triangle, price climbs to the HCR region (the area between the red lines) and then reverses.

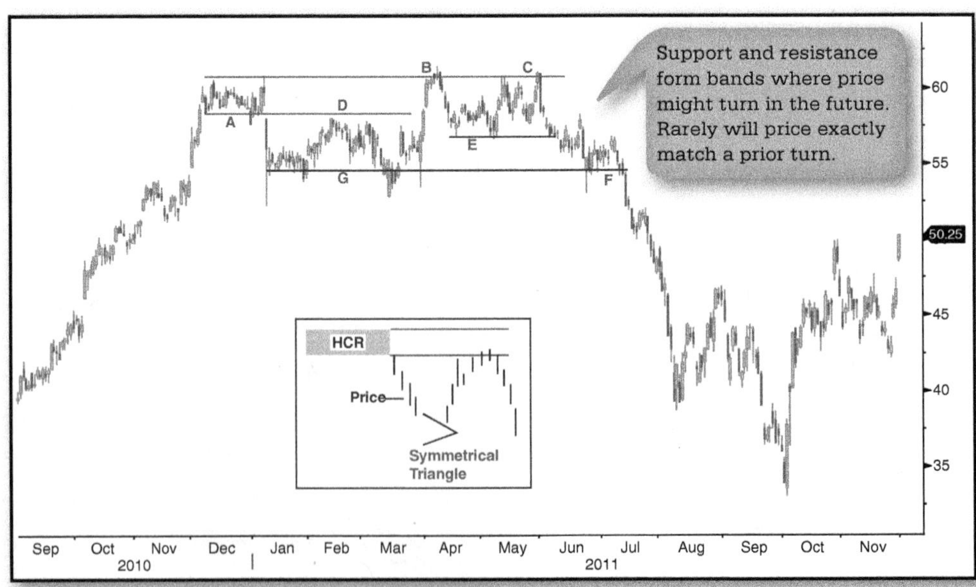

FIGURE 47.3 AYI US Equity (Acuity Brands Inc).

The rest of Figure 47.3 shows how HCRs can act. For example, at A, price forms an HCR about a month long, and I show it bounded by two red lines extended into the future. At D, the HCR is a ceiling that acts as overhead resistance. At B and C, price stops at a new level of overhead resistance.

The area between D and G is a weak HCR because price tends to meander. Area E finds support in the DG region.

I drew the blue trendline, starting at F, toward G, just to see where it was in relation to the DG horizontal consolidation region. Notice that F finds support at the bottom of the DG area.

Round Number SAR

Support and resistance is a product of fear and greed, and round number SAR fits into that definition as snugly as a bug in a rug.

When novice traders buy a stock, they ask their brokers to buy at $10 and not at $9.91. Those round numbers—numbers that end in a zero—tend to show support and resistance. When traders set price targets, they choose round numbers at which to sell—$50 and not $49.87. When investors pick the same round number at which to trade, their buying and selling creates overhead resistance or underlying support. Figure 47.4 shows examples of this behavior.

Circled in red are areas that either touch or come close to the blue lines. The blue lines are round numbers like 20, 30, 40, and so on.

A good example of round number SAR is at A in the upper middle of the chart. Price bumps up against 80 from May to December before throwing in the towel and giving up.

Since people will be selling at round numbers, get in ahead of them. Instead of selling at 80, sell at 79.93.

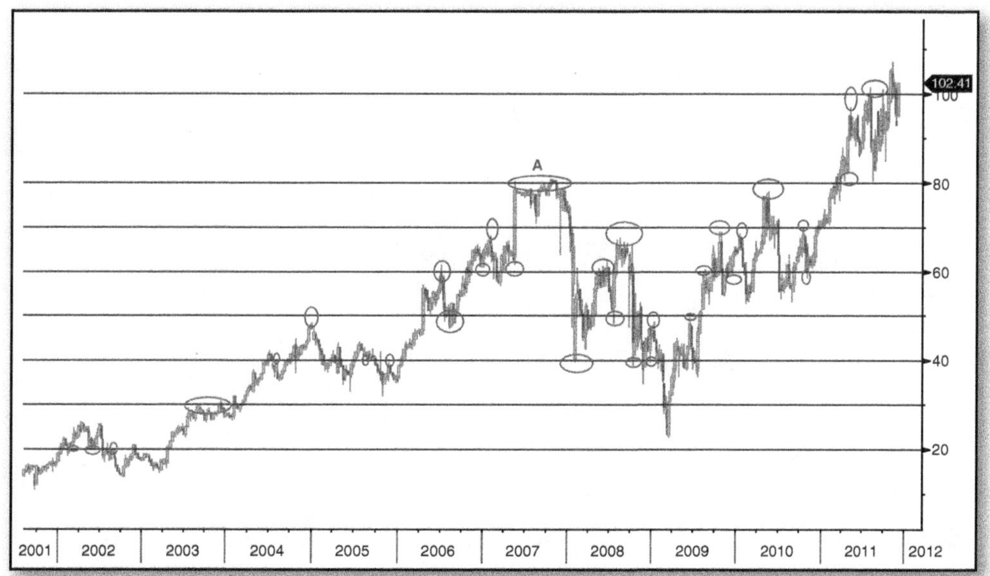

FIGURE 47.4 ADS US Equity (Alliance Data Systems Corp).

> **Smart Investor Tip**
>
> Do not place orders to buy and sell, or place stop loss orders at numbers ending in zero. That is where everyone else will place their orders, perhaps triggering unusual price moves.

Apply the same logic to stop placement. Avoid round numbers because that is where many novice traders will position their stops. If those stops trigger, it can start an avalanche where price drops, triggering more stops, and so on. The selling pressure forces price to tumble in what is called running or gunning the stop. If this happens to your stock, do not shoot yourself. Aim for something less valuable.

You can use round numbers to guess where price is going to stall, even if it has never reached that high before (no apparent overhead resistance).

For example, if a stock is breaking out to new highs at 17, you can guess that it will run into overhead resistance at 20. Traders and investors will use 20 as a sell point, and if enough actually sell, price will reverse there. Beat the crowds and sell at 19.95.

Day traders can use round numbers, too, as targets. When price reaches a round number, consider selling.

> **Smart Investor Tip**
>
> Use the next closest round number (a number ending with a zero) to guess where price is going to stall or reverse, even if the stock has never climbed that high.

SAR at Peaks, Valleys, and Chart Patterns

Support and resistance forms at peaks, valleys, and chart patterns. Figure 47.5 shows examples of all three.

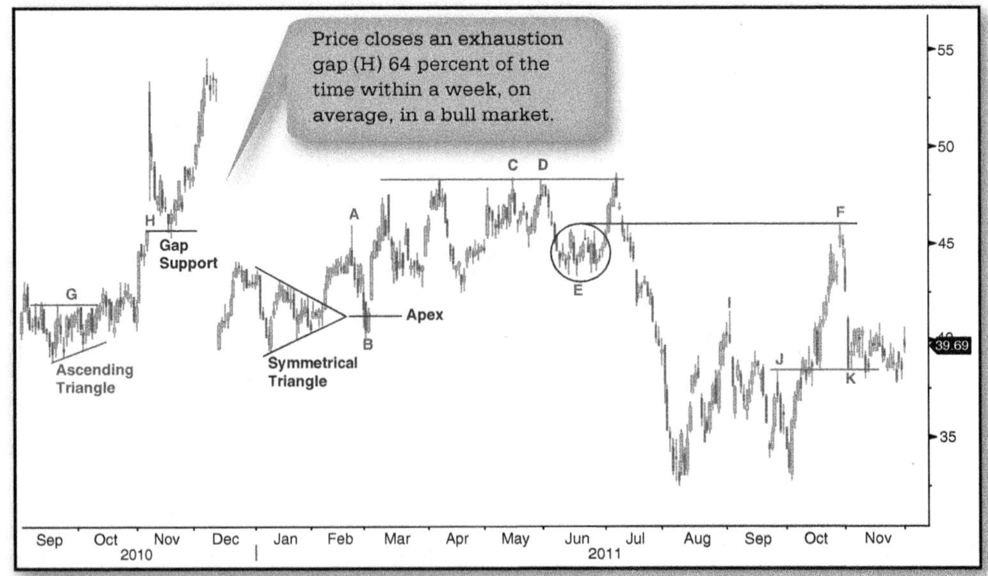

FIGURE 47.5 AWI US Equity (Armstrong World Industries Inc).

Starting on the left, an ascending triangle appears at G. The horizontal consolidation region has a flat top, but it looks loose with price wandering up and down between the two red trendlines. That region should show support or resistance in the future, and it does. The symmetrical triangle forms in the middle of the HCR and point I on the far right also peaks near the top of G.

H is an **exhaustion gap**. Notice that price later finds support at the bottom of the gap.

> **DEFINITION:**
> **Exhaustion gap**
> An exhaustion gap appears at the end of a trend. Price usually closes the gap within a week or two.

The symmetrical triangle is a delight because it is a perfect example of the chart pattern. Price bounces from trendline to trendline, filling the pattern with movement. The tops and bottoms of the pattern touch each trendline without leaving whiskers behind for your shaver.

Notice that price turns at A, directly above the triangle apex.

The apex is also a place of future support and resistance (as is the entire triangle, for that matter). Although valley B slides below the apex, it does reverse within the triangle.

The horizontal red line joining peaks C and D show peak SAR. Price bumps up against a ceiling there. During an advance, expect price to reverse at the level of a prior peak (it may not, so keep that in mind, too).

> **Smart Investor Tip**
> Objects that show support will often show resistance in the future and vice versa.

This idea also applies to valleys. Circled in blue is a loose horizontal congestion region at E. When price attempts to exceed this level at F, it hits the HCR and finds overhead resistance.

Finally, price drops to find support at K setup by peak J (and the loose congestion area to its left).

When looking at price trends, imagine where price may stall or reverse. Those reversals can happen at the price level of prior peaks, prior valleys, horizontal congestion regions, gaps, trendlines, chart patterns, and round numbers.

It sounds like I am covering every possible number on the price chart, right? Have faith that price will reverse at support or resistance and when it fails, squeal like a stuck pig.

The next section discusses four types of gaps. Traders love gaps. Why? I have no idea. I prefer women.

Test Yourself

Answer the following to test your knowledge of support and resistance.

1. Which of the following do not usually show support or resistance?
   A. Trendlines
   B. Gaps
   C. Chart patterns
   D. Horizontal consolidation regions
   E. Peaks
   F. Valleys
   G. Whole numbers
   H. The kitchen sink
2. True or false: Support is always beneath price.
3. If price peaks at $10, at what price can you expect resistance in the future?
   A. $10
   B. $10.50
   C. $9.50
   D. None of the above.
   E. All of the above, including D.
4. True or false: To help avoid stop running, never place a stop loss order at a round number.
5. What is meant by support?
   A. Price rises only to bump up against a ceiling and stop rising.
   B. Price drops and then bounces upward as if it has found a floor.
   C. A stock moves in a manner similar to other stocks in the same industry.
   D. Price peaks at $10 and a month later, it forms a minor high at $9.50.
6. True or false: Support areas can also act as resistance areas.

Answers: 1. G and H; 2. True; 3. E; 4. True; 5. B; 6. True

Gaps

There are several types of gaps, but we will cover only four of them. Others, like the ex-dividend gap and the opening gap, are inconsequential or too advanced.

Gaps are exciting! Those that appear at a chart pattern breakout can push a stock like a booster stage does to a rocket. For example, breakout day gaps in symmetrical triangles (bull markets, up breakouts) show gains averaging 36 percent compared to 28 percent for those without gaps.

Sometimes the booster stage fails to ignite as it does in ascending triangles. There, gaps hurt performance: 29 percent versus 35 percent gain for those with and without gaps, respectively.

Being able to tell the gap type can help traders decipher what will happen with the stock. Will a stock begin a new price trend as it does after a breakaway gap, or will an exhaustion gap signal the party is over faster than champagne left uncorked?

Four Types

I show a bar chart to find examples of the four major gap types: area, breakaway, continuation, and exhaustion. The bar chart makes finding gaps easier. (See Figure 47.6)

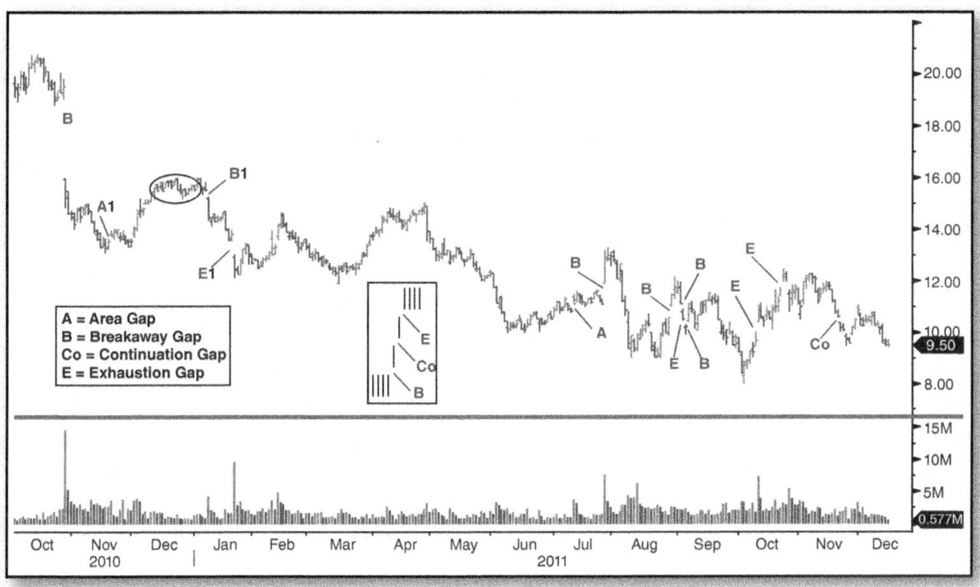

FIGURE 47.6 JNY US Equity (Jones Group Inc/The).

Look at gap B1, located to the right of the circled congestion region. A breakaway gap always leaves a congestion area. A congestion area is where price moves sideways for a time. It can be just a few days wide—or more—like that circled. The breakaway gap breaks away from the area, hence its name.

Slaloming downhill, we find gap E1. This is an example of an exhaustion gap. The gap exhausts the trend, thus its name. After an exhaustion gap, expect to see a quick reversal, sometimes a powerful one, but also one that does not last long.

Gap A1, on the far left of the chart, is an area gap. These little stinkers carry a load in their pants. They look like breakaway gaps, but a trend does not develop. The **gap closes** quickly by curling around and filling the gap.

DEFINITION:

Gap closes

A gap is said to close when future price action covers the same price level as the gap. Price fills the gap, closing it.

The inset shows an ideal example of the last type of gap, a continuation gap. A trend develops with a breakaway gap (B) that appears after a congestion region. Then a continuation gap appears (Co) during the trend. An exhaustion gap (E) ends the trend.

A continuation gap is also known as a **measuring gap** because it sometimes forms midway in a price trend. Continuation gaps are rare, and I found only one on the far right of the chart.

DEFINITION:

Measuring gap

A continuation, measuring, or runaway gap is one that appears midway in a price trend. Measure from the start of the trend to the gap and project from the gap onward to determine how far price might move.

Gap Type	Discussion
Area, Common, or Pattern:	Occurs in areas of congestion (trendless markets) and close rapidly. Volume on the day of the gap can be high, but returns to normal in a day or two. No significant highs (in uptrends) or lows (in downtrends) occur immediately after the gap. A distinctive curl as the gap closes is a key indication of this gap type.
Breakaway:	Identifies the start of a new trend and occurs on breakout from a consolidation region. Is accompanied by high volume on the day of the gap and continuing for several days. The trend continues long enough for several new highs (for uptrends) or new lows (downtrends) to occur after the gap.
Continuation, Measuring, or Runaway:	Happens in the midst of a straight-line advance or decline. Price continues making new highs or lows without filling the gap. Volume is usually high, propelling price in the direction of the trend.
Exhaustion:	Occurs at the end of a trend on high volume. The gap is not followed by new minor highs or minor lows and the gap itself may be unusually tall. After the gap, price consolidates. Commonly occurs after a continuation gap. The gap closes quickly, usually within a week.

Identification Guidelines

What differentiates gaps? The above table describes what to look for.

I studied each gap type and found that area gaps close in an average of 3 days.

Breakaway gaps take an average of 136 days to close in a bull market, upward trend, and 168 days in a downward trend.

Continuation gaps close in an average of 98 days (uptrends) and 77 days (downtrends).

Exhaustion gaps close in 9 days (uptrends) and 14 days (downtrends).

Exercise

When I visit my dentist every year, I pull out the *Highlights* magazine and search the drawing for a comb, rake, toothbrush, and other utensils hidden on the page. These exercises are just like that search except that here you are looking for chart patterns.

The next chart tests your knowledge of gaps, based on the earlier table and discussion. Try to identify each gap. The numbers point to the gaps and the associated volume. All four gap types appear in Figure 47.7.

Figure 47.8 shows the answers.

Breakaway gaps exit a congestion area as if it were on fire, so they are easy to spot. Sometimes, however, they become area gaps. Continuation gaps are rare and will appear only in strong price trends. It took a while to find a chart that had them. Exhaustion gaps end a trend, so look for a strong trend, and find a gap that leads to a consolidation region.

Trading Gaps

If you are a day trader, the only gaps important to you are opening gaps. Other intraday gaps that may appear happen because of low volume. Ignore them.

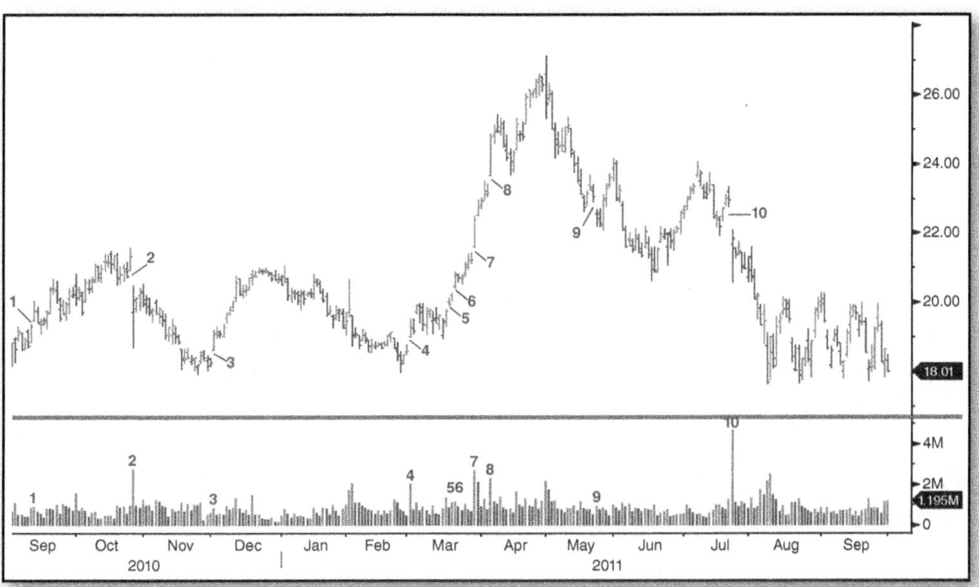

FIGURE 47.7 OLN US Equity (Olin Corp).

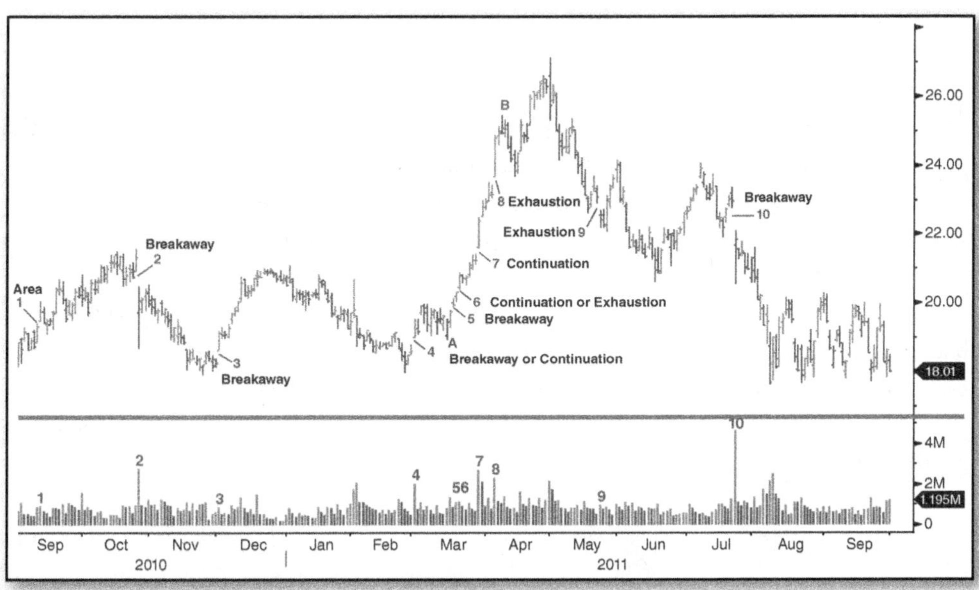

FIGURE 47.8 OLN US Equity (Olin Corp).

If you are a swing trader, then gaps are important. When a gap forms out of a consolidation region on high volume, you know that a trend is underway. It is a buy signal (but not one you should necessarily take).

If a trend fails to appear, then the gap becomes an area gap. That situation should become clear if the gap closes in two or three price bars. If the gap closes, exit the trade immediately.

Area gaps show a hook as price curls back to the gap. That hook should happen within a handful of price bars of the gap. If it does not, then it is a breakaway gap.

> **Smart Investor Tip**
> Very large gaps, especially well into a trend, are usually exhaustion gaps.

When a gap appears in a strong price trend that is already underway, it is probably an exhaustion gap. It could be a continuation gap, so waiting another price bar or two should provide confirmation, and perhaps a better exit price. If you see lots of overlap between one gap bar and the next, then it is an exhaustion gap and time to sell. If the trend continues with little overlap, then it is a continuation gap.

Since continuation gaps are rare, a gap in a trend already underway is most likely an exhaustion gap.

Gap Measure Rule For continuation gaps, measure from the start of the trend to the middle of the gap and project upward from the middle of the gap to get a price target.

For example, in Figure 47.8, continuation gap 7 shows a trend start at A that ends at B. The gap is about midway in the trend. To put numbers to this, the low at A is at 18.95 and the middle of the gap is at 21.57 for a height of 2.62. That gives a target of 21.57 + 2.62 or 24.19. The high at B is at 25.45.

Some say that continuation gaps follow breakaway gaps (I have not verified this). If the trend is already underway, but a breakaway gap did not appear, then you are probably looking at an exhaustion gap. Also, exhaustion gaps can be very large. If the gap you are seeing is tall, then it is probably an exhaustion gap.

If you do see an exhaustion gap, consider trading the new direction. Violent reversals can accompany an exhaustion gap. Gaps 8 and 9 in Figure 47.8 are examples. Notice that the new trend lasts for about a week, so you have to be nimble trading these.

Now that we have filled the *gaps* in your knowledge, what comes next? Throwbacks and pullbacks. Do you know the difference between them, besides spelling? Hint: Chart patterns that have throwbacks often perform worse than patterns missing them. What about pullbacks? Are pullbacks to stocks what fullbacks are to football? I have no idea what that means.

> **Smart Investor Tip**
> After an exhaustion gap ends, the trend reversal can be violent and offers a trading opportunity.

Test Yourself

Answer the following questions to test for gaps in your knowledge.

1. What does closing the gap mean?
   A. The window of opportunity to trade a gap is dwindling.
   B. Price covers the gap within a month.
   C. Price in the future retraces far enough to fill the gap.
   D. None of the above.

2. A breakaway gap has the following characteristics:
   A. Is accompanied by high volume.
   B. Is accompanied by low volume.
   C. Usually closes quickly.
   D. Often remains open a long time.
   E. Leaves a congestion region.
3. True or false: Exhaustion gaps close quickly.
4. True or false: The appearance of an exhaustion gap means the stock is tired, hence the name exhaustion gap.
5. True or false: A continuation gap always appears midway in a price trend.
6. The differences between a breakaway gap and an area gap are:
   A. Only one occurs on high volume.
   B. The breakaway gap is unusually tall.
   C. The breakaway gap closes quickly.
   D. The area gap closes quickly.
   E. The breakaway gap remains open longer.

Answers : 1. C; 2. A, D, E; 3. True; 4. False; 5. False; 6. D and E

Throwbacks and Pullbacks

Throwbacks and pullbacks are important patterns. Why? Because they happen about half the time after the breakout from a chart pattern. Not knowing about them invites disaster when the stock returns to the breakout price and continues lower. You sell for a loss only to watch the stock recover.

Figure 47.9 provides a typical example of what a **throwback** looks like.

> **DEFINITION:**
> Throwback
> A throwback occurs after an upward breakout when price returns to the breakout price or chart pattern boundary within 30 days.

FIGURE 47.9 **AMTD US Equity (TD Ameritrade Holding Corp).**

Imagine that you have a buy stop placed a penny above the top of this ascending triangle. The order triggers at A. Since you are a seasoned pro, you always use a stop and decide to place it below the prior minor low, at D.

Price rises for a few days and then the company announces earnings before the market opens, at C. The stock opens below the bottom trendline and then plummets far enough to catch your stop and take you out of the trade. By day's end, the stock has closed *higher*!

The injury to your ego continues when the stock performs like a killer bee chasing a bird, soaring 38 percent to B.

Congratulations! You have just been stung by a throwback.

Pullbacks

You learn from your mistake and decide that you placed the stop too close. In your next trade, you are looking to boost income so you select the dividend paying utility stock shown in Figure 47.10, and buy at A.

Since ascending triangles break out upward 67 percent of the time in a bull market, you feel confident that this stock will do well. You place a stop loss order further away this time, a penny below the bottom of the triangle, at B.

The day after you buy the stock, it breaks out downward and a day later, it stops you out (C). Then price recovers almost as quickly and begins the move up that you expected. In fact, at D, the stock has climbed 32 percent above your buy price. Not only did you take a loss, but you missed out on all of those dividend checks.

The drop to C and the recovery is called a **pullback**.

> **DEFINITION:**
> **Pullback**
> A pullback occurs after a downward breakout from a chart pattern when price returns to the breakout price or chart pattern boundary within 30 days.

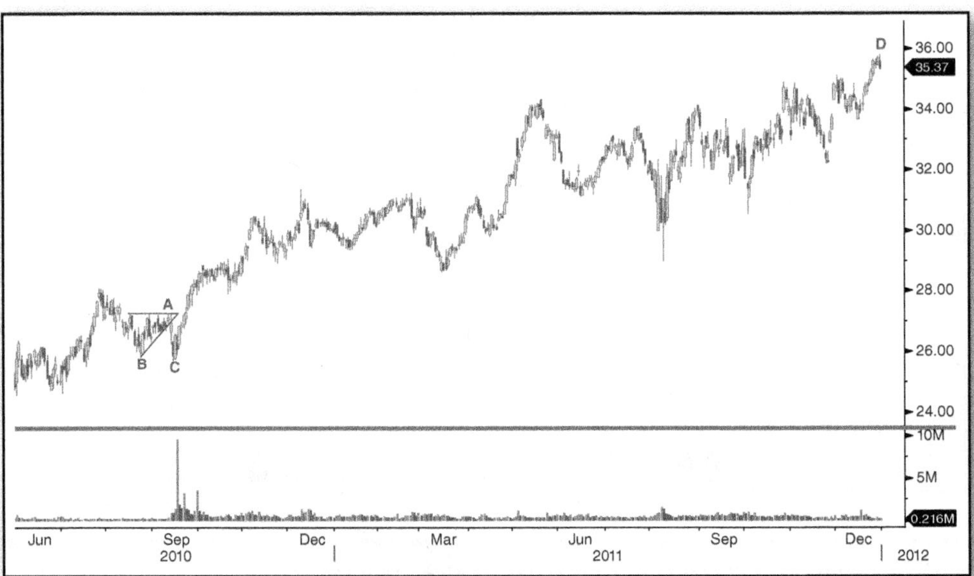

FIGURE 47.10 UIL US Equity (UIL Holdings Corp).

Identification Guidelines

What should you look for when trying to identify throwbacks and pullbacks? The following table provides the answer.

Characteristic	Discussion
Chart pattern breakout	From a chart pattern, price breaks out upward in a throwback and downward in a pullback.
Loop	Price continues in the direction of the breakout for a few days, but then loops back to the breakout price.
White space	After the stock returns to the breakout price, it leaves white space on the chart between the breakout and return.
Time	The stock must return to the breakout price or trendline boundary within 30 days.

Look at Figure 47.11, which helps explain the *average* behavior of throwbacks and pullbacks.

The left panel shows a throwback. Buying enthusiasm pushes price upward until it explodes out the top of any chart pattern. However, that buying demand slowly fades in the face of mounting selling pressure. In an average of six days, the stock has peaked after climbing 8 percent. Then it begins the return trip to the chart pattern.

The return takes only four days to either touch or come near the trendline boundary or breakout price, for a total of 10 days to make the round trip.

From there, price may continue lower or it may rebound immediately. In 65 percent of the cases, price resumes the upward breakout direction and rises. The other 35 percent close below the bottom of the chart pattern.

Pullbacks show a similar pattern except they apply to downward breakouts from any chart pattern. Price shoots lower at the breakout when excessive selling overpowers weak buying demand.

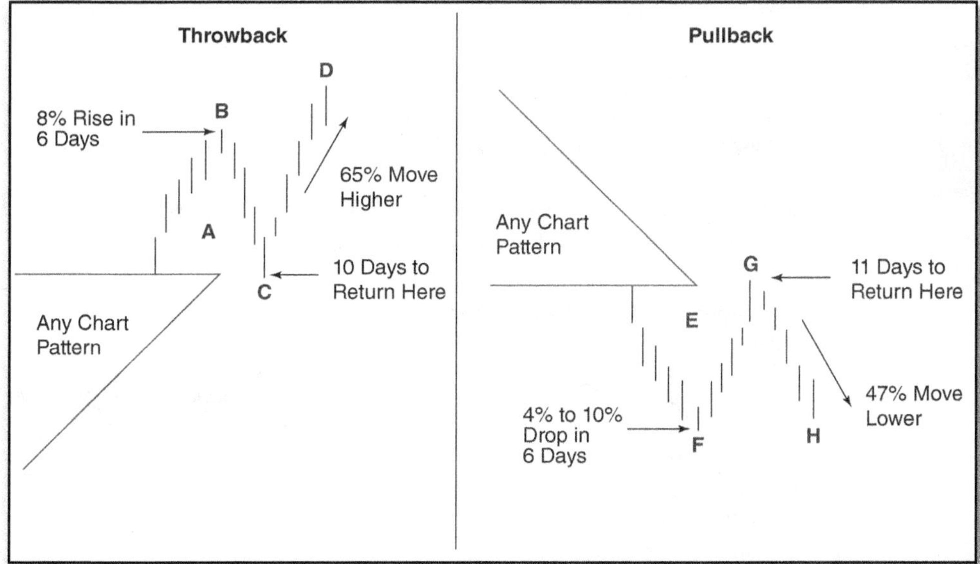

FIGURE 47.11 The Typical Behavior of Throwbacks and Pullbacks.

In an average of six days, the stock has bottomed and buying demand reverses the downtrend. The return journey takes 5 days for a total of 11 for the round trip from breakout to pullback.

Price may continue rising from there, and in 53 percent of the cases it does by closing above the top of the chart pattern. The remaining 47 percent of the time, the stock drops.

Figure 47.11 shows averages of thousands of chart patterns, so each individual case may vary.

Not all chart patterns will throwback or pullback, either. The following table shows the throwback and pullback rates for popular chart patterns.

Chart Pattern	Throwback Rate	Pullback Rate
Ascending triangles	60%	56%
Descending triangles	50%	55%
Double bottoms	56%	N/A
Double tops	N/A	57%
Head-and-shoulders bottoms	57%	N/A
Head-and-shoulders tops	N/A	59%
Rectangle bottoms	59%	59%
Rectangle tops	64%	54%
Symmetrical triangles	58%	58%
Triple bottoms	58%	N/A
Triple tops	N/A	63%

N/A: Not applicable

The highest throwback rate is for rectangle tops, and triple tops have the highest pullback rate. Descending triangles have the lowest throwback rate and rectangle tops have the lowest pullback rate.

This chapter ends the boot camp. The next chapter begins playing with live ammo by discussing individual chart patterns. It is an exciting time, so gather the children, and you may want to make popcorn.

Test Yourself

Answer the following questions.

1. True or false: A pullback occurs when price pulls back to the chart pattern from above.
2. True or false: A throwback never happens after a downward breakout.
3. If price breaks out downward from a descending triangle at $10 and 31 days later it is at $10, what has happened?
   A. A throwback has occurred.
   B. A pullback has occurred.
   C. Nothing.
4. Price completes a pullback after a breakout. What is the probability that price will continue higher?
   A. Over 50 percent.
   B. Under 50 percent.
   C. 50 percent.
   D. Unknown.

Answers: 1. False; 2. True; 3. C; 4. A

CHAPTER 48

Triangles, Pennants, and Flags

From Thomas N. Bulkowski, *Visual Guide to Chart Patterns* (Hoboken, New Jersey: John Wiley & Sons, 2002), Chapters 7–11.

Pattern Identification

This chapter focuses on identifying individual chart patterns. How do you find them? What should you look for, and why do they form? I answer these questions and others, as well as ask you to find patterns in the exercises in each section.

Rectangles

Now that we are experts at identifying minor highs and lows, drawing trendlines, and knowing what support and resistance look like, let us begin by finding our first chart pattern: a rectangle.

Think of a rectangle as a sewer pipe snaking through a construction site. It has a flat top and flat bottom, and price is a rattlesnake winding its way through the pipe. Figure 48.1 shows an example of a rectangle bottom.

After trending downward, the stock bumped up against an invisible ceiling of overhead resistance and stood on a floor of underlying support from October to December, forming a rectangle bottom.

That ceiling and floor I show as two horizontal trendlines in red. Notice that price touches each trendline three times on the top (1–3) and three on the bottom (4–6). Also notice that price enters the pattern from the top, trending down.

The exit from the chart pattern, called a **breakout**, is downward in this example, but can be in any direction for rectangles. I highlight the breakout location in the figure. Price must *close* below the bottom of the rectangle to stage a downward breakout.

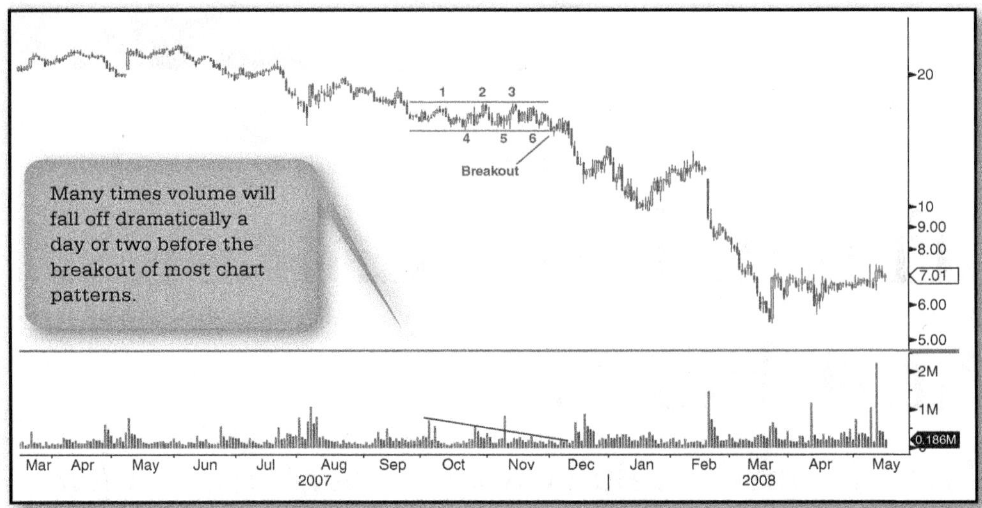

FIGURE 48.1 **ACMR US Equity (AC Moore Arts & Crafts Inc).**

Notice the volume trend. Just before the breakout, volume recedes to a low level. Many times volume will fall off dramatically a day or two before the breakout of most chart patterns (not just rectangles).

KEY POINT:

In a rectangle, price moves horizontally between overhead resistance and underlying support.

DEFINITION:

Breakout

A breakout occurs when price closes outside the boundary of a chart pattern.

Identification Guidelines

Rectangles are rare, so finding them is about as common as seeing a hummingbird in the middle of a housing subdivision. The following table lists the identification guidelines.

Characteristic	Discussion
Price trend	The short-term price trend leading to the rectangle is downward for bottoms and upward for tops.
Horizontal trendlines	Two horizontal, or nearly so, trendlines bound price along the top and bottom of the rectangle.

Characteristic	Discussion
Touches	There should be at least two touches of each trendline.
Volume	For rectangle bottoms: Volume tends to follow the breakout direction: upward for upward breakouts, and downward for downward breakouts. For rectangle tops: Volume usually recedes until the breakout.

When searching a chart for rectangles, begin looking for a congestion region where price moves horizontally, often for weeks. In fact, the average length of 1,228 rectangles in a study I did using daily price data from 1991 to 2011 was 71 days (about 2½ months).

Price should bounce between a support zone at the bottom and resistance at the top.

Connect the minor highs with a horizontal or nearly horizontal trendline. A similar line drawn below the minor lows forms a parallel trendline. Occasionally, one of the trendlines will not be horizontal. That is fine providing the slope is not too steep to disturb the overall picture. Consider the varying **trend lengths**.

DEFINITION:

Trend lengths

A short-term trend lasts up to three months. An intermediate-term or secondary trend lasts between three and six months. A long-term trend or primary trend lasts longer than six months.

At least two touches (but three is better) of each trendline are required for a valid rectangle. The touches need not alternate from top to bottom, but should have at least two clearly defined minor highs and two minor lows coming close to or touching each trendline.

In the ideal case, the trendline touches should be spaced evenly along the pattern, not bunched together on one end only. In other words, the trendline should not appear like a diving board, with one end unsupported.

To determine whether the rectangle is a top or bottom, look at the price trend leading to the start of the rectangle. Rectangle bottoms have price trending downward into them, but tops have price trending upward. Ignore any overshoot or undershoot in the price bars within a week or so before the start of the rectangle.

For rectangle bottoms, the volume pattern tends to track the breakout direction. For tops, volume often recedes over the length of the rectangle. Do not discard a rectangle because the volume pattern is wrong.

For example, Figure 48.2 shows a rectangle top on the weekly scale. Price bounces between two horizontal trendlines B and C, touching each plenty of times, spread along its length. No diving board here!

Price begins the uptrend at A and although price bobbles up and down in early 2004 (before the start of the rectangle), it is clear that this rectangle is at the top of the trend and not at the bottom.

Volume trends upward during the first half of the rectangle and recedes thereafter.

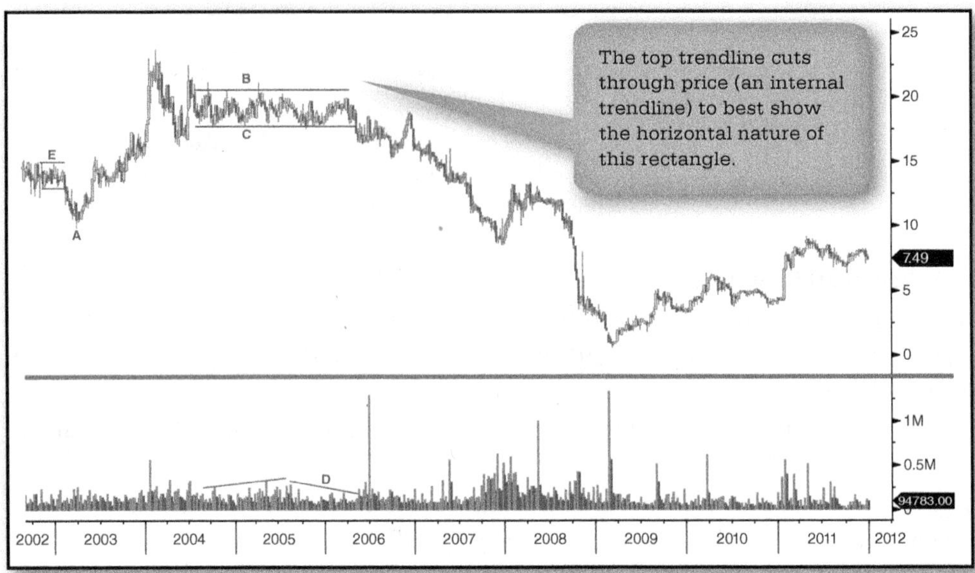

FIGURE 48.2 **BSET US Equity (Bassett Furniture Industries Inc).**

A smaller rectangle appears at E. The price trend off the chart to the left shows that this is a rectangle bottom because price trends downward into it.

Figure 48.3 shows a rectangle bottom on the weekly scale. Price trends higher at B, peaks at A, and drops into the rectangle bottom. There, price slides between two horizontal trendlines before breaking out upward.

Notice that the exit trend, C, nearly matches the slope of trendline B. In fact, the exit velocity of price leading out of a chart pattern nearly matches the velocity going into a pattern. That behavior applies not only to rectangles, but to all chart pattern

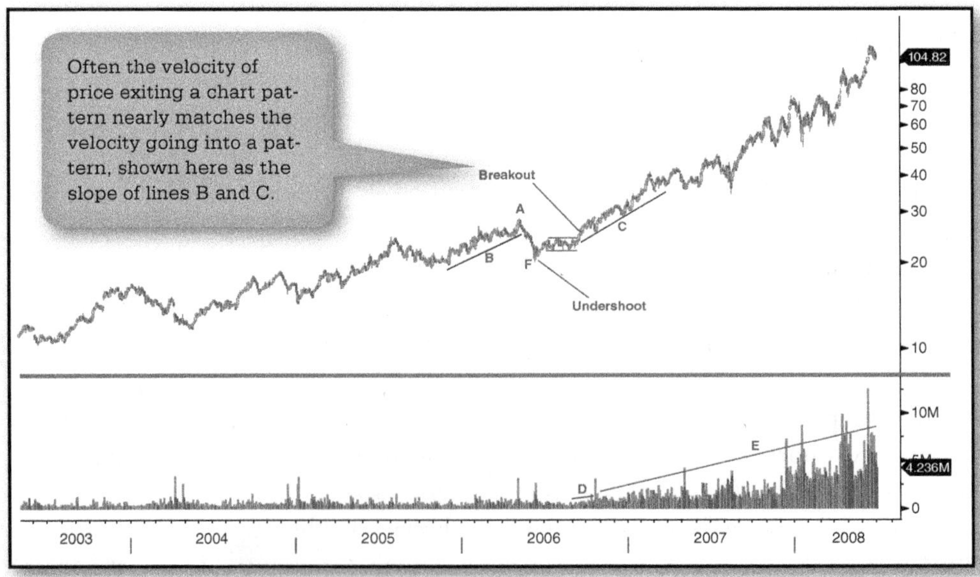

FIGURE 48.3 **AGU US Equity (Agrium Inc).**

> **SMART INVESTOR TIP**
>
> Tops have price trending into a chart pattern from the bottom, and bottoms have price trending into a chart pattern from the top.

> **SMART INVESTOR TIP**
>
> The price velocity leading to and exiting from a chart pattern are often similar even if the direction is reversed.

varieties. If you have limited dollars to spend and find two stocks showing chart patterns, choose the one with a higher velocity (cents per day).

Notice that volume, D, slopes upward. This upward slope grows dramatically as price climbs, forming a long hill at E that would scare bicyclists like me trying to climb it.

I also show price undershoot (F) a few weeks before the rectangle begins. Ignore it. **Undershoot or overshoot** is a short dip or rise, respectively, before the start of a chart pattern. The only influence they have is to confuse novices and give authors like me something to write about.

> **DEFINITION:**
>
> **Undershoot or overshoot**
>
> Both undershoot and overshoot occur before a chart pattern begins. Undershoot happens when price briefly dips below the entrance of a chart pattern. Overshoot happens when price briefly soars above it.

The inbound price trend is downward leading to this rectangle bottom (starting from A), not upward starting from the undershoot (F).

Rectangle Psychology

Why do rectangles form? Imagine that you run a small mutual fund and your fundamental and technical analysis says that Friedman Industries is a steal at 5.50. You order the trading department to buy the stock at that price. (See Figure 48.4.)

Since you want to own several hundred thousand shares and the stock averages only 16,000 shares traded daily, it could take weeks to buy all that you want. Why? Because if you hit the market with an order for 450,000 shares, it will likely send price soaring. That would boost the average cost of ownership.

One tip I learned is that your buying or selling should not be for more than 1 percent of the average daily volume. In this example, that would amount to 1,600 shares. Recently, I had to use a limit order to exit a stock for fear that my selling would punish price—it was that thinly traded.

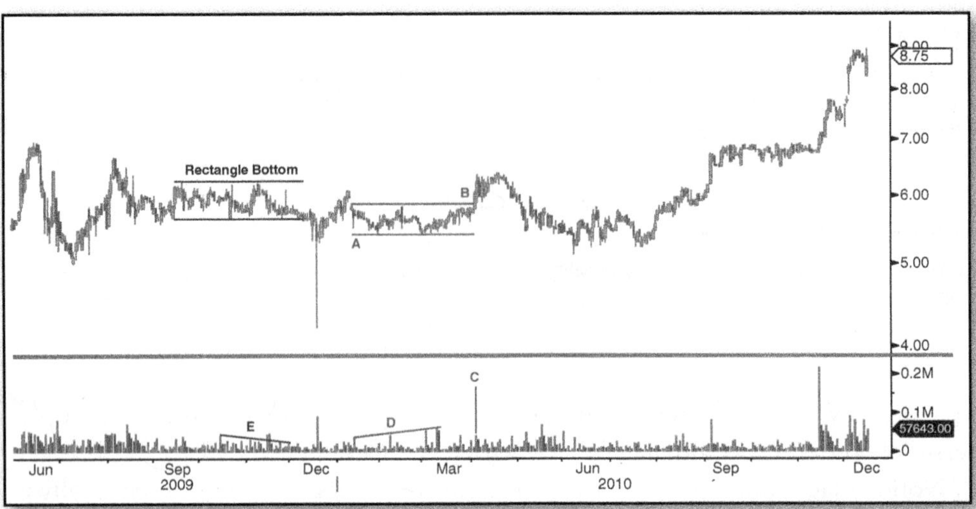

FIGURE 48.4 **FRD US Equity (Friedman Industries Inc).**

Beginning in early January, point A in the Figure, the trading department starts buying the stock. That buying demand causes price to rise, and your traders stop buying because the stock is too expensive. Price floats up to almost 6.

Another fund wants to dump the stock since they believe that the company will suffer in the coming economic slowdown. But they want to sell at a price no less than 5.75. Other institutional investors and retail traders join both sides. The result is that price hits a ceiling near 6 and a floor at 5.45.

> **SMART INVESTOR TIP**
>
> To help limit adverse price movement, avoid buying more than 1 percent of the average daily volume.

When price bubbles up to the sell price, the mutual fund jumps in and sells as many shares as they can before forcing the price back down. When it drops to the buy price, the other mutual fund begins buying, sending the price higher.

Eventually, one side fulfills their mission to either establish a position or liquidate one. The price will either drop out of the bottom or rise through the top.

> **KEY POINT:**
>
> A rectangle forms because traders want to own the stock at two fixed prices, one low and one high, setting limits (for a time) on how far price moves.

In this example, an upward breakout happens like a cork flying off a champagne bottle. C is the breakout day and 40,700 shares trade that day. The prior day saw only 12,200 shares traded.

Variations

This section looks at variations that you may come across in your quest to find rectangles. For example, Figure 48.5 shows an unusual chart pattern, but is it a rectangle?

Starting from A, the stock plunges like a bungee jumper whose cord breaks, splashing into the water, and slowly sinking into the top of the chart pattern. That means this rectangle is a bottom and not a top.

Our jumper surfaces three times near B, touching the top trendline. The guidelines say that at least two touches are necessary, preferably widely spaced. Does this qualify, or is it a diving board?

Since the chart pattern is so long, the three clustered touches are a problem. However, it helps that C is there to hold up the far end of the trendline.

Consider redrawing the top trendline parallel at F. It will slice through price as an internal trendline, but that is fine. Draw the line where it best shows overhead resistance.

> **SMART INVESTOR TIP**
>
> Volume is not an important *identification* feature of most chart patterns, including rectangles. Volume plays a bigger role in performance.

Now look at the bottom trendline. How many trendline touches do you see? The chart shows one at D, but the line is drawn incorrectly. Ignore that touch and move the line higher until it hugs the price valleys, connecting E. If you do that, the support area becomes clearer.

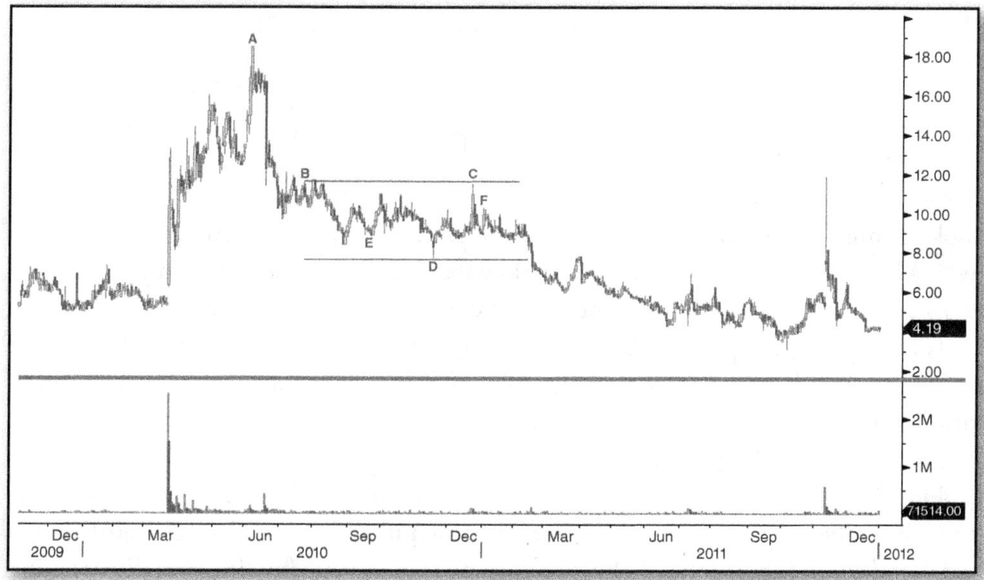

FIGURE 48.5 ARWR US Equity (Arrowhead Research Corp).

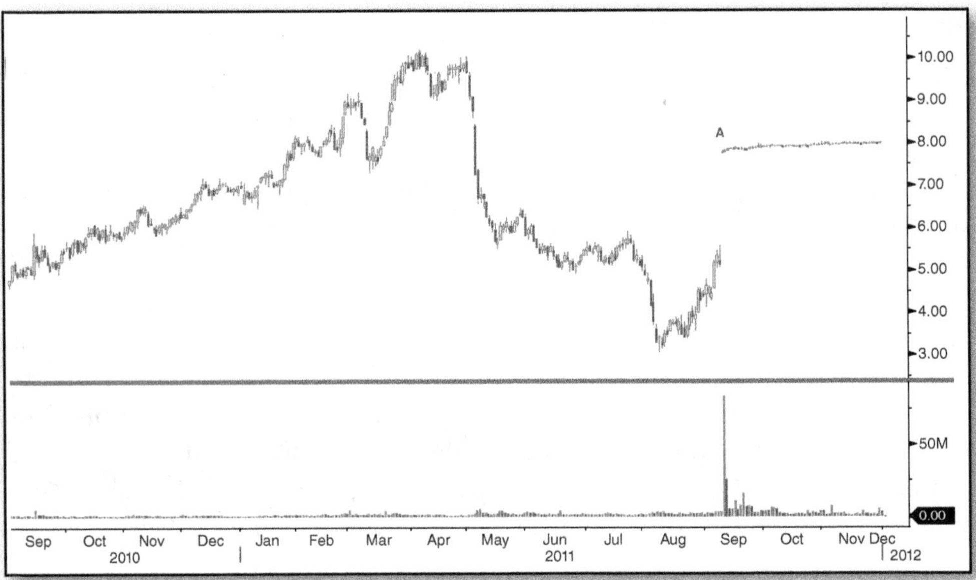

FIGURE 48.6 GLBL US Equity (Global Industries Ltd).

This is a rectangle bottom, but not a pretty one. If it helps, keep in mind what you are looking for—price moving sideways in a horizontal congestion region.

The next chart is one that reminds me of an e-mail that read as if the sender had overdosed on his medication. "Is this a flat base? Is this a rectangle? What kind of chart pattern is it? Price gaps up and then goes horizontal!" (See Figure 48.6.)

One glance at the chart told me all I needed to know, but I checked the news anyway. At A, the company received an offer to merge their operations with another company. These types of buyout offers make the stock soar and then flatline like a dead animal until the merger completes.

I do not consider the pattern to the right of A to be a rectangle. Why? Because of the news surrounding the stock. This is an example of an event pattern—how a stock behaves after it receives a buyout offer.

Exercise

This section presents two exercises. Find the rectangles on each chart. It will help if you look for minor highs that peak near the same price. In your mind, connect those peaks with a horizontal trendline. Then look below that line for minor lows that bottom near the same price. If you find that combination, then you have a rectangle.

Is it a rectangle top or bottom? Look at the short-term price *trend* leading to the rectangle. Tops have price trending upward into the chart pattern and bottoms have price trending downward.

Figure 48.7 has at least two rectangles. Find them.

Figure 48.8 shows the answer. The pattern highlighted in red is a rectangle bottom. Price begins sliding after A, trending down into the chart pattern, just as it is supposed to do for a rectangle bottom. Then it begins moving horizontally, forming minor highs (1 through 5) and minor lows (6 through 11).

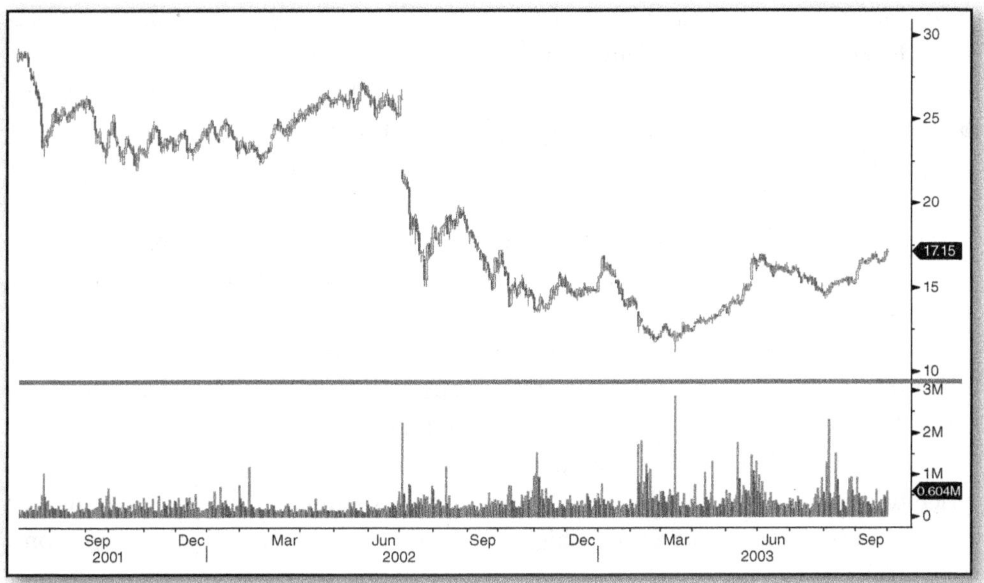

FIGURE 48.7 DPL US Equity (DPL Inc).

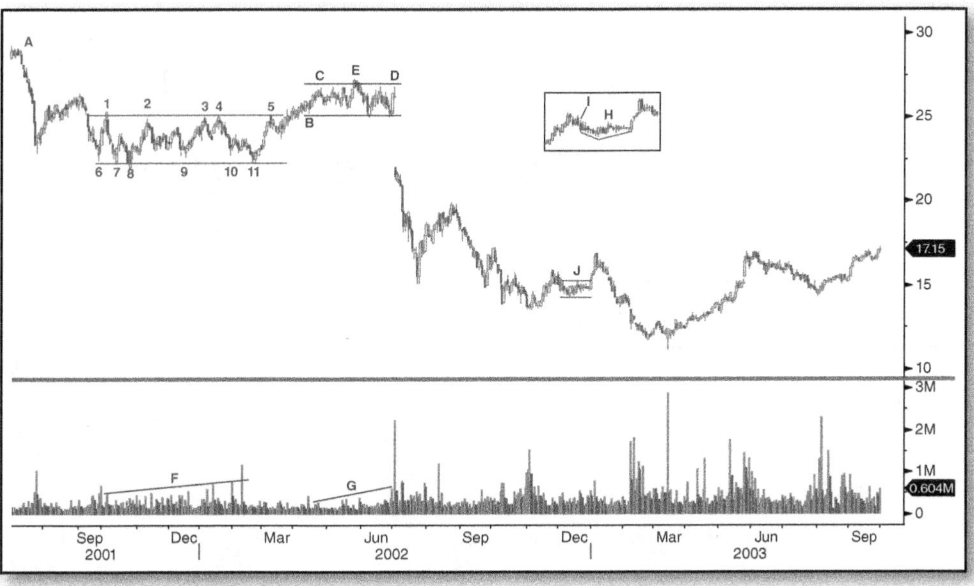

FIGURE 48.8 DPL US Equity (DPL Inc).

The peak at 1 slices through the top trendline, but does it matter? No. Why not? Because by the time you recognize the price pattern as a rectangle bottom, that peak ceases to have any significance. Drawing the top trendline above peak 1 would make the other top touches seem too far away.

The same argument applies to valley 8. Price pokes below the red trendline but is not important to the overall picture.

The volume trend (F) rises and price breaks out upward.

Pattern CED is a rectangle top because price trends upward into the chart pattern. Price touches the bottom trendline three times and several times along the top. I drew the top trendline through E to show how price touches the top trendline better. Also, the first bottom touch, B, is part of a straight-line run. It is a minor low, but one that is not easy to see without a trendline connecting it. This is not a perfect example of a rectangle top, but be flexible.

The volume trend (G) is upward even though this rectangle breaks out downward. Rectangle tops often have a receding volume trend, but do not let that throw you off.

Look at pattern J. Did you find this one? The bottom trendline touches only one point. I show it redrawn in the inset as a V-shaped price trend. This V shape more accurately represents the trend, not a horizontal line.

The top trendline rests on one peak, H. Point I is not a minor high. It is just a price bar on the side of a hill, not an individual peak (minor high). Avoid counting a trendline touch that is not a minor high or minor low. Pattern J is just squiggles on a chart and not a rectangle.

Figure 48.9 also shows at least one rectangle. Find as many as you can, and have tissues ready in case you get it wrong.

Figure 48.10 shows the answers. Let us begin with the red one (C) on the far right, since that is the only rectangle bottom on this chart.

Price trends downward into the chart pattern and then bounces up and down between two horizontal trendlines, touching each at least twice.

Look at peak B. This is an example of overshoot that I mentioned earlier. Price trends upward into the chart pattern, but overshoots the entry for a week or so before sliding into the rectangle. This is a rectangle top.

For rectangle top E, the price trend is horizontal leading to this pattern but upward before that (sharing the same inbound trend as rectangle D). Notice that point

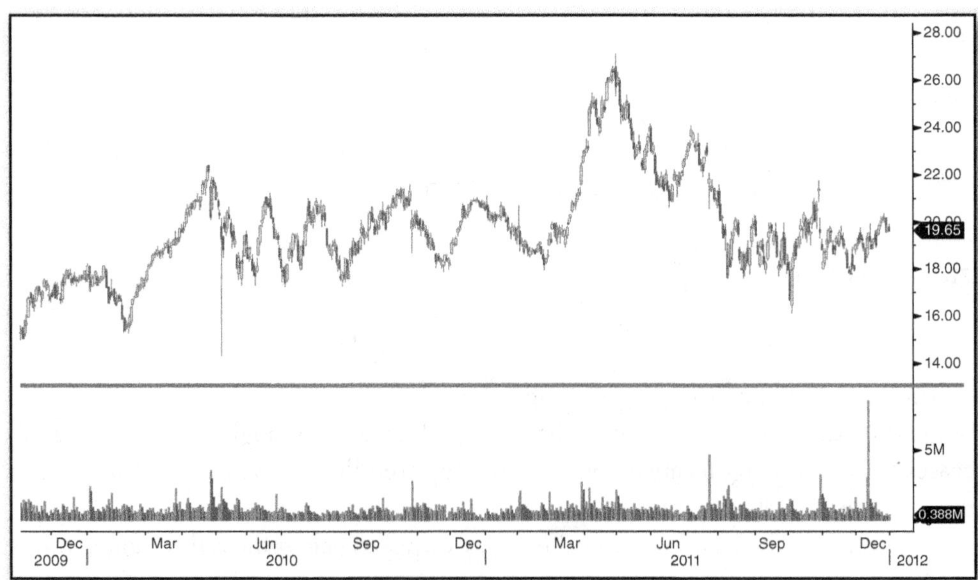

FIGURE 48.9 OLN US Equity (Olin Corp).

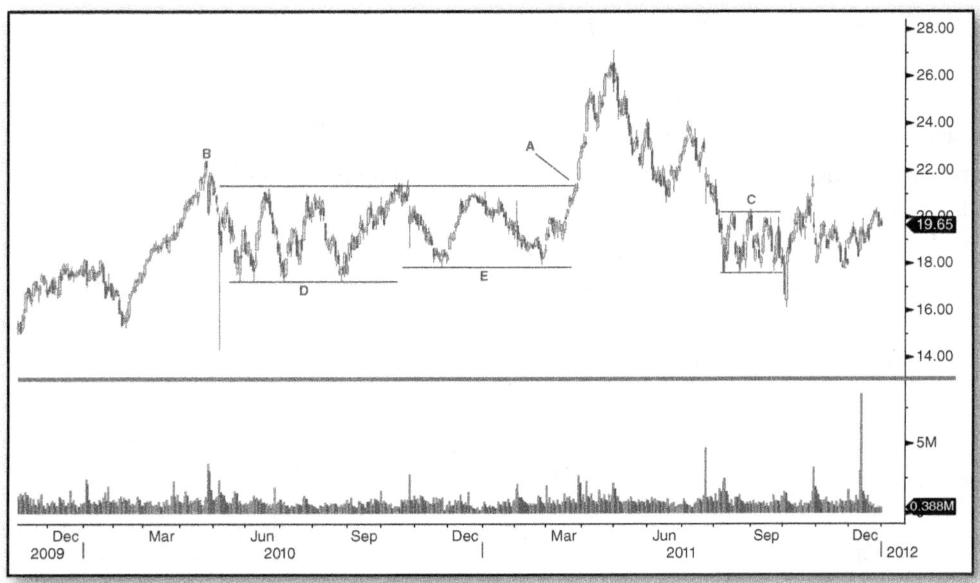

FIGURE 48.10 **OLN US Equity (Olin Corp).**

A is NOT a minor high so it does not qualify as a top trendline touch. Be careful about touch counts and include only minor highs or minor lows.

Pattern E is a rectangle top. However, I prefer to call pattern DE one long rectangle top instead of thinking of it as two separate ones.

The next section discusses ascending triangles. I used to love trading them until I discovered that they did not perform well. In other words, I lost my shirt. Have you seen it?

Test Yourself

Answer the following statements or questions.

1. True or false: A rectangle bottom *always* has price trending down into the chart pattern.
2. True or false: It is fine if *one* of the trendlines bounding the rectangle bottom is almost horizontal.
3. True or false: It is fine if *both* trendlines are not horizontal, providing they are not too far from level.
4. True or false: A down-sloping volume trend is a key factor in determining whether the chart pattern is a rectangle bottom.
5. True or false: A breakout occurs when price pierces one of the horizontal trendlines.
6. How is a rectangle bottom different from a top (pick all that apply)?
   A. Rectangle bottoms are shorter in duration.
   B. Rectangle bottoms have price entering the chart pattern from the bottom, and tops have it entering from the top, hence the bottom and top names.
   C. They have different names because the volume pattern is different.
   D. A rectangle bottom is a horizontal consolidation region but a top is not.
   E. By definition, price enters tops from the bottom and enters bottoms from the top.
7. True or false: A rectangle top is a horizontal congestion region.

Answers: 1. True; 2. True; 3. True; 4. False; 5. False; 6. E; 7. True

Ascending Triangles

This section begins looking at chart patterns not bounded by twin horizontal lines. Triangles use a more complicated shape: diagonal trendlines. Training your eye to recognize them is still easy, though, because the technique builds on what we have learned.

Figure 48.11 shows an example of an ascending triangle, highlighted by red trendlines.

Price overshoots (A) the entry to this chart pattern, but who cares? There are no ascending triangle top and bottom variations to worry about (where the inbound price trend is important); there are only ascending triangles.

The stock breaks out upward at B, which happens the majority of the time, but this one sees price quickly turn down, closing below the bottom of the chart pattern at C. When that happens, it **busts the ascending triangle**.

KEY POINT:

Ascending triangles are wedge-shaped patterns that break out most often upward. The triangle can act as a reversal or continuation of the existing price trend.

DEFINITION:

Busts the ascending triangle

A busted ascending triangle occurs when price breaks out in one direction, moves less than 10 percent before reversing, and continues in the new direction to close above the top or below the bottom of the triangle.

The popularity of ascending triangles stems from the belief that price will start a robust uptrend. However, I stopped trading most of them because too many looked like this chart. Price climbed a few percent and then died, killing my trade as well.

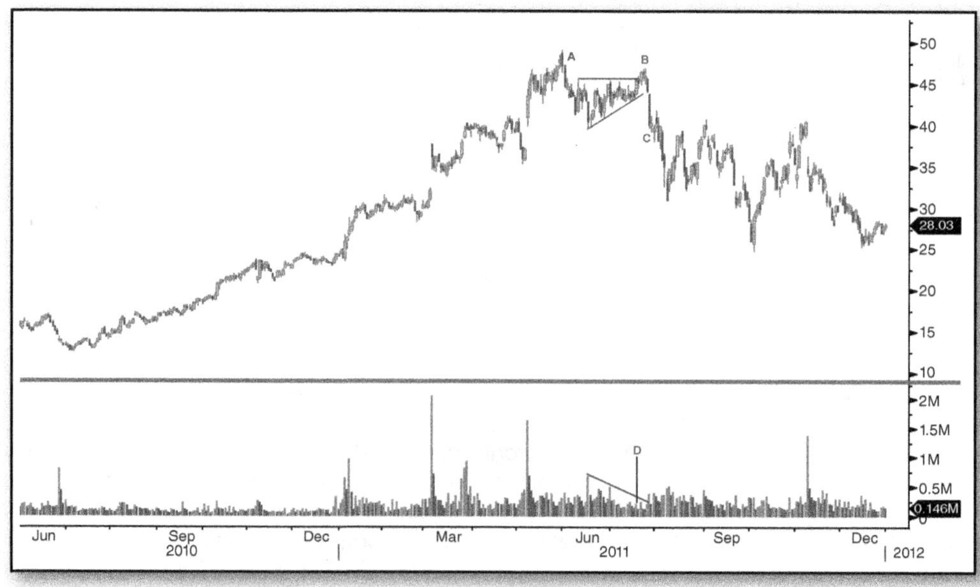

FIGURE 48.11 **LXU US Equity (LSB Industries Inc).**

Some volume disciples will look at the chart and say, "Look at volume! It should be well above average, but it isn't!" Point D shows the breakout day's volume, and they are right. Volume was well below average, but I have seen profitable trends start on mediocre volume, too. In fact, I do not even show volume on my charts. It is as useful to me as asking if fish like seafood. I am a vegetarian: I eat weeds.

Identification Guidelines

When searching for ascending triangles, look for minor highs close together (weeks apart, but usually not months between tops) that peak near the same price. Then look directly below those peaks to see if the valleys trend upward following a straight line.

Sometimes I will see an up-sloping line of valleys following a trend. Then I look above them and see a horizontal line of peaks. That combination spells triangle.

The accompanying table lists the important characteristics of ascending triangles.

Characteristic	Discussion
Horizontal top line	Price along the top follows a horizontal trend.
Up-sloping bottom line	Price makes a series of higher valleys, following a trendline. The two trendlines converge.
Price crossing	Price must cross the pattern from side to side, filling the triangle with movement. Avoid patterns with excessive white space in the center of the triangle.
Volume	Volume in the pattern recedes and can be especially low the day before the breakout.
Breakout	Can be in any direction, but is upward the majority of the time.

Price along the top of the ascending triangle follows a horizontal or nearly horizontal trendline. Along the bottom, the minor lows bounce off an up-sloping trendline drawn connecting them.

Look at Figure 48.12.

Minor highs A through D stop near the same price. Minor lows E through G touch the bottom trendline. Together they form an ascending triangle, only this one has a downward breakout.

Make sure that price crosses the chart pattern plenty of times. What you do not want to see is white space in the middle of the pattern. I show an example of that later in this chapter.

Volume tends to recede over the life of the triangle, but that varies from triangle to triangle. The chart shows volume trending higher in the first half of the pattern and then downward leading to the breakout. Do not discard an ascending triangle simply because of an abnormal volume trend.

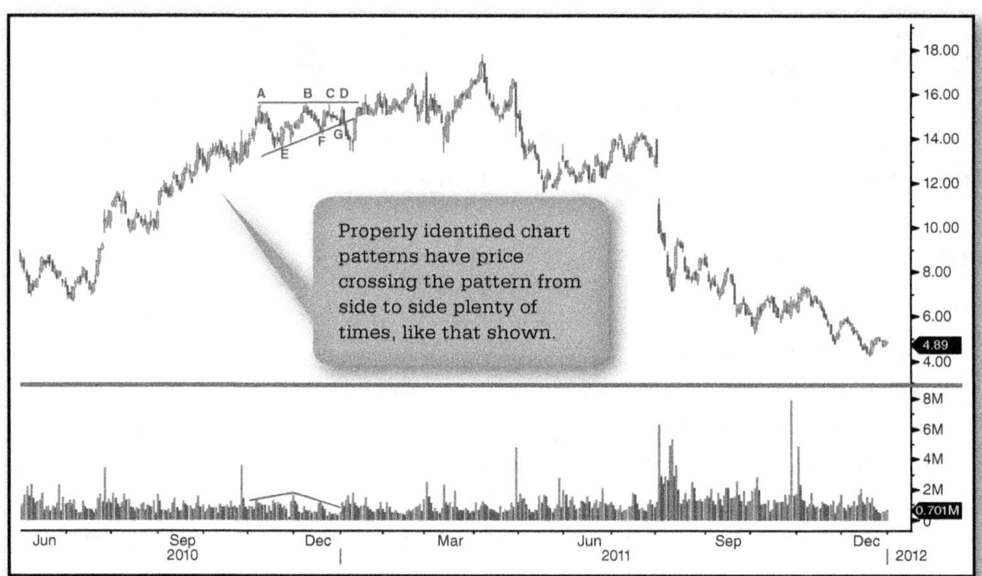

FIGURE 48.12 FOE US Equity (Ferro Corp).

The breakout from an ascending triangle can be in any direction, but is usually upward.

This is another example of a busted ascending triangle. Price breaks out downward and does not drop far (less than 10 percent) before reversing and closing above the top of the triangle. When that happens, it busts the downward breakout.

Unfortunately, this bust did not result in a tasty move upward. That might be because of the extended rise leading to the triangle. In fact, the downward breakout was a clue to weakness to begin with.

Ascending Triangle Psychology

In ascending triangles, price peaks for the same reason it does in rectangles: Traders sell when the stock reaches their target price.

Suppose that Molly runs a mutual fund and wants to sell several hundred thousand shares of ABC Chewing Gum. Every time the stock reaches $35, she sells some. Her selling creates a ceiling on the stock.

KEY POINT:
When searching for ascending triangles, make sure price crosses the chart pattern from side to side several times. Price should not be bunched up near the start nor near the end with an empty white hole in the middle.

KEY POINT:
An ascending triangle forms because of increasing demand at lower prices matched with selling at a constant price.

Harry runs the trading department of a hedge fund, and he loves ABC Chewing. When the stock drops to 30, he buys as many shares as he can, but the stock runs away from him and becomes too expensive to chase.

Johnny is a rich swing trader. He watches Mutual Fund Molly create overhead resistance at 35 and sees Hedge Fund Harry put a floor in the stock at 30. When the stock drops to 30.25, he starts buying, knowing that he can probably sell when it approaches 35. "Easy money," he says and smiles.

Harry sees volume tick up and believes that others are buying ahead of him. He raises his buy price to 30.50 and starts eating as many shares as he can before they disappear from his plate.

On the next cycle, Harry has to raise his buy price to 31 to stay ahead of the other cannibals. The hunt continues until Molly sells all of her shares or Harry bags his quota and quits. When one side gives up, the other side yells, "Tag! You're it!" and snatches the stock; then a breakout ensues, ending the pattern.

Variations

Figure 48.13 shows an example of an ascending triangle on the weekly scale.

Price touches the top trendline (A) three times at three minor highs and the bottom trendline (B) also three times, although the individual spikes may be hard to see.

Notice the white space at C. I would prefer that A slide to the left a bit, filling some of that white space, but I also think this pattern works as an ascending triangle. It is not perfect, but few chart patterns are.

You will notice that if I changed the time scale to days or intraday, the pattern shape would not change. An ascending triangle on the 1-minute scale would still have a flat top and an up-sloping bottom.

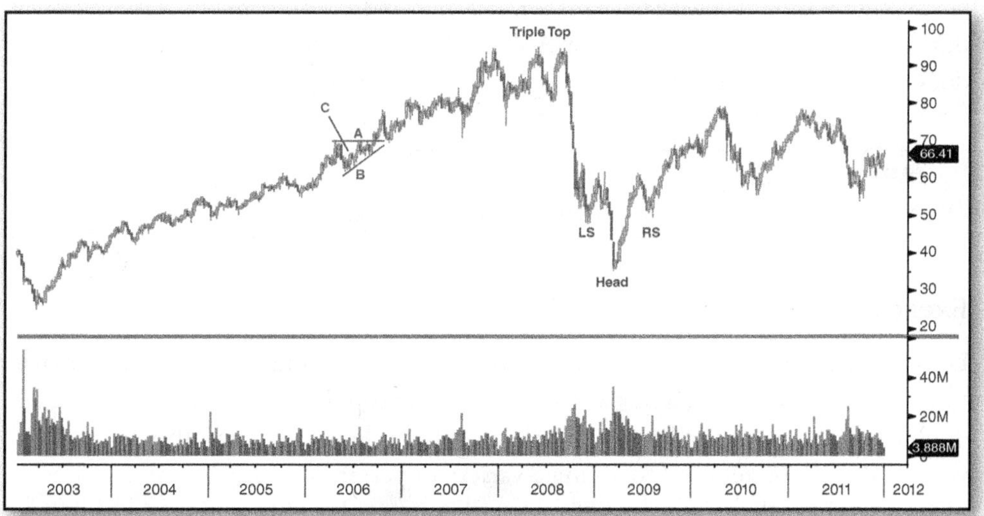

FIGURE 48.13 GD US Equity (General Dynamics Corp).

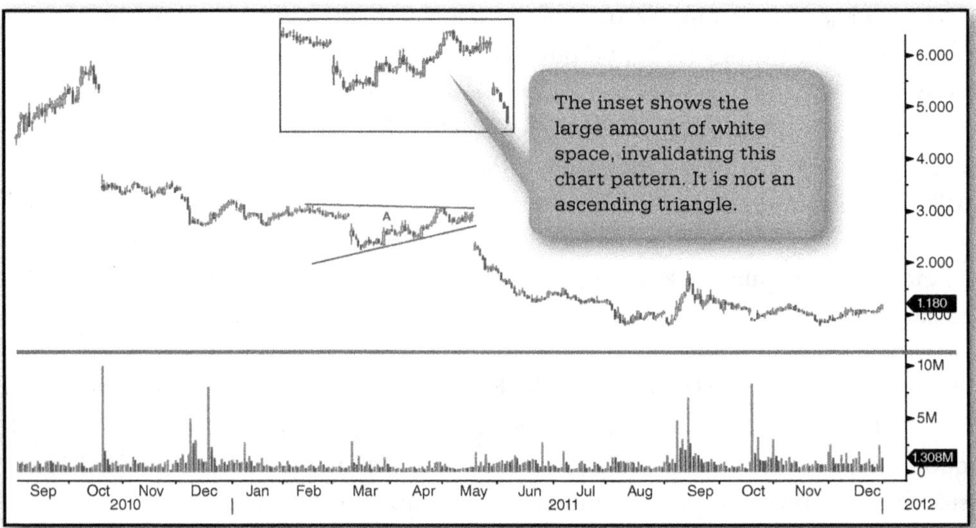

FIGURE 48.14 CWTR US Equity (Coldwater Creek Inc).

Before we move on to the next figure, notice the head-and-shoulders bottom that appears. The pattern is a wonderful example of a reversal that signaled the turn from bear market to bull.

FAST FACTS

The breakout from an ascending triangle is upward 64 percent of the time based on research completed in 2011 using over 1,600 ascending triangles in both bull and bear markets.

The left (LS) and right (RS) shoulders look fine. The stretched head and neck, however, warn us to never play tag with black holes.

Figure 48.14 shows an invalid ascending triangle.

Price touches the top trendline twice and the bottom line multiple times, just as the guidelines require. The top trendline is horizontal and the bottom one slopes upward. But the gaping hole of white space at A seems large enough to fly a 747 through. Price does not cross the triangle often enough to qualify this as a valid ascending triangle.

SMART INVESTOR TIP

Well-formed chart patterns have small amounts of white space.

Exercise

Look for ascending triangles in Figure 48.15. You should find two of them, maybe three if you are creative, along with a broadening top, head-and-shoulders top, and double top. If you do not know what the non-triangle patterns are, that is fine. I just want your eyes to get used to seeing a variety of patterns.

Figure 48.16 shows the answers, including examples of how the triangle's apex aligns with price.

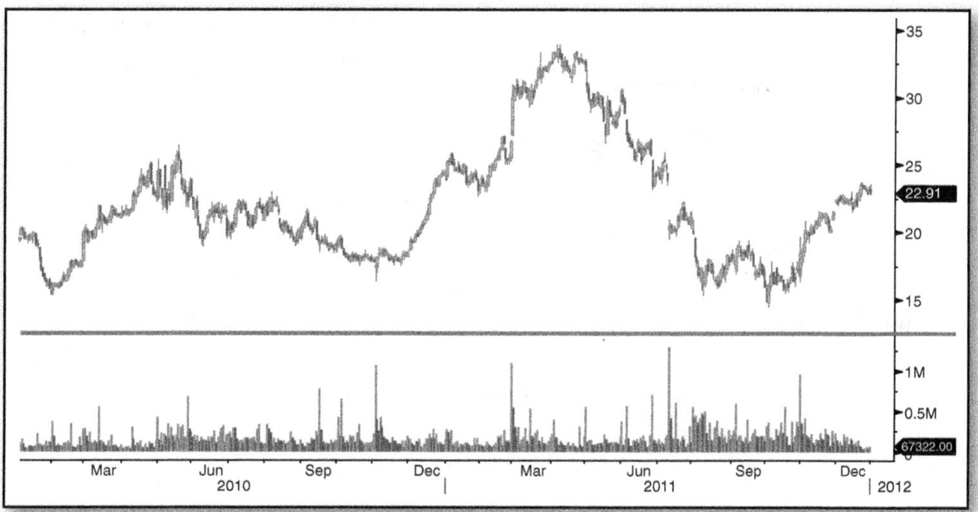

FIGURE 48.15 TREX US Equity (Trex Co Inc).

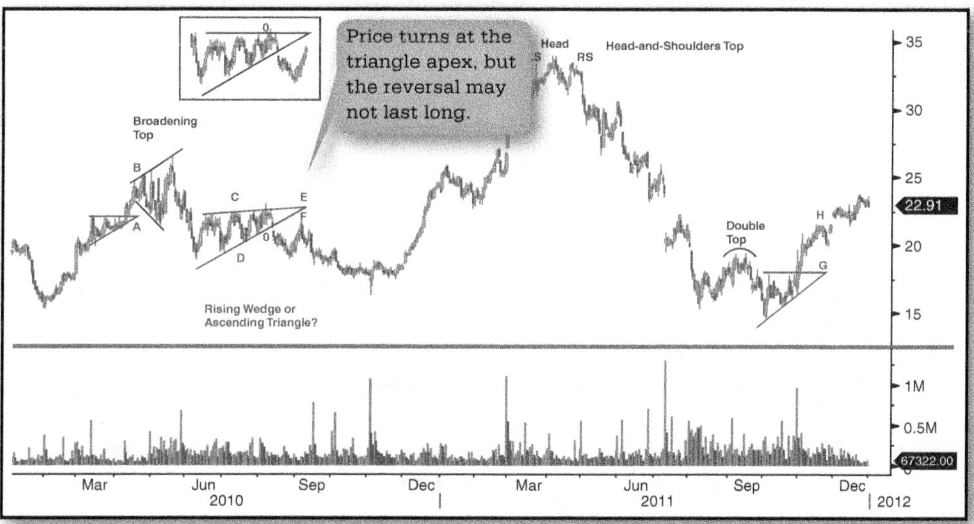

FIGURE 48.16 TREX US Equity (Trex Co Inc).

Compare apex A with turn B, apex E with F, and G with H. Above or below each apex is a corresponding price turn. The turn may not last long or it could start a new trend. The duration of the turn is unknown, but this technique does highlight short-term turns.

Look at pattern C. Price along the bottom of the pattern (D) touches the trendline three times (the end point does not count since price plunges through the pattern there). Along the top, it also touches the trendline multiple times, but there is a problem. The top line is not horizontal.

Does it have to be level? No. Now look at the blue inset directly above the triangle. This depiction makes the top line appear horizontal. Is it an ascending triangle or not?

> **FAST FACTS**
>
> The apex of a triangle is where price tends to form a short-term peak or valley.

Depending on how you draw the top trendline, the blue outline appears to have an upward breakout whereas the red depiction shows a downward breakout (a small red circle in each case).

I believe that the red image better represents a rising wedge and not an ascending triangle.

Before moving on to the next figure, look at the other chart patterns so that you can become accustomed to finding them, too.

Search Figure 48.17 for two ascending triangles, a double bottom, and a head-and-shoulders top and bottom. We have not covered many of those patterns, but do your best anyway.

Figure 48.18 reveals the locations of these chart patterns.

Hopefully, you were able to pick out the ascending triangles in February and April.

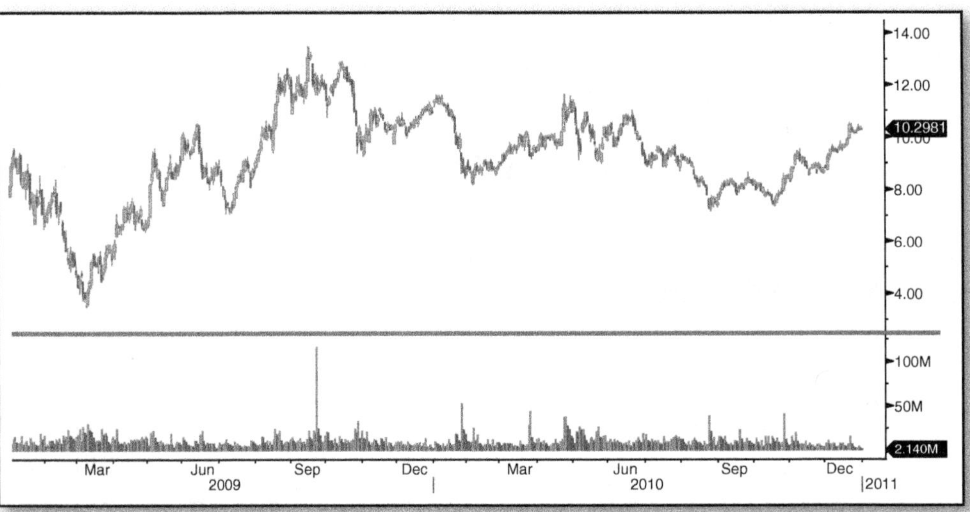

FIGURE 48.17 CX US Equity (Cemex SAB de CV).

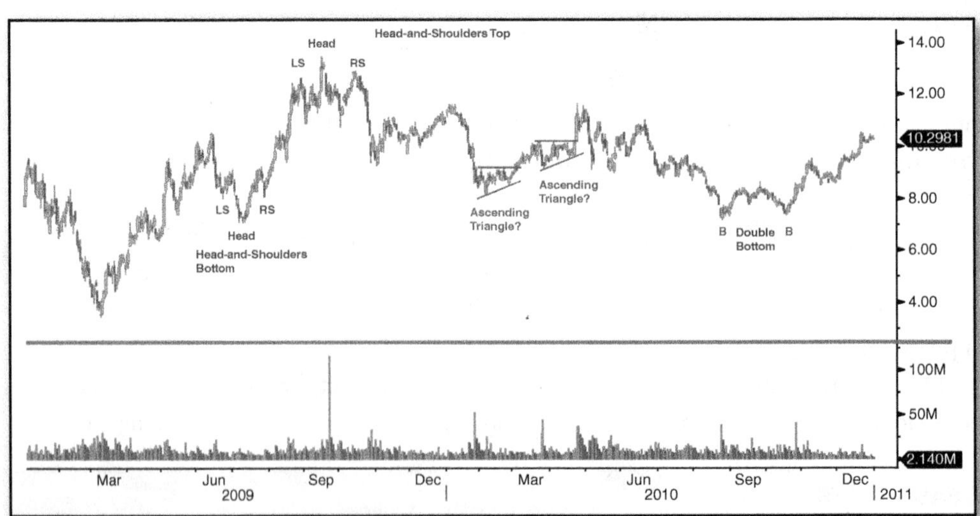

FIGURE 48.18 CX US Equity (Cemex SAB de CV).

The next section discusses descending triangles. Think of them as ascending triangles who forgot to refill their anti-depressant medication.

Test Yourself

Answer these questions with true or false.

1. The bottom trendline of an ascending triangle has a horizontal slope.
2. The top trendline can slant, but not too much.
3. The apex is where the trendlines converge.
4. Directly above or below the triangle apex is a likely turning point.
5. Ascending triangles break out upward most of the time.

Answers: 1. False; 2. True; 3. True; 4. True; 5. True

Descending Triangles

Descending triangles share characteristics of their ascending brothers including one horizontal trendline and another sloping.

Figure 48.19 shows two examples in red.

Starting in May, the stock drops like a Texas hailstone and slams into support at A, bounces several times and forms a descending triangle.

Points A, B, and C highlight valleys that align along a horizontal bottom trendline. Along the top, peaks D, E, and F touch another line, but this one slopes downward. The two trendlines merge at the triangle's apex.

Volume trends downward (G) until spiking on the breakout day, and that behavior is typical of many chart patterns.

Be still my heart: This is an example of a trading setup that I love. Price breaks out downward but reverses, pushes upward, and closes above the top of the triangle. When it does that, it busts the pattern. Busted patterns can lead to good performance, as this example shows.

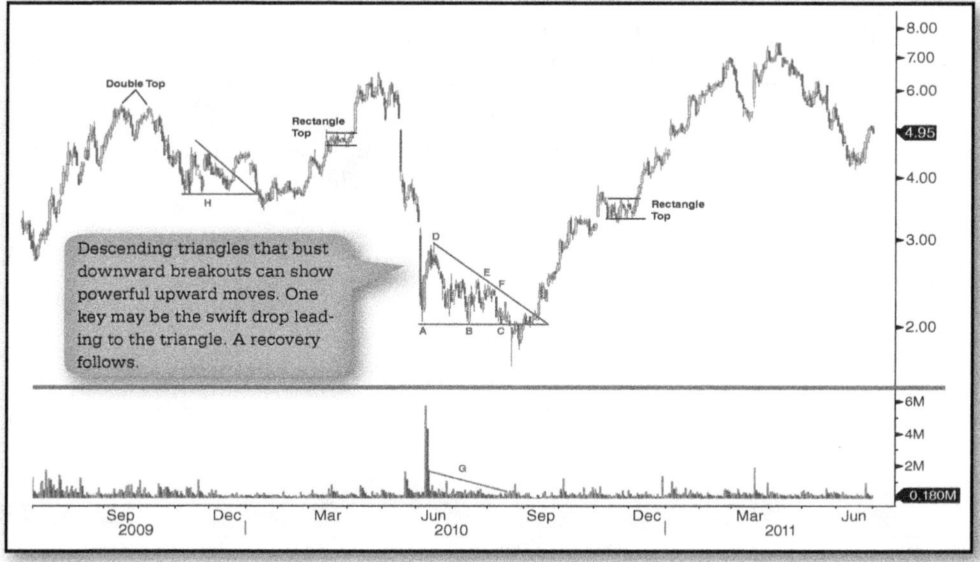

FIGURE 48.19 **NWY US Equity (New York & Co Inc).**

I was hesitant to show triangle H because the bottom trendline, although shown flat, is probably better drawn sloping upward. If you redraw it, the pattern becomes a symmetrical triangle, the subject of the next section. However, the bottoms are close enough to the trendline that the pattern qualifies as a descending triangle, too.

KEY POINT:
A descending triangle is a wedge-shaped chart pattern that breaks out downward most often. It can act as a reversal or continuation of the price trend.

Identification Guidelines

The following table lists the important characteristics that help identify descending triangles.

Characteristic	Discussion
Horizontal bottom line	Price along the bottom follows a horizontal trend.
Down-sloping top line	Price along the top slopes downward, following a trendline.
Price crossing	Price must cross the pattern from side to side, filling the triangle with movement. Avoid patterns with excessive white space in the center of the triangle.
Volume	Volume in the pattern recedes and can be especially low the day before the breakout.
Breakout	Can be in any direction, but is downward the majority of the time.

SMART INVESTOR TIP
If price touches the bottom trendline only twice, it should touch the down-sloping trendline at least three times. This is not a requirement, but five touches for many chart patterns works well to help avoid selecting boneheaded ones.

To help explain the guidelines, look at Figure 48.20.

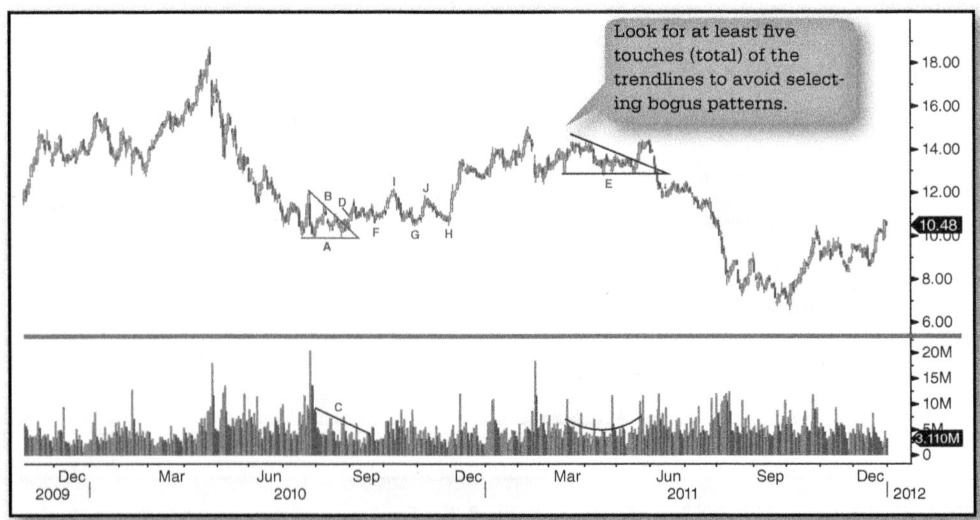

FIGURE 48.20 MAS US Equity (Masco Corp).

The bottom of triangle A shows three touches of a horizontal trendline. The valleys do not bottom at exactly the same price, but they come close. They *look* as if they belong on the same trendline.

Along the top, B, another trendline connects peaks that form at successively lower levels and yet still touch the trendline. I look for three touches along the diagonal if only two touch the bottom. That is a safety measure to prevent selecting triangles that are just random squiggles on the price chart.

Price crosses the triangle from side to side, leaving no room for white space. This is another important safety tip to avoid selecting bogus patterns.

> **SMART INVESTOR TIP**
> Avoid excessive white space between the two trendlines when selecting descending triangles. Price should cross the triangle plenty of times to fill the area.

Volume typically recedes in the chart pattern, but do not discard a descending triangle just because the volume pattern shows increasing volume. Triangle E has U-shaped volume and yet it is a valid descending triangle.

Price can break out of a descending triangle in any direction, but most often, it will be downward.

Look at points F through J. Is this a descending triangle? Yes. I dislike only two touches on the top, and the bottom trendline could be straighter, but the combination works.

There is another descending triangle on the chart that is not marked. Where is it? Go look for it before I tell you where it is.

Hint: Look on the far left of the chart.

In mid-November 2009, the stock began forming a descending triangle that extended to early January, breaking out upward. It has three touches on the top and three on the bottom.

Descending Triangle Psychology

Suppose you are a large institutional investor that wants to own Cemex, pictured in Figure 48.21, at $5 a share.

When the stock drops to $5, you buy (A). Notice the associated rise in volume.

I watch the ticker tape and see large blocks roll across my screen at $5 and below, so I conduct research and discover that the stock represents a compelling value. I buy too. Together, along with other buyers, we send the price moving up.

When the stock hits $6, I dump the turkey, pass Go, and collect my $200. Other sellers that view it as overvalued decide to cash in as well (D).

This selling pressure causes price to ease lower and eventually trigger more buying at a lower price (B). When the stock rises, those that missed selling as the stock approached $6 sell now.

The cycle of buying and selling continues at E, C, F, and G. At G, well into the traditional worst performing month of the year (September), selling pressure

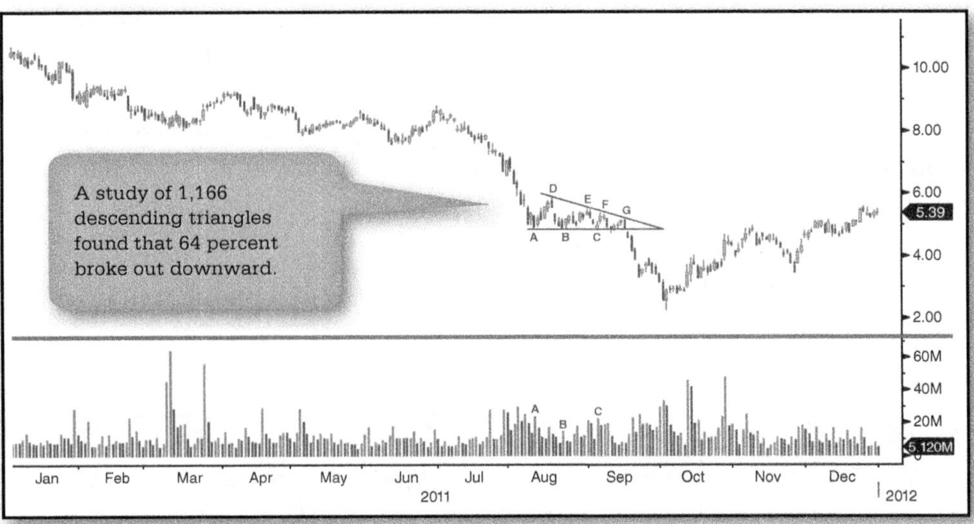

FIGURE 48.21 CX US Equity (Cemex SAB de CV).

increases, overwhelming buying demand, forcing the stock to push through support. The stock tumbles.

The footprint that remains on the chart outlines a descending triangle.

Variations

Look at Figure 48.22 because it reveals a flaw in pattern identification.

Price anchors the bottom of the chart pattern at A and B with minor low trendline touches at the same price. Along the top, price touches the trendline multiple times on the way to C. The peak at C pokes up through the top of the triangle, staging a breakout.

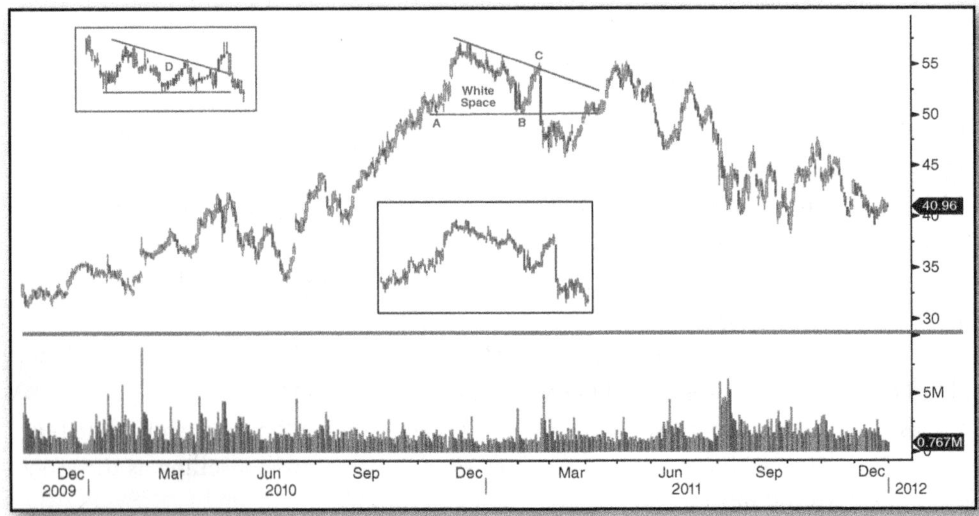

FIGURE 48.22 EXPD US Equity (Expeditors International ofWashington Inc).

What is wrong with this triangle? It contains too much white space in the middle of the pattern. Price does not cross the triangle from side to side, filling the chart pattern with price movement.

KEY POINT:
A descending triangle forms when buyers acquire the stock at a fixed price, forming a line of support. Others sell when the stock becomes overpriced.

If you look at the blue inset, with the triangle boundaries removed, you can see that this is nothing more than the stock climbing to a peak and withdrawing. It is not a triangle.

SMART INVESTOR TIP
It is helpful to look at a price chart without any trendlines connecting the pattern boundaries to make sure that what you are seeing is really a chart pattern. Can you draw each trendline a different way, by connecting other nearby peaks or valleys? Will others see the same pattern as you? If there are doubts, then skip the pattern and look for another one.

Compare pattern ABC with the one in the red inset at D. The D triangle shows plenty of price crossings as well as trendline touches spaced throughout the triangle. Image D is how a descending triangle should look.

Exercise

You will likely have difficulty finding a descending triangle in Figure 48.23. Here is a hint: Look for the down-sloping trendline first. You should also find a double bottom. Another hint? Both are large patterns.

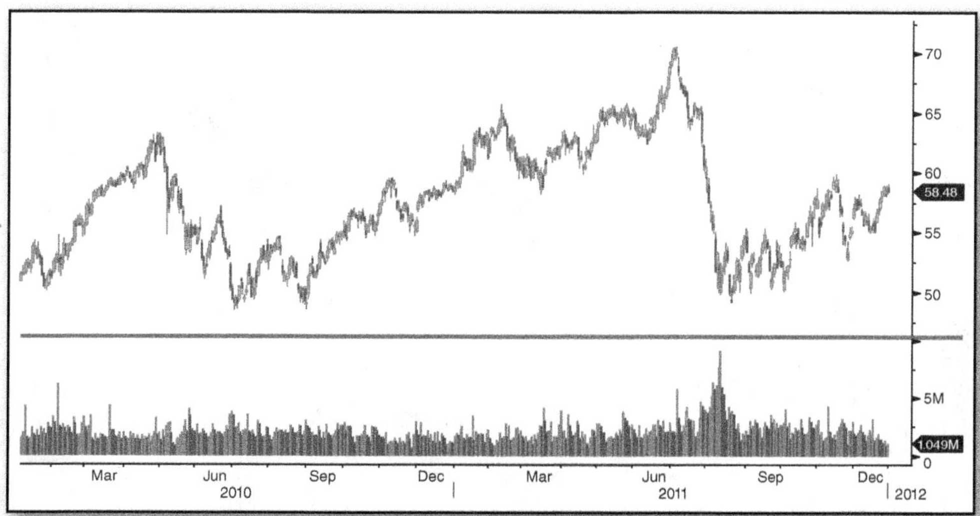

FIGURE 48.23 NOC US Equity (Northrop Grumman Corp).

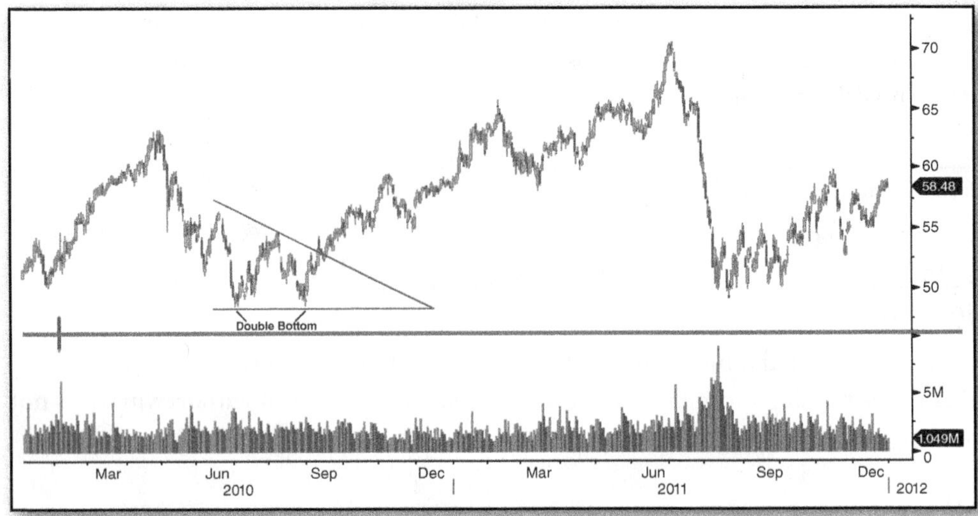

FIGURE 48.24 NOC US Equity (Northrop Grumman Corp).

The next chart (see Figure 48.24) reveals the descending triangle. It has three touches on the top and two on the bottom. Price crosses the pattern and fills the white space, but because the triangle is so large, it may look like too much white space. It takes time for price to cross the pattern, so it is fine.

Notice that the double bottom shares the triangle's space. Both are valid chart patterns.

I think that the next exercise is easy, but then I know where to look. You will find a descending triangle, two double tops, one double bottom, and a symmetrical triangle. Try to find as many of those as you can. (See Figure 48.25.)

The descending triangle is at A, in red. Price touches each trendline, forming a beautiful wedge shape. It reminds me of the rubber doorstop I use to keep the wind from slamming the door shut in summer. (See Figure 48.26.)

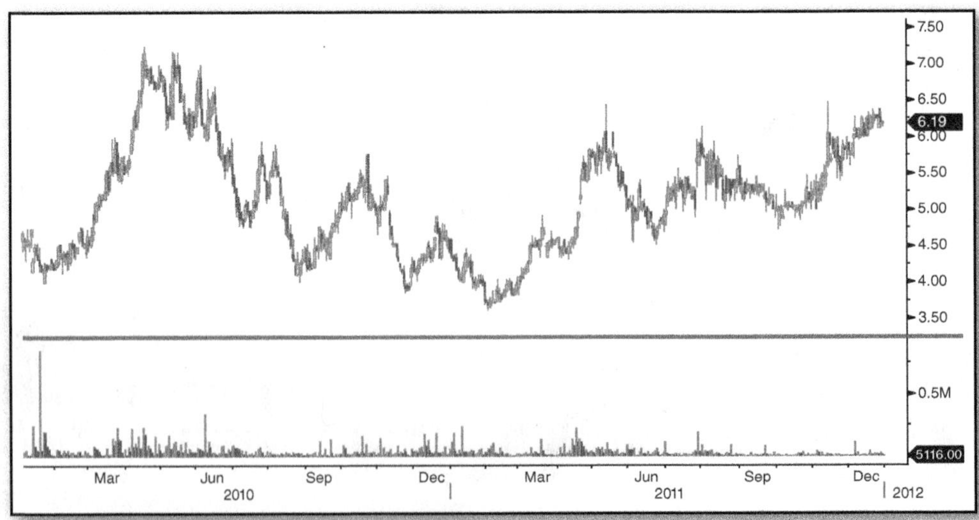

FIGURE 48.25 CACH US Equity (Cache Inc).

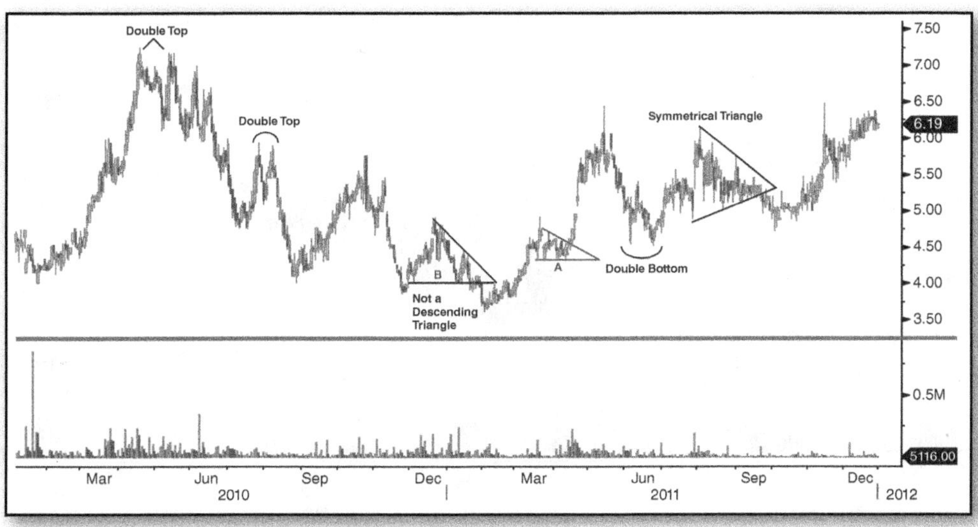

FIGURE 48.26 CACH US Equity (Cache Inc).

You probably did not select triangle B, and that is good because it is not a descending triangle. There is too much white space between the trendlines to qualify this as a valid triangle.

On the right of the chart is a symmetrical triangle. It is a more complicated shape, with two converging trendlines. Unlike ascending and descending triangles, the shape of the pattern does not hint at the breakout direction. Symmetrical triangles are as plentiful as fleas on a dog, and can be just as annoying. They are the subject of the next section.

Test Yourself

Answer these statements with true or false.

1. An ascending triangle has a horizontal top trendline.
2. A descending triangle has a down-sloping top trendline.
3. At least four touches, total, of the two trendlines are required, but five or more is better.

Answers: 1. True; 2. True; 3. True

Symmetrical Triangles

Symmetrical triangles take pattern recognition to a new level. We ditch horizontal trendlines and use diagonal ones to outline the pattern.

Figure 48.27 shows a pair of symmetrical triangles swimming in a price sea. They remind me of angelfish I had in my 55-gallon aquarium when I lived near Boston.

I like the red triangle at C. Price touches two sloping trendlines that merge at the triangle apex. Directly above the apex, in this example, is a price peak. I have

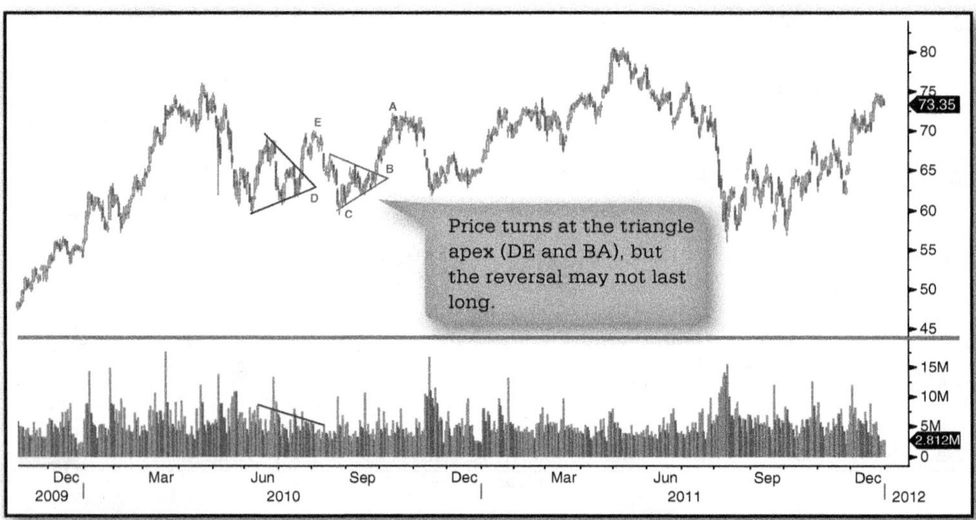

FIGURE 48.27 **BA US Equity (Boeing Co/The).**

mentioned this apex and turning behavior before because it works well and gives traders a clue where the trend might shift.

Notice that the blue triangle apex (D) sits beneath peak E. It is not as timely (it comes late as price is about to slide) as the other triangle's prediction, but it is valuable, too.

Triangle D cuts through price on both trendlines, so it is not ideal. Volume trends lower as it does in many symmetrical triangles.

Identification Guidelines

The following table lists important characteristics that help identify symmetrical triangles.

Characteristic	Discussion
Two sloping and converging trendlines	Price follows two sloping trendlines that join at the triangle apex.
Price crossing	Price must cross the pattern from side to side, filling the triangle with movement. Avoid patterns with excessive white space in the center of the triangle.
Volume	Volume in the pattern recedes and can be especially low the day before the breakout.
Breakout	Can be in any direction.
Duration	Should be longer than three weeks; otherwise, they could be pennants.

KEY POINT:

A symmetrical triangle appears like an angelfish bounded by two converging trendlines. The breakout can be in any direction.

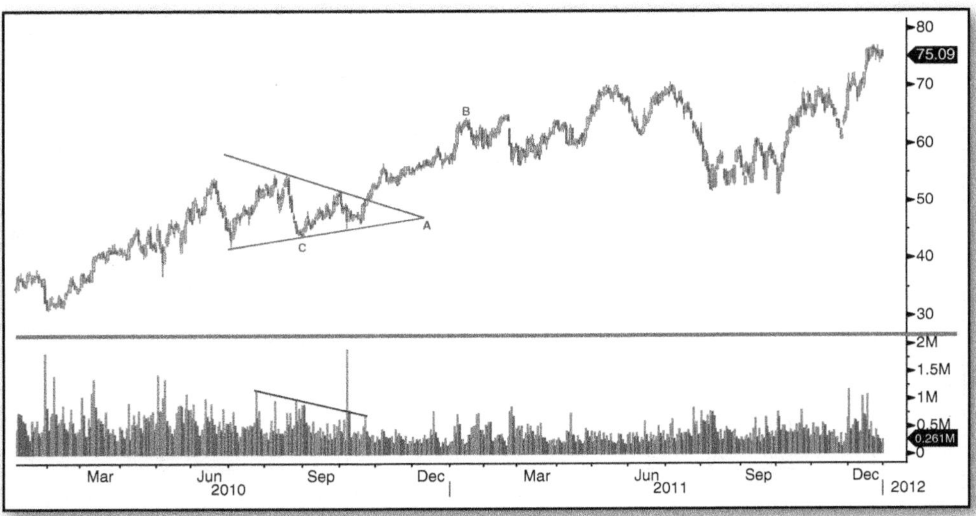

FIGURE 48.28 ALK US Equity (Alaska Air Group Inc).

To help explain the guidelines, look at Figure 48.28.

This is an example of a large symmetrical triangle at C, bounded by red trendlines. Price touches each trendline three times (twice is a minimum, but I like to see three) in distinct minor highs and minor lows. As price crosses the chart pattern from side to side, it fills the white space. Since this is a large example, do not expect price to fill the entire area. White space will be present, but should not look like a cavity too large for a dentist to fill.

Volume recedes, but is often irregular looking. Do not discard a symmetrical triangle because the volume pattern is wrong.

The breakout can be in any direction, including horizontal where price oozes out the front of the triangle.

Most symmetrical triangles should be longer than three weeks to help distinguish them from pennants. The exception is when a pennant is missing a flagpole. In that case, the pennant is really a small symmetrical triangle.

FAST FACTS

The breakout often occurs 70 to 75 percent of the way to the triangle's apex according to a study of 1,347 symmetrical triangles.

SMART INVESTOR TIP

Symmetrical triangles should be at least three weeks long; otherwise, they are pennants. Pennants always rest upon a flagpole (a straight-line price run), so if the pole is missing, the pattern is a symmetrical triangle.

Symmetrical Triangle Psychology

Symmetrical triangles are the epitome of confusion. Price does not know which way to trend. Figure 48.29 shows another example of a symmetrical triangle.

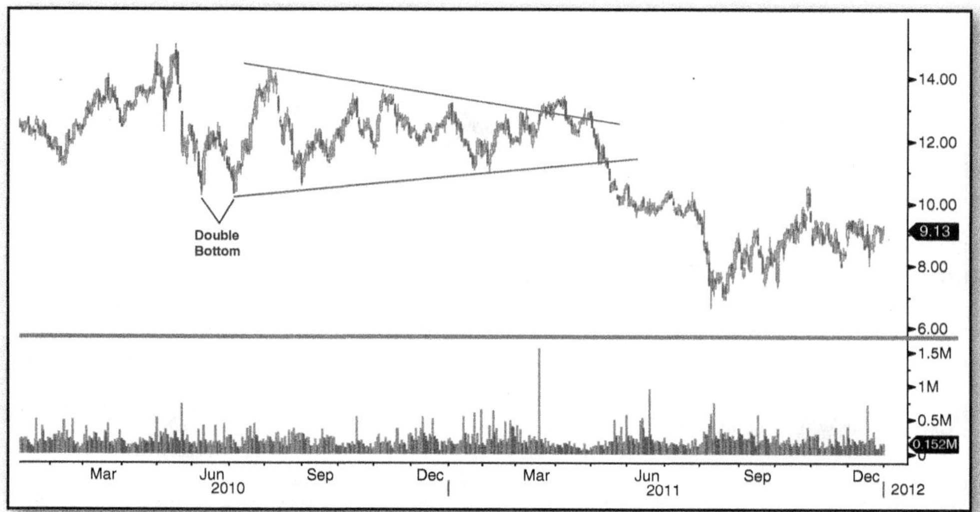

FIGURE 48.29 **GFF US Equity (Griffon Corp).**

At the start of the pattern, bulls push price up in the hopes that the double bottom will **confirm** as a valid chart pattern. That means price must close above the highest peak between the two bottoms, which it does.

> **DEFINITION:**
> **Confirm**
> Price confirms many patterns when the stock closes outside the pattern boundaries. For example, in a double bottom, price must close above the highest peak between the two bottoms; otherwise, it is not a double bottom.

The straight-line run continues until meeting overhead resistance set up by bears wanting to dump the stock at a price they believe is too rich.

Their selling forces price back down. When it approaches the price level of the prior minor low, eager bulls who missed their opportunity to buy do so now. Others may add to existing positions. That buying demand pushes price up until meeting bears wanting to take profits.

The oscillations continue, with bears taking profits earlier and bulls buying sooner, tightening the coil. Eventually, buying demand outpaces selling pressure and the coil releases, springing upward in this example.

Almost as soon as that happens, the bears regroup and force price back down, and they keep selling until the stock bottoms in August. What remains on the chart is a long symmetrical triangle.

Variations

Figure 48.30 shows several chart patterns, including some that hint of being symmetrical triangles, but are not.

Look at triangle A. What attracts me are the three touches of the bottom trendline. However, the top shows only two touches. That is not optimum.

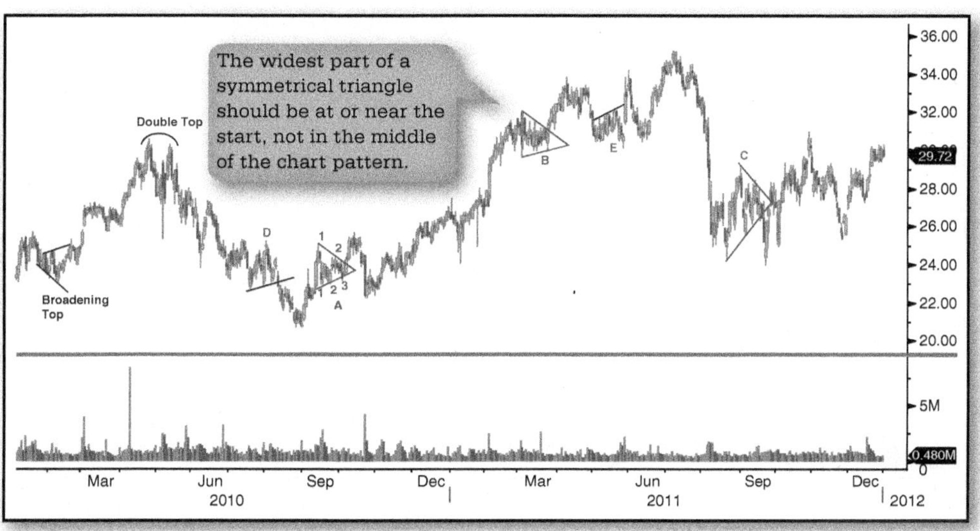

FIGURE 48.30 ASNA US Equity (Ascena Retail Group Inc.).

Triangle B is flawed because erasing the first touch on the bottom makes the line horizontal (but it may be difficult to see).

The top of triangle C is near the middle of the chart pattern instead of the start, making it difficult to approve as a valid triangle, too. Nevertheless, all three qualify as symmetrical triangles even though none is perfect.

Now look at pattern D. Along the bottom is an up-sloping trendline with three touches. Peak D is in the middle of the pattern. Using D as the start of the triangle would make it look too lopsided, too unbalanced. It is not a symmetrical triangle.

Confused? If any chart pattern looks questionable, look for another one. They are as plentiful as ants at a picnic.

Pattern E has many touches along the peaks, but too much white space on the bottom. It is not a symmetrical triangle.

Figure 48.31 gives a warning of how not to draw a symmetrical triangle.

Price along the bottom touches points A and B, widely separated. Along the top are two minor high touches.

Look at C. The white space is obvious. This is not a symmetrical triangle. It is just a peak with red lines drawn to resemble one. The inset shows the peak without the lines.

Exercise

In Figure 48.32, I found three symmetrical triangles, two double tops, and a head-and-shoulders top, but no partridge in a pear tree. See if you can find the chart patterns as well.

Figure 48.33 shows the answers. The symmetrical triangle at A is the easiest to find, probably because it is large with so many trendline touches.

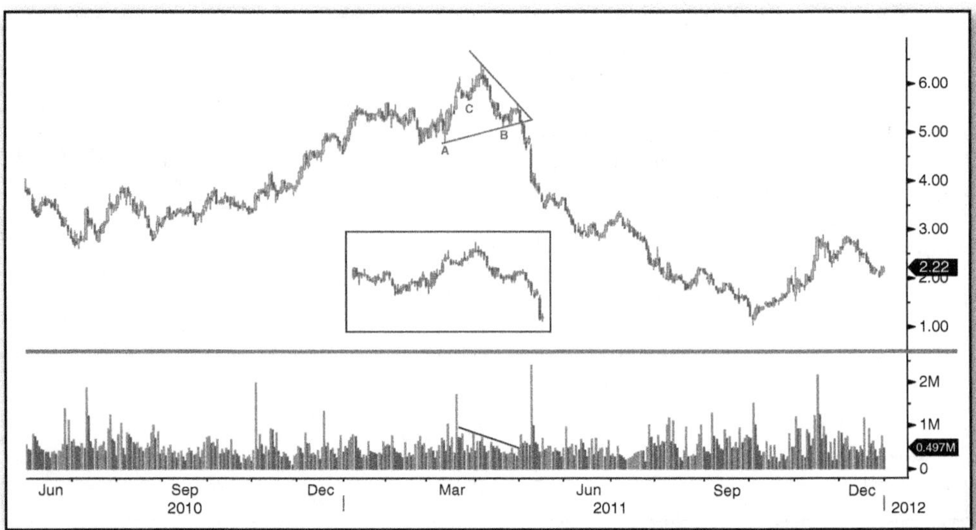

FIGURE 48.31 HW US Equity (Headwaters Inc).

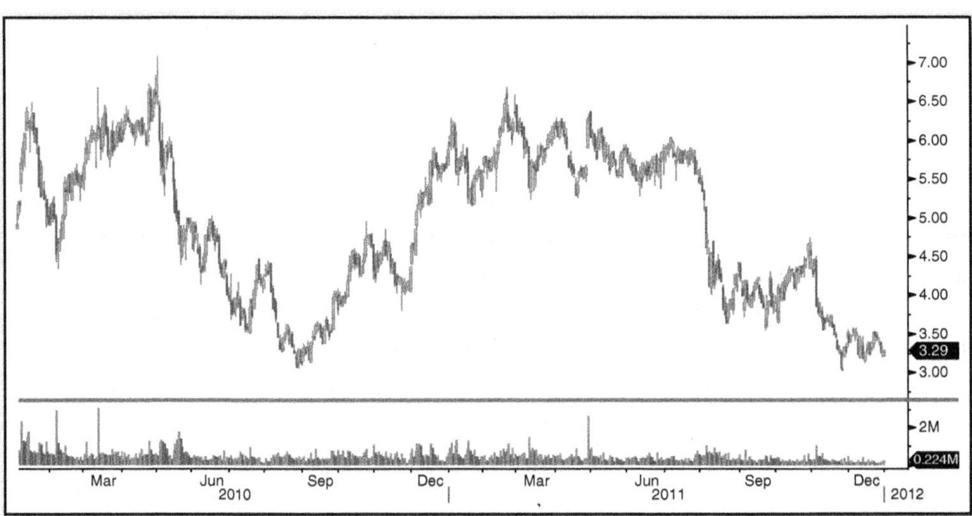

FIGURE 48.32 MEA US Equity (Metalico Inc).

FIGURE 48.33 MEA US Equity (Metalico Inc).

Triangle B is harder to spot because the top spike upward at the start might not register as a minor high touch. Without it, the pattern would resemble an ascending triangle.

Triangle C is the hardest to find. It seems buried in an area where price is directionless. There are three touches along the top trendline, but only two along the bottom. Notice that D does not qualify as a touch since it is not a minor low. D is part of a straight-line run downward that just happens to gap where the trendline touches.

SMART INVESTOR TIP

To avoid selecting bogus symmetrical triangles, look for at least three touches of each trendline.

Figure 48.34 has three symmetrical triangles. Also look for a descending triangle, head-and-shoulders bottom, and Big W, which is a type of double bottom with tall sides.

Figure 48.35 shows the answers. If you picked A as a symmetrical triangle, be careful because candle A is not a minor low and should not be used to anchor the start of the pattern. However, the pattern does appear wedge shaped. It is a symmetrical triangle.

Triangle B is large with plenty of trendline touches and should have been easy to spot.

Point C is the same height as D. That means the down-sloping trendline does not quite touch C. Even so, I think it is fine as a symmetrical triangle.

I hope you found the descending triangle. The Big W, even if you did not know what to look for, has an evocative name that just speaks to me. Perhaps it did to you as well. If you left your hearing aid turned off, then you could be talking to yourself.

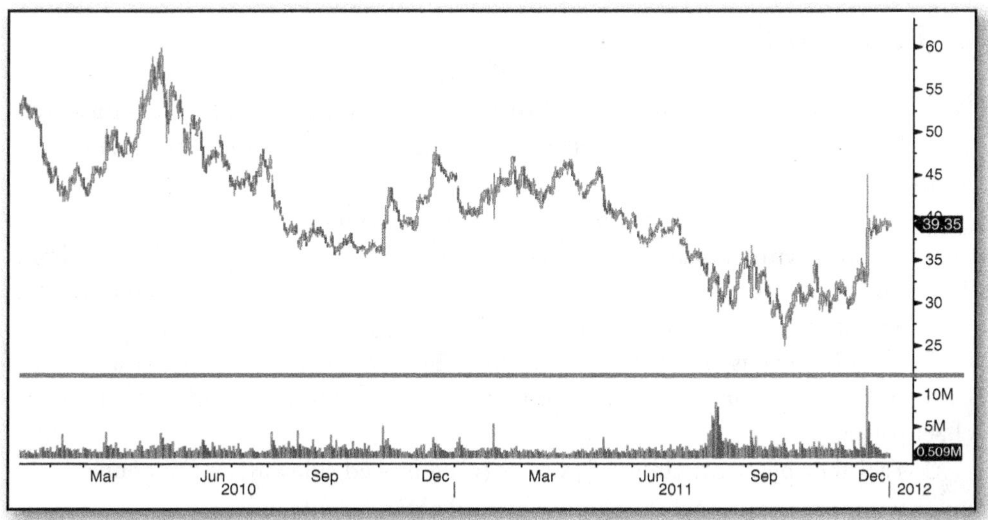

FIGURE 48.34 VMC US Equity (Vulcan Materials Co).

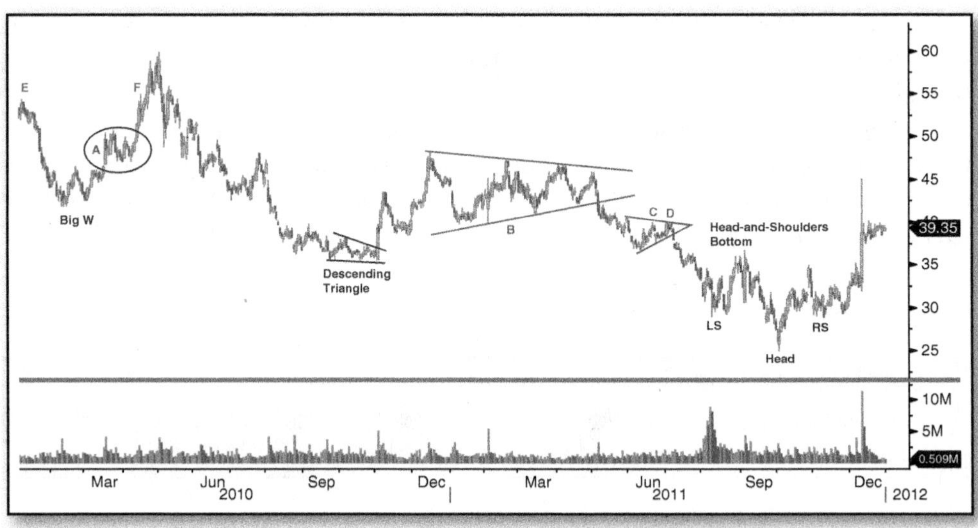

FIGURE 48.35 VMC US Equity (Vulcan Materials Co).

The next section discusses flags and pennants, so we will have a better understanding of those patterns and what a flagpole is. Why is there no such thing as a pennantpole?

Test Yourself

Answer these statements with true or false.

1. Ascending and descending triangles have only one slanted trendline, but symmetrical triangles have two.
2. Symmetrical triangles longer than three weeks are called pennants when they rest upon a flagpole.
3. If price does not confirm a chart pattern, you are looking at squiggles on a price chart and not a chart pattern.
4. Price confirms a symmetrical triangle when it first pierces the trendline border.

Answers : 1. True; 2. False; 3. True; 4. False

Flags and Pennants

Pennants remind me of those pointed streamers that line roped-off areas at festivals. They are the same as flags except that the trendlines bounding the pattern converge. In flags, they are parallel.

Figure 48.36 shows a sprinkling of flags and pennants.

Let us start with pennant B. This is the kind of pennant that traders dream about. The trend begins at A in a straight-line run up to the pennant (B). Price consolidates, forming a triangle shape (the pennant). After that, price resumes a strong move up to C. The AB move is about the same as BC. Thus, the pennant can act as a half-staff pattern; it can appear midway in a price trend. The same is true of flags and other chart patterns, too.

C is another pennant. Unlike B, where price moved sideways in the pennant, this one has a more traditional slope—downward against the trend.

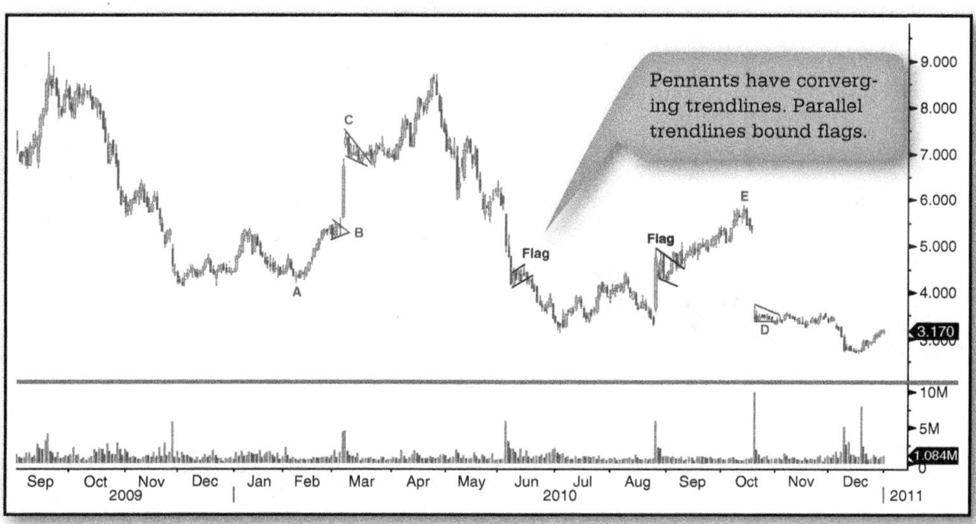

FIGURE 48.36 CWTR US Equity (Coldwater Creek Inc).

Pennant D, on the far right of the chart, looks like a small version of a descending triangle, a pattern that has a flat bottom and down-sloping top.

Flags have parallel trendlines whereas pennants converge. The flags appear in blue, but not because they have been holding their breath like a child throwing a tantrum.

> **KEY POINT:**
> **Flags and Pennants**
> Flags are short chart patterns that appear as small rectangles in a strong price run. They can act as reversals, but are usually continuation patterns.
>
> A pennant is a short triangular-shaped chart pattern. It can act as a trend reversal or continuation pattern.

Identification Guidelines

The following table lists important characteristics to help identify flags and pennants. For such simple patterns, why does it seem so complicated?

Characteristic	Discussion
Price trends	Flags and pennants always rest upon a flagpole, so look for a strong price run leading to them.
Two converging trendlines	For flags, price follows two parallel or nearly parallel trendlines. For pennants, price follows two converging trendlines.
Volume	Volume in the pattern recedes.
Breakout	Can be in any direction.
Duration	Flags and pennants are shorter than three weeks.

The easiest way to find a flag or pennant is to begin with the flagpole. Look for a straight-line price run. Price will consolidate along that run. When it does, it can take the shape of a flag or pennant.

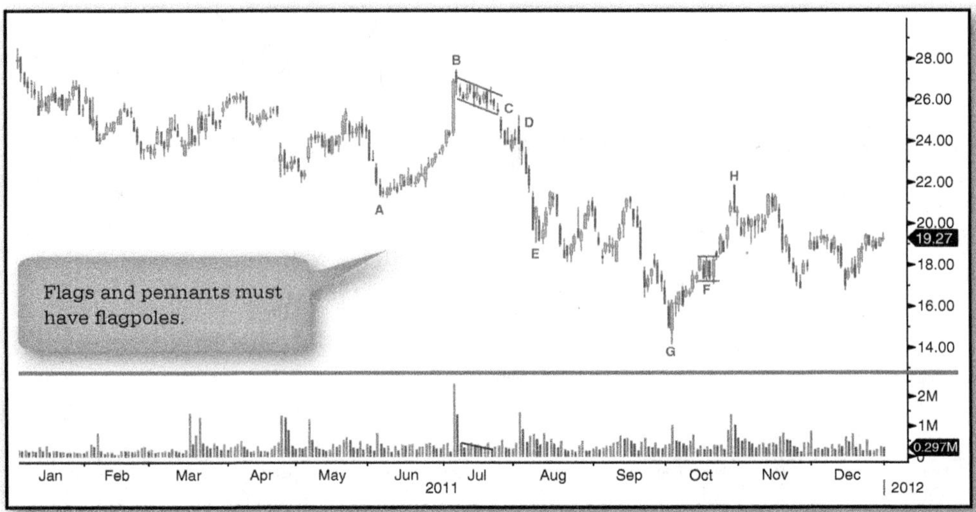

FIGURE 48.37 ABFS US Equity (Arkansas Best Corp).

To help explain the guidelines, look at Figure 48.37.

The flag pattern begins with the flagpole, AB. If a strong trend (a straight-line price run) does not exist, then look elsewhere. Atop the pole, price consolidates and forms flag BC. After that, price breaks out downward (C) and drops, pulling back briefly at D, but then powering down to the launch price and digging a crater (E).

SMART INVESTOR TIP

A flag or pennant appears atop a flagpole. For easy identification, look for the flagpole first—a strong straight-line price run.

Flags should form between two parallel or nearly parallel trendlines. The two lines do not have to be exactly parallel. Pennants should form between two converging trendlines. For both flags and pennants, trendline touch count is not important.

SMART INVESTOR TIP

How often price touches the trendline borders is not important for flags and pennants.

Price in the flag or pennant can slope in any direction, including sideways, but is usually against the prevailing trend. In this case, the trend is up from A to B and the flag slopes down from B to C.

Volume typically recedes in a flag or pennant just as it does in many other chart patterns. The breakout can be in any direction, too, but usually follows the trend leading to the flag or pennant.

SMART INVESTOR TIP

A flag or pennant can slope in any direction, but most often, it will lean against the prevailing price trend.

Flags and pennants are short, no longer than three weeks. This is an arbitrary value. What you are looking for is a small knot of congestion in a strong price run. Once the knot unties (breaks out), price should continue on its way.

Flag F is notable because it rests in the middle of the GH move.

Flag and Pennant Psychology

Figure 48.38 highlights one pennant and one flag.

At A, the smart money began buying, believing or knowing that a good earnings report was coming.

Two days later, the company announced earnings and raised their outlook to the top end of the target range while increasing the dividend.

Buying demand propelled the stock higher like an overly excited kid gobbling Halloween candy. Then the bears returned to the trading table and started a food fight with the bulls. The fight between evenly matched opponents pushed price sideways, forming the pennant. This one had a flat base and down-sloping top, suggesting a group of investors wanted to buy the stock at a set price (49.50) but stopped buying when price climbed too high. Their buying put a floor underneath the stock.

After the bears digested the news and ran for the exits, the bulls took over and sent the stock moving higher again, rising from C to D. Notice how one good earnings report can launch a stock toward the heavens. Or maybe it was the candy.

> **SMART INVESTOR TIP**
>
> If the chart pattern does not have a flagpole, then it is not a flag or a pennant.

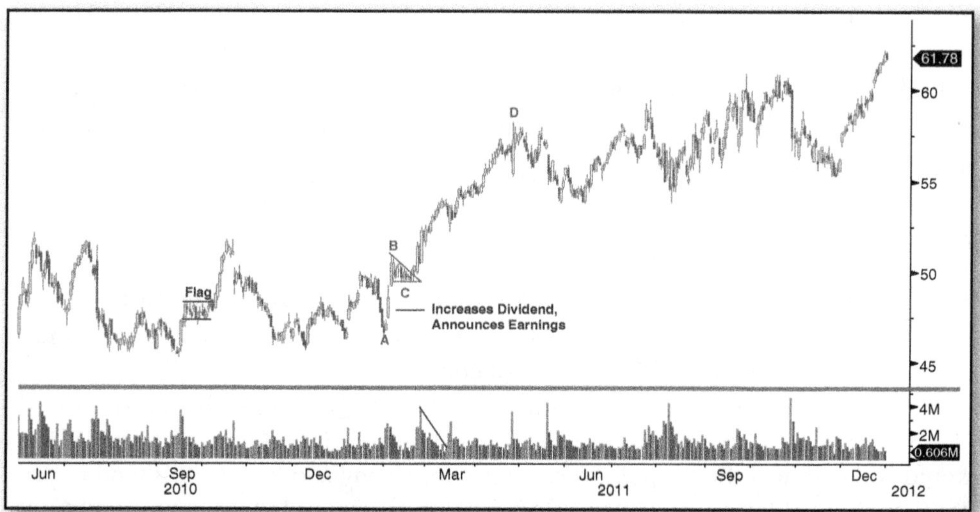

FIGURE 48.38 HSY US Equity (Hershey Co/The).

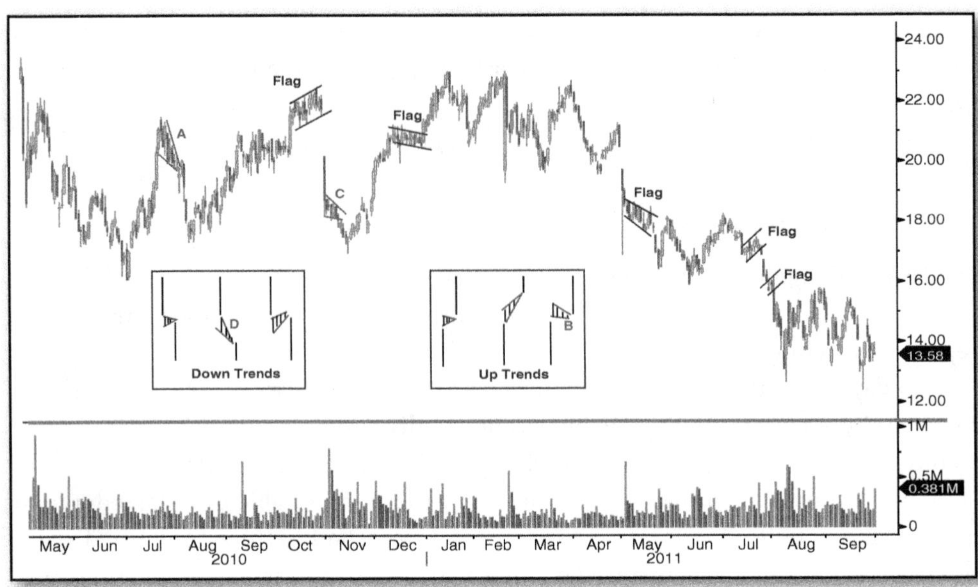

FIGURE 48.39 CKP US Equity (Checkpoint Systems Inc).

Variations

Figure 48.39 shows five flags (blue) and two pennants (red) with four additional variations in the inset. Although the insets show pennants, use your creative mind to redraw the pennant trendlines as parallel lines for flag variations.

Pennant A forms after a mediocre uptrend. I would call it powerful if price broke out of the pennant upward, but it does not. Rather, the pennant slopes downward, which is typical, but then price continues down, oozing out the end of the pennant like caulking. That configuration follows pattern B (except for a downward breakout, of course).

Pennant C forms after price gaps lower. The pennant boundary is irregular in shape, but highlights a small congestion region where price gathers its strength for the coming drop. That drop occurs, completing the configuration like that shown at D.

In the two insets, I show various pennant shapes in up and down trends. Be aware that pennants can break out in any direction, so expect that. I show only the patterns acting as continuations of the prevailing price trend and not reversals.

Exercise

Figure 48.40 has a multitude of flags. Try to find as many as you can that obey the identification guidelines discussed earlier. I found eight and stopped there. One is large and may not qualify. That is a hint, of course.

Figure 48.41 shows the answers. I numbered the flags, making them easier to see. Flag 5 is the likely offender to the three-week rule. It is about a month long. That would still be fine if the flagpole were long, too. Strong and long trends tend to precede extended sideways movement. This flag has the extended sideways movement, but the flagpole height is unexciting.

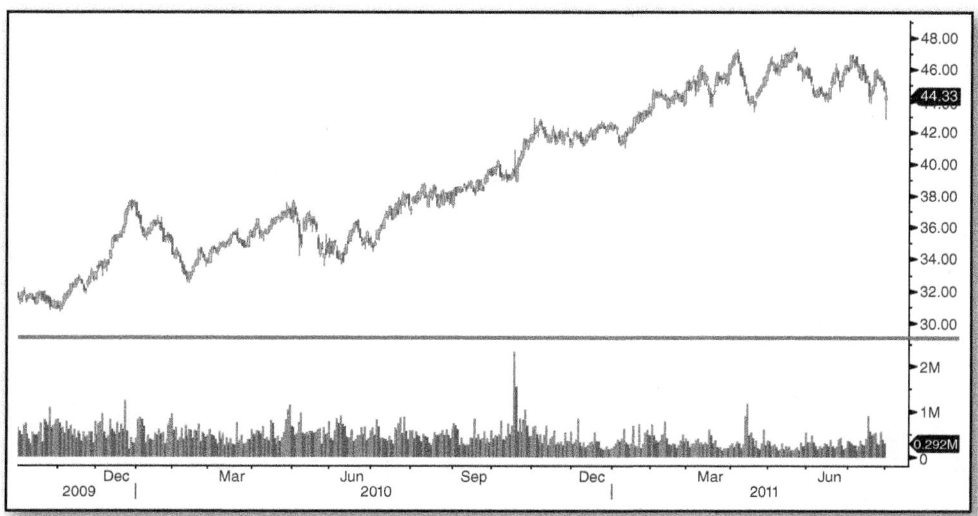

FIGURE 48.40 NST US Equity (NSTAR).

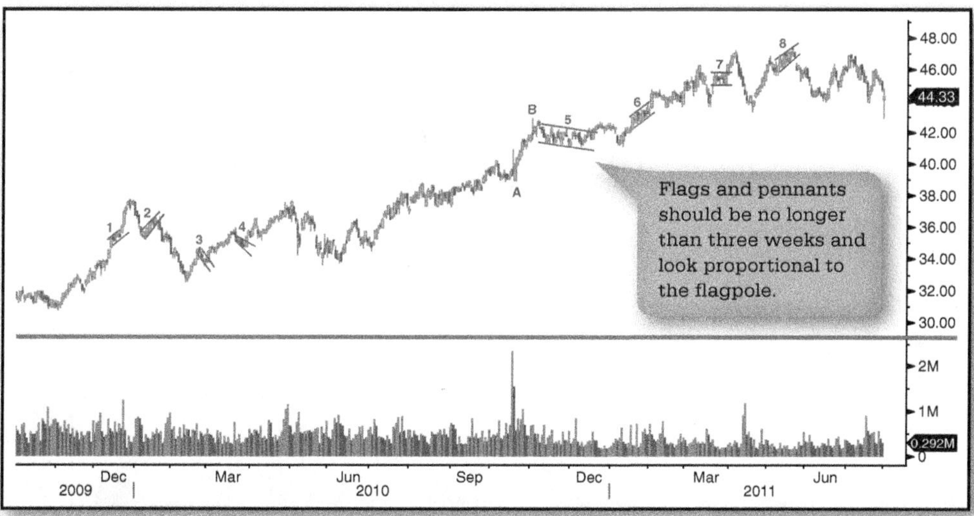

FIGURE 48.41 NST US Equity (NSTAR).

In other words, the flag or pennant should be proportional to the height of the flagpole. This pole begins at A and ends at B, which looks too short for the flag.

Are you rested enough to try again? Figure 48.42 shows pennants. Find as many as you can.

Hint: I found five.

Figure 48.43 shows the answers. Starting from the left at A, price begins trending to pennant B, breaking out upward and ending at C. The trend start (A) is important when the pennant acts as a half-staff pattern, as in this case.

SMART INVESTOR TIP

When looking for flags and pennants, try using a bar chart instead of a candlestick chart.

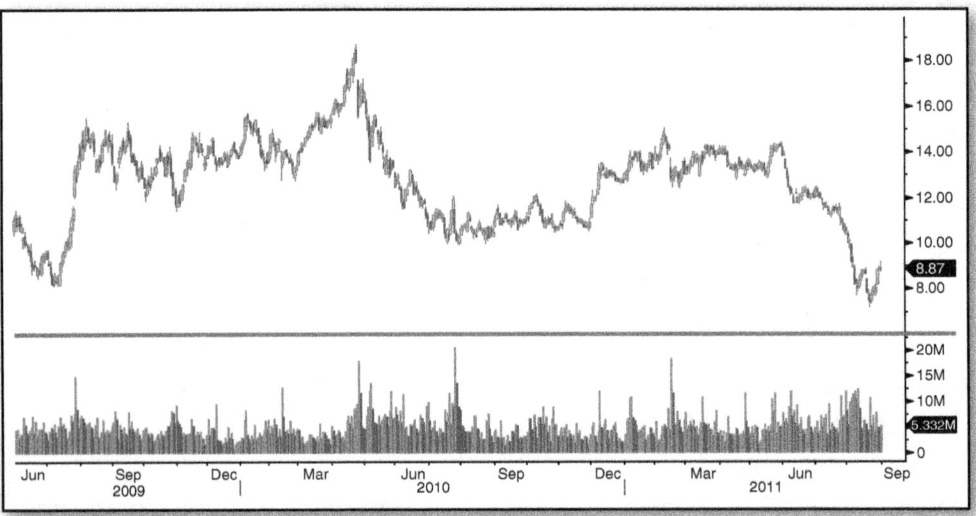

FIGURE 48.42 MAS US Equity (Masco Corp).

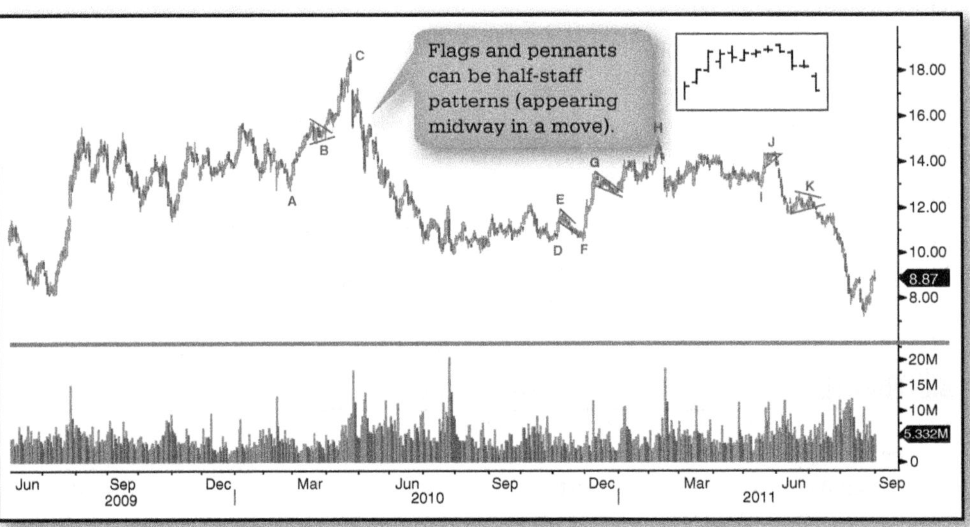

FIGURE 48.43 MAS US Equity (Masco Corp).

The rise from D to E matches the decline from E to F, only EF takes more time.

Pennant G is perhaps the prettiest on the chart. The trend begins at F and goes to H. The stock, from the bottom of G to H, only climbs about half the FG move.

You may argue that J is a flag and not a pennant, so I show the price action in the inset. The pattern resembles a small ascending triangle, but due to its size, becomes a pennant.

Pennant K is large and loose looking. Price meanders up and down within its boundaries. The straight-line run down from J looks proportional to the pennant size.

The next chapter shifts the focus from drawing trendlines to finding potholes that bottom near the same price. We call them double bottoms.

Test Yourself

Answer these statements with true or false.

1. One pennant variation happens when parallel trendlines form the pennant.
2. A pennant must have a flagpole; otherwise, it is not a pennant.
3. Pennants always appear midway in a strong price trend.
4. Since the duration of a flag has a maximum of three weeks, it appears only on the daily or intraday charts.
5. In a flag, price most often slants against the prevailing price trend.
6. A flag without a flagpole is like peanut butter without jelly (meaning they go together).
7. The flag and pennant size should be proportional to the flagpole length.

Answers: 1. False; 2. True; 3. False; 4. False; 5. True; 6. True; 7. True

CHAPTER 49

Tops and Bottoms

From Thomas N. Bulkowski, *Visual Guide to Chart Patterns* (Hoboken, New Jersey: John Wiley & Sons, 2002), Chapters 12–15.

Double Bottoms

This chapter begins discussing chart patterns not bounded by trendlines. How can you find them if not looking for straight or diagonal trendlines? You find them by looking for two potholes that bottom near the same price.

If I were to ask my brother to find a double bottom on a price chart, he might pick AB shown in Figure 49.1. Price from peak C forms a hill filled with moguls that my brother would love skiing down. At the bottom of that hill, the double bottom at AB acts as a reversal.

Is there more to correctly identifying a double bottom than finding two valleys? Yes.

Identification Guidelines

The following table shows the identification guidelines.

Characteristic	Discussion
Downward price trend	The short-term price trend leading to a double bottom is down.
Two valleys	Look for two valleys that bottom near the same price. Near means within about 5 percent. The bottoms should look as if they are at the same price.
Valley separation	The time between bottoms varies, but two to seven weeks results in the best performance.
Peak	The peak between the two bottoms should measure at least 10 percent, but exceptions are numerous, making this guideline almost useless.
Volume	Volume is higher on the left bottom than the right, but this is an observation, not a requirement.
Confirmation	Price must close above the highest peak between the two bottoms. If price closes below the lowest bottom before confirmation, it invalidates the double bottom.

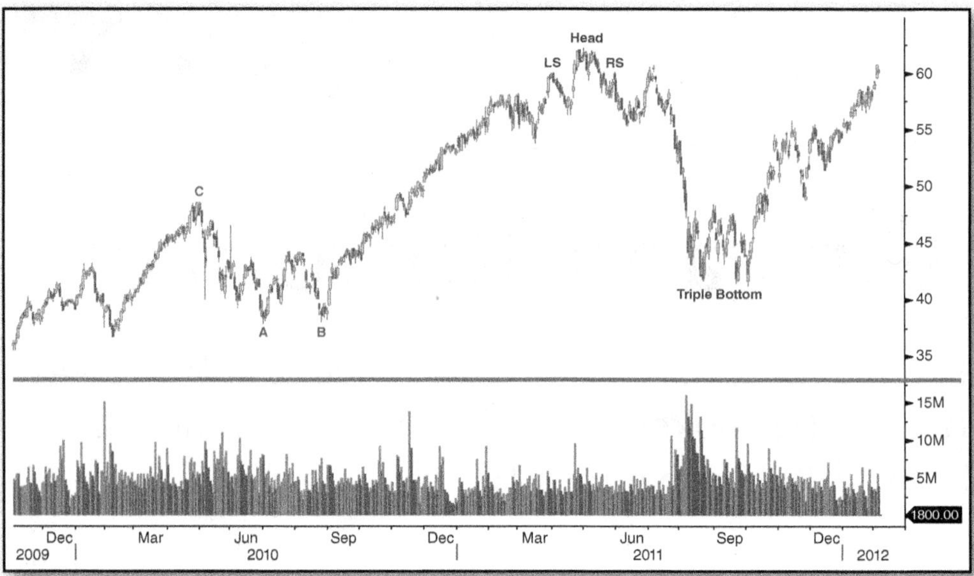

FIGURE 49.1 HON US Equity (Honeywell International Inc).

> **KEY POINT:**
> A double bottom is a twin valley pattern with valleys that bottom near the same price. The double bottom acts as a bullish reversal of the downward price trend.

Look at Figure 49.2 while we discuss identification guidelines.

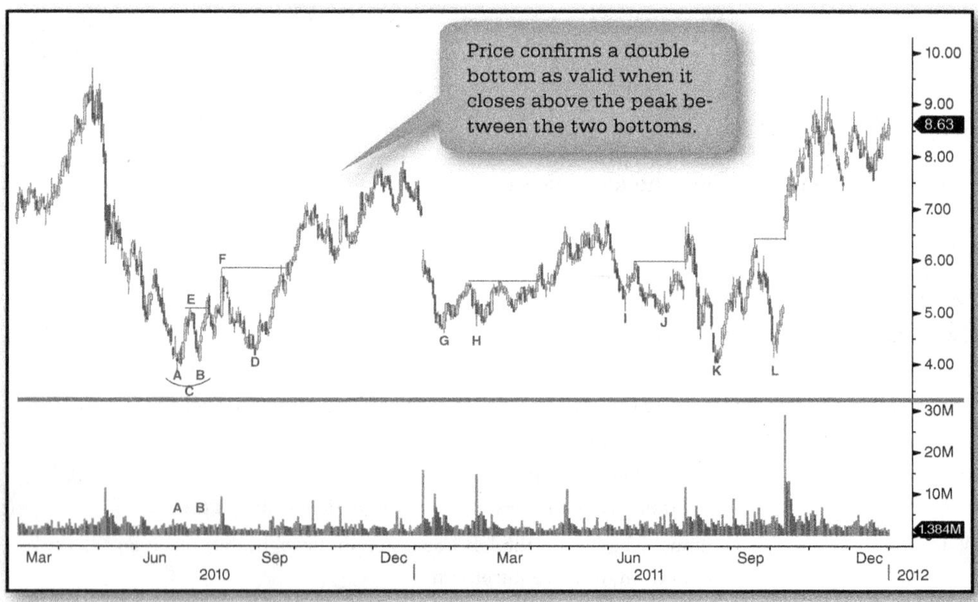

FIGURE 49.2 LIZ US Equity (Liz Claiborne Inc).

After trending down from the April peak, the stock bottoms at A, bounces up to E and down to B. The two valleys do not bottom at the same price, but they are just 17 cents apart (4 percent). On this scale, though, it looks as if an earthquake shifted the pavement.

The time between bottoms is about two weeks, but after studying thousands of double bottoms, the separation is not a concern.

The peak between the two bottoms, E, is supposed to be at least 10 percent above the lowest bottom. I do not even measure this nor do I care. What I am looking for is a reversal of the downward price trend.

SMART INVESTOR TIP

The time between bottoms and the price variation is less important than confirmation. An unconfirmed double bottom is just squiggles on a price chart.

Volume is often higher on the left bottom than the right, as in this case.

Confirmation is the key to double bottoms. Price must confirm the chart pattern. By that, I mean price must *close* above the highest peak (E) between the two bottoms (AB). If price closes below the lowest bottom first, it is not a double bottom. AB is a valid double bottom.

The figure also shows additional double bottoms at GH, IJ, and KL. If you consider AB as one bottom (C), then CD is also a double bottom. In all cases, the horizontal red line starting from the peak between the two bottoms marks confirmation. They point to where the stock closes above the peak.

SMART INVESTOR TIP

Reversal chart patterns, such as double bottoms, must have something to reverse. If the price trend leading down to the double bottom is shallow, do not expect a large rise after confirmation.

Double Bottom Psychology

Why do double bottoms form? Look at Figure 49.3 while I discuss one possible answer.

The figure shows a stock that I love to own. Why? Because it pays a tasty dividend while it bounces between the 30s and 50s. I buy below 40 and sell above 50 while collecting 5.5 percent in between. Yum!

Imagine that you are a big game hunter searching for income, and decide that when double bottom CD confirms, you will buy.

Unfortunately, price hides by tunneling down to A, invalidating the double bottom. The decline comes as a shock, so you sit paralyzed and just watch it weekly, wondering if the slide is over.

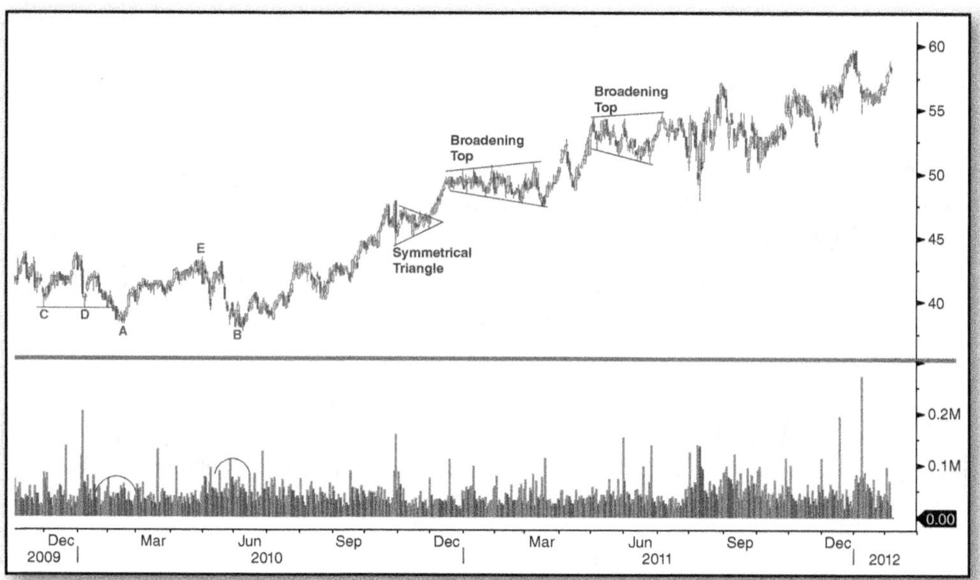

FIGURE 49.3 CHG US Equity (CH Energy Group Inc).

Eventually it bottoms at A, but you wait because you are not sure the decline has ended. When you look again, the stock has climbed too far to chase, despite the power of your hunting rifle.

At E, you vow that if the stock ever returns to the price level of A, you will bag it. The stock cooperates, reaching B. You shoot and score some shares!

Others do the same, putting a floor on the stock. Price rises, eventually confirming the twin valley pattern as a valid double bottom.

Who actually hunts like that? I do. I bought at 39.72 on June 3 (B) and sold it at 54 a year later, pocketing a 5.4 percent dividend along the way.

Variations

Double bottoms have several variations and Figure 49.4 shows three of them.

Pattern A is called an Eve & Eve double bottom. B is an **Eve & Adam**, and C is an Adam & Adam double bottom.

> **DEFINITION:**
> **Eve & Adam**
> Adam bottoms are narrow, often single-day price spikes. Eve is wider, more rounded looking. If Eve has price spikes, they are shorter and more numerous. Adam tends to remain narrow vertically whereas Eve broadens out.

The difference between Adam and Eve is the shape of the bottom. Adam bottoms are thin, narrow price spikes, often composed of a single day or two. Eve is wider and more rounded looking. If Eve has price spikes, they are more numerous and stubby.

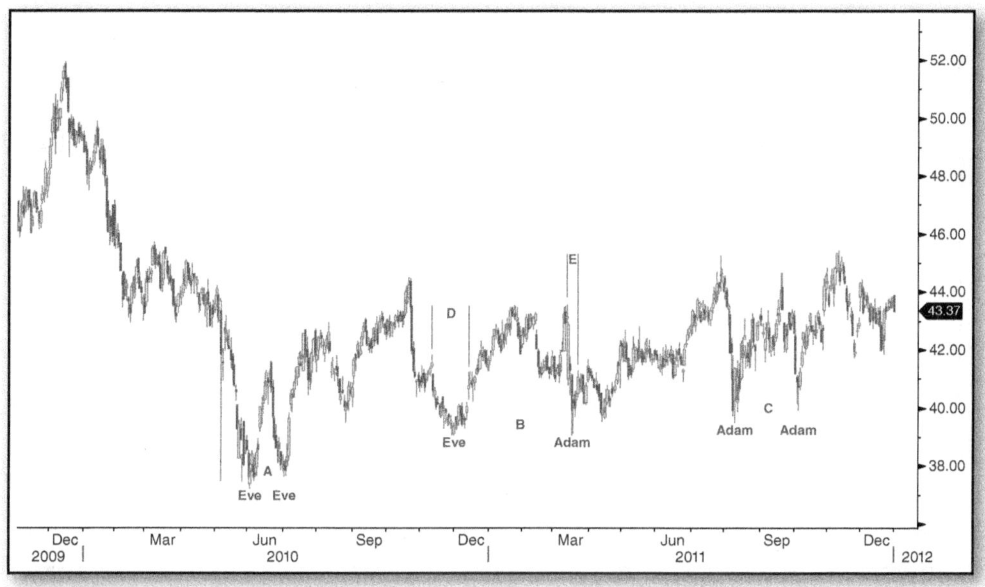

FIGURE 49.4 EXC US Equity (Exelon Corp).

Eve bottoms tend to be wide and widen out as price climbs. Adam bottoms tend to remain narrow.

For example, look at the width of Eve at B. The two vertical red lines at D show how it widens out. Compare that to the Adam bottom at E. The lines remain narrow.

I often use the width of the bottom in this manner to determine whether I am looking at an Eve or Adam bottom.

Another way to determine the type is to ask if the two bottoms look alike. If so, then you have Adam & Adam or Eve & Eve. Otherwise, it is a mix of the two: Eve & Adam or Adam & Eve.

SMART INVESTOR TIP

To differentiate between Adam and Eve bottoms, ask if the two bottoms look the same or different. If they look the same, then they are either Adam & Adam or Eve & Eve. If they look different, then they are either Adam & Eve or Eve & Adam.

Why the emphasis on Adam and Eve? Because the various types perform differently. Figure 49.5 shows the last two variations.

An Adam & Eve double bottom appears in February and it has a narrow bottom (three days wide) followed by a wide one. The chart pattern confirms as a valid double bottom when price closes above the peak between the two valleys.

The other double bottom variation is probably one you have never heard of. I call it an ugly double bottom. Price bottoms at A and then bounces to form a higher

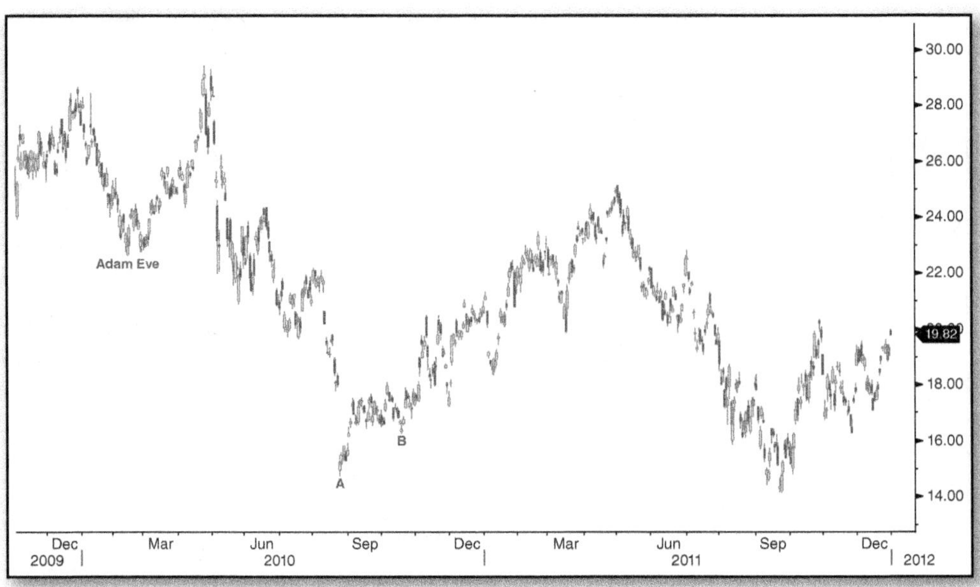

FIGURE 49.5 CRH US Equity (CRH PLC).

bottom, B (at least 5 percent higher, by the way). When price confirms the chart pattern by closing above the peak between the two bottoms, it indicates that the trend has changed from down to up.

Exercise

Find as many valid double bottoms as you can in Figure 49.6. Do not concern yourself with any of the identification guideline numbers, such as two to seven weeks

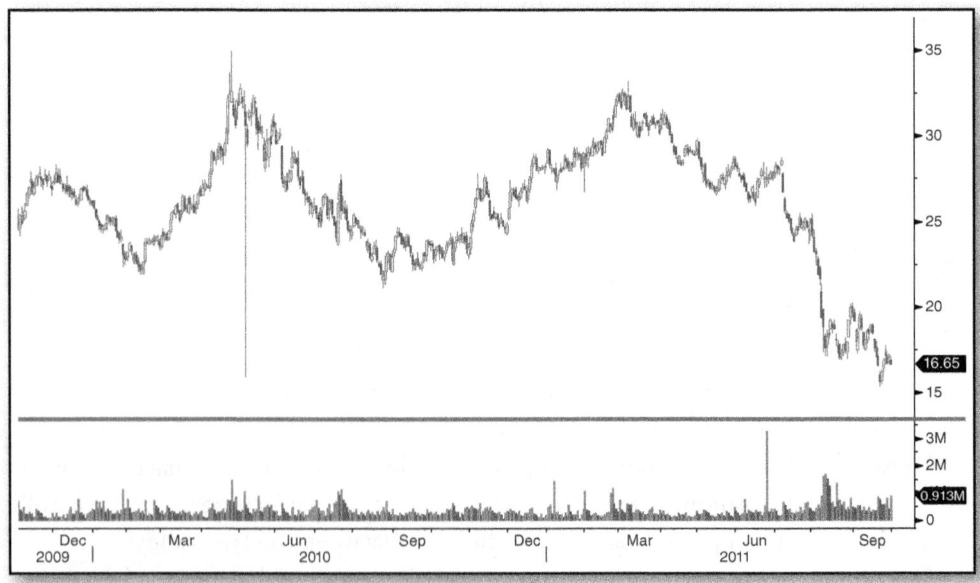

FIGURE 49.6 EXP US Equity (Eagle Materials Inc).

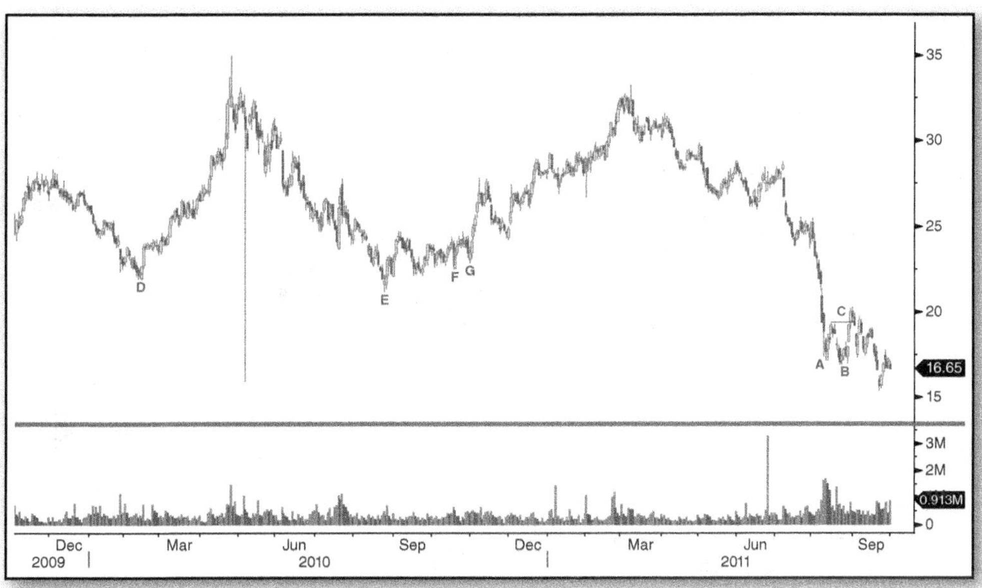

FIGURE 49.7 EXP US Equity (Eagle Materials Inc).

between bottoms, or 5 percent apart, and so on. Just look for two valleys that bottom at or near the same price and confirm as valid patterns. Do not look for ugly double bottoms, and do not worry about the Adam and Eve variations. Also pretend that the long green downward spike in May does not exist.

Figure 49.7 shows what I found. First, in the lower right of the chart is the only valid double bottom, AB. Price confirms it when the stock closes above the top of the pattern, at C.

If you marked DE, that would be wrong because it does not confirm.

Bottom FG confirms, but it is not a bottom. Price must trend downward into the chart pattern, not rise up from the grave. The rule I use is that in-bound price must be higher than the peak in the middle of the double bottom to guarantee that it is indeed trending down into the chart pattern. That does not occur on the FG bottom.

Confused? I explain it again in the next section.

All of the other potential double bottoms on the chart have one or both of those flaws. They do not confirm or are located in an uptrend.

Figure 49.8 has multiple double bottoms in it. Find as many as you can, but do not look for those narrower than about two weeks and forget about ugly double bottoms, too.

Figure 49.9 shows the answers. I drew a line connecting the bottoms for your viewing pleasure. Bottom A confirms as a valid pattern in a downward price trend. If you excluded it because the two valleys did not bottom at the same price (they are 72 cents apart or 1.7 percent), then, good. I still consider it one.

G is one of those double bottoms I told you not to worry about because the valleys are too narrow. If you found it anyway, wonderful! It is a double bottom. Price makes a third bottom, but that happens after the double bottom confirms.

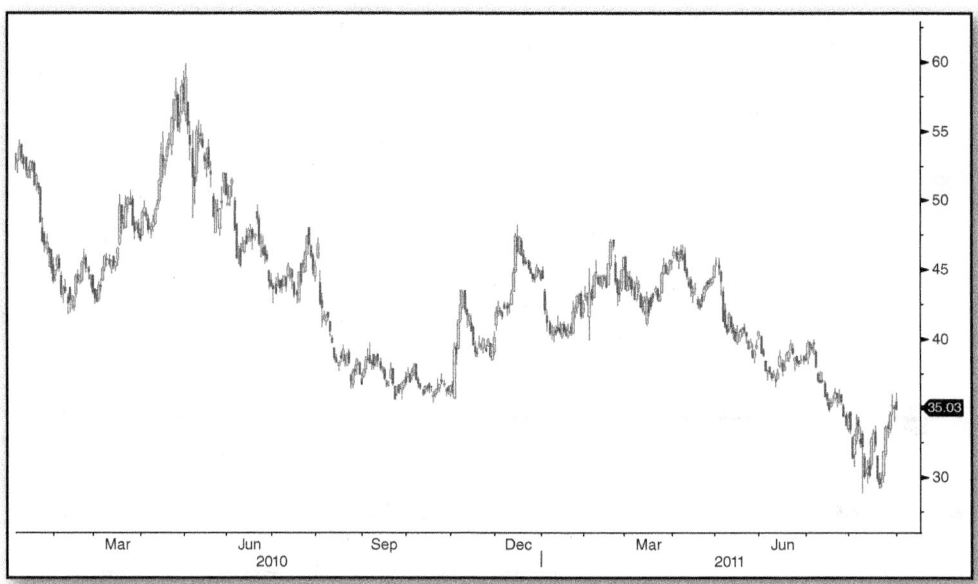

FIGURE 49.8 VMC US Equity (Vulcan Materials Co).

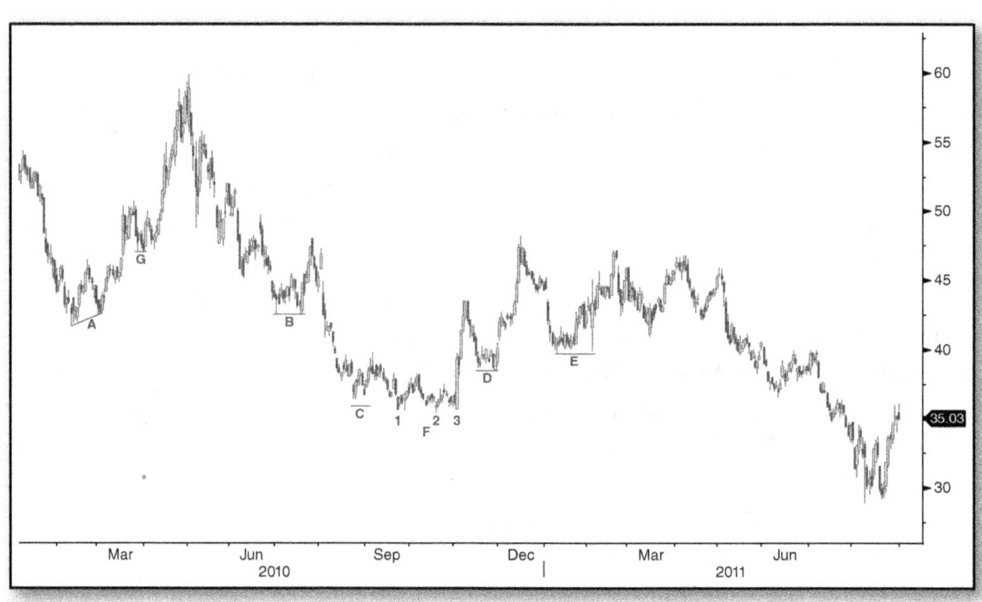

FIGURE 49.9 VMC US Equity (Vulcan Materials Co).

B, D, and E should have been easy (maybe C, too). E is especially delicious since the Eve bottom is so much wider than Adam.

What about bottom F? That is not a double bottom. Why? Look at bottoms 1 and 2. They do not confirm until *after* bottom 3 forms. This is an example of a triple bottom, the subject of our next section.

If you found bottoms 2 and 3, you should have looked to the left and found bottom 1, again, forming a triple bottom.

By now, you probably hate me. Are you going to remove me from your will? Do that after you die, and after you read the next section on triple bottoms.

Test Yourself

Answer true or false to the following statements.

1. A double bottom is just squiggles on a price chart until it confirms.
2. Confirmation of a double bottom is when price rises at least 10 percent above the lowest bottom.
3. Price must trend down into a double bottom.
4. The peak between the two bottoms should rise at least 10 percent above the lowest bottom, but if it does not, who cares?
5. If price closes below the lowest bottom before confirming the double bottom, it invalidates the chart pattern.

Answers: 1. True; 2. False; 3. True; 4. True; 5. True

Triple Bottoms

Now that we have trained ourselves to find two bottoms that line up at the same price, let us look for triplets: three bottoms in a row. It is as easy as it sounds, except that triple bottoms are sometimes confused with head-and-shoulders bottoms. Maybe it is not so easy . . .

Triple bottoms are considerably rarer than double bottoms, but the technique used to find them is the same. Find a double bottom and then look to the left and right to see if a third bottom exists at the same price.

KEY POINT:

Triple bottoms are three valleys that bottom near the same price. The chart pattern acts as a bullish reversal of the downward price trend.

Figure 49.10 shows an example.

Based on what you have learned in this book, which of the three patterns are triple bottoms (guess)?

Look at bottom ABC. Price trends downward into the chart pattern. If you do not see a downward price trend, then it is not a bottom reversal. The pattern has three price spikes, with A slightly above the other two. Price confirms the pattern by *closing* above the highest peak between the three bottoms.

It is a triple bottom.

KEY POINT:

Price must *trend* downward into a bottom and upward into a top. That trend is what qualifies the chart pattern as a bottom or top, respectively. Without the trend, then you do not have a reversal pattern.

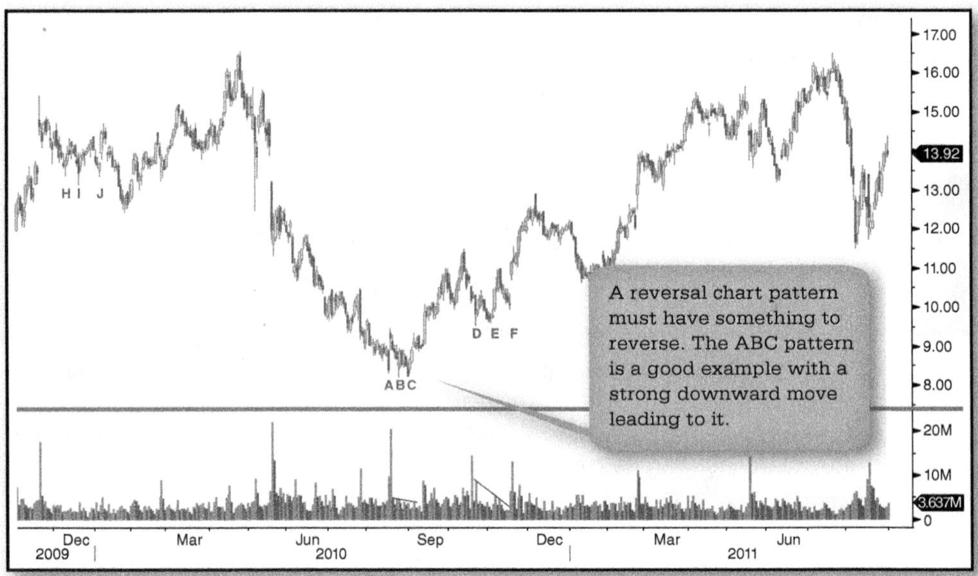

FIGURE 49.10 CHS US Equity (Chico's FAS Inc).

DEF is similar to ABC in that two of three bottoms are near the same price. However, F is much higher than DE, so this would work better as double bottom DE with throwback F.

HIJ has a center valley (I) below the other two. That is a dead giveaway. It is a head-and-shoulders bottom, a chart pattern I will be discussing later in the book.

Identification Guidelines

What is involved in identifying triple bottoms? You can probably guess most of them, but the following table provides a list.

Characteristic	Discussion
Downward price trend	The short-term price trend leading to the triple bottom is down.
Three bottoms	Three minor lows are involved in a triple bottom. Sometimes they can be one-day price spikes or wider, more rounded turns. Each valley tends to look similar to the others.
Same price	Each minor low should bottom *near* the same price. Rarely will all three bottom at exactly the same price, so be flexible.
Volume	Volume recedes, meaning it is higher on the left than the right, but each bottom can show significant volume. Do not exclude a pattern because it has an unusual volume shape.
Confirmation	Price must confirm the triple bottom by closing above the highest peak between the three bottoms.

SMART INVESTOR TIP

If the middle peak of an alleged triple bottom is *significantly* below the other two, then it is probably a head-and-shoulders bottom.

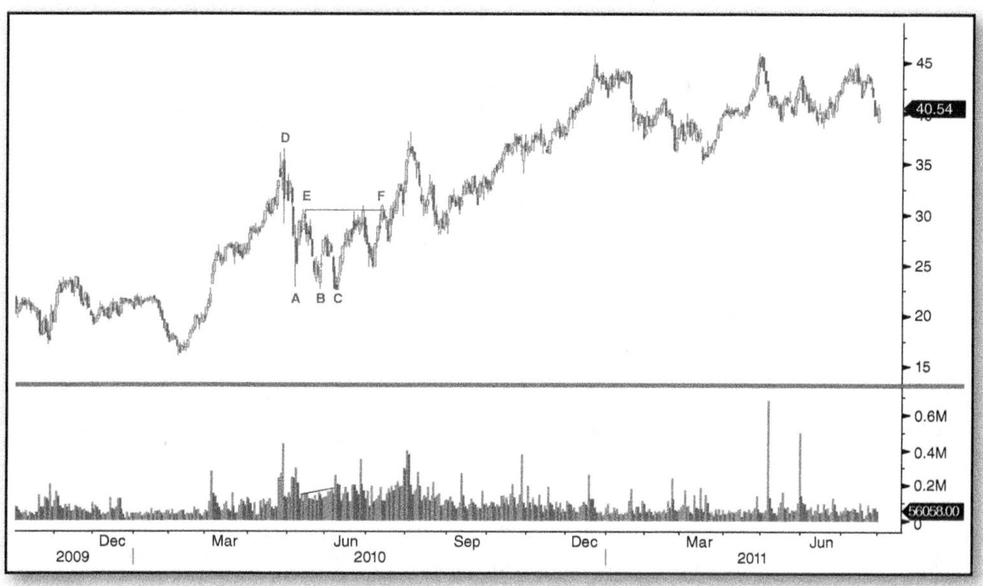

FIGURE 49.11 KWR US Equity (Quaker Chemical Corp).

Figure 49.11 shows an example of a triple bottom.

Price climbs a cliff to D and then turns into a waterfall, tumbling to the stream below and forming triple bottom ABC. The D peak is too far away to be an example of overshoot.

Three valleys appear similar in shape, all of them narrow and bottoming near the same price. Volume trends upward, which is odd for triple bottoms.

The pattern confirms as a valid triple bottom when price closes above the highest peak (E) between the three bottoms. Confirmation happens at F.

Figure 49.12 occurs on the weekly scale.

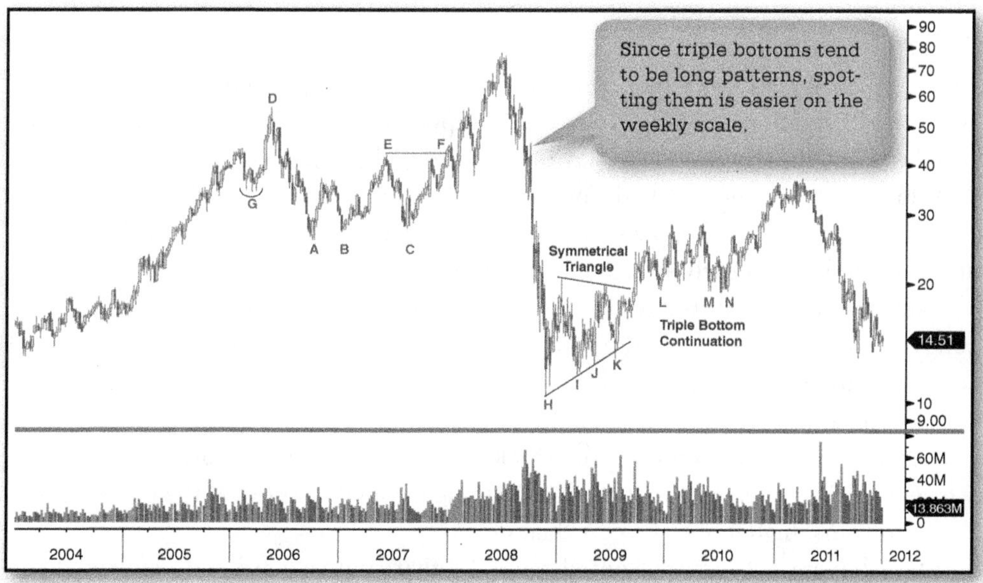

FIGURE 49.12 ACI US Equity (Arch Coal Inc).

KEY POINT:

Price must close above the highest peak between the three bottoms. If it closes below the lowest bottom first, then it is not a triple bottom.

I chose this chart because of its similarity to the prior one. Price climbs to D and then tumbles to the triple bottom reversal at ABC.

This time, though, the valleys are wider and more rounded looking. If you were to flip to the daily scale, you would see them expand as if they overdosed on potato chips.

Price confirms the triple bottom at F when it closes above peak E. Price must *close* above the highest peak in the pattern, or else it is not a triple bottom.

Look at G, the three brief spikes down in early 2006. This is also a triple bottom, but due to the weekly scale, it is harder to spot.

FAST FACTS

Longer triple bottoms are often easier to identify on the weekly chart. In a study of 602 triple bottoms, the average length was between two and three months long.

Valleys H, I, and J form three bottoms—and you can throw in K for another triple (IJK)—but the valleys do not bottom at or near the same price. They are better classified as a symmetrical triangle, shown outlined in blue.

Triple L, M, and N form three bottoms near the same price, but it is not a reversal. Price climbs into the start of the chart pattern from the bottom, not trends lower as required. However, some may call this a triple bottom continuation pattern. Price rises going into this chart pattern and continues rising on exit.

Triple Bottom Psychology

Why do triple bottoms form? Consider Figure 49.13.

In April 2010, pharmaceutical company Baxter International was facing hard times. How do I know this? Because they announced quarterly earnings that were worse than expected. The stock jumped out the window. When it splattered against the pavement in May, it had plunged 31 percent. Bet that hurt.

Value investors, when given the opportunity to grab the stock on sale, snatched it up like a horde of holiday shoppers bursting into an electronics store. The stock bounced at A and climbed to nearly 43 from mid 40 then retreated and formed valley B.

Value investors returned to the market and scooped up the stock. Seeing the first valley bottom near 40, technical players recognized the support area and bought, too. That buying demand pushed the stock back up to 43, but selling pressure cut it down a third time, to C.

Institutional investors bought the stock or added to their positions. It is as if they whispered "Buy BAX, but do it quietly." Volume trended lower over the course of the three bottoms, higher at bottom A than C.

At C, buying enthusiasm ignited a missile that shot upward and confirmed the triple bottom at D, but within a week was parachuting back down in a throwback.

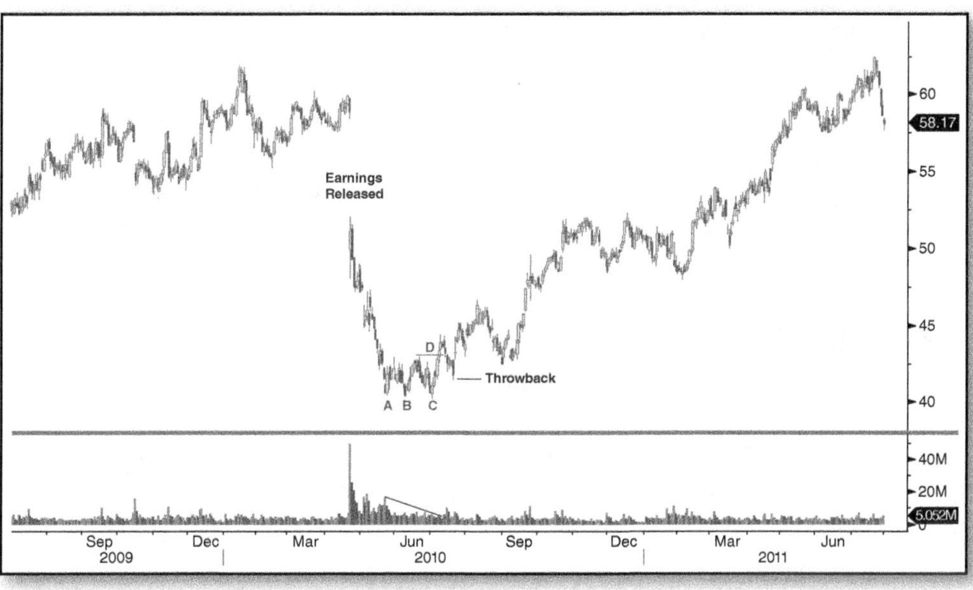

FIGURE 49.13 BAX US Equity (Baxter International Inc).

Months later, market enthusiasts could look back and see the triple bottom for what it was: a reversal that marked a significant bottom for the stock.

Variations

Variations in triple bottoms center around the price level of the three valleys. Look at Figure 49.14, starting with A on the far left.

This triple bottom has a middle valley (red dot) that is well above the other two. The triple bottom appears in a downward price trend and acts as a reversal. Price

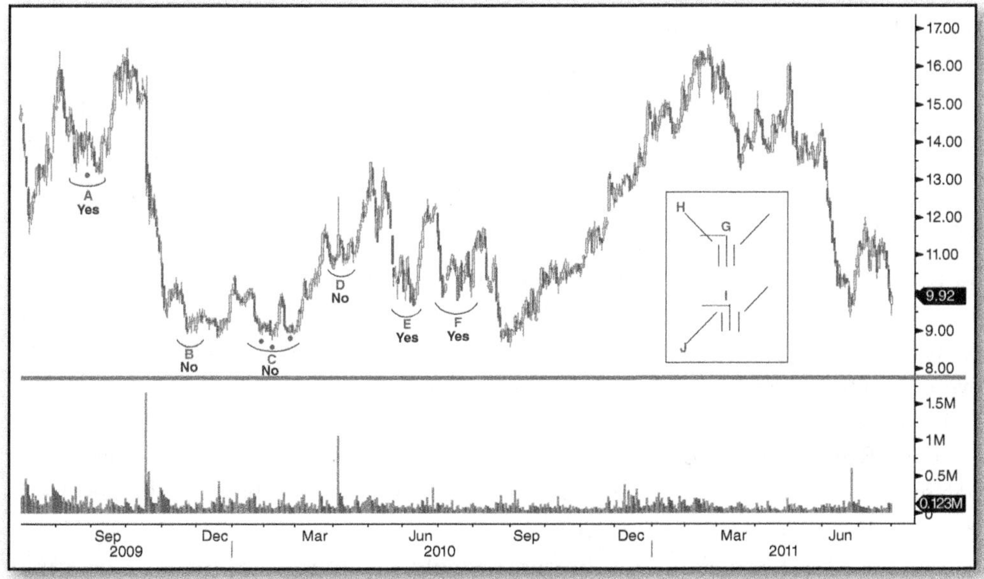

FIGURE 49.14 PMTI US Equity (Palomar Medical Technologies Inc).

confirms the chart pattern as a valid one when it closes above the peak between the three valleys. I consider it a valid triple bottom.

> **FAST FACTS**
> Tall triple bottoms tend to outperform short ones (gains averaging 39 percent versus 27 percent, respectively), according to a study of bull market patterns from mid-1991 to 2011 using 609 samples.

B shows three spikes near the same price level. Everything looks good except for one thing. Price closes below the bottom of the pattern first, so it is not a triple bottom.

Pattern C looks like a head-and-shoulders bottom because the middle red dot is much lower than the other two. When pattern A showed a higher middle, that was fine, but a lower middle often qualifies the chart pattern as a head-and-shoulders. C is not a triple bottom.

D is also not a triple bottom reversal because price rises into the chart pattern (starting at C) instead of trending downward. The rule I use is that the price mountain to the left of the chart pattern must be above the highest peak in the triple bottom.

I show what I mean using the two variations in the blue inset. The blue lines represent price. G has price trending downward (H) into the triple bottom from above the red line. The triple bottom acts as a reversal of the downward trend.

I has price rising (from J) into the three bottoms. The inbound price trend remains below the middle peak. This triple bottom acts as a continuation pattern, not a reversal. Pattern D resembles scenario I, so it is not a triple bottom reversal.

E is a triple bottom even though the right valley is lower than the other two. When looking at this on a historical basis, which we are, the triple bottom is a reversal with price rising above the three valleys on either side. It *looks* like a reversal. It *acts* like a reversal. It even quacks like a reversal.

Pattern F also has a lower middle valley but if this were a person, he would have the nickname "No neck." It is a valid triple bottom and not a head-and-shoulders bottom.

Exercise

To test what you have learned in this section, the first exercise (see Figure 49.15) is easy. There are only four patterns on the chart that I want to highlight. Two are triple bottoms and two are head-and-shoulders bottoms. See if you can find all of them even though we have not yet covered the head-and-shoulders.

Figure 49.16 shows the answers.

A and B are the triple bottoms. They exist in a downward price trend, form three bottoms near the same price, and confirm when price closes above the highest peak between the three valleys in each pattern.

The two head-and-shoulders bottoms would be difficult to confuse as triple bottoms since the heads are much lower than the surrounding valleys.

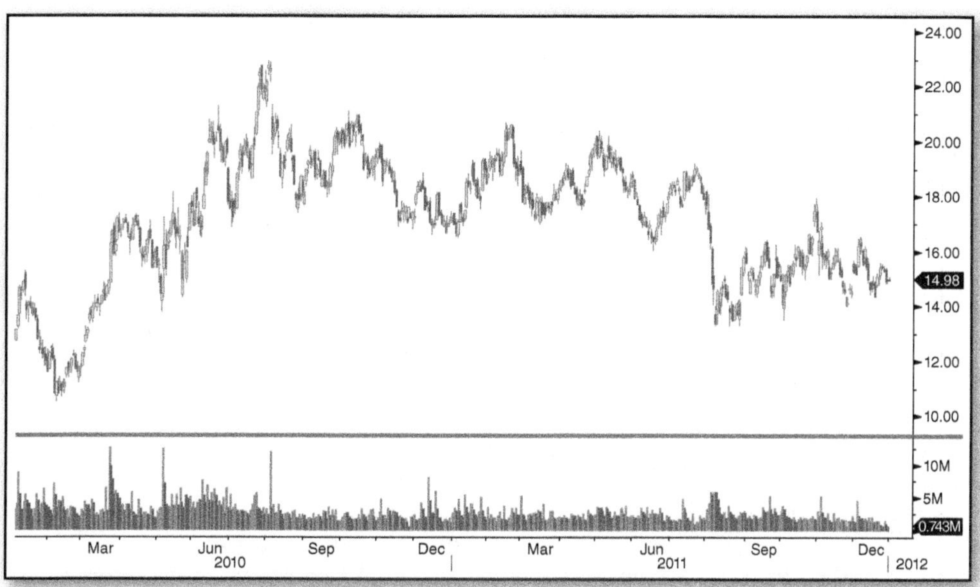

FIGURE 49.15 TIE US Equity (Titanium Metals Corp).

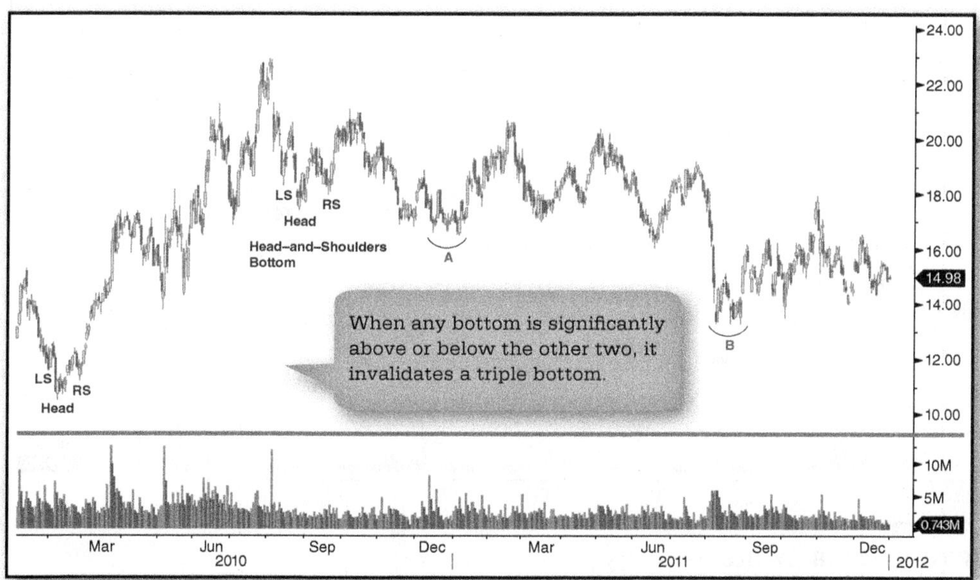

FIGURE 49.16 TIE US Equity (Titanium Metals Corp).

This next exercise (see Figure 49.17) is trickier than the last one. Look for three triple bottoms and one head-and-shoulders bottom.

Figure 49.18 shows the answers. Triple bottom A has a right bottom below the other two, but it still acts as a reversal of the downward price run. Price on the right valley does not sink too far below (just 20 cents) the other two to invalidate the triple bottom.

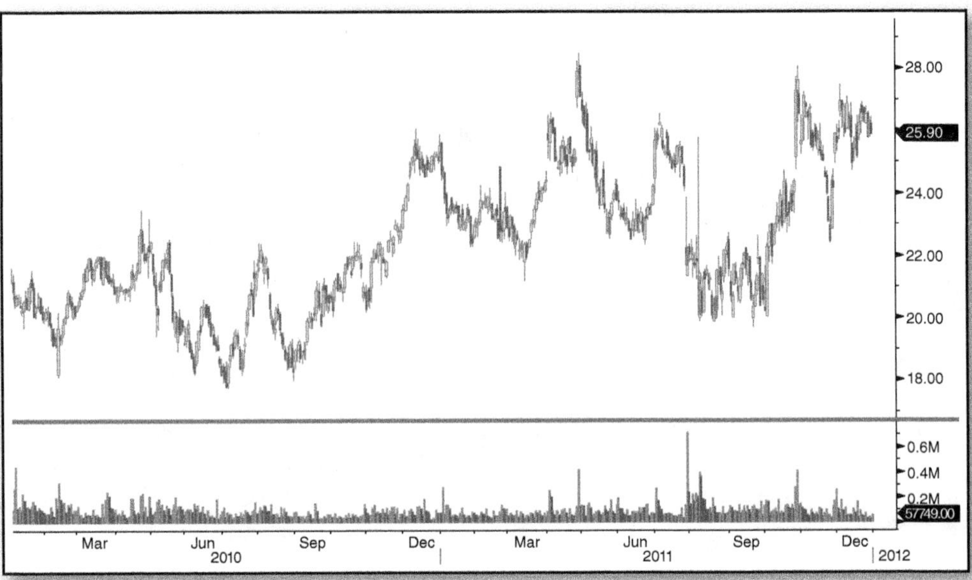

FIGURE 49.17 WIRE US Equity (Encore Wire Corp).

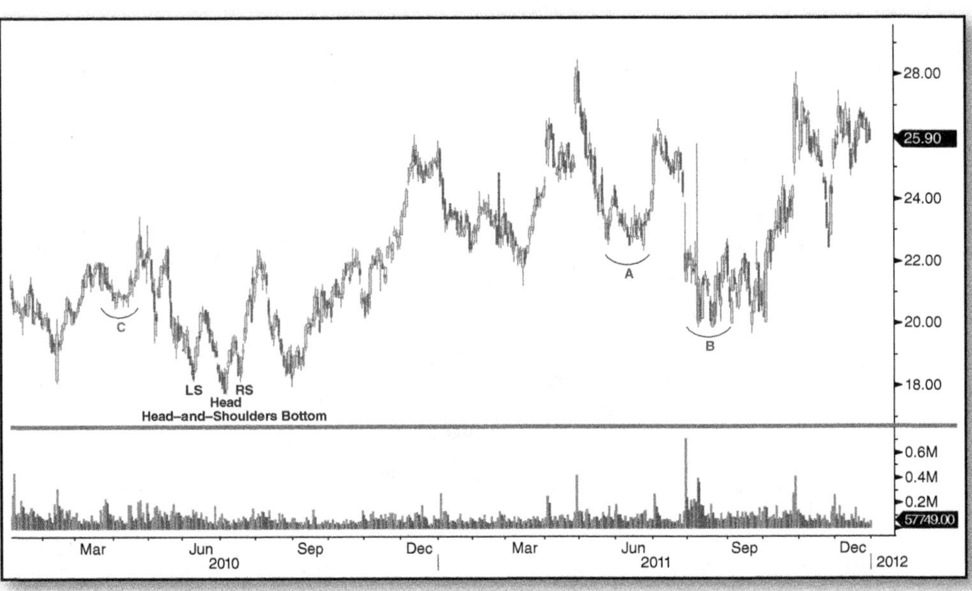

FIGURE 49.18 WIRE US Equity (Encore Wire Corp).

You might quibble with pattern B, and this is certainly a hard triple bottom to find. Cover up the additional valleys after the right one and it looks like a triple bottom. Price confirms this, too, by closing above the highest peak between the three valleys. Once the pattern confirms as a triple bottom, it does not matter if the stock nosedives into the ground or flies to the stars. The pattern remains a valid triple bottom.

Triple bottom C is a small one that you may have overlooked. It is valid, too.

The head-and-shoulders is a three valley pattern, but the head is well below the surrounding shoulders. It is not a triple bottom.

In the next section, we abandon bottoms and switch to tops: double tops. I like my double tops shaken, not stirred.

Test Yourself

Answer the following.

1. How many bottoms in a triple bottom need to be at exactly the same price?
   A. None
   B. One
   C. Two
   D. Three
2. True or false: If price does not close above the highest peak between the three bottoms, it is not a triple bottom.
3. True or false: If the middle bottom is well below the other two, the chart pattern could be a head-and-shoulders bottom.
4. In a triple bottom, price should bottom near the same price. What does "near" mean?
   A. Within 25 cents of each other.
   B. It depends on the price scale.
   C. It depends on the height of the triple bottom.
   D. It should look like they bottom near the same price.
   E. B and D.

Answers: 1. A; 2. True; 3. True; 4. E

Double Tops

Double tops are dual price mountains that peak near the same price. They are the same as double bottoms except flipped upside down. In this section, we will discuss what to look for when searching for double tops.

Figure 49.19 shows two examples of double tops on the daily scale. At F, price begins the steep march up the sides of the double top. It peaks at A, withdraws to G, and then forms another peak, B, at a price similar to A.

When price closes below G, it confirms the twin peaks as a valid double top.

I chose this chart because the long climb up reminds me of a trek up K2. The double top acts like storm clouds, warning of the coming decline.

Look at CDE. This is a triple top, but is CD also a double top? Yes. CD confirms as a double top before peak E forms. When E appears, the double top also becomes a triple top, but only when the trio confirms.

What do I mean by confirmation, and what should you look for in double tops? That question brings us to identification.

KEY POINT:
Double tops are bearish reversals of an uptrend formed by twin peaks near the same price.

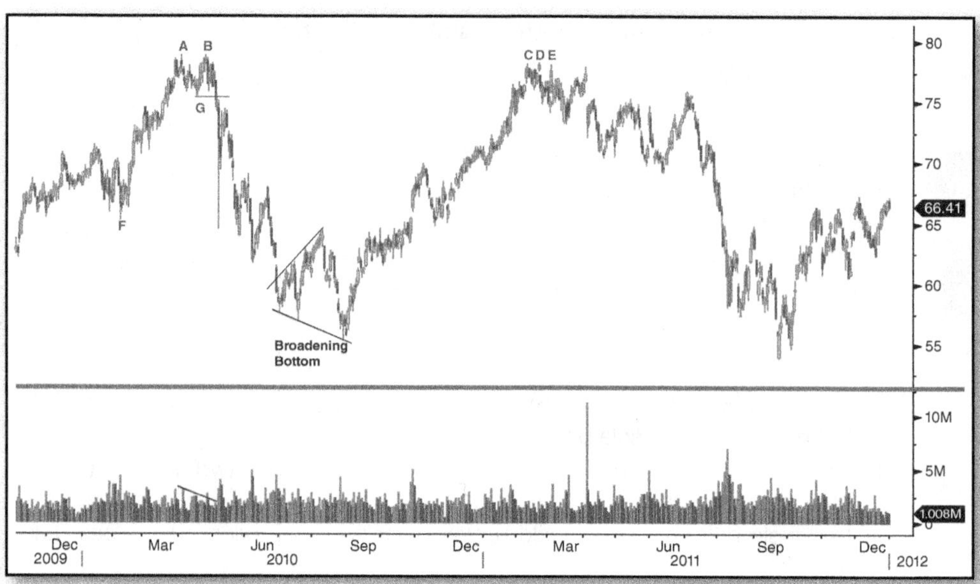

FIGURE 49.19 GD US Equity (General Dynamics Corp).

Identification Guidelines

The following table lists the criteria that double tops share.

Characteristic	Discussion
Upward price trend	The short-term price trend leading to the double top is up.
Two peaks	Look for two peaks that top out near the same price. Near means within about 3 percent. The tops should *look* as if they are at the same price.
Peak separation	The time between peaks varies, but two to six weeks is typical.
Valley	The valley drop between the two peaks should measure at least 10 percent, but allow exceptions. The drop should look proportional to the width of the double top.
Volume	Volume is usually higher on the left top than the right, but this is an observation, not a requirement.
Confirmation	Price must close below the lowest valley between the two peaks. If price closes above the highest peak before confirmation, it invalidates the double top.

Consider the double top shown in Figure 49.20.

Price begins the upward trend at F, leading to the double top. Twin peaks appear as an Adam & Eve double top at the cleverly chosen letters A and E. The double top begins to reverse the FA climb.

> **SMART INVESTOR TIP**
>
> A reversal chart pattern must have something to reverse. If the rise leading to a double top is small, then do not expect a big drop. The stock might try digging to the earth's core, but do not count on it.

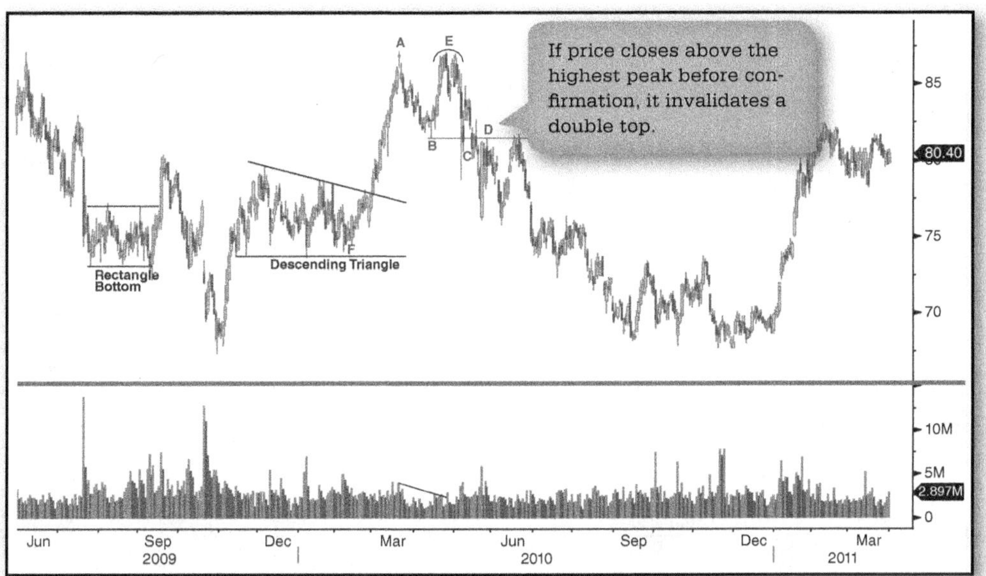

FIGURE 49.20 **LMT US Equity (Lockheed Martin Corp).**

The time between the two peaks is usually less than two months, frequently ranging between two and six weeks. They can be further apart, especially when using the weekly or monthly scales, or narrower for day traders.

The valley between the two peaks sees price drop, but the depth should be proportional to the width of the peaks. Peaks separated by two weeks probably will not see a massive plunge between the two tops. Usually the drop measures in the 10 to 20 percent range, but allow exceptions, especially when using other time scales (like intraday).

Volume tends to be higher on formation of the left peak than the right, which this example shows.

The twin peaks become a valid double top when price closes below the valley between the two peaks. The valley bottom is at B and it confirms at C when the red candle closes below the price of B. A pullback to the breakout price at D gives traders another opportunity to exit before the decline resumes.

> **FAST FACTS**
> A study of 2,333 double tops shows that a pullback occurs 58 percent of the time.

Double Top Psychology

Why do double tops form? The answer is the same as it is for other chart patterns: fear and greed, sometimes powered by fundamentals.

Figure 49.21 shows an example of a double top standing like a castle overlooking a sea of prices.

At C, the company released first quarter earnings and announced the completion of a merger with Amrep Inc., a chemical supplier. The stock went nowhere that day.

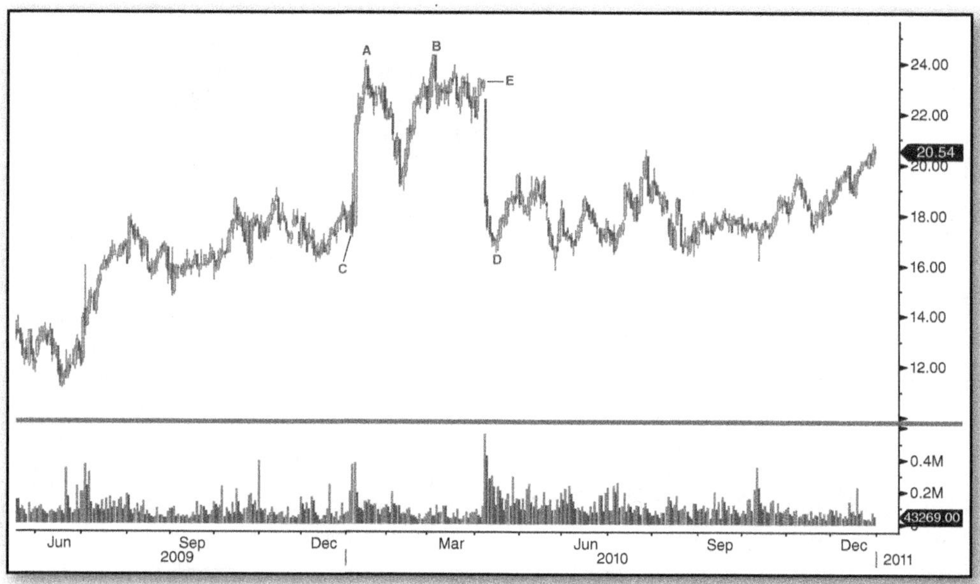

FIGURE 49.21 ZEP US Equity (Zep Inc).

Two days later, the institutions finished digesting the news and decided the stock represented a good value. Their buying pushed the stock up the price mountain to A where traders encountered a group of angry bears. The bears pushed them off the cliff, forcing the stock back down.

Since the bears remained at the top of the cliff, the bulls bought the stock at the bottom and their buying demand made it climb back up a new slope to B, forming a second peak.

FAST FACTS

Double tops show their best performance in bear markets, not bull. Adam & Adam performs best in a bull market, but worst in a bear market.

A day later, a brokerage firm downgraded the stock.

The bulls and bears fought again, tearing into each other, but not making or losing much ground. Even so, the smart money started selling ahead of the second quarter's earnings announcement.

At E, the company reported earnings and had a conference call to discuss them the next day. The news herded some of the bulls into the slaughterhouse and bears pushed the rest over the edge. The stock did a cliff diver plunge back to the sea at D.

Variations

I show variations of the basic double top, beginning with Figure 49.22.

I have already discussed Adam and Eve double bottoms, and the top variety is similar to the bottoms. Adam peaks are narrow, often one-day price spikes. Eve peaks look more rounded. If she has price spikes, they are numerous and short.

FIGURE 49.22 POL US Equity (PolyOne Corp).

FAST FACTS

Of the four combinations of Adam and Eve double tops in a bull market, Adam & Adam show the largest average decline after confirmation.

The figure shows an Adam & Adam double top at AA. Following that, an Eve & Adam top appears. Notice how wide Eve appears compared to Adam. Another Eve & Adam double top appears about a year later.

Figure 49.23 shows the two missing varieties of Adam and Eve.

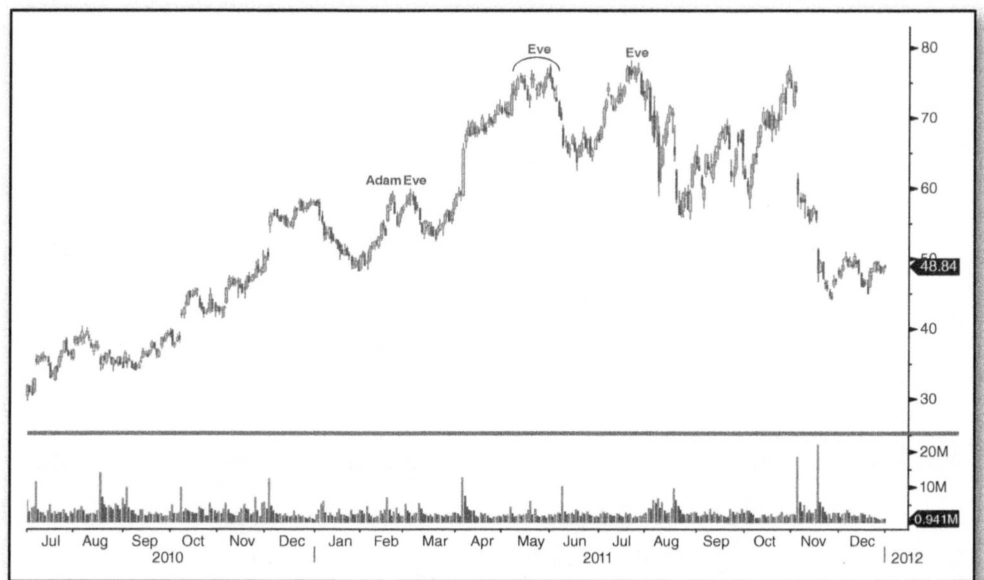

FIGURE 49.23 ANF US Equity (Abercrombie & Fitch Co).

An Adam & Eve double top appears in February, and you may be scratching your head because the two peaks look similar. That is the problem with labeling the various peaks. Recall that Adam tends to remain narrow whereas Eve widens out, which appears to be the case here.

The Eve & Eve tops look more rounded, especially when you consider the entire top on the left (blue arc) as part of the turn.

> **FAST FACTS**
>
> The failure rate can almost double from one type of double top to another, depending on the Adam and Eve combinations compared.

Exercise

The Adam and Eve combinations of double tops can confuse even the experts, so I am not going to test you on them. Look at Figure 49.24 to find three double tops, four flags, and a symmetrical triangle. Here is a hint for the flags. Look for the flagpole first (a straight-line price run), and then see if a flag is attached to it.

Figure 49.25 shows the locations of the chart patterns. A is an Eve & Eve double top. B is an Adam & Eve and C is an Eve & Adam. These should have been easy to locate, and I hope you found the flags and triangle as well.

This next exercise is more difficult because I chose a chart in which you may select some bogus patterns. Look for three valid double tops. (See Figure 49.26.)

FIGURE 49.24 COH US Equity (Coach Inc).

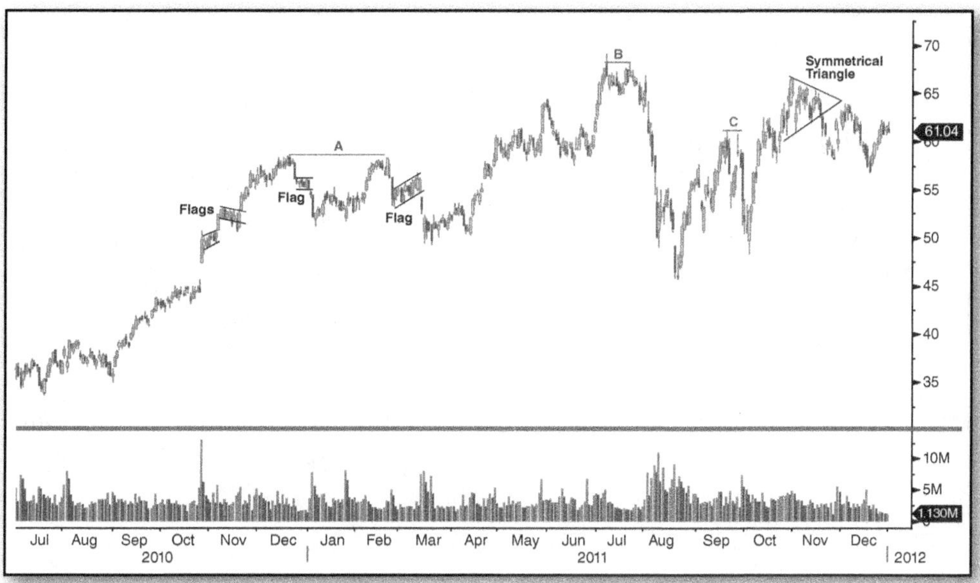

FIGURE 49.25 COH US Equity (Coach Inc).

Figure 49.27 shows the answers. Twin peak A is not a double top because it does not confirm (price does not close below line B).

C, D, and E are the correct choices for double tops. F, however, is an unconfirmed double top (at least so far).

The next section extends the twin peak pattern to three to create a triple top.

FIGURE 49.26 XLB US Equity (Materials Select Sector SPDR Fund).

FIGURE 49.27 XLB US Equity (Materials Select Sector SPDR Fund).

Test Yourself

Answer the following.

1. True or false: A double top is composed of two peaks near the same price.
2. A double top has how many valleys between the two peaks?
   A. 1
   B. 2
   C. 3
   D. At least 1
3. True or false: An unconfirmed twin peak pattern is not a double top.

Answers: 1. True; 2. D; 3. True

Triple Tops

A double top can become a triple after growing another peak near the same price. Let us take a closer look at this medical miracle to see how traders recognize it.

Figure 49.28 shows two examples of real triple tops and one implant.

The triple top at A has three peaks near the same price after the stock trends upward into the chart pattern. The stock becomes a base jumper and confirms the chart pattern on the way down through the horizontal red line.

The middle triple top, at B, is also a triple top with the same features as A. The skydiver pops his chute, and the drop ends soon after.

C is not a triple top because it does not confirm. You can guess what that means, but the next section makes the various components of a triple top clear.

KEY POINT:

A triple top is a three-peak pattern with the three minor highs topping out near the same price. The pattern acts as a reversal of the upward price trend.

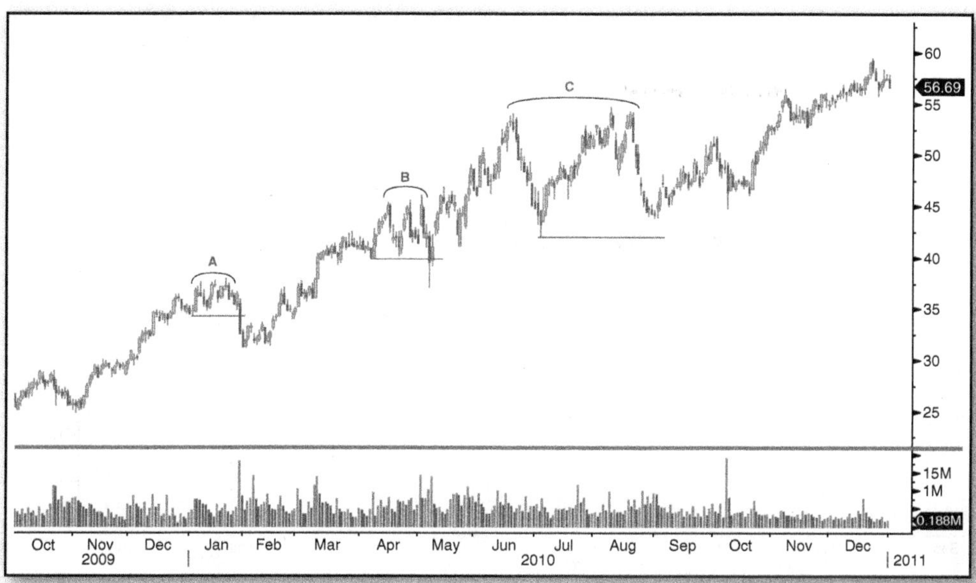

FIGURE 49.28 ALK US Equity (Alaska Air Group Inc).

Identification Guidelines

The following table lists guidelines for finding triple tops.

Characteristic	Discussion
Upward price trend	The short-term price trend leading to the triple top is up.
Three peaks	Look for three minor highs. Sometimes the peaks can be one-day price spikes or wider, more rounded turns. Each peak tends to look similar to the others, but allow variations.
Same price	Each minor high should peak near the same price. Rarely will all three top out at exactly the same price, so be flexible. In fact, the middle peak is sometimes lower than the other two.
Volume	Volume recedes, meaning it is higher on the left than the right, but each peak can show significant volume. Do not exclude a pattern because it has an unusual volume shape.
Confirmation	Price must confirm the triple top by closing below the lowest valley between the three peaks.

Figure 49.29 shows another example of a triple top.

I chose this one because the middle peak is depressed and needed cheering up. Do not trash a valid triple top because the middle peak is slightly lower than its neighbors.

Price trends upward from below the chart pattern at E. Peaks A and C have more rounded-looking turns than does needle B, but that is fine.

To confirm a triple top, price has to close below the lowest valley in the chart pattern. That happens at D.

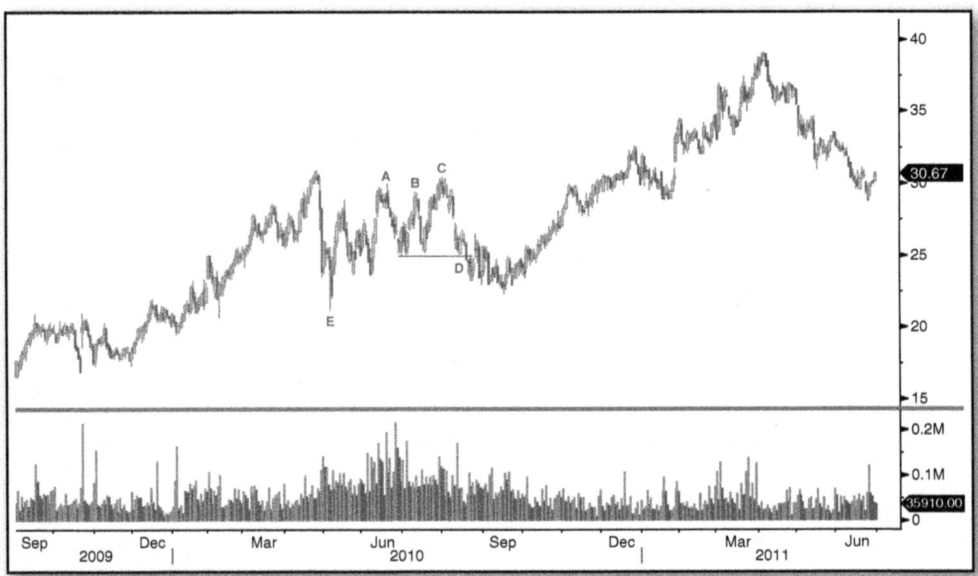

FIGURE 49.29 SXI US Equity (Standex International Corp).

Volume trends downward as the blue line shows. Receding volume is typical of triple tops, but do not discard a potential triple top because of unusual volume.

> **FAST FACTS**
>
> When the middle peak has higher volume than the last peak in the triple top, performance tends to be better.

Triple Top Psychology

Figure 49.30 shows selling near a fixed price that halts the upward movement in the stock, forming triple top ABC. It might play out something like this.

Imagine that you run a hedge fund that bought the stock at 18 in 2009 just after the bear market ended (not shown). At A, the stock reached 38 and change, more than double what you paid. Based on your analysis, it is time to sell.

> **FAST FACTS**
>
> The average length of a triple top on the daily chart is about three months in a bull market.

However, since you own a large position, you cannot just dump your shares on the market all at once. That would force the stock down into the Hudson faster than an airliner striking a flock of birds.

FIGURE 49.30 **HAYN US Equity (Haynes International Inc).**

At A, you let loose your first volley, but since the stock is thinly traded (less than 40,000 shares), you have difficulty selling 10,000 share blocks. You have to break it up into smaller chunks each day.

At B, you are having a bad day. You feel frustrated because other trades are going badly and you need to raise cash to cover redemptions. Your selling punishes the stock. Others see the panic selling and join in, sending the stock tumbling below 30.

At C, the stock is once again at your sell price, but you still have plenty of this lame turkey left in your portfolio. You sell as quietly as you can, as quickly as you can, but others sense the weakness and sell, too. Together, that sends the stock plunging quicker than a submarine during a crash dive. Momentum grows, keeping the stock trending down.

The stock reaches a long-term trendline (shown in blue) and bobbles up and down along that line for months. When the stock recovers to D, you sell more shares and finish dumping them when the stock powers higher at E.

Now that you have sold your position, the stock doubles, which really pisses you off.

FAST FACTS

Triple tops have the same performance and failure rate as the best-performing double top—Adam & Adam.

Variations

Only one variation needs to concern you: a head-and-shoulders top. In the next chapter, we discuss head-and-shoulders patterns but until then, just avoid picking triple tops in which the center peak rises too far above the other two. It should not look like a person's bust.

For example, consider Figure 49.31.

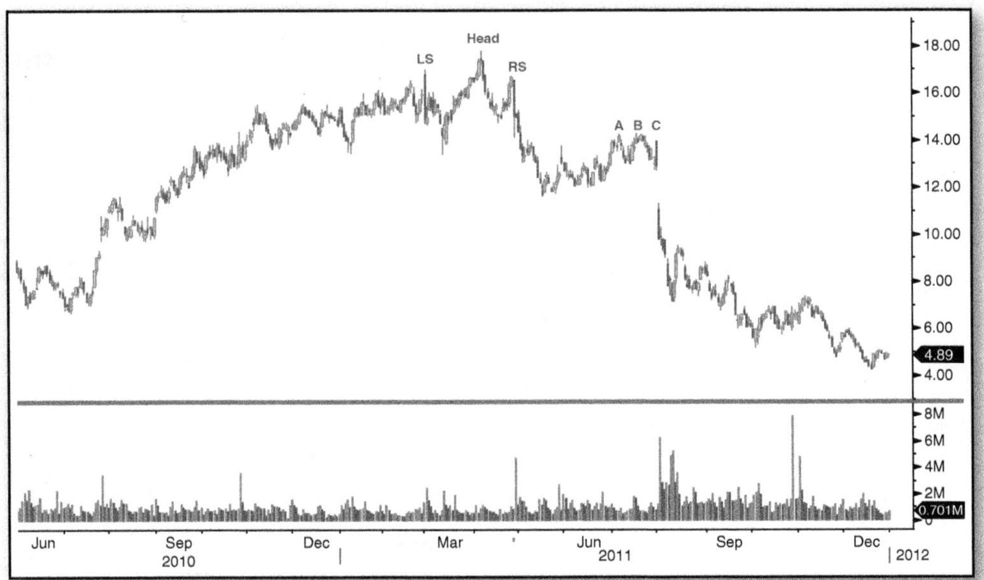

FIGURE 49.31 **FOE US Equity (Ferro Corp).**

The head-and-shoulders has a head above the shoulders (LS and RS) far enough to make it look like a person's bust.

> **SMART INVESTOR TIP**
>
> Select three peak patterns in which the middle peak is not too far above the other two. If the pattern resembles a human bust, then the pattern is better described as a head-and-shoulders top.

Compare that to the triple top ABC. B is slightly above A and C, but hardly enough to notice. It *looks* like a triple top and not a head-and-shoulders top.

Exercise

The first exercise is easy (see Figure 49.32). Find at least one triple top, a head-and-shoulders top (guess), and a double top. Except for the head-and-shoulders top, you should be able to identify the other patterns.

When searching for a triple top, imagine the outline of a mountain range. Three of the mountains line up at the same height to form a triple top.

Figure 49.33 shows the answers.

The head-and-shoulders top has a head sticking above the other two peaks, helping to differentiate it from a triple top.

The triple top at ABC forms three peaks near the same price. It confirms when price closes below the lowest valley in the chart pattern.

The double top may have given you some trouble because the two peaks are not at the same price (45 cents difference, or less than 1 percent).

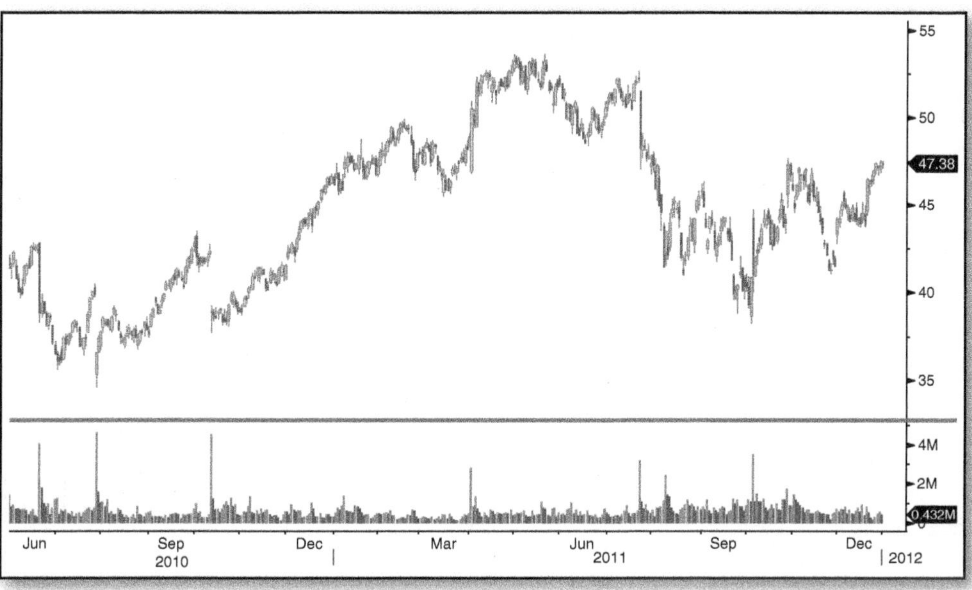

FIGURE 49.32 GPN US Equity (Global Payments Inc).

FIGURE 49.33 GPN US Equity (Global Payments Inc).

Peak D is not a triple top. I shy away from peaks that align like this one does, forming a diagonal trend downward. Often that is a clue to a symmetrical triangle.

Figure 49.34 shows a target-rich environment. In it you should find at least two triple tops, two flags, a pennant, a double bottom, and a head-and-shoulders top.

Figure 49.35 shows where the chart patterns are located. Starting on the left, a small head-and-shoulders top appears in April. Since the price difference between the first two peaks is just 15 cents, if you want to call this a triple top, fine.

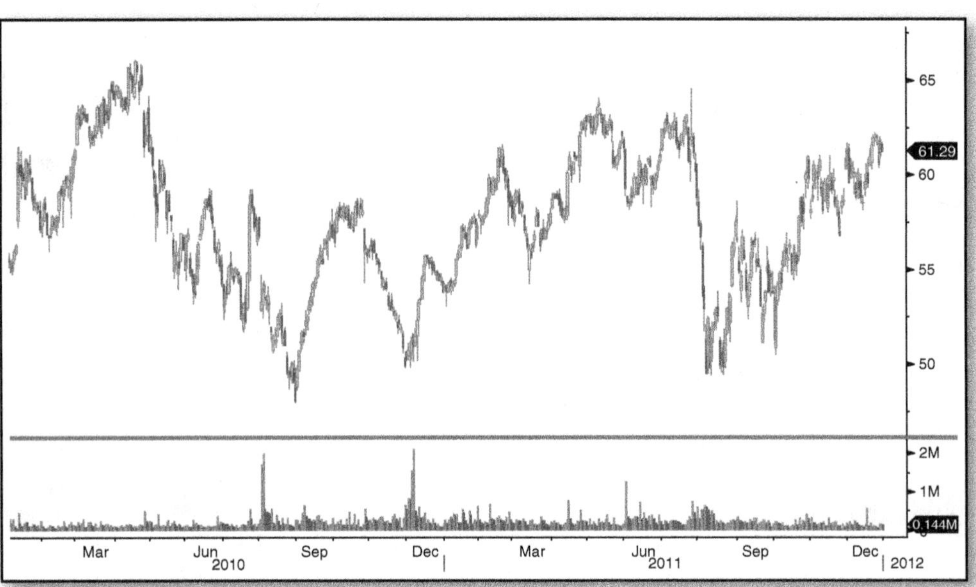

FIGURE 49.34 TFX US Equity (Teleflex Inc).

FIGURE 49.35 TFX US Equity (Teleflex Inc).

Next is the large pattern ABC. Although these three peaks line up near the same price, the chart pattern does not confirm, so it is not a triple top.

The flag in July is difficult to spot because it acts as a reversal of the uptrend.

The December flag and February pennant follow price higher surrounding the holidays.

D is the first triple top. The upward spike that occurs after the third peak also occurs after confirmation. The chart pattern reversal leads to a huge drop that sees a double bottom form as another reversal.

Following that is the second triple top, at E.

In the next chapter, I discuss head-and-shoulders bottoms. Just two days ago, I received an e-mail asking why I have not discussed the inverted head-and-shoulders pattern. I do not call them by that name. It has something to do with the federal eyewitness protection program.

Test Yourself

Answer the following.

1. If a fourth peak appears at the same price as the other three, what does it mean?
   A. If price closes below the lowest valley in the triple top before the fourth peak appears, you have a valid triple top.
   B. If the triple top is unconfirmed, it becomes a quad or multiple top pattern.
   C. If the four-peak pattern confirms, it suggests price is going down.
   D. Overhead resistance is strong.
   E. All of the above.
2. True or false: If price trends lower into a three-peak pattern, you have a triple top.
3. How close do the peaks have to be from each other to qualify as a triple top?
   A. It depends on scaling.
   B. No more than 25 cents.
   C. Within 4 percent.
   D. It does not matter providing they appear near the same price.
   E. All of the above.
4. True or false: Triple tops tend to be wide patterns with many lasting from two to three months.

Answers: 1. E; 2. False; 3. A or D; 4. True

CHAPTER 50

Head-and-Shoulders Patterns

From Thomas N. Bulkowski, *Visual Guide to Chart Patterns* (Hoboken, New Jersey: John Wiley & Sons, 2002), Chapters 16–17.

Head-and-Shoulders Bottoms

The head-and-shoulders is perhaps the best-known chart pattern. It has an evocative name, but recognizing a valid one takes an understanding of the rules. Let us begin by looking at a few samples. (See Figure 50.1.)

In this figure, I show three head-and-shoulders patterns. Pattern A is a head-and-shoulders bottom. The right shoulder (RS) bottoms at a price above the left (LS), but not too far. If this were the bust of a real person, yes, they might be in need of medical attention.

Notice that the head is below the adjacent shoulders. That is a key feature of a head-and-shoulders bottom.

Pattern B is similar to A. The two shoulders bottom close to the same price and they are almost symmetrical about the head in terms of time. Symmetry is important to head-and-shoulders patterns.

KEY POINT:
A head-and-shoulders bottom is a three-valley chart pattern that resembles a person's bust, inverted. The head is below the adjacent shoulders, and it acts as a reversal of the downward price trend.

C is a good example of a head-and-shoulders top. That chart pattern is the subject of the next section.

Besides a miracle, what does it take to find a valid head-and-shoulders bottom?

Identification Guidelines

The following table lists the identification guidelines.

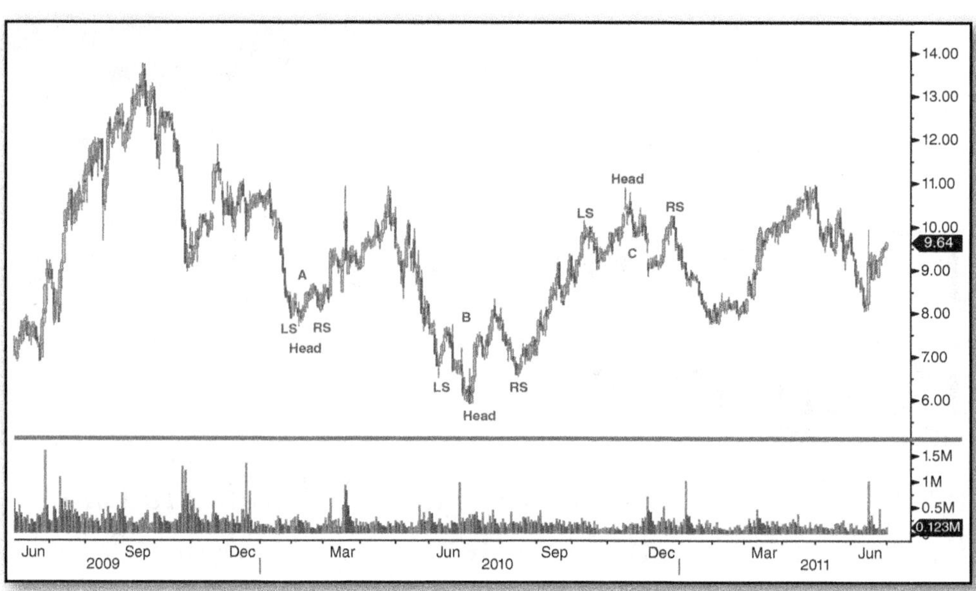

FIGURE 50.1 **SMRT US Equity (Stein Mart Inc).**

Characteristic	Discussion
Downward price trend	Look for a short-term price trend leading down to the head-and-shoulders bottom.
Three valleys	The head-and-shoulders is a three valley pattern with the middle valley bottoming below the other two. The three valleys and two armpits (peaks between the valleys) should be well-defined minor highs and lows.
Symmetry	The entire pattern has a symmetrical feel to it. The left and right shoulders should have similar distances to the head; both should bottom at or near the same price, and be positioned on either side of the head.
Volume	Weakest on the right shoulder and often highest on the left shoulder, but head volume can be high, too. Do not exclude a head-and-shoulders bottom because of an unusual volume pattern.
Neckline, confirmation	The neckline is a line drawn across the two armpits. A close above this line confirms the head-and-shoulders as a valid chart pattern. For up-sloping necklines, use a close above the right armpit as the confirmation price.

Figure 50.2 shows one valid head-and-shoulders bottom and a wannabe. Let us determine the differences.

> **FAST FACTS**
> The average length of a head-and-shoulders bottom is over two months.

Pattern AB is a valid head-and-shoulders bottom. From the peak in February, price tumbles down a waterfall into the chart pattern and forms the left shoulder as a minor low. Following that, a lower valley appears as the head. After recovering from the head, price makes a higher low that becomes the right shoulder.

FIGURE 50.2 CF US Equity (CF Industries Holdings Inc).

> **FAST FACTS**
> On average, when volume is highest on formation of the right shoulder, performance is worse than when volume is higher on the left shoulder or head.

Points A and B are the armpits. Connecting those is the neckline, shown in red.

The two shoulders are almost the same distance from the head, but hardly bottom at the same price. It is hard to tell which of the three valleys have higher volume.

In other words, the guidelines are just that, guidelines, not firm rules. Be flexible when prospecting for head-and-shoulders bottoms since wide variations are common.

Pattern DEF would seem to be a better example of a head-and-shoulders bottom. The two shoulders are more symmetrical looking both in price level and head distance. The pattern confirms when price closes above the neckline.

What is the flaw? Answer: The left shoulder is not a valid minor low. Recall that a minor low should be the lowest price from five days before to five days after. The left shoulder appears to be just a small blip in a rising price trend and not a minor low.

Head-and-Shoulders Bottom Psychology

Why do head-and-shoulders bottoms form? The chart pattern represents the struggle to find the lowest price at the best value. (See Figure 50.3.)

> **FAST FACTS**
> Head-and-shoulders bottoms in bull markets with down-sloping necklines tend to perform significantly better than do those with up-sloping necklines.

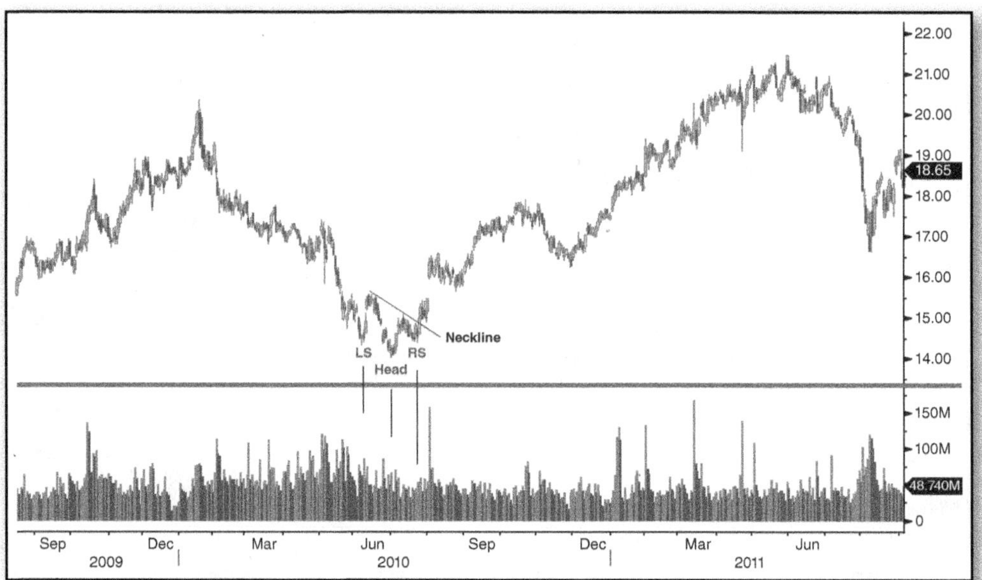

FIGURE 50.3 PFE US Equity (Pfizer Inc).

For example, the chart shows volume spiking even as the stock descends, going into the left shoulder. That higher turnover is a sign of a bottom, but one the stock has seen plenty of times as it rolled down the hill from the January high. What is different this time?

Buying demand puts a crimp on the downward slide and price moves up, but only for about a week. Then, the downtrend resumes, going into the head. Volume on formation of the head is less than on the left shoulder, but that configuration is typical for head-and-shoulders bottoms.

The smart money is accumulating the stock in anticipation of a change in the fundamentals and a rising price. The stock finds support and bottoms at the head low. Then the stock begins recovering, taking volume with it, signaling the change from bear to bull.

Price rounds over at the right armpit and drops to form the right shoulder. Volume is subdued here as if the smart money knows a good value when they see it, but are keeping it quiet. Their buying sends the stock moving higher again, above the neckline, confirming the turn from bear to bull.

Now firmly entrenched in their positions, the smart money can sip margaritas while others do the hard work of pushing the stock higher.

Variations

I show Figure 50.4 because of the right head-and-shoulders bottom (the one with measles). What is so special about this one compared to the others? It has multiple shoulders.

The right shoulder has two small valleys and the left has three. I show four of them as red dots. Strictly speaking, only two of these five are minor lows because of the five-day count on either side of the low to qualify it as a minor low.

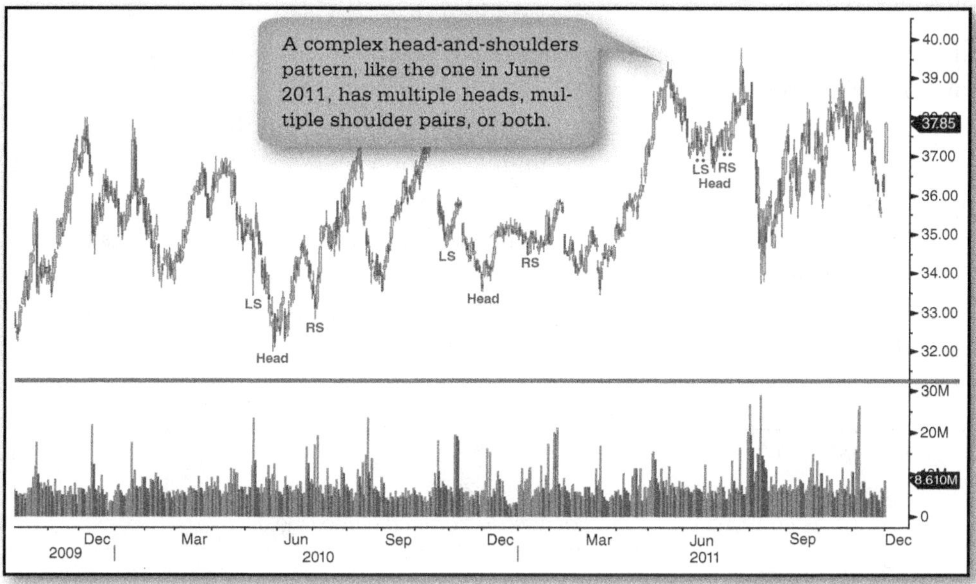

FIGURE 50.4 **LLY US Equity (Eli Lilly & Co).**

This variation is called a complex head-and-shoulders bottom. Those are chart patterns with multiple shoulders, multiple heads, or both (rarely). As you scan for head-and-shoulders bottoms, look to the left and right and check for additional shoulders or another head. Treat the more complex pattern as a simple head-and-shoulders bottom.

As for the other two head-and-shoulders bottoms, notice the higher left shoulder bottom in each case. Irregularities such as these will cause doubt until you become accustomed to identifying flawed patterns.

Figure 50.5 shows a chart pattern that you may think is a head-and-shoulders bottom, and you would be wrong. This one has two twists. What are they?

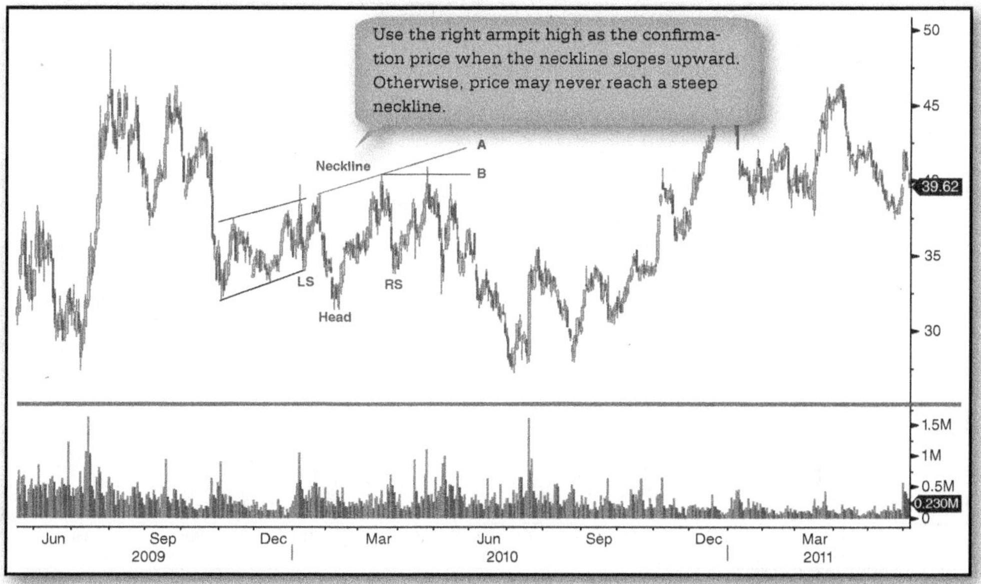

FIGURE 50.5 **TXI US Equity (Texas Industries Inc).**

First, price does not trend downward into the chart pattern as the blue channel lines show. Price rises instead. This head-and-shoulders acts as a continuation of the upward price trend and not a reversal.

One might argue that point, saying that price drops from the peak in July 2009 and bottoms a year later with the middle section being a retrace of that downtrend. Fine.

The second "flaw" is that it never confirms as a valid head-and-shoulders bottom. That means price did not *close* above the neckline (A) or right armpit high (B) before closing below the bottom of the pattern. The armpit measure is the correct one to use when the neckline slopes upward, as in this case.

> **SMART INVESTOR TIP**
> If the neckline slopes upward from a head-and-shoulders bottom, use a close above the right armpit as confirmation instead of a close above the neckline.

Exercise

The first exercise shows three head-and-shoulders bottoms, but one you may disagree with. See if you can find all three. (See Figure 50.6.)

Figure 50.7 shows the answers. The questionable head-and-shoulders bottom is at A. Why? Because price trends upward into the chart pattern. It does not act as a "bottom" reversal but as a continuation pattern.

The other two chart patterns are valid head-and-shoulders bottoms. They reverse the short-term downtrend.

Note the horizontal red confirmation line in patterns A and B where the neckline slopes upward.

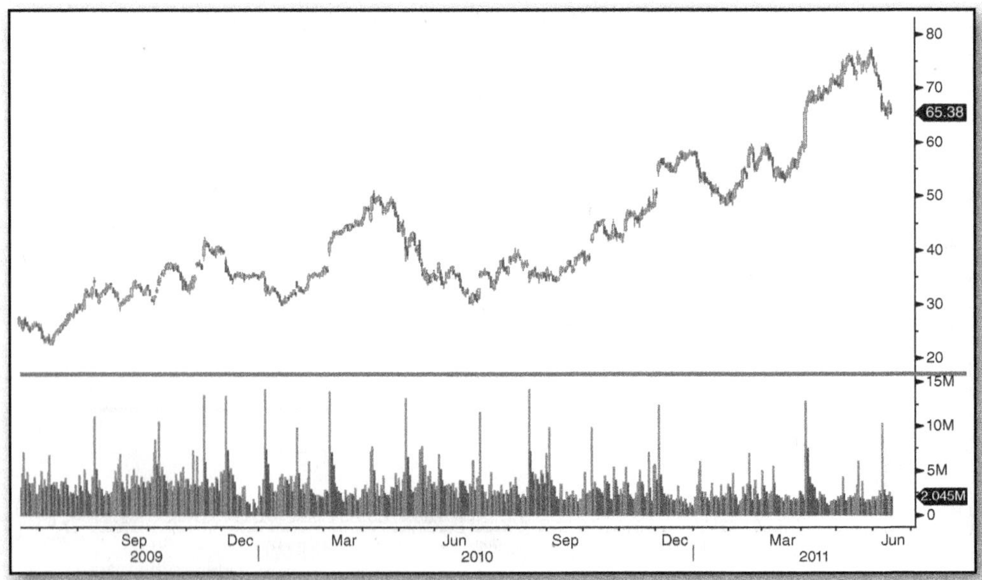

FIGURE 50.6 ANF US Equity (Abercrombie & Fitch Co).

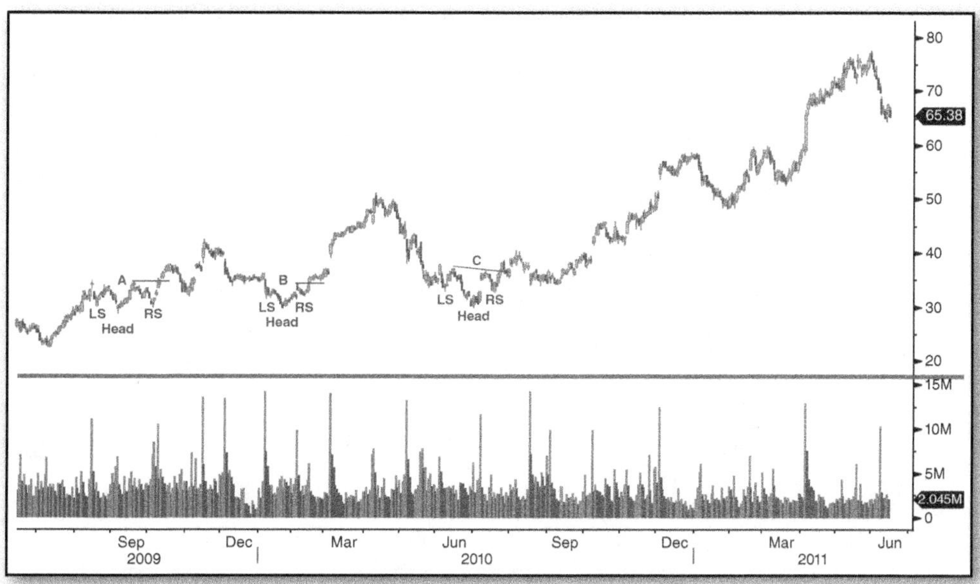

FIGURE 50.7 ANF US Equity (Abercrombie & Fitch Co).

The next exercise is easier, but just as tricky. There is at least one head-and-shoulders bottom in Figure 50.8. See how many you can find.

Figure 50.9 shows the answers. Pattern A is not a head-and-shoulders bottom. Why? Because it is not symmetrical. The right shoulder is just too far away from the head compared to the left shoulder–head distance.

Pattern B is a valid head-and-shoulders bottom chart pattern.

The next section discusses another variation of the head-and-shoulders pattern: a top! If you had trouble finding the bottom variety, then spotting tops may be easier.

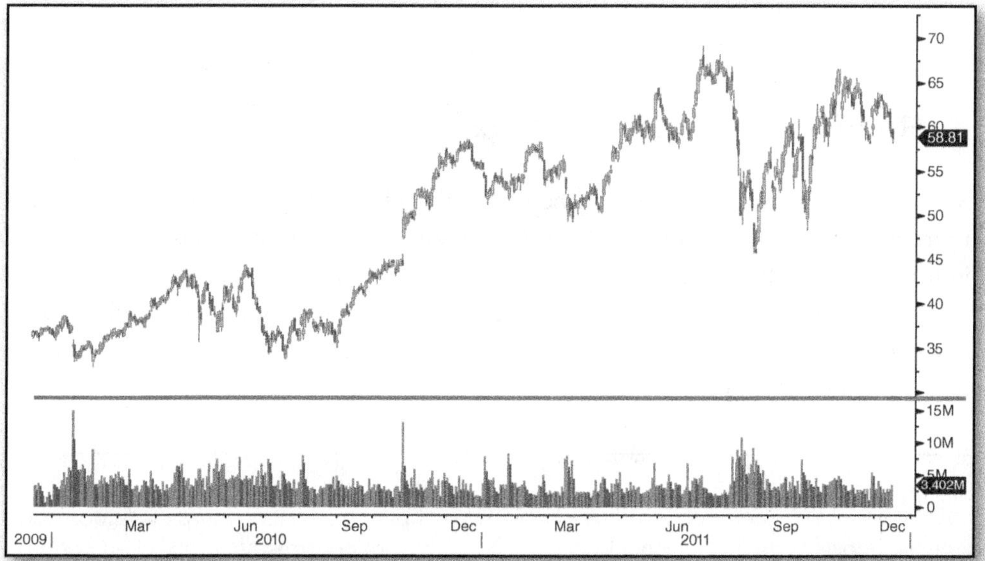

FIGURE 50.8 COH US Equity (Coach Inc).

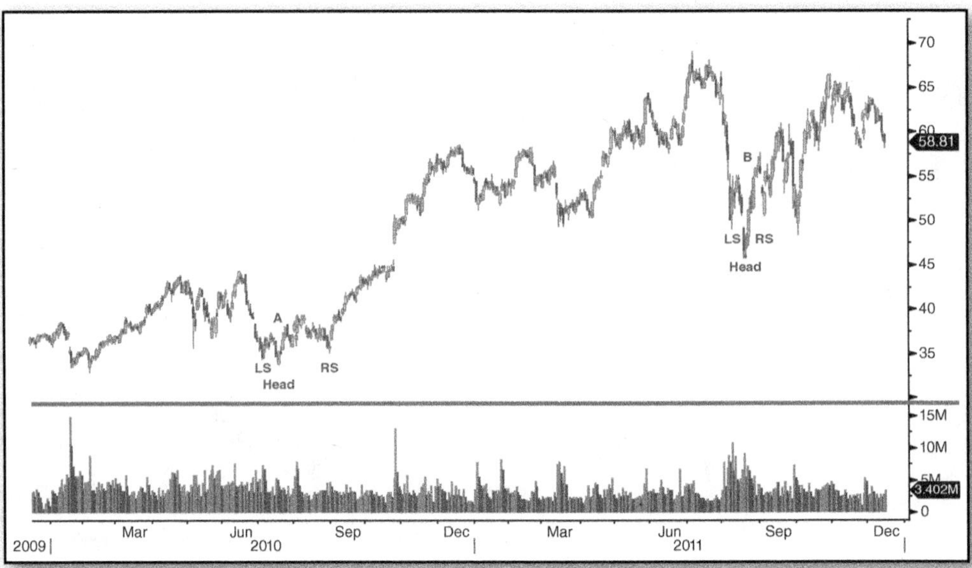

FIGURE 50.9 COH US Equity (Coach Inc).

Test Yourself

Answer the following.

1. True or false: A chart pattern acting as a reversal has price trending higher into the pattern and exiting out the top.
2. True or false: Draw a neckline connecting the two valleys in the head-and-shoulders bottom for confirmation.
3. Even though a head-and-shoulders bottom is a reversal chart pattern, it can act as a continuation pattern.
4. When the neckline slopes upward, use the left armpit to determine the confirmation price.
5. Price confirms a head-and-shoulders bottom when it pierces a down-sloping neckline.

Answers: 1. False; 2. False; 3. True; 4. False; 5. False

Head-and-Shoulders Tops

Spotting tops is easier for me. Perhaps it is the idea that preservation of capital is more important than profit. Whatever the reason, let us look at the last chart pattern in this section of the book.

The head-and-shoulders top appears on the chart just as it sounds, and Figure 50.10 shows examples. In both chart patterns, a head towers above the shoulders, making it look like a person's bust.

KEY POINT:
A head-and-shoulders top is a three-peak reversal pattern with a centrally located head priced above two adjacent (shoulder) peaks. The pattern confirms as a valid chart pattern when price closes below the neckline or right armpit.

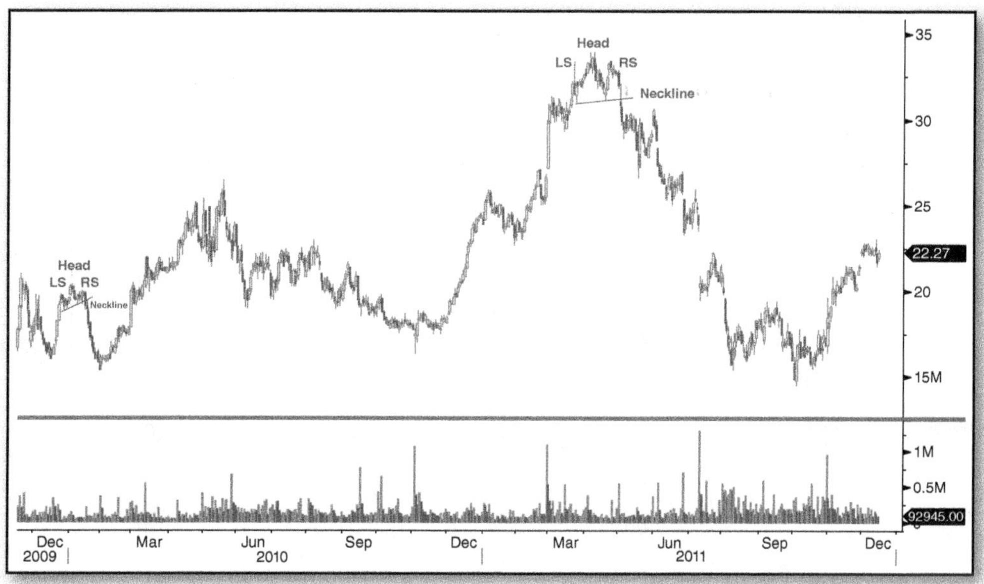

FIGURE 50.10 **TREX US Equity (Trex Co Inc).**

Price trends upward into the head-and-shoulders reversal. Then a left shoulder forms (LS), followed by a head and right shoulder. When price closes below the neckline, it confirms the chart pattern as valid. Price drops like a falling climber whose pitons have released.

Identification Guidelines

The following table lists guidelines for identifying head-and-shoulders tops.

Characteristic	Discussion
Upward price trend	Look for an upward price trend leading to a head-and-shoulders top.
Three peaks	The head-and-shoulders top is a three-peak pattern with the middle peak above the other two. The three peaks and two armpits (valleys between the peaks) should be well-defined minor highs and lows.
Symmetry	The entire pattern has a symmetrical feel to it. The left and right shoulders should have similar distances from the head; both shoulders should top out near the same price and be positioned on either side of the head.
Volume	Weakest on the right shoulder and often highest on the left shoulder, but head volume can be high, too. Do not exclude a head-and-shoulders top because of an unusual volume pattern.
Neckline, confirmation	The neckline is a line drawn across the two armpits. A close below this line confirms the head-and-shoulders as a valid chart pattern. For down-sloping necklines, use a close below the right armpit as the confirmation price.

Figure 50.11 shows a head-and-shoulders top on the weekly scale. It appears as a three-bump pattern sitting atop a hill as if it were playing King of the Mountain.

FIGURE 50.11 **HOV US Equity (Hovnanian Enterprises Inc).**

Notice that the chart pattern on the weekly scale appears similar to ones on the daily chart or any other scale.

FAST FACTS

The head-and-shoulders top, in a bull market after a breakout, has the best average decline of 21 chart patterns tested.

Two shoulders appear at similar distances from the head, but not quite at the same price, with a head that towers above the shoulders.

This head-and-shoulders top has a down-sloping neckline in red (A). The blue line (B) shows how much sooner price validates the pattern when using a close below the right armpit instead of the neckline.

Volume is higher on the left shoulder than the right.

Head-and-Shoulders Top Psychology

Why do head-and-shoulders tops form? Pretend that you represent the smart money—high wealth individuals, financial institutions, hedge or mutual funds. You are searching for a stock to buy and believe that Hovnanian, shown in Figure 50.12, represents an intriguing situation.

You start buying at A, and that buying pressure sends the stock exploding out of a loose consolidation region that ended in March.

FAST FACTS

When volume is highest on the right shoulder in a bull market, the average head-and-shoulders top underperforms.

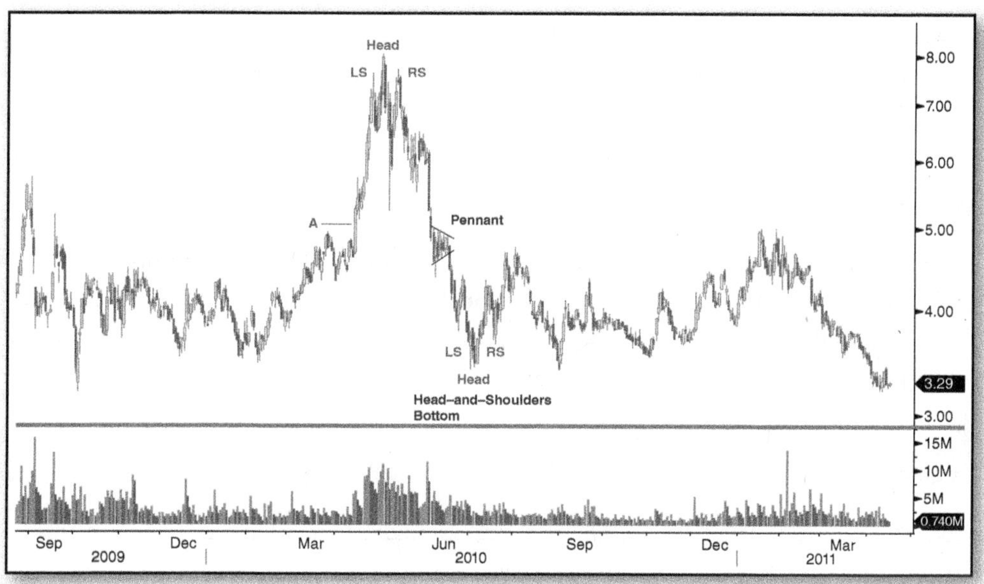

FIGURE 50.12 HOV US Equity (Hovnanian Enterprises Inc).

Others join in and buy the stock, sending the price into orbit like a shuttle launching.

As stars appear out the shuttle's window and the stock rises above 7, you have made 40 percent in about two weeks. Time to sell.

Your selling causes the stock to halt its upward move and begin a retrace, forming the left shoulder.

Sensing weakness, you stop selling but monitor the situation. Buy-the-dip players, believing that this is a chance to get in on a mission to deep space, buy the stock on the retrace. The decline halts, and the stock begins rising again.

As the stock moves up, momentum players join the trend. Once the stock rises above 8, you resume selling, not heavily at first because you have a large number of shares to dump. Still, the market players notice your selling and the stock heads back down.

You dump your remaining shares as the stock begins tumbling. Volume rises as other players sell their shares to unsuspecting buyers. The stock continues moving down and slides back below 6. Believing the stock oversold, demand picks up and sends the price moving up again for the last time.

You watch from the sidelines. The stock climbs to form the right shoulder. Lacking support for a continued rise, the stock turns down.

Investors versed in technical analysis see the head-and-shoulders top for what it is: a reversal. They quietly take profits. Others initiate short sales by selling high and hoping price hits zero.

The stock moves lower and forms a pennant before breaking out downward, leading to a head-and-shoulders bottom reversal.

FAST FACTS

When the left shoulder peak is above the right one, the average head-and-shoulders top tends to outperform.

Variations

Figure 50.13 shows a variety of head-and-shoulders tops. Let us begin on the left.

The head-and-shoulders at A is a traditional-looking pattern because it has wide, rounded shoulders and deep recessions that form the armpits. The pattern confirms when price closes below the horizontal line.

FAST FACTS

Head-and-shoulders tops with horizontal necklines tend to outperform.

Pattern B is an outlier. The left and right shoulders do not qualify as minor highs because they are not wide enough, and yet the head-and-shoulders acts as a reversal of the uptrend. It confirms when price closes below the up-sloping neckline.

Pattern C has a spike for its head with unevenly priced shoulders, but they are close to symmetrical about the head. The pattern also confirms when price closes below the up-sloping neckline.

Pattern D is the only invalid head-and-shoulders top. The left shoulder is much wider than the right one, and the two shoulders are not symmetrical about the head.

Notice that the stock closes above the top of the head (E) before price closes below the red confirmation line, invalidating the chart pattern.

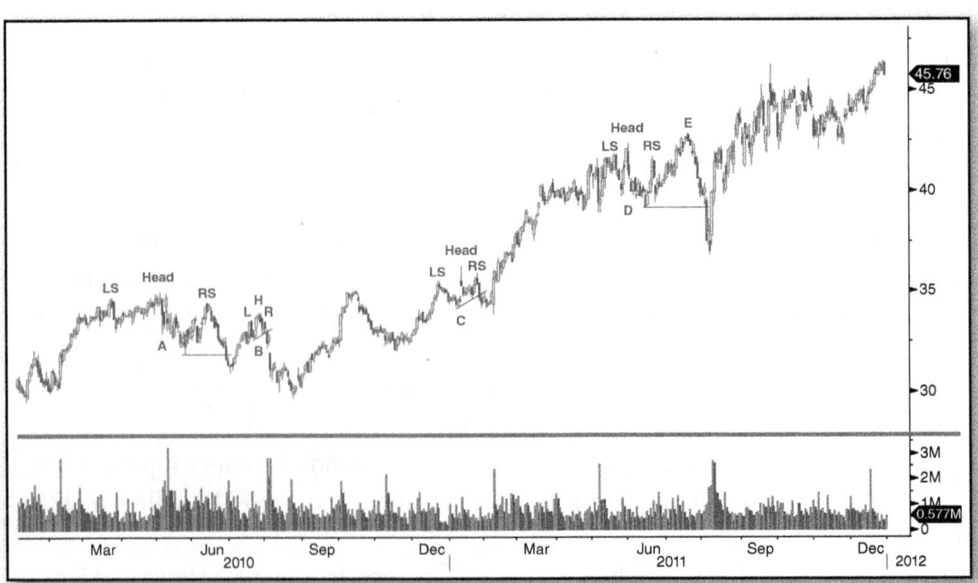

FIGURE 50.13 CHD US Equity (Church & Dwight Co Inc).

When searching for head-and-shoulders tops, I have found it beneficial to ask if the pattern *looks* like a person's bust. If the neck is unusually long or if the two shoulders are crooked, then look for another head-and-shoulders top.

SMART INVESTOR TIP

If a head-and-shoulders top does not resemble a human bust, then it is not a head-and-shoulders top.

Exercise

In this exercise, find as many head-and-shoulders tops as you can. Also, look for double and triple tops and bottoms, ascending and descending triangles. (See Figure 50.14.)

The answers appear in Figure 50.15. I show the patterns spread out like peanut butter across bread, but there are other patterns that may qualify (like additional double bottoms or double tops).

Head-and-shoulders tops A, B, and C are all valid. Pattern D confirms as a head-and-shoulders top, but the trend is downward leading to the chart pattern. It is not a reversal, but a continuation head-and-shoulders top.

Notice that since the head-and-shoulders pattern appeared at the end of the trend, the downward breakout did not amount to much. That is a trading tip you might want to remember.

SMART INVESTOR TIP

Chart patterns that form well into a price trend may signal the end of the trend.

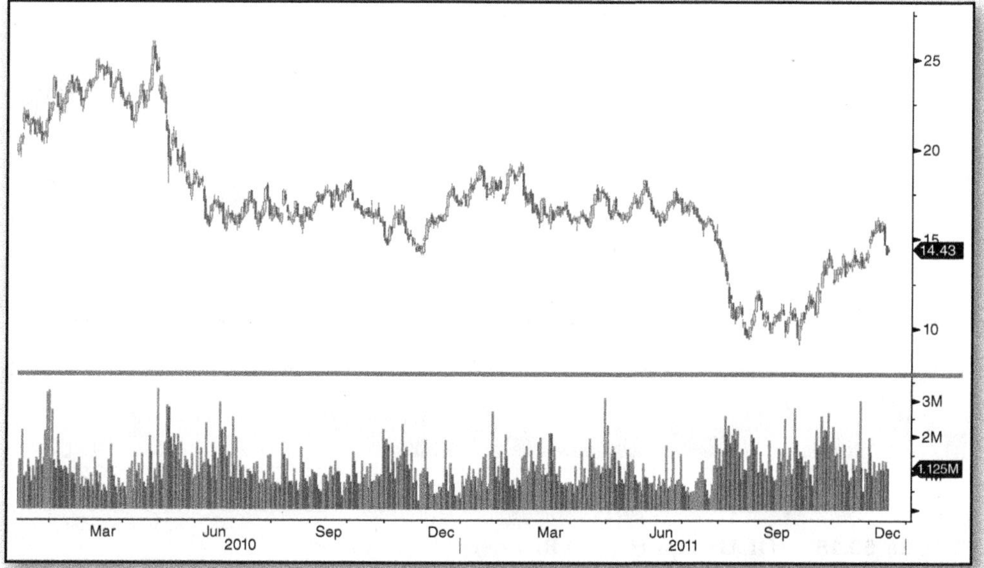

FIGURE 50.14 RYL US Equity (Ryland Group Inc/The).

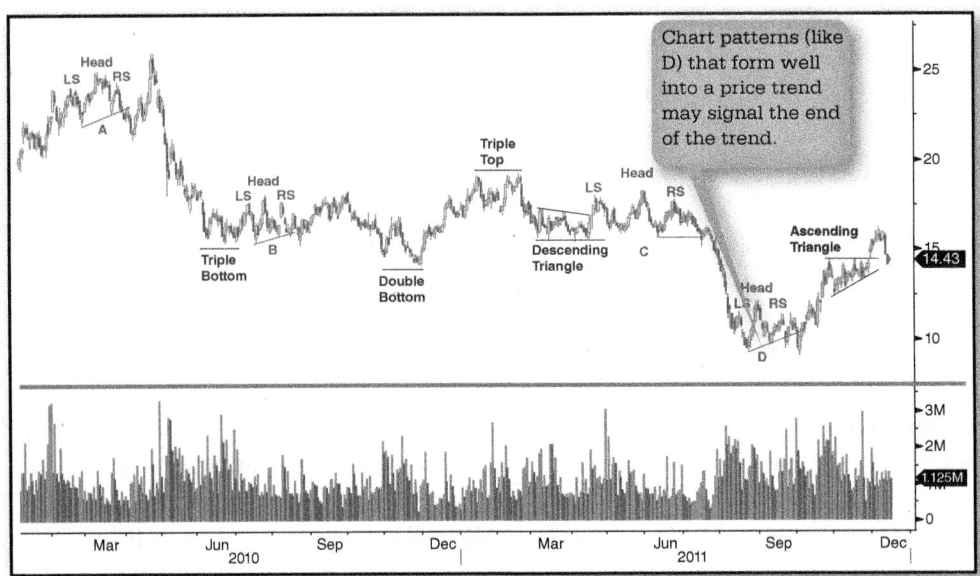

FIGURE 50.15 RYL US Equity (Ryland Group Inc/The).

As for the other chart patterns, the double bottom in November 2010 has uneven bottoms (3 percent apart), making the pattern difficult to identify.

Figure 50.16 has many patterns that look like head-and-shoulders tops, but are not. Find two valid ones.

Figure 50.17 shows the answers. The valid head-and-shoulders tops are marked A and B, flavored with red necklines. The other chart patterns do not confirm before price rises above the top of the chart pattern.

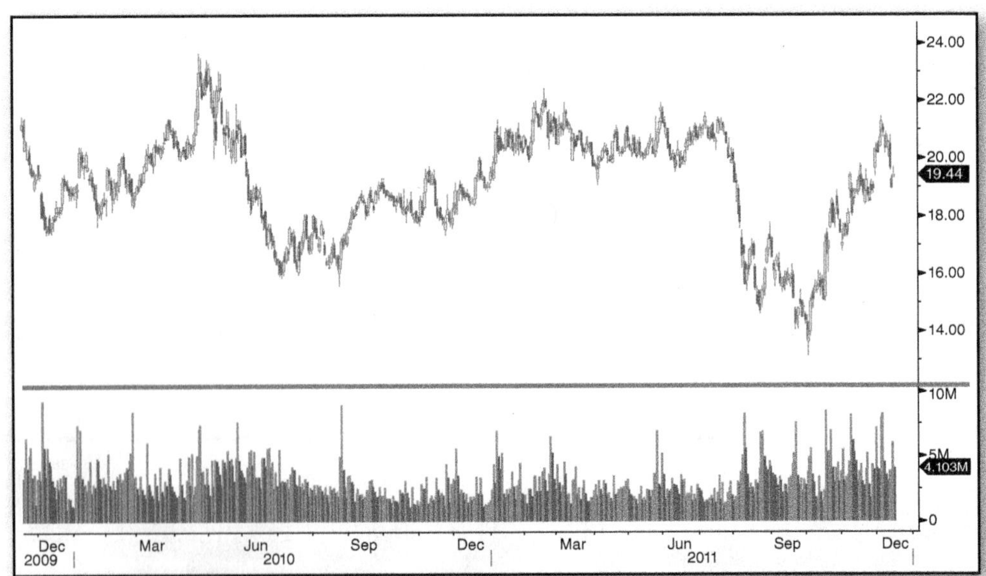

FIGURE 50.16 TOL US Equity (Toll Brothers Inc).

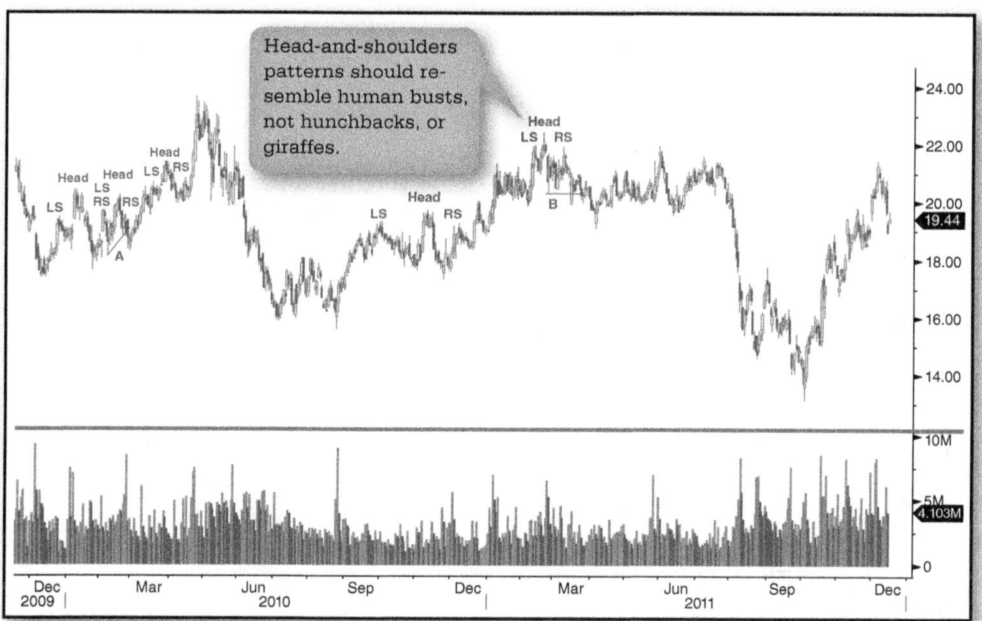

FIGURE 50.17 TOL US Equity (Toll Brothers Inc).

It's a Wrap

This chapter completes the introduction to chart pattern identification. We learned to use horizontal trendlines to highlight rectangles. Then we sloped one of the lines to find ascending and descending triangles. Two converging trendlines outlined a symmetrical triangle.

After that, we switched to peaks and valleys to find double and triple tops and bottoms. Completing the group were the head-and-shoulders, a complex pattern that is not much different from a triple top or bottom.

Now that we know what to look for, we can use the patterns as buy signals. The next section describes how.

Test Yourself

Answer the following.

1. How close must the two shoulders of a head-and-shoulders top be in price?
   A. Within 25 cents
   B. Within 50 cents
   C. It does not matter.
   D. It does not matter providing the entire pattern looks like a human bust.
   E. All of the above.
2. True or false: In a head-and-shoulders top, the chart pattern confirms when price closes below the left armpit.
3. True or false: To qualify as a top, price must trend upward into the bottom of a chart pattern.
4. True or false: In a triple top, the middle peak can be slightly below the other two.

Answers: 1. D; 2. False; 3.True; 4.True

CHAPTER 51

Understanding Implied Volatility

From Russell Rhoads, *Trading VIX Derivatives: Trading and Hedging Strategies Using VIX Futures, Options, and Exchange Traded Notes* (Hoboken, New Jersey: John Wiley & Sons, 2007), Chapter 1.

In this book, we will discuss the ins and outs of a popular market indicator, or index, that is based on implied volatility. The indicator is the CBOE Volatility Index®, widely known by its ticker symbol, VIX. It should come as no surprise that a solid understanding of the index must begin with a solid understanding of what implied volatility is and how it works.

Implied volatility is ultimately determined by the price of option contracts. Since option prices are the result of market forces, or increased levels of buying or selling, implied volatility is determined by the market. An index based on implied volatility of option prices is displaying the market's estimation of volatility of the underlying security in the future.

More advanced option traders who feel they have a solid understanding of implied volatility may consider moving to Chapter 52. That chapter introduces the actual method for determining the VIX. However, as implied volatility is one of the more advanced option pricing concepts, a quick review before diving into the VIX and volatility-related trading vehicles would be worthwhile for most traders.

Historical Versus Forward-Looking Volatility

There are two main types of volatility discussed relative to securities prices. The first is historical volatility, which may be calculated using recent trading activity for a stock or other security. The historical volatility of a stock is factual and known. Also, the historical volatility does not give any indication about the future movement of a stock. The forward-looking volatility is what is referred to as the implied volatility. This type of volatility results from the market price of options that trade on a stock.

The implied volatility component of option prices is the factor that can give all option traders, novice to expert, the most difficulty. This occurs because the implied volatility of an option may change while all other pricing factors impacting the price of an option remain unchanged. This change may occur as the order flow for options is biased more to buying or selling. A result of increased buying of options by market participants is higher implied volatility. Conversely, when there is net selling of options, the implied volatility indicated by option prices moves lower.

Basically, the nature of order flow dictates the direction of implied volatility. Again, more option buying increases the option price and the result is higher implied volatility. Going back to Economics 101, implied volatility reacts to the supply and demand of the marketplace. Buying pushes it higher, and selling pushes it lower.

The implied volatility of an option is also considered an indication of the risk associated with the underlying security. The risk may be thought of as how much movement may be expected from the underlying stock over the life of an option. This is not the potential direction of the stock price move, just the magnitude of the move. Generally, when thinking of risk, traders think of a stock losing value or the price moving lower. Using implied volatility as a risk measure results in an estimation of a price move in either direction. When the market anticipates that a stock may soon move dramatically, the price of option contracts, both puts and calls, will move higher.

A common example of a known event in the future that may dramatically influence the price of a stock is a company's quarterly earnings report. Four times a year a company will release information to the investing public in the form of its recent earnings results. This earnings release may also include statements regarding business prospects for the company. This information may have a dramatic impact on the share price. As this price move will also impact option prices, the option contracts usually react in advance. Due to the anticipation that will work into option prices, they are generally more expensive as traders and investors buy options before seeing the report.

This increased buying of options results in higher option prices. There are two ways to think about this: the higher price of the option contracts results in higher implied volatility, or because of higher implied volatility option prices are higher. After the earnings report, there is less risk of a big move in the underlying stock and the options become less expensive. This drop in price is due to lower implied volatility levels; implied volatility is now lower due to lower option prices.

A good non-option-oriented example of how implied volatility works may be summed up through this illustration. If you live in Florida, you are familiar with hurricane season. The path of hurricanes can be unpredictable, and at times homeowners have little time to prepare for a storm. Using homeowners insurance as a substitute for an option contract, consider the following situation.

You wake to find out that an evacuation is planned due to a potential hurricane. Before leaving the area, you check whether your homeowners insurance is current. You find you have allowed your coverage to lapse, and so you run down to your agent's office. As he boards up windows and prepares to evacuate inland, he informs you that you may renew, but the cost is going to be $50,000 instead of the $2,000 annual rate you have paid for years. After hearing your objections, he is steadfast. The higher price, he explains, is due to the higher risk associated with the coming storm.

You decide that $50,000 is too much to pay, and you return home to ride out the storm. Fortunately, the storm takes a left turn and misses your neighborhood altogether. Realizing that you have experienced a near miss, you run down to your agent's office with a $50,000 check in hand. Being an honest guy, he tells you the rate is back down to $2,000. Why is this?

The imminent risk level for replacing your home has decreased as there is no known threat bearing down on your property. As the immediate risk of loss or damage has decreased tremendously, so has the cost of protection against loss. When applying this to the option market, risk is actually risk of movement of the underlying security, either higher or lower. This risk is the magnitude of expected movement of the underlying security over the life of an option.

When market participants are expecting a big price move to the upside in the underlying security, there will be net buying of call options in anticipation of this move. As this buying occurs, the price of the call options will increase. This price rise in the options is associated with an increase risk of a large price move, and this increase in risk translates to higher implied volatility.

Also, if there is an expectation of a lower price move, the marketplace may see an increase in put buying. With higher demand for put contracts, the price of puts may increase resulting in higher implied volatility for those options. Finally, if put prices increase, the result is corresponding call prices rising due to a concept known as put-call parity, which will be discussed in the next section.

Put-Call Parity

Put and call prices are linked to each other through the price of the underlying stock through put-call parity. This link exists because combining a stock and put position can result in the same payoff as a position in a call option with the same strike price as the put. If this relationship gets out of line or not in parity, an arbitrage opportunity exits. When one of these opportunities arises, there are trading firms that will quickly buy and sell the securities to attempt to take advantage of this mispricing. This market activity will push the put and call prices back in line with each other.

Put and call prices should remain within a certain price range of each other or arbitragers will enter the market, which results in the prices coming back into parity. Parity between the two also results in a similar implied volatility output resulting from using these prices in a model to determine the implied volatility of the market.

TABLE 51.1 Put, Call, and Stock Pricing to Illustrate Put-Call Parity	
Stock/Option	**Price**
XYZ Stock	$50.00
XYZ 50 Call	$1.00
XYZ 50 Put	$2.00

Stated differently, increased demand for a call option will raise the price of that call. As the price of the call moves higher, the corresponding put price should also rise, or the result will be an arbitrage trade that will push the options into line. As the pricing of the option contracts are tied to each other, they will share similar implied volatility levels also.

For a quick and very simple example of how put-call parity works, consider the options and stock in Table 51.1.

Using the XYZ 50 Put combined with XYZ stock, a payout that replicates being long the XYZ 50 Call may be created. The combination of owning stock and owning a put has the same payout structure as a long call option position. With the XYZ 50 Call trading at 1.00 and the XYZ 50 Put priced at 2.00, there may be a mispricing scenario. Table 51.2 compares a long XYZ 50 Call trade with a combined position of long XYZ stock and long a XYZ 50 Put.

The final two columns compare a payout of owning XYZ stock from 50.00 and buying the XYZ 50 Put at 2.00 versus buying an XYZ 50 Call for 1.00. Note that at any price at expiration, the long call position is worth 1.00 more than the combined stock and put position. With this pricing difference, there is the ability to take a short position in the strategy that will be worth less and buy the strategy that will be worth more at expiration. The payout diagram in Figure 51.1 shows how the two positions compare at a variety of prices at expiration.

The lines are parallel throughout this diagram. The higher line represents the profit or loss based on buying the 50 call. The lower line represents the payout for the spread combining a long stock position and a long 50 put position. At any price at expiration, the combined position has less value than the long 50 call. Knowing this outcome, it is possible to benefit from the 1.00 spread, which will exist at any price at expiration for two positions that are basically the same.

Due to put-call parity and the mispricing between the 50 Call and 50 Put, the call may be purchased combined with a short position in the stock and put option. A quick

TABLE 51.2 Payout Comparison for Long Call and Long Stock + Long Put Trade

XYZ at Expiration	Long XYZ Stock	Long XYZ 50 Put	Long Stock + Long Put	Long XYZ 50 Call
45.00	−5.00	3.00	−2.00	−1.00
50.00	0.00	−2.00	−2.00	−1.00
55.00	5.00	−2.00	3.00	4.00

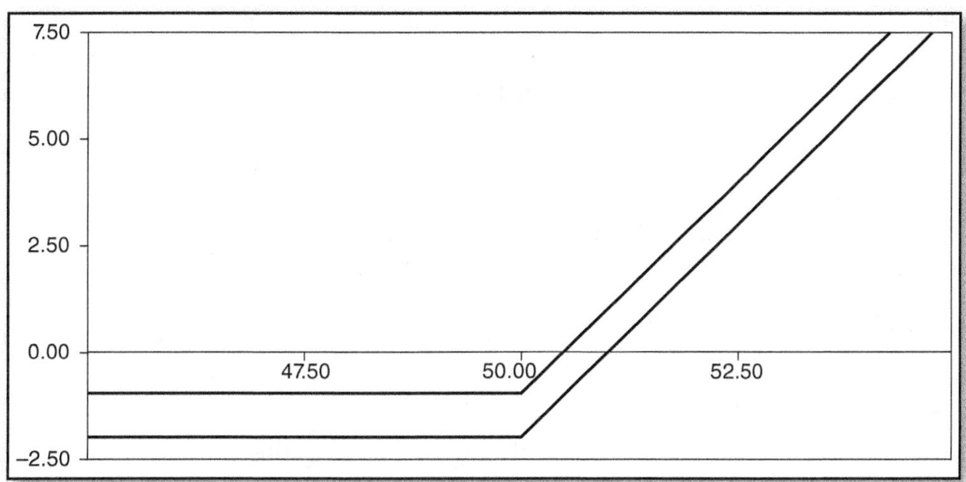

FIGURE 51.1 Payout Diagram Comparison.

transaction using the prices in the example would result in a profit of 1.00 upon options expiration. This 1.00 profit would be realized regardless of the price of the stock at expiration. Firms would attempt to take advantage of this opportunity through buying the cheaper call option and selling the comparable more expensive put option. The market activity of these participants is what keeps put and call option prices in line with each other and the implied volatility of both put and call contracts at the same level.

Estimating Price Movement

What the implied volatility of an option projects onto the underlying security is the expected range of price movement over a certain period of time. This estimation of price movement is based on statistics and the bell curve. The implied volatility of an option is the projection of an annualized one standard deviation move in the underlying stock over the life of the option. According to statistics and using implied volatility as a guide, the price of a stock should land between up and down one standard deviation at option expiration. The closing price should land in this range 68.2 percent of the time.

This 68.2 percent comes from statistics and what is referred to as a normal distribution. Statistics like this reveal that 68.2 percent of the time a stock should be between up one standard deviation and down one standard deviation a year from today. A formula may also be used to take this annualized number and narrow down the projection to a single day. The normal distribution also indicates that there is a 95.4 percent expectation of the stock landing between up two standard deviations and down two standard deviations. Finally, at three standard deviations, the probability reaches 99.7 percent.

With a stock trading at \$50 and the underlying option prices indicating 20 percent implied volatility, the result is a one standard deviation price move equal to \$10 (20 percent of \$50). In other words, the stock is expected to close between \$40 (down \$10) and \$60 (up \$10) with 68.2 percent certainty a year from today. A two standard deviation price move would be equal to \$20. This is calculated by simply multiplying 2 times a single standard deviation. Using two standard deviations, it can be projected out that the stock should land between $30 and up $70, with a confidence of 95.4 percent. At three standard deviations, there is a 99.7 percent chance of the stock closing between $20 and $80 a year from the date of the calculation.

Valuing Options: Pricing Calculators and Other Tools

An option pricing calculator is a tool that allows a user the ability to input the pricing variables that determine the value of an option with the result being a theoretical option price. Ultimately the market determines the price of an option through buying and selling forces. However, when analyzing and investigating option trades, using an option pricing calculator with certain assumptions gives an idea where an option may be trading in the future. Also, using an option pricing calculator is an excellent way to become familiar with the price action of option contracts. The CBOE has a free option calculator available on its website at www.cboe.com/tradtool; it is a valuable tool for option pricing.

The value of an option contract is derived from a variety of inputs. Inputs into an option pricing model include the price of the underlying security, the strike price of the option, the type of option, dividends, interest rates, and time to option expiration. The final input into an option pricing model is the implied volatility of the option. These inputs may be used in a model to determine the value of an option.

Table 51.3 demonstrates how an option pricing model is used to determine the value of an option. The inputs are at the top of the table, with the value of the option showing up as the only output. Option pricing models calculate a variety of pieces of useful information, such as the impact of changes in pricing factors. These outputs are known as the option Greeks. However, to keep focus on the topic at hand, implied volatility, only the necessary outputs are going to be demonstrated in this example of an option calculator.

TABLE 51.3 Option Pricing Calculator–Option Value Output

Factor	**Input**
Call/Put	Call
Underlying Price	44.75
Strike Price	45.00
Implied Volatility	30%
Days to Expiration	30
Interest Rate	1.00%
Dividends	0.00%
Output	**Result**
Option Value	1.45

The option price in the model is determined from a stock trading at 44.75 with implied volatility of 30 percent and a risk-free interest rate of 1.00 percent. The result is a call option value with a strike price of 45 and 30 days to expiration would be valued at 1.45 based on the inputs used in this model. Keep in mind that this is a pricing model, not the actual market trading price of the option. Again, the inputs in the model are assumptions, not just the market price. Just because using these inputs results in a value of 1.45 for this 45 Call does not mean it can be traded at this level. In fact, the market price of this option will vary if the market consensus differs from the inputs used in this model.

The real value of an option at any given time is actually determined by the price that it may be bought or sold in the market. In the case of this 45 Call, even though the inputs into the model result in a 1.45 value, when checking market quotes for this option we find that the current trading price is 1.70. The reason for the difference between our model's value and the market price is the result of different implied volatility levels being used. The previous model, in Table 51.3, takes inputs and the result in a difference in option values based on the inputs.

The pricing factors in an option pricing model are for the most part set in stone. The exception of this is the implied volatility input. For the model, the assumption of 30 percent implied volatility was used. However, the market is pricing in a higher implied volatility level. This is determined before any numbers or formulas have been run just by comparing the option market price and the option value assumption that resulted from the model. The market price of the option is higher than the pricing model output. Seeing this, it is pretty certain that the implied volatility based on market prices is higher than what was entered into the model. There is a direct correlation between high and low relative option prices and higher or lower implied volatility.

Table 51.4 is an option pricing model that uses the market price as an input with the sole output being implied volatility. This implied volatility level is being indicated by the 1.70 market price of the 45 Call. The higher option price here is a higher implied volatility than what was used in the first pricing model. As the option price in this model is higher than the option value that resulted from a 30 percent implied

TABLE 51.4 Option Pricing Calculator—Implied Volatility Output

Factor	**Input**
Call/Put	Call
Underlying Price	44.75
Strike Price	45.00
Option Price	1.70
Days to Expiration	30
Interest Rate	1.00%
Dividends	0.00%
Output	**Result**
Implied Volatility	35%

TABLE 51.5 Impact of a 5 Percent Increase in Implied Volatility		
Implied Volatility	30%	35%
Option Price	1.45	1.70

volatility, the expectation would be a higher implied volatility result. Using 1.70 as the price of the option actually results in the implied volatility that is being projected by this option price to be 35 percent. Professional traders generally start with the market price of an option to calculate implied volatility as that is where the implied volatility of an option is ultimately determined.

Another method of demonstrating the impact of different implied volatility levels on option prices appears in Table 51.5. Instead of a comparison of what the model output was versus the option price based on model outputs, consider the previous option prices in a different way. Consider the two option prices and implied volatility differences as changes based on an increase in demand for the option. Both prices represent the market and the option price increases from 1.45 to 1.70. This option price rise occurs due to an increase in buying of the call option while all other factors that influence the option price stay the same.

Since the price of the option contract has increased, the resulting implied volatility output from an option model has also increased. Higher option prices, whether put or call prices, will result in a higher implied volatility output with no changes in any of the other option pricing factors.

To recap, there is a direct link between the demand for option contracts and their prices in the marketplace. This is regardless of changes occurring in the underlying stock price. With demand in the form of buying pressure pushing option prices higher or an increase in selling occurring due to market participants pushing option prices lower, the implied volatility of an option is dictated by market forces.

Fluctuations Based on Supply and Demand

As mentioned in the first section of this chapter, implied volatility does fluctuate based on supply and demand for options. This leads to the question, "What exactly causes the supply and demand for options to fluctuate?" The short answer is the near-term expected price changes that may occur in the underlying stock. These moves are usually the result of information that has influenced the fundamental outlook for a stock. The best example of this type of information would be a company's quarterly earnings reports.

Every publicly traded company in the United States reports its earnings results four times a year. The date and timing (generally before the market opens or after the market closes) are usually known well in advance of the actual announcement. Along with the earnings results, other information is disseminated, such as the company's revenues and the source of those revenues. Many companies offer a possible outlook regarding the prospects for their business conditions, and most will hold a public conference call to answer professional investors' questions. These events often have a dramatic impact, either positive or negative, on the price of a stock.

Again, the date that these results are announced is public knowledge and often widely anticipated by analysts and traders. As the date draws near, there is usually trading in the stock and stock options that is based on the anticipated stock price reaction to the earnings announcement. The result is usually net buying of options as there is speculation regarding the potential move of the underlying stock. The net option buying results in higher option prices and an increase in the implied volatility projected by the options that trade on this stock. Usually this increase impacts only the options with the closest expiration and strike prices that are close to where the stock is trading. An excellent example of this can be seen in the option prices and resulting implied volatility levels for Amazon stock shown in Table 51.6.

These are market prices from just before the close of trading on July 22, 2010. Amazon's earnings were reported after the market close on the 22nd with weekly options that expire on the 23rd having only one trading day until expiration after the news was released. The difference in implied volatility between the options that have one trading day left and those that have just under a month left is pretty significant.

This difference stems from the options that market participants would use as a short-term trading vehicle related to Amazon's earnings announcement. This would be the same for hedgers and speculators alike. Both would focus on the strike prices that are closest to the trading price of the stock as well as the options with the least amount of time to expiration.

Option contracts that have the closest expiration to a known event that occurs after the event are the contracts that will have the most price reaction before and after the event occurs. With Amazon reporting earnings the evening of July 22 and an option series expiring on July 23, the July 23 options are the contracts that will see the most price action based on the stock price reaction to the earnings release.

TABLE 51.6 Amazon Option Implied Volatility and Option Prices Minutes Prior to an Earnings Announcement

			AMZN @ 120.07	
Call Strike	**July 23 Call**	**July 23 Call IV**	**Aug 21 Call**	**Aug 21 Call IV**
115	7.00	163%	9.25	48%
120	3.92	156%	6.25	45%
125	1.82	148%	4.05	45%
Put Strike	**July 23 Put**	**July 23 Put IV**	**Aug 21 Put**	**Aug 21 Put IV**
115	1.92	159%	4.05	48%
120	3.82	155%	6.20	47%
125	6.75	148%	8.90	45%

The stock price is very close to the 120 strike price when the option first listed and just before the earnings announcement. Using the 120 strike options, implied volatility for both the put and call options that expire the following day is around 155 percent. This indicates that on an annualized basis the option market is pricing in a 155 percent price move over a single day. This is much more dramatic sounding than it is in reality. Annualized implied volatility of 155 percent for an option with a single trading day left translates to a one-day move of around 9.76 percent. The math behind this is (see the following feature on calculating single-day implied volatility):

$$9.76\% = 155\%/15.87$$

This single-day implied volatility can be interpreted as being a single standard deviation range of expected price movement of the stock on that day.

CALCULATING SINGLE-DAY IMPLIED VOLATILITY

Assuming there are 252 trading days in a year, the denominator of this formula turns out to be the square root of the number of trading days for the year.

1 Day Movement = Implied Volatility/Square Root of 252

Amazon did report its earnings, and the initial price reaction was pretty close to what the option market was pricing in. The NASDAQ opening price the day after the company reported earnings was down 11.76 percent from the previous day's close. The market was forecasting a 9.76 percent move based on option pricing.

As a refresher from college statistics: One standard deviation in statistics indicates there is a 68.2 percent chance that an outcome is going to land between up and down one standard deviation. So this single-day implied volatility indicates the market is expecting Amazon's stock to trade within up or down 9.76 percent with a 68.2 percent level of confidence in the next day.

Table 51.7 shows the increase in the implied volatility of the 120 Call projected by Amazon option prices as the earnings announcement approaches. Implied volatility for other options rises in the same way, since 120 is the closest strike to the stock price when the option started trading and just before earnings were announced. Also, the options contract is a weekly expiration option that begins trading on a

TABLE 51.7 Implied Volatility Changes Approaching Amazon Earnings

Date	AMZN	120 Call	120 Call IV
July 15	120.13	4.80	71%
July 15	122.06	5.92	78%
July 16	118.49	4.00	84%
July 19	119.94	4.33	87%
July 20	120.10	3.95	90%
July 21	117.43	2.73	111%
July 22	120.07	3.92	155%

Thursday morning and expires on the following week's Friday close. This particular option started trading on July 15 with the last trading day being July 23 or what is called a weekly option that has only eight trading days from listing to expiration.

The first row is the opening price for the weekly option and underlying price for the option. When the option first traded it had an implied volatility level of 71 percent. This compares to non-earnings-period implied volatility levels, which are usually in the mid 30 percent range for Amazon options.

Over the next few days, the earnings announcement draws closer and the stock stays in a fairly tight range. The implied volatility of the option contracts continues to rise as time passes. By the time the announcement is imminent, the implied volatility of the 120 Call has more than doubled.

This illustration of how implied volatility climbs in front of a potentially market-moving event is a bit magnified by the options only having one day of time value remaining before the announcement. However, it is a good illustration of how option prices, through the implied volatility component, discount a potential market-moving event when the timing of this event is a known entity.

The Impact on Option Prices

Implied volatility is commonly considered an indication as to whether an option is cheap or expensive. This determination may be made through examining past implied volatility levels for the options of a particular stock or index and comparing present values.

Demand for options pushes up the price of an option contract and results in higher implied volatility. However, other factors such as the underlying price, time to expiration, and interest-rate levels also determine the price of an option. These other factors are not impacted through the buying and selling pressure on option contracts. Only implied volatility will fluctuate based on market buying and selling pressure.

The goal of any directional trading strategy should be to buy low and sell high. If the market considers any trading vehicle inexpensive, there will be participants that take advantage of this through purchasing the instrument. On the other hand, if something appears expensive it may be sold. Implied volatility is a measure that option traders use to define whether options are overvalued or undervalued.

As a simple example, take the option prices and implied volatility levels in Table 51.8. The data in this table represent a stock trading at 24.00 per share, and the value of a 25 Call with 90 days until expiration. The different option prices are based on various implied volatility levels. Note that as the option price increases so does the implied volatility of the 25 Call.

TABLE 51.8 Implied Volatility Levels and Option Prices

Stock Price	25 Call	Implied Volatility
24.00	0.80	20%
24.00	1.05	25%
24.00	1.30	30%

If options for the underlying stock usually trade with an implied volatility of 25 percent, then when the option could be purchased for 0.80 it may be considered undervalued or inexpensive. At 0.80 the option had an implied volatility level of 20 percent. When implied volatility rose to 30 percent and the option was trading for 1.30, the option may be considered expensive. At 1.05 with an implied volatility of 25 percent, the historical norm, the 25 Call may be considered fairly valued.

Of course, using implied volatility as a measure of how expensive or cheap an option is must be done in the context of some external factors. Remember, if the company is preparing to announce quarterly earnings, the implied volatility would be expected to be high relative to other periods of time. In that case, a comparison to implied volatility behavior around previous earnings announcements would be a more accurate analysis of whether the options appear cheap or expensive.

Implied Volatility and the VIX

The VIX will be further defined in the next chapter, but the concepts in this chapter should be tied to the VIX before moving forward. The VIX is a measure of the implied volatility being projected through the prices of S&P 500 index options. The VIX can be used to indicate what type of market movement option prices are projecting on the S&P 500 over the next 30 days or even a shorter time. Since the VIX is measuring implied volatility of S&P 500 index options and since implied volatility is a measure of risk projected by option pricing, the VIX is considered a gauge of fear in the overall market.

CHAPTER 52

About the VIX Index

From Russell Rhoads, *Trading VIX Derivatives: Trading and Hedging Strategies Using VIX Futures, Options, and Exchange Traded Notes* (Hoboken, New Jersey: John Wiley & Sons, 2007), Chapter 2.

Officially known as the CBOE Volatility Index, the VIX is considered by many to be a gauge of fear and greed in the stock market. A more accurate description of what the VIX measures is the implied volatility that is being priced into S&P 500 index options. Through the use of a wide variety of option prices, the index offers an indication of 30-day implied volatility as priced by the S&P 500 index option market.

Before diving further into the calculation that results in the VIX, this chapter will cover the history of exactly how this index was developed followed by an overview of how the VIX is determined. Then for interested parties there is a more in-depth discussion of how the VIX is calculated. The VIX index has historically had an inverse relationship to performance of the S&P 500, and this often results in questions from traders who are new to the VIX. This relationship will be discussed in the context of put-call parity, which was mentioned in Chapter 51.

Finally, there are a handful of VIX-related indexes based on other equity-market indexes. The S&P 100–related VIX is still calculated using the old method to maintain some continuity for historical comparisons. Finally, there are also VIX indexes calculated on options based on the Nasdaq 100, Russell 2000, and Dow Jones Industrial Average, which are discussed toward the end of the chapter.

History of the VIX

The concept behind the VIX index was developed by Dr. Robert Whaley of Vanderbilt University in 1993. His paper "Derivatives on Market Volatility: Hedging Tools Long Overdue," which appeared in the *Journal of Derivatives*, laid the groundwork for the index. The original VIX was based on pricing of S&P 100 (OEX) options and used only eight option contracts to determine a volatility measure.

TABLE 52.1 S&P 500 Industry Weightings

Industry	Weighting
Consumer discretionary	9.10%
Consumer staples	11.70%
Energy	11.40%
Financials	15.40%
Health care	13.40%
Industrials	10.00%
Information technology	18.50%
Materials	3.40%
Telecom services	3.30%
Utilities	3.80%

At the time, OEX options were the most heavily traded index option series that reflected performance of the stock market in the United States. This volatility index was based on a limited number of options and was slightly disconnected from the overall stock market due to the narrower focus of the S&P 100 versus the S&P 500.

In 2003 there was a new methodology for calculation of the VIX index that was developed through work done by the CBOE and Goldman Sachs. Although the calculation was altered, the most important aspect to this change for individuals is that the underlying options changed from the OEX to options trading on the S&P 500. Another significant change was an increase in the number of options that were used in the index calculation. Through a wider number of option contract prices feeding the formula to calculate the VIX, a true 30-day implied volatility level that is being projected on the S&P 500 by the options market is realized.

The S&P 500 index is considered by professional investors to be the benchmark for the performance of the stock market in the United States. The members of the index are 500 of the largest domestic companies in the United States that meet criteria based on market capitalization, public float, financial viability, liquidity, type of company, and industry sector. Companies are usually dropped from the index when they have violated membership criteria or have ceased to operate due to a merger or acquisition.

The industry representation of the S&P 500 index appears in Table 52.1. With a broad distribution of companies in the index, there is no industry that dominates the index's performance. This diversification across industries is a major reason the S&P 500 is considered a performance benchmark by most professional investors.

Calculating the VIX

After the VIX index was introduced, the CBOE moved forward with the first exchange listed volatility derivative instruments. Through the CBOE Futures Exchange (CFE®), the CBOE introduced futures contracts based on the VIX. Other instruments have followed, and more are in development.

There are two ways to explain how the VIX is determined. First, it can be explained using simple nonmathematical terms. Then, for those interested in an in-depth discussion of the formula and calculation, a more detailed overview will follow. Having a basic understanding of how the VIX is determined is more than enough to move forward with trading. However, for those with more interest in the VIX calculation, the more comprehensive description is included.

The Nonmathematical Approach

The VIX is an indicator of 30-day implied volatility determined through the use of S&P 500 index option prices. The option price used in the formula is actually the midpoint of the bid-ask spread of relevant at and out of the money actively traded S&P 500 index options. Using the midpoint of the spread is a more accurate price description than the last price for an option contract. Also, the contracts used are the S&P 500 index options that trade to the next two standard expirations with at least eight days to expiration. When a series reaches this eight-day point, it is not used anymore in the calculation and the options that expire farther in the future then start to contribute to the VIX calculation.

All of these S&P 500 options are then used to create a synthetic at the money option that expires exactly 30 days from the very moment of the calculation. This time variable to the formula is constantly being updated to weight the balance of the two expiration series in the formula. Using a wide number of actively quoted S&P 500 index options, a synthetic 30-day option is created and the VIX is the implied volatility of that option. This results in implied volatility of the synthetic option contract, which is then reported as the VIX.

The Formula and Calculations

It is possible to trade the VIX with a cursory understanding of how the index is determined. Those who are satisfied with their understanding of the VIX and what it represents may skip ahead. However, readers who are more interested in how the VIX is calculated should be interested in the remainder of this section.

The input for calculating the VIX index comes from all actively quoted S&P 500 index options for the next two standard option expirations that have at least eight days remaining until expiration. Eliminating the nearer term expiration options that have only a week to expiration takes out some of the end-of-contract volatility that can occur in the market.

The option contracts from these two expiration series are the at and out of the money put and call options. The series of options used extends out of the money until there are two consecutive option strikes that have no bid-ask market posted. Again, the midpoint of the bid-ask spread for the options is used in the calculation.

The time to expiration part of the calculation is very specific, down to the second. This is constantly being updated to change the weighting between the two series of options feeding into the calculation. Although S&P 500 index options cease trading on a Thursday for Friday morning settlement, the time to expiration is based on the market opening time, 8:30 A.M. central time, on the Friday of expiration.

There is also a forward price for the S&P 500 that is calculated using the closest at the money options in conjunction with put-call parity. This S&P 500 forward price is the underlying security price and strike price used to price the synthetic option used in the calculation. The implied volatility of that option is what is quoted at the VIX.

Finally if there is interest in using Microsoft Excel© to replicate calculating the VIX, a paper produced by Tom Arnold and John H. Earl Jr. of the University of Richmond is useful. In a very short study, 10 pages, they lay out the groundwork for using Excel to replicate the calculation of the VIX (to read the full paper, go to http://papers.ssrn.com/sol3/papers. cfm?abstract id=1103971). Also, once the template has been set up, changing the time frame and underlying instrument is simple. Using the template, the VIX methodology may be applied to a variety of instruments or time frames with little effort.

The VIX and Put-Call Parity

Many traders and investors often ask why there appears to be an inverse relationship between the direction of stock prices and the VIX. The relationship may be broken down to the nature of purchasing options. When the market is under pressure, there is a net buying of put options, which will result in higher implied volatility. This rapid increase in demand for put options pushes the implied volatility for both put and call contracts higher; the reason behind this is called put-call parity.

Put-call parity states that the prices of put and call options that have the same strike price and expiration are related. This relationship exists due to the ability to create synthetic positions in one option through combining the other option with the underlying stock. With this possibility, if the price of one option differs enough from the price of the other, an arbitrage opportunity may present itself.

For instance, in a zero-interest-rate environment, a put and call price should have the same value if the stock is trading at the strike price. As the options are related in price, the implied volatility of these options is also related. This is unrealistic, but it is a good method of demonstrating put-call parity. The prices in Table 52.2 may be used to demonstrate what can happen when put-call parity breaks down.

It is possible to replicate the payout of a long call through combining a put option and a stock position. Stated another way, a long stock position along with owning a put will result in the same payout structure as being long a call option. So, if the same payout may be created in two methods, the pricing of these two should be equivalent. If they are not equal, the lower priced one may be bought

TABLE 52.2 Prices to Demonstrate Put-Call Parity

Security	Price
XYZ Stock	45.00
XYZ 45 Call	2.50
XYZ 45 Put	2.00

TABLE 52.3 Long XYZ 45 Call versus Long XYZ 45 Put + Long XYZ at Expiration

XYZ	Long XYZ Stock	Long XYZ 45 Put	Long Stock + Long Put	Long XYZ 45 Call
35	−10.00	8.00	−2.00	−2.50
40	−5.00	3.00	−2.00	−2.50
45	0.00	−2.00	−2.00	−2.50
50	5.00	−2.00	3.00	2.50
55	10.00	−2.00	8.00	7.50

while the higher priced one is simultaneously sold. This is known as an arbitrage trade, in which an instant profit may be realized through a pricing difference in two equivalent securities.

If the XYZ 45 Put is purchased and shares of XYZ stock are also bought, the resulting position at expiration will be the same as owning the XYZ 45 Call. Above 45.00, the call option would result in a long position in XYZ; below 45.00, the call would not be exercised and there would be no position in XYZ. With a long 45 put position combined with a long position in the stock, if the stock is below 45.00 at expiration, the put option will be exercised and the stock sold. The result would be no position in XYZ. Above 45.00, the stock would still be owned, as the XYZ 45 Put would not be exercised. Regardless of the stock price at expiration, the resulting position in XYZ will be the same. Due to the different prices between the 45 Call and 45 Put, there is a difference in profit or loss of the position at expiration. Table 52.3 demonstrates this at a variety of price points at expiration.

The column Long Stock + Long Put represents the position payout at expiration of the combined long stock–long put position. Note at all price levels the combined long stock and long put position is worth 0.50 more than the long call position. If at all price levels at expiration the long call position will be worth less than stock plus put position, then an arbitrage opportunity exists.

The arbitrage trade would be to purchase the stock and put option while taking a short position in the call option. At any price level for XYZ at expiration, this trade would result in a profit of 0.50. Table 52.4 displays the outcome through buying XYZ at 45.00 and purchasing the XYZ 45 Put for 2.00 along with selling the XYZ 45 Call at 2.50.

TABLE 52.4 Long XYZ Stock + versus Long XYZ 45 Put + Short XYZ 45 Call at Expiration

XYZ	Long XYZ Stock	Long XYZ 45 Put	Short XYZ 45 Call	Combined Profit/Loss
35	−10.00	8.00	2.50	0.50
40	−5.00	3.00	2.50	0.50
45	0.00	−2.00	2.50	0.50
50	5.00	−2.00	−2.50	0.50
55	10.00	−2.00	−7.50	0.50

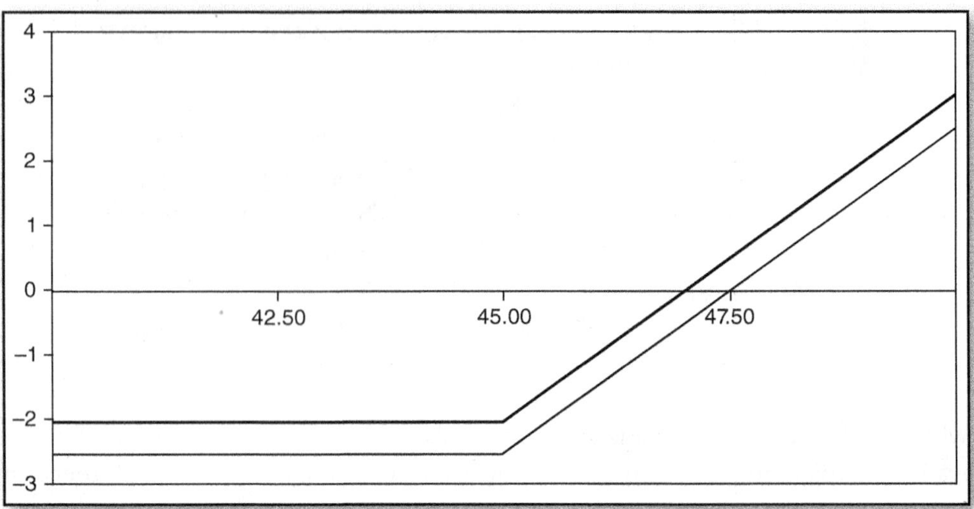

FIGURE 52.1 **Payoff Comparison.**

Admittedly this is an overly simplistic example, but the hope here is to get across the idea of put-call parity and what happens when put and call prices get out of line relative to each other. Execution of this combined position with the result of a riskless profit would involve transaction costs and a cost of capital. For individuals this might be prohibitive, but for professional trading firms this is an opportunity. When option prices get out of line to a point where a professional firm may take advantage through placing orders to buy and sell the instrument that are mispriced, then orders to take advantage of this mispricing will be executed. These trades will quickly push markets back into line and eliminate the arbitrage profit.

Figure 52.1 is a payoff diagram that compares the payout of the long call and combined long put–long stock position. The higher line represents the combined long put–long stock position. The lower line shows the profit or loss for the long call position. Note the lines are parallel—the only difference is the profit or loss. This difference shows an arbitrage profit that may be realized by shorting the long call and buying the other two instruments, then holding the positions to expiration.

The put-call parity formula has many components and is beyond the scope of this book. However, the formulas in Table 52.5 illustrate on a position basis what the equivalent single-position result is from different combinations of a put, call, or stock.

TABLE 52.5 **Variety of Positions Created through Put-Call Parity**

Position	Combination
Long call	Long stock + long put
Short call	Short stock + short put
Long put	Short stock + long call
Short put	Long stock + short call
Long stock	Long call + short put
Short stock	Short call + long put

A comparable payout of any single long or short position with a put, call, or stock may be created using a combination of the other two securities. Although it may seem like this does not relate to the VIX, there is a point to this exercise.

The relationship between put and call prices that results in put-call parity does have an impact on the VIX index. The level of the VIX is based on the implied volatility of a variety of both put and call options. The indicated implied volatility of option contracts rises and falls based on market forces. The specific market force that impacts implied volatility is the net buying or selling of options. This increase in demand is not necessarily purchase of either all call or all put options buy just net buying of option contracts. Since strong demand for call options will result in higher put prices and demand for puts will result in higher call prices, higher demand for either type of contract results in higher implied volatility for both put and call contracts.

The VIX has historically had an inverse relationship with the S&P 500 index. The reason behind this inverse relationship relates to the type of option activity that occurs during bullish markets versus bearish markets. When markets rally, there is rarely a rush by investors to purchase call options. Therefore when the market is rising, there is rarely dramatically higher options purchasing versus options selling.

When the S&P 500 comes under pressure, especially in very turbulent times, there is often a panic-like demand for put options. This demand for protection results in increased purchasing of put options. The result is a fast move higher in implied volatility for both S&P 500 put and call options. This higher demand then results in an increase in implied volatility and finally a move higher in the VIX index.

In summary, the VIX moves higher when there is more demand for S&P 500 options, this demand tends to increase when there is nervousness about the overall market. This concern about the market will result in increased demand for put options. Put-call parity is the reason the implied volatility of both types of options moves together. The result of this increased demand for puts is higher implied volatility indicated by the pricing of S&P 500 options and a move higher in the VIX.

The VIX and Market Movement

Again, the VIX is a measure of 30-day implied volatility as indicated by the pricing of S&P 500 index options. The VIX is expressed as an annualized volatility measure, but it may actually be used to determined shorter-term market-price movements. Recall the example with Amazon reporting earnings in the previous chapter. The implied volatility of the at the money options that only had a day left to expiration could be used to determine the magnitude of movement expected from Amazon stock the day following the company's earnings release. The implied volatility of those options was expressed as an annualized number.

The VIX is the 30-day implied volatility of the S&P 500, but it is also expressed as an annual figure. When the VIX is quoted at 20, this can be interpreted as SPX options pricing in an annualized move, up or down, of 20 percent in the S&P 500 index over the next 30 days. Using the VIX index, the anticipated movement of the underlying market may also be interpreted. The formula for determining the expected magnitude of market movements based on the VIX index is shown in the following section.

CALCULATING EXPECTED 30-DAY MARKET MOVEMENT

The formula for determining expected 30-day market movement is simple:

30-Day Movement = VIX/Square Root of 12

To determine the anticipated 30-day movement of the stock market as defined by the VIX involves dividing the VIX by the square root of 12. In the previous chapter the implied volatility for a stock was used to interpret the expected one-day move for the stock. The square root of 12 is a convenient number as 30 days is the average month and there are 12 months in the year. In a similar manner to breaking down what implied volatility was indicating about movement in Amazon stock, the VIX may be used to determine the anticipated 30-day move for the S&P 500.

If the VIX is quoted at 20, the result would be the market expecting movement of about 5.77 percent over the next 30 days. Following the formula for determining 30-day market movement, the math would be:

$$5.77\% = 20/3.46$$

At times the VIX has reached some extreme points with the index actually reaching over 100 intraday. Table 52.6 shows what different VIX levels indicate about anticipated stock market movement.

The VIX may also be used as an indication of what magnitude of daily price movement is being expected for the S&P 500. Much like the formula used in Chapter 51 for Amazon stock, the VIX can be taken down to a single-day estimate of market movement. Instead of repeating the formula from the previous chapter, a trader's rule of thumb about the VIX will be discussed.

TABLE 52.6 VIX and Expected 30-Day Movement of the S&P 500

VIX	Expected 30-Day Move
3.46	1%
6.92	2%
10.40	3%
13.85	4%
17.32	5%
20.78	6%
24.25	7%
27.71	8%
31.18	9%
34.64	10%

In the VIX trading arena, the option and futures traders take the level for the VIX and divide it by 16 to get a rough estimate of what sort of daily move is expected in the stock market based on the level of the VIX. Remember, the denominator of the formula in Chapter 51 was the square root of 252 or about 15.87. The traders round this up to 16 to get their denominator. So the VIX at 16 would indicate S&P 500 index options are anticipating daily price movement of 1 percent (16/16). A VIX of 32 would be interpreted as the S&P 500 option market anticipating a daily price move of 2 percent (32/16).

The math behind this method is not exact, but this is a pretty good rule of thumb. In 2008 when the VIX was trading in the mid-60s, this may be taken as the option market expecting a daily price move of 4 percent. Using a more common stock market index, this translates to the Dow Jones Industrial Average (DJIA) at 10,000 points being expected to trade in a 400-point range on a daily basis. Four-hundred-point days in the DJIA usually result in the stock market getting more than just professional investor's attention during the day. Those sort of moves generally grab headlines.

Equity Market Volatility Indexes

In addition to an index based on S&P 500 volatility, the CBOE has developed a handful of other volatility measures based on other common stock market indexes. Table 52.7 is a list of indexes based on index volatility that the CBOE has developed. There are also some quotes and strategy based and alternative-asset-based volatility indexes the CBOE has developed.

CBOE DJIA Volatility Index

The CBOE DJIA Volatility Index is calculated in a similar fashion as the VIX. Quotes for this index are disseminated using the symbol VXD. The index was created in 2005, and the index was introduced on March 18 of that year. The index indicates the market's expectation of 30-day implied volatility based on index option prices on the Dow Jones Industrial Average (DJX).

The DJX is one of the oldest stock indexes and is one of the most commonly quoted indicators of the overall stock market. Charles Dow, the publisher of the *Wall Street Journal*, created the index in order to bring more attention to his newspaper. The DJIA was first quoted on May 26, 1896. On days the stock market is open, at some point on the national

TABLE 52.7 CBOE Equity Market Volatility Indexes

Index	Ticker	Underlying	Website
CBOE Volatility Index	VIX	SPX	www.cboe.com/vix
CBOE DJIA Volatility Index	VXD	DJX	www.cboe.com/vxd
CBOE NADSAQ-100 Volatility Index	VXN	NDX	www.cboe.com/vxn
CBOE Russell 2000 Volatility Index	RVX	RUT	www.cboe.com/rvx
CBOE S&P 100 Volatility Index	VXO	OEX	www.cboe.com/vxo
Amex QQQ Volatility Index	QQV	QQQ	www.nyse.com

Sources: www.cboe.com and www.nyse.com.

news how the DJX did on the day will be mentioned. Some other common names for the DJX are the DJIA, Dow Jones, or just the Dow. For a person who pays little attention to the stock market or even for most investors, the Dow Jones Industrial Average is what they think of when they think of the stock market.

The DJX is composed of 30 stocks that represent a wide variety of industries and some of the largest companies in the United States. The stocks appear in Table 52.8. The small concentration of companies does take something away from the index being representative of the overall economy, but it continues to be the most commonly quoted index.

TABLE 52.8 Members of the Dow Jones Industrial Average

Company	Symbol
Alcoa Inc.	AA
American Express Company	AXP
AT&T Corp.	T
Bank of America Corp.	BAC
Boeing Co.	BA
Caterpillar Inc.	CAT
Chevron Corp.	CVX
Cisco Systems	CSCO
Coca-Cola Co.	KO
E.I. Du Pont de Nemours	DD
Exxon Mobil Corp.	XOM
General Electric Company	GE
Hewlett-Packard Co.	HPQ
Home Depot Inc	HD
Intel Corp.	INTC
International Business Machines Corp.	IBM
Johnson & Johnson	JNJ
J. P. Morgan Chase Company	JPM
Kraft Foods Inc.	KFT
McDonald's Corp.	MCD
Merck & Co. Inc.	MRK
Microsoft Corp.	MSFT
Minnesota Mining & Mfg. Co.	MMM
Pfizer Inc.	PFE
Procter & Gamble Co.	PG
The Travelers Companies	TRV
United Technologies Corp.	UTX
Verizon Communications Inc.	VZ
Wal-Mart Stores Inc.	WMT
Walt Disney Co.	DIS

TABLE 52.9 Dow Jones Industrial Average Industry Weightings

Sector	Weighting
Basic materials	3.75%
Consumer goods	10.52%
Consumer services	13.24%
Financials	10.80%
Health care	7.78%
Industrials	22.46%
Oil and gas	9.83%
Technology	17.64%
Telecommunications	3.98%

Note that although the index is referred to as an industrial index, a variety of industries are represented by the DJX. For example, Wal-Mart and Home Depot are major retailers, Pfizer is a pharmaceutical company, and The Travelers Companies specializes in financial services. The industry weightings for the DJX appear in Table 52.9.

The highest weighting of stocks in the DJX is represented by industrial companies, but only about a quarter of the performance of the index will be attributed to this market sector. A variety of other industries contribute to the DJX, which does result in an index that is representative of the overall economy in the United States. For instance, when consumer goods and services are combined, this area of the market represents about another quarter of the index's performance.

Finally, the CFE does not currently trade futures based on the VXD. However, from April 2005 to the middle of 2009, futures contracts based on this index did trade at the exchange.

CBOE NASDAQ-100 Volatility Index

Using quotes for options that trade on the NASDAQ-100 Index (NDX), the CBOE NASDAQ-100 Volatility Index is an indication of implied volatility on the NASDAQ-100 index. Trading with the symbol VXN, the index displays 30-day implied volatility for the NDX.

The NASDAQ-100 is an index composed of the 100 largest companies not involved in the financial sector that trade on the NASDAQ. The NASDAQ marketplace opened in 1971 as an alternative exchange to the traditional floor-based exchanges like the New York Stock Exchange. In 1985 the NASDAQ developed two market indexes to promote their exchange, one of which is the NASDAQ-100.

Table 52.10 shows the industry sector weightings that comprise the NDX. What is unique regarding this market index is the lack of financial and health care stocks in the index. The result is a focus on other industries with a very large weighting in the technology sector. In fact, the index is dominated by technology- and communications-oriented stocks, which when combined make up almost 75 percent of the index. Also, the SPX has approximately a 20 percent weighting in the financial sector, which results in the NDX and SPX having disparate performance at times.

TABLE 52.10 NASDAQ-100 Sector Weightings	
Sector	**Weighting**
Basic materials	0.40%
Consumer cyclical	8.40%
Communications	24.40%
Consumer noncyclical	16.80%
Energy	0.50%
Industrial	3.10%
Technology	46.40%

Futures were also traded on the VXN from 2007 to 2009. As this index may experience higher volatility than some other market indexes, the demand for a return of these contracts may result in them being relisted at some point.

CBOE Russell 2000 Volatility Index

The Russell 2000 Index is composed of the 2,000 smallest companies that are in the Russell 3000 Index. Although representing two-thirds of the companies in the Russell 3000, which is composed of 3,000 of the largest publicly traded companies in the United States, the Russell 2000 only represents about 8 percent of the market capitalization of the Russell 3000. The Russell 2000 index is composed of small-cap companies, which mostly focus on domestic markets. This index has a great niche as a representation of domestic economic trends in the United States.

Russell Investments also calculates the Russell 1000 index, which consists of the 1,000 largest companies in the Russell 3000. The top third of those companies represents 92 percent of the market capitalization of the Russell 3000.

The ticker symbol RUT represents option trading on the index and, like the previous volatility-related indexes, the Russell 2000 Volatility Index (RVX) attempts to show what the market is pricing in 30-day implied volatility for the index. At times the Russell 1000, Russell 2000, and Russell 3000 names are not entirely accurate. When, due to an acquisition, merger, or dissolution, a company ceases to exist as it had in the past, it may be replaced by a new company in a market index. These Russell indexes are actually reconfigured once a year at the end of June, with the number of stocks in each index taken back to the proper number.

Also, there is a minimum capitalization level for a company to be a member of the Russell 1000. When the indexes are rebalanced, the number of stocks in the Russell 1000 and Russell 2000 is very close to their respective numbers, but it may not be equal to the expected number of stocks in each index. For instance, after the 2010 rebalance, the Russell 1000 consisted of 988 stocks and the Russell 2000 consisted of 2,012 stocks. The total of the two indexes results in all the stocks that make up the Russell 3000. The Russell 3000 makes up 99 percent of the market capitalization of the U.S. stock market.

Between the index restructuring dates, companies that cease to exist will be deleted from the indexes, but no replacement will necessarily be put in their place.

However, company spinoffs and initial public offerings may be added between the June reconstruction dates. Those stocks are added on a quarterly basis.

RVX futures traded at the CBOE from 2007 through early 2010.

CBOE S&P 100 Volatility Index

When the VIX was originally quoted by the CBOE, the calculation was based on the implied volatility of the S&P 100 Index (OEX), not the S&P 500. When the calculation was altered in 2003, it was done so with part of the revision resulting in a focus on the S&P 500 as opposed to the S&P 100 index.

The CBOE S&P 100 Volatility Index (VXO) is actually the original VIX index, which was created in 1993. It continues to be calculated using the original methodology based on OEX options. Introduced in 1983 by the CBOE, OEX was the first equity index option product. Originally the index name was the CBOE 100 Index. Loosely translated, OEX could mean Option Exchange 100. The OEX and options listed on the index were so innovative that entire books were written on trading OEX options.

The OEX represents 100 of the largest companies in the United States. This results in the combined components of the OEX being close to 45 percent of the total market capitalization of publicly traded stocks in the United States. Also, almost 60 percent of the S&P 500 market capitalization is represented by the 100 stocks in the OEX.

Even with just 100 names, the OEX is a diversified index with all industry sectors being covered. Table 52.11 is a summary of the industry weightings of the OEX. Note the industry weightings of the OEX are as diversified as the S&P 500 even though there are fewer stocks in the index.

Amex QQQ Volatility Index

The Amex QQQ volatility index is another measure of implied volatility of the Nadsaq market. The method behind this index is similar to the original volatility index calculation used for the VXO. The index indicates the forward-looking volatility for

TABLE 52.11 S&P 100 Index Industry Weightings

Industry	Weighting
Consumer discretionary	6.25%
Consumer staples	15.32%
Energy	15.86%
Financials	11.06%
Health care	15.40%
Industrials	10.59%
Information technology	17.35%
Materials	1.03%
Telecom services	5.30%
Utilities	1.86%

the QQQ based on option prices. To get a true option contract value, the midpoint of the bid-ask spread is used as the option price input for the calculation.

The CBOE and CFE currently trade options and futures only on the VIX index. However, these alternate VIX indexes may be used to gain insight into market activity. The VIX and other index-related volatility indexes are excellent representations of what sort of near-term volatility is expected from the overall stock market according to the implied volatility of index options. Each of the indexes that have VIX representation have slightly different components and may indicate that there is higher expected volatility in one sector as opposed to others.

CHAPTER 53

Seasonality and Calendar Patterns

From Perry J. Kaufman, *Trading Systems and Methods, + Website,* 5th edition (Hoboken, New Jersey: John Wiley & Sons, 2013), Chapters 9 and 10.

In this chapter, we turn our attention to two other principal components, the seasonal and cyclic movements.

Seasonality is a cycle that occurs yearly. It is most often associated with the planting and harvesting of crops, which directly affect the feeding and marketing of livestock. Normally, prices are higher when a product is not as readily available, or when there is a greater demand relative to the supply, as often occurs with food or heating oil during the winter months and electricity during mid-summer. For grain, cotton, coffee, and other agricultural products, the crop year is dominated by planting, harvest, and weather-related events that occur in between. Most abundant crops have been produced in the northern hemisphere, but South American soybeans and orange juice have become a significant factor since the early 1980s, as have Australian and New Zealand beef and lamb, resulting in a structural change in seasonal patterns. Globalization has not only affected financial markets, but nearly everything we purchase.

Consumer habits can cause a seasonal pattern in metals and some equity markets as weather does for agricultural products. Passenger airline traffic, along with the travel and hotel industry, is much more active in the summer than in the winter, and profits of those companies that are not diversified reflect that seasonality. Gasoline is in high demand during the summer, when most of the population in the northern hemisphere makes room for each other at the beach. Eastman Kodak once had a classic pattern caused by much more active picture-taking during the summer months, which was also reflected in the price of silver, used to make film. Not anymore.

Many commodities are priced in U.S. dollars, such as gold, oil, and even metals traded on the London Metals Exchange (LME), but for investors not in the United States, purchasing in their own currency, the fluctuations in foreign exchange rates significantly change the price of the commodity. Looking at it from the view of a U.S. consumer, if the U.S. dollar falls, then American buyers will expect to pay more. Commodities that have worldwide demand maintain a world price, so that everyone essentially pays the same amount, regardless of their currency. When studying seasonality, it is sometimes necessary to separate the underlying price move of the commodity from the move in its denominated currency.

A Consistent Factor

Even when the impact of seasonality on agricultural products is not clear from the price patterns, it is still there. Consider the following factors that do not change:

- More corn, wheat, and soybeans are sold during harvest than at any other time of year because there is not enough available storage to hold all of the new crop. Rental storage, when available, requires a minimum 3-month charge. Lack of storage and the need for immediate income result in greater sales and cause prices to decline.

- Because feed grains are harvested only once each year, forward contracts include a storage cost as part of the total carrying charge. Therefore, each forward delivery price should be higher within the same crop year.

Sometimes the price pattern of forward months does not seem to reflect the added costs of carry. Occasionally these markets even invert, and the nearest delivery trades at a price higher than the deferred months, a situation familiar in crude oil and copper. The cost of carry, however, still exists in an inverted or *backwardation* market. Extreme short-term demand pushes the nearest delivery much higher, while the events causing price disruption are expected to be temporary. The normal carry is still there; it is just overwhelmed by temporary demand.

Seasonal equity shares reflect the same factors as agricultural products. While holiday travel may vary by 10% in a given year, there is still a strong seasonal pattern in the travel business. The profitability of a company may decline during a poor travel year, sending share prices lower, yet the seasonality is still there.

It is important to be able to identify seasonal patterns. Seasonal patterns can bias the size of the positions traded throughout the year, they can identify changes in risk, they can affect the direction of prices, and most important they can be exploited for profit. The methods for finding them are simple, and made more so by the use of a spreadsheet program or statistical software. These will be discussed in this chapter along with some practical applications.

The Seasonal Pattern

Seasonal patterns are easier to find than the longer-term cycles or economic trends, because they must repeat each calendar year. Although any 12-month period can be used to find the seasonal pattern, academic studies in agriculture usually begin with the new crop year for grains, just following harvest, when prices tend to be lowest. This approach makes the carrying charges, which increase steadily throughout the new crop year, more apparent. For uniformity, the examples in this chapter always begin with a calendar year, which assumes no knowledge of where the season starts, and can be equally applied to stocks. Carrying charges are always reflected in the market price.

U.S. agricultural production is considered to be the standard for "seasonal," even though a wheat crop is harvested continuously throughout the year in different parts of the world. Prices are expected to be lower during the U.S. harvest and highest during the middle of the growing season. The influence of world stocks and anticipated harvest from other major producers in South America or Russia will cause an overall dampening or inflating of prices, rather than change the seasonal pattern. There is a constant flow of agricultural and industrial products throughout the world. The seller of a product will always choose the highest price as denominated in the local currency, so that a buyer with a weaker currency will appear to pay more than one with a stronger currency. But the seller gets the same price from everyone, net of shipping costs. The fact that any buyer can go to any seller creates the competition that produces a *world market price*. The interchangability of product is called *fungibility*.

Industrial commodities have seasonal price variation based on demand. Silver and gold, although increasingly used in electronics as high-end conductors, are still mostly consumed for jewelry but during unstable economic times, they serve as a hedge against inflation by the general public. Almost half of all copper is used in electrical and heat conductivity, with much of it in the form of an alloy with nickel and silver. Its seasonality is heavily related to the housing industry, where it is required for both electrical and water systems. New sources of ore are introduced infrequently, and the possibility of discovery or expansion is rarely seen in price movement as short-term anticipation. The primary supply problems in copper are related to labor as well as social and political changes in producing countries. More recently, growth in China and India has spurred a demand for copper. It is said that China has warehoused large quantities of copper in anticipation of future needs. This might distort the seasonal patterns, but they will return to normal as seasonal consumption becomes the driver.

There are many businesses with finished products that have seasonal demand, and their publicly traded stock prices will reflect that tendency. Because the shares in a company are far removed from buying and selling the raw materials that they use, changes in the price of raw materials may have a small effect on the bottom line, or the share price. Yet some industries, such as airlines, still show seasonal patterns, and the same procedures given here can be used to find them.

Cycle Analysis

The cycle is another basic element of price movement, along with the trend and seasonality, but as a mathematical problem it can be more difficult to evaluate and is often avoided. But there are many different types of cycles, from agricultural to presidential election, and many of them are simple to evaluate and can improve trading.

Cycles come in many forms—seasonality, production startup and shutdown, inventory or stocks, behavioral, and even astronomical. Seasonality is a special case of a calendar or annual cycle. Seasonality was covered in the previous section, and its special features are not considered here. Some of the cycles are clearly *periodic*, having regular intervals between peaks and valleys; others are more uniform in their *amplitude* or height but irregular in period. The most definitive and regular cycle remains the seasonal, which is determined by periodic physical phenomena, the changing of the year.

This section will discuss the major commodity and financial cycles that most likely result from business decisions, government programs, and long-term market characteristics and phenomena. Short-term cycles are usually attributed to behavior.

There are a few important ways to find the cycle, the most common being *trigonometric curve fitting* and *Fourier (spectral) analysis*. Both will require a computer and will be explained in the following sections. John Ehlers introduced *Maximum Entropy Spectral Analysis* (MESA), which finds price cycles based on small amounts of data, at the same time avoiding some of the problems inherent in other methods. Examples of solutions will be included in the explanation of the methods and applications that follows.

Cycle Basics

The cycle, along with the trend and seasonality, comprise the three orderly components of price movement. The fourth is noise, which includes everything not accounted for in the first three. To find any one component, we must remove the others. We have found that we can eliminate the trend by taking the first differences of the data; that is, subtracting the previous value from the current value. In the previous section on seasonality, we used the simple technique of subtracting a 1-year moving average (a 12-period average applied to monthly data) from the original price series to remove the seasonal pattern. Alternatively, statistical software will subtract this month's average price from that of 12 months ago, or today's daily price from that of 252 days ago in order to detrend the data. By finding the first differences and then subtracting the 1-year average, or by removing the 1-year differences, we are left with the cycle and the unaccountable price movement, which we call *noise*.

Even when the seasonal pattern is eliminated, most cycles are still based on the periodic effects in our Universe. After the 1-year orbit of our planet around the Sun, there is the 28-day lunar cycle; converted to business days, this gives the very familiar 20-day reference that remains overwhelmingly popular among all analysts (also corresponding to four weeks). The possibility cannot be eliminated that planetary motion may account for, besides seasonality, the effects of mass behavior, which can produce a consistent cycle that repeats with a fixed period.

Cycles can be complex and difficult to see because there is often a combination of larger and smaller patterns, and cycles within cycles, all acting at the same time. Nevertheless, they exist, and they are real. The cycles that appear to be most important are either long-term or the sum of a number of subcycles that come together at peaks or valleys. This gives us a way to identify one point on a cycle; we must remember that, when the individual components are found, there may be a number of smaller patterns that cause this effect. Thinking about it as *harmonics*, just as in music, means that a smaller cycle is a fraction of the larger cycle, for example, its cycle length is ½, ½, ¼, . . . of the larger. When two cycles are *synchronized*, their peaks or valleys occur at the same time. Any price series can be decomposed into individual cycles, and represented as the sum of multiple cycles.

Observing the Cycle

Before selecting a market for cycle analysis, it is necessary to observe that a dominant cycle exists; it is also useful to know why it exists in order to avoid uncovering spurious patterns. This is most easily done for markets in which you can clearly identify the fundamental or industrial reasons for cycles. The basis for a cycle could be a pattern of holding inventory, the fixed time needed for breeding and feeding of livestock, seasonality, the time necessary for closing a mining operation then starting it up again, expansion or contraction of business based on disposable income, the effects of government interest rate policy, or other economic factors.

The Cattle Cycle Using cattle as an example, Figure 53.1a shows a clear 9- to 11-month cycle in futures prices[1] over a 6-year period from 1980 through 1985. The peaks and valleys vary by up to one month, making the pattern reliable for use as part of a long-term trading strategy. Although feedlots in the Southwest have made the supply of cattle more evenly distributed throughout the year, there are still a large number of ranchers in the North who send their cattle to market in the early fall to avoid the difficulties of feeding during a harsh winter. This causes generally lower prices in the Fall and higher prices in the mid-Winter when supplies are low.

A similar pattern can be seen more recently in Figure 53.1b. During the past six years the peaks of the cycle are consistently 12 months apart, although the valleys are not as consistent, most often coming within a few months after the peaks. The overall picture shows that cattle prices continue to have a clear cycle, driven by the fundamentals of production.

The Swiss Franc Cycle The Swiss franc cycle (denominated as Swiss francs/U.S. dollars on Chicago's International Monetary Market) shown in Figure 53.2a is quite different.[2] There are two likely cycles: the primary one (shown using letters at the

[1] Jacob Bernstein, "Cycle and Seasonal Price Tendencies in Meat and Livestock Markets," in Todd Lofton, ed., *Trading Tactics* (Chicago: Chicago Mercantile Exchange, 1986).

[2] Jacob Bernstein, *The Handbook of Commodity Cycles* (New York: John Wiley & Sons, 1982).

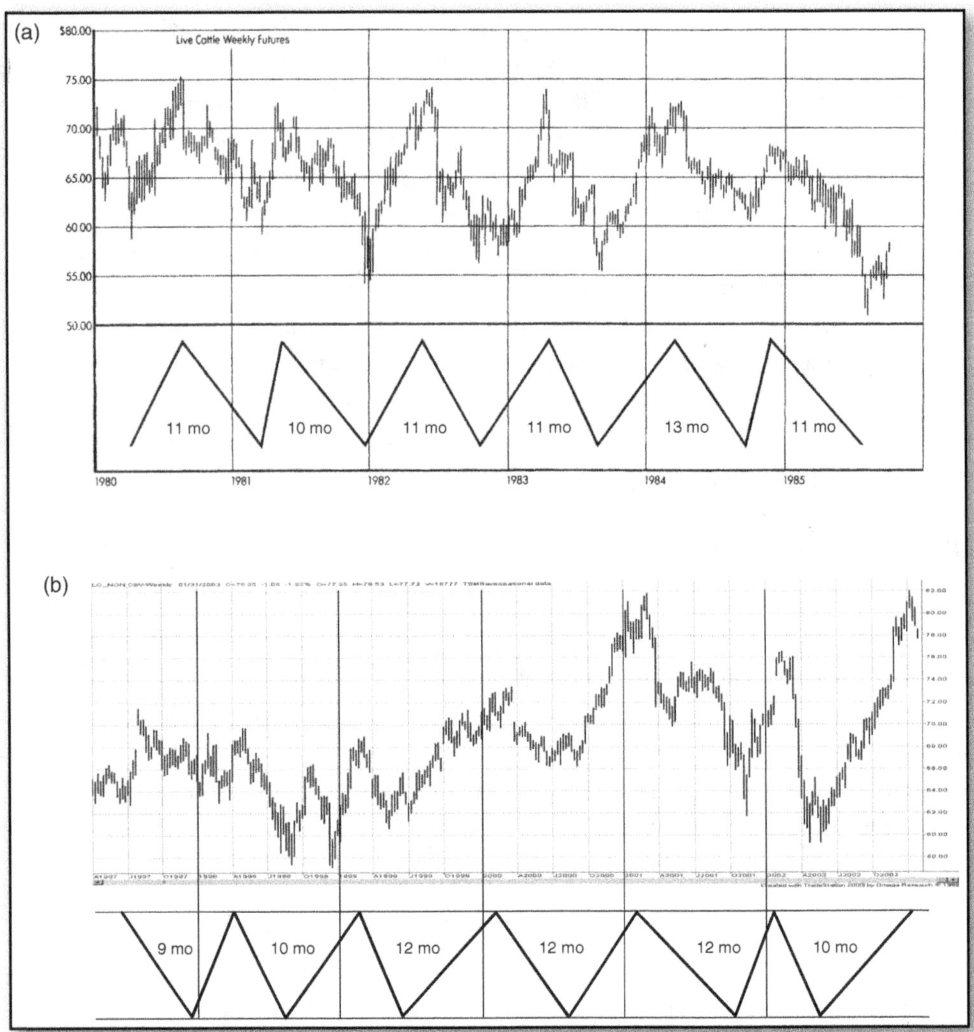

FIGURE 53.1 (a) 9- to 11-Month Cycle in Live Cattle, 1980–1985 Futures Prices. (b) The Cattle Cycle, 1997–2002.

peaks and valleys) and a subcycle (marked with numbers). The subcycle ranges from 24 to 35 weeks with a 40% variance compared to 20% for cattle. Most important, the cycle in the Swiss franc cannot be attributed to any specific fundamental cause. There is certainly a long-term cycle based on the strength and weakness of the U.S. economy with respect to the Swiss economy, or the relative attractiveness of U.S. interest rates. There is also the general ebb and flow of the U.S. trade balance and, of course, investor behavior. Unlike cattle, these patterns do not need to be rigid.

Looking at Swiss franc prices from 1997 through 2002 there are obvious peaks and valleys that continue a cyclic pattern (see Figure 53.2b). Although they are crisp in appearance, the cycle now has an average period of about 38 weeks with a range from 30 to 52 weeks. The new cycle falls about midway between the periods of the previous primary and subcycles. Although the cycles seem clear, the change in period and the variance between cycle tops will make a systematic strategy difficult.

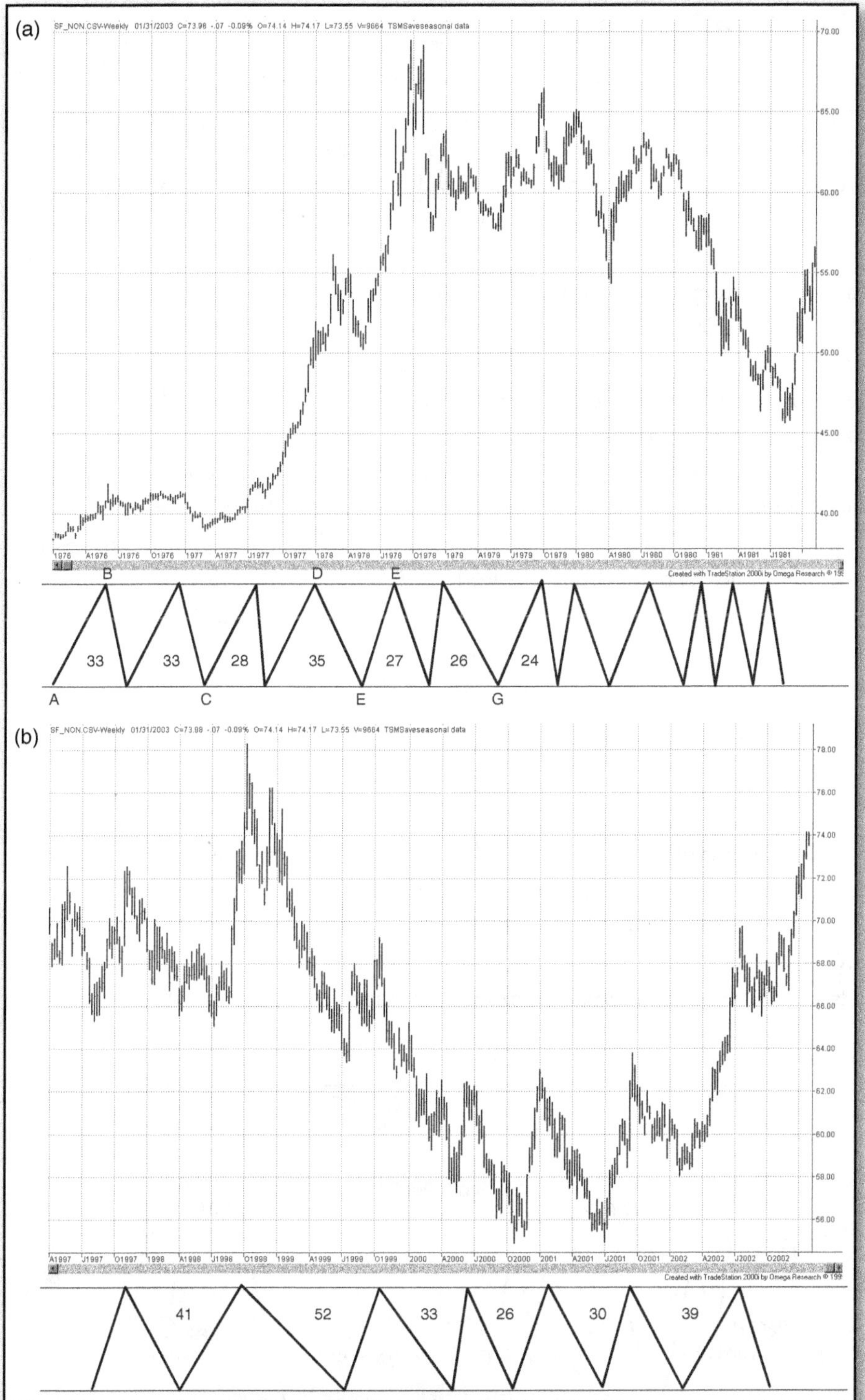

FIGURE 53.2 (a) Cycle in Swiss franc futures, 1975–1979. The lettered peaks and valleys show the choice for a primary cycle; the numbered peaks and valleys show a likely subcycle. (b) Cycle in Swiss franc futures, 1997–2002.

Basic Cycle Identification

A simple way to begin the search for major cycles is to look at a long-term chart, displayed as weekly rather than daily prices. The dominant half-cycle can be found by locating the obvious price peaks and valleys, then averaging the distance between them. A convenient tool for estimating the cycle length is the Ehrlich Cycle Finder.[3] Developed in 1978, it is an expanding device with evenly spaced points, allowing you to align the peaks and valleys and to observe the consistency in the cycle. For finding a single pattern, it is just as good as some of the mathematical methods that follow. It is best to have at least eight cycle repetitions before concluding that you have a valid cycle.

Cycles can be obscured by other price patterns or market noise. Strong trends, such as the ones in Swiss francs (Figure 53.2a) or the seasonal movement of crops, may overwhelm a less pronounced cycle. Classic cycle identification requires that these noncycle factors first be removed by detrending and then by deseasonalizing. The resulting data will then be analyzed and the trend and seasonal factors added back once the cycle has been found. To find a subcycle, the primary cycle should be removed and a second cycle analysis performed on the data. This can be a tedious process. In order to bypass these steps, the methods that follow (trigonometric regression and spectral analysis) can locate the dominant cycle and subcycles at one time using an integrated process.

The Business Cycle

The global business cycle, as distinguished from industry cycles, is the result of macroeconomic events, such as recessions, inflation, and government economic policy. Figure 53.3, a product of the Princeton Economic Institute, shows that this cycle is about 8.6 years, or about 4 years from top to bottom in each cycle. Although this chart dates from 1997, it seems remarkably accurate in capturing the tech bubble

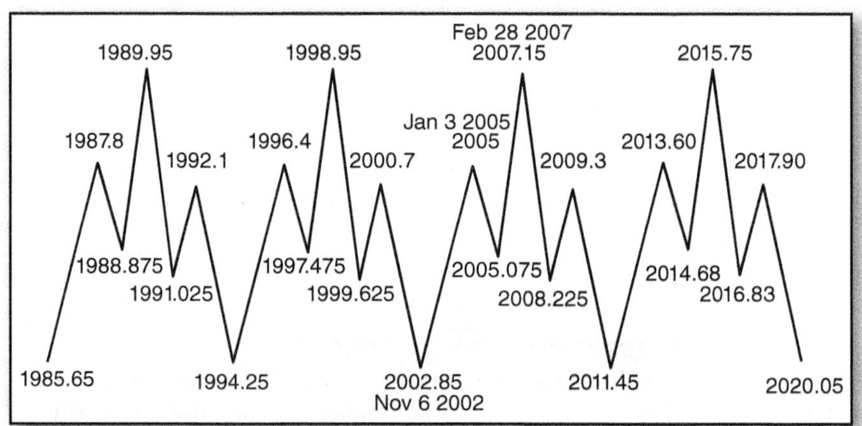

FIGURE 53.3 The 8.6-Year Business Cycle.
Source: The Princeton Economic Institute, available on www.financialsense.com.

[3] More information and a cycle-finding tool can be found on www.stanehrlich.com.

that ended in 2000, the downturn that followed, ending in 2003, the rally preceding the 2008 subprime crisis, and the extreme fall of the market and the economy afterward. It shows the bottom of this cycle in 2011, which we all hope is true.

The Kondratieff Wave

Much of the popularity of cycles is due to the publicity of Nicolai Kondratieff's 54-year cycle, known as the *K-wave*, or more recently, the *long wave*. During its documented span from about 1780 to the present, it appears to be very regular, moving from highs to lows and back again. In Figure 53.4 the Kondratieff wave is shown with major events (particularly wars) that have contributed to its pattern.[4] With only three full cycles completed, it is difficult to tell if the overall trend is moving upwards, or whether the entire pattern is just a coincidence.

The forecast of the *K-wave*, shown in Figure 53.4, corresponds to a sharp decline in wholesale prices due at about the year 1990, the millennium's equivalent to the depression of the 1930s. In fact, the 1990s posted remarkable gains in the stock market, peaking at the beginning of 2000. According to the chart pattern, this peak should be followed by 10 to 20 years of downturn in the economy, in which case we are in the middle, having experienced a major correction in 2008. It should be noted that the peaks of the four waves are of different duration, 1870 being the shortest and the recent one in 2000 the longest.

Although we all accept the existence of an economic cycle, pinpointing the peaks and valleys is impractical. Even if the 54-year period varied only by 10%, we could be entering an investment position 5 years too soon or too late. Determining long-term cycles for any market has the same problem—the actual price pattern will

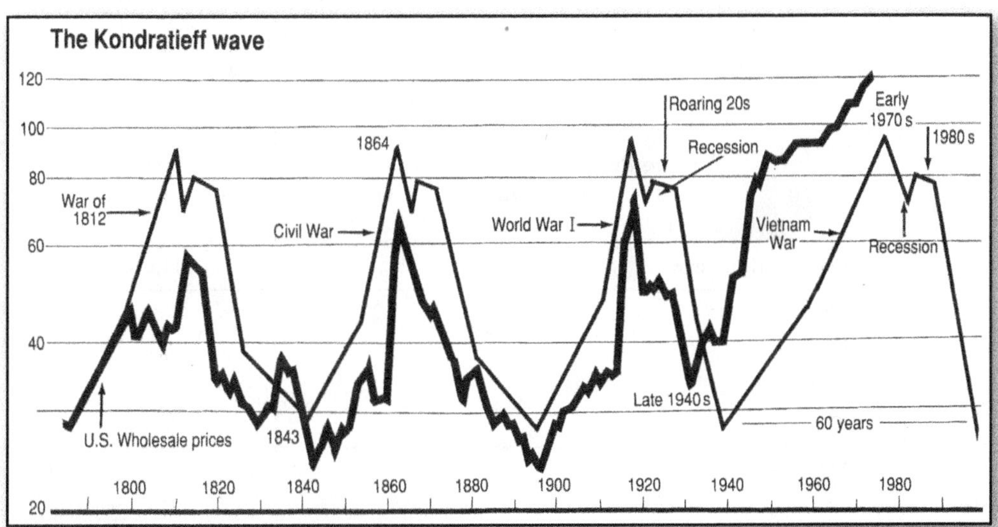

FIGURE 53.4 The Kondradieff Wave.
Source: Walker, Jeff , "What K-wave?" *Technical Analysis of Stocks & Commodities* (July 1990).

[4] Jeff Walker, "What K-Wave?" *Technical Analysis of Stocks & Commodities* (July 1990).

never correspond exactly to the predicted peaks and valleys that most often come at regular intervals. Fortunately, there are other choices. Shorter-term cycles do not need to have the same constant period, and the way in which cycles interact with other strategy components will make them more flexible. However, some investors will want to keep this big picture concept, both the business cycle and the Kondratieff wave, as a general guide to investment timing.

Presidential Election Cycle

Of all the events that move the market, the presidential elections have been the most consistent. The patterns stem from the motivation of the incumbent party to provide good economic news to the voters prior to the election year, and as far into the election year as possible. Stock market action during the election year is always more erratic, as parties battle over the value of each other's actions.

Typically, the year preceding the election (year 3 in the president's term) posts the strongest gains for the market, followed by a reasonably strong election year. (See Table 53.1.) Some analysts have been more specific by starting on October 1 of the previous year. The two years after the election show returns below average as the reality of politics reasserts itself and the new administration tries to implement campaign promises that turn out to be unpopular. More recently, it is only in the first year that the president can push for serious reform. Beginning in the second year, the mid-term elections of members of Congress become more important.

There is the additional possibility that there is an eight-year cycle that should be watched;[5] however, the eight-year period should be most informative if it represented only those years in which the same president was in office. Actions by a president who cannot be reelected are likely to be different from one who seeks another term; therefore, we should expect a different pattern. This can be made more intricate by studying the patterns preceding and following a change of party, all of which have a fundamental basis in the behavior of the political parties and the voters.

TABLE 53.1 The Presidential Election Cycle, 1912–1992, Based on the Percentage Returns of the Dow Jones Industrial Averages

Pre-election year	11.0%
Election year	7.0
Post-election year	4.7
Mid-term year	2.3
Average year	6.3%

Source: Adam White.

[5] Articles by Adam White, "The Eight-Year Presidential Election Pattern," *Technical Analysis of Stocks & Commodities* (November 1994); Arthur Merrill, "The Presidential Election Cycle," *Technical Analysis of Stocks & Commodities* (March 1992); and Michael J. Carr, "Get out the Vote and into Stocks," *Futures* (February 1996), all show very similar results for the four-year election pattern.

TABLE 53.2 **Election Year Analysis for Years in Which the Stock Market Began the Year within 8% of the Previous 2-Year Highs**

Year	1. Previous Year	2. First 2 weeks (1–10)	3. Primaries (10–83)	4. Pre-convention (83–161)	5. Pre-election (161–195)	6. Election to year-end (195–253)	7. (2) + (4) + (6)
1936	41.82	2.76	4.64	11.91	−0.62	5.85	20.52
1944	19.45	1.63	−0.84	9.27	−0.86	3.14	14.04
1952	16.15	1.60	−2.82	8.02	−2.49	5.47	15.10
1956	27.25	−1.78	5.42	3.16	−6.65	2.38	3.76
1960	8.48	−2.49	−5.75	2.94	−7.13	8.49	8.95
1964	18.89	1.79	4.44	3.03	2.52	0.06	4.88
1968	20.03	0.26	−0.10	1.44	4.39	4.25	5.95
1972	10.82	1.41	3.39	5.30	−1.78	4.88	11.59
1980	12.31	2.26	−5.42	18.57	−0.20	7.66	28.49
1984	17.53	1.27	−5.01	4.27	0.41	0.63	6.17
1992	26.30	0.80	−2.72	2.14	−0.23	5.87	8.82
Average	19.91	0.86	−0.44	6.37	−1.15	4.43	11.66

Source: Michael Carr, Logical Information Machines.

More sophisticated computer software, such as that provided by Logical Information Machines,[6] a Chicago firm, can produce a very interesting, closer view of how voters respond to election politics. Table 53.2 breaks the election year into seven periods between the key events for those years in which the stock market began the election year within 8% of its 2-year high price (*days* refer to business days):

1. The returns of the year preceding the election year.
2. The first 10 days of the new year, typically a strong period (days 0–10).
3. Through the State of the Union address and the primaries (days 10–83).
4. Waiting for the conventions (days 83–161).
5. Preelection blahs: the actual campaign (days 161–195).
6. The election to year-end reaction (days 195–253).
7. Combined periods (2) + (4) + (6).

Combining the three periods (2), (4), and (6), which have strong upward biases, gives consistently positive results. Even if the newly elected party fails to deliver on its campaign promises, traders could have already converted those marketing gimmicks into stock market profits.

Presidential Cycle from 1983 to 2010 In our rapidly changing world, it is always interesting to see if the market reality continues to support expectations. In fact, using the S&P futures and calculating the year-end returns, the results (in Table 53.3)

[6] See www.lim.com.

TABLE 53.3 Updated Presidential Election Cycle Based on S&P Futures

Cycle	S&P Total Returns
Preelection	16.4
Election	69.5
1st year	(30.0)
2nd year	48.3

confirm our new expectations of the presidential cycle. There are moderately good returns in the preelection year, but excellent returns in the year of the election as all candidates and parties promise whatever is necessary to get elected.

Reality follows in the first year of office, when the president attempts to fulfill campaign promises but also takes this one opportunity for economic reforms that are likely to be unpopular, such as budget reductions and tax increases. A better year follows ahead of the mid-term elections, which have become a more important political event than in the past.[7]

[7] Gerald Appel states, "There is a clear election-year cycle, where the election year is +10%, year after +4.5%, 2 years before next −1.25%, and the year before +20%." *Technical Analysis: Power Tool for Active Traders* (Upper Saddle River, NJ: FT Prentice Hall, 2005), 94.

CHAPTER 54

Relative Strength as a Criterion for Investment Selection

From Robert A. Levy, "Relative Strength as a Criterion for Investment Selection," *The Journal of Finance* 22, Issue 4 (1967): 595–610.

President, Computer Directions Advisors, Inc., Silver Spring, Maryland

I. Introduction

An extensive body of literature has recently emanated from scholarly sources stating that successive stock market price changes are statistically independent (i.e., that the study of past price trends and patterns—known in the trade as technical analysis—is no more useful in predicting future price movements than throwing a dart at the list of stocks in a daily newspaper). Most of the empirical tests to date of this random walk theory have employed some variation of serial correlation or runs analysis. The results have been both consistent and impressive. As stated by Eugene F. Fama:

> I know of no study in which standard statistical tools have produced evidence of *important* dependence in series of successive price changes. In general, these studies (and there are many of them) have tended to uphold the theory of random walks.[1]

There is, however, at least one important technique of technical analysis which has not been extensively tested—correction for the "co-movement" of stock prices. Benjamin F. King, Jr., in his unpublished Ph.D. dissertation, concluded that a large

[1] Eugene F. Fama, "Random Walks in Stock Market Prices," *Financial Analysts Journal, XXI, No. 5 (September–October, 1965)*, 57.

TABLE 54.1

	Price at Beginning of Time Period			
Stock	1	2	3	4
A	$10.00	$12.00	$10.00	$11.00
B	10.00	15.00	14.00	18.00

part of the movement of the price of a stock can be viewed as co-movement, not independent of what happens to the prices of other stocks.[2] King's conclusion was supported in a statement by John M. Birmingham, Jr.

> One . . . analysis, as yet only privately circulated, does indicate that the portfolio planning students are on the right track when they talk about intercorrelation of stock prices. It strongly suggests that the majority of individual stock price changes are controlled by more dominant "general market" and industry tendencies. In other words, successive changes in GM may be independent of previous changes for GM stock, but they are not independent of simultaneous changes in all other stocks or, in particular, other auto stocks.[3]

The intercorrelation or co-movement of stock prices could conceal existing dependencies in successive price changes. Perhaps an overly simplified example will illustrate this phenomenon more clearly. Table 54.1 sets forth the prices of Stocks A and B at the beginning of four consecutive time periods.

A serial correlation study (Table 54.2) might attempt to measure the relationship between successive first differences for each stock.

The limited data above certainly offer no preliminary indication that any significant degree of correlation exists between successive price changes.

Notice, however, that Stock B was relatively stronger than Stock A in all three periods. This fact might be revealed by computing the period-by-period percentage change in each stock's price and then ranking these percentage changes, assigning a rank of 1 to the stock with the greatest percentage appreciation (or least percentage depreciation) and a rank of 2 to the stock with the opposite characteristics. The outcome of this process is reported in Table 54.3

TABLE 54.2

	Successive First Differences by Time Period		
Stock	1–2	2–3	3–4
A	+$2.00	−$2.00	+$1.00
B	+ S.00	−1.00	+ 4.00

[2] Benjamin F. King, Jr., "The Latent Statistical Structure of Security Price Changes" (unpublished Ph.D. dissertation, University of Chicago, 1964). Cited by Lawrence Fisher, "Outcomes for 'Random' Investments in Common Stocks Listed on the New York Stock Exchange," *Journal of Business,* XXXVIII, No. 2 (April, 1965), 159.

[3] John M. Birmingham, Jr., "Random and Rational: Stock Price Behavior and Investment Returns," *Financial Analysts Journal*, XXI, No. 5 (September-October, 1965), 53.

TABLE 54.3

	Percentage Change in Price by Time Period		
Stock	1–2	2–3	3–4
A	+20.0%	−16.7%	+10.0%
B	+50.0	−6.7	+28.3
	Performance Ranks by Time Period		
Stock	**1–2**	**2–3**	**3–4**
A	2	2	2
B	1	1	1

Significantly, a serial correlation study of performance ranks offers far more promise of indicating a close relationship over time than would the same study using successive first differences.

By using ranks which measure *relative* strength, the co-movement of stocks is filtered out. This technique for eliminating the effects of the "general market" will be used for the empirical tests in this study.

II. Construction of the Data File

Raw Data The raw data for the tests which follow were the weekly closing prices of 200 stocks listed on the New York Stock Exchange for the 260-week period beginning on Monday, October 24, 1960 and ending on Friday, October 15, 1965.[4] The time period chosen was the most recent and lengthy period for which data were economically available in a form usable on the IBM 7090 and 7094 computers. The stocks were chosen according to the following criteria: (1) as previously mentioned, they had to have been listed on the New York Stock Exchange for the entire test period; (2) they must have been listed in the May 1965 edition of *Moody's Handbook of Widely Held Common Stocks;*[5] and (3) they must have been included as component stocks in Standard and Poor's Industry Stock Price Indexes as published in the 1964 *Security Price Index Record*.[6] In an effort to assure a representative sampling of the market, the stocks meeting the above three criteria were divided into industry groups, as determined by Standard and Poor's Industry Stock Price Indexes. The final selection of 200 stocks was then made in such a manner that the relative distribution of stocks by industry was approximately the same as in the Standard and Poor Industry Stock Price Indexes. (Although the sampling procedure was *ex post*, the author considers it unlikely that the test results have been materially biased.)

[4] Price data were supplied by Arnold E. Amstutz, Assistant Professor of Management at the Massachusetts Institute of Technology, and were checked extensively against the following sources: "Statistical Section," *Barron's,* October 1961 (Vol. XL, Nos. 44 through 52, and Vol. XLI, No. 1); *ISL Daily Stock Price Index: New York Stock Exchange* (Palo Alto, California: Investment Statistics Laboratory, Inc., 1961 annual edition and quarterly editions from 1962 through 3rd quarter 1965); "New York Stock Exchange Transactions," *The Wall Street Journal*, October 4, 11, and 18, 1965.

[5] *Moody's Handbook of Widely Held Common Stocks* (New York: Moody's Investors Service, Inc., May 1965).

[6] *Security Price Index Record* (New York: Standard and Poor's Corp., Inc., 1964). Of the 200 stocks, four were not included in the Industry Stock Price Indexes at the beginning of the test period.

TABLE 54.4

Ratio Designation	Description
C/A26	The price for the current week divided by the average of the series of prices ending with the price for the current week and including the prices for the 26 weeks immediately preceding. (Computed for weeks 27 through 260.)
4/C	The price for the current week divided into the price 4 weeks subsequent to the current week. (Computed for weeks 27 through 256 only.)
26/C	The price for the current week divided into the price 26 weeks subsequent to the current week. (Computed for weeks 27 through 234 only.)

Price Ratios All price series were adjusted for splits, stock dividends, and for the reinvestment of both cash dividends and proceeds received from the sale of rights.[7] It was then possible to compute various price relationships. Beginning with the 27th week (in order to allow for the compilation of 26 weeks' historical data), the following price ratios were computed weekly for each stock (Table 54.4).

One of the above ratios (C/A26) is "historical" (i.e., it is based upon data originating prior to and including C) and so may be used for purposes of investment selection. The remaining two ratios, 4/C and 26/C, are "future" (i.e., they are based upon data originating subsequent to and including C), and so may be used for purposes of measuring the results of investment selection.

The specific time periods covered by the ratios were chosen because of their familiarity (i.e., approximately one month and one-half year), and in the case of 26/C, because of the possibility that there might be some measurable effect evolving from the six-month long-term capital gains provision of the Federal income tax law.

Moving averages were used for computation of the historical ratio because of their tendency to smooth over temporarily exaggerated price movements, and because of their popularity with market practitioners. Moving averages were not used, however, for the future ratios since the future ratios are intended for the measurement of investment performance rather than for investment selection. Performance measures must be convertible into dollars and cents, and should express the relationship between cost of a given security and proceeds which would have been received upon sale of that security.

[7] Information on splits, stock dividends, cash dividends, and rights offerings were obtained from the following sources: *ISL Daily Stock Price Index, op. cit.,* 1961 annual edition and quarterly editions from 1962 through 3rd quarter 1965; *Moody's Handbook, op. cit.,* quarterly editions, 4th quarter 1960 through third quarter 1965; *Stock Guide* (New York: Standard and Poor's Corp., Inc., monthly editions, October 1960 through November 1965). The adjustment for reinvestment of cash dividends and proceeds received from the sale of rights ignored income taxes and brokerage fees.

TABLE 54.5

Week No.	Stock Number	Price Ratios		
		C/A26	4/C	26/C
027	001	1.306	0.906	1.101
027	002	1.212	0.990	0.802
027	003	1.269	1.023	0.918

Relative Strength Ranks As explained above, three price ratios were computed, as permitted by available data, for each of 200 stocks for each of 234 weeks (from week number 27 through week number 260). Next, on a week-by-week basis, each set of ratios was ranked by stock. The highest ratio was given a rank of 000 and the lowest a rank of 199. The following illustration, dealing with three stocks for one week, should facilitate an understanding of the ranking process. Price ratios for three stocks at week number 27 could have appeared as in Table 54.5.

Assuming that only three stocks were included in the study, the ranking process would have produced the additional information (shown in Table 54.6).

This same ranking process would have been extended to weeks number 28, 29, 30, etc. (each set of ratios for each week being ranked separately). Of course, 200 stocks were actually included in the study rather than only three, so that the ranks were inclusive over the range 000–199.

Volatility Ranks Several of the tests which follow make reference to the comparative volatility of the price movements of the individual securities. A measure of volatility known as the coefficient of variation was utilized in this study. The coefficient of variation is the ratio of the standard deviation of a set of numbers to the arithmetic mean of the set. For purposes of price volatility measurement, the relevant "set of numbers" was taken to be the 27 consecutive weekly prices ending with C for any given security.

For each week separately beginning with week number 27, and for each of the 200 stocks, the coefficient of variation for the 27 latest weekly closing prices was determined. On a week-by-week basis, these coefficients were then ranked by stock from 000 to 199, with the highest ratio receiving the lowest rank (a ranking process identical to that used for the price ratios).

TABLE 54.6

Week No.	Stock Number	Relative Strength Ranks		
		C/A26	4/C	26/C
027	001	000	002	000
027	002	002	001	002
027	003	001	000	001

Market Ranks In order to test certain techniques of market timing, long-term (i.e., 26-week) historical market ranks were included in the data file. The computation of these market ranks was relatively simple. The 200 stocks in total were considered to be representative of the entire market. Each week, the sum of the 200 C/A26 ratios was determined in order to indicate the market's performance over the preceding six months. There were 234 C/A26 sums computed (one for every week from week number 27 through week number 260). The long-term market ranks were then arrived at by ranking the C/A26 sums (i.e., the performance of the sample over 234 holding periods) from 001 through 234.

It may be correctly contended that the process described above resulted in the use of hindsight. For example, the rank for week number 27 was only determinable after the results for week number 260 were known. While this is true, it is considered unlikely that the dispersion of six-month market results would be significantly different over say one 234-week period of time as opposed to any other. In other words, the market ranks would probably be about the same no matter whether hindsight were used or whether some time period prior to the period of this study were adopted as a standard of dispersion of six-month market performance. Of course, the use of hindsight solved the critical problem of data availability.

Divergence Ranks Whereas the market ranks described above measure the historical strength or weakness of the market as a whole, they do not permit a determination of the extent of "speculative excesses" prevalent in the market at any given point in time. To accomplish this purpose, additional market measures, to be called divergence ranks, were computed for each week of the test period.

A possible indicator of speculative excesses, employed by many practitioners, is the comparison of the price movements of the strongest and weakest stocks against the price movements of all stocks in total. The two divergence ranks (long-term strong divergence and long-term weak divergence) were designed respectively to detect exaggerated market conditions by measuring the difference between the performance of the strongest, or weakest, stocks and the performance of the average stock, over 26-week historical time periods.

To illustrate, the computation of the long-term strong divergence rank was as follows: Each week, the average of the C/A26 ratios for the 20 strongest securities was compared to the average of the C/A26 ratios for all 200 securities. The absolute difference (divergence) between the two averages, week by week, was determined. These differences were then ranked, by week, from 001 through 234 with the largest difference receiving the lowest rank. Thus, a long-term strong divergence rank of 001 would indicate a wide divergence between the historical 26-week average price movements of the 20 strongest stocks and the historical 26-week average price movements of all 200 stocks. A rank of 234 would, of course, indicate just the opposite (i.e., a narrow spread between the two averages).

The long-term weak divergence ranks were computed in an identical manner except that the C/A26 ratios of the 20 weakest stocks were substituted for the C/A26 ratios of the 20 strongest stocks. Upon completion of these computations, every week from number 27 through number 260 was assigned two distinct divergence ranks, each ranging from 001 through 234.

The criticism of market ranks, as presented above, also applies to divergence measures. The method utilized for both computations involves hindsight. However, as explained earlier, this criticism is not considered to be of major importance.

III. Relative Strength Continuation: Empirical Results

(The reader should note that the word "historical," in the context used herein, refers to events occurring prior to the time at which a stock is considered for selection; the word "future" refers to events occurring subsequent to selection; the labels "long-term" and "short-term" refer respectively to 26-week and 4-week periods of time; and the words "strong" and "weak" refer to the trend of a stock's price movement relative to the movement of all other stock prices.)

Table 54.7 lists the short-term (4/C) and long-term (26/C) average ratios, by groups of stocks, for the entire test period. The groups were determined by classifying the stocks in accordance with their historical (C/A26) relative strength ranks. Also tabulated are the 4/C and 26/C ranks, listed in the same manner. The 4/C and 26/C average ranks are not affected by extreme price movements of one or more securities. This is not true, however, of the average ratios. Moreover, as discussed above, the computation of average ranks eliminates the sometimes confusing effect which the trend of the general market has on measures of investment performance. Ranks, being a relative measure, are free of general market influence. This applies whether the ranks are historical (C/A26) or future (4/C and 26/C).

Technical analysts contend that stocks which historically have been relatively strong tend to remain relatively strong for some significant period of time. Analysis of the

TABLE 54.7 4-Week and 26-Week Average Investment Performance by Stock Group as Classified According to Historical Relative Strength Ranks

	4-Week Performance		26-Week Performance	
C/A26 Relative Strength Rank	Average 4/C Ratios	Average 4/C Ranks	Average 26/C Ratios	Average 26/C Ranks
000–019	1.009	102.0	1.096	90.8
020–039	1.009	99.6	1.074	94.2
040–0S9	1.010	98.0	1.066	97.2
060–079	1.009	99.8	1.060	99.3
080–099	1.009	99.1	1.062	98.5
100–119	1.010	99.4	1.057	101.4
120–139	1.009	99.4	1.061	99.2
140–159	1.010	97.9	1.061	99.5
160–179	1.010	98.0	1.057	101.6
180–199	1.008	101.8	1.029	113.3
All Stocks	**1.009**	**99.5**	**1.062**	**99.5**

4/C (short-term) average ranks and ratios in Table 54.7 provides no evidence that this contention is correct. There seems to be no discernible pattern to the results.

However, the 26/C average ranks and ratios clearly support the concept of continuation of relative strength. The stocks which historically were among the 10 per cent strongest (lowest ranked) appreciated in price by an average of 9.6 per cent over a 26-week future period. These same stocks had an average 26/C rank of 90.8. On the other hand, the stocks which historically were among the 10 % weakest (highest ranked) appreciated in price an average of only 2.9 per cent over a 26-week future period; and the average 26/C rank of these latter stocks was 113.3.

There appears to be good correlation between past performance groupings and future (26-week) performance groupings. This is easily discerned when the C/A26 relative strength rank group numbers are compared to performance indicators based upon 26/C average group ratios and ranks (Table 54.8).

The correlation coefficient between the C/A26 rank group numbers (column 1) and the 26/C ratio group numbers (column 2) is .87. The correlation coefficient between the C/A26 rank group numbers and the 26/C rank group numbers (column 3) is .92.

The relationship tabulated above was not confirmed when weekly correlation coefficients between C/A26 and 26/C ranks were computed. The 208 correlation coefficients ranged from .37 to –.21, with an average of .08. (The corresponding range of 230 correlation coefficients between C/A26 and 4/C ranks was .51 to –.47, with an average of .00.) This minimal degree of relationship is not, however, inconsistent with dependence of the kind argued.

The conclusion to be drawn from Table 54.7 is that relative strength does, as technicians have claimed, tend to continue over the longer (26-week) period. This does not appear to be the case, however, for the shorter (4-week) period. The apparent unpredictability of the short-term (4/C) results seems to corroborate the results of

TABLE 54.8

C/A26 Relative Strength Rank Group Number	Group Performance Indicator Based Upon: 26/C Average Group Ratios	Group Performance Indicator Based Upon: 26/C Average Group Ranks
1	1	1
2	2	2
3	3	3
4	7	6
5	4	4
6	8	8
7	5	5
8	6	7
9	9	9
10	10	10

the numerous serial correlation studies and runs analyses which have shown *short-term* price movements to be random.

The average price appreciation of the historically strongest securities (9.6% over 26 weeks, or approximately 20.1% per annum) provides some preliminary evidence of non-randomness in price changes. The annual price appreciation of all stocks, computed from the average 26/C ratio at Table 54.7, was 12.8%. Even allowing 4% per annum in brokerage fees (assuming a 1% one-way transaction cost, and two turnovers of the portfolio per year), the profits attainable by purchasing the historically strongest stocks are superior to the profits from random selection.

IV. The Effect of Stock Price Volatility

In an effort to delve deeper into the data presented in Table 54.7 and in order to improve the potential investment results, several subclassifications of Table 54.7 were made. One of these subclassifications was to first divide the securities each week into three groups based upon their historical volatility ranks. Those stocks with a volatility rank of 000 through 049 (the 25% most volatile stocks) were placed in the first group. Those stocks with a volatility rank of 150 through 199 (the 25% least volatile) were placed in the third group. All other stocks (50% of the total) were assigned to the middle group.

After subclassifying the stocks in this manner, computations identical to those reported in Table 54.7 were performed for each of the three volatility groups. The results are set forth at Table 54.9. (The 4/C results are omitted in Table 54.9 and in succeeding tables in this paper. There does not appear to be a discernible pattern in these short-term results.)

The best results were obtained when dealing with the most volatile stocks. The average 26-week price appreciation for the most volatile group ranged from 10.4% for those stocks with the 10% strongest C/A26 relative strength ranks, to 2.5% for those stocks with the 10% weakest C/A26 ranks; and the respective 26/C average ranks ranged from 85.7 to 117.3.

As shown in Table 54.9 the most volatile stock group shows a wider dispersion of both 26/C average ranks and 26/C average ratios than either of the less volatile groups. Clearly, the employment of the continuation of relative strength concept appears to be most effective with regard to the most volatile securities. Moreover, the historically strongest stocks in the most volatile group realized an implied average annual appreciation of 21.9% (based upon their average 26/C ratio). (Of course, the market practitioner interested in risk aversion may prefer not to invest in those stocks which historically have been most volatile.)

Table 54.9 also indicates an excellent spread in 26/C average ratios as between the historically strong stocks and the historically weak stocks in the least volatile group. However, the 26/C average ranks for that group show no discernible pattern. In fact, the 10% historically strongest stocks in the least volatile group have both a high 26/C ratio (1.100) and a high 26/C rank (110.3), thus implying that the market was extraordinarily strong for the 26 weeks succeeding those time periods during which the strongest stocks were also the most stable.

TABLE 54.9 **Average Investment Performance by Stock Group as Classified According to Historical Relative Strength Subclassified According to Historical Volatility Ranks**

Volatility Ranks						
000–049		050–149		150–199		All
Average 26/C Ratios	Average 26/C Ranks	Average 26/C Ratios	Average 26/C Ranks	Average 26/C Ratios	Average 26/C Ranks	Average 26/C Ratios
1.104	85.7	1.063	103.7	1.100	110.3	1.096
1.078	90.7	1.063	97.4	1.107	93.9	1.074
1.081	93.2	1.057	99.0	1.078	96.8	1.066
1.060	99.4	1.064	99.1	1.046	100.1	1.060
1.073	96.1	1.071	98.3	1.038	99.7	1.062
1.069	103.4	1.069	99.1	1.035	104.3	1.057
1.076	105.6	1.071	97.3	1.046	100.3	1.061
1.090	103.5	1.064	98.0	1.048	100.4	1.060
1.068	111.1	1.050	98.6	1.061	101.3	1.057
1.025	117.3	1.030	109.1	1.036	115.4	1.029
1.076	97.2	1.061	99.6	1.051	101.7	1.062

The general conclusion to be drawn from Table 54.9 is that, over the entire test period, the selection of securities which historically had been both relatively strong and relatively volatile produced profits superior to those attainable from random selection.

V. Market Ranks: A First Attempt at Timing

The second subclassification of the results reported in Table 54.7 was by historical market ranks. All of the stocks at those weeks which had a market rank of 001 through 058 (the weeks at which the strongest historical market trends had been recorded) were placed in the first market group. The stocks at those weeks which had a market rank of 177 through 234 (the weeks at which the weakest historical market trends had been recorded) were placed in the third group. Remaining stocks (approximately 50% of the total) were assigned to the middle group.

The purpose of this subclassification was to indicate the extent to which historical market ranks could be used to facilitate market timing. The results of the subclassification by long-term historical market rank are presented in Table 54.10.

The stocks which had the 10% strongest C/A26 relative strength ranks, and which were in the strongest (lowest-ranked) long-term historical market rank group, recorded an average 26/C ratio of 1.150 and an average 26/C rank of 83.8. An average 26/C ratio of 1.150 implies an average annual price appreciation of 32.3%. However, the weeks included in this first market group covered only about 25% of the test period. The average annual rate of return for the entire test period would depend on the results achieved during the remaining 75% of the time (i.e., for the second and third market rank groups).

TABLE 54.10 Average Investment Performance by Stock Group as Classified According to Historical Relative Strength Subclassified According to Historical Long-Term Market Ranks

Long-Term Market Ranks						
001–058		059–176		177–234		All
Average 26/C Ratios	Average 26/C Ranks	Average 26/C Ratios	Average 26/C Ranks	Average 26/C Ratios	Average 26/C Ranks	Average 26/C Ratios
1.150	83.8	1.086	88.6	1.056	104.4	1.096
1.102	95.8	1.060	93.7	1.075	93.7	1.074
1.101	97.0	1.043	98.9	1.077	93.4	1.066
1.085	102.1	1.042	99.5	1.072	95.6	1.060
1.088	100.2	1.044	99.0	1.074	95.2	1.062
1.087	102.0	1.033	103.3	1.076	96.0	1.057
1.090	100.1	1.042	99.3	1.072	98.0	1.061
1.084	102.3	1.043	99.2	1.071	96.9	1.060
1.090	99.5	1.044	99.9	1.048	108.0	1.057
1.061	112.2	1.011	113.6	1.034	113.9	1.029
1.094	99.5	1.045	99.5	1.065	99.5	1.062

The second long-term historical market rank group (covering approximately 50% of the time period) supported the continuation of relative strength concept as did the first group. The 10% historically strongest stocks in the second group yielded an average 26/C ratio of 1.086 and an average 26/C rank of 88.6.

The third long-term historical market rank group (covering the weeks at which the weakest historical 26-week market trends had been recorded) did not support the concept of relative strength continuation. The most profitable stocks (based on average 26/C ranks and ratios) in the third market group were those stocks with a C/A26 rank ranging from 020 through 159. The historically strongest stocks did not produce the most satisfactory 26/C results. It is noteworthy, however, that even during the 26-week period following those weeks in the third market rank group, the stocks with the poorest C/A26 ranks (180–199) continued to produce the poorest C/A26 ranks and ratios.

Table 54.10 leads to the conclusion that the utilization of the continuation of relative strength concept produces superior profits during all periods except those periods immediately succeeding a comparatively weak market. Stocks with moderately strong C/A26 ranks seem to perform better during these latter periods.

It is also indicated by Table 54.10 that the best results are attainable by buying stocks in a market which historically had been comparatively strong. This implies that strength in the market tends to be followed by additional strength (i.e., continuation of relative strength seems to be applicable to the market as a whole as well as to individual securities).

VI. Divergence Ranks: A Second Attempt at Timing

The two divergence ranks described above also served as the basis for subclassifying the information presented at Table 54.7. The subclassifications were determined as follows: (1) all stocks at those weeks which had a divergence rank of 001–058 (the weeks at which the greatest historical divergence had been recorded) were placed in the first of three groups; (2) the stocks at those weeks which had a divergence rank of 177–234 (the weeks at which the least historical divergence had been recorded) were placed in the third group; and (3) remaining stocks (approximately 50% of the total) were assigned to the middle group. Table 54.11 sets forth the results of the subclassification by the long-term strong divergence ranks; and Table 54.12 presents the outcome of the subclassification by long-term weak divergence ranks.

Tables 54.11 and 54.12 indicate that the greatest 26-week rates of return are attained when selecting the 10% historically strongest stocks from the third divergence rank group; and the poorest returns (among the 10% historically strongest securities) arise from selecting those stocks in the first divergence rank group. With respect to Table 54.11 this principle is borne out by the average 26/C ratios (although not by the 26/C ranks); whereas, for Table 54.12 the average 26/C ranks are more indicative.

The stocks in the first divergence rank group do not appear to adhere very closely to the continuation of relative strength concept. Perhaps the historically strongest stocks which had shown the greatest divergence may have temporarily exhausted their upward momentum. On the other hand, those securities in the middle and third groups are quite consistent in following the patterns forecasted by their C/A26 relative strength ranks.

As between the two tables, the long-term weak divergence ranks at Table 54.12 produce the most outstanding results. For the 26-week periods following those weeks which evidenced least historical divergence (the third group), the 26/C average ratios ranged from 1.156 for the 10% historically strongest stocks to 1.029 for the 10% historically weakest; and the 26/C average ranks had a corresponding range of 77.6 to 122.0. This represents the best of the results yet investigated. However, since they are only attainable for approximately 25% of the time, the over-all rate of return would depend upon the profits achieved for the remaining 75%.

Also of significance, the sum total of all securities in the first divergence rank group at Table 54.11 yields an average 26/C ratio as low as 1.010. This implies that long-term strong divergence ranks might be an effective means of forecasting long-term (26-week) market weakness. The 1% average return over a six-month period, for all stocks in the first group, is quite low when compared to the over-all averages at Tables 54.10 and 54.12. Yet this was the return achieved for the 26 weeks immediately following those periods during which performance of the historically strongest stocks diverged by a relatively large amount from the performance of all 200 stocks. The possibility that long-term strong divergence ranks may possess forecasting significance is a familiar one to the many market practitioners who regularly advise caution whenever the market becomes "speculative" (i.e., whenever a few "high-flyers"

TABLE 54.11 **26-Week Average Investment Performance by Stock Group as Classified According to Historical Relative Strength Ranks and Subclassified According to Historical Long-Term Strong Divergence Ranks**

	Long-Term Strong Divergence Ranks							
	001–058		059–176		177–234		All Stocks	
C/A26 Relative Strength Rank	Average 26/C Ratios	Average 26/C Ranks	Average 26/C Ratios	Average 26/C Ranks	Average 26/C Ratios	Average 26/C Ranks	Average 26/C Ratios	Average 26/C Ranks
000–019	1.032	96.5	1.116	86.1	1.123	95.4	1.096	90.8
020–039	1.008	102.7	1.088	90.5	1.116	93.4	1.074	94.2
040–0S9	1.010	99.6	1.071	97.2	1.119	94.7	1.066	97.2
060–079	1.008	99.7	1.064	100.0	1.110	97.2	1.060	99.3
080–099	1.013	96.8	1.064	100.4	1.114	95.8	1.062	98.5
100–119	1.005	100.5	1.061	102.0	1.106	101.0	1.057	101.4
120–139	1.021	92.4	1.063	101.7	1.102	101.2	1.061	99.2
140–159	1.011	96.8	1.064	100.7	1.105	99.8	1.060	99.5
160–179	1.008	98.8	1.065	101.3	1.093	105.3	1.057	101.6
180–199	0.981	111.2	1.032	115.1	1.078	111.3	1.029	113.3
All Stocks	1.010	99.5	1.069	99.5	1.107	99.5	1.062	99.5

TABLE 54.12 26-Week Average Investment Performance by Stock Group as Classified According to Historical Relative Strength Ranks and Subclassified According to Historical Long-Term Weak Divergence Ranks

	Long-Term Weak Divergence Ranks							
	001–058		059–176		177–234		All Stocks	
C/A26 Relative Strength Rank	Average 26/C Ratios	Average 26/C Ranks	Average 26/C Ratios	Average 26/C Ranks	Average 26/C Ratios	Average 26/C Ranks	Average 26./C Ratios	Average 26/C Ranks
000–019	1.086	104.7	1.080	88.3	1.156	77.6	1.096	90.8
020–039	1.081	101.4	1.062	91.7	1.097	91.0	1.074	94.2
040–059	1.080	100.7	1.049	96.4	1.092	94.6	1.066	97.2
060–079	1.077	101.8	1.046	97.9	1.074	99.8	1.060	99.3
080–099	1.088	96.7	1.044	99.0	1.075	99.4	1.062	98.5
100–119	1.080	100.9	1.039	101.4	1.071	101.9	1.057	101.4
120–139	1.090	95.8	1.046	99.0	1.062	104.7	1.061	99.2
140–159	1.092	94.2	1.038	101.7	1.073	101.0	1.060	99.5
160–179	1.093	95.3	1.034	104.3	1.068	102.8	1.057	101.6
180–199	1.076	103.5	1.008	115.2	1.023	122.0	1.029	113.3
All Stocks	1.084	99.5	1.045	99.5	1.079	99.5	1.062	99.5

or "glamor" issues begin to record extraordinary gains relative to other securities). Of course, these market practitioners do not think in terms of divergence ranks; but they do express conceptually what the long-term strong divergence ranks seek to measure quantitatively.

It might also be expected that, if significant divergence (as measured by the long-term strong divergence rank) precedes a weak market, then a small degree of divergence (measured in the same manner) should forecast a comparatively bullish market. In fact, this supposition is borne out by Table 54.11 where the average 26/C ratio for all stocks in the third divergence rank group is 1.107—higher than any of the overall averages at Tables 54.10 and 54.12.

To summarize, the utilization of divergence ranks appears to facilitate market timing. Tables 54.11 and 54.12 (subclassifications of the information presented at Table 54.7) indicate that return on investment can be significantly improved by selecting the 10% historically strongest securities in the third divergence rank group (i.e., the group covering those weeks for which comparatively little divergence was noted). In the case of the long-term weak divergence ranks (Table 54.12), the results of following this strategy were superior to any results yet investigated. And in the case of the long-term strong divergence ranks (Table 54.11), it was discovered that comparatively weak market periods usually followed those weeks included in the first divergence rank group; and comparatively strong market periods tended to follow those weeks included in the third divergence rank group.

Any conclusions regarding the validity of using market ranks or divergence ranks to facilitate market timing must, however, be of a tentative nature. The studies in this paper fail to relate the various average 26/C ratios to the number of dollars which would be available for investment at various times in the market.

VII. Limitations

Although it appears that superior profits can be achieved by investing in securities which historically have been relatively strong in price movement, the random walk hypothesis is not thereby refuted. To the extent that the superior profits are attributable to the incurrence of extraordinary risk, the prices of individual securities could still be said to fluctuate randomly about a trend which is related to the opportunity cost of capital (a function of risk). Thus, only when a technical investment strategy can produce profits which are superior to those attainable by random selection, a risk which is less than that of random selection, can the random walk hypothesis be disproven.[8]

It is therefore necessary to determine the riskiness of the various technical measures tested above. Volatility ranks, while indicative of price stability, are unsatisfactory measures of risk for two reasons. First, since they are based upon the coefficient of variation of *prices* rather than *price changes*, they are more properly related to price

[8] For a further discussion by the author of the theory of random walks, see "The Principle of Portfolio Upgrading," *Industrial Management Review*, IX, No. 1 (Fall, 1967); and "Random Walks: Reality or Myth," *Financial Analysts Journal*, XXIII, No. 6 (November-December 1967).

action than to risk. While price action is an important variable for technicians to determine, it is not equivalent to risk. For example, stock prices rising sharply and rapidly would have a large coefficient of variation. But if the price series adhered closely to a linear trend, this coefficient of variation would bear no relationship to any common definition of risk. The relevant measure in this case would be either the coefficient of variation of *price changes* or the coefficient of alienation of price regressed on time. However, even these two measures would share with the volatility ranks a second weakness if applied to risk determination. Namely, prospective risk may not be a function of historical risk. It is the realized variance of the resultant rates of return rather than the predictability of past prices which better reflects risk.

Why, then, have the realized variances of the future returns and ranks not been computed? The answer is that there is no satisfactory method of doing so. To illustrate, comparisons of C/A26 ranks and 26/C ranks were made over 208 holding periods, each one commencing and terminating one week later than the previous one. Thus, it is clear that there are only eight non-overlapping 26-week periods analyzed. Consequently, the results are extensively intercorrelated; and the use of standard statistical measures becomes suspect. Only if each holding period were treated independently could the variances be relied upon; and under these circumstances, we would have 208 variances for each historical rank grouping, with no satisfactory method of combining them for analysis.

As a result, this study is limited by omission of statistical tests of significance, and omission of measures of return variability among individual securities and individual holding periods. However, as Paul Cootner commented in discussing his work on the random walk model:

> . . . my own tests . . . suffer from lack of a good statistical test of significance; on the other hand, they come closer to testing for the kind of non-randomness which stock market traders claim exists. It is a foolish sort of statistical reasoning which would suggest we limit our investigations to those hypotheses which are easy to investigate.[9]

[9] Paul H. Cootner, "Stock Prices: Random vs. Systematic Changes," *Industrial Management Review,* III, No. 2 (Spring, 1962), 43.